MOUNT MARY
Milwaukee, W   W9-BAU-805

SAM ADAMS

MOUNT MARY COLLEGE LIBRARY
Milwaukee, Wisconsin 53222
WITHDRAWN

SAM ADAMS

Pioneer in Propaganda

JOHN C. MILLER

STANFORD UNIVERSITY PRESS
STANFORD, CALIFORNIA

70-1643

921
Ad19M

To my Mother and Father

In the course of my research I have been accorded many kindnesses by the librarians of the Massachusetts Historical Society; the Massachusetts Archives; the Harvard College Library; the New York Public Library; the New York Historical Society; and the Congressional Library in Washington, D. C. I am deeply indebted to Professor Samuel Eliot Morison of Harvard University, and to Professors Lawrence J. Henderson and Charles Pelham Curtis, Jr., of the Society of Fellows of Harvard University, for their stimulating criticism of my work.

The substance of this book was delivered in lectures at the Lowell Institute during October 1935.

JOHN C. MILLER

CONTENTS

ILLUSTRATIONS

SAM ADAMS

I

A BOSTON ADAMS

THE character of Sam Adams is so unlike that of other members of the Adams Family that it is difficult to find him a place within the family circle. In that distinguished gathering there seems no room for a propagandist, democrat, and backstairs politician. Still, Sam was an Adams, although not, it is true, of the Quincy breed. During the eighteenth century, there were two distinct branches of the Adams Family in New England — the town and the country Adamses; and there were striking differences in talent and temperament between the townsmen and their country cousins. Most of the descendants of Henry Adams, the founder of the Adams Family in New England, remained obscure yeomen almost a half century after the Boston Adamses had become prominent merchants and politicians. While the Quincy clan were still not far removed from the dirt-farmer stage, the Bostonians gave promise of becoming one of the most influential families in Massachusetts Bay. Although the country Adamses outstripped the Boston branch before the century was out, it is significant that when rank in Harvard College was determined by social position, Sam Adams, a Bostonian, was placed fifth in his class, while his country cousin, John Adams, the first important Adams to come out of Quincy, ranked sixteenth on his graduation a few years later — and such prominence as he enjoyed was owing to the fact that his mother was a Boylston.[1]

Sam Adams, the greatest of the Boston Adamses, was born on the "sixteenth day of Septbr at twelve of the Clock at noon, being Sabbath day, 1722." His father, Samuel Adams, Senior, was a prosperous brewer and merchant, whose trim house,

[1] John T. Morse, Jr., *John Adams* (1885), 3.

brewery, and wharf on Purchase Street marked him as one of the substantial citizens of Boston's South End. Beside manufacturing beer, the elder Adams was a pillar of the Congregational Church. By the time of Sam's birth, "Deacon" Adams, as he came to be known, had acquired a comfortable estate and made a reputation as a "godly man." [2]

Little is known of Sam Adams until he reached middle age. Even the Tories who went over his career with a fine-tooth comb, determined to show he was a scoundrel, were unable to prove that he had spent an abnormal childhood. For eight years he attended the Boston Latin School, where little more than Latin and Greek was drilled into the students. Whatever its shortcomings, this instruction admirably fitted them for Harvard College. When the Reverend Mr. Thacher delivered Sam Adams's funeral sermon many years later he said that Sam had distinguished himself in his youth as one of the best scholars of his day. Although it is doubtful if he really shone so brilliantly in the classroom, he did well enough to give his parents high hopes for him in the ministry. Admitted to the class of 1740, Sam was packed off to Harvard College at the age of fourteen, where it was expected he would prepare himself for the Church. But here Deacon and Mrs. Adams suffered the first of many disappointments in their son. Sam's morals were good and he was seldom missing from the family pew on Lord's Days, yet he showed little interest in theology or metaphysics. He had not been long at Harvard College before it was clear that Deacon Adams would never have the gratification of seeing his son in a pulpit.

Such rebellion did not spare young Sam the torments of metaphysics, which was crammed into students at Harvard during the eighteenth century regardless of their choice of profession. But Adams put to good purpose in Cambridge all the Latin and Greek he had learned at the Boston Latin School. Freshmen studied Cicero, Virgil, the Greek Testament, and Hebrew. Although the curriculum was heavily weighted with

[2] William V. Wells, *The Life and Public Services of Samuel Adams* (1865), III, 427–428 (Appendix).

Greek and Latin, the college fulfilled in a great measure its purpose of instructing in "ye Learned Languages, ye Liberal Arts & Sciences"; and Adams became well grounded during his seven years at Cambridge in geography, arithmetic, geometry, astronomy, physics, logic, rhetoric, and natural philosophy. Only in English literature was he conspicuously ignorant — a fault common to most educated New Englanders of his generation.[3]

After his junior year at Harvard College, Adams was permitted to live "wholly out of Commons," which allowed him to board at a private home in Cambridge — a privilege accorded to delicate students who required different fare from that served in the Commons or to "swells" who turned up their noses at college food. Then Deacon Adams lost his money in the Land Bank crash and young Sam was forced to come down in life and serve as one of the waiters for the lower table in the college dining hall, where his duties consisted in being ready "when the Bell tolls at meal time to receive the Plates and Victuals at the Kitchen Hatch & carry the same to the severall tables." Although Adams seems to have taken no part in the "shamefull & scandalous Routs and Noises" in the college yard, — such as whittling lead from the roofs of the college buildings, tearing up the yard fences for bonfire fuel, and setting off "Squibs or Crackers" at midnight, — he was hardly a classroom saint.[4] Harvard College demanded that its scholars lead "sober, righteous & godly Lives," and the drinking of brandy, rum, or other distilled liquors in college rooms was strictly prohibited. Those detected in such revels were fined, degraded in class, or rusticated. During his senior year, Sam Adams was caught drinking rum; and, while he escaped with a five-shilling fine, several of his less fortunate companions were both rusticated and degraded.[5]

[3] *Records of the College Faculty*, I, 178, MS. Harvard College Library. *Harvard College Records, Publications of the Colonial Society of Massachusetts*, II, 557.
[4] *Records of the College Faculty*, I, 116, 132, 162. *Publications Col. Soc. of Mass.*, II, 543, 544, 568, 598.
[5] *Records of the College Faculty*, I, 123, 124.

Life in New England was certainly not humdrum during Sam Adams's youth. While he was at Harvard College, the Great Awakening swept over the country and Harvard became "a new Creature" filled with devout young men who had experienced the "New Birth." George Whitefield was welcomed in New England as "an Angel of God and Messenger of Jesus Christ," and there were few students at Cambridge able to resist his hot gospeling. Harvard again became a citadel of righteousness and the clergy exulted over "the sweet Work going on at Cambridge." When Whitefield first visited the college he was dismayed by the laxity he found: tutors did not pray with their pupils and their favorite theologian was Tillotson, whom Whitefield declared "knew less of Christianity than Mahomet." [6] But after the religious awakening of 1740, it was said that only "Voices of Prayer and Praise" were to be heard in students' rooms and Tillotson and Clark were cast aside for Flavel and the Mathers. Indeed, the piety of the college became so formidable that even "divers gentlemen's Sons" who came to Harvard prepared to spend four years in sloth and pleasure were suddenly seized with remorse and became so "zealous for Christ's Cause as to devote themselves entirely to Studies of Divinity." [7] In Boston, where the Congregational clergy had for many years past seen the Devil making long strides, the Great Awakening brought about a "Week of Sabbaths": taverns, dancing schools, and assemblies "which have always proved unfriendly to serious Godliness" were deserted for prayer meetings and sermons, and religious conversation became "almost fashionable." At every opportunity, Whitefield put "a Damp upon Polite Diversions" and beseeched his hearers to shun the snares Satan had laid for them in fashionable dress. His exhortations produced startling changes in Boston. Young men and women cast off their finery and walked along the fashionable Boston Mall, built in

[6] *Christian History* (1740), II, 282. *Massachusetts Historical Society Proceedings*, LIII, 214. Benjamin Colman to Dr. Benjamin Colman to Dr. Watts, *Ibid.*, LIII, 196. *Christian History*, II, 282. *New England Weekly Journal*, May 20, 1740.
[7] Benjamin Colman to George Whitefield, July, 1741, *Mass. Hist. Soc. Proceedings*, LIII, 196.

imitation of St. James's Park in London, wearing the sombre dress seen in the heyday of Puritanism.[8]

But this revival of Puritanism proved exceedingly short-lived. George Whitefield was followed in New England by a host of lesser "New Lights," such as Gilbert Tennent of New Jersey, who edified his audience by "roaring out and bellowing *Hell* and *Damnation*" at the top of his lungs, and by James Davenport of Long Island, who shrieked hell-fire on the Boston Common until his followers were tumbling and howling "more like a Company of Bacchanalians after a mad Frolick, than sober Christians."[9] The Congregational clergy soon found that instead of bringing back the days of Cotton and Winthrop, the Great Awakening had ushered in a wild, disorderly religious frenzy which split the Congregational Church into bitterly hostile factions — the "Old Lights" and the "New Lights." Far from harking back to Puritanism, the Great Awakening was the first of the backwoods revivals that were to sweep America during the eighteenth and nineteenth centuries.[10] But, as will be seen, this "Puritanism" of the early period of the Great Awakening left a profound impression upon Sam Adams.

Despite his repute as a merchant and staunch Congregationalist, Deacon Adams's liveliest interest was in neither rum nor religion, but in Boston politics. After accumulating a moderate fortune in business, the elder Adams turned his attention almost wholly to politics and became one of the most prominent public men in Massachusetts Bay — "a true New England Man; an honest Patriot." Beginning at the bottom of the political ladder, he ascended the stages of tithingman,

[8] Benjamin Colman to Dr. Watts, 1740, MS. Mass. Hist. Soc. *Christian History*, II, 282. *Diary of Paul Dudley, New England Historical and Genealogical Register* (1881), 29. Jonathan Belcher to Richard Waldon, Oct. 27, 1740, Belcher MSS., Mass. Hist. Soc.

[9] George Whitefield, *Vindication and Confirmation of the Remarkable Work of God in New England* (1741), 8. *Boston Evening Post*, Aug. 2, 1742.

[10] John C. Miller, "Religion, Finance and Democracy," *New England Quarterly*, March 1933, 29–58. Charles Chauncy, *Seasonable Thoughts on the State of Religion in New England* (Boston, 1743), 184. Chauncy, *Religious Commotions in New England* (Preface), 18.

constable, assessor, and selectman, to become at last one of the
Boston representatives in the General Court.   Only the veto
of a royal governor prevented him from reaching the Massachusetts Council, which was regarded as the particular preserve
of the first families of the province.[11]   Whenever a vigorous
statement of colonial rights was required, Deacon Adams's pen
was pressed into service.   In 1731, for example, he urged the
Boston representatives to use their "utmost Endeavor that the
Great Priviledges we Enjoy by the English Constitution & the
Royal Charter may be preserved from all Enchroachments"
— words which his son was to reëcho in his revolutionary
manifestoes.   Deacon Adams drew up Boston's declarations of
grievances against the British government and the royal governor; wrote the town's instructions to its representatives; and
denounced British impressments of New England seamen as
"breaches of Magna Charta, the Charter of this Province, and
an Act of Parliament." [12]

Deacon Adams's political success was owing to his influence
in the Boston Caucus, of which he probably was a charter member.   This club of small shopkeepers, mechanics, and North
End shipyard workers (it is possible that "caucus" is a corruption of "caulker") held a tight grip on town offices and filled
with its nominees all the snug berths, from hogreeve to selectman and representative.   Bostonians nominally decided their
concerns in the town meeting, but under Deacon Adams, and
still more under his son and successor in the leadership of the
Caucus Club, the political bosses laid their plans and thoroughly
cut and dried all the town's important business long before the
citizens met in the town meeting — there usually to do as the
Caucus Club bid.   During the eighteenth century, the Caucus
became so powerful that Sam Adams turned it into a revolutionary machine and with its aid made himself "Dictator" of
Boston.

Sam Adams grew up in an atmosphere heavily charged with

[11] *Boston Records*, 8th Report of the Record Commissioners of the City of
Boston (1879), 70, 77, 170. William Bennett, *History of New England*,
Sparks MSS., Harvard College Library, 145.

[12] *Boston Records*, 12th Report of the Record Commissioners (1885), 23–
24; 14th Report, 84–85.

politics and, from his earliest years, the dangers that threatened
New England's liberties were deeply impressed upon his mind.
Deacon Adams made his house a gathering place for Boston
politicians, from petty "bosses" to such leaders as Elisha Cooke,
"the greate Darling of his Country" and standard bearer of the
Massachusetts Country Party. When the Crown demanded a
fixed salary from the Massachusetts General Court for the
royal governors, Elisha Cooke and Deacon Adams led the
colony's resistance, with the result that the King and the governor were worsted in the struggle. Sam's biographers have supposed that he was allowed to sit at Elisha Cooke's feet; if so, no
rebel could have had better schooling. Governor Jonathan
Belcher, who certainly had no reason to love Cooke, said he
had "a fixt enmity to all kingly government" and "endeavoured,
to poyson the Minds of His Countreymen, with his republican
notions, in order to assert the Independency of New England"
— the accusation later brought against Sam Adams by the royal
governors of Massachusetts.[13] There is little doubt that had
Cooke lived two generations later, he would have been a leader
in the struggle for American independence. His attitude
toward the mother country reveals strikingly on what uncertain
tenure Great Britain held the allegiance of the chiefs of the popular party in New England. Elisha Cooke expressed the traditional spirit of Massachusetts that had taken root when the
colony was virtually an independent state recognizing only a
shadowy sovereignty in the mother country. This heritage of
the seventeenth century was handed down from one generation
to another, and it was chiefly through Elisha Cooke that Sam
Adams became imbued with the spirit that was to make him
a revolutionary leader.

During the struggle between aristocrats and common people
to establish a Land Bank in Massachusetts, Sam Adams was
brought into direct contact with political radicalism. In 1740,
shortly after he had graduated from Harvard, the colony
reached the crisis of an economic depression. Throughout the
greater part of the century, the lack of a stable currency em-
bittered Massachusetts politics and divided parties on class

[13] C. K. Shipton, *Sibley's Harvard Graduates*, IV, 352, 353, 354.

lines: debtors against creditors, and inflationists against the "sound money" mercantile aristocracy. As commerce began to decline and farmers and town artisans found themselves in a "pretty Pickle" because of the currency shortage, hostility mounted everywhere in the colony against the wealthy Boston merchants who, by paying their debts in England with colonial silver, made the scarcity more acute at home. The common people denounced them as "griping and merciless usurers" who "heaped up vast Estates" and made themselves "Lords of Mannors" by profiteering at the small farmers' expense. Another excellent reason for hating the Boston aristocracy was that they were creditors in the colony to the tune of "Hundreds of Thousands" and were not inclined to ease their debtors' burden by accepting payment in depreciated paper money.[14] Under these circumstances, the merchants became almost as unpopular in Massachusetts as did the Tories in the next generation. It was widely believed that they would "swallow up thousands of Families" and strip half the farmers in the province of their property; if they continued to dominate Massachusetts, it was said that yeomen would be forced into the degradation of "Husbandmen, Laborers and Tenants." Even a French invasion and the rule of "Papists" were pictured as preferable to remaining as the "Slaves and Vassals" of these mercantile overlords.[15]

In 1740, it was clear that a popular upheaval was imminent in the colony. The crisis led to the resurrection of an old scheme known as the "Land Bank" which promised hard-pressed farmers and town mechanics a Utopia of paper money backed by real estate. The promoters of the Land Bank were frankly inflationists who proposed to bring back prosperity by flooding the country with paper bills and, at the same time, to "humble the Merchants" by taking the control of currency out of their hands. With these rosy promises attracting thousands of distressed yeomen and mechanics, the Land Bank

[14] *Boston Gazette*, Jan. 28, 1740. *Colonial Currency Reprints*, edited by Andrew McFarland Davis, *Publications Prince Society*, IV, 223. *New England Weekly Journal*, Sept. 23, 1740; Aug. 19, 1740. *Boston Evening Post*, Sept. 22, 1740.
[15] *Colonial Currency Reprints*, IV, 42, 78, 79.

reached portentous dimensions. It quickly became the rallying point of a political party whose objective was to bring the government within the grasp of the common people. The "numerous swarm of the village" everywhere menaced the power of the aristocracy; and the metropolis fell under the sway of the "Boston Chaps who rule the roast." In the House of Representatives, the Land Bankers piled up a large majority and threatened to take possession of the Council, leaving only the royal governor as a brake upon the people's fury against the merchants. To the dismayed gentlemen of Boston it was clear that the question which lay at the root of the struggle was whether the common people or wealthy gentry were henceforth to control the political life of the colony; in their eyes, the balance trembled between the "Idle and Extravagant who want to borrow money at any bad Lay" and "our considerable Foreign traders and rich Men." [16]

One of the most important of those "Boston chaps" who held the metropolis for the Land Bank was Deacon Adams. As a director of the bank, Adams sunk most of his fortune in the scheme and was among the first "martyrs" to be deprived of office by the royal governor for activities in the Land Bank. Immediately after Governor Belcher's proclamation threatening all officeholders under the governor's commission with removal if they passed Land Bank money, Adams resigned as justice of the peace and sent a scorching letter to Belcher, in which he declared that upon the Land Bank "the Interests of our Native Country so much depends as to Require the Utmost of our Endeavours" to promote it. For this defiance, Adams was promptly dismissed from office, along with a large number of militia officers and justices of the peace who did business with the prohibited bills. Adams continued to accept Land Bank money at his shop, although it was rumored that he was wary of overloading himself with large sums. When stories began to circulate that Adams was refusing to take Land Bank bills,

---

[16] Thomas Hutchinson, *History of the Province of Massachusetts Bay* (1767), II, 394. *Colonial Currency Reprints*, II, 46; IV, 257, 258, 305. *Belcher Papers, Mass. Hist. Soc. Collections, Sixth Series* (1894), II, 222. Massachusetts Archives, 102, *Pecuniary Papers*, 29, 90.

a disastrous panic was threatened because if the most prominent
director of the scheme and deepest plunger had lost confidence,
it behooved the rank and file to make sure they did not scorch
their fingers with worthless currency. Adams immediately advertised in the newspapers that he would give five pounds to
the person who pointed out the author of this slander. To
Adams's consternation, his offer was accepted; one Benjamin
Pollard declared he had spread the story and volunteered to
produce his proof. To crown the Deacon's embarrassment,
Pollard claimed the five pounds reward.[17]

The mercantile aristocracy regarded the Land Bank as
nothing more than a scheme of "desperate and fraudulent"
debtors to cheat their creditors after they had firmly seated
themselves in the political saddle. Governor Belcher in particular "exerted himself to blast this fraudulent undertaking" by
means of royal authority. In spite of his labor, the Land
Bankers continued to gather up the threads of power so rapidly
in Massachusetts that Belcher and the Boston merchants became
convinced that nothing less than Parliamentary intervention
could prevent the "ruin of government and people" at the
hands of Deacon Adams and his followers. In Boston, the
"quarrelsome, mobbish Spirit and Impatience under Government that has so long been growing" gave rise to fears of outright insurrection. The House of Representatives, which now
swarmed with Land Bankers, treated the Crown with "all
possible rudeness and ill-Manners" by flatly ignoring royal
instructions regarding paper money. Indeed, the popular
party in the colony seemed inclined to pull the royal beard so
lustily that Belcher doubted whether it would leave "Jupiter
a hair upon his face, but will bid defyance to his imperial resentment." Outside the General Court, yokels and town laborers
screwed up the politicians' courage by declaring that free-born
New Englanders could do as they pleased since they were
"pretty much out of the reach of the government at home."
Few Crown officers doubted that unless Parliament came to
the rescue, royal authority would crumble and the colony would

---

[17] *Boston Evening Post*, Feb. 16, 1741. Mass. Archives, 102, *Pecuniary Papers*, 29, 90.

soon be "ripe for a smarter sort of government" in which republicans such as Deacon Adams would hold the reins.[18]

Unquestionably, two distinct social classes were arrayed against each other by the inflationist sentiment that had swept over the colony. The bulk of the Land Bank Party was composed of that class which Boston gentlemen called "the Mobility," "the Idle and Extravagant," "the needy part of the Province," or "the Rabble." The Land Bank's rolls show that wharfingers, shipwrights, bricklayers, weavers, tanners, and yeomen predominated, with a thin sprinkling of "Gentlemen" and physicians.[19] It was from these materials that Sam Adams later built the revolutionary Whig Party in Massachusetts; and the social cleavage in 1740 was very similar to that of 1775. In both, a small aristocracy stood at bay against a large majority of the common people; and in both, the aristocracy appealed to the King and Parliament for protection against colonial radicalism. In leading the Land Bank Party, Deacon Adams foreshadowed his son's later career, and even the quarrel with Parliament was not lacking to complete the resemblance.

In May 1741, the Land Bank Party reached the "height of its Malignity." The clergy were still dreaming of the new Puritan Age that was to emerge from the Great Awakening, but there was little in the temper of the people to remind one of the days of Cotton and Winthrop. "They are grown so brassy and hardy," wrote Governor Belcher, "as to be now combining in a body to raise a rebellion." It was said that thousands of farmers would march to Boston on election day to join forces with the town Land Bankers. The embattled farmers, assisted by their urban allies, would then "force the currency of the Land Bank Bills" and demand grain from the merchants; "if corn was there and the merchants would not let them have it they would throw them into the dock." [20]

[18] *Belcher Papers*, II, 349, 364, 386, 387, 388; Rev. William Williams to Benjamin Colman, July 1, 1740, MS. Mass. Hist. Soc.
[19] Hutchinson, II, 394. *Colonial Currency Reprints*, II, 46; IV, 305. Mass. Archives, 102, *Pecuniary Papers*, 103; a list of all such Persons as have mortgaged any part of their Estates in the County of Suffolk to the Directors of the Manufactory Company, Dec. 19, 1740.
[20] *Belcher Papers*, II, 388. *Publications Col. Soc. of Mass.* (1910), IV, 20.

What might have gone down in history as the Great Massachusetts Rebellion was nipped in the bud. Governor Belcher, who had been busily ferreting out radicals, learned that certain extremists were planning a desperate attempt to beat down opposition to the Land Bank. He struck quickly and hard. The leading conspirators were rounded up and jailed. Election day passed without a sign of the threatened uprising. But though the people did not openly revolt, they gave the Land Bankers such an overwhelming victory at the polls that when the new House of Representatives met, Deacon Adams and other prominent members of the popular party were elected to the Council and were prevented from entering that aristocratic stronghold only by the governor's veto. There was no question that the Land Bank had the support of the vast majority of Massachusetts voters and that the leadership of the Boston aristocracy had been completely repudiated. Yet just as the Land Bank Party was taking the reins of government in Massachusetts, it was learned that Parliament had responded to the pleas of Belcher and the merchants and had outlawed the Land Bank by extending the Bubble Act to the colonies.

The first impulse of the Land Bankers upon learning that the House of Commons had signed the death warrant of their bank was to defy Parliament. The people were "ripe for tumult and disorder" and confident that Parliament could not execute the act in the face of determined opposition. The severity of the Bubble Act was a strong argument for resistance. Parliament struck down the popular party in Massachusetts with so little regard to justice that for a generation the memory rankled in the colony, and particularly in the Adams household. The Bubble Act of 1720 had never applied to the colonies and certainly had nothing to do with the Massachusetts Land Bank, which was not a joint stock company. Yet Parliament declared in 1741 that the Bubble Act had been in force in the colonies from the beginning, thus making the Land Bank illegal *ab initio*. When Deacon Adams and his fellow directors established the bank they had no reason to suppose they were acting unlawfully, for as late as 1734 a New Hampshire Land Bank had been approved by the Board of Trade.[21] Nevertheless, Parliament now declared them criminals and liable to the punishments of the Statute of Provisions and Praemunire. All the directors were made personally responsible for the face value of all the Land Bank money that had been issued, on pain of forfeiture of estate or imprisonment. By this means, Deacon Adams and other directors were put at the mercy of any enemy who could gather up bills, demand payment, or insist they be punished according to the letter of the law. It was no wonder, then, that the Land Bank was dissolved with great difficulty and that many directors "appeared very stout" for disobeying Parliament. The Land Bank was brought to an end by the vote of a bare majority of moderates; but it was not until Governor Belcher, who had been chiefly responsible for Parliament's intervention, was removed and William Shirley put in his place that a serious clash between Massachusetts and the mother country was averted.[22]

Had the Bubble Act been carried out in its full severity in Massachusetts Bay, Deacon Adams would have been utterly ruined. The greater part of his fortune was in the Land Bank, and he had many enemies, particularly among the mercantile aristocracy, who would have been overjoyed to assist the royal authorities in clapping him in irons and confiscating his estate. Fortunately, the Massachusetts General Court eased the penalties prescribed by Parliament for the Land Bank directors. But even with this mitigation, the Adamses, father and son, were forced to withstand for twenty years the efforts of the Land Bank Commissioners to seize the remainder of Deacon Adams's estate to pay his obligations as director.

Sam Adams remained at Harvard College during the months when the Land Bank and Great Awakening were threatening the social and religious foundations of New England. After his graduation in 1740 he continued at Cambridge until 1743, when he received his degree of Master of Arts. Already his preoccupation with politics and government had begun to

[21] A. McF. Davis, *Publications Col. Soc. of Mass.*, III, Transactions 1895–97, 29, 31, 32, 41. Mass. Archives, 26, *Hutchinson Corr.*, II, 370.
[22] Mass. Archives, 26, *Hutchinson Correspondence*, II, 370.

crowd all other interests from his mind. Adams read deeply in Locke, Harrington, and Pufendorf; and in his choice of subject for his Master's degree he revealed strikingly in what channel his mind was running. He undertook to debate the affirmative of the question "whether it be lawful to resist the Supreme Magistrate, if the Commonwealth cannot be otherwise preserved." It is probable that Adams's choice of subject was inspired by the resistance to Great Britain contemplated shortly before by the Land Bankers, whose plans he had no doubt heard discussed in his own household. It has been supposed that Adams showed remarkable courage in defending a point so unpalatable to the Crown officers and blue-blooded conservatives who attended Harvard commencements. These gentry are pictured as thunderstruck by the young orator's "bold denial of British power." [23] But such subjects were not uncommon at Harvard College commencements; in 1738, for instance, a candidate had argued a question even more explosive than Sam Adams's: "Are we bound to observe the mandates of kings, unless they themselves keep their agreements with their subjects?" [24] Conservatives frequently found their toes trod upon by Harvard commencement speakers; and Sam Adams's political radicalism was in the best Harvard manner. Unfortunately, no copy of his thesis has been found: evidently it was not remarkable enough to be preserved in hearers' notes or in the newspapers. But if this early work was like his later political tracts, Adams probably began with the Greeks and Romans and ran the whole course of political theory down to John Locke. Although his address may not have struck his audience as "incipient 'treason,'" doubtless it showed that in Deacon Adams's son the Massachusetts patriot party possessed a promising recruit. Had his audience been composed of Land Bankers instead of Boston bigwigs, no doubt those disgruntled financiers and politicians would have cheered to the echo young Adams's premise that the supreme magistrate could be resisted.

Having fired this parting shot at political conservatism, it

[23] Wells, I, 10, 11.
[24] Edward J. Young, *Mass. Hist. Soc. Proceedings* (1881), XVIII, 125. Subjects for Master's Degree at Harvard College, 1655–1791.

S.A. Schoff

JOHN ADAMS AS A YOUNG MAN

THOMAS HUTCHINSON

PAINTED BY EDWARD TRUMAN, IN THE POSSESSION OF THE
MASSACHUSETTS HISTORICAL SOCIETY, BOSTON

became necessary for young Sam to find a profession. His mother's opposition prevented serious study of law; but the Whig Party in the colonies was so well provided with lawyers during the American Revolution that Adams's lack of legal training was not missed: he was, indeed, far more valuable to the Whigs as a popularizer of political ideas and as a man who possessed deep "understanding of liberty and her resources in the temper and character of the people." [25] Adams's first venture was as a businessman, and here he had the blessing of both parents. He was sent to Thomas Cushing's counting-house with high hopes of becoming a prosperous merchant. But Sam was not happy in trade and he soon showed that although he had inherited his father's passion for politics, he was woefully lacking in business ability. He lasted only a few months in Cushing's offices before his employer broke the news to the Deacon that his son would never make a merchant. Mr. Cushing remarked somewhat starchily that he was training young men for business, not for politics — which gives an inkling where Adams's wits had been woolgathering while he was expected to be conning figures and accounts. Decidedly, Sam was becoming a problem to his parents, and no doubt there were numerous worthies who solemnly shook their heads and prophesied a bad end to a young man who did not like business. When his father loaned him a thousand pounds with which to go into business for himself, Sam Adams prodigally loaned most of his money to a friend, who, in turn, promptly lost it. Sam never attempted to get his money back; and Deacon Adams provided in his will that his son should not be compelled to repay the loan. This unlucky incident ended Sam Adams's career as a financier: his father took him into the malt business and, under Deacon Adams's watchful eye, Sam settled down to the life of a merchant and brewer.

But his heart was not in beer, rum, and molasses. He had drunk in so much political talk at home and among friends that he was bursting with ambition to follow Elisha Cooke's footsteps and lead the Massachusetts Country Party in its struggle against the royal governors. In 1748 Sam made his

[25] *The Works of John Adams* (1850), II, 163.

first appearance as a political writer. He and a few close friends of similar political views swore themselves to secrecy, organized a club, founded a newspaper called the *Independent Advertiser*, and began to pepper the royal governor, William Shirley—a popular English-born politician whose chief anxiety was to keep the colony quiet and establish an "era of good feelings" while he made his reputation fighting French and Indians on the frontier. During King George's War (1741–1748) a truce had been patched up between the governor and the popularly elected legislature in order to meet the menace of an attack from Canada. In 1748, when the war came to a close, Sam Adams believed the time was ripe to renew the quarrel between royal and popular authority in the colony. Although he failed in his first attempt to kindle a flame in Massachusetts Bay, his work in 1748–1749 sheds significant light upon his later career as a revolutionist.

Throughout his life, Sam Adams was strongly disposed to "view with alarm," and his friends of the *Independent Advertiser* club shared his apprehensions to a man. They feared that the growing wealth and luxury in Massachusetts Bay were snuffing out the "good old *New England* Spirit" of the early settlers.[26] By 1748, all signs of the Puritanism of the Great Awakening had been swept away by a wave of materialism that reached its peak in Boston and other large seaports. Sam Adams and his friends were in revolt against the commercialism and money-making spirit that followed the religious excitement of the early 1740's, not only because it led to a sharp deviation from puritan morality, but because they believed it sapped the love of liberty that had enabled the early settlers to defend their liberties against the assaults of the British government. They did not doubt that, when Puritanism declined, "our Morals, our Constitution, and our Liberties must needs degenerate," and that New England would fall an easy prey to its enemies. The first of Sam Adams's many efforts to revive Puritanism was made in the *Independent Advertiser* when he was a young man of twenty-four years.

At Harvard College, Sam had read deeply in Roman history

[26] *Independent Advertiser*, Dec. 5, 1748; March 20, 1749.

MOUNT MARY COLLEGE LIBRARY
Milwaukee, Wisconsin 53222

and literature: and it was later said of him that he began "by the Greeks and Romans, to get at the Whigs and tories."[27] He was thoroughly familiar with Plutarch, Cicero, and the Roman historians. Because of this saturation in the learning and history of antiquity, even his political writings, designed to rouse the common people of New England against British oppression, are heavy with classical allusions that no present-day revolutionist would inflict upon his followers. But Sam Adams was appealing to an audience which, like himself, had been educated in the shadow of the Latin world and which knew the literature of Rome far better than it did that of England. In the *Independent Advertiser*, he repeatedly revealed the influence of his classical education. Characteristically, he used the decline of Rome as a "dreadful example" of what New Englanders might expect if they lost the puritan virtues, and he drew a close comparison between the best days of the Roman Republic and the early period of New England settlement. In Adams's mind, a Roman Senator would have quickly made himself at home in seventeenth-century Puritan New England because Rome and New England were spiritually built upon common ground. Adams became known as the "Cato" of the American Revolution because from youth to old age he preached the necessity of returning to an earlier and simpler way of life: his first revolt was against materialism and his first hatreds were against those whom he believed hostile to the rebirth of the Puritan or "Old Roman" spirit in New England.

For New England's moral decay, Sam and the *Independent Advertiser* club held Governor Shirley responsible. Instead of combating the evils they protested against, Shirley allied himself with the mercantile aristocracy and encouraged the growth of the colony's commercial prosperity at the expense of its religious well-being. Moreover, the governor entrenched himself in power by means of a political machine which effectively kept the Country Party, or popular party, out of office. Because the legislative body in Massachusetts was popularly elected, the royal governor was compelled to fight the leaders of the Country Party with their own weapons

[27] Marquis de Chastellux, *Travels in North America* (1787), I, 275.

70-1643

and to create by means of patronage a political following of
his own in the General Court. Adams and his friends exclaimed that Governor Shirley had used his powers of granting commissions in the militia, and nominating judges, justices,
and sheriffs, to the injury of the people; and they urged that
the governor's influence be curbed to make way for a more
democratic form of government.

It was in the pages of the *Independent Advertiser* that Sam
Adams fired his first shots at the "prerogative party" of town
gentlemen and country squires who had "an Itch for riding the
Beasts of the People." [28]   He was to have the satisfaction, many
years later, of driving these gentry from the province, but in
1748 he was unable to raise a storm against them.   He had no
potent economic grievances from which to manufacture political capital such as his father had had during the Land Bank.
Indeed, the attack upon Shirley gave Adams no more than some
valuable practice in shooting at royal governors; he gained no
reputation as a political writer from it because the meetings of
the *Independent Advertiser* club were kept secret: members
boasted that their identity was "utterly unknown" to the public
and even to their best friends.   And, in spite of young Sam's
gloomy forebodings of the decline and fall of New England,
popular liberty did not appear to be threatened.   There were
few indeed who became enthusiastic over his plan of turning
back to Puritanism and adopting the frugality of the founding fathers.

The *Independent Advertiser*, although it closed shop a little
more than a year after beginning publication, did keep alive
the principles of the Massachusetts Country Party at a time
when the power of the aristocracy and royal governor seemed
to have reached a new high-water mark.   Tories feared Sam
Adams because he never permitted the people to lose sight of
the struggle for liberty; and his work in the *Independent Advertiser* was similar to his efforts during the darkest days of
the revolutionary period.   Moreover, Adams's newspaper did
good service in popularizing John Locke's political thought in
New England by giving its readers extensive quotations from

[28] *Independent Advertiser*, May 8, 1749.

his works. A large part of Sam Adams's contributions is based directly upon Locke. Even more significant was Adams's interpretation of the Massachusetts Charter of 1691 as a "Sacred Ark" against all encroachments by the British government. Sam and his friends were wholehearted New England patriots, and it is clear that as early as 1749 they believed the Massachusetts General Court possessed authority in the colony similar to that exercised in England by the British Parliament. Because the Massachusetts Charter gave the royal governor the power of negativing elections of members of the Council, or upper house of the legislature, the *Independent Advertiser* demanded that the governor be stripped of this right, since "the KING AT HOME cannot *negative* or *suspend* any Member of the upper House called the House of Lords." [29] Sam Adams and his followers already regarded the Massachusetts General Court as a local parliament, and they insisted it be given equal dignity with the British Parliament. They justified their demand that the royal governor's power be curtailed in Massachusetts on the ground that the King did not have as extensive authority when dealing with the British Parliament. But most Englishmen put the Massachusetts General Court on no higher plane than a local corporation, and few of them suspected that Bostonians were nourishing the idea in the public press that it was a parliament. Thus, in England and Massachusetts, two irreconcilable theories of imperial government were slowly taking form. The *Independent Advertiser* contains the germ of the ideas for which Adams was to fight for the greater part of his life, ideas which were later to form the political testament of the Whig Party in the American Revolution.

[29] *Independent Advertiser*, Jan. 23, 1749.

II

SAM ADAMS AND THE MASSACHUSETTS
COUNTRY PARTY

WHILE Sam Adams was familiarizing New Englanders with colonial rights and John Locke's political theory by means of his newspaper, he was also playing an active part in politics, although until the outbreak of the revolutionary movement in Massachusetts his progress was painfully slow. It is true his father's influence in the Caucus Club opened for him that select circle of bosses and wire pullers, but, like the Deacon, Sam was forced to content himself with humble offices for many years. He won his first political office in 1746 when, at the age of twenty-four, he was elected one of the clerks of the Boston market, where he served with two other future members of the Massachusetts House of Representatives. After the death of Deacon Adams in 1748, however, Sam fell upon lean years, and he held no office in Boston until 1753, when he was elected a town scavenger — hardly one of those political plums on which he had his eye. Finally, in 1756, he was elected collector of taxes for the town of Boston, which led to one of the worst scandals attaching to the name of a signer of the Declaration of Independence.[1]

For nearly a decade after his election as tax collector, Adams seemed destined to remain an obscure Boston politician to the end of his days. He failed to rise higher in politics at this time, not because his ability was inferior, but because the period was one of almost continuous war. While French and Indians were burning up the New England frontier, ambitious politicians like Sam Adams, whose success depended upon picking quarrels with

---

[1] *Boston Town Records,* 14th Report of the Records Commissioners (1886), 110, 287.

Parliament and the royal governor, found themselves in bad
odor. With the province straining every nerve to muster
enough men and money to drive the French out of Canada, it
became a patriotic duty to bury the hatchet with which Elisha
Cooke had harassed the King's government and scarred more
than one royal governor. Moreover, when French and Indians menaced the colonies, Americans always displayed a sudden burst of loyalty to the mother country. During the
Seven Years' War in particular, British protection was highly
prized in New England because a flood of money and supplies
was poured into the Northern colonies by the home government. As a result, scarcely a ripple disturbed Massachusetts
politics, and Sam Adams was forced to bide his time until peace
should resurrect the Country Party and permit him to face the
royal governor upon the ancient battleground of colonial rights.

Sam Adams was nevertheless fully occupied during this period
in defending his estate against seizure by the Land Bank Commissioners. In 1758, a decade after Deacon Adams's death,
these officials put the estate up at auction for the fourth time.[2]
Owing to Sam's mismanagement and indifference to business,
precious little remained of it besides the house and brewery on
Purchase Street, now sadly weather-worn and in disrepair.
His only defense against the Commissioners was his pen, which,
as most of his enemies were to find, was an uncommonly sharp
weapon. Thomas Hutchinson, who felt its sting more than
any other man, declared that Adams was at first "but an indifferent" writer who learned the art by dint of hard work and
native skill in "artfully and fallaciously insinuating into the
minds of his readers a prejudice against the characters of all
whom he attacked."[3] His first move was always to win the
support of public opinion; and the Land Bank affair gave excellent training to a man who was to spend the greater part of
his life working with the popular mind. He employed the

[2] "To be sold at public Auction at the Exchange Tavern in Boston. Tomorrow at noon. The Dwelling House, Malt-House, and other buildings, with
the Garden and lands adjoining, and the Wharf, Dock and Flats before the
same, being part of the estate of the late *Samuel Adams*, Esq., deceased. . . ."
(Wells, I, 26.)

[3] Hutchinson, III, 295.

same methods against the Land Bank Commissioners that he
later used against royal governors: "Put your adversary in the
wrong," he said, "and keep him there." He swore that the
Commissioners had admitted privately that the money which
they now demanded from him was an unjust debt and that he
was not "truly indebted" to the Land Bank. They not only
were hounding him for debt, he protested, but were bleeding
the public for large salaries and wasting time in order to pro-
long their work. Indeed, this propaganda was so forceful that
the Commissioners lost their jobs as a consequence.

Adams's shrewdest defense against this confiscation of his
estate was to demonstrate to those who had no interest in the
Land Bank controversy that one of the most vital principles of
the British Constitution was at stake. If his property was forfeit, Adams said, a dangerous blow would be struck at the
"Security of English Property." He attempted to show that
the Land Bank Commissioners' action was an invasion of
property rights in which every property holder had vital interest. Adams knew that his misfortunes would not catch the
public eye unless they appeared as wrongs done to a principle,
not to an individual: hence his portrayal of himself to the public
as a "good and loyal" subject of King George II, who was
threatened with the loss of his rights and estate "contrary to all
Reason, and the Spirit of common Law, by which British Subjects are secured in the *quiet* Possession of their own Property." [4]
Perhaps even more timely was his warning to prospective buyers
of the Adams estate of his intention to prosecute the sheriff and
all purchasers who attended the sale. He reminded Bostonians
that although his property had been advertised for sale four
times, no one had been so ill-advised as to attempt to buy it.
As a result, the sale fell through and Adams was allowed to
enjoy what remained of his brewery.

Although Adams was thus subjected by the British House of
Commons to ten years of persecution for a debt he had not
personally incurred, this harsh treatment is not a touchstone
by which to explain his later career. He became a revolutionary leader in 1765 because he was a New England patriot who,

[4] *Boston Gazette*, Aug. 14, 1758; Aug. 21, 1768. Hutchinson, III, 294.

having received the torch from Elisha Cooke, carried on New England's traditional attitude toward imperial authority. To understand his rebellion against the mother country it is necessary to take into account the history of New England from its settlement, and the rapid growth in the colonies, after the fall of Canada, of an assertive, independent spirit toward Great Britain — a spirit to which Adams himself gave full expression.

Another cause of Adams's inability to make headway in politics until the beginning of the revolutionary movement in 1765 was the domination of Massachusetts by the "Shirlean Faction" — a "motley mixture of high Church men, and dissenters" who monopolized public office at the expense of the Country Party.[5] Governor Shirley had made his position in the colony almost invulnerable by entrenching himself behind the "Court Party," composed largely of wealthy merchants, country squires, and political appointees. The steady growth of Shirley's influence in Massachusetts Bay aroused Sam Adams's fears that the governor was plotting to destroy the colony's charter rights. Although Boston — always the hotbed of opposition to royal governors — quarreled with Shirley, Adams and his friends were unable to pry him from office and put a more easily managed governor in his place. Shirley remained in power in Massachusetts for sixteen years; and during this period the New England patriots, Sam Adams among them, cooled their heels outside political office.

Thomas Hutchinson, the "Prime Minister" of the Shirlean faction and leader of the party that later fought desperately against Sam Adams and American independence, was one of the finest examples of the pre-revolutionary aristocracy of Massachusetts. A scholar whose *History of the Province of Massachusetts Bay* marks the beginning of modern historical writing in New England and whose private collection of manuscript was one of the largest in the colonies, he was no recluse, but an active politician, merchant, and judge. In person he was "a tall, slender, fair-complexioned, fair-spoken, 'very good Gentleman,' " whose good looks, his enemies lamented, had "captivated

[5] Jasper Mauduit, *Letter Book, Mass. Hist. Soc. Collections*, LXXIV (1918), James Otis to Jasper Mauduit, Oct. 28, 1762, 76–77.

half the pretty Ladies in the colony" and whose polished manners had won him "more than half the pretty Gentlemen." [6]
Beside cutting the finest figure in Boston and setting "female"
hearts fluttering, Hutchinson was an aristocrat and the most
resolute of Massachusetts conservatives in keeping his class in
power.   The greater part of his life was spent in holding the
lid tightly on colonial radicalism.   By means of appeals to
Parliament, he and his father had crushed Deacon Adams and
the Land Bank in 1741; and in 1750 Hutchinson gave the
Massachusetts inflationist party its death blow by outlawing
paper money through Parliamentary legislation.   In later years,
Hutchinson had reason to take pride in calling himself the
father of the Massachusetts currency system, but the immediate
effect of the suppression of paper money was to bring upon him
the rage of colonial radicals.   A "great part of the people was
in a fury" and he was forced to barricade his house against the
Boston mob; when his house caught fire, the citizens stood by
cursing him and crying, "Let it burn!" [7]   In the House of
Representatives he joined the Court Party and opposed his
colleagues, who, like Deacon Adams, took the popular side; and
after his conservatism had cost him his popularity in Boston and
his seat in the House of Representatives, he moved to the Council, where he became a pillar of strength to the royal government
in the colony.   Thomas Hutchinson made it abundantly clear
that he stood for everything that Sam Adams opposed: the rule
of a few, well-born gentlemen over the lower classes; the suppression of colonial radicalism; the placing of loyalty to Crown
and Empire above local patriotism; and the existence of a
privileged aristocracy barred tightly against Sam Adams and
his kind.

By 1760, Thomas Hutchinson's office grabbing had aroused
Sam Adams's fears that Massachusetts was to be ruled by a
narrow oligarchy.   Hutchinson was president of the Massachusetts Council, lieutenant governor of the province, captain

<hr/>

[6] *Boston Gazette,* Jan. 31, 1763.

[7] *Publications Col. Soc. of Mass.,* III, Transactions 1895–97, 16.   *The
Diary and Letters of Thomas Hutchinson,* edited by Peter Orlando Hutchin-
son (1883), I, 53, 54.   *Mass. Hist. Soc. Proceedings* (1899), XII, Second
Series, 449.   Mass. Archives, 26, *Hutchinson Corr.,* II, 87.

of Castle William, and judge of probate of Suffolk County. Moreover, he had used his influence to load the Supreme Court, the inferior courts, and most of the choice political jobs in the colony with his friends, relations, and political followers, until the Hutchinsons and Olivers had become the ruling families of the province. Hutchinson sincerely believed that the people were never happier than when they were ruled by gentlemen of birth and ability. But his power rankled Sam Adams and James Otis, who found themselves excluded from all share in the government. For twenty years, Otis exclaimed, the province had "groaned under his Tyranny" as he made "enormous strides in power." This "amazing ascendency of one family" violated the principle, highly prized by the Massachusetts patriots, that legislative, judiciary, and executive powers should not be placed in the same hands. James Otis believed that when the same person held judicial and executive powers, as did Thomas Hutchinson, the government was "hastening fast to its ruin, and the mischiefs and miseries that must happen before that fatal period, will be as bad as those felt in the most absolute monarchy." Sam Adams had no doubt that Hutchinson planned to destroy "the Democratical part" of the Massachusetts government; and he feared Hutchinson the more because he used "soft words, a smiling countenance, fair promises, and other tickling blandishments" to gain his purposes. Whatever differences existed between leaders of the popular party in Massachusetts, they stood upon common ground in their conviction that Thomas Hutchinson and his fellow "oligarchs" must be overthrown.[8]

If Sam Adams could not be a political leader of Massachusetts Bay, he set his countrymen an example of an "Old Roman" who lived austerely, despised money, and neglected his own business for the public's. He had run his father's brewery to the ground and had allowed the remainder of his small estate to slip through his fingers, until by 1760 he was as

[8] Mauduit, James Otis to Jasper Mauduit, Oct. 28, 1762, 76, 77. *The Works of John Adams*, II, 150, 151. Thomas Cushing to Dennys de Berdt, Dec. 6, 1766, MS. Mass. Hist. Soc. *Boston Gazette*, Jan. 11, 1762; Feb. 28, 1768; May 4, 1772. *The Writings of Samuel Adams*, II, 165.

bereft of worldly goods as any of the "Old Romans" he venerated. The Tories later ridiculed his incapacity for business and nicknamed him "Sam the Maltster," but it would have been far better for them had Sam Adams become a contented brewer instead of a frustrated, restless politician. With the death of his wife in 1757, Adams was left with two small children and a meagre income eked out by his salary as tax collector, which, at best, was hardly equal to that of a country clergyman. Unlike Elisha Cooke, who had piled up a sizable fortune outside of politics, Sam Adams remained a poor man, dependent upon his political job for a living. But Adams was incorrigibly indifferent to money-making and, instead of tending his brewery, he was constantly running off to the Caucus Club or electioneering in the town meeting.

In 1757, the Shirlean Faction's long domination of Massachusetts came to an end. Shirley was removed as governor and Thomas Pownall was sent out by Pitt to put vigor into the lagging French War. This young Whig politician, who later became a stout defender of the colonies in Parliament, determined to win the support of the popular party in Massachusetts .in order to fight the war more effectively. Much to the patriots' surprise, they found themselves courted by a royal governor and invited to honeymoon with the Crown while important business was being settled with the French and Indians on the frontier. It was a rare royal governor who left Massachusetts without feeling the sting of Sam Adams's slings and arrows, yet Pownall's conciliatory methods made him the most popular governor since the granting of the charter. Even Adams left off attacking the governor and joined the rest of the patriots in basking in the unaccustomed warmth of court favor. Bostonians praised Pownall's "tender regard" for Massachusetts' civil and religious liberties, and James Otis spoke of him as "that truly good and worthy gentleman, almost the only governor whose fate I ever knew much lamented in the colonies." [9] Pownall's fate that so deeply grieved Otis was his removal in 1760 as governor of Massachusetts to make way for Francis Bernard, a gentleman with very different opinions of how royal colonies should be governed. Years later, when

[9] *Boston Gazette*, April 4, 1763; Aug. 12, 1765.

Massachusetts was caught in the full tide of the revolution, many colonists looked back to Pownall's administration as the happiest period of their lives and declared that if the British government would restore the liberties they had enjoyed under Pownall and give them another such governor, they would be the most peaceable of His Majesty's subjects. Indeed, this desire to return to Pownall's day became so strong in 1770 that Sam Adams, who then believed the colonies had gone too far to turn back to the old imperial system, and who considered Pownall at best a lukewarm supporter of colonial rights, felt compelled to destroy his old friend's reputation as a friend to Massachusetts Bay.

When Francis Bernard became governor of Massachusetts in 1760, the colony seemed to be one of the most loyal of His Majesty's American provinces. In contrast to the indifferent support given by many other colonies during the Seven Years' War, Massachusetts maintained a large army and made immense expenditures to crush the French.[10] Massachusetts might well have been chosen by a royal governor, who, like Bernard, being none too well grounded in the colony's history, wished to enjoy his salary and be "easy and quiet." Indeed, for a time, Bernard believed he had at last found a haven: "This people," he wrote shortly after his arrival in the colony, "are better disposed to observe their compact with the Crown, than any other on the Continent that I know." The Country Party was in such complete abeyance that the governor need have no fears of encountering serious opposition. Boston was noted for its observance of the laws of trade; it was, wrote Bernard to William Pitt, "the most commendable in that respect of any in N America." The people were satisfied with their charter and the Massachusetts House of Representatives "kept more within the Bounds of Moderation & Decency than most other Assemblies on the Continent." [11] Yet, in fact, Massachusetts was one of the unlikeliest spots in which a royal governor would

[10] *The Necessity of Repealing the American Stamp Act Demonstrated* (London, 1766), 11.
[11] Mass. Archives, 26, *Hutchinson Corr.*, II, 30. Hutchinson, III, 199, 254. *Bernard Papers*, II, Sparks MSS., Harvard College Library, Francis Bernard to the Lords Commissioners for Trade, Aug. 18, 1760; Bernard to William Pitt, Oct. 3, 1761; IV, Bernard to John Pownall, July 20, 1765.

find rest and quiet. In 1721, the Lords Commissioners for
Trade and Plantations had complained to the Crown that the
House of Representatives had such vast power that the province
was "and is always likely to continue in great disorder." [12]
Massachusetts seldom let slip an opportunity to make her Crown
officers as uncomfortable as possible, and the people were so
jealous of their charter liberties that the governor and House
of Representatives were almost constantly at odds.   Sam Adams
boasted that in Massachusetts "a governor's station is very
slippery"; and none were as adept as Sam at greasing the
ways on which royal governors were skidded out of the province.[13]

But what chiefly damped Bernard's hopes of a peaceful administration was the close of the Seven Years' War and the removal of the menace of French and Indian attacks from Canada.
As long as French "papists" forced the colonists to look to England for military protection, provincial ambitions were effectively swaddled; but when Canada became British, one of the
strongest bonds that held the colonies to the mother country
was snapped.   After 1760, the colonists began to entertain
high notions of their own importance: a great territory to the
North and West now lay open to their expansion; population
was increasing so rapidly that the colonies seemed destined soon
to outstrip the mother country; and wealth was increasing among
all classes.   These changes produced in America a "higher
sense of the grandeur and importance of the colonies." [14]   The
Seven Years' War enriched Americans because the British
government was forced to pour thousands of pounds into the
colonies to fight the French — thus creating some of the large
colonial fortunes, such as John Hancock's, that were used by the
colonists to fight the British themselves during the Revolution.
"You cannot well imagine," wrote a visitor to Boston in 1760,
"what a Land of health, plenty and contentment this is among
all ranks, vastly improved within these ten years.   The war on

[12] British Museum, King's MSS. 205, Library of Congress Transcript, *Report of the State of American Colonies* (1721).
[13] *Independent Advertiser*, Jan. 23, 1749.
[14] Hutchinson, III, 85.

this Continent has been equally a blessing to the English Subjects and a Calamity to the French." [15]   It was not surprising therefore that New Englanders began to demand that they be made "co-equal in dignity and freedom with Britons." [16] Even if the British government had not attempted to centralize the administration of the Empire and tax the colonies, it would have encountered great difficulties in ruling British America after 1760.   But, to aggravate the dangers that threatened the Empire, British statesmen chose this critical period in colonial development to unleash that "terrible menacing monster the writs of assistance" upon Massachusetts Bay. [17]

During the Seven Years' War, American merchants found it highly profitable to supply the Spanish and French West Indian islands with necessities which enabled them to resist British sea power.   This practice of putting profit above patriotism outraged Englishmen and led to stricter enforcement of the laws of trade and navigation.   It was clear that if American supplies could be cut off, the foreign West Indies would be quickly starved into submission; and, since Massachusetts was one of the offenders, customhouse officers were ordered to use writs of assistance in stopping the prohibited trade.   These writs enabled the customhouse officers to enter warehouses and private dwellings in search of contraband.   Because Massachusetts was singled out by the British government in its effort to crush illegal trade, while Rhode Island and the neighboring colonies were allowed to smuggle almost at will, a movement was soon on foot — particularly in Boston, where mercantile interests were strongest — to nullify the writs of assistance.   "We want nothing," declared the Boston merchants, "but to be as free as others are, or that others should be restrained as well as we."   Massachusetts would have no complaints, it was said, if smuggling were suppressed generally: "It is because *we only* are severely dealt with, that we complain of unreasonable treatment." [18]

[15] *The Letters of James Murray, Loyalist* (1901), III.
[16] *The Writings of Samuel Adams*, I, 288.
[17] *The Works of John Adams*, X, 247.
[18] *Boston Gazette*, Dec. 7, 1761; Jan. 4, 1762. *Bernard Papers*, II, Bernard to the Lords Commissioners for Trade, Aug. 6, 1761.

It was not Sam Adams but James Otis, Junior, who, as the Tories said, "first broke down the Barriers of Government to let in the Hydra of Rebellion" by attacking the writs of assistance. The Otises of Barnstable were one of the oldest and most conservative families in the province. Colonel James Otis, the father of the revolutionary patriot, was such a staunch supporter of the royal governors in the House of Representatives that he was singled out by the *Independent Advertiser* as one of the leading reactionaries in Massachusetts Bay. Nevertheless, this family was to begin the struggle against the British government and the Massachusetts aristocracy that Sam Adams finished by exiling the aristocrats and separating the colonies from the mother country.

The Otises took their first step toward radicalism in 1760 when Colonel James Otis saw the political plum on which he had set his heart — an appointment to the Supreme Judicial Court — snatched from his hands by Thomas Hutchinson. Otis had been promised the office by Governor Shirley as a reward for his political services, and when it became vacant in 1760 he assumed his appointment would follow at once. Otis had high qualifications for the Supreme Court; he was leader of the bar in the three southern counties of Massachusetts and speaker of the House of Representatives. Hutchinson's legal knowledge, on the other hand, was scarcely greater than that of many lawyers' clerks. He had been trained as a merchant, not as a lawyer, and his only legal experience had been gained as Judge of Probate for Suffolk County. But Hutchinson never permitted his shortcomings to stand in the way of his ambition. Before Colonel Otis knew fairly what his rival was about, Hutchinson secured his own appointment as Chief Justice of the province.

The Otises were enraged to be done out of office by what they firmly believed to be Hutchinson's double-dealing. Colonel Otis quit the governor's party in high dudgeon, and his son, James Otis, set himself up in Boston as a politician, swearing, it is said, among other things, to "set the province in a flame" to be revenged upon Hutchinson. It was indeed galling to Massachusetts patriots and lawyers that the Chief Justice of the province was still studying elementary law while many able lawyers found their talents unrewarded. By taking an office for which he seemed utterly unfitted, Hutchinson convinced his enemies that he was determined to make himself the "Cæsar" of New England. "It has been his principle from a boy," exclaimed Sam Adams, "that mankind are to be governed by the discerning few, and it has been ever since his ambition to be the hero of the few."

James Otis stepped forth as a champion of colonial liberty when Massachusetts patriots celebrated the fall of Canada and the end of the French and Indian War by launching a vigorous attack upon the writs of assistance in 1760. Rather than assist the Crown officers in rounding up smugglers with writs of assistance, Otis resigned his lucrative office as King's advocate general of the vice-admiralty court at Boston, and appeared as attorney for the merchants who had united to resist the writs. Otis was "chief Director, Chamber Council, Councellor at the Bar, popular Haranguer, & Assembly Orator" of the popular or smugglers' party in the colony.[19] In his great speech before the Supreme Judicial Court in the Council chamber in Boston he denied the right of the British government to employ writs of assistance in Massachusetts Bay, basing his argument upon natural law. Although Otis spoke with "such a profusion of learning, such convincing argument, and such a torrent of sublime and pathetic eloquence, that a great crowd of spectators and auditors went away absolutely electrified," he could not prevent the use of writs in the colony.[20] Here again Thomas Hutchinson proved he was the Massachusetts patriots' worst enemy, for it was owing to Hutchinson's efforts alone that the writs were pronounced legal in Massachusetts Bay. Most of the judges of the Supreme Judicial Court before whom Otis spoke were inclined to believe he had the best of the argument and were ready to refuse to grant writs in the colony. But Hutchinson exerted his influence as Chief Justice to persuade them to continue the case until the next term in order that he might write to England to secure a copy of the writ and evidence

[19] *Bernard Papers*, IV, Bernard to Lord Shelburne, Dec. 22, 1766.
[20] *The Works of John Adams*, X, 183.

of the Exchequer's procedure in the mother country. This delay allowed the friends of the British Ministry to rally, and writs of assistance were issued in the province the following year. Thus Hutchinson added another black mark to his record on which Otis and Adams had already noted the Land Bank, the Currency Act of 1751, the theft of the Chief Justiceship, and the domination of the province by a few oligarchic families.

Because Otis launched his attack upon the writs of assistance shortly after Hutchinson made away with the Chief Justice-ship under Colonel Otis's nose, his enemies declared he had become a patriot solely out of spite. This Otis stoutly denied, and during the next decade he showed that he was actuated by higher motives than a grudge against Thomas Hutchinson for stealing a political job, although it is true that he began his political career by making such a violent attack upon Hutchinson and the royal government "that he satisfied the People in Boston he was a proper person to represent them in the General Court." [21] It was no wonder that conservative gentlemen swore, when they learned that Otis had been sent to the House of Representatives, that "out of this election will arise a d——d faction, which will shake this province to its foundation." [22] Otis's election meant the revival of the Country Party after decades of inactivity. Massachusetts was running true to form: as soon as the war on her frontiers ceased, the scene of battle was transferred to the State House in Boston, where long-suppressed political hostilities began to explode with more violence than at any time since the Land Bank controversy.

When James Otis became the leader of the Massachusetts Country Party he stepped into the rôle Sam Adams longed to play. But a decade of failure had tempered Adams's ambition, and by 1761 he was prepared to serve in the ranks. His ability, however, soon made him Otis's right-hand man, chief newspaper agitator and ablest abettor in keeping the flame lighted by the

[21] "Because a Son felt the ungrateful treatment of a Father, real or imagi-nary," asked Otis, "ought it to be presumed that every Part of his Conduct flows from the foul Sources of Envy and disappointed Ambition?" (*Boston Gazette,* April 4, 1763.) Mauduit, Edmund Trowbridge to William Bollan, July 15, 1762, p. 66.
[22] *The Works of John Adams,* X, 248.

writs of assistance burning briskly in the colony. Between Otis
and Adams, Boston was filled with such "mad rant, and
porterly reviling" against Hutchinson and his party that the
lieutenant governor exclaimed it would put "even a Billingsgate matron to the blush." Pious countrymen who came down
to Boston were horrified to find that "downright scurrility and
gross impudence, was really the most exalted Patriotism, the
most perfectly refined, disinterested Amor Patriæ." For its
part, the Shirlean Faction attempted to convince the people that
Otis was "a Rakoon" and "a filthy skunk." His patriotism, it
was said, sprang solely from "ungoverned passion, disappointed
ambition, and implacable envy of superior merit." [23]
At the beginning of his administration, Governor Bernard
resolved to steer clear of all alignments with factions in the
colony. The governor was given no opportunity to carry out
his plan. He was immediately informed by Adams and Otis
that he must join forces with them or be driven from the colony.
They attempted to convince him that they could easily ruin a
royal governor; no Crown officer, they declared, could stand his
ground after they had "opened the trenches against him."
They reminded him of the long list of governors they had sent
packing out of the colony and boasted they had removed three
of the last four governors entirely by their own efforts. It
was made perfectly clear to Bernard that unless he favored the
Country Party in Massachusetts Bay he would find arrayed
against him some of the best politicians in the colony, particularly
that formidable Boston politician and newspaper writer, Sam
Adams.[24] But Bernard had not yet felt Adams's sting sufficiently to rate him at his true worth, and he attached little
weight to the patriots' threats. Hutchinson appeared to be the
most powerful man in the province and Bernard preferred to
cast his lot with him rather than with Otis and Adams. The
governor therefore went over to Hutchinson so wholeheartedly
that Otis gave up hope of ever weaning him from the lieutenant

[23] *Boston Evening Post*, Feb. 14, 1763; March 28, 1763.
[24] *Bernard Papers*, XII, Bernard to Pownall, Aug. 28, 1773. Peter Oliver,
Origin and Progress of the American Rebellion (1781), Egerton MSS., Gay
Transcripts, Mass. Hist. Soc., 68.

governor; and, indeed, Bernard seemed to have placed himself at the head of the old Shirlean Faction. With his aid, Hutchinson's influence soared, a strong party of "Governor's friends" was built up by means of patronage, and the "oligarchy" in Massachusetts Bay began to fasten itself deeper upon the province. Otis and Adams needed no more evidence to convince them that all the real power in the colony was in Hutchinson's hands and that every royal governor "must submit to him or live in perpetual broils." [25]

In many respects the revived Country Party, headed by James Otis, was heir to the Land Bank Party which in the previous decade had given Massachusetts conservatives the worst fright they received from the days of Anne Hutchinson to those of Sam Adams. Otis appealed to the old guard of colonial inflationists by calling Hutchinson's destruction of paper money "that fatal shock." Like the Land Bankers, Otis denounced the wealthy mercantile aristocracy "who grind the faces of the poor without remorse, eat the bread of oppression without fear, and wax fat upon the spoils of the people." He declared that his only purpose in opposing Hutchinson was to awaken in his fellow citizens "the true Spirit of Patriotism, and to stir up a manly Opposition against the Attempt of any Governor or Lieutenant Governor whatever, to infringe the Rights of the People." He regarded himself as a defender of the common people against those merchants and politicians who were piling up large fortunes and power by taking advantage of fluctuations in the price of gold to ship colonial currency to England. These men, Otis said, were "forging chains and shackles for their country"; and Thomas Hutchinson, the most arbitrary of this oligarchical crew, must be shorn of his offices before popular liberty would be secure.[26]

Otis and Adams fanned the flames in Massachusetts Bay so vigorously that the "Rage for Patriotism" spread through New England until it was said there was "scarce a cobler or porter

---

[25] Mauduit, 39, 78, 97. *Boston Gazette*, April 4, 1763. Mass. Archives, 26, *Hutchinson Corr.*, II, 30. *Bernard Papers*, IV, Bernard to the Earl of Shelburne, Dec. 22, 1766.

[26] *Boston Gazette*, Jan. 11, 1762 (Supplement); April 4, 1763.

but had turn'd mountebank in politicks" and set himself up as a village Hampden. Through the *Boston Gazette,* which gained the reputation of being the "most factious paper in America," the Boston patriots "Spit their Venom" at the governor and Thomas Hutchinson. Governor Bernard soon saw the true nature of the opposition with which he was faced. He realized that he was dealing with the "genuine Descendants of the Faction" which had driven out governors Shute, Burnet, and Belcher, and which, "like a Body corporate," carried on the tradition of hostility to royal government. It was clear to Bernard that he would not find the "ease and quiet" he sought in Massachusetts while Otis and Adams continued to keep the colony in ferment.[27]

By arousing Massachusetts patriotism, Otis produced a remarkable burst of activity in the clubs and secret societies which abounded in Boston. The Merchants Club, which met at the British Coffee House, gave him valuable aid in opposing the writs of assistance and the vice-admiralty system. The Boston Masonic Society peppered Hutchinson and the royal government from its meeting place in "Adjutant Trowel's *long Garret,*" where it was said more sedition, libels, and scurrility were hatched than in all the garrets in Grubstreet.[28] Otis and his Masonic brethren became such adept muckrakers that Hutchinson's friends believed they must have "ransak'd Billingsgate and the Stews" for mud to sling at the Massachusetts aristocracy. No less active was the Monday Night Club, composed of radical politicians headed by James Otis and Sam Adams, where the talk ran to "curious anecdotes about governors, counsellors, representatives, demagogues, merchants, &c." One of Otis's first steps had been to make allies of those redoubtable "trumpeters of sedition," the "black regiment" of Congregational ministers; and scarcely a patriot club was without a divine who lent an odor of sanctity to what conservatives believed would otherwise have been rank treason. "The Garrets . . . were

---

[27] *Boston Evening Post,* March 7, 1763. *Bernard Papers,* IV, Bernard to Pownall, July 20, 1765; Bernard to the Earl of Shelburne, Jan. 24, 1767.

[28] *Bernard Papers,* II, Bernard to Pownall, July 6, 1761; Aug. 28, 1761. *Boston News Letter,* March 24, 1763. *Boston Evening Post,* March 14, 1763.

crowded with the Rabble in full Divan," wrote one of Otis's
enemies, "with a Clergyman to praeside, whose Part was to
declaim on Politicks & Sedition." Frequently, this "ghostly
father" who "huddled promiscuously" with mechanics, lawyers,
and porters in some snug attic in North Boston was the
Reverend Dr. Samuel Cooper, pastor of the Brattle Street
Church which Sam Adams attended.[29] Hutchinson's friends
declared the patriots had fooled no one by hiding behind clergymen's skirts while they concocted sedition in backstairs hide-
outs. They longed to smoke these politicians and priests out
of their garrets, but the patriots stoutly refused to come into the
open.

By far the most important of these patriot clubs was the
Boston Caucus, which was still, as it had been in Deacon Adams's
day, the ladder by which politicians climbed into town offices
and the General Court. This "venerable Company," of which
Sam Adams was among the most prominent, usually met in
the garret of Tom Dawes's house on Purchase Street, where they
drank flip, chose town officers, and smoked tobacco "till you cannot see from one end of the garret to the other."[30] Like other
"Garretters," many members of the Caucus Club were men
whom Thomas Hutchinson considered the "rabble" of Boston,
but Sam Adams loved democratic company and felt thoroughly
at home among the shipyard workers, masons, and politicians
who crowded into Tom Dawes's attic. Aristocratic gentlemen often lamented that Boston was a "complete democracy"
in which the people's thinking was done for them by Sam
Adams and a few other wily politicians who controlled the
town offices. At the Caucus Club, moderators, selectmen,
assessors, tax collectors, wardens, firewards, and representatives
were picked by Adams and his friends several weeks before the
election. The nominees were then sent up to the Merchants'
Club for approval. Rarely was this ticket agreed upon by the
"Grand Corkass" and Merchants' Club defeated in Boston

---

[29] *The Works of John Adams*, II, 162. Peter Oliver, 102. *Massachusetts Gazette*, Jan. 11, 1776. Mass. Archives, 27, *Hutchinson Corr.*, III, 122. Richard Frothingham, *The Life and Times of Joseph Warren* (1865), 15.

[30] *The Works of John Adams*, II, 144, 219.

elections. For example, when Sam Adams was chosen moderator of the Boston town meeting in May 1774, apparently by the spontaneous decision of the citizens, it had already been decided in the Caucus that Adams should be moderator.[31] The town meeting was little more than a rubber stamp for the Caucus, but Boston voters could not complain they were not given a good show when they cast their votes in Faneuil Hall. "For form's sake (as on College Commencement days)," Adams staged during the town meetings "a number of warm disputes . . . to entertain the lower sort, who are in an exstacy to find the old Roman Patriots still surviving." The people received oratory and Adams and his friends received the town offices — and both sides were satisfied with the exchange.[32]

In the eighteenth-century Massachusetts, a large tavern acquaintanceship was indispensable to a politician. As John Adams said, it was in taverns that "bastards, and legislators, are frequently begotten."[33] There political bosses bought votes with flip and rum and made themselves intimate with the tavern keeper, who himself was a political power to be reckoned with in every election. Travelers who put up at a Massachusetts tavern usually found it full of people "drinking drams, flip, toddy, carousing, swearing; but especially plotting with the landlord, to get him, at the next town meeting, an election either for selectmen or representative." Sam Adams discovered these taverns with their "tippling, nasty, vicious crew" excellent recruiting grounds for the mobs he later raised against the Tories and Crown officers. Adams himself was a familiar figure in Boston taverns; one of his choice nicknames among the Tories was "Sam the Publican." Indeed, Adams seemed equally at home in meetinghouse or tavern: he was as much at ease with deacons and parishioners as he was with the shipyard workers and artisans. From early life, Adams spent much time among the common people of North Boston and he gradually came to be regarded as their spokesman; but his family's social position and his own piety gave him great in-

---

[31] E. H. Goss, *Life of Paul Revere* (1891), II, 643 (Appendix).
[32] *Boston Evening Post*, March 21, 1763.
[33] *The Works of John Adams*, II, 85, 112, 126.

fluence among the middle-class townspeople. Adams dearly
loved a pot of ale, a good fire, and the company of mechanics
and shipyard workers of radical political opinions. Under Sam
Adams, Boston taverns became nurseries of revolution as well
as "nurseries of our legislators." He made the headquarters
of the Revolution the Green Dragon Tavern in Union Street,
where the Boston Caucus Club held its meetings and where
Sons of Liberty from the near-by shipyards, ropewalks, and
docks met to hear him hold forth against British tyranny and
the Tories. At the Bunch of Grapes in King's Street, Adams
and the Whigs discussed the British Constitution and the Massachusetts Charter, and in the Salutation Tavern in Salutation
Alley they plotted the downfall of the royal government.
Thus, the setting of much of the preliminary work of the
Revolution in Massachusetts Bay is under the roof of a
Boston tavern.

It is surprising to find that Sam Adams, who belonged to almost every liberal political club in Boston and carried the
heaviest schedule of "lodge nights" of any patriot, was not a
Mason. Many of his friends were high-ranking Masons and
the Boston lodge did much to foster the Revolution, but Sam
Adams never joined the Masonic Society. It is true there
is no evidence that he was ever asked to become a Mason, but
Adams was one of the most popular clubmen in Boston and it
is hardly possible that the Boston lodge, which was filled with
fiery Whigs, would have missed an opportunity to bring him
in. But Adams disliked secret societies where ceremonial
ritual was practised, and he always distrusted political organizations which he had not had a hand in creating. He preferred to
revolutionize New England through the Whig Clubs, committees of correspondence, and caucuses, — over all of which
his control was certain, — rather than by means of Masonic
groups where his schemes might be disapproved. Notwithstanding its services in the Revolution, Adams never showed
that he bore any love towards Masonry.

Despite Otis's early success in reviving the Massachusetts
Country Party, it soon suffered a sharp decline. Without a
supply of fresh grievances, Otis found it impossible to keep the

colony in a flame: writs of assistance lost their novelty, and, after an unpromising beginning, Hutchinson became a popular Chief Justice. Otis lost control of the Massachusetts House of Representatives, where the governor's friends outnumbered his party two to one, although Crown officers complained there were still too many "Inkeepers, Retailers, & yet more inferior Orders of Men" to listen to Otis's "mobbish oratory." [34] Governor Bernard again began to believe that Massachusetts Bay was a haven for a royal governor who sought peace and quiet; the government ran along "with the utmost harmony & good humour"; governor and Assembly never met without exchanging compliments and well-wishes; and Bernard seemed likely to become highly popular. He considered the people in general "extremely well disposed to Government." [35] The colony was still riding the crest of war prosperity; there was yet no evidence of British tyranny; and when Hutchinson declared that Massachusetts possessed "as great civil and religious liberties as any people under heaven," he seemed to have the better of the argument against Otis and Adams, who shrieked tyranny against the royal government. Most New Englanders wished to settle down to enjoy the good fortune brought them by the Seven Years' War rather than help Otis and Adams turn the province topsy-turvy because Hutchinson held too many political offices for the people's good. "When God in his mercy is delivering us from our foreign enemies," asked Thomas Hutchinson, "shall we be so ungrateful as to endeavour to raise animosities and civil wars among ourselves?" And most New Englanders answered with a hearty amen. [36]

Otis's failure was due largely to his inability to win control of the Massachusetts Council. Many years before, in the *Independent Advertiser*, Sam Adams had said that the Council was a great stumblingblock to political liberalism; and Otis's experience from 1763 to 1766 completely confirmed this judg-

[34] Peter Oliver, 36, 37.
[35] *Bernard Papers*, IV, Bernard to the Earl of Shelburne, Dec. 22, 1766. Hutchinson, III, 254.
[36] *Bernard Papers*, III, Bernard to Pownall, May 5, 1765. *Massachusetts Gazette*, April 7, 1763.

ment. The Council was a stronghold of conservatism manned
by the governor's supporters, who kept a tight rein upon the
unruly Lower House. Although its members were elected
by the House of Representatives, the governor's friends were
usually present in the Lower House in such force that the
Council was filled with those well-born gentry who formed the
backbone of the Massachusetts Court Party. During such
crises as the Land Bank affair, when the representatives elected
Deacon Adams to the Council, the governor kept the Council
loyal by negativing the radicals. Almost invulnerable in the
Council, the royal governor possessed a strong party in the
Lower House which, during periods of political tranquillity, held
the balance of power. As James Otis learned, it was no easy
matter for the Country Party to wrest control of the House of
Representatives from the governor's friends, for successive royal
governors had strengthened their political fences by handing out
offices in the judiciary and militia to their supporters, thereby
creating a machine which served to keep the patriots out of
power for many years. Militia regimentals had great attraction
for country squires and the governor purchased their loyalty with
commissions and special favors. Landowners like John Murray
of Rutland, whose estates were the largest in Worcester County,
received a colonelcy in the militia besides numerous other
bounties from the governor; and Timothy Ruggles of Hardwick, likewise a militia colonel and extensive landowner, was the
leader of the governor's party in the House of Representatives.
Scarcely a country town in Massachusetts was without the governor's appointees; and, as they were chosen from a highly influential class, western Massachusetts became the most loyal part
of the province and repeatedly forestalled the Boston Whigs
when they attempted to lead the colony into a quarrel with King
and Parliament.[87]

Even when the British government unleashed another
"menacing monster" upon New Englanders, — fully as terrifying as the writs of assistance, — Otis was unable to awaken
patriotic fervor in the province outside of Boston. In 1764,

[87] Jonathan Smith, Toryism in Worcester County, *Mass. Hist. Soc. Proceedings* (1915), XLVIII, 15, 16, 33.

George Grenville, Chancellor of the British Exchequer, began his fatal quest of a colonial revenue by clapping new duties on Spanish wines imported into the colonies and reducing the duty of Spanish, Dutch, and French West India molasses from six-pence to threepence a gallon. Considering New Englanders' well-known aversion to taxation, it might be supposed that the Sugar Act, as it was called, was warmly welcomed by the "Saints" because it lowered taxes. But this piece of legislation produced, Governor Bernard wrote, "a greater alarm in this country than the taking of Fort William Henry did in 1757." [88] Boston merchants exclaimed that it was an "unformed Monster that will Devour all before It" and compel every trader and businessman to "hold the Plough, The Syth and Reaping Hook." [39] New Englanders had no quarrel with the pro-hibitively high rates on foreign molasses established by the Molasses Act of 1733 because no attempt was made to collect them. His Majesty's officers of the customs in Boston had notoriously short memories of the laws of trade, and it required only a stiff swig of rum to make them forget the existence of the Molasses Act. Had the Molasses Act been enforced to the letter, New England's commerce would have been destroyed, because the British West India islands were alone unable to supply the New England distilleries with sufficient molasses. But as long as smuggling from the French and West Indian islands was winked at, New England prospered, although the royal revenue from American commerce dwindled until the ex-pense of maintaining the customs had become greater than the income. By reducing the duty until its collection was feasible, George Grenville proposed to give American customs officers something to do besides drink rum with smugglers and make pocket money by conniving at violations of the laws of trade. His policy spread greater consternation among New England merchants than had the French and Indians during their bloody frontier forays in 1757, because it was realized that he

[88] *Select Letters on the Trade and Government of America* (London, 1774), 9. *Bernard Papers*, Bernard to Pownall, Dec. 3, 1765.
[39] *John Powell Letters*, MS. Mass. Hist. Soc.; John Powell to Christopher Champion, April 9, 1764.

planned to tighten imperial bounds and centralize its administration. New England's economic well-being depended upon a continuation of the laxity and free play of the early eighteenth-century Empire; and it was apparent that if George Grenville reorganized the British Empire, New England would be forced to pay a heavy penalty for having permitted its maritime and commercial ambitions to overleap the restraints laid by British mercantile policy upon its colonies.

Sam Adams's preoccupation with politics and mismanagement had long since put his own business beyond the power of injury by the British government, but he could protest as a citizen if not as a brewer and merchant. He found ample cause for alarm in the Sugar Act, which, he pointed out, would bring trade "to the lowest Ebb, if not totally obstruct & ruin it," but his anxiety was chiefly caused by the broad lines of policy Grenville laid down in the preamble to the act. Here Grenville gave strong hints of the reorganization of the Empire contemplated by the British Ministry. The preamble states that "Whereas it is expedient that new provisions and regulations should be established for improving the revenue of this Kingdom . . . and whereas it is just and necessary that a revenue should be raised . . . for defraying the expenses of defending, protecting, and securing the same. . . ." It was a new departure for Parliament to lay duties on commodities for the purpose of raising a revenue; and the implication that the taxes realized from the Sugar Act were to be used to support a colonial military establishment was an abrupt break with the traditional policy of the mother country. Taxes on commodities had hitherto been laid by Parliament only for the regulation of trade, and the mother country had shouldered the expenses of the regular army in the colonies. In the instructions to Boston's representatives in the General Court written by Sam Adams in 1764, he denied Parliament's right to impose such taxes upon the colonies. Almost alone of his contemporaries, Sam Adams protested from the first against the Sugar Act on the ground that Parliament was overstepping its authority. If the House of Commons could compel New England to pay ruinous taxes upon such a staple as molasses, Adams believed that the colonies held their liberty on uncertain tenure indeed.   Once the tax on molasses were paid, he warned, the colonists would find themselves saddled with more taxes by Parliament: "If our Trade may be taxed why not our Lands?" he asked.   "Why not the Produce of our Lands & every thing we possess or make use of?   This we apprehend annihilates our Charter Right to govern & tax ourselves. . . .   It strikes at our British Privileges."   Thus, as early as 1764, Sam Adams raised the cry of no taxation without representation.[40]

The Sugar Act proved that Bostonians had in Sam Adams one of the best watchdogs of colonial liberty in New England, but this tax alone would not have produced a revolutionary movement in the American colonies.   Indeed, there was so little resistance that George Grenville was encouraged to believe Americans would tamely swallow all the pills he had prepared for them.   In Boston, it was said that the British government had sold Americans to the West India planters, but Bostonians found New England yeomen slow to rally to their aid.   In Massachusetts, as in other provinces, there was latent hostility between town and country which occasionally flared into open hatred.   This antagonism greatly embarrassed Boston patriots when they stood in need of country support, for without the aid of farmers and back-country politicians, Boston had little political influence.   Of the one hundred and twenty members of the Massachusetts House of Representatives, the metropolis sent only four.   This meagre representation made it necessary for Bostonians to look to the country for their principal strength in the legislature.   When Sam Adams spoke in 1764 of the danger of taxes on land if the Sugar Act were made a precedent, he was attempting to show landowners in the province their community of interest with Boston in protesting against taxes on commodities for the purpose of raising a revenue.   Although the Massachusetts House of Representatives petitioned Parliament to repeal the Sugar Act, the country was far slower than the seaport towns in catching fire against Parliamentary trade duties.   Bostonians complained that many of the country towns sent representatives to the General

[40] *The Writings of Samuel Adams,* I, 5.

Court "who are profess'd enemies to trade," and Sam Adams found that many rural voters were "so careless in the Choice of their representatives" as to send to Boston men who became Governor Bernard's tools against the patriots.[41]   Country delegates to the General Court, like Artemas Ward of Shrewsbury, who later became one of Adams's staunchest adherents in rural Massachusetts, showed little excitement over the Sugar Act.[42]   In attempting to arouse Massachusetts farmers against the British government in 1764, Boston agitators bumped their heads squarely against rural conservatism and the strong inclination of countrymen to regard trade as Boston's own concern.   It required the Stamp Act to unite town and country and, by giving every class a grievance against the British government, enable Sam Adams to create a formidable revolutionary party in Massachusetts with Boston at its head.

The ill fortune that had overtaken the Massachusetts Country Party deeply dismayed James Otis.   Early in 1765, he attempted to give his earlier radical doctrines such a conservative whitewashing that his friends suspected he had sold out to Hutchinson.   Otis had been completely unable to remove Hutchinson and the "oligarchs" from their political offices; and Governor Bernard had entrenched himself, in spite of Otis and Adams, behind a party built up by means of patronage and favoritism.   In 1765, on the eve of the Stamp Act, James Otis lamented that he had "contended so much in vain" against Hutchinson and the Governor's party; and Hutchinson's friends, believing themselves well out of danger from Otis, said he had never succeeded in raising a flame in the colony: "With all his puffing and blowing," they rejoiced, "he has been able only to raise a smoke."[43]   Throughout New England, farmers swore that Hutchinson had been "most damnably abused, and slandered, and belied"; and few had been shaken in their conviction that he was an honest man, a philosopher, an "eminent saint" of the Congregational Church.[44]   To so little purpose had

[41] *Boston Evening Post*, May 12, 1760.   *The Writings of Samuel Adams*, II, 165.   *Boston Gazette*, May 14, 1764.   Hutchinson, III, 109, 166.
[42] Charles Martyn, *Life of Artemas Ward* (1921), 33.
[43] *Boston Gazette*, May 13, 1765.   *Boston Evening Post*, March 28, 1763.
[44] *The Works of John Adams*, II, 189, 193.

Adams and Otis labored before the attempts of the British government to tax the colonies by means of the Stamp Act and Townshend duties brought about Hutchinson's downfall and destroyed the conservative party in New England.

III

SAM ADAMS AND THE STAMP ACT

IMPERIAL defense was the rock upon which the old British Empire split. The Seven Years' War demonstrated that the colonies were utterly unable to make concerted military effort even when French and Indians were on the warpath along their frontiers. The requisition system by which the colonies had for generations given aid to the Crown — when they felt so disposed — broke down under the strain of a prolonged war. After peace had been made at Paris in 1763, British statesmen might well feel there was acute need of imperial reorganization. Although Great Britain had carved out a huge empire during the war and defeated the combined forces of France and Spain, Englishmen feared that all that had been gained by seven years of war might be lost in a single campaign if the British American colonies were not given strong military protection.[1] Yet England had emerged from the war with a staggering debt and taxpayers groaned at the thought of supporting large armies in the colonies. Unlike modern taxpayers, eighteenth-century British taxpayers had a decisive voice in government, and they let it be known unequivocally in 1763 that however necessary a colonial military establishment, they would no longer foot the bill.

When the British government learned that Englishmen were unwilling to pay for imperial defense, it began to look for other sources of revenue. It was inevitable that British statesmen should turn to the colonies as a promising reservoir. The American colonies were yet untouched by direct taxation

[1] George Grenville, *The Justice and Necessity of Taxing the American Colonies Demonstrated, together with a Vindication of the Authority of Parliament* (London, 1766), 10, 11.

by the British Parliament; they had become wealthy during the Seven Years' War; and the money that the British government was seeking was to be used for the colonists' own defense and spent in the colonies themselves. Moreover, it was widely believed in England that the defense of the American colonies against a French invasion was the sole cause of the recent war — in which, it was said, all the profits had gone to Americans while Englishmen paid the bill.[2] The shortest way to put hard-pressed English squires into a good humor was to saddle the colonists with part of the burden. Englishmen imagined Americans to be prosperous farmers living on the fat of the land or rich merchants who made fabulous profits in smuggling; and few doubted that the colonists could easily afford to support the garrisons that were to be sent them. Even after Americans had pleaded poverty in protest against taxation, Englishmen were unshaken in their conviction that the colonists were miserly rascals whose bulging money bags were more than ample to pay their share of imperial expense.

George Grenville, the Chancellor of the Exchequer, who had begun his imperial housecleaning with the Sugar Act of 1764, proposed in Parliament in 1764 that taxes in the form of stamp duties be laid upon the colonies to support their armed establishments. In order to sugar-coat the pill, Grenville gave the colonies a year of grace in which to inform their London agents of a more satisfactory method of raising the desired revenue. But the colonies frittered away the year without suggesting any alternative to the stamp duty, other than reverting to the old requisition system — with the result that when Parliament met in 1765, Grenville again brought forward his scheme for colonial revenue. He believed a stamp duty on American newspapers, legal documents, and commercial papers to be "the easiest, the most equal and the most certain that can be chosen." Among its advantages — to which Americans were unfortunately quite blind — was that few collection officers were required, the burden was spread lightly over the

---

[2] Thomas Whately, *The Regulations Lately made concerning the Colonies, and the Taxes imposed upon them, considered* (London, 1765), 3, 102. Grenville, 12.

whole population, and it fell on the colonies in proportion to their wealth. Undoubtedly, Grenville considered he was doing the colonists a good turn by favoring them with such a faultless tax as the stamp duty.[3]

As a result, Grenville and the British Ministry were taken completely by surprise at the manner in which Americans received the Stamp Act. Instead of erecting statues to Grenville and hailing him as their benefactor, they burned him in effigy and promised to string him on the gallows should he ever set foot in America. Even more startling was the growth of colonial unity as a result of the Stamp Act. Although the colonial mind always remained a mystery to George Grenville, he had reason for bewilderment in seeing Americans uniting against the mother country in 1765 when a few years before they had displayed a "peevish reluctance to associate and unite" while the French and Indians were pounding at their frontier.[4] The Seven Years' War had led many Englishmen to believe that the provinces were beyond hope of federation, and the reports of English travelers in the colonies confirmed this conviction: "Fire and water," said Andrew Burnaby shortly before the passage of the Stamp Act, "are not more heterogeneous than the different colonies in North America."[5] Colonial union was almost as unexpected to the colonists themselves as to British statesmen. Before 1765, it was said, the provinces were "ever at a variance, and foolishly jealous of each other," and united action was "what the most zealous colonists never could have expected."[6] Clear-sighted observers on both sides of the Atlantic believed colonial unity impossible because of the great differences between the provinces in manners, religion, and interest. Nevertheless, when confronted by the Stamp

[3] Whately, 101. Joseph Galloway, *Historical and Political Reflections on the Rise and Progress of the American Rebellion* (London, 1780), 12.

[4] Grenville, *An Application of Political Rules to Great Britain, Ireland, and America* (London, 1766), 80.

[5] Andrew Burnaby, *Travels through the Middle Settlements in North America* (1798), 121.

[6] James Otis, *A Vindication of the British Colonies against the Aspersions of the Halifax Gentleman, in his letter to a Rhode Island friend* (Boston, 1765). Frothingham, 21.

Act, colonial particularism began to crumble and America was "awakened, alarmed, restless, & disaffected."[7]   "What a Blessing to us has the Stamp Act eventually . . . prov'd," exclaimed Sam Adams.   ". . . When the Colonys saw the Common Danger they at the same time saw their mutual Dependence."[8]   From the frontier to the seaboard and from Pensacola to Quebec, there was scarcely a family who had not heard of the Stamp Act and who did not regard it with dread, although, as Thomas Hutchinson said, many had little idea what it actually was.[9]

Within a year of the passage of the Stamp Act by the British House of Commons, the American colonies were covered with Societies whose purpose was to nullify the act.   The members of these clubs called themselves "Sons of Liberty" — a name derived from Isaac Barré's speech in Parliament in behalf of the colonies during the Stamp Act debate.   By forming military alliances between the colonies, driving out the stamp masters and burning the stamps, the Sons of Liberty prevented the execution of the Stamp Act and usurped much of the real power of government in America.   During the course of the Revolution they assumed many different names, but whether they called themselves committees of correspondence, committees of safety, or "true-born Whigs," the Sons of Liberty of 1765 were the radicals who led the colonies into revolution against the mother country.

When news of the Stamp Act reached the colonies, these patriotic societies spread rapidly over America.   "The whole continent," George Bancroft said, "rang with the cheering name of the Sons of Liberty."   But not all of the clubs that called themselves Sons of Liberty were founded spontaneously to resist the Stamp Act.   Many had been in existence for years and had been created with no thought of resisting the "tyranny" of the mother country: their purpose was rather to combat the colonial aristocracy and give the unprivileged class a share of political power.   The muster rolls of the "Ancient and Honor-

---

[7] George Bancroft, *History of the United States*, V, 241.
[8] *The Writings of Samuel Adams*, I, 109.
[9] Mass. Archives, 26, *Hutchinson Corr.*, II, 198.

able Mechanical Company" of Baltimore, which had been formed in 1763 and became the Sons of Liberty in 1765, show that its membership was made up almost entirely of small tradesmen and artisans.[10] In Charleston, South Carolina, the nucleus of the Sons of Liberty was the long-established Fireman's Association; in Philadelphia, it was the "Heart-and-Hand Fire Company." And in Boston, where Sam Adams became the leading Son of Liberty, the Sons of Liberty sprang from the Caucus Club, which had been in existence for a half-century. Thus, the political machinery with which American patriots opposed British oppression and seized power from the royal government was firmly established before 1765.

The Boston Sons of Liberty, led by Sam Adams, boasted some of the most fiery, unruly Whigs on the continent. They were recruited largely from the wharfingers, artisans and shipyard workers of North Boston — the class of men who had warmly supported Deacon Adams and his inflationary Land Bank in 1740 and who were eager in 1765 to punish the Tory upper class. Although many wealthy merchants were known as Sons of Liberty and made an impressive show with their chariots in parades and celebrations, most of them were patriots out of prudence: when Boston swarmed with patriot mobs, it was well to be known as a Son of Liberty. The true Sons of Liberty — those who controlled the mobs and Boston elections — were a small group of politicians from the Caucus Club who met in a counting room on the second floor of Chase and Speakman's distillery. This building stood in Hanover Square near the Tree of Liberty — a huge oak that had been planted, it was significantly pointed out, in 1646, three years before the execution of Charles I. Tories always believed it important that the Liberty Boys had their meeting place conveniently near a liquor supply such as that afforded by Chase and Speakman's distillery, since it was supposed their courage arose chiefly "from the steams of their poisonous rum." [11]

Those Sons of Liberty who met in Hanover Square were

[10] G. W. McCreary, *The Ancient and Honorable Mechanical Company of Baltimore* (1901), 13–19.
[11] *Pennsylvania Journal*, Nov. 21, 1765.

known as the "Loyall Nine." They were John Avery, a distiller and secretary to the club; John Smith, a brazier; Thomas Crafts, a painter; Benjamin Edes, printer of the *Boston Gazette*; Stephen Cleverly, a brazier; Thomas Chase, a distiller; Joseph Field, a ship captain; George Trott, a jeweler; and Henry Bass, a cousin of Sam Adams. When John Adams visited the "Loyall Nine" in their room above Chase and Speakman's distillery, he was entertained with "punch, wine, pipes, and tobacco, biscuit and cheese, &c"; and Sam Adams sat down with them to a "very Genteel Supper" topped off with patriotic toasts.[12] Although neither of the Adamses was a member of the "Loyall Nine," Sam Adams's connection with them was very close. He spent many convivial evenings and ate Sunday dinners with Henry Bass and other Sons of Liberty; and, since the "Loyall Nine" were for the most part young fire-eating Whigs, they looked to Sam Adams, an older and more experienced plotter against the royal government, for leadership. Adams and the "Loyall Nine" spirited up the mobs which terrorized Boston during the revolutionary period. Whenever a riot or meeting of the citizens at Liberty Tree was planned, it was the "Loyall Nine" who placarded the town with notices during the small hours of the night, urging the townspeople to be on hand for the event. They kept their identity secret and wished it to be believed that the mobs they set in motion were spontaneous outbreaks of violence from the "lower sort."[13] But it will be seen that Boston was controlled by a "trained mob" and that Sam Adams was its keeper.

After the full consequences of the Stamp Act were seen, George Grenville's critics accused him of having destroyed Great Britain's best security for keeping intact her colonial empire: the love of the colonists for the mother country and the differences in sentiments and interest that kept the colonies at variance. The Stamp Act did not work such a miracle in America, but it taught the colonists the value of united action against the mother country and began the revolutionary turmoil

---

[12] *The Works of John Adams*, II, 178, 179. *Mass. Hist. Soc. Proceedings*, XLIV (1911), 688, 689.

[13] *Mass. Hist. Soc. Proceedings*, XLIV (1911), 688, 689.

that was to disrupt the Empire within a decade.   What manner
of "menacing monster" was this that produced such far-reaching
changes in the colonies, hitherto hopelessly disunited and firmly
bound to the mother country?

Despite Grenville's assertion that the stamp duty was an
equable and easy form of taxation, it is true that Parliament had
never before laid a tax of its kind upon the colonies: the only
precedent for Parliamentary taxation was port duties for the
regulation of trade.   The experience of the British government in attempting to impose new forms of taxation upon English taxpayers should have been a warning of the fate of the
Stamp Act in America.   Wise after the event, Englishmen
saw that the novelty of the Stamp Act alone was sufficient to
have aroused the colonists' opposition.   Like all property
owners, New Englanders dreaded an increase in taxes, and
they were reluctant to give up such an admirable scheme as the
requisition system.   The revenue derived from the Stamp Act
was to be used to support armies in the colonies, but Americans
could see no necessity for maintaining a colonial military establishment: the only enemy visible in 1765, they said, was
"a few ragged Indians" and beaten Frenchmen.   It was remembered that in the seventeenth century when Massachusetts
was surrounded with foes the British government had left the
colony to defend itself alone against "the combined powers of
France, hell, Indian Savages, and the corrupt administration
of those times." [14]   It seemed probable to Americans, therefore, that a large share of the Stamp Act revenue would be
used by the Ministry to buy up the British House of Commons,
make jobs in the colonies for Court favorites, and keep "lazy
fellows in ease, idleness, or luxury, in mother Britain's lap."
If Great Britain had run itself into debt during the Seven
Years' War, the colonists believed themselves no more obliged
to assist her with their pocketbooks than was the "Great
Mogul." [15]

The Stamp Act required that all colonial newspapers, legal
documents, and commercial papers bear a stamp which could

[14] *Boston Gazette,* July 29, 1765; Aug. 12, 1765.
[15] *Ibid.,* Aug. 5 and 12, 1765.

be purchased at prices ranging from a halfpenny to upward of twenty shillings from stamp masters stationed throughout the colonies. Although the price of the stamps was not onerous, Grenville required that they be paid for in specie. Paper money as a political issue was almost dead in Massachusetts, but the necessity of paying for stamps in specie was certain to revive it in an acute form. There was so little hard money in the colonies that Americans denounced the Stamp Act as a "devouring monster" that would "inevitably pump and extort from us all the remaining coin of the continent" and plunge them into monetary chaos. It was believed in America that the supply would not last a year after the Stamp Act went into effect, and this dismal prospect gave Sam Adams a strong talking point in urging resistance.[16]

Grenville's argument for the stamp duty — that it fell equally upon all — was one of the chief reasons it produced an outburst in the colonies. By falling upon all, it gave all a grievance: unlike the Sugar Act of 1764, the Stamp Act brought home British "tyranny" to every class. Because deeds, wills, and legal documents were made subject to stamp duties, the cost of litigation was raised in the colonies. Americans of all classes were notorious in the eighteenth century for the frequency with which they haled one another into court; and since the common people were most often involved in lawsuits, it was argued that the Stamp Act would fall most heavily upon them. It was said that even the "meanest peasant" in America would feel the effect of the Stamp Act: James Otis declared the "middling more necessitous and labouring people" would bear its brunt; and Benjamin Franklin characterized it as a tax upon the poor "and a tax upon them for being poor." [17] Moreover, by increasing the expense of lawsuits, the Stamp Act threatened to destroy the practice of colonial lawyers. Thus, at the outset of its quarrel with the colonies, the British government aroused the enmity of one of the most influential classes of men in America.

[16] *Boston Gazette*, Sept. 16, 1765.
[17] *The Examination of Dr. Franklin Relative to the Repeal of the American Stamp Act* (London, 1767), 30.

Vigorous opposition to the Stamp Act did not spring up in-
stantaneously in the colonies, nor were the provinces equally
active in resistance. Although it was evident that New Englanders were alarmed when they first learned of the Stamp Act,
there was no reason to suppose they would resort to violence
to prevent its execution. Governor Bernard believed Massachusetts would save its dignity with a perfunctory protest
against Parliamentary taxation and would then swallow the
Stamp Act, albeit with a wry face. Hutchinson thought the
people would pay the duties, and several patriots were so certain the act would be obeyed that they tried to have themselves
or their friends and relations appointed stamp masters. Nor
was the Massachusetts House of Representatives' petition to
the House of Commons against the Stamp Act calculated to inspire fears of conflict between mother country and colony. Indeed, this petition was so moderate in tone that Sam Adams
considered it a serious blot upon the reputation of the Bay
Colony.[18]

The "alarum bell" to the Stamp Act was first sounded not in
Massachusetts but in Virginia, where in 1765, at the instigation
of Patrick Henry, the House of Burgesses adopted the "Virginia Resolves." In contrast to the mild protest made by
Massachusetts, the Virginians made a straightforward denial
of the right of the British government to impose internal taxes
upon the colonies. Indeed, the House of Burgesses went so
far beyond the position taken by New Englanders that James
Otis was at first shocked by the radicalism of the Virginia resolves and pronounced them treason. Sam Adams had anticipated in 1764 the Virginia doctrine of no taxation without representation, but most Massachusetts patriots seemed indisposed
to burn their fingers with the red-hot sedition now flung at the
British government by Patrick Henry. Yet it was not long
before Adams was joined by all New England patriots, including Otis himself, in praising the Virginians' stand against British tyranny and in lamenting that Massachusetts' protest had

[18] Hutchinson, III, 114–115. Mauduit, 163. *Bernard Papers*, III, Bernard to Richard Jackson, Nov. 17, 1764.

been written in milk and water.[19] Oxenbridge Thacher, the Boston representative in the General Court, whose seat Sam Adams was soon to occupy, exclaimed of the Virginians: "Oh yes — they are men! they are noble spirits! It kills me to think of the lethargy and stupidity that prevails here." The "frozen politicians" of Massachusetts Bay were contrasted with the fiery Southerners, who "first asserted their Rights with *decent Firmness.*" Not to be outdone by Virginians, the Massachusetts patriots launched a vigorous attack upon the royal government: "It is inconceivable," said Governor Bernard, "how they (the Virginia Resolves) have roused up the Boston Politicians, & have been the Occasion of a fresh inundation of factious & insolent pieces in the popular Newspapers." [20] Here began the race between Virginia and Massachusetts for the leadership of the American colonies against British "tyranny." As will be seen, this rivalry did much to precipitate the outbreak of war between the mother country and colonies.

It was not difficult for Sam Adams to raise a storm in Massachusetts against the Stamp Act, because post-war depression had begun to grip the colony. Times were hard in New England in 1765 and the citizens were complaining they were already "miserably burthen'd and oppress'd with taxes." [21] Governor Bernard admitted that Massachusetts was in no position to stand any considerable taxation by the British government because the taxpayers were carrying a heavy load from their expenditures in the recent war. In Boston, in particular, a series of business failures gave the townspeople a bitter taste of depression. A banker failed for 170,000 pounds; many merchants were forced to close shop; and a "general Consternation" spread through the province as substantial Boston mercantile houses began to go into bankruptcy. Even John Han-

---

[19] Peter Oliver, 70. Hutchinson, III, 119 (note). Mass. Archives, 26, *Hutchinson Corr.*, II, 143. *Boston Gazette*, March 25, 1765; Aug. 11, 1766 (Supplement). Harbottle Dorr files, Mass. Hist. Soc.

[20] *The Works of John Adams*, X, 287. *Boston Gazette*, July 8, 1765; Aug. 11, 1766 (Supplement). *Bernard Papers*, IV, Bernard to Pownall, July 20, 1765.

[21] *Boston Gazette*, Feb. 28, 1763.

cock, the wealthiest merchant in the province, felt "a most prodigious shock" and said it was "like an Earthquake, to the Town."
Creditors squeezed their debtors so tightly that the whole colony was brought to the verge of panic. Thus, when New Englanders learned they were to be taxed by the British Parliament,
they were already deeply indebted to their own provincial treasury and to each other. On the eve of the Stamp Act, there
seemed never to have been "a time of more general distress
and calamity since the first beginnings of the country." [22]

Sam Adams rode into power on this wave of political and
economic unrest that swept over Massachusetts in 1765. The
times were bad, Bostonians reasoned, and there was need of a
man like Sam Adams who had long been famous for his "great
zeal for Liberty." In 1765 he was appointed by the town
meeting to draw up instructions for the guidance of the Boston
representatives in the General Court. The death of Oxenbridge Thacher shortly after gave Adams the opportunity he
had awaited for twenty years. The Boston town meeting was
called to elect Thacher's successor and Sam Adams was among
the candidates. On the first ballot, Adams failed to win a majority, but the Caucus Club quickly rallied to his support and
on the next trial Adams was triumphantly sent up to the General Court. [23]

Boston was ready in 1765 to take a plunge into radicalism and
the citizens could not have found a better man than Sam Adams
to lead the way. The fact that a prison term for embezzling
public funds was hanging over Adams's head certainly had not
strengthened his love for the established order. In 1765, at
the time of his election to the Massachusetts House of Representatives, Adams stood a defaulter to the town of Boston and
county of Suffolk for over seven thousand pounds because of
shortages which appeared in his accounts as tax collector. He
had gotten himself into this predicament chiefly through lack

[22] *Bernard Papers*, V, Bernard to Richard Jackson, Oct. 22, 1765. *Letters
and Diary of John Rowe*, edited by A. R. Cunningham (1903), 75. A. E.
Brown, *John Hancock, His Book* (1898), 61. *Boston Gazette*, Sept. 16,
1765.
[23] *Boston Town Records*, 16th Report of the Records Commissioners
(1886), 157–158.

of business sense and his habit of keeping his financial affairs
in a baffling state of confusion.   When Sam Adams had been
named tax collector for the town of Boston in 1756, the citizens
should have taken warning from his record when, as a young
man, he had been financed by his father, but Boston, the Tories
said, was a "perfect Democracy" and a place had to be found
on the public payroll for such an influential member of the
Caucus Club as Sam Adams.   In his own defense, Adams
could truthfully boast that he had no extravagances and lived
as temperately as an old Puritan, although he did take a flyer
in Maine lands, like most Bostonians who could scrape a few
pounds together.   But Maine lands alone do not explain the
appalling arrears that began to appear in Adams's accounts as
tax collector.   Had he speculated in dozens of wildcat schemes
or lived in John Hancock's style, he could hardly have shown
a greater shortage than that which appeared in 1764.   Tories
suspected that Adams was a sanctimonious peculator and wondered how they had ever trusted him with a shilling.   Yet it
is probable that his defalcations were chiefly caused by the ease
with which money always managed to slip through his fingers.
Adams had already run through his father's estate, and had
he been given time, he probably would have brought Boston
itself to similar insolvency.

Sam Adams was everything a good tax collector should not
be: a kind-hearted, easy-going man who listened sympatheti-
cally to hard-luck stories and never pressed his debtors once convinced it would be a hardship for them to pay.   He was an
ideal collector from the taxpayers' point of view because he
seldom made an outright demand for money and was easily
put off for weeks, months, and even years.   When money was
promised on a certain day, Adams was rarely on hand to collect it.   Although such methods made him very popular in
Boston, they were sure to bring him trouble.   His shortages
grew alarmingly, and, to make matters worse, he began to take
money for his own use from the funds he had collected for
the town of Boston and Suffolk County.   It was clear that this
could not go on long before Adams would be compelled to account for his arrears, but he successfully postponed the reckon-

ing by mingling his last year's collections with those of the year following, thus keeping an apparent balance. But in 1764 the truth was finally discovered and his total deficit was shown to have reached the staggering total of seven thousand pounds. Bostonians liked him so well as a tax collector, however, that even after his defalcations had been exposed they enthusiastically reëlected him tax collector for another term.[24]

Just when Adams's prospects seemed blackest, news of the Stamp Act reached Boston and public attention was diverted from his financial irregularities. Had not the British government attempted to raise a colonial revenue at this critical juncture of Sam Adams's career, he might have stood trial in Boston for embezzlement. As a young man, he longed to change the social and political order in New England; and no doubt the exposure of his defalcations in 1764 reminded him sharply that he had nothing to lose and much to gain by driving out the "oligarchs" and seizing political power.

In the Massachusetts General Court, Sam Adams soon proved himself a thorn in the side of royal government. When the assembly met in October 1765, Bernard was dismayed to find that the "Faction in perpetual opposition to Government" swept everything before it and "what with inflammatory Speeches within doors, & the parades of the mob without entirely triumphed over the little remains of Government." In full possession of the House of Representatives, James Otis and Sam Adams began "driving on at a furious rate." [25] Under Otis's leadership, the House of Representatives appointed a committee of grievances which Governor Bernard uneasily observed was founded upon the precedent set by the last Parliament of Charles I. Within a fortnight of taking his seat, Sam Adams was elected to all the important committees and recognized as Otis's chief lieutenant. Because of his readiness to agree with others' proposals as long as no vital principle was sacrificed, Adams quickly became one of the most popular committeemen

[24] William Gordon, *History of the Rise, Progress, and Establishment of the Independence of the United States of America*, I, 348. *Boston Town Records*, 16th Report of the Records Commissioners (1886), 150.

[25] *Bernard Papers*, IV, Bernard to General Conway, Nov. 25, 1765; V, Bernard to Pownall, Oct. 26, 1765.

in the House; and this "pliableness and complaisance in these smaller matters" enabled him to succeed where a less adaptable man would have failed.[26] Whenever Adams was appointed to a committee he usually "pulled out a set of resolves, ready cut & dryed" for the edification of his fellow committeemen.[27] During his first term in the General Court, Adams produced so many resolves and wrote so many state papers that Hutchinson rightly blamed him for the House of Representatives' aggressive attacks upon the royal government. Although a newcomer to the House, Adams was the author of the Massachusetts Resolves of 1765 which were regarded in Boston as "the best digested, and the best of any on the continent" and which omit the acknowledgment of Parliamentary sovereignty usually found in the colonial state papers of this period.[28]

Virginia led the way in constitutional protest against the Stamp Act, but Massachusetts was foremost in riots. In the summer of 1765, Sam Adams determined to terrorize Andrew Oliver, Thomas Hutchinson's brother-in-law, who had been appointed stamp master of Massachusetts Bay, into resigning office in order that the stamps could not be distributed in the colony. During the night of August 14, 1765, the "Loyall Nine," probably acting under orders from Sam Adams, hung an effigy of Oliver on Liberty Tree, where it was found the next morning by the astonished citizens. The Crown officers at first supposed it was merely a boyish prank, but when the sheriff reported he could not take down the effigy without risking his life, they began to suspect that this was not altogether child's play. When one of the spectators at Liberty Tree asked Sam Adams, who was standing under the tree peering up at the effigy, who it was, Adams answered that "he did not know — he could not tell — he wanted to enquire."[29] Nevertheless, it soon became clear that Sam Adams and the Sons of Liberty

[26] Gordon, I, 206.

[27] *Bernard Papers*, V, Bernard to Pownall, Oct. 26, 1765.

[28] Hutchinson, III, 134.

[29] *The Works of John Adams*, II, 150 (note), 180. *Mass. Hist. Soc. Proceedings*, XLIV (1911), 688, 689. *Bernard Papers*, IV, Bernard to the Earl of Halifax, Aug. 15, 1765. *Letters from the Rev. Samuel Mather to his son*, 1759–1785, MSS. Mass. Hist. Soc., Aug. 17, 1765.

planned an eventful evening for Boston: the crowds that gathered on street corners throughout the afternoon grew by nightfall into a large mob that paraded around the Town House where the governor and Council were sitting, giving "three huzzas by way of Defiance" as it passed. After destroying a building recently erected near the water front by Oliver, which was believed to be designed as a stamp headquarters, the mob marched to Oliver's house and beheaded his effigy. After giving the stamp master this significant foretaste of what he might expect at their hands, the rioters built a huge bonfire on Fort Hill. The demonstration was now thought to be over, and the gentlemen and "persons of character" who had been in the mob to keep order, "disguised with trousers & Jackets," went home for the night, leaving the rest of the rioters around the fire. But a large number of the mob felt they had spent a very tame evening: therefore, no sooner were the gentlemen rioters out of sight than they rushed down Fort Hill to Oliver's house, led by Andrew Mackintosh, a cobbler and chief of the South End mob. After shattering Oliver's windowpanes with a hail of brickbats, several ruffians broke into the house and began to search for the stamp master, swearing they would kill him if he fell into their hands.[30] Governor Bernard could do nothing to restore order: when he called for his drummers to beat the alarm, he was told they were in the mob. Had not Hutchinson already persuaded Oliver to get out of harm's way, he probably would have been roughly handled indeed during the "furious Onset." But, although Oliver escaped unhurt, the riot accomplished its chief purpose, for the next day he promised to resign as stamp master.

The fourteenth of August, the day on which this riot took place, was celebrated in New England for many years to commemorate "the happy Day, on which Liberty arose from a long Slumber." Sam Adams said it "ought to be for ever remembered in America" because "the People shouted; and their shout

[30] *Bernard Papers*, IV, Bernard to the Earl of Halifax, Aug. 15, 1765. *Letters from the Rev. Samuel Mather to his son*, 1759–1785, Aug. 17, 1765. *Letters from Andrew Eliot to Thomas Hollis, Mass. Hist. Soc. Collections*, IV, Fourth Series, 406, 407.

was heard to the distant end of this Continent." [31] Tories remarked that it was singular to hold in such esteem a riot that had done little more than terrify an old man out of his wits, but the patriots continued to make August 14 a day of processions, feasts, and patriotic toasts. There was, indeed, good reason to set this day apart: it marked the first important outbreak of mob violence in British America against the Stamp Act; and, as the parent day of all the riots in revolutionary Boston, it possessed strong claims to renown. Inasmuch as it encouraged rioting in other colonies and provoked violent resistance to the Stamp Act, Bostonians' boast that "the RESISTANCE *of that Day* roused the Spirit of AMERICA" was justified. [32]

When the Whigs saw what a powerful ally they possessed against the Tories in the Boston mob they determined to use it against Thomas Hutchinson. Sam Adams had no intention of permitting colonial wrath over the Stamp Act to vent itself wholly upon the British government: his policy was to force the Tories and Crown officers to share the guilt of George Grenville and the British House of Commons. The odium of "British oppression" was always cast upon Hutchinson and his party by Sam Adams. In the House of Representatives, James Otis declared that he knew the very room in Governor Bernard's house where the Stamp Act was conceived, the time, and the company responsible. It was whispered in Boston by Sam Adams that Hutchinson was the blackest conspirator of all because he had planned the Stamp Act and sent it to England, where the British Ministry had eagerly leaped at so plausible a scheme for raising a colonial revenue. In backstairs gossip, Governor Bernard was said to wish to enforce the Stamp Act with his "dear friend" George Grenville "at the head of a hundred legions." [33] Adams and Otis poured their suspicions into the ears of the "black regiment," whereupon the clergy began to dwell in their sermons upon the iniquity of Thomas

[31] *The Writings of Samuel Adams*, II, 201.

[32] *Boston Gazette*, Aug. 11, 1766 (Supplement). *Bernard Papers*, V, Bernard to Pownall, Nov. 1, 1765.

[33] *Bernard Papers*, IV, Bernard to Lord Shelburne, Dec. 22, 1766. Mass. Archives, 26, *Hutchinson Corr.*, II, 151. *Boston Gazette*, June 1, 1767. *The Works of John Adams*, II, 336.

Hutchinson, Governor Bernard, and other contrivers of the
Stamp Act. Between the politicians and the preachers, the
Boston *canaille* was soon raging against the Tories and itching
for an opportunity to lay hands upon Hutchinson and the governor. No doubt their patriotic fervor was whetted by the
consideration that Hutchinson's cellar was extraordinarily well
stocked.

Adams and Otis had no reason to believe that Hutchinson
was behind the Stamp Act other than their conviction that "some
high or low dirty American" always had a hand in plots against
colonial liberty.[34] They were certain that Hutchinson and
Bernard were secretly undermining the Massachusetts charter
in order to clear the way for raising a revenue by Parliamentary
authority from which they would be enriched. Adams did not
doubt that Hutchinson hoped to destroy "the Democratical
part" of the Massachusetts government and forge "chains and
shackles" upon the colonists.[35] But Sam Adams was in search
of good propaganda rather than historical accuracy and he was
never troubled by the flimsiness of his proof of Hutchinson's
guilt. Could Adams find a scapegoat for the Stamp Act within
the province and turn hostility against Great Britain into a
crusade against the New England "oligarchs," he could hope
to drive Hutchinson and his friends from Massachusetts Bay.
The well-being of the Whig Party demanded that Hutchinson
be implicated in the authorship of the Stamp Act regardless of
whether he actually had had a hand in unleashing that "menacing monster" upon the colonies.

In reality, Hutchinson had had nothing to do with the
Stamp Act until its passage by the House of Commons made it
his duty as a Chief Justice of Massachusetts Bay to enforce it.
When the Stamp Act was first proposed, Hutchinson urged that
it be given up; at no time did he advise that it be put in force;
and he did not hesitate to express his fears of its results.[36] Governor Bernard might be acquitted with equal ease of any complicity in the Stamp Act. It had been conceived in England

[34] *Boston Gazette*, Aug. 12, 1765.
[35] *Ibid.*, Feb. 28, 1763. *The Writings of Samuel Adams*, II, 165.
[36] Mass. Archives, 26, *Hutchinson Corr.*, II, 139, 149, 153.

by British imperialists who hankered after a colonial revenue, and the entire blame for its passage can be laid upon the British Ministry and House of Commons.   But Hutchinson and Bernard were unable to convince New Englanders of their innocence after Adams's and Otis's propaganda had done its work; Otis once boasted that nine tenths of the citizens of Massachusetts Bay believed that Hutchinson and Bernard had instigated the Stamp Act in spite of their denials.[37]

After the attack upon Andrew Oliver, Boston continued to simmer and the mob restlessly awaited another opportunity to riot.   The day after Oliver's house was ransacked, Boston gentlemen were forced to protect the stamp master from the lower class.   Oliver's promise not to distribute the stamps and to apply for permission to resign was satisfactory to Sam Adams, but the "lower Part of the Mob" clamored for an immediate resignation and were "unwilling to lose their Frolick."   For a fortnight the tension in Boston continued to increase, until, on the night of August 28, boys and negroes began to build bonfires in King's Street and blow the dreaded whistle and horn that sent the Boston mob swarming out of taverns, houses, and garrets.   A large crowd immediately gathered around the bonfires, bawling for "Liberty and Property," which, said Bernard, "is the usual Notice of their Intention to plunder & pull down an House."[38]   After fortifying themselves with rum, the mob started out on its "frolick" by wrecking several houses belonging to the customhouse officers and Court of Admiralty.   This desultory rioting warmed the mob to its real work, and by the time it reached the home of Lieutenant Governor Hutchinson its appetite had been whetted by large quantities of rum and loot.   "The hellish crew fell upon my house with the rage of devils," Hutchinson wrote, and had he not already left the premises he probably would not have escaped alive.   The mob gutted the house, destroyed his furniture, emptied his cellar, robbed his strongbox, and scattered the manuscript of his *History of the Province of Massachusetts Bay* in the mud outside

---

[37] *Boston Gazette*, Nov. 24, 1766.
[38] *Bernard Papers*, IV, Bernard to the Earl of Halifax, Aug. 31, 1765. Peter Oliver, 125.

his door.[89]   All that night the mob ran amuck.   Not since the
impressment riots of 1748, when the mob stoned the General
Court and held possession of the town for three days, had Boston seen such a wild evening.

Hutchinson had so many enemies in Boston that he scarcely
knew whom to blame for this outrage.   But it is certain that
even his worst enemies, Otis and Adams, had not intended that
the mob should go to such lengths.   No doubt the demonstration planned by the patriots against the lieutenant governor got
out of their control by reason of the large rations of rum handed
out to the mob before it attacked.   Otis and Adams had no
wish to make Hutchinson a martyr, but the morning after the
riot he came to court "clothed in a manner which would have
excited compassion from the hardest heart."   With tears in his
eyes, Hutchinson called upon God as witness to his innocence
of any hand in the Stamp Act.   He swore he had striven "as
much as in me lay, to prevent it," and urged the people to close
their ears to evildoers who attempted to inflame them against
the men who loved the province best.   Many agreed with
Hutchinson that it was "the most barbarous outrage which ever
was committed in America," and for the moment the lieutenant
governor seemed likely to become the most popular man in the
colony, particularly in the rural districts where "mobbish Boston" was in low repute.   But the Boston patriots deprived
Hutchinson of the sweets of martyrdom by circulating a story
that letters had been found in his house the night of the riot
which proved he was responsible for the Stamp Act.   For good
reason, Sam Adams never produced these incriminating letters.

Adams was alarmed by the destruction of Hutchinson's house,
not because he believed the lieutenant governor had been un-
duly punished, but because he feared the British government
would take steps against Boston for having handled a Crown
officer roughly.   The morning after the riot Adams attended
the Boston town meeting and voted with the citizens to assist
the magistrates in keeping order in the metropolis.   Because
the townspeople publicly expressed their grief for Hutchinson's

---

[89] *Publications Col. Soc. of Mass.* (1927), XXVI, 33.   Hutchinson, III,
125.   Mass. Archives, 26, *Hutchinson Corr.*, II, 147.

misfortune and showed "universal Consternation" when dis-
cussing the riot, Adams believed Bostonians had completely
cleared themselves of all blame; but Hutchinson said many of
the "villains" who had wrecked his house the night before were
the loudest mourners in the town meeting.[40]   Sam Adams immediately wrote a letter to the Massachusetts agent in London
instructing him to ward off punishment from the mother country by showing the townspeople to be innocent of responsibility
for the outrage done the lieutenant governor.   Had George
III read Sam Adams's letter he would have been overjoyed to
learn that a metropolis of such purity as Boston existed within
his dominions.   Adams declared that the riot was a "high
handed Enormity" perpetrated by "vagabound Strangers" such
as were to be found in even the most peaceable seaports.
Hutchinson's house was attacked, he said, "remote from any
Considerations of the Stamp Act" and "solely with a View to
Plunder." [41]   Nevertheless, it was well known in New England
that Adams and Otis had inflamed the mob against the lieutenant governor by picturing him as the author of the Stamp Act.
Had the rioters been merely the town riffraff Adams described,
he would not have taken precautions to prevent their arrest.
However, when Mackintosh, the leader of the South End mob,
was thrown in jail for taking part in the riot at Hutchinson's
house, Adams and his friends informed the sheriff that unless
he was immediately released, no one would stand guard in Boston the next night.   Rather than see the town given over to
pillage, the sheriff released Mackintosh.   The attorney general
was intimidated for prosecuting the rioters and Mackintosh was
rewarded for his services with a Boston town office and command of the Whig "trained mob" that Sam Adams later turned
against the Tories.[42]

The looting of Hutchinson's house was a sharp reminder to
Sam Adams that the Boston mob must be disciplined and kept
under leash before it could be used as a Whig weapon against

[40] Hutchinson, III, 125.   *Mass. Hist. Soc. Proceedings* (1860), IV, 49–
50, Mass. Archives, 26, *Hutchinson Corr.*, II, 148.

[41] Mass. Archives, 56, 465.

[42] Hutchinson, III, 126.   Mass. Archives, 26, *Hutchinson Corr.*, II, 184.

Tories. After the rioters had whetted their appetite at the lieutenant governor's, it was rumored that they had made a list of fifteen prominent gentlemen whose houses they proposed to attack. Since it was plain that the mob now contemplated "a War of Plunder, of general levelling & taking away the Distinction of rich & poor," many of the gentlemen who had taken part in the riot of August 14 became fearful of their allies. Governor Bernard said of these that they had raised the devil and now they wished to lay him again.[43] Sam Adams could not afford to let the Whig Party take responsibility for the violence of water-front toughs: therefore he must either bring the mob under control or wipe his hands clean of any connection with it. Adams was unwilling to give up such a redoubtable ally, yet it was apparent that the Boston mob was not to be easily tamed. Had there been a single mob in Boston, his problem would have been simple, but there were two fiercely antagonistic mobs in the town that seemed more eager to be at each other's throats than terrorizing Tories. On every fifth of November — celebrated as "Pope Day" — gangs from the North and South End of Boston carried popes and effigies to King's Street, where they met in a pitched battle, each mob attempting to destroy the other's pope. Everything was fair in this "dirty Contest" and no blow too low: indeed, these zealous Protestants sometimes belabored each other so furiously with staves and cudgels that they were carted dying off the field of battle.[44] Nothing was to be heard in Boston on these eventful nights but "a confused medley of the rattlings of Carriages, the noises of Pope Drums and the infernal yell of those who are fighting for the possession of the Devill."[45] By 1765, the feud between North and South Boston had become a tradition carried on by rival gangs of battle-scarred veterans. Thus, before the Whigs could harness the Boston mob they had first to induce the North and South End mobs to settle their quarrel and belabor the Tories instead of wasting their talents by cracking each other's pates on Pope Days.

[43] *Bernard Papers*, IV, Bernard to the Earl of Halifax, Aug. 31, 1768.
[44] *Massachusetts Gazette*, Nov. 5, 1767.
[45] *Copley-Pelham Letters, Mass. Hist. Soc. Collections* (1914), LXXI, 201.

Sam Adams painstakingly began to bring these gangs of cudgel-boys together. Of the two factions, the South Enders were the most powerful and were expertly led by Alexander Mackintosh. Adams's large acquaintance among the mob — he was an intimate friend of Swift, the leader of the North End, and well known to the rank and file of both parties — made him an important intermediary in the reconciliation that took place shortly after the attack upon Hutchinson's house. It was probably due to Adams's influence that Mackintosh and Swift, with their respective lieutenants, were brought together, feasted, and entertained until they had been convinced that patriotism required them to forget their quarrels and turn their energies to politics. A huge banquet — called the "Union Feast" — was held to commemorate the burying of the hatchet: the two mobs sat down together with Whig merchants and politicians and joined "with Heart and Hand in flowing Bowls and bumping Glasses" until they had completely drowned all memories of their former differences.[46] On November 5, 1765, instead of the usual riot Bostonians were treated to a parade and military revue. Mackintosh led the procession, resplendent in a gilt uniform of red and blue, a gold-laced hat and cane, and a speaking trumpet to give orders to his "troops," who marched and wheeled with impressive proficiency. Arm in arm with "General" Mackintosh walked Colonel Brattle of the Massachusetts militia, complimenting him upon the order kept by his men and assuring him that "his Post was one of the highest in the Government." [47]

Governor Bernard rightly feared that Sam Adams had united the Boston mobs for other purposes than burning a pope. The demonstration in 1765 of "lovely Unity" between the North and South Ends marks the end of the mob as a free lance in the revolutionary movement. Henceforth Boston was controlled by a "trained mob" under Sam Adams's direction. Although the North and South Ends occasionally took up the cudgels against each other after the "Union Feast," it is remarkable how

[46] *Bernard Papers*, V, Bernard to Pownall, Nov. 6, 1765. *The Works of John Adams*, II, 177. *Massachusetts Gazette*, Nov. 14, 1765.
[47] *Bernard Papers*, IV, Bernard to Pownall, Nov. 6, 1765.

seldom the mob got out of control during the revolutionary period. A hierarchy of mobs was established during Sam Adams's rule of Boston: the lowest classes — servants, negroes, and sailors — were placed under the command of "a superior set consisting of the Master Masons carpenters of the town"; above them were put the merchants' mob and the Sons of Liberty, — known to the Tories as Adams's "Mohawks," — upon whom the more delicate enterprises against Tories and Crown officers devolved; and Mackintosh was given one hundred and fifty men "trained as regular as a military Corps" to act as storm troops.[48] Englishmen found the Boston mob very different from those in England because the Boston rioters acted "from principle & under Countenance" and openly defied the magistrates who attempted to bring them to trial. Whereas an English mob good-naturedly spared houses where lights were placed in the windows, the only safety for Tories in Boston was to get out of town before the mob attacked.[49]

Governor Bernard firmly believed that after the Boston mob had finished with Oliver and Hutchinson, his turn would be next. He had no desire, however, to be the first royal governor in the colonies to suffer martyrdom for King and Parliament. He prudently slipped out of town and hurried to Castle William, where the stamps had been stored for safekeeping, but even here he did not feel secure. Therefore, to prevent a surprise attack upon the Castle by the Boston Sons of Liberty, he strengthened its defenses as though he expected a foreign enemy to appear in Boston Harbor, locked himself in with the stamps, and wrote to England that the metropolis was in a state of outright rebellion. Adams and Otis ridiculed a royal governor who "skulked from one Hole to another" and feared his own shadow, but Bernard had good reason for his furtive behavior: he had no means whatever of defending himself should Adams decide that the King's representative was fair game for a "frolick" with the Liberty Boys.

The British "tyranny" against which Sam Adams protested in 1765 was not the oppressive rule of a strong government prepared to crush resistance with force. Because Parliament had not foreseen colonial opposition, it made no preparations to enforce the Stamp Act and was caught completely off guard when the Sons of Liberty began to terrorize the stamp masters and Crown officers. After it was seen that stamps could be forced upon the colonists only at the bayonet's point, the weakness of the British government naturally made it contemptible in Americans' eyes. Daniel Leonard, the Massachusetts Tory, rightly complained that "if any thing was in reality amiss in government it was its being too lax": instead of finding themselves opposed by a strong government, Americans were frequently permitted to ride roughshod over British authority. When the Sons of Liberty stormed the fort at Charleston, South Carolina, they found only one private awake and the other eleven members of the garrison sound asleep; at Fort Johnson, North Carolina, a garrison of two British troops were hotly besieged by five hundred heavily armed Sons of Liberty; and in New York, the headquarters of British military authority in the provinces, the troops were unable to keep order in the town.[50] General Gage informed royal governors who clamored for military aid against the patriots that no military force could be collected within a month, and even then it would be at the expense of strategic posts which would be seriously weakened if their garrisons were removed.[51] The colonial militia was useless to the Crown officers because its ranks were filled with Sons of Liberty who, if called to arms, would be more likely to attack the royal government than suppress patriot mobs. Governor Bernard considered the militia as "worse than no Soldiers at all," against the "incensed & implacable Mob" commanded by "General" Mackintosh.[52] The "long arm" of Great Britain was so palsied that until British troops were sent to Boston in 1768, Tories and Crown officers were forced to lie low

[50] John Drayton, *Memoirs of the American Revolution* (1821), I, 45. *Colonial Records of North Carolina* (1890), VIII, 169–171, Governor Tryon to General Conway, Feb. 25, 1766. *Pennsylvania Journal*, Nov. 14, 1765.

[51] *Bernard Papers*, X, General Thomas Gage to Bernard, Sept. 6, 1765.

[52] *Bernard Papers*, IV, Bernard to Richard Jackson, Aug. 24, 1765.

or run the risk of facing the Sons of Liberty alone; in 1766, Bernard said with only slight exaggeration that he was "fighting the King's Battles without protection, support or maintenance." [53]   The British government was utterly unable to punish even the fiercest rioters and libelers among the Sons of Liberty: when Alexander MacDougall of New York, "the American John Wilkes," was imprisoned in 1770 he became famed as the first Son of Liberty to be put in jail — at least, for patriotic activities.   This helplessness to quell the revolutionary movement in the colonies convinced Sam Adams and his followers that the British government was "so contemptibly weak, and the people so superior to the royal authority that they are not a little elated upon their triumph over the defenceless officers of the crown." [54]

With the royal governor "skulking" behind the ramparts of Castle William in terror of his life and the nearest British troops two hundred miles from Boston, Sam Adams and the Sons of Liberty easily made themselves masters of the metropolis.   It was not necessary for them to create new political machinery to rule Boston: the machinery was already in existence under the name of the Caucus Club.   The Stamp Act brought about little change in the personnel of the ruling clique in Boston, — the Sons of Liberty were simply the Caucus Club writ large, — but it did vastly increase the power of the political bosses.   Never before had they known such prosperity as descended upon them in 1765.   Petty politicians who had hitherto wrangled for small offices found themselves famous overnight as daring mob leaders and "true-born" Sons of Liberty.   Aristocrats who had sneered at them a few months before as "the scum" and "rabble" were now compelled to bow and scrape before them lest the mob be turned against their fine houses.   The sheriff's assistants were Sons of Liberty and would not move against their fellow patriots; justices of the peace were "great favourers of them" and paraded beside them through the

[53] *Barrington Bernard Correspondence*, edited by Ed. Channing and A. C. Coolidge, *Harvard Hist. Studies*, XVII, 115.

[54] Francis Bernard, *Select Letters on the Trade and Government of America, and the Principles of Law and Policy, applied to the American Colonies* (London, 1774), 30–31.

streets; juries were packed with Liberty Boys; and the Boston
selectmen stood in such awe of them that they did not dare to
attempt repression. Whoever was so foolhardy as to oppose
the Sons of Liberty in Boston in 1765 was sure to feel the smart
of "the Iron Rod of the popular Despotism." [55]

To show Bernard and Hutchinson that "they were as nothing
in the Eyes or the Hands of the People," Sam Adams and the
"Loyall Nine" ordered Andrew Oliver, the stamp master, to
make another resignation at Liberty Tree on the pretext that
his promise to give up his duties, made immediately after the
attack of August 14, was not sincere. The memory of the
riot was too fresh in Oliver's mind to permit him to disobey
this command; and in the presence of a huge crowd at Liberty
Tree he took the oath administered by Justice Dana. "And a
Glorious sight it was, which I beheld," exclaimed a Son of Liberty who watched Oliver — one of the "oligarchs" of the
colony — humble himself in the biting wind and rain before
Sam Adams and his Mohawks and swear that "he never would,
directly or indirectly, by himself or any under him, make use
of his deputation, or take any measures for enforcing the stamp
act in America."   Only by such abasement, Bernard lamented,
could His Majesty's servants in the colonies be sure of a whole
skin. [56]

Having forced the stamp master out of office and bottled up
the stamps, together with the royal governor, in Castle William,
Sam Adams proposed to treat the Stamp Act as a "meer nullity."
He therefore demanded that business be carried on in the colony
without stamps in open defiance of Parliament. The patriots
quoted Coke to prove that an act of Parliament against Magna
Charta and the rights of Englishmen was void, but even without
recourse to political theory it was clear that the Stamp Act could
not be obeyed in Massachusetts because the Sons of Liberty had
cleared the country of stamps and stamp masters.   Either business was to go on without stamps or totally cease for want of

[55] *Bernard Papers*, IV, Bernard to the Lords Commissioners for Trade,
Jan. 10, 1766. *Mass. Hist. Soc. Proceedings* (1923), LX, 282.
[56] *Boston Gazette*, Dec. 23, 1765, Note by Harbottle Dorr, MS. Mass. Hist.
Soc. *Bernard Papers*, IV, Bernard to General Conway, Dec. 18, 1765. *The
Works of John Adams*, II, 156.

them.   Adams was well aware that if business stopped, Parliament's right to tax the colonies would be implicitly acknowledged.   To prevent this surrender of principle, he determined to open all public offices, courts, and customhouses, regardless of the lack of stamps.   In the House of Representatives, Otis and Adams declared that "the courts of Justice must be open immediately, and the law . . . executed"; and although the Crown officers deeply resented the dictatorial tone assumed by the Whig chiefs in laying down the law to His Majesty's governor and Council, they were unable to keep colonial business at a standstill while Parliament deliberated the fate of the Stamp Act.   The customhouse officers were terrified into opening the port to shipping without stamped clearances; courts of common law and even the Court of Admiralty were compelled to transact business as though the Stamp Act had been repealed; and the whole colony jubilantly read unstamped newspapers, married on unstamped licenses, and sued their neighbors on unstamped legal papers.[57]

Tories believed Sam Adams insisted upon opening the courts without stamps simply "to shew ye Power of our new Gov[erno]rs" and to insult Parliament.[58]   Although most Massachusetts Crown officers were frightened into violating the Stamp Act, Thomas Hutchinson refused to give way to Adams and his mob.   When the House of Representatives sent a resolution to the Council declaring that the closing of the courts for want of stamps would "dissolve all the Bands of civil Society," Hutchinson urged the councilors to prove their loyalty to the Crown by withstanding the seditious demands of the Lower House.   Hutchinson was so bitterly attacked by Adams and Otis in the *Boston Gazette* for his speech in Council that he

[57] *Massachusetts State Papers*, edited by Alden Bradford, Answer of the House of Representatives to the Governor's speech, Jan. 17, 1766. *Boston Gazette*, Jan. 27, 1766.   Mass. Archives, 26, *Hutchinson Corr.*, II, 193. *Bernard Papers*, IV, Bernard to the Lords Commissioners for Trade, Jan. 10, 1766.

[58] Mass. Archives, 25, *Hutchinson Corr.*, I, John Cushing to Thomas Hutchinson, Dec. 29, 1765.   *Bernard Papers*, IV, Bernard to the Lords of Trade, March 10, 1766.   *Israel Williams Papers*, MSS. Mass. Hist. Soc., Thomas Hutchinson to Israel Williams, Feb. 20, 1766.

believed another mob was being raised against him; but he
escaped a second attack because there was nothing left in his
house to destroy.[59]   Nevertheless Adams and Otis soon saw
an opportunity to punish Hutchinson for his work in the General Court.   For many years, the patriot chiefs had attempted
to deprive Hutchinson of his numerous offices, but it was not
until the Stamp Act that they achieved their first success.   British "oppression" was fashioned by the Whigs into a lever with
which to pry the New England "oligarchs" from office.   Acting under Sam Adams's direction, the Boston town meeting
demanded that Hutchinson, as Judge of Probate for Suffolk
County, open his court for business without stamps.   Hutchinson's veneration for his oath of office was too deep to admit of
such flagrant violation.   Knowing that he must either resign or
flee the country, he chose to give up his office as Judge of Probate.   It was, however, one of the least important of his
places and he remained lieutenant governor and Chief Justice
of the province despite Adams's success in making him the
scapegoat of the Stamp Act.

One of the most striking results of the Stamp Act was the
congress of representatives from the various provinces which
met in New York in November 1765 to make a united protest
to King and Parliament.   As early as 1763, the Boston patriots
had urged the merchants to choose committees for intercolonial
correspondence in order to defeat the Sugar Act, and in 1764
Sam Adams had appealed to the Boston representatives in the
General Court to unite the colonies against the new molasses
duty.   "As His Majestys other Northern American Colonys
are embarked with us in this most important Bottom," Adams
said in his Boston instructions of 1764, "we . . . desire you to
use your Endeavors, that their Weight may be added to that
of this Province; that by the united Applications of all who
are aggrieved, All may happily obtain Redress." [60]   In 1765,
after the Stamp Act had given the colonies a common cause
of action, James Otis followed Adams's suggestion of the previous year by proposing in the Massachusetts House of Repre-

[59] Mass. Archives, 26, *Hutchinson Corr.*, II, 205, 206.
[60] *The Writings of Samuel Adams*, I, 6.

sentatives an intercolonial congress. Otis's motion drew sneers
from the conservatives, but it was adopted by a majority of the
House and sent to all the British colonies on the continent.

Although several colonies were not represented in the Stamp
Act Congress and others sent delegates with inadequate powers, it brought together men from all quarters of the colonies
and laid the foundations for the later Continental Congresses.
Many of the delegates were far more conservative than their
constituents, — even in the Massachusetts delegation it was
said there were three men "fast Friends to Government, & prudent and Discrete," — and their petitions to King and Parliament were far too moderate for Sam Adams's taste. Nevertheless, the shortcomings of the Stamp Act Congress could not
conceal the fact that "the united Colonies have Remonstrated."
"Who," asked the Boston patriots in 1766, "dreamt this time
twelve Months of such a UNION of the Colonies?" [61]

An even more significant manifestation of colonial unity was
the secret military alliances formed among the Sons of Liberty
against the British government. When rumors began to circulate late in 1765 that the Ministry would attempt to enforce
the Stamp Act with redcoats and men of war, the Sons of Liberty
made preparations to give the royal troops a warm reception.
On Christmas Day, 1765, the New York and Connecticut Sons
of Liberty ratified a plan of mutual military aid against the expected attack by a British army. The Connecticut and New
York patriots agreed to march to each other's assistance with
their entire force. They declared they would not be "enslav'd
by any power of earth without opposing force to force," and
promised King George's men a hot battle should they take the
field against American Whigs.[62] Colonel Durkee of the Connecticut militia boasted that he could bring ten thousand well-
armed men against the British; and a "noble possy of Jersey

[61] *Boston Gazette*, Jan. 13, 1766, Supplement (1873). Bancroft, V, 200.
Bernard Papers, IV, Bernard to the Lords of Trade, 1765. *Boston Gazette*,
May 5, 1766 (Supplement); May 12, 1765; Jan. 20, 1766.
[62] *Belknap Papers*, MSS. Mass. Hist. Soc., Letter from Boston Sons of Liberty, Feb. 3, 1766. *Lamb Papers*, MSS. New York Hist. Soc., N. Y. Sons
of Liberty to Middletown, N. J., Sons of Liberty, April 10, 1766. *Bernard
Papers*, IV, Bernard to General Conway, Jan. 25, 1766.

Folks" and "Eastern Lads" were prepared to march to New York's relief. These military covenants gave the New York patriots assurance of being supported by a yeoman army if the British military machine were turned against New York; and everywhere the people were told that colonial Whigs were a match for the British army and that, even if the seaports fell into the enemy's hands, the patriots could take refuge in the inland country where the British army could never penetrate.[63]

Englishmen had not anticipated such violent opposition from New York and the Southern colonies, but they were probably less surprised to find the New England Saints — "the spawn of Old Cromwellians" — plotting to massacre British armies.[64] To enlist Boston's aid in the coming struggle against British troops, the New York patriots sent agents to New England to stir up the war spirit and learn how many men could be counted upon to march to their defense. The New Yorkers found the Boston Sons of Liberty laying plans to cut off the British army before it could reach Boston overland. Like the Sons of Liberty in the Southern colonies, the Boston patriots felt "the Patriotic Flame glowing in their Bosoms and would esteem it glorious to die for their Country." A Providence Son of Liberty who came to Boston with credentials from his local chapter was admitted to "the most Honourable Privy Council" of the Sons of Liberty and given a seat "at ye Board," where he learned that the Bostonians had made thorough preparations to handle British invaders. The Whigs boasted that with two hours' notice they could bring three thousand men to Liberty Tree "who would go any where for ye preservation of ye Constitution," and that within a few days forty thousand New Englanders would be on the march to the metropolis.[65]

Despite their enthusiasm for a pitched battle with the King's

[63] *Lamb Papers*, Joseph Allicocke to John Lamb, Nov. 21, 1765. *Bernard Papers*, IV, Bernard to General Conway, Jan. 25, 1766. *The Montresor Journals*, *Collections of the N. Y. Hist. Soc.* (1882), 350. *Belknap Papers*, Boston Sons of Liberty to the New Hampshire Sons of Liberty, Feb. 13, 1766.

[64] *Considerations on the American Stamp Act* (London, 1766), 33.

[65] *Bernard Papers*, IV, Bernard to General Conway, Jan. 19, 1766; V, Bernard to Pownall, June 29, 1766. *Boston Gazette*, Aug. 19, 1765. *Lamb Papers*, Extract of a Letter from Providence, Feb. 17, 1766.

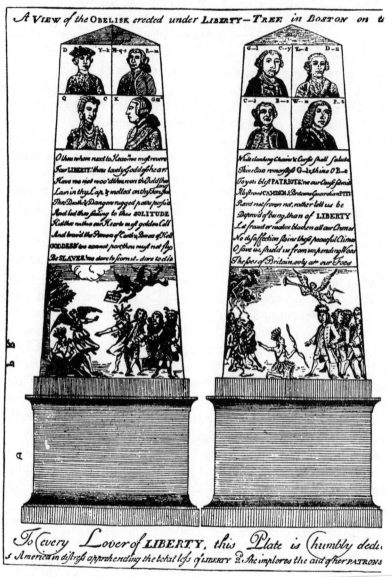

LIBERTY PYRAMID

ERECTED FOR CELEBRATION OF THE REPEAL OF THE STAMP

From an Engraving by Paul Revere

In the Boston Athenæum

ACT, MARCH 1776, AND DESTROYED BY FIRE AT THAT TIME

soldiers, Sam Adams and other Sons of Liberty did not regard themselves as disrupters of the British Empire, but as defenders of its constitution. The Sons of Liberty were the "King's Party" in the American colonies. They believed the Stamp Act was an encroachment made by the House of Commons upon George III's "Crown and Dignity," for the King alone was sovereign in the colonies. Royal requisitions and grants, they declared, were the only constitutional forms of colonial taxation: by means of the Stamp Act, Parliament was attempting to strip the colonists of their property and King George of his sovereignty. Thus, to oppose Parliament became the duty of all Americans who truly loved the King and the British Constitution. It is not uncommon to find the Sons of Liberty denying Parliament any power whatever over the colonies, although it required another decade for the mass of Americans to adopt this doctrine.[66]

While the Sons of Liberty were toasting King George in one breath and threatening to massacre royal troops in the next, it was learned in the colonies that the British government had repealed the Stamp Act. For the moment, at least, the crisis that had almost produced bloodshed between opposing armies of British and Americans seemed safely passed. But Englishmen always found it difficult to understand why the colonists should have organized themselves into Sons of Liberty, outraged Crown officers, and prepared to fight the British army. Granting that Parliament had made a serious mistake in imposing a stamp duty upon the colonies, it was not sufficient reason for Americans to make these warlike preparations against the mother country. The colonists seemed to be decidedly hot-tempered gentry, accustomed to reaching for their muskets on the slightest provocation. In reality, however, Americans were not as quick on the trigger as they appeared to Englishmen in 1765. The Stamp Act had almost precipitated an armed revolt in the colonies, not because Americans were particularly

[66] *Lamb Papers*, New York Sons of Liberty to the Middletown, N. J., Sons of Liberty, April 10, 1766; Resolves of the Sons of Liberty at Oyster Bay, N. Y., Feb. 22, 1766. *Belknap Papers*, Boston Sons of Liberty to the Sons of Liberty in New Hampshire, Feb. 13, 1766; Providence Sons of Liberty to the N. H. Sons of Liberty, March 24, 1766.

warlike, but because a century and a half of isolation had so completely estranged them from the mother country that they were prepared to take up arms in defense of their liberties on small aggravation.   The Stamp Act had awakened a militant spirit among men who, although in a minority, were the kind of minority that makes revolutions.   Particularly in the seaport towns of the North, the Sons of Liberty were recruited from the class that had everything to gain by a social and political upheaval.   These men, with Sam Adams at their head, were ready in 1765 to fight Great Britain.   And, as Governor Bernard said, it was apparent after the Stamp Act that the "weak patchwork government" in America had no power to prevent colonial independence, "one hour after the people have resolved upon it." [67]

Many years later, George III lamented Parliament's "fatal compliance" in repealing the Stamp Act.   It seemed to most Englishmen in 1774 that after Parliament had given way in 1766, the colonists had steadily raised their demands for self-government, made larger claims of exemption from Parliamentary authority, and even attempted to force the King out of his prerogative rights.   Looking back from this perspective, it appeared to many British statesmen that England would have done well to have had it out with the colonies in 1766 instead of giving them ten years in which to strengthen themselves for conflict with the mother country.   But it is probable that an attempt to enforce the Stamp Act would have proved fatal to the British Empire.   Americans were more united in 1766 than in 1776, and England had not yet recovered from the exhaustion of the Seven Years' War.   The British government chose to repeal the Stamp Act and blunder into civil war ten years later; but, if military force had been used to cram the stamps down the colonists' throats, it is probable the American Revolution would have begun in 1766.

[67] Bernard, *Select Letters on the Trade and Government of America* (London, 1774), 38, 39.

IV

THE BOSTON WHIGS

THE Stamp Act had brought Sam Adams out of obscurity and placed him in the General Court, where he was to remain for the next decade despite the Tories' best efforts to dislodge him. In 1764, Adams seemed destined to remain unknown except, perhaps, for the brief notoriety he had received for embezzling public funds. By 1766, when the Stamp Act was repealed, he had become one of the most important figures in Massachusetts politics, second only to James Otis in popularity. Decidedly, it behooved the Tories to look closely at this man whose rapid rise threatened to destroy their influence in New England.

They saw a middle-aged man, already stricken with palsy, whose clothing was invariably rusty from long use. There was little arresting in his appearance and even to his friends he seemed merely a "plain, simple, decent citizen, of middling stature, dress and manners," who lived frugally and took great pride in his poverty. Tories always professed to see in Adams's face strong traces of the "Malignity" of his heart. An American painter who knew him well is said to have remarked that "if he wished to draw the Picture of the Devil . . . he would get Sam Adams to sit for him."[1] It is singular that this resemblance to Satan which his enemies found so striking does not appear in any of Adams's portraits. It cannot be said that Tory painters did not have opportunity to expose Adams's diabolical qualities, for his best-known portrait is by John Singleton Copley, the greatest of Tory artists, but there is no sign of the cloven hoof in Copley's study of Adams. He has, indeed, long since

[1] *The Works of John Adams*, X, 251, 308; II, 164, 308. *The Writings of Samuel Adams*, IV, 226. Peter Oliver, 54.

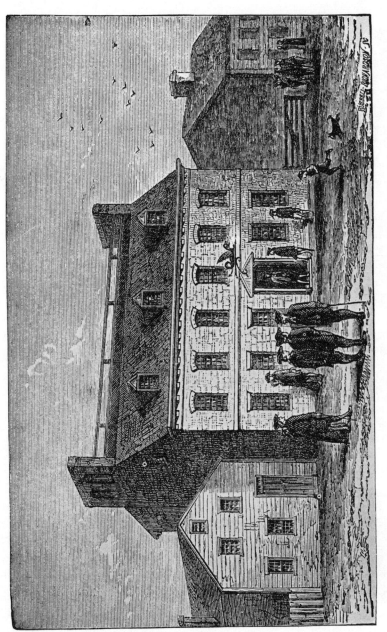

The Green Dragon Tavern

"headquarters of the revolution"

Mr. and Mrs. James Otis

painted by Blackburn

ceased to be a terror to conservatives; and those who to-day shriek that Lenin and Stalin are the very devil regard Sam Adams as a holy patriot.

The Adams household consisted in 1764 of Sam's two children by his first wife, a black slave girl, and a Newfoundland dog which, like its master, could not endure the sight of a British uniform. In that year, when his political prospects were darkest and a prison term for embezzlement hung over his head, Adams took as his second wife Elizabeth Welles, who, although she brought her husband no dowry, possessed a loyal spirit and such consummate skill in household management that the Adams family was kept in reasonable comfort even on Sam's meagre income. She was, in fact, said to be the best housekeeper in Boston and made Sam an almost ideal wife: she took upon herself the burdens he shirked, but made no effort to wean him from his first love, Boston politics. Whereas James Otis's wife was a high Tory who gave her husband stinging "curtain lectures" when he came home from the Whig Club, "Betsy" Adams was nearly as stout a Whig as Sam himself. Of Thomas Hutchinson, the leader of the Tory Party, she once wrote: "I believe the most Rancourous Envy and venom Swells the Contaminated veins of the fell tyrant . . . the infamous Hutchinson." [2] Undismayed by her husband's practice of making his home a gathering place for political friends, she made no protest either then or when he kept late hours at the Caucus Club or with the Sons of Liberty. Bravely she bore his long absences at Philadelphia during the Continental Congresses; and while they were separated she kept him closely informed of the latest political developments in Boston. "I am never more happy," she once wrote her husband, "than when I am Reading your Letters or Scribbling to you my Self." During the British occupation of Boston in 1774–1776 she quieted his fears that she would be harmed by telling him she could take care of herself among the redcoats. When Dr. Thomas Young, one of Sam Adams's henchmen, skipped out of Boston somewhat precipi-

[2] *The Works of John Adams*, II, 227. *Samuel Adams Papers*, Bancroft Collection, MSS. New York Public Library, Mrs. Adams to her husband, Sept. 12, 1774.

tately to escape the British dragnet, Mrs. Adams was unable to understand "why he should go just now."[3]

The Adamses were famous even in Boston for their strictness in religious matters. Prayers were said before meals; passages were read from the Bible at bedtime; and the Lord's Day was scrupulously observed in the Puritan manner. By Adams's day, however, the religious fervor that had made Puritanism a way of life had almost completely disappeared in New England; and, although Sam Adams has been called the last of the Puritans, it no doubt would be a shock to seventeenth-century Puritans were they told Sam Adams was one of them. Adams, it is clear, was a good, eighteenth-century Congregationalist who went to church regularly and observed all the formalities of his religion, but he was not a Puritan in the sense in which Winthrop and Cotton understood the name. Nevertheless, in revolutionary Boston, Adams passed as a devout, old-fashioned Puritan, except among the Tories, who believed he had "a religious Mask ready for his Occasions; he could transform his self into an Angel of Light with the weak Religionist, & with the abandoned he would disrobe his self." He was never more angelic than when singing hymns in Dr. Checkley's meetinghouse, where he displayed "an exquisite ear for music, and a charming voice." But Adams found a way of turning even this talent to politics. He organized singing societies among Boston mechanics at which, Tories complained, more revolutionaries were produced than songbirds, because Adams presided over the meetings and "embraced such Opportunities to ye inculcating Sedition, 'till it had ripened into Rebellion."[4] He never overlooked an opportunity to give a religious flavor to his political activities. During crises in the struggle between the House of Representatives and the royal governor, Adams set aside days of fasting and prayer to "seek the Lord"; and by this means he gave the American Revolution the character of a moral and religious crusade. No patriot leader had greater

[3] *Samuel Adams Papers*, MSS. Mrs. Adams to her husband, Sept. 12, 1774.
[4] Peter Oliver, 57, 58. *Chalmers Papers*, Sparks MSS., Harvard College Library, III, "A Key to a Certain Publication." *The Works of John Adams*, X, 251.

success than Sam Adams in convincing New Englanders that if they tamely surrendered their liberty to the British government, their religion was certain to be swallowed up by "Popery" or Episcopacy. Thomas Hutchinson said that he made religion a "stalking horse"; and Peter Oliver groaned that Adams had perverted the New England clergy, who, by making their pulpits "Foam with Politicks" and "Unceasingly sounding the Yell of Rebellion in the Ears of an ignorant & deluded People," incited them to revolt.[5]

Sam Adams never forgot those stirring days during the Great Awakening when George Whitefield "thunderd in the Pulpit against Assemblies & Balls" and New Englanders seemed to turn the clock back to the time of Winthrop and Cotton. The glimpse Adams caught of "Puritanism" in 1740 had profound influence upon his later career. It became one of his strongest desires to restore Puritan manners and morals to New England: in his eyes, the chief purpose of the American Revolution was to separate New England from the "decadent" mother country in order that Puritanism might again flourish as it had in the early seventeenth century. Adams hoped to do by means of a political revolution what George Whitefield had done through a religious awakening. Puritanism was his goal: revolution his method of attaining it. But, as Adams was to learn, it was far easier to make New Englanders rebels than "Old Puritans."

One of Sam Adams's most effective ways of arousing patriotic fervor in New England was to appeal to the example of the early Puritans who had lived frugally, loved their liberties, hated the devil, and looked with no friendly eye upon the British government. He always said his purpose was to revive the "ancestorial Spirit of Liberty" in the people rather than to indoctrinate them with newfangled revolutionary principles. Like many other leaders who have precipitated great changes, he regarded himself not as an innovator but as a restorer of the past. When the patriot cause seemed blackest and hardship began to turn the citizens from Whig principles,

[5] *New York Gazette and Weekly Mercury*, Oct. 10, 1774. Mass. Archives, 27, *Hutchinson Corr.*, III, 110. *The Writings of Samuel Adams*, II, 336.

Adams rallied his followers by reminding them of the sufferings their ancestors had undergone to establish liberty in the New World.   He firmly believed that New Englanders' best security against British tyranny was the Puritan spirit, which, although sadly weakened in the course of a century, might again be made a bulwark of colonial liberty.   Unwittingly, Thomas Hutchinson helped Adams turn New Englanders' eyes toward the past and acquaint them with the heritage they had received from their Puritan ancestors.   In the winter of 1764, shortly before the colonies were thrown into turmoil by the Stamp Act, there appeared the first volume of Hutchinson's *History of the Province of Massachusetts Bay,* which dealt with the early period of New England settlement when many of the Puritan colonists had regarded themselves as bound by only the slenderest ties to Great Britain.   Despite its Tory authorship, Hutchinson's *History* was widely read in New England, and Sam Adams frequently quoted it to prove his argument that the colonies had been independent of Parliamentary authority in the seventeenth century.   The Stamp Act awakened New Englanders' interest in questions to which they had previously paid little heed; and Thomas Hutchinson's historical work, in the opinion of Dr. Ezra Stiles, "contributed more than any Thing else to reviving the ancestorial Spirit of Liberty in New England on this Occasion." [6]

But few Boston Whigs shared Sam Adams's longing to bring back Puritanism.   James Otis seems not to have cared a whit whether New Englanders became "Old Puritans"; and his own life suggests that he would not have found the Cottons and Winthrops congenial company.   For Otis was a hearty soul who rapped out oaths and treated sacred matters so lightly that his friends complained he "very often bordered upon profaneness." [7]

In this respect, James Otis was a far more typical member of the Boston Whig Club than was Sam Adams.   The struggle

---

[6] *A True copy of the Manuscript Book entitled, the Stamp Act found among the Literary Remains of Dr. Ezra Stiles,* H. Stevens (1843), 64, MSS. Library of Congress.

[7] *The Works of John Adams,* II, 227.

between Whigs and Tories had cast Adams among strange bed-
fellows. He, the "holy man" of Boston, a dour Calvinist who
grumbled that New Englanders had lost their piety and were
"greatly degenerated," worked hand in hand with Dr. Thomas
Young, an avowed freethinker, and with William Molineux,
who went "neither to Mass, Church, nor Meeting." Dr.
Thomas Young had come from Albany to Boston in 1766 with
a reputation as an infidel, unsuccessful land speculator, and
passionate Son of Liberty. He was a close friend of Ethan
Allen and probably collaborated with him in writing *Reason
the only Oracle of Man, or a Compendious System of Natural
Religion.* William Molineux — known among the Sons of
Liberty as "Paoli" Molineux — was a small hardware merchant who became Sam Adams's lieutenant and "first Leader of
Dirty Matters" in Boston.[8] Although a notorious unbeliever,
Molineux was considered by the Tories to have a great deal
in common with Sam Adams inasmuch as both had "*fingered*
the public cash" and persuaded the "unthinking rabble . . .
to vote away the town's money." This singular mixture of
churchmen and infidels in the Boston patriot party was so striking that Hutchinson said it was composed of "mad, abandoned,
atheist fellows" and pious intriguers who, at heart, were no better than their companions. It is significant, however, that Sam
Adams did not permit his religious opinions to stand between
him and his fellow revolutionists. He judged men by their
political rather than by their religious creeds and catechized
his friends upon their Whiggery, not upon their Congregationalism. A man might be "a perfect viper, a fiend, a Jew, a
devil," but if he was orthodox in politics he was admitted into
the party.[9] Although John Wilkes was certainly no "Old Puritan" in private life, Adams reverenced him as a patriot struggling
"in the Cause of public Liberty, and Virtue, through the Rage
of Persecution." As became a follower of John Locke, Adams
believed all religious sects except those which taught doctrines

[8] *Boston Evening Post*, March 23, 1772. *Publications Col. Soc. of Mass.*,
Transactions 1906–07, XI, 17. *The Diary of John Rowe*, 286. *Massachusetts Spy*, Nov. 14, 1771.

[9] Mass. Archives, 26, *Hutchinson Corr.*, II, 514. *The Works of John
Adams*, II, 179; X, 262.

"subversive of society" should be tolerated. But during the
French Revolution, Tom Paine's irreligion became so brazen
that Adams felt obliged to rebuke his old friend of revolutionary days for contributing to the depravity of the younger generation.[10]

During the early period of revolutionary unrest in Massachusetts, James Otis was a far more important figure than Sam
Adams. Otis's name was well known in England: one of the
first questions put by the Marquis of Rockingham to travelers
returned from New England was whether James Otis still retained his influence; but Governor Shirley of Massachusetts
was unable to tell "where the Devil this brace of Adamses came
from." Crown officers dreaded Otis as the "director of all
the Councils of the town of Boston" whose "mobbish eloquence"
and "superior Powers of inflaming and distracting an infatuated
People" made him the most formidable enemy of royal government in America. When New Englanders toasted American patriots, James Otis's name was usually first on their lips:
throughout the country he was loved as the "American Hampden" by the patriots and feared as "the Great Leviathan" by
the Tories. Otis's popularity cast Sam Adams in the shade; and
it was not until Otis had been invalided by a crack on the head
in a tavern brawl that Sam Adams emerged as the leader of the
New England patriot party.[11]

Until 1769, Sam Adams acted as Otis's lieutenant and party
"whip" in the House of Representatives, and as proofreader for
Whig newspaper agitators. Since Otis disliked to revise and
polish his newspaper articles and state papers, he gave them to
Sam Adams, as he said, to "quieu whew" them. Adams had
a "correct, genteel, and artful pen" and was particularly adept
in polishing the work of others.[12] Josiah Quincy likewise sent
his manuscripts to the offices of the Boston Gazette with instruc-

[10] *The Writings of Samuel Adams*, II, 100–101; IV, 412–413.
[11] Mass. Archives, 25, *Hutchinson Corr.*, I, Thomas Hutchinson, Jr., to
Thomas Hutchinson, May 29, 1766. *The Works of John Adams*, II, 233,
367. *Bernard Papers*, IV, Bernard to Lord Shelburne, Jan. 24, 1767. *Massachusetts Gazette*, July 21, 1768. *Boston Gazette*, Aug. 18, 1766, Harbottle
Dorr Files, Mass. Hist. Soc.
[12] *The Works of John Adams*, II, 163; X, 367.

tions that they be corrected by Sam Adams. As a consequence, many of the newspaper articles in the *Boston Gazette* and the petitions and correspondence of the Massachusetts House of Representatives bear evidence of having been "smoothed with the oily brush of Sam Adams." [13]

Whereas Sam Adams was a popularizer of current political doctrines and a propagandist who was at his best in a rousing piece of sedition, James Otis was an original political thinker. When not lampooning Hutchinson and Bernard in the newspapers, Otis found time to write the *Rights of the British Colonies Asserted*, in which Sam Adams found most of his arguments against the Stamp Act ready-made. Although Otis was a stout imperialist who would have been horrified to learn that he was writing a textbook of rebellion, it was upon natural law, as conceived by Otis, that the American Revolution was ultimately defended.

Unlike modern centralized governments which pay scant respect to the laws of nature, Americans of the revolutionary generation regarded them as decrees of God, scarcely inferior to Biblical revelations. James Otis believed that natural law was superior to all man-made law. If an act of Parliament violated natural law, he said, it was contrary to "eternal truth, equity and justice, and consequently void." In Otis's eyes, the British Constitution was founded upon fundamental principles derived directly from nature; and, since Parliament drew its authority from the constitution, it was likewise bound by natural law. If Parliament attempted to break through the limitations imposed by nature, it overturned the constitution and destroyed its own authority. [14]

Natural law became a dogma among colonial Whigs because it afforded them a defense against British taxation. As James Otis said, the law of nature gave "to all men a natural right to be *free*"; and it was clear that Americans were not free if they were taxed by representatives from Old Sarum and the "cornish barns and ale-houses." Sam Adams proclaimed as one of the

---

[13] Josiah Quincy, *Memoir of Josiah Quincy, Junior* (1875), 21. *The Works of John Adams*, X, 361.

[14] Otis, *The Rights of the British Colonies Asserted and Proved* (1763), 70.

principles "upon which the *British empire is founded*" that no
money could be taken without the subjects' consent.   Since there
could be no rightful taxation without representation, natural
law ordained that the colonists could not be taxed by the British
Parliament in which they were not represented.[15]

Colonial lawyers and patriots never doubted they had been
taken into the confidence of the Almighty and privileged to
read His will in nature.   By their interpretation of these laws,
the colonies won every point in their controversy with the mother
country; indeed, nature seemed to work so exclusively for the
Americans that Englishmen complained that every usurpation
and attack upon government seemed sanctioned by God and
nature.   Americans appealed to the law of nature to prove
their equality to Britons.   Sam Adams believed that God had
decreed that New Englanders were "upon *equal* footing" in
point of liberty and privilege with the inhabitants of Great
Britain.   By thus basing his case upon natural law, Adams
escaped the pitfall which awaited those American patriots who
made colonial charters their chief defense against British oppression.   Without natural law there could have been no political theory common to all the colonies.   The charter-rights
patriots failed utterly to erect an effective barrier to Parliamentary taxation; on the contrary, they succeeded only in imperil-
ing colonial unity.   No common ground could be found in
colonial charters for resisting the mother country: the form of
government established under them differed greatly in the various colonies and some had no charters.   By relying upon natural law, however, Americans could boast that all the charters
in America could be annihilated without injuring their rights
as "men, citizens and British subjects."   For by the law of
nature every British subject was entitled to "all the natural,
essential, inherent and inseparable rights of our fellow subjects
in Great Britain."[16]

James Otis's cure for the ills of the British Empire was to give

[15] Otis, *Considerations on Behalf of the Colonists, Sent to the Publisher by
an unknown Person, from Boston, in New England, by F. A.* (London, 1765),
10.   Otis, *A Vindication of the British Colonies*, etc., 19.   *The Writings of
Samuel Adams*, I, 156, 190, 270, 288, 289.
[16] Otis, *The Rights of the British Colonies*, etc., 49, 51.

the colonists representation in Parliament. By this, Otis did not mean that a few "idle scurvey fellows" should be sent over to Westminster to sell themselves to the Ministry, but that there should be created a "thorough beneficial union of these colonies to the realm or mother country, so that all parts of the Empire may be compacted and consolidated, and the constitution flourish with new vigor, and the national strength, power and importance shine with far greater splendor than ever yet hath been seen by the sons of men." He did not believe that representation would greatly benefit his own generation, but to posterity it would be "an invaluable blessing" inasmuch as it would cause the colonies to "be united, knit, and worked into the very bones and blood of the original system." When Americans sat at Westminster, Otis said, British ministers would no longer be obliged to get their information of the colonies from "every vagabond stroller, that had run or rid post through America, from his creditors"; and the members of Parliament who knew no more of the affairs of British America than did "savages in California" would be able to hear colonial spokesmen from the floor of the House of Commons.[17] Yet Otis did not contend that the colonies had any legal right to representation in the British Parliament. At most, Americans had only reason and equity to support their plea that the House of Commons admit their representatives; and, Otis pointed out, if Parliament "indulged" the colonies by allowing them to return members to Westminster, it would be a favor, not the acknowledgment of a right. "Upon the reasonableness of an actual American representation," Otis said, "I placed my foot, and built my only hope and desire."

Sam Adams did not share Otis's eagerness for colonial representation in Parliament. While Otis urged that delegates from the provinces be sent to the House of Commons, Adams declared the scheme was *utterly impracticable* and no better than taxation without representation. By recognizing the practica-

[17] *Boston Gazette*, Aug. 26, 1765. Otis, *A Vindication of the British Colonies, etc.*, 20. Otis, *The Rights of the British Colonies, etc.*, 54. Otis, *Brief Remarks on the Defence of the Halifax Libel, Univ. of Missouri Studies* (1929), II, 174.

bility of such federation, Adams saw that he would throw away one of his strongest arguments for colonial liberty. He based his contention that the King had granted the right of taxation to the colonial assemblies upon the law of nature which made colonial representation in Parliament impossible. When America was separated from Great Britain by three thousand miles of ocean, nature had ordained that the colonies could not be represented in Parliament; and, because there could be no rightful taxation without representation, the British Parliament had no right to tax the colonies. Thus the colonial assemblies were made the sole taxing powers in America. Adams saw also that if American representatives were admitted to Parliament they would be too few in number to carry weight against the "King's Friends"; and, amidst the bribery and corruption of the House of Commons, he believed colonists would be hard put to preserve their virtue. Adams insisted that the only way to preserve the British Empire was to resume the form of government in effect before the passage of the Sugar and Stamp Acts. If the colonial assemblies were recognized as the sole taxing powers in America, Great Britain and the colonies would, he exclaimed, "long flourish in one undivided Empire." [18]

As radicalism gained strength in the colonies, much of Otis's political thought became antiquated and he was compelled to make apologies for his earlier conservatism. When his *Brief Remarks on the Halifax Libel* seemed likely to cost Otis his seat in the House of Representatives, Adams came to his rescue by declaring that there had been "almost a total Change of Opinion with Regard to our Rights" in the six months since Otis had written the *Brief Remarks*. Political theory had leaped forward so rapidly, it was said, that had Otis and other patriots "boldly asserted the truth, they would have been esteemed madmen, and their influence thereby wholly lost." Nevertheless, Otis's backsliding in the *Brief Remarks* could not be wholly explained away by this means. He had "*seemingly* carried the Parliamentary power and authority to the very *apex* of sublimity" and his enemies quoted it to prove that Otis was

[18] *The Writings of Samuel Adams*, I, 39, 40, 161, 171, 174, 175, 218.

really a Tory. Some of Otis's apologists suggested that his essay on the Halifax libel was a *"meer political Humbugg"* printed by the Tories to set honest Whigs by the ears. Otis himself attempted to make amends for having "rant it on the side of prerogative" by attuning his political theory to the radicalism of his followers. In particular, he was compelled to admit in 1765 that American representation in Parliament was doomed because of the colonists' opposition to federation.[19]

Between Sam Adams and James Otis there were differences in character and outlook that were to prove portentous to the peace of the British Empire. Unlike that of Adams, Otis's early background was conservative. Whereas Sam heard in his family circle denunciations of the British Parliament and the Massachusetts "sound money" aristocracy, James Otis was taught to praise the King, Parliament, and royal governors. Moreover, Otis was not born in Boston, the most fertile breeding ground of revolutionaries, but he made up for this shortcoming by attending Harvard College, which was second only to the metropolis in turning out future rebels against George III. Otis, however, never lost his reverence for the mother country. He was as stout a Massachusetts patriot as Sam Adams, but he was a British patriot as well, with a highly developed sense of the grandeur and power of the Empire. "If I have one ambitious wish," he exclaimed, "it is to see Great Britain at the head of the world, and to see my King, under God, the father of mankind." He believed the British Empire to be "founded on the principles of nature, reason and justice, and on the whole best calculated for general happiness of any that has yet risen to view in the world." [20]

James Otis represented an attitude toward the British Empire that was slowly dying in America, while Sam Adams expressed the assertive, independent spirit which, taking its rise from the early period of colonization, gained strength during the eight-

[19] *Boston Gazette*, May 5, 1766; Sept. 2, 1765; Jan. 13, 20, and 27, 1766; Dec. 30, 1765.

[20] James Otis to the Earl of Buchan, July 18, 1768; *Otis Papers*, MS. Mass. Hist. Soc., II.

eenth century and reached its full stature after the French had
been driven out of Canada. Sam Adams had little love for the
British Empire and, unlike most of his countrymen, he did not
regard the mother country as "home." John Adams once
said that although he had never been much of a John Bull he
had always been very much of a John Yankee. Sam Adams,
as well, was a John Yankee whose loyalties and loves were intimately bound up with New England and Boston. Indeed, later
in the Revolution, many Americans were to suspect him of
being too much of a Bostonian properly to guard the interest
of the United States. He was essentially a local patriot whose
sympathies had narrow range. Certainly he was not a traveled man: when he set out to attend the first Continental Congress in Philadelphia in 1774 it was the first time he had ventured far beyond Boston Neck.

To express the differences in temperament between Sam
Adams and James Otis, John Adams contrasted them with
Calvin and Luther, the leaders of the Protestant revolt. Otis,
said John Adams, resembled Martin Luther in that he was
"rough, hasty, and loved good cheer," while Sam Adams, like
Calvin, was "cool, abstemious, polished, and refined, though
more inflexible, uniform, and consistent." Tories made less
flattering comparisons, although their judgments of Whig leaders are more valuable as picturesque abuse than historical portraits. James Otis, said the Tory propagandist Peter Oliver,
was "rash, unguarded, foulmouthed, & openly spiteful," and
Sam Adams resembled no one so much as the Devil.[21]

Sam Adams's conduct as clerk of the Massachusetts House of
Representatives brought to view striking differences between
him and James Otis. The clerk enjoyed the privilege of taking part in the debates and casting his vote with the representatives. It was a post that could be made all-important by a
strong man: and none could say that Sam Adams did not take
full advantage of his opportunities. During the recesses of
the General Court, the London agent of the House of Representatives took orders from Sam Adams, who, as clerk of the
House or head of a recess committee, kept the colony's political

[21] *The Works of John Adams*, II, 163; X, 190. Peter Oliver, 57, 58.

waters almost as troubled as though the General Court itself were in session. By this means, Massachusetts Crown officers lamented, Sam Adams turned the blaze lighted by James Otis into a "perpetual flame." He had custody of all papers belonging to the House of Representatives and he published them freely in the *Boston Gazette* to keep the people informed of the struggle for freedom waged by their representatives. After Sam Adams had become clerk, Governor Bernard observed that all addresses of the House of Representatives to the royal governor were printed immediately in the newspapers with "the Air of a Manifesto much more than a Message to a Govr." [22] Moreover, it became difficult for the Crown officers to distinguish between Sam Adams's political tracts written for the *Boston Gazette* and the state papers he composed for the House of Representatives. Whether Adams was writing an address to King George or a squib at the Tories, his work seemed "in general designed for the Press & for that Purpose only."

Adams's fondness for publishing the proceedings and state papers of the House of Representatives in the newspapers soon brought him into conflict with James Otis. For many generations, the Massachusetts Assembly had not permitted its addresses to the King or Commons to be printed in the newspapers until they had been received and made public in the mother country. Sam Adams completely upset this traditional procedure. Instead of wasting valuable time waiting for King George and his ministers to ponder the petitions and remonstrances from Massachusetts Bay, Adams rushed them through the press and had them in the *Gazette* before they were stowed aboard ship for England. Such lack of respect for the King and Ministry deeply offended James Otis, who believed it very improper for petitions to be published in the colonial newspapers before they were received in England. When Adams proposed to publish a letter from the House to Lord Hillsborough before that minister had had opportunity to receive it in England, a stormy scene took place in the representatives' chamber between Adams and Otis. An eyewitness reported the dispute to Governor Bernard in the following manner: —

[22] *Bernard Papers*, VI, Bernard to Lord Shelburne, Feb. 7, 1767.

Otis. "What are you going to do with the Letter to Lord H[ills-borough]?"

Adams. "To give it to the printer to publish next Monday."

Otis. "Do you think it proper to publish it so soon that he may receive a printed Copy before the Original comes to his Hand?"

Adams. "What signifies that? you know it was designed for the People and not for the Minister."

Otis. "You are so fond of your own Draughts that you can't wait for the Publication of them to a proper Time."

Adams. "I am Clerk of this House & I will make what use of the Papers which I please." [23]

The letter to Lord Hillsborough appeared in the *Boston Gazette* a few days later.

When James Otis first entered politics in 1760 his enemies had sneered that he was insane and even his friends were soon compelled to admit that his conduct was disconcertingly eccentric. Level-headed John Adams thought Otis "fiery and feverous" and given to unseemly outbursts of passion. He was either very gay or very despondent; when melancholy, he reviled himself for ever having become a Whig; and when in high spirits he was apt to be rash and imprudent. Otis's love for the British Empire was constantly tormenting him with doubts which Sam Adams never experienced. Whenever Otis took a step forward on the slippery path to rebellion he was immediately conscience-stricken. When he returned from the Stamp Act Congress in 1765 he made such a violent speech at the Boston town meeting against Hutchinson that the mob would certainly have swooped down on the lieutenant governor's house again had there been anything left to demolish. Yet, within a few days, Otis outraged the Whigs by declaring that the only way to keep peace in the colony was to take away the Massachusetts Charter, fill the Council with royal appointees, and quarter British troops in Boston. His "mad pranks" at the town meetings began to prove costly to the patriots. At one time he is said to have called the Boston electors "*a pack of d——d stupid fools*" and he began to run off into such "incoherent ravings" that the Tories called him the "mad Dicta-

[23] *Bernard Papers*, IV, Bernard to Lord Hillsborough, July 9, 1768.

tor" of Boston. As moderator of a town meeting, Otis chal-
lenged George Grenville to single combat on the floor of the
House of Commons to decide whether the colonies were to be
free or enslaved by British "tyranny." No doubt the Boston
Sons of Liberty would have given heavy odds on the Whig
"gladiator," as Otis was called, against all comers in the British
aristocracy, but Otis soon lost his fancy to wrestle with English
statesmen. On the floor of the Massachusetts House of Representatives he was at times a wild-eyed radical, at others a strait-
laced conservative. As Thomas Hutchinson said, he often
seemed "more fit for a madhouse than the House of Representatives." [24]

Otis's singular conduct was the despair of patriots who, like
Sam Adams, made a virtue of consistency and "picqued themselves upon their Sanctity." [25] There was always danger that
when Adams was in the midst of a carefully planned coup, Otis
would give the game away by a passionate harangue or spill
the Whigs' secrets into their enemies' ears in a moment of repentance. Moreover, Otis did not share Adams's relish for
riots and the rough-and-tumble tactics used by the Whigs against
the Tories. Rather than turn loose the Boston mob, Otis
much preferred "dutiful and loyal addresses to his Majesty
and his Parliament, who alone under God can extricate the Colonies from the painful Scene of Tumult, Confusion, & Distress." [26] At one time he said in the Boston town meeting that
no possible circumstances could justify "tumults and disorders,
either to our consciences before God, or legally before men."
Repeatedly, Otis's moderation saved Adams and his hot-
headed followers from provoking a crisis between the mother
country and colonies. Unlike Adams, Otis never thought in
terms of American independence; even after Adams had become

[24] *Bernard Papers*, V, Bernard to Pownall, Nov. 5, 1765. *The Works of
John Adams*, II, 179, 180. *Boston Evening Post*, June 9, 1766 (Supple-
ment); May 19, 1766; March 31, 1766. Mass. Archives, 26, *Hutchinson
Corr.*, II, 235.

[25] Peter Oliver, 57–58. *American Stamp Act Papers*, 1765, 1766, MSS.
Lib. of Cong., James Otis to the Speaker of the House of Representatives for
the Province of New Hampshire, Nov. 8, 1765.

[26] William Tudor, *The Life of James Otis* (1823), 178 (note).

convinced that total separation from Great Britain was the only salvation of colonial liberty, Otis believed that "were these colonies left to themselves to-morrow, America would be a mere shambles of blood and confusion, before little petty states could be settled."

Despite Sam Adams's rapid rise in politics, it should not be forgotten that he was still under a cloud as a public defaulter. Since 1764, when his defalcations had first come to light, he had made many powerful enemies among the Tories, who were eager to bring him to trial. He was lampooned as "Jet" — one of the "pack of Cur-Dogs in Boston" — by Tory journalists. "This dog is very artful, loves babbling, especially when he gets into a very large Room," it was said; "has been taught to run into houses, to pick up money and run away with it directly to his kennel." Whenever Jet's master, the people, attempted to discover where he had hid this money, "one would imagine this sagacious cur realizes his Master's intentions for the moment he sees any of them, he runs to them, fawns, licks their hands and leaps upon them with so much cunning and good humour, that they forget all about the Money, spit in his Mouth, clap him on the side; and then away goes Jet, wagging his tail, and glad enough you may be sure." [27] The Tories gave the towns-people no opportunity to forget that unless Sam Adams made good his debt to the town the money would come from their own pockets. In March 1767, the citizens of Boston, now thoroughly aroused, appointed a committee to examine the books of the town tax collectors. The committee reported that Sam Adams owed the Province Treasury some £2300 and the town treasurer over £1700 — a total of nearly £4000 after deduction of salary. Sam Adams's prospects might have been dark indeed had he not already taken steps to defend himself against the irate citizens who were hounding him for debt.

For many years, Adams had made a practice of enrolling promising young men in the Whig Party. John Adams, himself one of Sam Adams's "boys," found that his cousin made converts by cultivating the friendship of likely young Bostonians, bringing them around to the Whig Club, and warning them of

[27] *Boston Evening Post*, Nov. 23, 1767.

the "hostile designs" of Great Britain against the colonies. Sam Adams had a keen eye for "every rising genius in the New England seminaries" and few good prospects escaped without a pressing invitation to attend the Whig Club, where they might be "embodied with the Whigs, and begin to taste of their spirit by being often in their company." Tories had a different name for Adams's missionary labors among the young: he was, said Peter Oliver, "ever going about seeking whom he might devour." [28] But there was no doubt of his success: Dr. Joseph Warren, Josiah Quincy, Jr., and Dr. Benjamin Church were among his pupils. Although Dr. Church came to a bad end by selling Whig secrets to the British in order to maintain a fine house and a fancy mistress, most of these young men became distinguished figures in the American Revolution. Close to the top of Adams's class of young rebels stands that eminent patriot, John Hancock.

In 1765, when Sam Adams first began to bring John Hancock to the patriot club, Hancock was a young man of fashion who possessed one of the largest fortunes in America. Although he was the son of an impoverished Congregational minister, his uncle, Thomas Hancock, was one of the shrewdest moneymakers in the colonies. Thomas Hancock made immense sums by smuggling and selling supplies to the British armies that served in America during the Seven Years' War. When he died childless in 1764, shortly before Sam Adams became interested in John Hancock, he left the bulk of his fortune of seventy thousand pounds to his nephew. Tory gentlemen had no liking for Hancock, whom they considered a man whose "brains were shallow and pockets deep"; and even the Whigs were compelled to admit that Hancock was not one of those "rising geniuses" of Harvard College for whom Adams was on the watch. Nevertheless, Hancock possessed what no precocious Harvard undergraduate could offer: money and prestige. Although he was overlooked by most as a makeweight between poor Whigs and rich Tories, Sam Adams quickly saw that his

[28] *The Works of John Adams*, X, 364. *Lamb Papers*, N. Y. Hist. Soc. MSS., Thomas Young to John Lamb, Nov. 19, 1774. Joseph Galloway, 110. Peter Oliver, 56.

eagerness for popularity and susceptibility to flattery might be
turned to advantage. Adams was desperately in need of powerful friends; and John Hancock, the wealthiest man in New
England, gave promise of rescuing him from his embarrass-
ments. That Adams expected to do himself a good turn at
the same time that he benefited the patriot cause can scarcely
be doubted, but it is questionable if Hancock realized that he
was expected not only to finance the Whig Party but to settle
the bills of its leader.

Tories were dismayed to find they had been napping while
Adams made a Whig of John Hancock, and they swore that he
had seduced Hancock "in the same Manner that the Devil is
represented seducing Eve, by a constant whispering at his Ear." [29]
Sam Adams did not underestimate the importance of his conquest nor was he backward in telling his close friends what use
he intended to make of Hancock. One day, while John and
Sam Adams were strolling along the Mall, Sam stopped before
Hancock's house and said that Boston had done a wise thing
by making "that young man's fortune its own." Hancock,
in other words, was to be made the financial godfather of the
Whig Party; or, as the Tories said, the "wretched and plun-
dered tool of the Boston rebels," the "Milch cow to the Faction,"
and the "poor plucked gawky" whom Sam Adams had stripped
bare.[30] It was observed that shortly after Hancock fell under
Adams's influence, Hancock began to branch out into new enterprises: by constructing warehouses and wharves and engaging
in trade on a larger scale he gave employment to so many workers
that John Adams estimated that a thousand New England
families were dependent upon him for support. It was not
likely that these laborers would offend their employer by voting
against his friend Sam Adams. The Tories were convinced
that Adams's "serpentine Cunning" was behind Hancock's new
ventures and that a policy of giving jobs in exchange for votes
had been adopted by the patriots. In any event, Sam Adams
determined to stand his ground in Boston and trust to Provi-

[29] Peter Oliver, 55.
[30] Tudor, 262. *Mass. Hist. Soc. Proceedings*, XII, Second Series (1899),
140. *Letters to Dr. Cooper* (Boston, 1775), 105, 112.

dence and John Hancock to deliver him from his difficulties
rather than to adopt the usual practice of defaulting tax collectors and skip out of the province.[31]

The story of how Adams escaped punishment for his defalcations properly belongs here.   In June 1767, suit was brought
in the Court of Common Pleas against him.   Adams was prose-
cuted by his friend James Otis, attorney for the town treasurer,
and although Adams won in the lower court, the appellate court
gave judgment against him for the whole penalty of the bond.
Execution was ordered to begin in March 1768 for £1463; and
Adams was given nine months in which to raise the money.

In March 1768, Adams appeared in the Boston town meeting,
not with cash, but with a petition.   He asked for more time to
collect his debts "that he may be enabled thereby to compleat the
Obligation of his Bond."   After this petition had been hotly
debated in the town meeting and Adams had promised to lay
a full financial statement before the people within six months,
the treasurer was ordered to stay execution.   This reprieve
was very unpopular with many thrifty townsmen who were unable to see why Adams's patriotic services should entitle him
to make away with the town's money.   Twenty Bostonians,
including Foster Hutchinson, the lieutenant governor's son,
petitioned that a town meeting be called to reconsider the respite
given Adams.   For an entire day, Adams's friend and enemies
debated furiously in Faneuil Hall, alternately picturing him as
a patriotic servant of the people and a rascally pilferer; but by
nightfall, the motion to reconsider was decisively defeated.[32]

Sam Adams spent this six months of grace in collecting small
sums from delinquent taxpayers, borrowing from John Hancock, and writing another petition.   In this second petition,
Adams dwelt upon the obstacles that had strewn his path as a
tax collector: the Boston fire of 1760, the smallpox epidemic,
and the poverty of the people.   If Adams's account were true,
he had served as a tax collector during a singularly catas-

[31] *The Works of John Adams*, X, 260.   Hutchinson, III, 298.   Peter
Oliver, 55.

[32] *Letters and Diary of John Rowe*, edited by Annie Rowe Cunningham
(1903), 157.   *Boston Town Records*, 16th Report of the Boston Record
Commissioners, 241, 242, 243.

trophic period of Boston's history and his only crime was in
being tender-hearted to the poor. But Adams might have
spared the citizens this lengthy catalogue of his virtues and
misfortunes. By 1769, Adams and Hancock were invulnerable
in Boston. The town meeting was now chiefly composed of
Adams's friends or those who looked to Hancock for their
livelihood. Indeed, Adams found the citizens so well disposed that he urged them to accept a small sum in full payment of his debt. He prepared a list of taxpayers who were
still indebted to him and he suggested that this list be turned
over to another collector, thus absolving himself of all responsibility. There was little opposition from the Tory Party,
now at its lowest ebb, and Adams's petition was granted by
the vote of a large majority. A few grumbled that patriots
were a costly luxury to Boston and agreed with John Rowe
when he wrote that it was "a very wrong step in the Town &
what they, I am afraid will repent." [33]   It was found impossible
to collect the money for which Adams was in arrears; and the
last chapter to this interlude in Adams's patriotic labors was
written in 1772 when a committee appointed to inspect the
state of the Town Treasury reported that Sam Adams still
owed fifty pounds to the Province Treasury and that there was
no hope of collecting the money owing to the town of Boston.[34]

[33] *Letters and Diary of John Rowe*, 183.
[34] *Boston Town Records*, 18th Report, 69.   Hutchinson, III, 295.   *Mass.
Hist. Soc. Proceedings*, XX, 213, 226.

V

THE MASSACHUSETTS CIRCULAR LETTER

In the history of the American Revolution there are many occasions when Sam Adams and the Whig Party, apparently about
to suffer defeat at the hands of colonial conservatives, were
rescued by the British government's timely blunder. Had
Massachusetts Tories been left to fight Sam Adams alone they
perhaps would have been able to stave off the Revolution for
years, but they could do little against the well-intentioned interference of the British government. Whenever Adams began
to founder in deep water the Ministry tossed him a life line in
the form of British tyranny. After 1766, the revolutionary
ferment in the colonies momentarily ceased; and radicals like
Adams who had been brought to the surface by the potent yeast
of the Stamp Act seemed about to slip back into obscurity. In
this crisis, the British government imposed the Townshend duties
upon the colonies. Instantly the cry of oppression was raised in
America; the Massachusetts circular letter revived colonial unity
against the mother country; and Sam Adams became one of the
most powerful men in New England.

In 1766 most Americans were too busy celebrating their
deliverance from British tyranny and raising statues to William
Pitt to ponder the problems raised by George Grenville's plan
of imperial centralization. Although the majority regarded the
repeal of the Stamp Act as proof of Great Britain's benevolence
toward America, Sam Adams believed George Grenville and
Parliament had created such ill feeling between mother country
and colonies "as it is to be fear'd will never wholly subside." [1]
He believed Parliament had repealed the Stamp Act more from
fear than from mercy: the colonial boycott of British manu-

[1] *The Writings of Samuel Adams*, I, 386, 387.

factures and the Stamp Act Congress had, he said, forced the
mother country to give way   In his eyes, Great Britain's mag-
nanimity toward the colonies was the result of American "firmness and resolution" rather than of Englishmen's sense of
justice.   Moreover, by passing the Declaratory Act at the same
time it repealed the Stamp Act, Parliament seemed to threaten
future oppression of the colonies.   The Declaratory Act was
a statement of the right of the British Parliament to legislate for
the colonies in all matters whatsoever; and by its terms the
sovereignty of the House of Commons over British America was
declared as absolute as that over Ireland.   It was not difficult,
therefore, for Adams to suspect the British government of
harboring plans to raise a colonial revenue in spite of its defeat
in the Stamp Act.   There seemed a multitude of ways by
which the British government could reach its goal of a colonial
revenue without awakening the colonists to their danger.
"Suppose for Instance," said Adams, "that some time hereafter
under the Pretext of Regulating Trade only, a revenue should
be designd to be raisd out of the Colonys, would it signify anything whether it be called a Stamp Act or an Act for the Regulation of the Trade of America?" [2]   Adams's fears were well
founded: within a year, the same thought was to occur to
Charles Townshend, Chancellor of the Exchequer, when he
took up the quest of a colonial revenue.

  With fresh British tyranny in the breeze, Sam Adams was not
disposed to relent in his struggle against the mother country and
the New England Tories.   But until overseas oppression again
became an actuality, Adams turned his attention almost wholly
toward strengthening the Whig supremacy in Massachusetts
Bay.   He was keenly aware that the Stamp Act was too valuable
to Massachusetts patriots to be thrown aside until the last drop
of propaganda had been squeezed from it.   His success in
linking Hutchinson with the Stamp Act led him to accuse the
entire Tory Party of being its abettor.   Adams and Otis drew
up a "Black List" of Tory representatives in the General Court
who, they declared, had favored the Stamp Act.   That the
Boston mob might know its enemies, the "Black List" was pub-

  [2] *The Writings of Samuel Adams*, I, 110.

lished in the *Boston Gazette*. In the House of Representatives, Adams demanded that votes be cast by name; and when Tories voted against the Whigs they found their names written in the House *Journal* by Sam Adams "so as to mark the Nays for resentment." Such measures utterly unnerved the Tory opposition: Boston's mobs kept many country Tories from taking their seats in the legislature and Sam Adams's intimidation muzzled those who had courage to come to the metropolis. Governor Bernard attempted to rally his followers by dismissing Whigs from militia posts and offering wavering conservatives their places, but desertions continued to weaken the Tory ranks. This browbeating of the conservative party resulted in a great Whig victory at the polls. Nineteen blacklisted Tories were "flung out & low and ignorant Men elected in their stead." [8]

As a result of this sweeping change in the House of Representatives, James Otis was elected speaker and Sam Adams clerk of the House in 1766. Their margin of victory was small: Otis could boast of a majority of only seven and Adams squeaked through with one vote to spare. Sam Adams remained clerk of the House for the next decade, but James Otis was immediately negatived as speaker by Governor Bernard. If Bernard had possessed the right of negativing the clerk of the House, he probably would have rejected Sam Adams as well. But because the governor's privilege of refusing to accept the representatives' choice of speaker had been used only once before in the colony's history, it was regarded as a weapon of last resort. Therefore, when Bernard revived this long-disused power to keep the most popular man in New England from the speaker's chair, he brought upon himself a torrent of Whig wrath. When it was learned that the governor had negatived James Otis's election, the Whigs rose to a man at this "signal to battle" and screamed for vengeance upon Bernard.

During a large part of the eighteenth century, the Country and Court Parties had struggled for possession of the Massachusetts Council. It was a prize worthy of the many sieges and battles that centred about it. The form of government

[8] *Boston Gazette*, March 31, 1766. Mass. Archives, 26, *Hutchinson Corr.*, II, 213.

established by the Massachusetts Charter made it impossible for
the royal governor to act effectively without the consent of the
Council, the members of which were elected by the House of
Representatives. If the Council were in opposition to the royal
government, the governor's hands were tied: consequently, most
Massachusetts chief executives urged the British government
to alter the form of government and pack the Council with royal
appointees. As long as the councilors were elected by the
House of Representatives Bernard declared the government
would be "like an open pleasure Boat, fit only for calm Seas &
favourable Gales." After the Stamp Act, there was very little
calm water or easy sailing for the royal governors of Massachusetts Bay. As long as the Council followed closely in the
wake of the governor and Crown officers, the mutinous representatives below decks could be kept under control, but if the Council
should begin to veer, nothing remained for the governor but to
"strike his Colours" and surrender the ship to Sam Adams,
who, Bernard suspected, navigated by the polestar of independency.[4]

Sam Adams nursed a deep grudge against the Council for
the part it had played during the Stamp Act troubles. Instead of siding with the popular party, the Council remained
loyal to the governor and planted obstacles in Otis's and Adams's
path. The Council had made it possible for Governor Bernard to store the stamps in Castle William; it had opposed opening the courts without stamps; and it had kept the House of
Representatives "within the Bounds of decency & moderation."
Because of these sins, Otis and Adams resolved to purge the
Council of Tories. Otis shrieked that the Upper House had
become an "infernal Divan" and swore to take the political scalps
of the sixteen Tories who paralyzed the Whig majority in the
House of Representatives. The governor's negation of Otis
as speaker of the House was made the signal for this purification
of the Council. Four judges of the supreme court, the
secretary of the province, and the King's attorney — Bernard's

[4] *Bernard Papers*, IV, Bernard to General Conway, Feb. 28, 1766; Bernard
to the Lords of Trade, April 10, 1766; Bernard to Lord Shelburne, March 28,
1767.

staunchest supporters — were ejected from the Council and men whom Hutchinson regarded as "little better than the scum" were put in their places.[5]   Although Otis failed to clear the Council of Tories, it had not undergone such a rigorous purgation since 1741, when the aristocrats were turned out by Deacon Adams and the Land Bank Party.

Having recovered from the panic in which "mobbish Bostonians" had plunged him during the Stamp Act riots, Governor Bernard was anxious to show his courage by sparring with Sam Adams in the General Court.   After the representatives had evicted the governor's best friends from the Council, he stormed down to the House to deliver two speeches which Sam Adams said were "as infamous & irritating as ever came from a Stuart to the English parliamt."[6]   Bernard accused the representatives of "oppognation" of the King's authority by turning out of the Council the friends of royal government merely because they supported the governor in his struggles to maintain the royal prerogative and authority of Parliament.   To this outburst Adams answered that the representatives were merely destroying a pernicious system by which the same persons held legislative and executive powers.   Bernard's fury did him no good and made it easier for Sam Adams to sink the royal government deeper into disrepute.   By allying himself to Hutchinson, Bernard had proved to Adams's complete satisfaction that he had "a deeply rooted prejudice against the people"; and Adams now began to look forward to sending the governor back to England with a chain around his neck.

A system of government such as existed in colonial Massachusetts, where an appointive governor represented the Crown and an elective house represented the people, inevitably bred contention.   Moreover, Whig supremacy in Massachusetts demanded a constant quarrel between governor and people: if the province should become quiet, Sam Adams could not hope to retain the influence he had gained by means of the Stamp Act.

[5] *Bernard Papers*, V, Bernard to Pownall, June 6, 1766; Bernard to Richard Jackson, May 31, 1766; Bernard to Lord Shelburne, Dec. 22, 1766.   Mass. Archives, 26, *Hutchinson Corr.*, II, 233.   Hutchinson, III, 149, 152, 156, 157.

[6] *The Writings of Samuel Adams*, II, 165.

After getting the worst of the quarrel with the House of Representatives in 1766, Bernard decided to avoid disputes with Adams in the future. He attempted to put the legislators in good humor by giving no provocation; but, no matter how precipitately he backed away from an encounter, Sam Adams always succeeded in bringing him into the quarrel. Whenever Bernard addressed the General Court, Adams read into his words such black meaning that the people were soon convinced that the governor was their worst enemy. If Adams and Otis could find nothing in Bernard's speech to turn into propaganda, they "filch'd a passage" from an address the governor had made five months before and, by distorting the meaning, "drew from thence an insinuation which has no foundation in truth." Finally, Bernard began to confine his speeches to bare formalities from which even Sam Adams could not squeeze a drop of propaganda. But Adams was revenged by fastening upon the governor the name of "Verres" — a tyrannical Roman governor of Sicily. It is no wonder that Bernard damned "that Adams": "Every dip of his pen," exclaimed the unhappy governor, "stung like a horned snake." [7]

Among those swept out of the Council by Otis's purge was Thomas Hutchinson. Even while the quarrel between mother country and colonies was hottest, Otis and Adams had not forgotten their feud with Hutchinson; and after the repeal of the Stamp Act they had no intention of ceasing their efforts to pull down the lieutenant governor and his fellow "oligarchs." Although Hutchinson had been forced to resign one of his offices during the Stamp Act, he and his family still held all the choice posts in the government and stood squarely in the way of Sam Adams's ambition. Moreover, it was chiefly through Hutchinson's efforts that the Council remained loyal to the governor and curbed the radicalism of the House of Representatives. Several years before, when Adams attempted to dislodge Hutchinson from the Council, he argued that executive and judicial powers should not be held by the same person. He now pointed out not only that Hutchinson's presence in the

---

[7] *Boston Gazette,* June 16, 1766. *The Works of John Adams,* II, 425, 426.

Council violated the principle of the separation of powers, but that Hutchinson was one of the bitterest foes of colonial liberty. Nevertheless, Adams succeeded by only a narrow margin in evicting the lieutenant governor from his seat in the Council. A majority of three voted not to return Hutchinson to the board.

Because the Boston mob had destroyed several thousand pounds' worth of Hutchinson's property during its "frolick" in August 1765, the question of compensation became a political issue. Sam Adams had no desire to reimburse Hutchinson for a loss he did not regard out of proportion to the lieutenant governor's deserts, and Bernard's blustering attempt to browbeat the Massachusetts Assembly made Adams even more resolute in opposing the compensation bill. Although Parliament had merely recommended that the Massachusetts General Court reimburse Hutchinson, Governor Bernard declared that Parliament had made a "requisition" which Massachusetts must obey. Such bullying hardly bore out Bernard's pious hope of restoring harmony in the colony because, as easily could have been foreseen, the Massachusetts House of Representatives refused to take orders from the British House of Commons on a money bill. Even without Bernard's blundering, there were serious obstacles in the way of Hutchinson's compensation. If the lieutenant governor were reimbursed from the Province Treasury, yeomen would be compelled to share the burden with Boston. Since "Boston Banditti" had done the damage, Massachusetts farmers said that the townspeople should be obliged to pay the entire bill. Bostonians thoroughly enjoyed a good riot, but they were dismayed by the prospect of paying for the wreckage. The Boston town meeting hastened to instruct the representatives to compensate Hutchinson out of the Provincial Treasury, thus distributing the expense between town and country. These instructions made Sam Adams as ardent as any Tory to do Hutchinson justice; and, paradoxically enough, it was largely through his efforts that the lieutenant governor was reimbursed from the Province Treasury for the damage done by the Boston mob.

Sam Adams was not satisfied with having made politics an

exceedingly hazardous career for Massachusetts Tories: he wished to silence all Tories whom the conservative rural districts sent to the House of Representatives. It had occurred to Adams that before the General Court could appear in its full dignity as the Parliament of Massachusetts Bay, a public gallery should be installed after the example of the British House of Commons. The chief benefit of a gallery, however, was not that it lent a Parliamentary atmosphere to the Massachusetts House of Representatives, but that it would practically drive the Tory Party from the floor. Even when the proceedings of the House were secret, proximity to the Boston mob cooled the most headstrong Tories; but with a gallery full of Adams's "Mohawks" listening to every word spoken in the House, few Tories would invite violence by openly opposing the patriots. As the Whigs said, the gallery would permit the people to see "who and who are together." The patriot leaders wished to seat the General Court in a building "equal to the most finished playhouse," where the people could hear Adams and Otis "thunder from the Rostrum." In this "School of Political Learning," asked Dr. Thomas Young, "how many would catch the fire" and emerge ardent Sons of Liberty? [8] It was well known that Sam Adams was more violent in speech than in print and that more treason was disseminated in the Whig clubs than in the newspapers. Although the proposal to open the House of Representatives to the public and transform it to all intents and purposes into a Whig debating club meant the virtual end of freedom of speech, the motion was carried and a gallery installed. The patriots immediately put it to good use: Adams crowded it with his "Mohawks & Hawcubites, to echo the oppositional Vociferations, to the Rabble without Doors" — to the acute discomfort of the already intimidated Tories.[9]

Massachusetts patriotism could not remain at the white heat to which Sam Adams had raised it without fresh tyranny from the British government. Yet the mother country made no

[8] Thomas Young to ——, Nov. 23, 1766, photostat copy in possession of Mr. George P. Anderson.
[9] Peter Oliver, 157. *Bernard Papers*, VII, Bernard to Lord Hillsborough, Sept. 9, 1768. *Boston Gazette*, Feb. 17, 1766.

effort to throw fuel on the embers left by the Stamp Act: there was a change of ministry favorable to the colonies; the molasses duty imposed by the Sugar Act of 1764 was reduced; and there seemed excellent chance that Parliament would relax the laws of trade. "The repeal of the Stamp Act," said John Adams, "has hushed into silence almost every popular clamor, and composed every wave of popular disorder into a smooth and peaceful calm." The people as a whole were not alarmed by the Declaratory Act of 1766: they regarded it as a "mere naked Form" and saw none of the latent tyranny perceived by Sam Adams. It was clear that unless Adams could keep up "the Clamour and Jealousy of the People by continuing to feed them with fresh Matter" he would lose the advantage he had gained over the Tories by the Stamp Act. Both Adams and the Tories were aware that tranquillity worked in favor of the conservative party — hence the Tories' rejoicing and Adams's dejection when calm water came into view in 1766. Many Boston merchants cut their connection with the politicians and began to look fondly in the direction of the Tory Party, which, Bernard said, included "almost every Person of Fortune and Fashion throughout the Province." Such fine company exerted powerful attraction at a time when Otis's influence was on the wane and little was to be feared from Sam Adams's mobs; and for the first time since the Stamp Act, Tories confidently looked forward to regaining the ground they had lost and bringing about the downfall of Otis and Adams.[10]

There could be no doubt that the Tory revival in Massachusetts Bay had assumed menacing proportions. In spite of Adams's efforts to fill the ranks at Whig assemblies, the meetings were "very thin & insignificant" and Bernard observed with satisfaction that there were few present who had "any pretension to converse with a gentleman." Although Sam Adams attended, his presence did not raise Bernard's low opinion of the company. In the General Court, the Whig Party was so riddled by desertions in 1767 that the Tories were

[10] *The Works of John Adams*, II, 202. Hutchinson, III, 147. *The Writings of Samuel Adams*, I, 109, 387. Mass. Archives, 26, *Hutchinson Corr.*, II, 344.

almost an even match. Even in the Boston elections, Sam
Adams and the other Whig members of the Boston Seat had a
stormy time before their ships, "remarkable for their steady
Sailing, being well mann'd with the best of Navigators and
true Sailors, got safe into Port." When Tories came within
inches of scuttling Adams and Otis in Boston, the safest Whig
anchorage in New England, it was clear that "Otis & his Gang"
were sinking fast. Otis himself was so frightened by the prospect of being caught in the rising tide of Toryism that he attempted to patch up a truce with Governor Bernard. The Whig
leader intimated that if Bernard would give up Hutchinson, he
would have no further trouble with the patriot party. But the
governor was so certain the Whigs were beaten that he rejected their overtures. Adams and Otis might "still mutter
threats," but Bernard felt certain he was safely out of their
reach.[11]

Massachusetts Whigs had fallen upon evil days, but Sam
Adams's skill in staging patriot parades, feasts, and celebrations
served to conceal most evidence of the patriot decline. He believed men were ruled by their emotions rather than by their
reason, and he knew that a display of fireworks on the Boston
Common or parades of marching Sons of Liberty were far more
effective ways of arousing popular enthusiasm than dry constitutional arguments. Unquestionably, he was a master of
stagecraft, deeply versed in the art of swaying the popular
mind. The Sons of Liberty celebrated the repeal of the Stamp
Act with "such illuminations, bonfires, pyramids, obelisks, such
grand exhibitions and such fireworks as were never before seen
in America." [12] Effigies of popular enemies were used to inflame the people's passion; cartoons exhibiting in easily understood form the wickedness of the Tories and mother country
were passed from hand to hand; stirring phrases were coined
and spread among the common people with greater effect than
whole volumes of political reasoning; and Whig newspapers

---

[11] *Boston Gazette*, May 11, 1767. *Bernard Papers*, VI, Bernard to Richard
Jackson, July 29 and Aug. 30, 1767; Bernard to Lord Shelburne, March 23
and May 30, 1767.
[12] *The Works of John Adams*, II, 179.

carried the radicalism of the seaboard towns to every corner of the province.   John Adams, too, saw the importance of Whig parades, fireworks, and propaganda: "Otis and Adams are politic in promoting these festivals," he wrote, "for they tinge the minds of people; they impregnate them with the sentiments of liberty; they render the people fond of their leaders in the cause, and averse and bitter against all opposers."   The Tories, on the other hand, knew nothing of influencing the common people; instead of attempting to wean them from Sam Adams, they merely sneered at them as "the rabble" or "the scum." The fatal error made by Massachusetts conservatives during the revolutionary period was their failure to recognize the importance of the common people in the coming struggle between mother country and colonies.   They looked to Great Britain for aid against the menace of colonial radicalism just as the mercantile aristocracy of 1740 had turned to the mother country for assistance against the Land Bank Party; but had the Tories actively combated radicalism and met the Whigs upon their own ground with their own weapons, Sam Adams would have found it far more difficult to overcome Toryism in Massachusetts Bay.   After the Revolution, the Massachusetts Federalist aristocracy held its own against Sam Adams's subversive Jacobinism because it won the support of a large part of the common people; the Tories of the revolutionary period were forced into exile partly because they ignored the masses.   After the full effects of Adams's propaganda began to be seen in New England, Daniel Leonard, a Tory pamphleteer, sorrowfully confessed that his party had made an irremediable mistake.   "I will do justice to their ingenuity," he said of Sam Adams and other Whig propagandists, "they were intimately acquainted with the felings of men, & knew all the avenues of the human Heart."

The most impressive of Sam Adams's celebrations was the annual festival held on August 14 to commemorate the founding of the Sons of Liberty and the riot against Andrew Oliver, the late stamp master of Massachusetts Bay.   Here the Sons of Liberty drank bumping toasts, roared out the chorus of the Liberty Song, and were edified by such choice mimicry as "the hunting of a bitch fox." [13]   The celebration of August 14, 1768, was typical of these Whiggish revelries.   The festivities were opened with the Sons of Liberty massing around Liberty Tree and singing the "American Song of Liberty" — "sublime entertainment" that drew applause and smiles from the "fair daughters of Liberty" who crowded all the windows around Hanover Square to watch their heroes.   After this performance, the wealthier Whigs climbed into their chariots and set off for Roxbury in a cavalcade that extended for over a mile and "surpassed all that had ever been seen in America."   At the Greyhound Tavern in Roxbury, the patriots sat down to a hearty dinner topped off with speeches and toasts.   After drinking forty-five toasts to the principal English and American Whigs, these stout patriots were still able to consecrate a Liberty Tree at Roxbury, make "an agreeable excursion round Jamaica Pond," and parade homeward through the streets of Boston. [14]

Fortunately for Sam Adams and the Whig Party, British squires still longed to tap the rich revenues they believed existed in the colonies and British politicians still pondered how Americans could be made to bear a share of the expense of imperial government and defense.   English landowners grumbled in 1767 that while they paid the war-time tax of four shillings to the pound, the colonists shirked their duties and rioted against the most equable form of taxation that George Grenville, the best financier in Great Britain, could devise.   Dissatisfaction gained such strength among the squires that the House of Commons mutinied against the party leaders and lowered the rate of taxation from four shillings to three shillings to the pound. Here, clearly, was an opportunity for a bright young man to save the Ministry and appease the truculent squirearchy by forcing the miserly colonists to make good the shilling which Englishmen had thrown over.   The hard-pressed taxpayers were not compelled to wait long before they found their man.   Charles Townshend, Chatham's Chancellor of the Exchequer, — known as "Champagne Charley" in London coffeehouses, — was one of the flashiest young politicians in England.   The revolt in

---

[13] *The Works of John Adams*, II, 218.
[14] Wells, I, 203. *Boston Gazette*, Aug. 22, 1768.

Parliament against high taxes had placed him in a very painful position: Chatham blamed him for having allowed the House of Commons to get out of hand and all parties awaited his resignation as Chancellor of the Exchequer after his defeat on a money bill. Rather than give up office, Townshend was prepared to risk the peace of the British Empire. He believed the colonies were still fair game for taxation by the British Parliament and he saved his place and hastened the Revolution by imposing new taxes upon them.

But Charles Townshend was far too clever a young man to send the Sons of Liberty scurrying for their muskets by repeating George Grenville's mistakes. He chose rather to take Americans at their word by giving them the sort of taxation they had acknowledged to be within Parliament's power. At the time of the Stamp Act, the colonists had distinguished between "internal" and "external" taxes. They had denied the right of the House of Commons to impose an internal tax such as the Stamp Act upon the colonies, but they agreed that port duties — external taxes — were constitutional. The distinction made by William Pitt was regarded in the colonies as a final solution of the problem of imperial government: Parliament could not tax the colonies, but it exercised "sovereign and supreme" authority over them. Parliament, said Pitt, had the right to restrict the colonies in their trade, navigation, and manufactures: it was sovereign "in every thing, except that of taking their money out of their pockets without their consent." George Grenville habitually pointed to the colonists' ready acceptance of this doctrine to prove his favorite argument that Americans were rascals who clutched at any absurdity to avoid paying taxes. Charles Townshend treated the distinction between external and internal taxation "as ridiculous in every body's opinion except the Americans'." But unlike most wits in the House of Commons, he was not content merely to jeer at the weakness of the provincials' reasoning: he sought for ways to take advantage of it. Since Americans admitted that external duties were binding, Townshend proposed to reach by means of port duties the same goal that Grenville had hoped to attain with the Stamp Act. By laying taxes upon paper, paint, tea, and lead imported from England into the colonies, Townshend told the House of Commons that at least forty thousand pounds in additional colonial revenue would be realized and the deficit resulting from the lowering of the tax scale in Great Britain would be considerably decreased. The scheme seemed safe: it was not to be expected that Americans would rise against port duties, the principles of which had been known in the colonies for a century. It was certain to raise a large revenue: by the laws of trade the colonists were compelled to import the duties commodities from Great Britain alone. Moreover, it eased British taxpayers by shifting part of the burden of imperial government upon the colonists' shoulders. Altogether, the plan put forward by the Chancellor of the Exchequer found such favor in the House of Commons that the "Townshend duties," as they came to be known in the colonies, were promptly enacted.

Colonial patriots were not slow to see that Townshend had forced them to seek new defenses against taxation by the British Parliament. Although the Townshend duties fell within the American definition of external taxes, the colonists were not happy that the British government had taken them at their word. It was the preamble to the Townshend duties which revealed to Americans that the mother country had sent another "menacing monster" swooping down upon the colonies. The preamble declared that the revenue realized from the Townshend duties was to be placed at the Crown's disposal to make governors and judges independent of the assemblies. This policy inevitably struck terror among Sam Adams and his followers, for all New England patriots regarded control of the purse by the local assembly as essential to colonial liberty. During the eighteenth century, Massachusetts had clashed with most of its royal governors over the issue of a fixed salary and had successfully resisted the British government's efforts to establish a civil list in the colony. But Charles Townshend seemed to have succeeded where a half century of British threats and stratagems had failed. Americans were no longer to be bullied into supporting a civil list: by placing taxes upon commodities which the colonists were forbidden to import from other countries, the British government made certain of a revenue ample to place colonial governors and judges out of reach of the assemblies.   And, after having accomplished this long-sought reform in colonial administration, enough money might remain to keep up a standing army to coerce refractory colonists and prevent the Sons of Liberty from stirring up a revolt.

Charles Townshend realized that laying new port duties was not in itself sufficient to produce the colonial revenue he had promised the House of Commons.   It was clear that before any considerable sums could be looked for from America, the colonial customs system must be completely reorganized.   The customhouse did not pay its own way: smuggling was still rampant and it was notorious that most customs officers had their price.   Townshend determined to put an end to this laxity by establishing new Vice Admiralty courts, authorizing writs of assistance, and appointing five Commissioners of the Customs to oversee the collection of colonial port duties.   These Commissioners were given powers similar to those exercised by the Commissioners of the Customs in England.   They acted under the authority of the Lords of the Treasury in the mother country; and all customs officials in the colonies were made responsible to them for the suppression of illicit trade and enforcement of the laws of navigation.   As if to give the Commissioners a taste of colonial intractability at its worst, Boston was made their headquarters.   It was believed in the mother country that since Boston had taken the lead among the colonies "in trade as well as politicks," the Commissioners should begin their labors among the "Saints": if Bostonians submitted, there seemed little doubt that the rest of the continent would follow suit.   With such high hopes were the heads of the Commissioners of the Customs thrust into the lion's mouth.

Sam Adams lost no time in mobilizing hostility in New England to the Townshend duties and Commissioners of the Customs.   To alarm the people for their liberty and property, Adams produced his most "dreadful scarecrows."   He pictured the colonies drained of their hard money by British taxation; townspeople and yeomen alike ruined by commercial stagnation; and governors and judges made arbitrary "overlords" of the colonies. Evil as the Townshend duties were, Adams did not suppose the British government would be long content with the revenue they yielded. The people were told that the taxes now imposed upon them were merely a "small specimen" of what they might expect after a standing army had been established in the colonies and the provincial legislatures deprived of authority. The Townshend duties, Adams exclaimed, were merely an entering wedge for British tyranny; they were fully as menacing to colonial liberty as the Stamp Act; and the Commissioners of the Customs, who had been sent to enforce them, merited no better treatment than the stamp masters. Reports were spread by the Whig chiefs that the Commissioners had been given power by the British government to tax land in New England in order to support the bishops who were to be set over New England. Because the Commissioners had authority to appoint underofficers to assist them in enforcing the laws of trade, Adams declared they would create "an host of pensioners" in the colonies to strengthen the Tories and Crown officers. As Adams roundly said, the Commissioners of the Customs were "the greatest political curses that could have been sent amongst us." [15]

This propaganda produced immediate results in Boston. Commerce was the mainstay of the town's economic life; and if the Sugar Act of 1764 had alarmed the citizens more than the Indian massacres on the frontier, the Townshend duties and Commissioners of the Customs seemed even more ill-omened. Bostonians were "set on boiling" by Sam Adams in 1767; and the Sons of Liberty of the metropolis strengthened their alliance with the New York Liberty Boys to prepare for possible military resistance to the British government. Adams planned to fall upon the Commissioners when they landed in Boston, march them to Liberty Tree, and give them a choice between resigning office or taking their chances with the mob. But Otis refused to join in provoking a quarrel with the mother

[15] *Letters of a Loyalist Lady*, 13. Mass. Archives, 26, *Hutchinson Corr.*, II, 327, 348. *The Writings of Samuel Adams*, I, 216. *Boston Gazette*, Oct. 12, 1767. *Boston Evening Post*, July 17, 1769.

country; New York gave the Boston hotheads no hope of military aid; and the other colonies seemed "perfectly easy and satisfied with what was done by the parliament." With great reluctance, the proposed reception at Liberty Tree for the Commissioners was given up. When they reached the town on November 5, — a day usually commemorated in Boston with a rousing riot, — the mob carried twenty "Devils, Popes, & Pretenders" through the streets bearing inscriptions of "Liberty, Property, & no Commissioners." Nevertheless, the Commissioners were not touched even when they passed close to the mob's bonfires on their way through the town. Boston was ruled by a "trained mob" which obeyed Sam Adams's orders; but the Commissioners were soon to learn that the Boston cudgel-boys were sorely disappointed at losing their "frolick" and restlessly awaited permission to drive them out of town.[16]

As Sam Adams had feared, the Commissioners of the Customs vigorously enforced the laws of trade, suppressed smuggling, and began to make the American customs profitable to the British government. It was soon evident to Bostonians that the British Ministry had revived the policy that brought Randolph to New England in the seventeenth century and had replaced the easy-going customs officers who winked at evasions and drank rum with smugglers by stiff, businesslike officials who collected taxes down to the last penny. Adams was as indignant as though smuggling were one of the rights of Englishmen which the British government unjustly denied Americans; and he quickly convinced most of the citizens of the province that tyranny was again flourishing in the metropolis. In reality, the Commissioners did more good to Sam Adams's party than to King George's exchequer. As long as the Commissioners collected port duties in Boston, Adams was under no necessity of appealing to abstract rights and imaginary grievances: he now had what he most sorely needed — visible tyranny imposed by the British government. Bostonians did

[16] *Bernard Papers*, VI, Bernard to Lord Shelburne, Sept. 21, 1767. Mass. Archives, 25, Thomas Hutchinson to Jasper Mauduit, Nov. 13, 1767. *Boston Evening Post*, Nov. 30, 1767; Dec. 21, 1767. *Letters of a Loyalist Lady*, 8. *Mass. Hist. Soc. Proceedings*, LVI, 348.

not have to "snuff the tainted breeze" for tyranny because, in
the persons of the Commissioners of the Customs and their
understrappers, it made itself felt constantly.   Sons of Liberty
throughout the colonies drank toasts to the "speedy removal of
the odious Board of Commissioners with all other vermin from
America." [17]

Sam Adams's grievance against the Commissioners of the
Customs was not only that they enforced unconstitutional laws,
but that they undermined Boston's morals.   Several of the Commissioners, being gay bloods out of England, attempted to enliven society in the metropolis, which they found insufferably
dull.   Their parties, balls, and concerts scandalized Sam
Adams and gave Boston its first taste of real night life: at a
"Turtle Feast" held at the Peacock Tavern, the Commissioners
and their friends celebrated until four o'clock in the morning,
when they were all carried home violently ill — which caused
Hutchinson to wish that the party had been composed of Otis,
Sam Adams, William Molineux, John Hancock, and "half a
hundred more of the same cast." [18]   The Commissioners en-
deavored to "mimic high life" by dressing in the height of
London fashion, retaining numerous servants, and "rolling
from house to house" in gilded carriages.   At first their balls
were unpopular, but Bostonians soon acquired a taste for these
"high frolicks"; and Sam Adams had the mortification of seeing Whigs, Commissioners, army officers, and Tories drinking
punch and dancing the minuet together.   Although the Commissioners found to their dismay that there were no eligible
"fortunes" in Boston, their assembly was so successful that the
patriots were forced to establish a rival "Liberty Assembly"
where Whigs might frolic without being exposed to the con-
taminating influence of the customhouse and royal barracks.
Concerts flourished as never before in the Puritan metropolis;
"grand Routs" and card parties became popular; cooks and
confectioners were brought over from London to satisfy the de-

[17] *Mass. Hist. Soc. Proceedings*, XLIII, 479.   Mass. Archives, 26, Hutchinson *Corr.*, II, 318, 319, 378.   *Newport Mercury*, Aug. 24, 1772.   *Lamb
Papers*, MSS. N. Y. Hist. Soc., Thomas Young to John Lamb, March 18, 1774.
Hutchinson, III, 345.
[18] Mass. Archives, 27, *Hutchinson Corr.*, III, 249.

mand for "luxurious and costly Feasting"; and the Whigs who scorned this prodigality were awakened at night by carriages rattling through the streets carrying parties on their way from carousals in the taverns.

Like many other strait-laced patriots, Sam Adams believed it was "a bad thing for Boston to have so many gay Idle people in it" whose example might spread to the citizens. If the citizenry became infected with fashionable London vices and conceived an appetite for "Turtle Feasts," Adams was certain New England would be undone; for when Whigs loved debauchery more than liberty, despotism would make an easy conquest of the colonies. After witnessing the conduct of the Commissioners of the Customs in Boston, Adams exclaimed that the British government was making war upon New England's morals as well as upon its liberties; and, with such unholy work going on in the metropolis, it is not strange that the clergy joined him in damning the Commissioners and the government that had sent them to Massachusetts Bay. The patriots and parsons looked upon the Commissioners of the Customs as sourly as the early Puritan magistrates had regarded those accursed sprites that danced around the maypole at Merrymount a century and a half before; and Adams yearned to smite the Commissioners as old Endicott had Thomas Morton and his crew.

In 1767, the winter session of the General Court opened so quietly that Governor Bernard began to believe the country had sent down enough moderate delegates to defeat the schemes of the "great Boutefeu," James Otis. But after Otis and Adams had harangued for several days upon the state of the colonies, the iniquities of the Townshend duties and Commissioners of the Customs, and the danger of a bishop being set over New England, the representatives' amiability rapidly disappeared. Within a short time they were in a "snarling humour." Otis and Adams were elected to all the important committees and, almost overnight, they seemed to recover the ground they had lost since the repeal of the Stamp Act. The House of Representatives obediently followed their directions by dispatching a letter of protest to the King, remonstrating to the Secretary of

State, and employing a separate agent in England "as if they were the States General of the Province, without a Governor and King's Council." [19] Bernard complained that the Whigs ignored him as though there were no royal governor in the colony: as clerk of the House, Sam Adams made no secret among his friends of the letters the representatives were preparing to send to the King and his Ministers, but he kept their contents hidden from the governor and the Tories. When the Crown officers learned that mysterious documents were being written in the House, they immediately suspected that Otis and Adams had some new trick up their sleeves to play against the King's government. It was widely believed that an effort would be made to call another colonial Congress. But, instead, Adams and Otis proposed that a circular letter be written to the other British-American colonies acquainting them with the measures adopted by Massachusetts against the Townshend duties. This scheme struck the delegates as a first step toward summoning a Congress; and few wished to invite punishment from the mother country by flinging such sedition in its face, particularly when they were uncertain of support from the other colonies. To the dismay of Otis and Adams, the House rejected the circular letter by a vote of two to one. Governor Bernard was overjoyed to see the Whigs soundly drubbed in their own back yard and he was certain the tide had begun to run swiftly in his favor: "The Faction has never had so great a Defeat as this has been," he rejoiced; "nor so great a disappointment, as it cuts off their hopes of once more inflaming the whole Continent." [20]

It was a source of great uneasiness to Massachusetts Crown officers that the upcountry Tory representatives in the General Court, among whom the royal government found its staunchest supporters, began to drop out of the House early in 1768. Believing all important business over for the session, the rural

[19] Mass. Archives, 26, *Hutchinson Corr.*, II, 284, 297. *Letters to the Ministry* (Boston, 1768), 7. *Papers relating to Public Events in Massachusetts, The Seventy-Six Society* (Philadelphia, 1856), 52. *Bernard Papers*, VI, Bernard to Lord Shelburne, Jan. 21, 1768.

[20] *Bernard Papers*, VI, Bernard to Pownall, Feb. 1, 1768. Mass. Archives, 26, *Hutchinson Corr.*, II, 287.

representatives returned to their farms, leaving the radicals in a majority. Governor Bernard observed with alarm that "the Friends of Government are allways tired out with the extended Length of the Winter Session, which the Faction lengthen for that among other Purposes. Hence it is that the Faction generally recovers Ground at the End of a Session." True to form, Adams and Otis seized this opportunity to secure a reconsideration of the circular letter. For a fortnight, they labored among the remaining delegates, convincing them of the legality of such opposition to British tyranny and quieting their fears that the circular letter would lead to a Congress. As a result, the legislature was thrown into the "most quarrelsome humour" that Hutchinson had ever seen in a Massachusetts Assembly. Since most of the "able Men on the Side of Government" were home congratulating themselves upon having tripped up the Whigs, Sam Adams's "private Cabals" soon whipped up a majority in favor of the circular letter. Shortly before the end of the session, it passed the House; and, to destroy all evidence of the difficulties encountered in securing its adoption, the first vote against the circular letter was erased from the *Journal*. Nevertheless, Tories continued to murmur that it had been "procured by surprise in a thin House" — a taunt which Sam Adams could not endure, probably because there was a large measure of truth in it.[21]

The Massachusetts circular letter formulated a new theory of colonial rights to combat the Townshend duties. Since the trade duties imposed by Parliament in 1767 made it plain to Americans that the distinction they had drawn between external and internal taxes was no barrier to oppression by the British government, Otis and Adams denied Parliament's right to impose external taxes, "with the sole & express Purpose of raising a Revenue." Although Parliament could lay taxes for the purpose of regulating colonial trade, it could not use the revenue to make governors and judges independent of the

---

[21] *Bernard Papers*, VII, Bernard to Lord Hillsborough, July 18, 1768; Bernard to Lord Shelburne, Feb. 20, 1768. *Letters to Dennys de Berdt, Col. Soc. of Mass. Collections*, XIII, Transactions 1910–11, 336. *The Writings of Samuel Adams*, 228, 231.

assemblies, as was contemplated by the Townshend duties,
without violating natural law. Thus, against Charles Townshend and the British House of Commons, Adams and Otis set
the law of God and nature which, by their interpretation, now
forbade even external taxes by Parliament. Englishmen exclaimed that all Adams and Otis were saying was that Parliament could lay a small but not a large tax upon the colonies;
and they rightly feared that the American Whigs would soon
deny its right to impose any taxes whatever. William Knox
said the powers Adams and Otis granted Parliament were
similar to those the Deists gave God over mankind: "He may
reward them with eternal happiness if he pleases, but he must
not punish them on any account." [22]

Both Sam Adams and James Otis could take this stand against
external taxes with perfect consistency. From the beginning,
James Otis had ridiculed his countrymen's distinction between
internal and external taxation. In 1765, he said that Parliamentary restrictions on colonial trade and manufactures were
no different from internal taxes; and after the repeal of the
Stamp Act, he told the Boston merchants they were fools for
submitting to trade duties and restraints on manufactures because Parliament had no right to confine American commerce
and manufactures. To the end of his political career, Otis
kept up a steady fire against Parliamentary legislation which
prevented the colonists from manufacturing iron "much beyond
the making a horse shoe or a hob-nail" and swaddled intercolonial commerce so tightly that the provinces were "scarcely
permitted to vend egg shells beyond their boundaries." Sam
Adams had said as early as 1764 that a tax on foreign molasses
laid by the British House of Commons to raise a revenue in
the colonies was a direct infringement of American rights.
Both Otis and Adams feared before 1767 that the British
government would renew the policy of the Sugar Act of 1764
and seek a colonial revenue by means of port duties: hence they

[22] William Knox, *The Controversy between Great Britain and her Colonies
Reviewed* (1769), 35, 38, 44. Hutchinson, III, 164, 165. *Remarks on
the late Celebrated Oration* (London, 1766), 28. *A Plain and Seasonable
Address to the Freeholders of Great Britain on the Present Posture of Affairs
in America* (London, 1766), 16.

were prepared in 1767 to receive the Townshend duties with a fully developed theory of colonial rights.

Nevertheless, the Massachusetts circular letter did not go beyond the point of denying Parliament's power to raise a revenue through external taxes.   Parliament was accorded the rights to regulate colonial trade and was recognized as the "supreme legislative Power over the whole Empire."   The letter written in the House of Representatives by Otis and Adams to the Marquis of Rockingham in 1768 admits the "superintending power" of Parliament over the colonies, and nowhere in the extensive correspondence, petitions, and remonstrances drawn up by them in that year is there a direct attack upon Parliament's sovereignty.   Its authority in the colonies was being cut away piecemeal, but the patriots were not yet aiming their blows at the root of Parliamentary jurisdiction.

John Adams was never able to understand why Sam Adams did not declare in the circular letter his conviction that Parliament had no authority whatever in America.   John Adams said he himself had already reached this conclusion; yet because the circular letter admitted Parliamentary sovereignty he believed it was entirely the work of James Otis and summed it up as "the rough cast of James Otis and the polish and burnish of Samuel Adams": "Every sentence and every word," he exclaimed, seemed to spring from Otis.[23]   But there is no reason to minimize Sam Adams's contribution to the circular letter merely because it acknowledged Parliament's sovereignty.   No realist such as Sam Adams could close his eyes to the fact that the time was not ripe in 1768 to throw off all Parliamentary authority.   Had Massachusetts taken the bold stand that John Adams favored, colonial unity would have been at an end and the Revolution set back many years.   The purpose of the circular letter was to unite the colonies against British oppression; and it was clear in 1768 that the colonies could be united only on conservative ground.   American political thought was dominated at this time by John Dickinson, the "Pennsylvania Farmer," who firmly believed that mobs, sedition, and ungentlemanly violence had no part in colonial resistance to the

[23] *The Works of John Adams*, 367, 374.

mother country. At the same time that Dickinson taught Americans devotion to Whig principles, he inculcated love of the mother country and reverence for King and Parliament — loyalties which did not seem incompatible in 1768. Although Dickinson denied Parliament's right to raise a revenue in the colonies by means of external taxes, he acknowledged its power to regulate colonial trade and legislate for the colonies. This doctrine, so distasteful to John Adams, became fashionable in Boston, where the town meeting in 1768 instructed the representatives in the General Court to "pursue the principles laid down by your worthy Farmer" and to state the colony's "constitutional subordination" to Parliament. As long as John Dickinson was regarded as the oracle of American political thought, no effort to throw off Parliament's sovereignty could hope for success.

John Adams ignored public opinion, frequently to his cost; Sam Adams was keenly sensitive to it. Many years after the passage of the circular letter, the latter is said to have remarked: "It is often stated that I am at the head of the Revolution, whereas a few of us merely lead the way as the people follow, and we can go no further than we are backed up by them; for, if we attempt to advance any further, we make no progress, and may lose our labor in defeat." [24] Sam Adams did not broach in 1768 so revolutionary a doctrine as complete freedom from Parliamentary authority because he knew he would isolate himself by outstripping public opinion. Had he rung the "alarm bell to a revolt" against Parliament prematurely, he would have destroyed the purpose of the circular letter and separated Massachusetts Bay from the rest of America, for not a single colony was ready to take so radical a step.

It is clear, nevertheless, that Adams believed in 1768 that Parliament had no lawful sovereignty in America. As early as 1748, in fact, Adams had regarded the Massachusetts General Court as the parliament of the colony; and he shared the conviction of the Sons of Liberty that the colonies had "no Superior upon Earth but the King." It was probably at Adams's instigation that the Massachusetts House of Represent-

[24] James Loring, *The Hundred Boston Orators* (1854), 13.

atives adopted resolves in 1765 which omit acknowledgment of the authority of Parliament. In these resolves the Massachusetts representatives declared they "venerated" Parliament, but nowhere do they grant Parliament specific authority.[25] Although Sam Adams called Parliament that "truly august body" in 1768 and said he felt "the greatest veneration" for it, William Knox pointed out that the patriots' reverence was merely "another subterfuge for seeming to respect its authority, whilst they *mean* to disavow it." Adams's recognition of the "superintending power" of Parliament when it was in accord with "the Enjoyment of our essential Rights as Freemen, and British Subjects," in effect stripped Parliament of most of its authority in America. If the colonists themselves were to be judges of the constitution, their "constitutional subordination" was worthless in the eyes of British imperialists. In every colony, Sam Adams said, the King, Council, and Assembly constituted the legislature of the province; and the British Parliament as "the Supreme Authority of the Nation" had a controlling power over the colonial legislatures so far as was consistent with the rights of Englishmen. But, he was careful to add, no Englishman was bound by laws made by a legislature in which he was not represented: "Thus," said Hutchinson, "in the same breath they give & take away all power of Parliament over the Colonies." Sam Adams gave a far clearer insight into his opinion of Parliamentary sovereignty when he exclaimed in the Boston town meeting in 1769: "Independent we are, and independent we will be." [26]

Hutchinson believed that Adams would soon interpret the law of nature to destroy completely Parliament's authority in the colonies: it was merely a matter of time, he said, before the cry of "no taxation without representation" would become "no legislation without representation" — an eventuality anticipated by many Englishmen as well. After the repeal of the Stamp Act, British statesmen feared the colonists would next demand the repeal of the navigation laws — the "Palladium of the Empire." It was hardly to be supposed that

[25] Hutchinson, III, 133–134.
[26] Mass. Archives, *Hutchinson Corr.*, II, 305.

Americans would consent long to pay 30 per cent more for
highly taxed British merchandise if they could buy untaxed
goods direct from the continent simply by throwing overboard
the mercantilist system. "Here," exclaimed an English writer,
"they are galled — *here* it is that the shoe pinches." [27]

No sooner had the Whigs pushed the circular letter through
the Massachusetts House of Representatives than a new Tory
menace sprang up in the colony. Thomas Hutchinson still
smarted from the humiliation he had suffered in 1766 when
Otis and Adams expelled him from the Massachusetts Council.
Early in 1768, however, having made careful plans to recover
his seat, he came within three votes of being elected to the
Council on the first ballot. It seemed impossible to prevent
his victory at the next vote. Adams and Otis, although they
were caught napping by Hutchinson's unexpected popularity
among the delegates, acted quickly. In the midst of the ballot-
ing, Sam Adams took the floor to ask the representatives if they
were sure the lieutenant governor was not a pensioner of the
Crown. Upon this signal, Otis leaped to his feet and exclaimed that he knew Hutchinson to be a pensioner paid by the
King from the "unconstitutional" taxes collected by the Commissioners of the Customs. Otis then ran round the House
"like an amazed Dæmon" furiously shouting "pensioner or no
Pensioner." Hutchinson's pension consisted of a small addition
to his salary as Chief Justice, which, he complained, was "scan-
dalously mean," but nothing was more calculated to arouse the
House against him than the name "pensioner" which Otis now
shrieked at the top of his lungs. Otis was well rewarded for
his effort. After the uproar had died down and the second
ballot had been counted, it was found that enough votes had
been turned away from Hutchinson at the last moment to
keep him from entering the Council. [28]

The Whigs had so narrowly averted defeat at Hutchinson's
hand that Sam Adams felt obliged to brace them with some

[27] *A Plain and Seasonable Address to the Freeholders of Great Britain, etc.*,
10, 16.
[28] *Bernard Papers*, VI, Bernard to Richard Jackson, June 6, 1768. Mass.
Archives, 26, *Hutchinson Corr.*, II, 306, 308.

particularly stiff doses of propaganda. James Otis had won the support of the "black regiment" of Congregational ministers, but it remained for Sam Adams to put the whole Tory Party under suspicion of Popery. As Adams was well aware, one of the surest ways of arousing New Englanders was to play upon their aversion to Roman Catholicism. Although Puritanism had disappeared, the hatred of Popery was still as strong as in the days of Winthrop and Cotton: the first book school children read was the *New England Primer*, embellished with a frontis-piece depicting the Pope "stuck around with Darts"; and Bostonians zealously burned "popes" on Guy Fawkes Day. A "papist" in eighteenth-century New England was not merely a Roman Catholic, but a boon companion of the devil and an abettor of all his works.

To crush the Tories, in 1768, Adams forced them to shoulder all the obloquy which "papists" carried in New England. Writing in the *Boston Gazette*, under the signature "A Puritan," he declared that Popery was abroad in Massachusetts and gaining ground so rapidly that it was more to be dreaded than British tyranny. He made Popery synonymous with the unwillingness shown by a large number of representatives in the General Court to support the Boston Whigs against the royal governor and British Parliament. He prepared lists of "Protestant" towns in the colony whose delegates voted with Boston, and "popish" towns whose representatives were "Governor's Tools" and worshipers of "graven images." The strongholds of Popery, by Adams's reckoning, were the Salem–Marblehead district and the western towns in the vicinity of Hatfield: the delegates from Salem, Hardwick, Hatfield, and Springfield were notorious Tories and the infection had spread even to Cambridge. Indeed, unless Adams exaggerated the danger, the Pope — presumably in the person of Governor Bernard — might take possession of Massachusetts at any moment, so alarmingly had his adherents grown; and many of those who were not outright "papists" were so shaky in their Protestantism that no good could be expected from them. "A man who Wavers," Adams exclaimed, "is but a step from a TOTAL APOS-TACY." Unless Massachusetts was to become the domain of

the Holy See at Westminster, the General Court must be filled
with "sound Protestants" who, it was implied, feared neither
the devil, the royal governor, nor the British House of Commons.[29]

Unquestionably, this skillful working with prejudice and
religious intolerance had great effect in solidifying the patriot
cause in the country where Tories found themselves regarded
by pious rustics as secret favorers of the "Romish" faith.
Tories denounced Adams for injecting religious passions into a
political struggle, but Adams was never nice in his choice of
methods when he believed the cause in danger. But despite
Adams's success in painting the Tory Party as bigoted to the
principles, if not the faith, of Roman Catholicism, there were
those who whispered that Adams himself was the real papist
because he insisted, with the Jesuits, that the end justifies the
means.

Adams's attack upon the Tories was well timed, for, soon
after his "Puritan" letters appeared, the British government
formally demanded that the Massachusetts House of Representatives rescind its circular letter on pain of dissolution; and Lord
Hillsborough's circular letter to the colonial assemblies ordered
them to discountenance the Massachusetts letter. But when
this command reached Massachusetts, the Tories were scattered
and made contemptible by Adams's propaganda and the moderate Whigs had been braced by the Boston radicals. Moreover, the dictatorial tone assumed by the British government
brought Massachusetts patriotism to white heat. Otis delivered a fiery oration in the Massachusetts House of Representatives against rescinding the circular letter; and the Tories
maintained a discreet silence because the gallery was crowded
with several hundred of Adams's "Mohawks." As a result,
the representatives voted 91 to 17 to defy the British government. Most of Governor Bernard's supporters voted with the
patriots, and their timeserving was fully justified by the treatment meted out to the seventeen members who voted to rescind
the circular letter: their names were posted on Liberty Tree and
they were branded as parricides to whom "the out done DEVIL
will resign his sway." Throughout the continent, Sons of

[29] *The Writings of Samuel Adams*, I, 203, 210, 212.

Liberty drank to the damnation of "the Seventeen of Massachusetts Bay," and few of them ever sat again in the General Court.

The efforts made by the British government to compel the colonies to renounce the Massachusetts circular letter raised patriotic fervor in America to a pitch it had not reached since the Stamp Act.   Instead of rejecting the circular letter as Lord Hillsborough demanded, the colonial legislatures enthusiastically adopted it and sent promises of support to Boston.   Sam Adams believed that "no one step . . . united the colonies more" than the Massachusetts circular letter unless it was Lord Hillsborough's own.   When answers from the Virginia and Maryland legislatures reached Boston, Adams declared it the most glorious day he ever saw.   During the Stamp Act days, Massachusetts had been laggard and Virginia had first rung the "alarum bell," but there could be no question that Massachusetts had taken its proper place of leadership in resistance to the Townshend duties.

The overwhelming majority in the Massachusetts House of Representatives that voted against rescinding the circular letter gave such clear indication of the patriots' strength that the Council gave up the struggle and deserted to the Whigs.   Ever since Otis's "purge" of 1766, the Massachusetts Council had shown an alarming inclination to run with the Whigs, but until the summer of 1768 it remained under the governor's control. After the colony had hurled forthright defiance at the British government, however, the councilors seemed to stand in greater fear of the people than of the King and governor.   Several years before, Bernard had said that as soon as Otis and Adams took possession of the Council, "the Governor has nothing to do but to strike the Colours."   Therefore, when he saw the Upper House of the legislature go over to the enemy, Bernard declared the royal government was "at length subdued" and he prepared to run up the white flag.   "After a three Years' War," he wrote Lord Hillsborough, the Council — the "Citadel" of royal government — had fallen and its garrison been made "Creatures of the People." [30]

[30] *Letters to the Ministry* (1768), 65. *Bernard Papers,* Bernard to Lord Hillsborough, July 7, 1769.

The theory of imperial government contained in the Massachusetts circular letter revealed how deep a gulf now divided British and American political thought. In Great Britain, the Massachusetts General Court was popularly supposed to be an assembly of Yankee rustics whose authority did not go much beyond making laws for the "yoking of hogs, or pounding of stray cattle." A colonial legislature seemed to Englishmen little more than "the vestry of a larger parish" or an "inferior licensed Corporation." The Massachusetts Charter, which Sam Adams believed to be "the Ark of God to New England," had little sanctity in England, where colonial charters were spoken of as "feeble Charters, these Divinities of their [the colonists'] own forming." As for the Rights of Englishmen and laws of nature upon which Adams based his arguments for colonial liberty, these seemed in the mother country to be merely "a synonymous Term for Blasphemy, Bawdy, Treason, Libels, Strong Beer, and Cyder." [31] The doctrine put forward in the circular letter that Parliament was sovereign in the colonies but could lay no taxes, internal or external, for the purpose of raising a revenue struck George Grenville, and, indeed, most Englishmen, as another proof that the colonists would swallow any absurdity. Sovereignty could not be thus parceled out, it was said; either the colonies were subject to Parliament and therefore obliged to obey its laws or they were completely beyond its jurisdiction. Even Benjamin Franklin, good American that he was, could not conceive of sovereignty divided. "I know not," he said, "what the Boston people mean by the 'subordination' they acknowledge in their Assembly to Parliament, while they deny its power to make laws for them." [32]

Unlike Sam Adams, Franklin was at this time under no necessity to conform his ideas to the slow progress of public opinion.

[31] John Dickinson, *Letters from a Farmer in Pennsylvania to the Inhabitants of the British Colonies* (1903), 91. *Boston Gazette*, March 17, 1766 (Britannus Americanus). *A Letter to a Member of Parliament* (London, 1765), 13, 16. Samuel Johnson, *Taxation no Tyranny* (London, 1775), 44. *Orations delivered at the Request of the Inhabitants of the town of Boston* (1807), 17.
[32] *The Writings of Benjamin Franklin*, edited by Albert Henry Smyth (1907), V, 114, 115.

Adams saw as clearly as Franklin the weakness of the principles set forth in the Massachusetts circular letter. Nevertheless, the danger of outstripping the people upon whom he depended for support compelled Adams to stand upon this halfway ground. As will be seen, he was merely biding his time until the people were ready to cast off all Parliamentary authority.

VI

THE MASSACHUSETTS CONVENTION OF 1768

THE frontier is not always a stronghold of political radicalism. During the revolutionary period, the spread of radical ideas in Massachusetts was from the town to the frontier, and the country was slowly brought to adopt the advanced political views that had already taken firm root in the eastern seaboard towns. Embattled farmers fought the Revolution, but Boston made it. British tyranny fell most heavily upon the commercial seaports; frequently the rural districts first learned they were oppressed when they heard the clamor raised by merchants and patriots in Boston or read Sam Adams's instructions to the representatives in the General Court. Had not Adams first brought about Boston's domination of the province, Massachusetts would not have taken the lead among the colonies against Parliament. If he had been unable to overcome the opposition of the western country which Tories regarded as "the most loyal part of the Province," a civil war might have broken out in Massachusetts with loyal western yeoman fighting for King George and the revolutionary eastern districts on the side of rebellion.[1] The battleground for which Whigs and Tories struggled was rural New England; Whigs attempted to impress Boston's ideas and spirit upon the country and Tories strove to keep it loyal to King and Parliament. Yet conservatism gave way so stubbornly that it required a decade of British misgovernment and Sam Adams's propaganda before the Tories were forced to surrender rural Massachusetts to the Whigs.

The policy of the Tory Party was to coop up sedition in Boston and to keep town and country apart. Tories recognized that it was the "fewel scattered from time to time by some of the

[1] Mass. Archives, 26, *Hutchinson Corr.*, II, 150.

Inhabitants of Boston" that kept the province in a flame: "If we could keep off the influence of Boston for one twelve month," said Thomas Hutchinson, "I think we could bring the rest of the Province to their senses."   In the Tories' eyes, the metropolis seemed to "collect and ferment the ill humour of the whole body" and to discharge the poisonous product throughout New England.   As "the source of all the disorders of the Government" and hatcher of "Cockatrice Eggs, which breed Serpents to poison the People," Boston was a bugbear to every well-wisher to royal government.   Thomas Hutchinson declared he would willingly sacrifice all his property in the town if Boston could be separated from the rest of the province, and Tories fervently prayed, "I wish to the Lord the whole town of Boston might sink this moment." [2]   The next best thing, in their opinion, to putting Boston at the bottom of the Atlantic was to see Sam Adams swing at Tyburn; but in spite of their efforts, Boston remained above high water and Sam Adams died at eighty-one in his own bed.

Tories regarded Boston as a wasps' nest because it was "an absolute Democracy" in which all real power was held by Sam Adams and the Sons of Liberty.   Few gentlemen of wealth and rank were inclined to mix in its rough-and-tumble political tussles or to rub shoulders with mechanics and ropewalkers at the town meetings over which Adams presided.   Although Massachusetts law required the payment of a property tax before voting in the town meetings, it was not enforced in Boston, where "any thing with the appearance of a man" was freely admitted.[3]   Consequently "the lowest mechanics" swarmed into Faneuil Hall on meeting days in such "shoals" that they far outnumbered the qualified voters; and on several occasions between three and four thousand people were present, although there were not more than fifteen hundred in the whole town

[2] *Bernard Papers*, IV, Bernard to the Lords Commissioners for Trade, Jan. 18, 1766; Bernard to Thomas Hutchinson, Dec. 5, 1769. Mass. Archives, 26, *Hutchinson Corr.*, II, 377; III, 175, 538, 579, 582. *Boston Evening Post*, Jan. 25, 1773. Octavius Pickering, *The Life of Timothy Pickering* (1867-73), I, 23.

[3] Mass. Archives, 25, *Hutchinson Corr.*, I, Thomas Hutchinson to Richard Jackson, Nov. 9, 1767.

qualified to attend.   Since these citizens were highly susceptible
to Sam Adams's demagoguery, Tories complained that the town
meeting fell under the control of "a few hot and designing
men" and thus became "a constant source of sedition."   Hutchinson lamented that the Boston Sons of Liberty were so insolent
toward their betters that a gentleman did "not meet with what
used to be called common civility." [4]   Because of this hard
treatment from the Boston "rabble," "men of Property & of
the best characters" — as the Tories described themselves —
kept a safe distance from Faneuil Hall and allowed Sam Adams
free rein in running Boston.

With Adams in the saddle and the Tories bent only upon
getting safely out of his way, the Boston town meeting made
such vast encroachments upon royal authority in Massachusetts that Governor Bernard believed Adams planned to bring
"all Authority down to the level of the People."   By province
law, the authority of the towns was strictly limited, but this
barrier did not hinder Adams and his "high flying" Sons of
Liberty.   Adams called the town meeting together for whatever purpose he chose and paid no heed to illegalities.   Even
when he summoned the townspeople to consider matters in
which they had no more authority "than to declare war against
France," Hutchinson was unable to prevent the assembly.
These encroachments became so menacing that the lieutenant
governor urged Parliament to stop the spread of Boston's influence in Massachusetts Bay.   "Let the Assembly do its worst,"
he exclaimed, it could never be as troublesome as the Boston
town meeting.   Bad as were the Boston mobs, Hutchinson
considered Sam Adams and his followers who controlled the
town meeting far more dangerous because they struck deliberately at the root of royal government in the province. [5]

Had Hutchinson succeeded in keeping the Boston town meeting within its constitutional limits, Sam Adams would have
found it far more difficult to revolutionize Massachusetts Bay.

[4] Mass. Archives, 26, *Hutchinson Corr.*, II, 464; III, 454.   *Mass. Hist.
Soc. Proceedings*, LV, 265.
[5] *Bernard Papers*, IV, Bernard to Lord Shelburne, Dec. 22, 1766.   Mass.
Archives, 27, *Hutchinson Corr.*, III, 573, 579.

Adams used the Boston town meeting to originate the measures which he hoped to see followed by the rest of the towns in the province. After the metropolis had set an example by making a daring attack upon royal government he urged the smaller towns to come to Boston's support. The result was that constitutional authority throughout the province was gradually undermined. To accomplish this rape of the Crown's sovereignty by a host of petty townships, Adams struck up an intimacy with the local political leaders who, like the members of the Boston Caucus Club, ruled the "Roast" and determined their town's policy. These men had to be handled skillfully and, in some instances, brought into the revolutionary movement against their own and their constituents' wishes. Lest, however, rural jealousy of the metropolis upset his plan of uniting town and country against the British government, Adams took care that Boston's leadership of the province was well screened. He seldom permitted rural New Englanders 'to see that they were being dominated by Boston politicians, but there are few instances of country people meddling with affairs outside their constitutional power until after Boston had led the way.

The cornerstone of Sam Adams's policy was to put New England in leading strings to Boston and make farmers as zealous Sons of Liberty as were the North End mechanics and shipyard workers. He knew that the metropolis could not oppose Parliament single-handed and that before Massachusetts could assume the leadership of the American colonies against Great Britain, yeomen must learn to look upon Boston as a bulwark of their liberties. Adams hoped to see town and country sink their differences when confronted by British tyranny. He found, however, that the long-established antagonism between town and country was not easily forgotten and was likely to reappear even in crises when Boston most needed rural support. There were many towns "principled against the Politicks of Boston" which refused to fall in line behind the metropolis. Marblehead and Salem, for example, strongholds of the Court Party, were little disposed to bow before the "Metropolis of Sedition"; and in some "remote parts of this Province which

have been friends to order," Tories cultivated antagonism to
Boston so successfully that the townspeople complained of the
countrymen being bigoted to the doctrine of nonresistance to
such an extent that they would not raise a finger against the
British "when they are graciously *instructed* to cut our
throats." [6]

Nevertheless, Sam Adams had much in his favor. Through
the *Boston Gazette* — printed by those "Trumpeters of Sedition," Edes and Gill — he continually drenched the country with propaganda. He filled its columns with such dire
prophecies of disaster and terrifying descriptions of "horred
slavery" at the hands of British overlords that many yeomen
were transformed into fiery Whigs. It was said of this journal
that if its readers were "not in the temper of the writer at the
time of publication, yet it is looked upon as the ORACLE, and
they soon bring their temper to it." Furthermore, it made
vastly more exciting reading than did the dull conservative
newspapers that attempted to keep the country people loyal to
King and Parliament; indeed, Sam Adams's journalism was
so lively that the *Gazette* became practically the only newspaper
read outside of Boston.[7] Although it was packed with sedition
and libel, it could not be suppressed by the Crown officers; when
Hutchinson attempted to induce the Suffolk Grand Jury to indict the author of a particularly "blasphemous Abuse of Kingly
Government," Sam Adams brought so much pressure to bear
upon the jury that the indictment was promptly quashed. During the Stamp Act, Tories had received a bitter taste of the
power of the patriot press. The Stamp Act riots in Boston
were so glorified by Sam Adams in the *Gazette* that rural patriots were sorely troubled because no mobs sprang up in rural
New England to harry the Tories. Upcountry Whigs asked
themselves "ye Reason *we* could do nothing when Such Great

[6] *Bernard Papers*, V, Bernard to Richard Jackson, Nov. 17, 1766. *Boston Gazette*, Nov. 29, 1773. *Israel Williams Papers*, MSS. Mass. Hist. Soc., II, Thomas Hutchinson to Israel Williams, Feb. 20, 1766. Peter Oliver, 59.
[7] *Copy of Letters sent to Great Britain by His Excellency Thomas Hutchin-son, the Hon. Andrew Oliver, and seven other persons, born and educated among us* (Boston, 1774), 27, 30. Mass. Archives, 26, *Hutchinson Corr.*, II, 535.

Things were done at Boston." Countrymen who bore a grudge against the local squire imitated Sam Adams by threatening to get up a mob, pull down the house, and give the "aristocrat" a coat of tar and feathers. Several gangs of Sons of Liberty, with an eye toward making patriotism profitable, raided the houses of their creditors and wiped out their debts by tearing up the ledgers and account books.[8]

A second circumstance which smoothed the way for the progress of the revolutionary movement in rural New England was the ineffectiveness of the Tory opposition. Whereas Boston patriots could be called together at a few moments' notice, the ablest Tory leaders such as Timothy Ruggles of Hardwick, James Putnam and the Chandlers of Worcester, the Winslows and Thomases of Plymouth County, and John Worthington of Springfield were too remote from each other to take concerted action. They were hampered, moreover, by poor support from the mother country and by Sam Adams's practice of making them the scapegoats of British "tyranny." Between Sam Adams and the British government, New England Tories were deprived of the greater part of their rural following and the country was revolutionized in spite of the people's distrust of "Boston Politicks."

In 1768, a sudden emergency made the country's aid vital to Boston. Before the metropolis was fully entrenched in its position of leadership, Adams's incompleted work was forced to withstand a severe attack. To punish Boston for its riots, the British government ordered several regiments of British regulars to the town. The question which Sam Adams anxiously asked himself during the summer of 1768 was whether the country would stand by quietly if British troops overran the metropolis. Would the people *away back* in the province" who were ill-disposed toward Boston and Whig principles make no resistance while the townspeople were forced to surrender their freedom at the bayonet's point? If Bostonians determined to fight the troops, would New Englanders answer a call to arms against the mother country? Adams found a conclusive

---

[8] Mass. Archives, 25, *Hutchinson Corr.*, John Cushing to Thomas Hutchinson, Dec. 29, 1765. *Bernard Papers*, V, Bernard to Pownall, March 31, 1766.

answer to his questions in the Massachusetts Convention of 1768.

It was the rioting that broke out in Boston early in 1768 against the Commissioners of the Customs that brought royal troops to the metropolis. After a hard winter, with unemployment rife and prices high, Hutchinson found Bostonians looking more "sowre and discontented" than he had ever seen them.[9] Since the people had been fully convinced by Sam Adams that their hardships were owing to acts of Parliament and the Commissioners of the Customs, the mob was spoiling to run the Commissioners out of Boston and stop the collection of "unconstitutional" taxes. When it was rumored that the mob would rise on March 18, 1768, the anniversary of the repeal of the Stamp Act which was celebrated in Boston as a "Day of Triumph over Great Britain," the Commissioners confidently expected to be attacked. But much to the mob's disappointment, the leading Sons of Liberty refused to permit a riot and even removed the effigies of the Commissioners that had been hung on Liberty Tree in anticipation of the evening's sport. The "great Opposers of Parliamentary Authority" came out strongly against terrorism and Sam Adams astonished his followers by declaring that there were to be "NO MOBS — NO CONFUSIONS — NO TUMULTS" in Boston. Adams was well aware that an uprising in Boston would defeat the purpose of the circular letter by turning the Southern colonies against "mobbish" Boston; as long as Massachusetts was attempting to unite America in protest against the Townshend duties, Adams put Boston strictly on its best behavior. He took the edge off the Liberty Boys' chagrin, however, by promising them speedy satisfaction against the Tories: "We know *WHO* have abus'd us," he said, ". . . but let not the hair of their scalps be touch'd: The time is coming, when they shall lick the dust and melt away." [10] Tories suspected that Adams meant that the patriots would have the pleasure of loading the governor and Commissioners aboard the next brig for England. By means of such promises, the mob

[9] Mass. Archives, 26, *Hutchinson Corr.*, II, 297.
[10] *Mass. Hist. Soc. Proceedings*, LV, 269. Mass. Archives, 26, *Hutchinson Corr.*, II, 296. *Boston Gazette*, March 14, 1768.

was held in leash; instead of riding out of Boston tarred and feathered on a rail, the Commissioners were untouched during the celebration and the evening passed with no greater disturbance than usually took place on a holiday.

Although both Hutchinson and Bernard, who had seen the Boston mob at close quarters in its ugliest moments, declared that no damage had been done, the Commissioners of the Customs were not disposed to take the matter so lightly. Sam Adams and his "Mohawks" had made the Commissioners feel that as long as they remained in Boston they were sitting on a volcano. At night, their houses were frequently surrounded by a mob of Liberty Boys lustily beating drums, blowing horns, and emitting the "most hideous howlings as the Indians, when they attack an enemy." [11] The Commissioners were unaccustomed to Boston mobs, which they found singularly lacking in the good humor of English rioters, and they firmly expected to be roughly handled before they had remained long among the "Saints." They saw that it was only because Adams held the mob in check that they were permitted to collect His Majesty's customs in Boston. They found living at the mercy of such a notorious riot lover as Sam Adams extremely uncomfortable; yet it was clear that if he gave the mob "the least hint" that the Commissioners were fair game, Boston would become too hot to hold them. The threatened assault of March 18 convinced them that they could not remain in Boston unless British regulars were sent to their protection. But garrisoning Boston with royal troops promised to be ticklish business: no soldiers had been stationed in the metropolis since the close of the Seven Years' War; the citizens were accustomed to having the nearest "Serjeant's Guard of real Soldiers" two hundred miles away; and it could easily be foreseen that Sam Adams would use British military tyranny to touch off an explosion. Nevertheless, two regiments of British regulars were ordered to proceed from Halifax to Boston. In the light of later events, it is important to remember that the British government first sent troops to the Puritan metropolis in consequence of a disturbance which Sam Adams himself had prevented from being

[11] *Letters to a Loyalist Lady*, II.

more serious than "a few disorderly boys hollooing before Mr. Inspector Williams' door." [12]

The riot of June 10, 1768, which led the Ministry to send two more regiments to Boston from Ireland, was an affair of more serious character. This outbreak occurred when the Commissioners of the Customs seized John Hancock's sloop *Liberty* and put it under the guns of *H.M.S. Romney* for running a contraband wine cargo into Boston. A mob of "sturdy boys & negroes" thereupon made its long-delayed attack upon the Commissioners, several of whom fled to Castle William for refuge. The morning after the "Liberty Riot" — so called from the name of Hancock's sloop — signs were hung on Liberty Tree urging the citizens to rise against the Commissioners if they again attempted to collect unconstitutional taxes. The metropolis was clearly no longer tenable and the Commissioners refused to return unless they were given a bodyguard of redcoats. "The Security of the Revenue, the Safety of its Officers, and the Honor of Government," they said, made imperative the speedy dispatch of men-of-war and British regulars. Governor Bernard, who, too, had had his fill of Boston and was preparing to get to England out of harm's way, urged the Ministry to send troops "to rescue the Government out of the hands of a trained mob." It seemed very unlikely that the British government would let slip an opportunity to rid itself of such a thorn in its side as Boston. Besides driving the Commissioners out of town, the Whigs had smartly rapped Lord Hillsborough's knuckles and defied the British government by refusing to rescind the circular letter. After such open bearding of the British lion, Sam Adams began to look forward to an attempt on the part of the Ministry to even the score with Boston. With the Commissioners screaming they were at the mercy of the Boston mob, it seemed probable that the British government would dispatch an army to tame the "Saints."

It was no secret to Sam Adams and his fellow patriots that the governor and Commissioners were outdoing each other in calling for British soldiers and men-of-war. With fear of

---

[12] *Boston Gazette*, Sept. 19, 1768. *Bernard Papers*, IV, Bernard to Richard Jackson, Aug. 31, 1767. *Mass. Hist. Soc. Proceedings*, LVI, 348.

military despotism as a spur, radicalism increased by leaps and bounds through the summer of 1768. During the debate on rescinding the circular letter in the Massachusetts House of Representatives, James Otis made "the most violent insolent abusive treasonable Declaration that perhaps was ever delivered." Otis declared that Lord Hillsborough's ultimatum to Massachusetts was written in such wretched style that in Massachusetts Bay it would pass for the "performance of School Boy" — which was to be expected from a member of an aristocracy who went to Oxford and Cambridge merely to learn the fine arts of "Whoring, Smoking and Drinking." There was not a man in England, Otis exclaimed, who was capable of writing "so elegant so pure & so nervous a Writing as the Petition to the King" which had been penned by Sam Adams and Otis himself. In his opinion, King George appointed "none but Boys for his Ministers" to administer the colonies; virtuous American statesmen could do nothing to restore harmony within the Empire as long as they were compelled to deal with such striplings and dullards in the British Colonial Office. Otis gave the British House of Commons — "those mighty Men that effect to give Law to the Colonies" — an even more severe tongue-lashing. He upbraided the members as "a parcel of Button-makers, Pin-makers, Horse Jockeys, Gamesters, Pensioners, Pimps and Whore Masters" — no doubt to the great joy of Adams's "Mohawks" in the galleries, who took democratic delight in seeing the whole British aristocracy dragged through the mud. After having shown up the scandalous illiteracy and immorality among the British peers, Otis turned the tables on Parliament and warned it to rescind *its* measures or be "lost for ever," and then passed "an Encomium upon Oliver Cromwell & extolled the Times preceeding his Advancement & particularly the Murther of the King." At the Boston town meeting in the Reverend Mr. Sewall's meetinghouse on July 14, 1768, Otis made a "Harangue from the Pulpit" in which he launched another violent attack upon British policy. If American grievances were not speedily redressed "and we were called on to defend our liberties and Privileges," Otis declared "he hoped and believed we should one and all resist even unto

Blood; but, at the same time, prayed almighty God it might never so happen." Should England use redcoats against the colonies, Otis believed there was "nothing more to do, but to gird the Sword to the Thigh and Shoulder the Musquet." [13]

The threat of British troops threw Sam Adams into a frame of mind even more warlike than James Otis's. The dissolution of the Massachusetts General Court after its refusal to obey Lord Hillsborough's "mandate" to rescind the circular letter convinced Adams that the British government was determined to leave the colony only a "vain semblance of liberty"; and when British regiments were reported on their way to Boston, he did not doubt that military law would be fastened upon the metropolis. The caution and reserve which Adams usually displayed in transforming American discontent into revolutionary fervor were characteristics acquired through many years of self-discipline. By nature, Adams was passionate, excitable, and violent, but he rarely allowed these qualities to appear in public. Bostonians usually saw him as a dignified, patient patriot who strove to keep the controversy with the mother country upon lofty constitutional grounds rather than as a hot-tempered revolutionist who spirited up mobs and longed to disrupt the British Empire. But the crisis of 1768 caused him to throw off the "serpentine cunning" which Tories dreaded more than the fire-eating of other patriot leaders, and to make a rash appeal to arms. Rather than allow a standing army to garrison Boston, Adams revived the plan which the Sons of Liberty had adopted during the Stamp Act of fighting off the British troops before they could gain a foothold in the colonies.

The morning after the Liberty Riot, Adams was seen in the South End of Boston "trembling and in great agitation" while he harangued a crowd of listeners to make a bold attack upon the royal government. "If you are Men," he exclaimed, "behave like Men; let us take up arms immediately and be free and Seize all the King's Officers: we shall have thirty thousand Men to join us from the Country." Boston was filled with "many wild and violent proposals" to prevent the landing of British troops, but Sam Adams's plan meant nothing less than

[13] *Chalmers Papers*, II, Speech of Otis, June 1768. *Bernard Papers*, VI, Bernard to Lord Hillsborough, June 25, 1768.

war with Great Britain. Rather than pay the Townshend duties and submit to military rule, Adams declared, "We will take up arms and spend our last drop of blood." To stir up Bostonians' war enthusiasm, he promised that thousands of embattled farmers "with their knapsacks and bayonets fixed" would swarm down from the country and cut off the British force to a man. Adams had no more hesitation in fighting King George's soldiers than Louis XV's "papists"; George III, he said, had no right to send troops to dragoon New Englanders and they should be regarded as foreign enemies.[14] Once before, Adams had prepared for war with the mother country, but no British army had been sent in 1766 to determine whether or not the Sons of Liberty were merely bluffing. In 1768, however, it seemed probable that the Massachusetts patriots would have ample opportunity to show their mettle.

With Sam Adams preaching war and sedition on Boston street corners, the Crown officers saw the metropolis becoming a hotbed of military fervor. While the country as a whole remained calm, Boston was caught up in the full stride of this radical movement. Instead of frightening Bostonians with threats of armed coercion, the British Ministry seemed to have stirred up a hornets' nest. Tories who observed the swift growth of the war spirit in Boston during the summer of 1768 expected to see England and Massachusetts at blows when the royal transports and men-of-war entered Boston Harbor. "The Promoters of the present Evils," wrote one particularly apprehensive conservative, "are ready to unmask and openly discover their long and latent Design to Rebel."[15]

Sam Adams had little fear of punishment from Great Britain even if Massachusetts patriots massacred the British troops sent to keep order in Boston. In the eyes of Boston Sons of Liberty, the British Empire was so "tottering" and rotten that it was almost beyond human aid; only John Wilkes seemed able to keep "the Great System from dashing to Pieces."[16] Because Englishmen were "degenerate" and the British Empire on the verge

[14] *Chalmers Papers*, III, Information of Richard Silvester of Boston taken before Thomas Hutchinson, Jan. 23, 1769.

[15] *Letters to the Ministry*, 104.

[16] Boston Sons of Liberty to John Wilkes, June 6, 1768, MS. Mass. Hist. Soc., Gay Transcripts, *Miscellaneous Papers*, III.

of destruction, Adams believed he had little to fear from a government that was busy with both hands in keeping itself afloat. Since the Stamp Act had first revealed the weakness of British colonial administration, the debility of government in England, the rioting and turbulence of the London mobs, and the corruption of English political life had been spread before New Englanders by Sam Adams in the *Boston Gazette*. This steady disparagement of British power led many colonists to believe America was more than a match for the mother country. It was difficult to respect the long arm of government which appeared "to totter on the brink of destruction from the unbounded licentiousness of the people" and which was unable to suppress "the great tumults and risings of the people all over England and Ireland." To encourage New Englanders to resist British demands, Sam Adams pointed out that the English government was harassed by "the Weavers mob, the Seamens mob, the Taylors mob, the Coal miners mob, and some say, the Clergys mob; and in short it is to be feared the whole kingdom . . . will unite in one general scene of tumult." If, as Sam Adams said, the ministry could not put down riots "at the very gates of the palace, and even in the royal presence," how could it deal, at a distance of three thousand miles, with the stout cudgel-boys of Boston after they had driven off the troops? Moreover, Adams believed that when the British government attempted to coerce America with military force, the mob would rise in England and paralyze its hands. He expected that the nonimportation agreement which Boston and New York had formed against British manufactures would lead to new working-class riots in England and cause serious embarrassment to the government. Boston patriots put great store in the laborers of the manufacturing towns, whom they hoped would "commit Riots and Tumults in their Favor." [17] After the American nonimportation agreement had begun to close English factories

---

[17] *Boston Gazette*, Jan. 27, 1766 (Supplement); Aug. 4, 1768. *Pennsylvania Journal*, Aug. 4, 1768. *Massachusetts State Papers: Speeches of the Governors of Massachusetts, from 1765 to 1775*, edited by Alden Bradford (1818), 170. Public Record Office: Colonial Office, Class or Series 5, LXXXVI, 266. General Gage to Lord Hillsborough, Sept. 26, 1768, Lib. Cong. Transcript.

and throw thousands of artisans out of employment, Sam Adams and his followers believed themselves well out of reach of reprisals.   Thus, as seen through the eyes of the Boston Sons of Liberty in 1768, England appeared so torn with dissension and the government so preoccupied with political squabbles and mob uprisings that American patriots felt free to settle affairs in the colonies to their own taste without risk of punishment.

With Bostonians in this highly inflammable state, Governor Bernard feared an explosion if definite news of the troops' coming were made public.   When he received information from General Gage in New York that two regiments had been ordered from Halifax to Boston, he held it back from the Council and people lest an insurrection should break out against the Crown officers before the troops arrived.   The governor preferred to let the bad news leak out gradually in order that the "*Heads* of the *Faction* might have time to consider well what they were about, and prudent men opportunity to interpose their advise." Accordingly, on September 3, Bernard told one of the councilors that he had private information that troops would soon reach Boston, but insisted that he had not received public orders.

Before night, all the citizens had learned that British regulars were coming to Boston and "nothing was to be heard among them but declarations that the troops should not enter the Town."   The Sons of Liberty declared that unless the people immediately took up arms there would be a bloody purge of Boston Whigs by the British: "some were to be pilloried, some whipped, some to lose their ears and others their heads." Adams pictured the troops as "dragoons and executioners" who had been sent out by the Ministry to cram unconstitutional acts of Parliament down the colonists' throats and bring them to "the very borders of slavery."   The citizens were told that their alternative was to resist the troops or tamely submit to a military despotism which would deprive them of all liberty. Confronted with this dilemma, the political temperature in Boston rapidly climbed to the bursting point.   The general expression among the people was "sullen Discontent on almost every Brow except where a panic fear seemed fix'd."   But what most alarmed the Crown officers and Tories was the report that two secret meetings had been held in Boston by the Sons of Liberty. At the first and larger of these meetings, it was believed that the patriots had laid a plan to raise the country against the troops and that at a smaller and more secret "meeting of the most violent" a plot had been hatched to surprise Castle William and garrison it with Sons of Liberty.[18]

As the key to Boston Harbor, Castle William must necessarily have played an important part in any attempt to prevent the landing of British troops. If the Castle should fall into the hands of the Sons of Liberty, it was believed there would be a good chance of beating off the British fleet when it attempted to enter the harbor, for "the Gunners could sink every ship that attempted the Castle" and force the men-of-war into the open sea. Moreover, the castle was not garrisoned by royal troops: Massachusetts soldiers were in possession, and Adams believed they would deliver up the stronghold with little, if any, resistance. Because this strategic point was in such vulnerable state, Governor Bernard was kept in a flutter of anxiety lest he should suddenly find the Liberty Flag run up over Castle William and the ramparts bristling with armed Liberty Boys. Bernard did his utmost to have the few royal ships in the harbor stationed in position to guard it from a surprise by the Boston Patriots. Therefore, when it was learned that the Boston town meeting of September 12, 1768, had brought forth such "inflaming Speeches" and "Treasonable Resolves" that there seemed real danger of an attack, Captain Corner of the *Romney* placed the *Magdalen* between Castle William and Boston — a precaution which he believed "disconcerted the Mobilities scheme" and prevented an assault by the Sons of Liberty.

Sam Adams had determined to call a town meeting when Governor Bernard first let it be known that British troops were expected. As in most Boston town meetings of the revolutionary period, the proceedings had been carefully prearranged by a small group of politicians who met secretly several days before

---

[18] *Boston Gazette*, Sept. 19, 1768 (Supplement). Public Record Office, Administrative Secretary, Letters, 483: *Diary of Captain Corner*, 215, Lib. Cong. Transcripts, 25. *State of Disorder . . . in Massachusetts Bay*, Mass. Hist. Soc., Gay Transcripts, *State Papers*, XIII.

the townspeople assembled. It was well known that Sam Adams, James Otis, and Joseph Warren gathered at Warren's house on September 10, where they "drew up the Resolves, Debates and other matter" for the town meeting which met on September 12.[19] By following the plans made by Sam Adams in this "caucus," the Boston town meeting came within a "hair's breadth" of treason and forced the British government to prepare for war with Massachusetts.

On the day of the town meeting, Adams and Otis came down to Faneuil Hall surrounded by the "Mohawks." No attempt was made to confine the meeting to lawful voters — there were "very few Gentlemen there," said Bernard, and "such as were, appeared only as curious, and perhaps anxious spectators." [20] So many Sons of Liberty had turned out, however, that, with James Otis in the moderator's chair, Sam Adams pushed through his schemes without difficulty. His first step was to demand that Governor Bernard summon the General Court immediately. Bernard knew from painful experience that the General Court planted thorns in the governor's chair at every opportunity, but rather than face the rising indignation in the province he would have risked even that acute discomfort had not royal instructions tied his hands. Bostonians had tried every means from petitions to threats to open the General Court; but even when the Boston town meeting in July 1768 put Hancock, Adams, and a score of other prominent patriots in chariots and sent them out of Roxbury to lay a petition before the governor that the legislature be called, Bernard refused to violate Lord Hillsborough's instructions. When the town meeting learned, on September 11, that Bernard had again rejected their demands, they adopted the doctrine formulated by Adams and Otis in the caucus, that the King could not impose a standing army upon Massachusetts without first securing the consent of the General Court, the parliament of the colony. The pressing danger of British regulars led Sam Adams to exalt acts of Parliament and to attack the prerogative, — a reversal

[19] *Diary of Captain Corner*, 217.
[20] *Papers Relating to Public Events in Massachusetts, the Seventy-Six Society* (1856), 102.

of his practice in 1765, — but few Whigs believed that constitutional arguments would prevent the troops from landing.
Sam Adams and his followers had sharper weapons with which
to keep Boston clear of redcoats.

When Sam Adams preached battle against the King's soldiers,
he did not entirely throw his habitual caution to the winds.   He
was keenly aware of the danger of attempting to stir up an
armed insurrection when troops were already on their way to
crush the revolt.   Adams never neglected to leave loopholes
behind through which he might beat a quick retreat; and when
advocating such barefaced sedition as taking up arms against
British troops, he kept a watchful eye to the rear.   By employing the fictitious danger of a French invasion of New England, he hit upon a stratagem which permitted the Boston patriots to denounce King, Parliament, and Ministry and threaten
to rise against the British "invaders," yet at the same time preserve the appearance of loyal, obedient subjects.   The Boston
town meeting adopted a resolution urging every householder
to carry out that "good and wholesome law of this Province"
which required that they should possess themselves of "a well
fixed Firelock Musket Accoutrement and Ammunition." [21]
Although everyone knew that these muskets and balls were to
be used against the British, the town meeting saved itself from
outright treason by declaring that the citizens should prepare
for war because "there is at this Time a prevailing apprehension,
in the minds of many, of an approaching War with France."
This pretext was put to good purpose by patriot orators who
used it to make their meaning clear without going to the length
of treasonable words.   When the Sons of Liberty in the Boston
town meeting enthusiastically approved these preparations for
war, the town arms, which had been removed from the store-
rooms for cleaning, stood ominously before the Whig speakers.
These weapons, it was said, were to be used against *their enemies;*
the motion to distribute the muskets among the people, which
was voted down as too radical a measure, was put in the form
of a resolve to oppose *the enemy.*   Occasionally, however, as
the patriot haranguers became more heated in their denuncia-

[21] *Boston Town Records,* 16th Report, 264.

tions of British tyranny, the "flimsy veil" was thrown off, and the true motive behind this military preparation exposed. One speaker forgot discretion so far as to exclaim that New Englanders "had a right to oppose with Arms military Force which had been sent to oblige them to submit to unconstitutional laws." In a crucial point of the debate, Otis is said to have declared that "they understood one another very well," and, pointing to the town arms, added, "There are the Arms, when an attempt is made against your Liberties they will be delivered, our declaration wants no explanation." In spite of this effort at dissimulation, not a Boston Son of Liberty expected to waste his powder on French "papists"; British regulars were the real enemy and it was against them that the citizens were urged to arm. This "disingenuous, canting, Jesuitical pretence" deceived no one, but it served as a convenient loophole through which the patriots later wriggled to escape treason trials. Indeed, it was so successful that Sam Adams used it as a blind to cover military preparations down to the eve of the Revolution.[22]

Because it was clear that Governor Bernard would not call the General Court before the troops reached Boston, Sam Adams proposed to summon the representatives of the people of Massachusetts Bay without the consent of the royal governor. Two years before, Otis and Adams had attempted to bring the legislature together over the governor's protest and had failed to shake the rural delegates from their conservative distrust of unconstitutional institutions and suspicion of the designs of Boston patriots. In 1768, however, Adams hoped for better things from New England farmers. There was no more effective way of sounding the country's disposition toward military resistance than to assemble delegates from the entire colony in Boston. If Sam Adams and his followers were given an opportunity to influence the country representatives, there was excellent prospect of sending them home with highly contagious cases of war fever which would spread over the entire colony. This meeting of popularly elected "committees" intended to

[22] *Boston Evening Post*, Oct. 31, 1768. *Papers Relating to Public Events*, 103.

fill the place of the dissolved General Court Adams suggested should be known as the "Convention."

Before inviting the Boston town meeting to touch off this train of explosives, the patriot leaders believed the townspeople needed to be spurred by new provocations against the Crown officers. There were few men more likely to arouse the citizens' wrath than the Commissioners of the Customs. Could some fresh outrage be laid at their doors, the patriots anticipated little opposition in pushing their plans through the town meeting. Unfortunately, however, the Commissioners were still in Castle William and showed no inclination to return to Boston until escorted by British regulars. Despite this obstacle, the patriot leaders contrived to manufacture an incident which set Boston in an uproar against the Commissioners and silenced all opposition to the Convention. The night before the Convention was proposed in the Boston town meeting, it was reported that an attempt had been made to cut down the flagstaff on the sacred Liberty Tree. The Sons of Liberty claimed to have caught the culprit, who, after a sound cudgeling, confessed that the Commissioners of the Customs had bribed him "and was to present him with a suit of Cloaths for that purpose." It is not likely that the Commissioners would have gone deliberately out of their way to make themselves more hated in Boston at a time when they were without the protection of British soldiers and rumors were abroad of a patriot plot to capture Castle William. It is more probable that Adams himself had fabricated the story, for it was by such means that Adams brought the people to approve his schemes and pulled the wires that set the Boston town meeting in motion against royal government in Massachusetts.[23]

But no Sons of Liberty doubted the Commissioners' guilt, and the town meeting obediently adopted Adams's proposal to call representatives to Boston. The selectmen were directed to send a circular letter to all the towns in the colony acquainting them with the dangers that threatened the metropolis and with the military preparations that had been made to prevent

[23] *Boston Gazette*, Sept. 19, 1768 (Supplement). Public Record Office, Colonial Office, Class or Series 5, LXXXVI, 276. *Diary of Captain Corner*, 218.

the impending French invasion. In order that "such Measures may be consulted and Advised as his Majestys service, and the peace and safety of his Subjects in this Province may require," it was urged that the towns elect delegates or committees to meet in Boston on September 22. This recitation of the innocent purposes behind the Convention did not allay the fears of the Crown officers. Governor Bernard believed that it was to be the signal for resuming the first charter, which Massachusetts republicans loved because it had "no ingredient of Royalty in it." He was certain that the real motive in calling this province-wide meeting was to make "an intended Insurrection more general." In the Boston selectmen's circular letter, the governor observed a sentence which quickened his apprehensions. The selectmen asserted that the proposed Convention "may happily prevent any sudden and unconnected Measures" which the people might take. "What," asked Bernard, "can *unconnected* be applied to, but to forcible Opposition to the King's Government?" [24]

Sam Adams certainly expected more from the country than appeared in the selectmen's circular letter. He had led the town artisans and laborers, from whom the war party drew its chief support, to believe that the country stood solidly behind the metropolis and would rush to arms at its call. The common people of Boston, who "were in a frenzy and talked of dying in defence of their liberties," did not intend to fight the British alone: they put up a bold front because they expected to be reënforced by thousands of yeomen. Sam Adams made every effort to extend the war spirit over New England and the neighboring colonies: emissaries were sent throughout Massachusetts Bay to rouse the country people to a fighting pitch and other provinces were sounded for military support against the British troops. It was never decided upon whom the command of this patchwork army of farmers and townsmen was to devolve. New England boasted many veteran Indian fighters, but the Boston Sons of Liberty exclaimed that the crisis called for another Cromwell. But there was no New England Crom-

---

[24] *Boston Town Records*, 16th Report, 263. *Bernard Papers*, VII, Bernard to Lord Hillsborough, Jan. 24, 1769.

well to fall upon the King's soldiers and the Boston patriots
were left to lament that "Oliver Cromwell was a glorious fellow and what a pitty it was that they had no such another to
espouse their Cause at present." [25]   Although lacking a commander, the Sons of Liberty continued to make preparations for
war.   In order that the town and country might be kept in
close communication, a beacon consisting of an empty turpentine
barrel was put on the pole on Beacon Hill, which, when fired,
was expected to send a host of armed farmers hurrying to the
town.   Tories believed that the beacon would be lighted the
moment the British transports and men-of-war were sighted off
the Boston lighthouse.   The Boston selectmen, who took their
orders from Sam Adams, refused to take down the beacon even
after being directed to do so by the Council, and it was not
until September 15 that the sheriff summoned up enough courage to remove it.

On September 19, however, when Governor Bernard finally
made public orders for dispatching troops to Boston from Halifax and Ireland, a large number of Adams's partisans began
to drop out of sight.   There could now be no question that
nearly one thousand redcoats would soon be in Boston Harbor
and that Adams would have to fight or eat his threats.   As
long as it was doubtful whether troops would actually come
to Boston the Liberty Boys boasted of their military prowess
and promised to make short work of the "invaders," but when
they learned that the regiments were within a few days' sail,
many lost heart.   One wing of the patriot party still favored
calling in the country and fighting the British, but the conservative Whigs fell back upon the plan of letting the troops land
unopposed and then devising means of getting rid of them.
Thomas Cushing, speaker of the House of Representatives
and one of the members of the "Boston seat," now said that he
had "always been for moderate Measures" and was in favor of
nothing more radical than putting Bernard and Hutchinson
out of the way.   This backsliding outraged the radical group

[25] Mass. Archives, 25, *Hutchinson Corr.*, I, Oct. 5, 1768.   *Chalmers Papers*, III, Sentiments of the Sons of Liberty.   *Bernard Papers*, VII, Bernard
to Lord Hillsborough, Sept. 9, 1768.

and Otis wrathfully told Cushing that "he was as great an Enemy to his own party as Frank Bernard, Thom Hutchinson, or the Commissioners." [26] Nevertheless, Otis himself had begun to waver. In spite of his war talk, Otis was unable to believe that the King would really send troops to Boston; and as their coming became increasingly certain he shrank from the prospect of conflict with the mother country. However, a large number of Bostonians were still eager for resistance, and although Sam Adams was losing ground he retained enough influence to make Boston's line of action uncertain when the British fleet should appear in the harbor. The decisive factor, however, in determining whether the metropolis would fight the troops or submit peaceably seemed to lie in the manner in which the country responded to Sam Adams's appeal to arms.

In England the Boston news became so alarming that stocks tumbled on the London Exchange. Rumors spread that Massachusetts was in arms and ready to pounce upon the British if they attempted to disembark. Although most Englishmen believed that British regulars would easily rout the Sons of Liberty, there were some who foresaw a hot battle on the Boston water front. Lord Hillsborough was said to be questioning closely every ship captain and passenger out of Boston, but their portentous accounts of New England's military preparations brought him small comfort. Excitement mounted when it was reported that the militia had been called out to fight the British "invaders." After long skirting the borders of treason, Massachusetts seemed finally to have slipped over into outright rebellion. War appeared certain, and the Ministry prepared to settle an old score with the New England "Saints." "It was justly esteemed a dreadful and destructive conflict which they were about to engage in, yet they were determined to undertake it at all hazards, and to rely upon the superiority of their arms for the support of their authority in America." Yet there was some trepidation in embarking upon this coercive policy because it was believed that the New England militia, one hundred and fifty thousand strong, were such expert marksmen

[26] *Chalmers Papers*, III, Nathaniel Coffin's Declaration to Governor Bernard, Feb. 6, 1769.

that they could shoot "a pimple off a man's nose without hurting him." [27]

But these sharpshooting New Englanders were far less eager than Sam Adams had imagined to test their marksmanship on British redcoats. Indeed, the country in general seemed strongly inclined to cool the Boston hotheads with dashes of cold water. "We are not to act like Rebels," said the *New Hampshire Gazette*. "Scorn the Thought — we have a good King and his royal Ear is not wilfully shut against us . . . we are represented as Rebels against his Crown and Dignity — But let us convince him by a dutiful Submission to his Government, and the British Constitution, that we are oppressed, and that we have a Right to Petition him thereon." In every town, Tories and lukewarm Whigs attempted to prevent participation in the Convention. Even in Cambridge, usually under the thumb of Boston politicians, the Tories mustered sufficient strength at the town meeting to carry, "with the aid of a *veering Whig*," an adjournment that kept Cambridge from taking part in the Convention. But the principal opposition to the metropolis came from the town of Hatfield, located in the heart of western rural Toryism. Here the proposed Convention was not only rejected, but denounced as a snare laid by Bostonians to involve the country in their quarrel with the mother country. The Hatfield voters declared that Boston's acts were "unconstitutional, illegal, and wholly unjustifiable, and what will give the enemies of our constitution the greatest joy; subversive of government, destructive of that peace and good order which is the cement of Society, and have a direct tendency to rivet our chains, and deprive us of our charter rights and privileges." Hatfield lectured Boston on the constitutional rights of towns in the province and gave Sam Adams instructions on how the metropolis should behave toward its smaller neighbors. In particular the townsmen ridiculed the pretense of a French war as a call to arms; if there was real danger of a French invasion, why did not Sam Adams and his fellow townsmen welcome the prospect of British troops being sent to their protection? It was singular, they said, that Boston should meddle with military matters before war had been declared against France and when the arrival of British regulars was expected at any moment.[28] Instead of promising to follow Boston dutifully, Hatfield urged that the metropolis be left to take its punishment alone, which, the Hatfield voters intimated, it richly deserved. If Boston had brought this storm upon its head by allowing the mob to run wild, its citizens should humble themselves in repentance before the throne and by "loyalty and quiet behaviour soon convince his Majesty and the world" that troops were unnecessary because all Bostonians were not rioters.

By hurling this defiant broadside at Boston, Hatfield made itself the chief opponent in western Massachusetts of the capital's domination of the colony, until the spread of Sam Adams's committees of correspondence forced out the ruling Tory clique in 1773. Not all the towns took a course so disconcerting to Sam Adams as that of Hatfield: in eastern Connecticut particularly, the citizens were zealous in Boston's cause and sent instructions to their representatives in the Connecticut General Court which, had they been followed by the Massachusetts towns, might have led to some lively fighting when the British fleet hove to in Boston Harbor. Sam Adams regarded the resolves of Lebanon, Connecticut, as a model which all towns should follow when the metropolis called upon the country for aid. Although the Lebanon townspeople found it convenient to threaten war upon the royal troops in the same cryptic language that had suddenly become fashionable in Boston, they made a forthright promise ·to "assist and support our American brethren at the expense of our lives and fortunes." [29] Norwich, Connecticut, was not content merely to approve the Boston Liberty Boys' war preparations, but called for a muster and review of the Connecticut troops "in order that the Militia be at all Times properly furnished" and ready to withstand an

[28] *Massachusetts Gazette*, Oct. 6, 1768.
[29] *Boston Gazette*, Oct. 10, 1768 (Supplement).

enemy attack.   Such pledges of aid were meat and drink to the Boston war party.   But outside eastern Connecticut Sam Adams found little to nourish his hopes that a yeoman army would rush to arms for Boston's support.

The Massachusetts Convention met in Faneuil Hall on September 22, 1768, with about seventy delegates present.   Adams had given such short notice in calling the meeting that some towns had not had time to elect representatives and many stragglers were still on their way when the Convention opened. Within a few days, however, the empty seats were filled by late-comers and the Convention began to assume a striking resemblance to the dissolved House of Representatives whose meetings had been forbidden by the British government.   Adams seemed to have called into being a close counterpart of the Lower House of the General Court, but would he be able to persuade it to usurp governmental authority and summon the country to fight the British troops?

The temper of the delegates who had been sent to the Convention from rural Massachusetts gave Adams no encouragement.   Most of them had been representatives in the last General Court who had little desire to add the fighting of British troops to the offense they had already given the mother country by refusing to rescind the circular letter.   "Some of the best men in the province" were sent down to Boston, and there was little likelihood of their being swept off their feet by town demagoguery.   Their attitude was that "waters not a bellows" ought to be used on fiery Bostonians.[30]   Even had they caught the war fever that raged in the metropolis, most of the country members were committed by their constituents' instructions not to join the town radicals.   These instructions were generally of the kind given Jedidiah Preble, who represented Falmouth in the Convention.   Preble was ordered to do nothing rash or unconstitutional; only a cautious and legitimate resistance was to be resorted to.   Such instructions made the outcome of the Convention a foregone conclusion and completely crippled the radicals' war plans.   Instead of rushing to Boston the thirty

[30] *Arthur Lee Papers*, Sparks MSS., Harvard College Library, I, 41; Peter Livius to his brother in London, Oct. 18, 1768.

thousand armed men Sam Adams hoped for, the country sent only a handful of conservative politicians who made it clear that they would do nothing more rash than write another petition to the King.

The open rift that began to appear among Boston patriot leaders gave great encouragement to these rural moderates. Thomas Cushing, the speaker of the Convention, committed himself to the conservatives by declaring that its purpose was to "bring together some prudent people who would be able to check the violent designs of Others." During the first three days, James Otis did not appear at the Convention. Nothing could be done without him, and the delegates sat in Faneuil Hall with open doors for three days while he played truant in the country. These desertions dismayed Adams, for he was unable to hold the radical fort alone; when, after being elected clerk of the Convention, he "attempted to launch out in the language used in the House of Representatives," he was silenced and compelled to give way to the opposition. But it is not probable that even Otis, with his great influence over the country members, could have made headway against the flood of conservatism that swept down from rural Massachusetts. He made no attempt to breast this current, for when he finally took his seat in the Convention, he was "perfectly tame" and content to let the country delegates have full sway.[31]

This unexpected moderation displayed by the Boston patriot leaders was partly owing to the refusal of the New York Sons of Liberty to join the struggle against the British government. At first, news that war was brewing in Boston aroused great enthusiasm in New York. "Peoples' Eyes here," wrote General Gage, "are now turned upon Boston and its feared too many rejoice at the Proceedings there, and encourage those People to proceed to every Extremity, tho' they might not chuse to venture so far themselves." But the New Yorkers never permitted their ardor for their hard-pressed Boston brethren

[31] *New England Historical and Genealogical Register*, XXII, 412. *Chalmers Papers*, III, Nathaniel Coffin's declaration. Thomas Cushing to Stephen Sayre, Oct. 7, 1768, MS. Mass. Hist. Soc. *Bernard Papers*, VII, Bernard to Lord Hillsborough, Oct. 3, 1768.

to carry them to the point of beating up recruits for the expected hostilities at Boston. And, after a report reached the colonies that "measures were taking at home, to bring the Bostoners to Reason," they were even less inclined to take a plunge with the "Saints" into rebellion.[32] Because it was clear that the British government intended to reason with redcoats and men-of-war, New York patriots left Boston to its fate.

Since New York and rural Massachusetts were overwhelmingly opposed to radical measures, the Convention surprised the Tories by acting "with more caution decency and order than could have been reasonably expected considering in what an extraordinary manner this famous Committee of Safety was called together."[33] After Sam Adams was satisfied that the popular pulse beat feverishly only in Boston, he made no further effort to uphold the radical cause; he abruptly threw in his lot with the majority and became such a wholehearted conservative overnight that his draught of a letter to the Colony agent stating the purposes of the Convention was accepted by the delegates. As a result, the Convention's public utterances fell far short of the seditious blasts that Governor Bernard had expected; and he remarked that they revealed a moderation "very different from the Tempers of those who called this Meeting."[34] Instead of opening a fresh controversy with the British government, the Convention merely sent the King another copy of the petition drawn up by the House of Representatives in February 1768. The delegates scrupulously avoided raking the coals left by the Boston town meeting of September 12, 1768, and dissociated themselves from the metropolis's warlike menaces by declaring they were "plain honest men, humbly consulting peace and order," whose purpose was to prevent "all tumults and disorders into which our present calamities may betray us." They asserted that the Convention was not a revolutionary body created at Boston's behest to deal a blow

[32] Public Record Office, Colonial Office Class or Series 5, LXXXVI, 263, Lib. Cong. Transcripts.

[33] *Arthur Lee Papers*, I, 41.

[34] *Bernard Papers*, VII, Bernard to Lord Hillsborough, Oct. 3, 1768. Andrew Oliver, *Letter Book*, Gay Transcripts, MSS. Mass. Hist. Soc., I, Andrew Oliver to Thomas Pownall, March 1, 1769.

at the prerogative; on the contrary, Sam Adams said that George III should regard it as "a fresh token of the loyalty of our respective towns to his Majesty, their attachment to his government, and love of peace and good order."[35]   Nevertheless, King George and his ministers always suspected that Sam Adams had called the Convention to fight the King's troops rather than to enhance the royal prerogative and demonstrate New Englanders' loyalty to the Crown.

No sooner had the Convention been called to order than Governor Bernard issued orders to disperse on pain of feeling the full weight of the royal prerogative.   He warned the delegates that juggling names did not conceal the fact that the Convention was an assault upon the Crown's constitutional authority: it was an illegal assembly of the people's representatives "and it is not the Calling it a Committee of Convention that will alter the Nature of the Thing."   Bernard greatly prided himself upon the boldness of tone he took in this counterblast to the Convention and he believed it kept the rural delegates in awe and "frightened them not a little."   But although there was a large party that was "fearful of the legality of their proceedings and would gladly break up without doing anything," the Convention did not scatter because of Bernard's bluster.[36]   The majority were determined to sit until the troops arrived in order to prevent the town hotheads from taking some reckless step that would involve the whole province in a quarrel with the mother country.   Yet all the delegates had one eye cocked on Boston Harbor lest they be found in session when the British fleet appeared.   None were disposed to run the risk of being dispersed at the point of bayonets: therefore, when British men-of-war were reported off the Massachusetts coast the Convention broke up without more ado and the representatives "rushed out of town like a herd of scalded hogs," swearing that "they were sent to keep the rest from doing mischief."[37]   They separated none too soon: that afternoon the British regi-

[35] Boston Chronicle, Oct. 3, 1768.

[36] Bernard Papers, VII, Bernard to Lord Hillsborough, Oct. 3, 1768. Mass. Hist. Soc. Collections, Fourth Series, IV, 428.

[37] Mass. Hist. Soc. Collections, Fourth Series, IV, 432.   Mass. Archives, 26, Hutchinson Corr., II, 333.

ments from Halifax reached Boston Harbor and a few days
later two more regiments from Ireland arrived in the metropolis.

On September 11, 1768, orders had been received in Halifax
for two regiments and an artillery company "to embark with
the utmost Expedition for Boston." A strict embargo was
immediately clapped upon the port and preparations were
pushed ahead with "more Caution used than in War Time,
when they were fixing out for to take Louisbourg." The British were taking no chances with the Boston Sons of Liberty and
came prepared to fight their way into the town, if need be.
When the fleet entered the harbor, it approached the town with
as much caution as though Boston were an enemy port. Keeping their guns trained upon the town, the ships "ranged themselves on the North East Side of the Metropolis, as if intended
for a formal siege," while the Commissioners of the Customs
set off skyrockets and roared the chorus of "Yankee-Doodle"
behind the walls of Castle William. The troops were landed
in Boston under the guns of the men-of-war and marched unopposed with drums beating and flags flying to Faneuil Hall,
"the School of Liberty," where they took up their quarters.
Not a Son of Liberty raised his finger against them.[38]

When it was learned that British troops had taken possession
of Boston without so much as seeing a rebel musket, the Boston
Sons of Liberty became the laughingstock of the "sticklers for
prerogative doctrines" throughout the colonies. In New York,
news that redcoats were in the Puritan metropolis was received
with "Glee and Triumph" by the Tories, who immediately began to "decry the behaviour of our oppressed brethren of Boston,
and maliciously and invidiously sneer at their not having opposed the landing of the troops." Even to some New York
Sons of Liberty, the quick collapse of the Boston war party
seemed to be an example of "the ridiculous Puff and Bombast
for which our Eastern brethren have always been but too famous." [39] But the backsliding of the Boston Sons of Liberty

---

[38] *Boston Gazette*, Oct. 10, 1768. Thomas Cushing to Stephen Sayre,
Oct. 7, 1768, MS. Mass. Hist. Soc. *Boston Evening Post*, Oct. 3, 1768.

[39] *New York Journal*, Oct. 20, 1768; quoted in the *Boston Evening
Post*, Oct. 31, 1768.

was no surprise to His Majesty's military officers stationed in New York. "I am very much of Opinion," said General Gage before the outcome of the Massachusetts Convention was known, "they will shrink on the Day of Trial. . . . They are a People, who have ever been very bold in Council, but never remarkable for their Feats in Action." [40]

To English politicians, as well, the war scare of 1768 was proof that New Englanders' threats need not be taken seriously. The collapse of the Boston war party showed that Sam Adams was unsupported by the bulk of the people; and as long as the memory of the Massachusetts Convention remained fresh, Englishmen had no difficulty in believing that the opposition party in New England was confined to a small clique of blustering Boston politicians whom a few redcoats could easily drive to cover. The Boston patriots were regarded in England "as having made a vain bluster and parade to no purpose," and the Convention was contemptuously spoken of as "that thing of Straw, which at last was afraid of its own shadow." [41] After Boston had been brought to its knees by two regiments of redcoats, it was difficult to believe the townsmen would really fight, no matter how much they clamored for redress of grievances and boasted of their readiness to die for American freedom. Many Englishmen considered the military occupation of Boston "as a trial of strength and courage between this kingdom and the Colonies," and the decision seemed to reveal that the mother country had little to fear from American courage. The conviction deepened among English politicians that all that was necessary to make a New Englander wilt was to show him a loaded musket in the hands of a British regular.

For England, however, the triumph at Boston was dearly bought. Never before had Great Britain seemed so much a "step-mother" to her colonies as when royal troops and men-of-war trained their guns on Boston to batter down the Sons of Liberty. Boston's recent riots had strengthened many

[40] *The Correspondence of General Thomas Gage . . . 1763–1775*, edited by Clarence E. Carter (1933), II, 488.

[41] *Trumbull Papers*, I, 301. *Bernard Papers*, XII, Thomas Pownall to Francis Bernard, Nov. 19, 1768.

Southern patriots' prejudice against "mobbish" New Englanders, but the British government's policy of military coercion
made Americans forget Boston's mobs and think only of its
martyrdom at the hands of royal troops. New Hampshire
patriots looked upon "the calm and serene Regions, once the
Seats of Ease and Contentment . . . now transformed into
gloomy and dismal Scenes."   The threat of military despotism
hung heavy over America. "Instead of the Civil," warned
the patriots, "we all see a military Government forming . . .
the Lives, Liberties and Fortunes of several Millions of his Majesty's most loyal and useful Subjects are in Danger." [42]   "We
are no longer strangers to the measures Great Britain is determined to use in treating with her loyal colonies in America,"
exclaimed a "British Carolinian."   "Already New England is
marked out as the place upon which she intends to lavish her
maternal affection in an extraordinary manner, by sending out
of Troops to bring them to compliance with all her measures
whether right or wrong." [43]   The taunt which the colonists
believed common in England that "Americans cannot endure
the smell of gunpowder" rankled among the patriots and
made them long for another opportunity to prove to British
regulars that American Whigs could stand their ground in the
hottest fire. Several years before, Benjamin Franklin had
told the House of Commons how to cause uprisings in the colonies: if British troops were sent to America, Franklin warned,
they would not find a rebellion, but they probably would make
one. Franklin's recipe was closely followed by the Ministry,
which, by throwing British soldiers into the same town with
Sam Adams, stirred together two of the principal ingredients
for producing a smacking rebellion.

The Massachusetts Convention of 1768 is an important mile-
stone in the history of Boston's gradual domination of New
England. The metropolis alone, acting under Sam Adams's
direction, had called into being a representative body which, to
all intents and purposes, was the dissolved Massachusetts House
of Representatives masquerading under a new name. The

[42] *New Hampshire Gazette*, Oct. 7, 1768.
[43] *Essex Gazette*, Nov. 23, 1768.

Convention was one of the first and most significant of those extra-legal institutions which Sam Adams was to bring forth with bewildering rapidity later in the Revolution. It was the precursor of the Massachusetts Provincial Congress and paved the way for linking together the towns of the colony under Boston's guidance and committees of correspondence. Thomas Hutchinson declared that in summoning the Convention, Boston had revealed "a greater tendency towards a revolution in government, than any preceeding measures in any of the colonies." [44] Governor Bernard believed that "so daring an assumption of the Royal Authority was never practiced by any city or town in the British Dominions, even in the times of greatest disorder, not even by the City of London when the great Rebellion was at the highest." [45] The crisis produced by the sending of British troops to Boston had brought forward the boldest and most radical of the patriots, who looked upon the Convention as a steppingstone to a later usurpation of governmental power. The curtain was drawn aside momentarily to reveal the existence of a formidable party headed by Sam Adams that was ready to take up arms against the mother country in defense of American liberties. Although Adams failed to find support for his plans in 1768, it was, wrote Hutchinson, "a bold attempt, and carried strong marks of that venturous spirit which has appeared in many stages of the American revolution." [46]

[44] Hutchinson, III, 205.
[45] *Papers Relating to Public Events*, 105.
[46] Hutchinson, III, 206.

THE BOSTON MASSACRE

BRITISH troops had marched into Boston unopposed, but Sam Adams did not propose to allow them to enjoy long the hospitality of the Puritan metropolis. Rather than provide barracks for the soldiers, Adams was resolved to let them freeze in their encampment on the Boston Common. Whigs were told to show redcoats the same courtesy they did "Serpents and Panthers," and Sam Adams felt that even the Common in the dead of winter was too good for them. Adams insisted that, since the General Court had not consented to receive the troops, they had no right whatever to be in Massachusetts; and he construed the Mutiny Act, by which Parliament had provided the manner and place of billeting royal troops in the colonies, to rule them out of Boston and station them in Castle William, three miles out to sea. Boston selectmen and the Massachusetts Council supported Adams in refusing to quarter the soldiers in Boston, but the British military authorities were determined to post them in the heart of town until the citizens had been thoroughly cured of their weakness for rioting. If the regiments were put in Castle William, Boston Sons of Liberty might tar and feather Tories and Commissioners at will before order could be restored. Consequently, Boston warehouses were converted into barracks and the metropolis was garrisoned with redcoats whose "spirit-stirring drum and ear-piercing fife" grated discordantly with the "sweet songs, violins, and flutes, of the serenading Sons of Liberty" until the Boston Massacre.[1]

With four regiments of British regulars in Boston, many of the Sons of Liberty began to cover up their attempts to incite resistance with a less stiff-necked bearing toward the "invaders."

[1] *The Works of John Adams,* II, 213; X, 199. *The Writings of Samuel Adams,* I, 249–250; II, 48, 49, 392.

After patriotically preventing the soldiers from being housed elsewhere in Boston, William Molineux tried to rent out for a garrison a warehouse on Wheelwright's wharf in which he had an interest; and James Otis sent Generpl Gage his card and an invitation to dinner which the general firmly declined. Parliament almost threw these uneasy patriots into a panic by reviving a statute of Henry VIII to transport Americans suspected of treason to England for trial. Adams felt safe with a Boston jury which was certain to be loaded with Sons of Liberty, but he knew that English jurors would show him small mercy. Tories and Crown officers hopefully awaited the "Doom of Boston"; and Thomas Hutchinson began taking depositions to speed Adams and his crew on their way to Tyburn. Wagers were offered in Boston that Adams, Hancock, and Otis would swing from the gallows, and it was whispered among Tories that Adams "shuddered at the sight of hemp." In London, the King's friends remarked "with a snear" that James Otis, the mad Bostonian, would soon have an opportunity to "defend the assumed rights of the New World at the bar of the House of Commons." [2] But a rude disappointment was in store for the British Tories who promised themselves huge diversion from this cargo of transported American Whigs. The Massachusetts patriots had been too cautious to run their necks into a noose. No treason could be proved against them, although the attorney-general found that they had come "within an hair's breadth of it." By this slim margin, Otis and Adams were spared the Tower. The Whigs quickly recovered from their fright and, when they saw that the Ministry intended to pocket the affront, they became "more assuming and tyrannical than before." [3] After the Massachusetts Convention, bluffing

---

[2] Andrew Oliver, *op. cit.*, Andrew Oliver to John Spooner, Oct. 28, 1768. *Chalmers Papers*, III, Sparks MSS., Harvard College Library; Thomas Hutchinson to Lord Hillsborough, April 27, 1770. *The Correspondence of Thomas Gage, 1763–1775*, edited by Clarence E. Carter (1933), II, 501. *Hess-Wendell Papers*, MSS. Mass. Hist. Soc., Edmund Quincy to John Wendell, Jan. 17, 1769. *Boston Gazette*, Jan. 23, 1769.

[3] *Debates in the House of Commons, Reports of Sir Henry Cavendish* (1841), I, 196. *Chalmers Papers*, III, Thomas Hutchinson to Lord Hillsborough, April 27, 1770.

was thought to be a besetting sin of Bostonians, but when the British government let the patriot leaders go scot-free after having threatened them with being drawn and quartered on Tyburn, it was clear that British Tories were as mighty blusterers as the Boston Whigs. By this unexpected change of policy, American patriots were encouraged to regard the menaces of the British government as empty gestures which would never be carried out.

As Sam Adams feared, the British "invasion" of Boston proved to be a thoroughgoing military occupation. Faneuil Hall — that "celebrated school for Catalines & Sedition" — remained in the troops' hands, and, until the middle of November, they overran the Town House. Guards were stationed at Boston Neck to challenge all who entered or left the town, and patrolling companies hovered near every ferry to Boston. So closely was the metropolis guarded that even the carriage of a member of the Massachusetts Council was stopped at the lines on Boston Neck. But the crowning indignity, in Adams's eyes, was the stationing of the main guard opposite the Boston Town House and the setting up of cannon whose muzzles pointed directly at the door of the legislative chambers. When Adams and other Massachusetts representatives left the General Court they found themselves looking squarely into the mouths of British guns. It would have needed only a well-aimed whiff of grape to put Sam Adams and several score of Massachusetts Whigs out of the way of Tories and Crown officers. And all this severity was owing to two riots, one of which Adams insisted was a parade and the other a justifiable demonstration against customhouse officers who had made an illegal seizure! [4]

No Bostonian smarted under these humiliations more deeply than did Sam Adams. Like his cousin John, he believed that when British troops took possession of Boston, the mother country had proved beyond doubt that its determination "to subjugate us was too deep and inveterate ever to be altered by

---

[4] *Boston Evening Post*, Jan. 9 and 23, 1769; Feb. 11, 1769. *New York Gazette and Weekly Mercury*, Nov. 7, 1768. *The Writings of Samuel Adams*, II, 239, 241.

us." John Adams dated Sam's determination to make America independent of Great Britain from the period of the military occupation of Boston. Unquestionably, he began to look forward to a speedy separation from the mother country after the failure of the Massachusetts Convention. He regretted bitterly that his plan of fighting the redcoats had been upset by rural conservatism. Even after having watched the regulars manœuvre and parade on the Boston Common, he was still convinced that New Englanders could have driven them back to their ships with "the greatest ease, for what was an handful of troops to subdue a large country?" [5] In his eyes, when New England farmers failed to march to Boston to meet the British, they merely postponed an inevitable crisis. Now that the troops were in Boston, the problem was to get rid of them before they could establish the rule of tyranny which Adams did not doubt was the real reason of their coming. He expected to find military law riveted upon the province, and Thomas Hutchinson and Governor Bernard with an "army of placemen and pensioners" kept in power by British arms. Although the troops had received strict orders from the Ministry to remain subordinate to the Massachusetts civil government and to act only at the command of magistrates, Sam Adams looked forward to an outright despotism and a "bloody career of the military." "Where," he exclaimed, "is the bill of rights, magna charta and the blood of our venerable forefathers?" [6] And how would New Englanders defend themselves against this new "menacing monster" — a British army? Although Adams did not receive his answer until 1775, he determined in the meantime to clear the Puritan metropolis of redcoats before they could gain a foothold.

Massachusetts Tories paid a heavy price for the luxury of British military protection. Although the "hideous Sound of Conch Shells" which warned Boston householders that the Sons of Liberty were abroad was no longer heard, and Hutchinson

---

[5] *The Works of John Adams*, II, 214; IX, 596. *The Writings of Samuel Adams*, I, 393.

[6] *The Writings of Samuel Adams*, I, 252, 253, 256, 258, 259, 392; II, 48–49.

and his friends slept for the first time in years without dread of
being turned out by a mob, few Tories could regard the troops
as an unmixed blessing.   It was clear that peace would endure
only as long as the soldiers kept order; the moment this "Interval or Truce procur'd from the dread of a Bayonet" was
over, Liberty Boys would fall to terrorizing Tories as never
before.   Temporary security from mobs was no compensation
for the rapid strides in power which Sam Adams made as a
consequence of the troops' presence in Boston.   Adams almost
ruined the Massachusetts Tory Party by linking it with British
military aggression.   Not ten men were left in the Massachusetts House of Representatives to oppose him, and the Council
was almost cleared of the governor's friends.   Adams dominated the Council so completely through his friend James
Bowdoin that he wrote its answer to the governor's speech;
although this paper purported to have come from the councilors themselves, Bernard recognized Adams's hand in the "barefaced Chicanery & Falsity of this Writing as well as the stile."
He exercised similar influence over the Boston selectmen and
wrote their address to Governor Bernard, which the selectmen
presented as their own.   With his hands tied by the Council's
defection and with the House of Representatives swarming with
Whigs, Governor Bernard was guilty of only slight exaggeration in saying that Otis and Adams were "in full Possession of
the Government." [7]   When Sam Adams declared that the
House of Representatives would do no business until the troops
were removed from Boston, the few Tories who still sat in
the House made no opposition.   In spite of the protection of
British bayonets which made Boston safer for country Tories
than it had been for many years, the governor's friends continued resolutely to remain at home and no amount of pleading could bring them to face Adams and Otis in the General
Court.   When Thomas Hutchinson pressed the stay-at-home
squires to come to Boston and give Adams a drubbing, they

---

[7] Andrew Oliver, *op. cit.*, Andrew Oliver to John Spooner, Oct. 28, 1788;
Andrew Oliver to Israel Mauduit, July 10, 1769. *Bernard Papers*, VII,
Bernard to Pownall, March 5 and June 1, 1769; Bernard to Lord Hillsbor-
ough, July 7, 1769; Bernard to Lord Barrington, May 30, 1769.

answered that it was "to no purpose — the whole Province must give way" to Sam Adams and the Boston Whigs.[8]

The security afforded by British soldiers and men-of-war did not tempt Governor Bernard to tarry in Massachusetts Bay. During the last years of his administration he held one fixed purpose — to escape from the colony before the Sons of Liberty put him through the "ordeal" at Liberty Tree. Bernard had been in mortal terror of "mobbish Bostonians" ever since the Stamp Act riots, and he felt certain each time the mob broke loose that he would never see England alive unless he made a quick getaway. He had not forgotten that the Liberty Boys had sworn to put to death all who were concerned in bringing troops to Boston, and he knew that Sam Adams held him, Hutchinson, and the Commissioners responsible for their presence. When the heart was cut out of his picture in Harvard College, Bernard's homesickness became more acute. He had so completely lost the popularity he enjoyed during the first five years of his administration that most New Englanders were as anxious to be rid of him as he was to be safe in England. By picking quarrels with the Assembly and writing alarmist letters to the British government, he brought the governorship into low repute and gave Sam Adams an opportunity to put royal government in bad odor throughout the colonies. British officials hoped for better things from Massachusetts Bay when Bernard should be removed: "His doubles and turnings have been so many," wrote Commodore Hood, commander of the British squadron in Boston Harbor, "that he has altogether lost his road, and brought himself into great contempt." [9] Yet Bernard might well have protested that he was being made the scapegoat of an unworkable system and the mistakes of the British Ministry and Parliament. After the Stamp Act, there was no middle course for a royal governor of Massachusetts: he must either favor the people, which would have brought him a prompt dismissal from the Crown, or defend the royal government, which meant endless conflict with the popular branch of the legislature. The difficulties faced by a royal

[8] Mass. Archives, 26, *Hutchinson Corr.*, II, 471.
[9] *Grenville Papers*, IV, 378.

governor of Massachusetts, always formidable, had become
staggering after 1765, when he became the embodiment of the
new policy of centralization attempted by British imperialists.
In reality, revolutionary forces were at work in the colony and
Bernard's successor had no better fortune in averting the crisis
which Sam Adams was doing his utmost to hasten.

Before Bernard could leave Massachusetts he felt the smart
of the shots with which Sam Adams usually sped a departing
royal governor on his travels. The Massachusetts colony agent
sent copies to Boston of a large number of letters written by
Governor Bernard, General Gage, and the Commissioners of
the Customs. There was little in this correspondence that the
Whigs did not already know and much less incriminating matter
than they had long since charged to Bernard, but Sam Adams
skillfully used it to convict the governor of plotting against
that "sacred ark," the Massachusetts charter. Bernard's letters were published in the *Boston Gazette* and sent to most of
the newspapers on the continent to put Americans on their
guard against all royal governors and to raise such a storm in
rural Massachusetts that the handful of Tories still in the
General Court would be blown out of their seats and replaced
by Sons of Liberty. In the Boston town meeting, Sam Adams
declared that "if all Records were to be Searched, no Instance
could be found of so much Malice and falsehood collected to
Injure as Loyal and Religious People, who were at that Time
really oppress'd, and under a Tyranny," as was to be found
in Bernard's correspondence. But when William Cooper, the
town clerk, began reading the governor's letters to the citizens,
interspersing Bernard's words with asides and cracking jokes
which "generally occasion'd a Grin of applause," Adams stopped
him before he had read halfway through because "so many plain
matters of Fact appear'd against them in the Course of the
Perusal." [10]   Indeed, Bernard's account of the patriots' activities proved so embarrassing that Sam Adams was directed by the
town to write an "Appeal to the World" to whitewash Boston's
reputation of all the governor's "slanderous *Chit-chat*." The

[10] *Chalmers Papers*, III, The Proceedings of a Town Meeting held at
Faneuil Hall the 4th October, 1769.

Suffolk Grand Jury indicted the governor, General Gage, and the Commissioners for libeling the inhabitants of the province; and Adams succeeded in persuading the General Court to petition the Crown for Bernard's removal on the ground that he had proved himself hostile to the liberties of His Majesty's loyal subjects in Massachusetts Bay.

So eager was Bernard to return to England that he left Lady Bernard behind in Massachusetts; but even this dispatch did not spare the governor the humiliation of witnessing the Sons of Liberty celebrate his departure. His ship lay becalmed outside the harbor, from where he could see the Union Flag run up Liberty Tree and Saint George's banner flying from Hancock's wharf and hear the bells and cannon that sounded throughout the day. That evening, while Bernard's vessel was still unable to get under way, huge bonfires were lighted on Fort Hill and in Charlestown to show the luckless governor how Massachusetts rejoiced to be free of "a Scourge to this Province, a Curse to North America, and a Plague on the whole Empire." [11] Massachusetts patriots had added another governor's scalp to their collection and had carried out to the full every threat they had made against him when he first came into the colony. As Bernard impatiently awaited a favorable wind and listened to the whooping Liberty Boys ashore, he well knew why he had been warned when he first arrived in Massachusetts Bay against Sam Adams, a "noted writer in the newspapers" and the terror of royal governors. But after his safe arrival in England Bernard had no difficulty in dismissing the impeachment proceedings of the Massachusetts House of Representatives as "Groundless, Vexatious & Scandalous." Instead of sending Bernard to the Tower, as Adams devoutly hoped, the persecution of the Massachusetts patriots so endeared him to King George that he was created a Baronet.[12]

Having turned out the royal governor, Sam Adams could give his undivided attention to ridding Boston of the royal troops. The British had scarcely landed in New England before Adams was at work drumming up hatred against them

[11] *Boston Gazette*, Aug. 7, 1769.
[12] *Collections Col. Soc. of Mass.* (1910–11), XIII, 386, 410.

throughout the length and breadth of the American colonies.
Boston patriots had connections with influential newspaper printers throughout the continent, and Sam Adams's political articles
not infrequently appeared in New York or Philadelphia papers
weeks before New Englanders saw them.   The patriots' purpose
was to educate Americans in "Boston politics" or to lead New
Englanders themselves to believe that the Southern colonies
were warm in their behalf and that Southern Whigs were
busily engaged in turning out political tracts which reëchoed
Adams's principles.   After the Massachusetts Convention had
failed to approve his war plans, Adams set out to make the British military occupation of Boston an intercolonial issue.   He
hoped to see the entire continent support Massachusetts in demanding the withdrawal of the troops and to raise such a storm
against "military tyranny" throughout the colonies that the
British government would be forced to hand Boston back to
the Sons of Liberty.   This undertaking required the aid of every
colonial printer on good terms with the Boston patriots.   Shortly
after the arrival of the British fleet in Boston Harbor, New
York printers received from Boston the first installment of
Adams's raciest propaganda, the "Journal of the Times" or
"Journal of Events."   From New York, the "Journal" was
sent to most newspapers on the American continent and even
to England, where it appeared in the *Gentleman's Magazine*
and was put to good purpose by the opposition in Parliament.
Probably none of Adams's work had a wider circulation or had
greater influence in laying the foundation for the intercolonial
support given Boston, "the antient Capital of North America,"
during the Port Bill days of 1774.

In the "Journal of Events," Sam Adams served colonial
Whigs with piping-hot "British atrocities" committed by the
soldiery in Boston.   It made a spicy dish indeed for countryfolk accustomed to a steady diet of almanacs and scripture.   The
"Journal" consisted of bloodcurdling descriptions of British
regulars brutally beating small boys on Boston streets; violating the Sabbath with gunfire, carousing, and horse racing; and,
above all, raping Boston matrons and young girls.   If Adams
and his fellow journalists were to be believed, scarcely a day

passed without a British soldier assaulting a woman; none were safe from these "bloody-backed rascals," and even the worthiest families were apt to share the grief of that venerable patriot who "the other morning discovered a soldier in bed with a favourite grand daughter." [13] That royal troops were the monsters Sam Adams painted was indignantly denied by the Crown officers. Thomas Hutchinson, who believed that Adams first published the "Journal" away from Boston because there was no one to contradict his "Infamous falsehoods," assured his friends that nine tenths of it was untrue and Governor Bernard said that "if the Devil himself were of the Party, as he virtually is, there would not have been got together a greater collection of impudent virulent & Seditious Lies, Perversions of Truth & Misrepresentations than are to be found in this Publication." The soldiers themselves swore there was no need to use force, since women of easy virtue were so plentiful in Boston that there was not an officer or private "down to a drummer, that cannot have his bedfellow for the winter; so that the Yankey war, contrary to all others, will produce more births than burials." [14]

Thomas Hutchinson was alarmed to find that Adams's propaganda was turning Americans against Crown officers and British troops in most of the colonies and making New Yorkers and Philadelphians, who "for some time past seem to have been cool," into fire-eating patriots. For, in spite of all denials, colonists eagerly swallowed the atrocities Sam Adams spread before them every week in the newspapers. He left unmentioned, of course, the riots that originally caused soldiers to be sent: Boston was overrun with "foreign invaders" who made the Iroquois seem tame in comparison, solely because the citizens had asserted the "just rights of Americans" in the teeth of the British government.

But it was in Boston itself that the "Journal of Events" raised

---

[13] *Boston Evening Post*, July 24 and 31, 1769.

[14] *Israel Williams Papers*, MSS. Mass. Hist. Soc., II, Thomas Hutchinson to Israel Williams, Jan. 26, 1769. *Bernard Papers*, VII, Bernard to Lord Hillsborough, Feb. 25, 1769. *New York Journal or General Advertiser*, May 4, 1769.

the most turbulent storm. By fanning Bostonians' hatred of
the British troops, Adams set the stage for the Boston Massacre, and his lurid descriptions of imaginary rapes, quarrels,
and insults led directly to real bloodshed.

In this highly charged atmosphere, it would have been
strange if the sparks Sam Adams struck off in the "Journal of
Events" had not quickly produced an explosion. The Sons
of Liberty rankled under the sneer that they lost their appetite for fighting as soon as they smelled gunpowder, and some
of the British troops who had been bitterly disappointed at not
finding the Boston Sons of Liberty in arms in 1768 were eager
to give them a trouncing. At the outset of the military occupation of Boston, the patriots had aroused the soldiers' resentment by their "low and spiteful devise" of attempting to freeze
the troops out of Boston by forcing them to remain on the Common all winter. Before the troops had settled themselves in
the town, a near battle was fought at the Manufactory House,
where the town paupers and Sons of Liberty prevented the
British from turning the building into a barracks. Unquestionably many of Adams's choice stories in the "Journal" were
true: a large number of British soldiers made a practice of jab-
bing patriots in the ribs with bayonets and hustling them off the
sidewalks, but the patriots in turn haled the soldiers into court
on every pretext and made their lives as miserable as creditors
can. Eighteenth-century British armies were composed in
large measure of scourings and scrapings, but the Twenty-ninth
Regiment, which the Ministry had sent to tame the Bostonians,
seems to have had more than its share of gallows birds. "They
are in general, such bad fellows, in that Regiment," said Thomas
Hutchinson, "that it seems impossible to restrain them from
firing upon an insult or provocation given them." Since the
Boston ropewalk workers were equally aggressive, a hot feud
sprang up between them and the "bloody-backed rascals" in
which both parties enthusiastically cracked each other's pates.
With such riotous allies, Adams had little difficulty in kindling
an "immortal hatred" between soldiers and his "Psalmsinging
Myrmidons." Thomas Young remarked that New Englanders needed "but a spark to set them all in flames," and Sam

Adams was sending out a shower of sparks every week in his "Journal of Events."[15]

In the summer of 1769 the British government planned to withdraw two of the four regiments of British regulars from Boston — to the great consternation of many Crown officers, who feared that the remaining troops would be unable to hold the Sons of Liberty in check. Governor Bernard believed that what was really required was "a Reinforcement of the King's Forces at Boston [rather] than a weakening of them." When Sam Adams learned that it was proposed to reduce the Boston garrison he immediately presented a set of resolves to the House of Representatives so seditious that Commodore Hood declared they were "of a more extraordinary nature, than any that have yet passed an American Assembly." Just as the Sixty-fourth Regiment was about to embark for Halifax, Adams published these resolves — which, in effect, denied all Parliamentary authority over the colony — in the *Boston Gazette*, although they had not yet passed the House of Representatives. This "alarm bell to revolt" so frightened the Crown officers that the embarkation was suspended and the troops were ordered back to their barracks lest the townspeople attempt to throw off British sovereignty and drive the remaining troops out of town. It was only after Adams's resolves had been repudiated by the House of Representatives that this alarm was allayed. When the town had quieted down, two regiments boarded the transports for Halifax, leaving less than five hundred effective regulars in Boston to keep order. The patriots were now more than a match for the troops and Hutchinson's misgivings deepened that there would soon be bloodshed in the metropolis.[16]

[15] Mass. Archives, 26, *Hutchinson Corr.*, II, 525. *Bernard Papers*, VII, Bernard to Lord Hillsborough, Dec. 26, 1768. *The Works of John Adams*, II, 230. *Chalmers Papers*, III, Thomas Hutchinson to Lord Hillsborough, March 12, 1770. *Mass. Hist. Soc. Proceedings*, XLVII, 202.

[16] *Bernard Papers*, VII, Bernard to Lord Hillsborough, July 7, 1769. Public Record Office, Admiralty Secretary, In Letters, 483, Lib. Cong., 25, Commodore Hood to Philip Stevens, July 10, 1769. Letters of Samuel Cooper to Pownall and Franklin, 1770–74, Bancroft Transcripts, New York Public Library, Samuel Cooper to Thomas Pownall, July 12, 1769. *Bernard Papers*, VII, Bernard to Lord Hillsborough, July 7, 1769. Hutchinson, III, 242.

Early in the spring of 1770 the situation in Boston passed entirely out of the control of the peace officers.   Sam Adams's "Mohawks" brawled with redcoats in taverns and back alleys while the ropewalkers picked quarrels with the Twenty-ninth Regiment — those guardians of law and order whose bad tempers were the terror of sober citizens whether Whig or Tory. Then, in March 1770, an incident occurred which led directly to the Boston Massacre.   Samuel Gray, one of the hardiest brawlers employed at Gray's ropewalk in Boston, asked a soldier of the Twenty-ninth Regiment if he wanted a job.   When the man answered that he did, Gray said he had a privy that needed cleaning.   This insult provoked an immediate fight between the soldiers and ropewalkers, but no serious clash took place until their pent-up animosity burst forth on March 5, 1770.

One morning shortly before that day, the citizens of Boston awoke to find the streets plastered with notices, signed by many of the soldiers garrisoned in the town, that the troops intended to attack the townspeople.   This startling news threw the town into a ferment, for apparently few citizens doubted the genuineness of these papers.   It is singular, nevertheless, that the soldiers should have given their plans away in this manner if they really contemplated an attack and that they signed their names to documents that might be used as damning evidence against them.   These notices were doubtless forgeries made by Adams and his followers and posted during the night by the "Loyall Nine" to produce an explosion that would sweep Boston clear of redcoats; for during the Massacre trials it is significant that the prosecution did not enter them as evidence of the soldiers' guilt.   The events of the night of March 5 bear out this explanation of their origin.   That evening a crowd of small boys began to snowball the British sentry in King's Street.   Pelting the redcoats had become a recognized pastime among the Whigs, but it was soon apparent that this was to be no ordinary evening in Boston, for both soldiers and civilians had been convinced by Adams's propaganda that they were in danger of massacre from their enemies.   After the sentry had sent his tormentors scampering, crowds of townspeople began to gather and head

for King's Street. The square before the customhouse was
soon filled with a swearing, turbulent mass of men, many of
whom were armed with clubs, staves, and formidable pieces of
jagged ice. Although Sam Adams and other patriots carefully avoided calling this crowd a mob, John Adams declared
the name too good for it — a "motley rabble of saucy boys,
negroes and mulattoes, Irish teagues and outlandish jack tars,"
he said, had turned out to fight the troops. Among them were
Samuel Gray, the ropewalker who had started a free-for-all
a few days before by inviting a soldier to clean his outhouse;
Crispus Attucks, a huge mulatto noted for his prowess with the
cudgel; James Caldwell, a ship's mate; and Patrick Carr, a
seasoned Irish rioter. These stout cudgel-boys had beaten up
so many redcoats that the sentry hastily summoned the main
guard, which, led by Captain Preston of the Twenty-ninth
Regiment, tumbled out eagerly for a fight. Consequently, the
mob found itself face to face with its worst enemies; pellets of
ice, sticks, and cudgels flew fast; and a large body of citizens who
had gathered in Dock Square, where a mysterious gentleman in
a red cloak and red wig harangued them to make a concerted
attack upon the troops, rushed to join the brisk work that was
going on before the customhouse. It was a wild scene even
to Bostonians hardened to "Pope Day" riots and patriotic dem-
onstrations; as John Adams later described it, "the multitude
was shouting and huzzaing, and threatening life, the bells ringing, the mob whistling, screaming and rending like an Indian
yell, the people from all quarters throwing every species of
rubbish they could pick up in the streets." [17] Meanwhile, the
ringing of bells all over Boston and the near-by towns was
bringing hundreds of reënforcements to the mob in King's
Street. Thus far, the soldiers had used their bayonets to keep
the mob at bay and no patriot had suffered worse casualty than
a smart rap on the shins. In spite of the hail of missiles, the
soldiers withheld their fire until the mob screamed that the
"bloody-backed rascals" did not dare to shoot. The troops
restrained themselves with difficulty from giving Adams's "Mohawks" a taste of powder and ball, but when one of them was

[17] Frederick Kidder, *The Boston Massacre* (1870), 255–257.

sent sprawling by a patriot brickbat he recovered his gun and fired directly into the mob. Most of the soldiers likewise opened fire, — at Captain Preston's order, many of the town's witnesses later testified, — and after they had emptied their guns five civilians had been killed or mortally wounded.

The victims were typical members of the Boston mob: Samuel Gray, Crispus Attucks, James Caldwell, and Patrick Carr all fell in the British fire. Samuel Maverick, the fifth victim, was an apprentice who had taken no part in the riot. John Adams said that those killed in the Massacre were "the most obscure and inconsiderable that could have been found upon the continent," but Sam Adams made them pure and holy martyrs to liberty.[18] Crispus Attucks, the Framingham mulatto, a veteran of a score of riots, was exalted with the rest, although it was common knowledge that he had led an army of thirty sailors armed with clubs in Cornhill on the night of March 5 and that it was chiefly his violent assault upon the troops that had caused bloodshed. Only one of the victims, Patrick Carr, was denied the sweets of martyrdom by Sam Adams, because his deathbed confession absolved the soldiers of all blame for the Massacre.

Sam Adams lost no time in making the most of the "Bloody Work in King's Street." The day after the Massacre, the town meeting was called in Faneuil Hall, where Adams made such a rousing speech from the rostrum that his hearers declared it was "enough to fire any heart with a desire to become a patriot." [19] Having thrown the citizens into this bristling frame of mind, Adams demanded the immediate withdrawal of the British troops from Boston. This, the townspeople agreed, was the only way to prevent further "blood and carnage." Adams thereupon placed himself and Hancock at the head of a town committee and marched to the Town House overlooking the scene of the Massacre, where, in the Council chamber hung with the portraits of Charles II and James II and "little miserable likenesses" of the Puritan magistrates, Adams laid his demands before the Council. At the head of the Coun-

[18] *The Works of John Adams*, IX, 352.
[19] *New York Journal or General Advertiser*, March 29, 1770.

"THE BLOODY MASSACRE"

PERPETRATED IN KING STREET, BOSTON, ON MARCH 5, 1770,
BY A PARTY OF THE 29TH REGIMENT

(*From the well-known engraving by Paul Revere*)

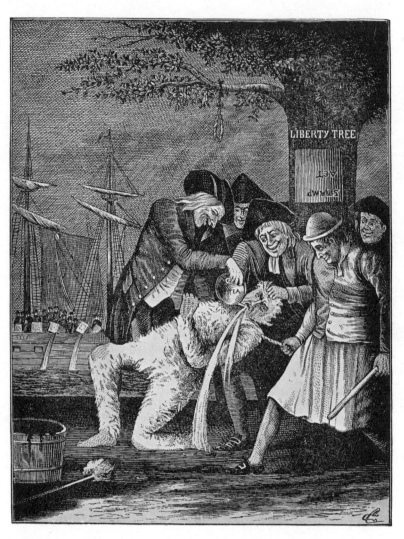

BOSTONIANS PAYING THE EXCISEMAN

cil table sat Lieutenant Governor Hutchinson; at his right,
Colonel Dalrymple, commander in chief of His Majesty's forces
in Boston; and around the table were seated twenty-eight councilors wearing "large white wigs, English scarlet cloth cloaks." [20]
Standing before these dignitaries as spokesman for the citizens
of Boston, Adams described the "dangerous, ruinous, and fatal
effects of standing armies in populous cities in time of peace,"
the hatred of New Englanders toward the troops who had
spilled patriot blood, and repeated the resolves of the Boston
town meeting demanding the immediate removal of the soldiers from the metropolis.   Hutchinson answered that since
he had no authority over the King's troops nothing could be
done until he had consulted the home government.   But Adams
was not to be put off so easily; he instantly appealed to the
Massachusetts charter by which Hutchinson was constituted
commander in chief of all the military and naval forces within
the province.   When Hutchinson and Dalrymple saw that
Adams was determined to force their hand, they laid their
heads together and, after much whispering, offered to remove
the Twenty-ninth Regiment, which alone had fired upon the
citizens, to Castle William and to keep the other regiment confined to quarters in Boston.   But here again Hutchinson played
into Adams's hands.   "In his venerable grey locks, and with
his hands trembling under a nervous complaint," Adams told
Hutchinson and Dalrymple that if they had "authority to
remove one regiment they had authority to remove two," and
that nothing short of a complete evacuation of the town by all
the troops would preserve the peace of the province.[21]   Unless
the metropolis were cleared of redcoats, Adams warned, there
would be more bloody work in Boston — this time with the
King's troops as the victims.   Fifteen thousand fighting men,
he exclaimed, were ready to pour into Boston to take revenge
upon the soldiers.   Dalrymple needed little persuasion: he
was well aware that he could not defend his position against
the New England militia with the four hundred men he could
bring into the field; and he had no desire to risk a disgraceful

[20] *The Works of John Adams*, X, 250.
[21] *Ibid.*, X, 252.

rout at the hands of farmers and Boston Sons of Liberty. When
Adams made these threats he believed he saw Hutchinson's
legs tremble and his face grow pale — "and," added Adams,
"I enjoyd the Sight." For a few hours, Hutchinson planned
to resist the townspeople, but when he saw "how artfully it was
steered" by Adams, whose strategy had placed the entire responsibility of keeping the troops in Boston upon his shoulders,
he acknowledged that he must either yield or leave the province. The Council assured Hutchinson that New England
would soon be in arms against the troops and that "the night
which was coming on would be the most terrible that was ever
seen in America." The danger of defying the people was too
great; before nightfall, Hutchinson struck his colors and Bostonians were promised the speedy removal of both regiments.[22]

The army of New Englanders with which Adams threatened
Hutchinson and Dalrymple was no empty menace. Had the
crisis been protracted, the metropolis would probably have
seen those embattled farmers that Adams had vainly looked
for during the Massachusetts Convention. The country people
were led to believe that Boston was to be given over to a general massacre and they were "on Tip toe" to rush in and save
the townsmen; "forty thousand men could have been brot
into the gates of this city at 48 hours warning," boasted a
patriot. The "Bloody Work in Boston calls loud for VENGE-
ANCE," exclaimed the Portsmouth Sons of Liberty, who talked
of marching ten thousand strong to help drive the redcoats
into Boston Bay; and the Salem Liberty Boys, not to be outdone, promised that thousands of Essex yeomen would turn
out to help Boston destroy a "licentious and blood-thirsty
Soldiery." Never before had Boston stood higher in the
estimation of New Englanders: the metropolis was now hailed
by countrymen as "the capital of British America," pledges of

[22] But the troops were not immediately removed from Boston. The delay
greatly alarmed the Whigs, who continued to threaten Hutchinson and other
Crown officers with an attack upon the troops. When the soldiers finally
marched out of their barracks to the wharf from which they took ship to
Castle William, it was necessary for William Molineux to march beside them
to protect them from the hooting citizens. *The Works of John Adams*, X,
252, 253.

support poured in from every side, and military fervor spread so rapidly over the country that Sam Adams began to believe his countrymen were in fact "Old Romans."

Adams's first thought was to convince the world that Boston was innocent of any blame for the Massacre. There was need of quick action, because immediately after the bloodshed, Robinson, the Commissioner of the Customs, who had been most active in counterworking the Whigs, secretly left Boston for England with papers which the patriots suspected were to be used to prove Boston's guilt. To offset this Tory propaganda, Adams had himself, Hancock, and the Boston selectmen appointed a committee by the citizens to take *ex parte* testimony from witnesses and draw up an account of the Massacre for public consumption. Adams and his followers fell to work with such enthusiasm that they were soon attempting to prove that the Commissioners of the Customs had fired upon the citizens the night of the Massacre and were as guilty as the soldiers of murdering unarmed Whigs. The patriots were eager to pin some fresh atrocity upon the Commissioners to render them more hateful to the people: therefore Adams proclaimed that he had ferreted out a conspiracy between the military officers and Commissioners of the Customs to slaughter Bostonians. "Some of the Banditti," remarked a Tory, referring to Adams and his fellow committeemen, "prevailed on a little French Boy belonging to Mainwaring [a customhouse officer] to swear he actually fired three Guns from the Custom House window under his Master's Directions." Moreover, Adams's examination of the witnesses seemed to prove conclusively that the soldiers and Commissioners were the sole aggressors and that the townspeople had been treated with "unexampled Barbarity"; but Tories said that Adams was forced to stoop to perjury and falsehood to save Boston's reputation. Had Hutchinson possessed authority to enforce his orders, he would have stopped Adams and the selectmen from taking testimony because he believed they were attempting to fasten the witnesses to signed affidavits before the trial took place — a procedure which would put the soldier's defense under a serious disadvantage. But before Hutchinson could act, the damage was done: the evidence was turned over to Adams and Bowdoin to be put into literary form. Robinson was already on his way to England, but Boston chartered a speedy vessel to carry its "Narrative" to the mother country; and although Robinson won the race, the patriots were not far behind with a cargo of red-hot propaganda with which to avert punishment by the British government.

Sam Adams was keenly aware of the necessity of bringing the soldiers to trial while the memory of the Massacre was still fresh. He bent every effort therefore to secure an early trial; and when it was reported that the illness of two judges would force a postponement until June, he headed a town committee to demand that Hutchinson appoint special judges immediately. At court, Adams made a "very *pathetic* Speech" in which he used such strong language that the Tories perceived that "the plain design of this Speech was, that gentlemen, you must comply with our demand." [23]   The spectacle of Massachusetts royal judges "overawed and insulted" by such a raw plebeian as Sam Adams spurred Hutchinson to action.   The governor knew that by opposing Adams he was risking another explosion in Boston: popular hostility toward the troops still blazed so fiercely that the patriot leaders themselves had difficulty in preventing another mob attack upon the soldiers before their final removal to Castle William, and there was constant danger that Preston would be dragged from prison for a lynching party at Liberty Tree.[24]   Nevertheless, Hutchinson encouraged the judges to resist the patriots and, as a consequence, the trials were delayed until October 1770, over six months after the Massacre. Yet, even with this respite, it seemed unlikely that anything short of a royal pardon would save Preston and his men from a gibbet on the Boston Common.[25]

Despite Adams's eagerness to see the soldiers declared guilty, he urged John Adams and Josiah Quincy, two of the best

[23] *Chalmers Papers*, III, Narrative of Events in Boston.   Peter Oliver, 123. *Boston Gazette*, March 19, 1770.

[24] *The Works of John Adams*, X, 252, 253.   Mass. Archives, 26, *Hutchinson Corr.*, II, 497, 525.

[25] Thomas Gage to Thomas Hutchinson, April 30, 1770, MS. Mass. Hist. Soc.

lawyers in the patriot party, to undertake their defense. Preston's friends advised him to "stick at no reasonable fee" to secure the services of lawyers friendly to the Whig leaders, but it was Sam Adams's persuasion and John Adams's high sense of duty rather than the prospect of a fat fee that brought Josiah Quincy and John Adams to Preston's aid. Since 1768, when John Adams had yielded to Sam's importunities and entered Boston politics, he had risen high in the patriot party. His law partner, Josiah Quincy, was a promising young patriot who many Whigs believed would eventually step into James Otis's place at the head of the Massachusetts Country Party. It is singular that Sam Adams, who was never known to give his enemies an advantage, should have bestowed this array of legal talent upon men he hoped to convict of murder. Certainly, Adams had lost none of his rancor toward the "bloody-backed rascals" who had shed patriot blood in King's Street, nor had he failed to perceive that an acquittal would be a disastrous blow to the Boston Whigs. Adams's action sprang from his conviction that if patriot lawyers defended Preston and his men, the town's witnesses would not be cross-examined so closely as to bring to light evidence which proved Bostonians responsible for the Massacre. In John Adams, Sam did not mistake his man.

The younger Adams saw as clearly as did his cousin that Boston's reputation was at stake and that the town's witnesses should not be pressed too warmly: when Josiah Quincy's ardor for his clients caused him to interrogate sharply the prosecution's witnesses, John Adams quickly stopped him by declaring that unless Quincy ceased he would resign as counsel. Although John Adams encountered a "torrent of unpopularity" from the rank and file of the patriot party for defending the soldiers, it is significant that Sam Adams, far from bearing him resentment, praised him in the Boston newspapers for his conduct during the trial.[26]

Undoubtedly Sam Adams had much to conceal. The Tories' suspicions were early aroused by the readiness of the country towns about Boston to march to the aid of the metropolis im-

[26] Gordon, I, 291. *Boston Gazette*, Jan. 7, 1771, Harbottle Dorr Files, Mass. Hist. Soc.

mediately after the Massacre. It was observed that the bells
had been set ringing simultaneously at Boston, Charlestown, and
Roxbury to call out the patriots the night of the Massacre, and
that the next day expresses were sent to Boston from Marblehead, Dedham, Milton, and other near-by towns promising
armed assistance at a moment's warning. This preparedness
seemed to point to a well-laid scheme to rouse the country when
the Boston Sons of Liberty struck at the British troops. Andrew
Oliver, later lieutenant governor of Massachusetts Bay, said
that one of the Massachusetts councilors had declared in Council
that a plot had been made by "men of estates, and men of religion" to drive the British out of Boston; and Hutchinson
wrote that "you cannot find one Man in fifty who makes any
doubt of ye determined design to remove the Troops." John
Adams was convinced that the Massacre was an "explosion
which had been intentionally wrought up by designing men,
who knew what they were aiming at better than the instruments
employed." [27] Of these "designing men," Sam Adams was
probably the chief and the instruments he used to bring about
the Massacre were his "Mohawks" from North Boston. Lord
North made no mistake when he dubbed the regiments forced
out of Boston by the patriots "Sam Adams' Regiments."

The six months' delay in bringing Preston and his men to
trial worked greatly to the disadvantage of the Boston patriots,
who had counted upon a jury passionately determined to take
revenge upon the murderers of their countrymen. When the
trials finally took place, the people were dispirited and fearful
they had already gone too far, and Boston Harbor was filled
with royal ships and troops to remind them that the "long arm"
of the mother country still extended to New England. Sam
Adams complained that the long postponement made conviction
difficult because many of the town's key witnesses were no longer
within reach, but his anxiety was chiefly caused by the character

[27] *Chalmers Papers*, III, Narrative of Proceedings in Boston, 1770. Francis
Maseres, *A Fair Account of the Late Unhappy Disturbance at Boston* (London,
1770), Appendix, 26, Deposition of Andrew Oliver. Mass. Archives, 25,
Thomas Hutchinson to Francis Bernard, March 12, 1770. *The Works of
John Adams*, II, 230.

of the jury that had been chosen to decide the soldiers' fate.
The prosecution was lukewarm — the Crown officers in Boston
had no wish to convict Preston and thereby throw him to the
mercy of the Boston Liberty Boys — and the defense was quick
to seize every straw that promised an acquittal.   As a result,
John Adams and Josiah Quincy were permitted to pick a jury
which consisted entirely of countrymen — every Bostonian was
carefully weeded out by challenge.   Sam Adams's dismay was
great when he found that not a single town Son of Liberty was
to try Preston and his men.   He had hoped for a jury of townsmen who knew at first hand the evils of military despotism,
yet he now found himself forced to cope with rustics who had
not yet learned to hate the sight of a British uniform.   With
good reason, Adams believed that the outcome of the trials was
decided when the defense was allowed to load the jury with
countrymen.

In spite of John Adams's care not to probe too deeply into
Whig activities, evidence was brought out at the trial which
raised serious doubt in New England whether the Boston
Massacre had not been precipitated by Sam Adams and the
Sons of Liberty in a desperate effort to turn the troops out of
the metropolis.   Thirty-eight witnesses testified that there
had been a civilian plot to attack the soldiers, and the defense
put forward evidence proving the townspeople were the aggressors.   From the beginning, the case began to turn against
the patriots and, with a jury so little to Sam Adams's taste, the
result was not long in doubt.   The proceedings proved so painful to the patriot leaders that few of them attended the trials
and the people behaved "remarkably decent" for Bostonians.
Judge Lynde's speech to the jury clinched the case for the
defense: "I feel myself deeply affected," said the judge, "that
this affair turns out so much to the disgrace of every person concerned against him [Preston], and so much to the shame of the
town in general." [28]   Preston was promptly acquitted on the
ground that there was not sufficient evidence that he had given
orders to fire.   Of the soldiers who had fired upon the mob,
only two were found guilty of manslaughter, and their punish-

[28] Mass. Archives, 27, *Hutchinson Corr.*, III, 47.   Gordon, I, 291.

ment was mitigated to burning on the hand when they pleaded
with their clergy.   The trial of Mainwaring, the customhouse
officer who was accused of firing upon the people from the windows of the customhouse the night of the Massacre, blew up
when the jury acquitted him without leaving the courtroom.
All the Commissioners of the Customs were proved to have been
miles away from King's Street on the evening of March 5, and
the "little French boy" — the patriots' star witness in proving
the Commissioners and soldiers had hatched a plot to murder
civilians — was shown to be a perjurer whose falsehood had been
encouraged by divers high Whigs, William Molineux among
them.

Adams and his followers felt themselves cheated by the
court: was this, they exclaimed, to be the only punishment for
men who had butchered Whigs until the very dogs were seen
"greedily licking human Blood in King-Street"?   The townspeople grumbled that no one had been condemned to death and
it was common to hear lamentations that a slight burning on
the hand was "ye only satisfaction the Public has got for the
Murder of 5 Men." [29]   Judges and jury were exceedingly unpopular in Boston, where the people spoke of the judges with
"atrocious impudence" and where even the pulpits "rung their
Peals of Malice against the Courts of Justice."   The patriot
leaders had difficulty in keeping their resentful followers within
bounds: one of Sam Adams's admirers posted a notice on the
door of the House of Representatives urging the people to
assassinate the judges who had betrayed them.   This rousing
bit of sedition was not carried out because the people as a whole
were thoroughly weary of bloodshed.   No explosion followed
the soldiers' acquittal and Hutchinson observed with satisfaction that the Whig leaders were rapidly falling out of public
favor. [30]

Sam Adams attempted to save Boston's reputation by trying the soldiers over again in the *Gazette* under the signature
"Vindex."   He set out to convince New Englanders that, re-

---

[29] *Boston Gazette,* Nov. 26, 1770; Dec. 10 and 17, 1770.
[30] *Boston Evening Post,* May 11, 1772.   Peter Oliver, 129, 130.   Mass.
Archives, 27, *Hutchinson Corr.,* III, 73.

gardless of the jury's verdict, the soldiers were murderers of innocent Whigs.   It did not trouble Adams that he was forced to sidestep all the evidence that had been brought forward at the trial and rely entirely upon the testimony gathered by himself and the Boston selectmen.   Between the two sets of evidence there was enough discrepancy to convict or acquit the soldiers, for even the testimony of the same witnesses differed materially when they were examined *ex parte* by Adams and the selectmen and when they were cross-examined in the witness box by John Adams or Josiah Quincy.   Adams explained the soldiers' acquittal not by the evidence brought forward in the trial, but by the shortcomings of the jury.   A jury of countrymen, he said, was unable to judge the credibility of witnesses who were almost all townsmen; had a jury of Boston mechanics been impaneled, he did not doubt the citizens would have gotten satisfaction.   To open New Englanders' eyes to the miscarriage of justice that had taken place in Boston, Adams conjured up all the horrors of the Massacre: redcoats firing wantonly into a throng of peaceably disposed Whigs; the dogs lapping the patriot blood in King's Street; and the soldier Kilroi brutally attacking the ropewalker Gray, who, by Adams's account, stood with his arms "folded in his bosom," although the evidence produced at the trial showed that Gray was wielding his cudgel with great effect until he was stopped short by a bullet.   British atrocities alone, however, were not sufficient to convince the people that murder had been done on the night of March 5: there was the deathbed confession of Patrick Carr, that the townspeople had been the aggressors and that the soldiers had fired in self-defense.   This unlooked-for recantation from one of the martyrs who was dying in the odor of sanctity with which Sam Adams had invested them sent a wave of alarm through the patriot ranks.   But Adams blasted Carr's testimony in the eyes of all pious New Englanders by pointing out that he was an Irish "papist" who had probably died in the confession of the Roman Catholic Church.   After Sam Adams had finished with Patrick Carr even Tories did not dare to quote him to prove Bostonians were responsible for the Massacre.

Sam Adams's "Vindex" articles contributed to stamp the

fray of March 5, 1770, as the "horred Massacre" in the minds
of nearly all New Englanders in spite of the jury's verdict and
the weight of evidence.   Better to remind the people of British
atrocities, a Boston town committee of which Adams was a
member proposed that an annual oration and celebration be held
every year on March 5 to commemorate the Massacre.   This
annual observance gave Whig orators an opportunity to vent
their wrath against the mother country and keep the memory
fresh of the "bloody work in King Street"; "The wan tenants
of the grave," shrilled one patriot, "still shriek for vengeance
on their remorseless butchers." [31]   On Massacre days, bells
tolled mournfully in Boston until far into the night; lighted
pictures of dead and dying patriots were exhibited from a window in the North End of town; and portraits of Hutchinson
and Oliver were shown in the select company of Empson and
Dudley.   Neither of the Adamses ever gave a Massacre oration: John Adams because he believed that by defending the
soldiers he had made it impossible for him to denounce the
"bloody-backed rascals" in the true Whig style; Sam Adams
because he distrusted his oratorical powers.   Still, Sam Adams
undoubtedly wrote a large part of the oration John Hancock
delivered on March 5, 1774, to a "crowded audience of Narragansett Indians" fresh from the second Boston Tea Party.
Hancock was quite incapable of writing that "hash of abusive,
treasonable stuff" which so delighted the redskins who swarmed
into Faneuil Hall on that occasion; it was really Adams speaking when Hancock called upon every father in New England to
gather his children about his knees and tell them the story of the
Massacre "till tears of pity glisten in their eyes, and boiling
passion shakes their tender frames." [32]

Sam Adams used the Boston Massacre not only to embitter
Americans toward Great Britain but to prove the necessity of
fighting British troops before they had opportunity to gain a

---

[31] *Orations, delivered at the Request of the Inhabitants of the town of
Boston* (Boston, 1807), 37.   *Boston Town Records*, 18th Report (1887),
47, 48.
    [32] *Orations, etc.*, 43.   Gordon, I, 300.   Lorenzo Sears, *John Hancock,
the Picturesque Patriot*, 143.

foothold in the country. The Massacre seemed to bear out Adams's contention that the King's soldiers should have been resisted when they reached Boston. It was futile, he preached in 1770, to look to the courts for redress; the militia, not judges and juries, must save New Englanders from military despotism. After the Massacre, Adams was joined by a host of amateur generals who proposed to save New England by bringing the militia to full fighting strength and replacing the "ancient methods of bushing fighting" with modern strategy and formations. The seat of danger was no longer the frontier and redskins but the seaboard and redcoats; military tactics which were effective against Indians would be useless against British regulars — therefore, New Englanders must henceforth practise manœuvres in open fields and train themselves to meet large bodies of troops fighting in European fashion. The fiction of an impending French war that had proved so useful during the Massachusetts Convention was again employed to screen these preparations to wage war against British troops; and Sam Adams and his followers still talked of grappling with France while they prepared to fight England.[33]

Like other Whig leaders after the Boston Massacre, Sam Adams painted war as glorious and fostered those "generous and manly Sentiments, which usually attend a true Military Spirit." He was overjoyed to see how eagerly New Englanders cleaned their muskets and drilled in militia companies to prepare for the day when they should be compelled to fight for their liberties. Boston led the movement to build up a militia capable of holding its own against British regulars, and plans were laid to give the next army of British "invaders" a warm reception. When it was rumored that troops would be sent from England to punish Boston for attacking British soldiers on the night of the Massacre, the Sons of Liberty held a meeting in William Molineux's house to decide whether to oppose their landing; and Hutchinson did not doubt that if the force sent out from England were small, the patriots would fight. To set an example for New Englanders, Bostonians went through their

[33] *Boston Evening Post*, April 30, 1770; June 11, 1770. *Boston Gazette*, Jan. 27, 1771; Feb. 24, 1772. *The Writings of Samuel Adams*, II, 68, 69.

military exercises every evening on the Common and declared openly that no royal troops would ever again land in the metropolis. "Innocence is no longer safe," exclaimed Adams and his followers, "we are now obliged to appeal to GOD and to our ARMS for defense." [34]

[34] *Boston Gazette,* April 12, 1770.

VIII

THE NONIMPORTATION AGREEMENT

THE Townshend duties brought about the riots in Boston which compelled the British government to send troops to preserve order in the metropolis; and the presence of royal soldiers, in turn, led to the Boston Massacre. It is now necessary to turn to other consequences of the Townshend duties: the colonial nonimportation agreement and the growth of American unity.

Almost a decade before Americans began to think of political separation from the mother country, the idea of economic independence had become widespread in the colonies. While the colonists still remained subjects of the mother country they began to cut the economic ties that bound them to the Old World. Stimulated by Charles Townshend's scheme of taxation, the colonists were seized with a fervor for economic self-sufficiency that matches present-day nationalistic aspirations. This spirit manifested itself in an intercolonial boycott of British manufactures and the establishment of home industries designed to free America of dependence upon Great Britain. Although the immediate origin of the nonimportation agreement of 1768 was Parliament's attempt to tax the colonies, in a deeper sense it was the first concerted attempt made by the colonists to escape from the swaddling clothes which British colonial policy had fastened upon them. It was a step toward the fulfillment of America's "manifest destiny" as a "Great Empire" politically and economically independent of Great Britain.

Although it has been supposed that Sam Adams originated the idea of coercing Great Britain by boycotting her manufactures, he actually played small part in its early develop-

ment.[1]   During the height of the Stamp Act excitement, while
the Sons of Liberty were tightening their military alliances and
cleaning their muskets for use against the King's troops, New
York merchants were taking surer means of procuring the repeal
of the Stamp Act.   One of Great Britain's most profitable
branches of trade was with the American colonies, and British
merchants had extended them credit to the tune of four million
pounds.   Provincial patriots regarded this bumping commerce
and immense debt as levers with which to pry concessions from
the mother country, but the New York merchants were the first
to demonstrate their true value in a controversy with Great
Britain.   By canceling orders for goods and refusing to make
further purchases until the Stamp Act was repealed, the New
Yorkers began in October 1765 the first of three colonial boycotts of the mother country's manufactures designed to redress
American grievances.   Early in November, Philadelphia followed New York's example, but it was not until December 9,
1765, that Boston belatedly joined the movement.[2]   The result
was a complete victory for the American merchants.   British
traders were panic-stricken at the prospect of seeing colonial
trade and debts slip through their fingers and they lobbied so
vigorously in Parliament that the Stamp Act was repealed in
1766, largely through their efforts.

   This easy success set the fashion for every subsequent attempt
by the colonies to force the mother country to grant their demands.   Having found the Englishmen's weakness, American
patriots hammered it until the outbreak of the Revolutionary
War, confidently expecting to see the mother country give way as
it had done in 1766.   Sam Adams, in particular, became convinced that the only way to reason with Englishmen was to
pinch them in their pocketbooks, and he believed that American
boycotts would so terrify Great Britain that everything the colonies asked would be given them.   When the Townshend duties

[1] Wells, I, 82, 149.
[2] *Publications Col. Soc. of Mass.*, Transactions 1919, 159–179. *Lamb
Papers*, MSS. N. Y. Hist. Soc., New York Sons of Liberty to the Providence
Sons of Liberty, April 2, 1766. *Boston Gazette*, Dec. 6, 1765; May 5, 1766
(Supplement). *Bernard Papers*, VI, Bernard to Lord Shelburne, Aug. 31,
1767. Gordon, I, 194.

were imposed upon America, Adams remembered how the excited merchants had stormed Parliament during the Stamp Act and he began to urge that pressure again be brought against the mother country.   It is as the instigator of the second colonial boycott rather than as the originator of the scheme that Sam Adams should be remembered.

Adams particularly relished a boycott of British manufactures because he regarded it as a step towards Puritanism.   He believed the nonimportation agreement was a double-barreled gun which would mow down luxury and high living in New England at the same time that it made Great Britain smart for its "tyranny" over the colonies.   The first move, in Adams's opinion, to clear the ground for Puritanism was to stop the importation of British "Baubles" which he believed Cotton and Winthrop would have cast out as snares of Satan.   Adams looked sourly upon the homes of rich Boston merchants with their expensive "Decorations of the Parlor, the shining Side Boards of Plate, the costly Piles of China," and compared their ostentation with the simple frugality of the founders.[3]   He saw a grain of good even in British oppression because he expected it to hasten the return of puritanic simplicity in New England; after the Sugar Act had pricked the bubble of war prosperity, Adams and his friends declared that "Nothing but FRUGALITY can now save the distress'd northern colonies from impending ruin."[4]   The heavier the taxes with which the British government loaded New Englanders, the more like Puritans the people were forced to become in order to survive.   Probably George Grenville and Charles Townshend would have been the last to suspect that they were making the rowdy New England Saints "old Puritans" once more.   Nevertheless, Sam Adams hoped to use the colonial revenue acts to put the people on the highroad to Puritanism.

In characteristic fashion, Sam Adams set the nonimportation agreement in motion.   After the passage of the Townshend duties, the Boston town meeting was called and the citizens were persuaded to forgo an elaborate list of British imports

[3] *Boston Gazette*, Oct. 1, 1764.
[4] *Ibid.*, Oct. 8, 1764.   *Massachusetts Gazette*, Oct. 29, 1767.

which Sam Adams had decided were unfit for Whigs and "Old
Puritans." To secure signatures to this pledge, a subscription
paper was carried from house to house in Boston. At first,
signing was entirely voluntary, but the names came in so slowly
and the scheme was so firmly "rejected & discountenanced by
the Principal Gentlemen of the Town," that Tories began to
believe Adams had overshot the mark. Governor Bernard suspected that the agreement was another piece of patriot bluff;
and conservatives ridiculed the Whigs, who in their eagerness to
add names to the subscription paper induced "Porters & Washing
Women" to sign a promise not to buy silks, velvets, coaches,
and chariots. In spite of this unpromising beginning, the proceedings of the Boston town meeting were sent to every important town on the continent and Adams began to demand that
the Boston merchants set the colonies an example of a boycott
against British goods to repeal the Townshend Act.[5]

As has been seen, opposition to the Townshend duties was
primarily political; in contrast to the Sugar and Stamp Acts,
they did not immediately menace the well-being of colonial
merchants. When Sam Adams began to agitate a boycott of
British imports among Boston merchants he found them deeply
alarmed by the political consequences of the Townshend duties
but little concerned with economic grievances against the mother
country: money and credit were abundant in the metropolis
and there had never been "a more apparent Ballance of Trade"
in favor of Massachusetts Bay.[6] Rather than permit the merchants to enjoy this prosperity, Adams proposed to throw them
into the thick of the political struggle that was raging around
the Townshend duties. If they proved unwilling allies, Adams
had a whip to crack about their ears. After patriot spell-
binders and newspapers had aroused the common people's enthusiasm for a boycott, the merchants were told that if they
wished to remain in the citizens' good graces they must cease
to import; and those who displayed obstinacy were reminded

[5] Peter Oliver, 84. *Mass. Hist. Soc. Proceedings* (1923), LV, 266.
[6] *Bernard Papers*, VI, Bernard to Lord Shelburne, Oct. 8, 1767; March 21,
1768. *Boston Evening Post*, Nov. 9, 1767. *Letters to the Ministry* (1768),
16.

of the unpleasant consequences of attempting to oppose "the Stream of the People." With the threat of Adams's "Mohawks" hanging above their heads, Whig principles rose remarkably in the favor of "gentlemen in trade" and converts to nonimportation began to appear on every side.[7]

But even without the aid of such forceful persuasion, Adams had many friends among the smaller merchants who were ready to carry out his plans. Those who were considered merchants in pre-revolutionary Boston were not usually wealthy aristocrats who looked down upon Sam Adams with the patrician disdain of Thomas Hutchinson; on the contrary, it was said that seven eighths of the Boston merchants were "more properly forestallers, retailers, pedlars, milliners, hawkers, squeezers, and grinders." Every shopkeeper in Boston was regarded as a merchant because the London traders dealt directly with them rather than through a middleman. As a result, whenever the merchants held their meetings in Faneuil Hall, it was difficult to distinguish them from the attendants of the Boston town meetings because "every master of a Sloop & broken Shopkeeper or Huckster" was admitted as freely as were the rich merchants and had an equal voice "in ordering the Property of the first Trader in the Province." [8] Hancock carried in his train many small traders who, when joined with Adams's supporters, could easily outvote the "mercantile overlords" who opposed the patriots' schemes. Thus, when the Boston merchants finally adopted a nonimportation agreement in March 1768, Thomas Hutchinson remarked that two thirds of those who voted in favor of the boycott were small shopkeepers who imported little or nothing from Great Britain.[9]

It was a more difficult matter to induce other colonies to erect a barrier against British commodities. Philadelphia refused to join Boston in April 1768 and for several months Adams's scheme seemed stillborn. But in August 1768, the New York

[7] *Letters to the Ministry* (1768), 16. *Bernard Papers*, VI, Bernard to Lord Shelburne, March 21, 1768.

[8] *Boston Evening Post*, Dec. 14, 1767. Peter Oliver, 101. Mass. Archives, 26, *Hutchinson Corr.*, II, 361.

[9] Mass. Archives, 26, *Hutchinson Corr.*, II, 322, 514.

merchants, hotly pressed by the Sons of Liberty, united with
Boston in prohibiting the importation of British and European
goods, with the exception of certain "enumerated" articles, to
force the repeal of the Townshend duties.   Committees of inspection were appointed by the merchants to oversee all imports; refractory merchants were threatened with the loss of
customers and credit; and the colonists consoled themselves for
the loss of British manufactures with the hope that this "bloodless" war with the mother country would quickly redress all
American grievances.

At the outset of the nonimportation agreement, Sam Adams
saw that the colonies could not go on indefinitely without British
and European commodities unless home industries were established.   Therefore Adams became one of the most enthusiastic promoters of colonial manufacturing in America.
He believed that nothing would be more alarming to the British
merchants than the sight of colonists trooping to factories and
producing all their necessities — Adams never envisaged them
turning their hands to luxuries — by their own efforts.   He
dreamed of America as a "Great Empire" permanently freed
of dependence upon Great Britain for both political and economic
guidance.   He set the clergy to work "to preach up Manufactures instead of Gospel"; and under his inspiration Boston
Whigs nursed tea leaves and mulberry trees in their gardens
and hopefully looked forward to the day when the course of
trade would be reversed and Massachusetts Bay would export tea, silk, linen, and iron to Great Britain.   Thomas Young,
that redoubtable freethinker and right-hand man of Sam Adams,
exhorted New England farmers to turn their oak plains into
sheep pastures and produce enough wool to clothe every American colonist.   To be clad in homespun became the mark of an
American patriot; and Harvard and Princeton seniors delighted the Sons of Liberty by taking their degrees at commencement in clothing manufactured in the colonies.   "Female
Patriots" spun and drank home-grown "Labradore" tea instead of wasting their time in "idle conversation" over cups
of British bohea.   Public-spirited Whigs attempted to establish factories to supply colonial needs, particularly in com-

modities taxed by the British government; and optimistic patriots believed that America would soon be able to manufacture all its necessities while "superfluities will be wholly given up."[10]

Few Crown officers were frightened by Adams's efforts to create colonial manufacturing. "For New England to threaten the Mother Country with Manufactures," said Governor Bernard, "is the Idlest Bully that ever was attempted to be imposed upon sensible People."[11] Tories who attempted to run down the stories in patriot newspapers of the rapid strides being made toward economic self-sufficiency remarked that the Whigs had given their imaginations free rein. Even James Otis ridiculed Adams's plan: "I can never hear American manufactures seriously talked of," he remarked, "without being dispos'd to a violent fit of laughter." Otis pointed out that the high price of labor and scarcity of raw materials in America were insuperable obstacles. Although Massachusetts had more sheep than any other colony, Otis showed that it could not produce enough wool to keep New Englanders even in stockings, much less supply all British America with woolen clothing; and he damped his followers' enthusiasm for economic independence by demonstrating that unless New Englanders bought British or European hose they would be compelled to go barefoot.[12] In fact, colonial manufactures were to play little part in bringing about the repeal of the Townshend duties and Adams did not live to see America reach the goal of economic freedom of Europe. It was not until after the War of 1812 that New England began to take its place in the industrial world and shut out those "British Baubles" which Adams exclaimed against in 1768. But Adams did not foresee that Americans would promptly begin to manufacture the same "Baubles" for themselves.

Nevertheless, the attempt to foster American manufactures

[10] *Chalmers Papers*, III, Information of Richard Silvester. Peter Oliver, 87. *Boston Gazette*, April 3, 10, 23, 1770; June 27, 1768; Jan. 4, 1768. *Boston Evening Post*, Nov. 16 and 23, 1767.

[11] *Bernard Papers*, VI, Bernard to Lord Shelburne, March 21, 1768.

[12] *Boston Evening Post*, Nov. 23, 1767. *Boston Gazette*, Aug. 12, 1765. Otis, *Brief Remarks on the Defence of the Halifax Libel, etc.*, II, 170, 171.

behind the protection of a boycott brought to light significant differences between Sam Adams and other leading colonial Whigs. John Dickinson, the foremost patriot of the Southern colonies, looked upon the nonimportation agreement as a mixed blessing because he feared that it might succeed in producing such a powerful "spirit of manufactory & Oeconomy" in America that the mother country would be seriously injured. "My Heart bleeds at the Prospect of our Success," Dickinson wrote; "How mournful a Reflection is it, that a just Regard for ourselves, must wound Great Britain, the Mother of brave, generous, humane Spirits, the chief Bulwark of Liberty on this Globe, and the blessed Seat of unspotted Religion." [13] Sam Adams, on the other hand, never showed concern for the suffering he might be bringing upon England — his attitude was that the mother country richly deserved to be punished for attempting to enslave the colonies. Unlike James Otis and John Dickinson, Adams felt little loyalty toward the mother country; in his eyes, America must become a "Great Empire" regardless of the well-being of Great Britain.

At the outset, Sam Adams added an ominous note to the nonimportation agreement which might well have disturbed English Whigs who believed that Americans would not go beyond constitutional opposition to the mother country. The Boston Sons of Liberty declared the boycott was "the only *pacifick* method of recovering our lost Liberties" — if defeated in their economic war with the mother country, Americans must fight in earnest for their liberties. Sam Adams said the nonimportation agreement was the only means outside of a "deluge of blood" by which the colonists could gain redress of grievances; and declared that the fate of *"Unborn Millions"* hung in the balance between peace and war.[14] Had Englishmen taken the Boston Liberty Boys' threats seriously in 1768 they would have seen they must do one of two things: either concede the colonists'

[13] *Arthur Lee Papers*, Sparks MSS., Harvard College Library, I, John Dickinson to Arthur Lee, June 26, 1769. *Chalmers Papers*, III, Information of Richard Silvester.
[14] *Lamb Papers*, New York Sons of Liberty to the Philadelphia Sons of Liberty, May 11, 1770. *Boston Gazette*, Oct. 9, 1769; Feb. 5, 1770. *The Writings of Samuel Adams*, II, 7.

demands or prepare for war. Unfortunately for the British Empire, they chose to do neither.

Even without this menacing chorus from Sam Adams and the Boston Whigs, the nonimportation agreement was a manifestation of colonial unrest which augured ill for the peace of the empire. By 1769, almost all the colonies had joined the boycott and a wall had been raised from Massachusetts to Georgia against a large number of proscribed British manufactures. The movement toward colonial unity which had produced the Stamp Act Congress and the corresponding committees of the Sons of Liberty appeared to have culminated in the nonimportation agreement. "One spirit," Sam Adams exclaimed, "animates all America . . . to *quench* the spirit, all the colonies must be absolutely *destroyed*." [15]   By 1769, Adams believed the provinces had fully learned the importance of concerted action — an achievement he called "a pleasing *omen* in favor of the great American cause" and the most hopeful sign of eventual success against the mother country. Never before had American affairs appeared more rosy in his eyes. While Tories groaned that the "Dementation" that had first seized Massachusetts Bay had now spread to all the colonies, Adams exulted that "the *tighter* the cord of unconstitutional power is drawn round this bundle of arrows, the *firmer* it will be." [16]   The New York and Boston Sons of Liberty were in as close communication as during the Stamp Act period: when Nathaniel Rogers, a Boston importer, attempted to escape from the mob in Boston, the Sons of Liberty sent an express to their New York brethren to give him a warm reception if he came their way. When Rogers reached New York he was hunted down by the Liberty Boys and barely got out of town in time to escape a coat of tar and feathers. [17]

When the Boston Sons of Liberty found themselves sup-

[15] *Boston Evening Post*, April 10, 1769; April 25, 1769 (Supplement). *Boston Gazette*, Jan. 29, 1770.

[16] *Miscellaneous Papers*, MS. Mass. Hist. Soc., Letter from —— to ——, Aug. 10, 1770, p. 76.

[17] *Boston Gazette*, May 21, 1770.   Mass. Archives, 26, *Hutchinson Corr.*, II, 488, 491.   *Lamb Papers*, New York Sons of Liberty to Philadelphia Sons of Liberty, May 11, 1770.

ported by most of British America they became almost as warlike as in 1768 before British troops entered Boston.   Indeed,
they grew so bumptious that some Tories feared they were
"ripe for Rebellion" in 1769 and ready to fight Great Britain
single-handed.[18]   If the patriots were to be taken at their word
there was good reason for apprehension.   Whig newspapers
stiffened the patriots' courage by declaring that as long as the
colonies remained united "it is not in the power of all the world
to enslave us."   At the Boston town meeting, William Molineux
assured the citizens that the entire British army and navy could
not compel them "to act against their Wills"; and it became a
common saying in the metropolis that "no Act of Parl[iament]
against the mind of the people shall ever be executed here." [19]
Just as in 1768, when Sam Adams attempted to stir up resistance
to the British troops, the degeneracy, debt, riots, and political
disorders of the mother country were contrasted with the vigor,
purity, and courage of the colonies.   It was said that Great
Britain was so corrupt that the moment "their high mightinesses
the manufacturers" saw their precious pounds and shillings
jeopardized by the nonimportation agreement they would storm
Parliament and buy back American business with offers of
political freedom.   Those who feared punishment from Great
Britain were told they were out of the reach of Parliament.[20]
Undoubtedly, the success of the nonimportation agreement
was heady wine to many patriots who, like Sam Adams, took
such deep draughts that they began to think America invincible.

The Whigs' high spirits were dashed, however, by the opposition to the boycott which started to spring up in the colonies.
The success of the nonimportation agreement required support
from all importers of British goods, yet there was in every seaport a clique of Tory merchants who continued to trade with

[18] *Chalmers Papers*, III, George Mason to Joseph Harrison, Oct. 20, 1769.
[19] *Boston Gazette*, March 27, 1769; July 19, 1770.   Mass. Archives, 26,
Hutchinson Corr., II, 389, 465, 492.   *Bernard Papers*, VI, Bernard to Lord
Shelburne, March 21, 1768.   *Grenville Papers* (edited by W. J. Smith, 1853),
IV, 439.
[20] *Chalmers Papers*, III, Narrative of the Events in Boston, 1770.   Mass.
Archives, 25, Thomas Hutchinson to Francis Bernard, May 3, 1770.

the mother country.   Much to the patriots' consternation, these British manufactures found a ready market in the colonies. It was clear that if the boycott was observed only by Whig merchants, the Tories would gobble up fat profits and put their self-sacrificing competitors out of business.   This circumstance alone was sufficient to arouse the Whigs against violators of the boycott: but in Boston hatred of importers was particularly strong because most of them were relatives or close friends of Thomas Hutchinson.   The lieutenant governor and his sons were themselves prominent merchants, and their refusal to sign the nonimportation agreement encouraged others to resist the Whigs.   It was widely believed that Hutchinson was the backbone of Tory opposition to the nonimportation agreement; and certainly, at every turn, the patriots found themselves face to face with the lieutenant governor, who, instead of yielding to mobs and threats, rallied his followers and undermined the boycott with imported British merchandise.   As long as Hutchinson encouraged the Tories, the nonimportation agreement was in danger of collapse.   It is no wonder, therefore, that Sam Adams railed at Hutchinson in the Boston town meeting with "peculiar pleasure" and became one of the most relentless hounders of importers in the colonies.[21]   At the town meeting held in Faneuil Hall in October 1769, Adams produced a list of violators of the nonimportation agreement who, he said, should be "Stigmatiz'd & declar'd Enemys of the Country, and to be recorded in the Town Books as such to the latest posterity." When it was learned that several importers were ready to sign the agreement, Adams refused to allow any last-minute recantations: it was too late, he declared, for them to make peace because by resisting the people they had committed an unpardonable sin — "no atonement could be made on this Side the Grave; God perhaps might possibly forgive them, but He and the rest of the People never could."   This intractable policy endeared Adams to the common people of Boston, who enthusiastically resolved in the town meeting to denounce the

[21] Mass. Archives, 26, *Hutchinson Corr.*, II, 384, 528.   *Chalmers Papers*, III, Journal of Transactions at Boston; Proceedings of the Town Meeting, Oct. 4, 1769.   *The Writings of Samuel Adams*, I, 395.

Tory merchants as "obstinate and inveterate Enemies to their Country" who had severed themselves from the commonwealth and the protection of its laws. Every importer, declared the citizens, was to be regarded as a public enemy to whom the people were forbidden to show any "Act and Office of common Civility . . . *for ever* hereafter" on pain of similar ostracism.[22] The offending merchants, it was clear, were now fair game for the mob.

With the exception of Thomas Hutchinson, no Massachusetts Tory was more feared by the Whigs than was John Mein, printer of the *Boston Chronicle*. Unlike most New England conservatives, Mein was not afraid to beard Sam Adams in his own den. He deliberately set out to wreck the nonimportation agreement by spreading suspicion throughout the colonies of Boston's good faith in enforcing the boycott. Mein secured copies of the manifests of all vessels that had entered Boston since the beginning of the agreement and discovered that a number of Boston merchants, John Hancock among them, were secretly importing British commodities which were retailed to the people at a large profit. These manifests were printed in the *Boston Chronicle* and in a pamphlet entitled, *Account of the late Importations &c in the port of Boston*. Mein scattered hundreds of copies over the colonies with the result that an uproar was produced not only "in the very heart of the Boston Faction, but between that Faction and the other combining colonies." [23] Even while exposing the "trickery" of the New England "Saints," Mein continued to remain in Boston openly defying Sam Adams and the "Mohawks," although he was given ample warning of what was in store if he persisted in his efforts to break up the boycott. Sam Adams said that Mein had "set himself in Opposition to an *awakened,* an *enlightened,* and a DETERMINED Continent," and so many threats were made by the Sons of Liberty that he was compelled to arm himself with

---

[22] Mass. Archives, 26, *Hutchinson Corr.*, II, 384. *Boston Gazette*, Jan. 29. 1770.
[23] *Chalmers Papers*, III, Extract of a Letter from Mr. Fleeming, Printer at Boston, to his Partner, Mr. John Mein, now in London, July 1, 1770. *Publications Col. Soc. of Mass.*, Transactions 1916–17, XIX, 229.

pistols when he walked the streets of Boston. It was evident
that Mein had sunk his shafts into too many prominent Boston
patriots to remain long unmolested. As the "common enemy
of America," he was in daily danger from the mob; and one day
he was attacked on the Boston Exchange by twenty Liberty
Boys "armed with Spades, Canes & Clubs." Through rare
luck, Mein escaped into the near-by guardhouse where the
soldiers kept the mob at bay. The magistrates immediately
swore out warrants for Mein's arrest; and Adams and Molineux
personally assisted the peace officer in searching for him. But
even Adams and Molineux, expert as they were in ferreting
out Tories, could not find Mein. The disgruntled patriots were
compelled to admit that "the Bird was flown" to England.[24]
Thus, with the aid of the mob, Sam Adams removed a serious
menace to the success of the nonimportation agreement, but, as
he was soon to learn, it was far easier to hustle Mein out of
Boston than to heal the wounds his sharp pen had inflicted upon
the reputation of the Puritan metropolis.

Even more destructive than John Mein's pamphleteering was
the conciliatory policy adopted by the British government.
Thoroughly alarmed by the formidable league against British
manufactures created in the colonies by the Townshend duties,
the Ministry quickly took steps to redress American grievances.
In 1769, Lord Hillsborough announced in a circular letter to
the American colonies that, for "commercial reasons," the
Ministry proposed to repeal all the Townshend duties with
the exception of the tax on tea and to renounce all plans of drawing a large revenue from the colonies.

In Boston, the British government's tempting "Sugar Plum"
had disastrous effect upon the nonimportation agreement: the
Whig merchants became lukewarm; the committees of inspection stopped work; and even the Sons of Liberty began to grow
dispirited. It was now apparent that Adams must delve deep
into his bag of tricks if the boycott was to be saved and Hutchinson and the Tories crushed. Adams met this emergency by

[24] *Boston Gazette*, Aug. 28, 1769; Jan. 15, 1770. *John Hancock Papers*,
MSS. Mass. Hist. Soc., John Longman to John Mein. *Chalmers Papers*, III,
George Mason to Joseph Harrison, Oct. 20, 1769.

making sweeping changes in the nonimportation agreement.
Although from the beginning the guiding spirits of the boycott
were Boston politicians, it was nominally in the hands of the
merchants, who, by holding meetings separate from the people's
and enforcing the agreement by means of committees of inspection chosen from among themselves, made its success or
failure dependent upon their efforts.   By 1770, these "gentlemen in trade" had proved to Adams's satisfaction their unfitness
to play a leading part in the commercial war against Great
Britain.   They were slow to harass importers; they were jealous
of interference by the Sons of Liberty; and, after Lord Hillsborough's circular letter of 1769, many were eager to call a
truce in their quarrel with the mother country.   Moreover, they
were utterly unable to cope with Hutchinson and his friends.
Startling proof of the merchants' laxity came to light early in
1770, just before the Boston Massacre, when it was shown that
Hutchinson's sons had secretly removed and sold some of the
tea they had been compelled to store for safekeeping with the
committee of inspection.   There was no longer any doubt that
the Whig traders lacked the vigilance and zeal necessary for the
success of the nonimportation agreement.   New vigor was required, and Adams undertook to supply it by throwing out the
merchants and putting the politicians and common people in
direct command.

Immediately after the Hutchinsons' double-dealing had been
discovered, Boston was plastered with notices urging the merchants "and all others who are concerned in or *connected* with
trade" to meet in Faneuil Hall.   This meant that, for the first
time, the people as a whole were to control the nonimportation
agreement, because, as the patriots pointed out, Boston lived
by trade and every person in town could be regarded as *"connected* with trade." [25]   To make sure of a thumping majority
over those who favored halfway measures against the importers, Sam Adams and other patriot leaders went about Boston
"trotting from house to house, to engage the master workmen, to suffer their journeymen and apprentices to attend at
Faneuil Hall, and to make what they called a respectable ap-

[25] *Boston Gazette,* Jan. 22, 1770.

pearance." [26] The meetings were henceforth open to all citizens regardless of legal requirements for voting: when a motion was made to exclude unpropertied townspeople the speaker was shouted down with cries from the floor that "if they had no property they had Liberty, and their posterity might have property." [27] Such staunch democrats might be expected to show small mercy to importers and to disregard the interests of the wealthy merchants whose lukewarmness had brought the nonimportation agreement to the verge of ruin.

Adams had long been clamoring for "spirited" measures to enforce the boycott and, after the people had displaced the merchants, he lost no time in giving the Tories a taste of true Whig spirit. For several years, Tories had feared that Adams would use the mob to beat down opposition to the boycott: when the agreement was first proposed in Boston, Governor Bernard declared it could not be carried out without the aid of Sam Adams's "Mohawks." [28] In 1770, these apprehensions were fully realized. To prepare the citizens for violence, Adams raised the cry that Boston's inactivity was undermining its reputation as a patriot stronghold: "Our brethren in the other Governments Complain'd of our want of Spirit," he said, "that our measures were too lax & in short began to grow very jealous of us." New Englanders whose fame extended "not only throughout the Colonies but throughout the world" were in danger, the Boston Sons of Liberty warned, of making their names "for ever detested & abhorred." [29] There was no more certain way of arousing Bostonians than reproaching them as laggards in the struggle for liberty, and the mob soon gave Americans convincing proof that there was still life in the Puritan metropolis. Adams's "Mohawks" fell upon the Tory merchants with such good will that Boston soon became the most uncomfortable spot on the continent for violators of the nonimportation agreement. At night, their houses were surrounded by "the most diabolical crew that are upon the face of the earth," bawling

[26] *Boston Chronicle,* Feb. 5, 1770.

[27] Mass. Archives, 26, *Hutchinson Corr.,* II, 492.

[28] *Bernard Papers,* VI, Bernard to Lord Shelburne, March 21, 1768.

[29] *Massachusetts Papers,* MSS. Mass. Hist. Soc., Committee of Merchants to Dennys De Berdt, Jan. 30, 1770. *Boston Gazette,* Feb. 5, 1770.

threats and "calling out with a Loud Voice kill that dog . . .
he is a Governours man a Bastard of Liberty." [30]   The patriots
stationed small boys before the importers' shops to pelt the
owners and customers with filth.   McMasters, a prominent
Tory merchant, was carted out of town to a gallows, where he
was forced to swear never to return to Boston on pain of hanging; and the "lawless banditti" of the metropolis who acted
on Sam Adams's orders gained such strength that terror-
stricken Tories expected "to hear of Blood and Murder every
hour."   Many of Adams's enemies fled to Castle William for
refuge or slept with loaded pistols beside their pillows in anticipation of a visit from the "Mohawks."   Yet, in spite of the
Tories' groans that the patriots had begun a reign of terror,
Adams believed the Boston Sons of Liberty displayed great
restraint in their treatment of the importers.   "Good God!"
he exclaimed.   "How much longer is it expected that the
patience of this injured Country shall hold out!" [31]

Another of Sam Adams's "spirited" measures to terrorize the
importers was to marshal hundreds of Bostonians into ranks and
files and march at their head to the merchants' shops.   As soon
as the people had been called into the merchants' meeting, the
whole body, one thousand strong, — composed, Tories said,
"of the very refuse of the town," — marched out of the town
hall up King's Street to the importers' shops and demanded
that they deliver their goods into the hands of the committee of
inspection. [32]   But even the forbidding spectacle of a thousand
Sons of Liberty outside their doors and the threat of the
"ordeal" at Liberty Tree failed to shake the merchants as long
as they believed themselves supported by Hutchinson.   It was
clear that the lieutenant governor must first be terrified into
submission before his followers would give way to the Whigs.
But when Sam Adams and William Molineux proposed in the

[30] *Chalmers Papers*, III, Journal of Transactions at Boston; and Extract of
a Letter from Mr. Fleeming, Printer at Boston, to his Partner Mr. John Mein,
now in London, July 1, 1770.   Mass. Archives, 25, *Hutchinson Corr.*, I,
Robert Jamieson to Thomas Hutchinson, May 30, 1770.
[31] *The Writings of Samuel Adams*, I, 395.
[32] *Chalmers Papers*, III, Journal of Transactions at Boston.   *Boston Gazette*,
Jan. 22, 1770.

town meeting that the people be led to Hutchinson's house to demand that he order his sons to surrender their goods to the committee, they brought a hornets' nest about their ears. Josiah Quincy, Jr., the young Whig lawyer who was shortly to defend the soldiers in the Massacre trials, declared the procedure illegal and called upon James Otis to confirm his opinion. But poor "Muddlehead" Otis spoke so unintelligibly that no one could tell whether he opposed or favored Adams's plan.[33] Sam Adams, however, made very clear his belief that there was nothing illegal in the step; and he spoke so plausibly that he soon had the people clamoring to be led to the lieutenant governor's. Nevertheless, when Hancock, Otis, and William Phillips were nominated to serve on the committee that was to march at the people's head, they declined the honor. A wave of consternation passed over the patriot ranks. Adams and Molineux were dismayed to find themselves deserted by most of their friends. "It would be impossible, sir," wrote a Tory spectator, "to describe the looks of Mollineaux . . . he drew his hand across his Throat, and declar'd he was ready to Die that Minute, that for his part he scorn'd to have any thing more to do with them," and, jumping down from the platform, began to walk out of the hall. Dr. Thomas Young caught him before he had reached the door and begged him "for God's sake to stay" unless he wished to ruin the patriot party. After "much perswasion and a great deal of pulling," Molineux was brought back to his seat. Otis and Phillips then consented to join the committee and Otis was "Clapp'd by the People universally." [34]

With Otis once more among the radicals, the people streamed out of Faneuil Hall, formed their ranks in the market place, and marched two thousand strong to Hutchinson's house. But, to the patriots' chagrin, Hutchinson faced the crowd without wavering. He warned the people that they were acting illegally, that "Mr. Otis as a Lawyer knew it," and'that they must go back instantly to their homes. Hutchinson's firmness disconcerted Sam Adams and his followers, and when they

[33] *Chalmers Papers*, III, Journal of Transactions at Boston; A Key to a certain publication.

[34] *Ibid.*, III, George Mason to ——, Jan. 24, 1770.

returned to Faneuil Hall they were "considerably non plus'd." [35]
Yet in reality the lieutenant governor was on the point of surrender: he had made a brave show before the crowd, but he
was rapidly becoming convinced that he could no longer withstand Sam Adams and the "Faneuil Hall patriots." He had
failed to form any party capable of opposing the Whigs: in spite
of their eagerness to free themselves from mob rule, the Tories
were made helpless by fear "for their fine Houses." Conservatives thought only of getting out of the way of the patriot steam
roller. "Few among us," they lamented, "are hardy enough to
dare assert their just rights, but timidly submit and tacitly be-
wail their hard fate." [36] Instead of setting out to destroy the
Whig "courts of inquisition" they sought to keep in the good
graces of the Liberty Boys lest the mob be turned against them.
Hutchinson could do nothing to break up the meetings in
Faneuil Hall where the patriots made such deep inroads upon
royal authority that he feared the time would come when "every
town every Parish & every particular club will meet & Vote &
carry their votes into execution just as they please." [37] The
Boston patriots' usurpation of constitutional power was, in the
lieutenant governor's eyes, far more menacing than riots and
tumult because it blotted out all notion of subordination from
the people's minds. Nevertheless, the Council refused to support him in defending imperial authority in Massachusetts Bay;
his entreaties failed to rouse the Tories; and his commands were
disregarded by the Sons of Liberty. Undoubtedly, further
opposition would merely provoke greater violence from the
patriots' "trained mob": therefore, early in 1770, Hutchinson
ordered his sons to surrender their merchandise to the committee of inspection. And after the lieutenant governor had
given way, the importers quickly made terms with the patriots
rather than risk an attack by the "Mohawks."

Although Sam Adams seemed to have won a crushing victory
over the Tories and the British government, there were many

[35] *Chalmers Papers*, III, George Mason to ——, Jan. 24, 1770.
[36] Mass. Archives, 26, *Hutchinson Corr.*, II, 385, 492, 495. *Boston
Chronicle*, Jan. 15, 1770.
[37] Mass. Archives, 26, *Hutchinson Corr.*, II, 391.

disintegrating forces at work that threatened to destroy the nonimportation agreement.   There was no uniformity among the colonies with regard to the number of British commodities boycotted: some imported almost without restraint, while others shut out practically all manufactures from the mother country. Consequently, sectional jealousies were inflamed and each colony suspected it was being overreached by the sharp practices of its neighbors.   John Mein had succeeded in putting most of the continent on its guard against the secret importations of the New England "Saints."   Moreover, with the exception of a few Whig leaders, there were few in the colonies who realized that firm union was essential to the American cause.   Even in Boston, the hotbed of the movement toward colonial union, the people dreaded incorporation in a large government because they believed that New York "being near the center & having other natural advantages would be the Capital." [38]   The American union which Adams believed invulnerable in 1769 was really exposed on every side and in imminent danger of falling apart before the purposes of the nonimportation agreement had been achieved.

Moreover, the British Ministry's promise of a partial repeal of the Townshend duties drove a wedge between the colonies and brought the boycott to a premature end.   New York was the first to respond to Lord Hillsborough's circular letter of 1769.   The New York merchants, thoroughly weary of the bullying of Sons of Liberty who had nothing to lose by economic war with Great Britain, threw off their control in the spring of 1770 — a step which Bernard said the Boston merchants might have taken long before had they not been guilty of "extreme Pusillanamity." [39]   After having freed themselves from the radicals, the New York traders proposed that a congress of merchants be held at Norwalk, Connecticut, where the nonimportation agreement might be revised and the British government met halfway in conciliation.

Instead of inclining Sam Adams toward reconciliation with

[38] Mass. Archives, 26, *Hutchinson Corr.*, II, 442.   *New York Gazette and Weekly Mercury*, Aug. 6, 1770.
[39] *Bernard Papers*, VII, Bernard to Thomas Hutchinson, Aug. 20, 1770.

the mother country, Lord Hillsborough's peace offering of 1769
led him to raise his demands.   The original purpose of the nonimportation agreement was to repeal the Townshend duties,
but when Sam Adams believed he had put the British government in retreat, he began to regard the boycott as a means of
redressing all colonial grievances.   As Hutchinson said, "Gaining one point makes them [the Boston Whigs] more sure of
another & more restless until they obtain it." [40]   Besides the
repeal of the Townshend Act, Adams now demanded that the
mother country remove the Admiralty Courts, clear Boston of
redcoats and Commissioners of the Customs, and put the colonies
back in the situation they occupied "before the late extraordinary
Measures of Administration took Place." [41]   Adams hinted that
the boycott should be prolonged until Parliament had repealed
all commercially oppressive acts from the reign of Charles II
to George III, but most Whigs were not disposed to drive such
a hard bargain with the mother country: the redress of grievances
imposed since 1760 was in their eyes a sufficient price for ending
the boycott.   Still, all of Sam Adams's followers agreed that
Lord Hillsborough's offer of a partial repeal of the Townshend Act was merely a sop cast to unwary Americans to
break up the nonimportation agreement and destroy colonial
unity.

Sam Adams saw that the British government's conciliatory offer left untouched the principles that lay at the root of the
struggle between mother country and colonies.   Although the
American cause was based upon the doctrine of "no taxation without representation," Lord Hillsborough's circular letter of 1769
made clear that the mother country had no intention of receding from its claims.   Parliament still held fast to its right to
tax the colonies — "and it is the right," exclaimed the Boston
patriots, "we contend against."   Sam Adams believed the real
purpose of the nonimportation agreement political rather than
economic: it was intended not merely to remove a few taxes but

---

[40] Mass. Archives, 26, *Hutchinson Corr.*, II, 397, 487.
[41] *The Writings of Samuel Adams*, I, 441.   British Museum, King's MSS.
203, Lib. Cong. Transcript, Samuel Cooper to Thomas Pownall, Jan. 30, 1770.
Grenville Papers, edited by W. J. Smith (1853), IV, 456.

to establish the principle that all taxation of the colonies by the British House of Commons was illegal.   Until the Declaratory Act of 1766 was repealed Adams believed "we acquire nothing, and all our labour is in vain."   In proposing to abrogate part of the Townshend duties on the ground of commercial expediency, the British government revealed to Sam Adams how little it understood the causes of colonial discontent: while "even a Pepper Corn" was taken by Parliament from the colonists without their consent, there could be no hope of peace between mother country and provinces.   "It is not the Quantum of the Duty, nor the Number of the Articles taxed," exclaimed the Boston Whigs, but the tax itself that kept the Empire in discord.[42]

Even without recourse to these "higher Principles" which Sam Adams kept always in view, there was good reason to believe the Ministry's "Sugar Plum" contained a bitter core. Lord Hillsborough let it be understood in his circular letter that the tea duty, which alone of the taxes laid by Charles Townshend yielded a considerable revenue, would not be repealed.   In revoking the duties upon glass, paint, and paper, the British government was really surrendering nothing of value because these taxes brought only small sums into the Exchequer.   The tea duty, on the other hand, was so profitable that if the price of tea were reduced to half what it brought in England, there would still remain a revenue larger than the sum of the salaries of all the Crown officers which were intended to be paid from it.[43]   And, because the preamble to the Townshend duties was left intact by the Ministry in its "conciliation gesture" of 1769, the tea duty continued to be a tax laid expressly for revenue purposes.   Its proceeds might be used to support armies in the colonies and make governors and judges independent of the legislatures.   Therefore it was said that every pound of British tea purchased in the colonies would further enable the Ministry to take American money and property and "daub them in gold lace on every dirty rascal, who has a scullion wench of a sister, inviting enough to make

[42] *New York Gazette and Weekly Mercury*, July 30, 1770.
[43] *Boston Gazette*, Aug. 15, 1768.   Hutchinson, III, 351.

a whore to a commissioner." [44]   Even more harrowing to apprehensive colonists was the fear that the tea duty would be
regarded by the British government as a precedent for taxation
of the colonies and would be extended to "the necessaries of life
among us, and the very land that produces them."

As a result, Sam Adams flatly rejected the New York merchants' proposal of a congress at Norwalk.   "The least altera-
tion in the present agreement," he declared, ". . . might shew
a levity of disposition probably injurious to the common cause." [45]
Whereas the New Yorkers saw a favorable opportunity in Hillsborough's circular letter to make terms with the mother country,
Adams and his followers considered it "the most unlucky Season" to talk compromise because they believed the Ministry
would soon be forced to give way completely to American demands.   Moreover, Adams thoroughly distrusted the merchants whose lukewarmness had caused him to put into the
common people's hands the enforcement of the nonimportation
agreement.   Rather than risk "so dangerous an Experiment"
as "committing the whole State of American Freedom, to a small
Deputation of Merchants," the Boston radicals intended to uphold the patriot cause by their own efforts. [46]   If a deputation of
merchants were given ambassadorial power and packed off to
Norwalk, it seemed likely to Adams that the "gentlemen in
trade" would sell out American liberty for the first mess of
pottage offered by the British government.

But despite Sam Adams's determination "firmly [to] ad-
here to the nonimportation agreement," the New York merchants began to import all British merchandise with the exception of tea, after a house-to-house canvass of the metropolis had
revealed that a majority of the people favored breaking the
boycott.   Although this method of ascertaining public opinion
was recommended by the New Yorkers for trial in Boston, Sam
Adams preferred to settle the question in Faneuil Hall, where
his power was overwhelming and no Tory dared raise his voice.

[44] *Massachusetts Spy*, May 23, 1771. *New York Gazette and Weekly
Mercury*, July 30, 1770.
[45] *Boston Gazette*, June 11, 1770.
[46] *New York Gazette and Weekly Mercury*, July 30, 1770. *New York
Gazette or Weekly Post Boy*, June 25, 1770.

Boston town meetings had an unsavory reputation among New York gentry, who said that even a child would laugh if told that these "doughty Meetings" really expressed popular opinion. Certainly, the citizens who assembled in Faneuil Hall left no doubt of their sentiments. When the letter from the New York merchants announcing the end of the boycott was read in the Boston town meeting, the people were so enraged they tore the letter to pieces and threw it "to the Winds as unworthy of the least Notice." [47]

New York's desertion of the nonimportation agreement did not immediately dishearten Sam Adams. He hoped to see the New York mechanics force the merchants to resume the boycott; and as long as Philadelphia, Boston, and Charleston remained firm, there was a prospect that New York could be brought back into the movement. Adams and his followers urged Bostonians to forget the "fancied Miseries" for which they held the nonimportation agreement responsible and to think only of the hardships endured by their ancestors to establish a government based upon "the generous Plan of Liberty." Adams still promised that the boycott would reëstablish colonial liberty "without the Risque of Blood" and warned the Boston merchants that, regardless of what had happened in New York, it was not yet safe in Boston to anger "the BODY of the people" by importing prohibited British merchandise. [48] Popular enthusiasm was kept warm with rosy pictures of the miracles the nonimportation agreement was to work. Those who protested it was taking an unconscionable long time to bring relief were met with the answer that "one year more will do the business & bring Parliament to what terms we please." In the Boston town meeting, Sam Adams exclaimed that if the boycott were continued for another twelve months a storm would be raised in England such "as would endanger the heads and necks" of the British Ministry. [49]

[47] *New York Gazette and Weekly Mercury*, Aug. 27, 1770. *Boston Evening Post*, July 30, 1770.
[48] *New York Gazette and Weekly Mercury*, July 30, 1770. *Boston Gazette*, July 23, 1770; Aug. 6, 1770.
[49] Mass. Archives, 26, *Hutchinson Corr.*, II, 492. *Chalmers Papers*, III, Narrative of Events in Boston, 1770.

One of Sam Adams's most persistent errors was his conviction that Englishmen would sacrifice their political principles for the sake of preserving the wealth they drew from the colonies. On the contrary, instead of frightening the mother country into surrendering to the colonists' demands, the nonimportation agreement solidified public sentiment in Great Britain against Americans and stiffened the people's determination to see the quarrel through to the bitter end. When news reached the mother country that the Boston town meeting had declared a boycott of British manufactures it was said that "the Bostonites could not by any other means have so forcibly inculcated upon their countrymen, that the essence of American virtue consists in distressing, affronting and starving Britain." The New Englanders seemed disposed to turn "this island into a desart"; and it was whispered that "those who would starve us would cut our throats, if they could effect that carnage." [50] Never before had Bostonians appeared in Englishmen's eyes so much like scoundrelly republicans who wished to strip the mother country of all sovereignty over the colonies except the privilege of protecting them at British taxpayers' expense.

But after the New York merchants threw the Sons of Liberty overboard and opened the port to British merchandise, Sam Adams and his crew of "Mohawks" struck rough water in Boston. When the common people were put in control of the boycott, the merchants, smarting from their humiliation by the politicians, went over to the opposition. After the separate merchants' meetings had been swallowed up in the gatherings of the townspeople, few prominent Whig merchants, with the exception of John Hancock and William Phillips, attended the "mob meetings" where patriot policy was decided. Most of the wealthy traders of the metropolis were eager to "shake off their Faneuil Hall friends" and to follow New York's example in coming to terms with the mother country: they were weary of protracting the boycott until the British government should recognize the principle of no taxation without representation, and they were fearful of the growing power of the mob. Whig

[50] *New York Journal or General Advertiser*, July 7, 1768 (Supplement).

merchants had no more love for mobs and riots than had Tory gentlemen once it had become clear that the "Mohawks" were ready to turn upon them. But, as Hutchinson said, the merchants had raised the Devil and now they could not lay him.

The outbreak of open hostility between Boston merchants and politicians was hastened by Sam Adams's efforts to crush all signs of opposition to his policies. In 1770, when the Philadelphia merchants proposed to revise the nonimportation agreement, a number of Boston traders called a meeting at the British Coffee House and voted to import all British goods except tea if the Philadelphians did likewise. No sooner had Adams gotten wind of this mutiny than the bells were set ringing for a meeting of the townspeople and Dr. Thomas Young was sent with orders to the merchants to disperse immediately. While Young was delivering this command he was asked how he presumed to dictate to gentlemen in trade since he himself was no merchant. Young replied that, though he was no merchant, "he was one that the Merchts had called in to their assistance & he would not leave them." [51] Meanwhile, at Faneuil Hall, Molineux and Adams were damning the merchants as "Rebels & Usurpers" so forcefully that had they not obeyed Young's orders and broken up their meeting they probably would have found a mob of Sons of Liberty at their doors. Swallowing their humiliation, the merchants gave way to the politicians; their meetings were forbidden by Sam Adams, the sovereign of Faneuil Hall; and "Tom, Dick & Harry" compelled the traders to maintain the boycott of British merchandise.

In order to prove Boston's loyalty to the nonimportation agreement in spite of "Sugar Plums" from Great Britain and treachery from New York, Sam Adams demanded that the British goods stored in Boston by the committee of inspection should be shipped back to England. By this gesture, Adams hoped to whitewash Boston's reputation of the blots left by John Mein's pen and to set the colonies an example that would, if

[51] Mass. Archives, 25, *Hutchinson Corr.*, I, Thomas Hutchinson to ——, May 3, 1770; Mass. Archives, 26, II, 492, 494. *Chalmers Papers*, III, Narrative of Events in Boston, 1770.

followed throughout the continent, greatly increase the distress
felt in England from the boycott. It was apparent, however,
that this expedient, although pleasing to the politicians, was
highly distasteful to the merchants. But "the lower Sort of
People who were called in as Servants" were now masters and
they insisted that the merchants reship the goods or risk "a
meeting in the evening" from the Sons of Liberty. The citizens
exclaimed that "if a Ship was to bring in the plague nobody
would doubt what is necessary to be done with her," and there
were few who disagreed with Sam Adams that British manufactures were a plague to New England. When Hancock
offered the free use of one of his ships to carry the merchandise
to England, his offer was immediately accepted and a cargo
placed aboard. "Our Zealots have no bowels," cried the merchants; and Hutchinson compared the position of people and
merchants to that of a highwayman who had his pistol pressed
against the ribs of a defenseless traveler.[52]

By resorting to such rough methods, Sam Adams alienated
the conservative patriots and split the Whig Party. By 1770,
the left wing of the patriot party, of which Sam Adams and William Molineux were the guiding spirits, had taken command
of the nonimportation agreement. Only the most violent
Whigs held influence among the people: Molineux raised himself in popular favor by declaring that he had no scruple in
putting to death with his own hands every violator of the nonimportation agreement; and Sam Adams won applause by relentlessly hunting down importers and refusing to temporize
with the British government until all colonial grievances had
been redressed.[53] And when Sam Adams vaulted into the leadership of the patriot party, he brushed aside all conservative
Whigs who stood in his path. Among the first to fall was
James Otis, the "American Hampden" of the earlier revolutionary movement.

In 1769 Otis had been severely clubbed in a Boston tavern
by John Robinson, one of the Commissioners of the Customs.

---

[52] *Chalmers Papers*, III, Thomas Hutchinson to Lord Hillsborough, April 27,
1770; May 18, 1770; Narrative of Events in Boston.
[53] *Ibid.*, III, Journal of Transactions at Boston.

Sam Adams manufactured rare propaganda from this brawl by screaming that the Commissioners had deliberately attempted to assassinate Otis, but Hutchinson said it was a "very pretty drubbing." [54]   In any event, Otis never entirely recovered from his encounter with Robinson.   The eccentricity and mental instability which his enemies had ridiculed earlier in his career now flared into outright insanity.   At the Whig Club, his conversation degenerated into such a steady stream of "trash, obsceneness, profaneness, nonsense, and distraction," that no other member could get a word in edgewise — a hardship that seems to have been particularly distressing to John Adams.[55] He became so talkative that he could not be trusted with secrets lest Hutchinson learn of them; and, in frequent fits of repentance, he lamented his incendiarism and blamed himself for all the evils of the day.   "I meant well," he exclaimed to Hutchinson, "but am now convinced I was mistaken.   Cursed be the day I was born." [56]   Such behavior cost Otis the last shreds of influence with the Whigs.   He was left out of the Boston seat in the elections of 1770 and Sam Adams stepped into his place as leader of the Whig Party.

Otis took his dismissal hard.   When he learned that Sam Adams had dished him, Otis told John Adams that he was "a d——d Fool for not taking Warning by his Fate" — advice which may have had something to do with Lawyer Adams's decision to wash his hands of Boston politics and beat a retreat to Braintree.[57]   Harassed by doubts, tortured with the realization that the revolutionary movement had passed beyond his control, and nagged by a Tory wife whose "curtain lectures" probably hastened his insanity, Otis became the most pathetic figure in the Whig Party.   In the spring of 1770, he was seized with a "mad freak" in which he fired guns from his windows and broke the windows in the Town House.   He drank himself into a frenzy, although, as Hutchinson said, "the partition was al-

---

[54] *The Writings of Samuel Adams*, I, 380–386.

[55] *The Works of John Adams*, II, 227.

[56] *Bernard Papers*, XII, Thomas Hutchinson to Francis Bernard, Nov. 27, 1769.

[57] Peter Oliver, 117.   Hutchinson, III, 339.

ways very thin." The man whose writings and oratory had
set fire to the colonies now became a local nuisance whose
"drunken distracted frolicks" scandalized his neighbors. He
was the sport of young Tory lawyers; and his own practice
steadily dwindled until finally he was bound hand and foot,
loaded into a chaise, and carted out of Boston, an apparently
hopeless maniac. Hutchinson, believing he had seen the last
of Otis, wrote an epitaph: "He has been as good as his Word,"
said the governor, "set the Province in a flame and perished in
the attempt." [58]

Many of Otis's former followers were not sorry to see him
out of the way. The revolutionary movement in Massachusetts had long since swept past him and left him far in its wake:
by 1770, his views were considered so conservative that Tories
used his writings to support their arguments. "I shall rely
solely on him [Otis]," declared a Tory partisan. "He avows
the right of Parliament, full as extensively as I would carry it,
and that an imperium in imperio is a solycism in politics." As
Hutchinson said, James Otis had always opposed "in his calm
Moments" schemes to separate the colonies from the mother
country, and even "in his ravings . . . stopped when any thing
was said like denying the authority of an Act of Parliament &
pronounced it High Treason." [59] Otis had begun the revolutionary movement, but, as the struggle against the mother
country became fiercer, he clearly showed that he was not of
the stuff of which revolutionists are made. Among such company as Sam Adams, William Molineux, and Dr. Thomas
Young, Otis's reverence for the mother country and insistence
upon orderly, constitutional change seemed the voice of an earlier
generation. Had Otis continued sane, he might have played
the part of a Mirabeau in the American Revolution; but after
his banishment there was no patriot leader in New England
capable of opposing Sam Adams and preserving the people's
loyalty toward the mother country. And whatever satisfaction Tories derived from Otis's fall was turned to gall and

---

[58] Mass. Archives, 27, *Hutchinson Corr.*, III, 231, 260. *Bernard Papers*,
XII, Andrew Oliver to Francis Bernard, Dec. 3, 1769.

[59] *Boston Chronicle*, March 5, 1770. Hutchinson, III, 339.

wormwood by the rise of "that more pernicious Devil Adams." [60]

Shortly after Otis disappeared from Boston, rumors began to spread of wholesale desertions of the nonimportation agreement by New England seaports. From the beginning of the boycott, Portsmouth, New Hampshire, and "the little, filthy, nasty, dirty colony of Rhode-Island" had been thorns in Sam Adams's flesh. [61] In Portsmouth, a "swarm of stupid Tories" kept the port open to British merchandise, thereby gaining a large part of Boston's trade in western Massachusetts. In Newport and Providence, Jews and Tories made huge profits by openly flouting the nonimportation agreement. [62] To dam these gaps through which British goods poured into the colonies, Sam Adams proposed that Boston break off all commercial intercourse with Portsmouth, Newport, and Providence until importations from the mother country ceased. The citizens quickly adopted his plan and so watchful were the Boston patriots that commerce stopped as completely as though the plague were raging in New Hampshire and Rhode Island. Nevertheless, the recalcitrant merchants continued to make inroads upon Boston's trade by selling British manufactures to rural New Englanders. In 1770, to Adams's consternation, it was reported that Salem, Marblehead, and Newburyport were likewise secretly importing prohibited British commodities. Because the embargo against New Hampshire and Rhode Island had failed to achieve its purpose and was regarded as the "meer impotent malice" of the Boston patriots, Sam Adams saw that he must use sharper weapons against the mutinous Massachusetts merchants. [63] At a meeting in Faneuil Hall it was voted to send a committee of inspection headed by William Molineux to visit all the suspected seaports and drive out the importers. By this stroke, Sam Adams hoped to strike terror among the Tories and put Boston in control of the nonimportation agreement throughout New England.

[60] *Chalmers Papers*, III, Extract of a Letter from Boston, Dec. 30, 1769.
[61] *Boston Gazette*, May 7, 1770.
[62] *Samuel Adams Papers*, Joseph Ward to William Cooper, July 13, 1770. *Boston Gazette*, Dec. 11, 1769.
[63] Mass. Archives, 26, *Hutchinson Corr.*, II, 484.

But the results of Molineux's inquisitorial tour of New England were a bitter disappointment to Sam Adams. In Salem, Molineux and his party were awakened in the dead of night with news that a mob was assembling at the Long Wharf with enough tar and feathers for the entire Boston delegation. Although the mob failed to attack, Salem was obviously not a healthy spot for the Bostonians, who resolved to move on to Newport to inspect the warehouses and throw out the "infernal cabal" that made the town a Tory stronghold. But Molineux was given no opportunity to ferret out the guilty Rhode Islanders: the citizens of Newport were prepared to give him a warmer welcome than he had expected and "nothing was heard talk'd of but tarring and feathering of Molineux and his Party." [64] Indeed, Molineux thought himself fortunate to escape from Newport unscathed on the first boat to Providence. After these rebuffs, it could no longer be doubted that nonimportation was a lost cause; and the unhappy Molineux admitted to the Providence Sons of Liberty that unless Boston was supported by other seaports, the boycott was doomed. Boston alone could not hold out against Great Britain, yet New Englanders seemed so little disposed to aid the metropolis that they brought out for the visiting Boston committee of inspection the tar and feathers they usually reserved for Tories and customhouse officers.

Even the most uncompromising boycotter could now see that Boston was doing itself an injury by carrying on after New York and other seaports had been opened to British trade. Whigs as well as Tories began to raise the cry that Boston's folly was driving commerce to other towns. Thanks to the politicians' obstinacy, the merchants lamented, the "antient channels of Commerce" were being diverted to enrich smaller ports at the metropolis's expense. "Providence, which was the other day but a straggling village," they said, "does now bid fair to rival this town in greatness." [65] The boycott had brought privation and distress to the common people of Boston: hundreds of workmen were unemployed and so restive that Tory gentlemen feared they would soon begin to "plunder the Rich"

[64] *Boston Gazette*, May 7, 1770; Aug. 20, 1770; Sept. 3, 1770.
[65] *Boston Chronicle*, Feb. 5, 1770.

and cut their throats.[66]   Though Sam Adams said business was good and the suffering in Boston trifling, the depression created by the boycott was steadily undermining his power.   The small shopkeepers whose loyalty to Adams had made possible the nonimportation agreement were the greatest sufferers: the wealthy merchants had laid in such large supplies of goods before the agreement went into effect that they made large profits from the boycott and drove their smaller competitors out of business. In the eyes of an increasingly large number of Bostonians, the town was "tottering on the brink of ruin" and Sam Adams and his fellow politicians were solely to blame.

Nevertheless, Adams made a last effort to continue the boycott by proposing to the Philadelphia merchants that a congress be held to form a new nonimportation agreement.   The Philadelphians' refusal to take part in a congress was the deathblow to the boycott: the Boston merchants met at the British Coffee House and, without interference from Sam Adams, voted to import all British commodities except tea.   Thus the agreement came to an end before any of the purposes Sam Adams prized most highly had been attained: Parliament had made no renunciation of its right to tax the colonies; the Commissioners of the Customs still collected "unconstitutional" taxes; and the tea duty remained a precedent for future taxation by the mother country.   Throughout the colonies, Crown officers exulted over Sam Adams's discomfiture: "The Pride of the Bostonians is lowered," said General Gage.   ". . . After a fair Struggle between Patriotism and Interest, the latter seems to have gained a compleat Victory." [67]   Here was more proof for His Majesty's Ministers of State that the disturbances in the colonies were the work of a few blustering politicians and that the mass of the people were unalterably loyal to the mother country.

Englishmen might well believe they had little further to fear from American patriots.   The union of the colonies was

[66] Mass. Archives, 26, *Hutchinson Corr.*, II, 359, 500.   *Letters of James Murray Loyalist*, edited by N. M. Tiffany (1901), 132.   *Boston Chronicle*, Feb. 5, 1770.   Andrew Oliver, *op. cit.*, I, Andrew Oliver to Francis Bernard, Nov. 21, 1769.

[67] *The Correspondence of General Thomas Gage*, edited by C. E. Carter (1931), II, 561.

completely at an end. At no time since the Stamp Act had Sam Adams's dream of a united America appeared more remote than in 1770 when the provinces fell to quarreling among themselves over the blame for the failure of the nonimportation agreement. The Philadelphia Sons of Liberty upbraided New York's "abandoned Perfidy and Parricide" in importing British merchandise and voted to break off all commercial intercourse with New York and avoid the town "as they would a poisoned City, lest they should be scabb'd with their Principles, as well as corrupted with their Goods." [68]   At a huge meeting under their Liberty Tree, the Charleston, South Carolina, patriots declared they would not trade with New York until the citizens atoned "for their treacherous Separation from their Countrymen." [69]   The quarrel between New York and Boston was particularly bitter: as Hutchinson said, "our People are in a perfect Rage against New York." [70]   Bostonians railed against the "perfidious Yorkers" who, in turn, denounced the "vile and scandalous Behaviour of the Town of Boston . . . the *Common Sewer of America.*" [71]   Each town accused the other of secretly breaking the agreement and making profits behind a screen of patriotism and self-sacrifice: when it was shown that over five thousand packs of playing cards had been imported into Boston during the nonimportation agreement, New Yorkers asked "whether ALL those VIRTUOUS PLAYTHINGS were imported for the *sole* Use of the few CHURCHMEN who are in that Colony?" John Mein had sown suspicion throughout the colonies that the "saintish, canting, puritanical, grace-pouring-down countenanced" New Englanders were pious rogues. Sam Adams failed to convince Americans of Bostonians' honesty by shipping the merchants' goods back to England, for it was widely believed that Hancock's ship had been loaded with "billets of wood, shavings and brick bats." In spite of Adams's efforts to clear his fellow townsmen's skirts, it was said that the "Boston way" of storing prohibited British merchandise was to

[68] *Boston Gazette,* July 30, 1770.
[69] *New York Gazette and Weekly Mercury,* Oct. 1, 1770.
[70] Mass. Archives, 26, *Hutchinson Corr.,* II, 523.
[71] *New York Gazette and Weekly Mercury,* Aug. 27, 1770.

place the goods in a warehouse with a convenient back door that might be opened unobserved in the small hours of the night.[72]

For this calamitous ending of the nonimportation agreement, Sam Adams blamed the merchants — those recreants who, "like a Spaniel meanly cringed & kiss'd the rod that whip'd them." [73] The lesson Adams learned from his failure in 1770 was that no trust could be placed in merchants whose eyes were fixed upon the profit-and-loss columns of their ledgers rather than upon colonial liberty, and who fell easy victims to "Court Influence." Adams now said he had expected the agreement to fail from the beginning because the merchants were guided by self-interest; it had, indeed, lasted longer than he hoped.   But its results were so disastrous that he wished to forget the colonies had ever entered upon an economic war with Great Britain: Americans, he said, must again turn their attention to "our first grand object" — the union of the colonies — in order to repair the damage done by the merchants.   Adams was wary of the trap in which he had once been caught: the merchants, he declared, had shown themselves "unworthy of any future Confidence" from colonial patriots.[74]   He saw that the only way to make nonimportation effective was to place it entirely in the hands of yeomen and townspeople who, by refusing to buy from merchants handling prohibited British merchandise, would quickly put all importers out of business.   "We can live without the baubles of Britain," said the Whigs.   "If there are no purchasers there can not long be Importers; we shall save our money, and save our Country."   Henceforth, Adams said, the "Edge of Resentment" against Great Britain must be kept sharp in order to encourage Americans to establish colonial manufactures and live as frugally as Old Romans.   Thus, as early as 1770, Sam Adams outlined the plan of nonimportation adopted in 1774 after the passage of the Boston Port Bill. From 1770 until the end of the Revolution, Adams acted upon

[72] *New York Journal or General Advertiser*, July 19, 1770.   *Massachusetts Gazette*, Jan. 11, 1776.   *Boston Gazette*, Sept. 3, 1770.
[73] *Publications Col. Soc. of Mass.*, Transactions, XIX, 255.
[74] *The Writings of Samuel Adams*, II, 65, 307.   William Pepperell to Arthur Lee, MS. Mass. Hist. Soc., Nov. 21, 1770.

the principle that it was the common people "who must, under GOD, finally save us." [75]

In reality, Sam Adams had no one but himself to blame for the plight in which the colonies found themselves in 1770. Nonimportation was an effective weapon against the mother country, but it could not work the miracles Adams demanded of it. It could not bring Parliament to abandon its claim of right to tax the colonies, nor could it procure the repeal of all Parliamentary legislation distasteful to the Whigs. Had the nonimportation agreement been confined merely to the removal of economic disabilities it might well have succeeded in its purpose, but Adams and his fellow politicians added so many political demands that failure was inevitable. Moreover, by hanging out the sign "No Compromise," Adams exposed himself to certain defeat and made it impossible for the colonists to withdraw with honor from the economic struggle with the mother country.

[75] *Boston Gazette*, Sept. 11, 1769; Oct. 15, 1770. *The Writings of Samuel Adams*, II, 58, 65.

IX

THE DECLINE OF THE PATRIOT PARTY

THE collapse of the nonimportation agreement and the acquittal of the British soldiers in the Massacre trials were the sharpest defeats yet suffered by the Massachusetts Whigs. For the first time in many years, Tories could toast Sam Adams's downfall with prospects of speedy success. An era of good feelings succeeded the five years of turbulence ushered in by the Stamp Act, and the revolutionary movement was brought to an almost complete standstill in the colonies. America was more peaceful than at any time since George Grenville first prodded the hornets' nest, and, although Sam Adams continued to shriek "oppression" and "tyranny" as lustily as ever, there were few to heed him. The Whig man-of-war, rigged for stiff gales, became becalmed in this unwonted tranquillity. Adams and his crew of "Mohawks" kept their eyes glued hopefully to the barometer for signs of storm, but the mass of colonists were content to drift with the tide and enjoy the calm. Adams was compelled to wait so long for a breeze — for fully two years the American colonies were not so much as mentioned in debates in the House of Commons — that mutiny broke out among the crew and skipper Adams came perilously near being thrown off the quarter-deck. And while the Whig leaders wrangled for the command and Whig principles went out of favor among the countrypeople, the Tories began to regain the ground they had lost since 1764. Even in Boston, Adams narrowly averted defeat at the hands of the revived Tory Party. But just when Sam Adams and the Whig Party seemed to have reached the lowest point of their fortunes, the British government again came to the rescue with a timely blunder.

In 1770 there was still a strong conservative spirit in New

England which the British government would have done well
to cultivate.   The greater part of the people were thoroughly
weary of quarreling with the mother country and their demands
were so moderate that most of the generation that fought the
Revolution to establish American independence would have
been satisfied in 1770 if Great Britain had returned to the
colonial system in force before the Sugar and Stamp Acts.   They
were overwhelmingly in favor of "recurring to first Principles
— the old Establishment upon which they have grown & flourish'd," rather than following Sam Adams along a slippery path
that led no one knew where.[1]   "We wish nothing remov'd but
Innovations," they exclaimed: the Commissioners of the Customs should be withdrawn; the revenue acts should be repealed;
and the money collected from port duties for the regulation of
trade should not be used to make judges and governors independent of colonial legislatures.   The charter of William and
Mary was regarded as the basis of a permanent union between
mother country and colony because it gave "ev'ry reasonable
Security to ye Nation & Government, for our Subordination."[2]

Although Sam Adams reëchoed his countrymen's longings to
return to the old colonial system, his sincerity is open to question.   Because Adams always strove to be the spokesman of
the common man, he was forced to adjust himself to the slow
pace at which public opinion moved.   The mass of the people
wished nothing more in 1770 than the "good old days" of
Pownall; hence, Adams took the stand that if Great Britain
reverted to its former imperial policy, the mother country
would "lose Nothing which she ought to retain" and Americans
would again become loyal, obedient subjects of King George.[3]
Yet it is probable that Adams would have been dismayed had
the British government taken him at his word.   In spite of
his insistence that he wished to go back, not forward, Adams

[1] British Museum, King's MSS. 203, Lib. Cong. Transcript, Original Letters from the Rev. Dr. Cooper and Dr. Franklin, Samuel Cooper to Thomas
Pownall, Jan. 1, 1770.   Letters of Thomas Cushing, *Mass. Hist. Soc. Collections* (1858), IV, Fourth Series, 357.
[2] British Museum, King's MSS. 203, Samuel Cooper to Thomas Pownall,
Jan. 1, 1770.
[3] *The Writings of Samuel Adams*, II, 57, 58.

already had visions of a new political and social order.   Since the landing of British troops in Boston in 1768 he had regarded independence as the only escape from British "tyranny."   Because he supposed "degenerate" Great Britain on the point of slipping into the worst vices of the declining Roman Empire, he was anxious to sever the ties between colonies and mother country before the contagion spread to America.   Furthermore, a return to the old colonial system would not settle the domestic quarrels of Massachusetts or bring the high-flying Hutchinsons and Olivers down to the dust where Adams hoped to see them. Adams was far too astute a politician to believe his struggle against Hutchinson would be made easier if the discord with the mother country was brought to an end: tranquillity always works in favor of the conservative party and strengthens the grip of "oligarchs."   His pious hankering for the "good old days" of good will between colonies and mother country was merely a pose struck to win public support.   To veil his real aggressions upon British authority in the colonies, Adams pretended to be a peace-loving colonist, desiring nothing so much as peace and quiet, reluctantly driven by intolerable grievances into rebellion.   Adams's true element was rough water — not the calm seas he professed to seek — and at heart he was a revolutionist who longed to overthrow the Tories and sever the bonds between mother country and colonies.

Perhaps the bitterest draught Sam Adams was forced to swallow after the failure of the nonimportation agreement and the acquittal of the British soldiers was the appointment of Thomas Hutchinson as royal governor of Massachusetts Bay.   Many years before, James Otis had said that Hutchinson's elevation to the governorship would be "as terrible to the honest part of this Province as a Volcano or an Earthquake," and, since Otis had made this dire prophecy, Hutchinson had made himself even more feared by the Whigs.[4]   None of the Massachusetts patriots seriously believed that the British government would force their worst enemy upon them as governor.   But whoever the Massachusetts Whigs opposed in Boston was certain to have

[4] Mauduit, LXXIV (1918), 76, 77. *Boston Gazette,* June 18, 1770. Peter Oliver, 133.

his fortune made at Westminster: Bernard had been made a baronet for the persecution he suffered at Sam Adams's hands and Hutchinson was appointed governor of the colony because it was recognized that for two decades he had been a bulwark of the royal government against Adams. Furthermore, Hutchinson had been well seasoned as lieutenant governor for the part he was expected to play in restoring order in the province. He was deeply ambitious of succeeding Bernard in the governor's chair and he had undertaken a vigorous campaign among his English friends to procure him the post. But after the Boston Massacre and its ominous foreshadowing of conflict between Great Britain and the colonies, Hutchinson abruptly changed his mind and wrote to England to withdraw his name from consideration. He was reluctant to enter the arena against Sam Adams and his "Mohawks" without even the support of a loyal Council. Rather than undertake what he feared might prove a hopeless task, Hutchinson preferred to remain as Chief Justice — a comparatively safe haven against the storm he saw brewing in the colonies. But before his letter expressing this decision reached England his commission as governor had already been dispatched. Unable to flinch publicly by resigning, Hutchinson accepted the office and the quarrel with Sam Adams that had by 1771 become an inescapable part of its responsibilities.[5]

As Hutchinson had foreseen, his assumption of the governorship raised a tempest in the Whig teapot. It availed him nothing to say that he had attempted to avoid the office: John Adams said in public that Hutchinson, far from declining, had schemed deliberately for the prize; and Sam Adams ridiculed the notion that he could have rejected an office "which his Soul is every day panting after & without the Possession of which his Ambition & Lust of Power will perpetually torment him." [6] The cause of the Adamses' alarm was the healthy respect they entertained for Hutchinson's ability as an "oligarch" and tyrant. Unlike most royal governors of Massachusetts Bay, Hutchinson

---

[5] Hutchinson, III, 257.

[6] *Israel Williams Papers*, MSS. Mass. Hist. Soc., Thomas Hutchinson to Israel Williams, Jan. 10, 1771.

had been born in the colony and, outside Boston, was popular among the people as a "native son" who had made good. It touched the pride of many yeomen that the King had appointed one of their countrymen as governor. Pious rustics who could not forget that Bernard had been a member of the Church of England were endeared to Hutchinson because of his strict Congregationalism. Indeed, Hutchinson enjoyed the reputation in the colony of being an "eminent saint." [7]   Like Sam Adams, the "Saint" of the Whig Party, Hutchinson gained his ends by tact and subtlety. He would have none of the forthright methods Bernard had unsuccessfully used in Massachusetts Bay; unlike that blunt English country gentleman who imagined that New Englanders could be bulldozed into loyalty to the Crown, Hutchinson knew how to handle the "Saints."

No sooner had Hutchinson taken the governor's chair than Sam Adams set out to prove he was the worst tyrant since the fall of the Roman Empire. For the benefit of country people who were well disposed toward Hutchinson because he had been born in the province, Adams raked up "horrible examples" from Roman history calculated to terrify the most complacent; natives of Rome, Adams demonstrated, had always shown themselves to be the worst tyrants of their home town. It was understandable that a "foreigner" like Bernard should join heartily in the British government's plan to snuff out colonial liberty, but when a man who was "bone of our Bone, & flesh of our flesh" aided the unholy work, he was a double-dyed villain.[8]   For colonists who believed Hutchinson a staunch friend to the Massachusetts charter there was, exclaimed Adams, a sharp awakening in store: the charter had no more dangerous enemy than Thomas Hutchinson, who was ready to undertake any oppression "for the sake of rising a single step higher," and who had already given notable proof of his real intentions by plotting the Stamp Act.[9]   There was no difference, Adams believed, be-

[7] *The Works of John Adams*, II, 189, 361, 362. *The Writings of Samuel Adams*, II, 276.
[8] *Ibid.*, II, 67, 175, 207.
[9] *Ibid.*, II, 67, 201. *The Works of John Adams*, II, 361, 362.

tween Hutchinson and Bernard except that they worked with different methods: where Bernard blustered and fumed, the "soft
& oily tongu'd" Hutchinson attempted to persuade New Englanders to do what they "would not be *driven* into by fleets &
armies." Of the two, Adams much preferred to deal with a
swaggering tyrant whose arbitrary acts kept the people sweating
for their liberties rather than with a despotically-minded "oligarch," such as Hutchinson, who worked in the dark with
gloves. In comparison with Hutchinson, Bernard was a blessing: "Happy indeed it was for the Province," Adams cried, that
Bernard had been governor, because his bullying had aroused
"such a Jealousy & Watchfulness in the people as prevented
their immediate & total Ruin." Instead of being a flattering
concession to New England, Hutchinson's appointment was
simply a step forward in the British government's new scheme
to tax the colonies: Hutchinson was expected to keep the people
calm and lull them "into that *quietude* and *sleep* by which
slavery is always preceeded." [10] Adams did not even spare
Hutchinson's repute as a Congregational saint. Because the
governor was present at an Episcopal christening, Adams in-
sinuated that he was about to go over to the Church of England; and, with a characteristic play upon New Englanders' religious prejudices, he said that Hutchinson venerated royal
instructions "as ever a poor deluded Catholic reverenc'd the
decree of Holy Father at Rome." [11]

But despite this abuse heaped upon the new governor, Sam
Adams was sorely disappointed to find how unshaken Hutchinson's "unbounded popularity" in the country remained.[12] In
the House of Representatives Adams was able to win a majority
of only one vote in preventing a congratulatory address being
sent to the governor; but the Convocation of Congregational
clergy — the "black regiment" that had done Otis and Adams
good service in spreading patriotic fervor over New England

---

[10] *Boston Gazette*, Sept. 13, 1773. *The Writings of Samuel Adams*, II, 58,
165, 203, 245.
[11] *The Writings of Samuel Adams*, II, 41, 188. *Boston Gazette*, April 1,
1771.
[12] *The Works of John Adams*, II, 295.

— outraged the Whigs by publicly complimenting Hutchinson upon his accession to the governorship. Adams was at first at a loss to explain the divines' backsliding, but he finally concluded that a few Tories had crept into the Ministry, where they were up to their old tricks of counterworking the Whigs. Because only a small minority of the Congregational clergy attended the convocation that voted to send its well-wishes to Hutchinson, Adams declared their address was nothing more than "the foul breath of sycophants and hirelings" which, had the whole body of clergy been present, would have been easily voted down.   Nevertheless, Adams was dismayed to find the ministry riddled with Toryism and he urged that those who were responsible for the convocation's work be regarded in the same light as were the seventeen Tories who had voted to rescind the Massachusetts circular letter in 1768.   It was not until 1773, when Benjamin Franklin put into Sam Adams's hands the means of destroying Hutchinson's popularity in New England, that the governor ceased to be a constant threat to the Whigs' power.

At the beginning of his administration, Hutchinson succeeded in putting a British garrison into Castle William behind the patriots' backs.   Castle William, as has been seen, was held by Massachusetts troops whose questionable loyalty to Great Britain during such crises as the Massachusetts Convention of 1768 kept the Crown officers in chronic uneasiness.   Late in 1770, Hutchinson received instructions from the British government which, he realized, could they be carried out without producing an explosion in the colony, would regain much of the ground lost when Boston Whigs had hustled British regulars out of the metropolis in the previous March.   The governor was ordered in these instructions to exchange the colonial garrison at Castle William for British regulars.   Hutchinson worked with such caution that, before Adams knew what had happened, the Massachusetts soldiers had been discharged and the fortress put in possession of redcoats.   Moreover, as a further precaution, the British Ministry designated Boston as the headquarters of the royal men-of-war in North American waters. Thus, a permanent British garrison was placed within striking distance of Boston, and the Sons of Liberty, who hoped to see no redcoats or men-of-war closer than New York and Halifax, found themselves within range of British cannon and bayonets.[13]

Because Castle William had been built by Massachusetts, Adams regarded it as the colony's property to be used by the Crown only after permission had been secured from the General Court. Yet Hutchinson had seized it for the King by distinctly underhand methods: no pretense whatever had been made of consulting the General Court. With Boston "environ'd with ships of war" and the fort surrendered to "foreign" troops who had recently shed patriot blood, Adams again lost his self-command as he had when British soldiers were reported on the way to Boston in 1768. At a merchants' meeting in Boston, Adams interrupted the proceedings with a fiery speech in which he accused Hutchinson of breaking the Massachusetts charter by handing over the castle to the British government, but the merchants cut him short by protesting that this "was not the business of the Meeting and repeatedly stopped him from going on." This rebuff so little discouraged Adams that he was soon going about Boston urging that twenty thousand men be raised in the country to retake the fort.[14] Had the need for such action arisen shortly after the Massacre when Boston was regarded in the country as a martyred town, Adams might have found embattled farmers pouring into the metropolis from every side; but by November 1770, when Hutchinson tricked the colonial garrison into surrendering Castle William and Sam Adams began to talk war, New England yeomen were in no mood to follow Boston into hostilities with the mother country.

The evidence unearthed at the Massacre trials gave New England countryfolk a glimpse of "mobbish Bostonians" at work — a spectacle that Adams always took great pains to conceal. Proof of the mob's eagerness to scuffle with the soldiers, the serious provocation given by Gray's ropewalkers, and the suspicion that Sam Adams had deliberately planned an attack upon the soldiers put the Massacre in very different light from

[13] Mass. Archives, 27, *Hutchinson Corr.*, III, 10, 14, 24, 392, 393.
[14] *Ibid.*, III, 3, 60. *Massachusetts Spy*, June 13, 1771; Nov. 26, 1773.

that shed by Adams's *Narrative*.   To counteract these damaging disclosures, Adams wrote his "Vindex" articles in the *Boston Gazette* and sent copies of the *Narrative* to New England innkeepers in order that their guests might be provided with racy literature — "And bitter reading they were," said a Tory, "for they were wrote with a Pen dipped in the Gall of Asps." [15]

Despite Adams's energetic whitewashing, country people began to suspect that Boston was not as pure and holy as the Whigs painted it; and the Tories were at their ears whispering that "the Town has by its rashness bro't all this Mischief upon us." [16] It became common to hear yeomen openly declare that Bostonians were to blame for the Massacre; and in most parts of New England the bitterness that had been heaped upon the soldiers was now turned against the townspeople.   "From the Borders of Connecticut all the Way to Boston," countrymen denounced the metropolis for their misfortunes and threatened to throw off its leadership.[17]   John Mein's exposure of Boston's secret importations during the boycott deepened rural distrust: "I hate them [Bostonians] from my very soul," exclaimed a countryman to John Adams.   "Great patriots! were for non-importation, while their old rags lasted; and, as soon as they were sold at enormous prices, they were for importing; no more to be heard about manufactures, and now, there is a greater flood of goods than ever were known."   Once Boston's spell over the country was broken, the delighted Tories found the old reverence for government reappearing and the people beginning to "look round them with astonishment and . . . willing to hear with both Ears."   Many feared to plunge into the "savage state" toward which the patriots seemed headed; unless the colony was to feel the "terrible effects of a state of Anarchy," it was said, royal authority could no longer be treated with contempt.   Hutchinson reported to the British ministry that there was more "general appearance of Contentment" in Massachu-

[15] Peter Oliver, 100.

[16] *Boston Gazette*, Sept. 24, 1770.

[17] Mass. Archives, 25, *Hutchinson Corr.*, I, Henry Young Brown to Thomas Hutchinson, Nov. 28, 1770, III, 72.

setts Bay than at any time since the Stamp Act.[18]   The tide ran
so strongly against Boston that Hutchinson had hope of dam-
ming up Whiggery in the metropolis and making Tories of New
England farmers; the time had come, he believed, to strengthen
royal government in Massachusetts by changing the Massachusetts charter and abolishing Boston's "pestilential" town meetings for a corporate form of government such as New York's.[19]

The Tories' strategy was to stir up antagonism between Boston and the interior by painting the metropolis as a hotbed of
irreligion and the patriots themselves as blasphemous free-
thinkers.   Boston put men in power not because of their morals
or religion but because they bawled loudest for liberty, cried
Tory partisans; the only standard in the metropolis was whether
candidates hated King and Parliament.   Had Massachusetts
Bay preserved the high ideals of the Puritans, conservatives
believed, Boston would be at "the tail instead of the head of
the province."   They were at a loss to explain how New Englanders, the descendants of Puritans, came to be guided by such
"thorough-paced infidels, and virulent opposers of Our holy
RELIGION" as Dr. Thomas Young and William "Paoli" Molineux.   Pious yeomen were frequently reminded that Molineux
"ridicules and sets at nought" all religion and that Dr. Young
was a notorious scoffer; indeed, the doctor was raked over the
coals so frequently for infidelity that he complained the Tories'
inquisitorial methods were more fit for "the meridian of Madrid
than Roxbury or Boston." [20]   Sam Adams rushed into print
with a rousing defense of Dr. Young, proving by illustrations
from Greece and Rome that pagans could be as great statesmen
as Christians.   Dr. Young, Adams exclaimed, was an "un-
wearied assertor of the rights of his countrymen" who should

---

[18] *Boston Gazette*, Dec. 24, 1770. *The Works of John Adams*, II, 265,
266.   Mass. Archives, 25, *Hutchinson Corr.*, I, Henry Young Brown to
Thomas Hutchinson, Nov. 28, 1770. *Boston Evening Post*, June 3, 1771;
April 6, 1772.   *Mass. Hist. Soc. Proceedings* (1882), XIX, 132.   *Chalmers
Papers*, III, Thomas Hutchinson to Lord Hillsborough, Jan. 24, 1772.
[19] Public Record Office, Colonial Office, Class or Series 5, 245, Lib. Cong.
Transcript, Thomas Hutchinson to ——, Jan. 22, 1771. Mass. Archives,
27, *Hutchinson Corr.*, III, 150.
[20] *Boston Evening Post*, March 16, 1772.   *Boston News Letter*, Nov. 26,
1772.   *Boston Chronicle*, Feb. 19, 1770.

be judged by his patriotism, not by his religious opinions.[21]   Sam
Adams himself was too pious to be open to attack on the score
of irreligion, but Tories made the most of his shady record as
a tax collector.

While painting Boston in the blackest colors, Tories pictured
Massachusetts Bay as a prosperous, thriving colony, disturbed
only by a "few gloomy discontented mortals" who croaked dis-
mally of tyranny and oppression.   Whereas Adams summed up
the grievances of Massachusetts, Tories weighed its blessings:
the low indebtedness of the province; the light taxes; the flourishing state of commerce; and the roads crowded with "Coaches,
Chariots and Chaises" whose well-to-do occupants had no desire to reopen the controversy with the mother country.   Conservatives pointed out that the mother country had dropped its
quarrel with the colonies: Parliament seemed to have forgotten
their existence and the Ministry had promised not to attempt
to raise a large revenue from America.   At no time since the
Stamp Act had Great Britain appeared more inclined to use
leniency towards the colonies; and many loyal provincials believed that Parliament kept up its claim to the right of taxation
solely to prevent Americans from making good their demand
that they be exempt from Parliamentary taxation.[22]   Tea was
cheaper in Massachusetts than in England, and the clamor raised
by Boston merchants and patriots against the Sugar Act of 1764
had been silenced by reducing the duty on molasses to one penny
per gallon.   As for those Boston Whigs who still continued to
groan of British tyranny, Tories declared that they would be
satisfied only when Massachusetts had been made "totally
democratical" and independent of Parliamentary sovereignty.[23]
Hutchinson and his friends appealed to all supporters of royal
government to muzzle these grumblers who disturbed Massachusetts' honeymoon with George III; conservatives, they
claimed, should go to the polls with the slogan, "All 's Well in
Massachusetts Bay" and sweep Adams and his crew out of
office because they were kindling discontent at a time when all

[21] *The Writings of Samuel Adams*, II, 376, 378.
[22] *Massachusetts Gazette*, Jan. 2, 1772.   Hutchinson, III, 332.
[23] *Boston Evening Post*, May 27, 1771.

good citizens should be quietly enjoying the prosperity brought them by King George's benevolent rule.

But when the Tories congratulated themselves upon the end of the Whig "tyranny" and the "expiring efforts" of Sam Adams's party, they rejoiced too soon.   However peaceable the country, in the seaport towns where the revenue acts and the Commissioners of the Customs were standing grievances, Sam Adams still held his own.   Hutchinson said that if the patriot party was dying, it was dying hard; and it took such an unconscionable long time that he began to suspect that what he had at first thought was good will toward royal government was in reality merely "sullen discontent." [24]   Even the cessation of intercolonial correspondence between the Sons of Liberty did not make all Tories feel safe: Hutchinson said there could never be real security because the provinces were not distinct islands and Boston was not placed far out in the Atlantic.[25] Adams and other Whig chiefs had escaped unscathed for their work in the Massachusetts Convention and the nonimportation agreement in spite of the Tories' warnings that there would be no lasting peace in Massachusetts until the patriot party had been forcibly broken up.   "If Parliament dont give us a flogging," said a conservative, "we shall be as rampant as ever." Most disquieting of all to the Tories was the fact that there was no sign of weakening in Sam Adams: he kept on dealing out "malicious Strokes" in the newspapers, and passers-by who saw a light burning late at night in his room knew that he was writing against the Tories.   "If it was not for 2 or 3 Adamses," said Hutchinson, "we should do well enough."   Although the governor was unable to understand John Adams's obstinacy because he seemed "when he began life to promise well," there was nothing surprising in Sam Adams's stubbornness.   "He never appear'd different from what he does at present," Hutchinson said, and added grimly, "I fear never will."   It was useless to tempt Sam Adams with bribes and there was no office at the governor's disposal which seemed likely to purchase his silence.   Yet it was clear that he must be quickly put out of the

[24] Mass. Archives, 27, *Hutchinson Corr.*, III, 172 236.
[25] *Ibid.*, 243.

way. "I doubt," said Thomas Hutchinson, "whether there is a greater Incendiary in the King's dominions or a man of greater malignity of heart, or who less scruples any measure ever so criminal to accomplish his purposes; and I think I do him no injustice when I suppose he wishes the destruction of every Friend to Government in America." [26]

Sam Adams could not remain idle while Tories sowed suspicion of Boston in the country and bottled up Whig principles in the metropolis. "That Fiend Hutchinson" might attempt to separate town and country, but Adams believed that New England yeomen were too wise "to be catch'd in such a snare." [27] Nevertheless, Adams saw that the country was rapidly cooling and that farmers were becoming "too unconcern'd Spectators" of the British government's attacks upon colonial liberty. [28] Before rural New England was entirely weaned away from the metropolis by the "contemptible wretches" who were busy with their "old Tricks to divide the Country from the town," Adams proposed to administer some particularly stiff doses of counter-propaganda. He and his assistants in the *Boston Gazette* attempted to convince the country people that Bostonians were orderly, long-suffering patriots who mobbed only when their oppressions became intolerable; who were zealous for the rights of New England, not merely of Boston alone; and who were on "*one bottom*" with their rural supporters. [29] But it was apparent that if yeomen were to become as fiery Whigs as were the Boston Sons of Liberty it was necessary to bring the menace of tyranny to their very doors. Bostonians had borne the brunt of the British government's severities: while Commissioners of the Customs and British army officers enforced acts of Parliament in the metropolis, the rural population derived most of its ideas of tyranny from reading the Boston newspapers. The townspeople really tasted British despotism over the colonies: it was the countryfolk who, inspired by Sam Adams, "snuffed tyranny in every tainted breeze." Adams set out to arouse the farmers

[26] Mass. Archives, III, 102, 104, 437.

[27] *The Writings of Samuel Adams*, II, 111.

[28] *Ibid.*, II, 334.

[29] *Boston Gazette*, Sept. 24, 1771; March 23, 1772. *Massachusetts Spy*, Sept. 3, 1772.

by predicting that their lands would be heavily taxed or forcibly taken from them by the British government and handed over
to court favorites and "King's Friends." If Great Britain
could take money out of the pockets of colonial merchants, it
could dispossess farmers of their land — and Adams had no
doubt that the Ministry would do so the moment it saw an
opportunity. The stage properties with which Adams usually
terrified his countrymen were the clanking chains and groans
of slavery to British "tyranny," but to convince New Englanders that their homesteads were in danger of confiscation or
ruinous taxation he was forced to turn on his horrors full blast.
He declared that as soon as port duties had been saddled upon
the colonists quitrents would follow: "If the breath of a british
house of commons can originate an act for taking away all our
money, our lands will go next or be subject to rack rents from
haughty and relentless landlords who will ride at ease, while
we are trodden in the dirt." [30] A British minister might seize
colonial lands to give huge estates to hangers-on at the court,
and New England yeomen be compelled to choose between serf-
dom or the repurchase of their farms from royal favorites.
Those who remained in possession of their estates would find
themselves in worse plight than those who gave up the struggle: such a plague of taxes would descend upon them that
they would soon be degraded into "mere Hewers of Wood and
Drawers of Water" to English landlords. There would be
window taxes, hearth taxes, land taxes, poll taxes, and these
oppressions were simply a prelude "for reducing the country
to lordships." [31]

Although this "perpetual incantation" brewed in Boston by
Sam Adams was one of the most powerful means of transforming rural conservatism into rebellion against Great Britain, the
patriots had little proof to support their fears of crushing taxation and colonial baronies. They attempted to raise an alarm
over the activities of Governor Tryon of New York in ejecting

[30] *The Writings of Samuel Adams*, II, 359. *Boston Gazette*, Dec. 23,
1771; Aug. 17, 1772. Hutchinson, III, 351.
[31] *Independency the Object of the Congress in America* (London, 1776),
18.

settlers in the New Hampshire grants, but the situation there was unique and could hardly be regarded as an instance of British land grabbing that endangered the security of Massachusetts farmers. Adams emphasized the grievances that still existed in Massachusetts Bay to expose the pitfalls in British policy. He pointed out that the Massachusetts charter was still unrecognized by the British government as a "Sacred Ark" of liberty; Admiralty Courts and Commissioners of the Customs continued to enforce "unconstitutional" laws; a fleet and army were stationed in the province without the consent of the House of Representatives; and Parliament kept up its claim to the right of taxation.[32] The root of all colonial grievances, in Adams's eyes, was Parliamentary taxes — "as arbitrary a tribute as ever the Romans laid upon the Jews" — which made the colonists' property insecure.[33] But the tea duty was the only considerable source of revenue that remained of the revenue acts, and Parliament showed little inclination to make further experiments in colonial taxation. Furthermore, however dangerous in tendency, the tea duty was deprived of most of its sting by the smugglers who swarmed in every colonial seaport and supplied the market with Dutch contraband. Indeed, Adams was hard pressed to discover evidence of British oppression with which to arouse the apprehensions of his readers in the *Boston Gazette*. He was forced to go back as far as the Stamp Act in search of padding for those "dreadful scarecrows" which had made Americans tremble for their liberties. Tories rejoiced to see how low Adams was running in propaganda: he was, said Hutchinson, dusting off his old bugbears and "raking the Ashes of Old Newspapers" in quest of a fresh supply of "Chaff & stubble" for his followers.[34] Unquestionably, he needed new tyranny and violent aggression from the mother country before he could hope to regain the ground lost by the nonimportation fiasco and the acquittal of the soldiers. But in only one significant instance did the British government

---

[32] *Massachusetts Spy*, June 4, 1772. *The Writings of Samuel Adams*, II, 33, 53, 76, 184, 312, 313, 316, 317.

[33] *The Writings of Samuel Adams*, II, 184.

[34] Mass. Archives, 27, *Hutchinson Corr.*, III, 126. *Massachusetts Gazette*, June 4, 1772.

oblige Adams by giving him a burning grievance with which to
keep warm the controversy between mother country and colonies.

By means of royal instructions, the Massachusetts General
Court was moved from Boston to Cambridge. Massachusetts
Crown officers had urged for many years that the legislators be
bundled out of the metropolis to some quieter spot where mobs
and Sons of Liberty were rarely seen. Although both Hutchinson and Bernard preferred Salem or Concord to Cambridge as
being farther away from Boston, the British Ministry designated Cambridge as a meeting place for the General Court.
Its removal promised a real-estate boom to Cambridge, but
Harvard College authorities did not welcome the Massachusetts
legislators with open arms: they were reluctant to turn the
college into an arena for Adams's and Hutchinson's squabbles
and to make politicians of a student body "already enough taken
up with politics." [35] Adams himself regarded the removal to
Cambridge as bitterly as though the General Court had been
banished to the wilderness. He declared that the Legislature
had been torn out of its "ancient, established and only convenient
Seat in Boston" and sent to Harvard College "to the great
Inconvenience of the Members, and Injury of the People,
as well as Detriment to that Seminary of Learning." When
the General Court sat in Boston, the country delegates were
so lavishly "dinnered & supper'd" by the town Whigs that
Tories complained they were lured into the radical ranks, and
Hutchinson at one time even considered having the influential
members of the House of Representatives at his table every
day in order to give them an antidote to the "Poison" Adams
and Hancock dished out.[36] In Cambridge, however, the patriots were unable to regale the rural delegates; and the
countrymen were disgruntled to find themselves prevented
from transacting their usual trading business in the metropolis
and saving living expenses by being "treated & caressed" by

[35] Letters from Andrew Eliot to Thomas Hollis, *Mass. Hist. Soc. Collections*, Fourth Series, IV, 447. *Chalmers Papers*, III, Thomas Hutchinson to
Lord Hillsborough, April 9, 1770.
[36] Thomas Cushing to Benjamin Franklin, Nov. 6, 1770, MS. Mass. Hist.
Soc. Peter Oliver, 140. Mass. Archives, 27, *Hutchinson Corr.*, III, 340.

the Boston Whigs. Adams complained that the representatives lost the benefit in Cambridge of listening to "the Reasonings of the People without Doors," but Tories suspected that his discomfiture was principally owing to the fact that he had lost the aid of his "Mohawks" in influencing the voting. But few delegates, whether townsmen or countrymen, relished exchanging their snug quarters in the Boston Town House for the cold, fireless Harvard chapel.[37]

In protesting against the removal of the General Court to Cambridge, Sam Adams struck the shrewdest blow against royal authority that had ever been delivered in the colonies. Because Hutchinson acted under royal instructions in calling the assembly to Cambridge, Adams put forward the doctrine that the royal prerogative could be used only for the good of the community and that whenever it injured the people it was not binding. What stiffened conservatives with alarm was that the community itself, in Adams's eyes, was to judge whether the exercise of the prerogative was beneficial or harmful and to support or nullify as it saw fit. Clearly, Adams argued, the King as well as Parliament was bound by natural laws "antecedent & paramount to all positive Laws of Men."[38] Without the aid of natural law, Adams would have been unable to justify his theory of a prerogative limited by popular consent. Positive law yielded him nothing because royal instructions, in the eighteenth-century British Empire, were regarded as the constitutions of the American provinces and paramount to colonial charters. Hence Adams was compelled to appeal directly to natural law without even a preliminary effort to argue from positive law. He declared that the vast distance between the colonies and mother country had made it impossible for statesmen at Westminster to judge provincial matters: such exercise of the prerogative as proroguing or removing the Massachusetts General Court should be decided by the Massachusetts governor on the spot, not by Lord Hillsborough, who knew

[37] Peter Oliver, 140. *The Writings of Samuel Adams*, II, 27. *Bernard Papers*, VIII, Bernard to Thomas Hutchinson, Oct. 7, 1770. British Museum, King's MSS. 203, Lib. Cong. Transcript, Samuel Cooper to Thomas Pownall, March 26, 1770.

[38] *The Writings of Samuel Adams*, II, 23, 24, 26.

nothing of local conditions and who acted upon stale second-hand information. Adams feared that if instructions were to be made "rules of administration," binding upon colonial legislatures, America would be under a despotism fully as oppressive as Parliament's: between the tyranny of the Crown and the House of Commons there was little to choose.[39] Once royal instructions were recognized as laws, Adams's theory that the constitution must be permanent and fixed was overthrown quite as effectively as though Parliament's enactments were accepted as the supreme law of the colonies: the constitution would be "as vague as the Will of a Minister" and the Massachusetts charter would be little better than a scrap of parchment. The General Court would be put in "a more humiliating state than even the parliaments of France" and the governor of the province would be a puppet moved by the Ministry at Westminster.[40]

Like other Sons of Liberty, Sam Adams was a staunch supporter of royal authority only as long as the King did not exercise his prerogative in the colonies. When the trial came, Adams showed no more reluctance in attacking the Crown's "unconstitutional" powers than Parliament's; and he spoke as early as 1770 of making an "Appeal to Heaven" against George III.[41] It is clear that Adams had little reverence for kingly power: when Parliament threatened colonial liberties, Adams exalted the Crown as the sovereign power, but when the royal prerogative in turn endangered American rights, he was prepared to destroy its jurisdiction. If George III wished to be "King of America" and remain on good terms with Sam Adams, he would have to keep his hands strictly out of colonial affairs and be content to remain a figurehead at the pleasure of Sons of Liberty who were ready to reach for their muskets the moment they believed he had overstepped his powers. After Sam Adams had whittled away the prerogative, George III would have had a slender rod indeed with which to rule his

[39] *The Writings of Samuel Adams*, II, 3, 31, 166, 167, 227.
[40] *Boston Gazette*, Nov. 5, 1770; June 17, 1771; March 4, 1772; March 23, 1772.
[41] *The Writings of Samuel Adams*, II, 22, 23.

American subjects. George soon made it clear that instead of the fragile birch proffered him by Sam Adams, he would be satisfied with nothing less than a stout club to beat loyalty into his seditious overseas subjects.

At the same time that Adams vigorously pared the royal prerogative he was careful not to touch the person of the King. The patriots still kept up the fiction that "good King George" dearly loved Americans and would set matters right in the colonies the moment he got out of the clutches of his ministers. Even Sam Adams solemnly declared that the instructions which sent the General Court to Cambridge were the "subtle Machinations, and daring Encroachments of wicked Ministers" to which the King was an innocent bystander.[42] The people were not yet ready to hear George III denounced as a scoundrel: had Sam Adams openly assailed the King in 1771, he would have alienated the greater part of his followers and convinced English Whigs who supported the colonies in the House of Commons that American Whigs were a set of rebellious republicans bent upon setting up an independent commonwealth. In throwing off Parliament's sovereignty, popular conservatism forced the Whig leaders to move so slowly that it was not until the eve of the Declaration of Independence that Parliament was denied all authority over the colonies. In the difficult operation of slicing away George III's sovereignty over the colonies, even greater delicacy was required. Popular veneration for the Crown compelled Sam Adams to handle George gently and to join in the cry raised by the Sons of Liberty: "We are rebels against parliament; — we adore the king." [43] Nevertheless, some Sons of Liberty had already begun to suspect that George III was the greatest rascal in the kingdom. As early as the Stamp Act days, Thomas Chase, a Son of Liberty and Boston brewer, had expressed the opinion that George was no better than Charles I and deserved the same end. There is no reason to suppose that Sam Adams entertained a much higher

---

[42] *The Writings of Samuel Adams*, II, 33, 34. *Boston Evening Post*, Aug. 20, 1770. *Boston Gazette*, April 27, 1772.
[43] *Orations, delivered at the request of the Inhabitants of the Town of Boston to commemorate the evening of the Fifth of March, 1770* (1807), 7.

regard for the King, in spite of his efforts to make the Crown the sole sovereign of America.   Adams was in close touch with correspondents in England who gave him good grounds for believing that King George was no righteous monarch led astray by his ministers, but a despotical-minded young man who had the Ministry securely in his own pocket.[44]

By denying the King's right to move the General Court about the province at will, Adams startled Hutchinson, who began to fear that royal authority in the colonies would go the way of Parliament's.   It seemed evident that men who denied the King's right to instruct his governors would soon begrudge him the right of appointing them.   Hutchinson was convinced that the struggle between himself and Adams had reached its crisis: if Adams succeeded in blunting the edge of royal prerogative, no Crown officer could stand against the Whigs.   Consequently, the governor was resolved to keep the legislature in Cambridge until the King's right to fix its place of meeting had been positively acknowledged by the General Court.   Sam Adams, on the other hand, was equally determined to march the assembly back to Boston and to take up the cudgels with King George after his successful bouts against George Grenville and Charles Townshend.

Unfortunately for Hutchinson's plans, the Tory revival in Massachusetts had not succeeded in wresting control of the House of Representatives from the Whigs.   Tories recognized that until Sam Adams's hold on the General Court was broken, Massachusetts Bay would not be "as decent & polite" as its neighbors, but few of them showed any eagerness to meet the patriot leader upon his own ground.[45]   Even Ruggles, Worthington, and Murray — redoubtable figures in the "Tory County" of Worcester — remained at a comfortable distance from the House of Representatives.[46]   Hutchinson declared

---

[44] *Chalmers Papers*, III, Information of Richard Silvester. *Samuel Adams Papers*, Arthur Lee to Sam Adams, Dec. 22, 1773. *Boston Gazette*, Aug. 31, 1772.

[45] Mass. Archives, 27, *Hutchinson Corr.*, III, 319. *Israel Williams Papers*, MSS. Mass. Hist. Soc., II, 167.

[46] *Massachusetts Spy*, June 25, 1772.   Mass. Archives, 26, *Hutchinson Corr.*, II, 514; *Ibid.*, 27, III, 332.

that so many of his supporters stayed away that the meetings of the General Court resembled a "rump," but his pleas failed to arouse any considerable number of Tories who were capable of bearding Adams in such a Whig den as the House of Representatives. On almost every question, the patriots were in a majority; the Massachusetts state papers were still filled with the same "seditious spirit" that Adams exhibited in the Boston newspapers; and conservatives continued to be driven out of public life and compelled to "quit the helm to the bold Adventurers." Hutchinson could not even regain possession of the Council, which remained under the control of James Bowdoin, who carried out the orders sent him by that "pale, lean Cassius," Sam Adams.[47]

Sam Adams endangered this Whig supremacy in the House of Representatives by his uncompromising demand that the royal governor return the General Court to Boston regardless of royal instructions. Because Hutchinson stubbornly refused to give way until the Crown's right to move the Assembly had been explicitly recognized, a deadlock was created which sorely tried the patience of the Whig rank and file, many of whom were eager to patch up a compromise which would leave the principle of royal prerogative untouched yet bring the legislature back to Boston. The legislators were anxious to leave their cheerless quarters in Cambridge, and the attack upon the King's authority did not prove as popular in Massachusetts Bay as had the struggle against Parliament. All these circumstances caused murmurings in the Whig Party against Sam Adams's leadership, but the first serious opposition sprang up in an unexpected quarter.

It was James Otis — the erstwhile "American Hampden" — who led the mutiny against Sam Adams. Otis had been carried out of Boston in 1770 in a strait-jacket, but early the next year he popped up again in the metropolis, apparently cured of his insanity, and was promptly elected to the House of Representatives. Otis's reverence for the British Crown had not been

[47] Mass. Archives, 26, *Hutchinson Corr.*, II, 522, 532, 547; III, 6, 164, 330. Andrew Eliot, *op. cit.*, II, Andrew Eliot to Francis Bernard, July 20, 1771.

swept away by the mounting revolutionary fervor in Massachusetts Bay: indeed, his quarrel with John Robinson, the Commissioner of the Customs who had clubbed him in a Boston
tavern, was caused by Otis's indignation upon learning that
Robinson was picturing him to the British government as an
enemy to the King. Such loyalty to the Crown made a break
inevitable between Adams and Otis. In 1771, when Adams
moved in the House of Representatives that no business be done
except in Boston and launched into a bitter tirade against Hutchinson, the patriot benches were startled to see Otis rise in the
governor's defense and declare that the Massachusetts General
Court could be moved anywhere the Crown pleased — even to
"Houssatonick" if it saw fit. Adams's motion was lost, and
although Otis was unable to bring the General Court to end
the quarrel and return to Boston, for a time it seemed that he
might lead a conservative reaction against his former lieutenant.
But the Tories soon saw that Otis was no great catch. Recur-
rent fits of insanity drove him permanently from politics within
a few years. In 1772, he became chairman of the Boston committee of correspondence, but the days when the "great Leviathan" of the Whig Party swayed New England were forever
ended.

Otis's revolt, however, was far less menacing to Sam Adams's
leadership than was John Hancock's flirtation with the Tories.
Hancock, as has been seen, was the financial backer of the
patriot party. But patriotism had proved expensive to him —
putting Adams's affairs to rights had been in itself a costly matter — and he was anxious to recoup his losses by minding his
business, which, in his preoccupation with politics, he had permitted to run down. He had come out of the nonimportation
fiasco with a badly battered reputation — for which he might
thank Sam Adams and other politicians who had egged him on.
Hancock's vanity was hurt and he began to feel that it was not
proper for a gentleman of his wealth and importance to be
on too close terms with politicians who had scarcely a shilling
to lose and who were willing to ruin every merchant in Boston,
himself not excepted, to gain their ends. Then, too, Adams
seemed to be losing ground and Hancock was ambitious of seiz-

ing the Whig command: in 1771, Ezekiel Goldthwait, a Tory, received more than double the number of votes cast for Sam Adams in the election for registrar of deeds for Suffolk County. Tories crowed "like dung-hill cocks" over this victory and Adams's lieutenants began to murmur that his attack upon the royal prerogative was breaking up the Whig Party.[48]   Early in 1771, Hutchinson learned that Hancock and other "heroes of liberty" were ready to turn against Adams and make terms behind his back to return the legislature to the metropolis by acknowledging the King's right.   But Hancock was too good a pupil of Sam Adams's to burn his bridges behind him and rush blindly into Hutchinson's hands: he chose rather to make alliances with both parties and sit safely on the fence as long as it remained doubtful which was to be the winning side.   Nevertheless, Hancock's actions aroused great anxiety among the Whigs: he broke with James Otis; took his legal affairs out of John Adams's hands; was "very civil" to Hutchinson and accepted from him the appointment of colonel of cadets; stayed away from the Whig Club for months at a time and got himself an entirely "new set of acquaintances"; and seemed on the verge of joining the Tory Club.   Still, Hancock did not go so far as to cause a total breach between himself and Sam Adams: even though he voted against Adams in the House of Representatives, he continued to give him occasional lifts in his chariot and left the door open for a future reconciliation.[49]

Hutchinson saw that Hancock was such a rare catch that it would require all his skill in angling to land the Whig leader safely in the Tory basket.   The governor had little hope of making Hancock a whole-hearted Tory because he knew Hancock to be too fond of popularity to choose the forlorn and thorny path trod by Massachusetts Tories.   His plan was rather to lead Hancock on until his reputation as a patriot had been

[48] The Works of John Adams, II, 259.
[49] Israel Williams Papers, II, Thomas Hutchinson to Israel Williams, Jan. 23, 1771.   Andrew Oliver, op. cit., Andrew Oliver to James Gambier, May 8, 1772.   The Writings of Samuel Adams, II, 296.   The Works of John Adams, II, 306.   Mass. Archives, 27, Hutchinson Corr., III, 286. Gordon, III, 20.   Mass. Hist. Soc. Proceedings, XIX, 139.

so utterly ruined that it would be impossible for him to join forces again with Sam Adams.[50]

Hancock probably did not suspect to what use he was to be put by Hutchinson. His only thought was for personal popularity; and in the widespread uneasiness over the deadlock between Adams and Hutchinson at Cambridge he saw his opportunity to make his reputation as a popular leader. He introduced a motion in the House of Representatives that the governor be petitioned to remove the General Court to Boston solely on the ground that Cambridge was inconvenient — thus surrendering the principle at stake between Sam Adams and the governor. Although Adams mustered a small majority to defeat this proposal, Hancock resolved to make another effort. Early in 1772, he and Cushing sounded Hutchinson on his terms for returning the legislature to Boston. They were bluntly told that if they still claimed the right to dictate to His Majesty where the legislature should meet, they would not sit in Boston while Hutchinson was governor of Massachusetts Bay. The governor then warned Hancock and Cushing to beware of Sam Adams's "art and insidiousness," which they would find pitted against them if they attempted to compromise the quarrel.[51] The two Whigs followed Hutchinson's advice, undermined Adams's following in the House of Representatives, and brought the General Court back to Boston in spite of Adams's insistence that it remain in Cambridge without doing business until the home government had acknowledged it had no right to move the legislature from the Boston Town House. Although the victory was not as clear-cut as Hutchinson had hoped for, it was unquestionable that the governor, with the support of the conservative Whigs, had won a two years' struggle against Sam Adams and the radicals.[52]

The radicals were dismayed by this defeat and many hastened to abandon the sinking ship. When it was rumored that the Boston Sons of Liberty were to be punished by the British gov-

---

[50] Mass. Archives, 27, *Hutchinson Corr.*, III, 260, 286, 340.

[51] *Mass. Hist. Soc. Proceedings*, XIX, 138.   Mass. Archives, *Hutchinson Corr.*, III, 342.

[52] Hutchinson, III, 357.

ernment, some of the patriots were heard whispering among themselves that they had indeed gone too far.   The growing antagonism to the metropolis in rural New England disheartened many others: Dr. Thomas Young took passage for North Carolina and Dr. Benjamin Church, another of Adams's trusted disciples, secretly switched to the Tories and began parodying in the Tory newspapers the patriotic songs and political tracts he wrote for the Whigs.   There were "a Languor and feebleness" in Massachusetts, said John Adams, which "discouraged almost every good man in it"; and John Adams himself bid politics farewell, and retired to "still, calm, happy Braintree," thoroughly disillusioned with public life and resolved to mind his farm and office rather than listen again to that siren, Sam Adams, who still attempted to lure him back to Boston politics.[53] Other patriots were so "flattened away" by adversity that they talked more like Tories than Whigs.   As Governor Bernard had said many years before, the Boston Whigs seemed to be an "expiring Faction."

The decline of the Whig Party in Massachusetts was merely a reflection of what was occurring everywhere in the colonies. The New York Sons of Liberty were humbled by the conservatives in 1770; and the Philadelphia patriots, notorious in Boston for their lukewarmness, were unable to breast the current that set in against them after the collapse of the nonimportation agreement.   Even in Virginia, little was heard from the Whigs. Sam Adams was dismayed to find that the Southern newspapers which formerly inculcated Whig doctrines upon the people now contained little more than "Advertisements of the Baubles of Britain for sale."[54]   When Adams urged John Dickinson, the "Pennsylvania Farmer," to rouse the people from "dozing upon the Brink of Ruin," Dickinson politely declined.[55] In attempting to define the limits of Parliamentary authority over the colonies, Adams found that "the Silence of the other Assemblies of late upon every Subject that concerns the joynt

[53] Mass. Archives, 27, *Hutchinson Corr.*, III, 102, 173.   *The Works of John Adams*, II, 256, 257, 260, 305.   *Warren-Adams Letters*, II, 399 (Appendix).

[54] *The Writings of Samuel Adams*, II, 267.

[55] *Ibid.*, II, 392; III, 14.

Interest of the Colonies" made it impossible to determine what principles they held in common. Colonial jealousy again made itself felt, and many Massachusetts patriots suspected that the other colonies were more inclined to take advantage of them than to join with them in defending American liberty. With greater truth than Sam Adams cared to acknowledge, Tories warned New Englanders that if they took a radical step against the mother country they would be deserted by the other colonies, every one of which had made its peace with the British government.[56]

Still, Sam Adams gave no sign that he believed himself to be upholding a lost cause. Even after many of his firmest supporters had begun to give way and rural Massachusetts had turned against the Boston Whigs, he continued to talk as boldly as though he had all British America behind him. "All of them except Adams abate of their virulence," said Hutchinson, but as long as he continued to hold the fort the Tories could not free themselves from the fear that a bombshell would explode unexpectedly in their midst.[57] Adams had already resolved to be the last defender of popular liberty to give up the struggle: the prospect of being outnumbered by his enemies had no terrors for him because he believed it "no Dishonor to be in a minority in the Cause of Liberty and Virtue." "Where there is a Spark of patriotick fire," he exclaimed, "we will enkindle it."[58] Years later, when King George III asked Thomas Hutchinson to what he ascribed Sam Adams's power in New England, Hutchinson replied: "A great pretended zeal for liberty, and a most inflexible natural temper."[59] Tories might doubt the sincerity of Adams's patriotism, but they could not question his tenacity of purpose when he doggedly kept fighting long after the greater part of his followers had found safe seats along the side lines.

Because there was no guarantee of peace while Sam Adams remained in politics, the Tories determined to drive him from the

[56] *The Writings of Samuel Adams*, III, 13. *Massachusetts Gazette*, Feb. 6, 1772.
[57] Mass. Archives, 27, *Hutchinson Corr.*, III, 246.
[58] *Warren-Adams Letters*, I, 9, 14.
[59] *The Diary and Letters of Thomas Hutchinson*, edited by Peter Orlando Hutchinson, I, 167.

House of Representatives. His failure to poll votes in recent elections encouraged them to hope that a full-fledged mutiny might be begun against him in Boston. Their first step was to turn upon Bostonians a deluge of propaganda that matched Sam Adams's best efforts. He was ironically hailed as the *"truly patriotic* DICTATOR*"* of Boston whose predatory raids upon the public treasury had resulted in the "insupportable Town Tax" that had been laid upon the townspeople.[60] Tory partisans reminded the citizens of Sam Adams's readiness to sacrifice the town's commercial prosperity during the nonimportation agreement in order to compel Parliament to grant his impossible demands. "Remember, my beloved Fellow-Citizens," said one of Adams's enemies, "the commercial Trade hath been violently expelled for four Years' past from this Metropolis" and diverted to other seaports by Adams's folly — which should teach the townspeople to be on guard against men who did not have Boston's mercantile prosperity closest to their hearts. Yet, while Boston's trade was sinking and its taxes mounting, Sam Adams, a public defaulter, was permitted to go scot-free, and his henchman, William Molineux, made off with more of the people's money. The rise to power of Adams and his satellites was, in the Tories' eyes, "the most extraordinary phaenomenon that hath appeared in this city, from its foundation"; even Andros and Randolph seemed benevolent in comparison with this "unrelenting Tyrant" who, with his "gang," would "monopolize every town office, suck its vital blood and churn its gore to satiate their unbounded ambition."[61]

Conservatives marched to the polls in 1772 resolved to oust Adams from his seat in the House of Representatives. They failed to achieve this long-desired purge, but they showed alarming strength against Adams. Almost one third of the total votes cast were against Adams, and he received nearly two hundred less votes than the other successful candidates. Thomas Cushing, the conservative patriot who had

[60] *Massachusetts Gazette*, Jan. 2, 1772; March 19, 1772. *Boston Evening Post*, March 23, 1772.

[61] *Massachusetts Gazette*, Feb. 6, 1772; April 19, 1772. *Boston Evening Post*, March 23, 1772.

opposed the war party in the Massachusetts Convention and had joined Hancock in bringing the General Court to Boston, received 699 votes, whereas Adams polled only 505.[62]   It could no longer be doubted that there was still life in "the *court* end of the town" and that Boston was not past saving by the Tories. Heartened by this promising beginning, the conservatives began to form themselves into a "firm, compact body" — a "Phalanx" that seemed likely to become increasingly formidable to the disorganized Whigs.[63]

But, in fact, the Tory Party had reached its high-water mark and a swift ebbing followed this effort to swamp Adams in the Boston elections.   The Tory menace now appeared so threatening that a cry was raised among the rank and file of the Whig Party that Hancock and Adams make peace and present a united front to their enemies.   After some persuasion, the two Whig chiefs were brought together; and to prove that the reconciliation was complete, Hancock commissioned John Copley to paint his and Adams's portraits.   As a final proof of friendship, Hancock hung the pictures side by side in his drawing-room.

Sam Adams blamed the Tories' "scurvy trick of lying" for his quarrel with Hancock.[64]   But Adams always saw Tories at the bottom of any mischief and he held them responsible for evils in which they had no hand.   It is clear that Tories had done no more in 1772 than "blow the coals" that smouldered between Hancock and Adams and hasten a disruption of the Whig Party that had already begun.[65]   As Adams was to learn, the differences between himself and Hancock had not been settled when Hancock hung their pictures together; for fourteen years after the Tories had been exiled and the colonies made independent of the mother country, the two men were to be the

[62] *Massachusetts Gazette*, May 7, 1772. *Boston Town Records*, 18th Report of the Record Commissioners (1887), 78.

[63] Andrew Oliver, *op. cit.*, II, Andrew Oliver to James Gambier, May 8, 1772. *Boston Gazette*, Nov. 18, 1771. Hutchinson, III, 356. *Otis Papers*, MSS. Mass. Hist. Soc., Samuel Allyne Otis to Joseph Otis, April 15, 1771.

[64] *The Writings of Samuel Adams*, III, 23.

[65] Mass. Archives, 27, *Hutchinson Corr.*, III, 260.

bitterest political enemies in New England. Actually there was little real friendship between Adams and Hancock: Hancock was eager to snatch the leadership of the patriot party from a man whom he secretly regarded as a plebeian wire-puller; and Adams, although he prized Hancock as a figurehead and financial godfather to the Whigs, distrusted him for a flighty young man of fashion whose life and ideals were decidedly un-Puritan. The two leaders had very different goals: Adams's purpose was to resurrect old-fashioned manners and morals and found a Puritan republic, whereas Hancock's dominant motive was to make himself popular and place himself at the head of a fashionable aristocracy. So divergent were Adams's and Hancock's aspirations that, after the Revolution, they were to pursue each other as relentlessly as they had once hounded Tories together.

X

THE COMMITTEES OF CORRESPONDENCE

HANCOCK was once more back in the patriot fold after his flirtation with the Tories, but the Whig Party was still in the grip of depression. British tyranny was essential to the prosperity of Adams and the Whigs, yet the mother country seemed to have buried its dispute with the colonies. It would have been fortunate for the British Empire had this policy of "let sleeping dogs lie" been continued in the colonies. Since 1768, significant changes had taken place in Adams's attitude toward Great Britain which boded ill for the peace of the British Empire if the schemes of Grenville and Townshend were again revived by British imperialists.

After Lord North and the Tory Party came into power in England in 1770, Adams lost all faith in the British government and people. With Tory squires and placemen swarming in the House of Commons and edging Whigs out of high office, Adams considered that England was well on the way to a "total Depravation of principles & manners," if not already "irrecoverably undone." He no longer believed, as he had in 1766, that the colonists should pin their faith to British parliamentarians who had "distinguished themselves as the Guardians, under his Majesty, of the Rights of British American Subjects."[1] Instead of urging Americans to trust to the Whigs at Westminster, Adams now deplored the state of mind which manifested itself in "anxiously waiting for some happy Event" in England, after it had become clear that no good could be expected from the mother country. If Americans were to wait for justice from England, Adams exclaimed, they would wait until doomsday or until they had become "so accustomed to bondage, as to forget

[1] *The Writings of Samuel Adams*, I, 178; II, 230–233.

they were ever free." He regarded the House of Commons, traditionally the guardian of English liberty, as a tool in the Ministry's hands, bought and paid for by King George. Rather than lean upon the broken reed of English Whiggery, Adams declared that "America herself under God must finally work out her own Salvation" and fight her battle for liberty unassisted by English liberals.[2]

The regularity with which the colonies' petitions to King and Parliament reached the wastebasket of the Colonial Secretary soured Adams toward further petitioning for redress of grievances. "For God's sake," he asked, "what are we to expect from petitioning?" When the matter of an appointment of an agent to represent Massachusetts in London came before the General Court in 1770, Adams favored dropping the colonial agent altogether and waiting the British government's moves "with a Sullen Silence" until the ministers should find themselves *"at the end* of their Tether." It was not merely "ye Inutility of all remonstrances & Negotiations" that prompted Adams to throw over colonial agents, but the character of the man Massachusetts wished to make its London representative.[3] Benjamin Franklin was always disliked by the Adamses: John Adams believed him to be a scandalous old rake and Sam Adams distrusted him as a Tory at heart. Franklin was suspected by Massachusetts radicals of being a tool of Lord Hillsborough or, at best, one of those lukewarm Whigs whom Sam Adams feared more than outright Tories. They exclaimed that he was "not for their turn" and published such violent squibs against him in the *Boston Gazette* that Thomas Hutchinson, whose friendship with Franklin dated back to the Albany Congress of 1754, became convinced that his old friend would find serving as Massachusetts agent very painful "unless he will go all their lengths."[4]

Adams soon saw that the Massachusetts House of Representa-

[2] *The Writings of Samuel Adams,* II, 190, 267.

[3] *The Writings of Samuel Adams,* II, 283. *Letters of Samuel Cooper to Pownall and Franklin* (1770–1774), Bancroft Collection, N. Y. Public Library, Samuel Cooper to Thomas Pownall, Oct. 12 and Nov. 5, 1770. *Samuel Adams Papers,* Samuel Cooper to Thomas Pownall, Sept. 8, 1769.

[4] Mass. Archives, 27, *Hutchinson Corr.,* III, 240, 241, 246.

tives could not be persuaded to sever itself completely from English affairs. Since the legislators wished to keep an agent in the mother country, Adams's choice fell upon Arthur Lee, a young Virginian resident in London who had convinced Massachusetts Whigs of his sterling patriotism by making virulent attacks in the newspapers under the signature "Junius Americanus" upon British and American Tories. Adams and his followers pushed Lee for office as "the only Man for he will go through with it." Franklin, in their opinion, would only go halfway. But in spite of their opposition, Franklin's friends in the House of Representatives were able to secure his appointment as agent with Lee as substitute in case of Franklin's death or absence. Sam Adams always preferred to correspond with the substitute rather than with the regular agent, and Lee soon became his most trusted adviser on English affairs. Lee possessed certain faults of temperament which made him an untrustworthy correspondent. He was a highly excitable young man, whose fiery Whiggish outlook distorted his view of British politics. His judgments of men were frequently at fault; he was constantly engaged in bitter quarrels; and he was suspicious of everyone's integrity except his own. His lively fancy pictured all British Tories, from the King down, as plotting deliberately to make the American colonists slaves. His letters put such black construction upon the acts of the British government that Sam Adams was kept constantly in alarm for colonial liberty and was convinced that nothing but oppression could be expected from the mother country. Adams paid no heed to the more reasoned judgments of cooler men; Arthur Lee appeared to him to be an "able and stanch Advocate for the Rights of America & Mankind" and he never ceased to place implicit reliance on Lee's opinion of British colonial policy.[5]

The British government was eager to believe that the Massachusetts Whig Party was an "expiring Faction," and Hutchinson's letters describing the steady progress of Toryism in the colony encouraged British imperialists to try fresh experiments. In 1771, the Ministry determined to make Governor Hutchin-

[5] *Boston Gazette*, April 6, 1772.

son financially independent of the colonial legislature by paying his salary as governor from the revenue collected by the Commissioners of the Customs.   From the standpoint of imperial efficiency, this was a highly desirable cure for the ills that beset colonial administration, but it touched New Englanders in a sore spot and raised again the spectre of centralization of the Empire.   Throughout the eighteenth century, successive British ministers had attempted to change the system in force in Massachusetts Bay, where an appointed governor and elected house wrangled almost without intermission for whole administrations.   In relieving Governor Hutchinson of financial dependence upon the Massachusetts legislature, Lord Hillsborough accomplished what most of his predecessors had attempted to do.   But even a smattering of Massachusetts history would have told Hillsborough that the power of the purse was one of the most jealously prized of colonial rights and that every effort to seize it immediately put the most radical colonial leaders in power.   With Sam Adams and his "Mohawks" famishing for want of grievances, Hillsborough's interference in Massachusetts Bay was uncommonly ill-timed.   Nothing was more certain to keep the revolutionary pots boiling than an independent governor paid by the Crown out of "unconstitutional" taxes collected by the hated Commissioners of the Customs.

When Adams learned that the power of the purse had been taken from the Massachusetts House of Representatives he exclaimed that Massachusetts was in the grip of a "perfect Despotism" and began to beat the old alarm that had made generations of New Englanders quake for their liberties.   If Hutchinson were permitted to draw his salary from Westminster instead of from the Commons at Boston, Adams warned, the checks and balances of the Massachusetts constitution would be utterly destroyed and the governor freed from all control by the people: the only thing that would then prevent Hutchinson from becoming the Cæsar of Massachusetts Bay was that Cæsar, "to do him justice, had learning, courage, and great abilities."   Adams was fully vindicated as a prophet of English oppression: the governor of New York was given a royal salary, and Benjamin Franklin wrote that there was no longer doubt of the intention

of the British government to make all colonial governors independent of the legislatures as soon as the expense could be
met from the American revenue. Adams's fancy pictured the
American colonies plunged into "abject slavery," ruled by
petty despots who looked to George III as satraps to an "Asiat-
ick Monarch." [6] The prospect was so dire that Adams could
find a parallel only in his favorite "dreadful example," the
Roman Catholic Church: the payment of royal governors by the
Crown was similar to the Pope's giving the King of England
an annual gift provided he turned "papist." Adams's apprehensions were not altogether groundless, for it seemed likely
that in putting the governors beyond popular control, the British government was merely taking the first step in a policy that
would eventually make judges, armies, fleets, and a host of petty
officials dependent only upon the Crown; and they, in turn,
would pave the way for such abominations as "episcopates &
their numerous ecclesiastic retinue; pensioners, placemen and
other jobbers, for an abandon'd and shameless ministry; hirelings, pimps, parasites, panders, prostitutes and whores." After
the colonies were swarming with this "vermin," the House of
Commons would begin in earnest to enforce acts of Parliament
in the colonies, "where they have no more Just Authority than
they have in Jerusalem." [7]

Adams gave Hutchinson little opportunity to enjoy the fruits
of royal bounty. He made the governor known the length and
breadth of the province as King George's "first American Pensioner" — with the result that even thrifty New England farmers who thought it would be a good thing for taxpayers if the
Crown paid the governor's salary were thoroughly frightened.
Hutchinson felt Adams's sting even in his own home. Better
to attend his official duties, Hutchinson moved from his Milton
house to the Province House in Boston, which had fallen into
a bad state of disrepair. At Hutchinson's request, the House of
Representatives appointed a committee to view the house to de-

[6] *The Writings of Samuel Adams*, II, 135, 252, 278, 280. *Boston
Gazette*, April 15, 1771.
[7] *The Writings of Samuel Adams*, II, 247, 280. *Boston Gazette*, Dec. 21,
1772.

termine what repairs were necessary, but unfortunately for Hutchinson Adams was made a member of the committee of inspection. Adams prevented the committee from handing in its report and forestalled every later effort to have the governor's house repaired in spite of Hutchinson's wails that it was "a dishonour to His Majesty's Commission that the Governor lives in it in its present state." Adams justified this treatment on the ground that, by accepting a salary from the Crown, Hutchinson ceased to be the constitutional governor of the province and merited no favors from the legislature. But, he let it be understood, Hutchinson had only to refuse the royal salary in order to enjoy a house "not barely tenantable, but elegant," at the expense of the Commons of Massachusetts Bay.[8]

In 1772, while Adams was making political capital out of Hutchinson's pension, a rumor reached Boston that the judges of the Massachusetts superior court were likewise to be made independent of the legislature for their support. The judges, like other public officers whose salaries were set by the General Court, were grievously underpaid: their wages, said one, were like "the Wages of Sin, for no Man could get a living by them."[9] The combined stipends of Hutchinson's three offices scarcely enabled him to maintain his household, but the judges of the superior court were so meanly paid that they got little more than a bare living. Peter Oliver's salary as judge of the superior court was inadequate to support his family, yet the Massachusetts House of Representatives ignored or denied his pleas for higher pay. Because of this niggardly aid from the General Court, the Massachusetts judges were overjoyed when it was reported they were to receive a fixed salary from the customhouse revenue.

The rumor that the Crown was about to pay the salaries of the Massachusetts judges gave Adams the opportunity he had long been waiting. It was true that he had only a rumor to work upon, but Adams had the gift of dressing hearsay and tavern gossip into fact in the pages of the *Boston Gazette*. His

[8] Mass. Archives, 27, *Hutchinson Corr.*, III, 60, 363. *The Writings of Samuel Adams*, II, 331, 332.
[9] Peter Oliver, 46.

strong inclination to believe the worst of the British government's
intentions toward the colonies wiped away any doubt that the
judges were to share in the revenue collected by the Commissioners of the Customs.   Adams was not disposed to wait
for confirmation of this latest tyranny, for it gave him fresh
supply of propaganda after the wearisome diet of "Chaff &
stubble" and hashed-over grievances he had been compelled
to foist upon his followers.   For the first time since the Boston
Massacre he had a stirring issue with which to reinvigorate the
Whig Party.   Since 1768, Adams had waved the bugbear before New Englanders of an independent, and therefore presumably arbitrary, judiciary.   The Massachusetts judges did
not hold office during good behavior as did English judges —
they were removable only at the Crown's pleasure.   But an
even more disquieting circumstance was that the Massachusetts
judiciary was filled with Hutchinson's relations: the Lyndes,
Olivers, Cottons, and Hutchinson himself occupied the most
important offices.   If such "oligarchs" were made independent
of the legislature, Sam Adams confidently looked forward to
seeing another Jeffreys riding a "bloody circuit" in New England.   It was no wonder, then, that the rumor of royal salaries
for the judges became a call to arms to Massachusetts patriots:
Boston Sons of Liberty raised the cry that the British government had aimed a "FINISHING STROKE" at American liberty
which would make the colonists "as complete slaves as the inhabitants of Turkey or Japan."   The Ministry appeared to
have created an emergency that made the do-nothing policy of
the "half-way Whigs" as dangerous as that of the Tories: Sam
Adams must again take command and "NOW strike a home blow,
or sit down under the yoke of Tyranny." [10]

Sam Adams's home thrust at British tyranny was the establishment of the committees of correspondence.   Corresponding committees had been used by American patriots from the beginning of the controversy with the mother country: merchants'
corresponding committees had organized resistance to the Sugar

[10] *The Writings of Samuel Adams*, III, 30.   *Boston Gazette*, May 5,
1771; Oct. 19, 1772; Nov. 2, 1772.

Act of 1764 and the Sons of Liberty had covered the colonies with a network of societies whose circular letters and secret correspondence were one of the most striking manifestations of colonial unity during the Stamp Act period. In 1770, Sam Adams had broached to confidential friends a plan of committees of correspondence which would embrace England as well as America, but his loss of confidence in English Whigs led him to drop the British connection in favor of a purely colonial institution which, originating in Massachusetts, would extend over all British America. The first step in this ambitious undertaking was to link the towns of Massachusetts Bay together so closely that they would present a solid "phalanx" to the British government — "a band of brothers, which no force can break, no enemy destroy." [11] Once Adams's radical followers — under the name of committees of correspondence — were in power in every Massachusetts town, the whole colony would act in concert with Boston and the rural representatives would be sent down to the General Court with instructions to join the metropolis in whatever measures it took to oppose the mother country. With committees of correspondence ruling the province there would be little danger of the country deserting Boston in an emergency. Such union between town and country would exhilarate the Whig morale, which, since the failure of patriot policies after the Massacre, had reached a low ebb. Those "timid sort of people" who made the country's antagonism to Boston a justification for inactivity would be silenced by proof that New England yeomen were ready to support the metropolis, and the radical Whigs promised themselves that a "plan of Opposition will be easily formed, & executed with Spirit." [12] Bernard's taunt that the Massachusetts patriot party was an "expiring faction" still rankled Adams and he was eager to show Americans that Massachusetts Whigs were still as fiery patriots as in the days of the Massachusetts circular letter. Lastly, Adams hoped to rout the Tories by means of the committees of correspondence. When they saw "the flame burst-

[11] *Boston Gazette*, Oct. 19, 1772.
[12] *The Writings of Samuel Adams*, II, 347.

ing in different parts of the Country" simultaneously, they could do nothing to check its spread.[13]

Yet few Whigs agreed with Sam Adams that the iron was sufficiently hot to strike such a heavy blow at British authority in Massachusetts. Almost single-handed, and against the opposition of most of his lieutenants, Adams brought forth the Boston committee of correspondence and thereby hatched the "foulest, subtlest, and most venomous serpent ever issued from the egg of sedition." [14] Most Boston Whigs regarded Sam Adams's plan of appointing a committee of correspondence "to state the rights of the colonists, and of this province in particular, as men and Christians, and as subjects," as political dynamite that was likely to explode in their own hands before they could plant it under the Tories; if the country failed to follow Boston's example in appointing a committee of correspondence, the patriot cause would suffer a setback that might permanently cripple it.[15] The more cautious patriots protested against risking the future of the Whig Party on a rumor that might well prove to be false: no one knew for certain that the judges were to be paid by the Crown, yet Adams was ready to gamble everything on the chance that the report was true. These arguments satisfied the majority of Sons of Liberty, and when Adams petitioned for a town meeting to establish the committee of correspondence, the Boston selectmen, John Hancock among them, flatly refused to consent to call the townspeople together for so seditious a purpose. Even after the town meeting had been summoned, Adams failed twice to win a favorable vote. At the third adjournment, Adams saw his opportunity: only a handful of citizens now remained in Faneuil Hall, and this rump consisted of a majority of his followers. While Adams held this momentary advantage the motion to appoint a committee of correspondence was rushed through the town meeting — an instance of how an aggressive minority triumphs over an unorganized majority. Nevertheless, throughout its existence,

[13] *The Writings of Samuel Adams*, II, 350; III, 43.
[14] *Massachusetts Gazette*, Jan. 2, 1775. Mass. Archives, 27, *Hutchinson Corr.*, III, 461.
[15] Gordon, I, 312–313.

the Boston committee of correspondence bore the stigma of having been midwifed into the world by Sam Adams while most
of the townspeople had their backs turned.[16]

Even this victory did not remove all obstacles from Adams's
path.   There remained the knotty problem of finding men
to serve on the committee of correspondence.   So few wished
for the honor that for a time it seemed not unlikely that only
Adams would accept.   Cushing, Phillips, and Hancock declined
their elections by pleading business — a lame excuse that failed
to conceal their real fears that the committee would come to
a bad end.   But Adams — the "grand Incendiary of the Province" who had carried the scheme to the verge of success on his
own shoulders — was not to be turned back by a few timorous
Whigs: a meeting of the leading patriots was hurriedly called,
the courage of the faint-hearted was screwed up by Sam Adams,
and a list of those willing to run the risk of serving on the committee of correspondence was sent down to the town meeting.

Twenty-one patriots, with James Otis as chairman, were
elected by the townspeople to serve upon the committee of
correspondence.   From the beginning, James Otis took little
part in the committee's work and most of the other members
delegated their authority to sub committees of radical Whigs
dominated by Sam Adams, William Cooper, and Thomas Young.
Hutchinson declared that this clique boasted "as black-hearted
fellows as any upon the Globe"; and he resolved to stay out of
dark alleys when members of the committee of correspondence
were abroad.[17]   These Whigs who struck such terror among the
Tories met in the Boston selectmen's chambers or at William
Molineux's house.   Their meetings usually lasted from six
to nine-thirty in the evening; and, no matter how urgent the
occasion, the committee scrupulously observed the New England
custom of ceasing work from Saturday until an hour after sundown on the Lord's Day.   All committeemen were sworn to
such strict secrecy that the citizens were kept completely in the
dark as to their doings.   By hedging itself behind this
mystery the committee laid itself open to suspicion that it was

---

[16] *Boston Gazette*, Nov. 9, 1772.
[17] Mass. Archives, 27, *Hutchinson Corr.*, III, 412.

making away with large sums of money belonging to the town
of Boston, as Sam Adams had done a decade before.   Stung by
this accusation, the committee voted to charge the town only
for "ye Candles & Firing" used during the meetings and
to tax the members a dollar apiece for the purchase of "Some
Rhode Island Beer."   As final proof of good faith, the clerk
was directed to bring in the account "of the Expence already incurred for Liquours." [18]   Having thus fortified themselves for
the business of combating tyranny, Adams and his friends proceeded to make the committee of correspondence the most formidable revolutionary machine that was created during the
American Revolution.

Sam Adams's first move was to draw up a declaration of colonial rights and grievances which, in his hands, swelled to such
a "great twelve-penny book" that Solicitor General Wedderburn said Adams told New Englanders of "a hundred rights,
of which they never had heard before, and a hundred grievances which they never before had felt." [19]   Had Wedderburn
been a Bostonian he would have found most of the grievances
familiar, but even a Bostonian might well have been startled
by Adams's boldness of tone in stating colonial rights.   As
Wedderburn said, Adams had produced "a set of ready drawn
heads of a declaration for any one colony in America, or any
one distant county in the kingdom, which shall chuse to revolt
from the British Empire, and say that they will not be governed
by the King and Parliament at Westminster."   Adams now
brushed aside all arguments from positive law and placed his
claim squarely upon natural rights "exclusive of all charters
from the Crown."   Conservatives had always dreaded the doctrine of natural law as a great cornucopia of revolutionary principles, but it remained for Sam Adams, delving far deeper than
had James Otis, to draw from it a full justification of American
rebellion.   It was indeed disquieting for British imperialists to
hear Sam Adams shouting in the colonies that by a law of
nature "all Men have a Right to remain in a State of Nature

[18] *Committee of Correspondence Papers,* Jan. 12, 1773; Feb. 1, 1773.
[19] *Letters of Governor Hutchinson and Lieutenant Governor Oliver*
(London, 1774), 113.

as long as they please: And in case of intollerable Oppression, Civil or Religious, to leave the Society they belong to, and enter into another." [20]   Sam Adams had already made an "Appeal to Heaven" against the British government and it was clear that if he were to judge when "intollerable Oppression" justified rebellion, an upheaval in the colonies was not far distant.

Sam Adams was keenly aware that rural New England was the battleground on which the fate of the committees of correspondence would be decided.   Far from sharing Adams's confidence that the committees would sweep the country, many Boston Whigs expected the scheme to meet with a resounding defeat at the hands of Massachusetts farmers because rural patriotism was dead "and the Dead cant be raised without a Miracle." [21]   As these cautious patriots feared, Tory squires did not give way to the committees of correspondence without a struggle.   "New made Colonels," stiff in fresh militia regimentals, came to town to persuade the farmers not to be dragged into rebellion by holding to Boston's skirts.   They swore that country people had been "too often imposed upon by Boston," where a few pushing Whigs were perpetually bearding King George and Parliament and were now trying to snare unwary New Englanders in a plan that had been approved by only a handful of the Boston "rabble." [22]   Edward Bacon, the Tory representative from Barnstable in the General Court, made a particularly bitter attack upon Boston patriots which promptly brought him into hot water with the Boston committee of correspondence.   Bacon said that William Molineux and Thomas Young were "men of no Principles and Infamous Characters" and urged that Barnstable refuse to correspond with "the Vilest of men." [23]   Bacon later remarked that he preferred to have his master three thousand miles away than in Boston and sneered

---

[20] *Letters of Hutchinson and Oliver*, 113. *The Writings of Samuel Adams*, II, 351.

[21] *Warren-Adams Letters, Mass. Hist. Soc. Collections*, LXXIII (1925); II, 401 (Appendix).

[22] *Boston Evening Post*, Jan. 18, 1773; Feb. 8, 1883.   Mass. Archives, 25, *Hutchinson Corr.*, I, Peter Oliver to Thomas Hutchinson, Dec. 12, 1772.

[23] *Committee of Correspondence Papers*, James Otis to William Molineux, March 11, 1773.

that "Adams was worth but little if his Debt was paid and that it was for his interest to contend with them in this way in order to get a Living." [24]   After having thus taken most of the leading Boston Whigs through the mud, Bacon incautiously came up to the metropolis. The Boston committee of correspondence was waiting for him to show himself in town and he was immediately haled before it. Behind the closed doors of the committee's chamber, Adams and Molineux procured from Bacon a written denial that he had ever slandered the high-ranking Whigs of the metropolis. This retraction was printed and sent to the districts where it was expected to do the most good, but its beneficial effect was largely nullified by a persistent rumor that it was either a forgery or had been bludgeoned out of Bacon while he was detained in the committee's chamber.[25]

Hutchinson had no better success than Tory squires in stopping the spread of committees of correspondence over New England. When he denounced the Boston committee for seizing authority that belonged rightfully to the Crown, Sam Adams quoted natural law to justify the usurpation: that "great and perpetual Law of Self preservation to which every Person or corporate Body hath an inherent Right" gave the people authority to establish committees of correspondence and adopt all other measures necessary to oppose tyranny.[26] Although at first the committees spread so slowly in rural New England that Hutchinson believed Adams had lured the Whigs into "such a foolish scheme that they must necessarily make themselves ridiculous," the governor soon realized his error. The propaganda with which Adams had steadily drenched New Englanders since the Stamp Act now brought forth a bumping crop. Plymouth was the first town outside of Boston to appoint a committee of correspondence, and it was followed by Cambridge, Marblehead, Charlestown, Newburyport, and a host of smaller towns throughout New England. By 1774, the Boston com-

[24]*Publications Col. Soc. of Mass.* (1894), XXV, 312.
[25] *Committee of Correspondence Papers*, James Greenleaf to James Otis, June 22, 1773; Bacon's Certificate, June 1, 1773. *Publications Col. Soc. of Mass.*, XXV, 265–348.
[26] *The Writings of Samuel Adams*, III, 5, 6, *Chalmers Papers*, VI, Thomas Hutchinson to Lord Dartmouth, Oct. 23, 1772.

mittee of correspondence was in communication with more than
three hundred towns in Massachusetts alone, besides carrying
on an intercolonial correspondence with Sons of Liberty as far
south as Charleston, South Carolina.   Thus, lamented Hutchinson, "was the Contagion which began in Boston" diffused
over the continent.   "All on a sudden," he exclaimed, "from
a state of peace, order, and general contentment . . . the province, more or less from one end to the other, was brought into
a state of contention, disorder, and general dissatisfaction." [27]

The committees of correspondence mark the rejuvenation of
the Whig Party in the American colonies and the reappearance
of Sam Adams as a serious menace to the stability of the British
Empire.   As Adams himself said, the committees diverted the
people's attention from "picking up pins, and directed their
Views to great objects" — with the result that politics again
became the besetting passion of New Englanders and "the Genius of Liberty" was once more "Roused after a Languor if not
a profound Sleep." [28]   Sam Adams was once more regarded as
the watchdog of New England's liberties, alert to all British
"Schemes to Subvert our happy Constitution."   With Adams
on the lookout, the Boston committee never lacked alarming
rumors of impending British tyranny which, when sent over
the network of corresponding committees, kept New Englanders constantly on edge for their liberties.   As soon as the local
committee received word from Boston of the plots being hatched
by British ministers against colonial freedom, the town meeting
was called and instructions were rushed to the representatives in
the General Court to uphold Sam Adams's policies against the
mother country.   For the benefit of backward towns, the Boston committee sent out circular letters containing political doctrines which Adams judged proper for rural patriots.   The
answers that poured into Boston from the interior were highly
gratifying to Sam Adams, who had gambled everything on the
hope that the rural districts would again become a hotbed of

[27] Mass. Archives, *Hutchinson Corr.*, III, 412, 431, 465.   Hutchinson,
III, 370 (note).

[28] *Warren-Adams Letters*, I, 245.   *Committee of Correspondence Papers*,
Boston Committee to the Sandwich Committee, March 9, 1774: Plymouth
Committee to the Boston Committee, April 8, 1773.

Whiggery; but Wedderburn found the resolves of the country
towns "full of the most extravagant absurdities, Such as the enthusiastic rant of the wildest of my countrymen in Charles the
2d's days cannot equal." [29]   In particular, the resolves of the
town of Pembroke horrified Wedderburn and delighted Sam
Adams.   "This people are warranted," the Pembroke citizens
declared, "by the laws of God and nature, in the use of every
rightful art and energy of *Policy, Stratagem,* and *Force.*" [30]

But while Adams thus educated New Englanders in "Boston
principles" he was careful to lead the country people to believe
that instead of being led by Boston they themselves were in
reality the leaders.   Bostonians had no wish, said Adams, to
"obtrude *their* Opinions upon their Fellow-Countrymen," and
he flattered the village Hampdens by assuring them that their
"resolution to oppose Tyranny in all its forms is worthy the
Imitation of this Metropolis."   In his letters to rural patriots
he skillfully soothed their distrust of the metropolis and over-
came their unwillingness to be led by town folk into a quarrel
with the mother country.   He always spoke of back-country
Whigs as his "sensible Brethren in the Country" or as his
"worthy & much esteemed Brethren." [31]   Indeed, if Sam Adams
were to be believed, the Boston Sons of Liberty were merely
responding to pressure from the country people in provoking
controversy with Great Britain.

As has been said, Sam Adams hoped to extend committees
of correspondence throughout the colonies if the experiment
succeeded in Massachusetts Bay.   At the first opportunity, he
planned to introduce a resolution in the General Court that a
circular letter be sent to all the provincial assemblies urging that
committees of correspondence be appointed. [32]   But here Adams
was anticipated by the Virginia patriots.   As early as 1768,
Richard Henry Lee of Virginia had suggested that the colonies
ought to establish committees for intercolonial correspondence.
Adams's success in Massachusetts convinced Lee, Patrick Henry,

[29] *Letters of Hutchinson and Oliver,* 113.
[30] *Ibid.,* 114.
[31] *The Writings of Samuel Adams,* III, 16, 17, 32.
[32] *Ibid.,* II, 380.   Mass. Archives, 27, *Hutchinson Corr.,* III, 437.

and Thomas Jefferson that the time was ripe to carry out this plan.   Early in 1773, therefore, they introduced resolutions in the Virginia House of Burgesses establishing a committee of correspondence and inviting the other provincial legislatures to do likewise.   This proposal met with instant favor throughout the continent and almost every colonial assembly appointed corresponding committees.[33]

The action of the Virginia House of Burgesses in initiating intercolonial committees of correspondence has provoked controversy between historians of the Old Dominion and the Bay State as to whether Virginia or Massachusetts can lay best claim to having created the mainspring which later pushed the colonies into revolution.   Sam Adams supposed that Massachusetts had inspired Virginia, but there is good reason to believe that the Virginia patriots were acting upon ideas that had been clearly formulated in their minds many years before.   But the matter is of slight importance.   The colonies were not revolutionized by the committees of correspondence that were created by the colonial legislatures acting upon the suggestion of the Virginia House of Burgesses: they corresponded little and most of the letters they interchanged are formal in nature and of relatively small interest.   The committees of correspondence that made the American Revolution possible were the town committees dominated by local "Sam Adamses" who were in close touch with Boston and other centres of radicalism.   These committees owed their origin to Sam Adams rather than to the Virginia Whigs.   Without their aid it is doubtful if the first Continental Congress would have been held in 1774 and the revolutionary movement in the colonies brought to its fruition in the Declaration of Independence.   They made possible the domination of a great part of British America by cliques of radical patriots who looked to Sam Adams for leadership against the mother country.   These committees were a direct outgrowth of the intercolonial unity that had been seen in the military alliances and corresponding committees of the Sons of Liberty during the Stamp Act.   After 1774, the colonies fairly bristled

[33] *Dictionary of American Biography*, Richard Henry Lee (1933), XI, 117–120.

with hot-tempered Liberty Boys, who, instead of calling themselves Sons of Liberty, were now known as the committees of
correspondence. But under whatever name these patriots
worked, their purpose remained the same: to defend colonial
liberty with arms rather than submit to British "tyranny."

The creation by provincial assemblies of committees of correspondence upon the Virginia model encouraged Adams to take
a bold step in political radicalism. The resolves of the Virginia
House of Burgesses in 1773 were the first sign given Adams
for several years that patriotism was reviving in the Southern
colonies. Instead of finding nothing but advertisements for
British "Baubles" in Southern newspapers, he was now overjoyed to see Whig political principles coming back into favor.
Once more he looked forward to colonial unity against the
British government: "There is now," he wrote after learning
of the Virginia resolves, "a fairer prospect than ever of an
Union among the Colonies." [34] Virginia gave him new hope
that "the Fire of true Patriotism" would sweep the colonies as
in the days of the Stamp Act, and he took the opportunity to
level a particularly aggressive attack upon the British government. It has been seen that as early as 1765 the Sons of Liberty regarded the King as the only bond between mother country and colonies and that only the slowness of public opinion
prevented Sam Adams from openly declaring that Parliament
had no authority whatever in the colonies. But in 1773, after
the committees of correspondence had begun to sow political
radicalism in the colonial mind, Adams judged the hour had
struck to speak frankly. He now declared that the King was
the sole sovereign of America and that each colonial legislature
was a parliament completely independent of the Lords and
Commons at Westminster. Indeed, Adams insisted that Parliament had never had any rightful authority in the colonies: if
Americans had submitted to its laws it was "rather from incon-
sideration, or a reluctance at the idea of contending with the
parent state, than from a conviction or acknowledgment of the
Supreme Legislative authority of Parliament." He denied
that the dissolution by Parliament in 1741 of the Massachusetts

[34] *The Writings of Samuel Adams*, III, 21.

Land Bank formed a precedent for Parliament's jurisdiction over the colonies: the Massachusetts House of Representatives had not carried out in its full severity Parliament's Bubble Act, but had passed an act of its own which, Adams insisted, was directly contrary to the intentions of the British government.[35] Had not Adams been so intent upon making out a case against Parliamentary authority, perhaps he would have remembered that the Massachusetts Land Bank had been destroyed solely by Parliamentary legislation and that, even after the Massachusetts House of Representatives had mitigated the Bubble Act, the Adamses had been harassed for two decades by the Land Bank Commissioners.   In keeping with the Massachusetts General Court's dignity as the "Parliament" of the province, Adams now called the House of Representatives "his majesty's commons"; the debates he styled "parliamentary debates"; acts of Parliament became "acts of the British Parliament"; and the province laws were termed "the laws of the land."[36]   By means of the committees of correspondence, Adams made the watchword in Massachusetts Bay: "Freedom from every legislature on Earth but that of the province." "Equal liberty" with Great Britain now meant that the power of the British Parliament be confined to the realm and its claim of authority in the colonies surrendered to a dozen or more provincial assemblies which exercised with the King full sovereignty within their borders.   Unless the mother country recognized this principle, Adams said that Americans ought to feel themselves treated "as bastards and not Sons."[37]   He had no doubt, however, that if Great Britain adopted his ideas of how colonies should be governed, the mother country and provinces would "live happily in that connection, and mutually support and protect each other."[38]   But before this Utopia could be attained, Parliament must repeal the Declaratory Act, acknowledge it had no authority over the colonies, and recognize King George as "King of America."

[35] *The Writings of Samuel Adams*, II, 423, 424, 451.
[36] Hutchinson, III, 413 (note).
[37] *The Writings of Samuel Adams*, II, 55.
[38] *Ibid.*, II, 424.

Adams's conception of the relationship between mother country and colonies foreshadowed the connection between Great
Britain and the Dominions in the modern British Empire; but
England was not prepared in 1773 to adopt Adams's revolutionary ideas of imperial government. The mercantilist system
under which Great Britain had developed her colonial empire
was based upon the principle that colonies were worth only
what the mother country received from them; and Englishmen
had not yet given up hope that a considerable revenue could
be extracted from the colonies. The problem, as Englishmen
saw it, was not to join hands with Sam Adams and leap into
untried schemes of government, but to keep closely to the
beaten path and devise means of compelling the miserly colonists to disgorge some of their wealth. Moreover, George III
was not flattered by his American subjects' devotion to the Crown
and anxiety to make him sole sovereign of the colonies. George
III had not bought and paid for part of the House of Commons and put himself at the head of the "King's Friends" to
see Americans declare themselves independent of Parliamentary
authority. He preferred to rule through Parliament because
its venality enabled him to "be a king" and yet remain within
constitutional limits. British Whigs were as determined as
King George to preserve Parliament's authority over the colonies. The traditional purpose of the Whig Party was to de-
base the power of the Crown — not to enhance it, as Sam Adams
proposed. Thus, when Adams laid his axe at the root of Parliamentary jurisdiction over the provinces, he cut the last tie
between British and American Whigs.

Unquestionably, Sam Adams had greater faith in American
independence as a barrier to British tyranny than in preserving
the connection with Great Britain through King George III.
He was well aware that George was not the man Americans
supposed him to be when they toasted him as the "Patron" of
colonial liberty. Adams was warned by his friends in England that the King "hates most cordially every American because he thinks they have an attachment to their Liberty."
Arthur Lee told Adams that "the Heart of the King is hardened,

like that of Pharoah," against the colonists.[39]   These disquieting reports of King George's villainy convinced Adams that he
was not fit to be "King of America": and rather than see such
a hard master set over the colonies, Adams hoped to make
America completely independent of Great Britain.   In 1772
it was said in Boston that the colonies ought to form a separate
commonwealth upon the model of the Dutch provinces and open
their trade to all nations.   "How shall the Colonies force their
Oppressors to proper Terms?" asked Adams in 1773, and he
replied to his own question by saying that only the formation
of a separate state — an "American Commonwealth" — would
"answer the great Purpose of preserving our Liberties."   He
told the people that Great Britain had no more right to their
money than had France or Spain and that there was no reason
why "robbers from one nation should have more indulgence
than from another."   Nevertheless, Adams still accompanied
his most rousing pieces of sedition with professions of loyalty
to the British government, and even when he appealed to the
"Law of Heaven" he hastened to disclaim any intention of
carrying out his threats.   But Adams's solemn assertions that
he was an obedient, peace-loving subject of King George III
carried no conviction with the Tories, who knew him far too
well to believe he reverenced either the King or the Empire.
And, indeed, their judgment of Sam Adams was not far wrong.
As the next two years were to show, Adams steered his course
not with George III, the "King of America," but with American
independence as a polestar.   "This country shall be independent," Adams said, "and we will be satisfied with nothing short
of it"; Great Britain might crumble, but America would "rise
full plumed and glorious from her Mothers Ashes."[40]

[39] *Samuel Adams Papers*, Mentor (William Lee) to Sam Adams, May 14,
1774; Arthur Lee to Sam Adams, Dec. 22, 1773.

[40] *Boston Gazette*, Nov. 2, 1772; Oct. 11, 1773.   Gordon, I, 347.   *The
Writings of Samuel Adams*, III, 21.

XI

THE BOSTON TEA PARTY

BECAUSE Sam Adams and other leaders of the American Revolution have handed down to posterity self-portraits in which they exhibit themselves as patient, peace-loving men driven to rebellion by intolerable British tyranny, the fact that they themselves made repeated aggressions upon the British government and did much to precipitate the Revolution is often overlooked. After the Massachusetts Convention of 1768, Sam Adams deliberately set out to provoke crises that would lead to the separation of mother country and colonies. He had scored his most notable success in the Boston Massacre, but, as has been seen, the consequences of the "bloody work in King's street" were not altogether happy for Adams or the Massachusetts Whig Party. A far greater triumph was the Boston Tea Party, which, by precipitating the American Revolution, deserves to rank as the masterpiece of Sam Adams's efforts to create an unbridgeable gap between Great Britain and her American provinces.

Intercolonial rivalry for leadership against Great Britain was one of the strongest forces that pushed the colonies, slowly but inexorably, into revolution. Many colonies hoped to distinguish themselves in the struggle against British "tyranny" by putting forward the most radical political doctrines or making the most violent resistance; and provincial patriots longed to make themselves the reigning toast among Sons of Liberty, whether as "the freedom loving Virginians," "the brave Carolinians," or "the patriotic Bostonians." In particular, Virginia and Massachusetts ran a hot race for colonial leadership and thereby hastened the eventual crisis between the mother country and colonies. If one colony took a step upon the slippery path to revolution, the Sons of Liberty in the other provinces immediately prepared to follow lest they be suspected of backwardness in the "sacred cause of Liberty." Sam Adams and other patriots never ceased to urge that "every colony still astern in the glorious cause, should advance close up to the foremost, that there may be no ground to suspect a disparity of sentiment upon any point of importance." By 1773, it had become apparent to the Crown officers in America that "every new advance upon government in any colony excites an emulation in the next," and that one "leading province" such as Massachusetts Bay could alone throw all British America into turmoil by "blowing up the general flame." [1]

Sam Adams's policy was to make Massachusetts the spearhead of American opposition to Great Britain and to weld the provinces into a solid phalanx behind the leadership of the Bay Colony. He believed that American liberty was safe only when Massachusetts was in the forefront of battle; it was as essential, in his eyes, that Massachusetts lead the American colonies as it was that Boston lead Massachusetts. Adams and the Boston Whigs never doubted that their boldness would serve as an example to Sons of Liberty elsewhere in the colonies and that, if they plunged Massachusetts into a quarrel with the mother country, the rest of British America would rush to their support: however deeply Dr. Thomas Young of Boston might lament the decline "of the noble spirit of the Yorkers," he was certain they could be depended upon to act vigorously if "a hard emergency" arose and New England called upon them for aid. [2] And, as the nonimportation agreement had shown, there was no surer way of producing quick action in Boston than to convince the citizens that they were being outstripped in patriotism by other colonies. Whenever Sam Adams wished to deal a particularly violent blow at British authority, he first aroused the townspeople's apprehensions that the Sons of Liberty in New York, Philadelphia, or Charleston were about to take into their own hands the leadership of the American col-

[1] Mass. Archives, 26, *Hutchinson Corr.* II, 184, 189.
[2] Thomas Young to Hugh Hughes, Aug. 31, 1772, MS. through courtesy of Mr. G. P. Anderson. *Boston Gazette*, Nov. 2, 1772. *Bernard Papers*, VI, Bernard to Richard Jackson, Aug. 24, 1765.

onies against Great Britain. Having once excited this fear,
Adams usually found the Boston Whigs eager to atone for their
backsliding with a riot or an attack upon royal government.
The Boston Tea Party — "the boldest stroke which had yet
been struck in America" — was a direct outgrowth of this intercolonial rivalry.[3]

Hutchinson's popularity in rural New England still remained a serious stumblingblock to Sam Adams's revolutionary
propaganda. The committees of correspondence had revived
Whig principles in the country, but rural patriotism had not
yet been highly spiced with hostility against Hutchinson and the
"oligarchs" — in great contrast to that of Boston, where Sam
Adams waged war on two fronts against local and overseas tyrants. Adams had waited many years to ruin Hutchinson,
but it probably had never occurred to him that the means of
achieving this ambition would come from Benjamin Franklin,
the "lukewarm Whig" whom Adams opposed in 1770 as the
colony's London agent. Since 1770, Franklin had strengthened the suspicions of Massachusetts Whigs that he was no
friend to colonial liberty by hobnobbing with Lord Hillsborough and running over to Ireland to visit that noble lord in his
Irish castle. Such intimacy with British ministers shocked
Adams and his radical friends, and they were about to write
Franklin down as a renegade Tory when he unexpectedly proved
himself a true patriot. Franklin was perhaps aware that his
conduct had raised misgivings in Massachusetts Bay and that
it was necessary to act quickly lest he be cast utterly out of
Adams's graces. He knew certainly that the surest way to pla-
cate Sam Adams was to put into his hands the power of pulling
down Thomas Hutchinson. By means he never explained,
Franklin got possession of a large number of letters Hutchinson
had written Thomas Whately, a former member of Parliament, and sent this "cargo" of private letters to Massachusetts
Bay in care of John and Sam Adams, James Bowdoin, Thomas
Cushing, Charles Chauncy, and Samuel Cooper. To protect
his own reputation, Franklin attached strings to his gift: no
copies of the letters were to be made; they were to be shown

[3] Hutchinson, III, 439.

only to a few confidential friends; and they were to be returned to England.[4]

Although Franklin settled all doubts of his patriotism in Massachusetts Bay by sending Hutchinson's letters to the province, it cost him much of his popularity in England and the office of postmaster general for the colonies. Franklin's misfortunes were caused by Sam Adams, who, by breaking all the instructions which had accompanied the letters, revealed Franklin's part in the affair. When Adams saw the governor's letters he immediately realized that he had in his hands a weapon which would infallibly work Hutchinson's downfall; and from that moment Adams determined to violate Franklin's orders. His first step was to announce that "a most shocking scene would soon open" in which it would be shown how certain "great persons" in the colony had attempted to destroy the Massachusetts charter and dragoon the citizens with British troops.[5] He hinted that incriminating letters had come to light which proved beyond question who was responsible for burdening the colony with taxes, soldiers, customhouse officers, and all other such "vermin."[6] By this means, the people were thrown into such excitement that Hutchinson declared if Adams "had bro't Chevy Chase into the House & proved it had been sent to England by the Governor they would have found some latent treasonable meaning against the Constitution & a Vote wou'd have passed accordingly."[7]

After having raised the citizens' apprehensions to this pitch, it was suddenly moved in the House of Representatives that the galleries be cleared and the doors barred to all messages from the governor. Sam Adams then informed the members that a number of letters written by "persons of rank in America" to gentlemen in England had reached his hands. These letters, Adams explained, were to be used only upon certain conditions to which the representatives must agree before they could be

[4] *Israel Williams Papers*, MSS. Mass. Hist. Soc., II, Thomas Hutchinson to Israel Williams, April 12, 1774. *The Works of Benjamin Franklin*, edited by E. D. Smyth, VI, 195.

[5] Mass. Archives, 27, *Hutchinson Corr.*, III, 514.

[6] *The Works of John Adams*, II, 319.

[7] Mass. Archives, 27, *Hutchinson Corr.*, III, 514. Hutchinson, III, 402.

read. The House quickly consented to be bound by these terms and Adams read the letters. But merely reading Hutchinson's correspondence to the Massachusetts legislators was not sufficient for Adams's purpose: the letters must be printed and scattered over the length and breadth of the province. Franklin had clearly stipulated that no copies were to be printed, but Adams overreached him with a trick that shocked even Hutchinson, hardened as he was to Adams's "knavery." "It was not in the power of Human Wisdom," exclaimed the governor, "to guard against this last Villainy." [8] Acting upon Adams's directions, Hancock rose in the House to say that "some body in the Common" had given him a manuscript which appeared to be a copy of Hutchinson's letters which the representatives were considering.[9] It was then moved that these letters be compared with the originals in Sam Adams's possession and, if identical, the clerk of the House (Sam Adams) should attest them and prepare them for publication. Everyone in the House knew that the letters which Hancock swore had been handed him on the Common were merely copies of the correspondence sent by Franklin. Despite its barefacedness, this stratagem enabled Sam Adams to print hundreds of copies of Hutchinson's correspondence without violating the letter of Franklin's instructions. As Hutchinson said, Sam Adams, the "Master of the Puppets," directed the business "with very great Art, as well as by sticking at no Falsehood, ever so glaring," and with "such baseness as no civilized people have ever countenanced." To the governor, it was clear that Adams was acting upon the principle which always guided his policy: "In political matters the Publick good is above all other considerations & every rule of morality when in competition with it may very well be dispensed with." [10]

Hutchinson was unable to understand how "a dozen harmless letters" written many years before when he was lieutenant

---

[8] Public Record Office, Colonial Office, Class or Series 5, 246, Lib. Cong. Transcripts, Thomas Hutchinson to Thomas Pownall, July 3, 1773.

[9] Mass. Archives, 27, *Hutchinson Corr.*, III, 509.

[10] Public Record Office, Colonial Office, Class 5, 246, Lib. Cong. Transcripts, Thomas Hutchinson to Thomas Pownall, July 3, 1773. Mass. Archives, 27, *Hutchinson Corr.* III, 516, 550.

governor of the province and addressed to an Englishman who held no political office could shatter the esteem in which he was held by rural New Englanders. Hutchinson had written little that might be used to incriminate him as an enemy to colonial liberty, but in one letter to Whately he had expressed his opinion that "there must be an abridgment of what is called English Liberty" and he had repeatedly urged that Parliament take vigorous measures to assert its sovereignty over the colonies before Sam Adams swept away all respect for government. But Hutchinson was convicted of plotting against colonial freedom not so much by his own words as by Sam Adams's interpretation of them. "It was not possible," grieved the governor, "for greater art to be made use of to inflame the people." [11] It had long since been observed that Sam Adams had only to accuse Hutchinson of bad faith to convict him in Bostonians' eyes; and it required merely the flimsiest of evidence to convince the people as a whole that the governor was secretly their enemy. By dint of frequently repeating that Hutchinson's correspondence revealed the "principal movers, in all the disturbance, misery, and bloodshed" in Massachusetts, and the governor's "Avarice & a Lust of power," Adams persuaded the people that there was more in these letters than met the eye. [12] Moreover, as Hutchinson said, in printing the letters Adams twisted their meaning by lifting passages from the text and omitting what preceded or followed. Another trick he used to expose Hutchinson's villainy was to jumble together his own and the governor's words in such a manner that readers were unable to distinguish whether it was Sam Adams or Hutchinson speaking. For example, Hutchinson was made to say in the *Boston Gazette:* "Nothing yet remains to compleat my wishes and *designs* but the arrival of the troops," and exult that his efforts had "at length prevailed on administration to conclude that all is in *anarchy* here." In reality, these words were put into Hutchinson's mouth by Sam Adams, but it was done so cunningly that the audience did not detect the deception. Adams seemed to have produced overwhelming proof that Hutchinson was re-

[11] *The Diary and Letters of Thomas Hutchinson*, I, 82.
[12] *The Writings of Samuel Adams*, III, 41, 42, 44.

sponsible for the Stamp Act, the Townshend duties, the Boston
Massacre, and the "plan of slavery" for the colonies which the
Ministry had been attempting to put in force for a decade. He
even convinced the people that Hutchinson was responsible for
bringing the troops to Boston in 1768, although it was clear
that his letters describing the crisis in the colony could not have
been received in England until long after orders had been sent
for the troops to embark for Massachusetts.[13]

Printed copies of Hutchinson's letters were sent by the Boston committee of correspondence to all the towns in the province
and to the Sons of Liberty outside New England. Everywhere
it was emphasized that Hutchinson had urged the restriction of
colonial liberty. The Boston committee of correspondence exclaimed that God, who had protected New England from its
earliest settlement, had brought to light a plot laid by its most
"malicious and invidious Enemies." [14] Having thus revealed
himself an instrument of the Deity, Sam Adams began to urge
in the House of Representatives that the King be petitioned to
remove Hutchinson as governor. The time had come, Adams
believed, to send Hutchinson on his travels because he had
shown himself to be one of the worst enemies of colonial liberty in America. During the debate that followed this motion,
Adams was asked what evidence he could present to support
his allegations. He replied that he and his followers "did
not trouble themselves about supporting them. the people of
the province would give credit to them. this would make the
Governor and Lieutenant Governor odious and the King would
always remove such a Governor. they had succeeded in this
way against Sir Francis Bernard" and Hutchinson would be removed "as was the case with Governor Bernard & would be with
all Governors who would not keep on good terms with the
people." [15] Adams's arguments carried conviction and a petition to the King was drawn up in which Governor Hutchinson
and Lieutenant Governor Oliver were pronounced the "chiefe

[13] *Boston Gazette*, June 21, 1773; Aug. 2, 1773. Hutchinson, III, 407.
[14] *Committee of Correspondence Papers*, MS. N. Y. Public Library, Circular Letter, June 22, 1773.
[15] Mass. Archives, 27, *Hutchinson Corr.*, III, 495, 522.

Instruments" in bringing a fleet and army to Massachusetts and therefore responsible for "all that Corruption of Morals in this Province, and all that Confusion Misery and Bloodshed" which followed.[16] But if Adams really expected that the King would remove Hutchinson on the strength of this arraignment, he was grievously disappointed. The Lords of the Committee of Council for Plantation Affairs declared that the Massachusetts petition was "groundless, vexatious, and scandalous, and calculated only for the seditious purposes of keeping up a spirit of clamour and discontent in the said province." [17] No evidence had been put forward by the colony, said the Lords, which in any way impeached the integrity of either Hutchinson or Oliver.

Although this attack failed to tumble Hutchinson out of the governor's chair, his reputation in New England was seriously undermined. Country people began to look upon him askance and to listen to Sam Adams's warnings that the worst tyrants were local boys who had made good by truckling to the British government. This sharp decline of Hutchinson's prestige in New England is especially important because it coincided with the appearance of another "menacing monster" in the colonies — the East India Tea Act.

Having seen what Sam Adams had done with a rumor that the Crown was to pay the judges' salaries, it might be expected that the British government would have avoided giving him fresh grievances. But Englishmen had not yet learned the folly of taxing Americans and the Ministry still hoped to appease the tax-ridden squires by means of an American revenue. Moreover, the financial muddle in which the East India Company had become mired made it essential that the British government take action in the colonies. The East India Company was heavily indebted to the government and immense quantities of its tea lay rotting in London warehouses. At the same time, the British American colonies, one of the principal tea markets of the world, smuggled in huge quantities of Dutch

---

[16] *The Writings of Samuel Adams*, III, 47.

[17] *The Letters of Hutchinson and Oliver*, 141. Mass. Archives, 27, *Hutchinson Corr.*, III, 564.

tea rather than pay the tax on British bohea. Thus, the most obvious course open to the British government was to unload the East India tea upon the colonies, lower the price, and take the profit out of smuggling by underselling Dutch contraband.

To British statesmen, there seemed an excellent chance that the colonists, thin-skinned as they were to British tyranny, would leap at the opportunity to buy tea at half the price it brought in London. At first, it is true, Americans were disposed to rejoice at the prospect of slaking their thirst with prime British bohea at low cost, but their joy was quickly damped by Sam Adams and other patriot leaders.[18] The British government had made East India tea cheap in the colonies, but it had not repealed the tax paid in colonial ports upon every pound of tea imported from the mother country. The tea duty, it will be remembered, was the only tax left untouched by Parliament in 1770 when it repealed the remaining Townshend duties in order to break up the nonimportation agreement in the colonies. As Sam Adams had then pointed out, the tea duty brought in a larger revenue than all the taxes combined that had been imposed by Charles Townshend. It was the sums collected by the Commissioners of the Customs from tea that permitted the British government to carry forward its policy of making colonial governors and judges independent of the legislatures: and if East India tea were permitted to pour into the colonies from the overstocked British warehouses, this revenue would be enormously increased. And, with the advantage of low price, the East India Company would possess a virtual monopoly of the American market because it would undersell the smugglers and cut out the colonial middlemen who had formerly bought their tea through London agents. When viewed in this light, the Tea Act was "more insidious than the Stamp Act" because, under the pretense of good will toward the colonies, it led directly to *"parliamentary despotism."* Instead of being compelled to pay unconstitutional stamp duties, the colonists were now to be tempted to drink themselves out of their liberties with cheap tea. Every time an American sat

[18] Hutchinson, III, 422.

down to breakfast, it was said, he would pay a duty to the British government.[19]

Although most colonists had patriotically patronized their local tea smugglers after the downfall of the nonimportation agreement in 1770, New Englanders continued to import British tea and pay the tax to the Commissioners of the Customs. Tea was not drunk merely by the upper classes of the towns: its use was general among all classes and far more was consumed in the country than in Boston. Sam Adams and other patriot propagandists vainly attempted to wean the people from tea. Because it was taxed by the British government, tea was said to be infected with a plague which destroyed colonial liberties, weakened the "tone of the stomach, and therefore of the whole system, inducing *tremors and spasmodic affections*," and turned strong men into "weak, effeminate and creeping valetudinarians." Nevertheless, "luxurious and enervating" tea continued to be so popular in New England that James Otis declared his countrymen would "part with all their liberties, and religion too, rather than renounce it." New Englanders gagged at home-grown "Labradore" tea — "that nauseous weed" — and were contented only with genuine British bohea.[20] To satisfy this thirst, — "the bane of New England," — John Hancock and other Whig merchants joined with the rankest Tories in importing British tea and paying the tax.[21] With good reason, the Boston Whigs believed that, in the matter of tea, New England was guilty of backsliding which called for atonement in the form of a particularly vigorous blow at British authority.

The loudest outcry against the East India Act came from Philadelphia and New York, where the Dutch smugglers were more numerous and the merchants better organized than in Boston. The Philadelphia citizens resolved on October 8,

[19] *Newport Mercury*, Nov. 22, 1773. *Boston Gazette*, Aug. 15, 1768; Oct. 25, 1773.
[20] *Essex Gazette*, May 19, 1772; Jan. 4, 1774. *Pennsylvania Chronicle*, Nov. 28, 1768. *Boston Gazette*, Aug. 15, 1768. *Pennsylvania Packet*, Dec. 13, 1773. *Rivington's New York Gazetteer*, Dec. 22, 1773. Mass. Archives, 27, *Hutchinson Corr.*, III, 610.
[21] *The Works of John Adams*, II, 381.

1773, that all who aided in the sale of East India tea were to
be treated as public enemies.   It was not until a month later
that the Boston town meeting voted to follow Philadelphia's
example in outlawing abettors of the East India Company.
The Philadelphia and New York Sons of Liberty also took the
lead in demanding that the company's consignees in the colonies
resign and publicly promise not to handle the tea when it arrived — a measure which Boston belatedly followed.   But
there were obstacles in the way of the Boston Sons of Liberty
which did not hamper the New York and Philadelphia patriots.
In the Southern colonies, the tea consignees hastened to resign
and treat the Whigs "in a soothing manner"; but the Boston
consignees were of a tougher breed and refused to be frightened
by the patriots' threats.[22]   The Boston Liberty Boys summoned
the tea importers to Liberty Tree and made elaborate preparations to receive their resignations: the flag was run up Liberty
pole; bells were rung in the meetinghouses; and a huge crowd
assembled in Hanover Square — but the show had to be called
off because the importers ignored the summons and refused to
appear. This unexpected resistance was owing to Thomas
Hutchinson, who, for a brief period, seemed about to worst
Sam Adams in one of the most crucial encounters of their long
quarrel.

Although his own popularity had been shattered by the publication of his letters, Hutchinson resolved to rally the Tories
and make a desperate effort to enforce the Tea Act in Massachusetts Bay.   Besides, he himself was a merchant and the tea
destined for Massachusetts had been consigned by the East
India Company to his sons and friends.   Because of the close
connection between the governor and the tea, Sam Adams exclaimed that Hutchinson had persuaded the British government to pass the East India Act in order that he might "finger
the profits" of the monopoly.[23]   But, in reality, the unlucky
job of selling the tea had been wished upon the Hutchinsons

[22] Hutchinson, III, 423. *Boston Gazette*, Nov. 15, 1772. *Letters of
Samuel Cooper to Pownall and Franklin, 1770–1774* (Bancroft Collection),
N. Y. Public Library, Samuel Cooper to Benjamin Franklin, Dec. 17, 1773.
[23] *Boston Gazette*, Dec. 13, 1773.

and their Tory friends by their English acquaintances, who mistakenly supposed they were making the enforcement of the Tea Act easier by giving a handful of Tory merchants a virtual monopoly of the trade, freezing out both honest tea merchants and smugglers. Moreover, Hutchinson had had nothing to do with the scheme conceived by the British Ministry of saving the government's investment in the East India Company and drawing a revenue from the colonies. Like Benjamin Franklin, Hutchinson had regarded the government's refusal to repeal the tea tax when the other Townshend duties were revoked in 1770 as poor surgery which left a splinter in an unhealed wound. He warned the British Ministry that in keeping up the tea duty it had left a powder keg in full view of colonial radicals who might kick it over at any moment. Hutchinson believed the East India Act of 1773 was an ill-timed and futile measure, but, because the British government had begun a new quarrel with the colonies, he saw that he must bear the brunt of the attack Sam Adams and the radical Whigs were certain to make upon royal government in the colonies.

Because Hutchinson encouraged the Boston tea consignees to resist the Whigs, Sam Adams and his "Mohawks" encountered an unexpected obstacle. They had anticipated no more difficulty in compelling the tea merchants to resign than they had experienced with the stamp masters, but in spite of menaces and mobs, the Hutchinsons and their friends would do no more than promise to store the tea when it landed and await word from England before taking further action.[24] Because of the failure of the Boston Sons of Liberty to bring the tea consignees to their knees, the reputation of the Puritan metropolis as a patriot stronghold began to sink rapidly throughout the colonies. "There are many fears respecting Boston," wrote a Philadelphian; "some even going to the length of asserting that tea was being imported and the duty paid; while in Philadelphia not an ounce of tea had paid duty." New Yorkers remembered that the "Saints" had imported dutied British tea

[24] Mass. Archives, 27, *Hutchinson Corr.*, III, 12, 14. *The Diary and Letters of Thomas Hutchinson*, I, 100. *Israel Williams Papers*, II, Thomas Hutchinson to Israel Williams, Dec. 23, 1773.

while the other colonists had patriotically drunk Dutch contraband; and the successful resistance of the Boston tea merchants was sneeringly contrasted with the speedy downfall of
the New York and Philadelphia consignees.[25] In New York,
the "Mohawks" were already threatening to destroy the tea
when it arrived and the Philadelphia Sons of Liberty were laying plans to set the tea ships on fire with burning rafts when they
appeared in the Delaware. "What think you, Captain," the
Liberty Boys asked the Delaware pilots who were expected to
guide the East India Company's vessels to Philadelphia, "of a
Halter around your Neck — ten Gallons of liquid Tar de-
canted on your Pate — with the Feathers of a dozen wild Geese
laid over to enliven your Appearance?" [26]   If the Boston patriots hoped to keep pace with these fire-eating Sons of Liberty
in the Southern provinces, it was clear that they must strike an
audacious blow directly at the British government.

Thus, in 1773, to kindle an explosion which would prove to
the Southern colonists that Boston Whigs were still fervent
patriots, Sam Adams began to beat the alarm he had sounded
during the nonimportation agreement. "Our credit is at stake,"
he told the people; "we must venture, and unless we do, we
shall be discarded by the sons of liberty in the other colonies."
Boston Sons of Liberty, he exclaimed, must "wipe off the score"
of irresolution by striking another home blow at British tyranny.[27]   How Sam Adams intended to make amends for Boston's backsliding was not long in doubt.

Adams did not believe that New Englanders would be able
to resist the East India tea if it were offered for sale in the
country: its low price was an almost "invincible temptation" to
thrifty yeomen addicted to bohea.[28]   Although he declared
the Ministry had infected the tea with a plague by laying taxes
upon it, he feared that New Englanders would shut their eyes

[25] *Boston Gazette*, Nov. 15, 1773; Dec. 13, 1773. Mass. Archives, 27,
Hutchinson Corr., III, 610. *Connecticut Courant*, Dec. 21, 1773.

[26] *Rivington's New York Gazetteer*, Dec. 2, 1773. Broadside, Lib. Cong.,
To the Delaware Pilots, Philadelphia, Nov. 27, 1773.

[27] Gordon, I, 336. *Massachusetts Gazette*, Dec. 20, 1773.

[28] *Mass. Hist. Soc. Collections*, IV, Fourth Series, 374. Hutchinson, III,
430, 433.

to the danger and swallow the bait.   For this reason, he determined not to permit the tea to be landed and stored in warehouses from which it might be smuggled into the country.   He insisted, instead, that the tea be sent back in the same ships in which it had arrived, before there was an opportunity to pay the duty or import it secretly into the country.   But in making this demand Adams came in conflict with British law.   By act of Parliament, no dutiable merchandise could be returned to Great Britain in the same bottom without a pass from the governor.   The governor, in turn, could not issue such a pass without a receipt from the customhouse that the duty had been paid.   Thus, if the tea were shipped back to England without payment of duty, the vessels that carried the tea would be liable to confiscation by the British government — but this objection carried little weight with Sam Adams because it was based upon acts of Parliament which New Englanders "had nothing to do with," since they "owed no Sybjection to yt Power & that thr Transactions might be carried on witht paying any Regard to It." [29]   In this manner, a deadlock was created between the patriots and tea consignees in Boston: the merchants offering to store the tea, which Adams regarded as a complete victory for the East India Company and the British government; the patriots demanding that when the tea arrived it be immediately returned, which the merchants knew would result in their financial ruin. [30]

Yet there was an escape from this dilemma which, had Sam Adams permitted it to be utilized, would have made unnecessary the Boston Tea Party.   If the tea ships anchored below Castle William instead of entering the port of Boston, they could return to England without a pass from the governor, payment of duty, or observance of any of the formalities required by Parliamentary law.   But if the ships came beyond Castle William, they could not again put to sea until the tea had been landed or the duty paid.   Hutchinson planned to avert the

[29] British Museum, Additional MSS. 35912, Hardwicke, Lib. Cong. Transcript, Extracts of Private Letters from Boston, Mr. H. to Mr. M., Jan. 6, 1774.

[30] Mass. Archives, 27, *Hutchinson Corr.*, III, 605.   *The Works of John Adams*, II, 324.   *Mass. Hist. Soc. Collections*, IV, Fourth Series, 374.

crisis he saw gathering in Boston by ordering the tea ships to
anchor below the Castle so that, if it appeared that the tea
could not be landed, they could set sail for the mother country.[31]
But Sam Adams had very different plans for the "plagued"
East India tea.

Adams had long hoped to produce an emergency that would
force Bostonians to show their mettle. Hutchinson saw that
Adams and the radical Whigs were eager "to engage the people
in some desperate measure" to clear Boston's skirts of all suspicion of remissness and bring the colonies nearer separation
from the mother country.[32] Sam Adams seldom let slip an
opportunity to plunge the colonies deeper into controversy with
Great Britain; and he soon showed that he had no intention of
allowing the crisis brought on by the East India Tea Act to pass
quietly. When the first tea ship anchored below Castle William, its captain was summoned before the Boston committee
of correspondence, where he was ordered by Adams and other
committeemen to bring his ship up to the Boston wharves and
land all the cargo except the tea on pain of being tarred and
feathered by the Liberty Boys. The captains of the two tea
ships which shortly after arrived in Boston Bay were given the
same alternative. In Philadelphia, where there was no Sam
Adams to evolve a desperate scheme to destroy the tea, the ships
were ordered by the Sons of Liberty to anchor below the port in
order that their cargo might not become liable to port duties.[33]
In Boston, on the other hand, three vessels laden with East India
tea were made fast at Griffin's wharf on a water front that
swarmed with Sons of Liberty. Sam Adams might well have
rejoiced in having created a dilemma which only his "Mohawks"
could solve.

If Sam Adams was planning, as the Tories suspected, to push
the metropolis headlong into a quarrel with Great Britain, he
did not intend that Boston should act alone. The reaction in
rural New England against Boston after the Massacre had shown

[31] *The Diary and Letters of Thomas Hutchinson*, I, 100.
[32] Hutchinson, III, 439.   Mass. Archives, *Hutchinson Corr.*, III, 609.
[33] *The Diary and Letters of Thomas Hutchinson*, I, 100–101.   Hutchinson, III, 425, 430. *Pennsylvania Gazette*, Dec. 29, 1773.

the Sons of Liberty the importance of country support, and they proceeded in 1773 to put the lesson to profit. The country, as well as the town, was to be involved in resisting the East India tea. Whenever a tea ship appeared in the harbor, the bells were set ringing for a "general muster" and handbills were posted throughout the country calling upon "Friends! Citizens! Countrymen!" to aid the metropolis. The Boston committee of correspondence dispatched circular letters to the Massachusetts country towns to inform them of the emergency in Boston; and rural committees of correspondence were summoned to the metropolis, where they sat as "a little senate" deliberating upon the disposition of the tea. When a tea ship was seen off the coast, Adams rushed expresses to the neighboring towns to meet the Boston committee in Faneuil Hall the next day to assist the townspeople in warding off British tyranny. He urged the country people to attend the meetings of "town and country" in Boston, and hundreds of the rural patriots flocked to Faneuil Hall to hear Adams thunder against the British government and the tea importers. Hutchinson remarked that the yeomen were brought to the metropolis "by the Artifices of Boston expecting them to share in the criminality to lessen their own share." At these gatherings of Boston mechanics and country farmers, Adams "never was in greater glory," and Tories observed with dismay that many country people were becoming more and more inclined toward violence as they rubbed shoulders with Boston Sons of Liberty in Faneuil Hall.[34]

The menace of East India tea revealed what a powerful revolutionary machine Sam Adams had created in the Boston committee of correspondence. The committee took complete charge in Boston and directed the patriots' activities, which culminated in the destruction of the tea. By means of the committees of correspondence, Adams kept the people in a state of feverish excitement: if the tea were landed, he told New Eng-

---

[34] *Mass. Hist. Soc. Proceedings* (1866), VIII, 324. *Committee of Correspondence Papers*, Boston Committee to Dorchester, Brookline, Cambridge and Charlestown Committees, Nov. 28, 1773. Mass. Archives, 27, *Hutchinson Corr.*, III, 581, 587, 605.

landers in his circular letters, taxes would be imposed upon
all necessities imported from Great Britain, and even the land
"purchased and cultivated by our hard laboring Ancestors"
would be taxed to support miscreants in office "whose vileness
ought to banish them from the Society of Men." [35] As a result, royal authority in the province became daily more power-
less: when Hutchinson attempted to disperse the meetings in
Faneuil Hall his proclamations met with "infinite Contempt"
and a "loud and very generall hiss." [36] Indeed, many of the
patriots were so infuriated that the Boston committee of correspondence was forced to appoint a military watch along the
water front to guard the tea against an attack.

There seemed, indeed, no alternative to destroying the tea or
experiencing the appalling taxes and wholesale confiscation of
colonial lands by British "overlords" which Sam Adams prophesied would follow payment of the tea duty.   Governor Hutchinson refused to give the ships permission to return to England
until the Commissioners of the Customs gave him a receipt; the
Commissioners declined to give the governor a receipt until
the duty had been paid; and the tea consignees refused to court
financial ruin by sending back the tea without a pass from the
governor and receipt from the customhouse.   Rather than trust
themselves further with the Boston mob, the tea merchants took
refuge in Castle William.   Their flight smoothed the way for
Sam Adams's plans.   Whatever now happened in Boston, he
could hold Hutchinson responsible.   The governor's obstinacy
in withholding a pass for the ships, Adams exclaimed, had made
desperate measures necessary.

The destruction of the tea struck Boston patriot leaders as
the only effective solution of the deadlock that Sam Adams had
created by ordering the ships to come beyond Castle William.
If the tea were thrown into the harbor, there would be no longer
danger of its being smuggled into the country to tempt the
patriotism of rural Whigs.   There was in Boston a large body
of men ready for any violence: several hundred "veteran Sons

[35] *Committee of Correspondence Papers,* Circular Letter, Nov. 22, 1773.
[36] *Mass. Hist. Soc. Proceedings,* IV (1860), 218.   Mass. Archives, 27,
Hutchinson Corr., III, 601.

of Liberty," it was said, were enrolled in the metropolis to destroy the tea or "perish in the Attempt." [37] Moreover, the British force in the vicinity was not likely to give trouble: only one regiment of royal troops was in Castle William, and the townspeople had no fears of the British fleet in the harbor because they believed that the admiral "might as well hang himself, as burn the town." [38]

If the tea were to be destroyed, the dead line for the business was December 17, 1773, when it would become liable to seizure by the customhouse officers for nonpayment of duty. After the tea had fallen into their hands and been stored in Castle William, Sam Adams had no doubt it would be either secretly imported into the country or left untouched until a British army could be sent to cram it down the colonists' throats. It was essential, therefore, that the Sons of Liberty strike before December 17. As this momentous day approached, it became clear that the Whig leaders were preparing for rough work: guns suddenly disappeared from all the shops in Boston. " 'T would puzzle any person to purchase a pair of p[isto]les in town," said John Andrews, "as they are all bought up, with a full determination to repel force by force." [39] The destruction of the tea had been agreed upon many days before the Tea Party; and on the morning of December 16, 1773, Sam Adams received a last-minute appeal from a Whig friend to spare the tea lest a rash attack "give yr Enemys a thousand Opportunitys against this Town." [40] But Boston's reputation as a patriot stronghold was in need of saving and Adams was not to be swerved from his scheme by the risk of retaliation from Great Britain. On the afternoon of December 16, several thousand people crowded into the Old South Meetinghouse to demand that Rotch, one of the owners of the tea ships, make a last effort to secure a clearance from Hutchinson. The candles were being lighted when Rotch returned to the Old South with

[37] *Boston Gazette*, Jan. 10, 1774. *Massachusetts Gazette*, Dec. 20, 1773.
[38] *Ibid.*, Dec. 20, 1773.
[39] *Mass. Hist. Soc. Proceedings*, VIII, 325. *Pennsylvania Packet*, Dec. 13, 1773.
[40] *Samuel Adams Papers*, Letter in old style handwriting, signed "W.T." to "Mr. Addams," Dec. 16 (1773).

Hutchinson's refusal. In the gathering dusk, Sam Adams arose and solemnly declared that "this meeting can do nothing further to save the country." His words were the signal for a wild war whoop from the galleries and the street outside the meetinghouse where several hundred "Mohawks," who had been fortifying themselves with punch and putting the finishing touches on their Indian make-up at Edes and Gill's printing shop, broke from the crowd and headed for the water front closely followed by a mob of spectators. As this howling procession approached the water front there was such an uproar that "you 'd thought the inhabitants of the infernal regions had broke loose." [41] Most of these "Narragansett Indians" were Adams's followers from the North End — shipyard workers, artisans, and ship masters — decked out in war paint and feathers.[42] Once aboard the tea ships, the braves worked quickly, and within a few moments three hundred and forty-two chests of the finest tea that ever tempted New Englanders' palates, pocketbooks, and patriotism were at the bottom of Boston Harbor.

After the Tea Party, Sam Adams and the Boston Whigs were in "a perfect Jubillee." For, as Hutchinson said, it was "the boldest stroke which had yet been struck in America" and fully restored Boston to the leadership of the American colonies.[43] The Puritan metropolis again stood forth as a citadel of patriotism: in New York, Philadelphia, and Baltimore, Bostonians were "highly extolled" by the Sons of Liberty, although the Tories railed against "ye wicked Bostonians, who have given it to the fishes!" [44] But most New Englanders were charmed, as was John Adams, by the "Sublimity" of the Tea Party; and in Massachusetts, the town and country were more firmly united than at any time since the Stamp Act. It now became a patriotic duty to follow Boston's leadership. "Many thought they

[41] *Mass. Hist. Soc. Proceedings*, VIII, 325; Wells, II, 122.
[42] Gordon, I, 341.
[43] *Essex Gazette*, Dec. 28, 1773. Hutchinson, III, 439.
[44] *Boston Gazette*, Jan. 3, 1774. *Essex Gazette*, April 5, 1774. *Pennsylvania Gazette*, Dec. 29, 1773. *Rivington's New York Gazetteer*, Jan. 27, 1774.

could not be Friends to their Country," lamented the Tories, "unless they trod in the same Steps, and imitated the Example of the Bostonians." [45]

Had British statesmen realized the strength of this determination in the colonies to stand by Boston — the "antient capital of America" — they might have been less ready to single out the metropolis for punishment. In England, news of the Tea Party provoked an immediate outburst against "the licentious Bostonians" who, it was believed, were making ready to rebel.[46] Englishmen were unable to see any cause for the destruction of the tea other than the zeal of the "Boston Fanatics" to pick quarrels with the mother country upon every occasion.[47] They regarded the Tea Party as "a downright thrashing from our own subjects" — an indignity which, it was pointed out, no European power would dare offer the victor of the Seven Years' War. If we can swallow this affront, Englishmen exclaimed, let the seat of Empire be moved from Westminster to Boston, since the New England "Saints" had shown themselves to be "the only people on earth who could trample on our once boasted spirit with impunity." Sam Adams and his "Mohawks" seemed to have brought the dispute between the mother country and colonies to a sudden head; the issue was now clearly defined: "Whether the Colonies shall give laws to England, or England to the Colonies?" The day of halfway measures had passed: the "Boston mutineers" must be deprived of their charter, "the spring and source of all their insolent and unjustifiable acts," and taught to respect the might of England before they rose in outright rebellion.[48]

Thus, by its achievement in forcing the British government's hand in the colonies and rallying colonial radicals to Boston's defense, the Tea Party might well be regarded as a crossing of

[45] *Warren-Adams Letters*, II, 403 (Appendix). *Letters of Samuel Cooper to Pownall and Franklin*, Samuel Cooper to Benjamin Franklin, Dec. 17, 1773.
[46] *New York Gazette and Weekly Mercury*, May 9, 1774. *Rivington's New York Gazetteer*, May 12, 1774.
[47] *Independency the Object of the Congress in America* (London, 1774), 2.
[48] *New York Gazette and Weekly Mercury*, May 9, 1774. *Rivington's New York Gazetteer*, May 12, 1774.

the Rubicon which left Sam Adams the desperate alternative
of "Neck or Nothing." [49]   It was a headlong plunge toward
revolt which set free the forces, long gathering in America, that
led to war between the mother country and colonies.   The
British government could not overlook the insult it had received at the hands of Sam Adams and his "Mohawks"; but
British statesmen were utterly unaware of the true strength of
the revolutionary movement in America.   And it was clear
that upon their decision hung "the FATE OF A GREAT EMPIRE." [50]

[49] Peter Oliver, 146.
[50] *Rivington's New York Gazetteer*, May 12, 1774.

XII

SAM ADAMS AND THE SOLEMN LEAGUE
AND COVENANT

SAM ADAMS was well aware that by serving the British government a dish of tea brewed with salt water, Boston was certain to be punished. It was widely believed in the colonies that Lord North was eager for an opportunity to send a fleet to America and blow the Sons of Liberty out of Faneuil Hall; indeed, it was said that American liberty had only to be mentioned to the Prime Minister to have him fall into a fit: "foaming at the mouth, and with eyes starting from their sockets," he would "vomit forth" horrid threats against the rascally American republicans. Rumors spread that he had ordered troops and men-of-war to Boston to collect damages for the tea and enforce a new stamp act; and Arthur Lee put Adams on his guard against a "particular stroke of revenge" from the British Ministry.[1] Sam Adams and his "Mohawks" seemed indeed to have brought a hornets' nest about their ears.

While the Boston Liberty Boys dug themselves in for the expected blow from England they proceeded to sweep away the last vestiges of Parliamentary authority in the colonies. For many years, Tories had pointed to the American post office as an example of Parliamentary authority which refuted the Whig argument that the British Parliament had no precedents for the internal taxation of the colonies. The American post office had been established by an act of Parliament, but it was so vital to the colonies that the patriots were reluctant to forgo

[1] *Newport Mercury*, Aug. 8, 1773 (Supplement). *New York Gazette and Weekly Mercury*, April 4, 1774. *Rivington's New York Gazetteer*, May 12, 1774. *Essex Gazette*, April 5, 1774. R. H. Lee, *The Life of Arthur Lee* (1829), I, 242.

its benefits by attacking it along with the Stamp Act. By 1774, however, Sam Adams believed the time had come to discard all Parliamentary authority; and when William Goddard, a Pennsylvania newspaper printer, popped up in Boston with a scheme for an independent colonial post office, he was warmly welcomed by Adams and the committee of correspondence. Adams was eager to make a fresh assault upon British authority, for he knew it would be fatal for the revolutionary movement in the colonies to appear to stand still after the Tea Party. Moreover, he foresaw that if matters came to the worst between the mother country and colonies, America would require a separate system of postriders to prevent a stoppage of intercolonial correspondence; hence his denunciations of the constitutional post office as "an usurpation of the Parliament no longer to be borne." [2]

At the same time that British statesmen watched colonial Whigs pulling up Parliamentary jurisdiction root and branch, Hutchinson exclaimed that Sam Adams was stripping the governor and Council of Massachusetts of all authority and setting up a new constitution by the "grossest falsities and misrepresentations." [3] By impeaching Chief Justice Oliver in the Massachusetts General Court, Adams took a long stride toward making the provincial legislature the complete "Parliament" of the colony. No Crown officer had ever before been impeached by the General Court, but lack of precedent was never an obstacle to Sam Adams: Oliver had accepted the salary proffered by King George and therefore he must be removed from office. From Thomas Hutchinson, however, Sam Adams encountered serious opposition. When Adams brought forward Chief Justice Oliver's impeachment in the House of Representatives, using the form and words of the British House of Commons, the governor attempted to stop the proceedings by refusing to attend the Council meeting before which Adams, as chairman of the House committee, was compelled to bring the articles of impeachment. As long as Hutchinson remained absent from the Council, the Chief Justice seemed out of reach of his enemies

[2] *Committee of Correspondence Papers*, Boston Committee to the Salem, Marblehead, etc., Committee, March 24, 1774; Boston Committee to the Newport and Providence Committees, March 29, 1774. *Lamb Papers*, MSS. N. Y. Hist. Soc., William Goddard to John Lamb, March 23, 1774.
[3] *The Diary and Letters of Thomas Hutchinson*, I, 140.

and the case against him was brought to a standstill. The Whigs exclaimed that not even the most arbitrary English King would have dared to protect his favorite from the House of Commons with such brazenness.[4] Hutchinson congratulated himself upon having tripped up the Whigs and exposed the Massachusetts House of Representatives as a mere "Mock Parliament," but he did not take into account Adams's resource. When it became evident that no persuasion or threats could bring Hutchinson to the Council, Adams declared the governor was "presumed" to be present and ordered the impeachment to be carried on with the governor "presumptively" in his seat at Council. This fiction enabled the patriots to enter upon the House *Journal* that the Chief Justice had been impeached before the governor and Council in spite of the fact that Hutchinson had not set foot inside the Council chamber during the proceedings.[5]

But Adams's efforts to purge the Massachusetts judiciary were rudely cut short by the measures taken by the British government to punish Boston for the Tea Party. By act of Parliament, the port of Boston was so effectively closed to trade that Lord North remarked he had shoved the metropolis back twenty miles from the Bay; and, by subsequent legislation, the administration of justice in the colony was reformed and the elective Council filled with royal appointees. British politicians expected the townspeople to wilt when confronted with these harsh measures, as they had in 1768 when British troops took possession of Boston. But much to the surprise of the Ministry, the citizens showed no sign of weakening. The Port Bill was denounced in the town meeting with "a freedom and energy becoming the orators of ancient Rome"; Sam Adams exclaimed that "for flagrant injustice and barbarity, one might search in vain among the archives of Constantinople to find a match for it"; Thomas Hutchinson was declared responsible for Boston's plight; and Paul Revere was sent galloping off to New York with an appeal for aid to the Sons of Liberty.[6]

[4] *Boston Gazette*, April 11, 1774. Hutchinson, III, 446.

[5] *Ibid.*, III, 447, 449, 453. *The Works of John Adams*, X, 238; II, 328–329.

[6] *The Writings of Samuel Adams*, III, 112, 117. Isaac Q. Leake, *Memoir of the Life and Times of General John Lamb* (1857), 84, 85.

Sam Adams saw in the Boston Port Bill another attempt by the British government to separate the colonies from Massachusetts Bay in order that the "leading colony" might be singled out for punishment. His course was clear: he must convince Americans that if they deserted Massachusetts in this crisis, the colonies would be beaten down singly and British tyranny imposed upon the whole continent. "This Attack, though made immediately upon us," said the Boston committee of correspondence, "is doubtless design'd for every other Colony, who will not surrender their sacred Rights and Liberties into the Hands of an Infamous Ministry. Now therefore is the Time, when *ALL* should be united in opposition to this violation of the Liberties of *ALL*." Sam Adams warned the Philadelphians: "*You* will be called upon to surrender your Rights, if ever they should succeed in their Attempts to suppress the Spirit of Liberty *here*." "It is not the Rights of Boston only, but of ALL AMERICA which are now struck at," declared the Boston Sons of Liberty. "Not the Merchants only but the Farmer, and every order of Men who inhabit this noble Continent." [7]

In the midst of the excitement over the Port Bill, Adams and the Whigs learned that "that damn'd *arch traitor*," Thomas Hutchinson, had been recalled to England. Just before he left Boston, Hutchinson was presented with addresses approving his administration as governor, signed by over one hundred and twenty of the principal merchants, lawyers, magistrates, and Episcopal clergymen of Boston. Sam Adams was dismayed by the number and prominence of Hutchinson's well-wishers, for he feared that if the addresses got abroad, the patriots in the neighboring colonies upon whom Boston depended for support against the British government would be led to believe that the Massachusetts Whig Party was in fact a small blustering faction discountenanced by the substantial citizens of the colony. Therefore, Adams told his friends outside Massachusetts that the greater part of those who signed the addresses

[7] *Committee of Correspondence Papers*, Boston Committee to the Westborough Committee, June 24, 1774; Boston Committee to the Philadelphia, New York, New Jersey, Rhode Island, etc., Committees, May 13, 1774. *The Writings of Samuel Adams*, III, 110. *Boston Evening Post*, May 16, 1774.

to Hutchinson belonged to the lowest class. "I believe," he said, "I could point out half a Score Gentlemen in Town able to purchase the whole of them." The only lawyers who signed, Adams declared, were obscure pettifoggers or young clerks who had recently purchased their books.[8] Yet, in fact, the names of many of the first families of the province appeared in these addresses; and Hutchinson sailed away from Boston on the day the Port Bill went into effect secure in the knowledge that he retained the support of the well-born and conservative. Most of these gentry, however, were exiled during the Revolution, and Hutchinson never returned to America. He did well to give Massachusetts a wide berth, for Sam Adams and John Hancock quickly came into power after the outbreak of war. And Sam Adams lost none of his hatred for Hutchinson: Bernard, he said, he could forgive, but Hutchinson's offenses were too great to be pardoned.[9]

For many years, Sam Adams had made it his policy to provoke the British government to attempt the punishment of the colonies — a step certain to put provincial radicals in power. Hutchinson and Bernard believed Adams baited the Ministry because he wished to see the Massachusetts charter under attack and British "tyranny" weighing heavily upon the colony.[10] Certainly, after the Tea Party, Adams was prepared to "make the best Improvement" of the expected British retaliation. The Boston Port Bill had been no more than received in New England before Adams produced his counterblast: a "Solemn League and Covenant" suspending all commercial intercourse with the "Island of Great Britain" until the privileges of the metropolis had been restored. This plan went beyond previous American nonimportation agreements inasmuch as both the exportation of colonial products to Great Britain and the importation of British commodities to the colonies were prohibited and the common people, rather than the merchants, were entrusted with its enforcement. Adams did not repeat his former mistake of

[8] *Mass. Hist. Soc. Proceedings*, VIII, 328. Hutchinson, III, 459. *The Writings of Samuel Adams*, III, 124–125.
[9] *The Writings of Samuel Adams*, III, 171–172.
[10] Mass. Archives, 27, *Hutchinson Corr.*, III, 40, 609. Hutchinson, III, 439.

putting "gentlemen in trade" in charge: the Solemn League and
Covenant provided that the boycott was to be wholly in the
hands of those "two venerable orders of Men stiled Mechanicks
& husbandmen the Strength of every Community." [11]   He had
learned from the ill-fated agreement of 1768–1770 to dread
"mercantile Avarice" and to pin his faith to the yeomanry and
town laborers whose firm patriotism, it was said, "must finally
save this Country." [12]   He believed that after the Solemn
League and Covenant had been accepted by these stout Whigs
it little mattered whether or not *"messieurs les marchands,* will
be graciously pleased to come into it," since they could not import when there was no one to buy.

To stir up enthusiasm for another economic war with Great
Britain, the Boston patriots declared the Solemn League and
Covenant to be the only alternative to "the horrors of slavery,
or the carnage and desolation of a civil war."   Although the
mother country had shown conclusively in 1770 that it was
not to be driven from its ground by the colonies' commercial
reprisals, Adams continued to tell the people that they could
bring Great Britain to terms merely by "a firm Resolution to
insist upon their Rights." [13]   He still said that "degenerate
Britons" would give up the struggle when they saw the provinces
swarming with "Old Romans" and Puritans who steadfastly
refused to touch British merchandise.   Adams attempted to
make Americans believe they were so important to the mother
country that Great Britain could not punish them without ruin-
ing herself.   Once England ceased to draw wealth and power
from the colonies, he prophesied her speedy end.   "Britain may
fall sooner than she is aware," he said; "while her Colonies who
are struggling for Liberty may survive her fate & tell the
Story to their Childrens Children." [14]   With over four million pounds of British money tied up in loans to American
merchants and planters, colonial patriots felt confident that the

[11] *Committee of Correspondence Papers,* MSS. N. Y. Public Library, "The
Solemn League of Covenant."   *The Writings of Samuel Adams,* III, 129.
[12] *Committee of Correspondence Papers,* Boston Committee to New York
Committee, June 18, 1774. Leake, 89.
[13] Mass. Archives, 26, *Hutchinson Corr.,* II, 305.
[14] *The Writings of Samuel Adams,* I, 447.

British government would hesitate long before endangering this investment by interfering in the colonies. Therefore, they regarded British menaces as mere bluff. "The consequences are feared by nobody," said Dr. Thomas Young when the mother country threatened to punish the colonies, because "every old woman" in America knew that Englishmen did not dare to jeopardize their credits and trade. Even such moderates as Thomas Cushing were convinced there was no need to fear coercion: when he was told by Hutchinson that the patriots' activities would bring down quo warranto proceedings against the Massachusetts charter, Cushing answered that "there had been none since the Reigns of the Stuarts and they dare not send one here." [15] As long as it was believed that Great Britain's "future glory" depended upon keeping in the good graces of her American subjects, all signs of yielding by the mother country merely aggravated the controversy with the colonies because Sam Adams had "art enough to improve them to raise the people higher by assuring them that if they will but persevere they may bring the nation to their own terms." [16] Indeed, until the outbreak of war, Sam Adams kept the people firm in the patriot cause by promising them a speedy, peaceful redress of grievances from the "tottering" British government.

From his experience in the last nonimportation agreement, Adams knew that the Solemn League and Covenant would be more warmly received in the country than in the seaport towns where the merchants were reluctant to begin another boycott. His plan, therefore, was to try the temper of New England yeomen before sending the Covenant among the townspeople. Adams and the Boston committee of correspondence worked so stealthily that few townspeople knew what was going on until they were startled to find the covenant sweeping the rural districts. Although it had scarcely been heard of in the metropolis, Adams told the Massachusetts farmers that it had already been adopted by an overwhelming majority of the citizens of

[15] Thomas Young to Hugh Hughes, Aug. 31, 1772, MS. through courtesy of Mr. G. P. Anderson. Mass. Archives, 26, *Hutchinson Corr.*, II, 530.
[16] *Boston Gazette*, Aug. 24, 1772. Mass. Archives, 27, *Hutchinson Corr.*, III, 550.

Boston.   This trick worked so well in the country that thousands of yeomen trooped to town to sign the Covenant, swearing they would support the patriotic Bostonians.   Nevertheless, many townsmen were outraged to discover they had been
hoodwinked by Adams and the committee.   Conservative
Whigs joined with Tories in wailing that to defend themselves
against British tyranny the people had created a far more oppressive tyranny at their very doors.   A vigorous effort was
made in the Boston town meeting to abolish the committee of
correspondence on the ground that it had exceeded its authority
by drawing up a nonimportation agreement and foisting it upon
the country behind Bostonians' backs.   For several hours, Sam
Adams and the committee of correspondence were in serious
danger of being thrown overboard by the irate citizens.   Although the storm was finally weathered, a large number of Bostonians showed themselves heartily in favor of destroying the
revolutionary steam roller which now threatened to flatten conservative Whigs and Tories alike.

The chief opposition to the Solemn League and Covenant
came from the Boston merchants, who denounced it as a hare-
brained scheme calculated to ruin New England's trade and enrich other colonies.   They protested that the whale and fishing
industry, the backbone of New England's commercial prosperity, would be completely destroyed because Adams had neglected to provide for the importation of many articles essential to
fishing which the colonies themselves could not supply.   They
believed that Massachusetts could not survive if cut off from the
West Indies as Adams proposed; and they groaned that they
would be put out of business because Adams had left nothing
to sell.   It became a common saying among Boston merchants
that Adams and his crew were "determined to bring total
destruction upon us" by plunging New England into a quarrel
with the mother country before making sure of support from
the Southern colonies.[17]   But Adams paid little heed to these
mutterings from "gentlemen in trade": all shortcomings of the

[17] *Massachusetts Gazette*, June 16, 1774; July 7, 1774.   *The Letters and
Diary of John Rowe*, edited by Annie Rowe Cunningham (1903), 276.
Mass. Hist. Soc. Proceedings, VIII, 329.   Gordon, I, 378.

Covenant he called mere "Punctilios" and reproached Bostonians for their "utterly unbecoming" behavior in complaining of hardships. "The Virtue of our Ancestors inspires us," he exclaimed, " — they were contented with Clams & Muscles." [18]

In spite of this unpromising reception in Boston, the committee of correspondence accompanied its appeals to the Southern colonies for aid against the Port Bill with copies of the Solemn League and Covenant. But instead of falling in with Sam Adams's plan to extend the boycott over America, most of the colonies gave him a point-blank refusal. The struggle, they declared, was against Great Britain, not against the American merchants, who would certainly be ruined by another nonimportation agreement. Jeremy Belknap in New Hampshire said the Boston committee of correspondence were "acting like persons out of their senses & blindly rushing upon their own Ruin," and he held the Covenant to be as arbitrary "as any Act of the British Parliament which it is intended to oppose." Philadelphia's answer to the Boston committee of correspondence was so cool that there seemed a "stroke of insulting pity in it." All "*moderate prudent* Measures" ought to be employed before resorting to economic war, the Philadelphians said, lest the "many Wise & Good Men in the Mother Country" who supported the colonial cause be alienated and the American Whig Party disunited. The Solemn League and Covenant was forwarded from New York and Philadelphia to Baltimore, Annapolis, Williamsburg, and Charleston, South Carolina, but everywhere it met with the same response: a nonimportation agreement was to be used only after all means of reconciliation had failed.[19]

This overwhelming rejection of the Solemn League and

[18] *The Writings of Samuel Adams*, III, 115, 128. *Boston Gazette*, June 27, 1774.

[19] *Mass. Hist. Soc. Proceedings*, Second Series (1886), II, 484–485. Lee, II, 318. *Samuel Adams Papers*, Thomas Mifflin to Sam Adams, May 26, 1774. *Committee of Correspondence Papers*, Philadelphia Committee to Boston Committee, May 21, 1774. Marblehead Committee to Boston Committee, June 18, 1774; Philadelphia Committee to Boston Committee, May 21, 1774. Peter Force, *American Archives*, Fourth Series, I, 303, 304, 323. Drayton, I, 128.

Covenant revealed how greatly Sam Adams had misjudged the
strength of his supporters in the Southern and middle colonies.
He depended upon "those worthy members of society, the
tradesmen . . . under God, to form the revolution of the
other ranks of citizens" in New York and Philadelphia.[20]   If
the merchants attempted to sell American liberty to the British
government in exchange for bounties and privileges, Adams
believed the mechanics would rise and "forbid the auction."
But in 1774, when Sam Adams set on foot the Solemn League,
the lower-class town radicals were not yet sufficiently strong
to force it upon the more conservative classes.   New York was
in the throes of a violent struggle for supremacy between the
merchants and Sons of Liberty; and, as conservatives or radicals
gained the upper hand, the complexion of the city changed
with bewildering suddenness from a stronghold of the "champions of liberty" to one of renegade Tories "hugging their
chains."   Pennsylvania — a province "which has hitherto been
distinguished for its moderation" — was under the sway of John
Dickinson, who declared, when he learned of Adams's scheme:
"Nothing can throw us into a more pernicious confusion but
one colony's breaking the line of opposition by advancing too
hastily before the rest." [21]   Until radicals like Isaac Sears of
New York and Charles Thomson, "the Sam Adams of Philadelphia," came into power, Adams's plans of revolutionizing America made slow progress in the Southern and middle colonies.

Rather than adopt the Boston-made Solemn League and
Covenant, the New York Whigs proposed that a Continental
Congress be held to petition for redress of grievances and to
determine by united counsel what steps should be taken against
the mother country.   Almost all the colonies supported a
Congress as against the Solemn League — many because it appeared less dangerous than riding on the tail of Sam Adams's
kite.

No American patriot had demanded more vigorously than

[20] Leake, 89.
. [21] Frothingham, 317. Quincy, 118, 148. *Sam Adams Papers*, Isaac
Sears and Alexander McDougall to Sam Adams, July 25, 1774. *Documents
relative to the Colonial History of New York*, VIII, 433.   *Correspondence of
Thomas Gage*, edited by C. E. Carter (1931), I, 361.

Sam Adams a Continental Congress to unite colonial opposition to Great Britain. In 1773, for example, he told Hutchinson that only a Congress of representatives from the various provinces could undertake to draw a line between the supreme authority of Parliament and the total independence of the colonies; and it was the fashion among Boston patriots to look forward to "some future Congress as the glorious source of the salvation of America." [22] His writings are filled with exhortations to Americans to unite: "The Colonies are all embark'd in the same bottom," he frequently said. "The Liberties of all are alike invaded by the same haughty Power." [23] Nevertheless, New York's proposal of a Continental Congress in 1774 left him cold. Adams feared that it would be too slow in bringing pressure to bear upon the mother country. "A Congress," he said, "is of absolute Necessity in my Opinion, but from the length of time it will take to bring it to pass, I fear it cannot answer for the present Emergency." [24] Delay, he exclaimed, would be fatal to Boston. And, indeed, the plight of the Puritan metropolis was deplorable: practically all business had ceased; hundreds of workmen had been thrown out of employment; and most of the inhabitants were "render'd wretchedly miserable." Moreover, quick action was necessary because the Tories were raising a storm against the patriots by whispering in the people's ears that it was "our Vile Sons" who were responsible for the town's misfortune.[25]

Sam Adams was well aware that the Tories and lukewarm Whigs expected to wield sufficient power in the Congress to prevent the use of economic weapons against the mother country. This prospect gave rise to many misgivings among the Sons of Liberty; and Sam Adams dreaded nothing more than being thrown in with a large number of "half-way Whigs" who were certain to clamor to go home as soon as they had dispatched a petition to the King and Parliament. Rather than run such risk, Adams wished the Sons of Liberty in each province to take

[22] Wells, II, 82.
[23] *The Writings of Samuel Adams*, II, 25.
[24] *Ibid.*, II, 115, 123–124.
[25] R. Lechemere to Messrs. Lane Son and Fraser, May 30, 1774, MS. Mass. Hist. Soc.

the reins in their own hands and follow Massachusetts into rebellion against the British government.   Therefore, the Boston
committee of correspondence protested to the New York and
Philadelphia committees against summoning a Congress before
adopting a nonimportation agreement.   The stoppage of British
trade to America, said the Boston patriots, would have "a
speedy and irresistable operation" upon hardheaded Britons
who ignored colonial petitions and remonstrances as long as
their pocketbooks were untouched.[26]

But it was soon made clear to Sam Adams that he would be
compelled to take his chances with a Continental Congress.
The colonies would not touch his Solemn League and Covenant,
yet they greeted the proposal of a Continental Congress with
enthusiasm.   Swallowing his disappointment, Adams quickly
set about securing the election of delegates from Massachusetts
Bay.   After General Gage, the new governor of the colony,
adjourned the General Court to Salem, Adams took care that a
report reached the governor's ears that the House of Representatives was preparing moderate measures for his approval, while
in fact it was taking steps to join the Continental Congress.   On
June 17, 1774, when all was in readiness, the doors to the
representatives' chamber were locked and the key pocketed
by Sam Adams.   Gage soon learned what was going on in the
House and dispatched the secretary to dissolve it.   The secretary pounded on the door in vain: no one would admit him and,
thanks to Adams's foresight, the key could not be found.   The
best that could be done was to dissolve the meeting by reading
Gage's proclamation outside the door.   But the Whigs inside
continued their work: the adherence of Massachusetts Bay to
the Continental Congress was agreed upon; and the "brace
of Adamses" were among those elected to represent the colony
at Philadelphia.

At the same time that Sam Adams was learning how greatly he
had overrated the radical strength in the Southern provinces he
was being made uncomfortably aware that Massachusetts conservatism was still very much alive.   In closing the port of

[26] *Committee of Correspondence Papers,* Boston Committee to New York
Committee, May 31, 1774.

Boston, the British government left a loophole by which the citizens might escape the full penalty of the law: if the tea destroyed at the Tea Party were paid for, royal clemency would be extended the town. When these terms were known in Boston, Adams remarked that if anyone should pay for the tea it was Thomas Hutchinson and his Tory friends whose obstinacy had made its safe return to England impossible. Nevertheless, a strong sentiment began to develop in Boston in favor of making full amends for the "Narrangansett" braves' work. Benjamin Franklin and John Dickinson of Pennsylvania urged payment, and Thomas Hutchinson made the offer more tempting by promising that if Boston paid the first cost of the tea "every thing else would be made easy." [27] The rapid fall in Boston real estate as a result of the Port Bill increased the clamor from the propertied class that reparation be made to the East India Company. Even the threats of the Sons of Liberty failed to silence the conservatives; and the frightened Whigs were forced to confess that the party in favor of paying for the tea was becoming too formidable for them.[28] A call was sent out to Sam Adams, then in Salem attending the General Court, to come to Boston and crush the Tories. Although Adams was busied in Salem laying plans for the first Continental Congress, he sent down to Boston a batch of propaganda calculated to overset the conservatives. He pointed out that Bostonians would make themselves contemptible in the eyes of their fellow colonists if they faltered after their "late glorious Behaviour" in the Tea Party and that, when the British government saw them in retreat, it would load the colony with taxes until the metropolis had been turned into a "poor fishing village." Massachusetts farmers listened eagerly to Adams because they feared that the tea would be paid for with money collected by means of a province tax — thus compelling yeomen to make good the damage done by the Boston Sons of

[27] *The Works of Benjamin Franklin*, VI, 179. Charles J. Stille, *The Life and Times of John Dickinson* (1891), 109. Peter Force, *American Archives, Fourth Series* (1837), I, 344.

[28] Frothingham, 317. R. Lechemere to Messrs. Lane Son and Fraser, Feb. 14, 1774, MS. Mass. Hist. Soc. *Chalmers Papers*, IV, Extracts of some Letters from New England, Dated in July and Aug. 1774.

Liberty. And at the Boston town meeting, Adams's supporters turned out in such numbers that the "better sort" who
favored reimbursing the East India Company were outvoted
"by a great Majority of the lower Class" which roundly damned
the British government and dared it to do its worst against the
"Antient Capital of North America." [29]

By pushing the colonies toward an open rupture with the
mother country, Adams terrified the conservative Whigs, who
believed with John Dickinson that the cause of liberty should
be left in the hands of lofty-minded patriots strongly averse to
the riots, sedition, and outright rebellion practised by Boston
Sons of Liberty. These cautious "half-way Whigs" were certain that America was not yet a match in war for Great Britain:
a premature struggle with the mother country, they exclaimed,
would prove so disastrous that the colonies would be "kept
down another Age." [30] They declared that there was no need
to hasten a quarrel with Great Britain: Americans had everything
to gain by postponing the day of separation, for within a few
years the colonies would be so powerful that the mother country would be unable to deny their demands. It was believed
that the rapidly increasing population in America would soon
outstrip that of Great Britain and that the balance of empire
would be shifted westward across the Atlantic. Some colonists
confidently looked forward to seeing good King George holding
court and opening Parliament in Philadelphia or New York,
and it is probable that George III would have found those
"polite cities" more suitable than Boston as the seat of his
American empire. Boston, he was informed, was inhabited
by rowdy Congregationalists who could no more bear a gentleman than a bishop and who planted their streets with Liberty
trees and broken glass. Dr. Franklin calculated that Americans doubled their population once every twenty years: therefore they had only to keep quiet for a few years more before
they could make their own terms with King and Parliament. [31]
James Otis believed the time was not far remote when one

[29] *Boston Gazette*, May 16, 1774; Aug. 8, 1774.
[30] *The Writings of Benjamin Franklin*, VI, 273.
[31] *Ibid.*, 3–4.

hundred million people would inhabit the colonies, and Dr.
Samuel Johnson lamented that His Majesty's overseas subjects were stiff-necked republicans who multiplied "with the
fecundity of their own rattle-snakes."[32] With abundant
natural resources and a birth rate that put the mother country
to shame, America seemed destined to become "the imperial
Mistress of the world" after the fall of the tottering British
Empire. This certainty of greatness by easy, natural means
convinced many colonists that it was foolhardy to take aggressive action against Great Britain. By waiting a few years,
war was certain to break out between England and France and
then the colonies could separate themselves from the mother
country without a struggle, if they chose. But if there was to
be fighting, they urged it be left to their children, who, millions
strong, would easily overwhelm the puny armies from the
"Island" of Great Britain.[33]

No patriot had firmer faith in the future greatness of America
than Sam Adams. As early as 1768 he said that America was
a great empire that would soon give laws to England; and his
conviction had since deepened that "providence will erect a
mighty empire in America" while the "Islanders," having lost
their colonies, would be "sunk into obscurity and contempt."[34]
But, unlike Benjamin Franklin, Adams did not draw the conclusion from the colonies' high birth rate that the Revolution
should be delayed in order to make the parting easier. He believed that the present generation of Sons of Liberty should
settle the controversy with the mother country rather than
hand it on to their descendants who might be "faint & languid"
in the defense of liberty.[35] By waiting quietly, Adams maintained, the British government would be encouraged to load
more taxes upon the colonists, who might soon become ac-

[32] Otis, *Considerations on Behalf of the Colonists*, 30–31. Johnson, 7.
[33] *Samuel Adams Papers*, Arthur Lee to Sam Adams, Dec. 24, 1772.
Lee, 237, 241. *The Works of Benjamin Franklin*, VI, 3–4. *Arthur Lee
Papers*, Sparks MSS. Harvard College Library, II, Thomas Cushing to
Arthur Lee, Feb. 1775. *Letters of Thomas Cushing, Mass. Hist. Soc.
Collections*, Fourth Series, IV, 362, 363, 420.
[34] *Boston Gazette*, Aug. 24, 1772; Nov. 2, 1772.
[35] *The Writings of Samuel Adams*, III, 66.

customed to such tyranny. Americans must challenge every step made by the British government, he said, and keep colonial rights always in the foreground. The very fact that America was gaining strength was "the strongest reason why we should be watchful over ourselves, lest for the sake of present peace, we *indirectly* or *implicitly*, or in any manner of way *inadvertently* make the least *appearance* of receding from our just claim of right." The colonies were already strong enough, Adams told New Englanders, to resist Great Britain successfully: if Americans formed an independent state, he said, "we certainly have no Cause to doubt of our Success in maintaining Liberty." Delay merely lessened the colonies' chances of victory because the Tories were entrenching themselves behind an army of officeholders independent of the provincial legislatures. "Every day," Adams exclaimed, "strengthens our oppressors & weakens us." If Sam Adams were to be believed, the wisest course for Americans was to prime their muskets and pray that the battle would not be long delayed. "It must come to a quarrel with Great Britain sooner or later," he said; "and if so, what can be a better time than the present?" [36]

[36] *Boston Gazette*, Sept. 13, 1773; Oct. 11, 1773. *The Writings of Samuel Adams*, II, 341. Gordon, I, 335, 336.

XIII

SAM ADAMS AND THE CONTINENTAL CONGRESS

SAM ADAMS was certainly not a dressy man; and it was a problem to his friends — although Sam himself seems to have given it no thought — how he was to make a proper appearance in Philadelphia at the Congress.   Adams had one of the slenderest wardrobes in Boston, yet he was so little troubled by its deficiencies that, had he been left to himself, he probably would have gone to Philadelphia in his everyday clothes.   To prevent this calamity, his friends resolved to send him southward in unwonted style.   One asked Adams to call at a tailor's shop to be "measur'd for a suit of Cloaths and chuse his Cloth"; another inquired politely about the condition of his linen; others questioned him concerning the shortcomings of his breeches and hose.   By this means, Adams was presented with an entire new outfit including: —

> a new whig
> a new Hatt
> six pair of the best silk hose
> six pair of fine thread ditto
> six pair shoes.

After he had been suitably arrayed for Congress, a friend "modestly enquir'd" of Adams "whether his finances want rather low than otherwyes."   Adams replied that although his pocketbook was empty, he was totally indifferent to money as long as "his *poor* abilities was of any service to the Publick." This answer seemed so worthy of an "Old Roman" that Adams's friend pulled out his purse and urged the patriot to accept a small present of "about 15 or 20 Johannes." [1]

[1] *Mass. Hist. Soc. Proceedings* (1866), VIII, 340.   Wells, II, 208.

Sam Adams and his fellow delegates set off from Boston in what, to Adams at least, was unaccustomed luxury. They rode in "a coach and four, preceded by two white servants who were mounted and arm'd, with four blacks behind in livery, two on horseback and two footmen." [2] This resplendent procession cantered by the Boston Common, where five regiments of British regulars lay encamped, and proceeded to Watertown, where they were met by gentlemen on horseback who treated them to "an elegant Entertainment." [3] Connecticut gave them a rousing reception: in every town, the people rang the bells and set off cannon with such fervor that John Adams said "no Governor of a Province, nor General of any army, was ever treated with so much ceremony and assiduity as we have been throughout the whole colony of Connecticut." In New York, the Bostonians sat down to the most splendid dinner John Adams had ever seen. Their hosts were the New York merchants and their meeting place the Exchange Tavern, where Silas Deane, the Connecticut delegate to the Continental Congress, found them late that evening "in the highest possible spirits," having passed the glass so briskly that they raised their good humor "just to that nice point which is above disguise or suspicion." [4] There was little in New York, besides excellent wine, to raise the spirits of Sam Adams and his friends: there was a strange "delinquency and backwardness" in the city; the Sons of Liberty, led by Isaac Sears, had been decisively defeated by the conservative merchants; and it was doubtful whether the party now in power in New York would support the Continental Congress.[5] Moreover, Philip Livingston alarmed the Bostonians by accompanying his remarks about "Goths and Vandals" with uneasy glances in their direction, which convinced the Adamses that he believed New Englanders at least as dangerous as British tyranny. Escaping from these un-

[2] *Mass. Hist. Soc. Proceedings*, VIII, 339.

[3] *Boston Gazette*, Aug. 15, 1774.

[4] *The Works of John Adams*, II, 343, 345–353. *Deane Papers, Collections N. Y. Hist. Soc.* (1887), I, 6.

[5] Josiah Quincy, 118, 173. *Documents relative to the Colonial History of New York*, VII, 433. *Deane Papers*, I, 6–7.

friendly surroundings, Sam Adams and his party hurried on to Princeton, where they were dismayed to find that the students sang in chapel as badly as did New York Presbyterians. But John Adams pardoned their discords because they studied hard and were all ardent Sons of Liberty.[6]

The antagonism the Boston delegates encountered in New York from Philip Livingston was merely a foretaste of the hostility and distrust which greeted them at Carpenter's Hall. Many Southern Whigs were not free from the fear that, if British rule were removed, Massachusetts would seize the hegemony of America and send governors to all the other provinces. "Boston aims at nothing less than the sovereignty of the whole continent," cried Southern Tories; and they declared that when King George had been turned out of America, Bostonians would overturn the political and social order and set up "a wild Republic of mad Independents."[7] To Southern patriots who already felt strong prejudice against New Englanders as "a parcel of Canting, Hypocritical, peculating Knaves" who loathed Episcopalians and all gentlemen regardless of denomination, these apprehensions were not altogether fantastic.[8] Bostonians had already done much to put Virginians and Carolinians on their guard. By assuming the leadership of the colonies in their quarrel with the mother country, Boston had aroused the suspicion that it was attempting to dupe the other colonies into fighting its battles against the British government. Colonists were jealous of the "big and haughty airs" assumed by Massachusetts men and feared there was "too great a nationality among the Bay-men" for the good of America as a whole.[9] Boston's political principles were too far advanced for most Americans: whereas Sam Adams and his followers had long since denied Parliament all authority over the colonies, the majority of Southern Whigs believed with John Dickinson that Parliament had a superintending power over

[6] *The Works of John Adams*, II, 350, 351, 356.
[7] *Mass. Hist. Soc. Proceedings* (1916), XLIX, 445.   Jonathan Boucher, *Reminiscences of an American Loyalist* (1925), 133.
[8] *Samuel Adams Papers*, William Palfrey to Sam Adams, Oct. 3, 1775.
[9] *The Works of John Adams*, IX, 344.   Gordon, II, 38.

them. Moreover, Sam Adams's doings in Boston led many Americans to conclude that the "Saints" were bent upon total independence of the mother country.

The full weight of this distrust of New Englanders fell upon Sam Adams. He was a poor man; he was more of a democrat than most members of Congress; and he was the embodiment of that New England spirit — or, rather, of "mobbish" Boston's spirit — upon which Southerners looked askance. It was remembered that Sam Adams had attempted in Massachusetts Bay to end the "insolent domination in a few, a very few, opulent monopolizing families" — a purpose that was not likely to endear him to monopolizing South Carolina and Virginia aristocrats.[10] It was supposed of Sam Adams, as of most Bostonians, that he was at heart a levelist who wished to lop off the Whig aristocracy after he had finished with the Tories. He was known in Congress as "the *Greatest Republican* in America" and as "the most extravagant partisan of the democracy"; and, when democratic leanings were coupled with lack of property, as in Adams's case, he loomed in Congress as the potential Wat Tyler of the Revolution against whom Whig gentlemen would do well to be on guard.[11] In the eyes of many of Adams's fellow rebels, it was essential that an American patriot be well stocked with material possessions in order that he might not be tempted to divert the struggle against British tyranny into a war upon American property rights. They believed the purpose of the Revolution was to protect property and that there was no room in the Whig Party for one who did not think the inviolability of all private property — except, of course, that which belonged to Tories — was one of the most sacred rights of nature. Furthermore, Adams was a stiff-backed "Bay-man," so partial to all things which concerned Massachusetts that it was said of him that he wished to see Massachusetts at the head of America, Boston at the head of Massachusetts, and himself dictator of Boston. Not only did

[10] *The Works of John Adams*, IX, 388.
[11] *Letters of the Members of the Continental Congress*, edited by E. C. Burnett, V, 400. Marquis de Chastellux, *Travels in North America* (1787), I, 276.

he epitomize the brawling, riotous metropolis of the latter-
day New England "Saints," but he was suspected of wishing to
"Bostonize" the whole continent and to throw his mobs against
the conservative Whigs who stood in the way of his levelism.

Southern gentlemen might well have dismissed most of their
fears of Sam Adams as fanciful. In spite of his meagre estate,
Sam Adams no more contemplated upsetting property rights
than did Virginia planters, and he was far too good a student
of John Locke to forget that the chief purpose of government
was to protect property. In 1768, Adams had pronounced
"Utopian schemes of levelling, and a community of goods" as
objectionable as the theory which gave the Crown and Parliament absolute power over the colonists' property. But as a
Bostonian and a democrat, conservatives had more reason to
dread him. His pride in his home town was so intense that he
frequently seemed to regard himself as more of a Bostonian
than an American. Adams himself admitted that he "showed
a Partiality in nothing so much as in regard to the Citizens of
that Place"(Boston), and even his fellow New Englanders complained that he had "too great an Idea of the Virtue of the
State of Massachusetts Bay." [12] And, until the Massachusetts
Constitutional Convention of 1780, he was an equally staunch
democrat. Even his cousin, John Adams, began to have
serious doubts about him when Sam championed unilateral
legislatures for the new states. One of John Adams's chief
grievances against Tom Paine was that *Common Sense* urged
the "crude ignorant Notion" of one sovereign assembly ruled
by means of appointed executive and judicial committees — a
scheme of government which destroyed the sharp divisions
between executive, legislative, and judiciary as well as the
checks and balances which John Adams believed essential in
a sound constitution. His fears for the future of the new
nation were visibly increased when he saw this political heresy
starting up in Sam Adams, who had so little respect for the
British Constitution, as interpreted by Montesquieu, that he

[12] *The Writings of Samuel Adams*, I, 137. *Samuel Adams Papers*, N. Y.
Public Library, Benjamin Kent to Sam Adams, Aug. 4, 1776; Sam Adams to
———, March 6, 1781.

was "always inclining to the most democratical forms, and even
to a single sovereign assembly." [13]   Sam Adams had none of
John Adams's fears that the people would abuse their power
by making it a "Cloke for Licentiousness."   But it was not
until after the French Revolution, when Sam became the Jacobin
governor of Massachusetts and John the Federalist President
of the United States, that the "brace of Adamses" split upon
the issue whether "Liberty, Equality, and Fraternity" should
become the political and social creed of the United States.

The New England delegates attempted to disarm the suspicion they encountered in Congress by saying little and keeping out of sight as much as possible.   They were "very modest"
in their conversation and acted with "uncommon prudence and
discretion." [14]   Among their friends, however, the Massachusetts men were less reticent, although even to them they
gave only "hints, which like straws and feathers, tell us from
which point of the Compass the wind comes." [15]   The Adamses
knew that if they showed their true colors in Congress and
openly agitated for complete independence they would produce a panic among timid congressmen who were ready to
stampede the moment they scented New England "republicanism."   Although they denied all desire for independence, their
prudence was wasted upon delegates who believed that a
Bostonian who did not publicly preach sedition was in sheep's
clothing for a sinister purpose.   These delegates were more
surprised than deceived by Sam Adams's studied mildness and
they continued to upbraid him as though he were ranting
political radicalism every day from the floor of Congress.

Nevertheless, Adams had in Congress a few staunch friends
with whom he could speak plainly and prearrange the proceedings of the Continental Congress in the same manner he
had controlled the Boston town meetings.   While the Bos-

[13] *The Works of John Adams*, II, 507–509; III, 17, 18.   *Warren-Adams
Letters, Mass. Hist. Soc. Collections*, LXXII (1917), I, 195, 196.
[14] *Aspinwall Papers, Mass. Hist. Soc. Collections*, Fourth Series (1871),
X, 706.   William B. Reed, *Life and Correspondence of Joseph Reed*, I, 78.
The Examination of Joseph Galloway . . . before the House of Commons
(London, 1779), 3.
[15] *Mass. Hist. Soc. Collections*, Fourth Series, X, 706.

tonians sat silent in their seats in Carpenter's Hall, their Southern supporters proposed the radical steps that had been agreed upon in the caucus and held Congress spellbound with their oratory. Christopher Gadsden of South Carolina declared that Massachusetts could not stand alone against British power and that Congress must act with vigor lest the country be "deluged in blood"; and Richard Henry Lee made the motion for a nonimportation and nonexportation agreement against Great Britain which partly fulfilled the purpose of Sam Adams's ill-fated Solemn League and Covenant.[16]

Christopher Gadsden, in particular, came to the rescue of the New Englanders when they found themselves arraigned in Congress as fire-eating republicans. Gadsden "thank'd God there was such a People in America" as New Englanders who had created "an Asylum that honest Men might resort to in the Time of their last Distress, supposing them driven out of their own States." He advised his countrymen to imitate the New Englanders instead of abusing them. From such "a Systematical Body of Men," Gadsden exclaimed, Americans had nothing to fear. The real danger to the American cause, he declared, came not from New England but from the frontier — the backwoods of Virginia, North and South Carolina, Georgia and Florida, where roamed "a numerous Sett of Banditti of no Property or Principles whatever & ready to be made the tools of power for the sake of plunder whenever they could do it with impunity." Why fear New Englanders, who were men of principle, Gadsden asked, when the frontier swarmed with "Catalines" who were ready to sell themselves to the enemy? Gadsden had no more than resumed his seat when a Pennsylvania delegate sprang up to urge him to include the Pennsylvania frontiersmen in his next denunciation of the enemies of American liberty.[17]

One of Sam Adams's most effective ways of putting his enemies in bad repute throughout New England was, as has been seen, to insinuate they were "papist," or, failing this, that they

[16] *The Works of John Adams*, II, 382 (note), 384.
[17] *Samuel Adams Papers*, Christopher Gadsden to Sam Adams, April 4, 1779.

were members of the Church of England. But Adams saw
that this method, although eminently successful in Faneuil Hall,
was not suited to Carpenter's Hall, which held a large number
of Southern delegates who were Episcopalians. It was clear,
moreover, that Bostonians had not raised their reputation in
the Southern colonies by using the Church of England as a
bugbear. To soothe these outraged religious sensibilities,
Thomas Cushing moved in Congress that the meeting be opened
with prayers by Dr. Duché, a prominent Church of England
clergyman. When Jay of New York and Rutledge of South
Carolina opposed Cushing's motion on the ground that the
members of Congress were of such divergent religious beliefs
they could not worship together, Sam Adams took possession
of the floor and roundly declared that "he was no bigot, and
could hear a prayer from a gentleman of piety and virtue, who
was at the same time a friend to his country." [18] Cushing's
motion was carried and the next day Duché appeared before
Congress in full canonicals. His prayer was an unparalleled
success: "even Quakers shed tears," it was said; one delegate
declared it was worth riding a hundred miles to hear; and
John Adams believed that not even Dr. Cooper of Boston, the
mightiest of the "black regiment," could have interceded with
the Lord for Boston's salvation with greater fervor. [19] Although Duché later became a Tory refugee, it seemed in 1774
that Adams had made a "masterly stroke of policy" by bringing him before Congress. For the moment, Southern Episcopalians' distrust of New England Congregationalists subsided.
But New Englanders had no need to fear that Sam Adams's
rigid orthodoxy was weakening in the lax atmosphere of
Philadelphia: he had championed Duché solely because he
recognized that "many of our *warmest Friends* are *Members*
of the *Church of England*" and suspicious of New Englanders'
attitude toward their sect. [20]

   Even before the opening of the first Continental Congress,

[18] *The Writings of Samuel Adams*, II, 188. *The Works of John Adams*,
II, 368–369 (note).

[19] *The Works of John Adams*, II, 369 (note). *Deane Papers*, I, 20.

[20] *Journals of the Continental Congress* (1904), I, 27 (note). *Boston
Gazette*, Sept. 26, 1774.

FANEUIL HALL, BOSTON

"THE CRADLE OF LIBERTY"

(From the Massachusetts Magazine for 1789)

The Old State House, Boston

LOOKING DOWN STATE STREET FROM WASHINGTON STREET

(From the Massachusetts Magazine for 1793)

Sam Adams had singled out Joseph Galloway as his most dangerous enemy. Galloway was speaker of the Pennsylvania Assembly, boss of the Quaker political machine, and the leader of
those "half-way patriots" who Sam Adams feared more than
outright Tories. When a Congress was first proposed, Galloway gave the Boston committee of correspondence fair warning of his intention to create a "political union" between the
colonies and mother country that would be proof against
colonial demagogues.[21] He earned the ill-will of the Boston
patriots by pointing out that the changes made by the Crown
in the Massachusetts charter, which Sam Adams was using to
stir up opposition to the mother country, immediately affected
only Massachusetts, Rhode Island, and Connecticut — the
charter colonies where the council was elective; Pennsylvanians,
he said, had no grievances in the abolition of the popularly
elected council because they had recently petitioned for a royal
charter in which the King was given power to appoint the members of the Upper House.[22] Moreover, Galloway hoped to
avert a nonimportation agreement against Great Britain by inducing Congress to send petitions and commissioners to the
mother country to plead for redress. He dreaded war between America and Great Britain as the certain ruin of the colonies and he set himself in opposition to "New England demagogues, educated under their democratical charter," because
he believed their policy led inevitably to a disastrous conflict
with the mother country. Sam Adams he regarded as the most
baleful of the New England "demagogues": the leader of the
irreconcilables, "the great director of their councils, and the
most cautious, artful, and reserved man among them."[23]

Sam Adams had brought to Philadelphia his bag of political
tricks from which he intended to serve Galloway as he had
Bernard and Hutchinson. From the outset, Galloway found
himself forced to breast a powerful current in Congress: he was
deeply offended when the delegates rejected his offer of the
Pennsylvania State House as a meeting place and chose instead

[21] Force, Fourth Series, I, 486.
[22] Galloway, 21, 22.
[23] Ibid. 8, 109. Journals of the Continental Congress, I, 47.

Carpenter's Hall, a less suitable building, in order to flatter
the Philadelphia mechanics; and his mortification became acute
when Charles Thomson, whom Galloway had successfully kept
from a seat in Congress, was elected secretary to the Continental
Congress.   Despite these disappointments, Galloway presented
to Congress on September 28, 1774, his plan for the firm "political union" of America and Great Britain.   This scheme might
well have come from the pen of a conservative patriot such as
James Otis, for, like Otis, Galloway acknowledged Parliament's
sovereignty over the colonies.   At the same time he saw the
iniquities of its exercise and the need of colonial representation
in Parliament.   He agreed with Sam Adams that it was futile to
attempt to settle the dispute by putting the colonies in the
position they occupied before 1763: the Empire could not be
preserved, he said, by resurrecting the old colonial system.
Galloway met the crisis, therefore, with a plan which he believed gave Americans the next best thing to representation in
the British Parliament: an American Grand Council in which
every province should be represented.   This Council was to be
an inferior branch of the British Parliament; and within America it was to exercise many of the rights and privileges enjoyed
by the British House of Commons in Great Britain.   But the
consent of the British Parliament was essential for the validity
of its statutes, and a Resident General, appointed by the King,
was to preside over its meetings.

Although Galloway framed his proposal so as to "leave no
room for any reasonable objection on the part of the republicans,
if they meant to be united to Great Britain on any grounds
whatever," neither John nor Sam Adams could swallow the
Grand Council and the Resident General, with Galloway's
heavy seasoning of Parliamentary sovereignty and royal prerogative.   But, in spite of their opposition, it was decided by
the Congress, six colonies to five, to resume debate on Galloway's plan at a later day.   With this understanding, the plan
was entered upon the minutes of Congress, and Joseph Galloway began marshaling his forces to drive the republicans out of
Congress, federate the colonies, and keep America within the
British Empire.

Yet Galloway's plan was never again considered by Congress. Sam Adams so inflamed the Philadelphia mob against the scheme that Galloway feared he would be attacked in the streets; and he became panic-stricken when he discovered a halter in his mail with a warning that unless he made use of it he would be put to death.   This threat, Galloway firmly believed, came from the "violent party" in Congress led by Sam Adams.[24]   By these means, Galloway was so thoroughly intimidated that he did not dare to reopen the debate.   Moreover, while Galloway was attempting to rally the conservative Whigs in Philadelphia to the defense of the Empire, the British government passed the Quebec Act, which, by threatening the colonists with a horde of "Popish slaves" in the North and West, disposed thousands of Americans to follow Sam Adams and his fellow radicals "should it be war itself."   Galloway's party was overthrown and his plan, which, had it been adopted, might have made possible the development of the United States within the Empire as a Commonwealth, was erased from the minutes of Congress "so that no vestige of it might appear there." [25]

Before leaving for Philadelphia, Adams had pressed upon his friends in Massachusetts Bay a plan to call a convention in Suffolk County to protest against British military rule and infringements of charter rights.   Adams's advice was followed: a meeting was called at Milton to evade the prohibition of town meetings and a set of resolutions known as the Suffolk Resolves were drafted by Joseph Warren and adopted by the delegates. The Resolves were immediately sent with Paul Revere, the Patriot "Express," to the Massachusetts delegates at Philadelphia, who, it was planned, were to secure their adoption by Congress.   But it seemed doubtful if the Continental Congress could be persuaded to sanction the boldness of the Suffolk patriots, who declared in their Resolves that no obedience was due the Boston Port Bill, urged the people to prepare for a defensive war against Great Britain, and ordered the committees of

[24] *The Examination of Joseph Galloway*, 59.
[25] Reed, I, 78. *Boston Gazette*, Dec. 5, 1774. *Journals of the Continental Congress*, I, 51 (note).

correspondence to summon the citizens to arms when the alarm
was sounded in Boston. Joseph Galloway exclaimed that the
Suffolk convention had made a "complete declaration of war
against Great Britain." [26]   Nevertheless, after a hot debate and
even hotter caucusing, the Virginia-Massachusetts "phalanx"
carried the field and the Suffolk Resolves were formally adopted
by the Continental Congress.

The Tories screamed that by upholding the republicans in
Suffolk County, Congress "gave such a blast from the trumpet
of sedition, as made one half of America shudder." [27]   The
military preparations made by the New England Whigs were
now fully approved by Congress, and they were led to believe
they would be supported by all British America if it came to
war with the mother country. Congress was pledged to the
hilt to aid Massachusetts in a defensive war; and, although
the delegates refused to promise aid if the patriots provoked
war with the British troops in Boston, it was well understood
that if the British sallied out of the metropolis with hostile intent or seized a patriot leader, hostilities would be justified in
Americans' eyes. Conservatives were terror-stricken at Congress's promise to support Massachusetts, but the Adamses were
in high spirits after the adoption of the Suffolk Resolves: Sam
Adams said it was now certain that America would aid Boston
"to the utmost" and John Adams declared that the day Congress had voted to accept the Resolves was the happiest day of
his life because the colonies had shown they would "support
Massachusetts or perish with her." [28]   War between the colonies and mother country now hung upon the question of
whether the fighting, almost certain to break out in Massachusetts, was defensive; and with a master of propaganda such as
Sam Adams at work, Americans were certain to be convinced
that New Englanders were fighting a defensive war against
British tyranny.

Nevertheless, the nonimportation and nonexportation agree-

[26] *Samuel Adams Papers*, Benjamin Kent to Sam Adams, Aug. 20, 1774.
Galloway, 68, 69.
[27] *What think ye of the Congress now?* (1775), 31.
[28] *The Writings of Samuel Adams*, III, 156. *Journals of the Continental
Congress*, I, 39 (note). Gordon, I, 392.

ment adopted by the first Continental Congress was not all Sam Adams had hoped for: although some of the spirit of the Solemn League and Covenant was retained, the colonists were permitted to import any amount of goods before November 1, 1774; wines and coffee, though still dutied, might be imported after the agreement went into effect; and each colony was obliged to carry out only such resolutions as had been assented to by its delegates — a concession to local sovereignty that Jefferson believed "totally destroys that union of conduct in the several colonies which was the very purpose of calling a Congress."[29]   But most Americans felt certain that the boycott of Great Britain and the West Indies would speedily bring the mother country to terms: Richard Henry Lee believed that the same ship that carried the news of the proceedings of the Continental Congress to England would return with the Ministry's promise of redress.   Adams did not believe Great Britain would be brought to terms so easily; had the government yielded in 1774, however, he would have been the first to exclaim that the colonies had driven a poor bargain with the mother country. Congress acknowledged Parliament's right to regulate colonial trade and refused to go beyond 1763 in enumerating American grievances.   Therefore Adams believed America's terms for reconciliation with England were far too low: as long as Parliament's sovereignty over the colonies was recognized, he said, there could be no lasting settlement of the quarrel.[30]

Thomas Young promised Sam Adams a pleasant surprise when he returned to Massachusetts Bay.   "You will perceive," wrote Young, "the temper of your countrymen in the condition your every wish, your every sigh, for years past panted to find it.   Thoroughly aroused and unanimously in earnest."[31]   New Englanders were indeed as warlike as an "Old Roman" could wish.   When "that illustrious Warrior and firm Patriot,"

[29] *The Works of Thomas Jefferson*, edited by Paul Leicester Ford (1904), II, 93.
[30] *The Works of John Adams*, II, 362–363; IX, 416, 453. *Journals of the Continental Congress*, I, 68–69. *Samuel Adams Papers*, Elbridge Gerry to Sam Adams, Oct. 15, 1774.
[31] Dr. Thomas Young to Sam Adams, Sept. 4, 1774, MS. Mass. Hist. Soc.

Israel Putnam, came down to Boston driving a flock of sheep before him for the relief of hungry Bostonians, he was welcomed as a savior; and both Putnam and Charles Lee, the English adventurer who became famous overnight by offering his services in the patriot cause, were "so much carressed" by Bostonians that they had difficulty in getting out of town. Throughout New England, the citizens were drilling as though war would begin within a few weeks; and "Old Louisbourgh soldiers" were laughing at the British fortifications on Boston Neck and swearing they could storm them as easily as a beaver dam. The "popular Fury" had spread from its source in Boston over the whole country: the British troops were no longer opposed by a "Boston rabble" that might quickly be dispersed with a few regiments, but by the "Freeholders and Farmers of the Country." [32] New Englanders had never before seemed so much like the founding fathers in Sam Adams's eyes: they prayed while they cleaned their muskets, and there seemed little doubt that in a crisis they would "shew themselves to be worthy of such Ancestors." [33]

But what chiefly led Adams to hope that New Englanders' fighting blood was up was their readiness to march to the defense of Boston. While Adams was at Congress a rumor that British soldiers had killed six Americans and that the fleet had opened fire on Boston put thousands of armed New Englanders, New Yorkers, and Pennsylvanians on the highroad to Boston. Since the news reached eastern Massachusetts and Connecticut on a Lord's Day, most of the citizens were in the meetinghouses, but clergy and congregations leaped out of their pulpits and pews, seized their muskets, and set off for Boston "cursing the King and Lord North, general Gage, the bishops and cursed curates, and the church of England." This false alarm, which perhaps was purposely set to "try the temper of the people," gave Massachusetts patriots "the most exalted idea" of the

[32] *Samuel Adams Papers, Dr. Thomas Young to Sam Adams*, Aug. 19 and 21, 1774. Frothingham, 357. Josiah Quincy, 175, 181. *The Correspondence of Thomas Gage*, edited by C. E. Carter (1931), I, 367, 371.
[33] *The Writings of Samuel Adams*, III, 163, 171.

willingness of New Englanders to fight for their liberties.[34] Sam Adams was told that if the British had marched out of Boston five miles they would have been cut off to a man; and on his way home from Philadelphia, he passed through districts where the entire able-bodied population had turned out to drive the "bloody-backed rascals" from the metropolis. Even at Philadelphia, it was believed that if the report that the British were cannonading Boston had not been almost immediately contradicted, forty thousand men would have been on the march to Boston. After this display of military ardor it was clear that "if blood be once spilled, we shall be involved in all the horrors of a civil war." [35]

Adams's joy upon finding New England yeomen preparing for war was sobered by the changes that had taken place in Boston while he remained in Philadelphia. "The once happy Boston is now become a den of thieves," wrote Mrs. Adams to her husband, "a Cage of Every unclean Bird — Consignees, Commissioners and tools of every denomination have made this town their ark of safety — they walk upon Change everyday with great insolence." The town that had begun the Revolution was now a Tory stronghold: rather than face mobs of Whig farmers, more dangerous than the Boston mob in its ugliest mood, New England Tories, from "Mandamus" councilors down to the petty squires, took refuge in the metropolis under the guns of royal troops and men-of-war. Although some Whigs left Boston for quieter parts, Mrs. Adams stoutly remained at her house in Purchase Street, where she was joined by her husband after his return from Philadelphia.

The Provincial Congress that had been called in Massachusetts during Adams's absence anxiously awaited his return in the autumn of 1774. Although it claimed no authority, taxes were paid into its treasury and it superseded the royal government of the province. But before the Congress took decisive

[34] *Boston Gazette*, Oct. 24, 1774. *The Correspondence of Thomas Gage*, II, 656. *What think ye of the Congress now?* 27. Frothingham, 356. *The Works of John Adams*, II, 404.

[35] Reed, I, 78.

action, the presence was required of "one who never failed to animate" — Sam Adams.[36] Having sounded public opinion in the middle colonies, Adams was well aware that no aggression could be undertaken against the British troops in Boston. The necessity of respecting the Southerners' prejudice against attacking the redcoats seriously hampered Adams's plans: he was certain early in 1775 that "the publick Liberty must be preserved though at the Expense of many Lives," yet he hesitated to risk losing the support of the Southern colonies by precipitating war.[37] Congress had agreed, however, that if the British marched out of Boston with hostile intent, resistance was justified. Therefore, Sam Adams urged that a New England army be created to lie in wait for the British outside Boston. The proceedings of the Provincial Congress were kept secret, but information leaked through to Gage which convinced him that Adams's plan was to put New Englanders on a war footing, yet at the same time to keep them from "being censured for their rashness by the other Colonies & that made a pretence for deserting them." [38] It was planned to establish a New England military confederation and to put an army of eighteen thousand men in the field, raised by quotas upon the members. Behind this army, New England was to be declared independent of Parliamentary authority and the King recognized as the only bond with the mother country. Many country delegates, however, were unwilling to burden themselves and their constituents with an expensive armament; the Essex members were fearful that the British would retaliate by laying waste the seaports; and it was difficult to convince the majority that there was any immediate necessity for a New England Confederation. Many rural representatives were so frightened by the radicals' war talk that they pleaded illness as an excuse to go home, but Sam Adams administered some strong physic by proposing that as soon as a sick delegate reached his home town he should be compelled to resign his seat in order that a more healthy representa-

---

[36] *Samuel Adams Papers,* John Pitts to Sam Adams, Oct. 16, 1774; Elbridge Gerry to Sam Adams, Oct. 15, 1774.
[37] *The Writings of Samuel Adams,* III, 180, 195.
[38] Allen French, *General Gage's Informers,* 20.

tive might take his place.   This immediately put an end to the epidemic of bowel disorders, agues, and rheums that threatened to invalid half the Congress, but it did not convince the country patriots that they should raise eighteen thousand men on the chance that the British would sally out of Boston.[39]   Adams, Warren, and a few other leaders gave Congress the appearance of "an assembly of Spartans or ancient Romans," but the greater number of delegates showed the virtues of thrifty, cautious New Englanders who thought more about the expense of war than its glory.   These men showed "great irresolution" in making military preparations against the British until they were certain of support from the other colonies.   As a result, the utmost Adams was able to get from the Provincial Congress was a promise that if General Gage marched out of Boston with artillery and baggage, the country should be called to arms to oppose the invader "to the last extremity," and that delegates should be sent from Congress to the New England colonies to learn their attitude toward the proposed confederation.   On the eve of Lexington and Concord, the Provincial Congress adjourned to await the response of the other New England colonies. Little had been done to create the army of which Sam Adams foresaw Massachusetts would soon stand in need.[40]

With Boston full of British troops, trouble was expected at the annual Massacre Oration in March 1775.   Because the soldiers regarded this commemoration as a deliberate insult, a large number of officers crowded with the patriots into the Old South Meetinghouse prepared to "resent any expressions made use of by the Orator, reflecting on the Military."   When Sam Adams saw the meetinghouse filling up with redcoats he immediately suspected they had come to "beat up a Breeze," but he took care, as moderator, to treat them civilly and invite them to take the best seats, in order that they might have no pretext to start a row.   Adams firmly believed that "it is a good Maxim in Politicks as well as War to put & keep the Enemy in the

[39] French, 20, 21, 23, 27.   *The Diary of William Pynchon*, edited by F. E. Oliver (1890), 43 (note).   Gordon, I, 416.

[40] French, 18, 21, 24, 27.   Josiah Quincy, 177.   *The Correspondence of Thomas Gage*, I, 388.

wrong." To begin the ceremonies, Joseph Warren, the speaker of the day, clad in a "Ciceronian Toga," mounted the black-draped pulpit, attended by "the most violent fellows in town" — the Adamses, Hancock, Church, Cooper, and the Boston selectmen. After taking uneasy note of the large number of officers in the audience, Warren threw himself into a "Demosthenian posture, with a handkerchief in his right hand, and his left in his breeches," and "began and ended without action." [41] Warren was careful not to risk a riot by waving the bloody shirt too brazenly and he particularly avoided mention of the *"bloody Massacre."* This restraint saw him safely through his oration: he was "applauded by the mob" and "groaned at by the people of understanding," but when he finally sat down, amidst cheers and hisses, all danger of a free-for-all between soldiers and civilians seemed past. But apparently Sam Adams was disappointed by this tame ending to a promising tussle with the redcoats, for, after Warren had finished, he came forward to propose that "the thanks of the Town should be presented to Doctor Warren for his Elegant and Spirited Oration, and that another Oration should be delivered on the 5th of March next, to commemorate the *Bloody Massacre* of the 5th of March, 1770." Adams's mention of the "bloody Massacre" was the spark that set off the explosive matter within the Old South: officers immediately leaped to their feet and began crying, "O fie, O fie," at the speaker. This created a panic in the galleries, where the Whigs, believing that the soldiers were crying, "Fire, fire," "bounced out of the windows, and swarmed down the gutters like rats, into the street." [42] To add to the confusion, a regiment of British regulars happened to be passing outside at this moment, and when the patriots indoors heard the beating of drums and tramping of feet they assumed they were about to be slaughtered in the meetinghouse. After a large number of Whigs had taken to cover, order was at last restored

[41] *Diary of Frederick MacKenzie* (1930), I, 9–10. Frank Moore, *Diary of the Revolution* (1860), I, 35. *The Writings of Samuel Adams*, III, 206.
[42] Moore, I, 35. *Diary of Frederick MacKenzie*, 9, 10.

and the meeting broke up peacefully.   Although the patriots
had suffered a severe fright, Sam Adams covered their confusion
by declaring that the soldiers, not the civilians, had been in
danger and that if it had not been for the Whigs' self-control
not an officer would have left the meetinghouse alive.[43]

Sam Adams had been frequently warned by his friends that
he was in danger of being seized by the British military authorities, clapped in irons, and taken to England to be tried as a
rebel.   It was said that the British officers who attended Warren's Massacre Oration planned to carry off Adams and other
Whig chiefs when the signal — throwing an egg into Warren's
face — was given.   The patriots believed they had escaped unscathed because the soldier who had been entrusted with the
delicate business of throwing the egg slipped and broke it on
his way to the meetinghouse.   Although Tories jeered that
Adams could not bear to look at a hemp rope and blanched at
the mention of Tyburn, his friends said he showed *"amazing
fortitude, noble resolution, and undaunted courage"* in his contempt of danger.   He voted with other members of the Boston committee of correspondence to "attend the business of the
Committee of Correspondence, as usual, unless prevented, by
brutal force"; and he continued to remain in Boston after the
military occupation, an easy mark for an assassin.   General
Gage was reluctant to lay hands on the patriot leader because he
feared such action would be the signal for hostilities against the
King's troops — which, he observed, New Englanders already
seemed "very ripe to begin." [44]   Nevertheless, as Sam Adams
continued to preach rebellion and prepare for war with the
mother country, it became clear that he "must be tucked up at
all adventures."   Most Massachusetts "top Tories" confidently
expected to see him safely stowed away in the brig of a royal
man-of-war before Congress met.   But when the British government dispatched orders to Gage to take up the leading Massachusetts Whigs, Adams knew of them before Gage; and he

[43] *The Writings of Samuel Adams*, III, 206.   *Mass. Hist. Soc. Proceedings*,
VIII, 340.   *Committee of Correspondence Papers*, July 5, 1774.
[44] *The Correspondence of Thomas Gage*, I, 376.

was in hiding at Lexington with John Hancock when the British general began the hunt.[45]

Because fighting usually broke out between New Englanders and British troops when Sam Adams was in the vicinity, it has been suggested that he may have had a hand in the fighting at Lexington and Concord. Parker and his men ignored the protection of forest and walls and took an open position along the Lexington road on April 18, 1775, as though inviting fire from the British; therefore it is said that Parker was acting under orders from Sam Adams, who was lodging near by with John Hancock at Parson Clark's.[46] It had already been agreed in the Continental Congress that if the British troops marched into the country, the people ought to be called to arms; and although it is certain that Adams was eager to see bloodshed hasten the separation of mother country and colonies, there is nothing to show that he was responsible for the military movements made by the embattled farmers at Lexington or Concord. Nevertheless, he was overjoyed when he heard the rattle of musketry on Lexington Common. "Oh," he exclaimed to Hancock, "what a glorious morning is this!" [47]

If Adams had by any chance planned to make patriot martyrs at Lexington, he did not intend to be one himself. He and Hancock slipped out of Massachusetts during the fighting around Boston and headed southward in Hancock's phaeton for Philadelphia. Since British and Americans had begun the "cutting of throats," it was now Adams's purpose to persuade Congress to adopt the New England army besieging the British troops in Boston and to involve the other colonies in the war against the mother country.

Until Sam Adams reached middle age, he was a very inexpert rider — as John Adams said, Sam "never would be persuaded to mount a Horse." This lack of equestrian skill greatly disturbed John Adams, who firmly believed horsemanship essential

[45] *The Works of John Adams*, IX, 345. *Mass. Hist. Soc. Collections* (1858), IV, Fourth Series, 371–372.

[46] Harold Murdock, *Historic Doubts on the Battle of Lexington*, *Mass. Hist. Soc. Proceedings*, XLIX (1916), 374.

[47] Gordon, I, 479.

"to the Character of a Statesman."   He determined, therefore, to make an effort while on the road to Philadelphia in 1775 to get Sam Adams on a horse and thereby complete his education in statesmanship before he reached Congress.   After much coaxing, Sam was induced to mount one of John's horses, — "a very genteel and easy little Creature," — and John taught him to mount and dismount without the aid of the two servants he usually required.   During the first few days of travel, Sam Adams suffered from the soreness inevitable to an inexperienced rider, but his cousin induced him to keep on, and to buy some linen cloth which their landlady made into "a Pair of Drawers" which eased the friction and "entirely healed the little Breach which had been begun."   Before the travelers had been many days on the road, their servants who rode behind in the carriage were commenting on Sam's superiority as a rider over John Adams; and when they reached Philadelphia, John had the mortification of hearing it said that Sam rode 50 per cent better than he.[48]   After this auspicious beginning, Sam Adams rode frequently, to the great benefit of his health.   And later in the war, when Congress was forced to flee from Philadelphia to escape capture by the British army, the full significance of John Adams's connection of horsemanship and statesmanship no doubt struck Sam Adams.   For certainly the ability to make a quick getaway on horseback was indispensable to American statesmen of the revolutionary period.

Although Sam and John Adams wished ardently in 1775 to see a New Englander in command of the troops about Boston, the prospect of a Northern army under a New England general brought visions to many Southerners of "Goths and Vandals" who, after finishing with the British, would turn upon their fellow colonists and make themselves the rulers of America. The prejudice against a New England general was, however, so strong in Congress that John Adams quickly saw it was useless to put forward even as redoubtable a warrior as "that Thunderbolt of War, the intrepid Putnam." [49]   Meanwhile, the situation in Massachusetts was daily growing more acute:

[48] *Warren-Adams Letters*, I, 110–111.
[49] *Samuel Adams Papers*, Benjamin Church to Sam Adams, Aug. 2, 1775.

appeals poured in to Congress to take over the besieging troops
and the Adamses were threatened with a serious loss of prestige
if they failed to spur Congress to action.   Sam Adams was ir-
resolute and hampered by his reluctance to see any but a New
Englander in command; when John Adams urged the necessity
of action to Sam, he received no more helpful reply than, "What
shall we do?" [50]   By his own account, John Adams alone had a
plan with which to meet the emergency.   The only member
of Congress who attended the meetings in military uniform was
George Washington, a delegate from Virginia.   Although his
military qualifications were not impressive, he caught the eye
of John Adams, who was in search of a general acceptable to
the Southern congressmen and yet capable of taking command
of the New England army and driving the British out of Boston.   John Adams believed that in George Washington he had
found his man; and, during a walk with Sam Adams in the State
House yard, he suggested Washington as commander in chief.
Sam Adams "seemed to think very seriously of it, but said
nothing." [51]

Sam's lack of enthusiasm for George Washington is easily
explained.   Washington was not that "Cromwell" Adams and
other Boston Sons of Liberty had vainly sought in 1768 when
British troops were sent to keep order in the metropolis.   His
military record was not such as to convince Sam Adams that he
was the long-awaited deliverer of America from British tyranny;
and his political opinions — always an important item in Adams's
judgment of military men — were decidedly not Bostonian.
Washington still thought in terms of reconciliation and redress
of grievances rather than of independence and war with the
mother country, and it was well known that he would oppose
the politicians in Congress who favored complete separation
from the mother country.   Nevertheless, the necessity of persuading Congress to take the New England army under its wing
forced the Adamses to act contrary to their convictions.   On
June 15, when Thomas Johnson formally nominated Washington as general, John and Sam Adams supported the motion,

[50] *The Works of John Adams*, II, 416.
[51] *Ibid.*, II, 416, 417.

and, after a few days of brisk caucusing, the army was adopted by Congress and put under Washington's command.[52]

The most deeply offended of the amateur generals who hoped to lead the American army was John Hancock, now, by grace of the Adamses, president of the Continental Congress. Hancock nursed a deep ambition for martial glory and thought himself a serious contender for the command of the Continental army, although his best claim to the post was that he knew how to put the governor's cadets through their manœuvres on the Boston Common and that he looked uncommonly well in gold braid. Yet, if the commander in chief were to be appointed on the strength of his services and sacrifices in the patriot cause, Hancock stood far above Washington and every other military man on the continent. With few prominent candidates in the field, Hancock considered his chances excellent, and when John Adams rose to speak in favor of Washington as commander in chief, he felt certain that Adams's long preamble was leading up to his own appointment. He sat in the president's chair listening with obvious pleasure until Adams came to the point where he suggested Washington as the best man to command the American army. Since Adams stood on the floor facing Hancock, he was able to observe the sudden change of expression that passed over Hancock's face: "mortification and resentment" flared in his eyes and revealed how deeply his vanity had been hurt.[53] When Sam Adams rose to second Washington's name, Hancock's wounded feelings received another stab. From that day, Hancock no longer even pretended friendship for the Adamses; and, as will be seen, he was not reconciled with Sam Adams until the rise of the Federalist Party in New England.

Sam Adams was not troubled because Hancock sulked when he was not allowed to play at being a general, but he was deeply alarmed to find him deserting the New Englanders and picking his friends from the aristocratic Southern and New York Whigs whom Adams distrusted as possible Tories. To repay Adams for his slight, Hancock favored all the enemies

[52] Gordon, II, 38.
[53] *The Works of John Adams*, II, 416, 417.

of the Massachusetts delegates in Congress: he courted Dickinson, Duane, and other leaders of the "cold party" and threw
his influence against Adams and Richard Henry Lee.[54]   The
estrangement between Hancock and Adams was made complete
when the president of Congress fell a victim to "the glare of
Southern manners and the parade of courtly living" and surrounded himself with all the "outlandish state and pageantry
of an Oriental Prince." [55]   Hancock had always been known as
a man of fashion, but even his closest friends were taken aback
by the finery in which he now burst forth.   Because he had not
been appointed general of the Continental army, Hancock determined to make his office of president of Congress do double
duty in reflecting splendor upon its occupant.   "King Hancock," as he was called, always appeared in public in an "elegant
chariot" attended by four servants dressed in livery mounted on
richly caparisoned horses and escorted by fifty horsemen with
drawn sabres, half of whom rode before and half behind his
carriage.[56]   This unrepublican ostentation outraged the Whigs:
Sam Adams spoke in private of Hancock "with great asperity"
and deplored his delight in seeing "the honest Country Folks
gapeing & staring at a Troop of Light Horse" and himself furiously tearing along the road.   Hancock and his entourage became the dread of tavern keepers for leagues around Philadelphia: when John Adams traveled through the country he found
innkeepers everywhere complaining that they had been cheated
out of their money by Hancock's cavalry, who usually pranced
off on their chargers in company with the president of Congress
without paying their bills.   The Adamses were at a loss to explain how a New Englander could turn out so badly and they
began to fear that Massachusetts had done itself a serious injury by giving "Such *Samples* of her Sons to the World." [57]

Hancock further scandalized the Adamses and made them
wish heartily he was not a New Englander by continuing to

[54] *Massachusetts Gazette,* Jan. 11, 1776.
[55] Gordon, III, 20.   Wells, II, 385.   Lorenzo Sears, *John Hancock, The
Picturesque Patriot* (1912), 226.
[56] *Ibid.,* 223.
[57] *The Works of John Adams,* III, 35, 441.   *Warren-Adams Letters,* I,
157.

occupy the chair of president of Congress long after he was bound by good manners to surrender it. He had been appointed to the presidency when Peyton Randolph, the first president, was called away to Virginia, it being understood that Hancock was to hold office only during Randolph's absence. Hancock had other plans, however, and when Randolph returned to Philadelphia the president of Congress made no move to step down. Although Randolph died shortly after resuming his place in Congress, the Adamses continued to demand that Hancock resign in order that a new election might be held. Sam and John Adams proceeded from hints to forthright denunciations of Hancock's conduct, but he paid no attention and remained in office until he grew weary of it. Only when, in 1777, it appeared to Hancock that he could better himself by going to Massachusetts, where a state government was being formed, did he determine to resign as president of Congress. Sam Adams was delighted to see him go, but he groaned throughout Hancock's farewell speech because the president took leave of Congress "with almost as much Formality as if he was on his dying Bed." [58] To show Hancock how little they thought of his work as president, Sam Adams and the other Massachusetts delegates voted not to thank him for his services on the ground that it was improper for Congress to thank a man for discharging the duties of office. But in spite of all that Adams could do, Hancock set out for Massachusetts with Congress's thanks in his pocket.

Sam Adams's habit of believing that conservative Whigs who opposed independence were enemies to America and in the pay of the British government brought the Massachusetts delegation into hot water during the second Continental Congress. Adams had been warned by his English correspondents to be on his guard against British spies and traitors in Congress who were selling the patriots' secrets to the Ministry. It could not be denied that there was a dangerous leak in Congress by which the British government learned of its proceedings; and Adams therefore immediately put certain delegates under suspicion. Among them were Philip Livingston, who was described as a "Sort of

[58] *The Writings of Samuel Adams*, IV, 178.

political Hermaphrodite," half Whig and half Tory, and his colleague, John Jay.[59] Jay, in particular, was suspect by Adams because Arthur Lee declared he was betraying the Whigs; and Adams always gave full credence to Lee's reports. Moreover, Jay had aroused Adams's distrust by advocating a conservative policy in Congress. Adams therefore leaped to the conclusion that Jay was a traitor and began to voice his suspicions to other members of Congress. But in fact Jay was guilty of nothing worse than attempting to keep the door open for the reconciliation of mother country and colonies. Instead of raising a storm in Congress against Jay, Adams succeeded only in strengthening the ill will with which the conservative majority regarded him and his fellow New Englanders.

Sam Adams had done much to turn a large part of Congress against the Massachusetts delegates, but John Adams fairly outdid his cousin in making enemies. In a letter to his wife which was intercepted by the British and made public, John Adams called John Dickinson, the leader of the conservative majority in Congress, a "piddling genius." Thus, the "brace of Adamses" succeeded in bringing down wrath from every quarter upon the delegates from the Bay Colony. No Massachusetts man sat upon important committees in Congress during 1775; and Sam Adams, in particular, was excluded from all except a few subordinate ones.[60] Sam, indeed, seems to have borne the brunt of both his and John Adams's mistakes. Jay apologized to John Adams for keeping him off the secret committees of correspondence and commerce and offered him an important place in Congress if he would drop Sam Adams and Richard Henry Lee. Although John Adams declined to purchase political advancement by giving up his friends, he and Jay were on good terms. No doubt Jay, an aristocrat to the core, wondered why John Adams nailed his colors to the mast and insisted on sinking with such a plebeian as Sam. For several months, the latter was almost an outcast in Congress. Even

[59] *Samuel Adams Papers,* "The Intelligencer" (Hugh Hughes) to Sam Adams and John Adams, Oct. 17, 1775; Stephen Sayre to Sam Adams, April 4, 1775; William Lee to Sam Adams, April 6 and 10, 1775. *The Works of John Adams,* III, 5.

[60] *Journals of the Continental Congress,* II, 53, 64, 67, 80, 102, 208.

his friendship with Richard Henry Lee made him enemies because Lee had antagonized many powerful Virginia aristocrats
by exposing their pilfering of the colony's treasury.[61]

John Adams was a much abler statesman than Sam Adams,
but he little understood how a propagandist like his cousin gradually brought public opinion to favor complete separation from
the mother country.   Had John Adams possessed some of Sam's
skill in influencing the public mind he would have been a more
effective force in American history, but too often he acted upon
the principle, "public opinion be damned."   In the Continental
Congress of 1775, John Adams displayed all of the unfortunate
bluntness and impatience with slow-moving majorities that
marked his later public career.   John Dickinson and the conservative majority in Congress refused to be pushed deeper into
opposition to Great Britain until another petition had been sent
the King humbly praying for redress of grievances.   Although
the radical minority believed that Americans ought not to waste
time on George III that could be spent in priming muskets and
gathering ammunition, it remained silent in the face of the
overwhelming majority that favored petitioning.   John Adams,
however, was no respecter of majorities and he was never silenced
by hostile public opinion.   He called the petition a "measure
of imbecility" and declared he dreaded further negotiations
with the mother country "like Death." [62]   His speeches in Congress against petitioning convinced the moderates that New
Englanders were so eager for independence that they would not
even give good King George an opportunity to restore peace
to his dominions.   Rather than be forced into war by Northern
republicans, Dickinson urged that New England be allowed to
go its own way while Pennsylvania and the loyal Southern
colonies made terms with the mother country.   One day, when
Dickinson caught John Adams outside Carpenter's Hall, he
exclaimed: "What is the reason, Mr. Adams, that you New
Englandmen oppose our measures of reconciliation? . . .
Look ye!   If you don't concur with us in our pacific system,
I and a number of us will break off from you in New England,

[61] *The Works of John Adams*, III, 5, 32.
[62] *Warren-Adams Letters*, I, 75.

and we will carry on the opposition by ourselves in our own way." [63] This "rude lecture" made it clear to John Adams that he must reconcile himself to the petition to the King or see American unity end in "Discord and a total Disunion." [64]

Sam Adams liked petitioning as little as did John, but he recognized that opposition was futile and even dangerous. He believed that the hope nursed by Dickinson and his party that the mother country would adopt a lenient policy toward the colonies was "the Rock which endangers the Shipwreck of America," because it caused a "total Stagnation of the Power of Resentment, the utter Loss of every manly Sentiment of Liberty and Virtue." [65] Among his friends, Sam Adams spoke enthusiastically of the approach of one of "the grandest Revolutions the World has ever yet seen," but he did not join John Adams in publicly attacking John Dickinson's plan of reconciliation. He saw that the petition must be agreed to before Pennsylvania would be ready to join the colonies in declaring independence. It was apparent that as long as hope remained of a change in British policy, the middle colonies would not unite with New England and Virginia in separating from the mother country. However unpalatable petitioning might be to New Englanders who hungered for immediate independence, it was necessary to convince conservatives that King George and Parliament would not have a last-minute change of heart. Moreover, Adams was too well informed on English politics to doubt that Dickinson's petition would go the way of all of Congress's petitions and remonstrances: into the Ministry's wastebasket.

The event proved the wisdom of Sam Adams's policy of waiting "till the Fruit is ripe before we gather it." [66] John Dickinson made the second petition to the King one of the masterpieces of revolutionary rhetoric; and, by avoiding all subjects that had irritated the King and Ministry in the first petition, gave George III an excellent opportunity to show his good intentions toward his American subjects. Nevertheless, Dickinson's peti-

---

[63] *The Works of John Adams*, II, 410.

[64] *Warren-Adams Letters*, I, 75.

[65] *Ibid.*, I, 280.

[66] *Ibid.*, I, 171. *Letters of Members of the Continental Congress*, I, 284.

tion fared no better than the truculent remonstrances written by Sam Adams in the Massachusetts General Court. Even after this rebuff, Pennsylvania was lukewarm toward the Revolution, but had New Englanders not agreed to the second petition to the King, the middle colonies might have been openly hostile and conservatives everywhere in the colonies would have been given a strong argument against independence.

Congress's delay in declaring American independence caused Sam Adams acute discomfort. He believed that when the British compelled the colonists to take up arms in self-defense at Lexington, America became independent of Great Britain; in fact all that was now required was formal recognition of the separation. Nevertheless, the Whig majority in Congress seemed so unwilling to face this reality that Adams believed the moderates would carry on the struggle against the mother country for a century before they would be able to make up their minds to declare independence and make war in earnest. "Every Day's Delay," he exclaimed, "trys my Patience." His friends in Massachusetts told him that the people were becoming suspicious of Congress: they anxiously asked each other, wrote Joseph Hawley, "what is our Congress about, they are *dozing* or amusing themselves." The postponement of independence, Hawley said, was making Tories saucy and Whigs disheartened, and he pictured to Adams "a Great Mobb" of New Englanders storming Philadelphia, dispersing Congress, and setting up a military dictatorship.[67] From England, Sam Adams received equally alarming news: the only alternative offered Americans was to declare themselves independent or become "Slaves to Scotchmen." Nevertheless, Adams saw he must work cautiously in persuading the timid members of Congress to take the plunge, and he made it his business to "remove old prejudices, to instruct the unenlightened, convince the doubting and fortify the timid." Rather than press the "halfway patriots" too hard, Adams preferred to wait until the efforts of the British government to suppress the rebellion by

[67] *Warren-Adams Letters*, I, 224, 225. *The Writings of Samuel Adams*, III, 276. *Samuel Adams Papers*, N. Y. Public Library, Joseph Hawley to Sam Adams, Feb. 5, 1776.

force had convinced them of the hopelessness of reconciliation. "We cannot make Events," Adams told his friends. "Our Business is wisely to improve them." [68]

But when a committee was appointed by Congress in 1775 to explain to the people that Congress had no intention of declaring independence, Sam Adams was so alarmed that he began to threaten openly a New England Confederation, independent of both Great Britain and the American colonies. The break-up of the American union was no empty menace hung over the heads of congressmen by Sam Adams to frighten them into separation from the mother country: thousands of New Englanders shared Adams's conviction that even alone they were a match for the British. As John Adams said, when New England exerted its full strength it would be found to be that of "a full grown Man, no Infant." [69]

Fortunately for the unity of the American Republic, the obstacles to independence melted away soon after Sam Adams began to threaten a New England Confederacy. Thomas Cushing, who opposed independence, lost his place in Congress to Elbridge Gerry, one of Sam Adams's followers. Henceforth, the Massachusetts delegation ceased to be hampered by internal conflicts: Gerry and the "brace of Adamses" formed a majority in favor of independence and, as a result, the Massachusetts vote was cast for an immediate declaration. [70] Washington was converted to independence; John Adams, — "the main pillar in debate," — Richard Henry Lee, Thomas Jefferson, and Patrick Henry advocated it in Congress; and Sam Adams's "intriguing arts" began to bear fruit. By transplanting the caucus from Faneuil Hall to Philadelphia, Adams overthrew the conservatives in Congress just as he had driven the Tories out of the Boston town meeting. The caucus directed every step taken toward independence: although Sam Adams was seldom seen in the centre of the stage, he was constantly at work behind the scenes. It was decided in the caucus what

[68] *Samuel Adams Papers*, William Lee to Sam Adams, Feb. 6, 1776.

[69] *The Writings of Samuel Adams*, III, 259, 260, 284, 304–305. *Letters of Members of the Continental Congress*, I, 438. *Warren-Adams Letters*, I, 175.

[70] *The Works of John Adams*, III, 25. Wells, II, 340.

parts Richard Henry Lee and Patrick Henry — known respec-
tively as the Cicero and the Demosthenes of the century — were
to take in the debates.   John Adams took little part in the caucus but he frequently acted under its orders: and it is significant
that George Wythe and Richard Henry Lee, two of the chief
members of the caucus, proposed in March 1776 that Congress
declare the King rather than the Ministry or Parliament the
"Author of our Miseries."   Without the aid of the caucus,
independence might have been long delayed by Dickinson and
his conservative followers; but with Sam Adams pulling the
wires backstage and marshaling the radical forces in Congress,
Dickinson was unable to prevent the separation of mother country and colonies.

By the time of the Declaration of Independence, Sam Adams
had attained celebrity as the foremost revolutionist in America.
"The whole Continent," cried a Tory, "is ensnared by that
Machiavel of Chaos," Sam Adams, and he was dreaded by all
conservatives as the "would-be Cromwell of America." [71]
Josiah Quincy, Junior, who had been sent to England on a
secret mission by the Massachusetts Whigs, found that in
London Sam Adams was considered "the first politician in the
world" and without a peer in the business of "forwarding a
Rebellion."   Adams was now recognized as the prime mover
of the Revolution — the man who, for many years, had worked
indefatigably to make America independent of the mother
country. Tories sometimes spoke of the Revolution as
"Adams's conspiracy"; and Lord North, with the Boston Massacre and Tea Party still fresh in his mind, nicknamed the
American patriots "Sam Adams's crew."   After Gage's proclamation excluding Adams from the general amnesty was known
in the colonies, no patriot could match Sam Adams's fame in
British America; as Thomas Jefferson said, Adams was "truly
the *Man of the Revolution*" — the greatest figure yet brought
forth by the upheaval. Many years before, Adams's friends
had begun to call him the "Father of America," and by 1775

[71] British Museum, Additional MSS. 35913 Hardwicke, Lib. Cong.
Transcript; —— to Governor Hutchinson, Sept. 14, 1774. *Independency
the Object of Congress in America* (London, 1776), 15.

he seemed to have proved beyond doubt his right to the name.[72]
"Would you believe it, that this immense continent from New
England to Georgia is moved and directed by one man," wrote
an English army officer, "a man of ordinary birth and desperate
fortune, who by his abilities and talent for factious intrigue, has
made himself of some consequence, whose political existence
depends upon the continuance of the present dispute, and who
must sink into insignificancy and beggary the moment it
ceases!"[73]   John Adams owed much of his early reputation
to the fact that he was "the creature and kinsman" of Sam Adams.
This reflected glory frequently was highly exasperating to John.
When he arrived in France in 1778, one of the first questions
he was asked was whether he was "the famous Adams" who
had been proscribed by General Gage and who had made himself
the ruler of Congress.   John protested that he was plain John
Adams and not "the famous" Adams, but his audience replied
in chorus: *"Oh, non, Monsieur, c'est votre modestie."*[74]   Obviously, the French did not know John Adams.

Yet, within a brief time, Sam Adams fell from his eminence
as the chief figure of the American Revolution.   His career in
Congress was marred by factiousness, intrigue, and broils; and,
unlike Jefferson and John Adams, he failed to reveal traits of
statesmanship.   Although Sam Adams was expert in overturn-
ing governments, he knew nothing of rebuilding them.   His
weaknesses are most apparent in his attempts to control the
American army during the war and in the protracted feuds he
carried on with his political enemies in Congress.

At the beginning of the war, Sam Adams wished to fight
King George with the American militia rather than with an enlisted regular army.   He dreaded an American standing army
almost as much as he had a British, for he suspected that American commanders were not free from ambition to establish a
military despotism.   Therefore, Adams praised the militia
system as a bulwark against militarism, and in 1775 he went so

[72] Josiah Quincy, 218. Moore, II, 144. Wells, II, 418 (note), 424.
Samuel Adams Papers, Christopher Gadsden to Sam Adams, May 23, 1774;
Stephen Sayre to Sam Adams, Sept. 13, 1770.
[73] *Letters of Captain W. G. Evelyn,* edited by G. D. Scull (1879), 46.
[74] Moore, II, 144. *The Works of John Adams,* III, 189.

far as to advise his friends not to entrust the Massachusetts militia to the command of Continental generals. Military power, he said, "has so often proved fatal to the liberties of mankind" that unless Americans made the militia the backbone of resistance to Great Britain they were in danger of losing their liberties to some aspiring general wearing the uniform of the Continental army.[75] But before many battles had been fought, Adams changed his mind about the effectiveness of the militia. Repeated defeat made him the champion of a strong regular army enlisted not for a year but for the duration of the war — an army that would cross state lines without haggling with their commanders and would remain in the field when the crops at home were ready to harvest.[76] Yet while Adams switched his faith from the militia to the regular army, he did not forget the peril of military dictatorship nor did he cease to be haunted with the fear that the American Revolution would have its Cæsar or Cromwell. Although most Americans seemed so unwilling to serve in the regular army that the real danger was not of military dictatorship but of submission to Great Britain for want of a sufficient number of effective troops, Sam Adams tormented himself, Congress, and the military leaders with apprehensions that "the Sins of America may be punished by a standing army." He proposed to avert such disaster by putting the generals securely in leading strings to Congress and making them instruments to execute the commands of the sovereign legislature. He joined in establishing the Board of War by which Congress intended to put itself in control of the Continental army; and he became exceedingly sensitive to slights cast upon the supremacy of Congress in both civil and military affairs. For example, when the King of France and George Washington were given precedence over Congress in the toasts at a public celebration in Boston, Adams said that he and other "old fashiond Whiggs" regarded it as a portent of approaching military tyranny.[77] But Congress's control of

[75] *The Writings of Samuel Adams*, III, 230, 247. *Warren-Adams Letters*, I, 198.
[76] *De Chastellux*, I, 275–276. *Samuel Adams Papers*, Sam Adams to Samuel Cooper, April 23, 1777.
[77] *Warren-Adams Letters*, II, 58, 67.

the army soon proved unworkable and Adams was compelled to give Washington practically dictatorial powers — a gift which Adams bestowed with many misgivings for American liberty.

Sam Adams once confessed that he knew nothing of military matters; and many American commanders would have found it easier to fight the British had Adams recognized that his ignorance unfitted him for meddling in the war department. His faculty for supporting mediocre generals was frequently detrimental to the American cause: through his influence, Charles Lee was appointed one of the major generals in command of the Continental army. Had Adams been able to dispel more of the "Dismal Bugbears" which hung thickly about Lee, that singular adventurer would probably have been given even higher rank. Lee had made strong converts in John and Sam Adams, who judged him largely upon the strength of his political opinions and tall stories of his exploits in the British army. Both "Sam and John fought for him . . . through all the Weapons" — with the result that Washington was given a subordinate who considered his abilities far superior to his chief's, and who refused in several emergencies to obey Washington's orders.[78] Nevertheless, Sam Adams continued to pass judgment upon commanders, strategy, and military matters in general as though he had spent a lifetime in the field. Like many amateur generals, he invariably blamed the commanders for reverses and overlooked the real causes of defeat, although many of them lay under his eyes in Congress. In 1778, after a succession of American defeats, he urged that there be a congressional examination of the "idle cowardly or drunken" general officers whom he held responsible. He saw treachery, intoxication, or gross incompetence in every American military setback: when Schuyler and St. Clair were forced to evacuate Ticonderoga, Adams said they were cowards or traitors who had acted upon "the worst of Principles."[79] He lent a willing ear to the defamatory reports which reached Philadelphia of Schuyler's generalship and he was one of the leaders of Gates's

[78] *Warren-Adams Letters*, I, 61, 64, 69–70, 331. *The Writings of Samuel Adams*, III, 387.
[79] *Ibid.*, III, 403, 404, 407.

party in Congress who intrigued for Schuyler's removal while Burgoyne was advancing upon Albany. Adams was told by Elbridge Gerry that Schuyler was the "evil Genius" of the Northern army, who was so heartily hated by the New England troops that unless he was displaced they would retreat to Philadelphia for the winter.[80] After the command of the Northern army had been juggled between Gates and Schuyler until it became a matter of doubt which was in command from one day to another, Gates's partisans in Congress finally triumphed. When Burgoyne surrendered at Saratoga to Gates (largely because of Benedict Arnold's attack), Sam Adams's estimation of his own wisdom in military matters began to soar and he was soon planning to bring down George Washington in the same manner he had worked Schuyler's downfall.

After the siege of Boston, Washington's strategy deeply pained Sam Adams. Adams was eager to give the British "a handsome Drubbing" and he was utterly unable to comprehend any military manœuvres that did not lead to a speedy annihilation of the invaders. He felt it intolerable that "a small Hand full of ragged discontented unpaid Mercenaries" should overrun the Jersies and Rhode Island, "plundering Houses, cruelly beating old Men, ravishing Maids, murdering Captives in cold Blood, and systematically starving Multitudes of Prisoners" while the American army rested on its muskets. Adams believed that it was the duty of the army to fight the British to a finish: in 1777, he considered that Washington could easily have driven the British into the Atlantic and put an end to the war had he made an energetic campaign.[81] As General Mifflin complained, the "Gentry at Philadelphia" who set themselves up for military geniuses loved fighting as long as they could remain in their cozy quarters in Philadelphia; and they longed for a smashing victory, forgetful of the raw, undisciplined troops and meagre stores with which the commanders were expected

---

[80] *The Writings of Samuel Adams*, III, 388. *Samuel Adams Papers*, Joseph Trumbull to Sam Adams, July 25, 1776; Roger Sherman to Sam Adams, Aug. 25, 1777; Elbridge Gerry to Sam Adams, July 21, 1776.

[81] *Warren-Adams Letters*, I, 278, 293, 331. *Samuel Adams Papers*, Sam Adams to Samuel Cooper, April 23, 1777. *The Writings of Samuel Adams*, III, 374.

to overwhelm the British.[82]   The situation appeared in very
different light when viewed from Congress and from the battlefield; and, because Adams could account for American defeats
only by the shortcomings of the officers, he soon fell out with
Washington.   In spite of much prodding from Congress,
Washington refused to hasten the end of the war by risking a
decisive battle.   He adopted, instead, the Fabian policy upon
which his military reputation is now based.   Sam Adams was
far too impatient for victory, however, to approve such dilatory
methods: Howe, he cried, was no Hannibal and, if Washington
would only stand and fight, the British would be swept out of
America.[83]

After Gates's victory at Saratoga, Adams thought he had at
last found the man to win the war.   When he called upon
Washington to give America another Saratoga at Howe's expense, Washington did no more than fight a few battles around
Philadelphia, evacuate the city, and retire to Valley Forge for
the winter.   Sam Adams wasted little sympathy on defeated
generals, but Washington lowered himself even further in
Adams's eyes by advocating half pay for officers in the Continental army — a scheme which the Massachusetts delegates
regarded as final proof of Washington's ambition to establish
a military dictatorship by means of a "set of haughty idle im-
perious Scandalizers of industrious Citizens & Farmers."
Adams now considered the removal of Washington and the
elevation of Gates to the supreme command essential to the success of the war.   He was already convinced that the only
soldiers in America who could be relied upon to do their duty
in battle were New Englanders.   Although Gates had not the
powerful recommendation of New England ancestry, his political opinions were as sound, in Adams's opinion, as though he
had been born and bred in Boston.[84]

Sam Adams always denied that he had attempted to throw

[82] *Collections N. Y. Hist. Soc.* (1878), 405.
[83] *The Writings of Samuel Adams*, III, 371, 374.   *Warren-Adams Letters*,
I, 64, 69–70, 331.
[84] *Samuel Adams Papers*, James Lovell to Sam Adams, Jan. 13, 1777;
Jan. 20, 1778.   Gordon, III, 57.   *The Writings of Samuel Adams*, III, 325,
329, 388.

Washington overboard during those stormy days that followed the British occupation of Philadelphia.   But every other member of the "Conway Cabal" later disavowed any parts in the conspiracy against Washington as vehemently as did Adams. The only question really in dispute is to what lengths Adams went in active intrigue to displace Washington.   Both Congress and the army were divided in the contest between the rival generals for supreme command, with most of the Northern delegates favoring Gates and the Southerners on the side of Washington.[85]   An important break in the Southern support of Washington was Richard Henry Lee, the Virginian, who was one of Gates's most active partisans in Congress and who put his head so close to John and Sam Adams's that they appeared "all so many heads under one bonnet."   General Thomas Mifflin, James Lovell, and Benjamin Rush were likewise eager to oust Washington.   Although it cannot be shown that Gates actively engaged in a plot to make himself commander in chief of the American army, he knew what his friends in Congress were about and kept in close touch with Sam Adams.[86]   Adams and Lee welcomed every defeat suffered by Washington and magnified his failures among their partisans in Congress: when news of Brandywine reached Congress, Adams and Lee could scarcely conceal their joy that he had met with such a signal reverse when his fate as commander hung in the balance.[87]   But even when undermining an enemy doomed as hopelessly as Washington appeared to be at Valley Forge during the winter of 1777, Sam Adams preserved all his customary caution.   Lest Washington unexpectedly recover his prestige, Adams carefully covered up all traces of his work in the Conway Cabal.   This prudence displayed by Washington's enemies eventually saved them from full exposure and it is not yet known precisely how they planned to make Gates the chief in command.   Undoubtedly, when Gates was put at the head of the Board of War,

[85] *New Materials for the History of the American Revolution*, edited by John Durand (1889), 23, 28, 173.   *Samuel Adams Papers*, Samuel Parsons to Sam Adams, July 9, 1778.

[86] *Ibid.*, Horatio Gates to Sam Adams, May 27, 1778.   *Dictionary of American Biography*, VII (1931), 184–190, "Horatio Gates."

[87] Edmund Quincy, *Life of Josiah Quincy* (1868), 415.

which had been given powers superior to Washington's, the
conspirators believed that Washington's downfall was inevitable.
Their next move was to attempt to induce the Massachusetts
House of Representatives and the Virginia House of Burgesses
to give their delegates in Congress instructions which would
either make Washington's resignation mandatory or shame him
out of the army. Although the leading members of Congress
from Massachusetts and Virginia, Sam Adams and Richard
Henry Lee, were important figures in the cabal, even such
proficient intriguers failed to dislodge Washington. Both
Virginia and Massachusetts refused to take part against Washington, and when Conway visited Congress at Yorktown in
June 1778 he wrote disconsolately to Gates that he had been
warmly received only by Sam Adams and Lee "and a few
others who are attached to you but who cannot oppose the torrent." Washington quickly regained his popularity; the
French alliance put a new complexion upon the war; and Gates's
bubble was pricked by the British evacuation of Philadelphia
and the battle of Monmouth.[88]

Another reason why Sam Adams's popularity steadily
dwindled during the Revolution was that he permitted his passion for intrigue, inherited from his early days in Boston, to
have full sway in Congress. If there was a plot being carried
on in his neighborhood, Sam Adams could not resist the temptation to get into the thick of it; and Congress gave him ample
opportunity to exhibit his talents in the cabal. His skill was
useful in bringing about Galloway's downfall and the declaration of independence, but unfortunately for his reputation as
a statesman he continued to use the same methods of attack
against all his numerous enemies in Congress. Although he
had earned the ill will of a formidable group of congressmen
through his own efforts, his friendship with Richard Henry
Lee and Arthur Lee vastly increased the number of his enemies.
Arthur Lee, the Virginia Whig whose letters from London
had been Adams's main source of information concerning the designs of the British government, was a man with amazing faculty

[88] Gordon, III, 57. *Letters of Members of the Continental Congress*
(1926), III, 278 (note). *New Materials, etc.*, 174.

for making enemies. He habitually assumed that other people acted from the worst motives: he had no sooner been made the confidential London correspondent of the congressional secret committee of correspondence than he began to calumniate the men who had appointed him. Through the influence of Sam Adams and Richard Henry Lee, Arthur Lee was made one of Congress's agents in France. In Paris, Lee made enemies by the score, the most important of whom were Luzerne, Franklin, Carmichael, and Silas Deane. Lee particularly distrusted Deane, the agent sent out by Congress to negotiate aid from the French government, and he quickly convinced himself that Deane was attempting to swindle the American government out of many thousand dollars by representing that the supplies furnished secretly by the French government through Beaumarchais's fictitious firm of Roderique, Hortalez & Cie were given with the understanding that they were to be paid for by the United States. To the joy of the parsimonious statesmen at Philadelphia, Arthur Lee declared that there was no necessity for payment, as the French government had intended from the beginning that these supplies should be a free gift to the United States. Both agents appealed to Congress for support with the result that Congress itself was soon divided into Deane and Lee parties. At the head of Arthur Lee's friends, opposing payment, stood Sam Adams and Richard Henry Lee.

All the jealousies and hatreds within Congress burst forth during the Deane-Lee controversy. Indeed, the delegates fell to quarreling with such good will that they expended almost as much time and energy upon Deane and Lee as upon the Articles of Confederation. Sam Adams was in a heaven of plots and counterplots. On the strength of the material sent him by Arthur Lee, Adams procured Deane's recall and John Adams's appointment as agent. But Arthur Lee continued to send alarming news across the Atlantic: corruption was still rampant; the French ministers were playing a double game with the United States; and there was a conspiracy in Congress to keep "all vigilant Patriots" off important committees in order that powerful merchants might monopolize the trade and

richest lands of America.[89]   Although Adams and Lee ruled
Congress "as absolutely as the Grand Turk does in his own
Dominions," their support of Arthur Lee cost them heavily.
After years of futile controversy, Arthur Lee was thrown over
by Congress; and the New York party, led by William Living-
ston, defeated him for the office of minister of foreign affairs.[90]

After six years of service in Congress, Sam Adams could still
boast that he was a poor man.   He was, indeed, in his usual
financial difficulties throughout his congressional career: salaries
were so low that John Adams complained the total amount he
had received for four years' labor at Philadelphia was not sufficient to pay a laborer on his farm; and when a story was cir-
culated by the Tories that a certain member of Congress was
"keeping Mrs. ——," the scandal was refuted by pointing out
that a congressman could not support himself, much less a
mistress.[91]   With this poor pay went long hours of drudgery
and extended periods of separation from Adams's "beloved
town": Sam was sometimes so busy he had not even time to write
his "Betsy" a love letter; and Elbridge Gerry was so over-
worked that he was said to be almost "past the salutary power
of Vegetables."[92]   Nevertheless, there were odd moments in
the hurry and bustle of Philadelphia, York, and Baltimore,
when the busiest congressman found relaxation.   Sam Adams
took pleasure in strolling with John Adams in the State House
yard; talking politics with other delegates over pipes and tea;
eating a Saturday night's dinner with his landlady, Mrs. Yard;
"smoaking a pipe in the political club at the Indian Queen";
holding a *tête-à-tête* at George Wythe's lodgings opposite
Israel's Garden; and "rambling towards Kensington" with a
few boon companions.[93]   When the Marquis de Chastellux
called upon Sam Adams he was shocked to find that redoubtable

[89] *Samuel Adams Papers*, Richard Henry Lee to Sam Adams, Nov. 23,
1777.   *Deane Papers*, III, 277; IV, 447.

[90] *The Writings of Samuel Adams*, IV, 113, 127.

[91] *The Works of John Adams*, 111, 89.   James T. Austin, *The Life of
Elbridge Gerry* (1828), I, 332.

[92] *The Writings of Samuel Adams*, IV, 238.   *Samuel Adams Papers*,
James Lovell to Sam Adams, Jan. 13, 1777.

[93] *Ibid.*, George Wythe to Sam Adams, Aug. 1, 1778.

Puritan *tête-à-tête* with a young girl of fifteen who was preparing his tea, but the Marquis dismissed all thought of scandal when he remembered that Adams was nearly sixty. Having thus acquitted Adams of any moral lapse, de Chastellux entered into a lively discussion with his host of the causes of the American Revolution, until they were interrupted by "a glass of Madeira, a dish of tea, and an old American General." [94]

Although Sam Adams shared comfortable quarters with John Adams in Philadelphia and found the atmosphere of intrigue in Congress to his taste, he liked neither the city nor its inhabitants. The true religion of Quakers, he said, was making money and sleeping in a whole skin. Even the "Mud & Mire" of Yorktown and the "infernal sink" of Baltimore, where even John Hancock, the president of Congress, had difficulty in living "tolerably decent," did not make Adams love Philadelphia the more. [95] He was incurably homesick for Boston; and, as most of his friends dropped out of Congress, he, too, found the only cure for his loneliness was long vacations in Boston with his Betsy. Moreover, he was disturbed by his failure to "Bostonize" Philadelphia by proscribing balls, theatres, and other entertainments frowned upon in the Puritan metropolis. Adams believed that congressmen should set an example for the people by praying often, watching their morals, and staying away from dances and horse races. During the early meetings of Congress, the New England delegates secured the passage of a law forbidding members of Congress to take part in public entertainments. Southern gentlemen who had diverted themselves at balls in Williamsburg and Charleston found this restraint irksome; and it was soon observed that the congressmen were seldom at their prayers but frequently at balls where they appeared in open violation of the law. To the mortification of the "rigid Republicans," many Northerners began to show they had been softened by daily contact with "Southern sensuousness." Sam Adams's puritanism had not been sweetened by

[94] De Chastellux, I, 267–276.
[95] *Warren-Adams Letters*, I, 280.   *Letters to Robert Morris, Collections* N. Y. *Hist. Soc.* (1878), 410, 413.   *Samuel Adams Papers*, James Lovell to Sam Adams, April 23, 1778.

Southern influences, however, and he demanded that further steps be taken to keep congressmen and army officers away from dances, theatres, and horse races. Congress agreed, but the day on which this legislation went into effect, the Whig citizens of Philadelphia and officers of the Continental army attended the theatre as usual; and on the next day, the ball given by the Governor of Pennsylvania was crowded. The contemptuous treatment accorded its moral code aroused Congress to such a pitch that it was ordered that every officer present at such revels should be cashiered.[96]   But Sam Adams's efforts to stamp out sin in Philadelphia were rudely cut short by news that the Devil was making long strides in Boston itself.

[96] *The Writings of Samuel Adams*, III, 414–416. *New Materials, etc.*, 166–167.

XIV

SAM ADAMS AND THE NEW REPUBLIC

AFTER the outbreak of war between the mother country and
colonies, Massachusetts failed lamentably to take the lead in
framing a new state constitution.   The Bay State was almost the
last of the states to adopt a settled form of government, although
its need had been urgent since the beginning of the Revolution.
The upheaval in Massachusetts completely destroyed the authority of the central government; and the towns became
petty sovereignties that clung tenaciously to the powers they
had usurped from the old royal government.   The towns had
already rejected one constitution, in fact, when in 1779 another attempt was made to establish a central government and
Sam and John Adams were elected to the Constitutional Convention.

The absence of a central government in Massachusetts was
far more disturbing to John than to Sam Adams.   The former
was greatly alarmed by the "rage for innovation" and levelism
which began to spring up in the state during the Revolution.[1]
He strove at all times to keep the Revolution in a well-defined,
conservative channel and to wage war against English oppression
rather than against English principles of government.   When
the two Adamses were undermining the royal government in
Massachusetts, John Adams was careful to blot out in Sam
Adams's state papers all reference to the principles of liberty,
equality, and fraternity.   He believed that the war was being
fought to protect property rights and ancient principles of
government which must be safeguarded against popular tyranny
in America as well as against overseas tyranny.   He wished no
violent break with the past: the old provincial form of govern-

[1] *The Works of John Adams*, II, 328; IX, 393, 410.

ment with its two legislative branches and separate executive
should, he said, be carried over into the state constitution.   If
Massachusetts followed Pennsylvania's example in establishing
a single legislative chamber, John Adams declared he would be
grieved "to the very soul" and would never be happy under
such a government.[2]

To broaden the franchise would, in John Adams's eyes, be
the surest way of undoing the work of the Revolution.   Prop-
ertyless voters, he exclaimed, would form a "Fountain of Corruption" which, in turn, would destroy the commonwealth.
Even slight alterations in the qualifications for voters he regarded as disastrous: if the franchise were tampered with,
women would demand the right to vote; boys over twelve
years old would insist they be given equal rights with their
mothers; and "every man without a farthing" would
clamor for the suffrage.   To prevent this train of evils,
Adams urged that the property qualifications for voting under
the royal government be preserved in the new state constitution.[3]

Although Sam Adams did not share his cousin's fears of giving the vote to the mass of the people, he had no deep conviction in its favor.   There was little crusading fire in Sam
Adams to enfranchise the unprivileged, and he certainly did not
believe it was a purpose of the Revolution.   He never made
suffrage extension a part of his revolutionary propaganda in
Massachusetts; he was no democrat in the Jacksonian sense because, although he wished to put power in the people's hands, he
was willing to accept the "people" as they existed in 1776.
The important business, in his mind, was to make certain that
the people doled out power cautiously to those they had appointed to govern.   He feared tyranny in rulers far more than
the discontent of the unenfranchised masses.   But, unlike John
Adams, he had little love for the old charter form of government under which such "oligarchs" as Thomas Hutchinson had
prospered.   Rather than revert to that system, he wished to
create a single-chamber legislature in Massachusetts on the

[2] *The Works of John Adams*, IX, 430.
[3] *Ibid.*, IX, 378.

Pennsylvania model which would execute its laws by appointed committees.[4]

At the Massachusetts Convention which met in Boston during the winter of 1779–1780, James Bowdoin and the "brace of Adamses" were appointed a subcommittee to draw up a constitution for the approval of the Convention and the Massachusetts towns.   Sam Adams and Bowdoin immediately gave full power to John Adams, who proceeded to write the entire Massachusetts Constitution with the exception of Article III. Several motives may have influenced Sam Adams in thus giving his cousin free rein: he was ill during the greater part of the Convention and his pet scheme of a single-chamber legislature met with little support from the delegates.   Bostonians made it clear that they wished to retain the fundamental principles of the old charter government; and, as he was to do a decade later when Massachusetts ratified the Federal Constitution, Sam Adams swallowed his own opinions, bowed to Boston's will, and abandoned "systems in which he loved to stray, for less sublime, but more practicable projects." [5]   The only part of the Massachusetts Constitution in which Sam Adams had a hand and which can be said to represent his true convictions was Article III, dealing with religion.   Because of his fame as a staunch churchman, Adams was placed at the head of the committee appointed to draw up the revolutionary religious settlement.   His work in Article III reveals how little he believed the Revolution had ushered in a period of religious liberalism. Even in the conservative Massachusetts Constitution of 1780, Article III stands out as notably reactionary: indeed, it makes the old provincial religious system seem lenient by comparison. Under the royal charter, Baptist, Quakers, and members of the Church of England were granted exemption under certain conditions from paying taxes for the maintenance of the Congregational Church.   In Article III, Sam Adams provided that the members of these sects were to pay taxes to their own pastors — with the result that unbelievers, non-churchgoers, and minorities too small to maintain a minister were compelled to

[4] *The Works of John Adams*, III, 18; IX, 618.
[5] De Chastellux, I, 275. *The Works of John Adams*, III, 18.

pay directly to the support of the Congregational Church.
Moreover, Article III obliged every new sect that appeared in
Massachusetts after 1780 to wage a costly legal battle to win
recognition as a religious body.   In spite of the opposition raised
against Sam Adams's work in many quarters, — four hundred
and twenty Boston voters protested against Article III and
clamored for a more liberal religious system, — it became a
part of the Massachusetts Constitution and endured until
1833.[6]

What Sam Adams did for vested religion in the Massachusetts Constitution, John Adams did for secular interests.   He
provided that the requirements for voting for governor, senator, or representatives should be 50 per cent higher than under
the charter.   Although the House of Representatives was supposed to represent the persons of the Massachusetts voters, the
ballot was confined to a propertied electorate.   Men "who
will pay less regard to the Rights of Property because they have
nothing to lose" were excluded from the franchise.   Certainly,
the Massachusetts Constitution of 1780 did not establish the
democracy which in 1776 the people were said "almost
universally & most ardently [to] desire & are now aiming at." [7]
Joseph Hawley, the Northampton patriot, declined his seat in
the Massachusetts Council in 1780 because of his dissatisfaction
with the civil and religious provisions of the Constitution.   The
old revolutionary watchword of no taxation without representation was thrown in the patriots' faces by soldiers who had fought
in the Revolution believing they were struggling for their own
liberty.[8]   But Sam Adams was not among these dissenting
voices: once the Massachusetts Constitution had been adopted by
the majority, he became one of its staunchest champions.   He
regarded it as a final settlement of the Revolution; and he told
the Marquis de Chastellux that the Constitution of 1780 had
been established in "the most legitimate manner of which there

[6] S. E. Morison, *The Struggle over the Adoption of the Constitution of
Massachusetts, Mass. Hist. Soc. Proceedings*, L (1917), 371, 379.

[7] *Sam Adams Papers*, N. Y. Public Library, Benjamin Kent to Samuel
Adams, May 24, 1776.

[8] *Hancock Papers*, MSS. Mass. Hist. Soc., Samuel Talbot and Lemuel
Gray to his Excellency John Hancock, Esq., Nov. 16, 1780.

is any example since the days of Lycurgus." [9]   He acclaimed it
as "truly *Republic*"; praised mixed government on the British
model; defended property qualifications for voting; and pleaded
the necessity of a governor and council "to check the human
Passions, and controul them from rushing into exorbitances." [10]
It is apparent that, with the adoption of the Massachusetts Constitution, Sam Adams ceased, for the time being, to be a revolutionist.

After Thomas Hutchinson and the Tories had been driven
into exile, Sam Adams hoped for great things from New England.   The chief obstacle to the return of Puritanism, he believed, was the old aristocracy which, by setting the people an
example of high living and loose morals, had attempted to
destroy their "Sense of true Religion & Virtue, in hopes thereby
the more easily to carry their Point of enslaving them."   As
one of the first fruits of the Revolution, Adams anticipated the
resurrection of "that Sobriety of Manners, that Temperance,
Frugality, Fortitude and other manly Virtues which were once
the Glory and Strength of my much lov'd native Town."   After
such "vermin" as the Commissioners of the Customs and
British army officers, whose balls and feasts had shocked Boston
Whigs for a decade, had been driven out of town for the last
time, Adams believed that he might look forward to "the ancient purity of principles and manners" again flourishing in
the Puritan metropolis.   Instead of dressing in the height
of London fashion as Bostonians had done during Hutchinson's
régime, Adams hoped to see British "frippery" banished from
the commonwealth and "that Simplicity which is the Ornament
and Strength of a free Republick" among all classes.[11]   In Sam
Adams's eyes, the American Revolution was to do far more than
establish an independent state: it was to purify society, revolutionize manners and morals, and pave the way for another
Puritan Age.   Its most important consequences were to be
felt in Boston, where another "Christian Sparta" would rise and
where "Old Puritans" and "Romans" would restore to the

---

[9] De Chastellux, I, 271.
[10] *The Writings of Samuel Adams*, IV, 348.
[11] *Ibid.*, III, 231, 286; IV, 68, 251.

metropolis its fame as a refuge for the virtuous.   But before
this transformation could be wrought, it was necessary that the
old pleasure-loving Tory aristocracy be succeeded by an upper
class of sober republicans who would guide the people to
Virtue.

Much to Adams's dismay, the "Happy Era of Republicanism"
was ushered in not by the righteous Whigs who had made and
fought the Revolution, but by men who had "Hid in Holes and
Corners" during the struggle for liberty.[12]   Profiteers, speculators, and privateers were the material heirs of the Revolution
in Massachusetts; the old merchants were driven out of business
and their places were taken by new men who amassed fortunes
and political power that put the Tories to shame.   Certainly,
this unforeseen result was due to no laxness on Adams's part in
sweeping the country clear of Tories: those who revisited Boston
after the war saw scarcely "any other than new faces" and found
a change in the upper classes "as remarkable as the Revolution
itself."[13]   Few of these "mushroom gentry" who moved into
the Tories' abandoned homes, bought up their confiscated
estates, and seized their places in society, could claim distinguished birth.   It was a bitter humiliation, exclaimed the Massachusetts republicans, to stand with empty hands on Boston
street corners and watch "the Scum of Creation Rideing in
State"; "fellows who would have cleaned my shoes five years
ago," said James Warren, now rode in chariots while he
drudged for "a Morsel of Bread."   In this "world turned
topsy turvy," the patriots complained, "one forfeits all title
to the respect of a gentleman, unless he is one of the privileged
order."   Was this, the old Whigs anxiously asked themselves,
to be the end of their labors: were the fruits of the Revolution
to be gathered by men who had started up from nowhere and
were for all the world like the exiled Tories?   None viewed
their rise with greater apprehension than did Sam Adams.
"The Seeds of Aristocracy," he said, "began to spring up before
the Conclusion of our Struggle for the natural Rights of Man,

---

[12] *Warren-Adams Letters, Mass. Hist. Soc. Collections,* LXXIII (1925), II,
20, 42, 147.
[13] *Mass. Hist. Soc. Proceedings* (1862), V, 245.

Seeds which like a Canker Worm lie at the Root of free Government." [14]   He was horrified to find the Massachusetts upper class imitating the British in "every idle amusement & expensive Foppery" which, Adams firmly believed, was invented by cunning Englishmen to sap American virtue.   Indeed, "British Frippery" was imported into Massachusetts in such large quantities after the Revolution that the General Court felt obliged in 1785 to dam the flood of foreign luxuries "unknown to our ancestors." [15]   It was clear that Adams could expect no aid from the revolutionary aristocracy in purging Massachusetts of "British gew-gaws, etiquette and parade" and restoring Puritanism.   From the standpoint of the puritanical "patriots of '75," there was little to choose between the old Tories and the new Whigs.

Had the banished Tories in "Hell, Hull, and Halifax" known the bitterness of the revolutionary patriots toward the new upper class, they might well have exulted that they had the last laugh on Sam Adams and his "crew."   But Adams had not yet tasted the sourest draught in his brimming cup of disappointments.   John Hancock, it will be remembered, had resigned as President of the Continental Congress to fish in Massachusetts waters.   Although his friends gave out that Hancock returned to Boston because "the Airs of Philadelphia doth not sute him," his real purpose in coming to Massachusetts was to angle for the governorship of the state — a prize which, in 1778, appeared far more desirable than the presidency of the Continental Congress. [16]   While Adams toiled in Congress, Hancock began to turn Massachusetts into an impregnable political stronghold.   To Adams's consternation, he quickly became the most popular man in the state and took Boston by storm: the citizens began to burn incense before a "Guilded puppet," as James Warren now described Hancock.   It was soon clear that Hancock intended to pay Sam Adams back for not having made him commander in chief of the Continental

[14] *Samuel Adams Papers*, N. Y. Public Library, Thomas Chase to Sam Adams, Jan. 26, 1781.   *Warren-Adams Letters*, II, 105.   Austin, II, 86. *The Writings of Samuel Adams*, IV, 325.

[15] *Ibid.*, IV, 315.   *Independent Chronicle*, Nov. 23, 1786.

[16] *Mass. Hist. Soc. Proceedings* (1910), XLIII, 333.

army: all who would not "Bow down and worship a very silly Image," it was said, were marked for ruin; and Sam Adams, in particular, was set apart as a fat offering for the sacrificial altar.[17]   As soon as he had consolidated his party in Massachusetts, Hancock began a backfire in Boston against Sam Adams that almost succeeded in driving Adams out of political office. Hancock spread a report that Adams was opposed to long-term enlistments in the army; that he was a factious meddler who distracted Congress by stirring up the Deane-Lee controversy; and that he was a secret enemy of George Washington who had been deeply implicated in the Conway Cabal.   In 1778, while Adams was attending Congress in Yorktown, he was informed that he had been "severely reprehended" by the Boston town meeting for taking part in an intrigue against Washington.[18] Adams immediately put his affairs in order and hurried to Boston, much to the relief of the French ministers, who welcomed a vacation from Sam Adams.   In Boston, Adams denied that he had plotted to remove Washington and asserted that the gossip on which the town meeting had condemned him was a "pityful Contrivance" of Hancock's to make him unpopular and ruin his political career.[19]   The only general he had removed from command, Adams said, was Schuyler — and in New England, where Schuyler was hated, this was regarded as a highly meritorious act.   Adams's speedy return to Boston saved his seat in Congress, but it was now apparent that he would be forced to keep a watchful eye on John Hancock, who was clearly determined to take his political scalp.[20]

Instead of making a stiff-backed "Old Puritan" first governor of the state of Massachusetts, the people elected John Hancock, who had no sympathy whatever for Sam Adams's somewhat querulous eagerness to restore the days of Winthrop and Cotton.   To Adams's great disgust, Hancock celebrated his inauguration with a round of parties and balls such as had not

[17] *Samuel Adams Papers*, N. Y. Public Library, Samuel A. Otis to Sam Adams, Nov. 10, 1780.   *Warren-Adams Letters*, II, 14, 87, 147, 150.

[18] *Ibid.*, II, 12.

[19] *The Writings of Samuel Adams*, IV, 140, 246.

[20] *Belknap Papers*, II, *Mass. Hist. Soc. Collections* (1877), Fifth Series, III, 151.   Wells, II, 466, 501.

been seen in Boston since the "routs" and "Turtle Feasts" of the Commissioners of the Customs.   Where Adams looked for republican austerity he found a lively night life topped with brilliant "Governor's Balls" which even the "sober Inhabitants" of Boston attended to pay court to Hancock.   The old Whigs groaned that "Addresses, Assemblies, Entertainments and Balls have ushered in the Happy Era of Republicanism" and bitterly exclaimed that Hancock was surrounding himself with "the Pomp and retinue of an Eastern Prince."   Hancock's example spread such a plague of feasts and entertainments over the metropolis that James Warren said Boston society was "more suitable to the effeminacy and ridiculous manners of Asiatic slavery, than to the hardy and sober manners of a New-England republic."   Sam Adams exclaimed that Bradford, Winslow, and Winthrop would have "revolted at the Idea of opening Scenes of Dissipation & Folly," but, actually, as Adams soon learned, Bostonians were little concerned how they might appear in the eyes of these puritanical worthies.[21]   Adams and his fellow Whigs scolded and fretted in vain: Massachusetts was possessed by such "a rage for Ease, Luxurious Living, and Expensive Diversions" that they got only jeers for their pains and were ridiculed "in polite assemblies as *rigid republicans*, men of contracted minds, only because they will not conform to gaming, sabbath breaking, drinking and every other vice practiced by persons of (What is called) the bon ton."   Boston was no longer regarded as a stronghold of patriotism: it became instead so notorious for fashionable reveling that the Whigs lamented that the love of liberty could be found only "in the sober and manly retreats of husbandmen and shepherds." [22]

James Warren said his ardor for the Revolution would have cooled very rapidly in 1776 had he known he was laboring for John Hancock's glory and the transformation of Boston into a haven for prodigals and *nouveaux riches* who aped British manner and fashions.   Boston's shaky puritanism aroused Sam

---

[21] *Samuel Adams Papers*, J. Scollay to Sam Adams, Jan. 17, 1781.   *Warren-Adams Letters*, II, 20, 147.   Lee, II, 273.   *The Writings of Samuel Adams*, IV, 238.

[22] *Boston Gazette*, Oct. 30, 1780; Jan. 24, 1785.   Lee, II, 273.

Adams's deepest anxiety: "I am greatly concerned for my dear
native Town," he wrote, "lest after having stood foremost in
the Cause of Religion and Liberty she lose her Glory." [23]
Each time he set off for Philadelphia to resume his duties in
Congress it was with greater uneasiness for Boston's "manly
Virtue" which, he feared, was being undermined by a "Torrent
of Vice." He longed to remain in Boston and again become the
"Gadfly" of the Puritan metropolis, buzzing warnings in the
citizens' ears and pricking them along the road to virtue. The
people had forgotten him and had given the highest regard to his
enemy, but Adams was not yet convinced that the citizens of
Boston were past saving and that he was not the man to save
them.

In Adams's eyes, it was necessary to take action against
Hancock because he felt that the first governor of the state of
Massachusetts would have decisive influence in forming the
people's manners and morals for at least a generation. If he set
the people a bad example, Adams believed the fruits of the
Revolution would be sour indeed. From the Greeks and
Romans to Bernard and Hutchinson, Adams said, all tyrants
attempted to destroy the people's love of liberty with luxury and
temptations to high living. He was convinced that Hancock
was using the same methods that Hutchinson had unsuccessfully employed before the Revolution; the question was
no longer whether Hutchinson would be able to keep the people
quiet while he forged "Chains and Shackles" upon them, it
was rather whether "the judicious Citizens of Boston be now
caught in the Snare, which their artful, insidious Enemies, a
few years ago laid for them in vain." "Should Levity & Foppery ever be the ruling Taste of the Great," Adams warned, "the
Body of the People would be in Danger of catching the Dis-
temper" and losing their liberties.[24] By bringing to the surface
these "mushroom Gentry" who now sat in the seats of the Tories
and by making such a bad example as John Hancock governor
of the commonwealth, Adams believed the Revolution had

---

[23] *Mass. Hist. Soc. Proceedings*, XLIII, 333.
[24] *Warren-Adams Letters*, I, 376. *The Writings of Samuel Adams*, IV,
229, 238.

made a return to Puritanism even more imperative than in George Whitefield's day.   Hancock's influence must be offset by a revival of puritan morality and the "old patriotick Feelings" that guided the Whigs of the first Continental Congress.[25]

Sam Adams's puritanism soon brought him into conflict with the "Coxcombs and Coquettes" of Boston.[26]   His direst forebodings of the metropolis's sinking virtue seemed fulfilled in 1784 when the establishment of the Sans Souci Club brought the depravity of the younger generation clearly into view. The Sans Souci or "Tea Assembly" was designed to give Boston a night life comparable to that of the "polite" cities of New York and Philadelphia.   Young men of fashion keenly resented that the metropolis of New England still forbade all forms of public entertainment except fortnightly assemblies where dancing was permitted and lectures where the gospel was expounded. In the winter of 1784, Adams was startled to learn that a plan was on foot to begin in Boston a club for dancing and card playing where girls over sixteen would be admitted.   He immediately leaped to the conclusion that Boston was to be given over to Roman orgies, and, although his pen had been idle for several years, this menace to morals again put it in motion.   He attacked the proposed Sans Souci Club in the *Massachusetts Centinel* with a flash of his old fire; and, as usual, he used the occasion to take a back-handed slap at England: "Why," he asked, "do you thus suffer all the intemperances of Great Britain to be fostered in our bosom, in all their vile luxuriance?"   [27]   This club, he gloomily prophesied, would work Boston's downfall: after the passion for gaming had seized the people, "every necessary restraint" would be cast aside; parents would set the example for their children by becoming hardened gamblers; and "those glaring spectres luxury, prodigality and profligacy" would rob the metropolis of its little remaining virtue.   He cited Greece and Rome as dreadful examples of how states declined when the citizens lost their habits of frugality.   The Sans Souci, he said, should alarm all the righteous in New England: it was "totally

[25] *The Writings of Samuel Adams*, IV, 251.
[26] *Warren-Adams Letters*, II, 120.
[27] *Massachusetts Centinel*, Jan. 15, 1785.

repugnant to virtue" and foreign to the principles of puritanism
and the Revolution alike. Rather than permit its existence in
Boston, he urged that the citizens follow New York's example
by forcibly breaking it up with a mob. "Be not behind your
sister States in extirpating vice," Adams said, "however marked
with the epithet of polite." [28]

Sam Adams apparently believed in fighting the Devil with
the same rough-and-tumble methods that had proved so successful against the British. Although he did not start a mob
uprising, he made the Sans Souci a storm centre for many
months and a "subject for farces, newspapers, broken heads
and legs." It is plain that Adams's proneness to view
with alarm greatly exaggerated the evils of the Sans Souci
Club: there was a twenty-five-cent limit on betting and, as one
of its defenders complained, its parties were "decent even to
dullness." [29] The gilded youth at Cambridge in particular
found Adams's moralizing sour and they rushed into print to
ridicule his fears. Harrison Gray Otis, the nephew of James
Otis, Adams's old political ally, made the liveliest of these
attacks upon Adams and his school of "rigid Republicans."
He peppered him with such stinging names as "a baleful comet"
and "son of sedition"; and he replied to Adams's use of Greece
and Rome as examples that the "reckless intrigues of disappointed ambition, and the seditious speeches of their popular
leaders, produced more important calamities in those Republics"
than had luxury and Sans Souci clubs. Adams was accused of
being a bigot, a would-be dictator of morals, and a riot lover
who was up to his old tricks of raising mobs. But if Otis and
his friends expected their invective to get under Adams's skin,
they were sorely disappointed: he had withstood so much abuse
from New England Crown officers during the revolutionary
period that he was able to disregard the Sans Souci boys and to
turn against them Calvin's words: "I KNOW BY THEIR ROARING
I HAVE HIT THEM RIGHT." His friends quickly came to his
aid: Dr. Benjamin Waterhouse and Ben Austin, Junior, railed

[28] *Massachusetts Centinel*, Jan. 15 and 22, 1785.
[29] Charles Warren, *Sam Adams and the Sans Souci Club in 1785, Mass. Hist. Soc. Proceedings*, LX (1929), 318, 344.

against the young upstarts who were "reviling an *old Senator*" and calling him Cato "by way of reproach!" [30] The quarrel was gradually dragged into politics, where it became one of the issues of the campaign of 1785 when James Bowdoin finally succeeded in bringing about the temporary eclipse of John Hancock.

Although Sam Adams believed the dissolution of the Sans Souci Club saved Boston from the worst vices of declining Rome, he found keeping watch and ward over the morals of the metropolis an increasingly arduous and thankless task. In spite of his vigilance, he was beginning to fear that "the poison of dissipation has choaked even the latent sparks of virtue" and entered into the very marrow of the citizens he hoped to make "Old Puritans." [31] Boston seemed to be a leaky vessel that kept its Puritan crew scurrying from stem to stern plugging its worn seams. After the Sans Souci affair, Adams made a desperate but futile effort to keep the theatre out of Boston. In 1792, a company of strolling actors fitted up a stable in Board Alley as a theatre and began performances under the name of "moral lectures." But Sam Adams was not to be deceived by juggling names: theatrical performances were going on in Board Alley and therefore the Devil was getting a foothold in Boston. Instead of rallying round their puritanical leaders, however, most Bostonians clamored that the theatre be continued: when Adams and Hancock attempted to jail the actors, the Suffolk Grand Jury refused to indict them. The republican leaders thereupon arrested an actor under an information *ex officio;* but when this was known in Boston, Hancock's picture was torn down from the stage box of the theatre and trampled underfoot and Adams was hooted down at the town meeting for speaking against what the citizens called their "natural Theatrical rights." [32] Three quarters of the voters in the metropolis demanded the repeal of the law prohibiting theatres and declared that the issue was between liberty and slavery —

[30] *Sam Adams and the Sans Souci Club,* 325, 329.
[31] *Massachusetts Centinel,* Jan. 15, 1785.
[32] Thomas C. Amory, *Life of James Sullivan* (1859), 271. *Independent Chronicle,* Dec. 27, 1792.

whether or not a remnant of "Feudal Tyranny and Despotic
Enthusiasm" and "an encroachment on the RIGHTS OF MAN"
should be tolerated in free America.[33] To Sam Adams and his
followers, on the other hand, the only question at stake was
whether or not morals and constitutional laws were to be
"trampled upon with impunity by Stage players." [34] Adams
proved himself too strait-laced for many of his warmest admirers: Charles Jarvis quarreled with him; and Elbridge
Gerry, who had moved to New York, married a rich wife, and
become an ardent theatregoer, expostulated warmly in favor
of a theatre in Boston.   Despite Gerry's assertion that the actors
scrupulously avoided everything that gave "offense to delicacy,"
Adams was not won over.[35] But Sam Adams was fated in
his old age to be the champion of lost causes and to go down
fighting staunchly against a less rigorous moral code.   In
1793, the Massachusetts General Court repealed the Act of
1750 and thereby legalized theatres in Boston.   Although this
act did not receive the governor's signature, the theatregoers
had so completely routed the old-guard Puritans that in 1794,
while Sam Adams was governor of Massachusetts, the Boston
theatre was formally opened.

John Hancock owed his power in Massachusetts not to party
machinery, — still in a very rudimentary stage, — but to his
personal popularity with the mass of the people.   He capitalized
on his early reputation as a patriot and loudly proclaimed himself
a champion of popular liberty: "I will not give up the Liberties
of the people to the last drop of my blood," he cried.[36] Hancock
had received his political training from Sam Adams and he now
showed how well he had learned his lessons: he stole most of
Adams's thunder and used all Adams's tricks to keep the people
in a ferment for their liberties.   But despite his pose as a
friend of freedom and the common man, it was said that he was
"an attentive listener to every popular *buzz*, & whirled about

[33] *Columbian Centinel,* Jan. 30, 1793.
[34] *Independent Chronicle,* Oct. 25, 1792.
[35] S. E. Morison, *Two "Signers" on Salaries and the Stage, Mass. Hist. Soc. Proceedings* (1930), LXII, 58, 60.
[36] *Samuel Adams Papers,* N. Y. Public Library, John Hancock to Sam Adams, Aug. 31, 1793.

by every wind of doctrine." [37]   John Adams called Hancock "an empty barrel," but John Quincy Adams saw that he had a "peculiar talent of pleasing the multitude" which made him "King of the Rabble," leader of the "true Republican party," and political boss of Massachusetts. [38] The tendency to look toward the aristocracy for political leadership, inherited from colonial days, was still strong in the state, but there were few men in New England who could claim to be blue-blooded aristocrats after Sam Adams had purged the country of Tories. John Hancock, however, was particularly acceptable to the people of Massachusetts, for not only was he a gentleman born, he was a patriot who talked fully as convincingly as did Sam Adams — the man of the people — of his love for popular liberties.

With Hancock upholding the radical cause in Massachusetts, Sam Adams turned perforce to the conservatives. He was convinced after the adoption of the Massachusetts Constitution in 1780 that the Revolution was at an end and that all men should devote themselves to making wise use of the liberties they had won during the struggle.   In 1781, his election as president of the Massachusetts Senate obliged him to turn his back upon his earlier radicalism.   The Senate was designed by the Constitution to represent the property in the state and to act as a check upon "the vices and follies" of the House of Representatives, which served the people.   Senators were required to have an estate of at least four hundred pounds — which, it was believed, would ensure their whole-hearted defense of property rights against democratic encroachments.   Sam Adams fell in so completely with the prevailing spirit in the Senate that he became a stickler for senatorial rights and demanded a rigid formality in intercourse with the Lower House that infuriated the democrats.   As president, Adams made the Senate a bulwark against the attempts of the refugees and "old Tories" to return to Massachusetts or repossess their land: when the House of

---

[37] *Samuel Adams Papers*, Samuel A. Otis to Sam Adams, Jan. 4, 1780.
[38] A. E. Morse, *The Federalist Party in Massachusetts to the Year 1800* (1909), 22 (note). *The Writings of John Quincy Adams*, edited by Worthington Chauncey Ford (1913), I, 31.

Representatives passed a bill for admitting loyalists according to the terms of the treaty with Great Britain, the bill was killed in the Senate by Sam Adams and his supporters who were "keen in their resentments and rigid in their notions." [39] Adams admitted that he was in a "Fit of Zeal against the Refugees"; indeed, his resentment was so strong that he used the Massachusetts committees of correspondence, inspection, and safety to keep the people in constant alarm for their liberty and the property they had confiscated from the Tories. John Adams protested against this "silly warfare" against the Tories, but Sam Adams endeared himself to the Massachusetts reactionaries by raising a hue and cry. Conservative leaders now spoke of Sam Adams as "the good, the worthy old patriot Mr. Adams." [40]

Adams's conservatism reflected the changing temper of the people after the close of the Revolution. Revolutionary zeal had slowly cooled in Massachusetts after 1776; and the war lasted so long that by the time the revolutionary settlement was made, conservatives were in complete control. When young John Quincy Adams returned to Massachusetts from Europe, he feared that his continental education had not made him sufficiently republican for the taste of his fellow countrymen, but he found himself the "best republican" at Harvard College and compelled to defend democratic principles against his classmates. [41] Before independence had been won, it was clear that patriotism and love of liberty, which "at first ran through the whole state like wild-fire," had burned themselves out. French officers discovered that Boston Whigs, "like the Carthaginians, know to a penny the value of life and liberty" and had learned to turn patriotism to profit. [42]

As a defender of the established order, Sam Adams was kept

[39] *Journal of the Convention for Framing a Constitution of Government for The State of Massachusetts Bay* (1832), 257. *Report of the American Historical Association* (1896), I, 757. *Massachusetts Centinel*, Nov. 23 and 26, 1785.

[40] *The Writings of Samuel Adams*, IV, 312. *The Works of John Adams*, IX, 548. Wells, III, 181. *Historical Collections of the Essex Institute* (1889), XXV, 18.

[41] *The Writings of John Quincy Adams*, I, 29.

[42] *Boston Gazette*, May 6, 1782. Morse, 15.

almost as busy as when he was undermining royal government
in the colonies.   Dangers seemed to loom on every side.   It
was feared by Massachusetts patriots that the Society of the
Cincinnati, founded by military officers of the Revolutionary
War, was a "political Monster" from which would be hatched
a government by kings, lords, and commons; as Sam Adams
said, the congresses held by the Cincinnati would take the place
of the constitutional assemblies of the states and a hereditary
military nobility would establish feudalism and military tyranny.
Although Adams himself had created more unconstitutional
institutions during the Revolution than any other patriot, he
now violently denounced all extra-legal political organizations.
In particular, he singled out for attack the County Conventions
which were beginning to spring up throughout western Massachusetts in protest against the inequalities and oppression to
which the Massachusetts Constitution had given rise.   These
County Conventions were no more illegal than were the committees of correspondence of 1773, but Adams now regarded with
dread all assemblies which brought the constitutional legislature
into contempt; men who "under any Pretence or by any Means
whatever, would lessen the Weight of Government lawfully
exercised," he said, "must be Enemies to our happy Revolution & the Common Liberty." [43]   Both John and Sam Adams
raged against these "pestilential county conventions" at which
the citizens resolved not to pay taxes, called for the abolition
of the Massachusetts Senate, and demanded the revision of the
Massachusetts Constitution.   Unquestionably, the religious and
political settlement made by the "brace of Adamses" in the
Constitution of 1780 was "not democratick enough in the opinions of these Geniouses" who summoned the County Conventions in western Massachusetts. [44]

Equally dangerous, in Sam Adams's opinion, with County
Conventions and the Society of the Cincinnati was the spirit of

[43] *Samuel Adams Papers*, N. Y. Public Library, Elbridge Gerry to Stephen
Higginson, March 4, 1784.   *The Writings of Samuel Adams*, IV, 296, 301,
305.

[44] *The Works of John Adams*, IX, 556.   *The Writings of Samuel Adams*,
IV, 296, 301.   *Historical Magazine*, 1869, *Thacher Papers*, 257.   *The
Diary of William Pynchon*, edited by F. E. Oliver (1890), 239.

levelism. He certainly did not believe it one of the purposes
of the American Revolution that all classes be placed on an
equal plane: he asked, he said, for no more equality than was
"consistent with the true design of government." Adams still
clung to the principles he had held before the Revolution.
"I am not of levelling principles," he said, in 1771. ". . . Subordination is necessary to promote the purposes of government."
Indeed, until he fell under the spell of the spirit of "Liberty,
Equality, and Fraternity" during the French Revolution, he
was so little of an equalitarian that he complained to John
Adams that luxury and easy wealth in post-revolutionary New
England were "confounding every Distinction between the Poor
& the Rich." [45]

In 1785, to the accompaniment of "indecent joy" on one
side of the House of Representatives and "unmanly blubbering"
on the other, John Hancock announced his intention of withdrawing from politics.[46] Although Hancock pleaded ill-health,
his enemies suspected that he was eager to vacate the governor's
chair before the storm he saw brewing in rural Massachusetts
burst upon him. In the election which followed, Hancock's
nominee for the governorship was defeated by James Bowdoin,
leader of the conservative party with which Sam Adams was
allied. Adams heartily rejoiced in Hancock's discomfiture and
the success of the conservatives: "I confess," he said, "it is what
I have long wished for." With men in office who set the people
an example of patriotism and piety there seemed hope that the
long-delayed Reign of Virtue was at hand.[47] Adams himself
was appointed to the Council which assisted the governor in his
executive duties. But Daniel Shays in western Massachusetts gave Adams and Bowdoin far greater problems than the
return of Puritanism to wrestle with.

Like other revolutionists, Sam Adams disapproved of revolutions when they were begun by other people; and in 1785
he shared John Adams's conviction that "it can never be the

[45] *The Writings of Samuel Adams*, II, 152; IV, 315.
[46] *The Life and Correspondence of Rufus King*, edited by C. R. King
(1894–1900), I, 81.
[47] *The Writings of Samuel Adams*, IV, 316.

Duty of one Man to be concerned in more than one Revolution." [48]   When Daniel Shays began to kindle the discontent in rural Massachusetts into open rebellion, Sam Adams denounced the Shaysites just as Luther hurled anathemas against the peasants during the Peasants' Revolt.   He regarded Shays as a rebel who richly deserved the halter, not as a defender of popular rights carrying on the principles of the Revolution. The struggle for liberty was over, Adams exclaimed; no people could be more free than those who lived under a constitution they themselves had established; and if the citizens of western Massachusetts had grievances, they should express them at the elections.   There was no justification of forcible resistance to law in a government where voting was free: whatever the provocation, citizens must remember that "republics could only exist by a due submission to the laws." [49]   Had Thomas Hutchinson heard Sam Adams inveighing against the Shaysites in 1786 he would scarcely have believed that it was the one-time incendiary of the colonies speaking.   But there was good reason why Sam Adams was to be found in the conservative camp in 1786.   Shays's Rebellion grew out of the unrest and privation in western Massachusetts and assumed the character of a movement of country against town: one of the insurgents' demands, in fact, was that the capital be moved from Boston.   Sam Adams was a staunch townsman who so little understood rural economic problems that, while western Massachusetts was drifting toward rebellion, he was far more concerned with immorality in his beloved Boston than with the economic breakdown in the country.   When the artisans and small tradesmen of the metropolis were quiet, Adams was apt to think all was well in the commonwealth; when the country people rose in revolt he was utterly unable to understand their grievance.

Sam Adams became one of the strongest advocates of the "passionate measures" taken by the government against the insurgents.   As president of the Senate, he pushed through a

[48] *Warren-Adams Letters*, II, 189.
[49] Wells, III, 235.   *The Writings of Samuel Adams*, IV, 373.   *The Works of John Adams*, IX, 551.

bill suspending the writ of habeas corpus during the crisis; he
served on the committee which urged Governor Bowdoin to
take energetic action against the Shaysites; and he attempted
to rouse Lieutenant Governor Cushing — called the "Old
Lady" because of his timidity — to show the Shaysites cold
steel. He hounded the insurgents so relentlessly and pleaded
so strongly that blood be shed in western Massachusetts that
his enemies later said he had shown himself "fitter for a
Venetian Doge than for the second Magistrate in a free
republick." After the rebels had been dispersed, Adams called
for the leaders' blood: in monarchies, he exclaimed, treason
and rebellion might be pardoned, but no mercy could be shown
in a popular government — "the man who dares to rebel against
the laws of a republic ought to suffer death." [50] By pardoning
the insurgent chiefs, Governor Hancock revealed himself a more
astute politician and a more humane man than Sam Adams.

Shays's Rebellion added strength to the demand for a revision of the Articles of Confederation. There were usually
portentous clouds on Sam Adams's horizon and in the proposal
for a closer federation of the states he believed he beheld the
certain approach of a tempest. He had sat on the committee in
the Continental Congress that drew up the Articles of Confederation; and the experiences of the "critical decade" had not
convinced him that they must be essentially changed. In
1785, he warned that a revision would endanger the hard-won
liberties of the Revolution through the "Artifices of a few designing Men & a general Inattention of the many." But, because he longed to retaliate against Great Britain for placing
restrictions upon American trade and refusing to carry out the
provisions of the peace of 1783, Adams proposed giving Congress a "properly guarded" control of trade. Adams made clear,
however, that revision ought to go no further. Outside the lack
of power in the central government to control trade, he found
the Articles of Confederation very much to his taste: under
them, the states were sovereigns which gave the federal government sufficient authority to maintain their "mutual Safety and

[50] Wells, III, 227, 228, 246. *Massachusetts Centinel*, March 31, 1787.
Columbian Centinel, April 2, 1794.

Happiness . . . and *no more.*" As he said to John Adams, only "petit politicians" could wish to decrease the powers of the states and make the Congress at Philadelphia an overweening sovereign.[51]   Sam Adams believed that the British Empire had been disrupted because King George and Parliament were bent upon "governing too much"; and he was resolved to prevent the national government of the United States from falling into the same error.   The best government, he said, played the least part in men's daily affairs; and, after the Revolution, his mind was never free from the dread of seeing a tyrant at Philadelphia who would rule America as George III and Parliament had ruled from Westminster.   His negative political theory of natural rights caused him to fear every increase in the central government's power; like Richard Henry Lee, Adams believed that "the first maxim of a man who loved liberty should be, never to grant to Rulers an atom of power that is not most clearly and indispensably necessary for the safety and well being of Society."[52]   Since his Harvard College days, Adams had been firmly attached to Locke's theory of the supremacy of the legislature; no principle of government was more fundamental to him than that "in a constituted commonwealth . . . there can be but one supreme power, which is the legislative, to which all the rest are and must be subordinate."   For every ounce of authority the people, represented in the legislature, doled out to the executive, they should keep a pound of checks and balances.   Instead of strengthening the executive as the Federalists proposed, Adams wished to keep it weak and to preserve the fences he had erected during the Revolution "to protect & cover the rights of Mankind" against the menace of a strong central government.[53]   To Adams, as to the most of the older revolutionary patriots, a "strong government" meant only one thing — tyranny.

With the menace of Federalism looming on the horizon,

---

[51] *The Writings of Samuel Adams*, IV, 322–327, 329.   *Samuel Adams Papers*, N. Y. Public Library, Sam Adams to Elbridge Gerry, Sept. 19, 1785.

[52] *Samuel Adams Papers*, Richard Henry Lee to Sam Adams, March 14, 1785.

[53] *Mass. Hist. Soc. Proceedings*, L, 383.   *The Writings of Samuel Adams*, IV, 322–327.

Sam Adams saw that republicans could not yet rest from their
revolutionary labors.   Although he had paid no heed when the
Shaysites cried that liberty was in danger, he regarded the proposed Federal Constitution as an alarm bell to the "patriots of
'75."   He never ceased to doubt that the United States was too
vast in extent and too divided by local differences to form a successful national government.   Under the Articles of Confederation, the separation of the states in education, manners, and
religion was clearly recognized.   But if an attempt were made
to override American localism, Adams believed the result would
be "Mistrust, Disaffection to Government and frequent Insur-
rections, which will require standing Armies to suppress
them," [54] if not wars between the different sections.   Seventy
years later, the Civil War was to bear out Adams's prophecy.

Adams's fears were strengthened by the outcry raised against
the proposed Constitution by some of his oldest friends.   Richard Henry Lee led the opposition in the Constitutional Convention, and Elbridge Gerry, one of the Massachusetts delegates,
refused to sign the Convention's report.   Gerry sounded the
alarm in Massachusetts by writing Sam Adams that the Constitution gave inadequate protection to popular liberty.   Having
thus put Massachusetts republicans on guard, Gerry returned
to the state and began to damn the Constitution by exclaiming
to the citizens: "Beware! beware! — you are forging chains for
yourselves and children — your liberties are at stake." [55]

Nevertheless, Sam Adams made no effort to denounce the
Federal Constitution openly.   As he later explained in the
Massachusetts ratifying convention, he withheld judgment until he had carefully weighed its advantages and shortcomings;
and, above all, he wished to take soundings in Boston to determine the townspeople's attitude.   His observations convinced
him that there was a serious backsliding from the "principles of
'75" in the metropolis.   As James Madison said, the seaboard
was everywhere in favor of the Constitution; the chief demand
for a strong central government came from the merchants and

[54] *The Writings of Samuel Adams*, IV, 324–325, 332.
[55] *Massachusetts Centinel*, Nov. 17, 1787.

traders who suffered from British commercial restrictions.[56]
The Boston mechanics and artisans were such strong Federalists
they could not be frightened by warnings that the metropolis
would lose its trade with Philadelphia if the Articles of Confederation were tampered with.   Far from sharing Sam Adams's
misgivings toward the Constitution, Bostonians were "in raptures
with it as it is, but would have liked it still better had it been
higher-toned." [57]   Boston's eagerness to ratify the Constitution had been foreseen by the Federalist leaders, who relied
upon the metropolis to turn the scales against rural opposition.
Resistance to the adoption of the Constitution in Massachusetts
came principally from the country districts where it was believed to be the work of rich men who hoped to create two social
orders, "one comprehending the opulent and great, the other
the poor and illiterate."   It was the "black cloud" rolling down
from the western counties that aroused Federalist apprehensions:
the seaboard would unquestionably vote for ratification, but
would it be able to overcome back-country anti-Federalism? [58]

Boston's enthusiasm for the Constitution caused Adams to
hold his fire against it.   His silence kept the Federalists in
great uneasiness, expecting every moment he would launch a
bitter attack upon the Constitution and start an anti-Federalist
backfire in the metropolis itself.   They anxiously scanned the
newspapers for signs of that pen "dipped in venom" with which
Adams upset so many of his enemies' best-laid schemes.   Although they believed Adams to be "Helvidius Priscus," the
author of a virulent arraignment of the Constitution, the writer
was in fact James Warren.[59]   Sam Adams gave the Federalists
no definite proof of his anti-Federalism until after his election
to the Massachusetts Convention.   At a banquet given the
Boston delegates it was found that all favored its adoption except Adams, who was "open & decided" against it, arguing that
"such a Govt. could not pervade the United States — that in-

---

[56] *The Writings of James Madison*, edited by Gaillard Hunt (1901), V,
8.   *The Life and Correspondence of Rufus King*, I, 69.
[57] Morse, 45.   *Mass. Hist. Soc. Proceedings*, LXIV, 149.
[58] *The Life and Correspondence of Rufus King*, I, 263, 266, 317.
[59] *Mass. Hist. Soc. Proceedings*, LXIV, 155.

ternal taxes ought not to be given to the Union — that the representation was inadequate," and that a large number of amendments must be made before liberty was properly safeguarded.[60]
This was no more than the Federalists had expected. Sam
Adams had at last come into the open and revealed himself an
enemy to the Constitution; and it could no longer be doubted
that he must be prevented from putting himself at the head of
the anti-Federalist forces in the Massachusetts Convention.

Although Adams was old and retained little of his former
political influence, the Federalists recognized that his sturdy
republicanism was a difficult hurdle in the way of Massachusetts' ratification of the Constitution.   They still entertained a
healthy respect for Sam Adams — an attitude that might well be
taken by aristocrats toward a revolutionist who had already overthrown one aristocracy.   The Federalist bugbear was the same
as the Tories': to be "entrapped by the craft of A[dams]." [61]
But the Federalists soon showed themselves quite as crafty as
Adams had been in his best days.   Because it was clear that
Adams's support of the Constitution could not be won by argument, the Federalists determined to convert him by other means.
Adams's habit of making the wishes of Boston mechanics his
guide in public conduct was well known to the Federalists.
Unlike the Tories, the Federalists carefully cultivated the
friendship of Boston mechanics and artisans, and by the time
of the Massachusetts Convention they had a strong following
among Adams's constituents.   It only remained, therefore, to
bring the men Adams looked upon as his political oracles to declare themselves in favor of the Constitution.   Clark, Rhodes,
and Freeman, three of the most powerful politicians in the North
End, who had kept the district loyal to Sam Adams for many
years, promised the Federalist leaders that they could call "the
most numerous caucus ever held in Boston" to rebuke Adams
for his anti-Federalist outburst at the delegates' banquet.
Early in January 1788, the mechanics assembled at the Green
Dragon Tavern and voted unanimously in favor of ratifying
the Constitution.   Resolutions drafted by Paul Revere and

[60] *The Life and Correspondence of Rufus King,* I, 311.
[61] *Ibid.,* I, 267.

Benjamin Russell were adopted by the mechanics, who declared their "warmest wish and prayer" was that the Constitution be ratified by Massachusetts. Sam Adams was given unmistakably to understand that if he opposed its adoption he would "act contrary to the best interest, the strongest feelings, and warmest wishes of the tradesmen of the town of Boston." [62] Adams was so stunned to find such heresy starting up among his followers that, upon learning what had been done at the Green Dragon, he is said to have exclaimed: "Well, if they must have it, they must have it." The story is doubtless false because Adams soon showed that even Boston mechanics could not immediately overcome his reluctance to part with the Articles of Confederation. Nevertheless, Adams's hands were henceforth tied by Federalist strategy and he was unable to play the part of an anti-Federalist leader in the Massachusetts Convention. [63]

The Green Dragon vote fairly muzzled Sam Adams, but the Federalists were well aware that he was at heart no friend to the Constitution. Moreover, there were signs that Adams might turn against his constituents and rally the anti-Federalists about him. Early in the Convention, he became an "Arch Devil" in the Federalists' eyes by moving that Elbridge Gerry, the Massachusetts delegate to the Constitutional Convention that had been held in New York, should be admitted to the Massachusetts Convention to give his reasons for opposing the Constitution. Sam Adams's proposal was carried and Gerry was brought in, much to the joy of the anti-Federalists. But the result was bitterly disappointing to Adams and his friends: Gerry was quickly silenced by the Federalists and forced to sit "biting the head of his cane" until he finally "left the Convention in dudgeon." [64] Adams's second fling at the Federalists was equally unsuccessful. When he interrupted young Fisher Ames to ask why biennial elections should be preferred over

---

[62] *Historical Collections of the Essex Institute* (1899), XXXV, 89. *Massachusetts Centinel*, Jan. 9, 1788.

[63] *Historical Magazine*, 1869, *Thacher Papers*, 263.

[64] *Historical Collections of the Essex Institute*, XXXV, 92, 93. *Belknap Papers*, II, *Mass. Hist. Soc. Collections*, Fifth Series (1877), III, 7. *Correspondence of the Revolution*, edited by Jared Sparks, IV, 204.

annual elections, Ames answered with a speech of such cogency
and force that Adams dropped the matter as though he had
touched a red-hot iron and meekly remarked that "he only
made the inquiry for information, and that he had heard sufficient to satisfy himself of its propriety." The haste with which
Adams backed away from an encounter with Ames disconcerted
the anti-Federalists, who had hoped to hear him attack the
Constitution. The Federalists, on the other hand, were exultant and they dated the turn of the tide in the Convention in
their favor from the day Adams was worsted by young Ames.
"This was the first dawn of the Triumph of Reason in the Convention," they exclaimed.[65]

Although John Hancock had been elected president, he had
not yet made his appearance in the Convention. Swathed in
bandages and keeping to his sickroom as tenaciously as Lord
Chatham, Hancock refused to take his seat until he was sure
which party in the Convention would triumph. It was well
known that as soon as Hancock was satisfied from which direction the wind was blowing his health would show immediate
improvement and he would be on hand to lead the winning
party to victory; but while the "balance of power was each day
vibrating, as the mercury in a thermometer," Hancock's ail-
ments kept him bedridden in Beacon Street.[66] There was nothing more fatal, in Hancock's eyes, than not to be on the winning
side; and had the Constitution been ratified or rejected without his aid he would have been a sick man indeed. If he can
be said to have had any convictions, they were anti-Federalist.
As the governor of one of the strongest states in the Union,
Hancock was reluctant to help create an office of greater dignity
and power than his own. Nevertheless, he was haunted by
the fear that the Constitution might be carried in spite of him
and that the rising Federalist tide would overwhelm him, as
it threatened to overwhelm all other enemies of the Constitution.
He was well pleased with the present order, but he had no in-

[65] *Massachusetts Centinel*, Jan. 19, 1788; Dec. 31, 1788.
[66] *Historical Magazine* (1869), *Thacher Papers*, 266. *Historical Collections of the Essex Institute*, 87. Theophilus Parsons, *Memoir of Theophilus Parsons* (1859), 78.

tention of lashing himself to the Articles of Confederation and
sinking with them should the Federalists' broadside strike home.

Shrewdly gauging Hancock's weakness, the Federalist caucus
leaders hit upon a plan to draw him out of his sickroom and
bring him into the Convention an avowed Federalist.   Hancock was willing to listen to offers and he soon learned that the
anti-Federalists had little to give in comparison with the tempting fruit the Federalists dangled before him.   In exchange for
urging the ratification of the Constitution, the Federalists promised Hancock their support for the presidency of the United
States in case Virginia failed to ratify the Constitution.   At the
same time, they convinced him that Virginia would not ratify —
thereby eliminating George Washington as a rival for the President's chair.   Hancock had no aversion to a strong central government provided he could be at its head and therefore he
eagerly swallowed the Federalist bait.[67]

While the Federalist chiefs were making certain of Hancock's
aid they were tampering with Sam Adams's devotion to the
Articles of Confederation.   Most of the work was done behind
the locked doors of the caucus, where Federalists worked "as
hard as in the Convention" and with far more important results.   In this secret meeting, Adams made his terms with the
Federalists.   Unlike Hancock, he could not be tempted with
political office, but the Federalists were well stocked with bait
to land even the stoutest anti-Federalist in their basket.   Adams
was promised that amendments would be added to the Constitution to protect the liberty of states and individuals under a
centralized government.   The Green Dragon vote had sown
the first seed of doubt in Adams's mind that perhaps he had
misjudged the Constitution; and the arguments of the Federalists began to convince him that even "old fashioned Whigs"
could swallow it if it were heavily seasoned with amendments.
It was agreed that the amendments drawn up by the Federalist
caucus should be introduced into the Convention by Hancock
as a "conciliatory proposition" to unite both parties in favor of
ratification, and that Sam Adams should second Hancock's pro-

[67] *The Life and Correspondence of Rufus King*, I, 319, 344.   Parsons,
78.   *Historical Collections of the Essex Institute*, XXV, 94.

posal.[68]   The delegates outside the caucus were kept in the dark
as to the way Sam Adams would vote, but it was known to the
Federalist chiefs that his opposition had been removed ten days
before he openly spoke for ratification in the Convention.   As
had been expected, Hancock's health quickly improved after he
had made his bargain with the Federalists and he was able to
take his seat as president of the Convention.   With Adams and
Hancock securely pocketed, the exultant Federalists believed
nothing more stood in the way of ratification.

The failure of the two leading revolutionary Whigs in Massachusetts to come to the aid of the anti-Federalists worked the
downfall of the enemies of the Constitution.   Although the
anti-Federalists were in a majority when the Convention opened,
they were unwieldy, poorly led, and unequipped with the
"whips" and caucuses possessed by the Federalists.   The anti-
Federalist leaders, Widgery and Bishop, were uneducated
back-country politicians who repeatedly allowed themselves to
be outgeneraled by the Federalist minority.   It was one of the
anti-Federalists' chief grievances that all the professional and
educated men in the Convention were in favor of the Constitution, leaving them only a handful of orators who, it was said,
were "very clamorous, petulant, tedious, and provoking."
There were so many Shaysites among them that Federalist
newspapers traced their genealogy from *"bankrupt tories* in
'74 — *fiery whigs* in '75 — *disappointed jockies* in '83 — *insurgents* in '86 and *antifederalists* in '88."[69]   Unquestionably,
most of the talent was on the side of Federalism; and the anti-
Federalists sorely needed a strategist such as Sam Adams to
counterwork the oratory of Judge Dana, who "thunders like
Demosthenes," and the skill of the Federalist caucus.   But
Adams made no effort to take command; and, as the Convention drew to a close, the anti-Federalists were panic-stricken to
see their strength melting away.   "The more the Constitution
is canvassed," wrote a Federalist, "the brighter it shines."
And, after Hancock made his "conciliatory proposition," seconded by Sam Adams, the anti-Federalists were so weakened

[68] *Belknap Papers,* II, *Mass. Hist. Soc. Collections,* Fifth Series, III, 15.
[69] *Massachusetts Centinel,* April 30, 1788.

by desertions that the Federalists began to believe themselves in a majority for the first time since the opening of the Convention.[70]

The Federalists flattered themselves they had taken Sam Adams securely in tow, but on the last day of the Convention he revealed how little to his taste was sailing in the wake of the Federalist man-of-war. Just when the Constitution seemed about to be ratified, Adams "almost overset the apple-cart" by unexpectedly introducing a set of new amendments to the Constitution in an effort to safeguard liberty further against the central government.[71] Both parties in the Convention were alarmed by Adams's motion; and a murmur ran through the anti-Federalist ranks that "such a man as Mr. A[dams] would not have guarded against these evils, if he had not seen a foundation for them in the Constitution." Indeed, he threw the meeting into such consternation that the Constitution's fate was in doubt for some hours. Finally, after it had become apparent that his amendments would create another protracted struggle between the weary delegates, Adams withdrew his motion. The damage was not repaired so easily, however, because some of the anti-Federalists revived the motion and Adams was compelled to vote against his own measure. Although it was ultimately defeated, it cost the Constitution precious votes and almost wiped away the small Federalist majority of seventeen that made possible the ratification of the Constitution. It was suspected by some that Adams introduced those last-minute amendments in order to keep Hancock from stealing the whole show "with *his* amendments and to increase his *own* popularity, as Hancock had his, by the midwifeing the other amendments into the world." [72] More probably, Adams acted from a sincere fear that individual liberty was not yet sufficiently protected from encroachments by the Federal government. The Federalists had silenced him for the greater part of the Convention,

[70] *Belknap Papers*, III, *Mass. Hist. Soc. Collections*, Fifth Series, III, 5, 17. *Historical Collections of the Essex Institute*, XXXV, 94.

[71] *Belknap Papers*, II, *Mass. Hist. Soc. Collections*, Fifth Series, III, 17. *Debates and Proceedings in the Mass. Convention*, 266.

[72] *Belknap Papers*, II, *Mass. Hist. Soc. Collections*, Fifth Series, III, 17. *Massachusetts Centinel*, Dec. 17, 1788.

but they had not succeeded in quieting his fears that the Constitution would undo the work of the Revolution by creating a despotism in Philadelphia. In Adams's justification, his friends later pointed out that most of the amendments he proposed in the Massachusetts Convention — particularly, the prohibition of standing armies, the guarantee of liberty of the press, the power of the people to petition Congress for redress of grievances, and the inviolability of "persons, papers, or possessions" against unreasonable searches and seizures — were later incorporated in the Constitution of the United States.[73]

In spite of Adams's filibustering, the Convention ratified the Constitution "to the great Joy of all Boston." The Federalists had transformed the citadel of Whig republicanism into a "federal metropolis" in which Sam Adams found few familiar landmarks. Boston mechanics who had been the staunchest friends of Sam Adams and the Revolution now paraded the streets in celebration of the Federalist victory, cheering the delegates who had voted for the Constitution and burning a longboat, called the "Old Constitution," on the Common.[74]

Sam Adams had gained no new laurels in the Massachusetts Constitutional Convention. Federalists scented treachery in his "insidious motion" for further amendments and believed his real intention had been to overturn the whole Constitution; and the anti-Federalists reproached him for precipitately withdrawing his amendments under the enemy's fire.[75] It was clear that Adams's reputation acquired in the American Revolution was wearing thin. He seemed completely out of touch with the new order that was being created in America; he could expect no honors under a centralized government; and even in his native state his influence had almost completely vanished. The new generation was as indifferent to most of the "heroes of '75" as it was to the old Whig principles and prejudices. The French traveler, La Rochefoucauld, found that the citizens of Boston retained little of the hatred toward Great Britain for

[73] *Independent Chronicle*, Aug. 6, 1789.

[74] *Historical Magazine* (1869), *Thacher Papers*, 270. *Massachusetts Centinel*, Dec. 17, 1788. *Independent Chronicle*, Feb. 14, 1788.

[75] *Belknap Papers*, II, *Mass. Hist. Soc. Collections*, Fifth Series, III, 17, 18. *The Writings of Laco* (1789), 49. *Massachusetts Centinel*, Dec. 17, 1788.

which they had been famous during the Revolution.[76]   Sam
Adams, it was plain, would receive no high political reward by
resting upon his fame as "the Man of the Revolution."

Misfortune had done much to show Sam Adams the futility
of further opposing John Hancock, the political "boss" of Massachusetts.   Adams had learned from his disappointments of
the past ten years that Hancock had power to make or unmake
any politician in the state and that, as long as he remained at
odds with Hancock, the highest offices would be barred against
him.   Moreover, in spite of the amendments, Adams regarded
the Constitution as a menace to popular liberty and he believed
that the republicans of the revolutionary period were now called
upon to make peace among themselves in order to combat centralized government and the new "Tory" aristocracy.   Hancock, as well, was eager for a reconciliation.   When Hancock
saw his chances for the presidency of the United States go glimmering with Virginia's ratification of the Constitution, he
abruptly broke off relations with the Federalists and, much to
the amazement of all parties, he and Adams went off arm in
arm on a new honeymoon, with Adams enthusiastically singing
the praises of a man whom for the past fourteen years he had
denounced as a wastrel and compared with Thomas Hutchinson.   Just as in 1772, when Adams and Hancock interrupted
their quarrel to make common front against the Tories, so in
1788 they erased old scores to make war against the Federalists.
But despite their parade of friendship, it was understood that
Sam Adams, the one-time leader of the patriot party, was now
merely a lieutenant in Hancock's party: "John is the first of the
tribe, and Samuel is second," it was said.[77]

Unfortunately, Sam Adams's humiliation in the Massachusetts Constitutional Convention at the hands of Fisher Ames
did not teach him that young Ames — soon to be known as the
"Colossus of Monocrats" — was a very dangerous political
opponent.   In 1788, Adams entered the race for the Federal
Congress from the Suffolk district, with Fisher Ames, the Fed-

[76] Duc de la Rochefoucauld Liancourt, *Travels through the United States
of North America*, I, 403, 404.
[77] *Independent Chronicle*, March 27, 1788.

eralist candidate, as his adversary. Ames was of the class of
1774, Harvard College, and his revolutionary service consisted in having once turned out with militia. It seemed incredible that such a stripling could defeat the veteran Sam
Adams; and, indeed, the Federalists apologized to each other
for having picked a novice to oppose him. Hopefully they
pointed out that Ames was as old as Sam Adams when he first
entered public life and that the Federalist candidate was older
than Pitt when he became Prime Minister of Great Britain.
But it was agreed that Ames's chances of winning the election
were slight.

The principal issue between Ames and Adams was the necessity of further amending the Constitution. Now an avowed
anti-Federalist, Adams ran as a "violent stickler for amendments," while Ames belabored the "disappointed jockies" who,
having failed to prevent the adoption of the Constitution, would
cripple it with amendments.[78] Although it had been a matter of
doubt where Sam Adams stood while the Constitution was being
debated in the Massachusetts Convention, there was no question
of his position now: there were far too few checks and balances
and safeguards to popular liberty in the Constitution, he exclaimed, to dispel his fears of despotism.[79] Adams now anxiously sniffed the breeze that blew from Philadelphia for whiffs
of tyranny; and he was as determined in 1788 as in 1775 to
resist the centralization of American government.

Fisher Ames and his friends pictured Adams as an enemy of
the Constitution who wished to enter Congress in order to wreck
the newly established Federal government. They urged the
Boston mechanics whose support had been vital to Massachusetts' ratification of the Constitution to elect to Congress a "*firm
decided* FEDERALIST" who would defend the Constitution
against the States' rights republicans.[80] Federalist propaganda
put Adams in the light of a destroyer of the Constitution and
Ames as its savior — to the great perplexity of the voters of

[78] *Massachusetts Centinel*, April 30, 1788; Sept. 27, 1788; Dec. 17
and 31, 1788.
[79] *The Writings of Samuel Adams*, IV, 337.
[80] *Massachusetts Centinel*, Sept. 27, 1788; Dec. 13 and 17, 1788.
Austin, II, 96.

the Suffolk District, who were torn between their loyalty to
the Constitution and their respect for Sam Adams. But their
desire to see a strong central government in the United States
ultimately prevailed and Ames was elected by a large majority.
Even Boston turned against Sam Adams and gave Ames 445
votes to Adams's 439. It was an impressive victory for the
Federalists; but Adams might well have comforted himself
with the reflection that he would have found, as did Elbridge
Gerry, that Congress was a very unhappy place for a republican of the vintage of '75.

Fisher Ames's victory was the result of the growing conviction among a large body of Massachusetts voters that Sam
Adams's ideas were more suited to solving the problems of
1775 than those of 1788. He seemed to belong to a past generation. "The spirit of '75 was a glorious spirit for *that period*,"
it was said, "but do its principles apply at the present day?" As
the Federalists pointed out, the question was no longer "Shall
we be free" but "How shall we use our freedom?" — and to
this last question Sam Adams could give no answer.[81] Since
the Revolution, Massachusetts had become a great commercial
state that demanded from its representatives in Congress wide
knowledge of commerce and finance rather than obsolete Whiggish hatred of Great Britain. It was well known that Sam
Adams had little interest in trade and that he was openly hostile
to commerce with Great Britain. He unhesitatingly confessed
his ignorance of commercial matters: "I get out of my Line
when I touch upon Commerce," he once wrote; "it is a Subject I
never understood." [82] This shortcoming might have been overlooked in 1775, but it was a serious handicap to a Massachusetts politician in 1788. Federalists saw Adams's vulnerability
and heckled him ceaselessly with questions concerning his fit-
ness to lead "this Commercial Commonwealth": "What," they
asked, "are his acquirements upon the great subject of Finance;
has he ever attended to System of Revenue; what are his ideas
of trade and Commerce; are they matter of great importance
in *his* estimation?" Sam Adams certainly did not seem to be

[81] *Massachusetts Centinel*, May 10, 1788.
[82] *The Writings of Samuel Adams*, III, 353.

the man upon whom Massachusetts businessmen should rely
to foster commerce and dispel the danger of *"Insurgents, Mobs,
Antifederalists, Paper Money, or Tender Laws."* [83]

Adams's greatest political weakness, however, was his unpopularity in rural Massachusetts. In the congressional elections of 1788, for example, he received only eighty-two votes
outside of Boston. Just as he had been looked upon with suspicion by many members of the continental Congress as representing too exclusively the interests of Massachusetts, so he was
distrusted by New England countryfolk as being too much of a
Bostonian. Like the Tories before them, the Federalists attempted to destroy Boston's influence in the country and to
keep the farmers "out of the power of the tempters in the seaports, and their mobs." Their policy was to create "an enlightened Yeomanry" that would stand firm against "all the
seditious, and desperate" Boston demagogues.[84] But, unlike
the Tories, they were not satisfied with merely winning the support of New England yeomen: by making allies of the "steady
going Mechanics" of the metropolis they cut the ground from
beneath Sam Adams's feet. Whereas the Tories had regarded
the artisan class of the metropolis as "the rabble" and "the
scum" and ignored their political importance, the Federalists
courted and flattered them as ardently as did Sam Adams. As
a consequence, Boston radicals found themselves opposed with
their own weapons: Federalists called town meetings, held
caucuses of mechanics and shopkeepers, and dispensed liberal
quantities of rum and flip among the electorate.[85] But it was
not until French Jacobinism had begun to infect Americans that
the true value of this missionary work among Boston mechanics
was clearly seen.

The Federalists were so successful in weaning Bostonians

[83] *Massachusetts Centinel,* Dec. 13 and 17, 1788.

[84] *The Works of Fisher Ames,* edited by Seth Ames (1859), I, 182.
Pickering Papers, MSS. Mass. Hist. Soc., XX, T. Williams to Timothy
Pickering, July 17, 1795, 21. *The Works of Alexander Hamilton,* edited by
J. S. Hamilton (1851), V, 571.

[85] *The Correspondence of Rufus King,* I, 361. *Federal Orrery,* April 6,
1795. *The Works of Fisher Ames,* I, 146. *The Works of Alexander
Hamilton,* 571.

away from Sam Adams and arousing hostility in the country districts against him that even John Hancock, the most powerful man in the state, had difficulty in putting his new ally into high office. Adams was defeated in 1788 when he ran for the lieutenant governorship; and it required all the strength the Hancockians could muster in 1789 to hoist Adams beside Hancock in the second highest office in the state.

In his political campaigns after the adoption of the Federal Constitution, Sam Adams was put forward as the "old tried republican" who would "preserve the republick of Massachusetts from being swallowed up in a merciless Aristocracy." He was declared to be the enemy of the "British Faction" in Massachusetts, "the black band of Tories," "British Agents," refugees seeking to recover their estates, and "the filchering gang of speculators" who robbed the people through the Bank of the United States.[86] Before elections the old hatred of Great Britain was turned into votes for Sam Adams by a prearranged British scare; King George's agents were said to be swarming in the state; Tories were plotting to regain their property and political influence; and republicans exclaimed that the British were beginning "to show their teeth" again because Americans had forgotten the men and principles of 1775. Readers of Massachusetts anti-Federalist newspapers might well believe that British redcoats would soon be camping on the Boston Common unless Sam Adams were given an overwhelming vote to prove to King George that New Englanders were still true to their "first love." Adams was not merely a bulwark against the British peril: he was, as well, a staunch opponent of encroachments from the national government and a guardian angel of local liberties. His favorite toast was, "The States united and the States separate"; and, the Federalists complained, he thundered against "every thing that is federal and rational."[87]

Had Sam Adams died before the adoption of the Federal Constitution and the outbreak of the French Revolution created new party struggles in the United States, he would have ended

[86] *Herald of Freedom and the Federal Adviser*, April 3, 1789. *Massachusetts Centinel*, March 14, 1789. *Independent Chronicle*, Jan. 15, 1795.
[87] Wells, III, 273. *Salem Gazette*, March 25, 1794.

his days in the conservatism that frequently comes upon revolutionists in their old age.   Like John Wilkes, Adams might
have exclaimed that he was an "exhausted volcano" and settled
down to the dreary business of repressing radicalism in the
younger generation.   Fortunately, the menace of a centralized
government and a Federalist oligarchy, together with the spread
of the spirit of "Liberty, Equality, and Fraternity" to the
United States, saved Adams from decaying in the conservative
backwaters into which he had fallen and plunged him again into
the centre of those revolutionary eddies which were his true
element.

Sam Adams's faith in the common people remained unshaken,
despite their preference for Hancock and high living.   For
many years, John Adams had felt doubtful of the success of
the republican experiment, but Sam Adams was firmly convinced
that democracy would flourish as long as education was extended
to the masses.   Sam Adams had much of the zeal for popular
education that his Puritan ancestors had carried to New England.   The way to perpetuate republican government, he said,
was to take the children young, clap them into a grammar school
run on sound New England lines, and instill Whig principles
into them until they emerged upright citizens who loathed British luxuries and monarchy alike.   As long as these "nurseries of
Virtue" kept turning out young Whigs, there was no danger
of dictatorship or monarchy in America because the people
would be wise enough to elect only the best men to office.[88]
Sam Adams's faith in the common man was fully as strong as
Jefferson's, but there was this significant difference between
these two staunch republicans: whereas Jefferson put his trust
in the American farmer, Sam Adams's common man was a
townsman and usually a Bostonian.   Far from being a Jeffer-
sonian democrat in the usual sense of the word, Sam Adams
represented that unruly town democracy which Jefferson later
took into the Republican Party with deep misgivings.

Adams's belief in the wisdom of the common people and devotion to a democratic form of government brought him again

[88] *The Writings of Samuel Adams*, III, 231; IV, 124, 125, 347. *Warren-
Adams Letters*, I, 171, 172, 197.

into the thick of the struggle when, in 1793, the French Revolution began to awaken a revolutionary spirit in the United States and divide the American people into Jacobins and anti-Jacobins. From the beginning, Adams believed the French Revolution to be "a war of Kings and Nobles against the equal Rights of Men," and he was eager to spring to the defense of popular liberty in the United States, jeopardized, as he supposed, by the Federal Constitution and the new aristocracy. "From my Youth," Adams said, "my mind has been strongly impressed with the Love of Mankind; and tho' I am old, the lamp still burns." [89]   Unlike his cousin, John Adams distrusted the French Revolution as early as 1790, when most Americans were strongly Francophile, because he suspected that the French people, like too many Americans, panted "for equality of persons and property." [90]   John Adams, it was clear, would have no sympathy with Sam Adams's efforts to preserve American liberty by making French Jacobinism a rallying cry.

The Federalists' opposition to the spread of French revolutionary principles in the United States sounded an alarm among the old guard of American patriots. The battles of the Revolution must be fought again, they cried, and the Tories once more struck down. "I am alarmed," wrote Hancock to Adams in 1793. ". . . It is time to step forth & oppose the torrent of opinions & pursuits that are attempting to establish a system foreign to your ideas & mine." Adams had lost none of his eagerness to do battle with Tories and he answered that Hancock's call to arms had "cheer'd the Spirit and caus'd the blood to thrill thro' the Veins of an Old Man." [91]   The Whigs forgot their internal quarrels and once more formed themselves into that "phalanx" that had struck terror among the Tories during the Revolution. As Elbridge Gerry said, Hancock, with all his faults, was still a Whig and sorely needed the help of his old comrades against the Federalist aristocracy. [92]

[89] *The Writings of Samuel Adams*, IV, 358. *Samuel Adams Papers*, N. Y. Public Library, Samuel Adams to Pierre Auguste Adet, July 28, 1795.
[90] *The Works of John Adams*, IX, 563, 564.
[91] *Samuel Adams Papers*, N. Y. Hist. Soc., John Hancock to Sam Adams, Aug. 31, 1793; Sam Adams to John Hancock, Sept. 3, 1793.
[92] Austin, II, 86.

After John Hancock's death in 1793, Sam Adams was given
an opportunity to become one of the chief apostles of Jacobinism
in the United States.   He inherited the leadership of the Han-
cockian party that had controlled Massachusetts politics for
over a decade, and, as Hancock's heir, seemed likely to dominate the political scene for the remainder of his life.   But to
the Federalists it was intolerable that Massachusetts, a strong
Federalist state, should elect a "doting antifederalist" to the
governorship.   They hoped to break up Hancock's party after
Adams had taken command and they made a vigorous effort
to tumble this "scapegoat of seventy-five" out of the governor's
chair in the elections of 1794.[93]   But Adams kept the loyalty
of Hancock's former followers by lauding the deceased governor in public and praising his "virtuous and patriotic example." [94]   With the Hancockians' support, Adams surprised
the Federalists by soundly beating their candidate for governor
in 1794, but the best John Quincy Adams could say of Adams
was that he "may do less harm than some others, but he will
certainly never do any good."   Conservatives seldom expected
good from Sam Adams; and when "all the wise, and good, and
the rich," as Fisher Ames characterized the Federalist Party,
saw Adams seated firmly in the governor's chair, they threw
up their hands in dismay and declared that all was lost.[95]   Sam
Adams, it was said, was looking forward to a second revolution
in the United States — this time with French Jacobinism as his
creed and the Federalist aristocracy as his victims.

During Shays's Rebellion, Sam Adams had inveighed against
all unconstitutional institutions as vigorously as the Tories had
once denounced his committees of correspondence.   But the
necessity of crushing Federalism in Massachusetts led Adams to
alter sharply his attitude toward unconstitutional organizations
and he enthusiastically gave his blessing to the Constitutional
Clubs — the "self-created Societies" that were designed to keep
alive the principles of the American Revolution and, the
Federalists suspected, to keep the United States abreast of

[93] *The Writings of John Quincy Adams*, I, 185.
[94] *The Writings of Samuel Adams*, IV, 354.
[95] *The Writings of John Quincy Adams*, I, 183.   Charles Warren,
Jacobin and Junto, 50.

France in the march toward "Liberty, Equality, and Fraternity." [96]   These Jacobin Clubs with their corresponding committees and secret caucuses — where radicals were as busy as "Old Nick and his imps" — bore strong resemblance to the machinery which Sam Adams had created during the American Revolution.   Like the earlier committees of correspondence they were the terror of the "Tories": Fisher Ames exclaimed they were "born in sin, the impure offspring of Genêt," and some apprehensive Federalists, who fancied they already saw the shadow of the guillotine on Boston Common, were unable to pass a lamppost without casting an uneasy glance in its direction. French tricolor cockades and liberty caps began to give Boston an uncomfortably Parisian atmosphere: "loud and saucy" Jacobins paraded through the streets and were heard to "yelp & howl and Trumpet sedition at every corner." [97]   Boston Federalists found to their dismay that they were unable to hoot down the republicans when they broke into the chorus of "Ça Ira" in Boston taverns and theatres.   But even more alarming than these portents of the Boston Jacobins' eagerness to see the metropolis play the part of an American Paris in the second American Revolution was the spectacle of the governor of Massachusetts, arm in arm with Jacobins and Frenchmen, surrounded by "Sattelites of Anarchy" and proclaiming the doctrine "Liberty, Equality, and Fraternity" from the governor's chair.

Indeed, Governor Adams seemed to be as enthusiastic a Jacobin as ever came out of "Equality Alley."   Whenever his failing health permitted, "Citizen" Adams was the guest of honor at the "Civic Feasts" where Boston democrats celebrated French military victories and indulged themselves in such disquieting sport as slaughtering an ox, labeled "Aristocracy," as a "PEACE OFFERING TO LIBERTY AND EQUALITY."   Federalists vainly protested against Governor Adams lending the sanction of his person to meetings which, they declared, consisted only of gallows birds and a few "hungry immigrants, happy to pick

[96] *Independent Chronicle*, Dec. 9, 1793.
[97] *The Works of Fisher Ames*, I, 148.   *Columbian Centinel*, Aug. 7, 1793; Nov. 1, 1794; Dec. 20, 1794. Parsons (Appendix), 472. Warren, 57. *Massachusetts Mercury*, Nov. 29, 1793. *Independent Chronicle*, April 25, 1793.

up a dinner." These gatherings, it was said, were properly
called tricolor festivals because the company was composed of
whites, mulattoes, and negroes.[98] But Adams continued to attend these Jacobin frolics regardless of the scandalized Federalists: at the great Civic Feast held in Boston in January 1793,
with Faneuil Hall decorated with French flags and mottoes of
"Liberty, Equality, and Fraternity," Citizen Adams sat beside
the French consul and led the toasts of France. He was present at the feast held in celebration of the abolition of monarchy;
and when news arrived of a great French victory, Adams ordered
that a collation be served in the Senate chamber and a military
corps parade through the streets. Adams took such prominent
part in these democratic revels and connected himself so closely
with the Jacobin Club that Federalists exclaimed he acted more
like a French agent than the governor of the commonwealth
of Massachusetts. But Adams's popularity with Jacobins
throughout the United States was so great that he ran Governor
Clinton a close race for highest honors. The French ministers
now found him greatly changed from the days of the Continental Congress when he had been a thorn in the side of every
French emissary. They were charmed by Adams's speeches
to the Massachusetts General Court, "every sentence, every
word" of which, they said, breathed "the purest republicanism"
and proved the governor a "friend of liberty and France."
Particularly exhilarating to the French ministers and perturbing
to the Federalists was Adams's address to the Massachusetts
legislature delivered in 1794, in which the governor pointed
out that liberty and equality were essential parts of the "political
creed of the United States" and that the American and French
Constitutions were based upon the same principles. Truly, said
the Federalists, Sam Adams had become a Frenchman.[99]

[98] Warren, 57. *The Works of Fisher Ames*, I, 146. *Salem Gazette*,
March 29, 1796. *Massachusetts Mercury*, Sept. 22, 1795. *Massachusetts
Centinel*, Jan. 17, 1794.
[99] Warren, 47. *The Correspondence of Rufus King*, I, 545. *Massachu-
setts Mercury*, Sept. 22, 1795. *Independent Chronicle*, April 2, 1795. *Salem
Gazette*, March 25, 1795. *Samuel Adams Papers*, N. Y. Public Library,
Antoine Charbonnet Duplaine to Governor Samuel Adams, April 10, 1794.
Report of the American Historical Association (1903), II, 893.

Sam Adams further outraged the Federalist aristocracy by surrounding himself with the boon companions of his revolutionary days and with Jacobins from the Boston Constitutional Society. After his election as governor, Adams's best friends continued to be Thomas Hewes, a constable; William Cooper, — "an old Baboon," — the former town clerk; Ben Austin, Junior, — "lank HONESTUS, with his lanthorn jaws," — and "birds of such sort, which," said the Federalists, "would disgrace the kitchen of any other Chief Magistrate." [100] Governor Adams was decidedly not a prize for fashionable hostesses and he was left as much alone by Boston society while he was governor as when he was plain Sam Adams, the South End rebel. The Adamses entertained little and continued to live in an ugly old-fashioned frame house off Winter Street which showed traces of once having had a coat of yellow paint. Sam still dressed in the style that had been popular before the war: his old-fashioned tie wig, cocked hat, buckled shoes, knee breeches, and red cloak were reminiscent of the last generation when Whigs had railed against finery in dress as unrepublican. With characteristic simplicity, Adams would have walked on foot when carrying out his official duties as governor had not his friends presented him with a horse and carriage. He was no longer a poor man, however, because his son's pension and his own lucky investments in Jamaica real estate had dispelled the poverty which pinched him throughout his earlier life. But lifelong habits of frugality were not easily broken and Adams showed how highly he prized his reputation for poverty by indignantly denying the Federalists' insinuations that he had become well-to-do.

That Governor Adams was an arrant Jacobin and no friend of orderly government, few Federalists could doubt after the rough treatment Jay's treaty received in Boston. The Boston mob, strongly anti-British in feeling, greeted the treaty with the cry that Jay had sold them to the British, and vented their anger by burning the treaty and effigies of Jay in the streets. Federalists saw the futility of appealing to Governor Adams to

[100] *Massachusetts Mercury*, Feb. 16, 1796; Warren, 62. Dr. John S. J. Gardiner, *Remarks on the Jacobiniad* (Boston, 1795), 15.

prevent indignities to Jay and the United States Senate, which, by ratifying the treaty, incurred the wrath of the Jacobins. "This weak old man," remarked a conservative, "is one of the loudest brawlers against the treaty, and the boldest in proposing schemes of opposition to the federal government."[101] Yet when the Boston mob got out of control and began to attack the houses of prominent aristocrats, it seemed possible that even Governor Adams might be persuaded to take action against his headstrong friends who were carrying matters further than most radicals approved. A body of frightened citizens rushed to Adams with news that the mob was loose in the metropolis and urged him to stop the riot. Governor Adams, however, seemed to relish a return to the days when the Sons of Liberty had fallen upon the Tories and he refused to act against the mob: "It was only Boys water melon frolicks," he told the townspeople. But Mrs. Adams, with a keener eye for the dangers of inaction, is said to have warned her husband that "it was time to look about, for the thing became serious and alarming." [102] When it was known that the governor had refused to restore order in Boston, the mob rioted for six nights, terrorizing Federalists and thoroughly intimidating the government. When the attorney general and sheriff attempted to disperse the mob by reading the Riot Act, they were "hustled" out of the way; and the rioters in Liberty Square made bloodcurdling threats to tear out and roast the hearts of any who tried to infringe their natural right to riot.[103] That the mob was finally driven off the streets was no fault of Governor Adams: it was only after the Boston citizens had organized themselves against the rioters that the town was quieted. The governor would have done well had he taken his wife's advice, for he did his reputation no good by openly countenancing disorder. Federalists immediately raised the cry that Adams was using the mob to satisfy his rancor against the Federal government and its supporters; and henceforth Adams's party was called the "Water Mellon Boys" and Adams himself was known as "our mob-loving Governor."

[101] *The Life and Correspondence of Rufus King*, II, 31.
[102] *Massachusetts Mercury*, Feb. 16, 1796.
[103] *Federal Orrery*, Sept. 28, 1795. Amory, 301.

But it was clear that Adams's influence was being gradually destroyed by the rising Federalist tide. The Federalists had long looked forward to making Massachusetts completely Federal: and with the rallying cry of "not a single Jacobin in the Senate," they purged the Upper House of all Adams's supporters in 1795, including the arch-Jacobin, "Honestus" Austin.[104] With the passing of the parent Constitutional Club at Philadelphia, the other clubs declined — with the result that in 1796 Austin lost political control of Boston and the Federalist nominees for the Boston seat defeated the Republicans. In spite of Adams's efforts to induce the Massachusetts General Court to adopt the Virginia Resolves, they were overwhelmingly defeated by the conservative majority. His assertion that Jay's treaty was "pregnant with evil" because it gave Great Britain an opportunity to carry out its plans to dominate the United States was greeted "with almost universal disgust" in the legislature, and the governor was rebuked by the representatives for interfering in the business of the Federal government.[105] Adams's Jacobinism cost him the support of the New England clergy, — that "black regiment" of revolutionary days, — who fulminated against the infidelity and license of the French Revolution as energetically as they had preached rebellion during the American Revolution. "Shall our Sons become the disciples of Voltaire and the dragons of Marat," exclaimed the Reverend Timothy Dwight; "or our daughters the concubines of the Illuminati?" And New England congregations answered with a hearty "Nay!" Moreover, Adams was .greatly embarrassed by the publication of a letter he had written Citizen Genêt. Although Washington had already demanded Genêt's recall, Adams assured him that his conduct as Minister Plenipotentiary would "greatly tend to promote the common cause of Liberty, and the Rights of Man" — an indiscretion that had the unfortunate effect of encouraging the French minister to appeal to the people over Washington's head.[106] New England Fed-

[104] *Federal Orrery*, April 6, 1795. *The Correspondence of Rufus King*, I, 511; II, 55.
[105] Morse, 158. *The Writings of Samuel Adams*, IV, 391.
[106] Morse, 171. *Columbia Centinel*, April 3, 1794. *Report of the American Historical Association*, II (1903), 277.

eralists were not slow to take advantage of Adams's mistakes and discredit the Republican Party in New England. It was made abundantly clear to Adams that Federalist domination of Massachusetts was inevitable. The "great Incendiary of the province" who had brought about the downfall of so many royal governors of Massachusetts Bay was well aware that he could not long remain the anti-Federalist governor of the strongest Federalist state in the Union.

Before he gave up the struggle against Federalism, Adams determined to fight one last pitched battle. In 1796, John Adams was the Federalist candidate for President of the United States to succeed George Washington. In Massachusetts, Sam Adams ran as a presidential elector opposed to John Adams's election; and the bitterly fought campaign that followed revealed how completely the "brace of Adamses" had parted company. The Republican newspapers warned the people that John Adams, "the advocate of kingly government, and of a titled nobility to form an upper house, and to keep down the 'swinish multitude,' would make Senate and President hereditary, and is to be your President unless you turn out THIS DAY and support the old tried patriot SAMUEL ADAMS, who is the friend of the people, a republican in principles and manners." Sam Adams believed John Adams had betrayed the "principles of '75," but the younger Adams was convinced that he alone had kept them pure and undefiled — Sam Adams, in his eyes, had cast the doctrines of the American Revolution into the sewer of French Jacobinism. "What is the reason," John Adams asked, "that so many of our 'old standbys' are infected with Jacobinism? The principles of this infernal tribe were surely no part of our ancient political creed." He declared that his ideal was the same in 1796 that it had been in 1775: a government "well ordered, mixed, and counterpoised." Unlike Sam Adams, John Adams believed that one revolution in a lifetime was enough.[107]

Despite the warm support of all the Jacobins in the Green Dragon Tavern, Sam Adams was defeated for presidential elec-

[107] *Independent Chronicle*, Nov. 7, 1796. *The Works of John Adams*, IX, 562, 584.

tor. Indeed, he was given such a drubbing by John Adams's
friends that the Republicans roared that the Federalists had
packed Boston during the election with "Foreigners and Strangers" who had voted illegally. To Sam Adams, governor of
the commonwealth, and to Sam Adams, the Boston rebel, illegal voting appeared in a very different light; and he now
complained as bitterly as had Hutchinson of frauds in Boston
elections. It made vast difference to Sam Adams whether the
unqualified voters who crowded into Faneuil Hall on meeting
days were Sons of Liberty or Federalist hirelings. Adams's
position was now similar to Hutchinson's during the Revolution;
and therefore he became as staunch a defender of purity in elections as any royal governor of Massachusetts Bay.[108]

Adams's failure to carry Boston as an anti-John Adams elector led him to take a step he had contemplated for several years:
to retire from the governorship before the Federalists had the
satisfaction of turning him out of office. Toward the close of
1796, therefore, Adams announced that he would not be a
candidate for governor at the next election; and his retirement
marks the virtual end of the early Republican Party in Massachusetts and the complete triumph of Federalism. As Ben
Austin bitterly exclaimed in 1797: "Every attempt to restore
the liberties of mankind, or to check the progress of arbitrary
power is now styled Jacobinism." Massachusetts had fallen
into the hands of a Federalist oligarchy; and the new aristocracy
so closely resembled the old Tories that John Adams lamented
a few years later that the Higginson family had more influence
than had Thomas Hutchinson at the height of his career, "and
upon the same Principles and by the same means." [109]

Sam Adams lingered on several years after his retirement
from the governorship — a broken-down old man who shuffled
wearily about his house on Winter Street and lived in the past
when he had been the foremost Son of Liberty in New England.
His old age was not happy or beautiful: it was John Adams's

[108] *Columbian Centinel*, Nov. 2, 1796. *Independent Chronicle*, Nov. 7
and 10, 1796. *The Writings of Samuel Adams*, IV, 400, 401.
[109] Benjamin Austin, Jr., *Constitutional Republicanism* (1797), 52. W. C.
Ford, *John Adams, Statesman and Friend*, 96.

prayer that he be spared the fate of Sam Adams, "a grief and distress to his family, a weeping, helpless object of compassion for years." [110]   Palsy, which attacked him early in life, had long since made it impossible for him to write, and he was forced to depend upon his "faithfull friend and amanuensis" John Avery, the one-time secretary of the Boston Sons of Liberty. He lived to see the triumph of Jefferson, which he regarded as a victory for the principles he had maintained throughout his life.   "The Storm is over, and we are in port," he wrote Jefferson when the Republicans came into power.   He still kept faith in the French Revolution and he looked upon the coalition against France as a league of "Tyrant Kings to exterminate those rights and liberties which the Gracious Creator has granted to Man."   He remained a "consistent Republican" to the end; although age and ill-health had made it impossible for him to aid in carrying on the principles of the Revolution, he wrote Jefferson, he could still give his blessing to the defenders of liberty.[111]

In 1803, Sam Adams died.   It was fitting that as his funeral cortege wound through the streets of Boston it passed the spot on which Liberty Tree had stood and Chase and Speakman's distillery, where Sam Adams and the Sons of Liberty had smoked their pipes, drunk flip, and plotted the overthrow of the Tories and the royal government.   He was buried in the Old Granary Burying Ground, near where "old Endicott lies."

Sam Adams was at last among the Puritans.

[110] *The Works of John Adams*, X, 100.
[111] *The Writings of Samuel Adams*, IV, 409–410.

BIBLIOGRAPHY

Since 1936, when *Sam Adams, Pioneer in Propaganda* was published, no full-length biography of Adams has appeared. There is no danger, however, that Adams will become a forgotten man of American history; thanks to the labors of historians and biographers, his stature as a revolutionary leader is rising steadily. Among the books published in the last twenty-three years which attempt to evaluate his contribution to the American Revolution, the following studies merit special mention:

Alden, John Richard. *The American Revolution, 1775–1783*. New York, 1953.

Bowen, Catherine Drinker. *John Adams and the American Revolution*. Boston, 1950.

Brown, Robert E. *Middle Class Democracy in Massachusetts*. Ithaca, New York, 1955.

Chidsey, Donald Barr. *July 4, 1776*. New York, 1958.

Davidson, Philip. *Propaganda and the American Revolution, 1763–1783*. Chapel Hill, 1941.

Douglass, Elisha. *Rebels and Democrats: the Struggle for Equal Political Rights and Majority Rule During the American Revolution*. Chapel Hill, 1955.

Falkner, Leonard. *Forge of Liberty*. New York, 1959.

Gipson, Lawrence H. *The Coming of the Revolution, 1763–1775*. New York, 1954.

Lengyel, Cornel. *Four Days in July*. New York, 1958.

Meigs, Cornelia. *The Violent Men*. New York, 1949.

Morgan, Edmund S., and Helen M. Morgan. *The Stamp Act Crisis: Prologue to Revolution*. Chapel Hill, 1953.

Rossiter, Clinton. *Seedtime of the Republic*. New York, 1953.

Sanford, Allan H. *John Hancock, Patriot in Purple*. New York, 1948.

Taylor, Robert J. *Western Massachusetts in the Revolution*. Providence, 1954.

Tourtellot, Arthur Benton. *William Diamond's Drum*. New York, 1959.

INDEX

America, 311–312; believes time ripe for quarrel with Great Britain, 312; at First Continental Congress, 313–315; senses distrust against New Englanders at Philadelphia, 316; lack of worldly possessions is detrimental in eyes of other colonists, 316–317; belief in property rights, 317; is a staunch democrat until 1780, 317–318; disagrees with John Adams's fears of abuse of power by the people, 318; splits with John Adams, on idea of "Liberty, Equality, and Fraternity" in the United States, 318; insinuates that his enemies are "papists," 319–320; chooses Duché as Chaplain for Continental Congress, 320; disapproves of Galloway's American Grand Council idea, 322–323; is in high spirits at adoption of Suffolk Resolves, 324; believes in fighting blood of New England, 326; other colonies hamper his plans against British troops in Boston, 328; creates disturbance at Massacre Oration of March 5, 1775, 330–331; is in danger of punishment by British military authorities, 331; hides at Lexington, 332; quoted on his remark to Hancock, 332; leaves for Philadelphia with John Hancock after Lexington fighting, 332; as an equestrian, 332–333; is reluctant to suggest George Washington as commander of Northern army, 334–335; John Hancock ceases to be friendly with, 335–336; suspects Philip Livingston, 337–338; makes enemies for Massachusetts, in Second Continental Congress, 338; agrees with John Adams in dislike of petitioning, 340; quoted on revolutionary movement, 340; feeling on delay in declaring American independence, 341, 342–343; agrees with New Englanders that they are a match for England, 324; as the

foremost revolutionist in America, 343–344; as "Father of America," 344; dreads thought of an American standing army, 344–345; as a hindrance to American commanders, 346; his opinion of Schuyler and St. Clair at Ticonderoga, 346–347; fights for replacement of Washington by Gage, 348–349, 350; loss of popularity, 350; with Richard Henry Lee, comes to support of Arthur Lee's political aspirations, 351–352; remains poor, after six years in Congress, 352; dislikes Philadelphia and its inhabitants, 353–354; differs from John Adams as to reasons for the Revolution, 355–356; is ill during the Massachusetts Convention, 1779–1780, 357; tells the Marquis de Chastellux his reasons for approval of the Constitution, 358–359; concern over laxity of morals in Boston, 363–364; strives against Hancock's bad influence in Boston, 365; attacks the Sans Souci society in the *Massachusetts Centinel*, 365–366; attitude on the franchise, 356; too strait-laced for his warmest admirers, 368, 387–388, 396–397; as governor of Massachusetts, in 1794, 368, 392; is kept busy as defender of Massachusetts, 370–371; as president of Massachusetts Senate, in 1781, 369, 370–371; wars on Tories, 370; fails to comprehend unrest in western Massachusetts, 373–374; disbelieves in national government, 376; withholds judgment on the federal constitution, 376–377, 381–382; stunned by heresy among his Green Dragon followers, 378–379; is a sturdy Republican, 379; confesses his ignorance of commerce, 387–388; defeated for lieutenant governorship, in 1788, 389; retains faith in the common people, 390; believes in the French Revolution,

391; fraternizes with Jacobins and Frenchmen, 393; attends collation in Senate chamber and military parade held on abolition of monarchy in France, 394; as Governor, entertains little, and lives simply with his wife in an old house off Winter Street, 395; is no longer poor, thanks to his son's pension and investments in Jamaica real estate, 395; drives about in horse and carriage furnished by his friends, for official purposes, 395; quoted on Jay's treaty, 397; writes an encouraging letter to the French minister, Gênet, 397; opposes John Adams's candidacy for President, 398; defeated as presidential elector from Massachusetts, 398–399; his retirement from governorship in Massachusetts marks the ending of the early Republican Party in Massachusetts, and marks the triumph of federalism, 399; picture of his last years and death, in 1803, in Winter Street home, 399–400; account of his funeral, 400. *See also under* Adams and Otis

Adams, Sam, and James Otis, excluded from share in government, 27; oppose Governor Bernard, 35, 70, 108; oppose Thomas Hutchinson, 63–64, 67, 74–75, 128; dispute in Representatives' chamber, 95–96; political views differ, 97–98, 118–119; resolve to purge the Council of Tories, 106; harangue in General Court over colonial wrongs, 121; recover lost ground in General Court, 121; propose circular letter on Townshend duties, 122; deny right of Parliament to impose external taxes, 123; letter to Marquis of Rockingham, 1768, 125; escape capture and imprisonment in London, 167; disagree over British authority in the General Court, 248

Adams, Deacon Samuel (senior),

father of Sam, business career, 3–4; title of "deacon," 4; as politician, 7; politicians gather at house of, 9; and the Land Bank, 11, 15; Belcher dismisses from office, 11–12; lends thousand pounds to son, 17; dies, 1748, 22; opposed by Hutchinson and his father, 26; member of Boston Caucus, 38; elected to Council, 42; successful attack on the Council, 1741, 107

Adams family, two branches in New England, Boston and Quincy, 3; influential Massachusetts family, 3; founded by Henry Adams, 3; John Adams first important member of Quincy Adamses, 3; religious strictness of, 84

Allen, Ethan, close friend of Dr. Thomas Young of Albany, 87

Americans, rights of as "men, citizens and British subjects," 90

Ancient and Honorable Mechanical Company of Baltimore, members as Sons of Liberty, 51–52

Aristocrats, Boston, at mercy of mobs and Sons of Liberty, 72

Assemblies, colonial, Sam Adams desires to make sole taxing power in America, 92

Avery, John, a Boston distiller, secretary of the "Loyall Nine," 53

BACON, EDWARD, Tory representative to General Court from Barnstable, attacks Boston patriots, 267; Adams and Molineux force him to retract his remarks, 268

Baltimore, life at, 353

Bancroft, George, quoted on Sons of Revolution, 51

Baptists, provisions in Massachusetts Constitution for tax exemptions, 357–358

Barnstable, residence of Otis family, 32

Baronies, colonial, alarm over, 240–241

Barré, Isaac, speech in Parliament during Stamp Act controversy, 51

dise to committee of inspection, 210

Hutchinson family, importance of in Massachusetts, 27; Sam Adams's effort to break power of in Massachusetts, 108–109

IMPORTS, to colonies, no united policy concerning, 325

Independence, American, and Sam Adams's strong desire for, 228–229; obstacles to, die away, 342

Independent Advertiser, short-lived, 20; Sam Adams used for propaganda, 21; against the Council, 41

Indian fighters, New England has many veterans left from the French and Indian Wars, 153

Indians, Iroquois tribe, Sam Adams on their ferocity, 175

Inflation party of Massachusetts receives death blow from Thomas Hutchinson, 26

Intercolonial Committees of Correspondence, and responsibility for American Revolution, 271

Ireland, is controlled by British House of Commons, 104; two British regiments from, sent to Boston, 142; rioting in, 146

JACOBIN MOVEMENT, effect on Boston mechanics, 388; Sam Adams as its chief apostle in the United States, 392; work of the clubs, 393

James II, of England, portrait of in Council Chamber, 180

Jarvis, Charles, quarrels with Sam Adams over theatres in Boston, 368

Jay, John, of New York, opposes Dr. Duché as chaplain of Continental Congress, 320; is colleague of Philip Livingston, and suspected by Sam Adams of giving away secrets of Congress, 337–338; an aristocrat, and friend of John Adams, 338; his treaty is roughly received by Governor Sam Adams in Boston, 395–396

Jefferson, Thomas, approves of inter-

colonial correspondence, 270–271; advocates independence, 342; calls Sam Adams "truly the Man of the Revolution," 343; great statesman, 344; Sam Adams lives to see triumph of his ideas, 400

Jeffreys, Judge, of England, mention of, 262

"Jersey Folks" prepared to aid New York, 76–77

Johnson, Dr. Samuel, on population growth in American colonies, 311

"Journal of Events," published weekly by Sam Adams, as political propaganda, 174–176, 177

Judges of Massachusetts Superior Court, salaries of, how paid, 261–262

Justices of Peace, parade with Boston Sons of Liberty, 72–73

KILROI, a British soldier killed at Boston Massacre by ropewalker Gray, 189

King George's War, and threat of attack on colonies from Canada, 18

King's Street (now State Street), Boston, the scene of Boston Massacre, 178–179; importers' shops located there, 208

Knox, William, quoted, 124; on ideas of patriots on authority of Parliament, 127

LAND BANK, of Massachusetts, crash of, 5; as a struggle between aristocrats and common people, 9; scheme for revival of, 10–11, 12–13; victory at the polls, 14; pronounced illegal, 14–15; trial is excellent political training for Sam Adams, 23–24; Hutchinson's part in destruction of, 26; dissolved by Parliament in 1741, 272–273

Land Bank, of New Hampshire, approved as legal by Board of Trade as late as 1734, 14–15

Land Bank Party, members of, 13; Sam's fight to prevent sale of his property, 23; called forerunner of

Milton, Massachusetts, Boston promised armed assistance by, 186; Thomas Hutchinson's home at, 260; Suffolk Resolves drafted at, 323

Minuet, at Boston balls, 120

Mobs, in Boston, and destruction of Thomas Hutchinson's house, 26, 109; bonfires and general destruction of, August 28, 1765, 65–66; out of control of Adams and Otis, 66–68; North End and South End gangs, 68–71; contrasted with English rioters, 70, 141; organized in country to keep Tories from taking seats in legislature, 105, 139; anxious to drive Commissioners out, 119; Hutchinson fears less than Sam Adams, 136. *See also under* Stamp Act, Whigs

"Mohawks," Adams's, composed of merchants' mob and Sons of Liberty, 70; in Council, 110; keep Commissioners of Customs uneasy, 141; delight at James Otis's condemnation of British colonial officers, 143; at Boston town meeting, 149

Molasses, imported from West Indies, tax on, 43; importance of to New England distillers, 47, 307; tax on, reduced, 111

Molasses Act of 1733, Crown makes no attempt to enforce in Massachusetts, 43

Molineux, William "Paoli," a freethinker, 87; tries to rent house on Wheelwrights' wharf for garrison, 167; encourages witness to make false testimony, 188; house of, as meeting place for Sons of Liberty, 191; speech on freedom in Boston town meeting, in 1769, 202; gains support of colony in demonstration against Hutchinson as an importer, 208–209; influence among patriots, 218; estimate of, 236; Tories oppose, 235; Committee of Correspondence holds

meeting at his house, 265; Edward Bacon's estimate of, 267

Monday Night Club, at Boston, James Otis and Sam Adams leaders of, 37

Murray, John, of Rutland, Massachusetts, landowner in Worcester County, made a Tory colonel, 42

Mutiny Act, revived to allow the billeting of royal troops in colonies, 166

"NARRAGANSETT INDIANS," disguise adopted by patriots in Boston Tea Party, 190; are really Sam Adams's North End followers, 294

Natural Law, as opposed to external taxes, 124; Sam Adams uses to appeal against Parliamentary dictation, 243–244

Navigation Laws, repeal of feared by British statesmen, 127–128

Negroes, mention of as belonging to Boston mob, 142

Newburyport, boycott at, is broken, 221; Committee of Correspondence at, 268–269

New England, activities in during the eighteenth century, 6; mention of good old New England spirit, 18; under Governor Shirley, 19, 25; attitude in, on imperialism, 25; makes demand to be as free as Britons, 31; desire of its people to enjoy prosperity following the Seven Years' War, 41; and George Grenville's tax policy, 43–44, 54; trade in, depended on leniency of British mercantile colonial policy, 44; farmers believe in Hutchinson, 46; conservative party destroyed by British taxation, 47; patriots praise Virginia for the stand taken there, 56–57; attitude toward British army, 77; love of James Otis, 88; Whigs and Tories fight for possession of rural sections, in 134, 137, 139–140; Sam Adams desires to make its farmers zealous Sons of Liberty, 137; encouraged to resist England,

against Hutchinson, 209; attends patriotic mob meetings in Boston, 216; refuses to serve on Committee of Correspondence, 265

Pitt, William, young Whig politician, defends the colonies in Parliament and sends Thomas Pownall to replace Governor Shirley in Massachusetts, 28; Bernard writes to, on Massachusetts, 29; statues of, in the colonies, 103; attitude on sovereignty of Parliament, 115

Plymouth County, Massachusetts, seat of rural Tories, 139; first place, outside of Boston, to have Committee of Correspondence, 268

Political life, in England, described by Sam Adams in the *Boston Gazette*, 146

Political theory, of equality of Americans and Britons, 90

Pollard, Benjamin, slanders Deacon Adams, 12

Pope Day, November 5, observance of, in Boston, 68–69

Popery, Sam Adams writes against, under signature "A Puritan" in *Boston Gazette*, 129–130

Population, rapid increase of, in colonies, 30; Benjamin Franklin on, 310; James Otis and Dr. Johnson on, 311

Port Duties, Townshend's aim concerning, 115–116

Portsmouth, New Hampshire, attitude at, on boycott of British goods, 221

Post Office, Colonial, establishment of, 297–298

Pownall, Governor Thomas, sent by Pitt to succeed Governor Shirley and put vigor into the French War, 28; removed from office, 1760, 28; most popular governor since Massachusetts Charter was granted, 29; people recall "good old days" under his governorship, 228

Preble, Jedidiah, instructed as to ac-

tion in the Massachusetts Convention, 158

Presbyterian faith, in New York, 315

Preston, Captain, in Twenty-ninth Regiment, British regulars, 179; as commander of British soldiers at Boston Massacre, 180; at Castle William, to avoid lynching, 184; acquitted of part in the Massacre, 187

Princeton College, colonial clothing worn at, 198; Sam Adams and Boston delegates received at, 315

Property rights, colonial, threatened by Land Bank controversy, 24

Providence, Rhode Island, sends Son of Liberty to Boston, 77; sale of British tea at, 221; Jews and Tories flout the boycott at, 222

Province House, Boston, dilapidated condition of, 260–261

Provincial Congress, Massachusetts, as outgrowth of Convention of 1768, 165; called in autumn of 1774, 327–328

Provisions and Praemunire, Statute of, and the Massachusetts Land Bank, 15

Pufendorf, Baron Samuel von, influence of his ideas on Sam Adams, 16

Purchase Street, Boston, Deacon Adams's house, brewery and business located there, 4; neglect of by Sam Adams, 23; Sam Adams lives there in 1774, 227

Puritan magistrates, portraits of, in Council Chamber, 180

Puritanism, revival of, under George Whitefield's teachings, 6–7; Sam Adams desires to restore to New England, 85, 195–196; not popular with the Whigs, 86

Putnam, Israel, drives flock of sheep to Boston for hungry inhabitants, 326; though the choice of Sam Adams, is not acceptable to Congress, 333–334

Putnam, James, of Worcester, a rural Tory leader, 139

tary alliance against Great Britain, 76; consider themselves as defenders of the British Constitution, 79–80; were the "King's Party," 80; condemn "the seventeen of Massachusetts Bay," 130–131; Massachusetts Committee of Correspondence in communication with by 1774, as far south as South Carolina, 269–270; and rivalry for supremacy in the colonies, 276–277

Sons of Liberty, in Massachusetts, growth of movement among farmers, 137; organize gangs, in country, to raid creditors' houses, 139

Sons of Liberty, in New York, ratify plan of mutual military aid against British army, 76–77; refuse to join in struggle against Great Britain, 159–160; lose ground in 1770, 251; take action against East India Company's consignees, 286; "Mohawks" of, threaten to destroy tea, 288; defeated by New York merchants, 314

Sons of Liberty, of Boston, meet at the Green Dragon Tavern, 40; their part in hanging of Andrew Oliver's effigy, 61–62; terrorize Crown officers, 71; leaders of, 72; plan to prevent entry of Boston, by land, of British army, 77; Sam Adams at gatherings, 83; Dr. Thomas Young, a passionate member of, 87; celebrate repeal of Stamp Act, 112; commemorate their founding, August 14, 113; seek alliance with the New York Liberty Boys, 118–119; possess Boston, 135; suppress attempted riot on March 18, 1768, 140; alarmed over fate of Boston Whigs, 147; hold two secret meetings in Boston, 147–148; arms for, 150; accept Adams's proposal to send circular letter to all towns in Massachusetts, 152–153; continue with war preparations, 154; become laughingstock throughout the colonies, 162–163;

use conch shells to call meetings, 169; are on bad terms with the British soldiers, 176; encouraged by support of most of the other American colonies, 201–202; threaten John Mein, 204–205; are within range of British cannon and bayonets, 234; attitude on royal prerogatives, 242; England hints at punishment for, 251; fail to bring tea importers to terms, 287–288

Sons of Liberty, of Connecticut, ratify plan for military aid against British army, 76–77

Sons of Liberty, of Philadelphia, break off commercial intercourse with New York, 224; take action against consignees of East India Company's tea, 286; plan to burn tea ships in the Delaware River, 288

Sons of Liberty, of Portsmouth, quoted on armed force, 182

Sons of Liberty, of South Carolina, storm fort at Charleston, 71

Sons of Liberty, Princeton, ardent spirits of, 315

Sons of Liberty, Providence, send member to Boston, 77

South End, Boston, gangs at, 4; mob under Mackintosh threatens Andrew Oliver, 62; most powerful mob, 69

Springfield, Massachusetts, a Tory stronghold, 129

Stamp Act, 1765, unites town and country against the British government, 46, 53–54; helps in Hutchinson's downfall, 47; scope of, 49–50; dreaded in colonies, 51; first direct tax laid on colonies, 54; levied and distributed, 54–55; Virginia and Massachusetts lead in protests and riots, against, 61; riot of August 14, 1765, reported in *Boston Gazette*, 62–63, 138; work of British imperialists, 64–65; stamps for, store at Castle William, 70; Great Britain not prepared

Flying Tigers

Smithsonian History of Aviation Series

Von Hardesty, Series Editor

On December 17, 1903, on a windy beach in North Carolina, aviation became a reality. The development of aviation over the course of little more than three-quarters of a century stands as an awe-inspiring accomplishment in both a civilian and a military context. The airplane has brought whole continents closer together: at the same time it has been a lethal instrument of war.

This series of books is intended to contribute to the overall understanding of the history of aviation—its science and technology as well as the social, cultural, and political environment in which it developed and matured. Some publications help fill the many gaps that still exist in the literature of flight; others add new information and interpretation to current knowledge. While the series appeals to a broad audience of general readers and specialists in the field, its hallmark is strong scholarly content.

The series is international in scope and includes works in three major categories:

SMITHSONIAN STUDIES IN AVIATION HISTORY: *works that provide new and original knowledge.*

CLASSICS OF AVIATION HISTORY: *carefully selected out-of-print works that are considered essential scholarship.*

CONTRIBUTIONS TO AVIATION HISTORY: *previously unpublished documents, reports, symposia, and other materials.*

ADVISORY BOARD: Roger E. Bilstein, *University of Houston;* Horst Boog, *Militärgeschichtliches Forschungsamt, Germany;* DeWitt C. Copp, *Author and air historian;* Tom D. Crouch, *National Air and Space Museum;* Sylvia Fries, *National Aeronautics and Space Administration;* Ben Greenhous, *Historian;* John F. Guilmartin, Jr., *Ohio State University;* Terry Gwynn-Jones, *Author;* Richard P. Hallion, *Secretary of the Air Force's Staff Group;* James R. Hansen, *Auburn University;* Von Hardesty, *National Air and Space Museum;* Robin Higham, *Kansas State University;* Lee Kennett, *University of Georgia;* Nick Komons, *Federal Aviation Administration;* William M. Leary, *University of Georgia;* W. David Lewis, *Auburn University;* Air Vice-Marshal R. A. Mason, CBE MA RAF (Ret.); LTC Phillip S. Meilinger, *HQ USAF/XOXWD;* John H. Morrow, Jr., *University of Georgia;* Dominick A. Pisano, *National Air and Space Museum;* Air Commodore H. A. Probert, MBE MA RAF (Ret.); General Lucien Robineau, *Service historique de l'armée de l'air, France;* Alex Roland, *Duke University;* F. Robert van der Linden, *National Air and Space Museum*

Claire
Chennault
and the
American
Volunteer
Group

Flying Tigers

Daniel Ford

ST CHARLES PUBLIC LIBRARY DISTRICT
ONE SOUTH SIXTH AVENUE
ST CHARLES, ILLINOIS 60174

SMITHSONIAN

INSTITUTION

PRESS

WASHINGTON

AND LONDON

Copyright © 1991 Daniel Ford
All rights reserved

Editor and typesetter: Peter Strupp/Princeton Editorial Associates
Designer: Linda McKnight

Permission to reprint copyrighted material was granted by Charles R. Bond, Jr., and
Terry Anderson for *A Flying Tiger's Diary,* © 1984; Kojinsha for *Tsubasa no kessen,*
© 1984; Konnichi no Wadaisha for *Hien tai Guramen,* © 1973; Robert T. Smith for
Tale of a Tiger, © 1986, published by Tiger Originals, 13624 Sherman Way, Box 457,
Van Nuys, CA 91405; and Tab Books for *With Chennault in China,* reprinted with
permission from book #23336, *With Chennault in China: A Flying Tiger's Diary,* by
Robert M. Smith, Assisted by Philip D. Smith, copyright 1984 by TAB BOOKS, a division
of McGraw-Hill, Blue Ridge Summit, PA 17294 (1-800-233-1128 or
1-717-794-2191).

Permission to quote from unpublished documents was granted by Helen Burgard, Anna
Chennault, James Donovan, David Lee (Tex) Hill, James Howard, Robert Keeton,
Robert Layher, Charles Mott, Robert Neale, Charles Older, Anne Marie Prescott,
Donald L. (Rode) Rodewald, Wilfred Schaper, Eriksen Shilling, and Thomas Trumble.

For permission to reproduce illustrations appearing in this book, apply to the owners of
the works as stated in the captions; the Smithsonian Institution Press does not retain
reproduction rights for illustrations nor maintain a file of addresses for photo sources.

Calligraphy: Eileen Chow

Library of Congress Cataloging-in-Publication Data
Ford, Daniel, 1931–
    Flying Tigers: Claire Chennault and the American Volunteer Group / Daniel Ford.
      p.   cm.
    Includes bibliographical references and index.
    ISBN 1-56098-011-7 (hardback).
    1. World War, 1939–1945—Aerial operations, American.   2. Chennault, Claire
Lee, 1893–1958.   3. China. K'ung chün. American Volunteer Group—History.
I. Title.
D790.F584   1991   90-26953
940.54′5973—dc20   CIP

British Library Cataloguing-in-Publication Data available

Manufactured in the United States of America

98 96 94 93 92   5 4 3 2

∞ The paper used in this publication meets the minimum requirements of the American
National Standard for Permanence of Paper for Printed Library Materials Z39.48-1984.

For Kate Ford

peripatetic student of Chinese history during the five years
I was writing this book, and volunteer researcher in
Cambridge, Washington, and London

3 0053 00323 4229

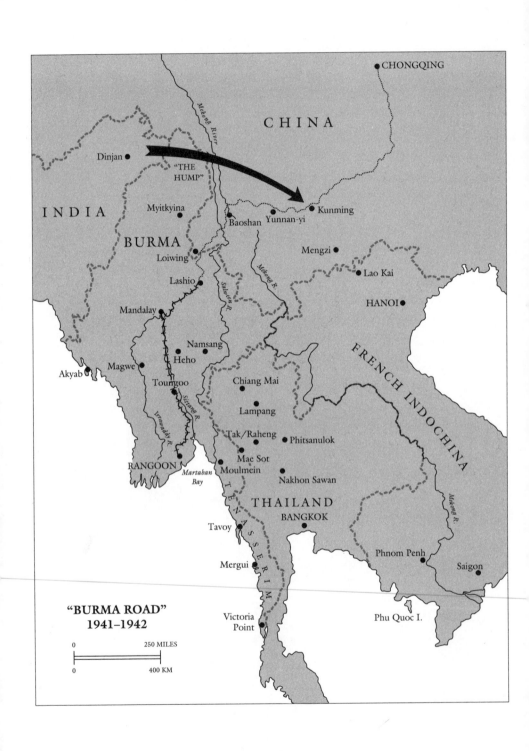

CHONGQING

CHINA

INDIA

Dinjan

"THE
HUMP"

Myitkyina

BURMA

Baoshan Yunnan-yi Kunming

Loiwing

Mengzi

Lashio

Lao Kai

Mandalay

HANOI

Namsang

FRENCH INDOCHINA

Heho

Magwe

Chiang Mai

Akyab

Toungoo

Lampang

Tak/Raheng Phitsanulok

Mae Sot

RANGOON Martaban Moulmein

Nakhon Sawan

Bay

THAILAND

Tavoy

BANGKOK

Phnom Penh

Mergui

Saigon

Phu Quoc I.

Victoria
Point

"BURMA ROAD"
1941–1942

0   250 MILES

0   400 KM

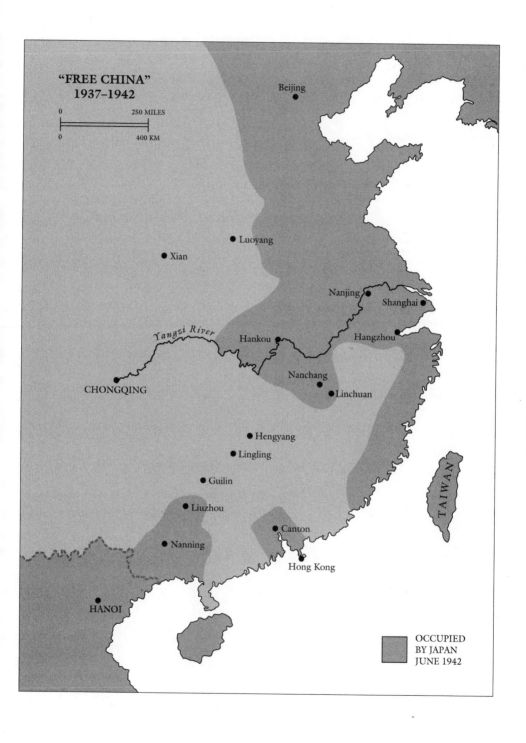

"FREE CHINA"
1937–1942

0   250 MILES
0   400 KM

Beijing

Luoyang

Xian

Yangzi River

Hankou

Nanjing

Shanghai

Hangzhou

Nanchang

CHONGQING

Linchuan

Hengyang

Lingling

Guilin

Liuzhou

Canton

Nanning

Hong Kong

HANOI

TAIWAN

OCCUPIED
BY JAPAN
JUNE 1942

Contents

Who is lonelier than the samurai?
The tiger in the jungle, perhaps.
— JAPANESE POEM

Wingman John Armstrong, accidentally killed, September 8 1941
Wingman Maax Hammer, accidentally killed, September 22 1941
Wingman Peter Atkinson, accidentally killed, October 25 1941
Flight Leader Neil Martin, killed by enemy fire, December 23 1941
Wingman Henry Gilbert, killed by enemy fire, December 23 1941
Wingman Lacy Mangleburg, accidentally killed, December 23 1941
Staff Secretary Joseph Alsop, interned, December 25 1941
Instructor Marion Baugh, accidentally killed, January 3 1942
Wingman Kenneth Merritt, accidentally killed, January 8 1942
Flight Leader Charles Mott, taken prisoner, January 8 1942
Flight Leader Allen Christman, killed by enemy fire, January 23 1942
Flight Leader Louis Hoffman, killed by enemy fire, January 26 1942
Wingman Thomas Cole, killed in action, January 30 1942
Squadron Leader Robert Sandell, accidentally killed, February 7 1942
Flight Leader Edward Leibolt, missing in action, February 25 1942
Crew Chief John Fauth, died of wounds, March 22 1942
Wingman William McGarry, taken prisoner, March 24 1942
Squadron Leader John Newkirk, killed by enemy fire, March 24 1942
Wingman Frank Swartz, died of wounds, April 24 1942
Wingman John Blackburn, accidentally killed, April 28 1942
Wingman Ben Foshee, died of wounds, May 4 1942
Wingman John Donovan, killed by enemy fire, May 12 1942
Vice Squadron Leader Thomas Jones, accidentally killed, May 16 1942
Vice Squadron Leader Lewis Bishop, taken prisoner, May 17 1942
Flight Leader Robert Little, killed by enemy fire, May 22 1942
Flight Leader John Petach, killed by enemy fire, July 10 1942
Wingman Arnold Shamblin, missing in action, July 10 1942

1

Tex, This Is Too Good To Be True
1941

In March 1941, a retired navy officer named Rutledge Irvine was touring U.S. Navy bases on the east and west coasts. Once an officer, always an officer, and Irvine is remembered by his serving rank—"the commander"—by the airmen he recruited. But not with clarity. All that survives of Commander Irvine is his shadow, moving from Norfolk to Pensacola to San Diego in the spring of 1941, when Europe was on fire, Asia smoldering, and America determined not to be burned again. He was a courtly man, as some recall. A scholarly gentleman, said one. A grizzled old fellow, said others . . . but they were youngsters, and they would have regarded anyone over forty as ancient.

Irvine's first prospects were a couple of dive-bomber pilots on *Ranger,* one of two aircraft carriers on the Atlantic coast. Twenty-two years old and fresh out of flight school, Edward Rector had joined the carrier the previous summer. He was a native of North Carolina, medium height, and handsome as a movie star. After his first tour with the fleet, supporting U.S. Marines who were practicing assaults upon the shore of Cuba, *Ranger* brought him back to Norfolk, Virginia. There, on New Year's day of 1941, he met a newly assigned pilot in the shower room. The newcomer was tall and lanky, with jug ears, a perpetually worried expression, and an unlikely background: born in Japanese-occupied Korea, the son of a missionary who later became chaplain to the Texas

Rangers. He introduced himself as David Lee Hill, but naturally he was called Tex.

Ranger took Rector and Hill to the Caribbean for further landing exercises, then back to Norfolk in March. "The word spread," Ed Rector said long after, "that there was this guy looking for people to go out and fly for China." He and Hill decided to look into it. In what would become a familiar script over the next four months, they went to a Norfolk hotel room and met Commander Irvine.

He offered them jobs in the Chinese Air Force. The pay was fabulous—$600 a month to start, plus a $500 combat bonus for each Japanese plane they shot down—and in a worthy cause. Japan had occupied Manchuria in 1931, had invaded China proper in 1937, and had now driven the government deep into the western highlands, from which its only port of supply was Rangoon in the British colony of Burma (now Myanmar). From Rangoon the stuff moved by barge, rail, and truck almost to the China border, thence by a twisting mountain road to Chongqing. The distance was 2,000 miles—in North American terms, the equivalent of supplying a U.S. capital in Denver from a port on the Pacific coast of Mexico.*

Rector and Hill were needed to stop the Japanese from bombing the "Burma Road," as this route was known to journalists. Though employed by China, Irvine explained, they would be equipped with the latest and best American fighters. Their commander too would be an American: Claire Chennault, U.S. Army retired, and China's air adviser since the first day of the Sino-Japanese War. As Rector recalled Irvine's pitch:

> He broke out a map and he said, "The only way the Chinese can keep fighting is to maintain the supplies that come up the Burma Road, and you will go over there under the command of Colonel Chennault and you will defend the Burma Road all the way up to Kunming, the capital of Yunnan province"—and he drew it out on the map. And we said, "Well, hell, we're interested."
>
> [But] when we left there and went back to our billets, I said: "Tex, this is too good to be true. This will never happen; they'll never let us go."

---

* Throughout, I have estimated distances as they were actually traveled, by boat, truck, or plane, and I have expressed these distances in land miles. For kilometers, multiply by 1.6; for nautical miles, by 0.87.

He said, "Well, I don't know."
And we went back to the fleet.

Their next assignment was even more tantalizing than their Caribbean duty. *Ranger*'s pilots served as scouts for British convoys while they were beyond a line drawn from Iceland to the Azores—the entire North Atlantic, for all practical purposes. Here, in what President Franklin Roosevelt with astonishing panache had defined as American waters, *Ranger*'s airmen swept out in front of the convoys, looking for German submarines. If they saw anything threatening, they radioed the information to the carrier, which informed the Royal Navy destroyers that would make the actual attack. Officially, this duty was "neutrality patrol." With greater honesty, American sailors called it "the secret war."

Whenever Rector and Hill returned to Norfolk, Commander Irvine met them with news of the fighter group being readied for service in China.

A recruiter named C. B. Adair—Skip to his friends—was doing similar work at U.S. Army airfields. Adair was thirty-two, tall and dark-haired, a sober man who had spent the last few years working for Chennault in China. He made an especially rich strike at Mitchel Field on Long Island, where he signed up nine pilots from the 8th Pursuit Group, all with experience in America's latest and best fighter plane, the Curtiss P-40, called Tomahawk by the British. Among the P-40 drivers was Parker Dupouy, an engineering graduate from Brown University, who years later claimed that he volunteered because Asian duty seemed less dangerous than being sent to Europe: "It seemed to me that sooner or later we would be in the war, and I would rather be shooting Japanese than Germans. That was wrong, but I didn't know it at the time."

The same thought occurred to Albert Probst, a red-headed second lieutenant at Maxwell Field, Alabama. Skip Adair turned up at Maxwell one day, looking for a pilot named Baumler (also first-named Albert, but more commonly known as Ajax) who in 1938 had flown as a mercenary in the Spanish Civil War. Red Probst explained that the former soldier of fortune was temporarily assigned to Eglin Field in Florida. "Adair then started talking to me," the plump young man recalled, "and the first thing I knew, he had recruited me." Probst was in debt, and he figured that shooting down Japanese bombers would be safer and more lucrative than fighting in Europe. He worked it out this way:

Let's see now, I am making $210 a month now, and you are going to pay me $600. I get a free trip to China, and if we go to war with somebody, I won't be on the first string, but the second string. I don't want to have anything to do with them Germans, so I'm going to get over there and help those Chinese.

Ajax Baumler did not wait to be recruited. According to Matthew Kuykendall, then at Eglin, the combat veteran knew "most of the brass in the Air Corps" because of his escapade in Spain. Hearing that somebody was hiring pilots for the Chinese Air Force, Baumler commandeered a Seversky P-35 and flew up to Washington to check out the rumor. He returned with a contract and assured Kuykendall that he too could qualify for service in China. A cautious type, Kuykendall did not commit himself until he returned to Maxwell Field and talked to his buddies. Then he signed up, along with Red Probst and two other pilots.

Ed Rector was perfectly willing to fly against the German air force, given the chance. But that did not seem likely, and by the end of June he too was ready to sign the contract Irvine was offering:

All I'd ever lived for since I was twelve years old was to fly airplanes, and I said, "If I'm going to fly combat airplanes, I want to smell a little cordite, and this is my opportunity to do so." But more important than that was the fact that I'd read everything Kipling had ever written, and I was just fascinated with that part of the world—Burma, India, China—*the old Moulmein Pagoda, looking eastward to the sea.* I thought, "This is my opportunity to see it, and I'll get paid for it. . . ." And I thought, "My God, I've come along in life at the proper time." And those two things are why I signed up.

Tex Hill signed, too. "I'd always wanted to go back to the Orient," he explained. "But the thing that motivated me to go to China was, more or less, adventure. I had no particular dedication to anything." Also joining from *Ranger* was Allen Bert Christman, who as a civilian had worked as a comic strip artist for Associated Press Feature Service, chronicling the adventures of Scorchy Smith, an American mercenary pilot who flew and fought in Latin America. When the three young men announced that they were resigning their commissions, the Norfolk base commander climbed aboard his personal seaplane and flew to Washington to register a protest with Admiral Harold Stark, chief of naval operations. As Rector recalled, the commander flew back to

Norfolk a chastened man, his protest rebuffed with the words: "This is presidentially approved, and that is *it*."

Across the continent in San Diego, the commander of *Saratoga* was similarly rebuffed when he tried to stop four dive-bomber pilots from resigning. One was Robert Neale. Tall and rugged, nervous and shy, Neale had three years of fleet duty behind him, and in the normal course of events he would be discharged in 1942—not a happy prospect for a lad who had joined the navy to escape the Great Depression. "And as far as knowing what I was getting into," Neale said, "the country or the people [or] the living conditions, I didn't have the faintest idea. It was an adventure, not motivated by patriotism or anything like that. . . . Looking back on it, actually, I don't know *why* I went out there." The navy owed him almost $1,500 in pay and accrued leave, so Neale took his discharge and used the money to finance his wedding on June 19.

Also on *Saratoga* was Robert Layher, who had tried to volunteer for the British, Dutch, and Canadian air forces—anything to escape the boredom of peacetime service. Each time, the navy refused to let him go. Layher's deliverance came in a telephone call from one of his shipmates, Henry Geselbracht, who told him in great excitement: "I've got a deal here!"

"What do you mean, a deal?"

"We can get out of the navy and go to China."

"Sign me up," Layher said.

But Commander Irvine was a tougher sell than the foreign recruiters. He wanted only experienced fighter pilots, as Layher recalled: "It cost us about three fifths of Scotch to get this nice guy [persuaded]. We wouldn't give up on him until he said he'd sign us up, about eight o'clock in the morning, and before he sobered up he had us signed up."

As a bonus, Irvine got a fighter pilot from *Saratoga*. This was James Howard, a gangling young man (in his wartime photographs, he bears a striking resemblance to the incumbent Prince of Wales) on temporary duty with the carrier. Like Tex Hill, Howard had been born in Asia (in Canton, where his father was a medical missionary) and he wanted to see it again. "But the overriding reason," Howard said, in words that echoed Hill's, "was my yearning for adventure and action."

At Randolph Field in Texas, R. T. Smith and Paul Greene were sweating through the summer of 1941 as flight instructors, hostages to the great military expansion that President Roosevelt had put into effect.

Just out of flight school, they had been kept at Randolph to teach new cadets, as the air force grew exponentially. Smith especially had little hope of becoming a fighter pilot: a recent edict had specified that no pilot taller than five foot ten could be assigned to fighters, and he stood well over six feet. He learned about the recruiting drive in the June 23 issue of *Time,* which reported that 100 Curtiss P-40s had been supplied to China, and that pilots to fly them were on the way. "For the past few months," the magazine reported, "tall, bronzed American airmen have been quietly slipping away from east- and west-coast ports, making their way to Asia." Actually, no pilots had left, but Smith and Greene were panicked that they might miss out on the great adventure. They asked around, got the recruiter's address, and sent him a telegram: "We each have a thousand hours flying time and are ready to go." Skip Adair met them a week later at the Gunter hotel in San Antonio, but turned them down when he learned that they had never flown anything hotter than a North American BT-9 trainer. Falling back on the same strategy as Bob Layher, they returned next evening with a bottle of I. W. Harper. When Adair was mellow enough, they put the case to him again, and this time he signed them up.

A likelier prospect was Charles Bond, whom the army had trained as a fighter pilot, then assigned to the Ferry Command. Movie-star handsome like Ed Rector—like Smith and Greene, for that matter—this stocky young man would fly a Lockheed A-28 Hudson bomber from Long Beach to Montreal, turn it over to a Canadian pilot, and himself board a commercial airliner for the trip back to California. It was a boring routine for a man who had set out to fly the hottest planes in the sky, so he was a ready listener when a friend called one night with the news that fighter pilots were needed in China. Bond asked around and got the number of a "Colonel Green" in Washington—probably the office of Claire Chennault at China Defense Supplies, an agency financed by the U.S. government but operating out of the Chinese embassy:

> The next day I called Colonel Green's office, giving name and duty station. In addition I told the secretary the names of two of my closest friends, who also were ferry pilots—George Burgard and James D. Cross. Within twenty-four hours a wire arrived at our headquarters, informing our commander that three of his pilots were resigning and were to be released immediately from active duty.

At Pensacola Naval Air Station in Florida, so many instructors wanted to fly for China that the base commander tore the list in half. John Gilpen Bright and John Donovan made the cut, along with a youngster named Henry Gilbert, fresh out of flight school, and a forty-three-year-old enlisted pilot named Louis Hoffman. Richard Rossi—in the wrong half of the alphabet—should have stayed behind with the training command. But Rossi went to the recruiter and signed up anyhow. "When you're young, you're looking for adventure, more than anything else," he explained long after. "Also I was put out because I'd been assigned as an instructor instead of to the fleet." Rossi was twenty-six, a former merchant sailor, with a fighting scowl and the beginning of a beer belly.

Tougher yet was Gregory Boyington, twenty-eight and a first lieutenant in the U.S. Marines—a regular officer, not a reservist like the others. Broad-shouldered, thin-hipped, with the moody face of a Cherokee setting out on the Trail of Tears, Boyington was a troublemaker. He drank heavily, through nights that ended with the challenge: "I'll wrestle anybody in the crowd!" His mother had remarried early, and he grew up believing his stepfather to be his natural parent; he graduated from the University of Washington, married, and became a draftsman at Boeing Aircraft Company under the name of Gregory Hallenbeck. When he discovered his birth name, he seized the chance to start anew as a bachelor and an aviation cadet. (Navy and marine pilots were not permitted to marry until two years after earning their gold wings.) The lie had since caught up with him, and the marines required him to report each month on how he had distributed his salary among those with a claim on it, including his ex-wife and three children.

Boyington did not identify his recruiter, except to say that he was a retired captain and a veteran of the Lafayette Escadrille. This would have been Richard Aldworth—like Irvine, a vice-president of the company that was hiring these mercenaries for China. The pitch was delivered in the usual downtown hotel room. "The Japs are flying antiquated junk over China," Aldworth assured him. (Boyington played the story for laughs, but his account was true in its essentials: the recruiters certainly scanted the dangers of the work.) "Many of your kills will be unarmed transports. I suppose you know that the Japanese are renowned for their inability to fly. And they all wear corrective glasses."

"Captain," said Boyington, "it's quite a setup, but how do you know the pilots wear glasses?"

"Our technical staff determines this from the remains after a shoot-down. . . . Best of all, there's good money in it—$675 [sic] per month. But the sky's the limit," Captain Aldworth went on, "because they pay a bonus of $500 for each Japanese aircraft you knock down."

Boyington sat there, entranced, calculating how rich this project was going to make him.

But of all the recruits, the strangest case was that of a navy pilot who had begun his life under the name of John Perry. After dropping out of San Diego State, Perry joined the army as an aviation cadet, but was washed out for buzzing his girlfriend's house. He therefore borrowed a friend's name and academic record and started again as a navy cadet. In time he earned his gold wings as a flying boat pilot, skippering a stately Consolidated PBY Catalina on patrols off the coast of California. Under the *nom de guerre* of Edwin Conant, he volunteered to fly for China, and was accepted, though he had never flown a fighter. For more than a year, in fact, he had not landed on a hard-surface runway.

Good, bad, and indifferent; mercenaries and idealists; fighter pilots, instructors, and flying boat skippers; one veteran and scores of green-horns; some eager to fight, some wanting only to escape from uniform—100 U.S. military pilots signed contracts in the summer of 1941. Those who survived the training regimen would serve a country they knew little about, in a conflict they understood not at all. Inside of a year, they would be America's darlings, and arguably the most famous combat force this country has ever produced.

2

May I Present Colonel Chennault?

1893–1937

The man who would command these adventurers was born in Commerce, Texas, on September 6, 1893.

Or was he? Commerce is right, though there is no documentary proof of Claire Lee Chennault's birth in Texas or anywhere else. As the story is told, his father left Louisiana after a horse trader tried to sell him an unbroken mustang as good farm stock. Mr. Chennault shot a hole through the man's hat, and a sojourn in Texas was thought advisable while the matter cooled.

But the year, the year! For most of his life, Claire Chennault claimed he was born in 1890, but his tombstone says 1893, and in this case death speaks the truth. Chennault lied in his memoirs, lied to *Who's Who in America,* lied to the U.S. Army, and lied to the admissions officer of each college he attended. More charitably, he saw a reason to make himself seem older than his chronological age, and—in a time and a place that had scant use for vital statistics—he made the change and then was stuck with it. The deception was all the easier because he looked older than his years. Not for nothing would his associates call him "Old Leatherface."

It is a small matter, this business of Chennault's birth year, but significant as the first of the ambiguities and deceptions that marked his career. Claire Chennault was a great man and a flawed one. It can be argued that the American Volunteer Group was not his idea, that another man did as much as Chennault to create it, that he did not invent its

9

tactics, and that when it was fighting most desperately, he was generally elsewhere. However that may be, it is also true that the AVG could never have succeeded without his passion and his remarkable ability to inspire devotion in young men—and women.

According to family legend, Chennault's great-great-grandfather came from France in 1778 to fight for American independence under the Marquis de Lafayette. He remained to plant tobacco in Virginia, and his descendants moved westward with the country. In the fourth generation, John Stonewall Chennault grew up in Louisiana and married Jessie Lee. Through him, Claire Chennault claimed kinship with the Texas hero Sam Houston; through his mother, he traced his lineage to Robert E. Lee of the Old Confederacy. The French connection, by this time, was all but forgotten, and the Chennaults pronounced their surname as any Southerner might, in a sort of hard-edged sneeze: *Sh'nawlt*. They settled in Jessie's home town of Gilbert. This was bayou country, woven with swampy tributaries of the Mississippi and forever threatening to return to wilderness. John farmed cotton, served as sheriff, and fathered a second son, William. Jessie died of tuberculosis in 1901, and the boys went to live with their maternal grandparents. The person who took care of them was their mother's sister, Louise Chase. Claire formed "an instant, strong attachment for his young aunt," and her sons became like brothers to him.

In 1904, John Chennault married Lottie Barnes, Claire's teacher in the ungraded Gilbert school. Far from resenting his stepmother, Claire became extremely close to her, as he had to his aunt. In many ways, his was an idyllic boyhood—Tom Sawyerish—though by his own account he was a loner, happiest when by himself or in the company of younger boys willing to follow his lead. He made his way through the one-room Gilbert school by the time he was fourteen, and in January 1909 he matriculated at Louisiana State University in Baton Rouge, in a freshman class of 146 men and 8 women. The university required incoming students to be sixteen "at nearest birthday," so Chennault pushed his birth month back to June, which is how it still appears on LSU records. At the same time (as he claimed) he applied to West Point and Annapolis, and during spring break took the train east to sit for the entrance exam for the Naval Academy. This may have been Chennault's occasion for falsifying the year of his birth, since a fifteen-year-old could not have applied to the military academies. He submitted a blank paper, he said, after considering what life would be like inside the walls. But why would he be dismayed by the regimentation at Annapolis? He was no stranger to drill; like all males living "in barracks" at LSU, he belonged to the Reserve Officer Training Corps and wore his ROTC garrison cap, high-buttoned tunic, and striped uniform trousers to class.

Of his own volition, he joined the Graham Literary Society. He showed some talent in that direction, according to his English teacher, Mercedes Garig, who later said of him:

> I remember his writing perfectly. . . . It had character and slanted to the right. It impressed you as though he knew what he wanted to say and how to say it. . . .
>
> He was also so silent. He would just sit and look and I never knew whether it was reserve or shyness. It seemed to me that it may have been just belief in himself—that he didn't have to go outside himself.
>
> He was slender, with dark hair and an olive complexion. But the most noticeable thing about him was his silence. I never got close to Chennault, mainly because his work was usually so good that I never had to have many "conferences" with him.

Chennault was an "aggie," a course of study that prescribed eighteen classroom hours a week in English, algebra, botany, comparative physiology, farm accounting, and elementary agriculture. Idle hands being the devil's workshop, LSU also encouraged its students to sign up for sports, and Chennault recalled that he competed at track, basketball, and baseball.

That summer, he farmed a cotton patch to earn money for his sophomore year. In November, his beloved stepmother died. Grieving—silently—Chennault dropped out of LSU in favor of the State Normal School at Natchitoches, where he followed a two-month regimen of physics, agriculture, arithmetic, algebra, grammar, and accounting before he again dropped out.

His second change of course may have had something to do with an epiphany at the Louisiana State Fair. In Shreveport, as Chennault recalled, he saw an early Curtiss biplane, the propeller mounted behind the wings and the pilot perched in front—a craft scarcely more sophisticated than the egg crate in which Orville Wright had become airborne at Kitty Hawk, North Carolina, seven years earlier. He was enchanted, but there seemed no way for him to pursue the fascination, and in September 1910 he went to work as teacher-principal of a school in

Athens, not far from Shreveport. When the school year was over, he attended commencement exercises at Winnsboro High, where the valedictorian (and only graduate) was Nellie Thompson, plump and pretty. They were married on Christmas Day. As a family man—the babies came as quickly as nature allowed—Chennault required more lucrative employment than presiding over an ungraded country school. When the United States declared war on Germany in April 1917, he was laboring in a Goodyear tire factory.

Chennault resettled his family near the home place in Gilbert, and went to infantry training school at Fort Benjamin Harrison, where he earned the silver bars of a first lieutenant. He was assigned to the 90th Infantry Division at Fort Travis, outside San Antonio. On the other side of town was Kelly Field, a former cotton plantation upon which the Signal Corps taught cadets to fly. Kelly asked Travis for the loan of an infantry officer, and Chennault joyfully accepted what he assumed was a billet in aviation, to find himself leading the cadets in parade-ground drill. No matter. If it was not flying, it was close, and he stayed at Kelly for nearly a year. He took a few bootleg flying lessons, and he dressed the part of an aviator: a 1917 photograph showed him togged out in puttees, riding breeches, shirt, tie, leather helmet, and round-lensed goggles like those worn on the Western Front. The man in the photograph was strikingly handsome, though with narrowed eyes and an uncompromising mouth. His companion, by contrast, smiled affably at the camera.

The war ended without Chennault's participation, but in 1919 he received the orders he had longed for, and he returned to Kelly Field as a cadet. Alas, his bootleg flying lessons had left him with habits that, combined with a rebellious temperament, caused him to be washed out by his civilian instructor, one Pop Liken. Chennault went up in the "washing machine" for the traditional second opinion by a military pilot. This was Lieutenant Ernest Allison, whose verdict was shrewder than Liken's: "This man can be taught to fly." Chennault earned his wings on April 9, 1919, but his only flying assignment was a stint on the Mexican border, and he was routinely discharged at the end of his tour. He went home to Gilbert, planted a field to cotton, and pined for the wings he had lost: "I have tasted of the air," he wrote to his father, "and I cannot get it out of my craw."

Happily for him, the National Defense Act of 1920 made the Army

Air Service a speciality like the infantry or the artillery, with 1,500 officers and 16,000 enlisted men. Before his crops were in, Chennault applied for one of the newly opened slots for flying officers. On September 14 he again received pilot's wings and lieutenant's bars—a reservist no longer, but an officer in the regular army. Again, however, he spent most of his time in nonflying assignments. By 1922, when he joined the 1st Pursuit Group at Ellington Field, Texas, he had logged just sixty-three hours in the air.

The 1st Pursuit was commanded by veterans of the Western Front. Chennault was assigned to the 94th Squadron, whose planes bore the hat-in-the-ring insignia made famous by Eddie Rickenbacker, America's "ace of aces" for shooting down twenty-six German planes. In this congenial environment, Chennault became the superlative pilot nature had intended him to be, and in 1924 he was sent to Hawaii as commander of the 19th Pursuit Squadron. It was a happy billet for Chennault, now thirty years old and the father of six sons and a daughter. He sported a waxed-tip mustache, luxuriant and black. His station was Ford Island in the middle of Pearl Harbor, America's mightiest naval base, where he absorbed the imperatives of Pacific geopolitics, including the emergence of Japan as an imperial power. During a war scare in 1925, Chennault ordered aerial patrols off the coast of Hawaii, and he improvised an early-warning system by posting men with binoculars on top of a water tower. By now, he was becoming hard of hearing, the result of long hours in an open cockpit amid the airstream and the roar of an unmuffled engine. He was obliged to fly on a medical waiver, but fly he did, logging 1,353 hours by the time he left Hawaii.

In 1929 the army promoted him to captain. Such a leisurely advance would be unthinkable today, but was standard for the underfunded U.S. Army between the wars. Chennault was on the accepted career track, and a year later he was selected to attend the Air Corps Tactical School, where future generals were trained. Among his instructors was Captain Clayton Bissell, three years his junior but credited with shooting down five German aircraft in World War I. As Chennault told the story, Bissell held that the best way to destroy the fast, heavily armed bombers of the 1930s was to fly overhead and entangle their engines in a ball-and-chain device. When not listening to such nonsense, Chennault studied the campaigns of Hannibal and Napoleon: though it had wings, this was the *Army* Air Corps.

When the Tactical School got a permanent campus at Maxwell Field, Alabama, Chennault joined the faculty as instructor of fighter tactics. He lived with his family in a large white brick house on the old Selma road, ten miles outside Montgomery. A neighbor recalled meeting him in 1934:

> Captain Chennault proudly showed us a giant scuppernong vine at the rear of his vegetable garden, explaining that he had been making some scuppernong wine which he wanted us to sample. Mrs. Chennault told me that the owner of the place had undertaken to harvest the grapes for himself, although the land on which they grew had been leased with the house. "It was simply a misunderstanding," she said, "but I thought Claire was going to shoot him. He's fiery."

The Tactical School was more than an in-service academy; its sixteen-man faculty also served as an incubator for air force doctrine. For his part, Chennault tried to devise something more effective than dangling chains to defend the country against enemy bombers. This he did in the air over the town of Waterproof, Louisiana, not far from where he had grown up. His cousin Ben Chase had settled there, and Chennault would fly in for the weekend, to fish and hunt. Chase had served in the Naval Air Service, and sometimes his friends flew in from Pensacola, where the navy had formed an acrobatic team called the Helldivers.

In 1929, the United States had adopted a fighter to replace its war-vintage machines. Built by Boeing, this darling biplane was known to the army as the P-12. Its cowling bulged like the head of a clothespin, and its landing gear and upper wing were so far forward that they almost met the engine, a 525-horsepower Wasp that drove the Boeing through the air at nearly 200 miles per hour—for the moment, the fastest and most manueverable fighter in the world. The navy flew it as the F4B. When the commander of the Tactical School saw the Helldivers perform in 1932, he asked Chennault to create a similar team at Maxwell Field. For his wingmen, Chennault picked Lieutenant Haywood (Possum) Hansell and Sergeant John Williamson, known as Luke. After their first performance, letting off steam in a Mississippi tavern, they sang the rollicking verse: "He floats through the air with the greatest of ease / That daring young man on a flying trapeze." Forthwith, they became the Three Men on a Flying Trapeze.

In their P-12s, the Three Men perfected their act in the air over Waterproof. In the end, they devised eighteen stunts, including a "collision" that brought the aircraft within eight feet of one another. At times they flew tied together with twenty-foot lengths of control cable, taking off, stunting, and landing again with the tethers intact. The results were awesome. "Chennault's 'Men on a Flying Trapeze' performed feats heretofore considered impossible," wrote a correspondent for the *Air Corps News Letter*. "Wingovers, slow and snap rolls, Immelmanns, and finally a turn and a half spin were executed with such precision and perfection that it seemed as if the three planes were activated by a single mind."

The Three Men were indeed activated by a single mind: Chennault's, mimicked to perfection by Luke Williamson and Possum Hansell. When Hansell left the act, he was replaced by Sergeant William McDonald. Photographed leaning against the lower wing of a P-12, they were three remarkably handsome men—all of a height, all of an age, all dressed in leather helmets, leather flight jackets, and sheepskin-lined leather coveralls held up by suspenders—and all happy. Even Chennault was grinning, although his smile was guarded, as if ready for an unfriendly move on the photographer's part.

In 1921, Colonel William Mitchell had proved that planes armed with 1,000-pound bombs could attack and sink the most powerful naval vessels afloat. This he did by cobbling together the 1st Provisional Air Brigade and sending it against a captured German battleship, anchored off the mouth of Chesapeake Bay. (Clayton Bissell was one of Billy Mitchell's pilots.) European strategists had reached a similar conclusion, most vividly expressed by General Giulio Douhet. The Italian argued that no city was safe from aerial bombardment, because no means existed by which a bomber could be stopped before it reached its target—that, even if intercepted, a heavily armed "battleplane" could outgun the puny fighters of the day. At the Tactical School, Douhet's writings were translated and mimeographed as a text. Experience seemed to prove the wisdom of his doctrine. In the war games of 1931, the 1st Pursuit Group failed to catch a single bomber, prompting Major General Walter Frank to conclude that "it is impossible for fighters to intercept bombers." That being so, it was clearly a waste of money to develop any more fighters.

The Boeing company had already designed the behemoth that would become the B-17 Flying Fortress, a "battleplane" that might have been sketched by Douhet himself. It weighed twenty-two tons; its four engines developed 3,720 hp and drove it through the air at more than 250 mph; and it was defended by machine guns at the nose, back, belly, and flanks. By contrast, the front-line American fighter plane of the day—the open-cockpit Boeing P-26, a monoplane version of the old P-12—boasted a top speed of 230 mph and mounted two machine guns. With the advent of the B-17 and sophisticated aiming mechanisms, air force doctrine became fixated on daylight precision bombing. "American Army or Navy planes," boasted a writer of the time, "can drop a bomb into a pickle barrel from 18,000 feet up." Altitude would protect them from antiaircraft fire, while high speed and close-formation flying—with their machine gunners providing mutual support—would fend off such enemy fighter planes as managed to locate them in the vastness of the sky.

Chennault was not convinced. He believed that the fighter plane's deficiencies could be overcome through teamwork, morale, concentration of firepower, and the speed built up in a dive. If a pilot "took the high perch," he could make a screaming pass through the enemy formation, climb back to altitude, and do it again. Chennault also argued that a fighter pilot should not have to keep track of more than one friendly aircraft at a time, and that a sensible commander would always keep some fighters in reserve, to be moved here and there as the situation changed.

He conceded that World War II would begin with a surprise attack from the air, and that the combat would be radically different from that of all previous wars, with bombers striking at the enemy heartland. "The ability of a nation to wage war," he wrote, "can be impaired if not wholly destroyed by an enemy who is able to employ, without opposition, a vast number of bombardment airplanes against factories, lines of communication, mobilization centers, centers of wealth and population, and harbors." The operative words were *without opposition*. What the fighter pilots needed (and what war games did not allow) was a continuous flow of information. Ergo: observers should be strung around the target and linked by telephone to a command post where the enemy's progress could be plotted on a map, enabling the fighter commander to know where and when to intercept. Drawing upon his service in Hawaii, he even suggested how to protect an island from attack: put the observers on picket boats or submarines.

He succeeded only in antagonizing the officers he most needed to convince. "The bombardment people were saying one thing," recalled a colleague at the Tactical School, "the attack people another, and Chennault was saying something else." In the end, the advocates of high-level bombing and low-level attack joined forces and "got Chennault where he was . . . lashing out," making enemies instead of converts.

He did strike one blow for the survival of the fighter plane in U.S. service. As an instructor in the Tactical School, he served on the Pursuit Development Board drawing up specifications for the nation's first 300-mph warplane. Modeled upon the sports racers of the day, it was to be a low-wing monoplane with an air-cooled radial engine, retractable landing gear, and stressed aluminum skin. Curtiss-Wright submitted the only entry, but the army extended the competition, and the contract (for seventy-seven aircraft) went to Seversky for a design that seemed to promise more maneuverability and longer range.

Chennault flew the competing fighters in August 1935, and for once he sided with the majority. Time proved him wrong: when it finally went into service as the P-36 (Mohawk, in British service) the Curtiss fighter proved to be faster, more reliable, easier to fly, and easier to maintain than the Seversky P-35. In the meantime, Curtiss-Wright set out to recoup its investment by working up a cheaper version of the Mohawk, with a smaller engine and nonretractable landing gear. This it hoped to sell to foreign countries—China, say.

The Three Men gave their farewell performance at the All-American Air Races in Miami in December 1935. Among the spectators was Colonel Mao Pang-chu of the Chinese Air Force. He cut a dashing figure, his face chubby and handsome beneath a wavy shock of hair, his uniform splendidly tailored and beribboned. Also in Miami was William Pawley, Curtiss-Wright representative in China, who had accompanied Mao to recruit flight instructors for the CAF and to inspect his company's new export fighter. Pawley threw a party on a yacht in Miami harbor. He invited the Three Men, and Mao offered them lucrative jobs at a flight school in Hangzhou. Williamson and McDonald "bought up" the time remaining on their enlistments and sailed for China in July 1936.

Even before *Empress of Russia* took his friends to Asia, Chennault had come to the conclusion that his argument was lost, his career in the air force effectively finished. His students devoted forty-one classroom hours to bombardment, forty-two to attack aviation, and only twenty-nine to "pursuit"—just ahead of naval operations. He wore the gold oak leaves of a major, but his commission was in the army reserve; his permanent rank was still captain. In 1936 he was reassigned as executive officer of the 20th Pursuit Group at Barksdale Field, Louisiana. He was forty-two. His face was pocked; crow's-feet radiated from the corners of his glittering black eyes; his nose was almost perfectly aquiline; razor-cut seams dropped from the corners of his mouth. Altogether, Major Chennault had the look of a weary eagle. "He's fiery," Nellie had said to her neighbor. Indeed: he was an uncomfortable presence, demanding and passionate, adored by his subordinates but impatient and sharp-tongued with his superiors.

"It is well to avoid a reputation for eccentricity," wrote Major General Henry Arnold in a manual to guide the young aviator from lieutenant's bars to general's stars. He may have been thinking of Chennault when he wrote that line. The story is told that, when he read the fighter advocate's critique of how war games were biased in favor of bombard-ment, Hap Arnold snapped: "Who is this damned fellow Chennault?" He sided with the bombardment advocates in that dispute, and he continued to do so even after World War II proved them wrong. "Bombers are winged, long-range artillery," he wrote. "They can no more be completely stopped once they have taken the air than the big shell can be stopped once it has left the muzzle." A major does not advance his career by arguing that the commanding general is wrong.

Then there was the problem of Chennault's health. He was tremen-dously active, tremendously eager, always ready for a roughhouse or a pickup baseball game with his sons or subordinates. But he was regularly laid low by bronchitis, the penalty for his addiction to Camel cigarettes. (He smoked up to three packs in twenty-four hours, chain-smoking through the day and sometimes through the night.) For years he had been flying on a waiver because of his deafness; now, at Barksdale, flight surgeons declared that he could fly no more. They sent him to the Army-Navy General Hospital in Hot Springs, Arkansas, to be treated for what appears to have been a physical and mental breakdown. In February 1937, the army suggested that he retire at his permanent rank of captain.

The Chennaults had bought a forty-nine-acre farm near Waterproof. The house was a one-story bungalow, shaded by tall pines. There was an

RFD mailbox, a white board fence, a black cook, and a pier reaching out into Lake St. John. Nellie took to rural life more eagerly than her husband. She was a portly woman by now, with a permanent, metal-rimmed glasses, black dress, and sensible shoes; she wore the benevolent but formidable expression of a Sunday school teacher—which she was, as well as president of the Waterproof Methodist Women's Society.

But Chennault had no intention of rusticating in Louisiana. Since meeting Colonel Mao aboard Bill Pawley's yacht in Miami, he had been bargaining with the Chinese. The assignment, as it finally evolved, was a three-month survey of the CAF, for which he would be paid $1,000 a month, three times what he earned as a major on active duty. On April 30, 1937, he retired from the U.S. Army. He boarded the train to San Francisco the next day, and from there set out across the Pacific on *President Garfield*. He began a diary when he embarked upon the "Great Adventure," but except for that revealing phrase he limited it to a recital of each day's events, with few personal reflections and no comments on what was happening in the world. So we do not know what he thought of the news that, on April 27, German and Italian bombers had destroyed the city of Guernica in Spain, killing 1,654 civilians in history's first terror bombing—the Douhet doctrine come to terrible reality.

Chennault's first stop in Asia was Kobe, on the Japanese main island of Honshu, where Billy McDonald met him for a day and a night of amateur espionage. (Chennault was impressed by the damage incendiary bombs would be able to inflict upon Japanese houses, built—as they seemed to him—of matchsticks and paper.) *Garfield* then took the two of them to Shanghai. Among the warships anchored in the sluggish river, Chennault saw HMS *Cumberland*, USS *Augusta*, and *Idzumo*, flagship of the Japanese 3rd Fleet. Shanghai was a "treaty port," governed and garrisoned by Britain, the United States, Japan, France, and Italy. The foreigners had their own police, courts, and prisons there, and the same was true of every important city within reach of their gunboats—even Nanjing, 200 miles inland, where Chiang Kai-shek supposedly ruled China. In fact, his was a theoretical and shifting domain, based on the valley of the Yangzi River (Chang Jiang). Japan occupied Manchuria, the Soviet Union controlled Mongolia and Xinjiang, there was a communist government in Shanxi, and the foreigners ran the treaty ports. Much of the rest was given over to warlords who levied their own taxes and fielded their own armies. In this fractured empire, Chiang was only the "generalissimo"—the ultimate warlord.

That Thursday (June 3, 1937) may have been the most important day in Claire Chennault's life, for it was then that he began his lifelong association with the first family of China:

> One sultry afternoon Roy Holbrook appeared and drove me to the high-walled compound in the French Concession to meet my new employer—Madame Chiang Kai-shek. We were told she was out and ushered into a dim cool interior to wait. Suddenly a vivacious young girl clad in a modish Paris frock tripped into the room, bubbling with energy and enthusiasm. I assumed it was some young friend of Roy's and remained seated. . . . Roy poked me and said, "Madame Chiang, may I present Colonel Chennault?"

Not for the first time, Chennault was bewitched by a handsome, youngish woman in a position of authority. "Granted interview by Her Excellency Madam[e] Chiang Kai-Shek," he wrote in his diary that night. Then he added a curious pledge: "who will hereafter be 'The Princess' to me."

Madame Chiang enchanted Americans from many backgrounds. They were impressed by her power, awed by her beauty, reassured by her Wellesley diploma, and charmed by her Southern drawl (as Chennault and others have characterized her speech, though in recordings her voice is clipped, authoritative, and without an accent of any kind). Madame was a chameleon, who could charm even a soldier of fortune. Among the American pilots hiring out to Chinese warlords in the 1930s was Royal Leonard, who flew the Chiangs to safety after a bizarre kidnapping that did not end until the generalissimo promised to lead communists, warlords, and his Nationalist army in a united front against the Japanese. Madame impressed Leonard as "the most beautiful Chinese woman I had ever seen," and he threw in his lot with the Chiangs. The generalissimo was a medieval man, who never felt entirely comfortable in his "flying palace." But madame was a modernist. She acquired a plane of her own and had herself appointed secretary-general of China's Aeronautical Commission, in which capacity she was interviewing Chennault.

His account of their meeting is notable in another respect. Chennault was a retired captain, who had never held a rank higher than major. If Holbrook introduced him as "colonel," the title either came from the Chinese or was cooked up by the Americans. The latter seems to have been the case. Chinese officers who worked with Chennault in the 1930s were unanimous in agreeing that he was not commissioned in the CAF. Chennault said the same, claiming he was never more than a civilian adviser in all the years he served the Chiangs.

His next interview was in Nanjing, where he met Brigadier General Chou Chih-jou, a somber-faced soldier whom the generalissimo had sacked for losing a battle with the communists, then put in command of the CAF. Chou's Italian adviser, General Silvio Scaroni, was there to brief Chennault.

His arm aching from typhoid and cholera shots, Chennault then took a train to Hangzhou, where the CAF primary flight school was staffed by Americans, including Luke Williamson and Billy McDonald. Chennault knew them all, and his first business was to have a "walla-walla" in their quarters. "Appalled by situation here," he wrote in his diary, but whether in reference to the flight school, the dreary weather, or a nagging head cold, he did not specify. He then set off on a whirlwind tour of airfields at Nanchang, Canton (Guangzhou), Hankou, and Luoyang—Scaroni's domain, where Italian airmen ran an intermediate flight school, assembled Fiat fighters and Savoia-Marchetti bombers, and kept the communists from breaking out of their base in Shanxi.

At Luoyang, Chennault learned that Japanese and Chinese troops were skirmishing near the Marco Polo Bridge, ten miles outside Beijing. The cause was obscure: Japanese troops on maneuvers, shells exploding in their bivouac area, and Private Kikujiro Shimura vanishing in the night. The supposed casualty was back on duty next day, by which time the regimental commander had decided to eject the Chinese troops from the area. His action came as a surprise to the government in Tokyo. However, as they had done with the occupation of Manchuria in 1931, and as they would do again in 1941, the politicians bowed to the wisdom of the generals. The skirmish became a battle, giving Chiang Kai-shek the option of surrendering Beijing—China's sometime capital—or going to war.

Chennault fired off a telegram to the Aeronautical Commission, offering his services in the emergency. The reply was vague, so he went on to Xian. There he received the hoped-for orders: go to Nanchang and take charge of final combat training. The CAF advanced flight school was commanded by Mao Pang-chu, the curly haired officer who had recruited the Three Men in Miami. Now a brigadier general, he tactfully removed himself to the capital when Chennault arrived. Thus the leading squadrons of the CAF came under the control of a man who had been in the country for six weeks, who did not (and never would) speak the language.

Nanchang was a dusty city in the interior, where many of the CAF's front-line pilots were so inept that they could not be trusted in a biplane Fleet trainer, never mind a Boeing P-26. (As the story is told, the cadets were mostly the sons of Chiang's bankers, generals, and legislators, and General Scaroni had not thought it politic to refuse them wings, whether or not they could fly.) Chennault vented his dismay and amusement in a letter to Billy McDonald: "What should I do, Mac, solo them on the Boeing and see if they break their necks or have them think I'm holding out on them? If the Commission is going to keep up sending greenhorns like these, it's no wonder the planes are all wrecks." On July 23, he went to Nanjing for his first meeting with Chiang Kai-shek, who was agonizing over whether or not to resist the Japanese occupation of Beijing.

The occasion for the meeting was Chennault's report on the war readiness of the CAF. It was delivered by General Mao, in fear and trembling, for he had to tell the generalissimo that, of 500 aircraft supposedly in the inventory, fewer than 200 were combat-worthy. For front-line fighters, the CAF had ten Boeing P-26s; for long-range bombers, it had six German-built Heinkels, six Savoia-Marchetti trimotors, and nine Martin B-10s from the U.S. There were some Italian biplane fighters (firetraps, in Chennault's opinion) and some ancient American light bombers and scout planes. But the backbone of the CAF squadrons was the Curtiss Hawk, a biplane fighter-bomber originally intended for the U.S. Navy. When the navy moved on to better things, Bill Pawley sold the design to China, the planes to be built at a factory in Hangzhou. Grandly called the Central Aircraft Manufacturing Company—CAMCO—this plant had been assembling Hawk IIs and Hawk IIIs since 1933. One hundred of these sturdy warplanes were now in service with the CAF, doing duty as fighters and as bombers.

Through the hot, wet weeks of summer, the Japanese drove Chiang's army south. On paper, the generalissimo had 1.7 million men under arms, but only 300,000 were in front-line units, and only 100,000 were first-class soldiers with modern weapons and foreign advisers. (The advisers were German. While Adolf Hitler rebuilt his army in violation of the Treaty of Versailles, he found China a convenient and profitable place to warehouse the officers Germany was not supposed to have.) This elite served first of all as Chiang's palace guard, and he did not want to have it destroyed by the Japanese. However, on July 31, he decided to honor the agreement that had been extorted from him at Xian. He would fight—but not at Beijing, where the Japanese could call upon their reserves of men and weapons in Manchuria. Instead, he sent his German-trained 87th and 88th Divisions into action at Shanghai, against marines dependent on the 3rd Fleet for supply, reinforcement, heavy guns, and air support. It was a clever move, except that it pitted the fledgling CAF against the Japanese navy air force, which was more formidable than the army's. The generals regarded the Soviet Union as their likely foe, so they wanted planes that could fight in the cold and barren reaches of Manchuria, in cooperation with the infantry. The admirals, by contrast, expected to fight the United States, so they developed planes that could fly great distances over water, and in a tropical climate. These were the qualities needed at Shanghai.

Chennault's first assignment was to silence the navy guns that were shelling Chiang's divisions. The order came on Friday, August 13. As he told the story, he and Billy McDonald stayed up until 4 A.M. Saturday morning, sketching the details of a raid that would send CAF bombers against the flagship *Idzumo,* anchored in the river off the Japanese consulate. The sky on August 14 was filled with rags of low-lying clouds, forerunners of a typhoon about to sweep the East China Sea. Scattered by the storm, the CAF bombers reached Shanghai in flights of two or three. At 10 A.M., *Idzumo*'s antiaircraft guns began to fire, alerting the foreign newsmen in the Cathay and Palace hotels, who saw three aircraft appear "with startling suddenness" over the harbor. The planes "dived and loosed one bomb each, the explosions reverberating through the city and engulfing [*Idzumo*] in smoke."

They missed. As Chennault explained the disaster, his pilots dropped to 1,500 feet to get under the clouds, but did not adjust their sights for the change in altitude and speed. As a result, their bombs sailed clear of *Idzumo* and landed in streets filled with civilians. "Oh, it was the most bloody catastrophe," recalled Tom Trumble, a young American seaman on USS *Augusta,* who went ashore to view the carnage. "There were arms, legs, torsos. The streets were running with blood." Only one Japanese ship was damaged, and that a merchantman, *Okinawa Maru.*

Nor did the Japanese cover themselves with glory on this first day of the air war in China. Twelve biplane bombers lifted off from the aircraft carrier *Kaga*, flew down to Hangzhou, and were cut to pieces by the squadrons Chennault had trained. CAMCO-built Hawks shot down eleven bombers and sent the twelfth limping back to the carrier. The survivor's report "astonished the officers of the fleet," as one of them recalled after the war. *Kaga* was ordered back to Japan, to take on a complement of carrier-based fighters—fast monoplanes that had been in service for a year, but had not been thought necessary to protect the fleet at Shanghai.

Meanwhile, the navy retaliated with a massive air attack on the Chinese capital (massive, anyhow, by the standards of 1937). On Sunday, sixteen twin-engined bombers appeared in the sky over Nanjing. They were of a type unknown to western observers, prompting the *New York Times* to report that the Japanese were flying German-built Heinkels. General Mao, after inspecting a downed bomber, conceded that it was Japanese, after all, though assembled from German metal, American engines, and British machine guns. An even greater mystery was where the bombers had come from, and Chennault sent out scouts to find the "secret base" he assumed the Japanese had built on Chinese soil. In fact, the raiders were Mitsubishi G3Ms, twin-engined navy bombers that western pilots later dubbed Nell. They were based on the offshore island of Taiwan, which Japan had seized in its first war with China (1894–1895). The round-trip distance to Nanjing was 1,250 miles, most of it over open ocean—a raid that could not have been duplicated by any other air force in the world. But without fighter escort, the G3Ms were "easy meat" for the defenders, as Chennault exultantly noted. CAF Boeings and Hawks tore into the raiders over the Chinese capital and damaged six so badly that they went down in flames or crashed on the way home. One of the survivors recorded the terror and anguish of that day:

> We have lost 30 men. . . . I wish to jump out and die with them, but how? My life is not mine. What can I do? The only thing I can do is hold the plane tight and pray God silently.

At the end of August, the first Japanese escort fighters appeared over Nanjing. "Jap pursuit reported superior in performance to Hawks," Chennault wrote gloomily. "Chinese pilots are most properly afraid of them." Like most westerners, he could not believe that the Japanese had built anything so formidable on their own, so he identified the new fighters as French Dewoitines. In fact, he was witnessing the combat debut of the Mitsubishi A5M, an open-cockpit fighter with nonretractable landing gear and two rifle-caliber machine guns firing through the propeller arc—like the Boeing P-26, though more agile.* Western pilots later called this plane Claude. About twenty had been shipped to China and based at coastal airfields scratched out by navy engineers.

On September 1, Chiang Kai-shek brought Chennault to the capital and put him in charge of CAF training and operations—in effect, chief of staff for air. Chennault set up shop at the Nanjing athletic stadium, with five officers to help him. The radio officer was Lieutenant Lee Cheng-yuan, with whom Chennault developed a control system for the CAF fighters. A Phillips radio was installed in each flight leader's aircraft, and Lieutenant Lee, in a radio-equipped station wagon, drove at breakneck speed through the streets of Nanjing, spotting for Chennault at the athletic stadium. The stadium was tied into an observer network consisting of a few army field radios and many hand-cranked telephones. Chennault configured them in a manner that the Chinese dubbed "the spider in the web," with each radioman serving as the center for a circle of eight or ten observers who reported to him by telephone. The radioman summarized their reports and forwarded them to the athletic stadium. Here the information was plotted on a map, with flags indicating the type, quantity, and direction of the enemy planes. The details were simple-minded to begin with: *much noise / little noise; one engine / two engines.* In time the observers became more sophisticated, and the system was expanded to cover the vital coastal triangle of Shanghai, Hangzhou, and Nanjing.

With Japanese fighters ruling the sky over China, Chennault switched

* The Japanese navy had two systems for designating aircraft. In the formal notation, the first letter indicated the aircraft type (*G* for land-based bomber, *A* for carrier-based fighter), and this was followed by a sequence number and a letter identifying the manufacturer (*M* for Mitsubishi). Informally, a plane was known by its year of adoption, using a calendar based on the mythical founding of the empire in 660 B.C. In this system, the G3M and the A5M were both "Type 96," since both went into service in the year 2596 (1936). Baffled western pilots bestowed feminine names on the Japanese bombers and masculine names on the fighters. I use the western pet names unless a better one is available from Japanese sources.

to attacks at dusk and dawn. He mocked up *Idzumo* with kerosene lanterns on the Nanjing airfield and drilled his pilots against this winking target from 3,500 feet. Then the CAF tried it live at Shanghai. Sure enough, the Japanese outlined their ships with searchlights and muzzle flashes, enabling the Chinese bombardiers to damage some of them— though not the charmed *Idzumo*. This sudden increase in accuracy aroused the suspicions of the American consul, Clarence Gauss, who cabled Washington:

> Recent Chinese night air raids over Shanghai are reported to have been carried out by pilots obviously more skilled than Chinese. One raider flew very low over foreign area to escape Japanese anti-aircraft fire and when passing over American Country Club dipped his plane and flashed on and off his lights. There is strong suspicion this plane was piloted by one of the American aviators [here].

Aboard *Augusta,* Tom Trumble shared the suspicion. As a yeoman (finance clerk) he saw dispatches identifying Chennault as a CAF adviser. "The name stuck," Trumble recalled, "and for a long time I thought that Chennault was the mysterious 'Mr. Wu' that used to fly by the *Augusta* at dusk every evening and try to bomb the *Idzumo*." Trumble later had a chance to question Billy McDonald on this point. No, McDonald assured him; Chennault was never the bomber pilot, but flew overhead as observer and critic. For this duty, Chennault flew a fixed-gear Curtiss Mohawk, brought to China by Bill Pawley in hopes of selling a new generation of fighters to Chiang Kai-shek.

Chennault did not mention such flights in his diary, but he hinted at it in a September 14 letter to Possum Hansell. "While there is *no* war going on at present," he archly told his former wingman, "some 2,000 Japanese airplanes are doing their annual bombing maneuvers all over China. . . . In view of this Jap activity, Chinese pursuit is conducting its annual gunnery practice." Chennault was particularly proud of that first interception over Nanjing. CAF fighters, he told Hansell, tore into the Japanese bombers and "had six of them burning in just 2 minutes, all six being visible from one spot in the sky." Was he suggesting that *he* was the airborne observer—or even one of the fighter pilots? The former may have been true, but the latter almost certainly was not. For more than half a century, American writers have claimed that Chennault flew as a mercenary in China, shooting down Japanese planes at $500 or $1,000

Curtiss P-36 Mohawk

The first plane off the drawing board of Curtiss-Wright designer Donovan Berlin, the Mohawk combined a rugged airframe with an engine that did not do it justice. Nevertheless, it was a sweet plane to fly, and durable beyond compare. Finally appreciating its virtues, the U.S. Army bought 210 in 1938—the largest single order it had ever placed—and took them into service as the P-36. They served as America's front-line fighter until 1940, and Curtiss built similar planes for the French, British, and Dutch air forces. Other countries (notably China) acquired a cheaper and lighter version with nonretractable landing gear. The Mohawk saw combat as late as 1942, but its most important role was to provide the platform upon which Curtiss-Wright would build a second-generation fighter plane, powered by a liquid-cooled engine. The specifications are for the fixed-gear H75-M model assembled in China and India by William Pawley's companies. Chennault's Mohawk would have been similar in performance.

Engine: 875-hp Wright Cyclone air-cooled radial
Crew: one
Wingspan: 37 feet 4 inches
Combat weight: 5,300 lb
Maximum range: 900 miles
Top speed: 280 mph at 11,000 feet
Armament: one .50-caliber and one .30-caliber machine gun in the nose, two .30-caliber machine guns in the wings

---

each. (Joseph Alsop, his sometime aide and lifelong advocate, called Chennault "the leading American ace of World War II" for shooting down fifty Japanese planes before the war began.) But CAF veterans scoffed at the notion that he performed any more hazardous duty than training and scouting missions.

His letter to Possum Hansell ended with a boast that in time became an obsession: "Boy, if the Chinese only had 100 good pursuit planes and 100 fair pilots, they'd exterminate the Jap air force!" In that sentence, he had sketched the outline of the American Volunteer Group he would bring to Asia in 1941.

We Are Not Choosers

1937–1940

The Chinese fought with suicidal gallantry at Shanghai, losing 270,000 men before retreating along the railroad to Nanjing. By the time they captured the capital, the Japanese had suffered losses nearly as terrible. The victors embarked upon an "orgy of looting, raping, drinking, and murder" in which at least 100,000 people died, making the Rape of Nanjing one of the bloodiest events of World War II. And for nothing, because Chiang simply moved his government upriver. Bureaucrats and soldiers, bankers and industrialists, teachers and students, peasants and workers—they moved up the mile-wide Yangzi by the thousands, scuttling boats behind them to slow the Japanese advance. The Central Aircraft Manufacturing Company was part of this immense hegira. At Hankou, CAMCO reconstituted itself in the shadow of the Japanese Concession, and from this safe haven repaired warplanes for the CAF, sometimes taking them out to the airfield in the morning and dragging them back at sundown, to make good the damage they sustained during the day.

Bill Pawley's order book was brimming: sixty more Curtiss Hawk biplanes, thirty new Mohawk fighters. He also persuaded the Aeronautical Commission to buy thirty Vultee attack planes to be used against Japanese facilities on the coast. With Shanghai lost, the planes came in through the British colony of Hong Kong, then went by rail to the dusty inland city of Hengyang, where Pawley built a satellite factory to assemble them. Also operating out of Hengyang in the winter of 1937–1938 was Harvey Greenlaw, a former flight instructor at Hangzhou who was assembling training planes for a Pawley rival, A. L. (Pat) Patterson. The factories became the target of Japanese raids, and Olga Greenlaw recalled how Chennault and her husband would sit on her garden wall, "oblivious of shrapnel falling near them, and discuss the Japanese methods."

Mercenary pilots flocked to China with claims of combat experience on the Western Front. The terms were enough to tempt anyone in those ·years of depression: $500 a month, plus $1,000 for each Japanese plane shot down. At Madame Chiang's request, Chennault organized the mercenaries into the 14th Volunteer Squadron, an elite unit to be equipped with the attack planes Bill Pawley was assembling in Hengyang. The Vultee A-19 was a low-wing monoplane with retractable landing gear, a 1,000-hp Pratt & Whitney engine, four wing-mounted machine guns, a flexible gun at the rear of the greenhouse canopy, and another in the belly. Such hermaphrodite warplanes—fighter and bomber in one—were popular with economy-minded generals of the 1930s, but in combat they performed neither job particularly well.

Chennault spent the winter shuttling between the CAF combat squadrons at Nanchang and the 14th Volunteer Squadron at Hankou. The mercenaries proved to have more zest for drinking than for fighting; Chinese pilots refused to work with them; the Chinese bombardiers were scarcely able to "hit a city even"—and the planes kept breaking down. The 14th Volunteer Squadron flew its first mission on January 23, 1938. Four Vultees took off; one crashed, two turned back, and one flew to Anyang but was unable to find the airfield that was its target. Soon after this, the Japanese attacked Hankou one morning when the Vultees were gassed and armed for another raid; a bomb exploded under one wing, and the entire row blew up in a ghastly crescendo. The squadron was then sent to Chengdu, in the far west of China, where the mercenaries trained their own replacements from among the CAF pilots.

After the fall of Nanjing, Chiang fired his Italian and German advisers and turned to the Soviet Union. The basic Russian fighter, battle-tested in the Spanish Civil War, was the stubby Polikarpov I-15 biplane; the bomber was the speedy, twin-engined Tupelov SB-2. They were sent by the Trans-Siberian Railway to Xinjiang province, thence by truck along the old Silk Caravan route, 1,700 miles to the Chinese railhead at

Lanzhou. Legions of Chinese snow shovelers kept the road open. Camel caravans brought gasoline to the way-points. Returning, the trucks brought out furs, antimony ore, tung oil, silk, and tea to pay for the Soviet aid. In this fashion, 300 planes arrived in the winter of 1937–1938, of which half were handed over to the CAF. The others came in the form of combat-ready units with their own pilots and mechanics. Royal Leonard flew the Soviet ambassador to Lanzhou to inspect the assembly plant, and afterward told the U.S. embassy that the Russians had the largest aircraft operation in China, with a mile-long runway and fifty planes in various stages of assembly.

Japan threatened the Soviet supply route by sending troops into Mongolia; Josef Stalin countered by sending an armored division to Xinjiang. Japan then tried diplomacy, protesting the presence of foreign pilots in the country—a complaint that might more reasonably have been lodged by the Chinese. Stalin paid no attention, but the U.S. State Department was more amenable. Consular officers stopped American pilots from entering China and urged those already in the country to leave it. (Luke Williamson was among those who went home.) More and more, the air defense of China depended on the Soviet "volunteers." Chennault's diary reveals him steaming over episodes when the Russians refused to go on missions or "sought safety in flight," but in his public statements he always spoke well of them:

> A fighting unit would go on duty just before dawn and would stay on duty all day long . . . without any relief, without lunch or any sort of rest except in the seats of their planes. The mechanics . . . stayed on duty with each of the fighters, in front of the wing, prepared to start the engine at any moment.

As he told the story, four high-ranking officers—General Asanov of the Soviet Union, generals Chou and Mao of China, and Chennault as the CAF adviser—worked as a team in the defense of Hankou. His young communications officer remembered it differently. "The Russians didn't like Chennault," Lee Cheng-yuan recalled, adding that Soviet officers would not even speak to Chou when the American was around, for fear Chennault would learn their secrets. They preferred to deal with Mao Pang-chu, who had studied in the Soviet Union and spoke some Russian.

Asanov was right to be suspicious. Like Royal Leonard and other American airmen in China, Chennault regularly reported to U.S.

authorities, though he bypassed the embassy and wrote instead to the adjutant general in Washington. In May 1938, he forwarded drawings and specifications of the open-cockpit Claude. When the Japanese army introduced a monoplane fighter of its own to China—the Nakajima *Ki*-27—Chennault filed a report on that as well.* And, as Asanov feared, he forwarded information on Soviet equipment and tactics. In the spring of 1938, the Polikarpov I-16 reached China. This was a stubby mono-plane fighter, faster than the I-15 though lightly armed and not as maneuverable. In a dogfight, Chennault reported, the Japanese pilot would execute a split-S and glue himself to the Russian's tail, from which position nothing could shake him. The Russians then turned to hit-and-run tactics, putting their Polikarpovs into a power dive when hard-pressed by the nimble Japanese, then zooming back to altitude and attacking from above. This was the same technique Chennault had once proposed for use against bombers, and it made no greater impact upon the U.S. Army.

A somewhat jaundiced portrait of Chennault in 1938 was sketched by Paul Frillmann, an American missionary at Hankou. They met at a July 4 baseball game between British and American teams, on the racecourse between the Lutheran mission and the Japanese Concession. The young missionary was greatly impressed, though he papered it over with disdain. "He was a smallish man . . . with a silk aviator's neck-scarf and other accessories," Frillmann wrote years later. "He was standing with a court of ambiguous-looking men—semi-adventurous, semi-commercial types whom I later found to be his perennial cronies." Chennault put Frillmann in left field and himself on the pitcher's mound. As the missionary told the story, the airman made a great show of spitting on his glove and putting flourishes on the ball, only to have the British players smash his pitches all over the lot—but especially into left field. Frillmann valiantly ran them down, until he finally missed one. "The glare Chennault sent me from his dark hawk face," he wrote with obvious sincerity, "was something I remembered years later."

Chinese tradition demanded a scapegoat for defeat, but did not go

---

* The Japanese army notation system was based on the airframe (*kitai*) number given to a plane when it went into the design stage, without regard to type. Like the navy, the army also designated equipment by the year it entered service, and Allied pilots had their own pet names for JAAF aircraft.

on to require that he forfeit life or honors. Just as Chou Chih-jou become CAF commander after losing an infantry battle, he was fired from the Aeronautical Commission when he could not defend Hankou from Japanese air attack. He was sent west to the province of Yunnan, bordering the British colony of Burma, to build a new flight school. Chennault went with him into exile, as did Billy McDonald and Boatner (Butch) Carney—one of Frillmann's "ambiguous-looking men." Carney had a widow's peak, a dainty mustache, and a long and disreputable face. But he came from Louisiana, and Chennault enjoyed his company.

Yunnan was a high and desolate country of brown mountains, green fields, and blue lakes. With 100,000 residents, Kunming was its principal city. The streets were cobbled with blocks of stone, grooved to improve the footing on the hills, of which there were many. The houses were so low that a two-story building stood no higher than Chennault's bungalow in Waterproof. The walls were brick, the roofs tile; in the poorer homes, these were fashioned from sun-dried mud, but in the more substantial buildings they were a cool and lovely gray-green, the result of firing a clay called "Yunnan blue." Chimneys were set into the walls at a jaunty angle, for all the world like Franklin Roosevelt's cigarette holder.

The mountains guarded Kunming to the south, the north, and especially the west, and the air was so clear that every wrinkle in their flanks could be seen from the city. Poplars bordered the road to the airfield. This road, with wooden-wheeled carts creaking along it in the mist of morning, reminded Europeans of France. This was no accident, for Kunming had long served as a hill station for French Indochina (now Vietnam, Laos, and Cambodia). The colonial authorities had muscled a narrow-gauge railway over the mountains to Kunming, whose 6,200-foot altitude made it a splendid retreat from the heat and humidity of Hanoi. Along this track ran a small rubber-tired train called the Michelin. French houseboats floated on Lake Kunming, French films played in the cinemas, and French bread and wine were sold in the shops. Even the constables wore the *poilu* helmet, like an inverted coal scuttle, traditional in French colonial outposts.

The Chinese gave Chennault a house in the European district, half a mile outside the wall, near Green Lake and the Hotel Grand du Lac. Later he acquired quarters at the CAF academy nearby. This was a beautiful building with red brick walls, two stories to the eaves, with a

Nakajima Ki-27 Nate

This gnat-like aircraft with fixed landing gear was the JAAF's first monoplane fighter. To meet the army's specifications, Nakajima produced a fragile craft with no starter motor, tail wheel, pilot armor, or self-sealing fuel tanks, and armed with two rifle-caliber machine guns. The resulting fighter had a wing loading of less than 18 pounds per square foot and was virtually impossible to stall. The Ki-27 went into service in the year 2597 (1937) and was therefore known as the Type 97 Army Fighter; western pilots would call it the Nate. It made its combat debut on April 10, 1938, when Captain Tateo Kato shot down three CAF biplane fighters. (The dashing Kato commanded the 64th Sentai, one of the few JAAF fighter groups privileged to serve in China proper.) The Nates then went to Manchuria—the cold climate in which they had been designed to fight. But Claire Chennault had seen enough to warn U.S. authorities that Japan had a new fighter that "climbs like a sky rocket and manuevers like a squirrel." The specifications are for the Ki-27B in service at the outbreak of the Pacific war.

Engine: 650-hp Nakajima air-cooled radial
Crew: one
Wingspan: 37 feet 1 inch
Combat weight: 4,000 lb
Maximum range: 500 miles (greater with drop-tanks)
Top speed: 290 mph at 13,000 feet
Armament: two 7.7-mm machine guns in nose; four 55-lb bombs

ridgeline as high again above that, and a dragon-tail dormer over the entrance. The CAF had commandeered it from the Advancing Intelligence Society, a fraternity of students and professors who migrated to Kunming and were melded into Southwest Union University.

Chennault's new post was "chief flying instructor" under the unsmiling General Chou. He established a primary flight school at Yunnan-yi (now Nanhua), 100 miles west of Kunming on the road to Burma; an intermediate school at Mengzi, on the Indochina border; and an advanced school at Wu Chia Ba airport, seven miles outside Kunming. Low, dirt-floored buildings were scattered around the perimeter of Wu Chia Ba. The only military touch was a flagpole, its trapezoidal base embellished with Chinese characters urging pilots to stop the enemy at any cost: *If not with guns and bombs, then with your plane and your body.* (The cadets told each other, however, that the better procedure would be to leap into their Hawks, take off, and fly as rapidly as possible in the opposite direction.) Eighteen Americans worked for the flight school over the next two years. Among the newcomers was Skip Adair, who came out with his wife to run the primary school at Yunnan-yi. Another was a radioman named John Williams, whom Chennault had known at Maxwell Field. Six-foot-four, with an intelligent face and engaging grin, Williams had impressed Chennault with his ability to talk pilots down to a safe landing at night. He sailed first to Hong Kong, then coastwise to Indochina, and rode the "two-bit tooter" to Kunming.

The flight school was a bitter pill for Chennault, who until the Russians arrived had been Chiang Kai-shek's factotum of the air. His health suffered in the chilly winters and damp summers, and he often took to his bed with bronchitis, colds, or pleurisy, whereupon Joseph Lee, a CAF flight surgeon, dosed him with sulfa drugs. Well or not, Chennault played bridge, dominoes, mah-jongg, cribbage, and poker with his fellow instructors or civilian friends, Chinese and foreign. He carefully noted his winnings and (less often) losses in his diary. He drank too much bourbon, sometimes ending up in a wrestling match in the early hours of the morning. In season, he hunted for ducks and doves. He played tennis obsessively—seven sets even on days when he was teaching cadets to fly. And he went wenching. Chennault in China was known as an "enviable cocksman," and one biographer hints at liaisons with Rose Mok (Carney's wife or girlfriend) and the wife of another instructor.

Flying was a never-failing solace. Chennault flew beautifully, whether driving a twin-engined Douglas transport to Chongqing or stunting a Mohawk over Wu Chia Ba—the latter, especially, a pretty thing to see. "Nobody flies a fighter like the Old Man," Butch Carney said. To John Williams, Chennault seemed to be the Mohawk's animating force, rather than its Wright Cyclone engine. "When he strapped on that plane," Williams marveled, "he just seemed to *lift* it into the air."

The Japanese captured Canton in October 1938, and Hankou was abandoned soon after. Most things Chinese have an epic quality, and the battle for the lower Yangzi was no exception: by their own account, the Chinese suffered 1,102,379 casualties. (The Japanese estimate was lower but equally precise: 823,296.) In the hagiology of Nationalist China, the retreat became known as "trading space for time," though in truth the commodity exchanged was Chinese blood. The Sino-Japanese War then fell into stalemate along a no-man's-land, 1,000 miles wide and 100 miles deep. Chiang's troops tore up the railroads, destroyed the bridges, and cratered the roads—the traditional Chinese defense against invaders, in contrast to the set-piece battles at Shanghai, Nanjing, and Hankou. On the coastal side of this roadless zone were 750,000 Japanese soldiers and as many camp followers. Inland were Nationalist armies far greater in size, but woefully lacking in arms, training, leadership, supplies, and morale.

Where Chiang Kai-shek had once pretended to rule China while controlling only the lower Yangzi, now the Japanese held the valley and left the western highlands to the generalissimo. China had room for both of them, and also for the communists in Shanxi province. Between and among these rival governments, millions of peasants grew their crops, endured famine and pestilence, married, begat, and died, unaware that war was ravaging the neighboring province or even the next village.

Chiang's final capital was Chongqing in Sichuan province, north of Yunnan. He brought the wealth of the nation with him: scores of banks and government bureaus, 400 factories, 40,000 university students, millions of soldiers, and tens of millions of refugees. Before they arrived, Sichuan had a population of 50 million—a Britain or a France—and its principal city had 200,000 residents. What did they know of Chiang Kai-shek and the Sino-Japanese War? They learned soon enough, as Chongqing's population doubled and redoubled, reaching a million by May 1939, when the Japanese began to bomb them. The city's torment was witnessed by Theodore White, a young Harvard graduate working for Chiang's Ministry of Information. The Chongqingese, he wrote, were "peasants born in the Middle Ages to die in the twentieth century." The city was shrouded in mist throughout its six-month winter; when spring came, the fog lifted and the bombers came over like vultures that had waited all winter to feed. The date was May 3, 1939. Teddy White watched them: "The bombers came from the north, out of the dusk, in serene, unbroken line-abreast formation, wing tip to wing tip, and laced their pattern through the very heart of the old city." Perhaps 5,000 people burned to death—at the time, the most successful massacre in the history of aerial warfare. Twenty raids followed. The twin-engined Nells came and went without escort, for the A5M Claude was too short-legged to make the trip and return to Hankou.

Teddy White sometimes dined with Chennault at the Methodist mission in Chongqing. Like Olga Greenlaw, he noted that Chennault, "taciturn and courtly," would not take shelter when the bombers came over, but stood in the open and studied the Japanese formations "as a football coach studies films of a team he expects soon to meet in the field." The details went into Chennault's notebooks, and from there to Major James McHugh at the American embassy. A U.S. Marine Corps officer, McHugh sent them to the Navy Department, where they made no greater impression than Chennault's reports to the army.

Among the industries following Chiang Kai-shek to the west was CAMCO. Bill Pawley had loaded his machine tools and Mohawk assemblies onto flatcars and sent them down to Hong Kong, and from there by steamer to Haiphong in French Indochina. He meant to use the Michelin to take them to Kunming, but—pressured by the Japanese—the French closed the railroad to war material. So Pawley shifted everything to Rangoon, in British Burma. From there it traveled by barge and rail to Lashio, and by plane, truck, and elephant back to a lovely plateau at Loiwing, just across the Chinese border in Yunnan province.

This route was now China's lifeline. From the Burmese railhead at Lashio, an ancient mule track (used by Marco Polo in the twelfth century) was straightened, widened, and paved with stone, by hundreds of thousands of forced laborers. American journalists called it "the Burma Road"—700 twisting mountain miles from Lashio to Kunming, over mountains that rose to 9,000 feet, and through the mile-deep gorges of the Mekong and Salween rivers. Crude but lovely chain suspension bridges were thrown across the rivers; on either side, climbing in and out of the gorges, the road folded upon itself like ribbons of Christmas candy, with terrifying turnouts at the outside of each loop. From Rangoon to Chongqing, the distance was 2,000 miles.

At Loiwing, 6,000 workmen built another CAMCO factory, financed by China but owned in part by Bill Pawley, to whom the Aeronautical Commission now awarded a $5.25 million contract for 55 Mohawk fighters, 75 Vultee attack planes, and 33 CW-21 Demon interceptors—Pawley's latest export marvel, a fighter plane derived from a Curtiss racer.

After spending $4 million on the factory, Chiang hedged the bet by ordering a fleet of U.S.-built planes from Pat Patterson. Chennault regularly flew to Chongqing to work on this contract, which finally included 120 trainers, 25 Vought dive bombers, and 54 Seversky P-35s. The total was $8.8 million, making it the largest aircraft contract ever awarded by China. But Pawley (as Patterson told the story) sabotaged the deal, and in the process bankrupted Seversky. In the end, only the trainers reached Rangoon, and they arrived too late, as Harvey Greenlaw discovered when he shifted his base of operations to Southeast Asia. He and Olga abandoned everything in Hengyang but their personal baggage, which they loaded into a 1928 DeSoto coupe and drove to Hanoi. From there they made their way to Rangoon, where Harvey tried to set up an assembly plant for Patterson's trainers. He found the British as nervous as the French, as mesmerized by Hitler's aggression in Europe, and as reluctant to offend Japan in the Pacific. No, Greenlaw could not assemble CAF planes in Burma. The Ryans and North Americans remained in their crates on the Rangoon wharf, among the growing piles of war material bound north to Lashio and Kunming.

Still hedging, Chiang asked Pawley to scout the possibilities of hiring American pilots for the CAF. (If war broke out in Europe, the Russian "volunteers" would almost certainly be withdrawn.) The presentation was made by Captain Bruce Leighton, formerly of the U.S. Navy but now a vice-president of Pawley's personal holding company, called Intercontinent. Leighton wangled an interview with Admiral Harold Stark, the chief of naval operations, in which he argued that it would be in America's best interest to frustrate the Japanese occupation of China. This could be done, Leighton said, by giving Chiang Kai-shek an air force of 100 fighters and 100 bombers. China would also need fifty American pilots, to be supplemented by the cadets Chennault had trained in Kunming. The cost would be $25 million, which China would borrow from American banks. Leighton promised to handle the entire affair as a commercial enterprise, "without any direct participation by the United States Government."

Chennault was also in Washington at this time, but apparently knew nothing of Leighton's presentation. His contract provided for a month's vacation in the year, and in the winter of 1939–1940 he took all that was due him and flew to San Francisco on the new "Clipper" service of Pan American Airways—a five-day, island-hopping voyage across the Pacific.

He visited his family, hunted for waterfowl in the Louisiana marshes, and with his son John (now an air force pilot) toured the Curtiss-Wright factory in Buffalo. He then went to Washington, where his only certain activities were to brief an army intelligence officer on the CAF and to ask about his chances for returning to active duty. (As he told the story, he was offered a job towing aerial targets for coastal gunners.) Next he joined Bill Pawley and Bruce Leighton for a tour of aircraft factories in Southern California. On February 1, they took off on a flight that revealed, with chilling clarity, how matters stood between the grizzled warrior and the dapper businessman, who had often clashed over China's aircraft purchases. After the plane took off from Los Angeles, the carburetors iced up and a crash seemed likely, as Pawley pointed out. Too bad, Chennault replied; he would hate to have his body found in the same wreckage as Pawley's.

It did not come to that. The pilot made a forced landing, cleared the carburetors, and flew on to San Francisco, where Chennault caught the Pan Am flying boat back to Hong Kong. From there he made his way home on the Douglas transports of CNAC, the China National Aviation Corporation.

That spring, German divisions overran Denmark and Norway, then Holland, Belgium, and Luxembourg. The French army and a British expeditionary force rushed into the Low Countries to stop them, only to have German tanks burst through the supposedly impassable Ardennes forest behind them. Cut off, 300,000 British soldiers were taken off the beach at Dunkirk, leaving France to swift and humiliating defeat. For all practical purposes, the war on the continent was lost in nineteen days, leaving Britain as the only country still opposing Adolf Hitler's hegemony in Europe. With patience and guile, President Roosevelt began to maneuver the United States into the position of Britain's savior.

Chiang Kai-shek quickly took advantage of the new thinking, sending his brother-in-law to Washington to speed the flow of American aid to China. Soong Tse-ven (T. V. to his friends) was the most endearing member of a large, clever, and unscrupulous family. Like Madame Chiang, his sister, he got along especially well with Americans. He was a Harvard man; he was more at home speaking English than Mandarin; and he was as neat as a doll, hair cut short and combed straight back, ears tucked against his head, and thin-rimmed spectacles reflecting the light. He wasted no time ensconcing himself in the hearts of Washington power brokers. On July 9 he met with Henry Morgenthau, Roosevelt's portly, balding treasury secretary. On the table, with luncheon, was a proposal that the United States lend China $140 million to stabilize her currency, improve the Burma Road, and buy military supplies, including 300 fighter planes and 100 light bombers. The Pawley-Leighton proposal had been doubled, and there was no more talk of borrowing money from banks.

Soong also cultivated Thomas Corcoran, Lauchlin Currie, and Joseph Alsop. The first was a lawyer, lobbyist, and member of Roosevelt's "kitchen cabinet" of informal advisers. The second was an economist and White House aide. The third was a bright young columnist published each week in seventy-four newspapers. Joe Alsop was also related to Eleanor Roosevelt, hence to the president—not an insignificant qualification in prewar Washington, where the work got done through a network of friendships, kinships, and raw talent. Morgenthau, for example, routinely made decisions that belonged to the war and state departments, and the pixieish, persuasive Tommy Corcoran sometimes overruled Morgenthau when it came to determining the size of the federal budget.

The United States had loaned China $25 million in 1939 and $45 million in 1940, to be repaid with exports of tin, tungsten, and tung oil. The transactions were handled by the Universal Trading Corporation of New York City, its staff composed mostly of bureaucrats detached from the government for that purpose. Though forbidden by the China Trade Act from dealing in war material, Universal was clearly the purchasing agent for a nation at war: 1,000 portable ten-watt radios, 48,000 scalpels, 72,000 forceps, 4 million blankets, 6 million yards of khaki cloth. . . .

To these mundane supplies—bound for Rangoon, Lashio, and the Burma Road—T. V. Soong was determined to add American military planes and American pilots to fly them.

Every day, sometimes twice a day, Japanese bombers roared up the Yangzi from Hankou to Chongqing. Each of the sleek, gray, twin-engined Nells was freighted with 1,000 pounds of explosives and fragmentation shards, and they were sometimes supplemented by army bombers—Mitsubishi *Ki*-21s—carrying twice the load. "This thing . . .

is beyond all description in its brutality," reported the American ambassador, almost incoherent in his dismay. "These daily visits of a hundred or more bombers swinging back and forth over a city of helpless people who cower for hours in dugouts where many are overcome just by the bad air, accompanied by the general migration into the country up over the hills, old and young, mothers carrying babies under the hot sun, up, up the hills. . . ." Yet the CAF exacted a steady toll on the raiders. Nine Nells were shot down and 300 were damaged—nearly 10 percent, the level regarded as prohibitive in Japanese service.

This problem was solved with the introduction of a long-range escort fighter. The Mitsubishi A6M was a slender, cigar-shaped monoplane with an enclosed cockpit and retractable landing gear. It was almost as nimble as the Claude, but it could fly faster and farther, and it was armed with two 20-mm cannon in addition to the usual rifle-caliber machine guns. In August, half a dozen A6Ms destroyed fifty-seven CAF interceptors over Chongqing, so easily that a navy pilot boasted: "When we chase the enemy, we must be very careful not to get in front of him!" The triumphant fighter was dubbed *Zero-sen,* for the year 2600, as the Japanese reckoned 1940.

In September, Japan took advantage of the new order in Europe by occupying northern French Indochina, on the border of Yunnan province. The Japanese now controlled the Michelin, some of the world's most productive rubber plantations, immense stores of rice . . . and Gia Lam airport outside Hanoi. From here, on September 30, navy bombers raided Kunming for the first time. Next day they destroyed the intermediate flight school at Mengzi. Six days later, they came out of the overcast to hit Kunming again: twenty-seven Nells and seven of the new long-range fighters. This was Chennault's first sight of the Zero, which he noted was "far superior" to the Japanese fighters he had observed in the Yangzi valley.

Later that week, Chennault received orders to report to Chongqing. He went out to Wu Chia Ba on Sunday morning to arrange for a seat on the next day's CNAC transport, only to have the warning net report another Japanese formation on its way: twenty-seven Nells, nine single-engined bombers, and half a dozen Zeros. Chennault fled the field in a battered Plymouth, the property of the new flight school commander, Colonel Wang Shu-ming. (General Chou had been restored to favor in Chongqing.) When bombs exploded on the road, they took shelter in a ditch. The raid lasted three hours, breaking plaster in the U.S. consulate, damaging Southwest Union University and the cotton mills, and wrecking buildings in the northern residential district, including Chennault's house. No CAF fighters managed to get into the air. When Chennault finally climbed out of the ditch—"literally covered with mud, blood and other items"—he snapped an order to John Williams: rebuild the Yunnan warning net so that it could be used to direct fighters against the enemy formations. This would be Williams's task for the next six months.

With General Chou again directing the Aeronautical Commission, the generalissimo intended to send Mao Pang-chu to Washington as air adviser to T. V. Soong. And to advise General Mao—who better than Chennault? The idea came from Soong, who had cabled on September 27: "It would assist in convincing authorities here if program . . . were supported by Colonel Chennault." Thus the airman's summons to Chongqing. He spent several days in the capital, but if the Washington assignment came up, he did not mention it in his diary. (Chennault was maddeningly enigmatic about important events, while detailing his victories at tennis and mah-jongg.) Certainly the generalissimo pumped him on the subject of American planes and pilots, for on October 18 Chiang had a proposal for the U.S. ambassador. "Japanese bombing goes unchallenged," Chiang explained in his grave fashion, "and the people are filled with disquiet." Therefore the United States must send China a Special Air Unit of 500 planes and pilots. This would relieve the pressure upon Chongqing and enable China to carry the war to the enemy's home islands, effecting a "fundamental solution" to the problem of Japanese aggression.

Bruce Leighton in Washington was an elusive presence, but he was working along the same line, to judge by a letter from the secretary of the navy to the secretary of state. "I am told," Frank Knox wrote Cordell Hull, "there are a considerable number of American aviators who would be glad to volunteer their services to China . . . if they could be absolved from any penalty for such action. Is it at all possible that we can handle this matter . . . as we have handled the same situation with respect to young men volunteering for service in Great Britain[?]" In other words, discharge the pilots from U.S. service and let them travel as civilians to a neutral country (Canada, in the case of the RAF) where they would join the foreign air force without taking a formal oath of allegiance.

In Kunming, Chennault was nursing a cold. On October 19—the

same day Secretary Knox dictated his letter to Cordell Hull—he was again summoned to Chongqing. This time, he paid off his servants before he set out for Wu Chia Ba, suggesting that he did not intend to return for some time. Two days later he dined with Chiang Kai-shek and General Mao. "Ordered back to U.S. for duty with Dr. T. V. Soong," he wrote in his diary. Late the following afternoon, a CNAC Douglas took them to Hong Kong, there to catch the Pan Am Clipper to the United States.

The Japanese army air force had now replaced the navy at Gia Lam airport, its mission to bomb the "aid-to-Chiang route" from the Burma border to Kunming. On October 26, fifty-nine Mitsubishi *Ki*-21s virtually demolished the new CAMCO factory at Loiwing. Dozens of half-completed Demons and Vultees were destroyed, along with some of the trainers brokered by Pat Patterson and since moved to Loiwing for assembly. But Bill Pawley had a genius for turning adversity into opportunity. He salvaged the machinery and aircraft assemblies and shipped them to Bangalore in India, where he reconstituted himself as Hindustan Aircraft Ltd., building planes for the Royal Air Force. (Indeed, he seems to have sold the RAF some of the same Mohawks and Vultees already purchased by China.) The Loiwing factory was rebuilt as a maintenance and repair facility for the CAF.

Pawley was about Chennault's age, though he looked a decade younger. A photograph showed him togged out in pinstripe suit, boutonniere, folded handkerchief, and what appeared to be a diamond stickpin—an impressive man, though perhaps a bit flashy. The British took to him, anyhow. They not only let him set up a factory in India, but they gave him what they had refused Harvey Greenlaw: permission to set up a plant in Burma to assemble the sixty-six North American and Ryan trainers that were still in their crates on the Rangoon wharf.

Chennault and Mao joined the infant China lobby at the end of October, beginning with dinner at T. V. Soong's home in Chevy Chase. Then they went to work in the Washington apartment of Arthur Young, financial adviser to Chiang's government, with Mrs. Young banished to the next room to preserve the secrecy of their discussions. (She heard most of what was said, nevertheless, for Young and Mao had to speak loudly if Chennault was to understand them.) They worked up a request for 250 air-cooled fighters, which Chennault knew and trusted from his own experience, plus 100 fighters with liquid-cooled engines—the type favored in Europe because it lent itself to a streamlined nose, providing more speed for the same horsepower. They would also ask for 150 bombers, 10 transports, and 190 training planes, plus parts, gasoline, antiaircraft guns, and materials to build airfields and landing strips. The plan also called for 350 flight instructors and technicians . . . but no pilots, unless the instructors were to be understood as such. (It is a curious feature of these dealings that the pilot Chennault seemed mostly interested in hardware, while the salesman Pawley focused on recruiting men.) T. V. Soong presented the revised shopping list to the President's Liaison Committee on November 25.

By the end of 1940, warplanes were pouring out of American factories at a prodigious rate—ten a day in the case of the Curtiss-Wright plant in Buffalo. (By contrast, Mitsubishi could build just one A6M Zero a day.) Roosevelt's "arsenal of democracy" had set out to build 6,000 military aircraft in 1940, 18,000 in 1941, and 50,000 in 1942, or more planes than all other countries of the world combined. They were destined in the first place for Britain, her own factories crippled by German bombing, labor strife, and outmoded facilities. In October 1940, the British had 11,000 planes under construction in the United States; in November, Prime Minister Churchill asked for 12,000 more; and in December he would request an additional 2,000 planes *per month*. After the RAF came the U.S. military, which was in the enviable position of taking small quantities of each design, after improvements had been made to British specifications, and after the unit price was driven down by British orders. Leftover planes were allocated to Allied air forces in the Pacific and to such potential allies as Sweden, Greece, and Brazil. In this pecking order, China had no priority at all. The Sino-Japanese War was regarded in the United States as a sideshow—"yellow man killing yellow man," as *Time* magazine put it—compared to the epic conflict among the white nations of Europe. It was difficult to get excited about the occupation of China when France had fallen, or about the bombing of Chongqing when London was threatened with destruction.

While his genial brother-in-law made the rounds in Washington, Chiang Kai-shek played the tough cop from Chongqing, warning Roosevelt that the Japanese were sponsoring a new and unfriendly government in Nanjing. In 1926, Wang Ching-wei had been a left-wing contender for the leadership of Nationalist China; losing to Chiang, he went on to serve him in a series of mostly ceremonial posts. In 1940, he defected to the Japanese, who set him up as head of the Reorganized National Government of China. If Wang's puppet regime attracted widespread support, it would free Japan to move south, seizing oil from the Dutch Indies and perhaps joining hands with Germany and Italy across the Indian subcontinent. The Pacific was not *that* much of a sideshow, and Roosevelt told his advisers to work up a loan for China. He also sent Lauchlin Currie to see the clever and useful Tommy Corcoran, now working out of an office at 1511 K Street, four blocks from the White House.

Corcoran's profession was an honorable one for the time, though it later fell into disrepute: he fixed things. He was expensive (he supposedly earned $1 million within a year of leaving the White House) but he gave value for the money. Nobody else had so many and such useful friendships in government, or maintained them so well. Corcoran eagerly performed such favors as the one Currie now asked of him: "to check with my friends on Capitol Hill—particularly the Senate side—and predict the reaction . . . if the president sent modest aid to China just to forestall Chiang's surrender. I reported back to Currie: there'd be very little trouble as things then stood and were likely to stand in the near future."

He also talked to Chennault. "If he had left in the first ten minutes," Corcoran mused, "I would have written him off as a fanatic." By the end of an hour, however, the aviator convinced the fixer, and word went back to Roosevelt that they had found a promising weapon to use against Japan. Corcoran warned, however, that Chennault must be allowed to run his own show. Their relationship, he said in an analogy that managed to flatter both men, would be that of Elizabeth I to Sir Francis Drake. The president was convinced: "Roosevelt sent back orders for me to take Chennault around town and introduce him to . . . influential men who could keep their mouths shut."

One such man was General George Marshall. On December 12, Chennault told the army chief of staff what he knew about the Mitsubishi Zero. Marshall was impressed, and next day he told Cordell Hull about the "new fast pursuit plane [that] has grounded all the Chinese Air Force." Marshall also warned army commanders in Hawaii and the Philippines about the Zero's capabilities, but they paid no attention, even to such an exalted source. If Chennault's description was to be believed, the new Japanese fighter was better than anything in the U.S. inventory—but that could not be. Everyone knew that the Japanese could only build inferior copies of western machines.

China could not export enough tung oil, tin, and tungsten to pay for the aid T. V. Soong was requesting. A cash loan would be needed, so Henry Morgenthau called his staff together on November 29. "The president just called me," he said—a man whose feet had been held to the fire. "He is worried about China and he is evidently worried about something going on between Wang and Chiang, and he wants me to make a . . . loan of $50 million to the Chinese in the next twenty-four hours."

On cue, T. V. Soong appeared next day, blinking benignly through his round lenses: the nice cop. Morgenthau haggled valiantly for the U.S. Treasury. "Well now," he began, "let me ask you, how much money have you in mind?

"General Chiang asked for between $200 million and $300 million, that is what he asked for."

"What will you take?"

"Well, we are not choosers, Mr. Secretary."

"But as to take care of the immediate situation, say for six months—"

"I should imagine $100 million," Soong said.

"I see. Well now, let me ask you this, if you will tell me this. Who else in Washington have you told this to, I mean officially?

"Of course, I saw the secretary of state. . . . I handed him a memorandum to be presented to the president."

Morgenthau did not like this. "Approximately what is in it?" he asked.

"Well, just two things in it," Soong replied. "One is for airplanes and the second is for stabilization."

"Well now, was there any time factor in there?"

"It is very urgent," Soong said, "because of the Japanese recognition of Wang Ching-wei." Let us not forget the tough cop in Chongqing: the generalissimo would have to come to terms with Wang, if the United States dragged its feet or made a demeaning counterproposal.

Morgenthau understood that they had reached the bottom line. "What would you call a minimum that might be helpful?" he asked.

"I should say $100 million," Soong repeated.

"Okay," said Morgenthau.

So it was settled, except for the problem of where to find the planes. Not even this was outside Morgenthau's jurisdiction, and a solution began to emerge at a meeting the following Sunday. Curtiss-Wright had contracted to build 630 liquid-cooled Tomahawk fighters for the Royal Air Force by March 1941, at which time the factory would switch to a more advanced model. But Curtiss had enough parts to build a few hundred additional fighters, and it wanted to do just that, to use up the inventory and keep the Buffalo plant running at full capacity. Thus, China's needs could be met simply by extending the production run. But Morgenthau did not mention this possibility to Soong when they met later the same day, December 8. Instead they talked bombers:

> After lunch at the White House, T. V. Soong was with me going back in the car and . . . I said that I had read General Chiang Kai-shek's memorandum. . . . I said, "Well, his asking for 500 planes is like asking for 500 stars." I then said that we might get him planes by 1942, but what did he think of the idea of some long range bombers with the understanding that they were to be used to bomb Tokyo and other Japanese cities? Well, to say he was enthusiastic is putting it mildly.

Enthusiastic, indeed. Soong understood, if Morgenthau did not, the difference between the twin-engined bombers Chennault had requested—defensive weapons, really—and the long-range missions now under discussion. He checked with the generalissimo, and within a week came back with a higher bid. What China really needed was that marvel of American aeronautical engineering, the B-17 Flying Fortress, so jealously guarded that not even the British had been able to get their hands on it. Chiang raised the bid again in a December 16 telegram to Morgenthau: "I am most anxious to acquire as many of your latest Flying Fortresses as you could spare . . . complemented by a proportionate number of pursuits and medium bombers." Thus armed, he would not only bomb Japan but recapture Canton and Hankou, forestalling a Japanese move against the British fortress at Singapore.

The Flying Fortresses came up at a December 19 meeting between Roosevelt and the department secretaries most concerned: Morgenthau for the treasury, Hull for the State Department, Knox for the navy, and Henry Stimson for the army. (Mrs. Stimson called this inner circle the

Plus Four.) They studied a map supplied by Soong showing 136 airfields in southern and eastern China, some in Japanese-occupied territory, and one just 600 miles from Nagasaki and Sasebo navy base. "The President was delighted," Morgenthau told Soong next day. But he wanted to discuss the details with a CAF representative: "This Colonel Chennault," he said, "where is he?"

"He is here now in Washington," Soong replied.

Morgenthau then related his conversation with the president: "I said, and I hope you will back me up, that if they could get [pilots] who knew how to fly these four-engine bombers, that China would be glad to pay up to $1,000 a month in United States dollars. Was that too high?"

"No," said Soong. "Not at all." Money was no object—after all, it was American money.

The China lobby assembled at Morgenthau's house on Saturday evening, December 21. The treasury secretary directed his questions to Soong, who deferred to General Mao, who deferred to Chennault. In this roundabout fashion, it was agreed that American crews would fly the B-17s to the Philippines, where the pilots and bombardiers would be released from active duty and paid $1,000 a month to take them to China . . . and eventually to Japan. Each B-17 would be accompanied by five American mechanics, but the CAF would provide gunners and radiomen. Then Morgenthau, his pince-nez glasses sparkling, advanced an idea of his own: "inasmuch as the Japanese cities were all made of just wood and paper," why not use incendiary bombs? A splendid idea, Chennault told him. In fact, Morgenthau's plan had the additional advantage (incendiaries being lighter than high explosives) of allowing the B-17s to carry more gasoline and thus to penetrate deeper into Japanese airspace.

Let there be no doubt of what was under discussion: that U.S. planes and U.S. pilots, in the employ of China, should set the Japanese home islands on fire. That the scheme got no further was due to the army chief of staff. Tall, aristocratic, and everyone's candidate for Washington's most honorable man, George Marshall on this occasion was moved less by principle than by logistics: he wanted the B-17s to go to Britain.

Stimson also had second thoughts. The bombing scheme was "half-baked," the army secretary decided, so he asked Marshall, Knox, and Morgenthau to his home that Sunday—a beautiful afternoon, virtually a second Indian summer—"to get some mature brains into it." The brains were Marshall's, and the treasury secretary immediately capitulated to the general's cool logic. By Monday morning, only fighter planes were still on the table.

Cordell Hull convened the next meeting in his office at the State Department. It was attended by the Plus Four and assorted civilian and military advisers, including General Marshall and Admiral Stark. As usual, Morgenthau opened the discussion. Curtiss-Wright, he said, could build 300 extra Tomahawks (P-40s, as they were called in U.S. service) in the spring of 1941. How should they be spread around? Like boys choosing sides in a baseball game, the great men haggled, their words recorded by a secretary who was clearly dazed by the possibilities:

> Secretary Hull suggested that . . . the 300 P-40's should be divided 150 to China, 120 to South America, and 30 for the Greeks. General Marshall said that he had a list of the various South American countries showing how the War Department thought planes should be allocated in that area. Secretary Knox stated that 150 would have to go to the British. To which Secretary Stimson added that the war was in Europe and the Far East, not in South America; therefore the planes would go to the British and the Chinese. . . .
>
> [I]t was resolved that the 300 P-40's should be divided equally between the British and the Chinese. . . .   [But] if the British gave up current deliveries to the Chinese, then the British should receive planes on a two for one basis. In other words, the British would give up to the Chinese fifty in January, twenty-five in February, and twenty-five in March, making a total of 100, but she would get back 300 later in the spring, giving her a net gain of 200. Secretary Morgenthau said he would get in touch with the British right away and ask them to place the order.

Actually, the RAF had already agreed to buy the fighters. Roosevelt approved the deal that same afternoon, December 23, and at 5:30 P.M. Morgenthau met again with the British to nail down such details as where the GFE—government-furnished equipment—was to come from. Warplanes were customarily purchased without engines, guns, or electronics. In this case, the engines would be diverted from another British order. Some machine guns could come from U.S. Army stores, Morgenthau thought, and the British would cannibalize the rest from fighters no longer fit for combat. As for radios, the RAF preferred to install its own, operating as it did on a frequency different from that of the U.S. Army. Neither Morgenthau nor the British thought to raise the question of GFE for the planes to be diverted to China.

4

Three Instruction and Training Units

January–July 1941

Sometime after Christmas, Chennault went to Buffalo "to see the Curtiss-Wright people and negotiate for the planes and see their performance." This may have been his first view of the Tomahawk, though he knew the airframe as well as his face in the mirror: it was his old friend, the Mohawk, fitted with a new engine, heavier guns, and protection for the pilot and fuel tanks. From the moment the U.S. Army had adopted the P-36, it was outclassed by liquid-cooled fighters coming on line in Europe: the Messerschmitt 109 in Germany, the Hawker Hurricane in Britain. The army therefore asked Curtiss to beef up its plane. Chief designer Donovan Berlin obliged by replacing its air-cooled engine (twelve pistons arranged around the propeller shaft like the spokes of a wheel) with an Allison V-1710 built by General Motors. The horsepower was the same, but the Allison's cylinders were arranged one behind the other, allowing Berlin to give the fighter a streamlined nose, greatly increasing its speed. At the same time, the appearance changed radically. Where the P-36 led off with the stubby, no-nonsense look typical of air-cooled fighters, the P-40 was as slender as a fish, its lines broken only by the air scoop beneath and behind the propeller cone. Ultimately, all engines are cooled by the outside air, but the Allison had a two-stage cooling system, the heat first soaked up by a bath of ethylene glycol (trade name Prestone) then dissipated through a radiator located in a stream of force-fed air. Berlin wanted the air scoop on the plane's belly, but moved it forward when a Curtiss-Wright executive thought it looked better there. The result was to give the plane a distinct *face*, the propeller spinner suggesting a nose, the air scoop a mouth.

Chennault did not like liquid-cooled engines, for a single bullet could pierce the Prestone tank or radiator, letting the coolant run out and disabling the plane. But he appreciated the tradeoff between frontal area and speed, and in his November want list he had asked for 100 liquid-cooled fighters, either the P-40 or the P-51 Mustang under development at the North American company. And he liked other features of the new design. The original P-40 boasted two fifty-caliber (half-inch) machine guns in its nose and two rifle-caliber machine guns in the wings. The Royal Air Force bought several hundred of this model and gave it the fighting name of Tomahawk. The British then asked for modifications: two more wing guns, a bullet-resistant windshield, half-inch armor plate behind the pilot, and a wrap-around membrane to keep gasoline from spilling out if the fuel tank were hit. This was the Tomahawk II—in U.S. service, the P-40B. By the time Chennault reached Buffalo, another refinement had been made: the fuel tanks had an interior membrane, which did a better job of stopping leaks. This was the Tomahawk IIB, which the U.S. Army would adopt as the P-40C.

The improvements added 800 pounds to the design weight and cut the rated speed to 340 mph. The rate of climb suffered, too, which was especially hard for Chennault to accept: his theory of "defensive pursuit" required a fast-climbing interceptor. A worse flaw, from the pilot's point of view, was that most of the extra weight was in front of the intended center of gravity; if the plane stalled, it could go into a spin so vicious that it seemed to be tumbling end over end. Still, the overweight Tomahawk IIB had one peculiar virtue. Nose pointed earthward, it was the fastest military aircraft in the world, with 500 mph possible in an all-out power dive.

Sprawling across twenty-eight acres in Buffalo, the new Curtiss-Wright factory applied Henry Ford's assembly-line principle to the building of aircraft. Most of its first-year production went to the Royal Air Force, though the British were not fond of the Tomahawk. Since its Allison engine was not supercharged, the plane was not much use above 20,000 feet, and combat at 30,000 feet was common over Britain. The Tomahawks therefore went to the Mediterranean theater, where fighting usually took place at lower altitudes.

Curtiss P-40C Tomahawk

This low-winged fighter with its distinctive profile was an update of the radial-engined Mohawk. Like all American fighters, it was intended to support the infantry and provide coastal defense, and thus was designed to "slug it out, absorb gunfire and fly home." In this environment, no American engine was available with a supercharger, meaning that the P-40 had to do its fighting below 20,000 feet. At low altitudes, it would prove the equal of such rivals as the Messerschmitt 109 and the Mitsubishi A6M Zero, if a pilot played from its strong points and refused to match the Japanese pilots turn for turn. Curtiss built 524 of the small-mouthed H81 series for the U.S. Army and 1,180 for the Royal Air Force, with many of the latter diverted to Russia, to Commonwealth air forces, and to China. Specifications are for the Tomahawk IIB, sold to Universal Trading Corporation under Curtiss designation H81-A3. Except for the paint job, the "armourglass" windscreen, and the caliber of the guns, this model was identical to the army's P-40C.

Engine: 1,000-hp Allison liquid-cooled in-line
Crew: one
Wingspan: 37 feet 4 inches
Combat weight: 8,000 lb
Maximum range: 700 miles
Top speed: 340 mph at 12,000 feet
Armament: two .50-caliber machine guns in the nose, four 7.92-mm or .303-caliber machine guns in the wings

---

As part of the deal for the Tomahawks, China had agreed to take the planes just as they came off the Curtiss assembly line. So their topsides were painted in RAF desert camouflage—alternating bands of tan and green, called "sand and spinach"—and their undersides pale blue. More significant, they had no wing guns, radios, or gunsights, items that were to have been provided by the Royal Air Force in North Africa.

The 100 airframes cost $4.5 million. In violation of the China Trade Act, the bill was paid by Universal Trading Corporation in New York. By this time, General Mao had flown back to China, taking Lauchlin Currie with him. (The White House aide, whose high starched collars, rimless spectacles, and thinning hair gave him the look of a clerk in a

Dickens novel, was to tour Nationalist China on behalf of President Roosevelt—his expenses paid, however, by Chiang Kai-shek.) This left Chennault to work out the details of acquiring the Tomahawks, equipping them, and finding people to fly and maintain them. He did not leave much of a paper trail, but in January he drafted a table of organization calling for 100 pilots and 150 ground crewmen. "American pilots," he argued, "cannot operate efficiently and successfully in China unless supported by American technical and clerical personnel." It was the first time anybody had raised the question of who would staff the Special Air Unit.

Bill Pawley must have seen that memo. He certainly knew about the deal for the Tomahawks, and as Curtiss-Wright representative in China he expected to receive a 10 percent commission on the sale. He also wanted CAMCO/Intercontinent (he used the names interchangeably) to assemble the planes in Burma. Indeed, who else could do it? Twelve miles north of Rangoon, his brother Edward had leased a plot of land at Mingaladon Cantonment, brought ninety Chinese technicians and their American foremen down from Loiwing, and was even now assembling the trainers left in Rangoon by Harvey Greenlaw. Ed's operation adjoined the runways of Mingaladon airport—Burma's largest, defended by the Royal Air Force—making it the obvious place to assemble the China-bound Tomahawks. Logically, too, CAMCO/Intercontinent would be hired to recruit American military personnel. On February 18, Bill Pawley cabled his brother in Rangoon:

> Negotiating extensive training program requiring employment by CAMCO of approximately . . . 100 pilots 150 technical including mechanics clerks radio operators doctors nurses. . . . [General Mao] possibly familiar with part of program. Diplomatically ascertain progress he is making in providing facilities such as quarters fields but do not disclose any information. One hundred P-40's purchased 35 being shipped immediately balance soon. Intercontinent signed contract covering assembly and flight test Rangoon. Special revolving fund being arranged New York payment of expenses this program.

If a contract existed, no trace of it survives, and it is curious that Pawley's manpower figures were identical to Chennault's. Was he really negotiating, or was he simply catching up with events?

The China-bound Tomahawks were taken at random from the Curtiss assembly line. A fuselage and engine were fitted into one crate, and the wing assembly, tail, and propeller into another. Railway flatcars took them to Weehawken, New Jersey, where they were loaded into the hold of a Norwegian freighter. The ship cleared Ambrose Light on February 19, bound for Rangoon via South Africa and the Indian Ocean. The easterly route involved three full months at sea, and T. V. Soong asked the State Department if the rest of the planes could be sent in U.S. bottoms through the Panama Canal. Impossible, he was told. Burma was a British colony, Britain was at war, and the Neutrality Act prohibited U.S.-flag carriers from touching at the port of a belligerent.

At the Treasury Department, Henry Morgenthau learned that his obligations would not end with the shipment of the planes. On February 21, a dreary Thursday in the capital, his telephone rang just after 9 A.M. Tommy Corcoran's voice came on the line, at once urgent, confidential, and soothing. After some preliminary banter, he got down to business: "Soong has asked . . . me to represent him in some things. . . . He said that this is not a trading business, this has to do with things after you get the planes." He had already broached the matter with Morgenthau's people, he said, and they had agreed that the best course was to bypass Universal Trading Corporation and its restrictions on military aid. What was needed was another company, controlled by Corcoran instead of some wheeler-dealer who might "bring all kinds of influence to bear and who might not play ball."

"Well, all those things are true, Tom," Morgenthau replied, "but you don't know what the nature of it is?"

"Well, may I talk on this line?"

"Yes, you can."

"What Soong wants me to do," Corcoran said, "is to help him recruit pilots. What he really wants me to do is to go over and wrangle for him with the army and the navy to have them practically order certain men to enlist in the Chinese Air Force."

Corcoran's company was China Defense Supplies, located in the Chinese Embassy. T. V. Soong was chairman, and Roosevelt's elderly uncle, Frederic Delano, signed on as its "honorary counselor." The work was done by youngsters from the Ivy League network: "My brother David took a leave of absence from Sterling Drug to become president," Corcoran recalled. (Sterling was one of the companies that employed him as a fixer.) "A friendly and influential congressman loaned me William Brennan to serve as our full time congressional liaison. . . .

The Marine Corps supplied an intelligence officer and Harvard Law man, Major Quinn [Shaughnessy], to be our eyes and ears around the War Department. . . . Finally, there was [Whiting] Willauer, my brother Howie's roommate at Exeter, Princeton, and Harvard Law." Tommy Corcoran was not on the payroll, but there was no doubt in anybody's mind that he was the man to know at CDS. "I remained nominally only the organizer of the firm," he said. "By design I took no title, and only earned a modest $5,000 fee for putting the company together."

Returning from China at the end of March, Lauchlin Currie leaked the "Special Air Program" to Joe Alsop. China needed a few dozen bombers and 200 fighter planes, wrote the syndicated columnist. "With this comparative handful of supplies," Alsop explained, "the Chinese think they could knock spots out of the Japanese invaders." Furthermore, they could "drop incendiary bombs on Japan's concentrated, almost undefended paper and matchwood industrial areas." There was no mention of who would fly the planes.

Currie took Chennault to see General Arnold at the War Department. Even with a presidential assistant in the room, Hap Arnold would not let his pilots go. It was not just that he preferred to have them flying American aircraft; he needed them, even more, to train 30,000 aviation cadets in 1941, as the U.S. Army geared up for the war that was sure to come. Chennault and Currie fared no better with Rear Admiral John Towers at the navy's Bureau of Aeronautics.

Tommy Corcoran had better luck behind the scenes. One Harvard man to another, he sent the president a copy of A. E. Housman's "Epitaph on an Army of Mercenaries," who "saved the sum of things for pay." As Corcoran recalled in later years: "If Roosevelt was troubled by the soiled label that Chennault's irregulars might wear, he was moved by the poem's wisdom. It bolstered his determination to act as forcefully as political constraints allowed." With the president's blessing, Corcoran met with the secretaries of war and the navy and promised that Chennault would not pillage any one service but would take a few men from each. The agreement was never more formal than that. Frank Knox approved a letter authorizing China's recruiters to visit navy bases, and Henry Stimson authorized Major General George Brett to provide the same courtesy at army airfields.

At the Colt factory in Hartford, Connecticut, Morgenthau's scouts had located 132 machine guns chambered for the 7.92-mm cartridge commonly used in Asia. Universal Trading Corporation bought these weapons, and after some arm-twisting the British agreed to release some of their own .303-caliber Brownings—altogether, enough wing guns to equip fifty Tomahawks. Universal bought 100 two-way radios from RCA, of a type intended to be installed in civilian sportsplanes, and it bought 150 Allison engines from General Motors (those installed in the Tomahawks at Buffalo, plus fifty spares). Universal also had to pay the U.S. Army for the fifty-caliber nose guns provided at the factory. With ammunition, the GFE seems to have doubled the price of the fighters: Universal spent $9.3 million for aircraft in the first half of 1941, and China bought no other planes during this time.

The guns reached Weehawken in time to accompany the second lot of Tomahawks, which were scheduled to sail in March. But Bill Pawley intervened, threatening to stop the shipment unless he was paid his $450,000 commission. Curtiss-Wright refused, arguing that Pawley had not brokered the planes, and that anyhow the payment would exceed its profit on the deal. Adjudicating the quarrel would have taken months, so Morgenthau called the principals to his office on April 1 and knocked heads together. Pawley withdrew his claim in exchange for $250,000 to be paid by the Chinese, plus a contract to assemble the planes in Burma. All obstacles cleared, the second lot of Tomahawks sailed for the long voyage around South Africa, and the final shipment followed soon after.

On April 15, CAMCO/Intercontinent was further employed as recruiter and fiscal agent for the Special Air Unit—not that any such organization was specified. Rather, Bill Pawley and T. V. Soong seemed to have joined hands in an educational enterprise:

> The [Chinese] Government intends to establish three advanced instruction and training units, each . . . equipped substantially as follows: eighteen American active trainers plus 50 percent reserves, plus necesssary complement of ground transport, field repair equipment, night landing floodlights, portable radio communication sets, clerical equipment, etc. The operation of these units in China shall be under the immediate direction of an American supervisor.

For "advanced instruction and training unit," read fighter squadron. For "active trainer," read Tomahawk IIB. And for "American supervisor," read Claire Chennault, though Pawley might well have refused to sign the contract if he had known about that understanding.

The youngest Pawley brother, Eugene, put a want ad in the *Los Angeles Times* for "aviation people for work overseas." Among those who responded were Byron Glover, a burly test pilot, and Walter Pentecost, a balding Allison engine specialist. They signed up at Vail Field, California, after an interview with two CAMCO foremen. (Pentecost's contract, when he received it, turned out to be with Intercontinent, indicating how porous were the boundaries between Pawley's holding company and the manufacturing enterprise he owned in partnership with the Chinese.) Later they met Gene and Bill Pawley, who treated them to a slide show of the Burmese countryside. Pentecost wasn't interested in local color: "I'd already made up my mind to go," he said. "I didn't care what they showed me. It was something different, and I was ready." He sailed from Los Angeles on April 24.

Byron Glover left later but flew by Pan Am to Hong Kong, thence by CNAC to Chongqing and Rangoon, and was the first to arrive. He was stunned by the heat: 115° Fahrenheit. He found that the CAMCO operation bordered Mingaladon airport but had no access to it, so that to go from one to the other involved a detour onto the main highway. A local contractor was building an assembly hanger of brick and bamboo thatch. It seemed flimsy to Glover, and he asked for the rafters to be trussed with steel, and for an outdoor U-frame hoist to be set up nearby, so assembly could start immediately.

Rangoon had several companies that fabricated truck bodies for the Burma Road. (The trucks came to Rangoon in knock-down form, were assembled as cab-and-chassis at a General Motors plant near the docks, and were finished locally.) Glover went to one of these entrepreneurs and ordered a trailer big enough for a fuselage crate: thirty-five feet long, ten feet high, and six feet wide. More Chinese technicians came down to Mingaladon, swelling the CAMCO crew to 130. Though passed through immigration as civilians, they were actually CAF mechanics from Kunming, where Colonel Wang had been led to believe that the Tomahawks were meant for him. They were bossed by the same American foremen who—at Hangzhou, Hankou, Loiwing, and Mingaladon—had assembled Hawk fighter-bombers, Vultee attack planes, Mohawk fighters, and North American and Ryan trainers for the CAF.

Following local custom, CAMCO hired Indians for the heavy work, muscling a four-ton fuselage crate onto a trailer at the docks and unloading it at Mingaladon. At the assembly area, forty or fifty Indians pried off the top and sides, put four-inch steel pipes under the floor, and rolled it to the outdoor hoist, which lifted the fuselage into the air. Next came the wing assembly, weighing a ton and a half. It was uncrated and picked up by "as many coolies as could conveniently get a grip on the wing without getting in each other's way." They walked it to the fuselage, set it on padded wooden supports, and lowered the body onto it, to be mated with forty-four large bolts. Chinese technicians hooked up the hydraulic system, cranked down the wheels, and rolled the Tomahawk away, making room at the hoist for another fuselage.

The CAMCO workers found that the Special Air Unit had already suffered its first losses. One fuselage lacked so many items that it could not be made airworthy, so it was set aside as a "Christmas tree" of parts (especially instruments) that had failed on other planes during the long sea voyage. The wing assembly of another plane had been dropped into Rangoon harbor, salvaged, and stacked with the rest. By the time it was uncrated at Mingaladon, salt water corrosion had ruined the aluminum skin, and that fuselage too was set aside for cannibalization.

After a fuselage and wing were mated, a truck towed the Tomahawk out to the main road, thence to the airport, where the British allowed CAMCO to do final assembly at one end of the main runway. Seen from the air, the gravel runways of Mingaladon suggested a sloping letter A, chalked upon a vast green slate, with the crosspiece extending beyond the right leg. The crosspiece was the main runway, with CAMCO at one end and the RAF at the other. When Glover took off in a literal cloud of dust, he ran the risk of meeting a twin-engined Blenheim bomber taking off in the opposite direction. Civilian airliners droned in from time to time from Kunming, Delhi, or Singapore, landing on the right leg of the A and crossing the military flight path halfway.

The monsoon was in full swing by now, bringing squalls so violent they could strip the paint from the leading edge of a wing. The Indians had to build a crushed-stone taxi strip from CAMCO's final assembly area to the runway, so the Tomahawks would not bog down. The temperature dropped to a more tolerable 95° F, but at the price of a humidity so high it rotted shoes, belts, and aircraft tires. Nor was that all, as Glover recalled:

When it is not raining the sun is shining brilliantly and the air is both very hot and very humid. . . . It was found necessary to drain the water from all fuel tanks and to drain the fuel strainers immediately prior to each flight. The sun shining on the unprotected airplanes caused the metal to get so hot that the workman could not touch them. This necessitated the construction of about eight mat sheds . . . under which the aircraft could be placed when it was necessary to work on them.

With all these obstacles, it was not until June 12 that Glover test-flew the first Tomahawk, bearing CAF serial number P-8113. (The serials were derived from "pursuit," the Curtiss model number, and the order in which the planes were uncrated at Mingaladon.) However, the assembly hanger was finished now, meaning that henceforth CAMCO would be able to work on two Tomahawks inside and a third at the outdoor hoist.

Meanwhile Chennault and Currie were searching for more fighters. Their first success was the discovery of 144 air-cooled, steel-and-wood Vultee Vanguards originally built for Sweden. The U.S. government had canceled the contract, and the Royal Air Force had agreed to buy the planes, for fear they might otherwise fall into German hands. Turning them over to China would save Britain millions of dollars while costing the Chinese nothing, since the transaction could be handled under the "lend-lease" program recently authorized by Congress. To satisfy the requirements of this law, the Vanguards were transferred to the U.S. Army, which gave them the designation P-66.

Then the army ("ever helpful in steering Chinese demands away from its own prospective equipment") let the China lobby know that Republic Aviation had some fighters available. This was the firm that had risen from the ashes of the Seversky company, bankrupted when China's order for P-35s fell through. The new management had updated Seversky's design as the P-43 Lancer, which the U.S. Army did not like because it had no pilot armor or self-sealing fuel tanks. (The Vanguard had the same flaws.) Republic sketched a larger plane that would meet these objections, but to keep its workers employed and to use its store of parts, it wanted to build 125 Lancers for anyone who would take them. Who but China?

Chennault and Currie drafted a "Short-Term Aircraft Program for

China," to include the Vanguards, the Lancers, and 100 twin-engined bombers diverted from British orders. With the Tomahawks already shipped, Chiang would receive 469 aircraft, nearly fulfilling his request for a 500-plane Special Air Unit:

> If this program were adopted, China would possess . . . a respectable air force, judged by Far Eastern standards, which should be sufficient to (a) protect strategic points, (b) permit local army offensive action, (c) permit the bombing of Japanese air bases and supply dumps in China and Indochina . . . and (d) permit occasional incendiary bombing of Japan. . . .
>
> Ships comprised in the above program would all be flown by American reserve officers and maintained by American technicians and mechanics. They would be under the command of an American reserve officer, Captain Chennault, directly under Chiang Kai-shek. To improve discipline and efficiency, 4 or 5 staff officers from the Army Air Corps are urgently desired. The opportunity for our men to acquire actual combat experience appears to be a factor that should be given some weight.

To recruit pilots and technicians, Bill Pawley had employed Richard Aldworth, widely but wrongly believed to be one of the American volunteers who had flown for France before the U.S. entered World War I. Captain Aldworth was bedridden that spring at Walter Reed Army Hospital, so another man was needed to do the legwork. As it happened, a flight of Zeros had strafed Yunnan-yi toward the end of 1940, burning up eighteen Fleet trainers and two CAMCO-assembled Ryans; and Skip Adair, who had not bargained on combat and who had just become a father, went back to the United States. Chennault caught up with him and signed him on as principal army recruiter, while Rutledge Irvine continued to scout naval bases as before. Supposedly there were other recruiters, and Chennault claimed that he was threatened with arrest at Hamilton Field while looking for pilots. But no AVG veteran remembers being signed up by anyone except Commander Irvine, Skip Adair, or (toward the end of the summer) Captain Aldworth with his aura of the Lafayette Escadrille.

They had three ranks to offer, but in almost every case the position was pilot-officer, paying $600 a month and supposedly equivalent to first lieutenant in the U.S. Army. Three men (Greg Boyington from the marines, James Howard and John Newkirk from the navy) signed on as flight leaders for $650 a month and the status of an army captain. There was also squadron leader, paying $700 a month and equivalent to major, but no pilot was hired with this rank.

Even at the lowest level, these were heady offers. Most of the pilots recruited by CAMCO were serving at the lowest commissioned level: second lieutenant in the army or marines, or ensign in the navy. Louis Hoffman was a navy chief—an enlisted man. Signing up with CAMCO thus meant instant promotion and a salary double or triple what the pilots were earning in U.S. service.* There was also mention of a $500 bounty for each Japanese plane they shot down, but in such vague terms that most of them did not believe it. Finally, some volunteers were promised (or managed to convince themselves) that their CAMCO tour would count as time-in-grade toward promotions and retirement.

One hundred combat pilots were recruited, though only ninety-nine would actually sail for Asia. Missing from the final roster was the name Chennault would most liked to have seen: Ajax Baumler with his record of four German and Italian planes shot down over Spain. Baumler ran afoul of "the redoubtable [Ruth] Shipley" at the State Department, who refused him a passport on the unarguable if foolish grounds that he had violated his previous travel documents by flying for a foreign government.

Reflecting Rutledge Irvine's early start—and perhaps the more enthusiastic support of Secretary Knox—fifty-nine of the successful volunteers were navy men, and seven more came from the marines. The army supplied only thirty-three pilots, though CAMCO later hired ten army flight instructors for the flight school at Yunnan-yi. Like the agreement between T. V. Soong and Bill Pawley, the contract they signed was a masterpiece of circumlocution. There was no mention of combat, bonus payments, or even cockpit time:

> WHEREAS, the Employer . . . operates an aircraft manufacturing, operating and repair business in China, and
> WHEREAS, the Employer desires to employ the Employee in connection with its business and said Employee desires to enter into such employment,
> NOW THEREFORE. . . .
> ARTICLE 1. The Employer agrees to employ the Employee to render such

---

* The pay was not exceptional for the work at hand. When Ajax Baumler flew as a mercenary for the Spanish government, he earned $1,500 a month plus $1,000 for each plane shot down. The civilians ferrying bombers to Britain also earned $1,500 a month, with a bonus of $2,500 after ten successful deliveries.

services and perform such duties as the Employer may direct and the Employee agrees to enter the service of the Employer who, in consideration of the Employee's faithfully and diligently performing said duties and rendering said services, will pay to the Employee a salary of _____ dollars United States currency. . . .

ARTICLE 2. The said employment shall become effective . . . from the date of the Employee's reporting in person to the Employer's representative at the port of departure from the United States . . . and shall continue for one year after the date on which the Employee shall arrive at the port of entry to China . . . unless sooner terminated as hereinafter provided.

CAMCO would supply him with travel documents, a train ticket to California, food and lodging while there, $100 in walking-around money, transportation to Asia, and $500 in lieu of return transportation at the end of his tour. If he were disabled or killed, CAMCO would make a lump-sum payment of six months' salary to him or his estate. (He was also required to take out a $10,000 life insurance policy, the premiums to be deducted from his pay.) There was no provision, however, for what would happen if he were taken prisoner. Nor was there any provision for him to quit, though he could be fired for insubordination, malingering, revealing confidential information, drug or alcohol abuse, or "illness or other disability incurred not in line of duty and as a result of Employee's own misconduct"—i.e., venereal disease.

To remedy such matters as that last, CAMCO hired a U.S. Army flight surgeon, Thomas Gentry, who in turn recruited two more army doctors, a dentist, and a male nurse. Gentry also wanted women nurses, so he went to Yale University, where somebody suggested he look up red-haired Emma Jane Foster. As an undergraduate at Pennsylvania State College, Red Foster had spent her junior year in China and resolved to return there as a nurse. (As she told the story, she decided that she was not spiritual enough for the missionary's life, nor patient enough to become a doctor.) There were no offers from China when she graduated from Yale, so Foster went to work in a Chicago "settlement house." Doc Gentry telephoned her father, who relayed the offer, figuring that *any* job was better than working in the slums. Foster signed up with CAMCO, along with an older nurse, Jo Buckner Stewart.

Then there were line chiefs, crew chiefs, mechanics, armorers, radiomen, propeller specialists, parachute riggers, photographers, weathermen, clerks, and orderlies—the men who would keep the planes and pilots in the air. The air force table of organization called for more than 1,000 ground personnel in a fighter group; CAMCO's quota was 200, and only 186 would actually sail for Asia. In contrast to the pilots, most were army men. Signing on for $300 a month was Sergeant Robert M. Smith, a twenty-six-old college graduate serving as a mechanic in the 20th Pursuit Group. Smith had caught the travel bug from *The Royal Road to Romance,* an immensely popular account of the around-the-world odyssey of Richard Halliburton, formerly of Princeton. The salary was less important: "I would have signed up for $100 a month," he wrote in his diary.

At Mitchel Field, Long Island, Skip Adair found a thirty-nine-year-old technical sergeant named Joe Jordan, who remembered Claire Chennault from the 1st Pursuit Group in the 1920s. Ten years later, as a finance clerk, he had paid off some of the pilots who had gone to China to work at the flight school at Hangzhou. Now he too signed up for Asia, mostly to oblige a buddy who wanted to go, and who asked Jordan to keep him company.

Among the navy men who signed up were Allen Fritzke, Donald Whelpley, and Randall Richardson, three young weathermen at Norfolk Naval Air Station. As Fritzke recalled, it was a Saturday morning in July, and he was hanging around the weather office for lack of anything better to do. When the phone rang, he picked it up. "This is Commander Irvine," said the voice on the other end of the line. "Does anybody there want to go to China?"

"Yes," said Fritzke, who had been applying for Asiatic duty since getting out of boot camp. "You're talking to one."

"Is there anybody else there?"

"Oh, there's a couple fellas here." He turned to Whelpley and Richardson: "You guys interested in going to China?"

"Sure," they said. They were young, they were bored—why not go to China? Following Irvine's instructions, they went to the customary downtown hotel and were offered $300 a month to work for CAMCO. They went back to the base, told the petty officer on duty that they wanted special-order discharges, and were sent over to talk to the base commander. The admiral was outraged. "What kind of nonsense is this?" he shouted, and telephoned Irvine to set him straight. To the delight of the three sailors, the admiral ended by eating humble pie: "Yes *sir*, commander, those men will be released within fifteen minutes."

Also signing on at Norfolk was Tom Trumble, who in 1937 had been a yeoman aboard *Augusta* while CAF bombs made a shambles of downtown Shanghai. He went AWOL to find Commander Irvine, looking for him in every hotel in town. Of all the reasons for joining the AVG, Trumble's was the maddest: he had left a Russian sweetheart in China. After completing his tour with CAMCO, he hoped to find her again.

But the armed forces would not release any staff officers for the Special Air Unit. Even more than pilots, these uniformed bureaucrats were needed to preside over the great expansion ahead. Forced to improvise a headquarters staff, Chennault tried to hire his brother Joe, then a college student, who turned him down. He had better luck with Skip Adair, who agreed to become Chennault's supply officer after his recruiting chores were done. Chennault next talked to the China hands at the State Department, who suggested Paul Frillmann—the Lutheran missionary who had played left field for him on July 4, 1938, and who was now unemployed and living with his family in Chicago.

Frillmann flew to Washington, reported to Chennault at the Chinese embassy, and was appointed chaplain and officer in charge of recreation, physical training, and liaison with the local populace, at a salary of $350 a month. That settled, Chennault set him to drawing up lists of what would be required by 300 Americans in China—coffee, ketchup, flour, peanut butter, canned meat, canned butter, mustard, mayonnaise, and sports equipment—for two years, omitting anything that could be purchased locally. Frillmann spent the morning on his lists and the afternoon in telephoning the orders to Washington wholesalers. He returned to Chicago that night. The experience left him bewildered and a bit resentful at the way Chennault had taken him up, wrung him out, and sent him packing. Indeed, Frillmann was a paradigm of the Chennault technique, whose distinguishing characteristic was to grab whatever lay at hand and to work a miracle with it. "He was a genius," mused Joe Alsop, "at doing things with string and chewing gum."

In June, the first contingent of technicians reported to Gene Pawley in Los Angeles. There were some epic transcontinental journeys. Joe Jordan and his buddy decided to fly, but left their airliner in Omaha so the finance clerk could visit his ex-wife in Sioux City. There being no other transport, they chartered a plane. Back in Omaha, they missed their scheduled flight and boarded a train, then abandoned that in Cheyenne to stretch their legs and buy a bottle of whiskey. No liquor seemed to be available, so they looked for a taxi to take them to Utah. (Jordan's memory, or his knowledge of geography, may have been playing tricks by this time). Failing in that, they boarded a train with a club car. This saw them safely to the Jonathan Club in Los Angeles, where they arrived on June 6, only to be sent north by bus to San Francisco.

Paul Frillmann chaperoned the advance party on *President Pierce,* her name painted over and her staterooms converted to barracks, crammed with reinforcements for General Douglas MacArthur's army in the Philippines. The CAMCO contingent consisted of thirty men, all technicians except the leader they called "Holy Joe." The senior army officer was annoyed by these former enlisted men who had been given cots in the first class lounge. He thought they should drill with his troops, stand for inspection, and snap to attention when he passed by. "Go away, soldier," they growled at him. "We're free men." In Honolulu, they tried to smuggle women aboard the transport. In Singapore, the city-state at the southern tip of the Malay Peninsula, they whistled at British customs officials in their tropical shorts. Quartered for sixteen days in the Raffles Hotel, they played golf in their rooms. James Regis, hired as a photographer, dunked the secretary of the English Club in the swimming pool. There was also a bogus beauty contest, for which prizes were promised but none awarded, and at which Regis, Jordan, and—yes—Frillmann served as judges. "Drove the Limeys wild down there," one of the men fondly recalled. "Bunch of crazy Americans, bringing all the native girls into the Class A dining room and drinking all their gin and tonic and everything." Somebody was indiscreet enough to leak their mission to a United Press correspondent, who filed this dispatch on July 9:

> Thirty United States airplane mechanics and maintenance men arrived here today from New York, and will go to Rangoon next week en route to [China], where they will aid the Chinese Air Force. It was understood that a number of American planes of various types already had arrived at Rangoon and that more were en route there.

The main contingent—thirty-seven pilots, eighty-four technicians, and two women nurses—meanwhile gathered at various hotels in San Francisco. They wore civilian clothes, and their passports described them as anything but what they were. Gil Bright, former flight instructor at Pensacola, put himself down as a hardware clerk in tribute to his father, a wholesaler in Reading, Pennsylvania. Robert M. Smith, the diary-keeping mechanic, went as a radio announcer, which profession he had practiced for two years at KFXJ in Grand Junction, Colorado. Robert Moss, a stocky P-40 driver from the 1st Pursuit Group at Selfridge Field, claimed to be an acrobat. Bob Neale from *Saratoga* was a rancher. As for their commander, Chennault's passport identified him as an "executive"—close enough in the circumstances. On July 4 he flew on a night plane from New Orleans to Washington, where he spent the next two days on last-minute details. Overnight on July 7—four years after the opening shots of the Sino-Japanese War—he flew to San Francisco. He paid a courtesy call on the Chinese consul, inspected the quarters on the Java Pacific liner *Jaegersfontein,* and conferred at the Mark Hopkins with Captain Aldworth and Doc Gentry. Among other concerns, they were dubious about sending two women on a ship full of lusty males. The nurses prevailed, but were given an above-decks cabin to keep them out of harm's way.

That evening, Chennault boarded the Pan Am Clipper for the overnight flight to Honolulu. It was a glorious moment for him: a flight instructor no longer but the almost-certain commander of the American Volunteer Group, as it had come to be called. The pilots and technicians sailed next morning, July 8, which was foggy and cold in the tradition of San Francisco Bay. Charles Mott, formerly a dive-bomber pilot on *Saratoga,* had been put in charge of the contingent. At twenty-six, he was older than most of the pilots, and he was also a married man, in violation of navy regulations. "When I left my darling wife at ten [A.M.]," Mott wrote in his dairy after *Jaegersfontein* motored under the Golden Gate bridge, "I was trying to be casual . . . but just about managed to do it without breaking down. Words can't tell of the void this parting has left in me." At sea, Mott did his best to keep discipline, policing the below-decks crap game, offering a bridge tournament as an alternative, and leading religious services each Sunday in the ship's dining room.

After Honolulu, *Jaegersfontein* was joined by the cruisers *Salt Lake City* and *Northampton.* The escort was the work of Lauchlin Currie, who feared that Japan might arrange to have the airmen kidnapped. The navy squirmed a bit, suggesting that the volunteers be distributed among several ships if Currie were concerned for their safety, but gave in when he replied that the liner was already at sea. The warships escorted *Jaegersfontein* as she swung south of the equator to avoid the Marshall and Caroline islands—former German colonies that had been seized by the Japanese during World War I. Off Australia, they were replaced by *Java,* a Dutch cruiser, which escorted the liner through the Dutch East Indies (now Indonesia) to Singapore. She docked on August 11, all her brandy drunk, along with 5,000 bottles of Coca-Cola.

En route to Chongqing, Chennault spent three days in Hong Kong, ingratiating himself with the RAF and recruiting staff officers. His likeliest prospect was Harvey Greenlaw, former aircraft salesman, who with Olga was about to go home to the United States. They were actually packing their trunks when Chennault came to their hotel room and offered Harvey a job as his executive officer—second in command of the American Volunteer Group. Chennault also signed up William Davis, an Anglo-Irishman known as Daffy. Davis claimed to have served with the Royal Flying Corps in World War I, but was now anxious to avoid being called to service. Also a salesman, and also at loose ends, he was living in Hong Kong with a married woman named Doreen Lonborg. She described herself as English, though she had been born in China and held a Danish passport, courtesy of her estranged husband.

Of this little band of expatriates, only Lonborg survived into the 1980s. She remembered Olga Greenlaw with particular awe: "She was a beautiful thing. She had green eyes and the longest lashes I've ever seen—the most exotic creature!—and her eyes were *literally green.*" In photographs, what is most striking about Greenlaw is her height: wearing heels, she stood eye-to-eye with the men who clustered around her. She had been reared in Mexico, where her father worked as a mining engineer.

Harvey graduated from West Point in 1920, on his second attempt, in a two-year program designed to speed the flow of officers for World War I; he ranked 246 in a class of 273. Something evidently went wrong in his military career, causing him to resign in 1931 and to wash up on the shore of China. He had never served at a grade higher than first lieutenant, but he liked to call himself Major Greenlaw, no doubt figuring he would have reached that grade if he had stuck around. A portrait from the AVG era showed him in a uniform cap and a khaki shirt open at the throat—a handsome man, though with an uncertain mouth and washed-out eyes. Snapshots were less flattering, showing him to be overweight, puffy, and tired. Olga looked half his age, though she was well into her thirties by this time, while Harvey was forty-three.

Chennault told the Greenlaws and Daffy Davis to wrap up their affairs and follow him as soon as they could. (Lonborg would come to Kunming after divorcing her husband, the Dane.) On July 18, he flew up to Chongqing on a CNAC Douglas—arriving at the same time as twenty-seven Mitsubishi bombers as they made their unopposed runs over the Chinese capital. The planes were new to him, twin-engined G4Ms with nearly twice the bomb load of the familiar Nells. The American Volunteer Group had already failed its first assignment: to defend Chongqing during the 1941 bombing season. Nor were there any Russian pilots to oppose the Japanese bombers. In a masterstroke of deceit and folly, Hitler had turned on Stalin the month before, and the Soviet air units had been withdrawn to bolster the crumbling European front. The G4Ms (Bettys, they would be called by Allied pilots) came and went without any opposition except from antiaircraft guns. Only a handful were shot down, and only one Zero, though that sufficed to blow the secret of Japan's deadly new fighter. From the wreckage and from Japanese prisoners, Chinese intelligence officers drew up a remarkably accurate data sheet for the Mitsubishi A6M, along with a set of recognition sketches—the first hard information about the new fighter.* Major McHugh at the U.S. embassy had sent this information back to the United States, and he now gave a copy to Chennault, so his pilots would know what they were up against.

The AVG's late start had another consequence. Its intended base, Wu Chia Ba airport outside Kunming, was sodden with the monsoon rains, making a training program there impossible. Anyhow, Kunming was no longer a safe haven, since it was regularly bombed from French Indochina.

---

* The side view drawing had one significant flaw. The Zero's tail was drawn out to a point, giving it a distinctive, cigar-shaped silhouette. But the tail of the salvaged fighter was too damaged for reconstruction, so the Chinese artist endowed it with the rounded empennage of its predecessor, the fixed-gear Claude. As it happened, the composite bore a strong resemblance to the *Ki*-43 then going into production at the Nakajima company.

Ed Pawley had a solution. (The Pawleys always had a solution.) He talked the British into giving him the use of Kyedaw airfield outside Toungoo, in southern Burma. This arrangement served everyone's purpose. For Pawley, it put the training base close to his Mingaladon assembly point. For Chennault, it enabled him to train his squadrons without fear of attack. For the Chinese, it ensured that AVG supplies would not compete for cargo space on the crowded Burma Road. As for the British, Air Marshal Robert Brooke-Popham felt that he had done a very fine thing to provide facilities for the AVG, but Kyedaw was no loss to the RAF. Toungoo in the summer was a petrie dish breeding malaria, dengue fever, and dysentery, and the only RAF planes in Burma were a few Blenheim bombers, which were more conveniently and comfortably accommodated at Mingaladon airport near Rangoon.

And if the Americans had a training base in Burma, they would certainly lend a hand in case of a Japanese breakout. According to Brooke-Popham, he actually discussed this possibility with the Chinese: "there was an understanding, amounting practically to an agreement . . . that, if Burma was attacked, part, or the whole, of this American Volunteer Group would be detailed for the defence of Burma." Chennault apparently knew nothing about the unwritten clause in his lease on Kyedaw airfield.

Toungoo was located in the broad valley of the Sittang River, 175 miles north of Rangoon. Its main street rumbled day and night with trucks bound for Lashio, while freight trains carried cargo to the same destination, whence it would be pushed over the Burma Road to Kunming. The highway was flanked with shops on one side and market stalls on the other. The village itself lay to the west, its narrow, twisting streets closely lined with bamboo shops and huts, including a liquor store and a building that purported to be a hotel but in reality was a brothel. The most notable building was the sprawling, red brick railroad station, containing Toungoo's only restaurant; the principal product was teak, hauled out of the rain forest by elephants and gangs of coolies under the supervision of young British "jungle wallahs." The population was 23,000, mostly ethnic Burmans, but including a few thousand Indians and some half-wild Karen tribesmen. Among the westerners were American and Italian missionaries, but Toungoo society was dominated by a dozen British families who made their homes on the outskirts of town. The men were army officers (Toungoo was headquarters of the recently formed 1st Burma Division) or managers for the MacGregor teak company. Off hours, they gathered at the Gymkhana Club (golf, tennis, billiards, and whiskey soda) and at dinner parties given by the wives in strict rotation. Black tie was obligatory, and afterward the ladies left the gentlemen to smoke cigars and discuss world affairs, which they did with unquenchable optimism. Sunday morning, they met again at St. Luke's, Church of England, which had more headstones in its graveyard than communicants in its pews. Southeast Asia was not a gentle land for European women and children.

Six miles north of Toungoo—past the hulks of trucks that had broken down on the road to Lashio, past a pagoda guarded by statues of *chintha*, the ferocious seated lion of Burmese mythology—was the side road leading to Kyedaw airfield. Its single runway ran north-south for 4,000 feet and was surfaced with asphalt, so it could be used during the rainy season. Eastward lay the Karen Hills, a sawtooth mountain wall, blue with haze and marking the Burma-Thailand border. Away from the squalor of Toungoo, the countryside had a wild tropical beauty, with gnarly trees and fantastic flowering shrubs.

The RAF had outfitted Kyedaw with a small control tower, several hangars, some office buildings, and—a mile from the field—barracks built from teak and bamboo according to the architectural fashion of Southeast Asia. That is, they had no interior partitions, and the outside walls were open from waist-height to the eaves, with the sunny side sheltered by a veranda. There were no screens. Instead, the occupants slept under mosquito netting, on slat-bottomed cots sternly labeled ON HIS MAJESTY'S SERVICE. Ceiling fans stirred the air, though only if the electric generator were functioning. The roofs were bamboo thatch, and the latrines were open pits with urine buckets on the side, attended by Indian "sweepers."

Chennault inspected Kyedaw on July 26. With him were Butch Carney, whom he had brought down from Kunming; Group Captain E. R. Manning, the cadaverous Australian who commanded the RAF in Burma; and Ed Pawley, who had laid on CAMCO's twin-engined Beechcraft for the tour. Chennault was not impressed by Kyedaw, but he had no alternative, so he approved Pawley's arrangements.

Skip Adair was still on recruiting duty; the Greenlaws and Davis were still in Hong Kong, waiting for visas. So Chennault left Captain Carney (that title too was probably a fiction) in charge of Kyedaw. Carney lived with an enterprising Chinese woman, Rose Mok, who among other things was a free-lance trader on the Burma Road, buying a truck in Rangoon, filling it with goods needed in China, and selling vehicle and cargo after a hired crew brought them through to Kunming. Mok followed Carney to Toungoo, to keep track of her dealings on the Burma Road and to see what opportunities this new venture might present.

In Washington, meanwhile, President Roosevelt approved the formation of a bomber group—the 2nd AVG—whose mission was to include "the incendiary bombing of Japan." Poor George Marshall. It was like keeping a cat off the couch: no matter how many times he put it down, it jumped up again.

5

Looks Mean As Hell

July–December 1941

A coastwise vessel, *Penang Trader,* took the AVG advance party from Singapore to Burma. On July 28 she crept up the tortuous channel of the Rangoon River, twenty miles of muddy estuary, the banks green beyond belief, broken only by the Burmah Oil refinery, the MacGregor teak mill, and clusters of drooping, lilac-like flowers. At Rangoon, the coaster tied to a float below the wharves—eleven concrete acres filled with cranes, warehouses, and tarpaulin-covered crates of war material, bound up the Burma Road to China. Behind this confusion, the men could see the stately white waterfront buildings, including the British embassy, the customs house, and the Strand Hotel. The avenues were broad and the side streets crossed them at right angles. This was European Rangoon, beyond which lay the native maze where lived 250,000 Indians, 40,000 Chinese, 90 Japanese (most of them spies), and—a minority in their own capital—160,000 Burmans. Towering over all was the golden dome of the Shwedagon Pagoda, holy symbol of Burmese Buddhism.

Chennault was standing on the float. He had spent the night at the Strand, en route to Singapore, and when he heard that the advance party was at the quay, he hurried across the street to greet them. "Hello, Frillmann," he said, as if he had planned their reunion just so. "I told you I'd be here first." Then he turned on his heel, as the chaplain recalled with his blend of admiration and resentment:

He was wearing some slapdash adventurous costume as usual—mosquito boots, officer's shirt with Chinese insignia, beat-up Air Force cap—which emphasized his gamecock look. . . . I don't think any of the men on our ship had ever seen him before, and as I looked down the rail where they were lined up, staring silently at him, I could see that [he] had them all in his pocket.

Chennault sent the mechanics out to Mingaladon Cantonment to help with the first lot of Tomahawks. He settled the others at the Strand—not the Raffles, perhaps, but lavish enough with its high-ceilinged rooms, parquet floors, brass-railed bar, and rattan furniture. To Frillmann he gave a new want list: parts for planes and automobiles, electrical and telephone supplies, musical instruments, screens, typewriters, rifles, coffins. . . . "Get the money from the Pawleys," he said, "and bring the stuff up to Toungoo when you come."

Then he left for Singapore, 1,200 miles south at the tip of the Malay Peninsula, where Air Marshal Brooke-Popham and his staff were not particularly interested in what Chennault had to tell them about Japanese tactics and equipment. "Hope their confidence in themselves is justified," he grumbled in his diary. Then he flew back to Rangoon. Instead of checking on Kyedaw airfield, he took the CNAC Douglas to Kunming and hired John Williams (the former CAF radio instructor, who was now free-lancing cargoes on the Burma Road) to transform the CAF flight school building into a hostel for the AVG. Chennault next flew to Chongqing, at a time of full moon and around-the-clock bombing. Between raids, he hammered out an agreement with the Aeronautical Commission that gave him command of the AVG—and of any Chinese squadrons that might work with it. Chennault was also promised first pick of the war material coming in from the United States. The agreement was codified in Order Number 5987, duly stamped with the generalissimo's "chop" (signature block) on August 1, 1941:

1. The First American Volunteer Group is constituted this date.

2. Col. Chennault will organize this Group with the American Volunteers now arriving in China to participate in the War. Additional personnel required to complete the organization of this Group shall be supplied by this Commission.

Chennault also recruited another staff officer. Now a navy intelligence officer assigned to a desk job in India, Joe Alsop had set out for his duty station by way of China, catching up with Chennault at a tea party given by Madame Chiang. Was there perhaps a slot for him in the AVG? Certainly, he was told: come to Burma as soon as you can get a special-order discharge.

The *Pierce* contingent, by this time, had taken the Up Mail to Toungoo. This was a typically British train with a piping whistle, a wood-fired boiler, and passenger cars with no interior aisles, each compartment instead having a door to the outside. (The technicians solved the visiting problem by climbing out the window and running along the roof.) It took all day for the 175-mile run to Toungoo, crossing and recrossing the muddy highway, stopping every hour to take on water and once for a box lunch provided by the Savoy company, caterers to the Burma railroad. The day was so hot, armorer Paul Perry recalled, that by the time he reached Toungoo, he was naked except for his shorts. A flatbed truck drove him and his mates to Kyedaw airfield. "And that's how we got there," Perry said, "twenty-nine wild military men who didn't give a shit, out in the middle of nowhere."

In Singapore, British officials remembered the *Pierce* contingent with distaste. Anxious to avoid another fortnight of wreck and riot, they told the captain of *Jaegersfontein* to take his passengers straight to Burma. This the good Hollander did, in a bad humor and without an escort, mooring at Rangoon on Friday evening, August 15. Next morning, Butch Carney cleared the 123 passengers through immigration and took them for breakfast—ham, eggs, and "corn flakes like cardboard"—at the Silver Grill, Rangoon's all-purpose restaurant, nightclub, and brothel. (A customer didn't even have to leave his booth for a tryst, since the partitions were six feet tall.) Then he put them aboard the Up Mail, but himself stayed in Rangoon to party with Charlie Mott, Jack Newkirk, and the two women nurses. Years later, Bob Neale recalled his arrival at Kyedaw airfield:

> We were met by [the advance party], who got us more or less assigned to quarters in large buildings about thirty feet long by twenty feet wide, with bunks in them and mosquito netting. . . . The latrines were around the back. . . . There were a considerable number of bugs, from mosquitoes to things falling off the ceiling and dropping on top of the mosquito netting.

The barracks were so uninviting that they piled into trucks and the AVG station wagon and drove into Toungoo. They found that the only drinking establishment was the railroad station buffet—named the Savoy, like all such establishments in Burma—and the only entertainment a cinema featuring Gary Cooper in *Beau Geste*. The technicians sat with the natives, feeling more comfortable in the pit stalls than in the boxes occupied by the British in evening dress. Afterward, they inspected the hotel-brothel, where they found that their arrival had doubled the price of a "black wench" to five rupees ($1.50). Back at the airfield, they cursed the bugs, the heat, the rain, the springless cots, the "slumgullion" (beef stew) served at the RAF mess, and the flavorless British cigarettes. Paul Frillmann went into a panic, convinced that the AVG was about to mutiny, and that Chennault would hold him responsible.

Butch Carney turned up next day with his gang of four, thoroughly hung over, and on Monday—apparently without looking at their personnel records—he announced the names of three squadron leaders. The 1st Squadron would be commanded by Robert Sandell, recruited at Maxwell Field in the same group with Red Probst and Matt Kuykendall. The 2nd Squadron went to Jack Newkirk, a homely and likeable man who had flown radial-engined fighters from the deck of *Yorktown*. The 3rd Squadron went to Arvid Olson, a P-40 veteran from the 8th Pursuit Group at Mitchel Field. Each of these men then chose a dozen pilots, for all the world like the captains of three sandlot baseball teams. Sandy Sandell chose army and navy pilots with an even hand, but Newkirk filled the 2nd Squadron almost entirely with navy fliers, and Oley Olson picked army fliers exclusively, including most of his friends from Mitchel Field.

Byron Glover had already delivered three Tomahawks to Kyedaw, and three more were ready at Mingaladon airport. Oley Olson and two of his P-40 drivers took the train to Rangoon to pick them up. Look for the railroad, Glover told them, and follow the rails 175 miles to Toungoo. The pilots came to know this style of navigation as IFR—not "instrument flight rules," as at home, but "I follow railroads."

The AVG technicians found that CAMCO had assembled the Tomahawks just as they came out of the box. "There were no guns in the airplanes," recalled armorer Don Rodewald, "and no gunsights. . . . There wasn't even a bracket for the gunsight." When Skip Adair signed him up, Rode had asked if he should bring his own tools to Burma. "Oh, no," he was told. "All the tools will be furnished—the best tools that you can get." But there were no tools, so Rode stole a kit from a truck bound for China, and with this began to install the guns that had been shipped with the second batch of Tomahawks. Mysteriously, there was now a surplus of fifty-caliber nose guns, but only enough rifle-caliber guns to equip thirty-one planes. To simplify maintenance, the armorers decided to outfit two squadrons with 7.92-mm Colt wing guns and the third with .303-caliber Brownings.

Then they found that they could not test-fire the guns. Burma in 1941 enjoyed a kind of independence, and the British considered that a ban on target practice was a reasonable price to maintain the fiction of self-government. (When the 60th Squadron at Mingaladon wanted to fire its guns or drop some bombs, it flew the Blenheims down to Singapore.) In time, a special dispensation was received from London, so the armorers could construct a firing range. Each Tomahawk was towed to a "gun butt," where its tail was jacked up level with its nose, and its nose guns aligned so that the bullets would converge upon a target 300 yards out; the wing guns were harmonized at 250 yards. Each pilot was then allowed a few practice runs against a target on the ground—but not in the air, for that would have offended Burmese sensibilities. In any event, the AVG had no tow targets.

The optical gunsight proved to be U.S. Army issue—a projection device whose image was distorted by the British "armourglass" windscreen. The armorers made do with the Curtiss-provided ring-and-post sight, less sophisticated than that on an infantry rifle, while Charlie Mott tried to build an optical sight of his own devising.

As for radios, the first task for Robert M. Smith was to rip the British radio harness out of the Tomahawks, working with a ball-peen hammer and a screwdriver through a small door in the tail of the aircraft. Only then could he begin the work of adapting the twelve-volt civilian radio sets to the Tomahawk's twenty-four-volt electrical system. It was a miserable job, and every day at midmorning, as the heat of the day began to build, Smith had to quit work long enough to vomit up his breakfast.

Chennault finally escaped to Kunming, where he was again bombed, and where he inspected the progress Williams had made on the AVG hostel. On August 22 he flew to Burma. As Frillmann had feared, he was not pleased by the situation at Kyedaw airfield. "Apparently agitators have stirred up resentment against mil. discipline and against volunteer combat service," he noted in his diary. Over the next several days, he talked to the men together and as individuals, smoothing the discontented and bawling out the rebellious. Even so, when he went to Rangoon on August 26 to confer with Bill Pawley, the main subject was what to do with the men who wanted to go home.

Returning from Rangoon, he brought Olga and Harvey Greenlaw with him. About the best that could be said of the executive officer was that he was a cut above Butch Carney. "Many of us couldn't tell just what it was he was supposed to do," one of the pilots afterward said of Greenlaw. "He usually dressed smartly in a khaki bush jacket and spent much of his time sucking on his pipe observing others at work." Olga, however, provided a fillip that had been lacking at Toungoo: "Her tight slacks and alluring makeup gave her a provocative look that suggested she was on the make." Perhaps the suggestion was no more than that, but Olga immediately became, and would forever remain, a sex symbol in the rain forest. Another pilot recalled his arrival at Kyedaw airfield, and how his first question—to Noel Bacon—was about the woman situation. "The executive officer has a wife," Bacon replied, puffing reflectively on his pipe, "that would make a dog strain on his leash."

His recruiting duties finished, Skip Adair reached Burma not long after the Greenlaws. Then Joe Alsop came in from India, a civilian once more. With this pickup staff, Chennault set out to whip the AVG into shape. He restricted the vehicles to official business, so the men had to bicycle to Toungoo if they wanted to see a movie, drink at the Savoy, or visit the hotel-brothel. On a heavy-duty British machine, the expedition required half an hour each way, meaning that for all practical purposes the town was off limits except on Sunday—and the Old Man did his best to fill that with church services and softball tournaments. If they persisted, at least they got some exercise.

Rations were a continuing problem. There were two mess halls—one for pilots and staff, the other for technicians—and after hours they served as drinking clubs on the same segregated basis. (Chennault liked to stress the democracy of the AVG, but his diary regularly spoke of "officers" and "enlisted men.") The RAF had contracted to supply food, cooks, and servers for 120 rupees ($36) a month, this sum to be deducted from each man's pay. The men were so unhappy with the results that Chennault demanded and got a rebate of 40 rupees on the first month's bill. Then he put William Towery, former army mess sergeant, in charge of the Indian cooks; and when Alsop showed up, he was put in charge of Towery. In the end, Chennault signed a new contract with the Savoy company. The meals improved, though they never ceased to evoke howls from men who had been spoiled by the bountiful food and skilled Javanese messboys on *Jaegersfontein*.

Henceforth, reveille came at 5:30 A.M. The technicians were on the job before sunrise, worked five or six hours, took a siesta, and if necessary worked a second shift in the evening—an arrangement that cured radioman Smith's morning sickness. For the pilots, the day began with a lecture by Chennault or a guest speaker. (RAF commander, Chinese ace, Allison engine specialist, U.S. Army lend-lease officer, war correspondent, Pawley brother: if he visited Toungoo that summer, he was shanghaied into the small teakwood classroom in the operations building, to add his expertise to the Old Man's.) As with the technicians at dockside, Chennault soon had most of the pilots in his pocket. "The more I see of the old boy," Charlie Mott noted, "the better I like him and the more I admire his talents. . . . We are indeed fortunate in having such a man as head of the project."

They were especially attentive to what he had to say about Japanese warplanes. With chalk, he would draw a Mitsubishi Nell or Zero on the blackboard, marking its vulnerable spots and advising them on the best angle of attack. (In the case of a bomber, for example, keep the propeller disc between you and the gun turret.) "He showed us these things," one of the later arrivals said, "and I got the very distinct impression from his lectures that he had actually engaged the Japanese Zero. Everything that he told us in his tactical lectures happened exactly. He knew. When we made our first contact with those enemy Zeros, they behaved exactly as he said they would." In fact, Chennault had only glimpsed the Zero from the ground: his lectures were based on the drawings and specification sheets recently given to him by Major McHugh.

Using a training manual captured and translated by the Chinese, Chennault explained the tactics that would be used by Japanese fighter pilots (attack from above; sow confusion; break up the enemy's formation; destroy his planes one by one). To counter them, Chennault instructed his pilots to forget what they had learned in U.S. service and instead use Royal Air Force combat rules, which had been battle-tested over Britain. Above all, he drew upon his own air force experience, what he had learned as China's chief air adviser in 1937–1938, and what he had seen Soviet pilots do. Take the high perch, he advised his men—dive on the Japanese planes, open fire with your fifty-caliber nose guns, add the rifle-caliber wing guns as you close the distance—then dive away and do it again. And harry them when they turn for home, low on fuel and ammunition. Destroy 10 percent of a Japanese bomber force, he assured them, and they'll go home to think again; shoot down 25 percent, and they'll quit—lessons hard won at Nanjing, Hengyang, Hankou, Chongqing, and Kunming.

Chennault did not write out his lectures, nor did anybody think to transcribe them. The nearest to a contemporary account was provided by George (Pappy) Paxton, debriefed by an air force intelligence officer in August 1942:

> Chennault told us that we had a sorry airplane, as fighters go. That it had two things: diving speed and gunfire. If we used those, we could get by with it. If not, we were going to get shot up, cold turkey.
>
> He told us: never stay in and fight; never try to turn; never try to mix with them. All we could do was to get altitude and dive on them and keep going—hit and run tactics. Never lose speed; never turn with them, or take for granted that the planes you could see were all there were because we would always be outnumbered.
>
> We flew a two-plane formation. Chennault told us to stick with our leader.

After the lecture, the pilots drove out to the runway for hands-on training. From cockpit checks they progressed to familiarization flights, acrobatics, and mock combat. For practice runs against an enemy bomber, another Tomahawk served as dummy, or Group Captain Manning might send a 60th Squadron Blenheim up from Mingaladon airport. For fighter training, they used each other. Whenever two pilots met in the air, they were supposed to have at one another—head-on if it came to that. In U.S. service, this practice was banned as too risky, but Chennault believed in the hard school of training: better to lose a few pilots than teach them to be timid.

Gil Bright, the "hardware clerk" from Pennsylvania, was a striking young man, with luminous dark eyes and a thoughtful face. He had prepped at Phillips Exeter and matriculated at Princeton, where off-campus flying lessons interested him more than his academic work; he quit college after two years to enroll as a cadet at Pensacola Naval Air Station.

Like many of the pilots in Jack Newkirk's 2nd Squadron, he had been trained to fly dive-bombers from the deck of an aircraft carrier.

On September 8, Bright was cruising over Toungoo when he saw another Tomahawk in the distance. Following protocol, he rocked his wings to challenge the other pilot to a dogfight. His opponent proved to be John Armstrong, slight of stature and boyish in appearance, but with more than a thousand hours on his logbooks. A week earlier, Armstrong had nearly rammed Charlie Mott in a dogfight. He tried the same tactic on Bright, approaching him head-on and forcing him to nose down. Armstrong did the same, so close now that his propeller seemed about to slice through the canopy. Bright made a quarter-roll to the right, expecting Armstrong to roll in the opposite direction, so they would pass belly to belly. But the other Tomahawk did not roll. "The collision," Bright wrote, "sounded like a very loud chop." Each plane lost a wing and began to spin. Bright slid back his canopy, unsnapped his harness, and was thrown out like a stone from a slingshot. The crippled plane spun earthward by his side, until he pulled the ripcord and his parachute opened.

Armstrong was not so fortunate. The "crash party" found him still strapped to his seat, and next day his body was prepared for burial by flight surgeon Sam Prevo:

> I . . . do hereby certify that on Sept. 9, 1941, the remains of John D. Armstrong were fixed in 10 percent formalin and wrapped in a formalin saturated sheet and placed in an hermetically sealed metal container. The metal container was placed in a teakwood casket. I further certify that I was present at the preparation of the body and the sealing of the metal container, and that the casket contains only the remains of the deceased.

Ed Pawley had sent the coffin and a truckload of flowers up from Rangoon, and Armstrong's body was laid out in the Greenlaws' parlor at 124 Steel Road, Toungoo. Paul Frillmann conducted the funeral in the pilots' mess, after which Armstrong was buried in the rain at the St. Luke's graveyard, with most of the local British colony accompanying the AVG to the plot on the south side of the village. "A Burma frontier guard played the ['Last Post']," Bright wrote his parents, "and we all went home." The lighthearted tone was adopted after the fact: on the day of the accident, Bright was hospitalized "with a bad case of nerves," too upset to explain what had happened. But those who do dangerous work quickly learn to distance themselves from tragedy, and never more quickly than in a fighter group, where pilots and planes are routinely stressed to the breaking point.

Chennault missed the accident and the funeral. With Butch Carney and Doc Gentry, he had flown to Kunming to certify fifty Chinese cadets for advanced training in the United States.

Ed Rector and Tex Hill were among seventeen pilots who reached Singapore on *Bloemfontein,* sister ship of the Java Pacific liner that had brought the main contingent to Asia. Also in the "Bloom Gang" were R. T. Smith and Paul Greene, formerly of Randolph Field. Like the *Pierce* contingent, they were stranded for a fortnight in Singapore before getting onward passage on *Penang Trader,* which delivered them to Rangoon early in the morning on September 15. They went up-country the same day, to be greeted at the Toungoo railroad station by a band playing "Stars and Stripes Forever." Next morning they were assigned to squadrons. Jack Newkirk made off with most of the navy pilots, including Hill and Rector, while Oley Olson took his pick of the army men, including the buddies from Randolph Field.

Few of the Bloom Gang had ever flown a Tomahawk. "That damn engine stuck out there so far," Ed Rector recalled, "I thought, if I step on my brakes this thing is going to tip over!" He was dismayed by the visibility, too, so restricted that the proper taxiing procedure was to weave the plane from side to side, like a crow turning its head to see what was in front of it. After a few takeoffs and landings, however, Rector realized that the length of its nose had little to do with a plane's flight characteristics.

It was the same with R. T. Smith, whom the army had barred from fighters because of the distance between his heels and his head. Neil Martin gave him a cockpit check on September 17. It was a tight fit, even with the seat bottomed out and the rudder pedals full forward. But from the moment he applied the throttle, R. T. began to think of his plane in the first person plural:

> I closed the canopy and turned onto the runway, got lined up, and firmly eased the throttle forward. The big prop began to bite into the humid air as eleven hundred horsepower thundered a message I'd never heard before.

We began to accelerate rapidly, manifold pressure gauge showing 48 inches, 3,000 rpm on the tachometer, now holding lots of right rudder to counteract the powerful torque. . . . Now there was a clear view over the nose . . . and in a matter of seconds the airspeed indicator was showing 100 mph . . . and we broke free of the runway . . . airspeed now up to 150 [mph], rate of climb indicator at about 3,000 feet per minute, altimeter needle winding steadily clockwise. . . .

At this point I was grinning and chuckling to myself like a kid with a beautiful new toy.

As each Tomahawk was ferried up from Mingaladon airport, it was given a fuselage number, painted two feet tall behind the cockpit. (The numerals enabled a pilot to jump for his own plane when the alarm went off, and in the air to recognize his squadron mates.) Numbers one through thirty-three were reserved for the 1st Squadron; thirty-four to sixty-six for the 2nd Squadron; and sixty-seven to ninety-nine for the 3rd Squadron. From the options available to him, R. T. chose No. 77—lucky sevens—for the Tomahawk assigned to him.

Not all the Bloom Gang did as well. On September 23, eight days after reaching Toungoo, Maax Hammer crashed to his death in the rain forest. The circumstances were "peculiar," as Chennault noted in his diary. (So was the spelling of Hammer's first name, but that was how it appeared on AVG records.) Charlie Mott concluded that the newcomer "got into an inverted spin and could not get out of it, probably because of faulty technique. He hit with tremendous force," Mott went on, "so naturally the remains are just so much meat. We decided to sell such of his effects as would be more valuable [here] than they would be in the U.S. bearing in mind of course that all bargain sale methods are to be avoided."

Chennault was discouraged, and not just by the deaths. "Six pilots want to quit," he wrote in his diary. "Rains go on daily and nightly." Curiously, most of the malcontents belonged to Oley Olson's 3rd Squadron. Olson later explained that they had joined the AVG to "get off of active duty with the Army and get into the more lucrative and immeasurably safer occupation of civilian flying"—an opinion shared by Chennault, though it failed to explain why most of the quitters were P-40 drivers from Mitchel Field. Altogether, seven pilots and a crew chief left Burma at the end of September. Another 3rd Squadron pilot went AWOL to visit a woman in Rangoon; he was grounded for the infraction, and in time he too resigned.

Not quite balancing the attrition, six more pilots arrived on October 10. With a handful of technicians, they had spent four weeks in
trains and coastwise vessels from Singapore, where *Zaandam* had
dropped them off in mid-September. Three were marine fighter pilots
from Quantico, and Olson grabbed them for the 3rd Squadron. Then,
on October 25, he lost another of his P-40 veterans. That morning,
Don Rodewald finished the guns on Tomahawk No. 1, and Peter
Atkinson volunteered to test it out, though it did not belong to his
squadron. He promised the armorers he would buzz the field, so Rode
(an acute observer, though his spelling was uncertain) watched for
him:

> He started to pull out of a long dive at terrific speed about a mile away to
> the south when the plane seemed to disintagrate and fall about 1500 feet.
> The motor fell free and wound up at a high rate till it hit. I went in a car as
> Armorer and got there to see the wreckage over a mile area. The motor was
> in a hole[.] Pete, still strapped in his seat, fell free of the plane so was still
> in one piece. His head was bad. The fuselage was along the RR tracks. The
> two wings were out in the rice fields about 300 yrds apart. I [salvaged] some
> of the ammunition and two wing guns so far. This is a sad occasion because
> Pete was so well liked.

There were conflicting theories about this third fatality. Chennault
grounded the Tomahawks in relays over the next few days in an effort
to discover a common defect, but none was found. (In all likelihood,
Atkinson had simply revved the long-pistoned, slow-turning Allison to
such a speed that vibration tore the plane apart.) David Harris—a close
friend of the dead man, and like him a P-40 driver from Mitchel
Field—now lost his appetite for flying. "If these guys can't do it,"
Harris said, *"I'm* sure not ready." Chennault obligingly added him to
the headquarters staff.

By this time, the AVG had developed a protocol for funerals. The staff
officers were "official mourners," while pilots from the dead man's
squadron were pallbearers. They wore khaki uniforms with black tie and
pith helmets, which they doffed during prayers; they saluted when the
coffin was carried between their ranks, and again when the bugler played
"The Last Post." As a Catholic, Atkinson received a requiem mass
instead of Paul Frillmann's modified Lutheran service, but he was
buried at the Anglican graveyard with Armstrong and Hammer.

Chennault at the controls of a Boeing P-12, probably at Brooks Field in 1930. "With his piercing black eyes and a small, fierce mustache," wrote his biographer, "he could strike fear into the hearts of the insecure." (Flying Tigers Association)

The Three Men on a Flying Trapeze, about 1935. Chennault's wingmen were Billy McDonald (left) and Luke Williamson (right), sergeant-pilots who resigned and sailed for China after they were turned down for commissions in the Army Air Corps. (National Air and Space Museum)

With hand tools and muscle, conscripted laborers built the "Burma Road" across China's mountainous western border. For three years it was the most famous part of a lifeline stretching 2,000 miles from the British port of Rangoon to the Chinese capital at Chongqing. (National Archives)

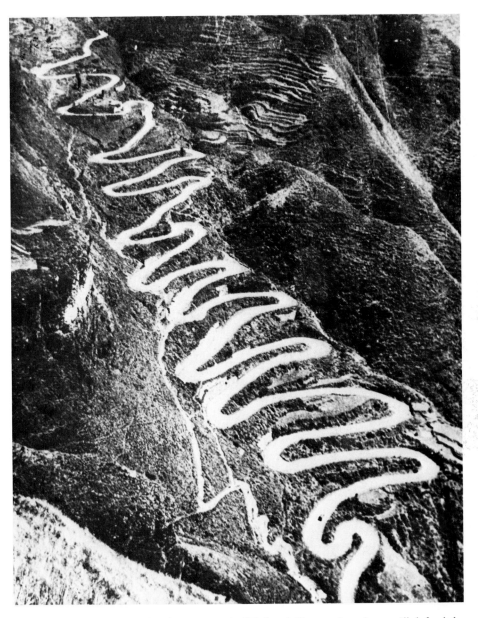

"You will go over there under the command of Colonel Chennault and you will defend the Burma Road all the way up to Kunming." In the mile-deep gorges of the Mekong and Salween rivers, the road looped upon itself like Christmas candy, obliging trucks to back and fill at every turn. (National Archives)

At Kyedaw airfield outside Toungoo, Noel Bacon posed in front of a Tomahawk before his maiden flight in a liquid-cooled fighter. He was one of the "water boys"—Jack Newkirk's Panda Bears, made up almost entirely of former navy pilots. (Courtesy of Noel Bacon)

The first man to die was John Armstrong, in a midair collision on September 8, 1941. At St. Luke's cemetery in Toungoo, his teakwood casket was supported by planks while Paul Frillmann (in uniform) read a modified Lutheran burial service. (National Air and Space Museum)

Air Vice Marshal Pulford of the Royal Air Force inspected Kyedaw in October. From left: Harvey Greenlaw, Pulford, Chennault, Sandy Sandell, Oley Olson, and Olga Greenlaw—as always, the center of their attention. (Flying Tigers Association)

After six months as a "Christmas tree," this Tomahawk was made whole with parts salvaged from planes wrecked in training. It was the ninety-ninth and last fighter off the CAMCO production line at Mingaladon Cantonment. (Walter Pentecost photo, National Air and Space Museum)

Oley Olson in the cockpit of his Tomahawk, bearing the Curtiss-supplied ring sight on the cowling, the AVG-built optical sight inside the windscreen, and the machine gun muzzles covered with tape to keep the barrels clean. (Flying Tigers Association)

隼戦闘隊長 加藤建夫

檜與平

誇り高き一軍人の生涯

An idealized portrait of Tateo Kato graced the cover of this 1987 memoir by Yohei Hinoki, who served under him in Burma. The plane is a Nakajima Hayabusa bearing a 64th Sentai arrow on its tail fin and the commander's diagonal stripes on its wings. (From *Hayabusa sentotai cho Kato* by permission of the publisher)

The Hayabusa's clean lines fooled the AVG pilots into believing that they were fighting the infamous Zero. The army plane was longer than the navy's, and the tail was rounded instead of being drawn out to a point. Note the weight-saving, nonretractable tail wheel, typical of Japanese fighters. (National Archives)

Kunming had not been raided for a month. The silence bothered Chennault, as he explained in a letter to the RAF commander: "Japanese tactics . . . can usually be counted on to repeat until a severe check is met with." He believed that Japanese bomber squadrons were being repositioned for a thrust to the south. If so, what country was weaker than Burma, and what target more helpless than Toungoo? Kyedaw airfield was only sixty miles from Thailand, a neutral kingdom that he suspected of having been infiltrated by the Japanese. Toungoo had no warning net such as John Williams had established around Kunming, nor a radar installation like that protecting Rangoon. And the Tomahawks had such a slow rate of climb that they had not yet managed to intercept any of the mock raids that Group Captain Manning had arranged at Chennault's request. It was not a happy position for the apostle of "defensive pursuit."

On October 24, Chennault sent the three squadron leaders on a patrol of Thailand. (The British forbade such overflights, along with anything else that might provoke Japan, but the RAF commanders knew about Chennault's patrols and even suggested where he might look for Japanese activity.) Sandell, Newkirk, and Olson crossed the sawtoothed Karen Hills at 20,000 feet and scouted as far east as Chiang Mai— Thailand's second city, the northern terminus of its railroad, and the logical place from which to launch a raid on Toungoo. Chennault had instructed the squadron leaders to stay high, dropping down only if they saw something suspicious. With the rice fields drained and the rainy season ending, a convoy could not move in Thailand without raising a plume of dust. But they saw nothing, because there was nothing to see.

Two days later, "a strange silver ship" returned the visit, seeming to scout Kyedaw from 6,000 feet. Five Tomahawks clawed for altitude and went into search formation, but could not catch the stranger. The same thing happened the following day, though Eriksen Shilling of the 2nd Squadron got close enough to count five of the silver ships. All Allied aircraft in Burma and Malaya bore RAF camouflage colors, so Chennault assumed that the intruders were Japanese scouts from Thailand. He was half right. In October, in an operation so secret it was kept from the high command of the Japanese Army Air Force, a flight of reconnaissance planes had been based in Hanoi, French Indochina, from which they flew across Laos and Thailand to photograph British installations in Burma—1,200 miles round trip.

Chennault asked the RAF to beef up the defenses at Kyedaw, and Group Captain Manning supposedly sent up a ship's bell to be rung in the event of a raid. He also agreed to provide a guard of Gurkhas, tough little mercenaries from Nepal, legendary for their exploits in British service. (The cost of their maintenance was billed to China.) But he refused to reinforce the border watch between Burma and Thailand, which consisted of Burmese civil servants with binoculars and field telephones, reporting over the easily tapped wires of Burma Post and Telegraph.

Ten more pilots arrived October 29 on *Klipfontein*. Several had previously flown Consolidated PBY Catalinas, so stately that they were equipped with bunks and hotplates. The flying boat captains had a lamentable tendency to "touch down" when they were nowhere near the tarmac, as if still seated in a cabin high above the harbor.

To fill the vacancies in the 3rd Squadron, Oley Olson got Robert Raine, who had logged ninety hours in navy fighters; Henry Gilbert, twenty-two years old and fresh from flight school; and the former PBY captain who had been christened John Perry, but who joined the navy and the AVG under the *nom de guerre* of Edwin Conant. In their maiden flights, Raine and Gilbert turned in creditable performances. Then it was the turn of Perry/Conant, who "leveled off at about twenty-five feet," as R. T. Smith recorded the disaster, "stalled, and dropped in. Bounced up, collapsed the landing gear, came down on one wing and the belly, and turned around 180 degrees on the runway."

A few days later, on November 3, Perry/Conant made another belly-flop. Thus commenced the worst shambles in the history of the AVG—"Circus Day," it was called. After Conant exploded a tire and ran off the end of the runway, Raine followed him into the greenery, collapsing his landing gear and damaging the propeller and a wing. Then Sandy Sandell—a squadron leader, no less—spun around on the runway while landing from a cross-country flight to Lashio. Shaken by this run of bad luck, the crew chiefs dispersed the Tomahawks for the evening . . . whereupon John Overly taxied one plane into another, chewing up its aileron; William Blackburn followed suit, damaging the propeller on his plane and on the one he hit; and Gale McAllister braked so hard that he stood a Tomahawk on its nose, with two frightened helpers clinging to the wings.

Two days later, Perry/Conant struck again, and the pilots began to joke that if he disabled two more Tomahawks, he would qualify as a Japanese ace. Chennault was not amused. He dictated a letter to CAMCO in New York, demanding more competent pilots and a more honest recruiting pitch:

> Typical of these problems is the case of pilot-officer E. S. Conant, who reported at this station with nine other navy pilots on October 29. Conant has the rating of a four-engine flying boat captain, [and] he has cracked up three planes in the first week of flying. . . .
>
> Two more [*Klipfontein* pilots] decided to go home within twenty-four hours after their arrival at this station. Their stated reason was that the conditions of service had been falsely described to them. . . . I request, therefore, that in future a more intelligent employment policy be followed.
>
> In telling the AVG story to pilots who may think of volunteering, nothing should be omitted. Far from merely defending the Burma Road against unaccompanied Japanese bombers, the AVG will be called upon to combat Japanese pursuits; to fly at night; and to undertake offensive missions when planes suitable for this purpose are sent out to us. These points should be clearly explained.
>
> Then, after the timid have been weeded out, the incompetents should also be rejected. . . . I prefer to have the employment quotas partly unfilled than to receive pilots hired on the principle of "come one, come all."

The letter would have been typed by Joe Alsop, to whom Chennault gave the title of "staff secretary" in addition to his duties as mess officer. "He is surely a great help in this work," Chennault wrote in his diary: the sigh of relief is almost audible. To the pilots and technicians, however, Alsop was a figure of fun, with his spectacles, his fussy manner, and his elevated speech, honed at Groton and Harvard and on the Washington dinner circuit. Tom Trumble, the yeoman striper who had left a sweetheart in Manchuria, and who was now clerking in the headquarters building, remembered him following the Old Man with an armload of papers: "Joe was always very much perturbed and anxious to get something signed."

Most of Alsop's documents had to do with supplies and spare parts. Cannibalization had become a way of life for the AVG mechanics, scavenging pieces of wrecked planes and installing them on those that could be made airworthy. But no amount of recycling could replace tires blistered by 100-mph landings on hot asphalt. Or propellers twisted by nose-overs, ground loops, and belly landings. (Wayne Ricks pruned one of these propellers back to unbent metal and used it for testing engines on the ground. When Erik Shilling had to ferry a propless Tomahawk to Loiwing for overhaul, Ricks put on the "club" for lack of anything better; it worked fine, Shilling reported, save that it screamed like a banshee during the 350-mile flight to the China border.) Or the E-1B solenoids that fired the Tomahawk nose guns when the pilot pressed a button on his control stick, but which usually failed after five hours of service. Alsop took over the paperwork entailed in ordering supplies from anyone who might have what the AVG needed. These requisitions went in the first instance to the CAMCO/Intercontinent office at 42 Phayre Street in Rangoon, around the corner from the Strand Hotel:

> We need six ounces of luminous paint for gun sights, which you should be able to get locally. We also need 100 Bausch and Lomb Ray-Ban sunglasses. The pilots were instructed to bring their own, but some failed to do so, and others have broken theirs. We find that the lack of good sunglasses appreciably lowers pilot efficiency, so I should like this order to be cabled to the United States and shipped by air express.

There was also a China Defense Supplies office in Rangoon. Alsop once visited it with a list of *one thousand* items, which required a day and a night to encrypt into the cable code used by everyone in Asia—civil and military, British and Japanese. This was a system of five-digit blocks, from which the sender subtracted or added a number known only to him and the recipient. There were standard abbreviations, but the codebook author had not anticipated solenoids, Ray-Bans, silver solder, or the items on another want list—432 packages prophylactics, 19 cases rye whiskey, 21 cases bourbon, 10 cases Camels, 5 cases Lucky Strikes—all of which had to be spelled out in full.

And ammunition! The Royal Air Force and the U.S. Army each believed that the other should meet China's needs, with the result that neither did. At the Raritan Arsenal in New Jersey, Lauchlin Currie found 900,000 rounds of .303-caliber ammunition and persuaded the Canadians (to whom they belonged) to give them up. He also wangled the release of 600,000 rounds of .50-caliber ammunition from U.S. stores in the Philippines. Pending the arrival of these shipments, Alsop scrounged odd lots from the British commando base at Maymyo, from the CAF, and from quasi-official Chinese dealers in Rangoon. Some of the Chinese ordnance dated back to 1938 and was given to hangfires that caused the pilots to shoot holes through their own propellers.

Chennault invited Jim McHugh to come down from Chongqing, to see for himself how shabbily the AVG had been treated. With Alsop's help, the major drafted a lengthy appeal to the Navy Department, beginning with a reminder of the hopes with which this enterprise had been launched:

> By its very nature, the war in China offers the United States a unique opportunity to strike a blow in self-defense with more effect and less expenditure than would be remotely imaginable anywhere else in the world. . . . [T]he defense of the United States could hardly be better served than by a crippling attack on Japan. . . . [But] without any staff officers competent to direct the enterprise; with less than a third of the material requested, and with less than half the pilots and men, the A.V.G. cannot be expected to attain the great objectives originally set for it.

McHugh then itemized what was needed to salvage the situation, from radio tubes to long-range bombers.

A similar message went to the War Department over the signature of Brigadier General John Magruder, head of the U.S. Military Mission to China—AMISSCA, it was called. General Marshall had sent the clerkish brigadier to Chongqing to monitor the flow of lend-lease supplies and incidentally to keep an eye on the AVG.* Magruder flew down to Toungoo and got the usual earful: without staff officers, without spare parts, and with just forty-two Tomahawks in flying condition, the AVG would be routed if it were thrown into combat, posing a "serious threat to American prestige in Far East and possible repercussions at home." To head off this debacle, the War Department must commandeer six

---

* On September 6, an Imperial Conference in Tokyo decided to widen the war unless the United States agreed to supply Japan with the war materials—especially oil—needed to subdue China. In the course of the debate, an army spokesman offered the U.S. Military Mission and the AVG as proof of a Sino-American coalition against Japan: "United States Army personnel . . . are going to China a few at a time and bringing weapons with them, particularly airplanes."

tons of parts (which Magruder listed in the same detail as McHugh) from RAF squadrons in North Africa and its own units in the Philippines. Magruder also urged that four air force officers be sent from the United States, assigned to AMISSCA but loaned to Chennault in Burma. Among the names was that of Lieutenant Ajax Baumler, the Spanish Civil War veteran who had been refused a passport to join the AVG.

T. V. Soong joined this campaign, and in suspiciously similar words, warning the White House that "if this air force tries to fight it may be destroyed with disastrous repercussions." Soong, however, did not trifle with spare parts. He wanted the United States to load eighty Douglas dive-bombers onto an aircraft carrier, take them to the Philippines, fly them to China, and turn them over to the AVG. "Would it be possible," he asked, "to direct the Army and the Navy to make these planes and ordnance available *now?*"

Bill Pawley had a more modest proposal. Two years earlier, he had imported three CW-21 Demon fighters to serve as prototypes for his assembly line at Loiwing. He now offered to assemble and deliver them to Kyedaw airfield "on the chance that some government authority could be found to pay for them" at the 1939 list price. This was a great bargain, as everyone agreed, and after much correspondence the U.S. agreed that China could use lend-lease funds to buy the flimsy but fast-climbing Demons, which Chennault hoped could accomplish what the Tomahawks had not: catch the mystery planes that kept passing over Toungoo.

On November 12, *Boschfontein* brought twenty-six more pilots to Rangoon. They were led by Curtis Smith, thirty-three years old, who had tried without success to enforce military discipline on the voyage. Smith had joined the army in 1928, jumped to the marines, back to the army, and finally to the marines again; when CAMCO signed him up, he was a reservist taking a refresher course at Pensacola. With 2,000 hours in his logbooks, he was an impressive catch, though overage for combat flying. Also on *Boschfontein* were Charlie Bond, Jim Cross, and George Burgard of the Ferry Command—and Greg Boyington, who caught the green eyes of Olga Greenlaw. "He was about five feet eight inches tall," she recalled, "with tremendous shoulders and narrow hips; his head held on by a strong neck. He had coarse features, large eyes, wide, flat nose, and heavy jowls." The other men, she thought, were afraid of him. (They had reason. Drunk as a skunk one night, Boyington roused Noel Bacon, who was serving as transportation officer, and demanded the keys to the AVG station wagon. Bacon complied when he found himself looking down the barrel of a .45 automatic.)

On November 15, a Saturday, the *Boschfontein* pilots were given their cockpit checks. Then, with some of the older hands, they drove into town for dinner at the home of Chester Klein, a Baptist missionary who often invited members of the AVG to his house for baked beans and conversation. On this particular evening, two Englishmen were also present. (They may have been covert-warfare agents, recruiting "left-behind" parties to harrass the Japanese if Burma was invaded and overrun.) After ice cream and cake, pilots and civilians sat in the living room, talking about the war in Europe and speculating on when it would spread to the Pacific. Bored with the talk, Erik Shilling thumbed through the *Illustrated London News* and found a photograph of a Royal Air Force Tomahawk in Egypt, its air scoop painted to represent the gaping mouth of a shark. The shark face motif had been used by pilots on both sides in World War I, though with an effect more comical than sinister; the first truly ominous version was painted by the men of the Luftwaffe 76th Group on their Messerschmitt 110 fighter-bombers in the spring of 1941. Over Greece and Crete, they had sliced through the Gloster Gladiator biplanes of the 112th Squadron, whereupon the RAF pilots were withdrawn to Egypt and refitted with Tomahawks off the same assembly line as those diverted to China. They adapted the shark face for their own use, and it was their variant that Shilling now admired and showed to his mates.

A former army test pilot, Shilling was one of the AVG's hottest fliers, an intense young man with jug ears and a shock of blond hair, bleached white by the tropical sun. With Ken Merritt and Lacy Mangleburg, he went out to the airfield next day, stole chalk from the lecture room, and drew a shark's face on his Tomahawk. He asked the Old Man if they could use it as a squadron symbol. "Chennault said no," Shilling recalled, "but would rather use it as a group marking."

And so it happened. All that week, pilots and crew chiefs busied themselves with chalk and paint, transforming Tomahawks into man-eating fish. They were delighted with the results: "Looks mean as hell," R. T. Smith gloated about the shark face on No. 77.

At the same time, they painted the CAF identification disc (a twelve-pointed white star in a blue circle) on each wing. Then they set about to find distinctive squadron emblems. For the 1st Squadron, Sandy Sandell's pilots chose an apple, in front of which a naked Eve chased a uniformed Adam, as mankind's "first pursuit." So they became the Adam & Eves. In the 2nd Squadron, Jack Newkirk's men chose a black-and-white panda, emblematic of China; they would be the Panda Bears. Oley Olson's 3rd Squadron opted for a scarlet nude with a halo and wings: Hell's Angels, they styled themselves, after a 1930 film starring Jean Harlow and celebrating the air war on the Western Front.

Chennault then asked the Royal Air Force to send up its best fighter pilot for a friendly joust with Shilling. Mingaladon airport had recently been strengthened by the addition of the 67th Squadron, transferred from Singapore with its lend-lease Brewster Buffaloes. (They brought some planes with them, took over the Buffalo flight formerly attached to the 60th Squadron, and had sixteen new planes shipped in.) Most of the pilots were from New Zealand, not Britain, but this distinction was lost upon the men of the AVG. Wrote Bill Schaper: "Shilling had a dog fight with a Limey in a Brewster and licked the pants off of him, so it should increase the confidence in our pilots quite a bit." Which was Chennault's intention, of course. Like the Sunday afternoon tournaments, and the shark face and the squadron emblems, the joust was one more technique for molding his irregulars into a fighting team. Insensibly, the 1st American Volunteer Group was becoming a combat force with its own heroes and heraldry.

The final contingent reached Burma on November 25. They had traveled from San Francisco to Singapore on *Zaandam*—the second voyage for that particular ship—thence by coaster to Rangoon. Only four pilots were assigned to the squadrons at Kyedaw airfield, including Louis Hoffman, who had joined the navy in 1915 and earned his wings in 1929. The rest of the *Zaandam* pilots were young army instructors who had signed contracts with the CAF flight school, and they were sent straight to China, to serve as check pilots at Yunnan-yi under the direction of Butch Carney. (It was not always clear where the AVG left off and the flight school began. On Chiang Kai-shek's direct order, several Chinese pilots had checked out in Tomahawks at Kyedaw; for a time, Carney was

---

Brewster Buffalo

Intended as America's first monoplane carrier fighter, this radial-engined warplane disappointed the navy when it went into service in 1938, and was supplied instead to Allied air forces in Southeast Asia. The British dubbed it Buffalo for its big-shouldered appearance, so different from their liquid-cooled Hurricanes and Spitfires. In Singapore on the way over, AVG pilots grumbled that the British had made off with the better plane, thanks to the lend-lease program. (Chennault may have thought so, too, for the Buffalo was one of the radial-engined fighters he had listed as suitable for the AVG.) In active service, it had continual problems with its radio, landing gear, and engine valves, sometimes leaking oil so copiously that a pilot had to throttle back, take off a sock, open the canopy, and reach around to wipe the windscreen. In Singapore, the British replaced the Buffalo's large-caliber guns with .303-caliber Brownings, thus reducing the hitting power of an already inferior plane. However, the 67th Squadron fighters at Mingaladon airport were not emasculated in this fashion.

Engine: 1,100-hp Wright Cyclone air-cooled radial
Crew: one
Wingspan: 35 feet
Combat weight: 6,500 lb
Maximum range: 650 miles
Top speed: 325 mph at 21,000 feet
Armament: two .50-caliber machine guns in nose, two .50-caliber machine guns in wings; two 100-lb bombs

---

carried on the rosters of both organizations; and Chennault monitored the flight school with such care that he could specify the equipment at Yunnan-yi: 150 desks, 450 chairs, 150 filing cabinets, 600 pen points, 300 erasers. . . .)

The AVG now prepared to follow the flight instructors, sending men and supplies not needed at Kyedaw up the road to China. The first convoy consisted of ambulances under the command of Joseph Lee, a CAF flight surgeon who had been hired to help the American medical staff. (He did not have a medical degree, and the technicians called him "Aspirin Joe" for his policy of treating every complaint with salicylic acid.) As a Chinese speaker, Lee was to assess the hazards of the Burma Road, including thieves, venal customs officials, and larcenous vendors of gasoline, food, and lodging. When he reached Kunming, he was to set up a hospital on the grounds of Hostel Number One, formerly the CAF flight school headquarters. Here, to judge by a complaint from the CAF liaison officer in Kunming, John Williams ran a rather loose ship:

> For the past few weeks, I have found that some of the personnel . . . are always drunk in the hostel, and this is not the worst. On several occasions they were badly drunk in the city, so much so that one of them lost his head completely and caught hold of a cook's chopper intending to kill a woman with it, but fortunately he was prevented from doing any injury by another person. . . .
>
> It is not customary that a military organization permits the bringing of girls into the sleeping rooms of the hostel. This may entail some misunderstanding among the public and, at the same time, spoils our reputation. Some amendments should be made along this direction and rules governing this should be circulated to enable an easier and better management of the hostel.
>
> Some of the Chinese here are planning to cooperate with a few Americans in the Volunteer Group in the hope that they could utilize the [AVG] trucks to smuggle goods into China from Burma and sell them here at market price. [This] is not only illegal, but profiteering at the country's expense, and as such, particular heed should be paid to nip it at the bud.

For bringing women into the hostel, Williams fined each man $25 "gold." (The Americans spoke of the U.S. dollar as precious metal, while scorning Chinese currency as "Mex"—no better than a peso.) The smuggling was more difficult to control. The second convoy from Kyedaw airfield contained great quantities of coffee, soap, and cigarettes not shown on the manifest, so Williams locked it inside the AVG compound until he could sort things out: cargo, trucks, drivers, and Chinese officer-in-charge. The hostage complained of "cruel treatment from bad feeding and poor beddings during the time of detention," and Williams had to apologize, no small concession in face-conscious China.

When not otherwise occupied, the Kunming detachment belted ammunition, built a softball diamond, set up a movie theater, and cared for two dogs. One was a dachshund named Joe, a Christmas present for Chennault; the other answered to the name of CAMCO. The animals got along fine together, Williams assured Chennault toward the end of

November, adding that the business of hardening Wu Chia Ba for the AVG was also progressing well, the Chinese having run a railroad spur to the airport to speed the delivery of crushed stone. On the other hand, a thief had made off with a clock from a parked Tomahawk. And for the first time in months, Japanese planes were scouting Kunming from their base in French Indochina, suggesting that air raids might soon begin again.

"We are preparing for an offensive war against Japan," General Marshall confided to a group of reporters on November 15. The American weapon would be the B-17 Flying Fortress, operating from the Philippines; if war broke out, squadrons of these huge bombers would "be dispatched immediately to set the paper cities of Japan on fire." So Marshall had bought into the plan proposed a year before by Morgenthau, Soong, and Chennault, and he had even adopted their language. (The confidential briefing was no slip of the tongue: four days later, he asked that plans be drawn up for "general incendiary attacks to burn up the wood and paper structures of the densely populated Japanese cities.") However, there would be no subterfuge in Marshall's offensive: the B-17s would bear U.S. Army markings, and the crews would wear American uniforms.

Since it was preparing to bomb Japan on its own account, the army was loath to release men for Chennault's bomber force, the 2nd American Volunteer Group. In the end, Lauchlin Currie had to draw up a formal directive for the president's signature, ordering Henry Stimson to let the men go. "In the next few months," the president wrote, "we are delivering to China 269 pursuit planes and 66 bombers. . . . I suggest, therefore, that beginning in January, you should accept the resignations of additional pilots and ground personnel as care to accept employment in China, up to a limit of 100 pilots and a proportional number of ground personnel." A similar directive went to Frank Knox at the Navy Department, the two letters providing the only documentary proof that Roosevelt actually knew about the fighter group now training in Burma.

When Currie protested that the letter did not allow recruiting to begin until 1942, Roosevelt gave him permission to reopen negotiations with Stimson. This was done, and CAMCO hired 82 pilots and 359 technicians for the 2nd AVG. The planes were already in the pipeline, diverted from British orders: thirty-three Douglas A-20 Bostons, which were loaded aboard freighters and sent to Africa, where they would be assembled and flown to Burma; and the same number of Lockheed A-28 Hudsons, which would be able to carry their own air crews across the Pacific, once the manufacturer installed additional fuel tanks. (The same tanks would enable the Hudsons to bomb Japan from CAF airfields in East China—fields that were even now under construction.) The ground crews and one pilot left California on November 21 aboard *Noordam* and *Bloemfontein,* the latter on its second voyage carrying U.S. airmen for service in China.

To equip the 3rd AVG—a fighter group like the one already in Burma—a shipment of Vultee Vanguards was already on its way to Rangoon. Under Tommy Corcoran's share-the-pain plan, the pilots would be navy men, but it was the navy that wanted recruiting put off until January 1942. As usual, Currie saw the way out: bring Chinese pilots to Toungoo and train them to fly the Vanguards. As it happened, Chennault had already agreed to turn these wood-and-steel fighters over to the CAF, while keeping the Republic Lancers for his own use. But Currie's brainstorm gave him a chance to obtain something he needed as much as planes. Yes, he replied, he would be happy to train a Chinese fighter squadron at Kyedaw airfield—if Currie sent him thirty American staff officers to manage the project.

The British too were coming on board. Prodded by Washington, Winston Churchill instructed Brooke-Popham to do what he could for China. The air marshal promised to send a Buffalo squadron from Singapore, complete with volunteer pilots and ground crews, and to investigate the possibility of releasing a bomber squadron as well. (Liquid-cooled Hawker Hurricanes were now reaching East Asia, but no new bombers were in prospect.)

Chennault was delighted. "Rush organization and equipment [Buffalo] unit fastest possible," he radioed Joe Alsop, whom he had sent to Singapore on a scrounging mission, "and explore possibility Blenheim volunteer squadron early date." But Alsop was not there to receive the radiogram. The British had authorized him to requisition parts and supplies, but there was little in Singapore of use to the AVG; then Bill Pawley turned up, saw Alsop's letter of authority, and realized that it would be much more useful in the Philippines. He took Alsop and the letter to Manila and managed to obtain a considerable stock of P-40 tires and parts, which the U.S. Navy loaded into three flying boats and sent to Rangoon.

So the logjam had broken. There was not a man of importance in Washington who did not understand that war in the Pacific was a certainty—that the only question was how it could be managed with the least damage to American interests. (As Henry Stimson recalled, Roosevelt on November 25 told his military advisers that the challenge was "how we should maneuver [Japan] into the position of firing the first shot without allowing too much danger to ourselves.") As a result of the new thinking, Lauchlin Currie was able to shake loose two tons of tires, ailerons, and miscellaneous spare parts for the AVG Tomahawks. The ailerons and half the tires were put aboard *Silver Star,* which sailed November 25. Currie requested space for the other tires and 2,300 pounds of emergency spare parts on the Pan Am Clipper flying to Hawaii overnight on December 3–4. Six army officers were bumped from this flight to make room for the cargo and the lieutenant in charge of it: Ajax Baumler, posted to AMISSCA but intended to serve with Chennault. Another 1,000 pounds would follow on the Clipper leaving San Francisco at sunset on Sunday, December 7.

At Mingaladon Cantonment, the Pawley brothers closed their assembly line. The last Tomahawk off the line was P-8101, which had been set aside because it lacked so many parts; it had since been made whole with pieces of the Tomahawks wrecked in training. Byron Glover took it up for a test flight, but was forced north by a squall, so he landed at Kyedaw airfield and handed it over without further formalities. The delivery brought the AVG's strength to sixty-two planes, including two without guns or radios.

One more Tomahawk, the one whose wings had been ruined by salt-water immersion, was still at Mingaladon. CAMCO workers loaded it onto a flatbed truck and sent it up the dusty road to Lashio and Loiwing, and the American supervisors and most of the Chinese technicians soon followed it. But Bill Pawley kept his office in Rangoon and a skeleton crew at Mingaladon, since he expected to be given the contract to maintain China's "International Air Force," as he called it. If every bet came up a winner, this would ultimately involve fourteen squadrons, of which nine would be manned by American, three by Chinese, and two by British Commonwealth crews.

At Kyedaw airfield, in these final weeks of peace, three more pilots left for home, leaving Chennault with eighty names on his pilot roster.* However, that number included at least twenty recent arrivals who had not been checked out in Tomahawks. By the most generous estimate, therefore, the American Volunteer Group in the first week of December had about as many combat-ready pilots as it had planes: sixty.

---

* Ninety-nine combat pilots and ten instructors had sailed for Burma. Of thirty-seven pilots on *Jaegersfontein,* two were killed, nine quit, and two took staff positions. *Bloemfontein* carried seventeen pilots; one was killed and another went home. The first *Zaandam* contingent included six pilots, all still with the squadrons on December 7. *Klipfontein* carried ten, of whom two quit and one joined the staff. *Boschfontein* brought twenty-six, including a flight instructor and a combat pilot who was assigned to the AVG Beechcraft. On her second voyage, *Zaandam* carried four combat pilots and nine instructors.

Flaming Till Hell Won't Have It

December 1941

unday, December 7, brought high winds and rain to Southeast Asia. On Phu Quoc Island, off the south coast of French Indochina, a starter truck nosed up to a fighter plane that any AVG pilot—harking back to Chennault's chalk talks—would have identified as a Mitsubishi Zero. In fact, it was an army plane, the Nakajima *Ki*-43 Hayabusa, so new that only fifty of these retractable-gear fighters were yet in service. This one had olive green topsides and a pale gray belly. The wings and fuselage were emblazoned with huge red disks, emblematic of the rising sun and Japan's imperial destiny; the rudder was slashed by a broad white arrow, showing that the Hayabusa belonged to the 64th Sentai; and a white band on the fuselage, behind the cockpit, showed that it was the commander's personal plane.*

If Japan had a Claire Chennault, he was Tateo Kato. They had crossed paths in 1938, when then-Captain Kato flew the fixed-gear Nakajima Nate in its first combat mission, shooting down three CAF biplanes near Hankou. A year later the 64th Sentai was in Manchuria for a full-scale border war between Japan and the Soviet Union. Kato was

---

* A sentai was the equivalent of a USAAF or RAF group, though with fewer planes (in the case of the 64th Sentai, three twelve-plane squadrons plus a small headquarters flight). Unlike his counterpart in American or British service, the group commander often led his pilots in combat.

credited with shooting down seven Russian planes, promoted to major, and hailed as the best of the "Imperial wild eagles." His fame (unusual in Japan, which rarely celebrated a hero who had not given his life in the emperor's service) may have been testimony to the army's need to glorify a war in which it had suffered huge casualties. Or it may been a tribute to Kato's dash and good humor, which made him a natural subject for Japanese reporters. A photograph from the time shows him as a full-faced and handsome man, with a broad nose and a full-blown mustache. The similarities to the young Chennault are irresistible: the mustache, the sheepskin flying suit, the gamecock stance, and even—as we are assured by Kato's eulogizers—his flair for leadership and his passion for baseball, which he played in roughhouse fashion with his men.

The starter truck had an auxiliary engine in its bed, which spun the Hayabusa's propeller through a rod-and-claw device extending over the cab. When the engine fired, the truck disconnected and moved to the next plane in line. When all engines had been started, the fighters rolled down the sod runway, taking to the air between rows of mechanics and clerks who waved their caps in farewell salute.

It was midafternoon when Major Kato sighted the gray troopships through the rain. In the leading vessel was General Tomioka Yamashita, commander of the 25th Army, a barrel-shaped officer with a piggish face and a genius for improvisation. The convoy had hugged the Indochina coast all morning, pretending to steam to Bangkok; at noon, it had turned and begun its dash across the Gulf of Thailand to Malaya. Kato and his men flew air cover until sunset. They could not communicate with the fleet. The Hayabusas had radios, but they were useless in the air; and even if it had been otherwise, the Japanese army and navy used different radio frequencies, just as they used different ammunition for guns that were nominally the same caliber. Kato had a logbook strapped to his thigh. "All the planes under my command are working according to plan," he wrote. Then, inspired by the glory of the moment, he cried out to General Yamashita: "Please make a clean job of it!"

In the fall of 1941, like two wheels turning, the two Japanese air forces had undergone a massive transformation. Navy fighter squadrons were withdrawn from China and mounted on the aircraft carriers that would take them across the Pacific Ocean to Hawaii. Other JNAF units, and especially the land-based heavy bombers, went to bases on Taiwan and French Indochina, from which they would support the army's move

---

Nakajima Ki-43 Hayabusa

When the Japanese army decided to acquire a retractable-gear fighter, it again turned to the Nakajima company. Like its predecessor, the *Ki-43* sacrificed durabiity for lightness, and had no pilot armor, self-sealing fuel tanks, or internal starter. For all that, it was clumsy and stiff in its combat trials, causing its development to be shelved. (Its remarkably efficient powerplant, however, was borrowed for the Mitsubishi Zero.) In the spring of 1941, butterfly combat flaps were added to the *Ki-43*, increasing the wing area and transforming a sluggish fighter into one that could actually turn inside a Zero. The modified version went into service in July, by which time the JAAF was giving pet names to its warplanes, to oblige journalists who found it difficult to write about aircraft identified only by their number and function. Thus the *Ki-43*, officially Type One Army Fighter, became *Hayabusa*—Peregrine Falcon. Because of its late start, only fifty planes were in service in December 1941. The specifications are for the early-model *Ki-43*-I.

Engine: 1,050-hp Nakajima air-cooled supercharged radial
Crew: one
Wingspan: 37 feet 6 inches
Combat weight: 5,000 lb
Maximum range: 750 miles (greater with drop-tanks)
Top speed: 305 mph at 15,000 feet
Armament: one 12.7-mm and one 7.7-mm machine gun in the nose; two 33-lb bombs

into the "Southern Treasure Chest"—Malaya, the Philippines, and especially the Dutch Indies. The navy had 1,300 warplanes in service, including 400 Zeros, and all of them were committed to the breakout scheduled for the night of December 7–8.

The army air force was nearly as large, but many JAAF squadrons were committed to the defense of the Japanese home islands, to the border watch in Manchuria, and to the continuing war in China. That left only 725 planes to support the landings in Malaya and the Philippines.

The Japanese breakout was an astonishing venture, ranging across 4,000 miles of ocean, against the combined might of the British Commonwealth, the Dutch colonial army, and the United States. Everything depended upon the success of the air strikes scheduled for the first hours of war, yet the defenders matched the attackers almost plane for plane. There was, therefore, no guarantee of victory, and the mood among the Japanese pilots was somber rather than joyous, as suggested by Major Kato's diary entry of December 6:

> Proceeded to headquarters to effect liaison on the matter of escorting a convoy fleet. . . . It occurred to me that this was one of the heaviest responsibilities ever thrown on my shoulders, but there is nothing to be done but to fulfill the task to the best of my ability and at all costs. . . . I saw [Lieutenant Colonel Hiroshi Onishi] in Saigon, who is detailed to lead the convoy fleet and to command a heavy bomber unit. I discussed details with him. Made up my mind to die with the heavy bombers, if need be.

The need did not arise. The only plane to challenge the invasion fleet was a British flying boat, a lend-lease PBY Catalina that blundered into the convoy's path on the afternoon of December 7. The Catalina was shot down by a Nakajima Nate from the 1st Sentai—first blood of the Pacific war.

Then night closed down, a better escort than the Nates and Hayabusas could provide. At 7:30 P.M., Kato dipped his wings and led his squadrons back across the Gulf of Thailand, navigation lights aglow. The nearer he came to Phu Quoc Island, the stronger the wind and the heavier the rain, and the Hayabusas began to drift apart. Unlike navy fighter pilots, Kato's men had no radio direction finders. Three Hayabusas were lost at sea—the 64th Sentai's worst hour in four years of war.

Just after midnight, the first shells exploded on Malaya's northeastern coast. The moment was brilliantly chosen. In Malaya, the troops had a high tide and a full moon to help them ashore. In Hawaii, beyond the international date line, it was daybreak on Sunday, lighting the target for the JNAF planes, while the American sailors and airmen were sleeping.

Nobody thought to alert Kyedaw airfield to the attacks on Malaya and Hawaii. The men of the AVG slumbered until their usual predawn reveille, got up, ate breakfast, and went to their duty stations. The news broke upon them at 7 A.M., by which time the war was seven hours old. "Somebody ran in to the ready-room and said the U.S. was now at war with Japan," wrote R. T. Smith in his diary. "We could hardly believe it even though it was confirmed on the radio. Everybody stood around laughing and kidding about it, although it was easy to see there was really plenty of tension." Harvey Greenlaw's first thought was to telephone his wife in Toungoo. (He had taken to sleeping at the airfield, while she remained at the house on Steel Street.) Olga wept, told her maid to make coffee, then tuned the radio to KGEI in San Francisco. The Japanese, she concluded from the short-wave bulletins, were "rushing up and down the globe like mad dogs, frothing at the mouth and biting everything in sight." So it seemed, with Japanese troops ashore in Malaya, the U.S. Pacific Fleet devastated in Hawaii, and bombs crashing on Hong Kong and Wake Island. Olga dressed and packed a bag for Harvey and another for herself: if the AVG was at war, she reasoned, she too would spend her nights at Kyedaw airfield.

Chennault had fallen into the habit of standing a dusk and dawn watch in the control tower, a bamboo box a few feet off the ground that provided Kyedaw's best view of the mountains to the east. On December 8, sunrise came without incident: dark one moment, and then, as if a switch had been turned, night gave way to blue sky and scattered clouds. Chennault climbed down from the tower and walked across the runway. Midway, he saw one of the radiomen running toward him and waving a piece of paper. Chennault snatched the bulletin, read it, and hurried to the headquarters shack, where he proceeded to put the AVG on a war footing. He designated Oley Olson's Hell's Angels as his "assault echelon," their planes to be gassed, armed, and parked at the south end of the runway, ready to take off. Jack Newkirk's Panda Bears would provide their "support echelon," while Sandy Sandell's Adam & Eves stood by in reserve. To protect Kyedaw airfield during the coming night, thirty-eight lanterns were filled with kerosene and placed in the operations building; if need be, they would be lighted and brought out to line the runway. Otherwise, Kyedaw was to be blacked out, while decoy lights burned at the RAF dispersal field four miles to the north.

What else? Chennault canceled all leaves, ordered the hospital to be evacuated to Kunming, and sent Oley Olson down to Rangoon to ask the British for steel helmets. When that was done, he drafted a radiogram to the Aeronautical Commission in Chongqing. Like all such communications, it was addressed to General Chou Chih-jou but intended for Madame Chiang Kai-shek, and through her the generalissimo:

Suggest moving Group into Yunnan at once as we are not prepared for combat operations here.

Olga Greenlaw reached the airfield at 10 A.M., in time to see the CNAC Douglas taking off with the AVG sick list and some of the medical staff. "Everyone was togged out in side arms," she recalled. "Gurkha guards with glinting bayonets walked their posts, and pilots and planes stood ready to take the air at a minute's warning. All our cars were being hurriedly camouflaged with green and yellow paint." The exec's wife was refused a weapon, though she badly wanted one. Annoyed, Greenlaw wandered over to the headquarters shack, where Chennault conscripted her to write the story of the AVG's first day at war. So Olga Greenlaw joined the staff. She closed the house on Steel Street, moved into the infirmary, and became keeper of the Group War Diary, for which she earned $150 a month, the same as a male clerk-typist.

Joe Alsop greeted the war on Hong Kong island. Having worn out his welcome in the Philippines, he had caught the last CNAC Douglas out of Manila, only to find himself bumped from his onward flight. Nationalist officials had parked their families in the British colony, safe from the bombing and deprivation of Chongqing, and now were grabbing every available seat to get them back again. The CNAC planes left at night, preferably when the moon was darkened by clouds or rain. Daytimes, Japanese planes roared over the colony, bombing and strafing, and Japanese troops encircled the perimeter. Against them, Hong Kong had virtually no defense, for its big guns—positioned by the Royal Navy—pointed uselessly out to sea.

Lieutenant Ajax Baumler had made it as far as Wake Island, where he awoke to Japanese bombs, shells, and bullets. The Pan Am Clipper, a sitting duck at her mooring in the coral lagoon, escaped with twenty-seven bullet holes, none in a vital spot. The cargo was dumped and the Clipper filled with refugees, including Baumler and a dozen civilian workers. At noon, the overloaded flying boat dragged herself clear of the lagoon, banked to the eastward, and retraced her path to shattered Hawaii. Left on the wharf to be captured by the Japanese were 2,300 pounds of Tomahawk tires and spare parts.

Also in mid-Pacific was *Silver Star,* bound for Rangoon with P-40 tires and ailerons; she was diverted to Australia. So were *Noordam* and *Bloemfontein*, carrying a hundred men of Chennault's bomber group, the 2nd AVG. In Australia, the armorers, crew chiefs, mechanics, and one pilot were taken back into the U.S. Army. The same fate befell their Lockheed Hudson bombers, still on the tarmac at Burbank, California.

In Washington next day, even as the U.S. Congress was declaring war on Japan, Lauchlin Currie drafted a memo for the president, pointing out there was no longer any reason to pretend that Chennault's airmen were volunteers in the service of China. Give them back the ranks they had formerly held, he reasoned, and the rogue pilots would be transformed into "an American task force" in the thick of the war.

Wednesday morning, December 9, the Kyedaw air raid alarm sounded at 3:30 A.M. The 2nd Squadron had the alert duty, and four Panda Bears took off and circled the base for more than an hour. At 5 A.M., no hostile aircraft having made their appearance, Chennault called them back in, and the ground crew lined the runway with lanterns. Guided by these faint pools of light, Tex Hill came in, overshot the runway, and piled his Tomahawk in a heap at the far end. "He was knocked a little goofy," one of the technicians recalled. "When we got there he was wandering around, his clothes soaked with gasoline. He had a cigarette in one hand and a match in the other. Luckily, he hadn't struck the match. Somebody took it out of his hand."

The ground crews then lined up all available cars and trucks, aimed the headlamps across the tarmac, and brought down the other three Tomahawks without mishap. "This was a true alarm," Olga Greenlaw noted in the Group War Diary, "but evidently the Japanese mistook the location of the Kyedaw aerodrome and no bombs were dropped." More likely, thunder and lightning from an electrical storm fooled the border watchers into thinking that a raid was underway: Japanese records do not mention any foray into Burma that night.

As soon as daylight came, Chennault told Lacy Mangleburg to take the AVG photo plane for another look at Chiang Mai airport. The photo plane was equipped with a Fairchild camera appropriated from the RAF and mounted in the baggage compartment. A hole had been cut in the bottom of the fuselage, the wing guns removed and the ports taped over, and the fuselage otherwise slicked up, giving the photo plane an edge over any likely interceptor. Six conventionally armed Tomahawks escorted it to Chiang Mai, tucked among steep mountains 175 miles east of Toungoo. No Japanese planes were in evidence, so Chennault scheduled a more ambitious reconnaissance for Thursday. With Ed Rector and Bert Christman flying shotgun, Erik Shilling took the photo plane down to the RAF airfield at Moulmein, directly across Martaban Bay from Rangoon. The Tomahawks refueled, flew south along Tenasserim province—a sliver of Burmese territory bordering on Thailand—then crossed the border and flew to Bangkok. Shilling photographed Don Muang airport from 20,000 feet; when his photographs were developed, they showed upwards of eighty planes on the tarmac.

A dozen Nates of the 77th Sentai had bullied their way into Thailand on the morning of December 8, shooting down three Royal Thai fighters that presumed to challenge them. They were followed later in the day by an equal number of Mitsubishi *Ki*-30 attack planes belonging to the 31st Sentai. These two groups set up headquarters at Don Muang airport, and over the next few days their remaining squadrons flew in to join them. There were probably some Royal Thai aircraft at Don Muang as well. In any event, 80 to 100 planes was the number Chennault reported to Chongqing, using it to reinforce his plea that the AVG be immediately evacuated from Burma. "No aircraft reporting net here," he pointed out, "and position very dangerous because impossible to prevent surprise." In the meantime, Ken Merritt took the train to Rangoon and brought back the first of Bill Pawley's CW-21 Demons. As an interceptor, the plane was "phenomenal," taking off in a few hundred feet and climbing almost a mile in sixty seconds, and it was supposed to give the AVG an edge that was lacking in its slow-climbing Tomahawks.

Chennault was not the only man lobbying Chongqing. From Singapore, Air Marshal Brooke-Popham was urging Chiang Kai-shek to make good on their "understanding, amounting practically to an agreement," that the AVG would help defend Burma, and especially Rangoon, where aerial reinforcements from India had to refuel before they could continue down the Malay Peninsula to Singapore.

Chiang shared Brooke-Popham's concern for the safety of Rangoon, though he was more interested in its harbor facilities. For all practical purposes, the Burmese capital was his only link with the outside world—

the cornucopia through which America would spill its lend-lease bounty into China. He therefore agreed to lend one AVG squadron to the Royal Air Force, stipulating that the pilots and planes remain under his command. The compromise was the generalissimo at his most devious: providing half the loaf, complicating the command structure, and retaining the leading string in his own fist.

Chennault cut the orders on Thursday, December 11, detaching a squadron for duty at Mingaladon airport outside Rangoon. Again, the assignment went to the 3rd Squadron, probably because so many Hell's Angels had been trained as fighter pilots in the army or the marines. Twenty crew chiefs, armorers, radiomen, and cooks went down to Rangoon on the overnight train. Four technicians and three pilots followed them next morning, driving the trucks and sedans that the squadron would need in Rangoon. And at 10:30 A.M. on Friday, the main group of eighteen Hell's Angels lifted off from Kyedaw airfield. Chennault duly reported the move to Chongqing, adding that the squadron had been sent to Mingaladon airport "for greater security"— not a word about helping an ally or shoring up Rangoon's defenses.

The pilots sent to Mingaladon included three detached from other squadrons, while nine Hell's Angels stayed behind at Kyedaw airfield. Chennault would come out of the Pacific war with a reputation as a gambler—always attacking, always taking risks—but in truth he did not gamble except with the best hand he could deal for himself. He would not send a pilot into harm's way until he judged him ready for combat, even if that meant permanent reserve status for pilots like the former flying boat captain, Conant/Perry. Among those deemed worthy were R. T. Smith and Paul Greene from Randolph Field. They were agreeably surprised by their billets at Mingaladon: two-man rooms in a barrack at the southern end of the airport. "After landing and dispersing our ships," R. T. wrote in his diary, "we went to our quarters in the officers' barracks. Nice quarters & good mess. A better setup than Toungoo."

Group Captain Manning assigned the Hell's Angels to Mingaladon's east-west runway—the crosspiece of the letter **A**—while his 67th Squadron used the north-south leg. Each squadron was further divided into two flights, one at each end of its assigned runway. Thus, when the alarm went off, upwards of thirty planes would bounce across the gravel from four different directions, blowing up a dust storm as they went, and take to the air at the midpoint of their intersecting runways. This system

was put to the test on Saturday, December 13, when the Burma
Observation Corps reported that Japanese bombers had entered Tenasserim province from Thailand. Fourteen Buffaloes and sixteen
Tomahawks made the rush across the gravel, sweeping past each other
in a maneuver that would have done credit to the Flying Trapeze—"the
damnedest rat race you ever saw," Curt Smith recalled. One Hell's Angel
had to slam on his brakes to avoid a Buffalo, but the thirty fighters got
airborne without damage, and faster than any other system would have
permitted. They then climbed to a chilly rendezvous, three miles above
the chalk-white runways and the green-brown rice fields that spread out
on all sides of the airport.

The Japanese air force assigned to Malaya and Burma was the 3rd
Hikoshidan, commanded by Lieutenant General Michio Sugawara. A
clerkish-looking man with a forage cap planted squarely on his head,
two broad patches for eyebrows, mournful eyes, and a mustache
trimmed to the exact length of his mouth, Sugawara had no interest
in Burma except as it posed a threat to his operations and those of
General Yamashita's 25th Army in Malaya. He had sent a scout to
Rangoon on Wednesday, and the report was reassuring: only four
aircraft, "type uncertain," had been seen in the vicinity of the Burmese
capital. Still, the Tenasserim district of Burma—that sliver of land
bordering on Thailand—must be neutralized, or the British would
use it as an assembly point from which to reinforce their army in
Malaya. Japanese commandos had already seized Victoria Point, the
southernmost town in Tenasserim. Now Sugawara ordered the
destruction of Mergui, the next town north. He gave the assignment
to two of his heavy-bomber sentais, the 12th and the 60th, with
fifty-one Mitsubishi Sallys between them.

They never saw the Allied interceptors. The Buffalo pilots returned
to Mingaladon when it became obvious that the raiders were not bound
for Rangoon. The Hell's Angels, however, could not make radio contact
either with the 67th Squadron or with fighter control at the airport; they
patrolled aimlessly for an hour and a half, until they were low on gasoline.
Then they too flew back to Mingaladon.

The Japanese air crews returned to their base at Phnom Penh and
reported that the mission had been a complete success, with all bombs
hitting the target. This was a considerable exaggeration: Group Captain
Manning sent three Buffaloes down to Tenasserim to protect it from

further attack, and the detachment apparently had no difficulty using the airfield at Mergui.

On Sunday, after an uneventful day, the RAF issued passes to the Hell's Angels, allowing them to drive the twelve miles into Rangoon—a drab city altogether, but with a half-dozen watering holes, from the raucous Silver Grill to the stately bar of the Strand Hotel, which was owned by a Swiss and managed accordingly. "Bad day for all men and lots of pilots," wrote Daniel Hoyle in the squadron log; "they went to Rangoon, Burma, on various amusement occasions, arriving back for duty at the aerodrome, in the wee hours of the morning." For Paul Greene, R. T. Smith, Percy Bartelt, and Lewis Bishop, that hour was 4:30 on Monday morning. Oley Olson was keeping sixteen Tomahawks on alert duty, so they were rousted out again at 5:30 A.M.

Lauchlin Currie's brainstorm of December 8—that the AVG be inducted into the U.S. Army as a task force already in place—was picked up by the War Department, and from there made its way to AMISSCA headquarters in Chongqing. On December 12, even as the Hell's Angels were settling in at Mingaladon, General Magruder drafted an appeal to Chennault, asking him to go back into uniform and to bring his pilots with him. At first, Magruder had Chennault returning to active duty as "brigadier general or colonel." Before sending the message, however, he crossed out those words and inserted these: "*if so, what grade?*" Not long after, he began a radiogram with an actual blank for the Old Man's rank: "If Chennault were commissioned immediately as _____ ," the AVG would be more easily reinforced through military channels.

Chennault would have been delighted to return to active duty—had twice tried to do so, in fact: during his Christmas furlough in 1939 and again in the fall of 1940—but not as a field-grade officer. His colonel's leaves may have been self-bestowed, but after four years he had exhausted the satisfaction to be derived from them. Now he wanted to wear a general's stars on his shoulder tabs. He composed a careful message for Madame Chiang, asking if the generalissimo would be willing to let the AVG return to American control. He scrupulously laid out the advantages: China would save money, reinforcements would be more likely, and there would be fewer disciplinary problems with the "enlisted men." (He called them that.) As for disadvantages, he mentioned just one: that the army might assign a commander who did not understand China or the Chinese—i.e., somebody other than Claire Chennault. There would also be a discrepancy between army pay and what CAMCO had promised the men, but China could finesse that problem by matching their service income with an equal amount in local funds, as had been done by South American countries that had hired U.S. military personnel. Over the long run, the men would come out as well as under their present contracts.

Nervous as a cat at Kyedaw airfield, Chennault ordered another patrol of Thailand. After touring Chiang Mai and nearby towns, the Tomahawks returned with the news that there were still no aircraft on the ground in northern Thailand. Chennault was not reassured. He sent another radiogram to Chongqing, asking for permission to move to Rangoon, leaving just one squadron at Kyedaw as a backup—not the best disposition, perhaps, but better than gambling most of his people, planes, and supplies at this crazily exposed location on the Thai border. There was no reply from Chongqing, so Chennault went back to plan one: let the AVG quit Burma and resettle in Kunming. This evoked a response, dictated by Chiang Kai-shek, signed by madame, and routed through General Chou. As always, it was a compromise. Oley Olson and the Hell's Angels would have to stay at Mingaladon airport, but the rest of the AVG could fall back on Yunnan province.

Kunming was 700 air miles from Toungoo—the outside edge of the Tomahawk's range—across one of the world's most inhospitable frontiers. The move was therefore more complicated than dispatching the Hell's Angels to Rangoon. The first step was to ferry a skeleton crew of technicians over the mountains to Kunming, which was done on Wednesday, December 17. (On the same day, the War Department radioed General Magruder that he could commission "all American pilots now serving in the AVG," but it gave him no guidance on what rank its commander should hold.) On Thursday, three CNAC transports picked up the headquarters staff and enough ammunition, oxygen, and supplies for two weeks of combat operations. Paul Frillmann was somewhat surprised to find himself on the list of "combat personnel." Similarly privileged were Olga Greenlaw, her dog Lucy, and a monkey belonging to the 2nd Squadron technicians, who were in the habit of getting the beast drunk on beer, for the fun of seeing him stagger about the barrack.

The Tomahawks would fly to Kunming under their own power. While they were rolling across Kyedaw's asphalt runway for the last time, Freeman Ricketts taxied into a Studebaker, destroying his propeller and the sedan's trunk, and George Burgard lost power and rolled off the end of the runway. That left thirty-four Tomahawks to make the move into China. In lieu of any better map, each pilot had been given a mimeographed sketch of the route, marked with distances and compass headings.

The Adam & Eves made the flight nonstop, navigating "IFR" to Mandalay and Lashio, then turning northeast over the mountains. They stayed at 21,000 feet to clear the summits and to lessen their chances of meeting a Japanese patrol. En route, John Dean's oxygen tube came loose; he passed out, drifted away from the formation, and regained consciousness at a lower altitude, whereupon he fixed the problem and flew on to Kunming without further incident. The city was easy to find: smoke was billowing into the thin, clear air. A few hours earlier, the JAAF 21st Hikotai—a mixed group of eight or ten Nakajima Nates, fitted with auxiliary fuel tanks and escorting a like number of twin-engined Kawasaki *Ki*-48 light bombers—had flown up from Hanoi to bomb and strafe the city. "The streets were strewn with bodies," said Fritz Wolf of his first sight of Kunming. "The Chinese . . . walked about the streets and picked up their dead, placing them in neat piles."

The Panda Bears made the flight in two stages, refueling at the brick-red airstrip at Lashio before following the Burma Road into Yunnan province.

The headquarters staff and the Panda Bears were billeted at Hostel Number One in the northern part of the city. The men were agreeably surprised to be given private rooms, each with a bunk, chair, table, bureau, desk, and charcoal brazier. (The charcoal was a mixed blessing. Without it the chill entered their bones; with it, they risked carbon monoxide poisoning.) The Adam & Eves were assigned to Hostel Number Two on the airport road, where the accommodations were more primitive but still more pleasant than at Kyedaw. Actually a cluster of brick buildings, the hostel was called "Adobe City" by the men of the 1st Squadron.

The AVG technicians had a more difficult route to travel. On December 20, eight trucks and two sedans left Kyedaw on the road to Mandalay, and another convoy left next day. They carried most of the ground personnel, the heavy supplies, and an undetermined amount of contraband. They were two weeks on the tortuous mountain road, dealing with officious Britons, obsequious Anglo-Burmans, corrupt Chinese, and exotic tribes whose women had necks stretched to giraffe-like proportions, and whose men tattooed their legs in lieu of stockings. The trip delighted radioman Smith, that fan of *The Royal Road to Romance:*

> We are driving on red roads through rolling, hilly forest. Great clumps of poinsettias grow wild at the side of the highway. . . . Red dust over green shrubs makes a purplish tinge; we ride over purple hills. There are no palm trees now; the people look more Chinese than Burmese. Their skins are lighter, and they wear trousers instead of skirts. . . .
>
> Yesterday we descended into a gorge and made 15 tight, steep hairpin curves to get out. I stopped the car halfway up and watched the seven trucks below. Several could not make the curves at the first try, and the drivers had to back up to get around. If they had backed up an inch or so too far, they would have rolled hundreds of feet to the river below.

Remaining at Kyedaw airfield—"Point A," as it was called—were twenty-seven men under Edgar Goyette, a former navy pilot now serving as staff officer. They would maintain Kyedaw as a backup field, repair facility, supply depot, and relay point for radio messages between Kunming and Rangoon. Their first task was to overhaul twelve Tomahawks that had been unable to make the flight into China.

In Kunming—"Point X"—Chennault picked up a few more volunteers. As if to make up for the loss of Joe Alsop, the U.S. Navy loaned him an officer named Robert DeWolfe. A lieutenant commander, his title was AVG intelligence officer, but his real work was in supply. The other addition was Gerhard Neumann, a German Jew whom Chennault had befriended in 1939, and whom he now hired as a mechanic. Neumann turned his Reliance Auto Service over to another refugee and moved into Hostel Number One. The culture shock was considerable. The technicians, he recalled long after, "were hard-drinking, poker-playing, rough and tough, yet they . . . went out of their way to teach me the American way of life."

> Never before had I heard of Log Cabin syrup, hotcakes or waffles. I didn't know what to expect when one of the Americans called at the breakfast table, "Shoot the jam, Sam!" I had never seen—or even heard of—a baseball game. . . . When [we] walked behind an attractive Chinese girl in a tight silk dress, my Texan friend sighed[:] "I'd like to bite her in the ass and let her drag me to death!" I couldn't imagine what this Texan had in mind: I

knew neither the three-letter word for posterior nor why he wanted to be dragged to death.

Neumann's name was too cumbersome for the Americans, who dubbed him "Herman the German." He repaid their friendship with concerts on his Hohner accordion, playing such 1941 favorites as "When the Lights Go on Again All Over the World."

Months of work and planning had preceded the move to Kunming, enabling Chennault to assign four pilots to alert duty their first night in Kunming. If the city had been bombed today, he reasoned, it would probably be bombed tomorrow. ("Japanese tactics . . . can usually be counted on to repeat until a severe check is met with.") But Friday passed without incident, and it was 9:30 A.M. on Saturday, December 20, before the warning net reported that ten bombers had crossed into Yunnan province from Indochina. At Wu Chia Ba airport, the yellow warning flag went up and Chennault hurried to his command bunker, located in a graveyard overlooking the airfield. Radioman Don Whelpley recalled the scene:

> Inside the dank, dark dugout . . . were gathered Chennault, his Chinese interpreter, the usual radio operators and Chinese personnel. . . . I watched Chennault's face as reports from the Chinese air raid net came in, tracing the progress of the attackers.
> "Heavy engine noise at Kaiyuan."
> The lines tightened about his mouth as he pulled a pipe from the pocket in his khaki jacket. I knew he was nervous by the way he crammed tobacco into it.
> "Unknown aircraft over Hwaning, headed northwest."

At Wu Chia Ba, the red flare went up and sixteen 1st Squadron Tomahawks rolled down the gravel runway and rose into the air. The Adam & Eves climbed to 15,000 feet and flew southeast. As the assault echelon, Sandy Sandell and his men would prowl fifty miles of railroad track from Kunming to Iliang, intercepting the Japanese bombers as they flew "IFR" to the target. The cold was numbing, despite the mittens, boots, jacket, and trousers that encased the pilot's body, and the helmet, goggles, and oxygen mask protecting his head. "It's strange how big the sky really is, once you get up there," Jim Cross wrote of this first combat patrol. "No trick at all to completely miss a bomber formation, even though it may be only a couple of miles or so out of the path. . . . It was bitter cold and my [wind]shield was already frosted."

Jack Newkirk's 2nd Squadron served as backup. Four Panda Bears circled directly above the airfield, while four others flew off to the northwest, meanwhile climbing to 15,000 feet. Newkirk led the second flight. Ten minutes after takeoff, he was astonished to see a formation of twin-engined planes coming toward him, eight miles out and 2,000 feet below. The intruders were arranged like migrating geese in a "vee of vees"—a diamond of four bombers followed by two flights of three, fanned out to port and starboard. In the AVG command bunker, Don Whelpley heard the Panda Bears debating whether this was the enemy formation:

"There they are."

"That can't be the Japs."

"The hell it can't. Look at those red balls!"

Indeed, it was the Japanese, following their long-established tactic of circling around the target and attacking from the far side. As on Thursday, the raiders were Kawasaki *Ki*-48s—speedy, twin-engined bombers of a type later known to Allied pilots as Lily. Apparently they had an escort upon leaving Gia Lam airport, but the Nates turned back at the Indochina-Yunnan border. Perhaps the fighter squadron had exhausted its supply of drop-tanks. Or perhaps the bombers were satisfied that they would meet no opposition over Kunming.

The Panda Bears attacked from out of the sun, opening fire so soon that even their fifty-caliber nose guns could not bridge the distance. The Lilys tightened formation, turned east, and jettisoned their bombs. Thus lightened, they were almost as fast as the Tomahawks. Jack Newkirk waggled his wings and led the flight back to Wu Chia Ba, explaining when he got there that his electrical system had failed him and his guns would not fire. ("It turned out to work perfect on the ground," Don Rodewald noted in his diary, "so we all had our ideas.") Writing home a few days later, Gil Bright explained that the Panda Bears had broken off because they were so few and so far from the field. But he must have known that the explanation sounded feeble, for he added: "We lost a bit of 'face' on that deal."

The Lilys were fleeing as fast as they could, circling around Kunming to pick up the railroad line at Iliang. Instead, they met the full strength

---

Kawasaki Ki-48 Lily

Encountering the Tupelov SB-2 in China in the fall of 1937, Japanese commanders were dismayed to find that the Soviet-built bomber was almost as fast as their best fighters. They immediately called for the development of a similar aircraft for the JAAF. Kawasaki undertook the project at the expense of its work on a new twin-engined fighter plane, the *Ki*-45 (see chapter 18). The lessons learned in the fighter project were applied to the new plane. Unique among Japanese bombers, the *Ki*-48 had a slender tail section behind the bomb bay, making room for a rear-facing belly gunner (otherwise the navigator) on a platform that swung down from the fuselage step, giving him a better range of motion than the porthole belly gunner on other bombers. The plane went into service in the year 2599 (1939) and was therefore designated Type 99 Light Bomber; Allied pilots gave it the pet name of Lily. By 1941 its comparative lack of speed, defensive weaponry, and armor made it an easy target. Specifications are for the *Ki*-48-I used in the winter of 1941–1942.

Engines: two 950-hp Nakajima air-cooled radials
Crew: four
Wingspan: 57 feet 4 inches
Combat weight: 13,000 lb
Maximum range: 1,500 miles
Top speed: 300 mph at 11,500 feet
Armament: three 7.7-mm flexible machine guns; 880-lb total bomb load

---

of the Adam & Eves, who had been patrolling over Iliang all this time. Sandy Sandell spotted the Lilys coming toward him at 16,000 feet: "single tail, aluminum construction," he wrote in his combat report; "red sun on wingtips [and] fuselage, dull gray color." (Another pilot reported that the bombers were pale green.) Hewing to the Chennault doctrine, Sandell told two pilots to prowl overhead as "weavers," guarding against enemy fighters. He divided the main force into three flights of four Tomahawks; two of these were to dive on the Japanese bombers from out of the sun, while the third remained in reserve.

Sandell was not a popular leader ("a small fellow," Charlie Bond described him, "with a mustache and a very cold manner") and his attack strategy was ignored by many of his pilots. So were the lessons

Chennault had drilled into them at Kyedaw airfield. Bob Little dove through the clouds to attack the Lilys from beneath, where their defensive armament seemed to be weakest—but Charlie Bond, who was in Little's flight, decided to attack from above and from the right. The Lilys were still in the porcupine cluster they had assumed after Newkirk's attack. As the Tomahawks swept down on them, each plane lowered its "dustbin"—a hinged platform upon which a gunner lay prone in the airstream, behind and below the thickest part of the fuselage. The bombers could now put out directed fire to the rear, but paid for the protection with a considerable drop in speed.

Bond charged his machine guns. For the wing guns, this was done by yanking three T-grips on either side of the seat, while the large-caliber nose guns were armed by pulling back on handles projecting from the instrument panel. Next he turned on the optical sight. The invention of armorer Roy Hoffman and pilot Charlie Mott, this consisted of a luminous dot inside a circle, engraved on a piece of glass that was mounted on the windscreen and lit from below. It was more accurate than the ring-and-post sight still mounted on some of the Tomahawks—unless, as had been known to happen, the pilot knocked it out of alignment while lowering himself into the cockpit.

Bond then flipped the toggle switch that readied the guns for firing. The actual firing button was located on the control stick, which he held in his two gloved hands:

> I rolled and started down. As the nearest bomber eased within the gunsight ring, I squeezed the trigger on the stick. Damn it, nothing happened! I took a quick look at my gun switch. In my excitement, I had checked it so many times that I had turned it off. . . . I broke off violently—down and away, and then back up to my original position for another attack.
>
> I went in for a second attack, and all guns were blazing this time. I saw my tracers enter the fuselage of the bomber. At the last second I broke off. . . . I attacked again and again. Two bombers began to lag behind, trailing smoke.

Also in the assault echelon was Fritz Wolf, a former navy dive-bomber pilot, who not long afterward recalled the engagement for a macho aviation magazine:

> My man was the outside bomber of the right-hand V. I dived down below him and came up from underneath. . . . At 500 yards I let go with a quick

burst of all guns. It was curtains for the rear gunner of the bomber. I could see my bullets rip into him and cut him to pieces. . . . At one hundred yards I let go with a long burst, and the bullets tore into the Jap plane's motor and gas tanks. A wing folded and a motor tore loose, then the bomber exploded in midair. I yanked back on the stick. . . .

I shoved Old Bessie into a dive for another attack. This time it was the inside man of the outside V. I came out of the dive quickly and straightened out level with the bomber. . . . I could see the tail gunner blazing away at me, but none of the bullets was striking home. At fifty yards I let go with a long burst. . . . The bomber exploded, but this time I was too close and managed to pull up just inches away from the flaming coffin as it dipped earthward.

Flying on his wing through both attacks was Jim Cross of the Ferry Command, who also wrote about the battle for a popular magazine:

There was the Jap plane, dead in front of me. I could see the sun glinting on the [dustbin] gunner's goggles. . . . I saw my own tracer fire almost before I realized I'd pressed the button. The sky above me was ribboned with criss-cross fire. I waited a split second before letting go with another burst. Waited until I saw the engines of the bomber right in front of my ring sight. . . .

Five hundred miles an hour is plenty fast. That's what I was doing as I passed the bomber. But I'd seen my tracers burying themselves in it. By the time I'd leveled off and then zoomed up behind [Fritz Wolf], the Japs were miles away. But we still had another crack at them. . . . Once more it was repeated. The confusion, the screams and the roar of racing, diving Allisons. Even the sounds of the guns were lost in that.

The reserve pilots were chafing in their assigned location. They were led by Edward Leibolt, a former army fighter pilot and a member of the Bloom Gang. His wingman was Camille Rosbert, called Joe, a stocky Italian-American from Philadelphia, to whom the combat seemed "like a bunch of swarming bees. I wondered why our planes did not collide with each other, they looked so close." Finally Leibolt signaled the reserve flight to join the attack, as Rosbert recalled years later:

I tensed myself and followed him down, with my pucker string performing some strange gyrations. As the rear bomber loomed large in front of us, I pressed the gun button almost at the same time as Ed. Debris flew by as we dove down and away.

As we started in for a second run, I saw only six bombers. Ed was in the midst of the other planes and I could not make him out; so I made the run alone. With a short burst, I knew the bomber had been hit, as I pulled away and down.

This free-for-all was now joined by Ed Rector of the Panda Bears. Rector was off-duty that day, for his plane was overdue for its twenty-five-hour engine check. So he had been forced to sit out the excitement, watching the Adam & Eves and his own squadron take off, then seeing Jack Newkirk's flight return with the gun barrels whistling—audible proof that they had been in combat. (The muzzles were taped over for flight, to keep water and dust from entering.) A crew under Henry Fox was still working on Rector's Tomahawk, but he sprinted out to the flight line and yelled: "Get that goddamned cowling back on!" While Fox and the others readied the Tomahawk for takeoff, Rector buckled himself into his parachute and climbed into the cockpit. He taxied out onto the field, awed by the sight of the billowing clouds that awaited him. "I fired up that P-40 and got out and chased them," Rector said years later, banking his hands to represent his plane, the fleeing Lilys, and the Tomahawks diving among them. "I saw eight damned airplanes out there engaging them. They were pulling up like this, and shooting, and it was bizarre beyond compare." But Rector remembered his navy gunnery practice and Chennault's lectures at Kyedaw airfield. He took the high perch and came down in a long, sweeping turn behind one of the Lilys:

> I came on in, right behind the guy . . . and I drove up his ass. I got target fixation—I just saw my shots going into him, and I said, *Why doesn't he blow up?* At the last moment I realized what I was doing. I looked, and I'd shot away the jaw of the rear dustbin gunner. I looked at him—right in the eye—and I'd shot away his whole jaw. And I can see him [now], and I can see the rivets and the camouflage pattern of that damned bomber. I know that I missed him by inches. . . . I pulled up and looked back, and he was on fire. I can see the flames. But he's still in formation, and I prepare myself for another run. And then I saw him do this: the formation goes ahead, and he gradually noses down . . . flaming till hell won't have it. All afire!
>
> And then I start my next pass. I go in, and I find out that there's only one thirty-caliber going *putt-putt-putt.* I pulled and I pulled [the charging handles]. I'd fired for three or four seconds, remember, going up the ass of that guy, and then I pulled out and they cooled, and the guns were so hot that they set.

And so it went. As the story was told at the time, Fritz Wolf accounted for two bombers, Sandell another, and Louis (Cokey) Hoffman a fourth. Afterward, there was a claim by Rector, and no doubt there were others (the individual combat reports have not survived). Yet each pilot, after telling how he knocked down a bomber or two, went on to say that the formation was mostly intact when he broke off. Sandy Sandell remembered that seven planes were aloft when the Adam & Eves headed for home. Rosbert thought there were six. And Bob Neale counted eight, with all the dustbin gunners dead on their platforms.

Almost certainly, this was what happened: the two outside bombers, and probably the lead bomber, were hit again and again by the full force of the AVG. For each engine that burst into flame, two or three pilots had been pouring machine gun fire into it—adrenalin pumping, sphincters twitching, vision tunneled down to that eruption of scarlet flame and oily black smoke. Diving clear, each man was understandably convinced that he alone had killed the bomber. . . . Except Bob Neale. He was that rarity among fighter pilots, a modest man. Asked in 1962 if he thought he had shot down one of the Lilys, Neale replied: "I didn't even know if I *hit* one. I could see them, all right, but you can see a lot better than you can shoot. . . . It was all new to me. I've never been a hero type, and I wasn't figuring on starting then, if ever."

In any event, more claims were lodged than there were Lilys on the ground. A Chinese listening post reported seven bombers aloft at 11:25 A.M., after Sandy Sandell had waggled his wings and led the Tomahawks home, low on fuel and ammunition. So three planes were shot down in the battle itself, as Sandell had reported. A few days later, however, the Aeronautical Commission decided (on what evidence, it is impossible to say) that a fourth bomber exploded in midair before reaching safety in Indochina. The pilots voted to share the credit among all those who had joined the fight: fourteen Adam & Eves plus Ed Rector of the Panda Bears. On the record, then, each man was credited with four-fifteenths of a *Ki*-48.

The Japanese had little to say about this battle. The 21st Hikotai was an administrative orphan, made up of two independent squadrons, and reporting neither to General Sugawara in Bangkok nor to the JAAF commander for China; it is consequently not much mentioned in Japanese accounts of the Pacific war. (The group "advanced toward Kunming," according to the semiofficial history of the air war in

Southeast Asia, "but realized that P-40 fighters were prevailing and a difficult foe"—so the bombers turned back. There was no mention of losses, nor the usual claims of enemy fighters shot down.) But if the formation did lose four *Ki*-48s on December 20, it was a disaster unprecedented since the first months of the Sino-Japanese War: sixteen airmen dead in a single action, plus whatever casualties were sustained among the crews that made it back to Hanoi.

In that teakwood classroom at Kyedaw airfield, Chennault had assured his pilots that if the Japanese were subjected to 25 percent casualties, they would not return. It fell out as he had promised: the 21st Hikotai never came back to Kunming, and it would be nearly a month before any other Japanese formation ventured across the Indochina border. In a single hour, the American Volunteer Group had won the battle for Yunnan province.

The cost was one Tomahawk washed out. Returning to Wu Chia Ba, Ed Rector ran out of fuel and made a wheels-up landing in a vegetable field. He spent the afternoon stripping the machine guns and ammunition out of his Tomahawk, then spent the night at an AVG listening post manned by Roger Shreffler. Next day, Rector hitched a ride on a Chinese army truck, bringing his guns with him.

The other damage was slight. Charlie Bond's plane had bullet holes in the right aileron, right tail fin, and rudder. Fritz Wolf's wing root fairing was damaged, and several planes had holes in tail assemblies and cowlings. But the resourceful crew chiefs had them airworthy with a few days.

The people of Kunming, who had suffered Japanese bombs since the fall of 1940, streamed out to the airport to show their appreciation. Joe Rosbert recalled the celebration:

> Soon we heard a band coming towards the field and a long procession appeared at the entrance. Led by the mayor were hundreds of people, each one carrying something. He made a speech while we all stood in line listening. . . . Little girls, with pretty faces crowned by neatly cut bangs, stepped up and placed long pieces of purple silk around our necks and bouquets of flowers in our hands. . . . [I]n town, our car was mobbed; everybody wanted to see the "*Meikuo-jen*" [Americans]. . . . Every time we went into a shop, there would be a dozen faces crowding the entrance just to get a glimpse of us.

Chennault was less impressed. He dismissed Jack Newkirk's performance as "buck fever"—the affliction of a deer hunter who freezes upon sight of his quarry. He was not much happier with Sandy Sandell, whose assault echelons had scattered in the first pass, and whose weavers too had been drawn into the melee. "The Old Man looked crestfallen," radioman Don Whelpley recalled. "But . . . he didn't say so. Instead, he sat his boys down, and with the kindness of a fond parent, explained their mistakes. He ended the discussion with, 'Next time, fellows, get them all.'"

With the advantage of the international date line, American newspapers published the story on December 21—next morning, as it would seem, but in fact nearly two days later. In a world resounding with gigantic clashes of arms, the Yunnan skirmish was not regarded as front page news. (The *New York Times* put it on page 27.) At *Time* magazine, however, Henry Luce saw more to the story. An authentic genius of popular journalism, Luce had been born in China; and his belief in America's manifest destiny in Asia was reinforced by a visit to Chongqing in May 1941, when he was deeply impressed by Generalissimo and Madame Chiang. His guide on that occasion was Teddy White, Chennault's sometime messmate at the Methodist mission in Chongqing. When Luce returned to the U.S., he took White with him as *Time* editor for East Asia. It was the perfect melding of talents, motives, and events: White knew the background of the AVG's victory, Luce had the political agenda to play the story large, and they had a catchy name to play with. The story was entitled "Blood for the Tigers," and it told how the Japanese had bombed hapless China for three years until "lean, hard-bitten, taciturn Colonel Claire L. Chennault" recruited American volunteer fliers and brought them to Asia:

> Last week ten Japanese bombers came winging their carefree way up into Yunnan, heading directly for Kunming, the terminus of the Burma Road. Thirty miles south of Kunming, the Flying Tigers swooped, let the Japanese have it. Of the ten bombers . . . four plummeted to earth in flames. The rest turned tail and fled. Tiger casualties: none.

Flying Tigers! It was the perfect conceit—but where had it come from? The credit belonged to the AVG "Washington Squadron," as David Corcoran, Quinn Shaughnessy, Whitey Willauer, and the others had styled themselves. Not knowing that the AVG had adopted the shark face as a group insignia, the men at China Defense Supplies decided to ask the Walt Disney studio to design a unit emblem. A dragon was the obvious choice—a *flying* dragon, with its connotations of China and aerial combat. As Tommy Corcoran remembered the session, his brother (who had worked in Tokyo for General Motors) vetoed the dragon because it was a favorable omen for the Japanese; if the idea was to demoralize the enemy, a tiger would be more effective. (If so, David Corcoran had it wrong: the tiger symbolized good fortune in Japan.) Others thought that T. V. Soong made the substitution, arguing that the dragon was an archaic symbol, unsuited to modern China. Soong then quoted a proverb about "giving wings to the tiger"—i.e., adding strength to an already ferocious beast—as speaking more eloquently to the relationship between the AVG and Nationalist China.

In any event, the request went to Hollywood, and in October a Disney cartoonist sketched a darling Bengal cat with wasp-like wings and extended claws, leaping from a V-for-Victory sign. So the conceit was ready when the news arrived from Chongqing, and the "Flying Tigers" made their debut in the issue of *Time* dated December 29, 1941.

7

Such a Bright Red!

December 1941

Lightly armed, moving fast, and living off "Churchill stores"—captured supplies—the Japanese drove the Commonwealth army down through Malaya. In the Philippines, they fared equally well against U.S. and Filipino troops. Meanwhile, their air forces softened the Dutch Indies for invasion. (Sparing the oilfields, however. With no petroleum resources of her own, Japan had hoarded enough oil for six months of war; after that, like General Yamashita in Malaya, she would have to fight on what she captured from the enemy.) Below this crumbling colonial barrier, Australia lay almost defenseless, her army and air force fighting for the Commonwealth on other fronts. And to the west lay India: the jewel in Britain's crown, her inexhaustible source of cannon fodder, and now the unacknowledged fulcrum of her war effort. If India were lost, Germany and Japan could join hands across the Middle East, turning their diplomatic "Axis" into a geographical fact.

Before that final triumph, the Japanese would have to pivot west through Burma. This was an impossible task, the British believed, with the Royal Navy to prevent a seaborne invasion and nature to guard the overland route from Thailand. The geography of Southeast Asia had a distinct north-south bias: mountains and rivers (and therefore roads, railways, and national boundaries) conspired to make east-west travel difficult. Thus Britain's long-established strategy for defending India and

Burma. The two colonies shared a 900-mile frontier, but no road crossed the mountains between them. Within Burma, the Irrawaddy and the Sittang rivers provided cheap and easy transport upcountry, while discouraging travel across it, and the east-west routes were little more than mule tracks. Even the Burma Road ran north for 450 miles to Mandalay, then northeast for 200 miles, before crossing into Yunnan province near Loiwing. The British *wanted* Burma to remain a cul-de-sac, never dreaming that they would be the ones trapped in it.

Convinced that Burma could not be invaded "across the grain of the country," the chiefs of staff had left its defense to a single division under the command of Lieutenant General Donald McLeod, headquartered at Toungoo. Olga Greenlaw remembered him as "a sweet old gentleman, tall, a bit heavy, with perfectly white hair and a ruddy complexion." McLeod was a paradigm of the British colonial officer: pompous, single-minded, and brave. His 1st Burma Division had 18,000 troops on the rations list, but most were native conscripts, border police, or militiamen. The serious fighting would have to be done by 1,000 British and 3,000 Indian soldiers, trained to fight in the desert, not in the rain forest of Southeast Asia.

McLeod reported to Brooke-Popham in Singapore—a ludicrous arrangement, for Singapore was 1,200 miles *southeast* of Rangoon. Two Japanese armies held the ground between them, and radio communications were so poor that messages had to be relayed back through India. Late in December, therefore, the chiefs of staff took the responsibility for Burma away from Brooke-Popham and gave it to the new commander-in-chief for India: General the Right Honorable Sir Archibald Wavell, a one-eyed veteran of World War I, the Boer War, and long-ago skirmishes in Afghanistan. Wavell immediately dispatched the 17th Indian Division to Burma, and he followed in person on December 21, flying into Mingaladon airport in a Douglas DC-2. After a conference with Burma's commanders, McLeod and Group Captain Manning, he decided to sack them both. He then radioed London that he needed two more fighter squadrons, two more bomber squadrons, and a quantity of antiaircraft guns if he was to defend Burma. That done, he flew to Chongqing to see what assistance he could wrest from Generalissimo Chiang Kai-shek. Accompanying him on this whirlwind tour was his American deputy, Lieutenant General George Brett of the U.S. Army Air Forces.

They found the generalissimo obsessed with keeping U.S. aid flowing north from Rangoon. To accomplish this, Chiang offered six Chinese divisions to shore up the Commonwealth army in Burma, but Wavell was not interested. ("Obviously," he wrote, "it was desirable that a country of the British Empire should be defended by Imperial troops rather than by foreign.") To mollify Chiang, he agreed to accept one division, but only on paper; the troops would stay in reserve around Kunming. Wavell then tried to exact a promise that "at least one of the AVG squadrons, which Colonel Chennault wanted to remove to China, remained in Burma for the defence of Rangoon." He also asked for a portion of China's lend-lease hoard, piled on the Rangoon docks or waiting to be unloaded. "To neither of these requests," he glumly noted, "did I get a definite reply." Which, in Chennault's view, was the answer he deserved: Wavell and Brett did not make a big hit with him, nor with Generalissimo and Madame Chiang Kai-shek.

At Mingaladon airport outside Rangoon, the Hell's Angels were calling themselves "the lost squadron." Except for Ed Goyette's detachment at Kyedaw airfield, they had no backup closer than Kunming, 900 miles northeast. As for the Royal Air Force, the 67th Squadron had thirty-two Buffaloes on its roster, but half were grounded with mechanical problems, while the 60th Squadron had just four Blenheims at Mingaladon, the rest having been sent to Singapore in November for live-fire bombing practice, and there drafted into the defense of Malaya.

The Hell's Angels had come down to Mingaladon without so much as a change of clothing, expecting the Royal Air Force to supply their needs. What they got was gasoline and three pallid meals a day. When they tried to refill their oxygen tanks, they found that the Tomahawk coupling was different from a Buffalo's; the British suggested that they nip into Rangoon and "get a fitting made." Nor would British .303-caliber ammunition fit their wing guns, for the 3rd Squadron had been equipped with the 7.92-mm weapons from the Colt factory in Hartford. After the mad scramble of December 13, Group Captain Manning had instructed the Buffalo pilots to use the AVG radio frequency when they patrolled together, but no effort was made to test this policy. On Sunday, December 21, the Buffaloes went on a strafing mission into Thailand, but the Tomahawks did not go with them. (To judge by his later actions, Olson probably refused the mission.) Later that day, a Japanese formation was spotted over Tenasserim; the Buffaloes and the Tomahawks scrambled, but the interception was called off when it became obvious that the target was not Rangoon.

Some days earlier, a Japanese reconaissance plane had brought back a new set of pictures from Burma, showing forty-four planes on the ground at Mingaladon airport, Kyedaw airfield, and the advance fields in Tenasserim—evidence, as it seemed, that the British were preparing to mount an airlift into Malaya. General Sugawara therefore ordered his 77th Sentai to occupy Phitsanulok, on the Thai railroad 300 miles east of Rangoon. The 77th was a redoubtable force, credited with destroying eighteen Chinese and Soviet aircraft in the Sino-Japanese War, but like most JAAF fighter groups in December 1941, still equipped with the fixed-gear Nakajima Nate. The commander was Major Hiroshi Yoshioka, who might have been picked for the job by a Hollywood casting office: a cold-looking man with a thin mustache and a narrow face. At Phitsanulok, Yoshioka commandeered gasoline, radios, telephones, and other necessities from the Thai air force. He was then reinforced by the 31st Sentai, equipped with the Mitsubishi *Ki*-30 Ann, an all-purpose warplane like the Vultees sold to China by Bill Pawley: nonretractable landing gear, a bomb load of 600 pounds, two rifle-caliber machine guns in the wings, and another at the rear of the greenhouse canopy.

Yoshioka next established a forward airstrip at Raheng, just 200 miles east of Rangoon. From this airstrip, on December 21, his Nates and the 31st Sentai Anns set out to destroy the RAF field at Tavoy, halfway down the Tenasserim panhandle. This was the raid (unsuccessful, as it turned out) that caused the Allied scramble that Sunday afternoon.

On Monday morning, December 22, Group Captain Manning asked the Hell's Angels to help guard a troopship taking reinforcements to the Tenasserim outposts. Oley Olson and Curt Smith worked out the route and calculated that by the time the Tomahawks were over Tenasserim, their gasoline reserve would be only forty-five minutes, so Olson refused the mission. But the 67th Squadron had no trouble with fuel. The Buffaloes returned in relays to Moulmein, refueled, and in this fashion escorted the troopship from dawn to dusk. Meanwhile, two Buffaloes stationed at Mergui nipped across the border into Thailand and strafed a train "travelling south with reinforcements" for the Japanese army in Malaya—just the sort of harassment that General Sugawara was determined to prevent.

So it came to Tuesday, December 23, when sixty Mitsubishi heavy bombers lifted off from the airports at Bangkok and Phnom Penh. The *Ki*-21, which Allied pilots dubbed Sally, was a big-tailed monoplane with two huge radial engines; carrying a metric ton of bombs, it had already helped to devastate Chongqing, Kunming, Hong Kong, Manila, and Singapore. Sugawara was supremely confident about the big plane's ability to defend itself from enemy fighters. (Because the 21st Hikotai did not report to him, he had no way of knowing that its bomber squadron had lost 40 percent of its aircraft over Kunming just three days before.) So he sent them to Burma without fighter escort. Furthermore, he assigned Mingaladon airport to the 62nd Sentai, commanded by the same Colonel Onishi who had conferred with Major Kato on December 6. (Onishi was another Hollywood stereotype, a brutal-looking man with jug ears, wide nose, and lantern jaw.) The 62nd Sentai was the smallest and least experienced of Sugawara's heavy bomber groups, and Onishi could muster only fifteen early-model Sallys, each with a six-man crew and five rifle-caliber machine guns. Sugawara bolstered them with the 31st Sentai Anns from Phitsanulok, which in turn would be protected by Major Yoshioka's Nates. The three groups were supposed to meet over Raheng, near the Burma border, then fly as one great formation to Mingaladon. But the Sallys did not bother to wait for the single-engined aircraft, and by the time they crossed the border they were two miles out in front. The day was beautiful, with a light southerly breeze and hardly a cloud in the sky.

Two other heavy bomber groups—the 60th Sentai from Phnom Penh and the 98th at Don Muang—were supposed to rendezvous over Bangkok, fly north until they were just below Moulmein, then turn west across Martaban Bay for Rangoon. But the Bangkok-based Sallys left before those from Phnom Penh came over, so this formation too was split by the time it reached Burma.

At Mingaladon airport, the 67th Squadron operations room logged the news at 9:30 A.M.: "two large waves of enemy aircraft approaching Rangoon, one from east and other from southeast." But nobody alerted the Hell's Angels. For them, the warning did not come until 10 A.M., and then it consisted of only three words: *Clear the field.**

Oley Olson had reorganized the Hell's Angels into four-man sections. From dawn to dusk, the "available" section patrolled over Mingaladon or waited in the alert tent, while the men of two "standby" sections worked around the airport, ready for takeoff within thirty minutes. The "release" pilots were off duty for the day. Thus, although the Hell's Angels had fourteen airworthy Tomahawks on December 23, only twelve had pilots assigned to them. In the air, they would operate as two elements, led by George McMillan and Parker Dupouy.

McMillan and R. T. Smith were in the bamboo-and-canvas alert tent at 10 A.M., when word arrived from the RAF. They sprinted to the flight line, fired up their engines, and thereby alerted the standby pilots that they were wanted on the flight line. The first to arrive was Robert Hedman, called Duke by his squadron mates. He scrambled into his cockpit and put on his earphones. "I heard McMillan over the radio saying we were taking off," Hedman said a few days later. "I took it as a joke." Tom Haywood arrived about the same time. Circling over the airport, waiting for the two standbys to form up on him, McMillan got further details on the radio: "Enemy bombers approaching from east." Two of his men were still missing, but McMillan decided not to wait. Instead, he took his four-plane flight to the eastward, meanwhile gaining what altitude he could. At 10,000 feet, Tom Haywood let out a yell: "Hey, Mac! I see the bastards!" Sure enough, to the east and high above him, McMillan spotted the Japanese formation: fifteen huge, twin-engined bombers, pale gray on their undersides, light brown with green splotches on top, with the red disks blazing on fuselage and wing. This was the 62nd Sentai.

Since crossing into Burma, Colonel Onishi's air crews had been able to see the white A of Mingaladon's runways, and as they passed over Pegu they actually saw the 67th Squadron Buffaloes taking off to intercept them. Spurred by the sight, the pilots advanced their throttles—an understandable reaction, but one that separated them even farther from the Nates that might have protected them. Years later, Duke

---

* To the Japanese pilots, their watches set to Tokyo time, the hour was high noon.

Mitsubishi Ki-21 Sally

The standard heavy bomber of the Japanese Army Air Force, the *Ki*-21 was adopted in 1937 and saw service over Hankou, Chongqing, and the Burma Road. Lightly built and highly flammable, it came to be scorned by Allied pilots as the "Flying Zippo," after their favorite cigarette lighter. The wings were mounted at midpoint on the fuselage and had a distinct dihedral, giving the aircraft the appearance of a soaring though overweight hawk. The rudder was huge. The *Ki*-21-I (Sally-1) was defended by a machine gun in the nose, a large-caliber gun at the rear of the greenhouse, a remotely controlled tail gun, and a drum-fed gun that was shifted from port to starboard to belly, depending on the plane's position in the formation. By the outbreak of the Pacific war, most bomber groups had converted to the *Ki*-21-II (Sally-2) with larger engines and additional armament. More than 2,000 of these bombers were built before production ended, some of them by the Nakajima company, traditional provider of aircraft for the army air force. The specifications are those of the Sally-2 generally encountered by the AVG over Burma.

Engines: two 1,500-hp Mitsubishi air-cooled radials
Crew: seven
Wingspan: 74 feet
Combat weight: 16,500 lb
Maximum range: 1,500 miles
Top speed: 300 mph at 15,500 feet
Armament: one 12.7-mm and four 7.7-mm flexible machine guns; 2,200-lb total bomb load

---

Hedman remembered how the Sallys bore down on Mingaladon in "vee" formation, followed by an apparently aimless swarm of fighters:

> There were hordes of fighters, going around in a kind of beehive formation—going around in circles, kind of looking out for each other, protecting each other, going up and down. It was a very peculiar formation.
> The bombers by contrast were in very tight, perfect formations, based on three-three-three. . . . And they would not deviate at all. But the thing that amazed me was the *numbers* of them—and that perfect tight formation—and that bright red rising sun. Such a bright red!

Hedman, like the other Allied pilots, assumed that all the single-engined planes were fighters. In fact, the formation that looked so peculiar from a distance was two different groups, with the Nates hovering protectively over the light bombers.

The 62nd Sentai settled into its bombing run, flying a course of 240 degrees toward Mingaladon airport. The Buffaloes struck first, damaging the Sally flown by Lieutenant Akira Niioka, who dropped behind the formation with his port engine smoking. Then McMillan's Tomahawks swept down. If Hedman was awed by the quantity of enemy aircraft, and confused as to their type, so were the Japanese air crews. One survivor reported that he was set upon by "thirty Buffaloes and Hurricanes," while others thought that the liquid-cooled fighters were Spitfires. Nobody identified them as U.S.-built planes, nor did anybody seem to notice the shark mouths on their prows: so much for psychological warfare!

McMillan led the attack, followed one at a time by his three wingmen. (So much for Chennault's tactic of the fighting pair!) Crammed into the cockpit of No. 77, R. T. Smith experienced for the first time the symptoms of combat—the cotton mouth, the pounding heart, and the bladder ready to burst:

> And now it was my turn, diving and turning to line up my gunsight . . . squeezing the stick-trigger and hearing the crackling sound of my four .30 caliber wing guns and the slower, powerful thudding of the two .50s in the nose . . . the pungent smell of cordite filling the cockpit, a good smell . . . the bombers were firing back, tracers crisscrossing the sky in every direction, black smoke and flames streaming from the left engine of a bomber up ahead, and all the while that creepy-crawling feeling at the back of the neck, knowing their fighters must surely be about to pounce down on us.

R. T. quickly learned two things about going to war in a fighter plane. First, that it was a lonely business: by the time he finished that run and porpoised back to fighting altitude, his companions were nowhere to be seen. Then there was the exquisite difficulty of hitting another plane from an angle: deflection shooting. It was not merely a case of "leading" his target, as the goose hunter aims in front of the bird, because in this case the hunter too was airborne. R. T. was traveling at 250 mph, trying to hit a Sally moving at 180 mph on a different heading—a problem in three dimensions instead of two. To help him aim, phosphorus-coated tracer bullets were mingled with his plane-killing rounds. (The usual mix was one tracer, one incendiary bullet, and three armor-piercing rounds.) The tracers now sailed out in front of him—lazy red fireflies, they seemed—to show whether the lethal rounds were on a collision course with the Sally. If not, R. T. could try to adjust the stream by jinking left or right, up or down. His feet worked the rudder, his left hand the throttle and trim tabs, his right hand the elevator, the ailerons, and the firing button. If a gun jammed, he had to clear it, yanking back on the pistol grips of the nose guns or pulling up on the T grips on either side of his seat. "And all this time," he wrote, "if the pilot is to live, his head is constantly turning in every direction"—looking for enemy fighters.

In the end, R. T. decided to attack from behind and below, avoiding the problems of deflection shooting while reducing his chances of being hit by return fire. (The Sally had no belly gun as such, merely a port through which a drum-fed machine gun could be thrust in case of need, while the tail gun was a "stinger," remotely controlled from the topside greenhouse.) So he "got directly behind him and just under his prop-wash, and opened fire at about 200 yards. I could see my tracers converging on the fuselage and wing roots . . . until he blew up right in my face." The concussion, he recalled, tossed his Tomahawk upward. Then he found himself under attack by three fixed-gear enemy fighters, who had left their own charges to come to the aid of the heavy bombers. He turned into the Nates, fired a burst at their leader, then split the scene by pointing No. 77 straight down.

Tom Haywood had a similar baptism, opening fire at 500 yards and pressing the attack until a Sally "fell off on one wing out of the formation," whereupon he was bounced by a Nate. Haywood swung toward the fixed-gear fighter, got off a burst, and found that the Japanese pilot easily out-turned him, so he too split the scene. Haywood went home with ten bullet holes in his Tomahawk and an aileron control wire shot away.

Meanwhile the Sallys dropped their bombs and turned south, a curious choice of direction, since it took them directly over Rangoon and its recently installed antiaircraft batteries. Probably the lead pilot was too frightened to think straight. Lieutenant Iwao Hayashi, flying a bomber in the 3rd Chutai, recalled the bombing run as a scene of "indescribable horror," as one friend after another was hit—first Niioka, then Shimada, then Sabe—each falling behind to be set upon by the Allied fighters, like a lone swimmer attacked by piranhas.

R. T. Smith was among the attackers. After making more runs on the bombers, and being again chased off by the Nates, he found a lone Sally under attack by George McMillan's Tomahawk and a 67th Squadron Buffalo. This appears to have been the Sally piloted by Lieutenant Niioka, his left engine crippled by a Buffalo in the first encounter. (None of the wounded Sallys had yet crashed, despite the claims of the Allied pilots.) McMillan reported that he shot one engine out of the laggard, and R. T. that he finished it off, running in again and again until the crippled plane dove away at a 30° angle, trailing smoke.

By this time, the battle had been joined by two of the release pilots, Charles Older and Edmund Overend. They were bicycling into Rangoon when the alarm went off; hearing the fighters start up, they wheeled around and pedaled back to Mingaladon, where they saw two unmanned Tomahawks on the flight line. "Why don't we hop in and go flying?" Older said. He was a Californian with the face of an East Coast preppie, who had joined the navy for a lark between UCLA and law school. He and Overend took off and made their way to the eastward, reaching an altitude of 8,000 feet before they brought McMillan's flight into view. Soon after, Older spotted the Japanese formations—a "huge conglomeration of airplanes," as he recalled, "more than I'd ever seen together at one time." He was still below them when the fight was joined, so he opened fire while he was climbing:

> I aimed at one of the wing planes on the left side of the formation and after my first attack, smoke began streaming from the port engine. I rolled out to the side . . . and came back. . . . I aimed again at the same plane and closed to about seventy-five yards. I gave it a long burst and the bomber suddenly nosed down out of the formation with smoke streaming behind. I saw it roll over into almost a vertical dive and disappear below.
>
> I continued making attacks from below, this time aiming at the leader of the formation. . . . I saw the bomber explode . . . and flame and smoke seemed to pour out from the bottom of the fuselage. I saw debris falling from this plane immediately after the explosion, and the bomber nosed straight down with flames and smoke pouring from it.

Eddie Overend worked ahead of the Japanese formation and made a frontal attack. His tracers went wide, so he turned with the Sallys and attacked from the side with no better luck. By now he too was below the formation. From this vantage he saw several Tomahawks and a Buffalo worrying the Sallys. Overend made three more passes to no apparent effect, but he saw two bombers go down, one with its port engine blazing and the other diving at a steep angle out of control—probably the planes flown by Lieutenants Niioka and Shimada. On his fourth and subsequent attacks, Overend concentrated on a Japanese straggler, at times joined by another Tomahawk. Finally the Sally's port engine caught fire, and it pitched over into a 70° dive—Lieutenant Sabe, in all likelihood. Overend followed the bomber down to 4,000 feet before he was driven off by three Nates, which forced him down to treetop level before he managed to lose them.

McMillan's late-starting standbys—Paul Greene and young Hank Gilbert—also caught up to the Sallys at about this time. Having closed their bomb bay doors, the remaining bombers had assumed a porcupine cluster, so the gunners (especially those in the topside greenhouses) could support each other. Gilbert was caught in this terrible crossfire. His Tomahawk blossomed into a ball of red and orange fire, hung suspended for a moment, then fell to the earth, trailing long fingers of flame and smoke. "I saw him go down," Paul Greene recalled long after. "He was just on fire, and he was right in front of me." Gilbert was two months past his twenty-second birthday. As the story was told, he had married just before embarking on *Klipfontein*, and his wife, who was pregnant, did not even have a photograph to remember him by.

Greene worried the bombers for four or five passes, then broke off to defend himself from the Nates. On a climbing attack he poured machine gun fire into a Japanese fighter from about 300 yards, saw the fixed-gear plane fall away, and immediately engaged another at close range. "Although I hit him plenty," Greene reported, "I did not see him fall, for about this time there were fighters firing at me and [they] evidently hit [my] controls for the ship went completely out of control." He slid back the canopy and jumped out, diving for the root of the wing so he would not be cut in half by his own tail fin. A six-footer, Greene had clambered into the Tomahawk wearing boots, shorts, and the parachute belonging to the much shorter Robert Brouk. When the chute opened, the harness bit into his crotch and shoulders, lacerating his skin and tearing a neck muscle. Then he looked up to check the canopy—only to see blue sky where white silk should have been: several panels were gone. (The parachutes were Chinese-made, and at Kyedaw airfield the Americans had joked about their reliability. Those ideograms on the pack? Why, they meant "umbrella insurance" . . . or else they instructed the wearer to return the parachute to the factory if it should fail to open.)

Greene's plane had been shot from under him. Then he had found himself hanging from two-thirds of a canopy. And now he saw one of the Japanese planes circling back toward him, its radial engine enormous behind the propeller blur. Yellow-white tracer bullets sailed toward him, but passed clear. Then the Nate roared by him, prop wash buffeting him in his harness. That plane did not return (observers on the ground said it was driven off by a Buffalo) but other Japanese pilots took up the sport. Hand over hand, Greene climbed up the shroud lines, to collapse the canopy and fall more quickly out of the combat zone. At the best of times, a parachute landing is like jumping from a second-story window. Greene hit so hard that he was knocked unconscious. When he came to, a gun muzzle was pressed up against his face, the weapon in the hands of a British major. Greene convinced him that they were on the same side, whereupon the major bundled him into a car and drove him to the hospital.

Greene was credited with shooting down one Nate—wrongly, it would seem, for all the 77th Sentai fighters returned safely to Raheng. However, one account has the 31st Sentai losing a light bomber on December 23.* In the adrenalin rush of combat, and attacking from below, Greene might well have mistaken the Ann for a Nate. As for the bombers, Chuck Older was credited with shooting down two Sallys, Ed Overend and Tom Haywood with one apiece, and George McMillan and R. T. Smith shared the credit for a fifth. The 62nd Sentai did indeed lose five bombers on Tuesday morning—one-third of its entire force—but it is unlikely that they all fell to the guns of the AVG, or at least not exclusively. The Buffalo pilots claimed six aircraft in this same engagement, without loss to themselves.

The other Hell's Angels had taken off in better order, six Tomahawks climbing "in string." Parker Dupouy was a thoughtful, stolid man with an engineering degree from Brown University and a remarkable set of

---

* "One of the wings collapsed," a Tokyo newspaper told its readers. "Lieutenant Ikura threw up his hands again and shouted something"—a *banzai* cheer for the emperor, as any Japanese reader would infer. "In the back, Sergeant-Major Hiwatari . . . continued firing while their plane was being consumed in flames. Finally he shot down the last enemy plane and . . . was all smiles when his plane blew up."

eyebrows: thick, black, and cocked like a pair of chevrons. Over the radio, RAF fighter control told him to circle Syriam, the oil refinery southeast of Rangoon, so Dupouy led his flight in that direction. Half an hour after takeoff, he spotted a "very tight" formation of twin-engined bombers approaching Rangoon from the seaward at 17,000 feet. The planes were camouflaged in shades of green, which his pilots variously described as light and dark, solid and two-tone. This was the 98th Sentai with eighteen late-model Sallys, more powerful and more heavily armed than those raiding Mingaladon airport. They were commanded by Colonel Shigeki Usui, who had flown to Rangoon as copilot of the plane assigned to Major Hikaru Atsumi. (The major dutifully moved down to the bombardier's compartment in the nose, while a younger officer flew the plane.) There were four enlisted gunners in the back, doubling as radioman, navigator, crew chief, and mechanic.

Dupouy divided his Tomahawks into three-plane flights—like Mc-Millan, paying no attention to the Chennault doctrine of the fighting pair. Then he rocked his wings and led William Reed and Ralph Gunvordahl in a front-quarter attack on the Sallys. They made no hits, and were agreeably surprised not to be hit in turn. The other trio—Neil Martin leading, with Robert Brouk and Kenneth Jernstedt on his wing—did not fare so well. "Martin broke away and scooted out in front," one of the Hell's Angels recalled. Boring into the 98th Sentai from the side, Martin was met by the massed fire of eighteen pairs of greenhouse guns, each consisting of one rifle-caliber machine gun and another with a bore of 12.7 mm, equivalent to the fifty-caliber nose guns on the Tomahawks. Martin suddenly pulled up, presenting his vulnerable underside to the storm of bullets. "I don't know if he had been hit," mused Ken Jernstedt years later, "or if he just made a terrible mistake." The Japanese air crews also vividly recalled the Allied pilot who "turned away, showing his belly to our gunners." Martin went down in flames. He was one of Olson's P-40 drivers from Mitchel Field, a gifted athlete, a graduate of the University of Arkansas, and not much older than Hank Gilbert.

Profiting by that fearful example, Jernstedt dropped below the level of the greenhouse gunners. "I made a below side approach to the rear quarter," he wrote in his combat report. "I saw the plane . . . falter, so I switched my aim to the other wing man. I gave him a short burst and must have hit his [engine] or an incendiary bomb because the bomber burst into flames and left the formation in a blazing dive." This was the Sally flown by Captain Iteya Mitsui, who crashed near the waterfront after his main fuel tank was exploded by incendiary bullets. Probably double-counting on Mitsui, Bob Brouk claimed a bomber at about the same time, and both claims were recognized.

The 98th Sentai had been aiming for the Rangoon docks, with their mountains of lend-lease goods bound for China. But when the formation was thrown into confusion by Mitsui's disappearance, Colonel Usui decided to regroup and to aim instead for the "British headquarters"—as if his bombardiers could pick out Government House from three miles in the air, or hit it with the unsophisticated Japanese aiming mechanism.

The remaining Tomahawks kept nibbling at the formation, five planes against seventeen. Parker Dupouy made repeated head-on attacks but, cautious engineer, put in no claim. Bill Reed worried the bombers from the beam and from below. Afterward, he reported that he had shot the port engine out of a Sally and saw the big plane fall out of formation. Using the same tactic, Gunvordahl also claimed a bomber. Again, the two Hell's Angels were probably double-counting on the same plane—the Sally piloted by Lieutenant Ryohei Nogami, whose left engine burst into fire, and who then made a choice unusual for a Japanese airman: he bailed out with two of his crewmen, and was taken prisoner. (It is also possible that Dupouy's pilots attacked the 62nd Sentai cripples, one of which crashed in Rangoon and another a few miles east.)

Though it did not go down, the commander's plane was badly hit. Machine gun bullets tore into the Sally from above and behind, stitching the copilot's seat and hitting Colonel Usui in the back and left shoulder. Hearing the crash of bullets, Major Atsumi scrambled out of the bombardier's compartment and tried to help his commanding officer. But the gallant Usui (as the Japanese told the story) waved the major back to his post, then died even as Atsumi loosed the Sally's bombs upon downtown Rangoon. Though the firefight continued for half an hour, the 98th Sentai returned to Thailand with no further casualties.

Ten minutes behind schedule, the 60th Sentai now droned over Rangoon at 23,000 feet. Its twenty-seven Sallys dropped their bombs on the city and returned to Thailand with only occasional interference from Allied fighters. No planes were lost, and only one airman was killed.

At the start of the raid, most of Rangoon officialdom had been in conference with General McLeod. When the screech of the air raid alarm interrupted him, the genial, white-haired officer merely glanced at his watch. "Plenty of time, gentlemen," he said, assuring his audience that the city's warning system was so good that they need not take shelter for half an hour. "Let us go on with the next item." Not entirely convinced, his listeners fidgeted and glanced at the clock. At last McLeod went to the door, where with ostentatious courage he chatted with the officials as they left the room. When they escaped, they found Rangoon in a carnival mood. The first Japanese formation (Colonel Usui's 98th Sentai) was approaching the city with fighter planes in hot pursuit. Few of the officials knew that a U.S.-supplied squadron was stationed at Mingaladon airport, and they naturally assumed that the raiders were being chased by the Royal Air Force, as one of them later wrote:

> Agleam in the sunlight the enemy bombers came on in arrow-head formation. Men climbed out of the trenches to watch them; people stood on the roads with uplifted faces. . . . Within a few moments they were clapping their hands and cheering. A British fighter on the tail of a bomber had shot up the Jap, from which streamed a trail of smoke. The bomber [Mitsui's plane] burst into flame, crumpled, fell. Another [Nogami's] flared like a spent rocket and dropped. Parachutes opened in the sky. We saw all this and cheered wildly; saw, too, that deadly arrow-head almost above the centre of the city; our fighters had not turned it.

Of Rangoon's 500,000 citizens, few had any love for the British Empire. An Indian shopkeeper afterward recalled that people cried, "There comes the enemy!"—pointing not to the Japanese bombers but to the Allied fighters. But the bombs made no distinction between masters and servants. Blasted and strafed, torn by flying glass, crushed by falling rubble, or trampled in the panic, more than a thousand civilians died in the streets of Rangoon that Tuesday, as the shopkeeper wrote:

> It was a pitiable sight to see women with dishevelled hair and babes in arms crying and running where their fear-laden whimsies took them. Children

and teen-agers having lost their parents were frantically searching for them.
. . . More pathetic were children who clung to running men and women,
mistaking them for their parents. The runners however discarded them as
dangerous nuisances and fled the more vigorously to escape the bombs and
save their skins.

Still they cheered. A clerk from Ceylon (now Sri Lanka) strolled up
and down, shouting to the Japanese bombardiers: "Oh, strike the
rascal, boys! Bravo! Strike hard!" Then he panicked and ran down
Phayre Street, to die in a burst of shrapnel outside Bill Pawley's office.

At Mingaladon airport, too, the first reaction was one of
pleasurable excitement. "None of the fellows thought a hell of a lot
about it," said Leo Clouthier, an operations clerk. "We just stood on
the porch at the barracks—just about all the ground crew were there.
Suddenly, somebody said . . . 'Good looking formation up there.'
Then we noticed . . . that they were two-engined Japanese bombers.
The porch was cleared in about twenty seconds flat." The technicians
ran to a nearby trench, where they cowered while a bomb fell on a
dummy fuel dump nearby and Japanese machine gun bullets whacked
the gravel. The strafing was brought on their heads by Paul Greene,
trying to escape his tormentors by going into free-fall. "We were all
watching Greene come down," Clouthier said. As he remembered it,
six fighters took turns shooting at Greene. "I think they followed him
almost to the ground. Then they figured they might as well strafe the
field."

Ten British and thirty Burmese servicemen died at the airport, including the medical officer, the crew of an antiaircraft gun, and a red-haired
private who happened to be in the 67th Squadron operations building
when a bomb came through the ceiling. (An AVG technician later saw
his body hanging on the barbed wire outside.) The same bomb destroyed
the air raid siren. Others fell on the main hangar, wrecking two Buffaloes
and wounding three mechanics who were working on them. The fuel
storage tanks were set afire, along with the decoys that were supposed
to deceive the raiders. The runways were pocked, the barrack windows
smashed, and the mess hall damaged. Two Tomahawks were shot up in
their dispersal pens, and another Tomahawk was wrecked when Bill
Reed, landing from his running fight with the 98th Sentai, hit a bomb
crater at eighty miles an hour.

On Wednesday—Christmas Eve—Neil Martin and Hank Gilbert were buried in the churchyard of Edward the Martyr at Insein Cantonment, two miles south of Mingaladon airport. They did not get neighboring plots, and none of the Hell's Angels could afterward remember the funeral, probably because they were too busy to attend. Mechanics tuned balky engines, patched control cables, and taped bullet holes. Armorers refilled ammunition boxes, tending first to the nose guns that gave the Tomahawks such an advantage over the lightweight Japanese fighters. Other technicians topped off fuel, oil, and coolant tanks. As each plane was restored to fighting condition, it went up to relieve a Tomahawk that had been patrolling over the airport, and that plane came down to take its turn in the maintenance pen. By nightfall, the AVG ground crews had brought the squadron's strength up to twelve planes, armed and ready to fight. But the margin was breathtakingly thin. The Hell's Angels had no rifle-caliber ammunition beyond what was actually loaded in the wing guns of the planes on the flight line. The RAF was marginally better off, with fourteen airworthy Buffaloes. By nightfall, a substitute operations center had been cobbled together, and the RAF servicing flight moved out of the wrecked hanger and into the Rangoon Country Club nearby. The mess hall had a lower priority, however, and the RAF and the AVG dined that evening on cold bread and warm beer.

Oley Olson sent a radiogram to Chennault, outlining his predicament and concluding: "Awaiting further orders." He must have been disappointed by Chennault's solution, which was to call upon Ed Goyette for replacements. Mess supervisor Clayton Harpold, his own job now superfluous, drove a truck the 175 miles to Toungoo and loaded it with 70,000 rounds of 7.92-mm ammunition for the Tomahawk wing guns, returning the following morning. To replace Gilbert and Martin, Goyette sent two of his pilots—Frank Adkins and Chauncy (Link) Laughlin—down to Mingaladon with the ammunition truck. "Hold on few more days," Chennault urged Olson. "Will move you soon if possible. Warmest Xmas greetings to all."

Photographs showed Arvid Olson as a good-looking man with black hair, narrow jaw, and sometimes fretful expression. Certainly he was fretting now—panicking may not be too strong a word. Squadron leaders in every air force are expected to fly in combat, but neither Olson nor his opposite number, Squadron Leader R. A. Milward, had left the ground on December 23. The Hell's Angels do not remember Olson unkindly for this. "He was always over with the British," one of them explained, "making sure they knew what they were doing—which they didn't."

For a week or two, Bill Pawley's CW-21 Demons had been stationed at Mingaladon airport under the command of Erik Shilling, the wiry photo specialist with his blond-white shock of hair. Shilling did not have the temperament of a fighter pilot: it was the *machine* that fascinated him, whether he was modifying a Tomahawk as a photo plane or rocketing to 20,000 feet in the overpowered and undergunned CW-21. His boon companions were Ken Merritt and Lacy Mangleburg, whom Shilling picked to fill out his Demon flight at Mingaladon.

Then Chennault decided to bring the Demons up to Kunming, intending to use them as high-altitude scouts, and the three men flew up to Kyedaw airfield on December 22. (That was probably just as well. In the Indies, Dutch pilots in these hyped-up Curtiss sportsplanes were being shot down like ducks.) They stayed put during the raid on Tuesday morning, probably for fear the Japanese might bomb Toungoo as well. In the afternoon, they flew north along the railroad line to Lashio. Shilling's engine kept misfiring, and at Lashio he discussed the problem with Glen Blaylock, an AVG crew chief who happened to be there. Blaylock speculated that the Wright Cyclone was running hot because of the 100-octane gasoline supplied at Kyedaw airfield. Try 87-octane fuel, he advised. Mangleburg's Demon was gassed first, and he took off to try it out, stunting over the field in a manner that convinced somebody—British or Chinese—that an enemy fighter was strafing the airport. Not knowing that his wingman had caused the alarm, Shilling decided to fly out of there without waiting for the usual briefing about the route and the weather. The three Demons flew northeast, crossing into China at 5:30 P.M., by which time Shilling's engine was sputtering again. Then it quit altogether, over the mountains sixty miles from Kunming, and Shilling glided down to a belly landing on a rocky slope.

The Demons had no radios, and only Shilling knew the route. That left Merritt and Mangleburg to fly aimlessly about (one AVG radioman reported that they passed his station twenty times). Eventually Merritt followed Shilling's example and made a belly landing on hard ground, which left him injured but able to walk. Mangleburg was not so wise.

He tried again and again to land with his wheels down, but each time lost his nerve and powered off. His final attempt was in a river. As soon as his wheels hit the water, Mangleburg again tried to lift off, but slammed into a terraced slope above the river. The Demon's fuel tanks ruptured, and the flimsy aircraft boiled with flame.

Shilling knew nothing of these disasters. Chinese mountaineers, believing him to be Japanese, kept him prisoner that night in his wrecked plane. Next day he persuaded them to take him to an army post, where he composed a cheery message for Chennault: "I am all right; Mangleburg and Merritt arriving together." But even before the radiogram arrived, a Chinese patrol had recovered Mangleburg's body—so badly charred that it could be identified only by the remnants of his passport—and Merritt had hobbled into a nearby village, where he was picked up a few days later by an AVG ambulance.

A board of inquiry charged Shilling with an armload of lapses: not providing maps for his wingmen, allowing Mangleburg to stunt over Lashio, taking off for Kunming in the late afternoon, and not finding an emergency field as soon as his engine began to falter. He was fined and reduced in rank to wingman, the AVG's new term for pilot-officer. But that was just Chennault, blowing his top at the loss of three planes and a pilot: he eventually forgave the fine and restored Shilling to flight leader.

He Just Went Spinning Away
December 1941

General Sugawara reached Bangkok late in the day on Tuesday, December 23, just as his heavy bombers were landing at Don Muang airport. Wing Commander Kenji Yamamoto had the unenviable job of explaining the disaster that had befallen the Sallys over Burma.* The 62nd Sentai was nearly wrecked as a fighting force: of the fifteen planes that had taken off, ten now returned, pockmarked with bullet holes and bearing crew members killed in the running battle. But by Japanese reckoning the 98th Sentai had suffered an even more grievous loss in the person of Colonel Usui. Altogether, Sugawara learned, his heavy bomber groups had sacrificed seven planes and fifty airmen in the attempt to bomb Rangoon—this in a force that had fought over Malaya for two weeks without losing a single plane.

Some of his staff officers wanted to cancel the raids planned for the next two days, and instead to send a swarm of fighters to Mingaladon airport, to lure up and destroy the Allied defenders. Others argued that the Buffaloes and "Spitfires" were no match for the Japanese fighters

---

* Yamamoto commanded the 7th Hikodan, including the 12th, 60th, and 98th heavy bomber groups, plus the Hayabusas of the 64th Sentai. The 62nd Sentai Sallys, the 31st Sentai Anns, and the 77th Sentai Nates belonged to the 10th Hikodan. Thus the makeup of the formations attacking Burma during the Christmas campaign.

(after all, the 77th Sentai had not lost a single *Ki*-27 over Mingaladon) and that Sugawara need only provide the heavy bomber formations with fighter escorts, as had been done for the light bombers at Mingaladon.

In the end, Sugawara scrubbed the raid scheduled for Wednesday. Then he called for reinforcements. From Phnom Penh came the 12th Sentai, a heavy bomber group. From Saigon came the 47th Independent Chutai, equipped with the Nakajima *Ki*-44 *Shoki*—Demon—an experimental fighter cobbled together from a Hayabusa airframe and a 1,500-horsepower bomber engine. In December 1941, the JAAF had nine Shokis in service, and three of these crashed en route to Bangkok. When the survivors landed at Don Muang, their commander had to admit that the Shokis were too short-legged to make the journey from Bangkok to Rangoon, and too unstable to stage out of the dirt fields at Raheng and Phitsanulok.

With better results, Major Kato's 64th Sentai was called up from Malaya. In one of those displays of tactical agility that so bewildered the Allies at the beginning of the Pacific war, twenty-five Hayabusas left Kota Baru at noon on Wednesday and flew the 450 miles to Bangkok. They refueled, spent the night, and were ready to leave for Rangoon on Christmas morning.

In the 62nd Sentai, ground crews had patched and repaired the Sallys damaged over Burma, and they reported that eight planes would be able to make the return trip. Their orders were unchanged from Tuesday: fly north to Raheng, rendezvous with the 77th Sentai Nates and the 31st Sentai Anns, and proceed to Mingaladon airport. In their bomb bays, along with the snout-nosed cannisters of explosives, each crew placed a bouquet of flowers to be dropped upon Mingaladon, to honor their comrades who had died on Tuesday.

The 60th Sentai had suffered no losses in the first raid and would be able to muster thirty-six Sallys, while the newly arrived 12th Sentai had twenty-seven planes. The 98th Sentai, in mourning for its commander, was excused from the raid, so the Rangoon attack force consisted of sixty-three heavy bombers, all heavily armed Sally-2s. Major General Yamamoto announced that he would lead them in person. Now a plump desk officer, Yamamoto had commanded the 12th Sentai during the Sino-Japanese War, so he selected the lead bomber of that group as his mount. Colonel Kumao Kitajima, the present group commander, would also make the trip, and in the same plane.

The 64th Sentai met the Rangoon-bound Sallys over the Menam River, west of Bangkok. Major Kato led the formation with ten fighters, while seven Hayabusas trailed behind and eight provided top cover. By JAAF standards, this was saturation coverage: twenty-five fighters to protect sixty-three bombers. It was another flawless day, and the air crews could see Rangoon and its shining lakes and rivers as soon as the armada crossed into Burma at 19,000 feet.

Then the formation came apart. The lead bomber, containing General Yamamoto and Colonel Kitajima, lost power in one engine and dropped out of the formation. The rest of the 12th Sentai followed it down to 18,000 feet. So did Major Kato—and all his Hayabusas dutifully followed him. Since the JAAF radios were almost useless for air-to-air communication, it was a time-consuming business to get the formation back on track. In the end, six bombers stuck with Yamamoto and Kitajima, as did Major Kato and his ten fighters. The main force—twenty Sallys and fifteen Hayabusas—climbed back to the assigned altitude, now under the command of Major Yoshikuma Oura. By this time, the 12th Sentai had fallen far behind the 60th, so Oura decided to fly directly to Rangoon instead of making the dogleg to Moulmein. The armada was thus divided into three parts, and the 60th Sentai—thirty-six Sallys under the command of Colonel Kojiro Ogawa—had been stripped of its escort.

Meanwhile, the eight battered Sally-1s of the 62nd Sentai flew north to Raheng and linked up with twenty-seven Anns and thirty-two Nates. The bomber crews had been given box lunches for the flight north, but they were too frightened to eat. After Tuesday's massacre over Mingaladon airport, they did not expect to return from this mission.

The AVG ground crews also continued their frantic patching on Christmas morning, and they now had thirteen Tomahawks ready to fight. The Hell's Angels, when not patrolling over the airport, retreated to the alert tent or dozed beneath the wings of their planes, dressed in boots and shorts. There was no more distinction between available, standby, and release pilots: every man was on alert, every daylight hour. This time, Oley Olson got the word as soon as the first Japanese formation crossed into Burma. He sent his Tomahawks into the air at 11:30 A.M., again in two flights led by George McMillan and Parker Dupouy. Their stations were reversed as compared to Tuesday:

McMillan circled the oil refinery at Syriam, while Dupouy patrolled over the airport. Pilots who had been sweltering in tropical heat now began to shiver at Himalayan altitudes. Far below, they could see the white triangle of Mingaladon, the green-and-brown rice fields, and the shimmering lakes and rivers surrounding Rangoon.

Also heading for Mingaladon airport at this moment was a Douglas DC-2 bearing the two highest-ranking Allied officers in Asia. Having done their bit to complicate inter-Allied relations in Chongqing, Sir Archibald Wavell and George Brett headed back to Burma by the usual route: Kunming to Lashio to Rangoon. They were lucky enough not to be shot down by the patrolling Buffaloes and Tomahawks, and they landed at Mingaladon airport minutes before the Japanese bombs began to explode. As the story was told, Oley Olson personally hustled them to safety in a slit trench.

Major Oura's twenty-plane formation was the first to reach Rangoon, his ostensible target the electric power plant. The bombing done, and each plane 2,200 pounds lighter, the Sallys steamed southeast, with fifteen Hayabusas pulling maximum manifold pressure to keep them in view. Soon after, General Yamamoto's seven-plane formation dropped its bombs from 14,000 feet and likewise headed for Martaban Bay.

George McMillan was over Syriam when he spotted Major Oura's formation returning from Rangoon with its escort of retractable-gear fighters, which he naturally identified as the Mitsubishi Zeros he had seen chalked on the blackboard at Kyedaw airfield. The Tomahawks sailed into the Japanese formation—seven planes against thirty-five. Again they attacked in string, then scattered all over the sky.

The star of this clash was Duke Hedman, an unprepossesing young man who until Christmas Day had been admired mostly for the way he attacked the keyboard of a piano: with considerable verve but little talent, and a cigarette dangling from the corner of his mouth. "I came up from low rear on the left flank," he wrote in his combat report for December 25. He kept firing until he was only 150 feet from the Sally, then dove out when it seemed to explode in front of him. Then:

> I fell behind so came up from direct rear firing . . . at the last bomber until
> it began flaming from the underneath of the forward part of the fuselage

and went towards the earth at a 45° angle. I stayed there, quickly charged my guns, and moved up and gave the next two in line good bursts . . . then half-rolled out.

On my next attack, I noticed three of them in a vee move away 45° to the left from the main formation. I came up from [below] and after short burst at 100 yards into the right wing plane, it began emitting heavy black smoke from the right motor and did a slow half roll to the right. I pulled up directly behind the leader and gave him a longer burst at 100 yards range. It went straight forward into a steep dive leaving a trail of heavy pitch black smoke behind. A bullet from the remaining bomber on my left broke my canopy and lodged to the left of my headrest. I half rolled sharply [and] saw a Navy Model "0" turning away from me on my right side at about 500 yards. I immediately turned inside him and at 300 yards range gave him a burst. He burst into flames and went straight down.

The Japanese fighter, Hedman realized, had been about to attack another Tomahawk. The near-victim was Curt Smith, the thirty-three-year-old former marine who had attempted to enforce military discipline on *Boschfontein*. "I had thirteen pursuit ships on my tail at one time," Smith boasted a few days later. However, his combat narrative for December 25 contained only one word: "None." That was an honest assessment of his part in the battle of Burma. He returned to Mingaladon with his ammunition boxes nearly full, and everyone thereafter pretended that there were only six pilots in McMillan's flight.

After knocking the fighter off Smith's tail, Hedman himself was bounced by a Hayabusa. He half-rolled and went into a power dive that dropped him from 20,000 to 5,000 feet, like falling down an elevator shaft. Taking sanctuary in a cloud bank, he flew on instruments to Highland Queen, the RAF satellite field at Hmawbi, where he landed with his gas tanks almost dry. He concluded his combat narrative by recalling a peculiar circumstance of the air battle—one mentioned by other pilots as well. "During my attacks," he wrote, "I heard them shouting over the radio on 6048 [kilohertz] . . . saying 'Hello, Hello, go home and land.'"

Hedman was credited with shooting down four Sallys and a Hayabusa, but they did not go on his official record. In the alert tent that morning, he had suggested that all members of the flight share credit for any planes shot down. He therefore missed the chance to become an AVG ace, ending the day with an official score of 3.83 enemy aircraft shot down. (The accounting was muddled when one of Hedman's kills was attributed to December 23, leaving seventeen planes to be divided among six pilots, or 2.83 apiece.) The same was true of Chuck Older, credited with two Sallys and a "Model 0" to add to his bag of December 23, for an official score of 4.83. R. T. Smith was credited with two bombers and a fighter, George McMillan with three Sallys, and Tom Haywood and Eddie Overend with two Sallys each. That was a considerable overestimate. The 64th Sentai lost no Hayabusas in this engagement, while the 12th Sentai lost five Sallys, three shot down over Burma and two crippled so badly that they crashed on the way home.

McMillan's flight lost two Tomahawks. After attacking his second Sally, Eddie Overend realized that his own plane had been hit. "I tried to pull away and found that my stick was jammed," he reported. "My right wing dropped and the engine was only just turning over. . . . I rolled full tab and held full left rudder and the wing came up." He made a belly landing in a rice field thirty miles east of Rangoon. The second victim was McMillan: with a flesh wound in his arm, and his right wing and his coolant tank blown open by the Sally gunners, he crashed in a dried-out rice field near Thongwa.

Parker Dupouy's flight had gone after Colonel Ogawa's 60th Sentai, whose thirty-six Sallys had circled around the target and were now bearing down on Rangoon from the northwest. But only Lew Bishop managed to get through to the bombers. The planes that had gathered over Raheng—Sallys, Nates, and Anns—were approaching Mingaladon airport from the east, and Major Yoshioka's fighters left their own formation to come to the aid of the 60th Sentai. In this they were soon joined by some of Major Kato's Hayabusas. The combat thereafter generally involved one Tomahawk versus several Japanese fighters. "One tries to draw you into attack," Bill Reed reported, "and the other two [climb] to gain a position of advantage should you attack the decoy." Bob Brouk claimed a Nate and was immediately bounced by four other fighters, which he fled by diving into the clouds. Ken Jernstedt likewise claimed a Japanese fighter and ran for home with two more on his tail. Fred Hodges (Fearless, he was called, in reference to his lively dread of the bugs at Kyedaw airfield) was caught three times in these Tomahawk traps before he called it quits.

Parker Dupouy had a similar experience when he made a head-on attack against a Japanese fighter "with square wing tips and an in-line engine." (He identified it as a Messerschmitt 109, and Flying Officer P. M. Bingham-Wallis of the 67th Squadron confirmed the sighting, though the JAAF had no such aircraft.) Dupouy watched his victim crash in the mudflats below Thongwa, then looked up and saw a Hayabusa coming down on him with its nose guns winking. Dupouy dove away. Three times he returned to altitude, tangled with an apparently isolated retractable-gear fighter, and was bounced by its companions.

Dupouy's persistent opponent may have been Tateo Kato. Flying to Rangoon, the major had worried that his other charge—Ogawa's 60th Sentai—had been stripped of its fighter escort. "Anxiety grew in my mind," he confided to his diary that night. So once the 12th Sentai had dropped its bombs, "I went back at top speed to meet the Ogawa bombing unit. On the way, I shot down two or three enemy planes." According to a 64th Sentai veteran, one of Kato's victims was Eddie Overend. Another may have been Dupouy, whose evasive tactics Kato interpreted as a knock-down. The Japanese too were guilty of wishful thinking.

But the bushy-browed engineer was still in the fight, which had drawn him well out over Martaban Bay. Here Dupouy spotted a formation of seven bombers running for Thailand—the formation Kato had abandoned—and he made a head-on run against the lead bomber. What a coup if he had shot it down! But he was driven off by the escorting Hayabusas, and Colonel Kitajima and Major General Yamamoto returned safely to Bangkok.

Bill Reed had been working along the same lines, claiming one "Model 0," engaging its companions, diving away, and chasing the Sallys offshore. There he came upon Dupouy dogfighting the escort. The skirmish continued for five minutes to no effect; then the two Tomahawks turned for home. They were jogging along at 20,000 feet when they spotted three Hayabusas below them and on the reciprocal course. The Japanese pilots had been among those escorting Major Oura to Rangoon. Years later, a 64th Sentai veteran recalled how they had let themselves be scattered: "1st and 2nd chutais did not follow orders to stay with [the bombers], leaving the formation after the bombs were dropped and dashing into combat, very much against the plan."

With their altitude advantage, Dupouy and Reed simply turned 180°

and dove upon the Hayabusas from behind. "I opened fire on one from point blank range," Reed reported, "and he burst into flame immediately and went into [the water]." His victim was Sergeant Shigekatsu Wakayama, the first of Major Kato's pilots to be killed by enemy fire in the Pacific war.

Like his partner, Dupouy had aimed first at Wakayama. When the Hayabusa burst into flame, Dupouy's Tomahawk had closed to within ninety feet—three plane lengths—and he kicked hard left rudder to swing onto the fighter on the other side of the formation, only to realize that his speed was so great that he was overrunning the enemy aircraft. Dupouy went into a half-roll, intending to pass to the left and below the other fighter. He almost succeeded. But the Tomahawk's right wingtip sliced into the Hayabusa at its weakest point, where its left wing was bolted to the fuselage. The wing folded "like a butterfly," in the words of a Japanese writer. The crippled falcon was piloted by Lieutenant Hiroshi Okuyama, twenty-three years old, from the southern island of Kyushu. "He just went spinning away," Dupouy recalled years later. "It was such an impact that I thought immediately that I had to get out." He watched Okuyama fall seaward in a tight, crazy spiral, while his own plane kept flying in the posture it had assumed before the crash, left wing pointing to the ocean, right wing to the sky. Looking up, Dupouy saw that his wing was missing four feet off the tip, including part of the aileron, without which the Tomahawk could not turn. Dupouy felt out the control stick and found that the aileron was still attached to the wing by its inside and middle hinges. Gingerly, he rolled the Tomahawk onto its belly. "When I found that the airplane would fly," he said, "I headed for the nearest shore." That was Tenasserim to the east, but after plugging along without incident for a few minutes, he decided he might as well go home:

I turned, and in three-quarters of an hour I was over Rangoon. When I got over the airport, everyone on the ground thought it was a one-winged airplane. So they all said, "Get out!" But I had no radio contact. I landed at 142 miles an hour. As far as I know, nobody ever landed [a Tomahawk] any faster. But I wasn't interested in that so much as dodging those bomb craters, because the airport at Mingaladon had been very heavily bombed. Well, I dodged those. And then—when I got out of the airplane and looked at it and started to think—*then* I started to shake.

With Dupouy's unorthodox kill, the Hell's Angels had run their claims for Christmas Day to twenty-five. The RAF was notably less successful. Taking off after the Tomahawks, fourteen Buffaloes had climbed toward Major Ogawa's 60th Sentai as it droned toward Rangoon from the northwest; still climbing, they were bounced by Major Yoshioka's Nates. Four Buffaloes were shot down and their pilots killed: Flying Officer Lambert and sergeants Hewitt, McNabb, and MacPherson. (The sergeant-pilots were New Zealanders while the officer was British.) The survivors claimed three Japanese fighters and half a bomber, bringing the total Allied claims to twenty-eight and one-half enemy aircraft.

But Kato's 64th Sentai lost only the two Hayabusas shot down or thrown into Martaban Bay by Reed and Dupouy. Yoshioka's 77th Sentai had lost three Nates over Mingaladon airport, whether to the AVG or the RAF. And Kitajima's 12th Sentai lost five Sallys, all to the Hell's Angels, and all from the twelve-plane formation led by Major Oura. To the incredulous joy of the men of the 62nd Sentai, no other bombers were lost: having dropped their bombs and their flowers upon Mingaladon airport, they were now eating a belated lunch over the mountains of Thailand. The chocolate, wrote a survivor long after, tasted "very, very sweet."

There was no joy in the 64th Sentai, which had been called up from Malaya to prevent another bloodletting over Burma, and which had lost five of its charges and two of its own pilots. "I felt terribly chagrined," Major Kato wrote in his diary, "while at the same time I felt a strong sense of responsibility for not having trained my men more thoroughly. I offered my apologies to [Colonel] Kitajima. . . . Spent the whole day in mortification tortured by the sense of responsibility." Fighting against the Chinese and Soviet air forces, Kato had allowed his men to perform victory loops and otherwise strut their stuff, in the way of fighter pilots everywhere. Now he bore down hard on such antics. Henceforth, he told his men, the 64th Sentai would function as a group, with each man working toward the larger purpose; there would be no more dashing off to individual combat. If his pilots smiled at that (Kato, of course, had done precisely the same) they did not mention it in their postwar recollections.

At Mingaladon airport, most of the AVG technicians had again been caught on the ground by the Japanese bombing. "The barracks were hit rather badly," Dan Hoyle noted in the squadron log, "and the men were rather scared and shook up, but they kept up their courage, as best they could." Leo Clouthier and Paul Perry were nicked by shrapnel. Though it drew no blood, another bomb struck forty feet from the trench in which Oley Olson and his two generals were crouching—as near a disaster as General Yamamoto's plane had experienced over Martaban Bay.

Legend has it that Bill Pawley brought Christmas dinner to the airport, loading a truck with groceries and driving out to Mingaladon for an impromptu feast. If so, it was his last service for the AVG in Rangoon. Leaving a skeleton crew to work on Olson's Tomahawks—most of them American-born Chinese mechanics, commanded by a CAF colonel—he closed the CAMCO office on Phayre Street and joined the general exodus, which by now had swept up most of the population of Rangoon. By car and on foot, refugees streamed past the airport in an endless line—"the crocodile," it was dubbed by the men at Mingaladon airport.

Oley Olson would have liked to follow them. At nightfall on December 25, having heard nothing from Eddie Overend and George McMillan, he concluded that he had lost two more men in addition to those killed and hospitalized on Tuesday—in all, a quarter of the pilots who had come down from Kyedaw airfield two weeks before.* Some of the 3rd Squadron technicians later claimed that they went to the

---

* Chennault also lost the services of his staff secretary on Christmas Day, when the Commonwealth garrison surrendered Hong Kong. Having burned his AVG identify card and swapped his cash for sapphires, Joe Alsop was interned at Fort Stanley. Doling out gems for food and a tutor, he not only kept himself alive but managed to read most of Confucius and Mencius in the original—"a quite useless but unusual accomplishment," as he put it, that "fills me with inordinate pride."

Also caught in Hong Kong was Doreen Lonborg, who had a Danish passport and the wit to convince the Japanese that she was a citizen of that neutral country. They let her book passage on a ferry taking refugees to Fort Baya (now Zhanjiang) on the South China coast, from where she set out to reach Kunming and her sweetheart, Daffy Davis of the AVG staff.

squadron leader, Curt Smith, and perhaps some other pilots, telling them to buck up and fight. If so, their advice was not taken. Before it closed for the day, Olson walked over to the RAF communications shack and sent the following appeal to Chennault in Kunming:

> Field hit badly. Two planes and pilots missing. Three more damaged. Have few ships left. Supplies short. Suggest move or reinforcements. Allied help in air doubtful. We doing work. Two ground crew slightly wounded. . . . Awaiting instructions.

But Overend and McMillan made their way back to Mingaladon next day, inspiring Olson to send a jaunty postscript to his after-action report. That Christmas battle had been "like shooting ducks," he boasted now—a phrase more often quoted by AVG historians than his gloomy appeal of December 25. Still, Olson hinted broadly that reinforcements would be appropriate: "would put entire Jap force out of commission with group here"—i.e., if Chennault would send the Panda Bears and the Adam & Eves to join him.

Meanwhile, high-flying Japanese planes showered leaflets on Rangoon, warning that an airborne invasion was imminent and sending more civilians fleeing from Rangoon. (The capital was already half empty, with no one to pick up the garbage or the bodies that were bloating in the streets; even the Strand Hotel had closed its doors.) The leaflets also spoiled the sleep of the Hell's Angels at Mingaladon airport. After all that had happened since December 8, even a night parachute drop did not seem beyond the capabilities of the Japanese army, especially with the moon coming on to full. Nobody who has not seen a full moon in the tropics can imagine its brilliance, turning midnight into cool silver day. At Mingaladon, as Dan Hoyle wrote in the squadron log, the Hell's Angels were "somewhat on edge, nervous and in a rather frayed condition as far as nerves" were concerned. The same was true of the 67th Squadron. "A jumpier lot of lads I have seldom met," a British reporter later recalled of the Commonwealth airmen at Mingaladon.

Clearly Chennault had to do something about his jittery squadron in Rangoon. He sent a radiogram to Olson, asking him to hold on for another twenty-four hours, when he would either reinforce the Hell's Angels or bring them up to Kunming. Group Captain Manning also did his best to calm the airmen at Mingaladon. As one of his last acts as Allied air commander in Burma, Manning sent this Churchillian communiqué to Oley Olson and Squadron Leader Milward:

> The result achieved during the two heavy raids we have experienced over the Rangoon area outstrip anything since the immortal defence of Great Britain in the Autumn of 1940. . . . Reinforcements are on the way, and the time will soon come when we shall hit back in full and overflowing measure.
>
> To all of you, R.A.F. and A.V.G., I say keep your chins up and your heads down, keep the aircraft flying at all costs. . . . It all depends on you and me, and how we honour the countries that have bred us.

Chennault was not inclined to chin-up defiance—not with respect to Burma. He would have been delighted to honor Olson's appeals and pull the Hell's Angels out of Mingaladon, without replacing them, and he so requested through the usual roundabout channel: General Chou to Madame Chiang to the generalissimo. But Sir Archibald Wavell had won that argument. Chiang Kai-shek was not about to lose his last supply route from the United States, if one of his American squadrons could keep it open. Had not Chennault been boasting since 1937 about the wonders that could be performed by a few good pilots in a few modern fighter planes? Then let him prove it now, by holding the seaward end of the Burma Road.

In Chongqing, the generalissimo had avoided any commitment to share his lend-lease bounty with the British. But the man on the spot was Lieutenant Colonel Joseph Twitty of the U.S. Army, who was not about to refuse a request from a Knight of the British Empire and a three-star general from his own service. Thus Wavell siphoned off forty China-bound antiaircraft cannon and a hundred machine guns for the defense of Rangoon. General Brett also dipped into the lend-lease hoard, to judge by this radiogram to Chennault in Kunming:

> Outfit at Rangoon doing superior work. Colonel congratulated by General Wavell. Have recommended to U.S. that they send you six planes per week, but feel that they should be used to defend Rangoon. Have asked Twitty to get spare parts on docks and help out Olson. Can't you send down six or ten planes and pilots to help out at this time? Feel that this area must be defended by AVG until British can get sqdn here.

Six planes a week! Chennault must have known that Brett was blowing smoke in his direction: an air force by July if only he would spare a few more Tomahawks right now. But he had to grasp at the straw, and he sat down and composed a message for President Roosevelt. It was an extraordinary gesture. Picture him, this bogus colonel in the badlands of China, writing to the president of a nation three weeks into the greatest peril of its history:

> The American Volunteer Group which was authorized by you is happy to report to the Commander in Chief that in three combats it has shot down twenty-nine Japanese airplanes and has lost only two of its own pilots. If furnished with a very small number of aircraft of proper types and models and a few more men immediately we are confident that in cooperation with the Chinese we can so damage and demoralize the Japanese air force that it will cease to be a factor in the China-Burma-Malaya theater of war. Any action taken must be immediate and must have the full support of the Allied powers. Be assured that the Group desires to be of the greatest service to the general cause in this brutal unprovoked conflict.

Chennault wrote in similar terms to the U.S. Military Mission in Chongqing, again pointing to the huge discrepancy between AVG losses and those inflicted on the enemy. "A study of these figures," he told General Magruder, "indicates that our pilots and planes are distinctly superior to those of the Japanese, and that with some additional forces we could quickly break the morale of the Japanese air force as well as destroy their aircraft and flying personnel." To accomplish this devastation, he needed fifty more fighter planes right away. They could be new or old, and they could be almost any type—the familiar Curtiss P-40; the cannon-equipped Bell P-39, now being used to great effect by the Soviet Air Force; or either of Republic's radial-engined fighters, the P-43 Lancer or P-47 Thunderbolt—but he needed at least fifty. Furthermore, not to repeat the mistake made with the first shipment of Tomahawks, they must be delivered with extra propellers, radios, instruments, oxygen tanks and masks, landing gear, windshields, canopies, generators, sparkplugs, and coolant tanks. Chennault also wanted twenty-five replacement fighters and fifteen replacement pilots per month, along with regular shipments of bombs and ammunition. Finally, he asked for thirty-six twin-engined bombers (the aborted 2nd AVG, in effect) manned by double crews of American pilots, gunners, and radiomen.

Then he returned to the immediate problem: the battered Hell's Angels at Mingaladon airport. On Saturday, December 27, Chennault told Jack Newkirk to get ready to replace Olson in Burma. Next day,

CNAC transports took the 2nd Squadron technicians and some of the Panda Bears down to Rangoon. "We were glad to see them," wrote Dan Hoyle. "Everyone wishing or rather anxious to leave and go to Kunming. . . . Today is Sunday and rather nice no activity something unusual I guess the Japanese feel they have had enough."

As it happened, Hoyle's estimate of the situation was exactly right. At General Sugawara's headquarters at Bangkok, the debate had continued without letup since Christmas Day. The Allied fighters on December 23 had been reported as stodgy, but now the JAAF officers were describing their speed as "incredible," an advantage compounded by their policy of "shooting and leaving" instead of doing the decent thing and making turns with the Nates and Hayabusas. Colonel Ogawa argued that his 60th Sentai had come home without loss because of its great numbers— that the Allied fighters went after Major Oura's formation because it was smaller. To this, Oura retorted that his losses had been due to the difficulty of reorganizing the 12th Sentai after its leading plane dropped out of the formation. Nobody drew the obvious lesson: that when the Allied interceptors hit them, the 60th Sentai was protected by fighters and the 12th Sentai was not.

In the end, Sugawara called off the campaign against Rangoon. Henceforth he would concentrate on Malaya and Singapore, where his heavy bomber sentais could come and go as they pleased. But it was a different version of the Christmas Day battle that was published in Tokyo:

> In large formations, the Japanese Army sky fighters swarmed over Rangoon on Christmas in the third [sic] devastating air attack on this British outpost, destroyed a power station and completely smashed the airfield besides sending down 40 enemy planes in a dog-fight while eight machines on the ground were blasted to pieces.

In any event, the changing of the guard at Mingaladon went forward without interference from the JAAF. Curt Smith, the ex-marine who had run away from combat on Christmas Day, took charge of the 3rd Squadron technicians as they staged through Kyedaw airfield to Kunming, where they arrived, bleary-eyed, on Tuesday morning. They were followed on Wednesday by ten Hell's Angels flying their own Tomahawks—the only planes able to make the trip, of eighteen sent to Mingaladon two weeks earlier. Oley Olson and four other pilots stayed behind to ease the transition from the Hell's Angels to the Panda Bears.

One of Chennault's missives must have hit the target, for Lauchlin Currie responded with the president's "intense admiration and appreciation" of the AVG's accomplishments. More to the point, Currie told Chennault to make arrangements to pick up 7,000 pounds of spare parts at Calcutta and 500 pounds at Karachi (now a seaport in independent Pakistan). Best of all, he had also managed to find the fighters Chennault wanted: fifty P-40E Kittyhawks, the big-jawed Curtiss model that had replaced the Tomahawks sold to China in the winter of 1940–1941. They were diverted from air force stocks in the belief that, by the time they reached Kunming, the AVG would already have been inducted into U.S. service. So China was not asked to pay for them, nor were they charged against her lend-lease allotment. Currie arranged for the Kittyhawks to be shipped on the freighter *Ferne Glen* to the west coast of Africa, where they would arrive toward the end of February. U.S. Army personnel would assemble the fighters and deliver them to Kunming, with fifteen of the pilots remaining in China (Chennault's first monthly allotment, in effect) while the others returned to Africa.

There was an ironic postscript to these appeals—Brett's to Chennault, and Chennault's to Roosevelt and Magruder. A freighter carrying thirty Vultee P-66 Vanguards dropped anchor in the Rangoon River on December 28, even as the 2nd Squadron technicians were landing at Mingaladon airport. This was the first shipment of the radial-engined, wood-and-steel fighters that had been ordered by Sweden, expropriated by the U.S., and allocated to China at Lauchlin Currie's request. Intended for the 3rd AVG, the Vanguards ought to have replaced the Tomahawks wrecked in Burma and China over the past six months. But Chennault did not like the Vultee fighter, and had already agreed that they should be turned over to the CAF. In any event, he had no way to assemble them, with the Pawleys having shut down their Rangoon operation. So the freighter weighed anchor and took the fighters on to India, still in their crates.

Meanwhile, Currie was proceeding with his plan to induct the AVG: "Army would like to convert A.V.G. into regular U.S. Army units," he radioed General Magruder in Chongqing. "I am inclined to favor this as insuring steady and increased flow of planes, supplies and men. It is almost impossible to secure this result working outside the army." On the last day of 1941, therefore, Magruder composed a lengthy radiogram to the War Department, outlining how induction might work in practice. The AVG would be reconstituted as the 23rd Pursuit Group, U.S. Army Air Forces. Chennault's people would receive lump-sum payments from CAMCO to make up the difference between their army salaries and what they would have earned by serving out their contracts. Those who refused induction or who failed the army's physical, intellectual, or moral standards would be replaced by qualified Chinese pilots and technicians, "thereby showing to the world a true spirit of mutual cooperation and consolidation of the democratic front." Having worked that out, Magruder still could not bring himself to grasp the nettle of Claire Chennault. He merely forwarded, without comment, the generalissimo's recommendation "that Colonel C. L. Chennault, in view of his past services and merits, be appointed commander" of all American air units in China. No rank was specified.

That December 31 radiogram was distinctly upbeat. All the more astonishing, then, that it was followed two days later by another on the same subject, which stands as the most pessimistic assessment ever made of the AVG's combat potential. (Perhaps Magruder had been reading Oley Olson's radiograms from Burma.) "Despite Chennault's personal accomplishments and the group's initial successes," Magruder told the War Department, the AVG "has no staying powers as now supplied and constituted." Its staff was "ineffective," its command "irregular," and its supply system "chaotic." Oley Olson, Jack Newkirk, and Sandy Sandell should be replaced by squadron leaders from the U.S. Army, and uniformed staff officers should take over from such amateurs as Harvey Greenlaw and Skip Adair. Chennault also needed a "complete enlisted staff" for his group headquarters and for each of his tactical squadrons. Unless the AVG were reorganized in this fashion, Magruder now believed, "its military value will deteriorate further." Nor was he the only American officer to conclude—despite three overwhelming victories in as many combats—that the AVG was no match for the Japanese air force. A few days after General Brett radioed his congratulations to Chennault, he gave an interview to a British war correspondent, O'Dowd Gallagher, who had rushed to Burma with two American colleagues to cover the story developing there. How many more such raids could

Rangoon withstand? "I give Burma three weeks," replied General Brett, the senior American officer in Asia, and the man who would command Chennault and the AVG if they were taken into the U.S. Army.

In Burma, to be sure, the AVG was fighting on a front never imagined by its creators. Rangoon was the whirlpool, and Kunming—intended as the AVG's main combat base—was a pleasant backwater of the war. That thoughtful observer, radioman Bob Smith, wrote in his diary:

> The valley of Kunming is an entrancing sight from the hills. One sees neat, small plots of ground, green with winter wheat and vegetables. There are clumps of pines, villages of adobe and tile. The lake is fifty miles long and the water is a deep blue. The cliff of the mountain of Si San rises about 2,000 feet above the valley floor. The winter climate is perfect—better in some ways than that of California or Florida. There is an occasional frost. The noonday sun is always warm and the air clear and pure. There is a scent of pine on the air.

The headquarters section and the newly arrived Hell's Angels were housed at Hostel Number One, a virtual fraternity house near Green Lake in the northern part of the city. In the rear courtyard they had a softball diamond, tennis courts, and a basketball hoop. Inside, they had a recreation room with ping pong table, Victrola, books—and a bar, of course. They also had a barbershop, where they discovered one of the luxuries long enjoyed by white men in Asia. "I could go down and get a haircut and a shave and a shampoo," Ken Jernstedt recalled in later years, "for the equivalent of eight cents American, when a Gillette blade would have cost ten cents. That was the life of Riley, to have somebody shave you every day." Three nights a week, they could take Chinese lessons from Peter Shih, graduate of George Peabody College in Nashville. In the dining room, Paul Frillmann screened movies from home. "Also," noted another pilot, "nicest thing of all, we have hot running water." The accommodations for the 1st Squadron—Sandy Sandell's Adam & Eves, billeted at Hostel Number Two on the airport road—were less sumptuous, but even Adobe City would have been a great improvement over the bullet-splintered barracks at Mingaladon airport.

On Monday, December 29, Colonel Wang Shu-ming made a tardy

appearance as Santa Claus, bearing presents from Chiang Kai-shek. Don
Rodewald described the festivities in his diary:

> Worked all day then the Chinese threw us a swell Xmas party tonight. The
> Col. was presented with a Air Force sword from the General Issimo.
> [Chennault] made an inspiring speech. We all got a silk scarf with the
> General Issimo's personal chop on it. We had wonderful entertainment by
> the Chinese.

John Donovan, a former navy pilot from Alabama, regularly wrote his
parents about life behind the combat zone, on subjects ranging from
China's inflation to Chennault's bronchitis, both of which had taken an
alarming turn. Donovan was almost bald, and one of his squadron mates
remembered him as "an abrasive, taciturn character always looking for
action." Yet his letters reveal a temperament so sweet that it is difficult
to reconcile with that description, or with his chosen profession. The
generalissimo's gift and the invigorating climate, Donovan wrote, made
him "feel good all over and every day seems like Xmas and I keep waiting
for something good to happen."

> We have wonderful food served in excellent style for which we pay $1,500
> per month. Since I did not bring a pistol, I need one and it would cost me
> several thousand dollars if I could find any for sale. . . . The price of a
> package of chewing gum is $20.

Those were Chinese dollars, of course. A U.S. greenback, which had
fetched three *yuan* when Chennault landed at Shanghai in 1937, now
bought fifty on the black market.

Donovan's major complaint was that he could not fly combat patrols,
because he had no single-engine experience . . . and he could not get the
experience without going on patrol. Thanks to this Catch-22, he had
logged just fifteen hours in a Tomahawk since he had been in Asia. (To
make use of his men who had not qualified in fighters, Chennault was
toying with the idea of loaning them to CNAC, which was due to
receive more transport planes from the U.S. In the end, this plan was
dropped, and most of the pilots—including Donovan—were eventually
assigned to combat squadrons.) Another, smaller regret was that he had
neglected to bring a uniform to East Asia:

> We wear flight clothing like that issued in the Navy. However, since we
> have no uniforms, we wear any combination of articles of clothing that

simulates a uniform. I certainly wish that I had brought my Navy greens, as some of the Army guys brought their uniforms and with the Chinese insignia on them they look real "snazzy."

There was another new touch: each pilot had been issued a silk panel to wear on the back of his flight jacket, containing the twelve-pointed Nationalist star and a message identifying him as a friendly airman who should be taken to the nearest army post. This "blood chit" had been inspired by Erik Shilling's misadventure with Chinese mountaineers on December 23–24.

I Commenced to Lean Forward

January 1942

Jack Newkirk was a lanky, coarse-featured man with a toothy grin, who at the age of twenty-eight was trying without much success to grow a fighter pilot mustache. Women found him immensely attractive—as he found them. The son of a lawyer in White Plains, New York, Newkirk had been an Eagle Scout, an office boy for *Time* magazine, a second lieutenant of infantry, and a civilian airline pilot before he joined the navy, which trained him as a fighter pilot and assigned him to *Yorktown*. He was much frustrated, upon reaching Mingaladon airport at the end of December, to find that the JAAF 3rd Hikoshidan had declared a truce in its campaign against Rangoon. For three days the Panda Bears waited for the enemy to come over. There was the occasional scramble, but the vast blue sky remained empty of Japanese planes.

So Newkirk called the Panda Bears together and said: "Let's take the war to the enemy!" In this, he was following the orders of Air Vice Marshal Donald Stevenson, who had arrived on New Year's Day to become Allied air commander in Burma. His air force consisted of two Blenheim bombers (the other two having been destroyed on the ground by Japanese bombs) and thirty fighters, RAF and AVG. Nothing daunted, as he boasted in his post-campaign dispatch, "I therefore commenced to lean forward with a portion of my fighters [to] attack enemy aircraft wherever found. . . . I hoped to make him disperse his

159

fighters by forcing protection for these widely separated points and so weaken him in the central sector opposite Rangoon. I gave instructions accordingly on January 2nd"—Stevenson's first full day in-country. His dispatch was in the best tradition of British military prose, in which all soldiers were brave, all combat glorious, and the whole business curiously bloodless. *Leaning forward.* For the Commonwealth pilots and the Panda Bears, Stevenson's strategy meant that they would fly into Thailand and attack the JAAF on the ground, against antiaircraft and small-arms fire, knowing that if anything went wrong they would be killed or captured—and that of the alternatives, death was easier.

In contrast to Oley Olson, who had not left the ground during his tour at Mingaladon, Newkirk led the first mission. The target was an airstrip near the village of Tak, fifty miles into Thailand, beyond the twin mountain ranges that guarded the border. This was the field the Japanese called Raheng. The usual garrison was a single hintai (three planes) but Captain Toyoki Eto of the 77th Sentai had spent Friday night there with nine Nates, in order to mount a dawn attack on the RAF base at Moulmein. The two raiding parties must have lifted off at about the same moment—Newkirk's from Mingaladon airport, Eto's from Raheng—just before sunrise on Saturday, January 3.

Newkirk set out with Bert Christman on his wing, but a balky engine forced the former comic strip artist to turn back to Mingaladon. That left three Panda Bears in the raiding party: Newkirk, Jim Howard, and Tex Hill. They flew east above the brown and green quilt of the South Burma delta, crossed the iridescent water of Martaban Bay, and reentered Burmese airspace north of Moulmein, whose airfield was now smoking from Captain Eto's attack. The three Tomahawks crossed the Dawna Range at 10,000 feet, the peaks only 3,000 feet below them, and flew into Thailand against the rising sun. Newkirk led his flight beyond the target, then circled back so they would have the sun at their backs. Dropping down at 250 mph toward the airstrip, the Panda Bears were elated to see several Japanese fighters like sitting ducks on the gravel field, their propellers turning—about to take off, as the Americans believed, but in fact just landed from their raid on Moulmein. There were spectators, too, in such quantity that Tak/Raheng seemed to be in the midst of an air show. Flush from their victory at Moulmein, where they claimed one Buffalo destroyed and two or three damaged, the Japanese pilots were landing by the hintai; as they told the story, three Nates were on the ground and three more touching down when the field was attacked by "Spitfires" from out of the sun.

"I got so preoccupied with seeing the enemy planes on the ground," Tex Hill recalled in later years, "that I didn't think about looking up. The three of us bent 'em over, and as we approached the field I looked up *and there were three more planes in the traffic pattern with us.* Like lightning, one Jap tacked onto Jim Howard's tail and was eating him up." The Nates belonged to Captain Eto's third hintai, coming down to land in their turn. Tex Hill had already followed Howard into the strafing run. That left Newkirk to deal with the Nates, as he wrote in his combat report:

> I saw two enemy aircraft circling the field at 2,000 feet and attacked the nearest plane . . . from astern. After two twists it turned to the left streaming smoke, rolled over, and crashed into the jungle. Vice Squadron Leader J. H. Howard at this time strafed the field and I saw a large fire as the result.

An AVG veteran later nicknamed Jim Howard "the automatic pilot" for the methodical way he carried out his duties. As he told the story years later, he knew there were Japanese planes in the air, but he chose to ignore them. "Our intended mission was to strafe the planes on the field," Howard wrote in his autobiography, "so I bore in to catch the prizes on the ground." He gave a five-second burst to a fighter that seemed to be taxiing for takeoff. (Actually it had just landed.) Then he glimpsed a surreal scene to his left. "Crowds of people on a grandstand," as he recalled, "were scrambling over themselves in a kind of wave to get out of the line of fire."

While Howard strafed the fighters on the ground, the airborne Nate clung to his tail with both machine guns chattering—eating him up, in Tex Hill's phrase. So Hill quit his own strafing run in favor of the live target and his endangered buddy. "I pulled around on him as quickly as I could and started firing as I did," Hill recalled. "I didn't even look through the gunsights—just watched the tracers like following a garden hose. With my diving speed built up, I came right up on him and he blew up. I flew through the debris and pulled up to come around and meet another Jap coming straight at me."

Hill thought he shot down the second Nate, too, but Jack Newkirk took the credit. Having dispatched his first quarry, the squadron leader went after another, which had to be the same plane that had just buzzed

Tex Hill. Newkirk got on its tail and fired several bursts, only to have it loop up and over "in the the most quick and surprising manner." The Nate rolled upright as it turned back on its former course, so that it was now heading straight for its pursuer. (Invented by the German ace Max Immelmann in World War I, this maneuver had fallen out of favor with western pilots, with their heavyweight machines, but it was still a favorite with the Japanese.) "Both of us were firing head on at each other," Newkirk wrote in his combat report, "and he pulled up over me. Several particles fell from his plane and he stalled and spun into the jungle." The squadron leader had redeemed himself for his "buck fever" near Kunming on December 20.

While these combats went on around and above him, Jim Howard finished his strafing run and returned for another. "I roared down the line of idling aircraft with my thumb on the firing button all the way," he wrote in his autobiography. "The machine guns ate a wonderful line of destruction the length of that array of fighters. I hauled back on the stick for the getaway. Nothing doing! As the nose came up, a dull thump shook my fighter. . . . Smoke poured from the cowling and the screaming Allison went dead. My prop idled to a windmill. I had been hit by ground fire."

Howard circled back toward the enemy airfield, intending to make a belly landing among the planes he had just been strafing. Then a miracle: the Allison coughed to life. Howard brought the nose up, and while he regained speed he actually flew for a time in formation with two Nates, their pilots evidently focused on the flame and confusion on the ground. Howard slipped away and headed for the border.

When the Panda Bears were reunited at Mingaladon airport, they relived the combat as pilots have done since the days of Max Immelmann—laughing, boasting, and weaving their hands and bodies like so many Oriental dancers. Hill yarned about shooting the Japanese fighter off Howard's tail, only to have his partner deny that anybody had been eating him up in that fashion. To settle the argument, they went out to the flight line, where Hill counted eleven bullet holes in the tail and fuselage of Howard's plane. Then it was Hill's turn for second thoughts: his own Tomahawk had thirty-three perforations in its wings. Evidently he had been hosed by a Nate whose guns were harmonized at such short range that the bullets had crossed in an X, with Hill untouched in the middle of the spread. "I began learning fast from that time on," he afterward said, "and I think my neck size increased about an inch—you know, keeping your head on a swivel, looking around."

Jim Howard was credited with destroying four planes on the ground at Tak/Raheng, while Hill was credited with shooting down one fighter and Newkirk with two.* However, Japanese records show that only two Nates were damaged on the field, and that only one was shot down. Indeed, the other Nates had to have survived the battle. Newkirk, Hill, and the Japanese all agreed that only three Nates were in the traffic pattern over Raheng—and Jim Howard testified that two were still flying when he left the scene, well after his buddies.

The JAAF now had about seventy-five planes targeted on Burma. They included the Nates of the 77th Sentai, the light bombers of the 31st Sentai, and the early model Sallys of the 62nd Sentai. These three groups belonged to the 5th Hikoshidan but had been attached to General Sugawara's forces for the opening weeks of the war; they were now waiting for their own headquarters to reclaim them. Meanwhile, they were to soften Burma for invasion. Thus the sunrise strafing of Moulmein airfield, and thus the predawn bombings of the Rangoon airfields that began on Sunday morning, January 4.

The siren wailed at 5 A.M. Under Stevenson's regimen, the AVG and the RAF had dispersed their planes for the night. Half the fighters remained at Mingaladon airport, hidden among the mango trees or protected by dirt-walled revetments, while the rest had been flown off to Highland Queen, fifteen miles north. (Royal Air Force engineers were building a network of dispersal fields in an arc beyond Mingaladon, naming most of them after favored brands of whiskey.) The raiders were three of Colonel Onishi's Sallys from Bangkok. They droned into Burmese airspace with their navigation lights gleaming, and they dropped their bombs after a burst of machine gun fire from the flight leader—signals made necessary by their lack of plane-to-plane

---

* Fighter pilots traditionally earn their victories in aerial combat. Chennault did not make this distinction, however, and the planes attributed to Howard on January 3 put him four-fifths of the way toward becoming an AVG ace.

radio communication. Their target was Highland Queen, where their bombs exploded without great effect.

Meanwhile, the on-duty Allied pilots were taking off from Mingaladon airport, while the standbys raced by sedan and truck to Highland Queen. But by the time the Buffaloes and Tomahawks were airborne, the raiders were well on their way back to Thailand. All the fighters then landed at Mingaladon. They were refueled, and the Panda Bears retreated to the shade of their wood-and-canvas alert tent.

The alarm howled again at 12:30 P.M. Each pilot ran to his plane, climbed the wing, slid into the cockpit, and buckled his seat belt and parachute harness. His fingers danced across the toggles and rotary dials in front of him and to either side: ignition switch at "battery"—fuel selector switch at "reserve"—generator on—propeller circuit breaker on—prop selector switch at "automatic"—throttle open—mixture control at "idle cutoff"—carburetor control at "cold." Okay. Open the coolant flaps, stroke the priming pump, and press the master switch to send twenty-four volts to the inertial starter. Listen to the flywheel whine, faster and faster. Turn the ignition switch from battery to both magnetoes. Engage the starter. Hear the whine-down as the flywheel takes the load, followed by the coughing and spitting of the big Allison engine, belching smoke from its twelve short exhaust pipes.

Then the clatter smoothed to a roar, and the Tomahawk began its perilous roll down the runway, weaving past the soft spots (bomb craters recently filled by coolie labor) while other Tomahawks jockeyed ahead and alongside, gray phantoms in the general storm of dust. At 100 mph they lifted off, the landing gear retracting and canopies closing as soon as they broke free of the earth. . . . To the ground crews watching them, the Tomahawks seemed both fragile and brave—little more than hummingbirds—bouncing and jittering in their eagerness to reach the sky.

Fourteen Panda Bears got off the ground. (The 67th Squadron logbook for 1942 was destroyed in the retreat from Burma, so it is not clear whether any Buffaloes got into the air that afternoon.) They climbed through the clouds to 20,000 feet, only to find that they had lost radio contact with Mingaladon. Eight planes kept to the high perch, while the others spiraled down in hopes of regaining communications with fighter control. The descending Tomahawks also divided. Frank Swartz led one three-plane element, with Gil Bright and Hank

Geselbracht as his wingmen. Bert Christman led the other, tailed by Pappy Paxton and Ken Merritt.

As Paxton recalled, they broke through the clouds at 11,000 feet, at which point the sky around them was clear and unmenacing. At thirty-nine, Paxton was the old man of the Panda Bears, with a face that seemed put together from slabs of raw clay. A graduate of Yale, he had worked as a banker before joining the navy, which trained him as a flying boat captain. Gene Pawley put him in charge of the *Boschfontein* contingent, and Chennault picked him to replace Butch Carney as AVG finance officer. All of which was poor preparation for what happened next to Pappy Paxton.

Thirty-one Nates swarmed in from the southeast, led by Major Hirose Yoshio, executive officer of the 77th Sentai. They were below the AVG top cover and therefore invisible to them, but they held the altitude advantage over the six descending Tomahawks. "The next second," Paxton said, "the air was full of little red and silver planes." (The impression of red came from the rising-sun identification discs, while the silver was the pale-green body paint of the 77th Sentai Nates.)

> I reached for the gun switch and all hell broke loose in my cockpit—awful thud of bullets hitting everything, glass, armor seats, everything. It was deafening. My plane seemed to hang still in the air under the pounding. Things got sort of cloudy. . . . I knew I had been hit—shoulder, leg, and arm. They all burned.
>
> Somehow I got over into a dive. Then I knew I was spinning. An awful smell of smoke filled the cockpit. I remembered wondering if I was going to burn. Then I was out of the spin and the pounding of the lead stopped. Thank God.

Paxton was shot through the left shoulder and right side. Another 7.7-mm bullet hit a joint in his seat armor, shattered there, and pierced his back with shards of brass and pellets of lead. By this time, Ken Merritt had tacked onto the Japanese fighter, hosing it with machine gun fire until it "burst into flames and dived to the ground"—too late for Pappy Paxton, his Tomahawk spinning out of control, his windshield and instrument panel covered with oil. Terrified that the Tomahawk would come apart, and that the Nate might still be behind him, Paxton leveled off and made a wide circle back to Mingaladon.

> The left side of the windshield fell out when I turned. I could see enough

to land then. Got the wheels down, but the plane veered off to the right as I went down the runway. Kicked left rudder and overcorrected. The rudder locked and the tail wheel seemed to fold.

The tail wheel did collapse, and the main landing gear too, so the Tomahawk screeched along on its belly until friction brought it to a stop. Paxton took a deep breath, decided that he was still alive, and (as one of his squadron mates recalled) vowed that he would never fly another combat mission. It would be hard to fault him. A fighter pilot requires quick reflexes and a firm belief in his own immortality, qualities that have faded by the time a man reaches thirty-nine.

Leading Paxton's element, Bert Christman had also come under attack. He dove away and tried to turn out of the stream of machine gun bullets, but without success. "The wings, fuselage, tanks, and cockpit of my plane were riddled," he reported. "The engine stopped after five minutes of flying. Smoke came into cockpit and the controls were damaged." Christman opened the canopy and jumped into the airstream. Below his heels, the Tomahawk spun away and crashed with a great wallop of dust, while he floated down to a safe landing.

In the second flight, Gil Bright counted twenty-seven Nates in the air around him—and "six or eight" bullet holes in the cowling of his plane. He dove away as he had been taught. Though his engine was on fire, Bright rode the Tomahawk down to a belly landing in a dried-out rice field near the railroad tracks. His face was scorched when he opened the canopy; when he stumbled out, he was shot at by his own fifty-caliber guns, triggered by the fire. Then a fuel tank exploded, knocking him to the ground. Bright got to his feet and staggered to the nearest building, which proved to be a station on the railroad leading north to Toungoo, Mandalay, and Lashio. Using the stationmaster's telephone, he rang the RAF duty officer at Mingaladon, explained his predicament, and asked for somebody to pick him up.

"Get on the train," he was told.

"But I don't have a ticket," Bright protested.

"Bugger the ticket, old boy," said the starched voice on the other end of the line. "Just get on the train."

In that flight, Frank Swartz and Hank Geselbracht managed to get some hits on the Japanese fighters, but only one claim was recognized: Ken Merritt's, for shooting the Nate off Paxton's tail. But the 77th Sentai lost no planes on January 4, while shooting down three of the defenders, for a clear victory—Japan's first—over the AVG. On the other hand, all the American pilots were still alive and would soon be able to fly again. (True to his vow, Pappy Paxton would limit himself to ferry trips and other noncombat flights.) That was the home-field advantage, such as the Royal Air Force had enjoyed in the Battle of Britain.

The bombers returned that night: half a dozen Anns of the 31st Sentai. At Mingaladon airport, they triggered the alarm at 2:20 A.M. The Tomahawks did not have instruments illuminated for night combat, nor were they equipped with exhaust shields. (So dazzling were the blue-white flames from the exhaust stacks that P-40 drivers joked about the new boy who took off on a night flight and immediately landed again, swearing that his engine was on fire.) Then too, their wheels were narrowly spaced, making night landings treacherous.

Nevertheless, three Panda Bears took off in the moonlight, determined to join the RAF in night interception. They missed the raiders over the airport, though they could see the bombs exploding in great lurid flashes, like sheet lightning against the clouds. The men on the ground took what cover they could find. "I jumped into a pit and crouched down," Noel Bacon wrote in his diary. "When the bombs started coming—wow! What a feeling! Each one felt like it hit me." Nine bombs hit the airport, one of them setting fire to General Wavell's DC-2.

The Brewster Buffalo had been designed to touch down on the heaving deck of an aircraft carrier, so it had the advantage of wide-track landing gear. And the 67th Squadron used a system that would have met with Chennault's approval: one pilot did the flying while another guided him by a portable radio transmitter on the ground. The result was the same, however, and all the Anns returned safely to Phitsanulok.

On January 7, after two weeks of traversing North Africa, the Middle East, and India, the 113th Squadron reached Mingaladon with fourteen twin-engined Blenheim bombers. Air Vice Marshal Stevenson immediately pressed them into his campaign against the Japanese in Thailand: they would bomb Bangkok that very night. To prep them for the 700-mile round trip, he had the 60th Squadron ground crews, stranded at Mingaladon airport while their own planes fought in Malaya. (Most of the 60th Squadron bombers had already been lost. Their air crews were straggling back to Burma by sea, and two of the Blenheims assigned to the Bangkok mission were crewed by these refugee pilots and bombardiers.) Still equipped with their ferry tanks and desert fuel filters, nine Blenheims took off at midnight, each carrying 1,000 pounds of fragmentation bombs and 100 pounds of incendiaries—half the load of Colonel Onishi's Sallys.

At Phitsanulok, meanwhile, a half-dozen Anns from the 31st Sentai lifted off for Mingaladon. The Japanese and British pilots were operating under the same imperatives: they wanted to bomb by moonlight, when interception was difficult, while returning to base after sunrise, when the touchdown was easy.

The Panda Bears had adopted the RAF system for night interception—one plane—and Pete Wright had drawn the duty for January 7–8. He arranged the signals with John Hauser, his crew chief, then went to sleep in the alert tent. Profiting by the example of generals Wavell and Brett, the AVG technicians had begun to help themselves to the treasures on the Rangoon docks, and high on their list were the little four-wheel-drive trucks recently adopted by the U.S. Army. Hauser had equipped himself with one of these creations (called "jeep" as shorthand for its designation of General Purpose vehicle) and in the event of a raid he would drive it to the far end of the runway, turn around, and aim the headlamps to guide Wright's takeoff. Then he would set kerosene lanterns along the runway—white to the right, red to the left—to be lit when Wright signaled his intention to land.

The siren howled at 3:30 A.M. Wright bounded off his cot, pulled on his flying clothes, and ran to his Tomahawk, which Hauser had warmed up hourly since sundown. The takeoff went perfectly, but Wright could not seem to position himself in the same part of the sky as the incoming bombers. He throttled back and adjusted his fuel mixture to lean, to make his exhaust flames as inconspicuous as possible, and he opened his canopy so he could hear and see better. Unlike the 67th Squadron night fighters, he had no buddy on the ground to direct him. Instead, RAF fighter control sent him conflicting messages: bombers to the east . . . bombers to the north. Then he saw some large yellow flashes. The raid appeared to be over, so Wright returned to Mingaladon:

> I let down to 2,000 feet and, flashing my running lights, I was rewarded a few minutes later by seeing the eight tiny pinpoints of light far below. . . . I was coming around the last turn now, concentrating on getting lined up

with the runway. As I straightened up, I threw the flap handle to "down" and pushed the button on top of the stick to lower my flaps.

Whereupon he was hit in the face by a jet of hydraulic fluid. He pushed his goggles up and leaned outside to escape the geyser of oil, which was coming from a ruptured gasket in his flap-control valve. Peering down, Wright saw Hauser's red lanterns vanishing beneath his left wing:

> I waited a split second, and then pulled back the stick. I hit the ground in a left skid, and the landing gear gave way with a lurch. . . . [T]he plane skidded along its belly. Suddenly there was a terrific crash, and I violently cracked my head against the windshield.

Wiping blood and oil from his face, Wright saw that his Tomahawk had rammed a Chevrolet sedan, tearing it apart. Much the same was true of the man inside: Ken Merritt, who had driven up at the last moment and aimed his headlamps along the runway, trying to be helpful. (Or so John Hauser explained the accident to Wright. Jack Newkirk reported it differently: worn out by lack of sleep, Merritt had simply taken a nap in the parked car.) The British buried him beside Hank Gilbert, in the graveyard of Edward the Martyr at Insein Cantonment.

After sunrise, the 113th Squadron returned from Bangkok. (The RAF communiqué described the raid as "very successful," while the Japanese with equal predictability claimed that most of the bombs fell on schools and hospitals.) Next day, the Blenheims flew off to Lashio for the inspection and overhaul that were due after their long journey from North Africa. One bomber, damaged when it taxied into a bomb crater, stayed behind at Mingaladon, to be destroyed in time by Japanese bombs.

The Panda Bears returned to Thailand that same afternoon— Thursday, January 8. Charlie Mott led the mission, accompanied by Robert (Moose) Moss, Gil Bright, and Percy Bartelt. Their target was Mae Sot, in the valley that marked the Thai-Burma frontier, where the Japanese were building another forward airfield, forty miles closer to the Allied bases in Burma. Leaving Bright to fly top cover at 6,000 feet, Mott and the others "went down to do the business." After his first screaming pass over the aircraft on the field, Mott spotted two more planes hidden in the rain forest. He lifted his wing and swung back to strafe this target of opportunity. Then his world fell apart:

> There was a big boom up in the engine, and the thing quit cold. I was [about] thirty feet off the ground. I had quite a bit of speed, naturally, and I pulled up and started to work on the engine, shifting fuel tanks and so on. But by that time I was out of airspeed. I rolled over—oh, I was 200 or 300 feet off the ground—and I kicked out.

Mott's parachute opened seconds before he hit, saving his life but leaving him with cracked ribs and breaks in an arm, a leg, and his pelvis. Japanese soldiers picked him up and took him to Raheng, where the 55th Division had set up a headquarters in preparation for its drive into Burma.

Moose Moss (the stocky pilot who had traveled as an acrobat to Southeast Asia) roared back again and again to strafe the Japanese aircraft. "I made three passes down the main line of the parked enemy aircraft," he reported. "The smoke and fire from burning aircraft was bad so I turned perpendicular to the line." He made six passes, estimating that eight planes were burning when he left the scene.

That tally was confirmed by Percy Bartelt. "My first run was made on an observation plane and carried on through the line of fighters," he wrote. He then made two runs on the fighters, a fourth on the plane that he believed to be a scout, and a fifth on some tents bordering the field. By this time, Bartelt had only two rifle-caliber guns firing, so he broke off and followed Moss to the westward. "There were eight burning when we left," he concluded. The eight planes were divided equally among the pilots in the raid, including Gil Bright and Charlie Mott.

Though not as devastated as the Panda Bears believed, the 77th Sentai had indeed taken a serious hit at Mae Sot, with four of Major Yoshioka's Nates destroyed. Three Nates and a transport (Bartelt's reconnaissance plane, no doubt) were also damaged in the raid.

Hardly had the Mae Sot survivors landed at Mingaladon than seven Tomahawks and six Buffaloes took off on another foray. (Two more Tomahawks were to have gone along, but Hank Geselbracht—blinded by dust—chewed up the tail of Tom Cole's plane during takeoff.) The raiders flew at 10,000 feet toward the Dawna Range, strung out in a loose line with "weavers" above to watch for enemy fighters. Their target was Tak/Raheng, as Jack Newkirk reported:

The first section dove straight into Tak Aerodrome out of the sun. The second dove from the southwest, and the third from the northwest in that order. On the first dive I was unable to distinguish any target, except the operations building. However, when reaching the field I saw four enemy aircraft, a few trucks and several ground personnel. On the next dive I attacked [a Nate] which was parked by the operations building. It was silver colored and had branches on it, and when I looked back it was in flames. On the same dive I fired on a truck which was driving across the field. The truck swerved and ran into the burning plane. On the next dive I fired on a plane across the field from the building, several pieces fell out of it and it collapsed on the ground. During this process I heard two "plunks" in my fuselage.

The plunks were rifle bullets. With the tenacity of samurai, Japanese riflemen stood beside the planes and emptied their guns at the screaming Tomahawks. John Petach saw them as he roared across the field: "Fired on a compact group of ground riflemen," he reported, adding that he "dispersed" them and shot up several tents and a truck. However, Petach saw no planes. Gil Bright had about the same luck: "Picked out a single enemy plane on the edge of the field and fired a long burst at it with no apparent results, although tracers were going into it. . . . Difficulty was experienced," he concluded, "in distinguishing camouflaged planes from buildings, truck, etc."

Noel Bacon (who "felt like hell" from a bout of diarrhea the night before) reported that he had shot up a fighter and a truck on his strafing run, in turn collecting two bullet holes in his own plane.

They returned to Mingaladon at 6:30 P.M. Leland Stowe, a white-haired reporter for the *Chicago Daily News,* was among the spectators peering through the evening light to count the Tomahawks and Buffaloes as they approached the field. "Across the airdrome," he wrote, "the umbrella-topped frames of trees suddenly stand inked out against the sky. Tropical twilight comes with a rush along the Irrawaddy Valley and the British–United States fliers are trying to beat it in. It is a pretty tight race but there are a succession of dust swirls off the lower end of the runway." (In his dispatches, Stowe liked to call the American squadron "the Scalpers," a name inspired by the Curtiss Tomahawk.) One of the 67th Squadron pilots did a victory roll, all but scraping the treetops. Then the usual chafing and boasting began. A pilot identified as Pete—John Petach, no doubt—kidded Newkirk about sending the truck into a plane that had already been hit: "You're a lousy billiards player. Why didn't you carom that truck into the plane that wasn't already on fire?" The RAF duty officer heard them out, slapped Newkirk on the shoulder, and gave him the ultimate British accolade: "Good show!"

In the debriefing that followed, Newkirk's flight agreed that they had destroyed three Japanese planes on the ground. (Again, it is impossible to know what the Commonwealth pilots were claiming.) The actual toll: one Nate burned, another disabled, and a starter truck destroyed—no small loss for a Japanese fighter group.

———————

And so it went, back and forth across Martaban Bay, the Japanese bombing Mingaladon at night, the Allied pilots strafing the Thai airfields during the day, and each side convinced that it was inflicting twice or three times the damage that was actually done.

And in Kunming, an AVG clerk changed Charlie Mott's personnel card to show him as missing in action. "Tokio radio claims one American pilot, badly burned, in Jap hospital," the notation read. "This apparently is Mott. His wife has been so notified."

Astonishingly, Bill Pawley and T. V. Soong had neglected to provide for the possibility that one of their "instructors" might be captured by the Japanese. In the end, Chennault arranged for Charlie Mott to be commissioned a captain in the Chinese Air Force. For the rest of the war, his wife in Alabama received a monthly check from China Defense Supplies: $650 until his CAMCO contract expired in July 1942, then the pay he would have earned as a captain in U.S. service.*

As for the pilots killed in action, their families received only six months' pay and $10,000 in insurance, the premiums for which were deducted from each man's paycheck. Perhaps as a consolation, the dead were commissioned in Chinese service at one grade above their serving

———————

* Mott's painful journey ended at Chulalongkorn University in Bangkok, which the Japanese had converted to a prison camp. He set his broken bones, taught himself to walk again, and by September was deemed fit enough to join the labor gangs building the "River Kwai" railway into Burma—work that killed 16,000 Allied prisoners and 60,000 native conscripts.

rank. So Hank Gilbert and Neil Martin, wingmen when they died, also became captains on the rolls of the CAF.

Jack Newkirk believed that his squadron was on a roll. "The more hardships, work, and fighting that the men have to do," he radioed Chennault, "the higher the morale goes. They seem to thrive on adversity. The squadron is becoming more unified every day." Perhaps, but the Panda Bears were as beat up as the Hell's Angels at the end of the Christmas campaign: Ken Merritt dead, Charlie Mott a prisoner, and five men hospitalized under the care of Sam Prevo, the AVG's chubby young flight surgeon. Four Tomahawks had been shot down and seven damaged on the ground. As a result, Newkirk could put only ten planes into the air—just what Oley Olson had mustered when he begged for relief. Squadron Leader Milward also had ten fighters, but the Buffaloes had to cover Mingaladon, Moulmein, Tavoy, and Mergui.

Chennault decided to send eight of Sandy Sandell's Tomahawks down from Kunming. In Adobe City on the airport road, the Adam & Eves drew slips of paper out of a hat to see who would fly them to Rangoon. Sandell did not go; instead, Bob Neale led the flight. Plagued by headwinds, balky engines, and inadequate maps, the Adam & Eves reached Lashio so late they had to spend the night. Indeed, they almost missed it altogether, as Neale recalled:

> The maps were Chinese maps and I couldn't read them too well, and they were very small scale. The main physical aspects of the country were the Mekong and the Salween. . . . I called one fellow up on the radio and said, "That was the Mekong River we just went over, wasn't it?" He said, "No, that was the Salween. . . ." [A]bout the time I was getting into a little panic, why, the little old field of Lashio showed up about ten miles to the north.

Dick Rossi did miss Lashio, finally putting down at an emergency field at Heho in the Shan Highlands. The field was defended by a British airman who had set up wooden ack-ack guns to frighten off the Japanese. He gassed Rossi's Tomahawk and pointed him toward Kyedaw airfield at Toungoo, where the ex-mariner spent the night.

When the Adam & Eves straggled into Mingaladon airport next day, they learned that the Allied airmen had moved off-base. The RAF servicing flight now operated out of the Rangoon Country Club, as did the mess. (The noon meal was prepared at the club, trucked to the airport, and served chuck-wagon style at the alert tents. Bully beef was the usual fare, served with bread, dried fruit, and tea whitened and sweetened with condensed milk.) The RAF bomber crews also lived at the country club, while the 67th Squadron occupied a "hostel"—an abandoned home, apparently—at Insein Cantonment. The AVG technicians were similarly assigned to a house north of the airport, which they named Eighteen Mile Ranch in tribute to its distance from Rangoon. The American pilots, however, were billeted in private homes, most of them in a compound occupied by executives of Burmah Oil Company.

The scattered accommodations, along with the dispersal system decreed by Air Vice Marshal Stevenson, made for a long day. For the on-duty pilots, morning came at 5 A.M. If they were lucky, wakeup came in the person of a manservant with a pot of tea, followed by a hearty English breakfast. Then they climbed into their purloined jeeps and drove to the dispersal field through the cool and misty darkness—a journey of fifteen miles, over a dusty gravel road that was sometimes no more than the dike between two rice fields. They picked out their Tomahawks in the glow of the headlamps, climbed into the cockpits, warmed their engines, and took off as soon as they could see the end of the runway. That brought them down to Mingaladon by 7 A.M., giving the crew chiefs time to top off the fuel tanks and finish the preflight check before the first alarm of the day.

In the evening, the ritual was reversed: just before sundown, the pilots flew north to the dispersal field, secured their Tomahawks, and drove home, where they arrived at about 8 P.M. Dinner was served by a houseboy who saluted them as "master," and afterward their host might provide whiskey soda on the veranda. "If you have to fight a war," Ed Rector said of his billet in the Burmah Oil compound, at the home of Basil and Joan Rigg, "that's the way to do it." But there was exhaustion, too, and tension, and the inevitable small diseases that afflict westerners in the tropics. Years later, Bob Neale remembered those dark tropical nights at Rangoon:

> A houseboy would serve me a quart of Mandalay beer with some cheese sandwiches. That was just heaven. We went into town a few times, but mostly we were too tired or too upset. I can remember times where I'd be sick to my stomach before combat, just from nervous tension.

The British families received a "feedback" (money or rations) for taking in the American pilots, but they did it gladly. To them, and to the mixed-blood residents of South Burma, the AVG Tomahawks were their best hope against the fate that had overtaken Hong Kong and that was now advancing upon Singapore. Dorothea Wilkins was among the young Englishwomen swept up in the general adoration. Nineteen years old, the daughter of a colonial bureaucrat, she had not yet been out without a chaperone, and in the ordinary course of events would not have done so for two years more. "Oh, we used to have wonderful balls in the Jubilee Hall," she recalled years later, "but always our parents would take us, and after the function they would take us home." Then the Hell's Angels performed their miracles in the sky over Rangoon, and the conventions began to fade.

Looking for girls one day, Bert Christman and Ed Rector knocked on the door of the Sacred Heart Convent and asked if they could look around. The Mother Superior—guileless woman—gave them a tour guide named Estre Healey, who taught at the convent school. As soon as the nun was out of sight, Christman asked if Estre had a friend, and why didn't they all go out to dinner? So Estre telephoned her young friend, whispering: "Dorothea, Dorothea, there are two pilots here—the AVG is here!"

"Where is here?" Dorothea asked.

"Here in the convent."

"What!"

"Yes, we're using the phone in Reverend Mother's study." She explained the plan, which Dorothea put to her father, who after some huffing agreed that she could make a fourth at dinner. Not even fathers were immune to the fame of the AVG. Dorothea relayed this incredible news to Estre, begging her not reveal that she was a child of nineteen, on her first date.

> Estre came at about seven with the two young men, and I knew from the way she took Bert Christman to my parents first, that he was her date for the evening. Eddie was at the back. And that beautiful person—I'll never forget—came up and shook my hand and said, "Sure glad to meet you!" We'd never heard that, you see.

Every genteel girl of the time had an autograph book, and Dorothea produced hers for the pilots to sign. On his page, Bert Christman sketched a Tomahawk, dated it—January 18, 1942—and wrote this caption: "Dorothea, may the American Sharks of the air keep you safe."

With the infusion of Adam & Eves, Jack Newkirk had more pilots than he could use, so the newcomers drew lots to see who would remain. John Croft and Greg Boyington lost the draw and rode the CNAC Douglas back to Kunming, where the AVG was about to have its first action since December 20.

The JAAF too was realigning its forces during the second week of January, though on a grander scale. In the Philippines, where American and Filipino troops were making their last stand on the Bataan Peninsula, General Eiryo Obata's 5th Hikoshidan had just about worked itself out of a job, so it was ordered to move to Bangkok. There Obata would resume command of the 77th, 31st, and 62nd Sentais, in addition to the units he would bring with him from the Philippines. These included two Nate-equipped squadrons of the 50th Sentai, commanded by Major Yasuo Makino. (His 3rd Chutai would continue to support the army's drive down the Bataan Peninsula.) Then there was the 8th Sentai under Major Mitsuo Honda, equipped with Mitsubishi Anns and Kawasaki Lilys like those the AVG had battled at Rangoon and Kunming. Finally, there was a heavy bomber group, the 14th Sentai under Colonel Magoroku Hironaka. With a total of about seventy-five planes, the three groups flew to Taiwan in the second week of January, underwent a modest amount of refitting and repair, then flew to Canton on the Chinese mainland. It was not lost on General Obata that his heavy bomber squadrons now had an opportunity to inflict some pain on the old enemy, Chiang Kai-shek, whose western redoubt had gone untouched for four weeks. Reconnaissance planes were reporting cloudy weather over Kunming, so Mengzi was selected as the target. Three Sallys were designated for this mission, with an escort of one chutai from the 50th Sentai. They flew down to Hanoi on January 16, while the rest of the division remained in China to mount a raid on Nanchang—Chennault's old stamping ground.

In one of those coincidences that seem commonplace in wartime, Chennault was planning a similar offensive. The Hell's Angels had recovered from their ordeal at Christmas, and most of the Adam & Eves were still at Wu Chia Ba airport, with nothing to occupy them but the occasional (and always fruitless) interception of reconnaissance planes. Why not send them against the Japanese installations in Indochina? Toward this end, Chennault had sent a three-plane flight across the border on December 31, but it ended in disaster: unable to spot the Japanese airfields through the clouds, the Tomahawks were equally hard put to find Wu Chia Ba on their return, and two planes were wrecked. Chennault tried again on Tuesday, January 13. This time the flight was to stage through Mengzi—more important to the AVG than the pilots realized. As the main source of tungsten for the U.S. war effort, the Mengzi mines stood behind the $100 million credit that had paid for their Tomahawks and was now paying their salaries. Furthermore, it had a gravel airfield (formerly the CAF intermediate flight school) seventy-five miles from the Indochina border. John Williams had accordingly established a radio station there and staffed it with Richard Ernst, two Chinese radio operators, a cook, and a squad of soldiers, whose job was not so much to fend off enemy attack as to protect the station from thieves. On Tuesday, when Ernst heard engine noises in his vicinity—three bombers, he thought—the AVG patrol was only twenty-five miles away. The three Tomahawks combed the sky for the intruders but could not find them. The enemy pilots must have seen them, however, for they jettisoned their bombs and turned back across the border. Japanese records do not identify this formation, but it may have been a probe by the 21st Hikotai, in preparation for the big raid scheduled for Saturday, January 17.

Chennault picked the same day for his next probe of Indochina. This time the patrol consisted of four Hell's Angels led by George McMillan. His wingmen were Chuck Older and Tom Haywood—like the vice squadron leader, veterans of the Christmas campaign over Rangoon—and Erik Shilling, who had never been in combat. Luckily for Shilling, he was flying Ben Foshee's Tomahawk instead of the stripped-down photo plane that was his usual mount.

For ten years Chennault had argued that a radio-equipped spotter network could guide fighter planes to an incoming bomber formation, destroying the intruders before they reached the target. In China, the CAF had never been strong enough to prove this argument, and the Burma Observation Corps was concerned only with warning that a raid was imminent, after which its job was done. But at Mengzi it all came together. On Saturday morning, Ernst again reported heavy engine noise near his station. The report was duly plotted on the map in the AVG command bunker, in the graveyard near Wu Chia Ba airport:

> Reports came in that loud noises were heard over Mengzi field. Reports also came in of noise heard overhead northeast of Yunnan Indo-Chinese border at Lao Kay. After receiving still another report of loud noises proceeding northeast, it was assumed that the Japanese had sent one or two bombers to reconnoiter Mengzi. . . . McMillan took off at 0950. About 1005 a report came that enemy aircraft [were] in the vicinity of [radio station] V-28. McMillan was given orders to proceed to P-27. At 1017 news came over the Plotting Room radio that McMillan's [flight] had contacted the enemy.

The formation consisted of the three heavy bombers that had spent Friday night at Gia Lam airport, outside Hanoi. Incredibly, they had arranged to meet their escort *over the target*. Somehow the fighters had missed the rendezvous, though from Hanoi to the border was an arrow-straight run: northwest along the railroad and the valley of the Red River (Song Hong Ha). In China, the terrain became more rugged, but still they had the gleaming river and the tracks of the Michelin to guide them. Nevertheless, the Nates got lost. It was probably their comings and goings that caused all the traffic on the AVG net.

George McMillan also followed the tracks of the Michelin, southbound from Kunming. After half of an hour of this, the Hell's Angels spotted the three big-tailed Sallys, twenty-five miles east of Mengzi at 16,000 feet. The Japanese bombers, Erik Shilling reported, wore a "fairly light colored camouflage" and were in the usual vee formation. But unlike the planes that had held such a steady course over Rangoon, they turned tail when the Tomahawks came into view. The Sallys were so fast, Shilling noted, that his manifold pressure gauge was showing forty inches of mercury by the time he caught up with them—at this altitude, for the early-model Tomahawks, a bit more than the "maximum boost" permitted by U.S. Army regulations. In a test pilot's clinical prose, Shilling described what happened next:

> We made two runs on them as they were heading north. Then they turned and went south. I made about two runs when I saw a thin stream of smoke coming out of the leader's plane but who shot it down I couldn't say. A little later it went down in flames. Then I saw thin smoke coming out of the second ship.

Shilling attacked from below and behind, while tracer bullets drifted toward him from the "stinger" in the tail—"Almost like they were dropping pieces of paper on fire out of the back." He had to charge his fifty-caliber nose guns before each run. Then his wing guns also began to jam. When the last gun quit firing, Shilling broke off and let the other Tomahawks finish the job.

Chuck Older reported that the Sallys were light gray on their undersides and "greenish tan" above, with red and white stripes on the rudder—"like the American Flag." (This was indeed the tail marking for the 14th Sentai.) Older's combat report continued:

> After one or two passes, two of enemy aircraft were trailing smoke, and I made attack on leader and he blew up in the air. . . . [The second bomber] glided down to overcast and dipped in and out. The [third] was trailing smoke and I ran out of ammunition except for a few in one .30-caliber gun. . . . Two enemy aircraft were shot down and one was pursued beyond border.

As the combat was recorded in the Group War Diary, the first Sally exploded when it hit the ground, killing all aboard; the second skidded in on its belly, with at least one crewman scrambling out; and the third bomber was found by Chinese ground searchers later the same day, the pilot dead and the big plane half-buried in the ground. So it appeared to be a clean sweep, and McMillan, Older, Shilling, and Tom Haywood were each credited with three-quarters of an enemy bomber. With his Rangoon victories, that made Chuck Older the first official ace in the AVG.

But Older had it right: only two Sallys had gone down over Yunnan province. According to a survivor, the first plane to fall was piloted by a Lieutenant Hironaka (no relation to the group commander), and so quickly did it drop out of the sky that the observer did not fully understood that his formation was under attack. Next to go down was the Sally flown by Captain Miki. The third bomber, flown by an officer named Fujiyoshi, was badly shot up, with gasoline pouring out of the main fuselage tank and two crewmen screaming from their wounds, but it stayed airborne long enough to cross the border and land at a small field belonging to the French colonial air force. Here Fujiyoshi commandeered a French transport to fly his casualties to Hanoi, where one man died in the hospital.

The Mengzi disaster left Colonel Hironaka with sixteen Sallys, which he used to bomb Nanchang the following day. That done, the entire group flew southwest across the rolling green mountains of Indochina and the rain forest of Thailand, to reinforce the 62nd Sentai in its campaign of attrition against the Allied airfields in Burma.

They All Fell in a Straight Line

January 1942

eneral Brett had given Burma three weeks, which time had now elapsed . . . but the port of Rangoon was still open, still pushing tons of lend-lease supplies up the Burma Road to China. Lieutenant General Thomas Hutton had taken charge of Burma's defenses, and the 17th Indian Division was arriving to bolster the hodgepodge battalions on the Thai frontier. More dispersal fields had been built beyond Mingaladon, in a layout suggesting a baseball diamond. (Running the bases, one came first to Zayatkwin, where the Blenheim bombers spent the night; then to Johnnie Walker, used as a dispersal field for the AVG Tomahawks; then to Highland Queen, used by the RAF Buffaloes; and so to Mingaladon again.) On January 16, *Neuralia* reached Rangoon with the ground crews and headquarters staff for three Hurricane squadrons—the 17th, 135th, and 136th—though the fighters themselves were still somewhere east of Suez and west of Karachi. An Indian Air Force squadron was also on its way to Burma, equipped with a dozen high-wing, fixed-gear Westland Lysander utility planes, for whatever purpose they might serve.

So Rangoon seemed more secure than at any time since December 23. The same could not be said of Tenasserim, that sliver of Burmese territory running 500 miles down the Malay Peninsula, with British garrisons at roughly 150-mile intervals. To secure General Yamashita's flank in Malaya, Japanese commandos had already seized the southernmost of these fields, at Victoria Point, and early in January they set out to cut Tenasserim at Tavoy, two-thirds of the way up the panhandle. "Wild elephants, leopards and venonmous snakes roamed this section of thick jungle," a Japanese officer recalled of the trek across the mountains to Tavoy. Cutting their way through the rain forest, and living on precooked rice, dried fish, and pickled plums, the commandos of Oki Detachment averaged only eight miles a day. But on the evening of January 16, on a mule-track outside Tavoy, they met two companies of Burma Rifles—native levies under the command of young British jungle wallahs from MacGregor Company and Burmah Oil.

The Burma Rifles greatly outnumbered Oki Detachment, but they had no stomach for close combat in the rain forest: they broke off, made camp, and attacked next morning with the support of yet another company, but ran for their lives when the Japanese opened fire. The officers and some troops made their way through the rain forest to Moulmein. But most found it more convenient—and more patriotic—to enlist in the Burma Independence Army.*

Oki Detachment attacked Tavoy airfield on Monday morning, January 19. The field was defended by a Frontier Force garrison: Indians trained as border police. They fared no better than the Burma Rifles, and six Blenheims were dispatched from Mingaladon "in an endeavour to evacuate 30 R.A.F. personnel . . . cut off by Japanese troops." Two Tomahawks and two Buffaloes flew shotgun. But the day was murky, the formation scattered, and when the bombers reached Tavoy they were bounced by seven Nates. When Dick Rossi caught up with the action, he was amazed to see a daisy chain in the air over Tavoy: a Blenheim under attack by a Nate, which itself was being chased by a Buffalo. This was Rossi's first combat, and the burly ex–merchant mariner roared into it with more zest than wisdom. He made four head-on passes against the Japanese fighter before realizing that another Nate had tacked onto *his* tail. Rossi escaped by diving into the clouds. Low on gasoline, he flew along the coast to Moulmein, where he landed

* The BIA was the creation of Colonel Keiji Suzuki, who recruited the "Thirty Comrades" in 1940 and took them to Taiwan for military training. They followed the Japanese army into Thailand, where they attracted hundreds of Burmese expatriates, and into Burma, where the BIA grew to 23,000 men.

to refuel, and where he met a Buffalo pilot who had been forced down with a ruptured oil line. The two men plugged the leak with rags, then kept each other company on the way home to Mingaladon airport.

Frank Lawlor (Whitey, he was called) reached Tavoy after Rossi had left the scene. He saw no Allied aircraft, nor the white cross that was supposed to show that the airfield was still in friendly hands. So, after a running scrap with the Japanese fighters, he too turned for home. No matter: Tavoy's defenders had already faded into the rain forest, leaving the RAF garrison to be captured by the Japanese.

Meanwhile, four other Tomahawks were strafing the Japanese forward airfield at Mae Sot. On their first pass, they saw no aircraft and had to be satisfied with shooting up a hangar, but on the next go-around they met a single-engine plane attempting to land—evidently a light bomber of the 31st Sentai. The Tomahawks chopped the unlucky Ann to pieces, with the credit shared by Jim Howard, Robert Layher, and John Petach.

Unseen by the Americans, two Japanese divisions—35,000 men— were trudging through the mountains on either side of Mae Sot. "As the war had progressed far more favorably than had at first been anticipated," a staff officer recalled, the Japanese had decided "to proceed with the Burma Operation without waiting for the completion of the other Southern Operations"—i.e., without waiting for Malaya and the Dutch Indies to fold. The 55th Division under Lieutenant General Yutaka Takeuchi was advancing on Moulmein, while the 33rd Division under Lieutenant General Shozo Sakurai would swing around Martaban Bay and into Burma proper. For them, too, the terrain was more difficult than expected, though not so formidable as the British had hoped. Unable to take motorized vehicles across the Dawna Range, Takeuchi reorganized his division into pack-horse units, which crossed the frontier on Tuesday morning, January 20.

Meanwhile the Allied air force was returning to Thailand: six Tomahawks shepherding a like number of Blenheims. Jack Newkirk led the escort, consisting of "self & Moss & Neale & Bartling & Christman & Gesel[bracht]." In the misty valley that marked the border, they tangled with half a dozen Nates. Newkirk claimed two Japanese fighters to become the Panda Bears' first ace. Bob Neale of the newly arrived Adam & Eves also tore into the Nates, though he needed a moment to understand that death was the expected outcome. "I was quite incensed," he admitted long afterward. "It seems a little strange for him to be shooting at you, and the first time you get shot at. . . ." His voice trailed away—this large and gentle man—unable after twenty years to express his wonder that the other pilot was actually trying to kill him.

> I can remember these tracers going by with this little plane on my tail. They were . . . much slower than us, and it was very easy to get away from them, but you couldn't turn with them. You could [only] make a pass at them and try to get them in your sights long enough to really hit them.

Neale put in a claim for one Nate, which Newkirk seconded, but the victory does not appear on his record.

Moose Moss also claimed a Nate, only to be bounced by two more. His engine caught fire, but he managed to keep the Allison ticking over until he was back across the Dawna Range. Then, 1,500 feet above the treetops, he opened his canopy and kicked out. The parachute fall left him with lacerations and broken teeth, but with charm enough to persuade a Burman to give him a ride in a buffalo cart. Bert Christman (lucky in love, unlucky in war) was also shot up in this engagement, returning to Mingaladon with a shattered windshield and twenty-seven bullet holes in his Tomahawk.

Meanwhile the Blenheims bombed Mae Sot "in a shallow dive from 2,700 ft," setting three fires and encountering heavy flak from anti-aircraft guns. At the same moment, the Japanese were bombing the RAF facilities at Moulmein. (Probably the Nates near Mae Sot were part of this mission.) Two Buffaloes were stationed at Moulmein, but were shot to pieces before they could struggle into the air. Moulmein, after all, was no safer than Tavoy. So when Moose Moss reached the airfield next morning, asking if he could hitch a ride to Rangoon, the Commonwealth airmen greeted him as an apparition. Didn't he know that the Japanese were across the border, and that he had passed through their lines during the night? "Well, I sure am surprised to hear that," Moss drawled. "I sure am." The British officers, who prided themselves on understatement, never tired of repeating that line.

General Wavell finally understood that "the grain of the country" would not protect Burma from invasion, and that he would have to accept Chiang Kai-shek's offer of troops. Hordes of sandal-shod infantry—without tanks or artillery, without trucks or field kitchens, without ambulances or even such homely prophylactics as mosquito nets and quinine—began the thousand-mile march down the Burma Road, from Kunming to Toungoo, where they would block any move into Central Burma. No exploit now seemed too daring for the Japanese army, and the British were terrified that Burma might be cut in half and the Commonwealth army trapped with its back to the sea. This threat seemed all the more likely when British intelligence picked up a rumor that 1,500 troops had been airlifted to Mae Sariang in northern Thailand. On January 22, Air Vice Marshal Stevenson sent six Blenheims with an escort of eleven Tomahawks to destroy the supposed invasion force. "Bad visibility marred bombing," the air crews reported, "mostly under-shooting." Which was probably just as well. There was nothing in Mae Sariang worth destroying, as Jack Newkirk observed:

> The bombers apparently aimed for the town but missed it and hit to the west and bombed some fields. No enemy planes in the air or on the ground. There wasn't much to straf, the town was deserted and there did not appear to be any troop concentrations or other activity. Eight (8) P-40s strafed the town and airdrome but caused no visual damage.

Newkirk also sent seven Tomahawks to support the 17th Indian Division, which was retreating through the rain forest toward Moulmein. This was the AVG's first experience with "ground cooperation," and the pilots did not care for it. Skimming the triple-tiered rain forest at 250 mph, there was not much chance of hitting anything on the ground, and a very real danger of being knocked down by rifle fire. And what would they accomplish thereby? The Indians probably thought that the Tomahawks were attacking *them,* for Japanese light bombers were also busy between Moulmein and the frontier, bombing and strafing in support of Takeuchi's 55th Division. For this dirty line of work, the Mitsubishi *Ki*-30 Ann—stodgy and slow, with three machine guns and 600 pounds of bombs—was a more effective tool than the high-powered Tomahawk.

Next day the AVG was back in business at the old location, on the terms it understood best. While the Blenheims and Tomahawks were trying to break up the ghost army at Mae Sariang, the newly arrived 8th Sentai had sent one of its twin-engined Lilys to have a look at Mingaladon airport. The scout brought back word that the airport was defended only by four bombers and twelve fighters. At his headquarters in Bangkok, General Eiryo Obata pondered this information and concluded that it provided an excellent opportunity to wipe out the Allied air force in Burma. For this, he would risk the first daylight bombing raid since Christmas Day. It would be on a more modest scale, of course, and (reflecting the lesson hard won over Mengzi) the bombers would be protected by large numbers of fighters. On Friday morning, January 23, six Sallys from the 14th Sentai would take off from Bangkok and fly to the usual rendezvous at Raheng. Here they would be met by the Nates of the 50th Sentai, which had settled into a new base at Nakhon Sawan, on the Thai railroad eighty miles south of Phitsanulok. In the afternoon, a different set of raiders would finish the job: the Anns of the 31st Sentai, escorted by their usual companions from the 77th Sentai.

General Obata was a chunky man with round-rimmed spectacles, a pith helmet, and an open-collared shirt, much more informal than the neatly turned out Sugawara. But he was no better at coordinating his raids. Major Makino's Nates took off from the rough airstrip at Nakhon Sawan, flew up to Raheng, refueled there, and took off again to meet the heavy bombers. But the Sallys could not find the airfield and so turned back to Bangkok. Makino went ahead anyhow, with the result that when the Japanese formation was spotted over Moulmein at 10 A.M., it seemed to be an exact repetition of the fighter sweep of January 4.

Mingaladon that Friday was defended by a mixed bag of fighters. Most of the AVG pilots were escorting the Blenheims on their daily commute to Thailand, leaving only a handful of Tomahawks at the airport, plus half a dozen Buffaloes. (The 67th Squadron fighters were now so decrepit that Air Vice Marshal Stevenson did not permit them to fly over enemy territory.) Three Hurricanes were also at Mingaladon that morning, having finished their 4,000-mile journey from North Africa, and Squadron Leader C.A.C. Stone—"Bunny" to his pilots—commandeered them for the 17th Squadron.

At the Thai border, meanwhile, the Blenheims ran into a squall and turned back before reaching their target: Tak, as they called it, but Raheng to the Japanese. Had they had pushed on, they might have caught the 50th Sentai in the act of refueling. As it was, the Blenheims flew back to their overnight base at Zayatkwin. Most of the Tomahawks landed to refuel, while one flight of Adam & Eves provided top cover. When his radio crackled the news of a Japanese formation coming across the border, Bob Neale steamed south with Bill Bartling and Bob Little. They brought Mingaladon and the Nates into view at the same moment. As the Americans watched, twenty-four Japanese fighters dropped their auxiliary fuel tanks—"like a bunch of confetti," Neale recalled.

On the ground at Mingaladon, Bunny Stone and two other 17th Squadron pilots scrambled into the newly arrived Hurricanes. Unlike the Japanese drop-tanks, the British version could not be jettisoned by the pilot in flight, so the Hurricanes went into combat with ferry tanks still bolted to their wings. At 6,000 feet, they were bounced by six of Major Makino's Nates. They managed to escape, but not before Stone's aircraft took bullets through the tail, fuselage, and starboard ferry tank.

Tex Hill and Whitey Lawlor also took off from Mingaladon, and to better effect. Lawlor made his attacks from out of a friendly cloudbank:

> I would spot an enemy from above, dive in on his tail and shoot and pull up again into the clouds for protection from the greatly superior numbers always present. I repeated this procedure in all of my attacks on fighters and succeeded in catching several completely unawares. I never experienced any difficulty in getting rid of attacking enemy aircraft as the Japanese seemed to be afraid to fly in clouds.

Twenty-seven, good-looking, with pale Nordic features—hence his nickname—Lawlor had graduated from the University of North Carolina in 1938. The navy trained him as a fighter pilot and assigned him to *Saratoga*, on which he served with Bob Neale and several other future AVG pilots. However, he did not reach Asia until *Zaandam*'s second voyage. As a latecomer, Lawlor had not made much of an impact on the Panda Bears, so he can be forgiven for his cocky account of ambushing the 50th Sentai on January 23. By the time he broke off, fifty miles east, he was claiming no fewer than four Nates.

Tex Hill, Bob Neale, and Bill Bartling each claimed one Nate in the running fight, for a total of seven Japanese fighters supposedly shot down that Friday morning. (In fact, only two of Major Makino's planes failed to return to Nakhon Sawan.) In the process, Bartling had his control cables shot away. He managed to ride the Tomahawk into the ground, the only Allied plane lost that morning.

George Rodger of *Life* magazine happened to be visiting Mingaladon that week, another of the journalists drawn to Burma by the dash and daring of Chennault's pilots. When the Americans landed, he posed them before a Tomahawk. The result was a marvelously evocative photograph, one of a series that did much to establish the legend of the jaunty and invincible "Flying Tigers." Its centerpiece was the rudder panel from a Nakajima Nate, bearing the stylized gull wing of the 77th Sentai. Hunkering on the gravel, Tex Hill and Ed Rector inspected the souvenir while Tom Cole and Whitey Lawlor looked on. They were togged out in helmets and goggles, and—despite the 95° heat—Rector and Lawlor were wearing leather flight jackets as well. Behind them, the shark-faced Tomahawk stared off-camera with its baleful painted eye, as if standing sentinel for these clowning, vulnerable young men.

The photo session was interrupted by the mournful wail of the air raid siren. This time, nine Tomahawks and three Buffaloes went up to intercept the raiders, the Hurricanes being sidelined while mechanics removed their ferry tanks. The Japanese formation consisted of twelve Anns. Heavy rain over Raheng had caused them to miss connections with their escort, so Major Yoshioka's pilots were far behind when Jack Newkirk spotted the Anns at 10,000 feet:

> We singled out the bombers and made an attack on them from three directions, dead ahead and the port and starboard beams. After several repetitions of this, the lefthand plane which I was following fell out of the formation about seventy-five feet, but joined up again. Then the formation turned, one plane gave several large puffs of smoke and flame and finally went down near the satellite field.

Newkirk probably meant Johnnie Walker, second base on the diamond of dispersal fields.

Gil Bright and John Petach each claimed an Ann in this encounter, and Noel Bacon may also have scored. Bacon had been serving as operations officer that day, so he was late taking off, and he caught up with the fight just as the light bombers were jettisoning their load. Fearing that he might be hit by one of the falling bombs—for a fighter pilot, a peculiarly distasteful way to die—Bacon turned away. As it happened, he turned right into the path of Major Yoshioka's Nates:

> Down they came, and I got one head-on. He spun in aflame. It was most encouraging to me. I dove out of the fighting maneuver and came back up, firing on the bomber formation, bow to stern. The other three [fighters] jumped me again, and the sky looked like it was full of them. Got another

Hawker Hurricane IIA

First flown in 1935, this liquid-cooled fighter was the mainstay of the Royal Air Force at the outbreak of World War II, and as late as January 1942 it had accounted for more enemy aircraft than its more famous cousin, the Supermarine Spitfire. Three different companies (Hawker, Gloster, and Canadian Car and Foundry) built 14,000 Hurricanes before production ended in 1944. Though slower than most front-line western fighters, the Hurricane was maneuverable, tough, forgiving of pilot error, and equipped for night fighting, with exhaust shields and a stable undercarriage. Except for its short combat radius (typical of British fighters, designed as they were for home defense) the Hurricane was technically superior to the Curtiss Tomahawk and should have outmatched the Nakajima Nate and even the Hayabusa. However, its record in Southeast Asia was poor. Thirty-six were dispatched to Rangoon in December 1941, across 4,000 miles of desert, snow-covered mountains, and tropical rain forest, but no more than twenty reached their destination. Altogether, 120 Hurricanes saw service in Burma, of which 109 were lost to accident, combat, and Japanese bombing.

Engine: 1,280-hp Rolls-Royce liquid-cooled in-line
Crew: one
Wingspan: 40 feet
Combat weight: 8,000 lb
Maximum range: 470 miles
Top speed: 340 mph at 22,000 feet
Armament: eight .303-caliber machine guns in the wings; two 250-lb bombs

one head-on and dove out with one on my tail. He put twelve slugs in me: one across the top of the engine, one through the cockpit at my right heel, and the rest in my gas tanks and wings.

Jack Newkirk by this time had been winkled away by the Nates, which drove him down 3,000 feet, broke off, and climbed back up. One Nate lagged behind, and Newkirk went after it with war-emergency power:

I caught him just past satellite, and after one burst his wing came off and he went down. Another bunch of fighters had been shooting at me while I fired on that one. My engine cut out and heated up and lost power, so I returned to the field where I crashed due to the fact that my flaps would not come down.

In another echo of the shootout on January 4, Bert Christman again had his Tomahawk shot full of holes by Major Yoshioka's pilots, and again he cranked open his canopy and jumped out of his crippled plane. But his luck had run out. Christman was shot through the neck, apparently while swinging from the shrouds of his parachute.

Also killed in that day's action was Flight Lieutenant Colin Pinckney of the 67th Squadron. Twenty-three years old, a graduate of Eton and Cambridge, with four German planes to his credit in the Battle of Britain, he had never scored against the JAAF. Still, Pinckney was proud of what his New Zealanders had accomplished in their hapless Buffaloes. "The squadron is doing well," he wrote his parents a few days before he died, "though we don't get the publicity given to the Americans."

Altogether, Major Yoshioka had reason to be delighted with that day's work. In what appears to have been the first Japanese reference to the Curtiss Tomahawk in Burma (though the pilots were still assumed to be British) a Tokyo newspaper told its readers:

> Staging an aerial duel with 10 British fighters which took to the air, Japanese fliers immediately shot down seven of them, including three P-40 aircraft, one Buffalo, two Spitfires and one medium-sized plane. The other British fighters managed to escape.

As so often happened, the Allied pilots also celebrated January 23 as a victory. Noel Bacon's claims cannot be proved from the documents now available, but the other Americans put in for eleven planes shot down, while the 67th Squadron was credited with one. But the *New York Times* reported next morning that twenty-one Japanese planes had gone down in "two terrific battles over Rangoon," while a Chinese observer, Captain C. P. Huang, radioed Chongqing that the Allied pilots had shot down no fewer than thirty-two planes, with twenty wrecks already counted on the ground. In fact, the Japanese lost only three planes—two Nates in the morning, an Ann in the afternoon—with ten Anns sustaining moderate or heavy damage. Major Yoshioka's pilots reported that "the enemy had a great will to fight," though they quickly added that "their technique in the air was not superior." Hedged though it was, this was a considerable compliment. Japanese fighting men, in every service and on every front, had been assured that westerners were effete, more interested in dancing than in fighting, and the events of the past seven weeks had done little to change their thinking.

Major Frank Merrill of the U.S. Military Mission set up shop in Rangoon about this time, his job to send daily reports to General Magruder in Chongqing. That for January 23 made sober reading. Merrill simply forwarded the RAF estimates of Japanese losses over Mingaladon, but he also reported (as did no one else at the time) how defeatist the British authorities in Burma had become, just three days after the Japanese 55th Division had crossed the Dawna Range:

> Jap casualties nine fighters three bombers. . . . Our loss one Buffalo one P-40. Govt leaving Rangoon and military stores being shipped north. Sinking two ships by gun fire enroute Rangoon has closed port until convoy system starts. Situation not critical yet as have local air superiority but main danger is attack in force on north and gradual attrition small air and ground forces available for defense Burma.

Colonel Hironaka's 14th Sentai tried again next day, January 24, and this time it stayed the course. There were six Sallys in Saturday's formation, consisting of an entire chutai under Captain Ryosuke Motomura.* Again the 50th Sentai flew from Nakhon Sawan to Raheng and refueled—and again the plan went wrong. Taking off from the rough field, Major Makino lost power, crashed, and was badly injured. Twenty of his pilots continued the mission under Captain Fujio Sakaguchi. Then, when the formation came in sight of Mingaladon airport, the bomber pilots reacted as others had done before them, shoving their throttles to the firewall and leaving the fighters far behind.

To intercept them, Jack Newkirk put seven Tomahawks into the air, while the British put up four Buffaloes and two Hurricanes. The Commonwealth pilots went after the bombers. So did Tex Hill, Ed Rector, and Bob Neale of the AVG. These nine fighters swept down on the Sallys, which for the first time in the Burma campaign they actually outnumbered. The results were terrible, as Hill drily reported:

> On first attack they released some bombs which fell short of the field. They maintained a westerly course and released more bombs which fell towards

---

* Allied accounts had seven bombers in the formation, but six is the number recalled by a 14th Sentai veteran who watched them take off on their one-way journey.

southwest side of the field. They then reversed course and we continued to make passes at the bombers with enemy fighters making passes at us. I saw the bombers crash one by one until there were three left. . . . I made a run on the one on right side and he blew up. Pieces of his plane blew against belly of my plane causing slight damage. One of the AVG shot down the remaining two bombers.

As he left that great hole in the sky, which moments before had been filled by six heavy bombers, Hill met a Nate coming toward him. "I attacked him and he went down in flames," he concluded—and with that became the second ace in the Panda Bears.

Ed Rector was credited with shooting down one bomber and a fighter. (According to a spectator, the Nate's pilot bailed out at 300 feet but was killed when he hit the ground.) And Bob Neale was credited with shooting down two Sallys, which he had approached with his usual deliberation:

Closed on one to about 100 feet from the rear and blew up his starboard engine. Only two left by now, so took after the leader. Closed on him although I was getting a hell of a lot of return fire. I didn't seem to be getting hit, so I closed to fifty feet and gave him a burst, and the whole damn plane blew up, part of it coming back and tearing up my right wing and aileron.

Neale was flipped upside down by the explosion, then sent plunging toward the ground. He felt out the controls, leveled off, and headed back for Mingaladon airport, hoping that the aileron would hold together. A Nate dove past his gunsights, and Neale hosed him but did not shoot him down. Then he was bounced by two more Nates, which disappeared almost as fast as they had come, leaving him with two bullet holes in his cockpit and the microphone shot away from his helmet. "Too damn close," Neale wrote in his diary.

The Commonwealth pilots, meanwhile, were convinced that they were scything the bombers out of the air. Bunny Stone and "Slug" Elsdon made their first attack from out of the sun. "Petrol streamed from one enemy aircraft after this attack and large pieces were seen falling from another," according to the 17th Squadron log. "S/Ldr. Elsdon's engine cut out but he succeeded in landing at Base safely. S/Ldr Stone carried out two more attacks. The starboard machine of the formation had large pieces falling from the engine and fuselage and brilliant flashes from the starboard motor. It was later seen to go down on its back." The flashes (better than tracer bullets when it came to confirming a pilot's aim) were

Stone's incendiary rounds, flaring when they hit the big radial engine.
Stone and Elsdon evidently claimed three Sallys, while the Buffalo pilots
put in for four. That made a grand total of eleven, which was manifestly
impossible. But however the credit was spread around, the Allied pilots
had made a clean sweep of the Japanese formation. Pappy Paxton (who
now sat out the combats on the ground) recalled how the huge bombers
had dropped out of the sky, like a flaming arrow pointing back to
Thailand. "They all fell in a straight line," he marveled, "as though
somebody was dropping smoke pots." Forty Japanese airmen died that
Tuesday, Captain Motomura included. In a month of combat over the
Philippines and Hong Kong, the 14th Sentai had not lost a single plane
to enemy action; it had left Taiwan ten days earlier in good spirits and
with nineteen planes. Only ten Sallys now remained—an attrition rate of
nearly 50 percent in two encounters with the AVG. Henceforth,
Hironaka would follow the example of Onishi's 62nd Sentai, and send
his bombers to Mingaladon under cover of darkness.

While this slaughter was taking place, three AVG pilots—Jim
Howard, Tom Cole, and Frank Schiel—went after the Japanese fighters,
and each was credited with shooting down one Nate. (In his autobiography, Howard recalled that his victim was a bomber, but the AVG
record says otherwise. In any event, the "automatic pilot" became an ace
in that day's battle.) With the victories of Hill and Rector, that made a
total of five Nates claimed by the American pilots. According to the
Japanese, the 50th Sentai actually lost three planes on January 24.
Among the dead was Captain Sakaguchi, who had taken command of
the formation after Major Makino crashed at Raheng.

The day ended with a fighter sweep by the 77th Sentai. Major
Yoshioka's Nates "sneaked in and made poor job of strafing field,"
Newkirk reported, while the Tomahawks patrolled unaware at 20,000
feet. Also in the air that afternoon was Pilot Officer Fuge of the 136th
Squadron, flying the only Hurricane still airworthy. Fuge landed at
Mingaladon in the middle of the raid. He not only escaped injury but
apparently scared the Nates away by his approach to the field, and the
only damage was six bullets through an already-disabled Blenheim.

Bert Christman was buried at dusk in plot C-93 at the church of
Edward the Martyr, making three in a row with Hank Gilbert and Ken
Merritt. (Neil Martin was nearer the gate.) Estre Healey and Dorothea
Wilkins were there: "It was the fourth row on the aisle, going into the

cemetery," Dorothea recalled nearly half a century later. "I could take you there today." As she remembered the funeral, Christman's cortege had to wait while the British buried a Japanese airman who had crashed near Mingaladon. The enemy pilot also received full honors, including an RAF bugler playing "The Last Post."

Nine Blenheims punched back at Bangkok that night. "The machines attacked singly at 10 minute intervals, bombing from 2,000 ft," according to the squadron log. "Large explosions and big fires resulted. . . . ACK ACK was intense over target area and search lights were numerous." The bomber flown by Sergeant Keeley must have been hit by flak, for it vanished with its three-man crew. Another Blenheim crashed upon landing at Mingaladon on Sunday morning, January 25.

Chennault never visited his squadrons in Rangoon—a curious lapse in a leader devoted to his men, and whose men were devoted to him. Poor health was certainly a factor: influenza, aggravated by Camel cigarettes and chronic bronchitis, had put him in bed at Christmas, and he was sick for the rest of the winter. "I alternated between brief spells in my airfield office," he wrote of this period, "and longer sieges in my sickbed" at Hostel Number One. Dealing with the Chiangs must have been equally debilitating. The Nationalist government combined elements of a civil bureaucracy, a military command, a personal fiefdom, and a marriage in which the wife was smarter than her husband. Most Americans soon lost themselves in this labyrinth. Chennault thrived in it, but not without cost. Among the trivia that filled his days in Kunming was the case of eight Chinese cadets sent down from Chengdu to be checked out in Tomahawks. The generalissimo specified how much flight time each should receive: two hours. Chennault had just forty-eight airworthy Tomahawks with which to defend western China, the Burma Road, and Rangoon—a line of communications extending 750 miles by air and twice that distance by land—and to go on the offensive in Indochina, as he intended to do. In such circumstances, it required an act of faith to give cockpit time to his own men. (John Blackburn, a flight instructor at Yunnan-yi, qualified in a Tomahawk on January 24 and was assigned to the Adam & Eves. John Donovan and Robert Raine, flying boat captains attached to the Hell's Angels, also got some fighter training at this time.) As tactfully as he could, Chennault explained the situation to General Chou at the Aeronautical Commission. Back came the order: do it anyhow. Seven Chinese were duly checked out, and only one Tomahawk was damaged in the experiment.

The generalissimo also fine-tuned the AVG presence in Burma. When Chennault tried again to bring his pilots back to Kunming, Chiang decreed that they remain in Burma "until British Air Force has arrived," meaning the Hurricane squadrons. A week later he announced that the AVG strength in Burma should be kept at eighteen planes, so Chennault had to tell another group of Adam & Eves to pack their bags for Rangoon. A few days after that, Chiang ordered Chennault to keep a full squadron at Mingaladon airport "until next Wednesday." All the national leaders of World War II—Hitler, Roosevelt, Stalin, and especially Churchill—were given to meddling in military affairs, but this was the generalissimo of 400 million people, determining the size and location of a single fighter squadron.

Then there was the question of induction. On January 20, in a radiogram to madame, Chennault predicted that the "combat effectiveness of AVG will be greatly lessened for months" if it became part of the U.S. Army. He personally would be happy to wear an American uniform again, since that would increase his chances of commanding any U.S. pilots or planes reaching China, but he now thought it best that the AVG continue as a mercenary force. "Urge this plan be sent to U.S. government," he radioed madame. A week later, Chennault went further. The AVG "cannot be inducted," he warned, "as majority of personnel prefer terminating contracts and returning home but it can be destroyed." In milder terms, he made the same argument to his friend at the White House. After thanking Lauchlin Currie for sending him thirty propellers, Chennault returned to the main irritant, as to a broken tooth: "Induction AVG into army will have bad effect." Only then did he list his current needs.*

---

* Including 100 solenoids, 50 relays, and 200 gunsight lamps; 4,000 sparkplugs and 1,000 feet of ignition cable; 1,000 generator brushes, 400 generator drive couplings, and 400 voltage controls; 400 RCA radio crystals; 25 carburetor diaphragms and 12 discharge nozzles; 20 oil coolers, 2,000 packing pellets, and 50 relief valve springs; 50 drive gears and 25 spool gears; 25 propeller switches; 50 hydraulic cups and gaskets, 12 hand pumps, and 12 selector valves; 12 master cylinders, 25 brake bands, 32 tires . . . and three staff officers.

Chennault also enlisted the U.S. Military Mission in his campaign for a commission. In a radiogram to the War Department, marked "personal" for George Marshall and Hap Arnold, General Magruder explained the situation with a frankness now unimaginable from a military officer:

> In China personal relations are predominant factors in all affairs and must so be reckoned with. Chennault is an extraordinary leader who has proved his worth. . . . He is probably the only man with qualities and experience who can effectively take operational command of both American and Chinese air forces. His fear of being superseded in this position by an officer inexperienced in China I believe arises from mixture of personal ambition and loyalty to generalissimo. He has suggested to me that he be made a general officer in order to be assured of command of air forces in China. . . . To what extent this view has politically been advanced by the sub-surface Chinese government in Washington I am not aware.

Magruder then grasped the nettle he had been avoiding so long: Chennault should be recalled to active duty with the rank of colonel, and immediately promoted to brigadier general.

At some point in these maneuverings, Chennault took the problem into his own hands, as he had done in Shanghai in 1937: he let it be known that he already was a general—in Chinese service. It was a long leg up, and no doubt the stars were as bogus as the colonel's leaves he had assumed on that earlier occasion. There is no commission among his papers, nor any correspondence from the Aeronautical Commission informing him of it. Nor does it seem likely that, five years after beginning his service with the Chiangs, and on the brink of achieving honors in his own service, he would now accept a commission in the Chinese armed forces. Finally, he did not put on the insignia—and he continued to use the old signature block: *C. L. Chennault, Commanding.*

Still, something happened in January to give the impression that he was entitled to wear a general's stars. Leland Stowe, in a dispatch from Rangoon in the first week of January, told his readers that Chennault had become a brigadier general in the Chinese Air Force "the other day." In his diary, Charlie Bond used the honorific from January 7 onward, and for a time Jack Newkirk began his radiograms from Mingaladon airport with the salutation "Gen. Chennault." (By the end of the month, however, Newkirk went back to addressing him as "colonel.") Even Bill

Pawley, when circumstances obliged him to write his old enemy, saluted him henceforth as "Dear General."

And Chennault was certainly thinking like an army officer. On the last day of 1941, two of Butch Carney's instructors at Yunnan-yi had handed in their resignations. Before December 8, if a man had wanted to resign, Chennault had let him do so, but he felt that the Japanese breakout necessitated a change in that easygoing policy. He ordered the names of Gail Stubbs and Henry Fuller "stricken from the rolls" of the AVG— dishonorably discharged. (Carney lost another instructor soon after, when Marion Baugh was killed in the crash of his Ryan trainer between Kunming and Yunnan-yi.) Chennault also issued a set of quasi-military regulations for the AVG and ordered each man to turn in a resumé of his previous military experience. This sent the Kunming rumor mill into high gear, as Dan Hoyle noted in the 3rd Squadron log:

> Personnel very upset about the possibility of joining the Army. Most of the Pilots and Technicians have already showed their dislike at the prospects by some of them tendering their resignations, but the resignations were refused acceptance by the Group Commanding Officer.

Not everyone felt this way. "I am willing to go back into the Air Corps right now," Charlie Bond wrote in his diary, "if they will give me a regular commission." But there was enough mutiny in the ranks that Chennault decided to clean house. In a gloomy letter to Lauchlin Currie, he noted that the AVG still had "a few members who are trouble makers or who lack the fiber to stay with us." These bad cases would be invited "to terminate their contracts before January 20."

Four pilots accepted the challenge. Leo Houle, Donald Bernsdorf, and Donald Knapp were among the Panda Bears who had not been sent down to Rangoon with the rest of the squadron, because Chennault did not think them ready to fly in combat. Perhaps they were troublemakers; perhaps they were discouraged by the Catch-22 that prevented them from getting Tomahawk time because they had no experience in Tomahawks. The fourth pilot was Ralph Gunvordahl of the Hell's Angels. The Gunner did not lack fiber—he had taken part in the Christmas combat over Rangoon and had a Japanese bomber to his credit—and there is no evidence in the AVG record that he had been more troublesome than anyone else.

Five technicians also accepted Chennault's invitation to leave. They included two clerks, Larry Moore and Kenneth Sanger, who were generally suspected of being romantically involved, in a time and in a profession that did not regard homosexual liaisons with favor. "Good riddance," was the reaction reported by Olga Greenlaw. "We don't want that kind . . . around here."

Like Stubbs and Fuller, these four pilots and five technicians received dishonorable discharges, though how that term could apply to civilians was never made clear.

Also consuming Chennault's energies at this time was his plan to raid Hanoi. General Mao Pang-chu (who now had operational control of the CAF, while General Chou ran the Aeronautical Commission) visited Kunming in mid-January. The two men went goose hunting, and afterward shared the bounty with the Greenlaws. The dinner began with oysters flown in from Calcutta by Billy McDonald, now a pilot for CNAC. The oysters were followed by roast Burma goose, washed down by French wine, a souvenir of the days when Kunming had been a summer resort for the colonial authorities in Hanoi. Afterward, Chennault and Mao huddled with a group of pilots to plan the raid on Hanoi, in which the Tomahawks would escort Soviet-built bombers of the CAF. The SB-3 was a midwing monoplane with two liquid-cooled engines, retractable landing gear, a large tail assembly, and a plexiglass nose for the bombardier and machine gunner. It had been a formidable weapon when introduced into China in 1937, but its day had long since passed, and the specimens in Chinese service were little more than flying relics.

On January 22, eighteen SB-3s flew down to Mengzi, where they were met by an escort of Adam & Eves. After refueling, the raiding party took off for Hanoi, flying a compass course with dogged fidelity, as Sandy Sandell reported:

> The bombers headed on a course of 135°, failing to make any corrections for wind. I dove down to the leader of the formation and indicated the direction of flight to be 150° because a very strong wind was blowing from the southwest. After a few minutes the bombers returned to 135°. . . . After flying for 1:35 hours on a haphazard course varying from 150° to 120° over a solid overcast without finding a single hole in the clouds, the bombing formation turned to a course of 240° and flew this course for several minutes, then they dropped their bombs through the clouds. I estimate the

position to be about twenty miles east of Haiphong because I saw one hole in the clouds that was near the Gulf of Tonkin. This hole was over the mouth of a wide river or a very marshy back bay region.

Sandell seemed to be saying that the Chinese had bombed the Gulf of Tonkin, or at best the port of Haiphong. At this point, the Tomahawks were 300 miles from Mengzi, near the outside limit of their combat range, so when the bombers took up a course of 340° for the return to China, Sandell wasted no fuel on shepherding them. He flew a direct course to Mengzi, where the Adam & Eves landed safely after three hours and five minutes in the air. One SB-3 was not so fortunate. Apparently hit by antiaircraft fire over Haiphong, the bomber fell back from the formation, lost altitude, and disappeared into the clouds, half an hour into the homeward flight.

Two days later, ten Hell's Angels under Oley Olson escorted a similar mission, with similar results, except that all the bombers returned to Chinese territory.

The JAAF retaliated for the raids by sending six Anns from the 21st Hikotai to bomb the airfield at Mengzi, and Chennault sent a flight of Tomahawks down from Kunming to intercept them. Hearing the English-language radio traffic, the 21st Hikotai scrambled its Nates to head off what seemed to be another Chinese raid. The French colonial air force likewise scrambled its interceptors: three Morane-Saulnier 406 fighters. Seen from a distance, the liquid-cooled French fighters were dead ringers for the Curtiss Tomahawk, and when the two flights met in the air, the Japanese pilots promptly shot the Frenchmen down. They were the only certain victims of the Chinese-American raids on Indochina.*

These inconclusive forays were transformed into great victories at home. "Bombers of the Chinese Air Force," reported the United Press on the first occasion, "struck inside French Indochina for the first time today, dropping twenty tons of bombs on a Japanese air base and other military installations, and inflicted heavy damage." But Chennault was

---

* Compounding the irony, the Morane-Saulniers had been sold to China in 1938, shipped to Haiphong, and seized by the colonial government as a favor to the Japanese. Formed into Escadrille EC2, they had resisted the Japanese occupation of northern Indochina in December 1940.

not after propaganda points. He was demonstrating that, even with antiquated bombers and Chinese crews, he could take the war to the enemy. This was part of his longstanding campaign for a bomber force, as he made clear in a January 26 radiogram to Lauchlin Currie at the White House:

> Can begin attacks on Japan's industries at once if you can send regular or volunteer bombardment group equipped with Lockheed Hudson as specified by me in June 1941 and American key personnel to operate under my command and control of the Generalissimo only.

This radiogram appears among Roosevelt's papers—proof that Chennault's backdoor appeals were getting through. The president also received a more subtle appeal from China about the same time, in the form of a Sung Dynasty tapestry, silk and gold, expressing the wish: "May your affairs prosper." It was a sixtieth birthday present from T. V. Soong.

Lauchlin Currie went into action, and on January 31 (the day after Roosevelt's birthday) he sent Chennault the good news:

> Hudsons will be ready by February 20. Probably accompanied by combat crews though no final decision yet.

Really, the man was a miracle worker. Like the fifty Kittyhawks he had recently acquired for Chennault, the thirty-six Lockheed A-28 light bombers were taken from U.S. Army stocks, and some or most of them would have been the bombers commandeered from the 2nd AVG on December 8. This time, however, the Hudsons were bound in the other direction—from the U.S. east coast south to Brazil, across the Atlantic, north again to Egypt, and through the Middle East to India, Burma, and China—a journey of nearly 18,000 miles from the Lockheed factory in Burbank, California.

11

Hoffman Shot Down and Dead

January–February 1942

Prefer no replacements," Jack Newkirk radioed Chennault about this time. "Situation well in hand." But even with his recent infusion from the Adam & Eves, Newkirk's planes were being chewed up at an alarming rate, and Chennault ordered Sandy Sandell to take twelve more Tomahawks down to Rangoon. The Adam & Eves again drew lots in Sandell's room at Adobe City on the road to Wu Chia Ba, and the winners flew into Burma on Sunday, January 25. They refueled at Lashio and landed at Mingaladon airport just before dusk. They refilled their tanks, dispersed their planes to Johnnie Walker, then repaired to the RAF club for drinks.

Sandy Sandell was a narrow-featured man who was cultivating a small English mustache. The face behind the mustache was shuttered—suspicious—or perhaps only shy. ("Gentle, sweet, serious Sandy," Olga Greenlaw wrote of him, in the fond language she reserved for pilots who were about to die.) In the army, he had been a flight instructor, not a fighter pilot, but he had acquitted himself well in the interception of December 20. (Better than Jack Newkirk, as a matter of fact.) But the victory had done nothing to endear him to his men.

The twelve newcomers naturally wanted to know what awaited them at Mingaladon airport. The RAF club was a partial answer, strafed as it had been on more than one occasion. Drinking at the bar, a man had to be careful where he planted his elbows, not to fill them with splinters.

Six Hurricanes had also flown into Mingaladon that day, so there were several groups of pilots to take each other's measure. "We stood there," an RAF officer wrote of his meeting with Chennault's mercenaries, "and frankly eyed one another, and in our association felt the pride of manhood—like members of friendly bandit gangs meeting." As usual, the American pilots were put off by the elevated speech and manner of the Englishmen. (They made another mistake when they assumed that the Commonwealth pilots were English. In fact, the 67th Squadron was dominated by New Zealanders, while the 17th Squadron had Irish, Scots, South African, Rhodesian, Canadian, and even American pilots on its roster.) Some of the newcomers then drove into Rangoon to eat at the Savoy and find beds at the Minto Mansions hotel. Others drank their dinner at the RAF club and slept in the derelict barracks. It would be a day or two before they found homes to take them in, because most European civilians had already left South Burma.

Monday morning, January 26, Newkirk and Sandell sorted their planes into four flights. The Panda Bears were designated "blue" and "green" and assigned to one end of Mingaladon's east-west runway—the extended crossarm of the A. The Adam & Eves were designated "red" and "yellow" and stationed at the opposite end of the same strip. The RAF used a similar system on the main north-south runway: Buffaloes at one end, Hurricanes at the other. Each squadron therefore had to take off in the face of another, and to cross paths with its allies on the other runway. "The takeoff procedure is a hell of a mess," Charlie Bond worried. "If we get our timing screwed up, there are going to be a lot of fighters in a tangled mess at the intersection." Wind direction was ignored . . . and in an emergency, the takeoff schedule was ignored as well. Recalling his wild sprints down the gravel runways at Mingaladon, one of the RAF pilots pointed out that "time was more than money" for a pilot on the ground. Their warning time was down to fifteen minutes. (The Burma Observation Corps had retreated with the army to Moulmein, and the RAF radar station had been brought back to Mingaladon airport to keep it from capture.) If a man got off the ground thirty seconds before his mates, he could grab an extra 500 to 800 feet of altitude before the Japanese arrived—an edge that could mean the difference between living and dying.

There were three false alarms that Monday morning. Each time, the pilots sprinted for their planes and took off in a lunatic race against the other Tomahawks and the RAF. From the torpor of Mingaladon to the thin, cold air of 20,000 feet—up and down, up and down—it was a torturous routine that left some of them weeping from sinus pain. Between scrambles, they tried to relax in the wood and canvas alert tent, while the sun climbed toward noon and the RAF armorers put wet cloths on the ammunition boxes of the Hurricanes, so they would not explode. (You could fry an egg on the aluminum surface of the wing, as an RAF mechanic demonstrated one day.) They talked, read, played acey-deucey, and waited for the siren to howl again, which it did for the fourth time at 10:45 A.M. This time the alarm was real: a low-altitude sweep by twenty-three Nates of the 50th Sentai.

Only one Panda Bear flight got into the air, consisting of Jack Newkirk Gil Bright, and Moose Moss. Climbing away from Mingaladon, Newkirk also picked up a flight of four Adam & Eves. Then his radio went dead, so he signaled the other flight leader to take charge, while he flew off to the northward. Bright and Moss likewise went off on their own. That left the interception to Red Probst, the plump young man from Maxwell Field who had joined the AVG so he would not have to fly against the German air force. Probst had been at Mingaladon for less than twenty-four hours; he had never been in combat; and his AVG career had been one damn-fool adventure after another. (Soon after these events, Sandell fined him $100 "gold" for not losing weight.) Followed by Cokey Hoffman, Greg Boyington, and Bob Prescott, he climbed gamely but stupidly toward the incoming swarm of Nates.

Boyington assumed that he was being led into combat by one of the veteran Panda Bears, until he realized that he was attacking from below and *into the sun*. Prescott, flying on Boyington's wing, was untroubled by this unorthodox approach. "You don't see anything except your leader when you fly in formation," he said years later. When he did spot the radial-engined fighters overhead, Prescott took them for the 67th Squadron Buffaloes:

> They were diving, looping, and just going nuts. I thought, "Silly bastards.
> . . . Hell, let's get these people out of here and we'll fight this war." Then
> I looked again. . . . Hell, that's no Buffalo—that's a Jap. He's diving at us!
> . . . I was on Greg's left wing, and this Jap was diving over my left shoulder.
> I couldn't leave the formation, but nobody said I couldn't move over and
> get on Greg's *right* wing, so he'd shoot Greg first.

Red Probst had already quit the scene. "The enemy jumped us while [we were] climbing up to attack," he rather lamely explained. "When they came within range I led my flight into a dive." He neglected to communicate his change of heart to Cokey Hoffman, who was his wingman if anyone was. In his AVG identification photo, Hoffman had the look of an Apache warrior: dark, scowling, and dangerous. On December 20 outside Kunming, he had earned a commendation for the way he had raked the 21st Hikotai Lilys at close range. He was no less determined when it came to attacking the 50th Sentai, and watchers on the ground theorized that he actually collided with one of the Nates. "Out of the whirling center of the battle," wrote the British reporter O'Dowd Gallagher, "came one in a spin. . . . A wing came off as it sped to the ground. The rest of the plane left it far behind. It raised a great cloud of dust as it hit the ground. I saw it bounce. Many seconds afterward the severed wing came switching down like a piece of paper and also raised dust as it lit in a paddy field." Hoffman's Tomahawk crashed near the railroad tracks, upside down, with his mutilated body half out of the cockpit. Forty-four years old, husband and father, he had spent more than half his life in the U.S. Navy, including thirteen years as an enlisted pilot.

By this time, Bob Prescott had succeeded in repositioning himself. "Once I moved over, Greg saw him," he recalled. "He rolled over with a split-S and said *foosh* and went down." Prescott followed, but in his excitement pushed the stick forward without first rolling onto his back, so that inertia pulled him *out* of his seat instead of pushing him into it. As a result, the safety belt nearly cut him in half.

> They said we could outdive these guys, but you never believe this stuff. I look around, and there he was, right on my tail. . . . At the last minute, I [pulled out]. And I forgot to take the throttle off. So by the time I pulled up, I was back up 13,000 feet. I looked over, and there's a P-40 diving down and a Jap shooting at him, going *boom boom boom*. I gotta go over and help him. You know, you can turn those sticks with your finger, but with all the strength I had, I couldn't turn that airplane around.

The other Tomahawk was Boyington's. The ex-marine had likewise climbed back to altitude and began making turns with a Nate—like everything else Probst's flight had done this morning, a flat violation of Chennault's teachings. As a college wrestler, Boyington had learned to tighten his neck muscles to keep the blood from leaving his head, and at Kyedaw airfield he had used the same trick to overcome gravity while dogfighting his squadron mates. But stiffening his neck muscles did him no good against the nimble Japanese; instead, he lost so much vision that he could not see where his incendiaries were going. "I had pulled myself plumb woozy," he wrote in later years. "All the time I was pulling this terrific 'g' load, tracers were getting closer to my plane, until finally I was looking back down someone's gun barrels. 'Frig this racket,' I thought, and dove away."

Prescott too was driven to the deck again. He decided that fate had not intended him to be a fighter pilot, and that the best thing to do would be to get out of the way. So he skulked around until he heard "free beer!" (the RAF recall signal) in his earphones. Then he flew back to Mingaladon, intending to take his partner aside, apologize, and promise to quit the AVG if Boyington would keep his cowardice a secret.

> So I just sat in the radio shack and waited, and Greg didn't come back and he didn't come back, and I thought, "Oh-oh, that Jap got him. . . . Well, thank God, he finally did land. Boy, I ran across that field. He whipped the airplane around and threw dust all over me. . . . I jumped up on his wing and pulled his canopy, and he looked at me with a big grin, and he said, "We sure screwed that one, didn't we?"

Gil Bright and Moose Moss had climbed above the Japanese fighters in order to make a more orthodox attack. "My wing man and I dove through a light cloud on two of them," Bright said in a letter home, "but they saw us and looped up, firing at us on their backs." Talking to a reporter the same afternoon, Moss reckoned that there had been *seven* Nates below them. "I was on a Jap's tail, firing," he said, "when my plane flopped over, out of control, probably from an attack from someone I never saw."

Bright fired on his target without effect, then looked around for his wingman. But Moss had been shot down for the second time. With plenty of altitude, he rode his Tomahawk down for nearly a mile, so the Japanese could not strafe him in his parachute as they had Paul Greene and Bert Christman. Finally he opened the canopy, unsnapped his seat belt, and kicked out. To his horror, a plane did drop down to look him over, but it turned out to be Gil Bright, who convoyed him down to a safe landing.

Moss landed near a waterhole, skinning his forehead, blackening an eye, and breaking several teeth. He waved to Bright to show that he was okay. Then a Burman came up to him and spewed a mouthful of water on his forehead, to wash off the blood. Another Burman stuffed his pockets with crackers to provision him for the trek back to Mingaladon.

With better success, Bob Neale had led the second flight of Adam & Eves into combat. "Picked up about 20 Jap fighters," he wrote in his diary that night. "Looked like a bunch of buzzards milling around." Neale led his flight toward the Nates, which immediately split up, with one group climbing above the Tomahawks. Whenever Neale tried to get at a Japanese fighter, one or two more would tack onto his tail, and he had to dive out. He lost contact for a time, but picked up the fighters again as they headed for Martaban Bay, evidently paying more attention to their gauges than to the air around them. With an altitude advantage of 2,000 feet, Neale dove on the rearmost plane and opened fire at 100 yards. As he watched, the Nate's engine burst into flame and it spun into the water. William McGarry—"Black Mac," he was called, a dark-haired, frowning P-40 driver from Selfridge Field—was also credited with downing a Nate in this engagement.

After escorting Moss to the ground, Gil Bright likewise chased the 50th Sentai to the eastward. He overhauled a Nate, fired a long burst into it, and later saw the same plane (as he believed) burning on a sandbank. "Like six others that I fired on," he wrote, "he was going home not watching out for planes. One stupe I surprised twice in the same way." Bright was disheartened because none of these later attacks amounted to anything, a failure he attributed to his lack of aerial gunnery practice in the navy. "I do a lot of shooting," he mused, "but it's all of questionable accuracy." He was credited with a shoot-down, however, to become the AVG's fourth ace.

Three 17th Squadron Hurricanes joined the combat over Mingaladon. They did not stay long, rolling out when they were bounced by three Nates. One of the RAF pilots fired "a short burst" at the enemy fighters but fled when he discovered that of his eight guns, only three were firing. (He later found that the others had not been loaded.) Another Hurricane was hit by enemy fire and came down with its starboard aileron cable shot away.

So the laurels for January 26 went to the enemy. The AVG was claiming three Nates shot down, but the 50th Sentai had lost only one, in exchange for which its pilots had knocked down two of the defenders.

Jack Newkirk's report to Kunming on Monday's action set a new standard for terseness:

> Combat with twenty enemy pursuit at 1100. Shot down three enemy planes. Hoffman shot down and dead.

That same afternoon, the 113th Squadron Blenheims trundled off to bomb Takeuchi's 55th Division near Kawkareik—on the near side of the Dawna Range, meaning that nothing now protected Moulmein but the bayonets of the 17th Indian Division. Two Hurricanes and six Tomahawks went along to guard the bombers and to do "a little straffing." Upon their return to Mingaladon, the Allied planes were flown off to the dispersal fields, except for two Hurricanes that Bunny Stone assigned to himself and Squadron Leader "Slug" Elsdon. A bandy-legged Englishman of the upper class, like most RAF officers, Stone may have struck the Americans as a dandy, but he had won the Distinguished Flying Cross in the last-ditch combat in France. As for his plane, the Hawker Hurricane was the best night fighter in the RAF inventory, thanks to its good cockpit vision, shielded exhaust pipes, and wide-track undercarriage.

Under the glow of a three-quarter moon, three 14th Sentai Sallys and three 8th Sentai Lilys made the long journey from Bangkok and rained high explosives and incendiary bombs upon Mingaladon airport. The two night fighters were caught on the ground, and one Hurricane was damaged beyond repair. But the raiders did not reach home unscathed: returning to Don Muang early Wednesday morning, they found the airport blanketed with fog, and one Sally crashed while trying to land.

The bombers were back the following night, January 27–28. Colonel Onishi's air crews had been pushed out of Don Muang by the arrival of the bomber groups from the Philippines, and they had spent the past two weeks finding new quarters at Nakhon Sawan and familiarizing themselves with the late-model Sallys that had been sent to make good their losses. Now they were ready, and four of the new bombers made the long trip to Mingaladon airport. This time, Stone and Elsdon got their Hurricanes off the ground before the Sallys came over. There was a veil of clouds above the airport. The moon shone through it with undiminished glory, but the watchers on the ground—who included Leland Stowe of the *Chicago Daily News*—could distinguish the dueling aircraft only by the sound of their engines, a booming noise for the bombers and a shriller sound for the liquid-cooled fighters:

> Now we stood alongside the sombrero-shaped kokobin trees, staring and staring. The buzzing Hurricane still remained invisible although a million stars winked at it. . . . So we listened to the double hums coming straight in and the other waspish buzz burrowing round. . . . Then we were yelling all at once, "The Hurricane's on her. . . ." Hundreds of crimson dashes chased each other madly in a straight line up and up. . . .
>
> Once more that slender, stabbing chain of red flashes. But this time it slashes diagonally earthward. . . . Then, well under the darkened sky where the machinegun bursts extinguished themselves, a great flame suddenly lights the sky. It hovers momentarily, then plunges straight down. Across the flat land, a mile and a half north of us, the horizon is illuminated with one huge flash.

The triumphant night fighter was Bunny Stone of the 17th Squadron, while the fireball was the brand-new Sally piloted by Lieutenant Akio Hirabayashi—himself new to the 62nd Sentai, having reached Thailand as a replacement sixteen days earlier.

The JAAF was baffled by the resistance it was encountering over South Burma, so unlike its experiences in Malaya, the Philippines, Hong Kong, and the Dutch Indies. "Crushing the enemy was like killing flies," a Japanese officer complained after the campaign for South Burma was over. (The speaker was probably Colonel Hironaka of the 14th Sentai.) "We thought we had . . . disposed of [the Allied air force] for once and all, only to find to our dismay 10 days or so later that the enemy was as strong as before in numbers of planes." With no better explanation for the Allied air resistance, the Japanese decided that spies had kept the enemy informed about the movements of the JAAF.

The Adam & Eves buried Cokey Hoffman on Wednesday morning, January 28, in plot C-97 at the church of Edward the Martyr. (Three graves separated his grave from Bert Christman's, so three Commonwealth servicemen must have been killed at Mingaladon in the interim.) The corpse was two days old, and the pallbearers gagged on the smell of rotten flesh. To make matters worse, the native diggers had made

Hoffman's grave too short, causing his coffin to jam halfway down. Afterward the pallbearers drove into Rangoon for strawberries and cream at the Silver Grill, to buy gems at Coombes's jewelry store, and to make an unsuccessful pass at two young Englishwomen.

The on-duty pilots had already scrambled once that morning, and now were sprinting for their Tomahawks again. The siren foretold a fighter sweep by twenty-seven Nates of the 77th Sentai from Phitsanulok, plus ten from the 50th Sentai at Nakhon Sawan. To intercept them, the Panda Bears put seven fighters into the air, the Adam & Eves nine, and the RAF two. This was Sandy Sandell's first combat in Rangoon, and he did himself proud:

> I, leading red-yellow squadron, engaged enemy fighters about twenty miles east of the field and continued fighting to about twenty miles west of the field. . . . On my first attack, one fighter caught fire and dived toward the ground from 17,000 feet, disappearing from sight still in a dive. After two more unsuccessful head-on runs, I hit one more ship that similarly went down. About twenty minutes later, I made a head-on run to very close range and could see parts of the plane coming off. The ship rolled away smoking, but it did not go down.

Sandell was credited with the first two victories, which were probably the Nates flown by Lieutenant Rine and Sergeant Nagashima of the 77th Sentai.

Also claiming victories were three Adam & Eves who had come down to Mingaladon earlier in the month. As the Japanese told the story, the Allied pilots—Bill Bartling, Dick Rossi, and Frank Schiel—ganged up on the Nate flown by Captain Mitsuhiro Matsuda, one of Major Yoshioka's squadron leaders. Seeing his captain hard-pressed by the enemy, Lieutenant Kanekichi Yamamoto dove to his rescue—to no avail. Matsuda's plane went down, and Yamamoto's was mortally hit. When his engine began to burn, the young lieutenant looked about for a target to take out with him. What he saw was the chalk-white **A** formed by the runways of Mingaladon airport, five miles east and two miles below.

At about the same moment, the yellow warning light came on in Sandell's Tomahawk, signaling that his engine was overheating from a bullet through the coolant system. With smoke pouring into his cockpit, Sandell headed down for a dead-stick landing at Mingaladon. He hit hard, bursting a tire, but managed to bring the Tomahawk to a stop without catching a wing on the runway. Then he glanced up and saw that his problems had only begun. Gliding down on Mingaladon to strike a last blow for the emperor, Lieutenant Yamamoto saw the enemy fighter roll to a stop, and he headed straight for it, his propeller windmilling. Sandell jumped out and sprinted for a ditch. Seconds later, Yamamoto's plane crashed so close to the Tomahawk that it tore off its rudder, and so close to Sandell that a piece of Nakajima engine rolled across the ditch in which he was crouching. Among those who ran over to help Sandell—and to gawk at the suicide pilot—was Greg Boyington. There wasn't much to be seen. "The largest part of the pilot I could recognize," Boyington wrote later, "was a tiny left hand with the severed tendons sticking out." Yamamoto, he guessed, had thrown up his arm in an instinctive attempt to shield his face from the impact.

In flight school, Japanese cadets practiced suicide dives as routinely as they worked on gunnery or formation flying. "It was taken for granted," one of them explained after the war, "that any pilot with a disabled plane would die in the samurai tradition. . . . He would dive into an enemy ship or plane, taking as many of his adversaries with him as possible." This was known as the *jibaku* death. (Japanese is rich in words describing the way in which a warrior might die, and especially rich in those involving self-destruction: a pilot might turn himself into a missile, join a scheduled suicide flight, disembowel himself, or otherwise commit suicide rather than suffer dishonor. There were other words to cover the usual hazards of combat, including death by enemy fire, by explosion, and by dying from wounds.) Even after the lapse of half a century, Yamamoto's death is still limned as beautiful in a Japan that has forsaken war but not its adoration of dead warriors. "The English general was impressed by this [gesture]," declared a 1977 history of JAAF fighter groups; "and Yamamoto's ashes remained there [at Mingaladon airport], buried carefully."

The contrast with Chennault's free-wheeling mercenaries could not have been greater. Among the Panda Bears in the air that Wednesday was Raymond Hastey, a former army pilot who had come to Burma on *Jaegersfontein*. Hastey's Tomahawk was hit; he bailed out; and according to one account he was strafed as he hung from his parachute. Like David Harris, Curt Smith, and Pappy Paxton before him, Hastey decided that his mother had not reared him to be a fighter pilot, and from that day forward he restricted himself to ground duties. Unlike the other three, he had one Japanese plane to his credit, whether for January 28 or some earlier combat.

After dinner, some of the AVG pilots sat on the veranda of the RAF club and watched the British bombers take off for their long, lonely journey to Bangkok. As the Americans looked on, the Blenheim piloted by Lieutenant J.L.B. Viney lost power and crashed at the end of the runway. (There were no fatalities.) Jack Newkirk, meanwhile, was composing a situation report for Chennault. The British, he predicted, would soon lose Moulmein, and he could use a few more technicians and a few more planes. Otherwise, the Panda Bears were fine where they were, without being pulled back to Kunming and certainly without being drafted into the U.S. Army:

> The planes that we have here now are beginning to look like patchwork quilts for the holes in them. The engines are also getting tired. . . . There are not sufficient ground crews for the job, and there is not enough time for them to teach the Chinese or other helpers which they steal from our neighbors [the RAF]. . . . There are four of my men who need a rest, they are [armorer Jack] Jones, who is getting over another bad attack of fever, [Pete] Wright, who is recuperating from appendicitis, [Moose] Moss who had some teeth knocked out when he was shot down and bailed out and [radioman Alex] Mihalko who has piles. . . .
>
> I am firmly convinced that . . . the A.V.G. does not need anything except cooperation from the army or any other organization, as far as we are concerned.

The 77th Sentai returned next day, Thursday, January 29. What kind of courage did it require to cross Martaban Bay—in a flimsy Nate with fixed landing gear, two rifle-caliber guns, and an unprotected tank of aviation gas—and over South Burma to meet the shark-faced Tomahawks of the AVG, which only yesterday had destroyed four of their comrades? The Buffaloes were no longer a factor in the defense of Mingaladon airport—never had been, really. The eight-gunned Hurricanes should have been more of a threat, although they had not yet managed to break even against the Japanese air forces, in Malaya or in Burma. But the Tomahawks were murder, with the power of their fifty-caliber nose guns, the toughness of Donovan Berlin's airframe, and the maverick intensity of Chennault's pilots.

To be sure, the Japanese pilots had their own list of virtues. They were at their best in a dogfight, not only because their planes were maneuverable but because they stuck together, while the Allied fighters streaked all over the sky. Their teamwork was superb, enabling them on occasion to lure a lone-wolf Hurricane or Tomahawk into their midst, to be overwhelmed and stung to death. And their courage was tremendous. It was institutionalized—religious—literally suicidal, as another of Major Yoshioka's pilots demonstrated on January 29.

There were twenty Nates in Thursday's formation. To oppose them, Jack Newkirk took off with a five-plane flight of Panda Bears, picking up two Adam & Eves as he climbed. Sandy Sandell was also in the air that day, as were two 17th Squadron Hurricanes—ten planes altogether.

Newkirk spotted the enemy swarm above him and to the east, so he turned west, to gain altitude before closing with them. One of his pilots was Noel Bacon, who wrote this account of the clash:

When the Japs dived on our planes Jack Newkirk and a wingman climbed and dove on them. The dives brought the Japs and Newkirk and his wingman under us, so my wingman and I jumped the Japs. I made a pass, went into a cloud, turned while in it and climbed again and attacked.

One Jap turned up at me and I got a 45-degree shot in his bow. His prop immediately began to windmill and he started to spiral down. I dove through the clouds and met him beneath them. He was still in a slow spiral. I dove on his tail and opened all guns, setting fire to his left tank. I went on past and saw the pilot was dead. I watched him crash and burn 10 miles northeast of the base, then I followed another little old devil out over the bay. He was running for home, and I got too eager and lost him.

Charlie Bond was one of the Adam & Eves who had followed Newkirk. He did not see the Japanese fighters until he was above them; then he charged his guns, flipped the switch to illuminate his optical sight, and went down in an almost vertical dive:

I missed him by a mile. I continued my dive on down a few thousand feet further. As I started pulling up I partially blacked out. I realized then that I had the throttle full up against the firewall and I was getting detonation in my engine. No one on my tail, so I stole a peek at the air speed indicator—over 400 mph. Using this speed I climbed back up to 18,000 feet.

Bond missed again on his second pass. He circled back, fired at one of the fixed-gear fighters, and finally found himself in a killing position behind another Nate. When he fired, the Japanese pilot dove into a cloud. Bond stayed above, confident that the Nate would emerge— which it soon did, climbing out of the cloud and squaring off for a head-on run against the Tomahawk:

> He must have been within two or three hundred yards as I closed in and opened fire with all six guns. He made no effort to turn; it was probably too late. My tracers tore into his cockpit and engine. Suddenly I was right on him. I had to raise my left wing to get over him as I zoomed past. His cockpit was flaming. I squealed in delight, laughing aloud. Enough for him. "Got one! There you are, Hoffman, old boy!"

Greg Boyington had also followed Newkirk's flight. As he remembered the day, he hit his first Nate "just right," setting it afire, then heard someone scream over the radio: "This is for Cokey, you son of a bitch!" That would have been Charlie Bond: the words may have been different, but the music was the same.

After his first pass through the Nates, Jack Newkirk had a head-on encounter with what he said was a retractable-gear fighter, though there were no "Zero types" over Mingaladon that month. "I held my fire and put a short burst in his engine at 300 yards," he reported. "A cylinder came off and the plane went down smoking. I fired three more bursts into him from above and behind him. Then he went into a cloud and I followed him through and saw him hit somewhere east of Dabein."

Meanwhile, Sandy Sandell—apparently alone—had tangled with a small group of Nates above a skim of clouds. He followed one enemy fighter down through the clouds, firing as he went, then turned away and watched it crash. He climbed back up and set another Nate aflame, then shot the engine out of a third. The second Nate was a likely kill, he wrote, and the third was "undoubtedly badly damaged but due to stress at the moment from other aircraft I could not follow them down to observe results." Stress!

The main swarm was now heading for home. Charlie Bond "firewalled everything" and charged after it, but each time he framed a Nate in his sights, the Japanese pilot doubled back in an Immelmann and met him head-on, two rifle-caliber machine guns against six. After sparring like this for a time, Bond saw that the clouds were filling in, and he decided to call it quits. He flew back to Mingaladon and executed "the first victory roll in my life." First, though, he radioed the control tower for permission to make the fighter pilot's traditional boast.

When he landed, Bond saw a crowd of airmen near one of the revetments that protected planes from being destroyed by a near-miss explosion. Another Japanese pilot had made a suicide dive on Mingaladon, this time trying to destroy a parked Blenheim. Bond taxied past the wreckage:

> An RAF airman held up a leather helmet with the pilot's head still in it and with parts of his throat hanging down in a bloody mess. With his other hand the airman pointed two fingers skyward in the usual V-for-victory sign. I returned the V-sign and taxied on. I could not, however, return his broad grin.

The dead pilot is not identified in Japanese records, suggesting that he was an enlisted man. Yet somebody saw his *jibaku* dive, for the attack on the Blenheim was remembered—and attributed to Lieutenant Yamamoto, who had died in the same manner the day before. According to a pilot who joined the 77th Sentai soon after these events, the group's first business upon moving to Rangoon was to locate Yamamoto's grave at the "Edward Church" in Insein. By then, the two *jibaku* dives had been merged into one. His engine dead but his controls still working (as the story was told) Yamamoto had dived upon Mingaladon and destroyed three Blenheim bombers with machine gun fire, then crashed his Nate into a hangar. He survived, climbed into a Brewster Buffalo, and tried to fly it off the field. Alas, the plane crashed and exploded, and the durable lieutenant was finally shot by British soldiers.

Sorting out the claims for January 29 is an impossible task, but Sandy Sandell was credited with shooting down three Nates to become the first ace among the Adam & Eves. Whitey Lawlor of the Panda Bears also became an ace that day, and seven other AVG pilots were credited with shoot-downs: Charlie Bond with two, and John Dean, Tex Hill, Bob Little, Jack Newkirk, John Petach, and Bob Prescott with one apiece. For the RAF, Squadron Leader Frank Carey and Pilot Officer Storey were also credited with kills. The Allied claims therefore came to at least fourteen. Fourteen planes on Thursday, five on Wednesday, three on Monday—twenty-two for the week, or nearly half of General Obata's total fighter strength.

Of course the figures were wildly exaggerated. The 77th Sentai actually lost four planes on January 29—which was bad enough, God knows. Since December 23, Major Yoshioka had sacrificed a dozen planes and a dozen pilots over South Burma, not to mention six *Ki*-27s burned on the ground in Thailand. In six weeks of combat with the AVG, Yoshioka had lost a third of the pilots and half the planes he had led into Thailand on December 8, 1941.

But the truth was not enough to satisfy an American public disheartened by the continuing defeats in the Pacific. The combat over South Burma that Thursday was witnessed by a wire-service reporter, who filed this breathless version of the carnage:

> Paced by three resolute Texans, the unbeaten American Volunteer Group's squadron and its Royal Air Force colleagues tore thirteen and possibly seventeen Japanese planes out of a mass enemy fighter sweep over Rangoon today and boosted their score of raiders destroyed over Burma and Thailand to at least 111 machines. . . .
>
> It was truly Texas day over the rice paddies of the Kipling country.
>
> Sandy of San Antonio got three Japanese for sure, a total of five in the two days since he was transferred here from China.
>
> Bill, also from San Antonio, got one for certain, increasing his bag to seven.
>
> Kirk of San Saba came down safely, drenched with oil from a broken fuel line and creased across his forehead by a bullet. "Now I'm really mad," he drawled. "Some guy got me while I was chasing another one at 20,000 [feet]. I'd have stayed up but oil was squirting all over the cockpit."

Sandell actually came from Missouri, though his army service may have given him a Texas address. "Bill" was Tex Hill. And "Kirk" was Matt Kuykendall, who was grazed across the forehead that Thursday afternoon, and who did indeed live in San Saba, the geographical center of Texas.

———

The pressure eased on Friday, so Jim Howard led Tom Cole and Ed Rector to the killing ground beyond Moulmein, to provide what relief they could to the 17th Indian Division. This was Howard's combat report for January 30:

> We were low over the ground when we arrived at the area of Kawkareik.

Seeing no enemy planes in the air Pilot Cole and I spiraled down to see if there was any troop concentrations to strafe. I saw a number of lorries in the road about 2 miles north of Kawkareik and went down and made a pass at them but did not fire. I made another pass and still did not fire, because I did not see anything of special importance nor did I know for certain that the particular lorries were ours or the enemies. I started to climb and headed for home, but looked back and saw Cole headed in a glide for the trucks presumably to strafe. The next thing I saw was an explosion and a flame shot up 100 feet into the air. Black smoke ensued. At first I thought that Cole had hit an ammunition truck but as I passed over the target I realized the pilot had crashed because there was a path cut thru the tall trees which bordered the road and bits of plane were visible scattered all over.

Howard was right to hold his fire, for there were no Japanese trucks in Burma. General Takeuchi's engineers were pushing a road across the Dawna Range, but the track was far from finished, and his troops were still fighting on what they had brought from Thailand, on their backs and those of their horses, plus the "Churchill stores" they had captured since crossing the frontier. Tom Cole had flown into the trees while strafing the 17th Indian Division.

A former PBY pilot, Cole had been the first of the "big boat" captains to make the transition to fighters. In his AVG identification photo—not always the most reliable record—he looked to be a glum, heavyset man, well on the way to baldness. He had one Nate to his credit, and Jim Howard remembered him as the animating spirit of the Panda Bears' softball team. His death made a great impression upon the pilots, and the AVG diaries for January 30 are raw with pain and anger. "Group wanted us for two other crazy missions," Noel Bacon wrote. "I told them to go to hell." There would be no more of the flip denials that had greeted the training deaths at Kyedaw airfield.

Even as Tom Cole was being consumed in his own fireball, Japanese troops were moving into position around Moulmein airfield. Like the field at Tavoy, Moulmein's was defended by the paramilitary Frontier Force, which held during the day but pulled out when night fell. Moulmein itself was defended by 2,000 of the porous Burma Rifles, on loan from McLeod's 1st Burma Division. That was bad enough, but on the same day Major General John Smyth, commander of the 17th Indian Division, got word that Japanese troops were operating "in strength" near Paan to his north. (This was General Sakurai's 33rd Division, advancing into Burma proper.) Since Moulmein was on the south bank of the Salween River, with the broad reach of Martaban Bay between it and Rangoon, this meant that Smyth's line of retreat was being threatened. He appealed to Rangoon for permission to withdraw, which was granted by General Hutton. During the night on Saturday, the Commonwealth troops commandeered all the boats they could find, and early next morning they rowed to the northern shore. Tenasserim now belonged to Japan, two weeks after Oki Detachment had fired the opening shots outside Tavoy.

February came in like thunder. At midnight, while Smyth's garrison was abandoning Moulmein without firing a shot, three 14th Sentai Sallys came from Bangkok to bomb Mingaladon airport. Unable to find it, they jettisoned three metric tons of bombs on Rangoon—the city's first raid since Christmas Day. Two hours later, six 8th Sentai Lilys made the same journey with better success, not only finding Mingaladon but putting its radar station out of operation. Finally, at 5:10 A.M., four 62nd Sentai Sallys bombed the dispersal fields to the north, hitting a Tomahawk at Johnnie Walker.

The bombers returned almost every night that week, though their aim got no better. Early Friday morning, six 14th Sentai Sallys raided Mingaladon, but their bombs missed by such a margin that they came close to hitting the Burmah Oil compound at Insein Cantonment, four miles south. The sound of the unsynchronized Mitsubishi radials was almost as bad as the bombs themselves; to a listener on the ground at Insein, the engines seemed to be beating out a personal threat: "*Doom*-ba-boom-ba-*doom*." Those Sallys were followed an hour later by six from the 62nd Sentai, and an hour after that by fifteen Anns of the 31st Sentai. In this last raid, the 17th Squadron managed to shoot down one of the light bombers, only to wreck a Hurricane when it ran into a bomb crater upon landing at Mingaladon.

The siren howled again at 10:30 A.M. Only six Tomahawks and two Hurricanes managed to intercept the enemy formation, which consisted of twenty-five Nates from the 77th Sentai, plus a flight from the 50th Sentai at Nakhon Sawan. Bob Neale led the interception. "I was in a good position," he wrote in his diary, "with eight planes about 2,000 ft. above and behind" the incoming swarm. Charlie Bond was among his pilots. With Greg Boyington on his wing, Bond caught a Nate "in my sights at about five hundred yards and let go with all guns." But he was foiled by the teamwork of the Japanese:

> My firing engulfed him. As I closed in, I misjudged my speed and had to pull up and away drastically to keep from hitting him. [Then] I had to dive out when a Jap got too close on my rear, and when I leveled off and climbed back up, I lost the enemy fighters.

He lost Boyington, too. Turning east, Bond searched the horizon for the retreating Nates. He spotted a lone fighter, went after it, and dove on it from behind. But only one of his machine guns was firing, so he rolled out and charged them.

> In I went again, and in my concentration I did not see another Jap who had come down on me but overshot me. He pulled around to get on my tail; I dove away. Just as I did, I got a glimpse of another P-40 whizzing past me—No. 23.

That was Bob Neale. Together, the two Adam & Eves cornered the Nate. "Bob and I fought that little devil some five to ten minutes," Bond marveled. "He must have known he was done for, but he was a game little guy." At one point, the Japanese pilot doubled back on his tormentors and attacked Bond head-on:

> All my guns were firing as we barreled on at each other. He started pulling up and I followed as long as I dared, then broke off in a screaming dive out. He flipped around in an amazing turn and followed me down. . . . I was in a vertical power dive and skidding like mad, since I did not bother [with] the rudder trim.

Neale was credited with shooting down the Nate, to become the second ace in the Adam & Eves. Also supposedly scoring that morning were Greg Boyington and Bob Little, each credited with two Japanese fighters; Bob Prescott, credited with one; and Mac McGarry, who claimed a bomber though there were none in the air that day.

This tally was enlarged by the war correspondents at Mingaladon, whose stories gave the impression that the entire American Volunteer Group had "ambushed" the Japanese air force over the airport. It was, the correspondents wrote, the "most spectacular of a long list of stunning victories" for the AVG. "But we were too busy to keep track of everything we shot at," Greg Boyington was quoted as saying. "The Japs split up their formation and tried to escape every which-way."

All of which is hard to reconcile with Japanese accounts, which show only one Nate lost over South Burma on February 6.

Three of the supposed Allied victories were scored by pilot-officers Storey and Underwood of the RAF 135th Squadron, activated on February 3 under Frank Carey. After more than a month in the pipeline, the planes from North Africa were moving into Burma in such quantity that there was talk of loaning eight Hurricanes to the Americans, "to tide them over until their own reinforcing aircraft arrived." Toward this end, Jack Newkirk checked out in a Hurricane, and some Commonwealth crewmen were loaned to the AVG. (Not always with happy results. Missing the distinction between British .303-caliber and Chinese 7.92-mm, an RAF armorer disabled Tomahawk No. 59 by loading it with the wrong ammunition.) But a disaster on February 3 put an end to this reverse lend-lease. Eighteen British fighters left Calcutta's Dum Dum airport at 4:30 P.M., bound for Lashio. Night overtook them above the mountainous Shan Highlands. The fighters lost sight of the "mother Blenheim" that was navigating for them, and one by one they crashed.

Some Westland Lysanders of the Indian Air Force made a more successful flight into Burma at about this time. These high-wing, fixed-gear planes were intended as artillery spotters, but there was little artillery on the Salween front, and not many targets to be seen in the rain forest. Group Captain Seton Broughall therefore ordered them to be used as bombers. The Lysanders had a rack on each wheel spat for a twenty-five-pound bomb, and these were adapted for 250-pounders, posing a serious risk of self-destruction as the planes clattered along the runways of Mingaladon airport. Nothing daunted, the Indians flew their first mission on February 5, bombing the Moulmein railroad station and docks under the protection of two 67th Squadron Buffaloes.

General Obata had also targeted Kyedaw airfield for destruction, and on February 3 six Anns of the 31st Sentai flew up from Phitsanulok to bomb the old AVG training base. Robert Keeton (called Buster in honor of the film comic) was stationed there as a test pilot, checking out Tomahawks as they were repaired. When the Anns came over, Keeton and two technicians jumped into a car, which they promptly careened into a ditch:

I, being in the back seat, the door jammed, and I couldn't get out. The bombs were whisteling and then hitting making a tremendous noise. I knew they were dropping awfully close from the impact and the car was being filled with dirt. I could hear the scharpnel falling and wizzing by sounding like machine gun bullets.

Thirty bombs hit the runway, by Keeton's count, but the only casualties were two Burmese soldiers injured and another killed. Somewhat shaken, the test pilot went back to work:

At 3:30 p.m. the siren went off and having a plane ready I jumped in and took off. Had reached about 300 feet altitude when they dropped their bombs. Circled field climbing until reaching 20,000 feet. Found out that I had no oxygen. . . . I began to feel dizzy and the lack of oxygen my head was hurting like the devil and I was breathing hard. I decided to come on back and land. I just nosed the plane over and started down when I saw a twin motored Jap plane practically flying formation about 1,000 feet below me and to my right. I switched on guns, and dove on him from above and the left side with all 6 guns going full blast. Passing under him and looking back I thought he was smoking but not certain.

The plane was an 8th Sentai Lily, returning from a raid upcountry. Keeton later persuaded himself that he had shot it down, but there is no mention of the loss in Japanese accounts.

Kyedaw was bombed again next day by six Sallys from the 62nd Sentai. Chennault's nightmare of the previous autumn had become reality: so close to the Thai border, and with no warning system except a few observers with heliograph mirrors, Toungoo could not be defended against enemy raids. Bus Keeton pronounced two of the Tomahawks airworthy, though not fit to fight, so Noel Bacon and Frank Swartz drove up from Mingaladon and flew them to Kunming—the first of the Panda Bears to move back into China. John Hennessy came down in the AVG Beechcraft and picked up some of the technicians, and the rest headed up the Burma Road in a four-truck convoy.

The 113th Squadron also abandoned Kyedaw, after moving there because of "persistent enemy bombing and strafing attack" at the Rangoon airfields. The Blenheims would continue to operate out of Zayatkwin, but the headquarters staff flew to Magwe, a desolate town on the Irrawaddy River that reminded Americans of a southwestern army post. However, Magwe had a substantial airport—Burma's second largest—and the incontestable advantage of being 250 miles north of Rangoon.

Let's Get the Heck Out of Here
February 1942

On Saturday morning, February 7, line chief Harry Fox pronounced Tomahawk No. 11 restored from the effects of Lieutenant Yamamoto's *jibaku* dive. Sandy Sandell took the Tomahawk up and put it through its paces, concluding with a barrel roll over the airport; trying to recover, he stalled the plane and augered in. All that could be salvaged from the wreck were its tail wheel and a main wheel assembly. "The boys had to dig Sandy out," one of the pilots recalled, "and it wasn't pleasant."

Unlike many of the Adam & Eves, Bob Neale had liked and respected Sandell. When Chennault radioed him to take command of the squadron, Neale tried to pass the job along to Greg Boyington, figuring that the ex-marine could "out-fly or out-fight" anyone in the AVG. Boyington declined, probably because he knew that Chennault would not tolerate any change in his orders. So Neale took the job and made Boyington his vice squadron leader, a decision he would soon regret.

Lanky, large-featured, and curly-haired, Neale could have posed for a recruiting poster as the all-American fighting man. One of the British pilots described him as "a well-built fellow of medium height, dressed in shirt and trousers"—i.e., not in uniform—"and having a revolver slung in an unorthodox, finely-worked leather holster. He looked dusty and tired, but his eyes were of a merry, friendly shade." But Neale's diary did not suggest a merry-hearted man. "No one will ever know the mental

221

anxiety I am going thru," he wrote, "for on top of losing a very close friend I have shouldered the responsibility of running the Squadron and assuring its safety." And again: "Chennault places full confidence in my decisions. I only pray that I will be deserving." Whereas Jack Newkirk actually seemed to enjoy the combat that surged back and forth across Martaban Bay, Bob Neale was that more typical warrior: the man who fights because he must.

To compound his problems, he had to replace not only Sandell but Newkirk as well. The Panda Bears were leaving South Burma at last: twenty-eight technicians left for Lashio that Saturday by train and truck, while twenty-one men from the 1st Squadron came downcountry by train. The pilots left more slowly (and Newkirk last of all) but within a week Bob Neale was senior American air officer in Burma.*

Fortunately for Neale, General Obata had concluded his extermination campaign, shifting his fighters and light bombers to the Salween front. (The 50th and 8th Sentais would support General Takeuchi's 55th Division as it advanced on Martaban town, while the 77th and 31st Sentais supported Sakurai's 33rd Division to the north.) As for his heavy bombers, Obata sent the 62nd Sentai home to refit. That left just twelve Sallys committed to the South Burma campaign: Colonel Hironaka's 14th Sentai, which moved to Nakhon Sawan to be closer to the front.

Like the Panda Bears at the turn of the year, the Adam & Eves were therefore granted a lull before battle. They buried Sandell in plot C-99 at the church of Edward the Martyr, and in the week that followed this was a typical radiogram to Kunming, with Bob Neale detailing the planes on hand, the Adam & Eves trickling down from Kunming, and the missions flown:

> Sixteen planes. Four pilots arrived. No enemy action six sharks combat patrol over Paan six sharks bomber escort to Paan.

Neale had twenty-two pilots in his squadron, but many had no combat experience—or weren't interested in having any more. To keep sixteen

---

* Among the Panda Bears flying to Kunming was John Petach, who proposed to Red Foster, his sweetheart almost since *Jaegersfontein* had cleared the Golden Gate Bridge. They were married February 17 at Hostel Number One, the bride with a black eye sustained in an arm-wrestling contest with Claire Chennault.

SOUTH BURMA ORDER OF BATTLE

RAF 221st Group
(Air Vice Marshal Donald Stevenson, Commanding)
AVG 1st Squadron (Sq Ldr Robert Sandell): 12 Curtiss Tomahawks
AVG 2nd Squadron (Sq Ldr John Newkirk): 8 Curtiss Tomahawks
IAF 1st Squadron (Wing Cmdr Karun Majumdar): 6 Westland Lysanders
RAF 17th Squadron (Sq Ldr C. A. C. Stone): 7 Hawker Hurricanes
RAF 67th Squadron (Sq Ldr R. A. Milward): 4 Brewster Buffaloes
RAF 113th Squadron (Wing Cmdr R. N. Stidolph): 10 Bristol Blenheims
RAF 135th Squadron (Sq Ldr Frank Carey): 4 Hawker Hurricanes
(51 aircraft in service, 3 Feb 1942)

JAAF 5th Hikoshidan
(Lt Gen Eiryo Obata, Commanding)
8th Sentai (Maj Mitsuo Honda): 10 Kawasaki *Ki*-48 Lilys, 10 Mitsubishi *Ki*-30 Anns
14th Sentai (Col Magoroku Hironaka): 12 Mitsubishi *Ki*-21 Sallys
31st Sentai (Lt Col Junji Hayashi): 22 Mitsubishi *Ki*-30 Anns
50th Sentai (Maj Yasuo Makino): 20 Nakajima *Ki*-27 Nates
62nd Sentai (Lt Col Hiroshi Onishi): 8 Mitsubishi *Ki*-21 Sallys
77th Sentai (Maj Hiroshi Yoshioka): 23 Nakajima *Ki*-27 Nates
70th Ind. Chutai (Capt Tateo Ohira): 7 reconnaissance aircraft
(112 aircraft in service, 3 Feb 1942)

planes on alert, he had to use almost every combat-ready flier on his roster. The others were given staff duties: Charlie Sawyer as liaison officer with the RAF, Ray Hastey as transportation officer, and Ed Goyette (who had moved his support team down from Kyedaw airfield) in charge of supply and maintenance. Neale also had an all-purpose aide in Paul Frillmann, the AVG chaplain, whom Chennault had sent down from Kunming for a taste of war.

The Adam & Eves took advantage of the interlude. They played golf at the Rangoon Country Club—four caddies to a pilot. They swam at the Kokine Swimming Club "and acted like rich kids." They bought sapphires. They caroused through Rangoon, brawling with the RAF and each other in disagreements that were potentially lethal, since everyone now went armed. One donnybrook began when the Silver Grill's proprietor tried to evict the Americans, whereupon they shot out his chandeliers, causing a panic among the prostitutes and their clients on the second floor. Another time, the Adam & Eves drank so hard and late at the brass-railed bar of the Strand (the bar remained open though the hotel was closed) that seven pilots missed roll-call next morning. One of the latecomers was Robert H. Smith, who finally showed up too drunk to fly. (Not to be confused with R. T. Smith of the Hell's Angels, this man was shorter and was usually distinguished with the nickname of Snuffy, after a comic strip character.) Greg Boyington was another casualty of the battle of the Strand—February 14, 1942. Still drunk when he reported for duty, he got into a bitter and public argument with Bob Neale, who never afterward placed any confidence in him.

Then there was the case of crew chief George Reynolds, who wrecked an AVG vehicle and shot some Burmans who seemed to be threatening him, killing one and wounding two. Reynolds spent the night in jail, but the British released him into Neale's custody next day, and no more was said about it. The feeling was general, among westerners in Rangoon, that the natives would gladly murder any white man they caught alone. That was a principal reason they went armed.

Another popular activity was to take a ten-ton truck, drive down to the waterfront, and order the dockworkers to load it with whatever took one's fancy. (The freebooting must have struck the laborers, many of them convicts working at gunpoint, as something of a double stand- ard. Looters were being shot in Rangoon at the rate of twenty-four per day.) As Paul Frillmann told the story, this dockside thievery was sanctioned by the authorities—that he was, in effect, AVG looting officer: "I spent every day," he wrote, "with whatever ground crewmen could be spared from the airfield, smashing open crates and barrels, loading our trucks with spare parts for planes and vehicles, tires, tools, radio equipment, guns and ammunition."

Much of this booty was converted to personal use. The technicians (including some who had quit the AVG in the fall of 1941 but who had remained in Rangoon) built up huge stores of contraband, which they meant to smuggle up the Burma Road to China. The pilots had less opportunity to play this game, but they helped themselves to the possessions in the houses where they slept, and which were now being abandoned by their owners. George Burgard and Ed McClure, pilot and crew chief, filled a truck with contraband—"so much stuff it would not be believed if I listed it," Burgard wrote in his diary—and consigned it to the convoy that would take surplus AVG supplies and personnel to Kunming. They hoped to sell the cargo for $1,500. Even Charlie Bond, the quintessential square-shooter, accepted the gift of a short-wave radio, knowing full well that it had been stolen from China's lend-lease stores. As for the staff officers, Ray Hastey was generally believed to be making a good thing out of his job as transportation officer.

An Australian journalist at the Burma-China frontier admired the style with which the Americans bullied their cargoes past the Chinese customs guards: "With 'AVG' in huge letters plastered across their windscreens, they drove straight through, every man bristling with [weapons]. Some of them were in the racket too, but their prestige and Tommy guns allowed their smuggled goods to pass through without hindrance." When Frillmann himself went north, he noticed that his convoy had a life of its own: the mounds of cargo were shrinking, as stuff was sold off the back—but the convoy grew longer, as the Rangoon free-lancers joined in to cross the border under the banner of the AVG.

Altogether, war was a great equalizer. For a month, the pilots had luxuriated in private homes, while the technicians clubbed together at Eighteen Mile Ranch, where there were no Indian servants with pots of tea. Don Rodewald described the routine at the hostel, beginning with wakeup by the line chief:

> [Harry] Fox calls us at 5:30. We have breakfast prepared by [Clayton] Harpold a former Army mess sgt. He usually has eggs and flapjacks, jam, syrup, coffee and bacon. We go to the field immediately. It usually gets light about a half hour after we get there. We preflight all ships right away then continue with our work on individual ships. At 8 A.M. Harpold brings us coffee, bread & jam. At noon Harpold brings us dinner. We usually have cold slaw, potato salad, cold meat bread & jam and Iced tea. We stay at the airdrome till 6:30 P.M. and then go like hell to the ranch to get a shower before dark. . . . We pay the native boy an anna to pump water for the shower. We then have chow and usually to bed by 9 P.M.

Now, as the pilots found themselves coming home to empty houses, with no whiskey soda ready and no dinner in prospect, they began to take their evening meal at Eighteen Mile Ranch. And with most of Rangoon's white women having taken passage to India, they even began to court the Anglo-Burmans and Anglo-Indians whom they had earlier left to the technicians. The British did not approve. "We don't mind you sleeping with them," they told the Americans, "but don't for God's sake drag them around in our hotels and restaurants."

Bassein was raided, starting the rumor that Japanese paratroopers had landed there, west of Rangoon, and the Adam & Eves began to joke that one fine morning they would drive out to Johnnie Walker and find Japanese pilots grinning at them from the cockpits of their Tomahawks.

But they saw no Japanese, neither preempting their planes, nor swarming over Mingaladon airport, nor even challenging their missions over the Salween front. At night in the abandoned Jensen house, Charlie Bond dreamed of combat in the sky. Daytimes too had a nightmarish quality, as a British pilot remembered: "We sipped at another mug of tea, and lay supine under the wings, eyeing with suspicion every speck of a bird soaring on high, and sweating—and sweating." Sometimes the siren wailed, at which they scrambled into their cockpits, roared down the runway in dust and confusion, and clawed for the altitude that could save their lives.

On February 18, during one of these false alarms, they climbed to 22,000 feet, eased back to cruising speed, and immediately heard "Snapper!" in their earphones. This was current RAF code for an immediate recall, so they pointed their noses back to Mingaladon, cursing the fools in the operations room. The AVG never learned the cause of the debacle, which was the work of Tex Barrick, an American pilot in the 17th Squadron. In North Africa, *snapper* had meant enemy aircraft approaching; seeing what he believed to be a Nakajima Hayabusa, Barrick sang out the accustomed warning and was astonished when everyone else (including the Buffalo pilot he had taken for Japanese) promptly dropped out of the sky.

The Commonwealth troops were in an unenviable position, holding a slab of land between two great rivers. The Salween provided them with a defensive barrier, but the Sittang was a mile-wide estuary with only a decked-over railway trestle connecting them with Burma proper. Through the Sittang, the ocean surged twice a day in a tidal bore—a horizontal waterfall that would sweep away any boat that tried to cross it. General Smyth wanted desperately to move behind this bottleneck, but General Hutton ordered him to hold as far east as possible, buying space and time for reinforcements to come up.

In the 17th Indian Division, Smyth had 8,000 men, or about half the strength of a textbook division. Fully trained, they would have ranked among the finest soldiers in the world, as Indians had often proved in Britain's wars, whether fighting for the crown or against it. On the Salween front, however, the newcomers had not finished their training, while the earlier arrivals were demoralized by their defeats in Tenasserim. They were bolstered by two British battalions, the Duke of Wellingtons and the King's Own Yorkshires. Finally, Smyth had four battalions on loan from the 1st Burma Division. (With about 500 men, the battalion was the basic unit of maneuver in the Commonwealth army.) Their morale was not improved when—on Sunday, February 15—the 100,000-man garrison at Singapore surrendered to a Japanese force one-third its size. Giddy with triumph, the Japanese renamed the city *Shonan,* or Radiant South.

Burma was now well and truly on the front line. In India, the civil and military authorities fretted that the troops in Burma were "not fighting with proper relish," so they did what came naturally to desk officers: they fired General Hutton. Burma's new field commander (her third in as many months) would be General the Honorable Sir Harold Alexander, who had presided over the evacuation of the British Expeditionary Force at Dunkirk. Perhaps there was a portent in that.

For the Adam & Eves, the string of eventless days came to an end over the village of Belin on February 21. Escorting four Blenheims to the Salween front, six Tomahawks ran into the full strength of the 77th Sentai. The Japanese fighters were on a mission similar to theirs: twenty-three Nates escorting light bombers of the 31st Sentai, off to silence a Commonwealth machine gun position. "They were on our tails in a split second," Jim Cross wrote of this combat. "Everywhere the sky seemed suddenly filled with orange suns. They kept no formation but came in like a flock of sparrows." (The rising-sun identification disc was usually described as red, but sometimes it seemed orange—paint fading in the tropical sun.) The Tomahawks dove out without returning fire, as George Burgard recalled:

> It was a lucky break but so sudden that it scared the pants off us. We were below them and I had to dive out the first time without getting a shot.

There were . . . Jap planes all over the sky. I tried to shoot them all down myself, but got only two in a full hour of fighting. It was a wild scramble. . . . [John] Farrell got a bullet through his canopy and I got one thru my wing that shot out my right tire. Some fun.

With pardonable enthusiasm, Burgard thought there were forty of the fixed-gear fighters in the air, and in his excitement he tore his gunsight rheostat off its mount, trying to brighten the illumination so he could aim better. Both his claims were recognized, and Farrell and Snuffy Smith were each credited with one Nate. (Japanese records show no losses for February 21, while Major Yoshioka's pilots claimed one Tomahawk "certain" and two more probable.) Farrell came home with cuts on his face and hands, inflicted by flying shards of plexiglass.

No sooner did they land at Mingaladon than the Adam & Eves were sent off again to attack a Japanese column of 300 vehicles on a track to the north of Kyaikto. Since the 17th Indian Division was falling back on this village, the Commonwealth troops seemed to be heading into an ambush. "For the first time in the campaign," Air Vice Marshal Stevenson exulted in his post-campaign dispatch, "the enemy provided a satisfactory bombing target. . . . The total fighter effort of the Rangoon defence and what bombers were at readiness were ordered to attack at 1625 hours." When Bob Neale called him out, Charlie Bond was still writing up his combat report from the previous action:

I was eager as hell and was hoping we would see [the Nates] again, since I didn't fare too well before. The Blenheims bombed the area, and then Bob went down with his flight to strafe the Japanese columns on the road. I counted over fifty trucks in the column heading northwest toward Kyaikto, which is the British Army headquarters.

But the Japanese column was supposed to be moving *south* upon Kyaikto, while the 17th Indian Division was heading north. Six Blenheims and an undetermined number of Tomahawks and Hurricanes did their best to destroy it. "Straffed a Jap motorized column," Bob Neale noted in his diary. "Did a lot of damage."

After an hour of flying top cover, Bond took his flight back to Mingaladon. He was immediately sent out with Snuffy Smith to find and destroy a Blenheim that had crashed in the rain forest—their third mission in as many hours. They searched for the bomber in vain, then Bond decided to go after easier game:

I headed north to the main road on which I had seen so many trucks in my previous mission. This time I was at treetop level, and then I found the Jap motorized column. I strafed it from one end to the other. Some vehicles already were on fire and bombed out. . . . I circled back to come back down the column again, and Smitty was right behind me. I came close to the treetops in my porpoising and jinking to get in bursts at choice targets.

Snuffy Smith's combat report was equally upbeat, and equally sure that this was the main Belin-Kyaikto track. "Falling into single file," he wrote, "we strafed up and down the road, until our ammunition was exhausted, paying particular attention to trucks and cavalry groups." Bond then spotted the crashed Blenheim and shot it up. His engine began to shudder, so he nursed the Tomahawk back to Mingaladon with the canopy open and his oxygen mask off, in case he had to jump. After landing, he found a one-inch hole through a propeller blade.

But there was no enemy motorized column, neither on the side road above Kyaikto nor on the Belin-Kyaikto track. What the Blenheims bombed—and what the Hurricanes and Tomahawks repeatedly straffed—was the 17th Indian Division. Roadbound by their vehicles, the Commonwealth troops were strung out for fifteen miles on either side of Kyaikto, while the Japanese filtered through the rain forest and rubber plantations to the north, in a slow-motion race to the Sittang Bridge. The day was astonishingly hot, and red dust choked the marching troops. In the morning they were attacked by the Japanese, in the afternoon by the RAF and the AVG. According to the scuttlebutt at Mingaladon, 160 Commonwealth troops died under friendly fire; officially, the losses were described as "numerous." Even more disheartening to a western-trained army was the loss of its transport and supplies. Vehicles (including ambulances full of wounded men) were blown up, machine-gunned, and run off the road. Pack mules broke loose and stampeded, taking weapons, ammunition, and radios with them into the rain forest.

The tragedy was just one bad moment in a ruinous three days. General Smyth's vanguard, a Frontier Force battalion and a company of engineers, reached the Sittang Bridge before the Japanese. The military policemen set up a bridgehead while the engineers prepared the trestle for demolition. At nightfall, the column's rearguard was still southeast of Kyaikto, and the twenty miles between were choked with an army that was exhausted, demoralized, and crazed with thirst. No one who has not made a forced march in the tropics can imagine what these men were suffering, having retreated for twelve hours without water, under a sun burning like an open furnace door. Night brought relief from the heat, but not from the drought: even where water was available, they could not drink enough of it to quench their thirst.

All through the night, the division's leading elements straggled across the railroad bridge. At daybreak, the bridgehead was seized by the Japanese—recaptured—lost again—and recaptured for the second time. Another Japanese force cut the Kyaikto road, and a Gurkha battalion fought all day to mend the break, losing its officers in the process.

The engineers finished their work at nightfall on February 22, but they did not have enough wire to put the blasting station on the western shore, where it would have been safe from capture. The troops coming down the road were stragglers, who told wild stories of being "ambushed, cut up and scattered" by Japanese commandos, and of jungle paths marked with paper arrows, presumably by Burman collaborators. The brigadier in charge—Hugh-Jones by name—tried to contact the main column but could not, its radios having been lost in the stampede set off by the Allied air attack. He concluded that the division had been destroyed. At 4:30 A.M., a junior officer explained the situation to General Smyth's headquarters over a bad telephone line. The question came back: was *Jonah* safely across? This referred to another brigadier, named Jones, who was preparing to fight his way to the river through a Gurkha position that he believed to be Japanese. To Smyth's question, the officer at the bridge answered yes, in the belief that they were talking about his own brigadier. Jonah, Jones, and Hugh-Jones: upon this muddle of names, half a division would be lost. The conversation was reported to Smyth, who concluded that most of his division was safe on the Burma shore. The charges were accordingly detonated at 5:30 A.M. on February 23. The division's third brigadier (who had the refreshingly different name of Ekin) described the scene when he reached the river:

> Here there was chaos and confusion; hundreds of men throwing down their arms, equipment and clothing and taking to the water. . . . As we crossed, the river was a mass of bobbing heads. We were attacked from the air and sniped at continuously from the east bank.

On the morning of February 24, the 17th Indian Division mustered

3,335 men—less than half its strength. Most were barefoot, and more than half had thrown away their rifles. They were little more than a rabble, as their commander himself described them: "ready to defend themselves doggedly but otherwise unfit for any of the normal operations of war."

Even before this disaster, the RAF had decided to follow the civil government out of Rangoon. On February 20, in an emergency meeting at Government House, Air Vice Marshal Stevenson proposed that his group headquarters be withdrawn to India. From this safe haven, he would maintain two operational wings in Burma: "Burwing" at Magwe in the Irrawaddy valley, "Akwing" at Akyab on the coast, each about 250 miles north of Rangoon. Mingaladon airport would then become a staging field, as the RAF had formerly used Moulmein, while a new airfield was built at Zigon, halfway between Magwe and Rangoon. Stevenson's proposal was accepted without argument.

Bob Neale had dinner with Seton Broughall that night, but the group captain did not mention the pullout, and the RAF kept working on a new clubhouse for Mingaladon, as if it planned to stay there forever.

Next day the authorities hoisted the "E" signal, telling nonessential personnel to leave the city. The telephone exchange shut down. Army engineers prepared the oil refinery and tank farms at Syriam for demolition, while the navy mined the river and prepared still-unloaded freighters for scuttling. When General John Magruder came down from Chongqing on February 22, he found the police gone, the city burning, dogs running wild, and looters operating with impunity. "Remembering previous British failure to effect destructions," as he phrased it, Magruder told Frank Merrill to destroy whatever he could. The major and his staff torched the General Motors truck assembly plant, destroying 972 vehicles, 5,000 tires, 1,000 bales of blankets, and a ton of jacks, chains, paint, and miscellaneous stuff.

There were jails in Rangoon and Insein, a lunatic asylum in Tadegale, and a leper hospital somewhere nearby. With their Indian warders fleeing to the north, the inmates seemed likely to starve to death. The dilemma was handed over to a junior officer, who ordered that the doors be opened and, in the case of the asylum, the inmates driven into the streets. (Afterward, his decision to release them was so widely criticized that the young officer shot himself to death.) The more rational joined the "crocodile" that was crawling past Mingaladon airport, but most became looters or firebugs, or roamed witlessly around the city. Driving through Rangoon one day, Bob Neale was flagged down by what seemed to be a white woman, but when he braked to a stop, he saw that what he taken for a fair complexion was actually the silvery skin of leprosy.

The Shwe Dagon pagoda was guarded by cadres of orange-robed monks, but elsewhere there was fire and chaos. The principal blaze was at the docks—a great column of black smoke and red flame—but smaller fires burned everywhere in the dying city. Sidewalks glittered with shards of glass, from shop windows and broken liquor bottles. On his last foray to the docks, before he took his convoy north, Paul Frillmann saw typewriters in the streets, along with clocks, cameras, clothing, and even jewels, while the looters who had abandoned them were chased down the alleys by rifle-bearing soldiers. This being the case, the chaplain felt justified in broadening his definition of essential war material: passing an abandoned automobile dealership, Frillmann and his assistants stepped inside, took the keys to three new Buicks, topped off their tanks with gasoline, and drove them back to Mingaladon airport.

On February 22, coastwise vessels began shuttling RAF ground personnel and heavy supplies around the west coast to Akyab, just as the transport carrying the 113th Squadron ground crews reached Rangoon. She stayed only long enough to take some wounded civilians and servicemen on board, then returned to India with the bewildered mechanics. Burwing was activated at Magwe the same day, The half-dozen Blenheims of the 113th Squadron moved back to this dusty, brick-red landing field, staging through Mingaladon or Highland Queen to unload their bombs on the Japanese army along the Sittang River. Local protection was provided by the four surviving Buffaloes of the 67th Squadron, joined a day later by four Hurricanes. Six Tomahawks also moved to Magwe, to provide air cover for the AVG convoy that would sooner or later leave Mingaladon by truck, jeep, and Buick sedan.

What the Adam & Eves found at Magwe was a base more interested in evacuation than in combat. Most of the multiengine planes in Burma—Douglas transports, ancient Valencia bombers, and six Lockheed Hudsons that had escaped from Singapore—were engaged in a day-long shuttle, flying RAF desk officers and high-priority civilians to India. Since there was no radar set at Magwe, a Blenheim circled all day as a "Jim Crow" sentinel, eighty miles south of the airport.

Fritz Wolf was one of the Adam & Eves at Magwe. He was supposed to carry on to Kunming, but when he asked for fuel he was told to wait: the evacuation took precedence. Trying again next morning, Wolf cooled his heels until 8:30 A.M., when the RAF arrived for work. Even then, nobody seemed to know whether the gasoline being pumped into his Tomahawk was 100 octane or not. Apparently it was, because Wolf made it to Kunming, where he informed Chennault that his Tomahawks in Burma were near collapse:

> The tires are baked and hard, and blow out on us continually. . . . [T]he battery plates are thin . . . and need recharging in a short time. There is no Prestone available at all. And there is no oxygen whatever. . . . The dust at Magwe and Rangoon fouls up the ship's engines considerably. It clogs the carbur[e]tion system to such an extent that it is dangerous to increase the manifold pressure of the [aircraft] as the engine quits cold. . . . This tendency of the engines to quit makes it impossible to dog-fight or strafe, especially at low altitude.

Wolf also talked to an American reporter, telling lurid stories of the death of Rangoon. Indian shopkeepers, he said, had given their keys to the Americans and told them to take what they wanted, rather than let the stuff fall into Japanese hands. Not to end his story on a downbeat note, the reporter had Wolf climbing back into his Tomahawk for the return to Burma. "It's hot in Rangoon," he supposedly said, "but all the fun is there."

Japanese propagandists also turned Wolf's story to account, reporting that "American volunteer pilots, who had been helping defend Rangoon and the Burma Road, fled to Kunming and reported that the city was in conflagration."

On the west bank of the Sittang, the Commonwealth army was defending a front that was also its best line of retreat. (If the 17th Indian Division fell back a few more miles, the Japanese would be astride the railroad and the highway from Rangoon to Mandalay.) At this perilous moment, the 7th Armoured Brigade reached Rangoon from North Africa with 114 lend-lease M-3 Honey tanks still bearing the symbol of the Desert Rat; they were immediately disembarked and sent to the Salween front. To the north, the leading divisions of the Chinese expeditionary force moved into the Shan Highlands. "All day long," wrote Leland Stowe, "you see them plodding the roads and bypaths, moving up and up toward the front, boyish little figures clad in worn, faded denim. With their visored hats of the same material, they look like coal miners in a child-labor district but they are carrying heavy packs and rifles and all sorts of equipment."

The Japanese, for their part, finished a 250-mile truck road from Phitsanulok to Moulmein, enabling them to bring supplies and bridging materials to the troops on the east bank of the Sittang. They mended the broken spans, mounted bicycles, and pedaled into Burma proper like Boy Scouts on summer holiday. Their only opposition was from the air. On February 24, the Adam & Eves crossed Martaban Bay to shoot up the Japanese airfields at Moulmein. An attack plane and two fighters were supposedly left burning on the ground, with the credit shared by Bill Bartling, George Burgard, Mac McGarry, Bob Neale, Bob Prescott, and Snuffy Smith. Four other Tomahawks escorted a flight of Blenheims to the infamous Belin-Kyaikto road, where they attacked a Japanese supply column that included artillery pieces drawn by oxen. The victims, according to press reports, were "thick as ants" on the road. Strafing was a gruesome business, and no American recorded the details, but a British pilot had this memory of it:

> There were horses, mules, dead and wounded Japs slumped on the road in all manner of grotesque attitudes, just as if they had been shoveled there by a giant spade. . . . I saw a number of them in their greeny-grey uniform scampering like mice for the cover of the trees. Squat bodies they appeared to have, and putteed bow-legs. . . . By the time I had wheeled on them they were almost under cover, but I caught the last dozen and with my fire jerked them to the ground where they sagged still. I'd never killed a man like that before.

The air strikes troubled the Japanese out of all proportion to the damage actually done. "Because of the gradual increase of the enemy's air strength," a Japanese officer complained after the war, "[and] its superiority in small planes, [our] divisions operated only at night." But why didn't the Japanese fighters provide air cover? The staff officer notwithstanding, they enjoyed a two-to-one advantage over the Allied fighters in South Burma.

Instead, General Obata was drawing up plans for another knockout blow on Mingaladon—an air superiority battle on the scale of those that had raged through the Burma sky during the first week of February. This time, he insisted on having some retractable-gear fighters that could match the Allied fighters for speed. Southern Army headquarters gave him the 47th Independent Chutai, the "Kingfisher squadron" that had been scheduled to take part in the Christmas raid on Rangoon. Alas, Major Toshio Sakagawa had lost even more fighters since December 25, and there were now only four *Ki*-44s on the squadron's roster. They flew to the main airfield at Moulmein, where Major Sakagawa and his pilots filled their tanks with aviation fuel left behind by the British. But on February 24 they were strafed by Tomahawks, which left one Shoki flaming on the field, along with a 14th Sentai Sally that had been forced down at Moulmein by a leaking fuel tank. (Bob Neale, George Burgard, Mac McGarry, and Bill Bartling were credited with destroying two fighters at Moulmein; Bob Prescott and Snuffy Smith shared credit for the bomber.) That left the 47th Independent Chutai with three Shokis to contribute to the attack on Mingaladon airport.

The battle began on February 25. To direct the campaign, Obata moved his headquarters that Wednesday morning to Lampang near the head of the Thai railroad, equidistant from Rangoon and Toungoo. His opening move would be a fighter sweep consisting of twenty-three Nates from the 77th Sentai (which had also moved to Lampang) plus twenty-one from the 50th Sentai, backed up by the three Shokis.

The Adam & Eves nearly missed the battle. Smoke from the burning city had combined with early morning fog to reduce visibility to half the length of John Haig field, a new dispersal field due north of Mingaladon. (On the baseball diamond that was the airfield layout outside Rangoon, John Haig would have been the pitcher's mound.) As was the rule in Burma, the Tomahawks took off from both ends of the sod strip, the pilots keeping as far right as they dared, and kicking more right rudder as soon as their wheels left the ground.

When the alarm went off at 10:30 A.M., the Adam & Eves put up only six Tomahawks, in two flights led by Bob Neale and Bob Little. "A hazy day made a will-o'-the wisp game out of it," Greg Boyington recalled. "Here they are. No, they aren't." Little, Boyington, and Charlie Bond charged after a phantom formation and missed the combat altogether. So did the RAF.

That left Neale and his wingmen to make the interception—three against twenty. Neale claimed two Nates, and two more were credited to Bob Prescott, but the identity of the other pilot is a mystery. So is the identity of their opponents. All the Japanese squadrons claimed to have been in combat, against twenty Allied fighters, of which they shot down sixteen! In fact, no planes were lost on either side.

At midday, some Blenheims came down from Magwe, circled Mingaladon while the Tomahawks came up, then flew across Martaban Bay and blasted the docks at Moulmein. The formation returned to Mingaladon, and in a fatal error of judgment the Blenheim pilots decided to stay put for the afternoon. They belonged to the 45th Squadron, which was replacing the 113th Squadron at Magwe.

The siren wailed again at 4 P.M. Again the Tomahawks and Hurricanes scrambled to intercept the Japanese formation. Soon after takeoff, Ed Leibolt's engine began to falter. At 6,000 feet he opened his canopy, either to bail out or to improve his vision for a forced landing. Dick Rossi took over Leibolt's flight, and did not see him again.

Bob Neale estimated that the Japanese formation contained twelve twin-engined bombers and more than thirty fighters. The bombers were Kawasaki *Ki*-48 Lilys of the 8th Sentai, escorted by the same troop of Nates and Shokis that had swept Mingaladon that morning. The bombers were "damn well protected," Neale grumbled in his diary. But some of the Allied fighters managed to get through to them, as reported by a Japanese war correspondent aboard the Lily piloted by Lieutenant Choji Onodera:

> About sixty enemy planes were proceeding toward our direction in a mass formation, their machine guns spitting blue flames menacingly. . . . I pictured the proud expressions of . . . my friends in the fighter craft as I saw the enemy planes being sent crashing toward the earth. . . .
>
> One of the enemy fighters . . . challenged the plane on which I was aboard. Blue flames spitting endlessly from eight machine guns . . . reminded me that we were in the midst of a hail of bullets. Fortunately none of them found their mark. As the enemy plane started to loop in order to get into a better attacking position, our gunner let fly and a second later it was commencing its death-descent, leaving a trail of black smoke in the air.

Bob Neale was credited with two more Nates that afternoon, putting him ahead of Jack Newkirk as top scorer in the AVG. Mac McGarry was credited with shooting down no fewer than four fighters. Charlie Bond, George Burgard, and Snuffy Smith were each credited with three kills, and Dick Rossi with one. John Blackburn (Blackie) also scored, the first of the former CAF flight instructors to be blooded. There were two other claims by the Adam & Eves, but the names of the pilots do not appear on Chennault's breakout of victories. The Hurricane pilots claimed six kills, making a grand total of twenty-five. Alas for legend! The Japanese lost only two fighters that afternoon, both from the 50th Sentai. Allied losses came to one Hurricane shot down and one Tomahawk missing— Ed Leibolt's.

The major damage to the Allied air force was done by the bombers. With line chief John Carter and some others, Don Rodewald was working on Tomahawk No. 33 that day, on a low hill 1,000 yards from the runway. When the siren went off, the technicians kept working. It had been weeks, after all, since Mingaladon was attacked during daylight hours. Then Carter yelled: "Look at that formation of bombers!" The technicians ran for shelter on the lee side of the hill, as Rode told the story in his diary:

> I went right thru briers and everything without stopping to put on a shirt. . . . About that time we saw all twelve bombers cut loose. . . . There must have been about 30 or 40 bombs at once. When they get close you can hear the wind whistle then the earth shakes and it's all over. We were about ten feet below the terrain so just stood and watched. Heard a little schapnel drop around us. We then came out of hiding and saw the airdrome ablaze. Those Japs hit direct.

Indeed they did, destroying an Indian Air Force Lysander, damaging five Blenheims, and killing one of the bomber pilots.

Curiously, none of the Adam & Eves mentioned fighting any "Zero types" that afternoon, though Lieutenant Yasuhiko Kuroe recalled that the Shokis had tangled with the Tomahawks. The three big-engined interceptors were flying in string, Major Sakagawa in the lead, followed by a lieutenant named Mitsumoto and then by Kuroe. (Because the 47th was a test-bed for the *Ki-44*, all its pilots were officers.) The major jinked wildly to avoid a Tomahawk boring in from the left, then went after another of the Allied fighters. Lieutenant Mitsumoto chased a third—and was himself pursued by a fourth Tomahawk, while Kuroe watched helplessly from a distance:

> This was the most dangerous enemy, because Sakagawa and Mitsumoto were attacking and could not look around, so they did not see the enemy

fighter, which was positioned outside of the battle area and now came to attack. . . . I went after him, but I was not fast enough. The enemy . . . fired at Mitsumoto, then turned upside down and got out of the battlefield by diving fast.

In other words, the Tomahawk executed a split-S, but not before putting several bullets through the Shoki. Though wounded in the back, Lieutenant Mitsumoto was able to return to Moulmein with his comrades.

The Sallys returned that night in their customary numbers: three planes, three metric tons of high explosives. In one of those displays of high-level bravado, Colonel Hironaka led the raid. His bombs finished the destruction of two Blenheims that had been too badly damaged to fly back to Magwe for the night.

The Tomahawks and Hurricanes were supposed to strafe Moulmein airfield next morning, February 26, but a false alarm sent the Adam & Eves aloft at 8 A.M. "Since we are already airborne," Bob Neale said, "let's go to Moulmein." Without the usual top cover of Hurricanes, he led the flight—consisting of himself, George Burgard, Bob Little, Mac McGarry, Bob Prescott, Joe Rosbert, and Dick Rossi—across Martaban Bay. They first hit the former RAF dispersal field at Mudon, an 800-meter strip south of Moulmein that now served as a forward base for the 77th Sentai and the 47th Chutai. As it happened, the Nates and Shokis had just returned from a raid on Zayatkwin. (This would have been the cause of the false alarm at Mingaladon.) As Joe Rosbert described the scene, there were only two planes on the airstrip, and the Adam & Eves required only one pass to put them out of action:

> We left the two planes in ruins as we quickly headed north. The east side of Moulmein was ridged with hills, so we made our initial approach over them directly out of the rising sun. As we came down from the ridge and neared the field, a wonderful sight met our eyes. The Japs had a little warning from the auxiliary field. Some of them were just getting into their planes and others were already making their takeoff runs.

These were the Nates of the 50th Sentai, now commanded by Major Tadashi Ishikawa. They too had just returned from the raid on Zayatkwin. With flak bursting all around them—the Japanese gunners "did not seem to have any regard for the safety of their own planes," Rosbert marveled—three Nates got into the air.

The first flight of Tomahawks swept down in a diving turn and hit the climbing Nates 400 feet above the runway. One of the Japanese pilots clawed up to escape Bob Neale's machine gun fire, only to make a perfect target for George Burgard, who claimed him as a kill. Meanwhile, the following Tomahawks strafed the field, but more Nates got off the ground and chased the raiders out over Martaban Bay. Two of the fixed-gear fighters glued themselves to Bob Neale's tail. Flying fifty feet above the water, he could not execute the customary half-roll and power dive, so he made himself small in front of his armor plate and prayed for the big Allison to haul him out of danger, which it eventually did. "Japs can't hit the side of a barn door," he said upon landing.

Paul Perry surveyed the damage. "Maybe not," the armorer said, "but they can sure hit a P-40." Neale's Tomahawk had seventeen rifle-caliber holes in the fuselage and tail, plus a fist-sized one that was probably the result of flak.

Later in the morning, Dick Rossi and Charlie Bond went out to look for Ed Leibolt, who had not reported in from yesterday's mishap. They flew a search grid over the rice fields west of the airport, but saw no wreckage, and after an hour they went back to Mingaladon. Before they could land, they saw alert crews sprinting to the flight line, so they circled around and waited for the other Tomahawks to come up. The Adam & Eves managed to put 18,000 feet of airspace below them before the raiders came into view. The Japanese formation was virtually the same as the day before—twelve Lilys of the 8th Sentai, escorted by about forty Nates from the 50th and 77th Sentais—and again the Tomahawks found it almost impossible to break through to the bombers. The only one to get any hits on a Lily was Snuffy Smith. It was a legitimate kill, as Japanese records show. (A second Lily crash-landed upon returning to Nakhon Sawan.) As for the Nates, the Adam & Eves claimed at least seventeen for the day, including the action on the other side of Martaban Bay. Bob Neale, Dick Rossi, and George Burgard were each credited with destroying three Japanese fighters; Bob Little, Mac McGarry, and Joe Rosbert with two apiece; and Blackie Blackburn and Charlie Bond with one each.

According to Japanese records, however, only one Nate had been destroyed that morning at Mudon, with another badly damaged.

Similarly, the toll over Mingaladon was one Nate shot down. All were from the 77th Sentai.

Late in the day on February 26, three Tomahawks were flown away from Mingaladon as unfit for combat. (One of them was flown by Jim Cross, who had taken a machine gun burst through his cockpit in the afternoon scrap, leaving him with a cut in his cheek and several bits of shrapnel in his shoulder. The injuries proved serious enough that Cross was eventually sent to India for treatment.) Three planes came down from Kunming to replace them, but one of these had to make a dead-stick landing when its engine quit on the final approach. It was a symbol of the Allied air force in South Burma: the men staggering with exhaustion, the planes flying wrecks. There was no oxygen at Mingaladon except for the bottles actually in the cockpits. The airport guards had left. The antiaircraft gunners were so jumpy that they had fired on the Adam & Eves taking off on the noon scramble.

Altogether, the claims that arose from the February 25–26 air battle were stupendous. The Adam & Eves eventually settled on forty-three Japanese aircraft destroyed. Several more were credited to the RAF, and by the time the newspaper correspondents were done with the story, the Allied tally stood at 104, which would have accounted for just about every aircraft under General Obata's command.

The Japanese pilots were every bit as optimistic. They too claimed forty-three enemy aircraft destroyed during the two-day air superiority battle.

At sundown on February 26, the Adam & Eves dispersed their Tomahawks to John Haig. They stopped at Eighteen Mile Ranch on their way home, to wolf down Clayton Harpold's chow and listen to the 14th Sentai blasting Mingaladon for the second night in a row. The rumor for the evening was that the Japanese had cut the road to Prome and Magwe—a serious matter, if true, for this was the escape route for the AVG technicians and the pilots who had no planes to fly.

Most of the men went to bed after dinner, but Bob Neale returned to the airport for his nightly conference with Group Captain Broughall. There he learned that the radar set had been disassembled and sent up to Magwe. As the story was told, the information was dropped ever so casually at the end of their meeting: "I say, Neale, you'll have a bit shorter warning tomorrow." Indeed, since the Burma Observation Corps was also pulling out of South Burma, the Adam & Eves could count on no warning whatever. Chennault had given Neale permission to leave Mingaladon on March 1—Sunday. Tomorrow was Friday, and it did not seem worth risking the squadron by a foolish regard for forty-eight hours. Shortly after midnight, Neale made the rounds of the billets and shook the pilots awake. "Let's get the heck out of here, fellows," he remembered telling them. "We don't have any air raid warning at all. There's no sense keeping a fighter bunch around here to get caught on the ground." The pilots then routed the technicians, as Don Rodewald recalled:

> About 2:30 A.M. today I was woke up and told we were moving out, that the Japs were in dangerous position to us and the British had taken out their radio direction finder. I rolled my bed and threw it on my truck with my one traveling bag (always packed). That took all of 15 minutes then I drove to the airdrome and loaded the remaining armament equipment. By 5 A.M. was ready to leave. [Mingaladon] was completely evacuated. . . . The Limeys sure do give up before they know they are licked.

Several Tomahawks had been left overnight at Mingaladon airport, including Jim Cross's shot-up No. 78. The technicians worked through the night to put them in flying condition. At daybreak, two Tomahawks were still unfit to fly. The others were flown up to John Haig. Another group of pilots drove through the morning mist for the last time and mounted the Tomahawks that had spent the night in dispersal. While they waited for the takeoff order, they heard antiaircraft guns barking to the northeast. The 14th Sentai was blasting Johnnie Walker, which the AVG had stopped using the week before.

The first to leave was Bob Little, with a flight of six Tomahawks bound for China. The AVG technicians assembled at milepost forty-nine on the Prome road, their convoy scheduled to depart at noon. After a lunch of canned pork and beans, Charlie Bond and three other Adam & Eves took off for Magwe. They buzzed the convoy in a gesture of goodwill that sent the technicians scrambling for the ditch; then they flew up to their new base. George Burgard and Mac McGarry immediately refueled and went back south to patrol the convoy route. The AVG trucks and cars reached Prome—safely above any Japanese cross-country thrust—at 5 P.M. From there to Magwe was a distance of seventy miles. They figured it would take them two hours, but the road was nothing more than a cart track, and they did not reach their new post until midnight. When they asked the RAF duty officer where they were to bunk, he told them to camp on the polo field.

The pilots also got to bed late, having checked out the American Club at Yenangyaung, an oilfield settlement where they found iced drinks and a swimming pool. Returning to Magwe in the early hours, they found bunks in the hostel belonging to the 67th Squadron. The Adam & Eves were pleased to discover that most of the RAF pilots were not Englishmen but sturdy New Zealanders, willing and eager to master the AVG pastime of acey-deucey.

Bob Neale and Snuffy Smith spent a nervous night at Mingaladon airport, hoping that Ed Leibolt would walk in as so many pilots had done over the past three months: George McMillan, Paul Greene, Eddie Overend, Gil Bright, Bert Christman, Moose Moss. . . . In the morning they took the radio out of the baggage compartment behind Neale's seat, figuring that Leibolt could squeeze in there if he had to. But Leibolt did not walk in. Neale and Smith finally voiced aloud what in their hearts they already believed—that he had been murdered by Burmese partisans. Twenty-five years old, a graduate of Miami University, Leibolt had been an army bomber pilot before coming to Burma with the Bloom Gang. When the AVG cashed in at the end of its tour, his CAMCO bonus account stood at the improbable sum of $133.33, representing his share from the December 20 firefight near Kunming.*

Late in the day, the two pilots took off for Magwe, only to miss the airport in the smoke haze that blanketed South Burma to an altitude of 15,000 feet. Smith bent a prop putting down in a river bed at Myingyan, 100 miles beyond Magwe. Neale made a flawless landing in a peanut field at Singu, closer in, but did not have enough gas to take off again.

That was Saturday, February 28. On the same day, the British hoisted the "H" signal in Rangoon, leaving only demolition teams in the city. A half-dozen Hurricanes ("X" wing, this rump unit was designated) still covered the Rangoon area, operating out of Highland Queen. At

---

* Leibolt never turned up. In later years, Neale came to believe that his missing pilot had recovered power, returned to the fight, and been shot down over Martaban Bay.

Mingaladon itself, only wrecks and dummies remained, artfully laid out to convince scout planes that the Allied air force was still guarding the capital.

On Thursday, March 5, Burma's new field commander finally reached Rangoon. General Alexander canceled the 17th Indian Division's withdrawal plans and told the 1st Burma Division to move south, but the time for such resolution had long since passed. On the west bank of the Sittang, the Japanese columns had crossed paths, the 55th Division driving north against Toungoo, the 33rd dashing west to cut the Prome road. As the Japanese bomber squadrons had so often done, General Sakurai intended to attack Rangoon from the far side.

On Saturday, March 7, the last charges were blown in the city. Toward midnight, launches took the demolition teams out to three steamers waiting in the river, while Rangoon burned luridly behind them. Indeed, the river itself was ablaze, as thousands of gallons of tung oil from China spilled from the docks and caught fire.

In one of those great coincidences of war, the 17th Indian Division found its retreat blocked by a Japanese force not far from Eighteen Mile Ranch. The Commonwealth column and the 33rd Division were crossing paths. But, rather than reveal his intention to attack Rangoon from the northwest, the Japanese commander ordered the roadblock out of the way, and the Commonwealth troops went by, mystified but relieved.

On Sunday morning, the 33rd Division drove into Rangoon, to find it empty and burning. The hour was 10 A.M., March 8, 1942—the first time in 118 years that nonwhites controlled the capital and major port of Burma. Despite the demolition work, and despite the looting, the Japanese recovered 19,000 tons of China's lend-lease supplies from the Rangoon docks.

Next day, the Dutch colonial army surrendered in Java. Except for the U.S. and Filipino troops still holding out on the Bataan Peninsula, the Pacific Rim was entirely Japanese, south to Australia and west to India.

Among the RAF units that quit Rangoon toward the end of February were the scavenger teams that inspected Japanese wrecks and gathered intelligence on the planes opposing the Allied air forces. (As a result of their work, the Commonwealth airmen knew the difference between the

Nakajima Hayabusa and the Mitsubishi Zero, and they did not confuse the army Nate and the navy Claude, as the Americans did.) In his post-campaign dispatch, Air Vice Marshal Stevenson summed up the results of the scavenger hunt:

> Although air fighting frequently took place over scrub or jungle country, 32 crashed enemy fighters and bombers were located on the ground up to the fall of Rangoon. Technical examination of these—although many were burnt or otherwise destroyed beyond recognition—established the quality of equipment about which little was previously known.

Thirty-two! To be sure, some Japanese aircraft had been destroyed over Thailand and behind enemy lines in Burma, and others probably lay undiscovered in the rain forest and beneath the waters of Martaban Bay. Whatever allowance is made for them, it remains a fact that a mammoth gap exists between the British scavenger count and the scores popularly attributed to Chennault's pilots. (The AVG romances often had the British locating thirty or more aircraft after a single raid.) At most, the pilots and antiaircraft gunners at Mingaladon airport may have destroyed fifty Japanese planes in the air and on the ground, up to the fall of Rangoon. Given that a large proportion were bombers, the JAAF may have lost 150 airmen in its effort to subdue the Allied air force in South Burma. By every account, the vast majority fell to the guns of the AVG.

For their part, five of Chennault's pilots were killed in action: Neil Martin, Hank Gilbert, Bert Christman, Cokey Hoffman, and Tom Cole. Two were missing: Charlie Mott and Ed Leibolt. Three were accidentally killed at Mingaladon or flying to Kunming: Lacy Mangleburg, Ken Merritt, and Sandy Sandell. About twenty Tomahawks were shot down or otherwise destroyed.

Even allowing for the home-field advantage, the AVG gave the JAAF far better than it got: two-to-one in aircraft, twelve-to-one in personnel. It was a magnificent victory, though small in comparison to the boasts that were current in the winter of 1941–1942, and that have been magnified at intervals ever since.

Did You Have Any Warning?

February–March 1942

While his squadrons fought the good fight in Burma, Chennault battled the military bureaucracy from Kunming. At the end of January, all the pieces of the grand compromise seemed to be in place: he would become a brigadier general, commanding U.S. air force personnel in China while continuing to lead the AVG by virtue of his parallel (if ambiguous) rank in Chinese service. In July, his mercenaries would be inducted into the U.S. Army, thus merging his two roles.

Then came the wrecking ball. General Marshall had never trusted Chennault or his schemes, and when the AVG was approved over the chief of staff's objections, he had set out to bring it under his control. This campaign now intersected Chennault's. Marshall needed someone to take command of the U.S. effort in China, Burma, and India. He picked Major General Joseph Stilwell, who as a colonel had served as U.S. military attaché in Beijing and Chongqing. Like Marshall, Stilwell was upright to a fault, but unlike Marshall he had no understanding of the role politics played in war. He was "Vinegar Joe," the quintessential infantryman, with a footsoldier's tough body, narrow mind, and salty tongue. To Stilwell, the wheelchair-bound American president was "Old Rubberlegs." His British allies were "bastardly hypocrites." Chiang Kai-shek was the "peanut dictator," the "little dummy," the "grasping, bigoted, ungrateful little rattlesnake," and the "stubborn, ignorant, prejudiced, conceited despot who has never heard the truth except from me." Altogether, to read Stilwell's diary is to be first amused, then sickened, by the venom of the man chosen to command U.S. forces in Asia—and not just American forces. Before he left Washington, Stilwell demanded and got a promise that he would command the *Chinese* army as well.

But his elevation was a minor annoyance compared to that of Colonel Clayton Bissell, who at the Air Corps Tactical School had maddened Chennault with his views on fighter tactics. Chennault learned of the appointment in a good news/bad news radiogram from Lauchlin Currie. Yes, he would command any U.S. Army fighter and light bomber groups sent to China. No, he would not be in charge of the heavy bomber groups. Another officer would be assigned to that job, with "Bissell over all."

Not if Chennault could help it:

> Personally am willing make any sacrifice for sake of China and Allied cause but cannot understand how either will be benefitted by superseding me as senior air officer China. Particularly when officer selected, Bissell, was junior to me until my retirement. In addition he has no knowledge of conditions in China. . . . Am most discouraged by attitude War Department and quite willing resume private life as health continues poor.

Currie responded with soothing syrup, which only encouraged Chennault to press the attack:

> Greatly appreciate your motive in sending wire because China's interest is of paramount importance. But I do not believe Bissell can handle situation out here. He is very headstrong and has always differed with me in regard to pursuit tactics.

Currie tried, pleading Chennault's case in a February 9 meeting in Washington. "I spoke for Bissell," Stilwell noted in his diary, "and insisted that he rank Chennault." As Stilwell told the story, Currie backed down and promised to tell Chennault "to get in the game and play ball"—a phrase that occurs again and again in Stilwell's diary. The good soldier did what he was told; the good soldier played ball. "They are acting like a couple of kids," he grumbled of Currie and Chennault, "and they'll both have to behave."

Currie phrased it more tactfully in his radiogram to Chennault, which he routed through T. V. Soong: "[Hap] Arnold is of opinion that you are A-1 as combat man and has fullest praise for AVG, but he wants member of his own staff to head larger show. . . . Bissell has now changed to your views on tactics and Stilwell adds you will have free hand regarding tactics." At the same time, Currie asked John Magruder to intercede with "Groco," as Chennault was known in radio traffic:

> Arnold and Stillwell [sic] insist on Bissell. . . . I wired Groco through T. V. informing him of decision and asking him to be content with full and free pursuit command. You could help in easing this difficult situation. Army is prepared to make Groco a B.G. shortly. His services must not be lost. Bissell can get equipment and in operation he will be under Stillwell and generalissimo.

Magruder did his best, but the result was not encouraging. On February 13, passing through Kunming on his way to India, he radioed Currie: "Groco told me confidentially . . . that if he had to work under Bissell he would resign." After returning to Chongqing, Magruder had the glimmering of a compromise: while Chennault "firmly believes that neither he nor Chinese officers can work harmoniously under Bissell because of latter's high-handed methods and way of accomplishing objectives," still, "he would welcome Bissell as his adviser if such step would facilitate equipment." But on March 2, he was back where he had started: "Groco insists he is willing to do anything for China's good, but feels under proposed organization [it is] best for him to resign."

Of course, there was no possibility that Chennault would let go of the AVG, now that parts, planes, and even pilots were moving toward China at last. Thirty Tomahawk propellers and fourteen Allison replacement engines had reached the CAMCO factory at Loiwing. *Silver Star* was overdue at Calcutta with a load of tires and gun solenoids. (To expedite the cargo, Chennault sent Lieutenant Commander Robert DeWolfe—his latter-day Joe Alsop—to open an AVG office in Calcutta.) Best of all, the first batch of Lauchlin Currie's replacement fighters had reached Accra on the Gold Coast of Africa, in what is now the nation of Ghana, and had been assembled there by U.S. Army personnel. However, the army reneged on its promise to fly the planes to China, forcing Chennault to detail six of his combat pilots to pick them up.

The ferry crew flew to Calcutta on CNAC, then to Cairo by British Overseas Airways, and finally to Accra on a U.S. Army Douglas flown under contract by Pan American Airways—7,500 miles in twelve days. "Our new ships are here on the field, ready to go," wrote R. T. Smith when he got there. "They look pretty good to us too." *Good* meant powerful. This was the jut-jawed fighter that had replaced the Tomahawk on the Curtiss assembly line, so earnestly desired by the RAF that it had given up 100 of the earlier model to China. "The ships are quite a little nicer than the Tomahawks," R. T. went on. "These are called Kittyhawks, and have better cockpit arrangement, six 50 cal. m.g.'s, more power, speed, etc." Trying them out, he and Paul Greene "put on a little show for the Pan Am boys" at the airport. Then they set out to the eastward, the Kittyhawks still emblazoned with the five-pointed star of the Army Air Forces. Before they reached Kunming, six more Hell's Angels would be on their way to Accra. Altogether, to fetch twelve replacement fighters, Chennault tied up half a squadron for most of a month.

He lost two more pilots to resignation, including Noel Bacon of the Panda Bears, with 3.5 enemy aircraft to his credit. Bacon went home on what was supposed to be compassionate leave, but actually to get married; and while he was home he rejoined the navy with the rank of lieutenant.

Attended by a lieutenant, three colonels, and a brigadier general, Stilwell flew to Africa on *Anzac Clipper*, a Pan Am flying boat that had been shifted to the South Atlantic run. He crossed paths with the AVG ferry pilots over Saudi Arabia, and in Calcutta had an interview with the Allied commander for Asia. Sir Archibald Wavell impressed him as "a tired, depressed man, pretty well beaten down" from his defeat in the Dutch Indies. (In Stilwell's lexicon of contempt, the general thereafter was "Bumble Wavell.") Also in Calcutta was Major General Lewis Brereton, "slapping his fanny with his riding crop and darting around importantly." As the designated commander of the U.S. 10th Air Force, with seven warplanes and the world's largest theater of operations, Brereton would be able to give orders to Bissell and Chennault—but not to Stilwell, as the latter took pains to inform him. The message did not get through: when Wavell set out for a conference with Chiang Kai-shek in Burma, he took Brereton but left Stilwell and his entourage to follow as best they could.

On his way to the inter-allied conference, the generalissimo and madame stopped off at Kunming. The occasion was memorialized by Dan Hoyle in the 3rd Squadron log:

General Issimo Chiang Kai Shek and the Madame were at the Hostel and
at 7:00 P.M. a Banquet was given in honour of the Generals visit and the
achievements of the A.V.G. . . . There was a play done in the Chinese
custom, we could not very well understand it as it was all in Chinese. The
master of ceremonies gave us a synopsis of the story which helped. Some
Chinese lady who had a music degree from Smith College . . . sang three
songs for us. The General, Madame and Colonel Chennault were the
main speakers.

Madame addressed the Americans as "my boys" and "angels with or
without wings"—words that might have been expected to send those
tough young men into fits of laughter. But they were enchanted, most
of them. "She absolutely captured our hearts," John Donovan told his
family. "We cheered her to the rafters time and again." Radioman
Robert M. Smith wrote in his diary: "We are all proud to fight for
China." Gil Bright, late of the Ivy League, was more skeptical. "Madame
gushed a bit," Bright reported. "She thinks airplanes are just too-o-o
romantic. One of the pilots from New England said she was just an old
Wellesley girl that was on fire with the cause."

Greg Boyington skipped this part of the program. Chennault had
taken the precaution of closing the bar in the recreation room, but
Boyington had his own supply, and with Percy Bartelt caroused in the
hall during the speeches. The two pilots then made a drunken entry,
falling over their chairs and loudly applauding the Chinese singer.

Accompanied by Chennault and an honor guard of six Tomahawks,
Chiang Kai-shek flew to Lashio next day to meet Wavell. He saw
Stilwell, too, but only in passing. Always quick to take offense, Stilwell
felt that the Chinese were snubbing him, and—an hour after arriving
in Lashio—he ordered his chartered plane to Kunming, where he
spent the night in Chennault's bed at Hostel Number One. Next
morning he installed Brigadier General Franklin Sibert as his local
representative, and himself went to Wu Chia Ba to wait for Chennault
to fly in from Lashio. "Had a talk," Stilwell wrote. "He'll be O.K. Met
a group of the pilots, they look damn good." Much relieved by the
encounter, he left for Chongqing and a briefing by "Magruder's
stooges" at the U.S. Military Mission.

The Chiangs also stopped at Kunming on their way to Chongqing.
There was another fete in their honor, and this time madame gave the
pilots something solid to cheer about. The $500 bonus, promised by the

CAMCO recruiters for each Japanese plane shot down, would indeed be paid, not only for shoot-downs but also for aircraft destroyed on the ground.

Harvey Greenlaw then detailed six pilots to put on an air show for the Chiangs. Led by Whitey Lawlor, they dove to near-ground level, rolled onto their backs, and screamed across the field upside down. Bob Layher was tail man. He became confused when the other planes disappeared from sight (his inverted position required him to push his stick *forward* in order to climb) and nearly flew into the ground. As the story is told, Layher's Tomahawk came so close to Chennault and the Chiangs that they had to throw themselves face-first on the gravel.

The honor guard accompanied the "flying palace" as far as Chanyi, with Greg Boyington now leading. (Lawlor aborted when he lost the door to his baggage compartment.) Alas, Boyington's compass was defective, and when he left the Chiangs he led his flight south instead of west. The Tomahawks eventually ran out of gas near the Yunnan-Indochina border. Boyington, Red Probst, and Gil Bright bellied in together; Hank Geselbracht crashed some miles away, and Layher more distant yet. "The Colonel," Bus Keeton noted in his diary, in what must have been the understatement of the month, "gave us a talk about the terrain . . . and a little bit on how to navigate in China." In time, Boyington flew one of the Tomahawks to Mengzi, but the others had to be written off.

In Chongqing, meanwhile, General Stilwell was having his first formal meeting with the Chiangs. It went very well, apparently. On March 7, even as the last-ditchers were leaving Rangoon, he composed this optimistic assessment for Marshall:

> Believe Chennault matter can be handled satisfactorily and AVG inducted within reasonable time. A short message of appreciation to Chennault from the Sec[retary of] War for his excellent work would help greatly. Request this be done.

On March 11, the Chinese Air Force gave honorary commissions to the four American pilots who had died in Burma since the beginning of the year. Each was promoted one grade from his rank-equivalent in the AVG: Sandy Sandell to lieutenant colonel, Bert Christman and Cokey Hoffman to major, Tom Cole to captain.

But the juicy promotions went to the U.S. Army officers in Chongqing. All through March, there was a blizzard of radiograms to the War Department on this pleasant subject, and on such related matters as insurance policies and family allotments. Stilwell was first, of course. No sooner did he reach Chongqing than he was promoted to lieutenant general—three stars. Then he arranged for Franklin Sibert to be bumped up to two-star rank. Promotions followed for most of the officers on his staff, though not for poor John Magruder. A high-strung officer with the temperament of a file clerk, Magruder was held in undisguised contempt by the newcomers.

By the time the promotion fever had run its course, the U.S. Army in China consisted of seventeen enlisted men under the direction of *sixty-seven* officers, and more were on the way. On March 19, three more colonels reached China, including the ball-and-chain advocate from the Tactical School. Three years younger than Chennault, Bissell was a prim, frail officer who dressed for East Asia in the British fashion, in pith helmet and khaki bush jacket. Stilwell immediately cranked the promotion engine to life on his behalf:

> Strongly recommend Colonel Clayton L. Bissell . . . be appointed temporary brigadier general according to my conversation with Arnold prior to my departure. Recommendation on Chennault will be submitted later.

Later. There was the rub: in military service, officers of the same rank fall into a pecking order determined by "time in grade." Bissell would be Chennault's superior if he ranked him by a single day.

When the new colonels were in place, Stilwell's headquarters asked for four majors and four captains. (This requisition was followed by an "urgent request" for four typewriter ribbons.) And when one of the colonels died in the crash of a CNAC Douglas near Kunming, the overriding concern was to replace him with more of the same. Rather overlooking Chennault's credentials, Bissell radioed Washington that the tragedy left him as the "only air officer in China-Burma area." To plug this terrible gap, he asked for three air force colleagues by name.

Chennault, to be sure, was not entirely uninterested in the trappings of command. Unable to requisition staff members, he picked them up where he could, as when Doreen Lonborg walked into the AVG radio station at Chanyi, having trekked a thousand miles from Fort Baya by foot, sedan chair, train, and truck. On March 17 she married Daffy Davis—China hand turned AVG staff officer—in a ceremony at Hostel

Number One, and the following day she went to work in Chennault's office at the airport.

One of Mrs. Davis's first tasks was to type Memorandum No. 20, in which Chennault set out a dress code for the AVG. Henceforth, on formal occasions, a wingman would wear a garrison cap with CAF star, an olive drab uniform jacket with Sam Browne belt and two blue shoulder stripes, a white shirt with a black tie, uniform trousers, and brown shoes. There were less elaborate schedules for "undress" and "service" duty, but a pilot was expected to wear his shoulder tabs even in the cockpit. The chaplain too was militarized: one silver stripe, consistent with his status as the lowest-ranking staff officer. By contrast, a pilot attached to headquarters rated two and a half stripes, putting him half a stripe ahead of a wingman on combat duty.

The best that could be said of Magwe was that the evenings were lovely. The sun went down in a rosy glow over the Arakan Hills, marking the Burma-India border, whereupon the mountains seemed to float like clouds in the dusk. The spectacular sunsets resulted from the dust and flame attending the collapse of the British Empire.

The Adam & Eves operated out of a small dirt airfield three miles south of town. It was surrounded by scrubby trees, cactus, thorn bushes, and a few rough buildings. There were no revetments or dispersal pens, and the mountains made it easy for aircraft to approach unseen. To improve security, RAF engineers built a secondary field (Maida Vale) north of Magwe, on the road to Yenangyaung, and they set up their peripatetic radar station at a third location, with radio links to the airfields. This tired old device could only scan an arc of 45°, so it was aimed southeast, to detect planes coming up the Irrawaddy from Rangoon as well as those traveling cross-lots from Chiang Mai in Thailand. The ground observer corps was similarly biased: watchers were stationed with the Commonwealth troops to the south, and with the Chinese army at Toungoo, but there were none to the north or west.

Group Captain Seton Broughall assigned the Adam & Eves to just one offensive mission during their fortnight at Magwe, and that one was a bust. Hearing that the Japanese were reshuffling their sentais in northern Thailand, Broughall laid on a spoiling raid for March 5. The target was Lampang, home base for Major Yoshioka's 77th Sentai.

Eight Blenheims, six Hurricanes, four Buffaloes, and an undetermined number of Tomahawks went along. The fighters flew 200 miles east to Namsang, an RAF outpost in the Shan Highlands, to refuel and wait for the Blenheims. But instead of circling the field until the fighters came up, the bombers barreled on through. The Adam & Eves flew down to the Thai border but saw neither the Blenheims nor the Japanese, so they returned to Namsang, thence to Magwe.

Bunny Stone's Hurricanes were still based at Highland Queen near Rangoon. There, on March 6, they were caught by the 77th Sentai, losing two planes on the ground. The squadron hid out at Mingaladon airport next day, among the wrecks and the dummies; then it moved 125 miles north to Zigon, a field so rough that it tore the tail wheels from their Hurricanes. The squadron fell back to Prome on March 10 and to Magwe a day later. By this time, the 67th Squadron had flown off to India, leaving the 17th Squadron with fifteen Hurricanes as the only RAF fighter unit in the Irrawaddy Valley. There were some RAF Lysanders at Magwe, too, along with a dozen Blenheims and eight Tomahawks. At Akyab on the coast, Group Captain Neal Singer commanded an even smaller force: six Hurricanes and some light bombers, including the Indian Air Force Lysanders and the Hudsons from Singapore. Altogether, the Allied air force in Burma came to about fifty planes, most of them long past their useful lives.

The only reinforcement in view was Lewis Brereton's 10th Air Force, consisting of six Boeing B-17 Flying Fortresses and the Consolidated B-24 Liberator that had flown Brereton and Wavell out of the Dutch Indies. They were based at Dum Dum airport in Calcutta, from which they could easily have supported the Commonwealth army in Burma. Instead, the huge bombers were used to move a battalion of Royal Inniskillin Fusileers into Magwe, bringing in 470 soldiers and taking out a like number of RAF personnel and high-priority refugees.

Despairing of finding a place in the airlift, hundreds of European and mixed-blood civilians drove on to Mandalay, hoping that by the time they got there the rescue operation would be better organized. The Indian refugees did not aspire so high. They had walked most of the way from Rangoon, and they kept on walking, by their thousands, over the Arakan Hills that looked so gentle in the twilight but were so brutal in reality.

Chennault made no effort to reinforce his half-squadron at Magwe, though Charlie Bond and Blackie Blackburn were allowed to fly two of the worst cases to Kunming and swap them for better aircraft. They brought back the news that the Hell's Angels would soon be down to replace them. The Adam & Eves were sorry to hear it: they had learned to enjoy life at Magwe, especially the nightly round trip to the Yenangyaung oilfields, where the American Club offered the only iced drinks in Burma. Furthermore, Bond and Blackburn also brought back word of the $500 combat bonus, which put a whole new light on the task of fighting the JAAF.

The correspondents who had celebrated the AVG victories at Mingaladon, and who had followed the Adam & Eves to Magwe, were on hand to greet the Hell's Angels:

AMERICAN VOLUNTEER GROUP HEADQUARTERS, Somewhere in Burma, March 7 (AP)—Guns loaded and motors tuned for combat, another American Volunteer Group squadron roared from out of the China skies today to take over their share of the Battle for Burma from the little band of Yankee aces who smashed the last big Japanese air offensive in Rangoon.

On a dusty, camouflaged field somewhere north of the actual front, tall, curly-haired Robert A. Neale of Seattle, with confirmed destruction of twelve enemy aircraft to his personal credit, relinquished command of the A.V.G.'s forces in Burma to Arvid Olson of Chicago and Los Angeles. . . .

The group's new Curtiss P-40 fighter planes bear as fuselage insignia a nude winged damsel painted in rollicking red.

Magwe was 200 miles from the front, Oley Olson was still in China, and the reinforcements consisted of four beat-up Tomahawks flown by Parker Dupouy, Moose Moss, Fred Hodges, and Clifford Groh.

The changeover was attended by an astonishing number of mishaps. Duke Hedman had set out with Dupouy, but turned back when his engine caught fire. He tried again on March 10 with four other Tomahawks, only to be waved away from Lashio when they came in to refuel, a false alarm having stirred up the field. The Tomahawks flew back toward Loiwing, but ran out of gas before they reached the CAMCO airfield. Bob Brouk and William Fish managed to belly in with superficial damage, but Hedman, Eddie Overend, and Bill Reed hit so hard that their planes could only be salvaged for parts.* Mac McGarry flew down from Loiwing to drop supplies to the stranded men, but he too ran out of gas and bellied in, for a total (with Boyington's farcical mission to Chanyi) of eleven Tomahawks on the ground in one week.

The day after this disaster, a U.S. Army Douglas took off from Kunming with the 3rd Squadron technicians aboard. The pilot was a green lieutenant, so a Chinese second officer went along to show him the route. The lieutenant used up the entire length of the runway, barely missing a granite roller and a parked Tomahawk as the Douglas lifted off. Then, as Dan Hoyle wrote in the squadron log, "the Chinese Co-Pilot lowered the flaps and that changed the flying characteristics of the airfoils and the plane just cleared the trees tops, the wing cutting off some of the branches." One engine vibrated so badly that the men demanded that the pilot return them to Wu Chia Ba. "We vowed that we wouldn't get in the plane again for all the orders in the world," Hoyle added. (Nor did they: a CNAC Douglas flew them down.) Oley Olson led three more Tomahawks into Burma that same day, losing one of them en route.

Olson had eleven pilots at Magwe, though five were borrowed from other squadrons. They lived in an abandoned house that also served as the AVG communications center. The technicians were billeted in another house, and Clayton Harpold agreed to stay on to cook for them, so it was Eighteen Mile Ranch all over again. Dan Hoyle found the setup much better than expected:

> We go swimming in the Irrawaddy River to get clean and some of us wash our clothes there. The food is good and we sleep well getting up early in the morning. Its so hot in the afternoon that one can hardly work. There was a dance at the American Club at Yenangyaung, Burma, about 30 miles from the field, last night, a number of our members attended but not much dancing due to lack of girls for partners.

But the accidents continued. Ken Jernstedt taxied into a jeep, and Dick Rossi collapsed the landing gear on No. 77—R. T. Smith's lucky

---

* The instruments and radio went into Tomahawk No. 100, its fuselage derived from P-8197 (whose wing assembly had been ruined by salt-water corrosion) and its wings from the wreck of P-8194. Einar (Mickey) Mickelson flew the composite to Kunming on March 18.

Tomahawk, which could not be salvaged. John Hennessy, ferrying the last of the 3rd Squadron technicians down from Kunming in the AVG Beechcraft, was forced down in the mountains.

At Magwe, the Hell's Angels were pawns in a four-way power struggle. Chennault, as always, wanted to conserve men and planes for the future; that, compounded by Olson's lack of fighting spirit, accounted for their generally passive role. The British wanted them to cover the retreat of the Commonwealth army, while Chiang Kai-shek thought they should serve as flying gun platforms for the Chinese 200th Division at Toungoo. And Stilwell had no use for them at all: "AVG equipment now reduced to point where operations must soon cease," he informed the War Department. At best, the good soldier thought, the Tomahawks might prove useful in reconnaissance. Stilwell won out, and the Hell's Angels went to work for the Chinese at Toungoo, carrying messages and scouting Japanese dispositions. This work began on Friday, March 13.

On Sunday, Parker Dupouy led a flight all the way down to Martaban Bay, and on the way back "shot up vehicles and personnel" near the pretty village of Nyaunglebin. Then Ken Jernstedt, leading the second element, spotted several uncamouflaged Nates a mile and a half to the east and 1,000 feet above him. His radio was dead, so he put the throttle to the firewall in an effort to overhaul Dupouy and warn him visually. In the process, he lost the Nates in the haze.

Cliff Groh had fallen behind with a balky engine. A navy pilot who had come over on *Boschfontein,* he had never been in combat; he neither saw the Nates nor understood the significance of Jernstedt's hasty departure. His first inkling that something was wrong came when Moose Moss did a half-roll and dropped out of the sky, then porpoised up behind him. "I then noticed the Japanese sitting on my tail," Groh reported—a nice understatement. For his part, Moss spotted four Nates above and behind the one that was after Groh:

> I picked out the one fartherest to the right and fired a long burst into him. He caught fire and turned earthward. The other three turned towards me and hooked on my tail. I out distanced them and they turned back one at a time, at about 15 seconds intervals. Seeing no other allied aircraft in the vicinity I went to Toungoo to refuel.

Groh escaped his pursuer by diving away. As he did so, he saw a billow of dust in the rice fields below, confirming Moss's shoot-down. (Japanese accounts do not mention this skirmish.)

On Monday, March 16, the 14th Sentai laced Toungoo with incendiaries and high explosives, turning the town into an inferno and wrecking the redbrick railroad station where the AVG had been wont to eat strawberries and drink Mandalay beer. The raid was Colonel Hironaka's farewell to Burma. He left his remaining Sallys at Nakhon Sawan to serve as transport planes, while the crews went home to refit.

Ken Jernstedt and Bill Reed announced that they were tired of driving up and down the Sittang Valley like errand boys. (Their impatience may have been whetted by Madame Chiang's promise that combat bonuses would indeed be paid.) All right, Olson told them: fly down to Moulmein and see what the Japanese air force was up to. So on Tuesday they flew over to Kyedaw airfield, deserted except for an RAF detachment with a single officer, who gave them a meal and took them on a tour of yesterday's damage. Among other sights, they inspected the bombed-out railroad station and the piles of bodies outside the Toungoo pagoda. Then they drove back to the airfield and went to bed.

Kyedaw had no takeoff lights, but they knew the runway of old. At 5 A.M. on Wednesday, they climbed into their Tomahawks and aimed them at the Little Dipper. "It was sitting right smack over the end of the runway," Jernstedt recalled nearly half a century later. "So I just gunned it and kept my eye right on the North Star, and when it felt like taking off, why, I pulled it back." He laughed at the young fool of 1942, rolling a narrow-gaited Tomahawk down an asphalt runway in the dark of night. "The only time I've ever done anything like that," he marveled. They flew south at 20,000 feet until they were abreast of Rangoon. The city was easy to spot at night, with Victoria Lake to the north and two rivers meeting to the south—so much water to catch the starlight. Then they turned east across Martaban Bay, heading first for the auxiliary field at Mudon. They reached it just as the tropical darkness lifted like a curtain, revealing fighter planes, transports, and bombers parked in neat rows on either side of the gravel field. "Those doggone planes were just lined up wingtip to wingtip," Jernstedt recalled. They split up to strafe, one screaming north while the other screamed south; then they changed direction, back and forth for a total of six runs. Jernstedt reported that he had flamed three fighters, a bomber, and a twin-engined transport.

So did Reed, though they agreed that only five planes were burning when they left the field.

They next flew up to Moulmein. The airstrip was boiling with pilots and planes, apparently trying to get off the ground. Spotting a fighter in the act of taking off, Jernstedt hammered it with machine gun fire. "I was never too proud of that poor guy," he said. Then a hangar loomed in front of him. The Tomahawk was equipped with a flare compartment, for night landings or for illuminating targets on the ground. Jernstedt had fitted a twenty-five-pound incendiary bomb into this compartment, and he now reached down with his right hand and yanked the flare-release lever beside the seat. "I missed the hangar," he wrote in his combat report, "and hit [a Sally] parked in front of the hangar. This ship was soon ablaze." Ack-ack guns were now blazing away, the black clouds bursting just 200 feet over the field, so he decided to call it a day.

Reed thought he flamed two bombers on his first run, then went back for more. "On my last dive across the field," he wrote in his combat report, "I had only one .50 cal. and 2 .30 cal. firing, but I succeeded in setting [a] fighter plane on fire."

Between them, Jernstedt and Reed put in for fifteen aircraft destroyed. (The JAAF did lose some planes at Mudon and Moulmein, but it is not possible to break out the figures.) Dan Hoyle, posting the squadron log next day, noted that Group Captain Broughall had agreed to the claims. "These pilots will probably get paid for same since they are confirmed," Hoyle wrote—the first mention of a combat bonus in any AVG document. It was also the most profitable mission ever flown by Chennault's pilots: $4,000 for Reed, $3,500 for Jernstedt.

On the retreat to Prome, the Commonwealth army was strung out for forty miles, but was never attacked from the air. For this respite, General Alexander could thank the commando mentality that so unnerved his men in the field. The Japanese took their objectives in a rush, then sat on their haunches for days or weeks until supplies and reinforcements caught up with them. General Obata's fighter sentais, for example, had used up their drop-tanks in the campaign for Rangoon, and could not engage the Allied air force until more arrived. Then too, Mingaladon and its satellites had been wrecked by Japanese bombs and British demolition teams, and the labor to repair them had mostly fled.

Over the course of two weeks, Mingaladon airport was rebuilt as Obata's headquarters and as a base for Major Ishikawa's 50th Sentai. At the town of Hmawbi, fifteen miles northwest, Highland Queen was refurbished for the 77th Sentai under Hiroshi Yoshioka, who now wore the pips of a lieutenant colonel. At Hlegu to the northeast, the Japanese were delighted with Zayatkwin's long runway and the 800 barrels of aviation gasoline that had been left there by the RAF. Hlegu/Zayatkwin was modified as a base for the 47th Independent Chutai and the Nate-equipped 1st and 11th Sentais, newly arrived in Burma. Thus, by the third week of March, Mingaladon and its two major satellites had been transformed into a defensive triangle against attack from the north. The smaller fields were ignored: "busily occupied with maintenance and repair work," a JAAF officer explained after the war, "we were contented with dispersing our planes within [these three] airfields, or taking simple covering measures. However," he went on, in the bloodless prose affected by military men of every nationality, "when the enemy's air attacks were intensified, our air division realized the disadvantage of these improvised defensive measures." By this he meant the strafing party put on by Jernstedt and Reed—an object lesson in the folly of parking planes in neat rows overnight.

In addition, two heavy bomber groups were detached from the 3rd Hikoshidan and sent to bases in Thailand: the 98th Sentai to Nakhon Sawan, the 12th Sentai to Lampang. (The Hell's Angels had fought these groups over South Burma at Christmas.) To protect them, Tateo Kato's 64th Sentai moved to Chiang Mai, due east of Toungoo. Kato too had been promoted to lieutenant colonel, and the group had left its original-equipment Hayabusas in the Dutch Indies, to be replaced with production-model *Ki*-43s with larger guns and more powerful engines.

For three months, Allied pilots and war correspondents had wildly overestimated the number of Japanese planes ranged against Burma. But now the wolf was at the door. On March 20, when Obata drew up his "Central Burma Attack Mission," he had a truly magnificent air force to carry it out: eighty fighters, seventy heavy bombers, and forty attack planes and light bombers. Their mission was to destroy the AVG and the RAF, so the Japanese army (also doubled in size during the lull that followed the capture of Rangoon) could drive north without interference from the air.

Meanwhile, Obata's reconnaissance planes had scoured Central Burma, searching for the airfield that had replaced Mingaladon:

On 9 March, we discovered the enemy air force, which we had not heard anything of for a while, secretly assembled at Magwe. However, we did not carry out any small scale attacks against it. Instead, in order to deceive the enemy, we supported operations in other areas, awaiting a greater assemblage of the enemy's strength.

The RAF nearly spoiled Obata's plan. The British too were trying to get a fix on enemy dispositions, and on Friday, March 20, an observation Blenheim reported an "extraordinary concentration" of planes in the Rangoon area. At Magwe, Dan Hoyle put the number at thirty-five aircraft, morosely adding: "We are prepared to be attacked tomorrow morning or at early dawn." But on Saturday morning, March 21, it was Group Captain Broughall who went on the offensive, dispatching every airworthy British plane to blast the JAAF before it could move: nine Blenheims from the 45th Squadron, ten Hurricanes from the 17th Squadron. As the Commonwealth pilots told the story, the Blenheims were intercepted forty miles north of Mingaladon and fought all the way in. The Japanese planes were identified as Zeros—i.e., the retractable-gear Shokis at Hlegu, their number now increased to five or six. Every Blenheim was damaged, but the turret gunners claimed two Japanese fighters shot down. Bunny Stone's pilots claimed nine "Zeros" in the air battle, plus sixteen enemy planes destroyed on the ground, for the loss of one Hurricane on the way home. It was, concluded Air Vice Marshal Stevenson, "a magnificent air action."

According to Japanese accounts, there were sixty aircraft at Mingaladon airport when the Blenheims came over. In addition to the fighters and reconnaissance planes actually based there, two light bomber groups were supposed to have staged in from Moulmein that morning, and at least one—the 31st Sentai with its Mitsubishi Anns—had already arrived. As the Japanese told the story, the Blenheims came in from the northeast at 13,000 feet and destroyed one Nate on the ground. Then three Tomahawks supposedly made a low-level strafing run from the south, and after that the Hurricanes strafed the field. (But there were no Tomahawks. Clearly, the strafing party at Moulmein was shifted forward in time, and the damage done by Jernstedt and Reed was mingled with that done by the RAF at Mingaladon.) Altogether, four planes were destroyed and eleven damaged, with the light bombers taking most of the hits. It was a setback, but not so severe that General Obata canceled his Central Burma Attack Plan. Or perhaps, given the fabulous detail with which it was laid out—nine combat sentais converging upon Magwe from six airfields in two countries—it was easier to go ahead than to call it off.

The 98th Sentai was the first to set out, for its Sallys had to cover a 500-mile dogleg from Nakhon Sawan to Chiang Mai to Magwe. Soon after taking off, the lead bomber fell out of the formation and crashed. Among the dead was Lieutenant Colonel Junji Osaka—the second commander lost by the 98th in its campaign against the Allied air force in Burma. There was the usual confusion before Captain Masato Kodam took over, with the result that the Sallys reached Chiang Mai too late for the scheduled rendezvous.

The first plane over Magwe was a Mitsubishi *Ki*-46 Dinah, a fast, twin-engined reconnaissance plane. It carried Major General Kenji Yamamoto, the plump wing commander who had nearly crashed going to Rangoon on December 25. Again his bravado nearly cost him his life. The Dinah's oxygen system failed over Magwe, the pilot blacked out, and Yamamoto's command post plunged 7,000 feet before the pilot regained consciousness. Meanwhile, the noise of its engines was heard at Magwe airfield. Two Hurricanes took off to intercept what seemed to be only a scout. They missed the Dinah and returned to the airport, where the Blenheim crews were again in the briefing tent, getting instructions for another raid on Mingaladon. The time was 1:23 P.M.

By now, the main Japanese formation had swung around Magwe to strike from the northwest: twenty-six Sallys from the 12th Sentai, escorted by fourteen of Colonel Kato's Hayabusas. They had passed north of the ground-watchers with the Chinese army, and now they were blind-siding the British radar station. . . . But the trap was prematurely sprung. In his rush to catch up, Captain Kodam led the 98th Sentai to Magwe by the most direct route. This formation was spotted from the ground, and the word was radioed to fighter control: "Bandits from the southeast at angels fifteen"—15,000 feet. Six Hurricanes and five Tomahawks took off to intercept them.

Parker Dupouy and Ken Jernstedt climbed to 13,000 feet before breaking out of the clouds and seeing the 12th Sentai Sallys bearing down on them from the northwest, with the Hayabusas following at the usual inexplicable distance, an armada very like the one they had fought at Rangoon on Christmas Day. Small wonder that the Hell's Angels came away from Burma convinced that the Japanese had limitless formations of heavy bombers and retractable-gear fighters to throw against them. Dupouy and Jernstedt kept climbing until they held the high ground, then made a rear-quarter attack on the Sallys. Jernstedt took a bullet through his windshield, a plexiglass shard cutting his eye and putting him out of the fight. Meanwhile, Dupouy was caught in a classic Tomahawk-trap:

> After the third similar attack I saw a lone fighter Model "0" circling in behind me. I headed for him and then saw seven more Model "0" slightly above me starting down. I turned toward the nearest one and fired at him head on. His engine caught fire before he passed me and one 30 calibre from his guns entered my cockpit directly below the wind shield on the left side. I dove straight for the ground and the other 6 followed for a few thousand feet. I saw the Model "0" on fire crash in the trees about 30 miles Northwest of Toungoo.

Dupouy was slightly wounded in this exchange, his hand laid open by a piece of shrapnel. As for his victim, the 64th Sentai admitted to no losses on March 21, but a Hayabusa crashed on the way home, its pilots showing up at Chiang Mai a day or so later.

The 12th Sentai Sallys had now reached their target, only to find it hidden by the clouds. Dropping 367 bombs by hunch, the bombardiers hit the airport dead on.

The other AVG flight included Bob Prescott, Fred Hodges, and Cliff Groh. They climbed away from the airport toward the southeast, so the first planes they saw were the Sallys of the 98th Sentai under Captain Kodam, flying a compass course from Chiang Mai. Prescott chased after the big-tailed bombers and damaged one of them. The 98th showed the same magnificent discipline it had maintained over Rangoon on December 23: the wounded Sally moved inside the formation, another bomber took its place on the flank, and the twenty-five pilots continued their approach without flinching. By now, the clouds over Magwe had cleared out, and the airport was marked as if by beacon fires from the 12th Sentai's bombs.

Thirty-one Nates (the newly arrived 1st and 11th Sentais, plus the headquarters flight from Mingaladon) blundered onto the scene at about

CENTRAL BURMA ORDER OF BATTLE

RAF Burwing
(Grp Capt Seton Broughall, Commanding)
AVG 3rd Squadron (Sq Ldr Arvid Olson): 8 Curtiss Tomahawks
RAF 17th Squadron (Sq Ldr C. A. C. Stone): 15 Hawker Hurricanes
RAF 28th Squadron (Sq Ldr P. N. Jennings): 6 Westland Lysanders
RAF 45th Squadron: 9 Bristol Blenheims
(38 aircraft in service, 20 Mar 1942)

JAAF 5th Hikoshidan
(Lt Gen Eiryo Obata, Commanding)
1st Sentai (Maj Kinshiro Takeda): 15 Nakajima *Ki*-27 Nates
8th Sentai (Lt Col Mitsuo Honda): 22 Kawasaki *Ki*-48 Lilys; 6 Mitsubishi
 Ki-30 Anns
11th Sentai (Maj Tadashi Okabe): 14 Nakajima *Ki*-27 Nates
12th Sentai (Col Kumao Kitajima): 35 Mitsubishi *Ki*-21 Sallys
31st Sentai (Lt Col Junji Hayashi): 16 Mitsubishi *Ki*-30 Anns
50th Sentai (Maj Tadashi Ishikawa): 13 Nakajima *Ki*-27 Nates
64th Sentai (Lt Col Tateo Kato): 18 Nakajima *Ki*-43 Hayabusas
77th Sentai (Lt Col Hiroshi Yoshioka): 15 Nakajima *Ki*-27 Nates
98th Sentai (Lt Col Junji Osaka): 37 Mitsubishi *Ki*-21 Sallys
Other units: 6 Nakajima *Ki*-44 Shokis; 3 Nakajima *Ki*-27 Nates; 17
 Mitsubishi *Ki*-15 and *Ki*-46 reconnaissance planes; 6 Mitsubishi *Ki*-21
 Sallys used as transports.
(223 aircraft in service, 20 Mar 1942)

this time. They were half an hour late, thanks to the damage and confusion wrought by the Blenheims that morning. But the delay was a lucky break for General Obata. If the Nates had swarmed up the Irrawaddy Valley on schedule, they would have been spotted at Prome, giving the Allied fighters the chance to intercept as a group instead of piecemeal.

The 17th Squadron Hurricanes joined the action about this time. One of them was flown by Pilot Officer Kenneth Hemingway, who in two months of combat at Rangoon had not seen a Japanese air armada. "Wherever I looked," he marveled, "I could pick out bunches of weaving Jap fighters protecting formation after formation of bombers."

Hemingway dove away as the second salvo of bombs began to burst on Magwe airport. "I saw a sudden storm of dust clouds and a thousand flashes erupt," he recalled, after which "black smoke gushed forth from a blitzed oil and petrol dump." Then he was bounced by a Nate—like a fly on his windshield, as he described it. He laced the Japanese fighter with machine gun fire and may have shot it down, but was himself hit badly enough to make a crash landing near the airport. A second Commonwealth pilot also claimed a Nate, and one Hurricane crashed near Prome, whence the pilot hitchhiked home on an army truck.

Cliff Groh also scored in the brawl. After chasing the Sallys almost to Toungoo, he was chugging home when he spotted a lone Nate at 4,000 feet:

> I got behind it without being seen and saw the markings on the wings. I turned on my gun switch and when in position pulled my trigger but the guns didn't fire as I had locked them. I dived underneath the Jap and turned towards the left. I charged my guns and made an approach from his port side. I gave a deflection shot and fired several bursts before he turned towards me. . . . I kept firing burst after burst until just before I passed him. I saw the plane lurch but dived down in case he was all right. As I pulled out of my dive I turned and saw the Jap plane crash in the vicinity of the fires (forest) that is SE of the Magwe airport about 15 or 20 miles.

Groh's victim was none other than Major Tadashi Okabe, commander of the 11th Sentai, whose service with the group went back to the Russo-Japanese border conflict of 1939.

Most of the Japanese fighters concentrated on strafing the airport. For this work, JAAF pilots employed a figure-eight technique that enabled them to fix on a single target. They dove down vertically, climbed straight up, executed a wingover, and dove down for another attack. It was a radically different approach than that used by western pilots, who generally swept across a target at rooftop height, spraying bullets at a flat angle before them.

His engine on fire, a 17th Squadron pilot chose this moment to land his Hurricane. Fritz Wolf was watching from a slit trench:

> He came in fast and skidded, throwing flame and smoke in every direction. . . . The pilot looked trapped for sure. But Crew Chiefs Johnny Fauth and

little [Henry] Olson jumped out of their shelters and rushed to the wreckage, breaking through and rescuing the RAF pilot from the burning mass.

The AVG technicians put the injured pilot into a jeep, which Little Olson (as he was called to distinguish him from the squadron leader) drove off the field. (Another account identified the driver as Lewis Richards, the AVG flight surgeon at Magwe.) Johnny Fauth then ran back toward the trench, but before reaching safety was hit in the shoulder by a machine gun bullet. Crazed with pain and fear, he began to run aimlessly across the field. Frank Swartz—one of the Panda Bears who had volunteered to fill out Oley Olson's roster at Magwe—left his trench to sprint after him. "One big bomb fell within fifteen feet of them," Wolf recalled, "and both were wounded badly." Each man lost part of his jaw, Fauth's arm was nearly torn off, and Swartz's throat was laid open. Also injured in the explosion was crew chief Wilfred Seiple.

Obata's final wave now reached Magwe. The 8th Sentai came over with seventeen twin-engined Lilys, followed by the 31st Sentai with ten Anns. Based at Moulmein and Mudon, these planes had staged through Mingaladon that morning, and there would have been more of them if not for Stevenson's spoiling raid and the Jernstedt-Reed strafing party. They were escorted by twenty-eight Nates from the AVG's old antagonists, the 77th and the 50th Sentais. Altogether, Obata put 151 bombers and fighters over Magwe that Saturday. It was the largest air armada ever mounted in Southeast Asia, and in their enthusiasm Japanese reporters assured their readers that it was the largest the world had ever seen.

It was 2:30 P.M. when the last Ann left the scene. Explosions continued to rock the airport for some time thereafter, making rescue and salvage impossible. The Americans believed that the Japanese had seeded the field with delayed-action bombs, but the cause was probably less sophisticated: the 45th Squadron had already gassed and armed its planes for a return trip to Mingaladon. Set afire by fragmentation bombs and incendiary bullets, the Blenheims were now being blown apart by their own bombs.

When the AVG mechanics finished their work, they pronounced four Tomahawks fit to fly. This number increased to six when Oley Olson and Duke Hedman flew in from Lashio just before dark. Olson was handed a radiogram from Chennault which, in two sentences, perfectly distilled the Old Man's approach to war, always trying to outguess the enemy, and always trying to ensure that his planes were not caught on the ground:

> Look out for follow up raid tomorrow. Did you have any warning of raid today?

Somewhat unfairly, Olson replied that the AVG had received one minute's notice of the raid. He added that the raiders were mostly "Model Zeros," which had flown back to Thailand in the direction of Chiang Mai.

There Is Always a Way

March–April 1942

Johnny Fauth died at 4:30 A.M. Sunday morning, March 22, the first AVG technician to lose his life in the service of China. An agreeable young man with a mop of dark hair, he was posthumously commissioned a second lieutenant in the CAF.

Within hours, General Obata's formations returned to Magwe. The first plot was made by the radar station at 8:04 A.M. and was confirmed a few minutes later. The screen kept showing new and better information at intervals thereafter—but to no result, for the radio link to the airfield had gone dead. Magwe was therefore reduced to what information it could garner by ear. Hearing radial engines overhead at 8:30 A.M., Kenneth Hemingway and another 17th Squadron pilot took off to intercept what they believed to be a reconnaissance plane. Instead, they met all the airworthy planes from Mingaladon and its satellites: twenty-three Anns and Lilys, escorted by sixty-one Nates. The Hurricanes gallantly attacked, perhaps damaged two planes, and were themselves shot up, though not fatally.*

---

* Officially, the JAAF lost no planes on March 22, but Lieutenant Sugiyama of the 47th Independent Chutai vanished on a flight to Toungoo. His Shoki was later found near Bassein with Sugiyama dead at the controls and bullet holes in the fuselage. His squadron mates decided that he must have flown a course of 300° instead of 30° (the JAAF compass omitted the final zero) and blundered into the Magwe combat.

No one else got off the ground. The first group of bombers droned over Magwe airport at 8:47 A.M., the second at 9:03. "Considerable damage was sustained," Air Vice Marshal Stevenson reported with British sangfroid. "The runways were rendered unserviceable, communications were broken down and a number of aircraft, both bombers and fighters, were destroyed on the ground." The Americans sustained no casualties for the good reason that they scrambled into vehicles and drove away from the field. Afterward, Oley Olson returned to the airport and radioed the news to Chennault:

> Absolutely no warning. . . . One shark burned up four hit badly. Three planes left now. Repairing and possibly have two others to fly away.

Chennault told him, in effect, to get out of there. Olson went to Group Captain Broughall and explained (in Stevenson's version) "that in view of the absence of warning and the scale of attack he was compelled by the terms of his instructions from General Chennault to withdraw his remaining flyable aircraft to refit." The implication is that Olson ran out on the RAF, but he did not. Instead, he kept the technicians working on the damaged Tomahawks, while he got the evacuation organized. For one thing, there was Johnny Fauth to bury. This was done without ceremony at the local Catholic church or (accounts conflict) in a mass grave at the British military cantonment. Early in the afternoon, a CNAC Douglas flew in from Lashio to pick up Frank Swartz and Wilfred Seipel, whom Doc Richards wanted to send to India for better care than he could give them.

No sooner had the ambulance plane taken off than Obata's second wave reached Magwe: fifty-three Sallys and eighteen Hayabusas from Thailand, twenty-three Nates from Rangoon. Again two Hurricanes took off, to no effect except to save themselves from destruction, and again the Tomahawks were caught on the ground. Olson's next radiogram was even more bleak:

> All sharks hit possibly fly three. . . . Proceeding with convoy to Loiwing. Radio will operate until 10 P.M. tonight.

The technicians did better than that. Working through the night, they patched and tuned and coaxed four Tomahawks into condition to fly the 300 miles to Loiwing on the China-Burma border. Frank Van Timmeran and Joey Poshefko, line chief and armorer, waved them off the cratered airstrip early in the morning of Monday, March 23. The two technicians then climbed into a truck and followed the squadron up the road to Mandalay.

The RAF followed suit. Eight Hurricanes flew to Akyab on Monday, to be cannibalized for the benefit of the 135th Squadron. Virtually no bombers or transports were airworthy, so the mechanics and the headquarters staff set off in a sixty-truck convoy to Mandalay.

They left twenty burned-out hulks at Magwe: half the AVG Tomahawks, half the 17th Squadron Hurricanes, and most of the 45th Squadron Blenheims. The Japanese, in their exultation, put the count much higher. After the war, one of Obata's officers assured the victors that no fewer than 120 planes were destroyed in the two-day blitz of Magwe, and this fantasy number still appears in Japanese accounts of the air war in Southeast Asia, much as the Flying Tiger romances repeat the fantasy scores attributed to the AVG. However that may be, the JAAF had at last succeeded in its campaign to destroy the Allied air force in Burma. Obata's triumph was only mildly tarnished by the fact that by this time his advantage in aircraft was five-to-one.

When he got the first news from Magwe on Saturday, March 21, Chennault was choking with bronchitis in his bedroom at Hostel Number One. His first thought was that Olson must get ready for the inevitable follow-up raid; his second, that the Japanese must be paid back in kind. From Toungoo, in the opening weeks of the war, he had sent out patrols to scout the airports in northern Thailand. More recently, British intelligence had reported a base-building effort at Lampang, and Oley Olson's after-action report had fingered Chiang Mai. On Sunday morning, not knowing that the Japanese were even then returning to Magwe, Chennault rose from his sickbed to plan his revenge.

Compared to the aerial armadas Obata was sending across Burma, the AVG counterstrike would have to be a puny affair. Chennault picked ten of the best pilots at Kunming. They included six Adam & Eves—Bob Neale, Greg Boyington, Charlie Bond, Mac McGarry, Ed Rector, and Bill Bartling—who would fly to Chiang Mai and strafe the "Jap Air Force headquarters in Southeast Asia." Meanwhile, four Panda Bears—Jack Newkirk, Whitey Lawlor, Hank Geselbracht, and Buster Keeton—would attack Lamphun to the south.

But Chiang Mai was a forward airfield with twenty aircraft, and Lamphun was a flat mistake. The Americans spelled local names any which way, and the Panda Bears variously recorded their target as *Lambhun, Lambhan, Lambhung,* and *Lampong.* The last was not a bad approximation of *Lampang,* the heavy bomber base that Chennault actually meant to hit.

Their ammunition boxes heavily laden with incendiary rounds, the Tomahawks took off from Wu Chia Ba on Sunday afternoon. Two hours later, they touched down at Loiwing, on a runway carved out of a hillside. Though China had paid for its construction, this was Bill Pawley's private domain. So unprepared was CAMCO to support a combat operation that there was no one at the field to gas and tune the Tomahawks. The AVG flights would have to wait until Monday morning, thus shifting their program by twenty-four hours. (The plan had been to refuel, fly down to Namsang, and there spend the night.) The delay had no effect on the drama at Magwe, which was even then in its final act, but it was otherwise for Group Captain Neal Singer at Akyab. On Monday, he was blasted by the Sallys from Lampang and strafed by the Hayabusas from Chiang Mai, in a raid that would have been spoiled if the Adam & Eves and Panda Bears had flown into Thailand on schedule.

The CAMCO factory was eight miles from the airstrip: a neat little compound of whitewashed buildings with camouflaged metal roofs. There was a nine-hole golf course and a clubhouse outfitted with electric lights, polished wood floors, wood-burning fireplace, jukebox, pool table, movie projector, a refrigerator stocked with Milwaukee beer, and a plate-glass window overlooking the pretty valley in which Bill Pawley had set out for the fourth time to assemble warplanes for China. The guestrooms had thick Chinese rugs and tiled baths. There was even a housemother-cook named Davidson, who told the pilots to call her "Ma."

The AVG convoy from Rangoon had reached Loiwing a few days before. Harry Fox, the line chief, had made it his business to inspect the CAMCO factory, and he now complained to Bob Neale that the Pawley brothers had accumulated thirty wrecked Tomahawks at Loiwing. Eighteen of the derelicts, Fox thought, could be put into combat condition. But no effective work was being done at the CAMCO factory.

Monday, March 23, dawned foggy and wet. Their Tomahawks serviced, the pilots sat around for the rest of the day, because they did not want to fly into Namsang until dusk. Thus they were on hand when the four pilots from Magwe flew in with harrowing accounts of the disaster. Moose Moss told about jumping into a trench with Fred Hodges, only to have Fearless try to dig himself deeper into the red earth—pushing the dirt under Moss and lifting him to the surface again. Wrote Bus Keeton in his diary: "They almost scared us out of going on our mission which to my way of thinking is the most dangerous undertaking the A.V.G. has done, going 120 miles into enemy territory where if you have to force land and the Japs don't get you the jungle will."

With these thoughts to keep them company, the raiders took off for Namsang at 3 P.M. They arranged for trucks and lanterns to light the runway in the morning, then ate a tense meal at the pilots' mess and washed up in the officers' billet. Combat literature is filled with omens and portents, and the Chiang Mai mission was no exception. An RAF sergeant supposedly warned the Americans that the water was polluted, so they shouldn't use it to brush their teeth, causing Newkirk to scoff: "After tomorrow, I don't think it'll make any difference." Certainly the mood was heavy. "Here goes *nothing*," Bob Neale wrote in his diary, underlining the final word twice.

A barrack-boy shook them awake at 4 A.M., and they were dressing when the duty officer bounded in with the cry: "All right, you curly-headed fellows, it's time!" Joking and gabbing to keep their spirits up, they wolfed breakfast and went to their planes. Takeoff was 5:45 A.M. —black night, broken only by truck headlamps, flickering kerosene lanterns, and the blue flames that washed along the cowlings of their Tomahawks.

Newkirk's flight set off for Thailand without waiting for the form-up over Namsang. As the Panda Bears gained altitude, daylight came down to greet them, though the ground was still hidden in darkness and the smoke haze from the fall of Rangoon. They flew on instruments until they reached Chiang Mai at about 7 A.M., by which time they could make out objects on the ground below them, but not off to the sides. By the same token, they could not be seen from the ground, which was the logic behind the timing of the raid. Newkirk tarried long enough to strafe the Chiang Mai railroad station—an astonishing breach of discipline, like poking a stick into a hornet's nest before his friends came along. Flying on, he found Lamphun but saw only a row of buildings that might have been warehouses or barracks. He laced them with incendiary bullets. So did Hank Geselbracht and Whitey Lawlor, but Bus Keeton decided to save his ammunition for a better target. Newkirk then scouted some auxiliary fields, but they were empty. At the third and largest field, the Panda Bears strafed more buildings, after which Newkirk turned north with the apparent intention of joining the Adam & Eves at Chiang Mai. In his combat report, Geselbracht told what happened next:

> The next target we dove on were two vehicles on the road south of [Chiang Mai]. Newkirk dove and fired and as he cleared the target I began to fire. I saw a flash of flames beyond the target and looked for Newkirk after my run. I realized he had crashed causing the flash. I pulled up and continued to the north on the way home.

Keeton also saw the explosion, and like Geselbracht did not at first understand its cause. "As I pulled up to the right," he wrote in his diary, "I noticed a large flame of fire burst up on a field to the right of me. The fire spread along the field for a 100 or 150 yards. Thinking Jack and Gesel had set fire to some oil dumps and not seeing anything to shoot at I proceeded to follow Lawlor."

Newkirk was one of the immortals, the "Scarsdale Jack" of so many upbeat dispatches from Rangoon. He died in a fireball that skittered and bounced and smeared itself along the ground—a napalm cannister with a man inside. Then the Allison engine broke loose and rolled 300 yards farther. Whitey Lawlor identified the vehicle upon which Newkirk had been firing, and which probably shot him down, as a Japanese armored car.

The Adam & Eves had since reached Chiang Mai. Charlie Bond saw a towering mountain that he recognized from a patrol on December 13, when he had scouted Chiang Mai from Toungoo, so he took the lead from Neale. If he remembered correctly, the airfield was a mile or so southeast of this landmark:

> I nosed downward in a gentle left turn and hoped I was right. At about six thousand feet, and as the haze thinned, I saw the field and the outlines of the hangars. I flipped on my gun switch, and another thousand feet lower I fired my guns in a short burst to check them and let the other guys know this was it—the main Japanese Air Force of Southeast Asia!

The plan called for Ed Rector and Mac McGarry to stay high as top cover, with the option of attacking the field if the sky proved to be clear. Bond led the other four Tomahawks onto the field:

> I made my first strafing run firing everything into the [Japanese fighters]. At the end I remained low and turned sharply to the left. . . . After turning 270 degrees I was in a position to strafe another line of parked aircraft. These were sitting practically wingtip to wingtip. Hell, I hadn't seen this many aircraft in years. Seemed like the whole Japanese Air Force had tried to crowd into this one little field.

He made four runs with tracer bullets streaking the air beside him and flak exploding overhead. Once he was so low that he thought he might decapitate the Japanese pilots scrambling into their cockpits. (They were shouting "*Mawase, mawase!*"—"Turn, turn!"—to the mechanics trying to start the engines by spinning the propellers.) On his last go-round, Bond concentrated on a larger plane that "seemed to shake itself to pieces" under his machine guns.

Greg Boyington made two passes over the field. "The aircraft on the field were parked mainly in two long lines," he wrote in his combat report. "All enemy planes were turning up and the pilots and crews were running about." After his first pass, he saw three transports burning in a single bonfire, with the flames shooting a thousand feet into the air; after his second, he counted ten fires on the ground.

Bob Neale made three runs, estimating that there were forty planes on the field, and that his pilots destroyed half of them before veering away in the face of antiaircraft fire, the "heaviest I have ever seen." Signaling the others to join up on him, Neale headed north for the Burma border. In his combat report, he mentioned eight or nine fires burning on the field, "two of them being very large."

But only Boyington was following him home. Coming up from his final strafing run, Charlie Bond linked up with Bill Bartling, Ed Rector, and Mac McGarry. The top cover had taken the worst of the flak, and McGarry's engine was spluttering. He waggled his wings to attract the attention of the other pilots, as Rector recalled in his combat report:

> I circled back & tried to rendezvous on his wing but his speed was too slow & I overshot. Bond & Bartling were circling now. I saw smoke coming from his engine intermittently & he seemed to be losing altitude.
>
> After continuing in this condition for five or ten minutes & losing more altitude, McGarry turned left over a canyon, turned the plane over & fell out. His 'chute opened instantly & he landed about 200 yards from his plane.

McGarry waved to his buddies, who dropped him a candy bar and a map with his location and time: thirty miles south of the Salween River at 7:41 A.M., March 24, 1942.

As they had flown into Thailand, so they returned, the Panda Bears and the Adam & Eves following separate routes to Namsang and Loiwing. At the American Club, Ma Davidson fixed lunch and the CAMCO foreman made drinks. "Soon we were in the bar," wrote Charlie Bond in his diary. ". . . Everybody was laughing and enjoying the moment. Yet Jack was gone and we weren't sure of Black Mac."

Starved as they had recently been for good news from Burma, American newspapers hailed the Chiang Mai raid as a magnificent victory, while playing down the disaster of Magwe. Even the *New York Times* gave the Adam & Eves top billing next morning, spread across four columns:

U.S. FLIERS IN BURMA SMASH 40 PLANES

The years have done little to dim that boast. As recently as 1987, an AVG chronicler was claiming that the Adam & Eves "destroyed most of an entire enemy air regiment" at Chiang Mai, causing the shattered sentai to be "returned to Japan for replacement pilots and planes."

The *Times* gave special attention to Jack Newkirk, whose portrait (in navy uniform) accompanied the story. Newkirk was described as a Tom Sawyerish lad who had impaled a sheriff with an arrow, and who had received his Eagle Scout badge from Admiral Richard Byrd, the Antarctic explorer. In Burma, the story continued, the British had awarded him the Distinguished Service Order for destroying twenty-five enemy aircraft. (Actually, the decoration was the Distinguished Flying Cross and Newkirk's score stood at ten and one-half planes—and some AVG pilots doubted those.)

In the end, Chennault settled upon fifteen planes as a reasonable tally for the Adam & Eves at Chiang Mai. The credit was shared by the six pilots taking part, including the top cover. That done, Chennault sent off a radiogram to Lauchlin Currie, exploiting the Chiang Mai victory and the Magwe disaster to pry concessions from the White House:

A.V.G. becoming ineffective due exhaustion equipment and personnel. . . .
Send spare parts by air. Personnel replacements now equally serious as

This Japanese photo shows a squadron of 12th Sentai Sallys under attack by a Tomahawk, suggesting that it was taken over Rangoon on December 25, 1941. Alas, it is a composite. Note the rear greenhouse gunner with his canopy raised like the visor of a helmet. (National Air and Space Museum)

Lieutenant Yamamoto's *jibaku* dive upon Mingaladon airport as rendered by a postwar Japanese artist. The Nakajima Nate was the fighter most often encountered by the AVG, and the 77th Sentai was its most persistent opponent. (From *Hien tai Guramen* by permission of the publisher)

Cigarette break at Wu Chia Ba airport. From left: Harvey Greenlaw, John Williams, and Chennault. Their uniforms are U.S. Army issue, but the insignia—including the wings over Chennault's left pocket—are Chinese. (Flying Tigers Association)

A Tomahawk with full AVG warpaint, probably at Mingaladon airport in January or February—the men appear to be wearing British army helmets. Note the coolant flaps, which are open to increase the airflow across the Prestone radiator. (National Air and Space Museum)

The Panda Bears. Kneeling from left: Ed Rector, Pappy Paxton, Peter Wright, Jack Newkirk, Tex Hill, Gil Bright, and Conant/Perry. Standing from left: Bus Keeton, Whitey Lawlor, Freeman Ricketts, Bob Layher, Hank Geselbracht, Tom Jones, and Frank Schiel. (National Archives)

The alert shack at Loiwing. Facing the camera from left: Herbert Cavanah, Tex Hill, Bill Reed, Oley Olson, Moose Moss, Parker Dupouy, Bob Prescott, and Cliff Groh, who went missing soon after. John Petach is visible behind Hill and Reed. (Flying Tigers Association)

Hell's Angels on the prowl over Baoshan, near the China-Burma border. The low-number Tomahawks were inherited by the Hell's Angels when the other squadrons were equipped with Kittyhawks. (Courtsey of Robert T. Smith)

Chinese workmen built decoys from bamboo and canvas, so convincingly that Japanese pilots reported that they had destroyed several Tomahawks at Baoshan airfield, several days after it was abandoned by the AVG. (National Air and Space Museum)

The Old Man in his office at Wu Chia Ba. Chennault appears to be wearing a mix of U.S. Army and CAF insignia, including (on his left shoulder only) one of the general's stars given to him by Jimmy Doolittle. (National Air and Space Museum)

Victorious Adam & Eves at Guilin. Standing, from left: Snuffy Smith, Corporal Honda, Bill Bartling, and George Burgard, who shot down the Kawasaki Toryu in which Honda was gunner-radioman. Joe Rosbert and Dick Rossi are kneeling on the wing of the Kittyhawk. (Flying Tigers Association)

Chennault conducts a briefing on the hood of an AVG jeep—one of those "liberated" from the docks at Rangoon. The pilots (including Bob Neale and George McMillan, in leather-brimmed garrison caps) are wearing CAF insignia. (Wide World photo, National Archives)

In August 1943, a grateful Britain awarded the Distinguished Flying Cross to Charlie Bond, Tex Hill, and Ed Rector for their services in the defense of Burma. No such recognition came from the U.S. government. (Courtesy of Charles R. Bond, Jr.)

equipment. Have great opportunity now if can get new airplanes, 30 pilots and 50 ground crew quickly. . . . Is induction A.V.G. still desired even if destruction of group results?

In truth, Chiang Mai was no victory. The 64th Sentai lost only three Hayabusas that Tuesday morning. Ten fighters were damaged—four of them seriously—but the Japanese mechanics were as industrious as their counterparts in the AVG, and by noon they had eleven planes fit to fly. (By way of comparison, the 64th Sentai had taken sixteen Hayabusas to Magwe on Saturday, eighteen on Sunday, and sixteen to Akyab on Monday.) Kato led this scratch force 350 miles across the width of Burma to strafe Akyab airport and a "secret runway" to the north. This seems to have been a spur-of-the-moment mission to erase the morning's loss of face. The bombing mission planned for that day was put forward to Friday, meaning that the loss of Newkirk and McGarry had bought a seventy-two-hour reprieve for Neal Singer at Akyab.

And the ground campaign was not delayed in the slightest. Even as the Adam & Eves and Panda Bears were downing whiskey soda at the American Club, the Japanese flanked Toungoo and captured their old training base, Kyedaw airfield. The battle for Toungoo raged through the week, with two divisions (Takeuchi's 55th, plus the newly arrived 56th under Lieutenant General Masao Watanabe) pitted against a small and lightly armed Chinese force. In the Irrawaddy Valley, Sakurai's 33rd Division rolled up the Commonwealth army at Prome. Despite what western historians have written about the lack of spirit in Chiang's army, Japanese accounts of the Burma campaign leave no doubt about who proved to be the tougher foe.

Obata's attack planes and fighters worked with the army during this climactic week. But he diverted his heavy bomber sentais to an operation that was the most important consequence of the Chiang Mai raid. Day after day, the Sallys bombed Allied airstrips at Heho, Loilem, Lashio, Mandalay, and (as they wrongly believed) Loiwing. Following each raid, observation planes monitored the target to see if Allied engineers were repairing it, hoping to discover if the base was in active use and therefore responsible for the attack on Chiang Mai.

This search was inspired by Mac McGarry. Thai policemen captured him before the week was out—perhaps the day he went down—and took him to Chiang Mai, where he was interviewed by Colonel Kato. The conversation took place over two or three days, with McGarry kept between times in a cage he entered by crawling under a fence, and into which the guards tossed food as to an animal. Kato's questions were phrased in Japanese, translated into Thai, and put to McGarry in English, with the answer coming back in reverse order. In this roundabout fashion, Kato determined that the AVG Tomahawks were based in China but, because of their short combat radius, had to stage out of fields in Burma. (McGarry apparently did not name the fields.) Kato also picked up some insights into the mentality of American pilots—for example, that they painted small Japanese flags on their planes to represent enemy aircraft destroyed. But the most important result of the interviews was to convince Kato that the "American air force" in Southeast Asia was a shadow of its old self, having lost many or most of its pilots since Christmas Day. Perhaps McGarry lied, or perhaps he simply told the truth about the AVG's losses, and the facts were twisted or exaggerated in the double translation. However it happened, Kato concluded that he no longer had anything to fear from the Americans.

For reasons that probably had to do with Japan's desire to appear as Thailand's ally, not her conqueror, McGarry was handed back to the local authorities. Instead of suffering the horrors of a Japanese prison compound, he entered upon a lonely but tolerable existence in a Bangkok jail.

Chennault realized that the Chiang Mai raid had put Loiwing in jeopardy, as he warned David Harris at the CAMCO compound: "Suggest repaired P-40's be flown here promptly. . . . Suggest all work be dispersed widely." (Harris was the ex-army pilot who went off flight status after Pete Atkinson was killed, and who had functioned since then as a staff officer.) Chennault also told Oley Olson to transform the CAMCO airstrip into a fighting field, from which the Hell's Angels could continue their reconnaissance and courier missions for the Chinese army. They would also fly "special missions on call"—a somewhat ominous provision—and defend Loiwing from attack. So the Hell's Angels commandeered a bamboo-and-thatch building for an alert shack, painting a crude sign over the door:

OLSON & CO., EXTERMINATORS
24 HR. SERVICE

To support this boast, Olson conscripted the ground crewmen (AVG and RAF) straggling up the road from Magwe. They had not entirely recovered from their trauma. "All of the technical personnel are rather jittery about a raid," Dan Hoyle wrote in the squadron log. "It seems to be this Squadrons misfortune to be in every raid thiere is." From Kunming, Chennault dispatched cooks and provisions in a convoy commanded by John Donovan, the balding pilot who wrote sweet letters to his family. He typed one now to his sister, explaining the setup at Loiwing:

> This is written as I sit in "my" truck. . . . I look up and see the P 40's on the runway. The alert shack is about 50 ft. away. In it, on days when we are on "alert," we play acey deucey, read, play ping pong or cards—or sleep.

Four Kittyhawks from Africa had reached Kunming on March 22, flown by George McMillan, R. T. Smith, Paul Greene, and Link Laughlin. Chuck Older and Ben Foshee were four days behind them, having been held up in Cairo by engine trouble. The Kittyhawks would need some work before they were ready for combat—their U.S. Army insignia replaced by the twelve-pointed Chinese star, their jaws decorated by the AVG shark face, and their machine guns harmonized at 300 yards—but the pilots were more flexible. Before the week was out, Chennault sent Smith, Greene, Laughlin, and Older down to Loiwing in Tomahawks, bringing the number of fighters there to an even dozen.

The first of the "special missions" called for the Hell's Angels to fly down to Toungoo and show the twelve-pointed star over the Chinese lines. The main object was to boost the morale of the Chinese, who were fighting a desperately mismatched battle against two Japanese divisions supported by the light bombers of the 8th Sentai and the Nates of the 50th. It was the longest set piece battle in the Burma campaign, and would be remembered by the Japanese as the bitterest fighting in their conquest of Southeast Asia.

With Newkirk's death still vivid in their minds, the Hell's Angels were not happy about this assignment. "We're all against it," R. T. Smith wrote in his diary. "[I]t seems senseless, with a good possibility of nobody coming back. This is to be just for one day, but it's mighty low grade, Lord, mighty low!" The mission was scheduled for Sunday morning, March 29. Oley Olson took off with eight Tomahawks but brought them back within the hour. The weather was too bad, he decided. It was a lucky call: the Hell's Angels had planned to refuel at Heho airstrip, which had just been bombed out of existence.

Hardly were the Hell's Angels back at Loiwing than an AVG listening post reported an observation plane flying in their direction. Paul Greene and Chuck Older took off to intercept the intruder, probably a Mitsubishi Dinah from the 15th Independent Chutai at Lampang, searching for new airports to bomb. Circling Loiwing at 27,000 feet, Older spotted the graceful reconnaissance plane flying on the opposite course and 5,000 feet below. He waggled his wings for Greene to follow, then put his Tomahawk into a power dive, opening fire at 500 yards and continuing until he was fifty yards from his target. "The enemy plane started smoking as I closed in," Older reported, "and burst into flames a few seconds later. One man bailed out. . . . The enemy plane disintegrated on the way down."

But the Japanese were getting their range. Tuesday morning, March 31, the Hell's Angels scrambled at 9 A.M. to intercept a bomber formation supposedly heading for Loiwing. Finding nothing, they returned to the field. Most of the pilots went to lunch, but Olson and Moose Moss stayed aloft to provide protective cover for the field. Then the alarm went off again. R. T. Smith led a flight of four to 28,000 feet, then heard over the radio that the Japanese were bombing Lashio, ninety miles south. Olson and Moss were heading in that direction, but they lost track of each other before bringing the Japanese formation into view. R. T.'s diary gives the outline of what happened next. Some of the rest can be read between the lines, including the growing feeling of mutiny among the pilots at Loiwing:

> Oley sighted 27 bombers and 9 fighters. He was alone so didn't attack. We went down to Lashio & joined him but they had left. Moss landed at Lashio, we think, but not sure.
>
> Message from Chennault [who] wants the Toungoo job done still, but we're all agin' it. Think we'll go down & strafe Jap fields instead.
>
> Expect a real raid here tomorrow.

But there were only false alarms on April 1. During one of the scrambles, Greg Boyington's engine cut out, leaving his Tomahawk to jump a twenty-foot ditch and hit the ground with such an impact that the seatbelt broke. Boyington slammed into the instrument panel, cutting his forehead and laming both knees. Next day, Moose Moss crashed upon returning from Lashio—two wrecks in as many days.

Between alerts, the Hell's Angels worked out the details of their strafe, which they planned as a repeat of the Chiang Mai affair. The motive was not revenge but the hope of getting out of the "Toungoo party." Oley Olson, R. T. Smith, and Paul Greene would hit one Japanese airfield, while Parker Dupouy, Eddie Overend, and Bob Brouk went after the other. This mission too was canceled because of the weather. The pilots had a blow-out night instead, and on Thursday they went one better and had a wedding.

The principals were Fred Hodges and a young woman named Helen Anderson. Greg Boyington recalled that Anderson had fled Rangoon on an AVG convoy with her Indian father. Others thought that her father was English and her mother Burman. Whatever her lineage, Anderson was about twenty, a small woman with a splendid body, an oval face, high forehead and cheekbones, long hair drawn back, and a smile calculated to break a pilot's heart, especially a skinny specimen like Fearless Fred Hodges. The pilots held a meeting in which they incorporated Loiwing and elected "Doc" Walsh of the CAMCO staff as mayor, reasoning that this would give him the power to marry people. The American Club was converted into a chapel. Greg Boyington attended in his bathrobe because his knees were too swollen for him to put on his pants. Duke Hedman played the piano—badly, as was his custom, and with a cigarette dangling from his lips. As Boyington told the story, the pilots substituted a genuine minister at the last moment, transforming the charade into a sacrament, but a version written closer to the time had the wedding solemnized a day or two later by a British army chaplain. Whatever the sequence of events, they left Anderson confused as to whether she was actually married or not.

The scrambles of March 31 and April 1 were caused by Colonel Kato, looking for the Tomahawks that had blistered his Hayabusas at Chiang Mai. But the sky was huge, the defenders had no radar station, and the two sides did not meet in the air. And because the Tomahawks had already scrambled, there were no planes on the ground at Loiwing when the 64th Sentai came over, causing Kato to write it off his list of suspects. On April 3 he scouted Mandalay, causing another scramble at Loiwing, but again the Hell's Angels and the 64th Sentai missed connections. Kato went home convinced that the American air force had indeed retreated into the interior of China, as McGarry had said.

The Hell's Angels attended Easter services in the American Club, with Duke Hedman at the piano and the British chaplain at a makeshift altar. The weather continued foul, so both the Toungoo party and the airfield strafe kept being postponed. Oley Olson flew to Kunming for a conference with Chennault—probably about the rebellious mood in his squadron.

Meanwhile, the CAMCO airstrip was looking more like a military base. Eight Hurricanes arrived from India on Easter Sunday, flown by some of the 17th Squadron pilots who had recently fled Magwe. Not to offend Chinese sensibilities, they were billeted across the border at Namhkam, on Burmese soil. The Hurricane pilots were impressed by the setup at Loiwing, especially "the excellent warning system provided by the wireless and telephone communications with Chinese lookouts on the surrounding hills." (Apparently such a precaution had never occurred to them.) Five 113th Squadron Blenheims also flew in, crewed by the men whom the Panda Bears used to escort to Thailand and the Adam & Eves to the Salween front. The RAF intended to use Loiwing as a rear base, with Lashio as their advance field, to support the Commonwealth army in the Irrawaddy Valley.

At 9:30 A.M. on Wednesday, April 8, a high-flying Dinah passed over Loiwing. Chuck Older and Eddie Overend scrambled but could not catch it, and the scout reported seeing "fifteen small planes" on the runway. That was about right. There were nine Tomahawks, four Hurricanes, and a Blenheim at the CAMCO airstrip that morning, plus two P-40Es that had spent the night en route to Kunming. The Kittyhawks, however, were not armed.

Colonel Kato had been scheduled to escort bombers to Maymyo that morning. Instead, he decided to go after the Allied air force before it vanished again. He therefore cut the escort to a single chutai, while the other two squadrons, plus his headquarters flight, set off for Loiwing. Japanese accounts are vague on how many Hayabusas were involved, but the AVG combat reports put the number at thirteen. The Tomahawks had been obliged to refuel between Loiwing and Chiang

Mai, going and coming, but the Hayabusas would be able to cover the 375-mile outbound leg on their external drop-tanks. They would then fight and fly home on their internal fuel supply.

But the Japanese were operating at an unaccustomed disadvantage. For the first time in the Pacific war, they were attacking an airfield protected by Chennault's early-warning system. Furthermore—also for the first time—some of Kato's pilots were without combat experience. In what would become an increasingly common practice in the JAAF, three 64th Sentai veterans had been called away to form the nucleus of a new fighter group, and their places had been filled by men fresh from flight school. This was a serious matter for an air force accustomed to overpowering its foes with the dash and skill of its pilots.

The Hayabusas crossed the China border at 20,000 feet, triggering warnings from Lashio onward. Meanwhile, three Kittyhawks flew into Loiwing from China, carrying AVG warpaint and piloted by Oley Olson, Ken Jernstedt, and Bob Little. They had scarcely landed when, at 12:30 P.M., word came into the bamboo alert shack: "many ships headed this way." The Tomahawks scrambled, as did the 17th Squadron Hurricanes and the three Kittyhawks just arrived from Kunming. The Blenheim stayed on the ground. So did the eastbound Kittyhawks. One of the fighters was being repaired, and their pilots (civilians in the employ of Pan Am) had left the field. If there was an extra Hell's Angel on the field, he did not think to fly the airworthy Kittyhawk away from danger.

Just before intruding the Loiwing airspace, Kato dropped down to 2,000 feet. He had instructed Captain Haruyasu Maruo to stay high with a top cover flight, but Maruo—having bought into McGarry's story that the AVG was a spent bullet—could not resist the temptation to join the strafing party. Since the Hayabusas had no air-to-air radio communication, Kato did not know that his rear was now exposed. The Japanese pilots dove upon the field, nose guns spewing a hail of incendiaries into the Blenheim and the U.S. Army Kittyhawks, whose unpreparedness seemed proof that the AVG was a sitting duck.

Word of the attack was flashed to the Hell's Angels at 22,000 feet: "Japs strafing the field." They screamed down on the Hayabusas, just as the Japanese pilots were climbing up for another strafe. Slow to get off the ground because the belly tank had to be removed from his Kittyhawk, and slow to climb because the plane had just been topped off with gasoline, Oley Olson may have been the first on the scene. He fired at a Hayabusa near the top of its climb. "He rolled over and I passed my fire to another climbing," Olson reported; "passed him and fired a long burst into a third at about 3000 feet [that] turned over shedding a few pieces of airplane and dived straight down into the ground and exploded" west of the field. First blood for the squadron leader—first combat, for that matter.

Then the Tomahawks arrived. "It was the most thrilling experience I've ever had," wrote R. T. Smith, who was credited with shooting down two Japanese planes in the melee, one of them while on his back. "The guys on the ground saw it all & are still raving. They say it looked just like a movie only better. Ha!"

Not everyone was jubilant. John Donovan, his radio dead, followed Fritz Wolf back to the field in the belief that the scramble had been a false alarm. Suddenly, two planes turned toward him with their nose guns winking. "Never have I been more scared," he confessed to his sister. "I felt more helpless than a baby and wouldn't have bet ten cents on my chance of getting out." Donovan was credited with a Hayabusa (his first) in the fifteen-minute battle. It fell, he reported, on the north edge of the field.

Cliff Groh tangled with several of the nimble fighters before catching one unaware, southeast of the field. "I kept firing burst after burst into him until I was about 10 to 20 yards behind him," he reported. The Hayabusa dove toward the ground, recovered momentarily, then augered in.

Fred Hodges met a Japanese plane climbing toward him. "I opened all guns on him with a head on shot," he wrote in his combat report. Without returning fire, the Hayabusa began to smoke, then dove to earth southwest of the field. First score for the bridgegroom, too.

Link Laughlin's combat report is notable for its clear-eyed description of the Japanese fighters. He even noticed that their armament was limited to two machine guns firing through the propeller arc—information that should have told Chennault that the AVG was not facing the cannon-equipped Mitsubishi Zero.* Laughlin shot one Hayabusa off a Toma-

---

* Laughlin reported that the enemy fighters had two large-caliber guns, and he may have been right. As compared to the *Ki*-43-I that fought the Hell's Angels at Rangoon, Nakajima had clipped the plane's wings (to 35′ 6″), slightly increased its power, weight, and speed (320 mph at 20,000 feet), and armed it with two 12.7-mm machine guns. This was the *Ki*-43-II. However, the large-caliber guns were so slow that at Chiang Mai the ground crews replaced the port-side weapon with a 7.7-mm gun.

Curtiss P-40E Kittyhawk

In July 1941 Curtiss-Wright produced a P-40 model so different from its predecessor that the company gave it a new designation: H83. As compared to the small-mouthed Tomahawk, it had a more powerful engine, larger airscoop, shorter nose, and higher propeller line, giving it a distinctly jut-jawed appearance. The addition of bomb racks and fifty-caliber wing guns made the new plane immensely effective in tactical ground support missions. Curtiss built more than 12,000, of which 6,800 went to the U.S. Army Air Forces, 3,100 to Britain, and 2,100 to the Soviet Union. However, the AAF and RAF transferred many planes to other countries, especially Canada and Australia, but also to Brazil, Turkey, and the "Free French" air force. They were used to great effect in climates ranging from the tropical heat of Burma, through the dust of North Africa, to the frost of Alaska and the Soviet Union. The specifications are for the P-40E supplied to the AVG in the spring of 1942.

Engine: 1,150-hp Allison liquid-cooled in-line
Crew: one
Wingspan: 37 feet 4 inches
Combat weight: 8,840 lb
Maximum range: 700 miles (greater with drop-tanks)
Top speed: 350 mph at 15,000 feet
Armament: six .50-caliber machine guns in the wings; six 35-lb bombs

---

hawk's tail, south of the field. He flamed another to the west, but lost sight of it between the shooting and the crash. They were the first and second kills of his combat career.

Fritz Wolf tangled with a Japanese plane and saw it crash west of the field. Then he shot another off a Kittyhawk's tail: "it started smoking in a glide. . . . I went down again and the Japanese did nothing to avoid me." Wolf fired again and saw more smoke. He was credited with both kills, though he saw only one Hayabusa go in.

Eddie Overend evidently came on the scene later than his comrades, for the Japanese were at 4,000 feet when he saw them. He skirmished with four Hayabusas without result, then caught a loner southeast of the field: "I fired from 150 yards until I was almost up on him, at which time he turned violently and I saw the canopy and upper part of the fuselage at this point tear away." The Hayabusa crashed without burning.

Bob Little, flying a Kittyhawk, was also credited with a kill, meaning that the Hell's Angels were claiming twelve out of thirteen Hayabusas. But a close reading of the combat reports shows that most of the Japanese fighters went down in four locations: three in the vicinity of the CAMCO airstrip, and one a few miles southeast by the river. That is significant because only three wrecks were found near the airport—and because the 64th Sentai lost only four Hayabusas on April 8.

Four was plenty, amounting as they did to nearly a third of the planes that went to Loiwing. Some of Kato's best pilots were among the victims, including the 3rd Chutai leader, Captain Katsumi Anma, credited with destroying upwards of twelve enemy planes in China, Manchuria, Malaya, and the Indies. Anma was the first of the great Japanese army pilots to die in the Pacific war—to the JAAF, a loss equivalent to Jack Newkirk's for the AVG. It was his Hayabusa that crashed in a paddy field two miles south of Loiwing, with four Hell's Angels (Wolf, Overend, Smith, and Groh) claiming it for their own. Another veteran to die that Wednesday was Sergeant Haruto Wada, whose first kill had been an I-15 biplane over Luoyang in January 1938. He crashed at the Loiwing airstrip, as did a young lieutenant named Tadao Kuroki. The other man to go down near the field was also a lieutenant, Muneyuki Okumura, thirty years old and evidently a sergeant-pilot commissioned in the fall of 1941.

Back at Chiang Mai, the mood was gloomy, lightened only by the confession of one of the green pilots—a lieutenant named Takehasi—that when the Tomahawks had swooped down he could think of no expedient but to loop-the-loop. This he did for more than thirty repetitions, around and around, until against all logic he waltzed himself out of harm's way.

Lieutenant Yohei Hinoki had been assigned to the Maymyo escort and thus missed the fight. At dinner, he so far forgot his manners that he attempted to console his commander. "There was nothing you could have done," Hinoki blurted. But it was not in Kato's nature to admit that a situation was past mending. "No," he told the presumptuous young pilot. "I will go back there and attack again. Whatever the hardship, we must not yield. *There is always a way.*"

Claire Chennault's reaction to the Loiwing fight was also perfectly in character. Olson's after-action report informed him that twelve "Zeros" had been shot down at the cost of one P-40E Kittyhawk destroyed on the ground, plus a Blenheim and the other grounded Kittyhawk lightly damaged. Note the priorities in Chennault's response, which read in full:

> Why were two P40Es left on ground during raid? Congratulations on fine work beating Model "0."

Terminate Our Contracts

April 1942

O n the night of April 2, the 10th Air Force flew its first combat
mission from India, bombing the Andaman Islands to the seaward
of Rangoon. "It was a beautiful night," wrote General Brereton,
who rode as copilot in one of the B-17s, "with a bright Indian moon
illuminating the sea for miles." Next day, the Flying Fortresses bombed
Rangoon. Stilwell was furious, perhaps because a bomber crashed on
takeoff, killing everyone aboard, but more likely because Brereton and
Bumble Wavell had cooked up the raid without consulting him.

By coincidence, Erik Shilling scouted South Burma that day, as part
of a plan by the Adam & Eves to make a moonlight raid on the Rangoon
airports. In Kunming, the Panda Bears also hoped to go on the offensive.
Chennault had replaced Jack Newkirk with the tall, jug-eared Tex Hill,
who planned to shoot up the Japanese airfields across the border in
French Indochina. While they prepared for this raid, the pilots at Wu
Chia Ba competed for the joy of flying the AVG's new Kittyhawks. With
three fifty-caliber guns on each wing, the Kittyhawk would actually slew
off course if the guns on one side fired and the others did not. Less
lovable was its tendency to "mush" in a power dive: it kept dropping
even after the pilot brought the nose up, posing the danger that it would
slam into the ground before it answered the controls.

Walt Disney's darling Bengal cat, leaping through a V-for-Victory
sign, reached Kunming at about this time. "My God, do we have to wear

those things?" a headquarters clerk is supposed to have said. But on Skip Adair's orders, the men at Wu Chia Ba pinned the symbol of their fame over the right pocket of their uniform jackets, and before long they were taking pride in it. Perhaps it was not so bad, after all, to be a Flying Tiger.

When not otherwise occupied, the Tigers fought the local populace and each other, as was their unfortunate custom. A crew chief assaulted a French doctor who would not perform an abortion on the woman he had brought up from Rangoon. Other men beat up the AVG police officer, Melvin Ceder, when he tried to search Adobe City for contraband. George McMillan and Skip Adair were punched in the same brawl, which ended with Ceder in the hospital and two technicians— Frank Metasavage and Glen Yarbery—under house arrest. (While Yarbery punched McMillan, John Petach guarded the crew chief's back, to keep anyone from interfering with what he viewed as simple justice.) Somebody tore the lock off the recreation room door to get a drink, with Greg Boyington the favorite suspect. Matt Kuykendall was fined $100 "for firing his gun in a reckless manner while intoxicated and off duty." An Allison engine specialist was hit by a ricochet. . . .

Chennault was in Chongqing that week, having flown to the capital to settle the matter of the AVG's induction. (He took two Flying Tiger pins with him, for madame and the generalissimo.) While there, he had a chat with John Davies of the U.S. Embassy staff. The young Foreign Service officer had just arrived from Washington with some advice from the War Department and the White House: "I told [Chennault] what Currie had to say about Arnold and the desirability of his playing ball." That metaphor again! If Chennault expected reinforcements for the AVG—if he hoped to put his military career back on track—then he must join the authorized team of George Marshall, Hap Arnold, and Vinegar Joe Stilwell.

He did so. In a private conference with Madame Chiang, Chennault agreed to accept induction for himself and his men, asking only that he be present when the decision was made. It was a face-saving request in the Chinese tradition, but it added another black mark to Chennault's already dark reputation at the War Department. Bissell forwarded the condition with the comment: "His value to China and the U S is recognized but the conclusion that he is playing personal politics is unescapable." For an army man, there was no worse sin than playing politics—or at least to be *seen* playing politics, because in fact they all did it, all the time.

The principals met with Chiang Kai-shek that afternoon, with Brereton putting in his oar by radiogram from India. After long discussion, they hit upon an induction date three months hence—time for the AVG to go out of existence and the 23rd Pursuit Group to move into China. The date was wonderfully symbolic, since it was the birthday of the United States of America. Madame radioed the good news to Lauchlin Currie:

> After hour's conference with Stillwell [sic], Bissell, Groco, Magruder, final decision reached induct A.V.G's. Formal induction July 4. Meanwhile, every effort maintain efficiency unit. Thank Heavens. Inform T.V.

Stilwell must have been equally pleased, but he did an admirable job of concealing it. His radiogram to the War Department laid out the proposal in businesslike fashion, and concluded: "Cardinal principal should be to maintain maximum effectiveness of AVG during induction. Approval requested." A few days later he turned to the matter of Chennault's place in the new scheme of things:

> It is recommended that Col Clayton L Bissell O-10474 be promoted to brigadier general Army of the US and that Col Claire L Chennault be promoted to brigadier general Army of the US, effective date of Chennaults rank to be one day subsequent to the appointment of Col Bissell. These recommendations have the concurrence of the generalissimo.

Having ensured that Chennault would be subordinate to Bissell, Stilwell turned to his goal of commanding the Chinese army in Burma. To achieve this goal, he did not shrink from trumping Chiang Kai-shek with his own air force: "Told him," Stilwell wrote in his diary, "I couldn't put American air units in support of troops in whose commanders I had no confidence." In other words, unless Stilwell commanded them, Chiang's troops in Burma would get no support from the planes their country had purchased and the pilots it had hired.

Chennault, Stilwell, the generalissimo, and madame then flew to Kunming, and the last three continued to Lashio. There Chiang made good on his part of the bargain, telling his officers "that I am the boss," as Stilwell put it, with "full power to promote, relieve, and punish any officer in the Chinese Expeditionary Force." He expressed his glee in one parenthetical word: "Jesus."

Watching the brass come and go, Bus Keeton observed: "There is something in the air about to happen." He was right. Chennault called a meeting at Hostel Number One, chewed out the men for their brawling ways, and told them a new policy in Washington prohibited them from resigning their CAMCO contracts. The men were unsure whether President Roosevelt or the Congress was responsible for this edict.

Chennault did not mention that he was returning to active duty, yet he must have known that he was due to be commissioned the following day with serial number O-10090. Bissell sent him a radiogram to that effect, Magruder sent two follow-up messages, and—when they evoked no response—Madame Chiang was asked to pass the word "through private channels." For a week Chennault made no reply, which may have been his most heartfelt comment on the rank that had been offered him. As the U.S. Military Mission understood the matter, however, Claire Chennault returned to active duty on April 9 as a captain (his retirement rank!) and was promoted to colonel the following day, legitimatizing the eagles he had assumed five years before. As for his general's stars, he would have to wait until Bissell got his.

In any event, he was back on the team. Tex Hill and five other Panda Bears had flown down to Mengzi, missing Chennault's lecture at Hostel Number One; they spent the night and may or may not have strafed their targets next day. When they straggled back to Wu Chia Ba airport, Chennault told them that their Indochina offensive was canceled. Instead, the Panda Bears were to go to Loiwing with seven Kittyhawks and three Tomahawks. ("There is definately something in the air," fretted Keeton in his diary.) With Lashio as their advance field, Tex Hill and his pilots would fly three missions a day over the Chinese lines at Pyinmana, on the railroad north of Toungoo. Thus did Stilwell make his payoff to Chiang Kai-shek, tit for tat.

Chennault flew down to Loiwing on a CNAC Douglas with some of the 2nd Squadron technicians—in four months of war, his first visit to his pilots on the front line. He wanted to keep an eye on how the Panda Bears performed their "morale missions," and he also wanted to deliver the word on induction and discipline to the Hell's Angels. Oley Olson's pilots were to have no part of the flights to Pyinmana. Their Tomahawks were weary and their spirit rebellious, so Chennault gave them the task of defending Loiwing from air attack.

At Chiang Mai, Kato was assembling pilots and planes for a predawn return to Loiwing. His mechanics managed to put eleven Hayabusas into condition to make the 750-mile round trip, but three were disabled when their pilots taxied into one another in the darkness. That left eight fighters to lift off at 3:45 A.M., April 10—and three of those turned back with engine trouble. Navigation lights glowing on wingtips and tail, the five remaining Hayabusas droned across the desolate Shan Highlands on the two-hour flight to China. If the listening posts heard them coming, the warning served no purpose. The AVG technicians were warming up the Tomahawks and Kittyhawks for the day, but the pilots had not yet reached the field when the Hayabusas came over. At 6:10 A.M., Kato waggled his wings, turned off his navigation lights, and dove to the attack. He rejoiced to see twenty-three planes on the ground, neatly lined up—a perfect reprise of the situation at Chiang Mai two weeks before. Like the Adam & Eves on that occasion, the 64th Sentai pilots actually saw the enemy airmen running across the field. "Some one hollered bombers," as Dan Hoyle wrote in the squadron log, "and everyone took to the best available cover."

The Hayabusas strafed the field repeatedly, but they failed to set any of the fighters alight. Finally Kato turned on his navigation lights and waggled his wings for the flight home. To the astonishment of his pilots, he then fired a burst from his machine guns. Back at Chiang Mai, Lieutenant Hinoki asked Kato about this unusual signal, and the colonel admitted that he had strafed Loiwing with dead guns. Reaching to turn off his navigation lights, Kato had hit the main switch instead, and did not realize the error until he tried to turn the lights on again; he had fired his guns to convince himself that he had really done this stupid thing.

Kato's pilots were convinced that they had torn a great swath through the enemy air force, though they were puzzled why the planes did not burn. (They finally decided that the Americans had drained the gasoline from their planes overnight.) In fact, the damage at Loiwing was even more trivial than what the 64th Sentai had suffered at Chiang Mai. Of twenty-three fighters on the field that morning—thirteen Tomahawks, seven Kittyhawks, and three Hurricanes—fewer than half were hit, and only one was so badly damaged that it could not be put back into commission. With just one hour's delay, Tex Hill, Pete Wright, and Bill Fish took off for Friday's morale mission, scouting Kyedaw airfield and showing the twelve-pointed CAF star over the Chinese lines.

Meanwhile, the 64th Sentai mechanics worked on the Hayabusas at Chiang Mai, and they told Kato that he could have nine planes for a knockout blow on Loiwing. The warning net picked them up at 2:30 P.M. near Lashio. (The AVG had seventeen listening posts on the China-Burma border and another near Lashio, each with a hand-cranked fifteen-watt transmitter; the British had stations at Heho, Namsang, and Lashio; and the Chinese had one at Pyawbwe.) At Loiwing, the alarm shrilled at 2:45 P.M. Seven Tomahawks took off, but one turned back with a loose oil cap; the others climbed through the clouds to 25,000 feet. They patrolled for half an hour, then got word that the Japanese fighters were over the field.

Again the 64th Sentai had come in below them—a fatal error. Lieutenant Hinoki, on his second trip of the day into China, watched with horror as four Tomahawks fell out of the clouds upon the flight led by Lieutenant Takeshi Endo. With no other means of warning his friends, Hinoki turned toward the enemy fighters and opened fire at the nearest pair, which dove away with Hinoki after them.

The Tomahawks were flown by Whitey Lawlor, Bill Reed, R. T. Smith, and Bob Brouk. With Sergeant Aikichi Misago on his wing, Hinoki went after the last two. As R. T. recalled the clash, he bounced several retractable-gear fighters and dove out when hard-pressed by two other Japanese fighters; he then went after one of the intruders while Brouk chased the second. Said Brouk in his combat report:

> I made three passes at the enemy ship hitting him each time. On the fourth pass, a head on attack, I hit him and he turned to my left; went over on his back, and flames shot from under his left gas tank. He started down and I followed him for several seconds, thousands of feet, while he was in flames.

If this was Sergeant Misago, then R. T. was chasing Hinoki. But as the Japanese lieutenant told the story, *he* did the chasing, and the two planes went into the clouds, dodging in and out of the murk at ever lower altitudes. At one point, he saw a ghostly wing in the clouds. He fired at it, and the American opened fire at the same moment. Hinoki heard bullets tearing through his fuselage; his face turned warm and sticky with blood, and gasoline spilled out of his right wing, turning immediately to white vapor. Almost certainly, his opponent was R. T.

Smith, who wrote in his combat report: "After firing at one, I observed heavy smoke pouring from his engine as he dove down."

Concluding that he was hit too badly to make it home, Hinoki "decided to die in the mountains." He turned toward the nearest peak. The Tomahawks kept after him but were driven off by two Hayabusas, to whom Hinoki signaled thanks and farewell. ("I fought two of them for 7 or 8 minutes," R. T. recalled, "and finally had to dive out as they both got the advantage.") Again a liquid-cooled fighter came at him, and more bullets tore through his plane. The Hayabusa's wingtips disintegrated, but at last the other plane broke off. Hinoki looked down and saw a river, which he recognized as the rendezvous for the trip home. Death no longer seemed quite so inviting, so instead of diving into the mountains he set out for Chiang Mai, where his tanks ran dry just as he was gliding down to land, after a total of nine hours in the cockpit. Hinoki had twenty-one bullet holes in his Hayabusa and one in his back, and he would spend a month in an army hospital.

Kato had meanwhile joined the battle and claimed one Tomahawk. Another was credited to Sergeant Yoshito Yasuda, who suckered an enemy plane into a dogfight but who kept being frustrated by the jamming of his guns. At last Yasuda broke off, out of ammunition—whereupon his opponent suddenly nosed up, fell off, and dove into the jungle. In both cases, the enemy fighters must have been Hurricanes. (The RAF lost four planes but no pilots in the combats at Loiwing. Among those who bellied in was Tex Barrick, the American who had bewildered the AVG by yelling "snapper!" on February 18.) As soon as he was able, Kato broke off and headed for home.

Knowing that the JAAF pilots tended to go slack when the heat was off, the other two Hell's Angels—Chuck Older and Duke Hedman—had flown south, hoping to intercept the Japanese planes as they headed for the barn. For twenty minutes they saw nothing, so they turned back toward the field. Almost immediately, they met a retractable-gear fighter. The two Americans pulled up sharply, made a positive identification, and dove on the enemy's tail. "He went wild," Older recalled in later years. "He went into a flat loop and went right over our heads. I could look right up and see him go by—upside down in the cockpit." This was Sergeant Yasuda, whose first warning of danger was the sight of red fireballs dancing on his cowling. His Hayabusa vibrated, and for a moment he believed that his own guns had spontaneously begun to fire.

Then he did go wild, trying to survive close combat with two enemy fighters when he had no ammunition. "All I can do is turn, turn," he recalled years later. "Oil is coming out of the exhaust pipes like white smoke, and oil is on the fuselage and windscreen." He opened the canopy in order to see, but oil covered his goggles, too, and he had to throw them away. At one point, he wrote, he gave up the fight and tried to ram one of his tormentors. Chuck Older's combat report told the story this way:

> For the next half hour Hedman and I engaged the enemy in a twisting and turning dogfight. We lost altitude and ended up right over the mountain tops. . . . We both got in several good burst after this, and finally saw the enemy going down steeply toward a hillside, apparently out of control, with black smoke streaming to the rear. We lost sight of the enemy after this, but after circling I noticed smoke rising from a spot on the hillside near where the enemy seemed to be falling.

But Yasuda was still airborne, though exhausted from the ordeal, eyes and throat burning from the 300-mph blast of air. Like Hinoki, he limped back to Chiang Mai, and like him made a dead-stick landing at the home field.

Meanwhile, R. T. Smith had also gone on the prowl for the retreating enemy. "I looked south and saw three of them heading for home," he wrote in his combat report. "I chased them and after about 5 minutes caught up with the last one. Closed to about 100 yards and opened up. He went into a dive and I followed, shooting on the way down. He crashed in a rice paddy on the side of a mountain about 30 to 40 miles down the valley." This Hayabusa was flown by Sergeant Chikara Goto, credited with shooting down two Hurricanes over Singapore on December 31. Afterward, R. T. was sorry he had wasted so much ordnance on a dead duck. "I could easily have slid in behind the other two," he wrote, "and picked them both off." But he was lucky to have settled for the sure bet. The flight was led by Colonel Kato. Wiser than Goto, Kato kept looking to the rear, and he had seen the Tomahawk come up. Like Hinoki earlier in the fight, the only way he could warn Goto was to turn back to help him, which he did. Before reaching an attack position, however, he saw that Goto was mortally hit, so he broke off. Had R. T. pressed his luck, he would have met the JAAF's most famous pilot head-on.

The second battle of Loiwing is remarkable for how closely the combat reports tracked reality. The Japanese claimed two fighters, and two Hurricanes had gone down. The Hell's Angels earned three combat bonuses—Bob Brouk for shooting down Misago, Chuck Older and Duke Hedman for their duel with Yasuda, and R. T. Smith for his after-action ambush of Goto—and the first and last were actual kills.

Remarkable too is the consistency with which Chennault's pilots were besting Kato's. The 64th Sentai had lost thirty pilots in four months of almost continual combat; of that number, the AVG had killed eight, and in only three encounters. For its part, the 64th Sentai had shot down Eddie Overend and ruined Parker Dupouy's day on December 25, with both Americans living to fight again. Stretching a point, Kato might also have taken the credit for Jack Newkirk's death and Mac McGarry's capture—though ground fire had knocked them down—but even that would have left the laurels on the other side. In nearly five years of war, against Chinese, Soviet, British, Dutch, and American pilots, this was the first time the 64th Sentai had come out second best.

On Saturday evening, April 11, pilots and technicians gathered at the American Club to hear Chennault on the subject of induction. He had smoothed his pitch since his lecture at Hostel Number One. If they did not want to join the army in China, he assured them, they would be allowed to serve out their year with CAMCO and go home. Furthermore, the morale missions over the Chinese lines would stop in just ten days. Afterward, Doc Walsh screened a film for them: *Varsity Show 1937*.

Tex Hill, Pete Wright, and John Croft missed the lecture, having flown down to Lashio to prepare for the next day's mission. (As usually happens in war, the headquarters dictate was modified in the field. Chiang's three missions generally came down to one, and often that one was scrubbed.) The three Panda Bears spent the night at the CNAC hostel, and at sunrise they warmed up their Kittyhawks on the red-clay runway. The plan was to follow the road and railway south to Pyinmana, make themselves known to the defenders, then fly on to Toungoo and see if the JAAF had moved into Kyedaw airfield. Not long after, Pete Wright told what it was like, showing the CAF star on the Burma front:

We hit our checkpoints without fail and in about an hour and a half the ranges of mountains dropped away and we were over a lush green valley floored with rice paddies. Running down the center, crisscrossing each other every few miles but never more than a few hundred yards apart, were the Rangoon-Mandalay railroad and the Burma Road.

Ahead of us we could see the village of Pyinmana smouldering in the distance. We went into a shallow dive which brought us over the town at about two thousand feet. . . . [W]e made two quick turns around it to make sure they recognized us. . . . We climbed as quickly as possible and started south down the railroad. By the time we reached 15,000 feet we could see the aerodrome of Toungoo.

As they watched, a twin-engined plane landed on Kyedaw's asphalt runway and taxied off to the side—probably a Kawasaki Lily of the 8th Sentai, which had moved to Kyedaw to support the Japanese troops around Pyinmana. Radioing Croft to fly top cover, Tex Hill dropped his wing and dove on the airfield. He was followed by Wright:

I was scared to death. . . . I had my eye on the plane that had just landed. As I came over the field at about 200 feet, I saw it parked out to the side with its engines still turning over. I eased over a bit to get it in my sights and squeezed the trigger. Pulling back on the stick, I flashed over it and made a steep climbing turn to the left. I looked back to see the results. As I did so . . . huge black balls exploded all around me. One went off under my tail. I gave my plane full throttle and did a series of violent maneuvers and miraculously got away.

Hill made two runs, in each of which he claimed a single-engined Mitsubishi Ann. Flak hit his Kittyhawk on the second pass, so he decided to call it a day.

The three men made their separate ways north. After a few minutes of flying, Pete Wright spotted a lone plane ahead of him. Thinking it was a Kittyhawk, he turned toward it with the intention of linking up. As he came close, Wright saw that the other plane had fixed landing gear and a greenhouse canopy:

It was a Jap! He was coming towards me, so I dove down and out to one side in order to swing around behind him. . . .

I kept expecting him to dive, turn, or use some kind of evasive action. Suddenly it dawned on me he was completely unaware of my presence. Both the pilot and his rear seat gunner had made the fatal mistake of believing they were safe simply because they were in sight of their home aerodrome. I closed in to about 200 yards and let go a long burst. As the slugs from my six heavy caliber machine guns poured into the tail of the bomber, pieces of the fuselage started coming off from the left hand side and a huge sheet of flame burst from the base of the right wing. . . .

As I flashed over it, I got a glimpse through the closed transparent canopy, not more than twenty feet below, of the figure of the gunner slumped forward in the rear cockpit. He had not even turned around, much less opened his canopy and fired his gun!

He was credited with both planes, the Lily on the ground and the light bomber (or observation plane) in the air. That made two kills in less than an hour for Wright, who had dropped out of Yale to join the navy, and whose only previous moment of glory had been his hapless night interception at Rangoon, when he had slammed into the car in which Ken Merritt was sleeping.

At Loiwing, Chennault and Bob Prescott were playing cribbage in the alert shack when they heard an engine over the field. The Old Man cocked his ear, announced that the roar was that of a Wright Cyclone engine, and went on with the game. (Chennault played to win; if he was behind, he tried to keep playing until the score was even.) The pilots loafing outside the alert shack did not hear this confident pronouncement. They saw a radial-engined plane swooping toward them with its wheels up, and they ran for the nearest trench, shouting *"Zero, Zero!"* The men inside the alert shack exploded off their chairs—positive identification be damned!—and raced for shelter. As the story is told, they jammed in the door and the windows of the alert shack: too many shoulders, not enough exits.

The intruder was Erik Shilling in a North American trainer, flying onto the clay runway without pausing to identify himself. Chennault "chewed his ass out royally," and within seventy-two hours the AVG adopted a formal protocol for pilots approaching a combat field. Make radio contact sixty miles out, lower your wheels ten miles out, come down to 1,500 feet one mile out, and make a circuit of the field before you land. The Old Man signed the order with the same enigmatic signature—*C. L. Chennault, Commanding*—that he had been using since the previous July.

Chennault had not yet been inducted into the U.S. Army, and the AVG still belonged to the Chinese Air Force, but Stilwell was now directing their operations. Witness his April 14 radiogram to Chennault:

> Request you arrange air recon road and railway Rangoon to Toungoo with mission are reinforcements from 40 ships reported Rangoon moving to Chinese end?

Stilwell was right to worry. Sakurai's 33rd Division was advancing up the Irrawaddy Valley, while Takeuchi's 55th Division was advancing up the Sittang. (Though Burma widened in the north, the rivers were now converging. If they continued to retreat, the Allied armies would eventually come together at Mandalay.) Meanwhile, Watanabe's 56th Division swung eastward into the Shan Highlands, on an end run to Lashio. This was "the hook," a favorite tactic of the Japanese army: set up a roadblock to the enemy's rear, draw off his forces to meet the new threat, then hammer him on the original front.

Stilwell's radiogram referred to yet another division, the 18th under Lieutenant General Renya Mutaguchi. As a colonel in 1937, Mutaguchi had commanded the regiment that had fired the first shots of the Sino-Japanese War; each July 7, to commemorate the glorious affair at the Marco Polo Bridge, he bowed toward the imperial palace in Tokyo.* Most of his troops were former coal miners, and in Malaya they had earned a reputation for brutality. As Stilwell feared, they moved up the Sittang Valley to reinforce the 55th at Pyinmana. In other words, while a single Japanese division was considered sufficient to deal with the Commonwealth army, three divisions were aimed at the "Chinese end." At that, the British borrowed Chinese troops to help hold the oilfields at Yenangyaung. When the Chinese arrived, they were mistaken for Japanese, throwing the Commonwealth army into such turmoil that the Inniskillins were cut off. As a result, the first task of the Chinese troops

---

* In 1943, commanding the Japanese defense of Burma, Mutaguchi would order his troops to die rather than yield: "If your hands are broken, fight with your feet. If your hands and feet are broken, use your teeth." Among the 30,000 men who gave up their lives in obedience to Mutaguchi's injunction was Private Kikujiro Shimura, whose disappearance at the Marco Polo Bridge had caused the first skirmish of an eight-year war.

was to rescue the British battalion, which they did with such dispatch that General Hutton was moved to write:

> They had on the average only one weapon for three men so that the fire power of a division was about equal to that of one of our brigades. The balance of men were used as porters . . . or for digging but were always available to replace casualties. The results of this organisation were not therefore as bad as might be expected.

In response to Stilwell's radiogram, Chennault sent a flight of Kittyhawks to scout the Sittang Valley below Pyinmana, and another to inspect the Japanese airfields in northern Thailand. Next day—April 15—he sent the Panda Bears to Pegu, 150 miles into Japanese-held territory. Of the three pilots on this mission, John Croft turned back when his engine cut out, and John Petach became lost on the way home, ran out of gas, and made a wheels-up landing in a dry river bed. Petach was rescued by the missionary doctor Gordon Seagrave, now a U.S. Army major serving with the Chinese army. Although the Kittyhawk was not damaged, it had to be burned to keep it from the Japanese.

Chennault had dispatched some Hell's Angels to Lashio as backup for this patrol. Oley Olson's men regarded this as a breech of their tacit agreement that the Tomahawks would be reserved for local defense, while the Kittyhawks did the dirty stuff over the lines. Chennault thought otherwise, as R. T. Smith wrote in his diary on Thursday:

> A mission was planned this p.m. for tomorrow morning—& is it a stinker. 4 Tomahawks & 4 Kittyhawks to escort 6 R.A.F. Blenheims on a raid to [Chiang] Mai. After the Blenheims dropped their bombs the Tommies are to strafe the field. It bristles with anti-aircraft & is about 160 miles inside enemy territory. Volunteers were scarce as hen's teeth, but finally some of the boys who haven't seen much action decided to go. . . . We figure two or three may get back.

Fortunately the Blenheims did not show up, and the raid was canceled.

Meanwhile, Chennault finally sent that radiogram to Chongqing, accepting the colonelcy that had been offered him. Twenty-four hours later, six U.S. Army Douglas transports flew in from India with supplies for him. It was as if the Old Man had sold the AVG for a mess of propellers and tires, and himself for a pair of gold eagles.

The rebellious mood was spreading. "It is believed," wrote Dan Hoyle in the 3rd Squadron log, "that about 10 or 15 members of the

Group . . . resigned a few days ago probably to work for Pan American Airways, Ferry Command. Pilots are disagreeing over some of the missions they go on as to the necessity and valuation of them."

Seven technicians had indeed decamped for India—"deserted," in Chennault's view, since he had decreed there would be no more resignations. (In the end, as he often did, he softened the punishment and gave them dishonorable discharges.) They included Glen Yarbery and Frank Metasavage, the crew chiefs who had put Melvin Ceder in the hospital. Clayton Harpold, the redoubtable mess sergeant from Eighteen Mile Ranch and Magwe, also quit at this time.

Several pilots would have followed them home if they could have done it honorably . . . including Bob Neale, squadron leader of the Adam & Eves. Among others, George Burgard planned to join Pan Am as a ferry pilot as soon as the AVG broke up, and he talked to some of the technicians about accompanying him to Africa. Chennault was so alarmed that he asked Bissell to put a finger in the dike:

> Please issue instructions to CNAC and Pan American not to employ former AVG personnel. Many AVG men quitting hoping to take better pay jobs with these companies. Also issue orders that U S Army air transports may not carry AVG personnel except by written request.

On Saturday, April 18, the Hell's Angels scrambled when a twin-engined reconnaissance plane came over Loiwing. Three Tomahawks bounced the intruder at 14,000 feet, with Bob Brouk and Bob Prescott sharing credit for the kill. That night, Chennault called a meeting in the American Club. He told the pilots that they must carry out the missions he gave them, or else be fired for cowardice. "If you want to show the white feather," he supposedly told them, "you can all quit." Then he reasoned with them: he had just accepted a commission in the U.S. Army, so he had no choice but to order morale missions if Stilwell asked for them. Finally, he appealed to their love of country. "You fellows have to remember," one of the Panda Bears remembered him saying, "that's an American general with his staff down there directing these Chinese armies, and we owe him all the support we can give him."

The pilots were astonished to hear that Chennault was back on active duty. (He told them he was a brigadier general, which was premature.) They were relieved, too, for if the Old Man were merely following orders, then perhaps his judgment was as sound as ever. But however much they loved and respected him, they despised the morale missions more. Caucusing afterward, they voted to go on strike—or so they termed the event that became known as the Pilots' Revolt. Actually, their letter was less a strike call than a mass resignation:

> We, the undersigned, pilots of the American Volunteer Group, hereby desire to terminate our contracts with the Central Aircraft Mfg. Co. and our services with the AVG.

Whereupon Tex Hill unhinged himself, got to his feet, and urged them not to sign. Of all the squadron leaders, Hill was probably the best-liked—raw-boned, shambling, dispenser of one-liners that could be sidesplittingly funny. Curiously for a Southwesterner, he did not tan, but burned and peeled under the tropical sun, until his face glowed like a ripe tomato. What motivated him at Loiwing was a mix of patriotism, affection for the Old Man, and a Chennault-like understanding that a soldier had to go along to get along.

Only four men followed his lead: Duke Hedman, Frank Schiel, Ed Rector, and Robert Raine. The rest signed, including four of his Panda Bears, fourteen Hell's Angels, and six Adam & Eves who were serving under Olson at Loiwing. The mutineers handed their letter to Chennault on Sunday morning. He never said how much it burned his fingers, but he could count, and he had fewer than sixty pilots on duty with the squadrons, including several who did not have the right stuff for combat flying. Of the men he could depend upon to fight the JAAF, twenty-four had announced their readiness to go home, including a squadron leader (Oley Olson) and six aces (Bob Prescott, Dick Rossi, Whitey Lawlor, Ken Jernstedt, Chuck Older, and R. T. Smith). It was an offer he simply could not accept.

Having dared his pilots to quit, Chennault fell back on the argument he had advanced at Hostel Number One. He called a meeting for 8 P.M. Sunday evening in the American Club and told the mutineers that he could not accept their resignations. If they went home, he said, they would go as deserters. The distinction between desertion and a dishonorable discharge might be hard for a civilian to grasp, but it was clear to these proud young men. "There wasn't much we could do but stay," Bus Keeton wrote in his diary. "Here we have fought tremendous odds and done a good job. Desertion would ruin everything."

There was a lot of brave talk among the pilots about calling the Old

Man's bluff, but in fact he had called theirs. Chennault's only concession in the Pilots' Revolt was to pretend it never happened.

At this lowest hour of the American Volunteer Group, another group of American airmen reached China, by a route that had been closed since December 8. Early in the morning of April 18, sixteen stripped-down B-25s under the command of Colonel Jimmy Doolittle roared across the deck of the carrier *Hornet*, lifted off with an ease that astonished their crews, and skimmed at low altitude toward the Japanese main island of Honshu. Appropriately, the pet name of this twin-engined bomber was Mitchell, after the iconoclastic officer who in 1924 had argued that American planes could set the cities of Japan on fire.

Like Chennault in the 1930s, the Japanese realized that the way to protect an island from surprise attack was to surround it with radio-equipped picket boats. The U.S. task force encountered one of these vessels and sank it, but had to assume that Japanese planes would soon be out to attack *Hornet* and her escort. As a result, the Mitchells were launched ahead of schedule, requiring them to travel hundreds of additional miles. After they bombed Japan, one B-25 diverted to Siberia, where its crew was interned. (Though allied with the United States in Europe, the Soviet Union maintained a cynical neutrality in the Pacific until the last days of the war.) The other fifteen bombers reached the China coast at nightfall and almost out of gas, and one by one they ditched offshore or crashed in Japanese-held territory. Three airmen were killed; eight were captured. Chinese partisans guided the rest to safety, but not one plane survived to become the nucleus of Chennault's long-promised bomber group.

Like the Flying Tigers, the Doolittle raiders became heroes in the United States, less for the damage they inflicted than for the proof that Americans could still strike back at their tormentors. In Japan, too, the greatest impact was psychological. The Nakajima and Mitsubishi aircraft factories were damaged, but the lasting hurt was the realization that for the first time in 2,600 years, enemy war machines had violated the Sacred Motherland.

Tex Hill, Ed Rector, Duke Hedman, and Robert Raine missed the Sunday evening showdown at the American Club, having flown down to Lashio for Monday's morale mission. After a 6:45 A.M. takeoff, they made the bread run to Pyinmana, as Rector related in his combat report:

> We arrived over the target an hour later and began circling at 8,000'. Shortly after we received a barrage of AA fire and turned north and continued our patrol. . . . We had circled for twenty minutes at 9,000' when I observed an enemy ship approaching from the south and two thousand feet above us. I informed Hill by radio then turned toward the plane and started climbing. The plane turned west on sighting us and poured on all gun to escape. I chased him . . . six minutes at 210 MPH indicated then finally started closing on him as he turned south. I gave him three bursts in the turn, one more long one as he straightened out eastward and started in a dive toward the ground. Hedman had meanwhile made a pass at him, and gave him a final burst setting him on fire.

Reporting the shoot-down to Skip Adair at Kunming, Chennault added what was even better news: "Situation here normal today with all hands working." But Monday's mission had been tailored to suit the mood at Loiwing. Not only did Chennault pick the pilots from those who had refused to join the mutiny, but he evidently instructed them to patrol at an altitude that would keep them safe from small-arms fire. Then, when ack-ack bothered them, they moved north and increased the distance between them and the ground.

Chennault had sent another group of pilots to Namsang, the British airfield nearest the Thai border, in the continuing effort to mount a joint AVG-RAF raid on Chiang Mai. Meanwhile, in a coincidence so perfect as to be spooky, General Obata was also repositioning his forces. He sent the 77th and 31st Sentais north to Magwe, to keep the pressure on the Commonwealth army in the Irrawaddy Valley. Then he moved his heavy bomber sentais into Burma, the 12th to Mingaladon and the 98th to "Toungoo South," as the Japanese called Kyedaw airfield. This last was a high-risk move, since the AVG had been active around Toungoo in recent days. So, to protect the Sallys, Obata sent the 64th Sentai to Kyedaw as well. Colonel Kato's Hayabusas were on the prowl Tuesday morning, April 21—and ten of them buzzed Namsang as Bob Brouk was returning from a test hop. Frank Schiel told what happened next:

As they approached the field they dropped to about 5,000 feet, and three of them peeled off to strafe Brouk who was landing. He was caught by surprise and hit by the first burst. With his airplane still rolling he jumped from the cockpit and dived head first into a trench. His airplane rolled a short distance and stopped. The Japs made about four passes each until the plane began to burn. It was completely burned, and Brouk was shot three times in the legs.

Gordon Seagrave, the missionary surgeon, drove to Namsang with a Karen nurse and operated on Brouk in the RAF billet. "One bullet had gone right through the thumb," Seagrave reported. "Two others were in his legs, and I recovered several bits of airplane metal from various parts of his body." The AVG Beechcraft was at Loiwing that day, having brought down a cargo of drop-tanks from Kunming. John Hennessy and Mickey Mickelson flew the battered transport to Namsang, picked up Brouk, and brought him to Lashio for treatment. Oddly, the Hayabusas had strafed only Brouk's Tomahawk, so the other pilots flew back to Loiwing under their own power, while the technicians evacuated Namsang by truck.

While this was going on, four Panda Bears flew down to Pyinmana, whose blackened embers were now occupied by the Japanese. Tom Jones skirmished with four Nates and took a 7.7-mm round through his wing. The enemy fighters probably came from the 1st or 11th Sentais, which moved to "Toungoo North" (the former RAF dispersal field) at about this time.

The following day—Wednesday, April 22—Chennault achieved his life's ambition, becoming a brigadier general in the U.S. Army. His delight may have been dimmed somewhat by the knowledge that Clayton Bissell had been promoted twenty-four hours before him. Furthermore, as a serving officer, Chennault now had to route his White House messages through the U.S. Military Mission. Thus, under the date of April 22, Bissell sent the following radiogram to the War Department, deftly fulfilling a request from Chennault while ensuring that news of the Pilots' Revolt was noised around Washington:

Following from Chennault: "Urge immediate appeal by president to all members of AVG to remain on duty here with promise early reinforcement. Group literally worn out—nerves and morale shot. Pilots quitting."

Another reliable report states: "Three or four individuals refused to go on scheduled mission. Twenty-four of best pilots have served notice of termination of contract."

The radiogram concluded with a personal assessment. "Many of AVG pilots are wild, undisciplined lot unsuitable for command of squadrons at present," Bissell told the War Department. "They fight well but are probably overrated." This was in response to a suggestion that Chennault's best pilots be sent to other theaters as squadron leaders, thus spreading their experience and panache throughout the air force. It was a pity that this scheme did not go forward. Bissell was no fool, and everything he said about the AVG pilots was right on target. They were wild. They were undisciplined. They fought well. And their exploits had been much exaggerated. But Bissell did not have the imagination to realize that many of these same pilots—including some of the wilder specimens—would eventually prove their worth as squadron leaders.

In any event, their ranks were shrinking. Sent back to Kunming after he tore up his knees a second time (he fell off a cliff in the dark, thinking it was a bomb shelter) Greg Boyington was flying "slow time" in Tomahawks whose engines had been replaced at the CAMCO factory in Loiwing. Evenings he got drunk and played around with Olga Greenlaw. (He never named the object of his affection, but he boasted of climbing the hostel wall, a bottle of Scotch under his arm, for a rendezvous on the second floor, where the Greenlaws had a two-room suite.) Of his few friends, Ralph Gunvordahl had quit in January, and Percy Bartelt in March. Now Boyington threw in the towel, flying to India on a CNAC Douglas, then by BOAC flying boat to Karachi, where he tried to get onward transportation from the U.S. Army. He was refused—apparently the first to be caught by Chennault's request that AVG "deserters" not be allowed to fly on military aircraft. Boyington finally took passage on a civilian liner. His shipmates, he said, included several hundred CAF cadets and some of the same missionaries who had come out with him on *Boschfontein*.

Then Cliff Groh went astray while ferrying a plane from Loiwing to Kunming. He landed on a sandbar in the Mekong River, far south of the route he should have followed. After the usual confusion—was he Japanese?—he was taken to the local magistrate, who allowed him to compose a message to be sent by runner to the nearest telegraph office. Some essential information must have been omitted, however, for the

AVG never learned Groh's location. After waiting two weeks for an answer, he destroyed his Tomahawk and set out on horseback for the long trek to Kunming.

And on April 24, Frank Swartz died in Poona, India, of a disease contracted in the hospital. Charlie Bond had visited the injured pilot in Calcutta not long before, while on a ferry mission to pick up more Kittyhawks and the first of the Republic P-43s that Lauchlin Currie had acquired for the 3rd AVG. Swartz had then seemed in good health and reasonable spirits, considering that he had lost part of a thumb, was undergoing skin grafts, and would need surgery to repair his mouth. A torpedo plane pilot in the navy, he had reached Burma in the first *Zaandam* contingent; he had served at Rangoon with the 2nd Squadron, but mostly in desk jobs, and he had no combat bonuses on his CAMCO account. Twenty-six years old, he was buried in the cemetery of St. Supulchre church in Poona.

Of the 109 pilots who had come to Asia in the summer and fall of 1941, eighteen were now dead or missing, twenty-one had gone home, ten were serving as staff officers or noncombat pilots, and six were stationed at Yunnan-yi as flight instructors under Butch Carney. With no other replacements in view, Chennault invited the instructors to join the combat squadrons, which they did at the end of the month.

For planes, the AVG had twenty Tomahawks and eight Kittyhawks in commission on April 22—about enough for a single squadron. This census included the Kittyhawks brought to Kunming by Charlie Bond's ferry crew . . . but not the Lancers. The AVG pilots were enthralled by the P-43, and Bond had great fun showing off its climbing ability: 200 pounds lighter than the Tomahawk and equipped with a turbo-supercharger, it was a "flying engine" on the lines of the Curtiss Demon or Nakajima *Ki*-44 Shoki. But the Lancers went to the CAF. Chennault was no fool, and he must have realized that, without pilot armor or fuel tank membranes, the P-43 was a deathtrap for the men who flew them in combat.

This May Screw Us Completely
April–May 1942

With bewildering speed, the focus of the Burma campaign now shifted to Lashio, the dusty town—an Asian Fort Dodge—where the railway ended and the mountain road to China began. On April 16, Lashio was so far behind the lines that Harvey Greenlaw thought it safe to have his wife join him there; she bunked at the CNAC hostel while he ran errands for Chennault. (Among other chores, he fetched Lieutenant Colonel Homer Sanders from Karachi to Kunming. Sanders had a fighter squadron that Chennault hoped to winkle away from the 10th Air Force, with the lure that he might then take command of the 23rd Pursuit Group.) The front was then 200 miles southwest of Lashio. The Commonwealth army was holding at Yenangyaung on the Irrawaddy River; the Chinese army, at Pyawbwe on the railroad line.

A second Chinese army was stationed in the Shan Highlands, its mission to block the long-feared Japanese invasion from northern Thailand. The leading division was the "Temporary-55th" under Chen Li-wu, an inept general even by the standards of Chiang's army. As the main Allied armies retreated, Chen simply kept pace with them, walking his 6,500 troops along dusty mountain tracks with only occasional skirmishes. The combat was so light that Stilwell concluded that the Temporary-55th was being prodded by a reinforced battalion.

In fact, Chen faced a reinforced *division:* the 56th under General Watanabe, whose mission was to seize Lashio and cut off Stilwell's line of retreat. To speed him on his way, Watanabe had been given two regiments of tanks, two of heavy artillery, and 400 British vehicles captured at Singapore. His first obstacle was a Karen guerrilla force led by Chester Klein, the American missionary who had treated the AVG to Saturday-night beans and conversation at his compound outside Toungoo. The Japanese quickly routed the lightly armed partisans, leaving their commander to walk to Mandalay and eventually to India (where he died of a heart attack). Watanabe then sent his motorized battalions driving north on roads the British had built for hauling coal, while his footsoldiers made forced marches over the mountains. On April 15, his leading elements surrounded part of the Temporary-55th, and for three days a desperate battle raged at a place the Japanese identified as Tzuchien. Watanabe's tanks broke through on the night of April 18, advancing twelve miles "through continuous enemy fire" before finding themselves on a clear road to the north.

Only then did Stilwell realize that he had been flanked. "Disaster at Loikaw," he wrote in his diary on April 20. "Wild tales of Jap tank division. . . . Aiming at Lashio? Jesus. This may screw us completely." In one of those audacious gambles that served Japan so well during the opening months of the war, Watanabe ordered that the trucks be used only for carrying troops. As for supplies, the men would manage with what the Chinese left behind. The gamble paid off. His tanks ran dry on April 22 but found 700 drums of gasoline abandoned at Taunggyi, and next day they rumbled into Loilem, a road junction a few miles from Namsang airfield, recently evacuated by the AVG. The Japanese were now *north* of the Allied armies, leaving them with no option but headlong retreat. "All fade for Mandalay and its one bridge," Stilwell wrote in his diary. "I hope it's still there."

On the road to Mandalay, Stilwell experienced a sudden conversion to the merits of air power, as the only weapon he could bring to bear against Watanabe's rogue division. The available forces consisted of five British bombers at Lashio and a dozen AVG fighters at Loiwing . . . when they were not grounded by rain. As always in Southeast Asia before the monsoon, the weather was impossibly hot and sultry, with frequent and vicious "mango showers" that reduced visibility to a few hundred feet. The RAF went to work on Friday morning, April 24, bombing truck convoys on the tracks radiating out from Loilem, and losing one Blenheim in the process. The pilots reported that tanks, armored cars, and trucks were strung out all along the highland tracks. To take advantage of this opportunity, Chennault sent six Kittyhawks down to Loilem, each carrying six thirty-five-pound bombs in its wing racks. This was the AVG's first bombing mission, so Tex Hill flew tail-end Charlie to assess the results:

> I could see bombs landing in a nice string about 50′ apart, some on the convoy and some to the right of road which was ideal for [hitting] the people who had left the trucks to take cover in the field. I came down the line of trucks strafing after the last man had bombed. The trucks were probably carrying gas as they burned readily. I counted 8 burning.

Then a Japanese reconnaissance plane blundered onto the scene. "We overtook him immediately and shot him down," Hill wrote. He identified the victim as a Mitsubishi *Ki*-15 Sonia, an ungainly fixed-gear observation plane often flown by chutais attached to the Japanese army; it resembled the *Ki*-30 Ann but carried no bombs. The credit was shared by Hill, John Petach, Ed Rector, and Pete Wright.

Five Hell's Angels provided top cover during the bombing run, and afterward went down to strafe, running the count up to ten trucks burned and five or six "broken up" by bombs and machine gun fire. Chennault was exultant. "The air activities of the AVG can have a serious amount of slowing down effect on the motorized equipment of the enemy," he declared in an intelligence estimate sent to Kunming. "The heavy armament of the P-40E's literally tore the trucks to pieces." He sent the Hell's Angels out again in the afternoon. The tacit contract—that the Kittyhawks handle the offensive operations, while the Tomahawks took care of local defense—had been forgotten.

"Perhaps someone got to sleep that night in Lashio," Olga Greenlaw recalled, "but I know I didn't. . . . The activity going on all over the dirty little town was frenzied and noisy. People shouting and running around in the rain, repairing tires and motors, loading trucks and all sort of vehicles in frantic haste and confusion. This was the last chance to escape. In a few hours, or less, it would be all over." By car and foot, the refugees set off again, as they had earlier set off from Rangoon and Magwe. Their destination now was Myitkyina in North Burma, the last airfield from which they might catch a flight to India.

The RAF sent its four surviving Blenheims back to Loiwing, the British and Chinese listening posts closed down, and even CNAC refused to land at the red-clay airfield. The last plane out of Lashio may have been the AVG Beechcraft. Before leaving, John Hennessy and Mickey Mickelson broke into the post office and made off with a bag containing mail for the AVG. Olga Greenlaw meanwhile stripped the curtains from the CNAC hostel, preparatory to escaping up the Burma Road with crew chief Henry Olson.

On Saturday, six Kittyhawks and five Tomahawks went down to Loilem, bombing and strafing a truck convoy and perhaps shooting down another of the unlucky Sonias. The last to leave the area was Robert Raine. Flying over Loilem, he saw two Japanese fighters flying in the opposite direction. "I . . . flew north till I was nearly even with second fighter," Raine reported. "I turned under him about 1000 ft. and caught him about 10 miles south of Loilem. Pulled up under him gave him a short burst [whereupon] he started smoking rolled over and went straight in bursting into flame on impact." Raine was one of the big-boat pilots who had come over on *Klipfontein,* and this was his first $500 encounter.

No sooner did they land at Loiwing than Chennault ordered them out again. Five Kittyhawks had just arrived from Kunming, bringing his detachment to seventeen planes—the most the AVG had mustered since December 20. To fly the new arrivals, Chennault drafted two of the ferry pilots and told Bill Reed to round up some off-duty Hell's Angels.

In three elements—the Panda Bears with their fragmentation bombs, the new arrivals as flying gun platforms, and six Hell's Angels as top cover—they took off at 3 P.M. Over Konhaiping, they spotted two Sonias. Bombs still hanging from their wings, the lead Kittyhawks went after the enemy aircraft, as Link Laughlin reported:

[I] dove on EA from about 5000 feet, hit him with a burst from about 250 feet, he turned under me and I noticed two or three other P-40's making runs on him. I caught him in a shallow turn close to the ground, started firing at about 300 ft. and closed up to about 50 ft. The rear gunner quit firing at me and I am certain he was killed. A trail of smoke was coming out of the starboard side of the engine when I turned off. My plane had been hit eight times by the rear gunner's return fire. I turned off to the right, the EA turned left, I got behind him and two P-40's. The first P-40 hit him with a short burst and the EA skidded from a 50 ft. altitude into the ground, cartwheeled, and burst into flames. The pilot was thrown clear of his plane, his chute opened on the ground. Pilot apparently dead.

When Robert Raine came on the scene, he saw six Kittyhawks making runs on one Sonia, so he went after the other:

I dove from 3000 ft., started firing from 200 yds. up to about 50 yards. The Jap burst into flames. As I pulled over him about 30 ft. the Jap looked as though he was trying to jump. The plane crashed just about 500 ft. from where he caught fire being about 50 ft. up when he caught flame.

Seven pilots were credited with a piece of this action: Laughlin, Raine, Pete Wright, R. T. Smith, John Petach, Lew Bishop, and Freeman Ricketts.

The Sonias had just finished strafing a Chinese column. As a Tokyo newspaper told the story, the rear gunners—corporals Nakayama and Sora—were killed early on. "Determined to avenge the death of their comrades," the story continued, "Captain Maruyama and Sergeant-Major Uyeda manned the machine guns and fired furiously at the enemy planes, shooting down several of them. But the two Japanese machines were badly hit and becoming completely disabled were dashed to the ground by the pilots in heroic acts of self-destruction." Increasingly, in the Japanese press, tales of suicide had begun to replace the earlier accounts of overwhelming victories.

It may have been on this flight that history repeated itself in Central Burma. Just as the 17th Indian Division had raced for the Sittang Bridge, so did the Allied armies race for the bridge at Mandalay—and again Allied warplanes attacked their own troops. The U.S. Army history of the Burma campaign puts the blame on the AVG, but the combat reports do not support the accusation. More likely, two RAF Blenheims were at fault. Using 250-pound bombs with rod extensions to make the bombs explode on the surface, the 113th Squadron blasted a truck convoy near Konhaiping that Saturday. Flying at 1,000 feet, the Blenheims would have been more likely than the ground-hugging Kittyhawks to mistake Chinese trucks for Japanese. The Chinese, in any event, were too polite to complain. The only message in the AVG record that might refer to the debacle was a plaintive radiogram from General Lin Wei at Lashio to Chennault at Loiwing: "Please do not attack Konhaiping and its rear region for the time being. Suggest that your group today concentrate effort in reconnoitering Loilem."

General Mao Pang-chu was supposed to send nine SB-3 bombers to Yunnan-yi, and from there to support the Chinese army in Burma. As always in the CAF, the assignment involved a great deal of planning and little in the way of action. Mao and Chennault had been exchanging radiograms on the subject for a week, and at one point the curly-haired general flew to Loiwing for further talks. But the SB-3s had not yet moved west of Kunming, and Chiang Kai-shek turned again to his American air force. "Use all available AVG strength to strike enemy trucks, troops, etc. in Lashio-Namian region," he ordered Chennault. "Establish close liaison with [Chinese commanders] and report daily operations to me." A few hours later, he was demanding *two* reports per day, with General Mao standing by at Kunming to relay them to Chongqing.

But Chennault wanted to leave the border region. "Enemy reported in Lashio," he replied. "No warning net. . . ." He asked for permission to pull back to Baoshan, 125 miles deeper into China.

Sunday morning, he sent the Hell's Angels down to Lashio to assess the Japanese advance. From the air, the town seemed deserted, though the road was crowded with "sand colored" trucks heading north. (They belonged to the retreating Chinese army, though the Hell's Angels seemed to think they were Japanese.) The four Tomahawks then flew down to Hsipaw, where the track being used by Watanabe's 56th Division intersected the main Mandalay-Lashio road. Circling at 8,000 feet, the Hell's Angels saw that Hsipaw was on fire, with twenty-eight twin-engined bombers heading away from the town.

Then they were bounced by a dozen Hayabusas. John Donovan was the first to see the Japanese fighters:

> I attracted the attention of [Bill] Reed by diving by him wobbling my wings. I pulled up in a cloud and came out where I thought I would be above the enemy fighters. As I came out I saw several other Model "0"s and fired at one. I was firing at another when I saw still other enemy fighters above and to my right. I saw a Model "0" climbing. . . . I dove toward him and fired a long burst. After diving away, I returned to Loiwing. Though I saw bullets entering one of the Model "0"s I do not know whether he went down or not.

He didn't, but the 64th Sentai turned for home without attacking Loiwing, which had been its destination. The skirmish had forced the

Hayabusas to drop their auxiliary fuel tanks, and anyhow the weather was deteriorating. Clouds and rain moved in at noon, causing the opposing air forces to shut down for the day.

This option was not available to the men on the ground. At dawn on Monday, April 27, Stilwell crossed the Mandalay bridge in a balky command car. In the charred city, he held a bad-tempered conference with the British. ("Reconnaissance? No got. Limeys as usual knew nothing.")

Chennault meanwhile was having his ears boxed by Madame Chiang:

> Your urgent message of 26th just received. At this moment twelve o'clock midnight we are still receiving messages from Lashio radio station. . . . Carry out morning bombing mission as usual. If by tomorrow enemy entrance into Lashio confirmed then generalissimo consents that you change to whatever fields you think best.

Chennault heard only the instructions he wanted to hear. He told the 3rd Squadron technicians to drive to Mangshi, eighty miles into China, and there prepare a fallback field for the AVG. The British too were winding down their operation on the China-Burma border, sending three Blenheims to India and keeping just one bomber and some ground crewmen at Loiwing. About the same time, a U.S. Army C-47 took off for Kunming—the first Ferry Command plane to make the trip into China. (Based at Dinjan, the easternmost airfield in India, the Ferry Command had been cobbled together the previous week, using army planes and some DC-3s leased from Pan Am. They were crewed by former Doolittle raiders and the men who had delivered General Brereton's B-17s.) Among those who hitched a ride on the army Douglas from Loiwing were Olga Greenlaw, stout Ma Davidson from the American Club, and two Anglo-Indian women put aboard by Moose Moss and consigned to Ray Hastey in Kunming.

Adding to Chennault's urgency was the date. In two days, the Showa emperor would celebrate his forty-first birthday. Four years earlier, Japanese navy planes had chosen April 29 for a great raid on Hankou, and Chennault believed there would be another spectacular on Wednesday. In Kunming, Don Rodewald recorded the warning in his diary: "We got as much done as possible today as we expect a birthday greeting from the Jap Emporer tomorrow. He will probably want to celebrate his birthday joyusly but we intend to have 18 planes to upset his plans."

Rode went on to note that John Blackburn "took off about 4 P.M.

and hasn't been seen since. . . . We fear for the worst. He was testing the guns for me on one of the new E's." A serious man with a pencil-thin mustache, Blackburn dove into Lake Kunming, the victim of target fixation or the Kittyhawk's reluctance to pull out of a dive. One of Butch Carney's check pilots at Yunnan-yi, he had transferred to the Adam & Eves on January 14 and was credited with downing two Nates over Rangoon.

The Japanese had their own idea of what would be suitable as a birthday spectacular. The 56th Division was to capture Lashio on April 29 with the help of parachute troops. To ensure the safety of the air drop, General Obata was anxious to neutralize the Allied air force. The Hayabusa probes of the past two days had been part of this effort, and the bombers that hit Hsipaw may also have been looking for Loiwing. Obata tried again on Tuesday morning. Like Chennault, Kato was receiving replacement fighters in the spring of 1942, and he was able to put twenty Hayabusas in the air. As with the AVG, it was the largest force the 64th Sentai had mustered since December. They would escort twenty-four Sallys of the 12th Sentai to destroy Loiwing on April 28, the day before the emperor's birthday.*

By coincidence, Chennault had sent fourteen fighters down to Lashio that morning in response to a plea from General Lin Wei, whose troops were still holding the city against Watanabe's tanks and artillery. He did not have enough oxygen for that many planes, so most of the Hell's Angels did without. Oley Olson led a flight of eight Tomahawks at 10,000 feet, with two oxygen-equipped Tomahawks as weavers a few thousand feet above them. Higher still, at 18,000 feet, were four Kittyhawks under Tex Hill. This three-step formation was southwest of Hsipaw when Hill spotted the Japanese formation on the reciprocal course. He called Olson but got no answer, so he told another Hell's Angel to relay the message, then led his own flight toward the bombers. At the same moment, a half-dozen Hayabusas dropped their auxiliary tanks and turned out to meet him. They were led by Captain Yasuhiko Kuroe, formerly of the 47th Independent Chutai, who had joined the

* Coincidentally, 10 million crude-rubber balls reached Japan from the Dutch Indies, to be distributed to schoolchildren on the emperor's birthday—just about the only tangible return to the Japanese people from their nation's conquest of Southeast Asia.

64th Sentai to replace the squadron leader killed at Loiwing on April 8. The Japanese pilots "tried to get into some semblance of a formation," Hill recalled, "but I couldn't tell exactly what type." His combat report went on:

> They were apparently trying to work in threes. I fired four short bursts at my first opponent before I got him. In the 4th burst he started off in a shallow dive [and] crashed into the jungle. From then on the fight was a rat race with "0"s and P-40s on each others tails. I got my second "0" on a head on approach with him having a slight altitude advantage. . . . The range was closing so fast that I had to haul back on the stick violently in order to [target] him.

Meanwhile, Lew Bishop shot a Hayabusa off Hill's tail and saw the Japanese pilot bail out. Bishop was climbing steeply at the time, and the tremendous recoil of the fifty-caliber guns caused his Kittyhawk to stall. He fell off in a spin, recovered, and chased after a Hayabusa that seemed to be leaving the fight. As he told the story, his bullets chopped a wing off the Japanese plane, which then burst into flame. Back in the fight again, he saw a retractable-gear fighter going down under the guns of Tom Jones. Bishop then laced another Hayabusa, which "fell off on one wing and started spinning." He followed his quarry down to 3,000 feet but was unable to set the enemy craft afire. Jones was credited with shooting down one "Zero," and so was Frank Adkins. For each man except Tex Hill, it was his first blood against a Japanese fighter.

The Hell's Angels, meanwhile, had scattered. Oley Olson had not received Hill's warning, but was put on the alert by a Japanese radio operator:

> I heard a strange tongue on the radio and looked about more intently. About two minutes later one of the planes in our formation sighted enemy planes above about twenty miles away. I turned to an interception course and called for the planes without oxygen to join on me and advised the others to join on R. T. Smith who had the enemy located and who was supplied with oxygen.

Olson's radio must have strayed off the AVG frequency, explaining why he failed to receive Hill's warning—and why the Hell's Angels did not follow him into combat. Olson reported that he skirmished without result, lost contact with the Hayabusas, and went back to Loiwing.

Meanwhile, his pilots chased the Japanese formation in flights of two or three. Chuck Older was the first to spot the bombers, and he went after them without waiting for a backup. Ken Jernstedt watched him go:

I saw Older give the attack signal but I did not see any enemy. He changed his course a little and struck out ahead of [our] formation. I then saw a large formation of planes a great distance away that I judged to be bombers. By this time Older was some distance ahead of [Eddie] Overend. . . . About that time I saw some enemy fighters coming up from behind and below Older. Overend dove on 3 of them. They split up and one pulled up sharply and apparently stalled as I made a run on him from above. I gave him two short bursts. He burst into flames and headed down.

This was Kuroe's squadron, catching up with the bombers after its skirmish with the Panda Bears. As Eddie Overend recalled the encounter, there were four Hayabusas, and two of them "pulled up and away." He closed on the other pair and gave the righthand plane a long burst at point-blank range. The Hayabusa burst into flame, clawed straight up, then dived for the ground. Following it down, Overend realized that the other two Hayabusas were on his tail. He shook them by running the Kittyhawk's indicated airspeed to 330 mph, but in the process lost sight of his quarry. Chuck Older claimed two Hayabusas in the same skirmish, in circumstances forever obscure because his combat report does not survive.

Parker Dupouy and Tom Haywood had almost overhauled the bomber formation when one of the escort turned back to give fight. The two Hell's Angels went after the Hayabusa. "After about three passes each," Haywood recalled, "the fighter started breaking up and crashed into the jungle out of control." They resumed their chase after the Sallys, catching them just as they reached Loiwing. Haywood made several runs on the formation before running out of ammunition, with no better result than to take several bullets through his Tomahawk.

R. T. Smith and Paul Greene (the oxygen-equipped weavers) started the chase with an altitude advantage over the other Tomahawks. They too went after the bomber formation, but before reaching it saw several retractable-gear fighters in what R. T. described as a "large sloppy Lufberry"—a squirrel-cage formation, each pilot protecting the tail of the man in front of him.

The two of us went into the Lufberry on the tail of one Jap. We both shot at it, and then Greene had to break off as another Jap came up. I followed the first one. . . . He pulled up sharply in a steep chandelle [clawed straight up], and I followed. Got a good rear quarter shot at him and he flew right thru a burst. He caught fire around the engine immediately, and crashed out of a long spiral.

Greene squared off with the intruder, but the Hayabusa declined the challenge. "I still had speed enough to get on his tail," Greene reported. "After several bursts he caught on fire." The two buddies then turned for Lashio, having heard on the radio that Japanese fighters were strafing the town. Seeing nothing, they flew on in hopes of intercepting the bomber formation, now returning from Loiwing. They gave up the chase when they realized they did not have enough fuel to follow the Sallys downcountry.

After the Hell's Angels and the Panda Bears had taken off from Loiwing, but before the Sallys came over, several Douglas transports arrived from Dinjan, including an army C-47 and some Pan Am DC-3s. Chennault ran across the runway and ordered them off the field. At the controls of the C-47 were colonels Caleb Haynes and Robert Scott of the Ferry Command, whose cargo included two Ryan trainers for the CAF, food and ammunition for the AVG, and a bottle of whiskey for Chennault. As Scott recalled the incident, Chennault drawled: "Guess we're going to have some Japs—you-all had better get those transports off the field." Trained as a fighter pilot but now considered too old for such work (he was thirty-four) Scott was desolate to leave the battle zone:

> I'd have given anything to trade my colonel's eagles and that "delivery wagon" that I flew for the gold bars of a second Lieutenant and one of those shark-nosed pieces of dynamite!
>
> But we started the Douglas and took off for China. . . . Even as we cleared the field and climbed towards the Salween, I heard the call "Tally-Ho" from the AVG. . . . Every now and then we could hear one of the AVG say to some unlucky Jap, "Your mother was a turtle—your father was a snake,"—and then the rattle of fifty-caliber guns over the radio.

One DC-3 failed to clear the field and had its tail blown off. As Scott told the story, Chennault's bottle of whiskey was another casualty, blown up with the jeep into which he had put it for safekeeping. The runways were also damaged, though not heavily enough to prevent the Panda Bears and Oley Olson from landing there.

The other Hell's Angels flew on to Mangshi, which was to be their

---

Douglas DC-3 / C-47

Arguably the finest aircraft ever built, this twin-engined transport was the brainchild of Donald Douglas, a graduate of the U.S. Naval Academy. In 1930, football coach Knute Rockne was killed in the crash of an airliner belonging to the company that became Trans-World Airways, causing it to ask manufacturers for a safer, all-metal passenger plane. Douglas responded with the prototype DC-1, which went into production as the DC-2; it became the DC-3 when American Airlines asked that the plane be widened to accommodate sleeping berths. Douglas built about 500 DC-2s and DC-3s by 1942, when the plane was adapted to military use, with a production run of 31,268 before the war ended. The U.S. Army flew these aircraft in ten variants from C-32 to C-54, the U.S. Navy used it as the R4D, the RAF took it into service as the Dakota, and Nakajima copied it for the Japanese navy as the L2D. Intended for twenty-one passengers, it sometimes carried up to seventy refugees out of Burma; designed to haul 2,500 pounds on civilian routes, it regularly lifted more than 7,000 pounds of cargo "over the Hump" to China. In 1991, as many as 2,000 of these incredibly durable planes were still flying, often in the most rugged and inaccessible regions of the world. The specifications are for the C-47A cargo version flown by the U.S. Army in 1942.

Engines: two 1,200-hp Pratt & Whitney air-cooled radials
Crew: two or more
Wingspan: 95 feet
Maximum range: 2,125 miles

---

new home. They landed safely except R. T. Smith, who ran out of gas over an empty field while trying to follow the directions of the Mangshi radio station. (The operator talking him down was looking at a different plane.) R. T. made a wheels-down landing, collapsed his gear in a gully, and hitched a ride into Mangshi with a truckload of Chinese casualties.

What are we to make of this carnage? Between them, the Panda Bears and the Hell's Angels claimed thirteen Japanese fighters. Yet of the twenty Hayabusas taking part in this battle, only two failed to return to Toungoo South.

The first Hayabusa to go down was that of an enlisted pilot of Kuroe's 3rd Chutai. Corporal Hirano was first "shot up by a P-40 and then collided with another pursuing P-40." He bailed out after the supposed collision—an unusual act for a Japanese pilot—so this had to be the encounter with the Panda Bears. Probably Hirano was winged by Tex Hill and finished off by Lew Bishop, who then claimed him a second time. (The Hayabusa whose pilot bailed out was the same one that lost a wing, leading Hirano's comrades to imagine a collision.) In any event, Hirano landed safely, walked south until he met the advancing 56th Division, and six days later turned up at Toungoo.

The second pilot to go down was Lieutenant Tadashi Kataoka of the 1st Chutai, who like Kuroe had left the main formation and come out to meet the enemy. Almost any of the Americans might have shot him down. Captain Kuroe recalled that his squadron's final brush with the enemy involved two enemy fighters, which then turned away in favor of Kataoka's plane. The likeliest candidates were Parker Dupouy and Tom Haywood (who met and attacked a lone Hayabusa) or Paul Greene and R. T. Smith (who were skirmishing with several fighters when Greene broke off to battle an intruder).

In any event, it was two-for-nought for the AVG, and the 64th Sentai was again obliged to mourn its dead. Kuroe was especially morose, for it was he who had broken formation and caused (as he then believed) the death of Corporal Hirano. His commander did not console him. "We knew you were battling the enemy," Kato said when they were reunited at Toungoo South, "but we did not come to help because the principle was to protect the bombers. . . . Forget those pilots," he said. "Work for the group."

While this epic and confusing battle was underway, 440 men of the 1st Parachute Brigade moved up to Toungoo by train. Before dawn on April 29, at the former AVG training base, they filed into forty twin-engined Lockheed Electra transports built under license by the Kawasaki company. At Toungoo North, the brigade's supplies were loaded into nine Sallys from the 98th Sentai. Then fate took a hand. A Mitsubishi *Ki*-51 ground-support plane took off from Toungoo South just as a Mitsubishi Dinah touched down from Magwe; the planes collided, destroying both. This was the Dinah that was to have reported on the weather around Lashio. But the brigade commander, a Major Mihara, decided to go ahead as planned. The transports and the cargo-Sallys took off and joined up with the light bombers of the 8th Sentai. The formation was guarded by the 64th Sentai. There were only sixteen Hayabusas in the escort, suggesting that in addition to the planes shot down the day before, two more had been damaged.

The weather deteriorated as the raiders flew north. At 8:42 A.M., when the transports were fifty miles from Lashio, Major Mihara gave the order to turn back. In the 64th Sentai, Sergeant Yasuda made a crash landing when his Hayabusa began to spill gasoline. (Like Hirano, he walked back to the Japanese lines.) A cargo-Sally crashed on the way home, and a second upon landing at Toungoo North. Of the 100 planes that had set out for Lashio, only four Anns managed to reach the target, which they did by flying below the storm. They were on hand to support the 56th Division when it swept into Lashio at noon. In the nine days since Stilwell had learned that he was being flanked by a motorized division, General Watanabe had advanced 300 miles, effectively doubling the Japanese penetration of Burma.

"Burma reporting net collapsed," Chennault radioed Skip Adair next day. (With Greenlaw in Burma, Adair was serving as AVG executive officer.) "Steady rains low clouds prevent operation. Field here and [at Mangshi] very muddy and unusable after few more rains. . . . Am sending 2nd Squadron to Kunming today." To the generalissimo, Chennault sent this brief and bleak report: "Jap took Lashio noon 29 April. Situation here very bad."

Stilwell was now in Shwebo, sixty miles north of Mandalay and beyond the point at which his divisions could have wheeled eastward into China. Still, he wanted to know how things stood at Lashio, and he ordered Chennault to send a plane so he could reconnoiter that "front." But there was no front toward Lashio, only a hundred-mile traffic jam of refugees and soldiers bound up the Burma Road toward China. It must have been with a private smile that Chennault radioed his boss that the Chinese staff had already left Loiwing and that the AVG would soon follow.

"With a resounding thump," as the latest British commander recalled, the bridge at Mandalay was dynamited during the night of April 30. "[I]ts center span fell neatly into the river—a sad sight, and a signal that we had lost Burma."

Colonels Haynes and Scott had spent the night in Kunming, so Bissell asked them to rescue the three American generals—Chennault, Stilwell, and Sibert—who were caught in Burma. No better crew for the mission could possibly be imagined. Haynes, as the saying went, "looks like a gorilla and flies like an angel," and Scott's dream was to escape the Ferry Command and join Chennault as a fighter pilot. (The bottle of whiskey had been meant to lubricate this process.) They "took off about 0545 and went to Loiwing," as Haynes described the flight, "but there was a heavy rain in the vicinity and I couldn't get into the field. While I was circling Loiwing I was in contact with Gen. Chennault and told him of my instructions to pick up . . . the 'Double-0 Man.'" This was a reference to Stilwell, whom the Americans in China called the Old Old Man, Chennault having preempted the title of Old Man. "He caught on at once and said he guessed maybe I should go take care of that job. I was beginning to run low on gas, so I told him I was going into the place I had been the day before [Myitkyina] and would come back for him."

Chennault radioed back that he would have "an auction sale" at two o'clock (i.e., would leave Loiwing) and if Haynes could not return before then, not to bother. Haynes refueled at Myitkyina and headed south. "The Japs had just bombed Myingatha," he recalled, "and it was a blazing inferno, with people jumping out of houses, animals running everyplace and masses of people streaming out of town." He landed at Shwebo and was taken to Stilwell's headquarters, where the Americans were burning their files. "I told the General that I was prepared to take practically all of them to Calcutta," Haynes wrote, "and that I would take him to China if he so desired. He agreed to the latter, providing we stopped by Loiwing and picked up Chennault." Haynes radioed Loiwing, to find that the station had already gone off the air. He then loaded twenty-nine officers for the flight to India, but Stilwell was not among them. He had decided on the spur of the moment to stay with the Chinese army—an act of great courage and even greater folly. Once the C-47 lifted off from the dirt airfield at Shwebo, the highest-ranking American officer in Asia ceased to have any influence on events beyond the sound of his voice.

That was Friday, May 1. Another Ferry Command transport had picked up Chennault at Loiwing, leaving Harvey Greenlaw to demolish the CAMCO factory and the twenty-two Tomahawks awaiting repair. Greenlaw and the wrecking crew then left for Mangshi by car and truck.

As in the retreat from Magwe, the AVG 3rd Squadron was now spread out over a hundred miles of mountain road, "at their leisure and at their own expense and best judgement," as Dan Hoyle put it. Ed Lussier and Robert King brought up the rear in a radio truck; at times, according to Lussier, the Japanese were so close that he had to discourage them with bursts from a submachine gun.

The last plane out of Loiwing was a Blenheim piloted by Flight Officer D. J. Hammond of the 113th Squadron. The bomber carried only its crew of three, plus the gunner who had parachuted from the Blenheim shot down on April 24. (Like Bob Neale and Snuffy Smith at Mingaladon, the Commonwealth airmen had lingered in hopes that the missing pilot and bombardier would turn up.) The Blenheim could have carried a dozen men, but Hammond did not evacuate his ground crewmen. Instead, they went on the road with the AVG.

Mangshi was a dismal billet where meals were eaten under the open sky, and where the pilots slept on bamboo cots with a single blanket. The technicians were billeted at the hotel in town—"very poor and filthy," according to Dan Hoyle—and two were already sick with malaria. Moreover, with Loiwing abandoned, Mangshi was perilously exposed. Chennault therefore called the Hell's Angels back to Kunming, where they landed late in the day on Friday, not having washed or shaved for three days.

Chennault's plan was to move the AVG to Chongqing, where the "bombing season" was due to begin. (Jim Howard had spent most of the spring checking out airfields at the capital and toward the coast, and the useful John Williams was already in Chongqing, attending to the details of setting up a new headquarters.) But he also had to support the Chinese army in Burma. Toward this end, he would establish a forward base at Baoshan, 125 miles from the Burma frontier, on the high ground between the precipitous gorges of the Mekong and Salween rivers. He gave the assignment to the Adam & Eves, and Bob Neale took eight Tomahawks to the soggy grass airstrip on Saturday, May 2. Before their engines cooled, they took off again in a rainstorm to escort nine SB-3s to Lashio. This was the CAF's first mission in Burma. The target was supposed to be a highway bridge near Lashio, but the SB-3s passed it by and bombed the railroad yards instead. The bombers then returned to Kunming, and the Tomahawks to Baoshan.

The Adam & Eves' new post was an ancient city jammed to the walls with refugees. Trucks were parked bumpers-touching in all the streets, with their occupants sleeping in and under them. The Americans were assigned to a monastery built against a mountain on the other side of town from the airfield. Dinner began with soup, which they gulped straight off, without pausing to wash their hands.

The Japanese advance had become a pincer. In the west, Sakurai sent a detachment up the Chindwin River, to prevent the Commonwealth army from escaping into India, while the rest of the 33rd Division joined the drive on Mandalay. In the center, Takeuchi and Mutaguchi marched their troops along the main road, the divisions taking turns so they could "advance by bounds." In the east, Watanabe's motorized units took advantage of the Burma Road, smoothed and hardened by Chinese labor. ("The Japanese," an AVG technician said in awe, "are making better time up the road than we did in convoy.") But before the 56th Division reached China, Watanabe diverted his main force toward Myitkyina, over the route used by the refugees from Lashio. By Japanese estimates, 150,000 Allied troops were caught in this great trap.

Chief among them was Lieutenant General Joseph Stilwell, who had refused the last flight from Shwebo to stay with his army, but who now had no army to command. There was only a rabble, as terrified of the approaching monsoon as of the Japanese. Stilwell decided to head for the wilds of North Burma, far enough and fast enough that when he turned west for India, he would brush past Sakurai's reaching fingertips. Thus the senior American officer in Asia—arguably one of the great fighting generals of all time—was unable to do more than save himself and his immediate party. They included three generals (Stilwell, Sibert, and a Chinese brigadier) and the Seagrave Hospital Unit with its Karen nurses and British Quaker drivers. A junior officer recalled the scene at the first village they passed:

> British stragglers walked aimlessly about, haggard, shocked, frightened. Punjabi soldiers twisted and turned through the mob, snatching food from helpless, unarmed families. . . . Turbaned, black-bearded Sikhs, aloof and sullen, their pride humbled, stumbled through the crowd. A dozen men of the Burma Rifles bickered over the loot of a house they had set afire, while

the owners clustered in a silent knot of misery. Fighting for the possession of a truck, gray-clad Chinese troops hauled the Burmese driver from the cab and pistol-whipped him until he lay bloody and still in the dust. Mountain tribespeople stealthily explored the sprawled body of a Chinese soldier with bare toes to be sure the man was dead before they stripped him.

In the general shame, there were flashes of courage. At a town identified as Wanlaikam, Mutaguchi's 18th Division overtook a group of Chinese stragglers, who dug trenches, piled vehicles across the road, built breast-works of teak, and put up such a fight that the Japanese finally passed them by.

Japanese engineers and conscripted native laborers rebuilt Lashio airport, and the Anns of the 27th Sentai—newly arrived from China—moved in to occupy the red-clay field. Also based at Lashio was the 71st Independent Chutai, attached to the 56th Division for reconnaissance. Presumably it was one of the squadron's Sonias that ran afoul of the AVG on Sunday, May 3.

The weather that day was too thick for the CAF bombers, so Chennault sent the Adam & Eves down to Loiwing to see if the CAMCO facilities had indeed been destroyed. Bob Neale led the six-plane flight to the border. At Loiwing, he reported, "no fires were noted except one at the west end of the long runway," suggesting that Greenlaw's demolition had been something less than total. Then Bill Bartling spotted a stranger through the clouds and went in chase. "I followed on a slightly different heading," Bob Neale recalled, "and after diving thru a cloud ended up to my surprise on the tail of a Jap observation plane." All he had to do was to press the button on his control stick. The Japanese gunner returned fire, but only managed to destroy the pitot tube that measured the Tomahawk's airspeed. The Sonia was on fire by this time. "My second burst was at very close range," Neale wrote, "after which he started a diving turn to the left finally ending in an inverted dive in which attitude it crashed on the edge of a small river approximately 10 to 15 miles NE of Lungling." Number fifteen for Bob Neale, who thereby became the first triple ace in the AVG.

The Japanese entered Loiwing Sunday evening, to find "a great many stores," including six planes on the production line and pieces of twenty more. Most were Tomahawks, accumulated by the Pawley brothers at Loiwing and never repaired. The Japanese were bemused by the decorations on their prows, and a Tokyo newspaper published a photograph with the caption:

Note the peculiar design painted on the wreckage—a shark's bared teeth. If these markings were found on a submarine, the significance could perhaps be understood; but on a plane? Suffice it to say that Japan's "Wild Eagles" will rule the skies regardless of what freaks the enemy may send up in his futile attempts to continue resistance.

Next day, General Obata sent his two heavy bomber sentais—the 12th from Mingaladon and the 98th from Toungoo—thundering north to the Burma-China border, then east to Baoshan. They were escorted as usual by the 64th Sentai. It was Magwe all over again, and most of the Adam & Eves simply jumped for the nearest trench. Charlie Bond ran in the opposite direction and was already in his Tomahawk when he realized that he was the only pilot on the flight line. Deciding that it was safer to go forward than back, Bond started his engine and took off without waiting to don his flying gear. Once in the air, he closed the canopy, put on his helmet, and buckled his parachute harness and seat belt. Only then did he remember to retract his landing gear.

By this time the 12th Sentai had finished its bombing run, which (fortunately for Bond) was directed at Baoshan city and not the airfield. At least one bomb hit the monastery on the other side of town. Ben Foshee, an off-duty pilot, was caught in the blast along with an AVG technician, a CAMCO employee, and some Chinese hostel workers.

Climbing to 18,000 feet, Bond found himself in a position to make runs on the 98th Sentai. He watched his tracers lick through one of the Sallys, but it would not burn. Instead, two nearby bombers gave off streams of blue-gray smoke. Deciding that this was a decoy—oil injected into the engines—Bond kept attacking the original target:

> On my third attack I saw his right engine disintegrate and ignite into a flaming torch. He went down and through the overcast. I turned on the bomber at the tail of the vee, but suddenly my guns quit firing. . . . Hell, I was out of ammunition!

He had made plenty of hits, however. Not only did the 98th Sentai lose a *Ki*-21 over the border, but three other Sallys came home damaged. Meanwhile, seeing no enemy fighters, the 64th Sentai had abandoned the formation in order to settle its account with the AVG. The Hayabusas screamed down upon Baoshan airfield, strafing the seven Tomahawks on the ground. Before they were done, Charlie Bond blundered into the line of fire. Hearing a terrible rattle in his cockpit, and believing that his hydraulic system had burst, he reached down to operate the landing gear manually . . . and put his left hand into a fire.

> I swung my head around and looked to my rear. . . . Three Jap Zeros right on my tail and firing like mad! The explosions were their rounds of ammunition hitting my armor plate behind my seat. . . . The fuselage tank had exploded, and the fire was whipping into my lower rear cockpit and then up around my legs.

When the flames reached his face, Bond decided to get out. He opened the canopy, unhooked his seatbelt, and pulled the plane up and over. When he stood up, the airstream yanked him free, and his parachute popped moments before he hit the ground in a Chinese cemetery. He hid behind a burial mound while the Hayabusas finished strafing the airfield.

Bond had burns on his hand, torso, and head, and two machine gun bullets had laid open his helmet and the skin beneath. Doc Richards gave him first aid and a shot of morphine, then some of his friends bundled him into a jeep and drove him to the monastery:

> There were bodies lying everywhere, in and under charred debris. Some were completely dismembered, and others were burned so badly the teeth were showing from fleshless faces. . . . Once Bob Little had to get out of the jeep to move a timber from our path. When he heaved it aside, a human head rolled across the road.

At the monastery, meanwhile, a Chinese doctor had tried to amputate Ben Foshee's torn leg. The pilot drove him away, calling for Doc Richards, but he died before the flight surgeon reached the hostel. A former navy pilot, Foshee was a Hell's Angel but had been attached to the Adam & Eves for his first combat tour.

The technicians worked feverishly to repair the damaged Tomahawks. Four planes were flown off to Kunming that afternoon, and another was made ready that night. In the end, two Tomahawks were written off and stripped of their guns and other useful gear, which was loaded aboard a U.S. Army transport sent over from Kunming on Tuesday morning. Also into the Douglas went Foshee's body, the wounded men, most of the pilots, and some of the technicians. The transport was so heavily loaded that the pilot (Lieutenant Jacob Sartz) had to bounce it off the runway. Bob Little flew shotgun in No. 33, which the technicians had put into fighting condition overnight.

The evacuees never knew what a narrow escape they had. A few hours earlier, while the 12th Sentai Sallys were warming their engines for a return visit, some of General Brereton's B-17s had dropped their bombs on Mingaladon airport. Two Sallys went up in flames and ten or more were damaged, delaying their return to Baoshan. That was the AVG's first stroke of luck for May 5. The second came when six Kittyhawks, assigned to escort the Douglas, were delayed while refueling at Yunnan-yi. Led by Tex Hill, they did not reach Baoshan until noon—just as the reorganized Japanese formations crossed the border into China. Frank Schiel recalled how Radioman Ralph Sasser, who was still at the airfield, talked the Panda Bears into attack position:

> Through the calm, accurate directions of the BC-5 crew we were able to quickly find the enemy. They consisted of 16 [Nates] circling at an altitude of about 18,000'. [Whitey] Lawlor led the flight into attacking position and started the first run. Lawlor got a flamer on his first run. . . . On my first rear attack I got in a good burst. When I looked back the plane was burning in a spin.

Lawlor was credited with two Nates, and every other member of the flight was credited with one: Tex Hill, Frank Schiel, Gil Bright, Freeman Ricketts, and Matt Kuykendall, the last two scoring for the first time against Japanese fighters. They described the Nates as reddish brown on their topsides, light gray beneath. These were the markings of the 11th Sentai, whose commander had been killed on March 21 by the still-missing Cliff Groh. Now led by Major Katsuji Sugiura, the group had moved up to Mandalay expressly to support the second Baoshan raid. According to Japanese records, it lost four planes on May 5—one-quarter of its strength—including the Nate flown by a popular enlisted pilot, Sergeant Sudo. In addition, the 27th Sentai lost two Anns over Baoshan, and these were no doubt included in the claims submitted by the Panda Bears.

As for the Kittyhawks, the only combat damage was suffered by Whitey Lawlor, his propeller and undercarriage dinged when he flew through the debris of a disintegrating Nate. But on the way home, Frank Schiel ran out of gas, bellied in, and temporarily joined the list of missing pilots.

Piss on Bissell

May 1942

On May 7, the starving remnant of General MacArthur's army—
9,500 Americans and 42,000 Filipinos—raised the white flag over
the fortress island of Corregidor, ending five months of resistance
in the Philippines. There was no such resistance in North Burma. "The
brave and gallant officers and men of the Japanese Forces are scoring
overwhelming victories," boasted a Tokyo newspaper, "leaving in their
wake the mercilessly scattered remains of the [Allied] forces to scatter in
all directions." The Commonwealth army escaped to India, in such haste
that it left 412 tanks, 8,254 cars and trucks, 420 heavy guns, 11,248
rifles and machine guns, 14,856 artillery shells, and 3,462,302 rounds
of ammunition to be picked up by the Japanese. (As each Southeast
Asian country fell to the imperial army, Tokyo newspapers ticked off
the weapons and raw materials thus captured, much in the manner of a
corporate report to the stockholders.) The Chinese left 44,000 tons of
lend-lease supplies in Burma . . . and 30,000 troops. Also left behind
were the 16 million inhabitants of Burma, along with its natural bounty
of oil, teak, and rice. Best of all, the "aid-to-Chiang route" had been
closed at last, or so it seemed in May 1942.

In the mop-up, the JAAF played only a small role. General Obata sent
his heavy bomber groups to French Indochina, where the Sallys were
fireproofed and their crews rested from their long ordeal. Of the fighter
groups, the 50th Sentai went home for refitting. Colonel Kato's

Hayabusas moved to Magwe, and the 1st and 11th Sentais to Rangoon, to protect occupied Burma from bombing attack. That left only the 77th Sentai—and all of Obata's light bombers and attack planes—still operating in North Burma.

Altogether, Obata did not have much reason to congratulate himself on the campaign now ending. He and his predecessor had lost 117 planes in Burma, Thailand, and western Yunnan—a quarter of the aircraft they had committed to subduing Burma. This was a terrible toll, not at all mitigated by the fact that the Allies believed it to be higher.* This embarrassment was well hidden by the Japanese press. Individual pilots might die heroically from time to time, and losses in specific combats were reported with reasonable accuracy, but overall Burma was presented as another unsullied victory for the Wild Eagles of the JAAF. The British air force had been defeated yet again, along with an American unit whose name was thought too menacing to be published. "Last autumn," reported one Tokyo newspaper, "American airmen calling themselves the 'Flying Corps' reached Kunming and temporarily relieved the Chinese fear by their tall talk. But before long, when the efficient Japanese airmen went into action, they proved to be no more than 'Flying Cats.'" As censored, the joke made no sense to anyone who did not know that the AVG pilots had been dubbed the Flying Tigers.

The job of the air units remaining in North Burma was to harass the lost Chinese divisions. At the same time, they supported a drive into Yunnan province by a motorized regiment under Major General Shizuo Sakaguchi, his mission to "pursue the enemy to the Salween River and if possible destroy him in one blow." Sakaguchi Detachment was an extension of the mop-up in Burma, and not an advance into China proper. But Chennault could not know that. To him, the Japanese column seemed a spear aimed at Kunming and Wu Chia Ba airport, without which there would be no further resistance in China. (The

---

* Air Vice Marshal Stevenson estimated that his 221st Group destroyed 291 Japanese planes in the Burma campaign, and of this number he attributed 217 to the AVG. The Chinese paid combat bonuses for 275 planes destroyed in Burma, Thailand, and western Yunnan. Though on the high side, these figures at least did not exceed the number of enemy aircraft taking part in the campaign. The same could not be said of the Japanese, who claimed 554 Allied planes destroyed in the conquest of Burma.

Douglas transports of CNAC and the Ferry Command could fly "over the hump" of the Himalayas, from Dinjan to Kunming, but their range did not permit them to reach Chongqing.) Chennault decided to commit the full strength of the AVG and the CAF against Sakaguchi Detachment, even if that meant bombing the refugees who choked the road from the border to the Salween River. On Wednesday, May 6, he sent an urgent radiogram to Madame Chiang:

> Japs meeting no opposition anywhere as soldiers civilians panic stricken and fleeing east along road. Consider situation desperate. . . . Japs may drive trucks into Kunming unless road and bridges are destroyed and determined opposition is developed. . . . [R]equest authority H.E. the generalissimo to attack targets in between Salween and Lungling city.

Chennault did not wait for His Excellency's approval. That same afternoon, he sent the Adam & Eves and six SB-3s to attack the Japanese truck convoys moving toward the Salween. Meanwhile, in the deep river gorge, Sakaguchi Detachment forced a crossing of the river against fierce resistance by the Chinese 36th Division. The twin-engined bombers could not get into the gorge, so Chennault gave that job to the Panda Bears. Tex Hill led the first mission on Friday morning, May 8, accompanied by Ed Rector, Frank Lawlor, and Tom Jones, all of them trained as dive bombers in the navy. Their orders were nothing less than "to destroy the Burma Road by blowing it up at a point where a landslide would result or repairs of the road would be difficult." Such an outcome was unlikely, to say the least, for the Kittyhawks carried nothing larger than thirty-five-pound fragmentation bombs—"weed cutters"—meant to kill troops, not to move mountains.

The Panda Bears tried again in the afternoon. By this time, Japanese truck convoys were massed on the west bank of the river, waiting for engineers to build a pontoon structure to replace the suspension bridge blown up by the Chinese. To reach them, the Kittyhawks had to thread their way between the steep walls of the gorge, one after the other, unable to deviate from the one line. This was sweaty-palm time, as Lew Bishop recalled:

> Made first pass at an angle of about 50 degrees, speed 300 MPH. Dived to within 100 ft. of trucks releasing bombs in string. Continued on down gorge gaining altitude and turned back. Noticed results of attack as 4 bombs burst amidst line of trucks [and] other two slightly beyond but close enough to do destruction by fragmentation. Made three straffing passes.

. . . On third and fourth attacks drew fire from anti-aircraft gun stationed near road. By the time I completed my last straffing attack, I noticed one extremely large fire and two smaller fires amid trucks. Believed to have destroyed about 50 trucks during the course of attacks made by the four planes. Estimate 200 casualties among personnel on ground.

Bishop's dive angle and airspeed were not radical by navy standards, but the Kittyhawk had been designed for a different line of work. Heavy in the nose and lacking dive brakes, it was inclined to pick up speed without limit. Bishop throttled the engine back to idle, so that the airstream had to drive the big, three-bladed propeller, while the prop in turn had to drive the engine—which caused the Kittyhawk's built-in rudder trim to pull the plane to the right. To fly straight in these conditions, Bishop had to *stand* on his left rudder pedal. Then there was the Kittyhawk's tendency to mush. When he hauled back on the control stick, bringing the nose up, Bishop could only hope that the plane would not keep plunging toward the water, as had happened to Blackie Blackburn on April 28.

On Saturday, rain put a stop to the dive bombing, but the Chinese 36th Division crossed the river to the north of the Japanese bridgehead, threatening Sakaguchi Detachment's supply line and sending its trucks scurrying back toward the China-Burma border.

At Wu Chia Ba, meanwhile, a plot from the warning net caused the Adam & Eves to scramble. They climbed to 18,000 feet before spotting the intruder over Lake Kunming: a twin-engined reconnaissance plane, flying high. Bill Bartling made the first hit. "His first burst caused the rear cockpit to blow up," Bob Neale reported, "and the Jap started down making gentle spirals." Two other Tomahawks then joined the fight. "I circled the fight area," Neale wrote, "and watched the 3 P-40's making individual runs for about 5 minutes at approximately 16,000 feet. [A] burst from one of the P-40's caused the enemy to burst into flames after which the plane went into a spinning dive and crashed about 60 miles southwest of the southern tip of the South Lake." Bartling was credited with the kill: a Mitsubishi Dinah of the 18th Independent Chutai, which for four years had reconnoitered China without a loss. Before crashing, Captain Hideharu Takeuchi radioed Hankou that there were twenty-seven enemy planes at Wu Chia Ba.

The weather cleared on Sunday, May 10, and Chennault sent the Panda Bears winging back to the Salween. Ed Rector led the mission.

Before reaching the gorge, he learned over the radio that Chinese troops were now across the river and that he should confine his attacks to the area beyond Mangshi, the soggy airfield used by the Hell's Angels in the last days of Loiwing. At Mangshi, Rector saw a Japanese reconnaissance plane on the ground, but he kept going west until he found a truck convoy to strafe:

> The trucks were so scattered that I directed the flight to make individual attacks. I dived down, levelled out at 300 ft. . . . and released my bombs at three trucks parked in a small village. They missed by twenty yards and hit in the village. We were back to the airdrome by then and I straffed the Jap reconnaissance plane setting it afire.

Rector spotted more trucks but did not have enough gasoline to attack them, and he flew back to Yunnan-yi with two of his wingmen. The other Kittyhawks—flown by Frank Schiel and Harry Bolster, a flight instructor who had made the transition to fighters—were equipped with seventy-five-gallon belly tanks, so they kept going to the Burma-China border. Here Schiel spotted a truck convoy entering Yunnan province:

> At about 0945 Bolster and I straffed about 10 trucks of the column moving east. Two or three were set on fire indicating that they were carrying gasoline. A few minutes later we saw the head of the column on a straight stretch of road. . . . Bolster and I each made two passes, raking the whole line and setting some of them on fire.

A few hours later, Schiel again flew to the border, accompanied this time by Jim Howard and Tom Jones. They strafed and bombed whatever they came across, which in Schiel's case was "a group of trucks and low buildings which looked like barracks," while Jones tore up a fifty-truck convoy passing through Wanding.

On Monday, Chiang's 2nd Reserve Division also recrossed the Salween. In a reversal of the situation in Burma, the lightly armored Chinese now put "the hook" on Sakaguchi Detachment, roadbound by its vehicles and tanks. In the confusion, crew chief Gale McAllister of the Hell's Angels made his escape from the refugee horde. Caught on the west bank when the Salween bridge was dynamited, McAllister took advantage of the new fighting to walk upriver, cross over, and hitch a ride to Kunming, the last of the AVG technicians to straggle in from Loiwing.

To join the American Volunteer Group, Ajax Baumler had twice resigned from the air force, but was frustrated once by Mrs. Shipley in the passport office and again by the Japanese at Wake Island. He now came around the world in the other direction as a designated member of the 23rd Pursuit Group. En route, Baumler was supposed to take charge of the Republic P-43s that were being assembled in a dirigible hangar at Karachi airport by a crew of U.S. Army mechanics and AVG technicians under the direction of line chief Jasper Harrington. But when this combat veteran of the Spanish Civil War reached Kunming on May 11, he was given a desk job in Chennault's headquarters.

Nor did Baumler bring any Lancers to China. Instead, Chennault had to detach men from his combat squadrons to pick up the planes, as he had done for his replacement Kittyhawks. There were at least three of these missions in May. The first took George Burgard, Jim Cross, Dick Rossi, and a dozen Chinese pilots to Karachi, where they spent two weeks on transition training. (Among those who assisted in this project was Elwyn Gibbon, who in 1938 had served in Chennault's 14th Volunteer Squadron at Hankou.) They spent another two weeks trying to fly the Lancers to China. One Chinese pilot was killed, four were hospitalized, and six Lancers were wrecked before Burgard led the survivors into Wu Chia Ba on May 23. Once there, Cross joined the growing list of AVG pilots who wanted nothing more to do with fighter planes. When Chennault asked him to fly a Tomahawk to Chongqing, Cross pleaded earache and went instead in a CNAC transport. He spent the rest of his AVG tour as a staff officer.

Two P-43s were commandeered by Caleb Haynes of the Ferry Command when Chinese pilots abandoned them at Dinjan, too terrified to fly any farther. Colonel Haynes used the Lancers to escort his transports and scout Japanese airfields in Burma. This was such a success that when Charlie Sawyer and Bob Layher came through Dinjan, ferrying Kittyhawks to Kunming, Haynes borrowed them, too. And when Sawyer and Layher decided that they really should get on the road again, Haynes persuaded them to ride a C-47 and leave their Kittyhawks behind. Thereafter, the Ferry Command pilots took turns on fighter patrol—especially Colonel Robert Scott. He appropriated one of the Kittyhawks for his personal use, named it "Exterminator," and was awarded a Silver Star for his exploits over Burma. (Though known at home as the "one-man air force," Scott shot down no Japanese planes on these missions.) Haynes wanted to borrow even more Kittyhawks, but Chennault protested that the planes were needed in China:

> Thanks very much for the quart of Old Schenley [sic] which you sent me. It reminds me of home a great deal. . . . I regret very much that I am unable to send you six more P-40's. Our squadron strength now averages about eight P-40's and we are still conducting very active combat operations against our little brown friends. . . .
>
> I have just sent Harvey Greenlaw to India to serve as our supervisor for distribution of supplies and as liaison officer to the 10th Air Force and the Ferry Command. . . . We have enough ammunition, fuel, armament, etc. to last several months, but we could use food and cigarettes. Of course we will always be glad to receive new airplanes complete also.

From mid-April to mid-June, the Ferry Command hauled two tons of cigarettes to Kunming, along with 698 tons of fuel, ordnance, and miscellaneous supplies. On the return trip, the Douglas transports brought out tin, tungsten . . . and hog bristles, prized by the U.S. Navy to make paintbrushes.

In Delhi, the Greenlaws moved into the suite at the Cecil Hotel that was reserved for Bill Pawley. (This at a time when hotel accommodations were so scarce that Bill Tweedy and Jim Adams—Greg Boyington's affluent hosts at Rangoon—had to share a bathless room in Calcutta.) But what did Harvey *do* to justify this billet? As liaison officer, he was nowhere near Dinjan, where the Ferry Command operated from a pierced-steel runway, or Calcutta, where the 10th Air Force bombers were based. As for expediting supplies, Commander DeWolfe handled that job for Chennault, and Pappy Paxton also spent most of his time in India on supply matters. AVG veterans later speculated that Greenlaw applied for a commission in the U.S. Army, was turned down because of some unsavory but unspecified activity during his time in service, and packed his bags for home. Harvey and Olga never returned to Kunming, though their suite at the Cecil became a favorite rest stop for AVG ferry pilots.

Tom Jones was the very model of an all-American lad, with curly hair, wide eyes, and open features. In the navy, he had been a dive-bomber pilot on *Yorktown*. He missed the Panda Bears' tour at Mingaladon airport, as a result of malaria contracted on a tiger hunt with Moose Moss; and Olga Greenlaw recalled that he suffered dizzy spells when he was stationed at Loiwing in April, but concealed the episodes from Tex Hill and Doc Richards. However that may be, he now emerged as one of the Panda Bears' most aggressive bomber pilots. Early in May, he flew down to Hanoi and spotted forty planes on the runway at Gia Lam airport. That appeared to be a buildup aimed at Kunming, so Chennault laid on a spoiling strike, only to cancel it when Sakaguchi Detachment reached the Salween.

Jones got a second chance on May 12, when Chennault let him take six Kittyhawks to Hanoi. They were to drop propaganda leaflets supplied by a French refugee in Kunming, then bomb and strafe Gia Lam airport. Long after, Link Laughlin recalled Chennault's briefing in the ready room at Wu Chia Ba:

> Chennault lays the raid out like a football plan in his terse, flat matter-of-fact briefing. "... and take-off from [Mengzi] at 1630. Cruise at 14,000. Your ETA over Hanoi will be around 1740. Twenty minutes out, start your letdown to come over the city at 1,000 feet. Drop your leaflets ... then hit the field. Approach will be from the north at 300 feet. Maintain a two-hundred yard separation. Bomb and strafe on the first pass. If ground fire is minimal, come back for a second strafing run. ...."

Reality seldom matches the briefing. As soon as they crossed the border, Laughlin's engine began to grumble. ("It always does that when we get into enemy territory.") Jim Howard experienced the same phenomenon, and he turned back to Mengzi. High, roiling clouds over Indochina forced the remaining Kittyhawks down to 3,000 feet, and they were spotted from an auxiliary airstrip. Some Nates came up and chased them to Hanoi, where the Americans ran into a firestorm of antiaircraft fire. Nevertheless they opened their canopies and threw the propaganda leaflets over the side. (Addressed *aux Français d'Indochine,* they appealed to the white population to rise against the Japanese.) In string formation, the Kittyhawks then swept down on Gia Lam airport with the sun behind them, strafing and dropping fragmentation bombs. Link Laughlin was fourth in line:

> I follow [Frank] Schiel down to 300 feet and over the airfield. [Tom] Jones and [John] Donovan are scudding down the runway unloading their fifty-calibers and dropping weed cutters like they were going out of style.

The field is erupting like it was the end of the world. Donovan's hit! He goes straight into the runway and skids clear off the end in a big rolling ball of flame. . . . I squeeze down in the cockpit looking for a place to hide. Retract my neck right down into my puckering rectal area.

Bringing up the rear, Lew Bishop saw Frank Schiel make a direct hit on the administration building and Laughlin riddle "a DC-3 type Transport"; in a cluster of eight fighters, four were burning. Bishop saw another group of fighters beyond that, and he jinked toward it with all guns blazing, spilling six bombs as he swept over at 300 feet. When he pulled up, he saw the transport on fire and bombs bursting among the parked fighters. Fifteen Japanese planes had been destroyed, Bishop estimated, and thirty damaged. "All the time," he reported, "the anti-aircraft fire was very heavy and I noticed four [Nates] in our midst. One was on Schiel's tail and I started after him when I noticed Jones roll over and go down on him. The Jap turned away then back at Jones, passing above him."

Laughlin saw the Japanese fighter, too. It blew up "like a gas well," he recalled, hit by Jones or antiaircraft fire.

North of Hanoi, the four Panda Bears went into a thunderstorm so violent they had to fly on instruments. Afterward, they picked up the Michelin and flew "IFR" to Lao Kai on the border, then up the green valley to Mengzi, where they landed at 6:43 P.M. When Bishop taxied off the runway, his low-fuel light winked on. Laughlin too was out of gas, the result of a machine gun bullet through his right wing tank.

It appeared to be Chiang Mai all over again, with the better part of a Japanese fighter group destroyed at the cost of one man shot down, and the raid was so reported in the American press. But as with the 64th Sentai, the death of the 21st Hikotai was greatly exaggerated. The group was made up of two independent chutais, one of light bombers and the other of fighters. Most of the fighters were Nates, but "Nagano Force" (as it was called after its commander) had also been equipped with the first nine *Ki*-45s off the Kawasaki assembly line. The *Toryu* (Dragon Killer) was a twin-engined interceptor with twice the heft of a Hayabusa, and it was probably one of these that Laughlin flamed on the ground. The Japanese recorded only that one Nate was shot down and "three or four planes"—type unspecified—destroyed on the ground by incendiary bullets and fragmentation bombs.

In Chongqing, the more optimistic estimate prevailed, and each

Panda Bear was credited with three enemy aircraft. "If we destroy fifteen Nippon planes every day," Madame Chiang exulted, "soon none will be left." The generalissimo promoted Laughlin to flight leader; Jones, Schiel, and Bishop to vice squadron leader; and Jim Howard to squadron leader, presumably for the work he had done at Chongqing and in East China, getting airfields ready for the AVG. (Since the top slots were filled, the practical effect of the promotions was a fifty-dollar raise.) John Donovan was not mentioned in the generalissimo's dispatch, though it was traditional to promote those killed in line of duty.

It was also a tradition that a man knew when he was flying his last mission. After all, if it is ordained that we are to have a presentiment of death, then without the premonition we can live forever. Among Donovan's belongings, the Panda Bears found support for this comforting fiction, in a message addressed to his parents in Alabama:

> Dear Folks
>
> You must not feel badly about my death the small part that I have played in the war though it has cost me my life I am glad to give that. Life has meant much to me but not so much that I am too distressed at leaving and neither must you be. I had only a few things planned for the future one of the most important was a nice home. Momma will please me much if she will live in a more comfortable home with many flowers and trees. I am happy and so must she be love to all =
>
> John Junior

They sent the message as written, without preamble or explanation. It reached Montgomery before his last letter home, in which Donovan had pondered his career options after July 4, and asked his mother to find out what rank he might receive if he came home and returned to active duty. "If the Navy thinks that I would accept a commission as an Ensign," he warned, "after the experience that I have had over here, they are crazy."

Madame Chiang wanted the AVG to fly close support for the Chinese divisions that were trapped in North Burma. Eighteen sorties a day would do nicely, she thought. Chennault gave the job to the Adam & Eves, and by the time the orders were filtered through him and Bob Neale, the missions generally came down to two Kittyhawks, once a day. In the vastness of North Burma, the Adam & Eves rarely saw the victorious Japanese army, never mind the Chinese. Chennault wrote a long and careful letter to madame, explaining that the distances were too great, the weather too foul, and his planes too undependable for him to follow the letter of her instructions. In the five years since he had enlisted in the service of the Chiangs, it was the closest he had come to insubordination.

The Panda Bears continued to harass the Japanese in Indochina. On May 15, Gil Bright led a four-plane mission to Lao Kai on the border. "The idea," he explained to his parents, "was to blow up the daily train that comes up from the south. . . . We were too late for the train, so went down the track twenty-five miles to make them think we were going to Hanoi, and then turned off into the mountains so that their net would get confused when the stations along the railroad stopped reporting us." Another flight caught the Lao Kai train on Saturday, as Link Laughlin recalled:

> With steam squirting out of the boiler from fifty caliber holes, the engineer runs it into a mountain tunnel. "Hooo man!" hollers [Lew] Bishop, "Let's catch him coming out the other side." [But] that train crew is endowed with some sense of survival. They aren't about to come out the other side. Tunnels are security. But Bishop hops over the mountain and hangs around for ten minutes waiting for the engineer to come out and commit suicide.

They returned to Kunming to learn that Tom Jones was dead. The dive-bombing enthusiast had crashed on the target range, a small plateau a mile or so from Wu Chia Ba. Two AVG armorers, Charlie Baisden and Roy Hoffman, had adapted the Kittyhawk's drop-tank mechanism to carry a 550-pound bomb, one of those sent down the Old Silk Road before the Soviet Union turned its attention to the war in Europe. Jones apparently was testing this system when he augered in, the second victim of the Kittyhawk's reluctance to follow its nose out of a dive. He was buried in the Chinese airmen's cemetery near the airport, between Blackie Blackburn and Ben Foshee.

Chennault sent the Panda Bears back to Lao Kai on Sunday. Bus Keeton was scheduled to go, but when Colonel Scott of the Ferry Command asked to go along, Keeton gladly gave up his Kittyhawk to further the cause of melding the army and the AVG. (The pilots did not like Homer Sanders, whom Harvey Greenlaw had brought over from India to audition for command of the 23rd Pursuit Group, so Scott was trying out for the job.) Lew Bishop led the flight with two Panda Bears and the thirty-four-year-old colonel as his wingmen, while two Hell's Angels provided top cover. Fifty miles inside Indochina, R. T. Smith spotted the locomotive steaming north. He radioed Bishop, who told him to strafe the train while the Panda Bears bombed the railroad station. So the Tomahawks made four passes on the train, and the Kittyhawks dove on Lao Kai from out of the sun, as Pete Wright recalled:

> We approached the freight yard from South to North. Bishop came down in a steep glide and released his bombs at about 500 feet. I was a few hundred yards behind him and just as I was releasing my bombs I saw him pull up in a steep climbing turn to the left. About four feet of flame was coming out of the tail of his plane. I called to him over the radio to jump and he rolled on his back and left the plane. His parachute opened immediately and his plane crashed and exploded a moment later. The wind drifted him towards the East. . . . He landed almost in the center of the town and was alive when he disappeared into the trees.

Bishop was captured three days later and questioned about his service in Asia. According to a Tokyo newspaper, he professed contempt for the CAF and admiration for the Japanese fliers he had faced in Burma. As for the AVG, Bishop gave this sketch: "At the time when the war of Greater East Asia started, there were about 300 American volunteer fliers and ground crew men in the [Chinese] Air Force. However, at the time when I was shot down, there remained only about 50 American fliers and 100 ground crew members and there were only 45 Curtiss P No. 40 type planes left." He was sent to a prison camp in China.

The AVG had lost four pilots in less than a fortnight—not a run of luck calculated to encourage the survivors to join the 23rd Pursuit Group. The reluctance was especially notable among the squadron regulars. They were at the breaking point, most of them, worn down by the stress of combat, by the nightmares that preceded and followed it, and by the alien food and climate. Diarrhea was an almost constant companion, and many of them had been felled at one time or another with dengue fever or malaria. ("Even my eyelashes were sore," one of the technicians said of his bout with malaria.) Bob Neale had weighed a strapping 170 pounds when he stepped off *Jaegersfontein* the previous August; now he was down to 138 pounds. As a rule, the more combat a man had seen, the more anxious he was to go home, or at least to settle into a billet that did not oblige him to fly into the guns of the Japanese.

(In his diary, George Burgard wrote of one pilot: "He is all through flying over here and nothing will change his mind. He is just plain scared—but so are we all.") Chennault understood fear. He had already found noncombat jobs for half a dozen men who developed a fear of flying, and he now extended the same courtesy to Hank Geselbracht, who had refused to go on the most recent Lao Kai mission.

In their diaries and letters, the men usually concentrated on more mundane concerns: their health; their wives, sweethearts, and parents; and especially their resentment against the army's policy of offering them commissions in the reserve. On May 18, Chennault took Bob Neale aside and asked him to become executive officer of the 23rd Pursuit Group, with the rank of lieutenant colonel. "Might do it," Neale allowed—"if he can get me a permanent commission."

On Thursday, May 21, Brigadier General Clayton Bissell flew to Kunming for a meeting in the auditorium of Hostel Number One. It was the first time the pilots and technicians had seen the man who would be cutting their orders if they accepted induction. They were not impressed. He seemed a womanish martinet, like the British officers they had encountered at Singapore, Rangoon, and Magwe, and whose manner and uniform Bissell liked to ape.

Chennault opened the meeting with a brisk explanation of financial matters. If they refused induction, their contracts would end on July 4, and they would be paid for leave not taken (as much as one month's salary) and $500 for travel expenses. Nobody seemed to notice, but this was an outrageous breach of contract, as Bissell had pointed out. "Do you not agree," he had radioed Chennault before this meeting, "that China should pay full amount due under the original contract whether personnel elect induction or not?" And if that was too generous: "Can you agree that those . . . who refuse induction shall be permitted to complete contract [as civilians] attached to 23rd Pursuit Group or used elsewhere by Chinese?" No, Chennault did not agree. He would accommodate a fearful man, but not one who refused to follow him into the army.

Those who accepted induction would receive the difference between their army pay and what they would have earned by serving out a year with CAMCO—and if this proved to be less than one month's salary, they would get the full amount due them on their contracts, without subtracting their army pay. In addition, they too would be paid for leave not taken, and even $500 for travel home.

So far, everyone was satisfied. Then Bissell took the podium to explain the induction terms. To the technicians who stayed on in China, he offered the rank of technical sergeant—four stripes—for most of them, little or no advancement from their grades in the peacetime army or navy. Don Rodewald was delighted with the bonus provisions, but he had no intention of returning to active duty as a four-striper. "They didn't offer [the technicians] a thing," he wrote disgustedly. "Looks like most of them will take their chances with the home draft board."

As for the pilots, they would receive commissions at an appropriate rank in the U.S. Army Reserve. They were furious, most of them, though reserve commissions were the norm in the wartime army. To understand their anger, it is necessary to remember that they had entered military service during the Great Depression, as reserve officers on a four-year tour of duty, and that many of them had joined the AVG precisely because their four years were running out, and they fully expected to be unemployed and unemployable after that. A regular commission had been the grail to them in 1941, and it remained so in 1942. They had no knowledge of a world in which jobs could be found for the asking.

When Bus Keeton stood up and insisted on this point, Bissell got his back up. Regulations were regulations! Furthermore, if Keeton or anyone else intended to pull a fast one by taking a job with CNAC or Pan Am—well, he could forget it. The army had already closed that avenue. "And for any of you who don't want to join the Army," Bissell concluded, "I can guarantee to have your draft boards waiting for you when you step down a gangplank onto U.S. soil."

But of course they would be drafted! Able-bodied men in their twenties, as most of them were, did they really think they could sit out the rest of the war? A few did, but most wanted only a few weeks of rest and recuperation before returning to duty with the army, navy, or marines. Yet it was Bissell's mention of the draft that offended them more than anything else. "Instead of keeping us here," Keeton wrote in his diary, "he changed a few minds to the contrary. There will probably be 3 or 4 pilots stay"—an ominous forecast, and one that turned out to be reasonably accurate.

It was a tragedy that Bissell was so stupid, Chennault so uninvolved (or so pleased to see Bissell with pie on his face), and the men so prickly that they could not have reached a compromise—higher rank, for example. For more than a month, Stilwell had possessed the authority to offer a commission "up to and including Colonel" to anyone he wanted to keep in China, even if that resulted in an organization top-heavy with oak leaves and eagles. Bissell knew that, for he handled the radio traffic while Stilwell was trekking out of Burma. As for regular commissions, they too were negotiable, as later events would demonstrate. But in their public pronouncements, Bissell and Chennault hoarded rank as if the money was coming out of their own pockets, generally bidding four stripes for a technician and a major's gold leaves for a pilot or staff officer.

After the meeting, Charlie Bond went up to Chennault and asked privately for a regular commission. The Old Man hewed to Bissell's line, telling Bond that he must return to duty as a reservist—and he might as well do it in China, where he could count on becoming a major. Furious, Bond went back to Adobe City and wrote letters to President Roosevelt and Senator Tom Connally of Texas, asking for their help in obtaining a regular-army commission.

There was something odd about this blow-up: Bissell, in his radio-grams to Washington, had undergone a change of heart with respect to the AVG. He sniped no longer at Chennault and his men; instead, he sang their praises in such terms that his radiograms were scarcely indistinguishable from those Chennault had been wont to send. "AVG has been at its best in past ten days," Bissell had told the War Department earlier in the month, "and can do a job of work if kept supplied with planes and parts." And when General Marshall forwarded the president's congratulations to the AVG—this in response to Chennault's plea—Bissell first showed the document to Madame Chiang, then sat down to improve its language. It was standard practice to paraphrase a radiogram, so that an enemy agent could not break the code by comparing the original to what was distributed at the other end. But Bissell's revisions were calculated to flatter the AVG. This was the first sentence of Roosevelt's message: "The conspicuous gallantry and daring of the AVG officers combined with their extraordinary efficiency is a source of tremendous pride throughout America." As touched up by Bissell, it read: "The *outstanding gallantry and conspicuous daring* of the American Volunteer Group, combined with their *almost unbeliev-able efficiency*, is a source of tremendous pride throughout *the whole of America*." It was the hyped version, not Roosevelt's more austere original, that went onto the AVG bulletin board and into the Flying Tiger romances.

Even after his sullen reception at Hostel Number One, Bissell continued to plead the AVG's case. "Chennault and others have done wonders with very little," he radioed Marshall toward the end of the month. "They cannot do the impossible. The wholesome effect of promises of help by the president and the WD is wearing off due to our failure to deliver a single man to replace steady combat losses."

And Bissell (though he probably never knew it) supplied the stars for Chennault's shoulder tabs. Early in May, Jimmy Doolittle passed through Kunming on his way home, stopping long enough to have lunch at Hostel Number One. He noticed that Chennault still wore the silver eagles of a colonel. Doolittle too had been promoted to brigadier, and Bissell had done the honors in Chongqing, pinning two stars from his personal supply on America's latest hero. (Had he brought them to China, or were they flown in with the typewriter ribbons and other necessities?) Doolittle unpinned the stars and gave them to Chennault, without saying where they had come from.

The Chinese counterattack west of the Salween was such a success that Mutaguchi's 18th Division had to be diverted to Yunnan, to stop what seemed to be a thrust into occupied Burma. Nevertheless, part of Sakaguchi Detachment still clung to the west bank of the Salween, and on May 22 the AVG was ordered to blast them out. Chennault gave the job to the Adam & Eves, who had received the latest Kittyhawks to come in from Africa. It would be their first attempt at dive bombing. The weather was clear when they took off, but deteriorated as they neared the Salween, and they had trouble spotting the cluster of tents on the bank that was supposed to hide Japanese artillery. Bob Little led the attack echelon of four Kittyhawks, with Snuffy Smith flying on his wing:

> After making several circles, Little peeled off and following him I saw he was diving on the target. At about 1,000 feet, before Little had levelled off, I heard an explosion. Glancing at his plane I saw a burst of flame and black smoke midway of his left wing. He immediately went into a tight spin, I now noticed half his left wing was missing. He made no attempt to jump, or pull out, and was on fire when he hit the ground, when his plane exploded.

Smith was next into the gorge, overshooting the target and blasting the hillside instead. He saw no antiaircraft guns. But Bob Neale, circling overhead with the escort, thought that a lucky hit from a Japanese gun had struck a bomb in Little's wing-rack, thus blowing him up. A P-40 veteran from the 8th Pursuit Group at Mitchel Field, Little had built up his score in unspectacular but steady fashion, and his bonus account stood at 10.5 enemy aircraft destroyed.

Almost at the same moment, the JAAF suffered its most grievous loss of the Pacific war. Even as the Kittyhawks were taking off from Wu Chia Ba, a 60th Squadron Blenheim took off from Dum Dum airport in Calcutta. Warrant Officer W. M. Huggard flew the bomber down the west coast of Burma and blasted Akyab airport. Five Hayabusas chased the Blenheim out over the Bay of Bengal. For twenty minutes, Huggard flew low over the water while his gunner—Sergeant J. S. McLuckie—fought off the Hayabusas from the Blenheim's dorsal turret. His first hit was on Sergeant Yasuda, who turned back to Akyab with a .303-caliber bullet in his arm. Next McLuckie holed the gas tank on the fighter flown by Captain Masuzo Otani, forcing him to retire as well. Then he hit the command Hayabusa with an incendiary round, and its right wing blossomed with orange flame. "Kato then made up his mind to die," as a Tokyo newspaper explained to its readers, "and plunged into the sea in self-destruction, thus dying a daring death and ending a glorious career." It was 2:30 P.M. on Friday, May 22, 1942. Too shocked to press the fight, the remaining pilots turned for home, leaving the Blenheim to escape to India.

Kato was posthumously promoted to major general—the first army officer to be jumped two grades—and Japan went into mourning for its "Hero God of the Air," who supposedly had shot down 200 Chinese, Soviet, British, Dutch, and American planes in four years of war. (A postwar Japanese historian put Kato's victories at eighteen.) Even more than the Doolittle raid, the loss of the JAAF's first and most famous ace brought home to the Japanese people the understanding that the Sacred Motherland was not invincible, and that their South Pacific adventure would not be concluded without pain.

On Sunday, May 24, Chennault took the Panda Bears off the Indochina run and reassigned them to the Salween front. The target was a town in which 300 Japanese troops were besieged by the Chinese 38th Division. The Panda Bears grumbled that they were drawing all the dirty jobs; Bus Keeton blamed "our two eager squadron leaders," meaning Tex Hill and Ed Rector. But Hill was in Delhi, enjoying the swimming pool at the Cecil Hotel with Duke Hedman, Olga Greenlaw, and Fred and Helen Hodges. It was Rector who assigned the missions, which were led in turn by himself, Frank Schiel, and John Petach. With twenty pilots and only eight planes on the 2nd Squadron roster, Rector filled the missions on a rotating basis. Butch Carney's flight instructors were blooded one by one: Arnold Shamblin on Monday, Van Shapard on Thursday, Lester Hall on Friday. Also flying his first combat mission was Conant/Perry, the former PBY skipper who had wrecked three Toma- hawks at Kyedaw airfield.

The CAF joined this campaign with its SB-3s and even some of its ancient I-15 biplanes, dating from the early days of the Sino-Japanese War. The weather was impossible, obliging the raiders to struggle over 12,000-foot peaks through clouds and blinding rain. More often than not, they turned back. On Thursday, May 28, Frank Adkins managed to get through and drop six weed-cutters on the defenders:

> Weather was very bad, cloudy and raining. Found objective and only had 1200 ft. ceiling. I dove to 800 feet and released bombs. I saw all six bombs hit in the center of the town. The bombs hit about 50 feet apart causing quite a bit of damage to wooden buildings in the small town. I saw no ground fire in return to my raid.

Next day, the AVG finally got through in force: eight Panda Bears loaded with fragmentation bombs, with the Hell's Angels flying top cover. "We passed through some fairly bad weather," Bus Keeton noted in his diary. They found the walled town and attacked it in pairs. "Ed Rector and I laid all of our bombs in the middle of the town and started a fire," Keeton wrote, adding that at least half the flight's bombs landed inside the walls, after which three Kittyhawks went down to strafe. With this boost, the Chinese took the town, and for the AVG that was the last shot in the Salween campaign.

On Saturday, May 30, it was back to Indochina. Gil Bright took the Kittyhawks down to Mengzi, then followed the Michelin seventy miles into enemy territory on what appears to have been another shakedown for inexperienced pilots. Bright's wingmen were Lester

Hall and Conant/Perry, each on his second combat mission . . .
and Curt Smith, the AVG adjutant, putting himself in harm's way
for the first time since his inglorious retreat to Mingaladon on
Christmas Day.

Seven pilots persisted in the quest for regular-army commissions,
though few of them met the posted criteria: four years of college or its
equivalent, a graduate of army flight school, and no older than twenty-
six. They flew to Chongqing, were interviewed by Bissell, and took a
battery of written and physical exams. As they understood the matter,
they were all turned down, for reasons varying from defective hearing to
genital chancres. But that was not what happened. Regulations were
regulations, Bissell had proclaimed at Hostel Number One, but behind
the scenes he would bend regulations with the best of them. He
recommended Robert Raine for a commission, though he had never
been near an army flight school: he was a former navy pilot. He also
okayed Charlie Sawyer, who failed the hearing test—and George
Burgard and Charlie Bond, specifically noting beside their names that
the age requirement should be waived for them. The other pilots to
pass muster were Frank Schiel and Ernest (Bus) Loane, formerly a
flight instructor at Yunnan-yi. These six, the induction board concluded, were "fully qualified and recommended for such commission." (The seventh applicant was presumably the man with venereal
disease.) The commission in question was second lieutenant in the
regular army, though each would also receive a reserve commission
as captain or major.

Incredibly, Bissell did not tell the six that he intended to support
their applications. They flew back to Kunming believing they had
been turned down—another insult, as it seemed to them, from the
officer who had come to represent that most unloved creature in any
organization: the son of a bitch from headquarters. This was an ironic
reversal of roles. Chennault had spent World War I in American training
camps, while Bissell was shooting down five German aircraft on the
Western Front; but now Chennault was the Old Man—the warrior—
and Bissell the staff officer making life miserable for fighting men. All
the frustration, bitterness, disillusion, fatigue, and weariness of the past
year was focused on this unfortunate man, who was only trying to do his

best for the U.S. Army and (as he saw it) for the AVG. As the story is told, Chennault's men got their revenge by teaching the gas coolie at Wu Chia Ba to chant: "Piss on Bissell!" Smiling and bowing, and believing it to be an American greeting, he shouted this pleasantry to the passengers of all incoming planes.

Far Worse Than You Know

June–July 1942

On June 1, forty-eight hours after Curt Smith's foray into French Indochina, Chennault put him in charge of the 23rd Fighter Group. (In May 1942, the army changed the "pursuit" terminology to "fighter," though the planes kept their P designations until the end of the war.) It was an extraordinary appointment: a civilian commanding U.S. Army personnel by authority of a unit of the Chinese Air Force. AVG Special Order 120 went on to specify that the detachment commander was to be "obeyed and respected as such." Obedience, certainly, but it was an eloquent commentary on his staff officers that Chennault felt it necessary to include respect in the package.

Seven army pilots arrived that day, without planes of their own. In the easy-rank year of 1942, when smooth-cheeked lads were walking about with silver bars on their shoulders, they were all second lieutenants, fresh out of flight school. But they accomplished what the Flying Tigers had not, checking out in the AVG Tomahawks with no worse mishap than a ground loop, and that in a pileup begun by Bill Bartling of the Hell's Angels. That done, the seven lieutenants were distributed among the AVG squadrons for seasoning.

A more formidable unit was on its way. Six North American B-25s had reached India under Major Gordon Leland, consigned to China as a down payment on Chennault's long-promised bomber group. The flight into China would have been hazardous enough, but somebody—

his identity unclear—decided that the Mitchells should bomb Lashio en route. Carrying cots and duffel for their crews, plus a full bomb load and extra cases of fifty-caliber ammunition, the B-25s took off from Dinjan airport on Wednesday morning, June 3. Dinjan was in the far northeast of India, so the Mitchells had to fly a dogleg of 700 miles instead of the usual 400 miles over the Hump. Caleb Haynes offered one of his Ferry Command pilots to show the way, but Leland refused. The planes were so overloaded that carrying the pathfinder would have required him to leave one of his own men behind.

The Mitchells bombed Lashio on schedule, tearing up the red-clay airfield and destroying a Mitsubishi Dinah on the ground. However, two Nates got off the ground and gave chase. Most of the Mitchell pilots headed for China at full throttle, burning up their fuel reserves and crashing in the mountains before they reached Kunming. Only two pilots had the nerve to stay at cruising speed. The Nates shot them up and killed radioman Wilmer Zeuske at his panel, but these Mitchells managed to reach Wu Chia Ba—two out of six.

As always, Chennault believed that a bit more attention to detail would have prevented the disaster, as he radioed Caleb Haynes in Dinjan:

Please forward following to [General Brereton:] "Request all B-25's be equipped auxiliary tanks giving minimum one hour additional endurance before coming China. Better bomb sight also required for flight leaders at least." Thanks. Please advise future bomber crews [about] AVG radio setup, frequency, call letters etc. Also need for getting frequent weather reports. . . . Sergeant Zeuske killed in action June 3. Require replacement urgently.

Meanwhile, thousands of miles to the east, two naval task forces were groping toward each other, preparing for a combat that would be the turning point of the Pacific war. The Battle of Midway had been inspired by Jimmy Doolittle's raid upon Honshu. Captured in China, his airmen claimed that they had taken off from "an island 500 kilometers west of Midway." The Japanese had to take the threat seriously: fleets of four-engined bombers taking off from a mid-Pacific island, bombing Japan, then continuing west to China or Siberia. So the navy set out to capture Midway with a task force that included four aircraft carriers and 261 planes. Losses were huge on both sides, but in the end American dive-bombers sank the Japanese carriers—and thereby doomed their planes—in the worst defeat ever inflicted upon the Empire of the Sun.

The army was more successful in its response to the Doolittle raid: to move inland and "destroy the air bases from which the enemy might conduct aerial raids on the Japanese Homeland." The Japanese committed 148,000 troops to Operation *Sei-go,* plus 30,000 soldiers and 10,000 porters contributed by the Wang Ching-wei government in Nanjing. They captured Zhuzhou airfield on June 6. The airfield had crushed-stone runways 4,600 feet long and an "underground hangar" large enough to hold forty or fifty bombers, so impressive a piece of work that the Japanese ascribed it to American engineers. To prevent it from being used again, they dug trenches eight feet wide and three feet deep the entire length of the runway. They gave the same treatment to other airfields, and summarily executed tens of thousands of peasants suspected of helping the Doolittle raiders. Like the other great battles that had raged in East China since 1938, *Sei-go* was all but ignored by the American press: yellow men fighting yellow men, after all.

Chennault already had the Panda Bears scheduled to move up to Beishiyi airfield outside Chongqing, to protect the capital during the summer bombing season. By the time the weather had cleared enough for them to make the move, he decided that he must also put a squadron in East China. He gave that assignment to the Adam & Eves. When they were in place, his squadrons would be scattered as never before—the Hell's Angels at Kunming in the west, the Panda Bears at Chongqing on the north, and the Adam & Eves at Guilin to the east—a triangle 400 miles to a side.

On Tuesday, June 9, Colonel Wang Shu-ming gathered the Americans in the main hangar at Wu Chia Ba. He decorated thirty-three pilots and three technicians with the Chinese Cloud Banner (4th, 5th, 6th, or 7th class) for "bravery and outstanding combat performance."* He also

---

* The decorations went to Bill Bartling, Blackie Blackburn (dead), Charlie Bond, George Burgard, John Dean, John Farrell, Cokey Hoffman (dead), Bob Little (dead), Bob Neale, Bob Prescott, Joe Rosbert, Dick Rossi, Sandy Sandell (dead), Snuffy Smith, and Fritz Wolf of the Adam & Eves; to Noel Bacon (on leave), Gil Bright, Tom Cole (dead), Tex Hill, Jim Howard, Ken Merritt (dead), Moose Moss, Jack Newkirk (dead), and John Petach of the Panda Bears; and to Parker Dupouy, Tom Haywood, Duke Hedman, Ken Jernstedt, George McMillan, Chuck Older, Eddie Overend, Bill Reed, and R. T. Smith of the Hell's Angels. Also decorated were line chief Harry Fox, radioman Mickey Mihalko, and armorer Herb Pistole. Evidently there was no Fifteen Star medal with which to honor Neale, the triple ace.

presented each ace and double ace with the appropriate Five Star or Ten Star Wing Medal. (Not many double aces were on hand to collect, so Wang rounded up Charlie Bond's score to qualify him for a Ten Star medal, and he did the same with some Five Star candidates.) Chinese troops provided an honor guard, and a band played martial music.

After the ceremony, the Adam & Eves and Panda Bears took off for their new stations. Wu Chia Ba was left to the Hell's Angels, with fourteen pilots including two army lieutenants and Cliff Groh, who reached Kunming that day after nearly four weeks on horseback and train. "We of the Third Pursuit Squadron," mused Dan Hoyle, "are here alone with the Chinese air force of P-43 airplanes which do not go into combat." Neither did the Hell's Angels, come to that. When the Japanese bombed on the Salween front, these heroes of Rangoon and Magwe sprinted to their Tomahawks as before, but after they clawed to altitude they did no more than maintain a protective umbrella over the airport. It was all their weary engines could manage. From time to time, more army pilots came from India, and the Hell's Angels checked them out in Tomahawks. When they had no better entertainment, they watched the CAF pilots crash their P-43s, as happened once or twice a week. On two occasions, a Lancer spontaneously burst into flame, the result of leaks in the plane's fuel system.

A CNAC Douglas flew the 1st Squadron technicians to Guilin on Tuesday afternoon. This was one of the forward airstrips Jim Howard had scouted for Chennault; it was located in a range of sugarloaf peaks, like 800-foot pylons sticking out of the paddy fields, so close together that the CNAC pilot could not circle the airstrip but had to thread his way among them. But the facilities were among the best in China. Guilin had a mile-long runway surfaced with crushed rock, and revetments large enough to hide a B-17 Flying Fortress. (For which purpose, indeed, Guilin and Zhuzhou had been built in the fall of 1940, the only tangible result of the Morgenthau-Chennault scheme to send heavy bombers to China.) The operations center and radio station were built into the sugarloaves, impervious to bombing. The hostel was five miles away: a cluster of dormitories tucked against the mountains, each with a stone foundation and camphor-wood sheathing—like "a small camp in the north woods," as Don Rodewald marveled. There was a shower room, a dining hall, a clubhouse with a pool table, and an air-raid shelter in a cave.

After breakfast on Wednesday morning, the technicians went outside to see a lone Nate circling Guilin. "We could watch him well with our glass," Rode wrote. He drove to the field with armorer Robert Neal (not to be confused with the squadron leader) and crew chief Robert Rasmussen, stopping at the radio station manned by Ralph Sasser:

> He has his transmitter in one large cave and his receiver in a small one. While there we got word of bombers headed this way. We went down to the field where Neal, Rass and myself got perched up on the ledge of one of the bluffs ready for the show. We didn't wait long before we heard them. The AcAc started in on them and then we started our cameras going. Three passed over on each side of us dropped their eggs and then left. We only saw two fighters but thought we could hear more.

The raiders came from Canton on the coast: Kawasaki Lily medium bombers, fixed-gear Nakajima Nates, and (though nobody identified them as such) the JAAF's new twin-engined Toryu fighters. They did little damage. As Chennault had long ago noted, an unoccupied airfield made a poor target, especially when built of native materials and maintained by coolie labor.

Chennault flew down to Guilin that evening—also by CNAC, since the army pilots at Chongqing would not fly through the fog and rain that shrouded the capital. The Japanese formation returned on Thursday morning. Even as the bombs exploded, twelve Adam & Eves tried to follow their commander down from Chongqing. Two planes were delayed by engine trouble, and another crashed midway. By dusk, however, eleven Tomahawks and Kittyhawks managed to reach their new station.

Chennault scheduled reveille for 3 A.M. Two hours later, his pilots were hunched over their cribbage boards when the usual scout came over the field. Who needed a warning net when the Japanese were so obliging as to telegraph their raids? The Adam & Eves ran for their planes, took off, and climbed to the positions Chennault had assigned them: George Burgard's flight at 21,000 feet, Bob Neale's at 18,000, and Charlie Bond's at 15,000, circling like hawks to the west of Guilin. It was just before 6 A.M. on Friday, June 12.

The JAAF in China was thinly spread. The bombers at Canton

consisted of one squadron from the 90th Sentai, whose main base was at Nanjing; there were five Lilys that morning. They were escorted by eight Nates of the 54th Sentai, which since the outbreak of the Pacific war had been the principal fighter group in China, and its planes scattered from Canton to Hankou. Finally, there were five Toryus of Nagano Force, the squadron that had opposed the AVG at Hanoi. The Toryus had moved to Canton under Sergeant Jiro Ieiri to lend some badly needed muscle to Operation *Sei-go*. For four weeks, they had escorted the Lilys to Liuzhou, Guilin, and other East China fields, and not once had the CAF come up to challenge them. Sergeant Ieiri had accordingly transformed them into attack planes, slinging 110-pound bombs beneath their wings and loading their nose guns with explosive shells, to destroy buildings, vehicles, and aircraft on the ground.

Droning in from the southeast at 16,500 feet, the Lilys bombed at 5:58 A.M. and turned for home. If attacked, the Nates were supposed to stay with the bombers while the Toryus dealt with the enemy; but as often happened with Japanese formations, the planes drifted apart before the Americans swept down on them. In the top flight, George Burgard saw four Nates, at a lower altitude than the Lilys had followed. He put his Tomahawk into a screaming dive, dropping 9,000 feet in a matter of seconds. "I fired several long bursts from a good position," he reported. He got some hits, as he saw from the flashes on the fuselage of his victim. "However, I observed no results as I was forced to recover sharply to avoid another Jap who was practicing his deflection shooting on me. The melee lasted for several minutes during which I fired at three Jap planes several times." Then he saw another Nate, chasing a Curtiss fighter that was streaming smoke from its engine.

The burning plane belonged to Allen Wright, formerly of the CAF flight school. His engine had been hit by the greenhouse gunner on a Lily, but he had gone on to attack three "light bombers." Luckily for Wright, the Nate drove him away before he learned that he was actually chasing three cannon-equipped fighters. And George Burgard took care of the Nate, dropping 2,000 feet and firing bursts at long range until the fixed-gear fighter turned away. Then he escorted Wright back to the airfield, where the ex-instructor bellied in, spraining his back and wrecking his plane.

Climbing back to altitude, Burgard set up a patrol to the south of Guilin. He was soon joined by Lieutenant Romney Masters. Spotting a

---

Kawasaki Ki-45 Toryu

Aware that the western powers were developing long-range, twin-engined escort fighters, the JAAF in 1937 staged a competition to build a similar plane. The successful designer was Kawasaki, whose prototype was powered by Bristol Mercury engines built under license in Japan. The plane was lovely to see, with a needle nose, two neatly faired radial engines, and a two-man cockpit with a rear-facing gunner; it boasted three machine guns and a cannon adapted from an anti-tank weapon. Performance was sluggish, however, and the project was shelved until the Hayabusa powerplant became available. Production began early in 1942, so the plane went into service as the Type Two Army Two-Seater Fighter. It was dubbed *Toryu,* meaning Dragon Killer. The independent fighter squadron at Hanoi received its first *Ki-45*s in February, but the June 12 shootout at Guilin seems to have been the Toryu's baptism of fire. Disappointed by its performance against the Kittyhawk, the JAAF began to reserve it for attacking ground targets and Allied shipping.

Engines: two 950-hp Nakajima air-cooled radials
Crew: two
Wingspan: 49 feet 3 inches
Combat weight: 11,600 lb
Maximum range: 1,400 miles
Top speed: 340 mph at 23,000 feet
Armament: one 20-mm cannon and two 12.7-mm machine guns in the nose, one 7.92-mm flexible machine gun; 1,100-lb total bomb load

---

Nate and a Toryu, Burgard went after the fixed-gear fighter and left the army pilot to take care of what seemed to be the easier target. The Nate wriggled out of the way, so Burgard made a run on the twin-engined plane. "The bomber was light, fast, and exceptionally maneuverable," he reported. "He dove sharply for the ground and made a sharp turn." The Nate came back, put a shot through the Tomahawk's left aileron, and dove away with Burgard after him, firing long bursts at an angle. "The fighter skidded badly and fell off on a wing," he wrote. "I pulled up and saw he had run into the side of a sharp peak and blew up." Lieutenant Masters was nowhere to be seen, so Burgard decided to finish off the twin-engined plane. His fifty-caliber guns were dead, however, and the "light bomber" strangely elusive:

I got back some altitude and picked up the bomber hedge-hopping through the sharp hills. Each time I got at him from the rear he would slip in and out of the peaks. . . . After about five or six runs I caught him in a valley and got right in behind him but he turned almost 90° and began making 360° vertical turns around a sharp cone. . . . We were never more than 150′ from the ground. On a pass from above my right fifty started working and in a brief interval his left engine caught fire. . . . I throttled back and continued to shoot until he dragged his wing on a small knob and mushed in.

This was the command Toryu. Sergeant Ieiri died in the crash, but the gunner-radioman climbed out and was captured unhurt by Chinese soldiers.

Joe Rosbert, flying a Kittyhawk in the low-level echelon, also attacked a Toryu thinking it was a bomber. The plane looped up and over him, then fled in the opposite direction. Rosbert used his dive speed to gain altitude for another attack. This time, "a quick burst of the six fifties tore off part of his wing and the Jap spun towards the sharp mountains below."

Charlie Bond tried to do the same, only to have the Toryu's rear gunner put a bullet through the Kittyhawk's coolant system. Bond's guns quit firing, the overheat light came on, and smoke poured out of his instrument panel. Then two Nates came up behind him. Bond put the Kittyhawk into a dive, made himself small in front of the armor plate, and wondered whether he should bail out or make a dead-stick landing. The Japanese pilots must have believed it was a death dive, for they peeled off and left him to belly into a flooded field. Bond was thrown against the gunsight, stunning him and gashing his forehead. The Kittyhawk did not burn, and after a minute he climbed out, gathered his flight gear, and made his way to a telephone. He was on the railroad twenty-five miles southwest of Guilin, and a priest picked him up and took him into Yongfu. "The reverend told me that this was the greatest moment in the life of the village," Bond wrote in his diary. "The Flying Tigers are heroes to them, and now they had seen one." Alas, they expressed their pleasure by strewing firecrackers in his path, giving him fresh burns to go with those from his Baoshan shoot-down.

Bob Neale was not having a good morning, either. The squadron leader got a few hits on the Lilys, then found himself with a Toryu on his tail. "Thought it was a Me 110," he wrote, referring to the twin-engined German fighter that had helped inspire the *Ki*-45. "Had a hell of a time getting away."

Altogether, the Adam & Eves claimed nine Japanese planes that Friday, attributed to George Burgard, Joe Rosbert, John Dean, Bill Bartling, and Dick Rossi. The actual tally was not much smaller. One Lily crashed near Guilin and two more had been shot up so badly that they had to be written off. Only one Nate was lost, but two Toryus went down over Guilin and another crashed on the way home—and the two survivors had wrinkles on the fuselage, revealing that the Toryu was not up to the high-*g* manuevers favored by Japanese pilots. After assessing this dismal result, the JAAF called off the campaign against Guilin.*

The Adam & Eves were still celebrating their victory when the Chinese brought in the radioman-gunner from the command Toryu, which had been suckered into a mountainside by George Burgard. The prisoner identified himself as Corporal Kei Honda, a member of Nagano Force since February, with two years' experience as a gunner in twin-engined bombers. Corporal Honda was not a dedicated samurai. "What are you fighting for?" he was asked.

"I don't know," he replied.

"Do you think the Japanese will win the war?"

"I have no opinion on that."

"What did you do before you went in the army?"

"Raised chickens," Honda said. He went on to tell the Americans everything he knew about the planes and antiaircraft defenses at Canton and Hankou. He identified his own plane as a "Model 45"—the first time Chennault had heard the *kitai* number of a JAAF plane. Then Honda described the large-caliber guns in the Toryu's nose, adding that every second round that Friday had been an explosive shell. The Adam & Eves were greatly sobered by this information. Not only had they attacked a fighter believing it to be a bomber, but they had been seriously outgunned. "No more head on runs for me," Bob Neale vowed.

* Until the Battle of Midway, the Japanese press had reported specific combats with reasonable accuracy. No longer: "Nine American aircraft of the Curtiss-Hawker P-40 type were downed by the Japanese Air Unit in a fierce combat," wrote a Tokyo newspaper of the Guilin action. "In the breath-taking aerial duel, the Japanese lost only two planes."

The Adam & Eves introduced George Burgard to Honda as the man who had shot him down. They posed with him in front of a shark-faced fighter, his crew-cut head scarcely reaching their shoulders, and they treated him to coffee and cream puffs. Then they gave him back to the Chinese. Since the usual fate of a prisoner was to be paraded from village to village in a bamboo cage, taunted and stoned by the peasants, Corporal Honda probably did not survive very long.

Chennault flew up to Chongqing on Sunday, June 14, for the conference that would determine the shape of American air power in China. Stilwell was back in town, having successfully marched his party across the Arakan Hills to India, then returned to China by flying over the Hump. He was sick with jaundice and worms, so General Brereton flew in from Delhi in his Consolidated B-24 Liberator bomber to take charge of the induction conference. Brereton explained that army policy allowed only one air force in each theater of operations, so Chennault would have to content himself with running a "China Air Task Force" as a stepchild of the 10th Air Force in India. As Brereton envisioned it, the CATF would consist only of fighters. Caleb Haynes of the Ferry Command would be promoted to brigadier general and put in command of the bombers now coming to China.

Bissell attended the conference but apparently was ignored. So too was the question of whether Haynes would report to Chennault in Chongqing or to Brereton in Delhi. "Deaf as a post," Brereton wrote of this meeting, "Chennault would sit around in conferences like a cigar-store Indian. However, he was a good lip-reader and his agile mind followed everything." Those who knew him better believed that the Old Man heard what he wanted to hear, using his deafness to excuse him from acknowledging the rest. He would outrank Haynes, so the command problem would take care of itself, if Bissell were kept out of the loop.

The immediate challenge was to persuade his pilots and technicians to sign on with the CATF. Toward this end, they set up an induction board consisting of Chennault, Caleb Haynes, Homer Sanders (whose planes Chennault still coveted, though he had decided against Sanders as his fighter commander), and a navy officer to pitch the pilots and technicians who had joined the AVG from that service.

That Saturday night, after eight days without an air raid, the Guilin authorities put on a "comforting party" at the AVG hostel. The refugee mechanic Gerhard Neumann remembered it fondly: "A bevy of beautiful, slim, English-speaking girls in slinky Chinese silk gowns and a flower in their black hair . . . took each of us by the arm and escorted us, one by one, into the large dining room to the applause of our hosts." The Americans were treated to cigars, souvenir tapestries (a flight of eagles attacking the rising sun), speeches, toasts, and a dramatic skit in Chinese. There were place cards, too, and a handbill celebrating the achievements of the AVG and those—quite fictional—of the Chinese Air Force at Guilin, which the handbill rendered in its then-customary spelling:

> Guardians of the air, you heroes of the American Flying Tigers and the Chinese Divine Hawks:
>
> After our long expectation and to our great cheerfulness, you have annihilated eight Japanese vultures in the air above Kweilin on June 12. This is the most brilliant merit of air combat that has ever been achieved at Kweilin. You have once more created your great glory of extinguishing the enemy in the air. . . .
>
> Today, we, the 300,000 citizens in Kweilin, are presenting you our heartiest congratulations and highest respects to your comfort. And we are expecting your continual achievements of greater and richer merits with your inexhaustible heroism and bravery.
>
> Let us yell:
>
> Long live the American Flying Tigers!
>
> Long live the Chinese Divine Hawks!
>
> Long live the co-operation between the U.S.A. and China!

With his "fifty-mission" cap crushed low on his brow, Caleb Haynes flew the induction board down to Guilin on Sunday, June 21. It was not the most propitious day to begin recruiting. "Everybody had a lot of party left in them yet," Don Rodewald wrote, adding that the recruiters "sure heard our vein on the subject" of going back in uniform.

Rode was willing—if the price were right. He went before the board on Monday and asked for a commission as first lieutenant. "The board didn't like the idea," he wrote, "but [Chennault] recommended me so there wasn't much they could do about it." Line chief Jasper Harrington struck the same bargain. He identified Colonel Sanders as the man opposed to giving silver bars to these former sergeants, while the Old Man argued that they would otherwise go to work for the Chinese as technical advisers. "Chennault was the one that decided what rank you were going to get," Harrington said. "The board was a formality."

If so, Charlie Bond had a legitimate complaint. He offered to stay in China on the usual condition—a commission in the regular army—and the board offered to commission him as a major in the reserves. Bond refused, and so did George Burgard when the offer was made to him. As for Bob Neale, the squadron leader felt altogether worn out, and the only thing he wanted out of life was to see his wife again. Nevertheless, he came away from the interview feeling that he had let the Old Man down. "It was the hardest thing I have ever done," he wrote in his diary. Neale took to his bed with what he assumed was dengue fever, but which he later diagnosed as a nervous breakdown.

And so it went. Half a dozen technicians signed up for continued service in China—but no pilots.

Two hundred miles northeast of Guilin was Hengyang, where in 1938 Chennault had perched on a garden wall and studied Japanese bombing tactics. After its defeat at Guilin, the JAAF turned its attention to this undefended airfield, so Chennault brought the Panda Bears down from Chongqing. They found another miracle of the Chinese base-building effort: a two-story hostel with sleeping quarters above and dining and recreational facilities below, nicely sited on a fast-moving tributary of the Yangzi. The food, however, was notoriously bad.

On Monday morning, June 22, Ed Rector led the Panda Bears from Hengyang to the Yangzi, where they strafed a Japanese gunboat and three smaller vessels. Their fifty-caliber bullets killed ten sailors, including the gunboat commander, a Captain Sumida. The JAAF struck back the same afternoon from Hankou and Nanjing: two squadrons of the 54th Sentai, with fourteen Nates between them. They winged south over the great oxbow of the Yangzi, to be picked up by the Chinese warning net at 1:20 P.M. Rector made the interception with six Kittyhawks and a mixed bag of pilots, including Charlie Sawyer of the Adam & Eves and Captain Ajax Baumler of the U.S. Army, flying his first combat mission since the Spanish Civil War. They took off at 1 P.M., climbed to 20,000 feet, and circled Hengyang, as Sawyer wrote in his combat report:

> We spotted 14 [Nates] 8,000 feet below us and attacked. My first attack was a headon run, after one good burst a large stream of smoke started coming out his motor. . . . Later I made a rear quarter attack on one and again smoke poured out of his engine. . . . Finally, I got in position to make

a direct stern attack; I came upon him slightly below and directly from the rear. I opened fire at approximately 500 yards and closed into about 250 yards with pieces flying off and smoke coming out. He turned 90 degrees to the left and I got in a good burst at close range and he seemed to explode and disintegrate.

Sawyer was credited with the kill—his first. Frank Schiel also claimed a Nate, though just one *Ki*-27 actually went down over Hengyang. (Another was badly damaged and may have crashed on the way home: Japanese accounts tend to pass over losses that took place away from the scene of battle.) As had happened on two occasions at Rangoon, the crippled Nate made a *jibaku* dive onto Hengyang airfield, trying to take out a Kittyhawk on the ground.

Major Yasunari Shimada, the 54th Sentai commander, was discouraged by his group's reception at Guilin and Hengyang. "Surprise attacks were very difficult," a JAAF officer wrote after the war, because of "the enemy's precise antiaircraft observation networks." Furthermore, the Nate was too slow to compete with the American fighters, and its maneuverability was offset by the enemy's "coming-and-go" tactics. Shimada therefore asked that the 54th be sent home and refitted with Hayabusas, as soon as replacements could be brought to China.

In a conference at Nanjing on June 24, the hikodan commander announced that henceforth the Allied airfields would be attacked only at night, and only by small groups of bombers. The idea probably came from the AVG's longtime antagonist, Colonel Onishi of the 62nd Sentai, which had been refitted and sent to China in the spring of 1942.

In North Africa, the German army launched an armored drive on Cairo, to such effect that General Brereton and most of the 10th Air Force were ordered to Egypt to shore up the crumbling British front. The planes thus diverted included the Lockheed Hudsons that Lauchlin Currie had acquired for Chennault. With exquisitely bad timing, the A-28s reached the Middle East just as the German tanks began to roll.

So the only bombers in view for China were the B-25s already in Kunming: the two survivors of Major Leland's flight, plus four brought in by Major Allen Fortune. On June 23, Chennault ordered the Mitchells to fly to Guilin, thus settling the question of who controlled their movements. (That was one motive. Another was to prevent their being sent back through the pipeline to North Africa.) On the same day, Chennault sent seven Adam & Eves up to Hengyang to reinforce the Panda Bears. The induction board followed them. Chennault was worried now, and even Colonel Sanders toned down the bluster that had irritated the Adam & Eves. As Jim Howard recalled the interview, he was warmly greeted, praised for his services as combat pilot and administrator, and offered command of a fighter squadron with the rank of major in the reserve. Two days out of three, Howard was so sick with dengue fever that he could not fly, and he refused. But Ed Rector, Frank Schiel, and Gil Bright accepted identical offers, and Charlie Sawyer, the late-blooming pilot attached to the Panda Bears, agreed to stay in China as a captain.

Then it was off to Kunming, where the induction board made the same dismal hit as at Guilin: a handful of technicians but no pilots.

If Chennault was heartbroken, he did not show it. He understood perfectly, he assured his pilots at the time and again in his memoirs: they were worn out, Bissell had handled them stupidly, and they deserved a rest. If genuine, it was one of the rare moments in his life that Chennault found it in his heart to forgive someone who had let him down. On the other hand, there was this radiogram to Stilwell:

> From present observations I deem it imperative that induction of AVG be deferred until October first and that present contracts etc be continued. Otherwise our operations are in serious jeopardy. Induction board strongly concurs in above recommendation.

Though signed by Caleb Haynes, the radiogram was logged into the Group War Diary as coming from Chennault. The scheme came to nothing. Stilwell had been down that path before, with General Marshall, and he did not forward the proposal to draft Chennault's pilots for three months' involuntary service in China.

Of the technicians, nineteen radiomen, crew chiefs, and clerks accepted commissions as lieutenants in the army or ensigns in the navy—a long step up for men who had enlisted during the Great Depression. Seven more agreed to join the army as sergeants, including Gerhard Neumann and a Chinese-American named Francis Yee, who had worked for Bill Pawley in Rangoon and Loiwing, then followed the AVG to Kunming. Two other Chinese-American mechanics enlisted as private soldiers.

The staff officers responded more eagerly to the induction board. Skip Adair agreed to return to active duty as a major, as did flight surgeons Tom Gentry and Sam Prevo. (Gentry, in fact, had already received his commission.) John Williams and Roy Hoffman would be commissioned as captains. Daffy Davis, the Anglo-Irish salesman from Hong Kong, would become a first lieutenant.

But staff officers could not fight a war. Nor could four former Flying Tigers, Captain Ajax Baumler, the seven lieutenants who had been attached to the AVG since the beginning of June, and the eight who reached Kunming on June 19. Some imaginative stroke was needed, and it was provided by Colonel Sanders, who took CNAC to India on June 27 to commandeer his old outfit, the 16th Squadron of the 51st Fighter Group. (It was not quite a theft, because the 51st had been in the pipeline to China since April. At that time, however, the group had no planes of its own.) He led the eight Kittyhawks across the Hump the same afternoon, reaching Kunming an hour overdue, and only after a heated argument with AVG radioman Robert King about whether he should fly north or south to find Wu Chia Ba. "God damn it," King finally said, "who's lost, you or me?"

Chennault was involved in two other projects that June. Larry Moore and Ken Sanger, former clerks and presumed lovers, had been hired by the Republic film studio as technical advisers to an AVG epic starring John Wayne. When he heard of it, the Old Man fired off letters to anyone who might intervene, and Republic obligingly fired Moore and Sanger. He would have done better to stay out of it. *Flying Tigers* gave a wildly inaccurate impression of the AVG as a collection of former transport pilots who fought in China *before* the outbreak of the Pacific war. Indeed, the movie ended with John Wayne and his sidekicks listening to news of the Japanese attack on Pearl Harbor.

Then there was Chennault's brothel. At a time when the only treatment was time, sulfanilamide, and aspirin, venereal disease was the AVG's most serious medical problem, with as many as seven men hospitalized at one time. "The boys have got to get it," Chennault reasoned, "and they might as well get it clean as dirty." So he asked the Ferry Command to fly twelve medically checked Indian women over the Hump to Kunming, to service the army personnel now occupying Hostel Number One. But Stilwell got word of the scheme and radioed Delhi: "No women to China." They arrived nevertheless, though from the other direction. Thirteen young women were recruited in Guilin, inspected by an army doctor, and airlifted to Kunming in a U.S. Army C-47. "I am afraid Chennault does not realize the difference between the AVG and the U.S. Army!" Stilwell wrote to General Marshall, as probably the only man who would appreciate the enormity of what Chennault had done. A few days after that, Stilwell radioed a bitter assessment of how the transition from the AVG to the 23rd Fighter Group was shaping up. Unlike Bissell, he had not mellowed in the slightest in his opinion of Chennault's mercenaries:

> Recommend no publicity at this time reference replacement of seasoned AVG group by American unit devoid of combat experience. . . . Fact is AVG is quitting under fire and walking out on United States in an emergency. They are placing personal interests before those of their country. This wont stand publicity.

At Hengyang, Chennault's fighters were only 260 miles from Hankou, giving him an opportunity to take the offensive against a highly symbolic target, the Yangzi port that had served as interim capital for Nationalist China. On June 29, he ordered the B-25s to move from Guilin to Hengyang. Bob Neale and Bill Bartling flew shotgun, and Don Rodewald took a supply of 220-pound bombs up the creaky railroad line. Next day, a CNAC Douglas flew Chennault to Hengyang to take charge of the operation.

First, though, he had a private word with Bob Neale. "He had information that the Japs were going to try and knock out the Army after the AVGs leave on the 4th," Neale recalled. To stave off disaster, Chennault went on, the generalissimo had authorized him to extend the tour of anyone who would stay two more weeks in China. Would Neale stay on? And would he put in a word with his pilots and technicians? Neale was feeling better now, and he hated to disappoint Chennault a second time. He agreed to stay, as he noted in his diary with no detectable emotion. Charlie Bond's diary was less guarded:

> Bob Neale came into the alert shack from a meeting with the Old Man and called in all of the First Squadron. I immediately sensed something wrong. Bob asked, "How many of you are willing to stay two more weeks beyond the fourth to permit the [air force] to arrive here and get in shape to replace

us?" There it was; I knew it! Several of the pilots and mechanics said, "Hell, no!"

I was mad as hell. I knew my conscience wouldn't let me do anything about it but say yes.

Which he did, along with a majority of the pilots and technicians at Hengyang—arguably the most heroic act they had performed during their year with the AVG.

On July 1, the B-25s at Hengyang were commissioned as the 11th Bombardment Squadron under Colonel Caleb Haynes. They immediately set off on their first mission. One Mitchell aborted with a broken hydraulic line, and another bogged down in the mud at the end of the runway. That left four bombers to make the run to Hankou, escorted by Ed Rector with five Kittyhawks. Twice the Mitchells went astray; twice Rector put them back on course. (Hankou was almost due north, with a river and a railroad to mark the route.) In the end, they dropped their bombs on a Yangzi village. Only then did the Mitchells find their target, the former CAF airfield at Hankou. The JAAF did not come up to challenge them, and the Mitchells did not expend any ordnance. It was a fiasco, as Charlie Bond noted in his diary. Next day the B-25s improved their navigation and managed to find and bomb the navy docks at Hankou.

That brought the American Volunteer Group to Friday, July 3—its last service day. Wake-up came at 2:30 A.M. with the familiar *doom*-da-*doom* of unscynchronized Mitsubishi engines. The bombs missed the runway by several hundred yards. At first light, Don Rodewald and his helpers (who included two RAF armorers who had followed the AVG into China) loaded bombs into the five airworthy Mitchells. They took off at noon to bomb the JAAF field at Nanchang. The flight was made in a clear zone between layers of clouds, with the undercast breaking just before the Mitchells and four Kittyhawks reached Nanchang. The B-25s dropped their bombs from 2,500 feet, then turned for home. At that moment, the Nates fell out of the sky, as Robert Raine reported:

I went after the fighters but was too low and too far behind to keep them from hitting the bombers, but I contacted the stragglers. One I fired head on, but never saw him after he rolled over to tell if I had hit him or not. Came on another one from behind that was trying to chase the B-25's. I fired a long burst into him at fairly long range. He rolled over and dove back under me trailing smoke. He pulled up in a steep turn off to one side and bailed out of his ship. There were other Japs diving on me so I ran for a cloud and came on home.

Harry Bolster was also in the escort. After the Mitchells dropped their bombs, the former flight instructor went down to strafe the hangars and a cluster of planes at the intersection of two runways. He left one Nate smoking, as he afterward reported. Then he set off after the Mitchells, catching up just as three Nates came down on them:

> I opened up on one of the planes and noticed it start into a spin. I then dove out and a shell exploded in my cockpit and a model "0" zoomed off my tail. I finally lost the Jap, but oil was covering the cockpit and constituted a very dangerous fire hazard. So after flying to friendly territory I bailed out.

Bolster was credited with two Nates, Raine with one, and a fourth was supposedly shot down by the turret gunner of a B-25.

As for the "Zero," Bolster may have made the first sighting in China of a Nakajima Hayabusa of the 10th Independent Chutai, commanded by Major Mitsuru Takatsuki. This squadron was one of the few army units taking part in the Yangzi campaign, 1937–1938; in December 1941, it supported the assault on Hong Kong, then returned to Japan to be refitted with Hayabusas. The squadron was rushed to China after the sorry performance of the Toryus and Nates against the AVG.

Takatsuki struck back at Hengyang that afternoon. The Americans scrambled to intercept a plane approaching at high altitude from the north. While they searched the clouds, seven Hayabusas came in below them and laced the field with machine gun bullets, as Don Rodewald recorded:

> While strafing one caught sight of [Dr. Sam] Prevo, [Morton] Bent and myself and he straffed us. The bullets really cracked around that hole we were in. I hope I don't come any closer. They got our No 22 [Tomahawk] which was out of commission and also our only good truck.

In Chongqing, meanwhile, Chiang Kai-shek gave his final order to Chennault as commander of the AVG: "You are directed to demobilize the American Volunteer Group and to discharge the personnel of that Group in accordance with plans which I have approved." Chennault sat down to write the AVG's valedictory in a letter addressed to Lauchlin Currie but intended for President Roosevelt—"the Boss." It was a gentler version of the resignation gambit Chennault had used so often and so effectively with Madame Chiang:

> After talking to General Brett here between December 16 and 24, I knew that the A.V.G. was doomed and that the entire program we had mapped out and worked so hard to put through was likewise doomed. . . . I accepted recall to active duty early in April in the hope of obtaining better coordination and more support. I regret this action now and believe that I should have returned to the U.S. and told the story of China to the public.
>
> I believe that the conditions out here . . . are far worse than you know or even imagine. I don't believe that the Boss knows about the mistakes and failures. I am sure that the American people don't. The things I told you in Washington about Air Force employment are true and our young pilots and excellent equipment are being needlessly sacrificed. We are also losing a great deal of the confidence and admiration of the people out here—two things which I have worked hard to retain. . . .
>
> My work with the A.V.G. has been the most wonderful experience of my life. Few individuals ever have the opportunity to do the things they want to do and be of service in such a great cause at the same time. . . . Despite bad health which continued until March, I have maintained long hours of work and have had no holidays. At the present time I am in excellent health but a bit fagged mentally.

He wrote a similar but more restrained letter to T. V. Soong, then went to bed.

The Fourth fell on Saturday. The fireworks began early at Hengyang and at the dispersal field at Lingling, each of which received a salvo of bombs from Colonel Onishi's Sallys. At first light, the warning net reported a third formation on its way. Bob Neale and another pilot had been stationed at Lingling overnight, and they flew up to Hengyang to lend a hand. Arriving over the airfield at 13,000 feet, they saw a dozen enemy fighters above them, as Neale reported:

> They saw me at approximately same time [and] dove down to attack. Dove away. They proceeded in climbing turn to west. Dove on fighters . . . when I reached altitude above and in the sun. Hit fighter I was aiming at, but saw no reason to believe he went down. Made another diving attack and my target started to smoke and started down. Did not see any further results. Followed flight north and picked out lone enemy fighter about 5,000 feet

below. Made diving attack from rear quarter and pulled up. 2nd attack was a front quarter after which fighter started to smoke and was losing altitude.

Before he could confirm the kill, Neale was bounced by two other Nates. He dove out, picked up four fixed-gear fighters, and followed them 100 miles north before giving up the chase.

The Panda Bears were patrolling at 18,000 feet when the Nates came in below them. Wrote Ed Rector in his combat report:

We sighted them west of the field at 13,000 feet as they dived on Neale's approaching flight. We immediately attacked and had enemy planes outlined against a white cloud layer at 7,000 feet. I fired a 4 second burst at [a Nate] in a slight diving turn, and he burst into flames and bits of debris flew from his plane as he dived through the cloud layer. I climbed up to the outside and made several more passes. . . . One [Nate] forced me to dive out, but in doing so I got in a head on burst at two fighters in close formation coming up at me. I got a fleeting glimpse of a wingman's engine letting out a large burst of smoke as I passed over them.

Rector was credited with one *Ki-27*, as were Jim Howard, Charlie Sawyer, and Van Shapard, the first of the newly attached flight instructors to make a kill. That made eight Nates claimed on July 3 and July 4. According to Japanese records, the 54th Sentai lost four planes in these two combats, the last before it went home to be refitted. The dead pilots included a popular officer named Akiyama.

Chennault spent July 4 at Beishiyi airfield, catching up on paperwork. That evening, Madame Chiang and her sisters put on a party for AVG personnel in the Chongqing area. It had been planned as a barbecue, but rain moved it indoors. The guests refreshed themselves with non-alcoholic punch, madame led them in a game of musical chairs, and Chennault was presented with an oil portrait of himself and the Chiangs. At 11 P.M., the Americans—with what relief can only be imagined—drove back through the rain and mud to their quarters at the airfield.

The AVG Passed into History

1942–1991

A t midnight," Chennault wrote of Independence Day 1942, "the AVG passed into history." But the American Volunteer Group was not so neatly written off. On Sunday morning, July 5, the CAMCO mercenaries still provided most of his combat strength. Even the pilots who had accepted induction were still civilians—including Tex Hill, back from India, who led nine Kittyhawks from Beishiyi to Guilin that Sunday afternoon.

Chennault followed on Monday, to do something truly extraordinary: he put Bob Neale in command of the 23rd Fighter Group. Why not Hill or another of the soon-to-be army officers? Well, Neale was going home; it would be easier for him to step aside when the designated commander reached Guilin. (This was Colonel Robert Scott, late of the Ferry Command. Scott was in Kunming, organizing group headquarters and an army squadron to replace the Hell's Angels. The squadron's first mission was to buzz Wu Chia Ba on July 4 for the benefit of photographers.) Besides, Hill was rested and eager, and he would be more useful in the cockpit of a Kittyhawk than in squadron headquarters.

Among the Panda Bears who came down to Guilin on July 6 was John Petach, who had won the heart of Red Foster on *Jaegersfontein*. Petach was a steady if unspectacular pilot, and Tex Hill picked him as part of the escort for a raid on Canton that afternoon. Five Mitchells made the run, bombed an oil refinery, and headed for home at 10,000 feet. A few minutes into the return flight, one of the bomber pilots radioed that he was under attack. "I dropped my belly tank," Petach reported, "and

367

looked about quite violently, but could see nothing." Then Petach spotted three Nates below him. He passed the word to Hill, waggled his wings, and dove upon the Japanese fighters:

> They must have seen me, because the last E.A. fired a [warning] burst and all 3 started to turn towards me. I opened fire at 500 yards but was shooting behind the last man so I pulled the nose of my plane well ahead of the E.A. and gave him a 1 second burst. Then the E.A. pulled into sight right in front of my nose so that my fire raked him as he passed. I saw large holes in his wings, the other 2 planes started to make a pass at me so I pulled up and took off. . . . I pulled away and saw two more [Nates] about 3 miles north of our combat. I turned towards them and this time they turned away and headed for a mountain. The first plane was just turning around the mountain top when I overhauled the second plane. I gave him about a one second burst and he burst into flame and was burning well. Just then Hill called all planes from combat, so I joined up.

He was credited with one of the Nates, bringing his CAMCO bonus account to $1,991.67—a nice shower present for Red Petach at Beishiyi, pregnant with their first child. Tex Hill likewise claimed one fighter shot down. That made him second only to Bob Neale as the AVG's leading ace, and for the moment the second-ranking American pilot of World War II.

On Tuesday, Bob Neale sent the new arrivals up to Hengyang, where Tex Hill resumed command of the outfit that the AVG regarded as the Panda Bears and the army pilots as the 75th Fighter Squadron. Whatever the name, it was grounded by squally weather for the next few days, though Hill did manage to lead a strafing run on Japanese shipping on the Yangzi. Meanwhile, Japanese scouts kept probing Guilin and Hengyang, trying to discover the true state of Allied air defenses in China. (Though Stilwell had ordered a press blackout on the transfer, it was no secret that the Flying Tigers were going home.) On Thursday, July 9, Pete Wright and Lester Hall took off from Hengyang in pursuit of a "reconnaissance bomber"—probably a 90th Sentai Lily from Canton. After a long search, Wright caught the twin-engined plane in a climbing attack:

> I opened up at about 150 yards directly behind him, at the first burst part of his tail came off and his left hand motor caught on fire. I gave two more bursts and he rolled over and went down. I did not see him crash as oil from his engines covered my windshield.

Wright was credited with the shoot-down. It was the last for the American Volunteer Group, bringing his personal score to 3.65 and the AVG's to. . . .

And here I must grasp a nettle of my own. How many planes *did* the AVG destroy, in the air and on the ground? Different documents yield different figures, but when they are sorted out it appears that the Chinese confirmed 296 kills, including those of Petach, Hill, and Wright in the week after the group was officially disbanded. (See Appendix I.) In many instances I have been able to disprove a claim—to my own satisfaction, anyhow—but not with such consistency that I can advance an equally precise figure of my own. In the first place, the JAAF did not celebrate the feats of individual pilots. After an air battle, the survivors were debriefed at group or squadron headquarters; a consensus of losses and victories was arrived at, and the unit totals were recorded by an enlisted clerk. In almost every case, these unit records were lost in the great retreat of 1944–1945. As for central records—if there were any—the jest in Tokyo in August 1945 was that the smoke from the final American air raid merged into the pall raised by military and civilian bureaucrats, burning documents before the victors arrived.

So all we have are reconstructions. Demobilized Japanese officers were interviewed by the occupiers; as time went on, JAAF veterans wrote their memoirs (the market was especially good for books about the 64th Sentai); and in the 1980s the Japan Defense Agency produced a series of campaign histories. Taken together, these accounts share two characteristics with their Allied counterparts: absurdly optimistic with respect to aerial victories, and quite persuasive as to losses. How could it have been otherwise? A soldier, after all, *knows* when his friend goes missing or is killed: the friend does not return; letters must be written and personal gear disposed of; a bunk is empty in the barrack, a chair vacant at the mess. . . . That on December 25, 1941, the 64th Sentai lost Lieutenant Okuyama and Sergeant Wakayama—and only them—is a fact burned into the memories of every man who served with them, who grieved for them, and who later wrote about them.*

---

* Among those who grieved for Okuyama and Wakayama was Lieutenant Yohei Hinoki, who had fought the AVG at Rangoon, Magwe, and Loiwing. Shot down over Burma in 1943, he lost a leg, went home, joined a training unit, and flew again as a combat pilot over Japan. In *Tsubasa no kessen,* Hinoki gave the names of 161 pilots of the 64th Sentai killed during the Pacific war, with the location and the circumstances of their deaths. Since the group seldom had more than forty pilots on its roster, its losses were therefore on the order of 400 percent—an utterly convincing admission.

Necessarily, the JAAF tallies are less precise than those of the AVG. Japan lost the war, after all, and lost a greater proportion of the men who would otherwise have memorialized the dead. In July 1944, Major Yoshioka's 77th Sentai—the AVG's regular antagonist in the campaign for South Burma—lost all its aircraft in New Guinea, and its pilots and mechanics were given rifles and reformed into infantry squads. But even when a unit was destroyed, like the 77th, its history survived in the memories of airmen who had previously been transferred out or invalided home. Their recollections are certainly conservative. Few Japanese combat accounts give the names of pilots who were taken prisoner, and they pass lightly over "forced landings" away from the combat zone. But on the whole I think they can be trusted, and what they show is this:

The JAAF lost about 115 aircraft to the AVG in Burma, Thailand, and China. (Or, for those who would like to take the measure of my certainty, no less than 110 planes but no more than 120.)

The toll in lives was far higher. Because they were the aggressors, the Japanese airmen generally fought over enemy territory, giving them less chance of making their way home after a shoot-down. There were more of them per plane (two men in a *Ki*-30 Ann, six or seven in a *Ki*-21 Sally) and they rarely used parachutes. . . . By my best calculation, the JAAF lost 400 men in its various combats with the AVG, including pilots, air crews, and ground personnel.

As for AVG losses, those were not yet finished. On July 10—a year to the day after *Jaegersfontein* sailed under the Golden Gate Bridge—Tex Hill sent four pilots winging northeast from Hengyang with orders to bomb the walled city of Linchuan (now Fouzhou). John Petach led the mission, with Lieutenant Leonard Butsch flying on his wing. The second element consisted of Captain Ajax Baumler and Wingman Arnold Shamblin, formerly of the CAF flight school.

Petach followed a heading of 68°, crossed the wide tributary south of Nanchang, and hit his checkpoint on the nose at 11:45 A.M., an hour after leaving Hengyang. He then changed course to the southwest, ordering the others to trail out behind him, and the formation reached Linchuan "in string" at 12:03 P.M.

Ajax Baumler's combat report was more formal than those filed by the AVG:

Careful scrutiny of air revealed no pursuit of enemy in vicinity. We started dive from 6,500 feet in formation. Mr. Petach had just reached the terminus of his dive at about 2,300 feet when his airplane burst into flames around the cockpit and main fuel tanks. His airplane went into a violent tumbling spin completely out of control and a portion of left wing separated from airplane. His airplane crashed in flames on river edge at north east side of wall around city. The pilot remained in plane and it is my opinion that his plane received several direct hits from 20 mm anti aircraft fire immediately after he had released his bombs.

A former navy pilot like most of the Panda Bears, Petach had graduated from New York University in 1939 with a major in aeronautical engineering. On the Wednesday following, he would have been twenty-four years old.

Baumler pulled out over the river, then followed its twisting course for several miles until he was safely away from the antiaircraft guns. Lieutenant Butsch did the same. Not until the two army pilots were reunited at Hengyang did they realize that Baumler's wingman was also missing. A red-haired former army pilot from Oklahoma, Arnold Shamblin too had been hit by flak over Linchuan; he bailed out of his Kittyhawk and evaded capture for several hours, but Japanese soldiers eventually caught him. He evidently died in prison camp, as happened to 27 percent of Anglo-American servicemen in Japanese hands.

So twenty-two of Chennault's mercenary pilots were now dead, captured, or missing in action, not counting the three who were killed in training. In absolute numbers, this was not an especially high toll. (For every airman lost by the AVG, the JAAF lost seventeen.) But as a proportion of the pilots who were on the squadron and flight-school rosters at the outbreak of war, the AVG losses were huge: nearly one out of four.

Material losses were also considerable. From December 8 to July 10, the AVG lost eighty-six planes to combat, accident, and abandonment. Of these, twenty-two were wrecked Tomahawks that had been accumulated at Loiwing by the Pawley brothers, and there captured by the Japanese 56th Division.

Also on July 10, Major John Alison and the 16th Fighter Squadron flew into Guilin with eight Kittyhawks—the planes that had been brought from India by Colonel Sanders. Bob Neale sent them up to the dispersal field at Lingling, containing the most dismal of the hostels that had been built for the American airmen in China. Charlie Bond went along to show them the ropes. As a result, he was among eighteen pilots and technicians poisoned when the squadron was served fish fried in tung oil, intended for the manufacture of paint and the reduction of China's war debt. Bond's misery was compounded when he took to his bed and found it crawling with bugs. "I am unhappy, disgusted, feeling ill, and just about at the end of my rope," he wrote in his diary. Bob Neale had to fly up from Guilin with castor oil, epsom salts, and insecticide.

Two more B-25s reached Guilin on Sunday, July 12. The Old Man followed on Monday, bringing belly tanks for the Kittyhawks, food and mail for the men, and Caleb Haynes to take charge of the 11th Bombardment Squadron. Chennault was desperate to go on the offensive before his AVG holdovers went home, but the weather was against him. Rain kept the Mitchells at Guilin until Thursday—twenty-four hours before the volunteers were scheduled to fly up to Chongqing and begin the trek home.

Thursday was rainy, too, but Colonel Haynes finally managed to get the Mitchells off to raid the docks at Hankou. They were escorted by a mixed crew of army and AVG pilots. "The flight was uneventful," Major Alison reported; "the bombs hit the dock area, no fighters were sighted and we all returned to [Hengyang]." Their engines were still tick-ticking—the metal contracting as it cooled—when the warning net reported an unidentified formation north of the field and closing in. (In fact, the control room was processing reports of the Mitchells and Kittyhawks that had just landed.) There followed a desperate race to fly the planes to safety. "Most of the P-40's on the field got in the air," as John Alison told the story, "and all the B-25's got off but not without some near collisions as we were scrambling like a bunch of geese."

Freeman Ricketts was flying one of the Kittyhawks. A former army pilot with more than 900 hours in his logbooks when he reached Burma, he had not seen much combat, but had been credited with one Nate over Baoshan and a piece of a Sonia near Lashio. Ricketts flew an aimless pattern while fighter control warned him that the "bandits" were north of Hengyang—no, south—then called him back to the field. Making his approach, he spotted a twin-engined plane to the west and three miles out. He turned toward it, whereupon the stranger turned away. Ricketts charged after it:

> I overtook this ship from directly behind and a very little below. . . . I opened fire at approximately 350–400 yards. My guns jammed, then I pulled off to the left and recharged my guns. The airplane again turned away from me. Apparently I slowed the ship down with the first burst for I overtook very easily and fired another burst. I then pulled off to the right and recognized the [U.S. Army] insignia on the B-25. I watched the B-25 to see if it could continue flight and about one or two miles later saw five parachutes. The ship was still under control and when last seen was flying towards Hengyang.

The Mitchell pilot rode his plane down. He crashed near Lingling, spent the night there, and telephoned Hengyang next day to report that he had been shot down "by two Zeros" but had survived the ordeal. So did his crew, and so did Ricketts, though not without a board of inquiry ordered by Chennault.

That was Thursday, July 16. A U.S. Army Douglas flew down to Guilin that afternoon with ten pilots and four mechanics for the 23rd Fighter Group. That was cutting it mighty fine, since the AVG holdovers were supposed to leave next morning. Two more transports came down on Friday. Colonel Robert Scott was among the passengers, but if Bob Neale met his successor he did not mention it in his diary, nor could he recall the meeting afterward. (Scott said he waved to Neale through the cabin door.) The same transports took the AVG holdovers to Chongqing. "Had iced tea," Neale wrote in his diary. "What a treat." As a reward for two weeks' additional duty in the combat zone, Chennault gave them letters requesting priority status on military flights heading toward the United States.

Back in Guilin, among the weird pinnacles, in the heat and the damp, Don Rodewald was also posting his diary:

> All the rest of the boys left today so it is "A.V.G. Finish." Sure rough to see them going home. Sometimes I wonder if I made a mistake. I only got two armorers and two Limey helpers. Sure hope the men get in.

They did, though in fits and starts, and Chennault carried on as if his boys had never left. (He even called the new men "Flying Tigers," to the lasting annoyance of the original AVG.) On Sunday, July 19, three more Mitchells reached Guilin and immediately went out to "bomb hell out of a town," as Rode noted. That same day, he and the other AVG veterans were inducted into U.S. service. The commissioning went off without ceremony. Jasper Harrington was walking to the dining hall when he was hailed by an army officer. "It was after sundown, about dark," the line chief recalled. "He wanted to know, 'Is your name Harrington?' I says, 'Yup.' 'Jasper J.?' I says, 'Yup, sure is.' He says, 'Hold up your hand.' I held up my hand, and he swore me in and shook my hand and says, 'Now you are a lieutenant in the Army Air Corps.' And I never saw the character before or since. . . . It didn't change my work any. I was still a line chief with a tool box, working."

Major Frank Schiel took command of the 74th Fighter Squadron at Kunming—the Hell's Angels reconstituted, right down to its ten weary Tomahawks. All his pilots were army men. At Hengyang, Major Tex Hill took command of the 75th Fighter Squadron, with Gil Bright (also a major, but "surplus in grade") to help him. And at Guilin, Major Ed Rector took command of the 76th Fighter Squadron, with Captain Charlie Sawyer as his only leavening from the AVG. Hill and Rector had twenty-four fighters between them. In addition, Major Alison had eight Kittyhawks in the peripatetic 16th Fighter Squadron, and Colonel Haynes had seven Mitchells in his 11th Bombardment Squadron. The China Air Task Force (CATF) thus began operations with a grand total of forty-nine aircraft, scarcely the infusion Chennault had been promised for bringing the AVG into the U.S. Army.

To pay for the planes taken over from the AVG, the U.S. Army gave China a $3.5 million credit on its lend-lease account. This was more than generous, considering that China had paid only $9.3 million for 100 Tomahawks with guns, radios, and extra engines, and nothing at all for the Kittyhawks. In the end, the net cost to China for the services of the American Volunteer Group was $5.8 million for aircraft and $3 million for salaries and combat bonuses, or a bit more than $75,000 for each Japanese plane destroyed. It was one of the rare instances in modern warfare where the instrument of destruction cost less than the objects destroyed. On the other hand, any calculation involving the lend-lease program must be taken with a grain of salt. There was no chance that China, Britain, or the Soviet Union would ever pay for the material they received from the United States during World War II—and not much reason why they should, considering that the war was largely fought on their territory, with their subjects doing most of the dying.

The last AVG contingent to leave China consisted of Bob Neale, Charlie Bond, and Red Petach. Chennault's priority letter counted for little in India, but after a week's delay it got them a flight to Khartoum in North Africa. (At this desert base, they saw great quantities of aircraft, including the Lockheed Hudsons that had been sold to Britain, twice diverted to China by Lauchlin Currie, and twice repossessed by the U.S. Army.) At 11:30 A.M. on August 7, Neale, Bond, and Petach touched down at Miami airport.

They were the lucky ones. Most of the AVG pilots and technicians were treated as civilians cluttering up a war zone, with no claim on military accommodations or transportation. They were given the choice of paying $1,200 for a ticket on Pan Am or a smaller but still considerable sum for transportation by sea. "The Army is out to get us," Bus Keeton wrote in his diary on July 11. A week later, his anger had become more pointed: "The Army has at least 15 transports sitting on the field here and won't [fly] us out, the bunch of bastards." A week after that, hearing about the priority letters Chennault had given to the AVG holdovers, he switched his anger to the Old Man: "If I ever had any respect for him I don't have any now."

In retrospect, the AVG veterans blamed their treatment on Lewis Brereton of the 10th Air Force or—their favorite goat—Clayton Bissell of Stilwell's staff. I have searched the files of the U.S. Military Mission for documents to support this belief, finding only the radiograms Chennault himself had sent to India throughout the spring, trying to block military transportation for AVG members who had quit early. Perhaps the army transportation officers assumed that every AVG veteran fell under this ban. More likely, they were simply unable to cope with the problem of processing men who had no uniforms, no travel orders, and no explanation for their presence in India except that they had served for a year in a foreign air force and now wanted to go home.

The largest number bought passage on *Mariposa*, an Italian passenger liner seized by the United States and converted to a troopship. The fare was $150 for a belowdecks bunk, $800 for a cabin in officers' country. *Mariposa* finally sailed from Bombay on August 7, even as Neale, Bond, and Petach landed in Miami. As on the Java-Pacific liners that had brought the AVG to Asia, many of their fellow passengers were missionaries; the AVG veterans ran a poker game on one side of the ship while the missionaries prayed on the other. They reached New York on

September 6. They were agreeably surprised to be greeted as heroes, and (in the case of the pilots) to learn that their combat bonuses had in fact been paid. "I knew you were doing all right," Ken Jernstedt was told by his banker in Hood River, Oregon, "because the money kept coming in."

Jernstedt had had enough of war, and with Parker Dupouy and Erik Shilling signed on with Republic Aviation as a test pilot. They were not alone. Pete Wright went to work for American Export, ferrying planes across the Atlantic. Sixteen pilots signed on with CNAC, flying Douglas transports over the Hump at $800 a month, plus up to $20 an hour for overtime. (Doc Richards and four technicians also went to work for CNAC.) Ironically, the hardest part of the transition to transport flying was learning to keep the plane heading in the right direction without benefit of the P-40's long snout—the same feature that had given them so much grief at Kyedaw airfield.

Chennault remained in China until August 1945, rounding out eight years of war against the empire of Japan. He continued to work miracles of improvisation and to win the love of his men, while infuriating the brass in Chongqing, Delhi, and Washington. In this, he was helped by many of the people he had recruited for the AVG. Foremost among them was Tex Hill, who was credited with shooting down five more Japanese planes in China, and who eventually took his well-deserved place as commander of the 23rd Fighter Group. He was a legend throughout the air force. A young army pilot, new in the theater, recalled his first combat briefing at Guilin. Expecting something on the order of *The Target for Tonight,* with jests, chalkboards, and weather reports, what he got was a tall, sunburned man who shambled into the briefing room and spoke three words: "Y'all follow me!"

The casualties among Chennault's cadre of loyalists were as high as they had been in the AVG. Major Frank Schiel, commanding the 74th Fighter Squadron, was killed in 1943 when his P-38 crashed on a reconnaissance flight. Captain Roy Hoffman, an AVG armorer and staff officer who accepted induction in China, was killed as a crewman in a B-24. George McMillan rejoined the army and returned to China, where he was killed in 1944. Bill Reed did the same, chalking up seven more aerial victories before he too was killed in 1944. Three AVG veterans who remained in China as CNAC pilots were killed in crashes: John Dean in 1942, Allen Wright in 1943, Mickey Mickelson in 1944.

As a colonel, Ed Rector served a second tour in China and likewise commanded the 23rd Fighter Group. Chennault's entire clerical staff— Tom Trumble, Doreen Lonborg Davis, and a Rangoon refugee named Eloise Whitwer—continued to work for him as civilians, their salaries paid by the Chinese government. Joe Alsop, repatriated by the Japanese, made his way back to China as a lend-lease official and finagled a transfer to Chennault's headquarters, where he served the Old Man as before. So did Paul Frillmann. Spoiled for the godly life by his year in the AVG, he joined the air force as an intelligence officer and was sent to China, where Chennault greeted him with his usual air of infallibility: "Hello, Frillmann. I thought you would be back." One of his missing pilots also turned up before the end of the war: in 1945, Lew Bishop escaped from the train that was supposed to take him to a new prison camp in Manchuria, and he too made his way to Kunming.

From further back, Luke Williamson returned to China as commander of the 322nd Troop Carrier Squadron, to become Chennault's personal pilot. Billy McDonald was CNAC's operations officer, so the Three Men could have a "walla-walla" from time to time at Chennault's new bungalow near Wu Chia Ba airport.

In August 1942, Clayton Bissell moved to India as commander of the 10th Air Force, having stayed in China long enough to receive the Legion of Merit for his "especially meritorious performance" in activating the 23rd Fighter Group. (Chennault was similarly honored, but as usual Bissell got there ahead of him.) From a distance of 1,800 miles, he made life so miserable for Chennault that the Old Man sometimes came down sick when his boss was scheduled to land at Wu Chia Ba on an inspection tour. This torture ended in March 1943 when the CATF was upgraded to the 14th Air Force. Independence brought a second star: Major General Claire Lee Chennault, one of the most colorful, controversial, and popular commanders in U.S. service.

The conflicts with Stilwell continued, though these were more elevated than the guerilla war with Bissell, stemming not from meanness but from an honest difference about the best way to defeat Japan. "It's the man in the trenches that will win the war," the good soldier was supposed to have said, to which Chennault supposedly replied: "God-dammit, Stilwell, there *aren't* any men in the trenches." They were both right. Stilwell warned Chennault that if the "air boys" ever seriously threatened the Japanese, the latter would simply take his airfields away from him—which they did, in Operation *Ichi-go* in the spring of 1944. Chennault predicted that long-range bombers based in China would devastate the Japanese home islands—which they did, in Operation Matterhorn that summer. (Chennault was not permitted to control the B-29 Super Fortresses, however, and the air force eventually found a better base for them on the Pacific island of Saipan.) Each in pursuit of his own agenda, Chennault and Stilwell kept quarreling until Chiang Kai-shek demanded and got Stilwell's recall in October 1944.

But George Marshall and Hap Arnold would not allow a China maverick to triumph over the old-boy network. When the U.S. Army began to gird for the invasion of Japan, they set out to get rid of Chennault—a campaign that was simplified by Chennault's loyalty to some of his less admirable associates. Butch Carney, "stoned out of his gourd," shot and killed an army sergeant in a poker game. Harry Sutter, another friend and former instructor, was the subject of a messy investigation into the smuggling of gold, drugs, and other valuables between India and China. (These scandals were compounded by the widespread belief that the women—Rose Mok/Carney and Kasey Sutter—were romantically involved with Chennault.) Altogether, the army investigators developed files on 300 smuggling cases involving members or ex-members of the AVG, CNAC, CATF, and 14th Air Force. Chennault stood by his friends to the point where his own reputation was tarnished, thus providing a lever to the men in Washington who wanted to remove him. After a four-month holding action, he accepted Hap Arnold's pointed recommendation that he "take advantage of the retirement privileges now available to physically disqualified officers." (Arnold's letter contained the explicit threat that if Chennault did not go gracefully, he would be busted back to colonel and *then* retired.) He left China on August 1, 1945. Two weeks later, Japan surrendered, with eighty of her cities so devastated by American air attack that they were not fit for human habitation.

Pappy Paxton calculated in 1945 that the AVG had 220 members when it was disbanded, and that 187—85 percent—returned to active duty with the U.S. armed forces. (Most of the others took jobs in war-related enterprises such as CNAC, and one joined the British army.) They served on many fronts and in every conceivable capacity, but a remarkable number made their way back to Southeast Asia. Major Oley Olson and Major R. T. Smith served in the air commando units that helped recapture Burma for the Allies. In 1944, still flying the Hump for CNAC, Dick Rossi ran into R. T. at a base in northeastern India, piloting a B-25 named *Barbie III*. The turret gunner was Charlie Baisden, former AVG armorer. For old times' sake, they took Rossi on a tour of the Japanese airfields in Burma, allowing him to sit up front and enjoy the view through the plexiglass bombardier's compartment. On the way home, R. T. bombed a railway yard and Baisden tested his guns, whereupon some of the plexiglass panels fell out. Rossi was still recovering from this shock when R. T. announced that *Barbie* had an unexploded bomb dangling from her belly. He put her down as gently as he could, but the bomb broke loose, skittered along the ground, and rolled into a ditch. Rossi thanked R. T. for an interesting day, then went back to the infinitely more calming work of driving an unarmed Douglas across the Himalayas.

After his China tour, Gil Bright moved on to North Africa, to become one of the few Allied pilots believed to have shot down planes from each of the three Axis powers. (Counting his victories in Spain, Ajax Baumler would have been another.) Jim Howard commanded the 354th Fighter Group in Europe and won the Congressional Medal of Honor—the nation's highest decoration—for breaking up an attack on a bomber formation. "I seen my duty and I done it," he told the war correspondents.

Greg Boyington rejoined the marines and formed the "Black Sheep Squadron"—VMF 214, a maverick outfit with many similarities to the AVG, with "Pappy" Boyington playing Chennault. He was credited with destroying twenty-two more Japanese planes before he was himself shot down. He too was awarded the Medal of Honor, but to the chagrin of the Marine Corps (as Boyington told the story) he emerged from prison camp in 1945 and drank his way through the ensuing publicity tour. Boyington felt that he had been treated shabbily by the AVG, and his revenge took the form of an achingly funny novel called *Tonya*, whose title character bore many similarities to Olga Greenlaw.

Harry Bolster and Robert Brouk rejoined the army, to die in accidents. Ralph Gunvordahl and Maurice McGuire (one of the pilots who had quit the AVG in the summer of 1941) became test pilots and were likewise killed in accidents. Altogether, of the 109 pilots and flight instructors who sailed for Asia in the summer and fall of 1941, at least thirty-six—*one-third*—lost their lives or freedom before the end of World War II. So much for Red Probst's theory that joining the AVG would be good for one's health.

At least nine former technicians went to flight school, and they became casualties at the same rate. Robert Rasmussen was killed in action in North Africa. Carson Roberts became a transport pilot, and after a tour on the Hump route was also killed in North Africa. Jesse Crookshanks was shot down over Germany and spent eighteen months in a prison camp, weighing 120 pounds upon his release—and Jesse was not a small man.

Whatever their later service, they received no official recognition for their time in the AVG. Charlie Mott escaped from a work compound in 1945 and joined a covert force that was building an airstrip in the Thai backcountry; the first plane to land brought the news that the war was over. Mott made his way to India, where like the AVG returnees in 1942 he was classified as a civilian and denied military transport. It was the same for all the AVG veterans. Their victories did not count toward qualifying them as fighter aces in the army, navy, or marines. Their CAMCO year did not count as "time in grade" for promotion, retirement, or the points that determined a man's priority for discharge at the end of the war. They did not receive veterans' benefits unless they earned them by their later service, and they were refused overseas ribbons on the basis of their time in the AVG. The army and navy even denied their petition to wear Flying Tiger pins on their military uniforms.

The U.S. government did award the Distinguished Flying Cross to John Petach for his mission to Linchuan in July 1942, on the theory that he was serving with the 75th Fighter Squadron at the time of his death. However, the air force did not deliver the medal for more than forty years. Joan Petach Randles—the daughter he never saw—was among those attending the award ceremony at McGuire Air Force Base in 1984.

The British government, which had recruited hundreds of American pilots for the RAF in 1940 and 1941, was more open-handed with Chennault's irregulars. In August 1943, Ambassador Lord Halifax awarded his nation's Distinguished Flying Cross to Tex Hill, Ed Rector, and Charlie Bond (and posthumously to Jack Newkirk) for their exploits in the defense of Burma.

After the war, Chennault continued in the service of the Chiangs. He organized a private airline, Civil Air Transport, with Whitey Willauer and others of the AVG's "Washington Squadron." CAT began with mercy flights and evolved into a paramilitary force during the civil war that ended with Chiang Kai-shek's defeat by the communists in 1949. Chennault also tried to form a mercenary fighter group—a new AVG— for service in China, but the scheme was vetoed by his old nemesis, George Marshall, now serving as President Truman's secretary of state.

Exiled with the Chiangs to Taiwan, CAT became a contract airline for the U.S. government, supporting American troops in Korea and French colonial forces in Indochina. Among the pilots who did this work were Erik Shilling of the Hell's Angels and Randall Richardson, a clerk who had quit the AVG in February 1942 to train as a navy pilot. Dropping supplies into Dien Bien Phu in the spring of 1954, Shilling and Richardson flew forty-five missions to that deadly valley—"hell in a very small place"—whose sides bristled with Vietnamese guns. But Chennault's plan to raise a group of F-84 Thunderjet fighter-bombers for service in Indochina was quietly shelved by the Eisenhower administration.

There was another airline, too. In California, a group of AVG veterans headed by Bob Prescott created the Flying Tiger Line, which in time became the country's largest air-freight carrier. Among its pilots was John Leibolt, son of the man who had disappeared over Rangoon in February 1942.

With his connection to the Chiangs, there was no doubt of where Chennault would stand in the anticommunist scapegoating of the 1950s. He had an unwanted ally in the person of Bill Pawley, who had become a millionaire with his aviation dealings in China and India, and who used his wealth to fight the Cold War as ambassador to Peru and Brazil, sponsor of commando raids on Cuba, and perennial witness before the U.S. Congress. On the other side, Lauchlin Currie found himself accused of complicity in the "Silvermaster spy ring." He fled the country, took up residence in Colombia, and had his American citizenship revoked in 1956. Many of the old China hands—Paul Frillmann among them—were similarly tarnished by their association, real or imagined, with the victorious communists.

Lieutenant General Claire Chennault died of lung cancer on July 27, 1958. (He had received the third star nine days before.) Among the last visitors at his bedside was Madame Chiang Kai-shek. With the Old Man gone, his airline was reorganized as Air America under the Central Intelligence Agency. Its gray cargo planes, with no national markings, carried out CIA missions all during the Vietnam War. Thus, the kind of covert air force proposed by Chennault in 1940 became an accepted instrument of American foreign policy more than twenty years later, with consequences that are still being felt. There were other guerrilla airlines in Indochina, including Bird & Son, which specialized in missions in Laos and Cambodia, and whose chief pilot was Erik Shilling. Call him the last Flying Tiger.

Chennault was buried in Arlington National Cemetery. In Lake Charles, Louisiana, an air force base was named in his honor. In Taipei, Taiwan, in a park where hundreds of citizens gather for their dawn exercises, the Republic of China erected a bust of a jut-jawed Chennault, the only westerner to be so honored in Chiang's capital. In 1987, he became the last major World War II figure to be dignified with a biography—and then there were two. (As if to confirm him as a man of contradictions, one gave his birth year as 1890, the other as 1893.) For a generation, Chennault's admirers in this country made a commemorative stamp the litmus test of his place in history. He got that, too, at a "first day of issue" ceremony at Monroe, Louisiana, on September 6, 1990, on what was wrongly believed to be the centenary of his birth. The denomination was forty cents—a suitably maverick sum.

Since the 1950s, veterans of the AVG have met every second year on July 4, most often at Ojai, under the burning sun and live oak trees of Southern California. (Until the FAA put a stop to it, Bob Prescott transported them gratis on the Flying Tiger Line.) Of the pilots and technicians who served to disbandment, about one hundred were alive at the most recent reunion, and half of them attended, along with wives, children, grandchildren—and sweethearts. Ed Rector turned up with Dorothea Dunsmore (nee Wilkins) on his arm, plump and beautiful, her voice as sweet as an English nightingale's. It was their first meeting since Rangoon in January 1942. Paul Greene was there, curly-haired and outrageous, flashing a photograph of *his* current project, a P-51 Mustang replica he planned to fly to the next reunion. And Parker Dupouy, hobbled slightly by a stroke—wondrous to recall that his hand-eye coordination was once so precise that he could land a fighter at 142 mph with a section missing off the wing. And Charlie Mott, an amiable buddha with a briefcase of documents, with which he hoped to persuade the navy that it would not set an undesirable precedent by recognizing him as a former prisoner of war. (He won the point.) And Doc Richards dancing with Red Hanks, nee Foster. . . . Some were in wheelchairs, including Don Rodewald, who lost the use of his legs when he crashed an air force trainer, but was not grounded by that. In 1985, Rode flew a small plane alone around the world, regretting only that the Burmese authorities did not permit him to land at Mingaladon airport.

For some, the reunion is the best part of their year, and the AVG is the organizing principle of their lives, one that has taken them back to China, and even to visit the Japan they fought but never saw. (They were hosted by veterans of the JAAF 24th Sentai—which, in one of those misunderstandings that seem to cluster around them, flew against the 14th Air Force but not the AVG.) Because they have met so often, and because the moment they celebrate happened so long ago, the reunion has come to bulk larger than their months as Flying Tigers. The only war stories they tell now are to outsiders. "That's five lies in five minutes," marveled a pilot of a technician making his first appearance at one of these events. But who knows any longer what was true, what was imagined, and what was only wished?

When somebody asks, they oblige with the same stories that were told in the winter and spring of 1941–1942: that the Flying Tigers shot down 300 (or 600 or 1,000) Japanese planes, that they outfought the Mitsubishi Zero, that they stopped one Japanese army in the gorge of the Salween River and another in East China. (All wrong, save possibly the last. Operation *Sei-go* did indeed evaporate after the AVG reached Guilin.) What they do not say is that for a few months, half a century ago, in their incandescent youth, they were heroes to a nation that needed heroes as never before and never since.

They fought magnificently in a losing battle, and their achievement is not at all diminished by the fact that they believed their accomplishment to be greater than they were.

They were there. Mercenaries, gamblers, innocents, black-market-eers, romantics, war lovers—they were there when the British empire was falling, and when America's future seemed nearly as bleak. "Did you ever regret joining the AVG?" a reporter once asked R. T. Smith. R. T. glanced off to the side, put his tongue in his cheek, and said: "Only on those occasions when I was being shot at." Yes. Frightened men in fallible machines, they fought against other men as frightened as themselves. All honor to them.

Appendices

Victories Attributed to AVG Pilots

20 December 1941–6 July 1942

Frank Adkins	1.00	David Lee Hill	11.25
Noel Bacon	3.50	Fred Hodges	1.00
Percy Bartelt	7.00	Louis Hoffman	0.27
William Bartling	7.27	James Howard	6.33
Lewis Bishop	5.20	Kenneth Jernstedt	10.50
John Blackburn	2.00	Thomas Jones	4.00
Harry Bolster	2.00	Robert Keeton	2.50
Charles Bond	8.77	Matthew Kuykendall	1.00
Gregory Boyington	3.50	C. H. Laughlin	5.20
J. Gilpin Bright	6.00	Frank Lawlor	8.50
Robert Brouk	3.50	Robert Layher	0.83
Carl Brown	0.27	Edward Leibolt	0.27
George Burgard	10.79	Robert Little	10.55
Thomas Cole	1.00	William McGarry	10.29
James Cross	0.27	George McMillan	4.08
John Dean	3.27	Kenneth Merritt	1.00
John Donovan	4.00	Einar Mickelson	0.27
Parker Dupouy	3.50	Robert Moss	4.00
John Farrell	1.00	Charles Mott	2.00
Henry Geselbracht	1.50	Robert Neale	15.55
Paul Greene	2.00	John Newkirk	10.50
Clifford Groh	2.00	Charles Older	10.08
Ralph Gunvordahl	1.00	Arvid Olson	1.00
Raymond Hastey	1.00	Edmund Overend	5.83
Thomas Haywood	5.08	John Petach	3.98
Robert Hedman	4.83	Robert Prescott	5.29

Robert Raine	3.20	Frank Schiel	7.00
Edward Rector	6.52	Van Shapard	1.00
William Reed	10.50	Eriksen Shilling	0.75
Freeman Ricketts	1.20	Robert H. Smith	5.50
C. Joseph Rosbert	4.55	Robert T. Smith	8.73
J. Richard Rossi	6.29	Fritz Wolf	2.27
Robert Sandell	5.27	Peter Wright	3.65
Charles Sawyer	2.27		

CAMCO evidently paid bonuses for 294 planes, omitting the July victories of Petach and Wright; the confirmed total is therefore 296 as shown above. However, Bolster was paid for two planes though he claimed only one "certain," while other records suggest that Boyington and Hill each had one more victory than was credited to their bonus accounts. Thus the range of victories attributed to the AVG, from 293 to 298.

Roster of the American Volunteer Group

Name	Assignment	Served to (later service)
C. B. Adair	HQ staff*	Commissioned in China (AAF)
Frank Adkins	Pilot	Served to disbandment (CNAC)
James Allard	Mechanic	Served to disbandment
Joseph Alsop	HQ staff*	Captured 25 Dec 1941 (AAF)
John Armstrong	Pilot	Killed 8 Sep 1941
Peter Atkinson	Pilot	Killed 25 Oct 1941
Noel Bacon	Pilot	On leave Feb 1942 (USN)
George Bailey	Crew chief	Enlisted in China (AAF)
Charles Baisden	Armorer	Served to disbandment (AAF)
Percy Bartelt	Pilot	Discharged Mar 1942
William Bartling	Pilot	Served two extra weeks (CNAC)
Marion Baugh	Instructor	Killed 3 Jan 1942
Edmund Baughman	Communications	Served to disbandment (USN)
Leo Beaupre	Clerk	Served to disbandment (AAF)
Donald Bell	Clerk	Commissioned in China (AAF)
Morton Bent	Clerk	Served to disbandment (USN)
Donald Bernsdorf	Pilot	Discharged Jan 1942
Lewis Bishop	Pilot	Captured 17 May 1942
John Blackburn	Instructor/pilot	Killed 28 Apr 1942
William Blackburn	Crew chief	Served two extra weeks
Harold Blackwell	Crew chief	Served two extra weeks
Glen Blaylock	Crew chief	Discharged Apr 1942
Morris Bohman	Pilot	Discharged Nov 1941
Harry Bolster	Instructor/pilot	Served two extra weeks (AAF)

Name	Assignment	Served to (later service)
Charles Bond	Pilot	Served two extra weeks (AAF)
Ernest Bonham	Communications	Commissioned in China (AAF)
Gregory Boyington	Pilot	Discharged Apr 1942 (USMC)
James Brady	Clerk	Served to disbandment
Kenneth Breeden	Clerk	Served to disbandment
George Brice	Crew chief	Served to disbandment
J. Gilpin Bright	Pilot	Commissioned in China (AAF)
Robert Brouk	Pilot	Discharged Apr 1942 (AAF)
Carl Brown	Pilot	To CAF flight school (CNAC)
Everett Bruce	Medical staff	Served to disbandment (AAF)
Alfred Bryant	Clerk	Discharged Oct 1941
Carl Bugler	Admin chief	Served to disbandment (AAF)
George Burgard	Pilot	Served to disbandment
Richard Buxton	Medical staff	Discharged Feb 1942
Michael Callan	Ground crew	Served to disbandment (USN)
Boatner Carney	HQ staff*	To CAF flight school
John Carter	Line chief	Served two extra weeks
Herbert Cavanah	Pilot	Served to disbandment (USN)
Melvin Ceder	HQ staff	Served to disbandment (AAF?)
Charles Chaney	Crew chief	Served to disbandment (USN?)
Claire Chennault	Commander*	Commissioned in China (AAF)
Keith Christensen	Armorer	Served to disbandment (USN)
A. Bert Christman	Pilot	Killed 23 Jan 1942
Leo Clouthier	Clerk	Discharged early (USN)
Thomas Cole	Pilot	Killed 30 Jan 1942
Leon Colquette	Crew chief	Discharged Mar 1942
Edwin Conant†	Pilot	Served to disbandment (USN)
Elmer Cook	Pilot	Discharged Sep 1941
Jack Cornelius	Crew chief	Served to disbandment (CNAC?)
Charles Cribbs	Medical staff	Served to disbandment (USN)
Albert Criz	Pilot	Discharged Dec 1941
John Croft	Pilot	Served to disbandment
Jesse Crookshanks	Crew chief	Served to disbandment (AAF)
Harvey Cross	Communications	Served to disbandment
James Cross	Pilot	Served to disbandment
John Crotty	Clerk	Discharged Apr 1942
George Curran	Crew chief	Served to disbandment
Albert Cushing	Clerk	Served to disbandment (AAF)
Otto Daube	Crew chief	Served two extra weeks (AAF)
Doreen Davis	HQ staff*	Worked for AAF in China

Name	Assignment	Served to (later service)
William Davis	HQ staff*	Commissioned in China (AAF)
John Dean	Pilot	Served to disbandment (CNAC)
Robert DeWolfe	HQ staff	USN attached to AVG Jan-May
Walter Dolan	Crew chief	Served to disbandment (AAF)
John Donovan	Pilot	Killed 12 May 1942
Francis Doran	Clerk	Served to disbandment (AAF)
Carl Dorris	Clerk	Served to disbandment (AAF)
Francis Dudzik	Clerk	Discharged Feb 1942
Parker Dupouy	Pilot	Served to disbandment
Eugene Durall	Clerk	Served to disbandment (AAF)
Estill Durbin	—	Discharged Sep 1941
James Dyson	—	Discharged Sep 1941
Charles Engle	Ground crew	Served to disbandment
John Engler	Communications*	Commissioned in China (AAF)
Richard Ernst	Communications	Enlisted in China (USN)
John Farrell	Pilot	Served to disbandment (AAF)
John Fauth	Crew chief	Killed 22 Mar 1942
William Fish	Pilot	Discharged May 1942
Edwin Fobes	Clerk	Served to disbandment (AAF)
Ben Foshee	Pilot	Died 4 May 1942
Henry Fox	Line chief	Served two extra weeks (USN)
Charles Francisco	Communications	Served to disbandment (USN)
Paul Frillmann	HQ staff*	Served to disbandment (AAF)
Allen Fritzke	Armorer	Served two extra weeks (USN)
Henry Fuller	Instructor	Discharged Dec 1941
Edward Gallagher	Crew chief	Discharged Mar 1942 (USN)
Robert Gallagher	Medical staff	Enlisted in China (AAF)
Joseph Gasdick	Crew chief	Served to disbandment (AAF)
Chun Yuen Gee	Engineering*	Served to disbandment (AAF)
Thomas Gentry	Medical staff	Commissioned in China (AAF)
Henry Geselbracht	Pilot	Served two extra weeks
Henry Gilbert	Pilot	Killed 23 Dec 1941
Lloyd Gorham	Crew chief	Served to disbandment (USN)
Irving Gove	Crew chief	Served to disbandment
Edgar Goyette	Pilot/staff	Served to disbandment (Army)
Richard Graham	Crew chief	Discharged Apr 1942
Paul Greene	Pilot	Served to disbandment (AAF)
Harvey Greenlaw	HQ staff*	Served to disbandment
Olga Greenlaw	HQ staff*	Served to disbandment
Clifford Groh	Pilot	Served to disbandment (CNAC)

Name	Assignment	Served to (later service)
Ralph Gunvordahl	Pilot	Discharged Jan 1942
Lester Hall	Instructor/pilot	Served two extra weeks (CNAC)
Maax Hammer	Pilot	Killed 22 Sep 1941
Lee Hanley	Armorer	Discharged Mar 1942
Martin Hardesty	Crew chief	Discharged Mar 1942
Clayton Harpold	Food service	Discharged Apr 1942
Jasper Harrington	Line chief	Commissioned in China (AAF)
David Harris	HQ staff	Served to disbandment
Edward Harris	Admin chief	Commissioned in China (AAF)
Raymond Hastey	Pilot/staff	Discharged May 1942
John Hauser	Crew chief	Discharged Apr 1942
Thomas Haywood	Pilot	Served to disbandment
Robert Hedman	Pilot	Served to disbandment (CNAC)
John Heller	Clerk	Discharged Mar 1942
George Henderson	Clerk	Discharged Jan 1942
John Hennessy	Pilot	Served to disbandment
Thomas Henson	Medical staff	Served to disbandment
David Lee Hill	Pilot	Commissioned in China (AAF)
Fred Hodges	Pilot	Served to disbandment (CNAC)
Louis Hoffman	Pilot	Killed 26 Jan 1942
Roy Hoffman	HQ staff	Commissioned in China (AAF)
Burton Hooker	Parachute rigger	Served two extra weeks (AAF)
Leo Houle	Pilot	Discharged Jan 1942
James Howard	Pilot	Served two extra weeks (AAF)
Daniel Hoyle	Admin chief	Served to disbandment
Marlin Hubler	Clerk	Commissioned in China (AAF)
Lynn Hurst	Pilot	Discharged Feb 1942
Frank Jacobson†	Crew chief	Served to disbandment
George Jaeger	Mechanic	Discharged Apr 1942
Edwin Janski	Prop specialist	Served to disbandment (AAF)
Kenneth Jernstedt	Pilot	Served to disbandment
Leon Johnston	Clerk	Discharged Oct 1941
Jack Jones	Armorer	Discharged Apr 1942
Thomas Jones	Pilot	Killed 16 May 1942
Joe Jordan	Clerk	Served to disbandment (Army)
Walter Jourdan	Weather	Served to June 1942
Albert Kaelin	Clerk	Served two extra weeks (AAF)
Robert Keeton	Pilot	Served to disbandment
John Kelleher	Pilot	Discharged Sep 1941
Daniel Keller	Crew chief	Served to disbandment (AAF)

Name	Assignment	Served to (later service)
Thomas Kelly	Communications	Served to disbandment (AAF)
Merlin Kemph	Crew chief	Served two extra weeks
Charles Kenner	Crew chief	Served to disbandment (AAF)
George Kepka	Crew chief	Served to disbandment (AAF)
Melvin Kiner	Communications	Served to disbandment
Robert King	Communications	Served to disbandment (CNAC)
Donald Knapp	Pilot	Discharged Jan 1942
Stephen Kustay	Armorer	Served to disbandment
Matthew Kuykendall	Pilot	Served to disbandment
Lawrence Kwong	HQ staff*	Served to disbandment
George Lancaster	Clerk	Discharged Feb 1942
C. H. Laughlin	Pilot	Served to disbandment (CNAC)
Frank Lawlor	Pilot	Served to disbandment (USN)
Robert Layher	Pilot	Served two extra weeks
Charles Leaghty	Parachute rigger	Served to disbandment
Joseph Lee	Medical staff*	Served to 28 Jun 1942
Pak On Lee	Engineering*	Enlisted in China (AAF)
Edward Leibolt	Pilot	Missing 25 Feb 1942
Robert Lindstedt	Communications	Served to disbandment (AAF)
Jack Linton	Armorer	Served two extra weeks (AAF)
Robert Little	Pilot	Killed 22 May 1942
Ernest Loane	Instructor/pilot	Served two extra weeks (CNAC)
Robert Locke	Prop specialist	Served to disbandment
Elton Loomis	Communications	Commissioned in China (AAF)
Frank Losonsky	Crew chief	Served to disbandment (CNAC)
George Lum	Engineering*	Served to disbandment
Joseph Lussier	Communications	Commissioned in China (AAF)
Gale McAllister	Crew chief	Served to disbandment
Edgar McClure	Crew chief	Enlisted in China (USN)
Mark McDowell	Crew chief	Discharged Apr 1942
William McGarry	Pilot	Captured 24 Mar 1942
Maurice McGuire	Pilot	Discharged Sep 1941
Sharon McHenry	Supply clerk	Served to disbandment (AAF)
Eugene McKinney	Armorer	Enlisted in China (AAF)
George McMillan	Pilot/staff	Served to disbandment (AAF)
Lacy Mangleburg	Pilot	Killed 23 Dec 1941
Neil Martin	Pilot	Killed 23 Dec 1941
Kenneth Merritt	Pilot	Killed 8 Jan 1942
Frank Metasavage	Crew chief	Discharged Apr 1942
Einar Mickelson	Pilot	Served to disbandment (CNAC)

Name	Assignment	Served to (later service)
Alex Mihalko	Communications	Enlisted in China (USN)
Arvold Miller	Communications	Commissioned in China (AAF)
Charles Misenheimer	Crew chief	Served to disbandment
Lawrence Moore	Clerk	Discharged Jan 1942
Kenneth Moss	Weather	Served two extra weeks (Army)
Robert Moss	Pilot	Served to disbandment (CNAC)
Charles Mott	Pilot	Captured 8 Jan 1942
Charles Mundelein	Crew chief	Discharged Mar 1942
Willard Musgrove	Crew chief	Served to disbandment
James Musick	Armorer	Enlisted in China (AAF)
Robert Neal	Armorer	Served two extra weeks (USN)
Robert Neale	Pilot	Served two extra weeks (AAF)
Gerhard Neumann	Mechanic*	Enlisted in China (AAF)
Ferris Newell	Admin clerk	Discharged Feb 1942
John Newkirk	Pilot	Killed 24 March 1942
Charles Older	Pilot	Served to disbandment (AAF)
Arvid Olson	Pilot	Served to disbandment (AAF)
Henry Olson	Crew chief	Served to disbandment (AAF)
Harold Osborne	Crew chief	Served to disbandment (AAF)
Edmund Overend	Pilot	Served to disbandment (USMC)
John Overley	Crew chief	Served two extra weeks (USN)
Preston Paull	Crew chief	Served to disbandment (AAF)
George Paxton	Pilot/staff	Served two extra weeks
Joseph Peeden	Crew chief	Served to disbandment (AAF)
Richard Peret	HQ staff	Served to disbandment (USN)
Paul Perry	Armorer	Served to disbandment (AAF)
Emma Jane Petach	Medical staff*	Served two extra weeks
John Petach	Pilot	Killed 10 July 1942
Joseph Pietsker	Photographer	Served to disbandment
Herbert Pistole	Armorer	Served to disbandment (USN)
Kee Jeung Pon	Engineering*	Enlisted in China (AAF)
Joseph Poshefko	Armorer	Served two extra weeks
John Power	Crew chief	Discharged Mar 1942
Robert Power	Pilot	Discharged Sep 1941
Robert Prescott	Pilot	Served to disbandment (CNAC)
Samuel Prevo	Medical staff	Commissioned in China (AAF)
Albert Probst	Pilot	Served two extra weeks (AAF)?
Carl Quick	Crew chief	Served two extra weeks (Army)
Robert Raine†	Pilot	Served two extra weeks (CNAC)
James Rasbury	Food service	Discharged Feb 1942

Name	*Assignment*	*Served to (later service)*
Robert Rasmussen	Crew chief	Enlisted in China (AAF)
Edward Rector	Pilot	Commissioned in China (AAF)
William Reed	Pilot	Served to disbandment (AAF)
James Regis	Photographer	Served to disbandment
Stanley Regis	Crew chief	Served to disbandment
George Reynolds	Crew chief	Discharged Mar 1942
Lewis Richards	Medical staff	Served to disbandment (CNAC)
Charles Richardson	Crew chief	Discharged Mar 1942
Randall Richardson	Weather	Discharged Feb 1942 (USN)
Rolland Richardson	Communications	Commissioned in China (AAF)
Freeman Ricketts	Pilot	Served two extra weeks
Wayne Ricks	Prop specialist	Served to disbandment
Clarence Riffer	Armorer	Served to disbandment (AAF)
Joseph Ringey	Mechanic	Discharged Nov 1941
Carson Roberts	Communications	Commissioned in China (AAF)
Donald Rodewald	Armorer	Commissioned in China (AAF)
Robert Rogers	Crew chief	Served to disbandment (AAF)
C. Joseph Rosbert	Pilot	Served two extra weeks (CNAC)
J. Richard Rossi	Pilot	Served to disbandment (CNAC)
John Rumen	Armorer	Served two extra weeks (AAF)
Edwin Rushton	Pilot	Discharged Oct 1941
Robert Sandell	Pilot	Killed 7 Feb 1942
Kenneth Sanger	Communications	Discharged Jan 1942
Ralph Sasser	Communications	Enlisted in China (USN)
Charles Sawyer	Pilot	Commissioned in China (AAF)
Wilfred Schaper	Crew chief	Served two extra weeks
Frank Schiel	Pilot	Commissioned in China (AAF)
Ralph Schiller	Armorer	Served to disbandment
Leo Schramm	Crew chief	Served to disbandment
Carl Schur	Crew chief	Discharged Sep 1941 (AAF)
Loy Seamster	Communications	Served to disbandment (CNAC)
Edward Seavey	Clerk	Served to disbandment (AAF)
Wilfred Seiple	Crew chief	Served to disbandment (Army)
Arnold Shamblin	Instructor/pilot	Missing 10 Jul 1942
Van Shapard	Instructor/pilot	Served two extra weeks (CNAC)
William Shapiro	Clerk	Discharged Jan 1942
John Shaw	Medical staff	Served to disbandment
Milan Shields	Prop specialist	Served two extra weeks
Eriksen Shilling	Pilot	Served to disbandment (CNAC)
Roger Shreffler	Communications	Served to disbandment (CNAC)

Name	Assignment	Served to (later service)
Corbett Smith	Food service	Discharged Nov 1941
Curtis Smith	Pilot/staff	Served to disbandment (USMC)
George Smith	Clerk	Discharged Dec 1941
Robert A. Smith	Crew chief	Served to disbandment (AAF)
Robert H. Smith	Pilot	Served to disbandment (AAF)
Robert M. Smith	Communications	Served to disbandment (AAF)
Robert T. Smith	Pilot	Served to disbandment (AAF)
John Sommers	Clerk	Discharged Mar 1942
Jo Stewart	Medical staff*	Served to disbandment
Edward Stiles	Crew chief	Served to disbandment (AAF)
Irving Stolet	Crew chief	Served to disbandment (AAF)
Gail Stubbs	Instructor	Discharged Dec 1941
William Sutherland	Mechanic	Served to disbandment
Frank Swartz	Pilot	Died 24 April 1942
Joseph Sweeney	Communications	Served to disbandment (AAF)
Estes Swindle	Pilot	On leave Sep 1941
William Sykes	Communications	Commissioned in China (AAF)
Julian Terry	Admin clerk	Served to disbandment
William Towery	Food service	Commissioned in China (AAF)
Thomas Trumble	HQ staff	Worked for AAF in China
Chester Tuley	Crew chief	Served to disbandment (USN)
George Tyrrell	Crew chief	Served to disbandment
John Uebele	Crew chief	Served to disbandment
William Unger	Armorer	Discharged Mar 1942 (Br army)
Frank Van Timmeran	Line chief	Served to disbandment
Morgan Vaux	Communications	Served to disbandment (USMC)
Hugh Viverette	Medical staff	Served to disbandment
Earl Wagner	Armorer	Served two extra weeks
Manning Wakefield	Crew chief	Served two extra weeks (CNAC?)
Harold Walker	Crew chief	Discharged Apr 1942
Stanley Wallace	Pilot	Discharged Sep 1941 (AAF)
Robert Walroth	Pilot	Discharged Oct 1941
Andrew Walsh	Clerk	Discharged Jan 1942
George Walters	Admin clerk	Served to disbandment (USN)
Eugene Watson	Pilot	Discharged Sep 1941
Donald Whelpley	Weather	Served to disbandment (USN)
John White	Crew chief	Discharged Mar 1942
Richard White	Pilot	Discharged Nov 1941
R. G. Whitehead	HQ staff*	Discharged May 1942
Eloise Whitwer	Clerk*	AAF civilian in China

Name	Assignment	Served to (later service)
Edwin Wiggin	Admin chief	Discharged Nov 1941
John Williams	HQ staff*	Commissioned in China (AAF)
Clifford Wilson	Mechanic	Served to disbandment
George Wing Shee	Engineering*	Served to disbandment
Harvey Wirta	Armorer	Served to disbandment
Fritz Wolf	Pilot	Served to disbandment (USN)
Melvin Woodward	Crew chief	Served to disbandment (CNAC)
Allen Wright	Instructor/pilot	Served two extra weeks (CNAC)
Peter Wright	Pilot	Served two extra weeks
Lem Fong Wu	Engineering*	Served to disbandment (AAF)
Louis Wyatt	Communications	Served two extra weeks
William Wyke	HQ staff	Discharged Mar 1942
Harold Wylie	Clerk	Discharged Jun 1942
Glen Yarbery	Crew chief	Discharged Apr 1942
Francis Yee	Engineering*	Enlisted in China (AAF)
John Young	Clerk	Served to disbandment

* Not recruited from military services

— Did not reach Burma

† Conant was born Perry, Raine was called Raines during his AVG service, and Jacobson later changed his name to Andersen.

Notes

What follows is a reasonably complete record of the sources from which this book was written. I am especially indebted to the general's widow, Anna Chennault; to his biographers, Martha Byrd and Jack Samson; to the AVG's volunteer historians, John Williams and Robert Andrade; to J. Richard Rossi of the Flying Tigers Association; to William Leary at the University of Georgia; and to John Fredriksen at Brown University. A Verville Fellowship from the Smithsonian Institution, under the guidance of Donald Lopez and Robert Mikesh at the National Air and Space Museum, enabled me to spend a year working with Japanese sources; my translator was Miyuki Rogers, and I was assisted also by Yohei Hinoki, late of the 64th Sentai, and by Yoshiko Yoshimura of the Asian Division, Library of Congress. With respect to the British effort in Burma, I am indebted to Philip Reed at the Imperial War Museum, London; to William Foot at the Public Record Office, Kew; and to Vice Consul Fraser Wilson at the British Embassy, Rangoon. In Taipei, my work was expedited by Ambassador Shah Konsin.

Except for Burma, where I follow British colonial usage, place names are spelled as they appear on the appropriate Operational Navigational Chart of the U.S. Defense Mapping Agency (in Britain, the Directorate of Military Survey). I use *pinyin* for place names on the mainland of China, but retain the old Wade-Giles spelling for the names of historical figures, and in all romanizations I eliminate diacritical marks.

These notes are the minimum that will enable a reader to find the source in the bibliography; if the source is clearly indicated in the text, I do not cite it again here. A few individuals could not or would not give me permission to quote them, obliging me to cite a secondary source or an anonymous author interview. When quoting unpublished diaries and letters (especially if transcribed by another hand) I sometimes correct minor lapses in spelling and punctuation.

The following abbreviations are used here and in the bibliography:

AFHRC: Air Force Historical Research Center, Maxwell Air Force Base, Alabama
AMISSCA: U.S. Military Mission to China
Author materials: Daniel Ford, Durham, New Hampshire
AVG Archives: San Diego Aero-Space Museum (64 numbered folders)
CDN: *Chicago Daily News*
CLC Papers: Claire Lee Chennault Papers, Library of Congress microfilm (65 numbered folders)
Columbia interviews: Oral History Research Office, Columbia University (conducted by Frank Rounds, Jr.)
FDR Library: Franklin D. Roosevelt Library, Hyde Park, New York
FRUS: *Foreign Relations of the United States* (followed by the year and volume number)
FTA Archives: J. Richard Rossi, Flying Tigers Association, Fallbrook, California
GWD: Group War Diary, American Volunteer Group
Japanese Monograph Series: Library of Congress microfilm
JDA: Japan Defense Agency
JT&A: *Japan Times and Advertiser,* Library of Congress microfilm
NASM: National Air and Space Museum
NYT: *New York Times*
PSF: President's Secretary's File
SEP: *Saturday Evening Post*
USAAF: United States Army Air Forces

CHAPTER 1: *Tex, This Is Too Good To Be True*

2 *The word spread,* etc.: Rector, author interview. Also Hill, author and Columbia interviews.
3 *It seemed to me:* Dupouy, author interview.
3 *Adair then started,* etc.: Cornelius & Short, 103–104.
4 *Most of the brass:* Kuykendall, Columbia interview.
4 *All I'd ever:* Rector, author interview.
4 *I'd always wanted:* Hill, Columbia interview.

5   *This is presidentially:* Rector, author interview.
5   *And as far:* Neale, Columbia interview.
5   *I've got a deal,* etc.: Layher, Columbia interview.
5   *But the overriding:* Schultz, 84.
6   *For the past few: Time,* 23 Jun 1941.
6   *We each have a thousand:* R. T. Smith, 17; also 8–22.
6   *The next day:* Bond & Anderson, 20.
7   *When you're young:* Love.
7   *The Japs are flying,* etc.: Boyington, 15. Also Walton, *passim.*
8   Perry/Conant: Joseph Brown.

CHAPTER 2: *May I Present Colonel Chennault?*

Chennault's autobiography is *Way of a Fighter* (hereafter *Fighter*), but the most reliable account of his early years is Byrd's 1987 biography. Members of his family were unanimous in agreeing that Chennault was born September 6, 1893, and his son Max assured me he had seen that birthdate in the family bible (letter, 10 Oct 1986). For the China years, I rely mostly on Chennault's diary, from which his unattributed quotes are taken.

10   *Instant, strong attachment:* Anna Chennault, *Thousand Springs,* 203.
10   Applying to military academies: *Fighter,* 6. West Point and Annapolis have no record of these applications.
11   *I remember his writing:* Abbott. Also 1910 LSU catalog; 1909 and 1910 volumes of *Gumbo,* the LSU student yearbook; *Fighter,* 4; Chennault's transcript from Natchitoches.
11   State Fair: *Fighter,* 7—but see Byrd, 370.
12   *This man can be taught:* Nancy Allison Wright, author interview.
12   *I have tasted:* Hotz, 55.
13   Chennault as army aviator: *Fighter,* 11–13; Byrd, 30.
13   Bissell: *Blue Book of Aviation,* 1932; *Fighter,* 20.
13   ACTS during Chennault's tenure: Finney, *passim.*
14   *Captain Chennault:* Frances Wright, SEP, 8 Aug 1942.
15   *Chennault's Men:* Hotz, 63. Also Anna Chennault, *Thousand Springs,* 65; Maurer, 421; *Fighter,* 21.
15   Bombardment doctrine: Craven & Cate, I:26–28, 51, 65; Maurer, 349; Douhet, 375–376, 393–394.
15   *It is impossible: Fighter,* 22.
16   *American Army or Navy:* Fletcher Pratt, SEP, 2 Dec 1939.
16   *The ability of a nation,* etc.: Chennault in *Coast Artillery Journal.* These articles formed the basis for *The Role of Defensive Pursuit,* published by

ACTS ca. 1933. For Chennault's fighter tactics, see his *N.A.A. Magazine* article and the monograph *Pursuit Aviation.*

17   *The bombardment people:* Nalty, 13–14.

17   Fighter competition: Rubenstein & Goldman, 146–149; Byrd, 52; Patterson correspondence.

17   Party on yacht: Byrd, 60.

18   *It is well to avoid:* Arnold & Eaker, *Army Flyer,* 73.

18   *Who is this:* Nalty, 13.

18   *Bombers are winged:* Arnold & Eaker, *Winged Warfare,* 144–145.

18   Retirement: *Fighter,* 3; *Life,* 15 Mar 1943.

20   *One sultry afternoon: Fighter,* 34–35.

20   *The most beautiful:* Leonard, 105.

21   No rank in the CAF: Fu, Wang, and Lee, author interviews.

21   Foreign missions: Burton; Jouett; Wagner; Leary, *Dragon's Wings,* ch 2; Tamagna, 19–21.

21   Outbreak of fighting: Hata, 241.

22   Combat training at Nanchang: *Fighter,* 39.

22   *What should I do:* AFHRC 248.211-24.

22   Strength of CAF: Griffith; Fu, Wang, and Lee, author interviews; Mao Pang-chu, Air Force interview.

22   Chinese army: Young, *Helping Hand,* 17 and 448; F. F. Liu, 198.

23   *With startling suddenness,* etc.: NYT, 14–16 Aug 1937. Also FRUS 1937, IV:255 and 295; Shah, author interview.

23   *Oh, it was the most bloody:* Trumble, Columbia interview.

24   *Astonished the officers:* Okumiya & Horikoshi, 24–25.

24   Raid on Nanjing: Hisazuma; NYT, 15 Aug 1937; *Time,* 30 Aug 1937; Hata, 268.

24   *We have lost:* "Diary of a Japanese Airman."

24   Arrival of A5M: Hata & Izawa, 25–26.

25   Training CAF: Lee, author interview; *Fighter,* 53–54.

26   *Recent Chinese:* FRUS 1937, IV:317.

26   *The name stuck:* Trumble, Columbia interview.

26   *While there is no war,* etc.: AFHRC 248.211-24.

27   *Leading American ace:* Alsop, author interview. Also Byrd, 86–88.
       Chinese view: Fu, Wang, and Lee, author interviews.

CHAPTER 3: *We Are Not Choosers*

28   Chinese resistance: Saburo Hayashi, 10–12; Crozier, 210–211; Hata, 241.

28   *Orgy of looting* (Frank Lockhart): FRUS 1938, III:243. The Inter-

national Military Tribunal (390) put the deaths at 200,000. Also Ienaga, 186.

28 CAMCO: *Curtiss Flyleaf,* Sep-Oct 1942; FRUS 1938, IV:234–235.

29 *Oblivious of shrapnel:* Greenlaw letter to army historian, 13 Feb 1947, AVG Archives 7. Also Bowers, 355–356; Greenlaw, 18–21.

29 14th Squadron: Chennault, *Fighter,* 70–71; Frillmann, 12; Wagner; 14th Air Force Association, I:60; McHugh report, 23 May 1938.

29 Soviet supply route: FRUS 1938, III:20, 165, 595.

30 Leonard's report on Lanzhou: FRUS 1939, III:160.

30 Discouraging American aviators: FRUS 1937, IV:520, 522.

30 *A fighting unit:* Chennault, "Air Warfare in China."

30 *The Russians didn't like:* Lee, author interview. But see Chennault, *Fighter,* 61–62.

31 Chennault's reports to Adjutant General: 21 May 1938; undated 1938.

31 *He was a smallish:* Frillmann, 19.

32 Changes in Aviation Commission: McHugh report, 7 June 1938.

32 Situation in Yunnan: Chennault, *Fighter,* 72; FRUS 1937, III:637; Wang, Lee, and Adair, author interviews; Williams, Air Force interview.

33 Aircraft profile: *Climbs like:* Chennault report, 1938.

34 *If not with guns:* album of Mao Chou-pin, who translated the inscription and told the joke about what to do if attacked.

34 *Two-bit tooter:* Williams, author interview.

34 *Enviable cocksman:* author interview.

34 *Nobody flies:* Samson, 55.

34 *When he strapped:* Williams, author interview.

35 *Trading space:* Wei et al., 17. Also F. F. Liu, 145; FRUS 1938, III: 561.

35 *Peasants born,* etc.: White & Jacoby, 20, 12.

35 *The bombers came:* White, 82. Also FRUS 1939, IV:41, 322, 420.

36 *Taciturn and courtly:* White, 74.

36 Factory at Loiwing: Johnstone, 92; *Curtiss Flyleaf,* Sep-Oct 1942; U.S. Senate, 38–39; Young, *Helping Hand,* 138–139; Gordon Seagrave, 124–133.

37 Aircraft contracts: Morgenthau Diary, 324:143; collection of A. L. Patterson, Hong Kong.

37 Olga and Harvey in Burma: Greenlaw, 23–24; FRUS 1941, V:598.

37 *Without any direct:* Fairbank, "Air Program." This useful document (hereafter "Fairbank ms.") was prepared in January 1942 by the China scholar John King Fairbank, then working for Lauchlin Currie at the

White House. For another version of the AVG's creation, see Pawley, *Americans Valiant.*

38 Chennault G-2 interview: Pickler.

38 Pawley and Chennault in California: Byrd, 120; that the year was 1940 is clear from Chennault's diary.

39 Soong's want-list: U.S. Senate, 178–179.

39 Universal Trading Corp.: U.S. Senate, 50–51.

39 Japanese air operations: Okumiya & Horikoshi, 33–34, 40.

40 *This thing is beyond* (Nelson Johnson): FRUS 1940, IV:887.

40 *When we chase,* etc.: Horikoshi, 100–103.

40 Raids on Kunming: Chennault's diary; FRUS 1940, IV:196, 903; Hata & Izawa, 428.

41 *Literally covered:* Williams, Air Force interview.

41 *It would assist:* Byrd, 106.

41 *Japanese bombing,* etc.: FRUS 1940, IV:673–674.

41 *I am told:* FRUS 1940, IV:671; also 677–678.

42 Loiwing bombed: FRUS 1940, IV:907; FRUS 1941, V:597–599; *Curtiss Flyleaf,* Sep-Oct 1942; JT&A, 2 and 12 Nov 1940.

42 Pawley's appearance: *Life,* 22 Mar 1943.

42 Assembling trainers in Rangoon: FRUS 1941, V:597196599.

42 Dinner at Soong's: Chennault, "Air Warfare in China."

42 Mao-Chennault conversations: Young, *Helping Hand,* 141–142.

43 Want list: Hopkins Papers 305, FDR Library.

43 British orders: Churchill, II:554, 565, 715.

43 *Yellow man: Time,* 26 Jun 1939.

43 Chiang's maneuvers: FRUS 1940, IV:697–699.

44 Corcoran as fixer: Official File 1560, FDR Library.

44 *To check with my friends,* etc.: Corcoran, "Pacific Wars."

44 *New fast pursuit:* Byrd, 111. Warned Pacific commanders: Bland, II:411–416. For how the U.S. military treated the information coming from China, see Leary in *Aerospace Historian.*

45 *The president just:* U.S. Senate, 243; talk with Soong: 274–277. Curtiss production: U.S. Senate, 293; Bowers, 481, 499.

46 *After lunch, I am most anxious, The president was, inasmuch as,* etc.: Morgenthau Diary 342-A.

47 *Half-baked,* etc.: Blum, II:368. Also Sherry, 102.

48 *Secretary Hull suggested:* U.S. Senate, 334–336.

48 British agreed to buy: Morgenthau Diary, 342.

CHAPTER 4: *Three Instruction and Training Units*

49   *To see the Curtiss:* Mao, Air Force interview.
51   Aircraft Profile: *Slug it out* (George Kenney): Craven & Cate, II:213.
51   Bill to Universal: Christy & Ethell, 27.
51   Mao returned to China: McHugh AVG history.
52   *American pilots:* Young, *Helping Hand,* 149.
52   Pawley assembling trainers: Morgenthau Diary 346:112.
52   *Negotiating extensive:* Pawley, letter to army historian.
53   Tomahawk shipment: Glover; Fairbank ms; FRUS 1941, V:593, 611, 617, 675; Morgenthau Diary 351:301.
53   *Soong has asked me,* etc.: U.S. Senate, 352–353.
53   Organization of CDS: PSF 105, FDR Library.
53   *My brother David,* etc.: Corcoran, "Pacific Wars."
54   *With this comparative:* Joseph Alsop & Robert Kintner, *Washington Post,* 25 Mar 1941.
54   *If Roosevelt was troubled,* etc.: Corcoran, "Pacific Wars."
54   Letters of entry: Byrd, 117.
55   Obtaining GFE: Morgenthau Diary 344:13; Fairbank ms.
55    $9.3 million: E. R. Stettinius letter, 9 Oct 1941, Hopkins Papers 305, FDR Library.
55   Pawley's commission: Morgenthau Diary 346:382; Chennault, *Fighter,* 100; CLC Papers 41; Pawley's letter to army historian.
55   *The Chinese Government:* CLC Papers 8.
56   *Aviation people,* etc.: Pentecost in AAHS *Journal.* Also his Air Force interview.
57   *As many coolies* and *When it is not raining:* Glover. Also Shah, author interview.
58   *Ever helpful* and *If this program:* Fairbank ms. Also McHugh AVG history.
59   Aldworth and other recruiters: Pawley, *Americans Valiant.* Also Adair, author interview; letter from Austin Brady, 8 Jan 1941, Morgenthau Diary 346:112.
59   Evicted from Hamilton Field: Chennault, Air Force interview.
60   Salaries in Spain: Sterling Seagrave, *Soldiers,* 50.
60   Skeptical about combat bonus: Jernstedt, author interview.
60   *Redoubtable Ruth Shipley:* Currie's cover letter to Fairbank ms.
60   *Whereas the Employer,* etc.: contract at FTA Archives.
61   Medical personnel: Richards and Hanks, author interviews.
62   *I would have signed:* Robert M. Smith, 16.

62   *This is Commander Irvine,* etc.: Fritzke, author interview. Also Jordan and Trumble, Columbia interviews; Byrd, 118.

63   *He was a genius:* Alsop, author interview. Also Frillmann, 51–52.

64   *Go away, soldier,* etc.: Frillmann, 57–59.

64   *Drove the Limeys:* Perry, author interview.

64   *Thirty United States:* NYT, 10 Jul 1941.

65   *Jaegersfontein* contingent: *Princeton Alumni Weekly,* 22 Jan 1943; Robert M. Smith, 10; R. T. Smith, 34; Neale, Columbia interview.

65   Chennault's passport: Byrd, 23, 122. Departure: Chennault, diary and *Fighter,* 104; Hanks, author interview.

65   *When I left my darling:* Mott diary. Also Robert M. Smith, 17–20; Howard, ch 6.

65   Navy escort: Fairbank ms.

66   *She was a beautiful:* Reynolds, author interview. Also Greenlaw, 1, 24; *West Point Alumni Register,* 1987; Williams and Alsop, author interviews.

67   Japanese effort against Chongqing: Okumiya & Horikoshi, 44.

67   Zero reconstructed: Bueschel, *Mitsubishi A6M;* McHugh report 29–41, 21 Jun 1941.

68   Ed Pawley in Burma: Romanus & Sunderland, *Mission,* 18–19.

68   *There was an understanding:* Brooke-Popham.

69   Carney and Mok: Chennault, *Fighter,* 107; Greenlaw, 67.

70   *The incendiary bombing:* Schaller, 80–81.

CHAPTER 5: *Looks Mean As Hell*

Daniel Hoyle, Olson's administrative chief, kept a "Diary of the Third Pursuit Squadron" (hereafter "3d Sq log") from August 1941 to June 1942.

71   *Hello, Frillmann,* etc.: Frillmann, 62–64. Also 57–59; Chennault, *Fighter,* 107; Harrington and Perry, author interviews; Pentecost in AAHS *Journal.*

72   Chennault in China: Williams and Alsop, author interviews.

72   *The First American:* CLC Papers 10.

73   *And that's how:* Perry, author interview.

73   *Corn flakes like cardboard:* Schaper diary. Also Mott diary; Howard, ch 7.

73   *We were met:* Neale, Columbia interview.

74   *Black wench:* Schaper diary ("wensh" in original).

74   Picking squadron leaders: Howard, ch 7; Frillmann, 69; Mott diary.

74   Tomahawks delivered: Pentecost in AAHS *Journal.*

74   *There were no guns:* Rodewald, Columbia interview. Also CLC Papers 8; Robert M. Smith, 21–24.

76   *Couldn't tell just* and *Her tight slacks* (James Howard): Schultz, 105, 103.

76   *The executive officer:* Jernstedt, author interview.

76   Regimen: Schaper, Columbia interview; Rodewald diary; Robert M. Smith, 21; Chennault, *Fighter,* 107–115; Olson notebook.

77   *He showed us:* Hill, Columbia interview.

77   British and Japanese manuals in CLC Papers 13.

78   *Chennault told us:* "Informal Report," AFHRC 863.539.

79   *The collision,* etc.: Bright. Also *Princeton Alumni Weekly,* 22 Jan 1943.

79   *I do hereby certify:* CLC Papers 30. Also Frillmann, 84; Greenlaw, 44, 46.

79   *With a bad case:* Rodewald diary.

80   *That damn engine:* Rector, author interview.

80   *I closed the canopy:* R. T. Smith, 67–68.

81   *Got into an inverted,* etc.: Mott diary.

81   *Get off of active:* Olson, "A Story."

82   *He started:* Rodewald diary. Also Greenlaw, 61; Chennault and Schaper diaries; Pentecost in AAHS *Journal;* R. T. Smith, 98–102; Ricks, author interview.

82   *If these guys:* Jernstedt, author interview.

82   Funeral protocol: CLC Papers 25.

83   *Japanese tactics:* letter to C. W. Pulford, 13 Oct 1941, CLC Papers 37. Also letter from Bruce Scott, 8 Nov 1941.

83   Chiang Mai patrol: Chennault and Rodewald diaries.

83   *Strange silver ship:* R. T. Smith, 99–100.

83   Japanese overflights: Ikari, 119–120.

84   Alert precautions: Chennault, *Fighter,* 120.

84   *Leveled off:* R. T. Smith, 104. Also Schaper and Chennault diaries.

85   *Typical of these problems:* CLC Papers 44.

85   *Joe was always:* Trumble, Columbia interview.

86   *We need six ounces:* CLC Papers 43. Also Alsop, author interview; Fairbank ms.; CLC Papers 39.

87   By its very: McHugh AVG history. For Marshall's maneuverings, see Fairbank ms.

87   *United States Army:* Ike, 153.

87   *Serious threat:* AMISSCA rad, 18 Nov 1941. These radiograms provide a fascinating side-view of AVG operations.

88   *If this air force:* PSF 37, FDR Library.

88   *On the chance:* CLC Papers 39.

88   *He was about:* Greenlaw, 61–62.

89   Incident of the keys: Bacon, author interview.

89   Rev. Klein: Schaper diary; Harold Klein to author, 23 Jul 1987.

89   Origin of the shark face: Ward; *Curtiss Flyleaf,* Apr-May 1942.

89   RAF 112 Sq: *Illustrated London News,* Sep 1941.

89   *Chennault said no:* Shilling, "Origin."

89   *Looks mean as hell:* R. T. Smith, 122. Also Bond & Anderson, 44; Schaper diary; Neale, Columbia interview.

90   Arrival of RAF 67 Sq: Brooke-Popham; *Aircraft Profile* 217 (Christopher Shores).

90   *Shilling had a dog fight:* Schaper diary.

90   Second *Zaandam* contingent: Cavanah, author interview.

91   Aircraft Profile: Sock story from Gallagher, 203.

91   Flight school: CLC Papers 18; CLC Papers 17.

92   *For the past:* Lin Wen-kuei to CLC, 6 Dec 1941, CLC Papers 30.

92   *Cruel treatment,* etc.: letters from Williams, CLC Papers 15, 44.

93   *We are preparing:* Blum, 676–678.

93   *General incendiary attacks:* Costello, 105.

93   *In the next few months:* Official File 150, FDR Library. Also FRUS 1941, V:683–685, 721–722, 725, 736.

94   Hudsons to bomb Japan: McHugh AVG history.

94   *Noordam* and *Bloemfontein:* CLC Papers 44; Hopkins Papers 305, FDR Library.

94   Chinese fighter unit: FRUS 1941, V:761; McHugh AVG history.

94   British squadrons: AMISSCA rad, 30 Nov 1941.

94   *Rush organization:* CLC Papers 52. Also Pawley, *Americans Valiant;* Alsop, author interview.

95   *How we should maneuver:* U.S. Congress, *Hearings,* 5433–5434.

95   Currie's shipments: CLC Papers 19; Hopkins Papers 305, FDR Library. Census of planes and pilots: AVG Archives 7.

CHAPTER 6: *Flaming Till Hell Won't Have It*

Greenlaw kept the Group War Diary (GWD) from December to March, taking a copy with her when she left China; this version appears at AFHRC and in the AVG Archives. When Lonborg took over the diary, she retyped most of Greenlaw's entries, with the result that the two versions differ slightly. Lonborg's GWD was retained by Chennault and appears in the CLC Papers. (Reynolds, author interview; letter from Greenlaw to army historian, 13 Feb 1947, AVG Archives 7.) Unless otherwise specified, I quote the version in the Chennault Papers.

97   Major Kato: Izawa in *Aero Album.*

98   *Imperial wild eagles:* JT&A, 5 Jan 1941.

98   Convoy route: Yamaguchi.

98　*All the planes:* Tateo Kato
98　War preparations: U.S. Strategic Bombing Survey, *Japanese Air Power;* Tomioka.
100　*Proceeded to headquarters:* Tateo Kato.
100　*Somebody ran in:* R. T. Smith, 144.
101　*Rushing up and down:* Greenlaw, 69. Also Chennault, *Fighter,* 122; GWD (AFHRC), 8 Dec; Keeton diary.
102　*Suggest moving:* CLC Papers 18.
102　*Everyone was togged:* Greenlaw, 71–72.
102　Events in Hong Kong: Alsop, author interview.
102　Baumler on Wake: Currie's cover letter to Fairbank ms.
102　Fate of AVG supplies and reinforcements: letter from Chou, 15 Dec 1941, CLC Papers 18; Currie memos of 8 and 22 Dec, in Harry Hopkins Papers 305 and 331, FDR Library.
103　*An American task force:* Secretary's File 37, FDR Library.
103　*He was knocked:* Moore & Sanger.
103　*This was a true:* GWD (AFHRC), 10 Dec.
103　Patrols to Thailand: Bond & Anderson, 53; GWD (AFHRC); Pentecost in AAHS *Journal;* Brooke-Popham.
104　*No aircraft reporting:* CLC Papers 18.
104　*CW-21 phenomenal:* Shilling taped memoir.
104　War preparations: GWD (AFHRC); Brooke-Popham; British General Staff, *ABDACOM.*
105　*For greater security:* CLC Papers 18. Also CLC Papers 25.
105　*After landing:* R. T. Smith, 148. Also 3d Sq log.
105　Disposition of AVG: GWD (AFHRC), 13 Dec.
106　*The damnedest rat race:* "Activities of Third Pursuit Squadron."
106　*Type uncertain:* JDA, *Nanpo,* 336.
106　Mergui raid: Kasuya, 62; RAF 67 Sq log.
107　Partying in Rangoon: 3d Sq log; R. T. Smith, 151.
107　Induction: FRUS 1941, IV:745.
107　*Brigadier general,* etc.: AMISSCA rad, 12 Dec.
107　*If Chennault were:* Hopkins Papers 135, FDR Library.
107　Chennault exchanges with madame: CLC Papers 18.
108　Reconnaissance of northern Thailand: GWD (AFHRC), 13 Dec.
108　*All American pilots:* AMISSCA incoming weekly report file, 17 Dec. Move to Kunming: Bond & Anderson, 55–58; Rosbert, 73; Greenlaw, 81; Frillmann, 91; Rector, author interview.
109　Raid on Kunming: Izawa & Hata, 73; JDA, *Nanpo,* 338.
109　*The streets were:* Wolf & Ingells. Also Bond & Anderson, 58.

110   *We are driving:* Robert M. Smith, 35.
110   Addition of DeWolfe and Neumann: GWD, 19 Dec 1941; CLC Papers 44. *Were hard-drinking:* Neumann, 80–81.
111   *Inside the dank:* Whelpley. Also GWD, 20 Dec.
111   *It's strange:* Cross.
112   *There they are:* Whelpley.
112   *We lost a bit:* Bright.
113   *Single tail:* GWD. But see Bond & Anderson, 62.
113   *A small fellow:* Bond & Anderson, 63.
114   Optical gunsight: CLC Papers 19; Mott and Rector, author interviews.
114   *I rolled and started down:* Bond & Anderson, 61.
114   *My man was:* Wolf & Ingells.
115   *There was the Jap:* Cross.
115   *I tensed:* Rosbert, 75–76.
116   *Get that goddamned,* etc.: Rector, author interview.
117   *I didn't even know:* Neale, Columbia interview.
117   Chinese reports: GWD, 20 and 25 Dec.
117   *Advanced toward:* JDA, *Nanpo,* 338.
118   AVG damage: Rector, author interview; Bond & Anderson, 62; Rodewald diary.
118   *Soon we heard:* Rosbert, 77.
119   *Buck fever:* Chennault, *Fighter,* 128.
119   *The Old Man:* Whelpley.
119   *Blood for the Tigers,* etc.: *Time,* 29 Dec 1941.
120   Origin of name: CLC Papers 43; Corcoran, "Pacific Wars"; Byrd, 136.
120   Emblem drawn in October: David Smith to author, 4 Oct 1988.

CHAPTER 7: *Such a Bright Red!*

For this and the following chapter, the individual combat reports are at FTA Archives, as is the December 31 debriefing entitled "Activities of the Third Pursuit Squadron" (hereafter "Activities"). Flight leader summaries are in CLC Papers 42.

121   *Churchill stores:* Tsuji, 187.
122   *Across the grain:* Wavell. Also British Government of Burma, *Burma Handbook;* U.S. Office of Strategic Services, *Survey of Burma.*
122   *A sweet old gentleman:* Greenlaw, 53.
122   Wavell: British General Staff, *ABDACOM;* FRUS 1941, IV:751.
123   *Obviously it was,* etc.: Wavell.
123   *Lost squadron:* R. T. Smith, 154. Also Brooke-Popham.

123   *Get a fitting* (Curtis Smith): "Activities."

124   JAAF moves on Burma: Ikari, 120; JDA, *Nanpo*, 335–337; Ishikawa et al.; Kasuya, 63; Izawa & Hata, 201–202.

124   Olson refused air cover: "Activities."

125   *Travelling south:* 67 Sq log.

125   Rangoon formations: Iwao Hayashi, 230; Izawa & Hata, 202; Izawa, *Jubakutai*, 166; JDA, *Nanpo*, 339–340.

125   *Two large waves:* 67 Sq log.

126   *I heard McMillan:* "Activities."

126   *Hey Mac:* R. T. Smith, 3.

127   *There were hordes:* Hedman, author interview.

128   *Thirty Buffaloes:* Hasegawa, 78. Also Kasuya, 64.

128   *And now it was,* etc.: R. T. Smith, 3 and 160.

129   *Fell off:* Haywood combat report.

129   *Indescribable horror:* Iwao Hayashi, 46.

130   *Why don't we:* Older, Columbia interview.

130   *Huge conglomeration:* Older, author interview.

130   *I aimed at:* Older combat report. Also Overend combat report.

131   *I saw him go down:* Greene, author interview.

131   Parachute fall: author interview; combat report; 3d Sq log.

132   *One of the wings:* JT&A, 28 Dec 1941.

133   *Very tight:* Dupouy, author interview. Also his combat report.

133   *Martin broke away* (Curtis Smith): "Activities."

133   *I don't know:* Jernstedt, author interview.

133   *Turned away* and Usui's death: Hasegawa, 80. Also Izawa, *Jubakutai*, 166–168.

134   AVG claims: combat reports; 3d Sq log; Olson to D. F. Stevenson, 17 Feb 1942, at FTA Archives.

135   *Plenty of time* and *Agleam in the sunlight:* Foucar, 116–118.

135   *There comes the enemy,* etc.: Omar.

136   *None of the fellows:* "Activities."

136   Damage to Mingaladon: 3d Sq log; 67 Sq log; Robert M. Smith, 48–49; R. T. Smith, 162; Gallagher, 123.

137   *Awaiting further, Hold on,* etc.: CLC Papers 7.

138   *He was always:* R. T. Smith, author interview.

138   Demons: GWD, 23–24 Dec; 3d Sq log; Shilling, taped memoir.

139   *I am all right* and disciplinary action: CLC Papers 28.

CHAPTER 8: *He Just Went Spinning Away*

140 JAAF attack plan: JDA, *Nanpo*, 341; Izawa & Hata, 176.

141 Limitations of *Ki-44*: Ikuhiko Hata to author, 29 Apr 1988.

141 Formations to Rangoon: Hinoki, *Hayabusa*, 103–106; Iwao Hayashi, 47; Izawa, *Jubakutai*, 136, 163, 168–169; Kasuya, 68–69.

143 Wavell landing at Mingaladon: Gallagher, 162.

144 *I had thirteen:* "Activities."

144 Sharing bonus: Hedman, author interview. Also Kasuya, 69–73.

146 *With square:* Dupouy combat report.

146 *Anxiety grew:* Tateo Kato.

146 *1st and 2nd Chutais* and shot down Overend: Hinoki, *Hayabusa*, 109. Pilots lost: ibid., 110–111; Hinoki, *Tsubasa*, 307.

147 *Like a butterfly:* Izawa in *Aero Album*.

147 *He just went spinning*, etc.: Dupouy, author interview.

148 RAF activity: 67 Sq log.

148 Japanese losses: Izawa, *Jubakutai*, 169–170; Izawa & Hata, 176, 202; Kasuya, 74.

148 *Very, very sweet:* Iwao Hayashi, 47.

148 *I felt terribly:* Tateo Kato.

148 Heroics forbidden: Yohei Hinoki to author, 19 Dec 1989.

149 Damage to Mingaladon: 3d Sq log and "Activities."

149 Pawley quitting Rangoon: CLC Papers 18. Also "Activities."

149 *A quite useless:* Alsop, SEP, 9 Jan 1943. Also Alsop and Lonborg, author interviews.

150 Olson's timidity: Rodewald and Schaper, Columbia interviews.

150 *Field hit badly:* CLC Papers 7.

150 *Like shooting ducks:* GWD, 26 Dec.

150 Situation in Rangoon: Gallagher, 111–112; *a jumpier lot:* 193.

151 *The result achieved:* Manning's letter at FTA Archives.

151 Seized guns: transcription of AMISSCA rad, PSF 37, FDR Library.

151 *Outfit at Rangoon:* CLC Papers 44.

152 *The American Volunteer Group:* CLC Papers 18.

152 *A study of these:* CLC Papers 36.

153 Japanese debate: JDA, *Nanpo*, 344.

153 *In large formations:* JT&A, 27 Dec.

154 *Intense admiration:* PSF 38, FDR Library.

154 P-40Es and Vanguards: Currie to Magruder, 8 Jan, PSF 38, FDR Library; Madame to Chennault, 19 Jan, CLC Papers 52; CLC Papers 18.

154 *Army would like:* PSF 38, FDR Library.

155 *Thereby showing*, etc.: AMISSCA rad.

155 *Despite Chennault's personal:* AMISSCA rad.

156   *I give Burma:* Gallagher, 125.
156   *The valley:* Robert M. Smith, 56.
156   *I could go down:* Jernstedt, author interview.
156   *Also, nicest thing:* John Donovan letter, 28 Dec 1941.
157   An abrasive: Laughlin in *Foundation*.
157   *Feel good,* etc.: John Donovan letters, 28 Dec 1941, 11 Jan 1942.
157   Pilots offered to CNAC: CLC Papers.

CHAPTER 9: *I Commenced to Lean Forward*

159   Newkirk: NYT, 25 Mar 1942; *Time,* 12 Jan 1942; AVG records.
159   *Let's take the war:* author interview.
159   *I therefore commenced:* Stevenson.
161   *I got so preoccupied,* etc.: Cornelius & Short, 140.
161   *I saw two enemy,* etc.: Newkirk letter, CLC Papers 38.
161   *Automatic pilot:* Boyington, 71.
161   *Our intended mission,* etc.: Howard, ch 10. Also GWD, 3 Jan 1942; JDA, *Nanpo,* 574.
162   *I began learning:* Hill, Columbia interview.
163   JAAF movements from Tanaka; Izawa, *Jubakutai,* 182; Izawa & Hata, 202; JDA, *Nanpo,* 574–575; Iwao Hayashi, 231.
163   Dispersal system: Newkirk letter, CLC Papers 38.
165   *The next second,* etc.: Hotz, 130–131. No more combat: Howard, ch 10.
166   *The wings:* Newkirk letter, CLC Papers 38.
166   *Six or eight:* GWD. Also Bright.
166   *Get on the train:* Frillmann, 103–104.
167   Night interception: GWD, 5 Jan.
167   *I jumped:* Bacon in NYSN.
167   RAF system: Gallagher, 196–197.
167   Blenheims: 113 Sq log; British General Staff, *ABDACOM.*
168   *I let down,* etc.: Peter Wright in *Flying.* Also GWD, 7 and 17 Jan.
169   *Went down to do,* etc.: Mott, author interview.
170   *I made three passes:* Newkirk letter, CLC Papers 38.
170   *My first run:* USAAF, "Informal Report." Also NYT, 11 Jan.
171   *The first section, fired on a compact,* and *picked out:* Newkirk letter, CLC Papers 38.
171   *Felt like hell:* Bacon in NYSN.
171   *Across the airdrome,* etc.: CDN, 12 Jan.
172   *You're a lousy,* etc.: NYT, 11 Jan.
172   Japanese losses in both raids: JDA, *Nanpo,* 576.

172   *Tokio radio claims:* CLC Papers 45. Status of casualties: Mott to author, 5 Feb 1986; CLC Papers 6, 18, 43.

172   Footnote: Mott, author interview.

173   *The more hardships:* CLC Papers 38.

173   *The maps were Chinese:* Neale, Columbia interview.

173   Rossi's flight: author interview.

174   *If you have to fight:* Rector, author interview.

174   *A houseboy:* Neale, Columbia interview.

175   *Oh, we used to have,* etc.: Dunsmore, author interview.

176   Movements of 5th Hikoshidan: Tanaka; Sato, Army interview.

177   Alarm at Mengzi: GWD, 13 Jan; 3d Sq log.

178   *Reports came in:* GWD, 17 Jan.

178   *Fairly light colored* and *greenish tan,* etc.: CLC Papers 38.

179   Japanese version: Kubo, 52–54; Izawa & Hata, 73, 132; and JDA, *Chugoku,* 273.

CHAPTER 10: *They All Fell in a Straight Line*

The Americans and British sometimes used different names for the satellite fields, and the Japanese labeled them by the nearest village, so it is not always possible to know which is meant in a given reference. See Stevenson.

181   Incoming squadrons: British General Staff, *ABDACOM;* Rawlings, 42–47; Wavell; Hemingway, 11–12.

182   *Wild elephants:* Terakura et al.

182   BIA: Ba Maw.

182   *In an endeavour:* 113 Sq log. Also GWD, 19 Jan; Love.

183   *As the war had progressed:* Hattori et al.

183   *Self & Moss,* etc.: CLC Papers 38.

184   *I was quite incensed:* Neale, Columbia interview. Also GWD, 20 Jan; NYT, 23–24 Jan.

184   *In a shallow dive:* 113 Sq log.

184   *Well, I sure am:* Gallagher, 142.

185   *Bad visibility:* 113 Sq log.

185   *The bombers apparently:* GWD, 22 Jan.

186   Raid on Mingaladon: JDA, *Nanpo,* 587; Izawa & Hata, 132, 202; Izawa, *Jubakutai,* 182; Tanaka.

186   Buffaloes and Hurricanes: Rawlings, 169; 17 Sq log.

187   *Like a bunch:* Neale, Columbia interview.

187   *I would spot:* GWD.

188   Rodger's photographs: *Life,* 30 Mar 1942; Bright.

188   *We singled out:* GWD.

188 *Down they came:* Bacon in NYSN.
189 Aircraft Profile: Mason, 234–265. Planes to Burma: British General Staff, *ABDACOM;* William Donovan Memoranda 427, 20 Apr 1942.
189 *I caught him:* GWD.
190 Christman's death: Rector, author interview; Hill, Columbia interview.
190 *The squadron is doing:* Cooke & Cooke, 94–96.
190 *Staging an aerial:* JT&A, 24 Jan.
190 67 Sq claimed one: *Aircraft Profile* 217 (Christopher Shores).
190 *Two terrific battles:* NYT, 24 Jan. Haung's report: GWD.
190 *The enemy had a great will:* JDA, *Nanpo,* 587. For Japanese racial attitudes, see Tsuji, appendix.
191 *Jap casualties:* AMISSCA rad, 26 Jan.
191 *On first attack,* etc.: GWD.
192 *Closed on one:* Neale diary.
192 *Petrol streamed,* etc.: 17 Sq log.
193 *They all fell:* Hotz, 146.
193 Japanese losses: Izawa, *Jubakutai,* 182; Izawa & Hata, 133.
193 *Sneaked in,* etc.: GWD; also 17 Sq log.
193 *It was the fourth,* etc.: Dunsmore, author interview.
194 *The machines:* 113 Sq log. Also AMISSCA rad, 27 Jan.
194 *I alternated between:* Chennault, *Fighter,* 137.
194 Training CAF cadets: CLC Papers 18; 3d Sq log.
194 Tomahawk census: CLC Papers 19. Blackburn: CLC Papers 28.
195 *Until British* and *until next Wednesday:* CLC Papers 18.
195 *Combat effectiveness* and *cannot be inducted:* CLC Papers 18. *Induction AVG,* etc.: PSF 38, FDR Library.
196 *In China:* AMISSCA rad, 28 Jan.
196 *The other day:* Stowe in CDN, 6 Jan. Also CLC Papers 12, 38, and 43; Bond & Anderson, 71.
197 *Stricken from the rolls:* GWD, 31 Dec.
197 Baugh killed: CLC Papers 7.
197 *I am willing:* Bond & Anderson, 69.
197 *A few members,* etc.: CLC Papers 19. Resignations from AVG personnel records.
198 *Good riddance:* Greenlaw, 127. Also R. T. Smith, 186.
198 Goose hunt and dinner: Greenlaw, 113.
198 *The bombers headed:* GWD, 22 Jan. Also 3d Sq log; GWD, 24 Jan.
199 Morane-Saulniers: GWD, 27 Jan; Izawa & Hata, 73; *Aircraft Profile* 147 (Gaston Botquin).
199 *Bombers of the Chinese:* NYT, 23 Jan.

200   *Can begin attacks:* CLC Papers 19; PSF 38, FDR Library.
200   *May your affairs:* President's File 2907, FDR Library.
200   *Hudsons will:* Currie to Chennault, 31 Jan, PSF 38, FDR Library.

CHAPTER 11: *Hoffman Shot Down and Dead*

201   *Prefer no replacements:* CLC Papers 38.
201   Drawing lots: Rosbert, 78.
201   *Gentle, sweet:* Greenlaw, 202. But see Bond & Anderson and Rodewald diary.
202   *We stood there:* Hemingway, 121. Also Bond & Anderson, 82; Boyington, 55; Burgard diary.
202   *The takeoff procedure:* Bond & Anderson, 82. Also CLC Papers 26.
202   *Time was more:* Hemingway, 69.
203   *You don't see anything,* etc.: Prescott, Columbia interview—one of the funniest combat stories ever told.
204   *The enemy jumped us:* GWD, 26 Jan.
204   *Out of the whirling:* Gallagher, 147.
205   *I had pulled myself:* Boyington, 59.
205   *My wingman and I* and *Like six others:* Bright.
206   *I was on a Jap's tail:* NYT, 30 Jan.
206   *A short burst:* 17 Sq log.
207   *A little straffing:* 17 Sq log.
207   Japanese version: JDA, *Nanpo,* 589.
207   *Combat with twenty:* GWD, 26 Jan.
207   Bunny Stone: Hemingway, 21.
207   Sequence and scale of raids from AMISSCA rad, 28 Jan.
208   *Now we stood:* CDN, 29 Jan. Also Boyington, 69; Bond & Anderson, 84; Iwao Hayashi, 48, 230.
208   *Crushing the enemy:* JT&A, 16 May.
208   Funeral party: Bond & Anderson, 85.
209   *I leading red-yellow:* GWD, 28 Jan.
209   Japanese version: Tagata, 118–121.
210   *The largest part:* Boyington, 62.
210   *It was taken:* Kuwahara & Allred, 99. Also Hata & Izawa, xii.
210   *The English general:* Izawa & Hata, 203.
210   Hastey shot down: Howard, ch 10; Burgard diary.
211   Blenheims: 113 Sq log; Bond & Anderson, 86.
211   *The planes that we have:* CLC Papers 38.
212   Japanese strength on 29 Jan: JDA, *Nanpo,* 590.

212   *When the Japs:* Bacon in NYSN.
212   *I missed him,* etc.: Bond & Anderson, 86–87.
213   *Just right,* etc.: Boyington, 63.
213   *I held my fire,* etc.: GWD, 29 Jan.
214   *The first victory roll,* etc.: Bond & Anderson, 88.
214   *Edward church:* Tagata, 118–121.
214   Claims: AVG Victories; 135 Sq log. Losses: JDA, *Nanpo,* 590.
215   *Paced by three:* NYT, 30 Jan.
215   *We were low:* GWD, 30 Jan. Also Howard, ch 10.
216   *Group wanted:* Bacon in NYSN.
216   *In strength* and Commonwealth withdrawal: Hutton.
217   Obata's offensive: JDA, *Nanpo,* 593–595; Izawa, *Jubakutai,* 183; Iwao
       Hayashi, 231; GWD; Neale diary; Bacon in NYSN.
217   Radar damaged: AMISSCA rad, 3 Feb.
217   *Doom-ba-boom:* Burchett, 300.
218   *In my sights,* etc.: Bond & Anderson, 94.
218   Boyington's kills from a commendation by Chennault (Samson, 130).
218   *Ambushed the Japanese,* etc.: NYT, 7 Feb 1942.
219   One Nate lost: JDA, *Nanpo,* 595.
219   RAF claims: 135 Sq log.
219   *To tide them over:* British General Staff, *ABDACOM.*
219   Newkirk checked out: 17 Sq log. Eighteen planes lost: GWD, 3 Feb.
219   Lysanders: Kirby, 43; *Aircraft Profile* 159 (Francis Mason); Bacon in
       NYSN. Raid on Moulmein: AMISSCA rad, 6 Feb.
220   *I being in the back,* etc.: Keeton diary; Keeton, author interview. Also
       JDA, *Nanpo,* 593–596.
220   *Persistent enemy bombing:* 113 Sq log.

CHAPTER 12: *Let's Get the Heck Out of Here*

221   Sandell's death: GWD, 7 Feb; Burgard diary; Bond & Anderson, 95.
221   *The boys had to dig:* Wolf & Ingells.
221   Replacing Sandell: Neale diary.
221   *Out-fly or out-fight:* Neale, Columbia interview.
221   *A well-built fellow:* Hemingway, 18.
222   Petach married: Hanks, author interview.
222   Japanese movements: Iwao Hayashi, 48; Kubo, 61.
222   *Sixteen planes* and makeup of 1st Sq: GWD, 9 Feb.
223   Allied O/B: Stevenson; British General Staff, *ABDACOM;* Kirby, 43;
       Young & Warne; CLC Papers; diaries and squadron logs. Japanese O/B:

Tanaka; Izawa, *Jubakutai;* Izawa & Hata; Sato interview; JDA, *Nanpo,* 607.

223   *Acted like rich kids:* Burgard diary. Also Bond & Anderson, 98–102; Hemingway, 54.

224   Reynolds jailed: Neale diary. Looters shot: Burchett, 156.

224   *I spent every day:* Frillmann, 114.

224   Contraband: Burgard diary; Bond & Anderson, 102; Howard, ch 10.

225   *With 'AVG' in huge:* Burchett, 80.

226   *We don't mind:* Burchett, 275. Also Bond & Anderson, 99.

226   *We sipped at another:* Hemingway, 85.

226   Snapper: Hemingway, 50; Bond & Anderson, 101.

227   *Not fighting with proper* (British Viceroy): Kirby, 81.

227   *They were on our tails:* Cross.

227   *It was a lucky:* Burgard diary. Also GWD, 21 Feb; JDA, *Nanpo,* 600.

228   *For the first time:* Stevenson.

228   *I was eager as hell,* etc.: Bond & Anderson, 104–106.

229   *Falling into single:* GWD, 21 Feb.

229   160 killed: Rodewald diary; *numerous:* Kirby, 67.

230   *Here there was chaos:* Kirby, 68.

231   *Ambushed* and *ready to defend:* Hutton.

231   Air force leaving Rangoon: British General Staff, *ABDACOM;* Stevenson; Hemingway, 59–61; GWD, 23 Feb; Burgard diary. The abandonment of the city is described by Hughes, 6–7.

231   *Remembering previous British:* AMISSCA rad, 6 Mar.

231   Destroying lend-lease stores: AMISSCA rads, 27 Feb and 19 May.

232   Chaos in Rangoon: Burchett, 156; Neale, author interview; Frillmann, 114–115.

232   Ground crews to India: 113 Sq log.

233   *The tires are baked:* GWD, 24 Feb.

233   *It's hot in Rangoon:* NYT, 26 Feb.

233   *American volunteer pilots:* JT&A, 27 Feb.

233   Armored brigade: Belden, 23–25, 245.

234   *All day long:* CDN, 13 Mar.

234   Crossing the Sittang: Toho newsreel, *Biruma.*

234   Raid on Moulmein: GWD, 24 Feb; CLC Papers 38.

234   *Thick as ants:* NYT, 25 Feb.

234   *There were horses:* Hemingway, 40–41.

234   *Because of the gradual:* Terakura.

235   New attack plan: JDA, *Nanpo,* 600; Shokis at Moulmein: 602.

235   Sally destroyed: Kubo, 66 (it was his plane).

235　*A hazy day:* Boyington, 71.

236　*About sixty enemy:* JT&A, 1 Apr 1942 ("crushing" in original).

236　Japanese formations: JDA, *Nanpo,* 602. Also GWD, 25 Feb; Neale diary; AVG Victories.

237　Blackburn: Bond & Anderson, 78; CLC Papers 28.

237　Leibolt missing: GWD, 25–26 Feb.

237　*Look at that,* etc.: Rodewald diary.

237　*This was the most dangerous:* Kuroe, 126–128.

238　Hironaka: Izawa, *Jubakutai,* 183.

238　Blenheims: Bond & Anderson, 113.

238　*Since we are already:* Dick Rossi to author, 26 Mar 1990.

238　*We left the two planes,* etc.: Rosbert, 81. Also GWD, 26 Feb; Neale and Burgard diaries; JDA, *Nanpo,* 602; Izawa & Hata, 133.

239　*Japs can't hit,* etc.: Perry, author interview.

239　Noon combat: Bond & Anderson, 114; GWD; Neale diary; CLC Papers 38.

240　Allied and Japanese claims: NYT, 27–28 Feb.

240　RAF withdrawal: British General Staff, *ABDACOM;* Stevenson.

240　*I say, Neale:* Hotz, 174.

241　*Let's get the heck:* Neale, Columbia interview.

242　Magwe: Bond & Anderson, 120; Burgard diary.

242　Waiting for Leibolt: Neale, author interview.

243　Abandonment and capture of Rangoon: Hughes, 7; Terakura; Young, *Helping Hand,* 242.

244　*Although air fighting:* Stevenson.

CHAPTER 13: *Did You Have Any Warning?*

245　Stilwell's epithets: his published diary and Schaller, passim.

246　*Bissell over all:* AMISSCA rad, 4 Feb.

246　*Personally am willing:* CLC Papers 19.

246　*Greatly appreciate:* PSF 38, FDR Library.

246　*I spoke for Bissell,* etc.: Stilwell, 39.

246　*Hap Arnold is:* Samson, 118.

247　*Arnold and Stillwell insist:* PSF 38, FDR Library. "Groco" may have been coined from "Group Officer Commanding."

247　*Groco told me,* etc.: PSF 38, FDR Library.

247　Supplies and spares: CLC Papers 8, 28, 52.

247　*Our new ships,* etc.: R. T. Smith, 231–232. Also 3d Sq log and CLC Papers 52.

248   Bacon on furlough: author interview.

248   *A tired, depressed,* etc.: Stilwell, 48–50. Also *Life,* 30 Mar 1942; AMISSCA rad, 5 Mar; USAAF, "Chronology."

249   *She absolutely captured:* John Donovan letter, 1 Mar. *We are all proud:* Robert M. Smith, 65. *Madame gushed:* Bright. Also Boyington, 79; Greenlaw, 159.

249   *Had a talk,* etc.: Stilwell, 49–50. Also Dorn, 31; AMISSCA rad, 4 Mar.

250   Chiangs in Kunming: Bond & Anderson, 122; Keeton diary; GWD, 5 Mar; 3d Sq log; Boyington, 80–88.

250   Chongqing conference: AMISSCA rad, 5 Mar.

250   *Believe Chennault matter:* AMISSCA rad, 7 Mar.

250   CAF commissions: GWD, 11 Mar.

251   The paperwork war from AMISSCA radiograms. Taking over from Magruder: 11 Mar. Promotions: 4, 13, 15, and 19 Mar. *Strongly recommend:* 21 Mar. Requisition officers and typewriter ribbons: 26–27 Mar. *Only air officer:* 26 Mar.

251   Lonborg: Robert M. Smith, 71; Greenlaw, 176–177; Reynolds, author interview.

252   Uniform regulations: CLC Papers 25.

252   Magwe: Stevenson; Moyes, 157; Rawlings, 47, 169, 275; Young & Warne, 142; GWD, 15 Mar.

253   Lampang raid: GWD, 5 Mar; Bond & Anderson, 124.

253   Retreat of 17 Sq: Hemingway, 113; JDA, *Nanpo,* 608.

253   67 Sq withdrawn: Rawlings, 169; Bond & Anderson, 125.

253   B-17s: USAAF, "Chronology."

254   *American Volunteer Headquarters:* NYT, 8 Mar.

254   Tomahawks crashed: CLC Papers 17.

255   Takeoff from Wu Chia Ba: 3d Sq log; Keeton diary.

255   Delivery of No. 100: CLC Papers 8.

256   *AVG equipment:* AMISSCA rad, 18 Mar.

256   *Shot up vehicles,* etc. (Dupouy); *I then noticed* (Groh); *I picked out* (Moss): combat reports at FTA Archives.

257   *It was sitting,* etc.: Jernstedt, author interview.

258   *I missed* (Jernstedt) and *On my last* (Reed): combat reports at FTA Archives.

259   5th Hikoshidan to Rangoon: JDA, *Nanpo,* 693–697; Izawa in *Aero Album;* Izawa & Hata, 25, 48, 124, 133, 176; Izawa, *Jubakutai,* 183.

259   *Busily occupied:* Tanaka.

260   *On 9 March:* Tanaka.

260   *Extraordinary concentration:* British Air Ministry, 9.

260   *Magnificent air action:* Stevenson.

260 Japanese version: JDA, *Nanpo*, 698–701; Izawa, *Jubakutai*, 183.

261 Bandits from the southeast: Hemingway, 149.

262 *After the third:* Dupouy combat report at FTA Archives. Also Dupouy, author interview; R. T. Smith, 257.

263 O/B: JDA, *Nanpo*, 694–695. Also sources cited in ch 12 above.

263 *Wherever I looked:* Hemingway, 157.

264 *I got behind:* Groh combat report at FTA Archives. Also Izawa & Hata, 48.

264 *He came in fast,* etc.: Wolf & Ingells.

265 Largest air battle: JT&A, 12 May.

266 *Look out for:* GWD, 21 Mar.

CHAPTER 14: *There Is Always a Way*

267 Fauth to 2nd Lieutenant: CLC Papers 18.

267 Sugiyama lost: Kuroe, 131–133.

268 *Considerable damage,* etc.: Stevenson.

268 *Absolutely no warning,* etc.: GWD, 22 Mar.

269 Evacuation: 3d Sq log; Hemingway, 162.

269 Japanese claims: Tanaka; Sekigawa, 120. The semiofficial JDA history makes the more modest claim of 34 planes destroyed and 50 damaged.

269 Revenge mission and his health: Chennault, *Fighter*, 147–148.

269 *Jap Air Force headquarters:* Bond & Anderson, 130.

270 To Loiwing: Rodewald diary; Greenlaw, 246–247; Neale diary.

271 *After tomorrow:* Boyington, 98.

271 *All right, you curly-headed:* Bond & Anderson, 132.

272 *The next target:* Geselbracht combat report at FTA Archives. Also GWD, 24 Mar; Keeton diary.

272 *I nosed downward,* etc.: Bond & Anderson, 134.

273 Japanese tried to take off: Yasuda, 140, 170.

273 *The aircraft:* Boyington combat report at AVG Archives.

273 *Heaviest I have ever:* Neale diary.

273 *Two of them:* GWD.

273 *I circled back:* Rector combat report at AVG Archives.

274 *U.S. Fliers:* NYT, 25 Mar 1942.

274 *Destroyed most,* etc.: Schultz, 224. In an unusually clear example of how the AVG legend grew over the years, Schultz was inflating Chennault's account in *Fighter,* 148.

274 Among those who doubted Newkirk's tally were Keeton (diary, 20 Mar 1942) and James Howard (letter to author, 15 Mar 1990).

274 *A.V.G. becoming ineffective:* PSF 38, FDR Library.

275   Damage to Chiang Mai and raid on Akyab: JDA, *Nanpo,* 698, 703.
275   *Secret runway:* Hinoki, *Hayabusa,* 240–241.
275   Raids on Heho, etc.: Izawa, *Jubakutai,* 183; JDA, *Nanpo,* 707.
276   McGarry as prisoner: Hinoki, *Hayabusa,* 244; Hinoki to author, 18 Dec 1989; McGarry, Andrade interview; U.S. Embassy memo, 22 Apr 1943, in CLC Papers 39.
276   *Suggest repaired:* CLC Papers 8.
276   *Special missions:* GWD, 24 Mar.
277   *This is written:* John Donovan letter, 6 Apr.
277   Kittyhawks arrived: CLC Papers 52.
277   *We're all against:* R. T. Smith, 260.
278   *The enemy plane:* Older combat report at FTA Archives.
278   *Oley sighted:* R. T. Smith, 263; *Toungoo party,* 261.
279   Wedding: Boyington, 107; Jernstedt, author interview; 3d Sq log; Greenlaw, 253.
279   Searching for AVG: Hinoki, *Tsubasa,* 64–66.
280   Events at Loiwing: R. T. Smith, 265–269.
280   *The excellent warning:* Hemingway, 185. Also 113 Sq log.
280   *Fifteen small planes:* JDA, *Nanpo,* 714.
281   64th Sentai to Loiwing: Hinoki, *Hayabusa,* 250–251.
281   *Many ships headed, Japs strafing,* etc.: R. T. Smith, 271.
282   *He rolled over:* Olson combat report at FTA Archives.
282   *Never have I been:* John Donovan letter, 9 Apr. Also his combat report in GWD.
282   *I kept firing:* Groh combat report at FTA Archives.
282   *I opened all guns:* Hodges combat report at FTA Archives.
282   Hayabusa: Laughlin combat report at FTA Archives; Yasuda, 147.
283   *It started smoking:* Wolf combat report at FTA Archives.
283   *I fired from:* Overend combat report at FTA Archives.
284   Three wrecks near field: John Donovan letter, 9 Apr.
284   Japanese pilots lost: Hinoki, *Tsubasa,* 309; Izawa in *Aero Album;* Izawa & Hata, 320; and JDA, *Nanpo,* 714.
284   *There was nothing,* etc.: Hinoki, *Hayabusa,* 254–255.
285   *Why were two:* GWD, 8 Apr.

CHAPTER 15: *Terminate Our Contracts*

286   *It was a beautiful:* Brereton, 116–117. Also USAAF, "Chronology"; Romanus & Sunderland, *Mission,* 116.
286   Planning raids: Bond & Anderson, 147; GWD, 8 Apr. Kittyhawk: Burgard diary.

286 *My God, do we:* Greenlaw, 209.
287 Assaults: Bond & Anderson, 158; Greenlaw, 214–215, 221; Rodewald diary.
287 *For firing his gun:* CLC Papers 28.
287 *I told Chennault:* Davies, 267. Also Greenlaw, 211; Stilwell, 77.
287 *His value to China:* AMISSCA rad, 31 Mar.
288 *After hour's conference:* PSF 38, FDR Library.
288 *Cardinal principal:* AMISSCA rad, 2 Apr; *It is recommended:* 4 Apr. *Told him I couldn't:* Stilwell, 78.
288 *That I am the boss:* Stilwell, 82–83.
289 *There is something,* etc., and mission to Mengzi: Keeton diary.
289 AVG meeting: Bond & Anderson, 150.
289 *Through private channels:* AMISSCA rad, 16 Apr.
289 Chennault's official file (AFHRC, 862.289A) contains no documents relating to his induction or promotions. Some AMISSCA radiograms give the induction date as 8 Apr. The War Department was confused, too, and on 17 Jul Stilwell sent a message summarizing Chennault's induction and promotions as given here (AMISSCA rad). Hill and Chennault to Loiwing: GWD, 9 Apr; 3d Sq log.
290 Return of 64th Sentai: Yasuda, 144–146; Hinoki, *Hayabusa,* 258–264; JDA, *Nanpo,* 715.
290 AVG activities: 3d Sq log; Keeton diary; GWD, 10 Apr.
291 *I made three passes:* Brouk combat report at FTA Archives.
292 *Decided to die:* Hinoki, *Hayabusa,* 265; return to Chiang Mai and Kato's actions: 267–270. Also Izawa in *Aero Album;* Smith's combat report at FTA Archives.
292 Hurricanes lost: GWD, 10 Apr; Hemingway, 187–188.
292 *He went wild:* Older, Columbia interview.
293 *All I can do:* Yasuda, 149.
293 *For the next:* Older combat report at FTA Archives.
293 *I looked south:* Smith combat report at FTA Archives.
293 *I could easily:* R. T. Smith, 275.
294 Japanese casualties from Hinoki, *Tsubasa,* appendix.
294 Events of Saturday from R. T. Smith, 276; 3d Sq log; Keeton diary; 113 Sq log.
295 *We hit our checkpoints,* etc.: Peter Wright in *Sportsman Pilot.* Also combat reports in GWD, 12 Apr.
296 Panic at Loiwing: Jernstedt, author interview.
296 *Chewed his ass:* R. T. Smith, 277. Also memo in CLC Papers 26.
297 *Request you arrange:* GWD, 14 Apr.

297   Mutaguchi: Hata; JT&A, 1 Jul 1942.

297   *If your hands are broken:* Moser, 156.

298   *They had on the average:* Hutton.

298   Petach crackup: GWD, 15 April; Gordon Seagrave, 206.

298   *A mission was planned:* R. T. Smith, 281.

298   Chennault commissioned: AMISSCA rad, 17 Jul.

298   Transports and morale: 3d Sq log; R T. Smith, 282; Burgard diary.

299   *Please issue instructions:* AMISSCA rad, 20 Apr.

299   *White feather:* Keeton diary. Also Greenlaw, 250.

299   *You fellows have to remember:* Rector, author interview.

300   *We the undersigned:* CLC Papers 28. Also Howard, ch 12. The pilot total
      excludes those in hospital or on limited duty.

301   Doolittle raid: Glines. Also Horikoshi, 134.

302   *We arrived over* and *Situation here:* GWD, 20 Apr.

302   Namsang mission: 3d Sq log; GWD, 21 Apr.

302   JAAF movements: Hinoki, *Hayabusa,* 271; JDA, *Nanpo,* 213, 215.

302   *As they approached:* GWD, 21 Apr.

303   *One bullet:* Gordon Seagrave, 218.

303   Jones skirmish: GWD, 21 Apr. Also JDA, *Nanpo,* 709.

303   Chennault to brigadier: *Army Directory,* 20 Oct 1942.

303   *Following from Chennault:* AMISSCA rad, 22 Apr.

304   Boyington in Kunming: Boyington, 110–117; Bond & Anderson, 158;
      Boyington to USMC historian, 23 Jul 1981, at AVG Archives. Most
      AVG veterans I interviewed were convinced that Greenlaw bedded
      Boyington and most of the other pilots mentioned in her book—each
      adding, however, that he himself was not so favored. As with combat
      scores, there may have been an element of wishful thinking with respect
      to the exec's wife.

304   Groh's story: GWD, 9 Jun; Robert M. Smith, 91; Bond & Anderson,
      161.

305   Swartz in Calcutta: Bond & Anderson, 153; DeWolfe letter in CLC
      Papers 7.

305   Instructors to squadrons: CLC Papers 20.

305   Aircraft census: CLC Papers 12. Forty-seven other fighters were sidelined
      for lack of parts. Lancers: Bond & Anderson, 158–159.

CHAPTER 16: *This May Screw Us Completely*

306   To Lashio: Greenlaw, 231.

307   Karen guerrillas: Harold Klein to author, 23 Jul 1987.

307   *Through continuous:* Terakura.

307   *Disaster at Loikaw:* Stilwell, 90; *all fade:* 92.
307   Blenheim raid: 113 Sq log.
308   *I could see* and *The air activities:* GWD, 24 Apr.
308   *Perhaps someone:* Greenlaw, 261. Also Hennessy, author interview.
309   *I flew north* (Raine), *I dove on EA* (Laughlin), and *I dove from 3,000* (Raine): combat reports at FTA Archives. Also GWD, 25 Apr; R. T. Smith, 291.
310   *Determined to avenge:* JT&A, 12 Jun.
310   Strafed Chinese: Romanus & Sunderland, *Mission,* 134.
310   Blenheims at Konhaiping: 113 Sq log.
310   *Please do not attack,* etc.: GWD, 26 Apr.
311   Chinese bombers: GWD, 21 Apr and 26 Apr.
311   *Use all available* and *Enemy reported:* GWD, 26 Apr.
311   *Sand-colored,* etc.: Donovan combat report at FTA Archives.
311   64th Sentai to Loiwing: Hinoki, *Hayabusa,* 271.
312   *Reconnaissance:* Stilwell, 93.
312   *Your urgent message,* etc.: GWD, 27 Apr.
312   Evacuating Loiwing: 3d Sq log; 113 Sq log; Hemingway, 188.
312   Army transport: Greenlaw, 275–276; Haynes letter to AF historian.
313   Rubber balls to Japan: JT&A, 24 Apr.
314   *Tried to get,* etc.: GWD.
314   *Fell off on one* (Bishop), *I heard a strange* (Olson), *I saw Older* (Jernstedt), *Pulled up* (Overend), *After about three* (Haywood), *Large sloppy Lufberry* (Smith), and *I still had speed* (Greene): combat reports at FTA Archives.
314   Japanese version: Kuroe, 163–166; Yasuda, 153–154.
316   *Guess we're going,* etc.: Scott, *God,* 75–76. Also Haynes letter. Returning to Mangshi: R. T. Smith, 294.
318   *Shot up by:* Izawa in *Aero Album.* Also Hinoki, *Tsubasa,* 309.
318   *We knew you were battling:* Kuroe, 168.
318   Airborne mission: JDA, *Nanpo,* 717–720; Yasuda, 156–158.
319   *Burma reporting net,* etc.: GWD, 30 Apr. Also 1 May.
319   *With a resounding:* Slim, 67. Slim was now the British field commander in Burma, the fourth since December.
320   *Looks like a gorilla: Ex-CBI Roundup,* Jul 1989.
320   *Took off about 0545:* Haynes letter.
320   Evacuating Loiwing: 3d Sq log; Robert M. Smith, 83; 113 Sq log.
321   Mangshi: 3d Sq log; Keeton diary; R. T. Smith, 296–298.
321   Adam & Eves to Baoshan: GWD, 2 May; Bond & Anderson, 161; Neale diary.
322   *Advance by bounds:* Terakura.

322   *The Japanese are making:* Robert M. Smith, 82.

322   *British stragglers:* Dorn, 145. Also Belden, 277, 285, 301.

323   Wanlaikam strongpoint: Terakura.

323   *No fires* and *My second burst:* GWD, 4 May.

323   *I followed:* Neale diary.

323   *A great many stores:* JDA, *Nanpo,* 722.

324   *Note the peculiar design:* JT&A, 24 May.

324   *On my third attack* and *There were bodies:* Bond & Anderson, 164–168.

325   Evacuation of Baoshan: Neale diary; Haynes letter.

325   *Through the calm,* etc.: GWD, 5 May.

325   Japanese losses: Izawa & Hata, 48; JDA, *Nanpo,* 722.

CHAPTER 17: *Piss on Bissell*

327   *The brave and gallant:* JT&A, 20 May. Also Iwao Hayashi, 92; Terakura; Young, *Helping Hand,* 242; JDA, *Nanpo,* 717–723; "Southern Area Air Operations."

328   Planes destroyed: "Japanese Air Losses," compiled for British Military Intelligence in 1953 by demobilized officers of the 5th Hikoshidan but including 3rd Hikoshidan losses over Burma. Allied claims: Stevenson; AVG Victories.

328   *Last autumn:* JT&A, 17 May.

328   *Pursue the enemy:* Terakura.

329   *Japs meeting no:* GWD, 6 May. Also Chennault, *Fighter,* 163.

329   *To destroy the Burma Road:* GWD, 7 May.

329   *Made first pass:* GWD, 8 May.

330   *His first burst,* etc.: GWD, 9 May. Also R. T. Smith, 305; Neale diary. Japanese version: Ikari, 122, 126.

331   *The trucks were, At about 0945,* and *a group of:* GWD, 10 May.

331   McAllister's journey: 3d Sq log.

332   Baumler's arrival: CLC Papers 52, 28.

332   Lancers: Harrington, author interview; "AVG Ends With Party," *Ex-CBI Roundup,* Nov 1989; CLC Papers 52; Bond & Anderson, 180.

332   Cross refused to fly: Burgard diary, 24 May and 10 Jun.

332   Ferry Command: Haynes letter; Scott, *God,* 66, 93; Layher, author interview.

333   *Thanks very much:* Chennault to Haynes, 11 May, collection of Martha Byrd.

333   Harvey wanted a commission: Jernstedt, author interview.

334   Tom Jones: Greenlaw, 62–63, 225; R. T. Smith, 300, 313.

334   *Chennault* and *I follow:* Laughlin in *Foundation.*
335   *A DC-3 type,* etc.: GWD, 12 May.
335   Japanese version: Izawa & Hata, 73.
336   *If we destroy:* GWD, 13 May. Promotions: CLC Papers 28.
336   Donovan radiogram at FTA Archives.
336   *If the Navy:* John Donovan letter, 3 May.
336   Support for Chinese army: GWD, 12–15 May; Neale diary.
337   Chennault's letter to madame: Samson, 146–147.
337   *The idea was:* Bright.
337   *With steam squirting:* Laughlin in *Foundation.*
337   Jones testing bomb: Greenlaw, 225–226; Howard, ch 12.
337   Lao Kai mission: Keeton diary; GWD; Scott, *God,* 106; R. T. Smith, 312; Bright.
338   *We approached:* "Statement of Peter Wright," at FTA Archives.
338   *At the time:* JT&A, 2 Jun.
338   *Even my eyelashes:* Harrington, author interview.
339   *He is all through:* Burgard diary, 10 Jun. The AVG war weariness was typical of airmen in all theaters.
339   Geselbracht refused mission: Keeton diary.
339   *Might do it:* Neale diary.
339   *Do you not agree,* etc.: AMISSCA rad, 10 May.
340   Financial terms: CLC Papers 18; Bond & Anderson, 178; Rodewald diary.
340   *And for any of you:* Chennault, *Fighter,* 172.
341   *Up to and including:* AMISSCA rad, 10 Apr.
341   Letters to FDR and Connally: Bond & Anderson, 182.
341   *AVG has been:* AMISSCA rad, 2 May.
341   *The conspicuous:* undated AMISSCA rad. Also GWD, 6 May (emphasis added).
342   *Chennault and others:* AMISSCA rad, 19 May.
342   Doolittle in Kunming: Greenlaw, 293; Byrd, 149.
342   *After making several:* GWD, 22 May. Also Neale diary.
343   *Kato then* and *Hero God:* JT&A, 23 Jul 1942. Also JDA, *Nanpo,* 731–733; Izawa & Hata, 284.
344   Salween and Indochina missions: GWD, 24–30 May.
344   *Our two eager,* etc.: Keeton diary.
344   *Weather was very bad:* GWD, 28 May.
345   Pilots to Chongqing: CLC Papers 28; Bond & Anderson, 184; Burgard diary.

345   *Fully qualified,* etc.: AMISSCA rad, 14 Jun. Stilwell also recommended
       regular commissions for six of his own officers.
346   *Piss on Bissell:* Byrd, 149.

CHAPTER 18: *Far Worse Than You Know*

347   23rd Fighter Group: CLC Papers 28; R. T. Smith, 330.
348   Lashio raid: Haynes letter; JDA, *Nanpo,* 730.
348   *Please forward:* GWD, 5 Jun. Also AMISSCA rad, 6 Jun.
348   *An island:* JDA, *Chugoku,* 281. Also Kori et al., 2:59–61; Wei et al.,
       239–248.
349   *Destroy the air bases:* Shiba.
349   Trenching and reprisals: Glines, 320–322.
349   AVG moving inland: GWD, 1, 2, 9, 11 Jun.
349   *Bravery and outstanding:* GWD, appendix. Also Bond & Anderson, 184.
350   *We the Third:* 3d Sq log. Also R. T. Smith, 337–338; Keeton diary;
       AMISSCA rad, 18 May.
351   *A small camp* and *We could see him,* etc.: Rodewald diary.
352   JAAF units and losses: JDA, *Chugoku,* 300–301; Watanabe, 64–66.
352   *I fired several* and *light bombers:* GWD, 12 Jun.
353   *The bomber was:* GWD, 12 Jun.
354   *A quick burst:* Rosbert, 86.
354   *The reverend:* Bond & Anderson, 188–190.
354   *Thought it was:* Neale diary.
355   Nagano Force to Hanoi: Nonaka; Watanabe, 66.
355   *Nine American aircraft:* JT&A, 15 Jun.
355   *What are you fighting:* "Questions Asked Japanese Prisoner," CLC
       Papers 13. Also Rodewald diary; R. T. Smith, 335.
355   *No more:* Neale diary, 20 Jun.
356   *Deaf as a post:* Brereton, 130. Also Stilwell, 114.
357   *A bevy of beautiful:* Neumann, 92–93; handbill: 85.
357   Induction procedure: Chennault, *Fighter,* 172; Haynes letter; U.S.
       Military Mission, "American Volunteer Group."
357   *Everybody had a lot:* Rodewald diary.
358   *Chennault was the one:* Harrington, author interview. Also Bond &
       Anderson, 197–198; Neale diary; Neale, Columbia interview.
358   2nd Sq at Hengyang: Bond & Anderson, 198–199; Neale diary; GWD,
       22–23 Jun.
358   *We spotted 14:* Samson, 152.
359   *Surprise attacks:* Nonaka.

359 *Coming and go* and Japanese activities at Hankou and Hengyang: JDA, *Chugoku*, 303. Also Izawa & Hata, 152.

359 Movement of planes: Romanus & Sunderland, *Mission*, 157–158; Brereton, 130; Samson, 149; R. T. Smith, 345, 348; Bond & Anderson, 199; GWD, 23 Jun.

360 Interviews at Guilin: Howard, ch 13; Neale and Keeton diaries.

360 *From present observations:* GWD, 23 Jun.

360 Induction ranks: GWD, 1 Jul.

361 *Goddammit* and 16th Sq: Perry, author interview. Also Keeton diary.

361 Moore and Sanger: Rodewald and Keeton diaries.

361 *The boys* and *That whorehouse:* White, 139.

361 *No women:* Stilwell, 116.

362 Women from Guilin and *I am afraid:* Samson, 154.

362 *Recommend no publicity:* AMISSCA rad, 26 Jun.

362 *He had information:* Neale diary.

362 *Bob Neale came:* Bond & Anderson, 200.

363 Raids: Bond & Anderson, 201–202; Neale diary; JDA, *Chugoku*, 304.

363 *I went after:* GWD, 3 Jul.

364 *I opened up:* GWD, 3 Jul.

364 10th Chutai: Izawa & Hata.

364 *While straffing:* Rodewald diary. Also Neale diary; Bond & Anderson, 202.

364 *You are directed:* CLC Papers 10.

365 *After talking to:* CLC Papers 19.

365 *They saw me:* GWD, 4 Jul.

366 *We sighted:* GWD, 4 Jul. Also Rodewald and Neale diaries; Bond & Anderson, 203; Izawa & Hata, 152.

366 Madame's party: Chennault, *Fighter*, 173–174; GWD, 4 Jul.

CHAPTER 19: *The AVG Passed into History*

367 *At midnight:* Chennault, *Fighter*, 174.

367 23rd Fighter Group: Neale diary; Scott, *God*, 115–117.

367 Formation flying at Wu Chia Ba: Cornelius & Short, 220.

368 *I dropped,* etc.: GWD, 6 Jul.

368 *Reconnaissance bomber,* etc.: GWD, 9 Jul.

369 JAAF losses: Izawa, "Japanese Aces"; Hinoki, *Tsubasa*, 307–317.

371 *Careful scrutiny:* GWD, 10 Jul.

371 Shamblin captured: JT&A, 15 Jul; CLC Papers 7. Fate of Anglo-American prisoners: International Military Tribunal, 385.

371   On 2 Jul, Stilwell reported that the AVG had lost 84 planes (AMISSCA rad), to which I have added the two lost on 10 Jul.

372   *I am unhappy:* Bond & Anderson, 205.

372   *The bombs hit, and all the, I overtook,* and *by two:* GWD, 16 Jul. Also Neale diary.

374   *It was after sundown:* Harrington, author interview.

374   *Surplus in grade:* AMISSCA rad, 1 Jul.

374   Squadron strength: AMISSCA rad, 4 Jul; Romanus & Sunderland, *Mission,* 200. $3.5 million: Byrd, 152.

375   Going home: Bond & Anderson, 208–211; Keeton diary; Wolf & Ingells; R. T. Smith, 357; Robert M. Smith, 108.

376   *I knew you were doing:* Jernstedt, author interview.

376   *Y'all follow:* Lopez, author interview.

376   *Hello, Frillmann:* Frillmann, 174.

377   Bissell as commander: AMISSCA rad, 17 Jul; Scott, *Sky,* 89.

377   *It's the man in the trenches,* etc.: *Time,* 15 Feb 1943.

378   *Stoned out of his gourd:* Brown, author interview. Also Byrd, 170, 277–278; Samson, 218, 288–290.

378   *Take advantage of:* Samson, 263–264. Also Byrd, 411.

379   The story of *Barbie III* is from Robert M. Smith, 110.

379   *I seen my duty:* New York *Herald Tribune,* 19 Jan 1944.

380   Denial of military benefits: Mott, author interview; Flying Tigers, Inc., *Bill of Rights.*

381   Chennault's airline: Leary, *Perilous Missions.*

381   Bird & Son: Sterling Seagrave, *Soldiers,* 145–165; Shilling, author interview.

381   Pawley's career: *Washington Star,* 8 Jan 1975.

381   Currie: NYT, 27 Mar 1956.

382   Chennault stamp: NYT, 13 Jan 1991.

384   *Only on those occasions:* Anscorp video.

Photos

With his piercing: Byrd, 30–31.
You will go over: Rector, author interview.

Bibliography

Abbott, Edythe. "Chennault's LSU Teacher." Louisiana *State Times,* 4 Oct 1945.

"Activities of Third Pursuit Squadron," 31 Dec 1941. FTA Archives.

Adair, Claude Bryant. Author interview (telephone), 1986.

Aircraft Profiles (Britain). Various issues. NASM.

Alexander, Harold. "Operations in Burma." *Supplement to the London Gazette,* 5 Mar 1948.

Allison, Ernest. Films from China, 1929–1937. Nancy Allison Wright collection.

Alsop, Joseph. Author interview (Washington DC), 9 Oct 1985.

American Volunteer Group [Daniel Hoyle]. "Diary of 3rd Pursuit Squadron," 1941–1942. AFHRC 863.059.

———. "Group War Diary," 1941–1942. AFHRC 863.305; CLC Papers 29–30.

———. Victories attributed to AVG pilots, 1942. CLC Papers 13.

Anscorp. *The Flying Tigers and 14th Air Force Story.* Video. Thousand Oaks: AAF Museum, 1985.

Arnold, Henry, & Ira Eaker. *Winged Warfare.* New York: Harper, 1941.

———. *Army Flyer.* New York: Harper, 1942.

Baba, Kazuo, ed. *Nihon gunyoki no zembo* (Japanese Warplanes in the Pacific). Tokyo: Kantosha, 1956.

Bacon, Noel. "Diary of a Flying Tiger." New York *Sunday News,* 2 Aug 1942.

———. Author interview (telephone), 1990.

Ba Maw. *Breakthrough in Burma.* New Haven: Yale University Press, 1968.

Belden, Jack. *Retreat with Stilwell.* New York: Knopf, 1943.

431

Blackburn, John. Letters, 1939–1942. Stanley Blackburn collection.

Bland, Larry. *The Papers of George Catlett Marshall.* Baltimore: Johns Hopkins University Press, 1986.

Blum, John. *From the Morgenthau Diaries.* Boston: Houghton Mifflin, 1965.

Bond, Charles, & Terry Anderson. *A Flying Tiger's Diary.* College Station: Texas A&M University Press, 1984.

Boorman, Howard. *Biographical Dictionary of Republican China.* New York: Columbia University Press, 1967.

Bowers, Peter. *Curtiss Aircraft.* London: Putnam, 1979.

Boyington, Gregory. *Baa Baa Black Sheep.* New York: Putnam, 1958.

Boyle, John Hunter. *China and Japan at War.* Stanford: Stanford University Press, 1972.

Brereton, Lewis. *The Brereton Diaries.* New York: Morrow, 1946.

Bright, J. Gilpin. "From a Flying Tiger." *Atlantic,* October 1942.

Britain. Air Ministry. *Wings of the Phoenix.* London: HMSO, 1949.

Britain. General Staff. *ABDACOM.* Delhi: Government of India, 1942.

Britain. Government of Burma. *Burma Handbook.* Simla: Government of India, 1943.

Britain. Military Intelligence. "Japanese Air Losses, Burma Operation," 1953. Imperial War Museum AL 5190.

———. Summary of Japanese documents, Burma invasion. Imperial War Museum AL 5191.

Britain. Royal Air Force. *Pilot's Notes: Tomahawk I.* Publication 2013A, n.d.

———. Log of 17 Sq, 1942. Public Record Office AIR 27/235.

———. Log of 67 Sq, 1941. Public Record Office AIR 602–603.

———. Log of 113 Sq, 1942. Public Record Office AIR 878.

———. Log of 135 Sq, 1942. Public Record Office AIR 949.

Brooke-Popham, Robert. "Operations in the Far East." *Supplement to the London Gazette,* 22 Jan 1948.

Brown, Carl. Author interview (Ojai CA), 4 Jul 1989.

Brown, Joseph. "Will the Real Flying Faker Please Stand Up?" *Argosy,* Sep 1963.

Bueschel, Richard. *Mitsubishi A6M1/2/2N Zero-Sen.* New York: Arco, 1970.

———. *Nakajima Ki.27A–B.* New York: Arco, 1970.

———. *Nakajima Ki.43 Hayabusa I–III.* New York: Arco, 1970.

Burchett, Wilfred. *Trek Back from Burma.* Allahabad: Kitabistan, 1943.

Burgard, George. Diary, 1941–1942. FTA Archives.

Burton, Wilbur. "Mandate from Heaven." *Asia,* Aug 1935.

Byrd, Martha. *Chennault: Giving Wings to the Tiger.* Tuscaloosa: University of Alabama Press, 1987.

Cavanah, Herbert. Author interview (telephone), 1986.

Chen, Moon. Author interview (Arlington VA), 11 Jul 1989.

Chennault, Anna. *A Thousand Springs.* New York: Eriksson, 1962.
———. *The Education of Anna.* New York: New York Times Books, 1980.
———. Author interview (Washington DC), 23 Oct 1986.
Chennault, Claire. *Pursuit Aviation.* Maxwell Field: Air Corps Tactical School, 1933.
———. "The Role of Defensive Pursuit." *Coast Artillery Journal,* Nov-Dec 1933, Jan-Feb 1934, Mar-Apr 1934.
———. "Pursuit Vs. Bombardment." *N.A.A. Magazine,* Dec 1936.
———. Reports to Adjutant General, 1937–1938. AFHRC 248.211-24.
———. Diary, 1937–1942. Anna Chennault collection.
———. *Way of a Fighter.* New York: Putnam, 1949.
———. Air Force interview, 5 Apr and 16 Apr 1948. AFHRC 105.5-11.
———. "Air Warfare in China." Lecture, 29 Aug 1952. AFHRC K239.716252-17.
China. Ministry of Information. *China Handbook.* New York: Macmillan, 1943.
Christy, Joe, & Jeff Ethell. *P40 Hawks at War.* New York: Scribner, 1980.
Churchill, Winston. *The Second World War.* Boston: Houghton Mifflin, 1949–1953.
Collier, Basil. *Japanese Aircraft of World War II.* London: Sidgwick & Jackson, 1979.
Cooke, Roger, & Ann Gresham Cooke. *Your Uncles.* Rochester, Kent: privately printed, ca 1950.
Corcoran, Thomas. "Pacific Wars." Typescript. Anna Chennault collection.
———. Columbia interview, 1962.
Cornelius, Wanda, & Thayne Short. *Ding Hao.* Gretna: Pelican, 1980.
Costello, John. *The Pacific War.* New York: Rawson, Wade, 1981.
Craven, Wesley, & James Cate. *The Army Air Forces in World War II.* Chicago: University of Chicago Press, 1948–1958.
Crookshanks, Jesse. Author interview (Ojai CA), 4 Jul 1989.
Cross, James. "We Kept the Tigers Flying." *Mechanix Illustrated,* Dec 1942.
Crozier, Brian. *The Man Who Lost China.* New York: Scribner, 1976.
Cruickshank, Charles. *SOE in the Far East.* Oxford: Oxford University Press, 1983.
Currie, Lauchlin. Memoranda & letters, 1941–1942. FDR Library.
Curtiss Flyleaf. Various issues. Yale University Library.
Curtiss-Wright Corporation. *Ways of the Warhawk.* Video. Eagan: Historic Aviation, n.d.
Davies, John. *Dragon by the Tail.* New York: Norton, 1972.
"Diary of a Japanese Airman," 1937. AFHRC 248.211-24.
Donovan, John. Letters, 1941–1942. FTA Archives.
Donovan, William. Memoranda, 1942. Secretary's File 163–164, FDR Library.

Dorn, Frank. *Walkout.* New York: Crowell, 1971.

Douhet, Giulio. *The Command of the Air.* New York: Coward-McCann, 1942.

Dower, John. *War Without Mercy.* New York: Pantheon, 1986.

Dunsmore, Dorothea. Author interview (Arlington VA), 11 Jul 1989.

Dupouy, Parker. Author interview (Providence RI), 22 Aug 1985.

Fahey, James. *U.S. Army Aircraft.* New York: Ships & Aircraft, 1946.

Fairbank, John King. "Air Program," 15 Jan 1942. William Leary collection.

Feis, Herbert. *The Road to Pearl Harbor.* Princeton: Princeton University Press, 1950.

Finney, Robert. *History of the Air Corps Tactical School.* Maxwell AFB: Air University, 1955.

Flying Tigers 40th Anniversary Reunion. San Diego: privately printed, 1981.

Flying Tigers, Inc. *Bill of Rights Requesting Veteran Recognition by Congress.* New York: privately printed, 1945.

Foucar, Emile. *I Lived in Burma.* London: Dennis Dobson, 1956.

14th Air Force Association. *Chennault's Flying Tigers.* Silver Bay: 14th Air Force Association, 1982.

Francillon, Rene. *Japanese Aircraft of the Pacific War.* New York: Funk & Wagnalls, 1970.

Frillmann, Paul. *China: The Remembered Life.* Boston: Houghton Mifflin, 1968.

Fritzke, Allen. Author interview (Piscataway NJ), 25 Jul 1985.

Fu Jui-yuan. Author interview (Taipei), 9 Dec 1986.

Gallagher, O'Dowd. *Action in the East.* New York: Doubleday, 1942.

Glines, Carroll. *Doolittle's Tokyo Raiders.* New York: Van Nostrand Reinhold, 1964.

Glover, Byron. "Assembling and Testing P-40's in Burma." *Aviation,* Dec 1942.

Green, William, & Gordon Swanborough. *Japanese Army Fighters.* London: Macdonald & Jane, 1976, 1977.

Greene, Paul. Author interviews (Ojai CA), 2–4 Jul 1989.

Greenlaw, Olga. *The Lady and the Tigers.* New York: Dutton, 1943.

Griffith, S. D. "The Chinese Air Force." 21 Aug 1937. AFHRC 248.211-24.

Hanks, Emma Jane. Author interview (Ojai CA), 3 Jul 1989.

Harrington, Jasper. Author interview (Ojai CA), 4 Jul 1989.

Hasegawa, Naoyoshi. *Rikuwashi nanpo sakusen* (Land Eagles in the South). Tokyo: Nihon Gunyo Tosho Kabushi Kigaisha, 1943.

Hata, Ikuhiko. "The Marco Polo Bridge Incident." In James Morley, *The China Quagmire.* New York: Columbia University Press, 1983.

Hata, Ikuhiko, & Yasuho Izawa. *Japanese Naval Aces and Fighter Units.* Annapolis: Naval Institute, 1989.

Hattori, Takushiro, et al. "History of Imperial General Headquarters." Japanese Monograph 45. Tokyo: U.S. Army, 1959.

Hayashi, Iwao. In *Shichi jusan butai kaisoki* (73rd Division Remembered). Tokyo: Reimeisha, 1980.

Hayashi, Saburo. *Kogun: The Japanese Army in the Pacific War*. Quantico: Marine Corps Association, 1959.

Haynes, Caleb. Letter to USAAF historian, 20 Apr 1943. Martha Byrd collection.

Hedman, Robert. Author interview (telephone), 1986.

Hemingway, Kenneth. *Wings Over Burma*. London: Quality, 1944.

Hennessy, John. Author interview (Ashland NH), 3 Dec 1988.

Hill, David Lee. Columbia interview, 1962.

———. Author interview (Ojai CA), 3 Jul 1989.

Hinoki, Yohei. *Tsubasa no kessen* (Desperate Winged Combat). Tokyo: Kojinsha, 1984.

———. *Hayabusa sentotai cho Kato* (Commander Kato's Falcon Corps). Tokyo: Kojinsha, 1987.

Hisazuma, Tadeo. "Air Operations in the China Incident." Japanese Monograph 166. Tokyo: U.S. Army, 1951.

Horiba, Kazuo. *Shina jihen senso shido shi* (Strategy in the China Incident). Tokyo: Jiji Tsushinsha, 1962.

Horikoshi, Jiro. *Eagles of Mitsubishi*. Seattle: University of Washington Press, 1981.

Holley, Irving. *Buying Aircraft*. Washington: U.S. Army, 1964.

Hotz, Robert. *With General Chennault*. New York: Coward McCann, 1943.

Howard, James. "Roar of a Tiger." Typescript. Author.

Hughes, Thomas. *The Burma Campaign*. Lahore: n.p., 1943.

Hutton, T. J. "Operations in Burma." *Supplement to the London Gazette,* 5 Mar 1948.

Ienaga, Saburo. *The Pacific War*. New York: Pantheon, 1978.

Ikari, Yoshio. *Shinshitei* (New Reconnaissance). Tokyo: Sankei Shuppan, 1981.

Ike, Nobutaka. *Japan's Decision For War*. Stanford: Stanford University Press, 1967.

International Military Tribunal for the Far East. *The Tokyo Judgment*. Amsterdam: University Press of Amsterdam, 1977.

Iriye, Akira. *Power and Culture*. Cambridge: Harvard University Press, 1981.

Ishikawa, Shin, et al. "Southwest Area Air Operations Record." Japanese Monograph 55. Tokyo: U.S. Army, 1946.

Izawa, Yasuho. "64th Flying Sentai." *Aero Album,* Summer 1970, Fall 1971.

———. *Nihon rikugun jubakutai* (JAAF Bomber Units). Tokyo: Gendaishi Shuppankai, 1982.

———. "Japanese Fighter Units and Aces." Typescript. John Fredriksen collection.

Izawa, Yasuho, & Ikuhiko Hata. *Nihon rikugun sentokitai* (JAAF Fighter Units). Tokyo: Kantosha, 1977.

Japan. Defense Agency. *Nanpo shinko rikugun koku sakusen* (Army Air Operations in Southeast Asia). Tokyo: Asagumo Shimbunsha, 1970.

———. *Chugoku homen rikugun koku sakusen* (Army Air Operations in China). Tokyo: Asagumo Shimbunsha, 1974.

Jernstedt, Kenneth. Author interview (Hood River OR), 1 Mar 1988.

Johnstone, William. *The United States and Japan's New Order.* Oxford: Oxford University Press, 1941.

Jordan, Joe. Columbia interview, 1962.

Jouett, John. "War Planes Over China." *Asia,* Dec 1937.

Kasuya, Toshio. *Yamamoto jubakugetai no eiko* (Glorious Yamamoto Bomber Corps). Tokyo: Futami Shobo, 1970.

Kato, Masuo. *The Lost War.* New York: Knopf, 1946.

Kato, Tateo. "Diary of Major-General Kato." *Japan Times & Advertiser,* 25 Jul 1942.

Keeton, Robert. Diary, 1941–1942. FTA Archives.

———. Author interview (Ojai CA), 5 Jul 1989.

Kirby, S. W. *India's Most Dangerous Hour.* London: HMSO, 1958.

Kori, Katsu, ed. *Nihon no koku gojunen* (Fifty Years of Japanese Aviation). Tokyo: Kantosha, 1960.

Kubo, Yoshiaki. *Kyunana jubakutai kusanki* (The 97 Heavy Bomber Story). Tokyo: Kojinsha, 1984.

Kuo Ju-lin. Author interview (Taipei), 9 Dec 1986.

Kuroe, Yasuhiko. *Aa Hayabusa sentotai* (Ah, the Falcon Corps). Tokyo: Kojinsha, 1969.

Kuwahara, Yasuo, & Gordon Allred. *Kamikaze.* New York: Ballantine, 1957.

Kuykendall, Matthew. Columbia interview, 1962.

Laughlin, C. H. "China Tiger." *Foundation,* Spring 1983.

———. "The Transition." *Air Classics,* March 1989.

Layher, Robert. Columbia interview, 1962.

———. Author interview (Ojai CA), 3 Jul 1989.

Leary, William. *The Dragon's Wings.* Athens: University of Georgia Press, 1976.

———. *Perilous Missions.* Tuscaloosa: University of Alabama Press, 1984.

———. "Assessing the Japanese Threat." *Aerospace Historian,* Winter 1987.

Lee Cheng-yuan. Author interviews (Taipei), 10–11 Dec 1986.

Leonard, Royal. *I Flew for China.* Garden City: Doubleday, 1942.

Lett, Tye. "We Learned War Maintenance With the AVG." *Aviation,* Dec 1942.

Liu, F. F. *A Military History of Modern China.* Princeton: Princeton University Press, 1956.

Liu, S. Y. Author interview (Taipei), 8 Dec 1986.

Lopez, Donald. Author interview (Washington DC), 11 Jul 1989.

Love, Syd. "To Old Hand Rossi." *San Diego Union,* 10 Jul 1986.

Lu, David. *From the Marco Polo Bridge to Pearl Harbor.* Washington: Public Affairs Press, 1961.

McGarry, William. Interview, 1989. Robert Andrade collection.

McHugh, James. Reports for 1938. AFHRC 248.211-24.

———. "The History and Status of the First American Volunteer Group," 1941; reports for 1939. Cornell University Library 2770.

Mao Chao-pin. Author interview (Taipei), 8 Dec 1986.

Mao Pang-chu. Air Force interview, 28 Apr 1948. AFHRC 105.5-10.

Mason, Francis. *Hawker Aircraft Since 1920.* London: Putnam, 1961.

Maurer, Maurer. *Aviation in the U.S. Army, 1919–1939.* Washington: Office of Air Force History, 1987.

Metasavage, Frank. Air Force interview. AFHRC 549-3.

Moore, Larry, & Ken Sanger. "We Fight With the Flying Tigers." *Cosmopolitan,* Aug-Sep 1942.

Morgenthau, Henry. Diaries, 1940–1941. FDR Library.

Moser, Don. *China-Burma-India.* Alexandria: Time-Life, 1978.

Mott, Charles. Diary, 1941–1942. FTA Archives.

———. Author interview (Arlington VA), 19 Jul 1988.

Moyes, Philip. *Bomber Squadrons of the RAF.* London: Macdonald & Jane, 1974.

Murano, Shinichi. Memoir of the 56th Division. Author collection.

Nalty, Bernard. *Tigers Over Asia.* New York: Elsevier-Dutton, 1978.

Neale, Robert. Diary, 1941–1942. FTA Archives.

———. Columbia interview, 1962.

———. Author interview (Ojai CA), 4 Jul 1989.

Neumann, Gerhard. *Herman the German.* New York: Morrow, 1984.

Nonaka (no first name). "Southwest Area Air Operations Record." Japanese Monograph 56. Tokyo: U.S. Army, n.d.

Ogawa, Toshihiko. *Nihon hikoki daizukan* (Encyclopedia of Japanese Aircraft). Tokyo: Kodansha, 1980.

Okumiya, Masatake, & Jiro Horikoshi. *Zero!* New York: Dutton, 1956.

Older, Charles. Columbia interview, 1962.

———. Author interview (telephone), 1986.

Olson, Arvid. Notebook, 1941. NASM, 1987-0075, roll 83.

———. "A Story of the American Volunteer Group." FTA Archives.

Omar, M. I. "First Bombing Day in Rangoon." Rangoon *Guardian,* Dec 1960.

Patterson, A. L. Correspondence, 1987. Author collection.

Pawley, William. *Americans Valiant and Glorious.* New York: privately printed, 1945.

————. Letter to army historian, 6 Jul 1950. National Archives, HIS 330.14.

————. *Wings Over Asia*. New York: privately printed, 1971.

Paxton, George. Air Force interview. AFHRC 863.549-2.

Pentecost, Walter. "Advance of the Flying Tigers." American Aviation Historical Society *Journal,* Summer 1970.

————. Air Force interview, 27 Apr 1942. AVG Archives 9.

————. Author interview (telephone), 1988.

Perry, Paul. Author interview (Ojai CA), 4 Jul 1989.

Phreaner, Alys. Author interview (Ojai CA), 2 Jul 1989.

Pickler, Gordon. "U.S. Aid to Chinese Nationalist Air Force." Ph.D dissertation, 1971. Ann Arbor: University Microfilms.

Poshefko, Joseph. Author interview (El Segundo CA), 5 Jul 1989.

Prescott, Robert. Columbia interview, 1962.

Quick, Carl. Author interview (telephone), 1986.

Raine, Robert. Author interview (Ojai CA), 3 Jul 1989.

Rangoon Times. Various issues. British Library.

Rawlings, John. *Fighter Squadrons of the RAF.* London: Macdonald & Jane, 1976.

Rector, Edward. Author interviews (Arlington VA), 7 May 1986, 21 Jul 1988, 11 Jul 1989.

Reynolds, Doreen. Columbia interview, 1962.

————. Author interview (Arlington VA), 7 May 1986.

Richards, Lewis. Columbia interview, 1962.

————. Author interview (Ojai CA), 4 Jul 1989.

Ricks, Wayne. Author interview (Ojai CA), 3 Jul 1989.

Rodewald, Donald. Diary, 1941–1942. Rodewald collection.

————. Columbia interview, 1962.

————. Author interview (Ojai CA), 2 Jul 1989.

Romanus, Charles, & Riley Sunderland. *Stilwell's Mission to China.* Washington: GPO, 1953.

————. *Stilwell's Personal File.* Wilmington: Scholarly Resources, 1976.

Roosevelt, Franklin. Memoranda, 1941. Official File 150, FDR Library.

Rosbert, C. Joseph. *Flying Tiger Joe.* Franklin: Poplar, 1985.

Rosholt, Malcolm. *Days of the Ching Pao.* Rosholt: privately printed, 1978.

Ross, Augustus. Author interview (Rangoon), 13 Dec 1986.

Rossi, J. Richard. Letters, 1986–1990. Author collection.

————. Author interview (Ojai CA), 3 Jul 1989.

Royce, Ralph. Report, 17 Jul 1939. AFHRC 248.211-24.

Rubenstein, Murray, & Richard Goldman. *To Join With the Eagles.* Garden City: Doubleday, 1974.

Samson, Jack. *Chennault.* New York: Doubleday, 1987.

Sato, Shoichi. Army interview, 1949. National Archives, Military Record Branch 319.

Schaller, Michael. *The U.S. Crusade in China*. New York: Columbia University Press, 1979.

Schaper, Wilfred. Diary, 1941–1942. AVG Archives 60–61.

———. Columbia interview, 1962.

Schultz, Duane. *The Maverick War*. New York: St. Martin's, 1987.

Scott, Robert Lee. *God Is My Co-Pilot*. New York: Ballantine, 1956.

———. *Flying Tiger*. Garden City: Doubleday, 1959.

———. *The Day I Owned the Sky*. New York: Bantam, 1988.

———. Air Force interview, 1942, 1943. AFHRC 142.052-174A/174.

Seagrave, Gordon. *Burma Surgeon*. New York: Norton, 1943.

Seagrave, Sterling. *Soldiers of Fortune*. Alexandria: Time-Life, 1981.

———. *The Soong Dynasty*. New York: Harper & Row, 1985.

Sekigawa, Eiichiro. *Pictorial History of Japanese Military Aviation*. London: Allan, 1974.

Shah Konsin. Author interview (Taipei), 8 Dec 1986.

Shamburger, Page, & Joe Christy. *Curtiss Hawk Fighters*. New York: Sports Car Press, 1971.

Sherry, Michael. *The Rise of American Air Power*. New Haven: Yale University Press, 1987.

Sherwood, Robert. *Roosevelt and Hopkins*. New York: Harper, 1948.

Shiba, Takejiro. "Air Operations in the China Area." Japanese Monograph 76. Tokyo: U.S. Army, 1956.

Shilling, Eriksen. "Origin of Shark Teeth." Typescript, n.d. AVG Archives 10.

———. Taped memoir, 1981. Author.

———. Author interview (telephone), 1990.

Shores, Christopher. *Fighter Aces*. London: Hamlyn, 1975.

Slim, William. *Defeat Into Victory*. New York: McKay, 1961.

Smith, Robert M. *With Chennault in China*. Blue Ridge Summit: TAB, 1984.

———. Author interview (Ojai CA), 2 Jul 1989.

Smith, Robert T. *Tale of a Tiger*. Van Nuys: Tiger, 1986.

———. Author interview (telephone), 1986.

"Southern Area Air Operations." Japanese Monograph 31. Tokyo: U.S. Army.

Stevenson, Donald. "Air Operations in Burma." *Supplement to the London Gazette*, 11 Mar 1948.

Stilwell, Joseph. *The Stilwell Papers*. New York: Sloane, 1948.

Sugita (no first name), et al. "Malay Operations Record." Japanese Monograph 54. Tokyo: U.S. Army, 1946.

Tagata, Takeo. *Hien tai Guramen* (Swallow vs. Grumman). Tokyo: Konnichi no Wadaisha, 1973.

Tamagna, Frank. *Italy's Interests and Policies in the Far East.* New York: Institute for Pacific Relations, 1941.

Tanaka, Masa. "Burma Air Operations Record." Japanese Monograph 64. Tokyo: U.S. Army, 1946.

Terakura, Shore, et al. "Burma Operations Record." Japanese Monograph 57. Tokyo: U.S. Army, 1946.

Thorpe, Donald, & Yasuo Oishi. *Japanese Army Air Force Camouflage and Markings.* Fallbrook CA: Aero, 1968.

Toho Motion Picture Company. *Aa Hayabusa sentotai cho Kato* (Ah, Commander Kato's Falcon Corps). Film, n.d. John Fredriksen collection.

———. *Aa Hayabusa.* Film, n.d. Fredriksen collection.

———. *Biruma* (Burma). Newsreel, n.d. Fredriksen collection.

Tomioka, Sadatoshi. "Political Strategy Prior to Outbreak of War." Japanese Monographs 144, 146, 147, 150, 152. Tokyo: U.S. Army, 1952–1953.

Trumble, Thomas. Columbia interview, 1962.

Tsuji, Masanobu. *Singapore: The Japanese Version.* London: Constable, 1962.

Tuchman, Barbara. *Stilwell and the American Experience in China.* New York: Macmillan, 1970.

United States. Air Force. "AVG Bibliography," 1960. AFHRC.

United States. Army. G-2 files, China, 1940–1941. National Archives, Military Field Branch 319.

United States. Army Air Forces. "Chronology of 10th Air Force," n.d. AFHRC 105.2-10.

———. "A.V.G. Fighter Tactics," 1942. FTA Archives.

———. "Informal Report on A.V.G. Activities," 1942. AFHRC 863.549.

———. *Pilots Manual for Curtiss P-40 Warhawk.* USAAF, n.d.

———. *Pilot Training Manual for the P-40.* USAAF, n.d.

United States. Department of State. *Foreign Relations of the United States: Diplomatic Papers.* Various volumes. Washington: GPO, 1943–1956.

United States. Military Mission to China (AMISSCA). Radiograms and weekly reports, 1941–1942. National Archives, Military Field Branch 332.

———. "American Volunteer Group," 1942. AFHRC 863.01.

United States. Office of Strategic Services. *Survey of Burma.* Washington: OSS, 1942.

United States. Senate Judiciary Committee. *Morgenthau Diary.* Washington: GPO, 1965.

United States. 79th Congress. Joint Committee on the Investigation of the Pearl Harbor Attack. *Hearings.* Washington: GPO, 1946.

United States. Strategic Bombing Survey. *Japanese Aircraft Industry.* Washington: GPO, 1946.

———. *Japanese Air Power.* Washington: GPO, 1946.

———. *Japanese Air Weapons and Tactics.* Washington: GPO, 1947.

Wagner, Ray. "The Chinese Air Force." American Aviation Historical Society *Journal,* Fall 1974.

Walton, Frank. *Once They Were Eagles.* Lexington: University Press of Kentucky, 1986.

Wang Shu-ming. Author interview (Taipei), 9 Dec 1986.

Ward, Richard. *Sharkmouth, 1916–1945.* New York: Arco, 1979.

Watanabe, Yoji. *Toryu.* Tokyo: Sankei Shuppan, 1983.

Wavell, Archibald. "Operations in Burma." *Supplement to the London Gazette,* 5 Mar 1948.

Wei Ju-lin et al. *History of the Sino-Japanese War.* Taipei: U.S. Army Military Assistance Advisory Group, 1967.

Whelan, Russell. *The Flying Tigers.* New York: Viking, 1942.

Whelpley, Don. "I'll Never Forget Chennault." *Ex-CIB Roundup,* May 1989.

White, Theodore. *In Search of History.* New York: Harper, 1978.

White, Theodore, & Anna Lee Jacoby. *Thunder Out of China.* New York: Sloane, 1946.

Williams, John. "Yunnan Warning Net." AVG Archives 29.

———. Air Force interview, 25 Jun 1980. USAF Academy Library.

———. Author interviews (San Diego CA), 11–12 May 1987.

Wirta, Harvey. Columbia interview, 1962.

Wolf, Fritz, & Douglas Ingells. "It's Hell Over China!" *Air Trails Pictorial,* Oct 1942.

Wright, Nancy Allison. Author interview (Ojai CA), 3 Jul 1990.

Wright, Peter. "A Fighter Pilot Learns a Lesson." *Sportsman Pilot,* Mid-May 1943.

———. "I Learned About Flying From That." *Flying,* May 1944.

Yamaguchi, Shiro. "Malaya Invasion Naval Operations." Japanese Monograph 107. Tokyo: U.S. Army, 1959.

Yasuda, Yoshito. "Muteki Hayabusa sentai" (Almighty Falcon Group). In *Eiko Hayabusa sentai.* Tokyo: Konnichi no Wadaisha, 1978.

Young, Arthur. *China and the Helping Hand.* Cambridge: Harvard University Press, 1963.

———. *China's Nation-Building Effort.* Stanford: Hoover Institution, 1971.

Young, A. J., & D. W. Warne. *Sixty Squadron.* Singapore: Eurasia, n.d.

Index

Planes are indexed under *Aircraft,* by manufacturer, with detailed profiles shown in **bold** type. Military units are indexed under the name of the parent service.